BOOK

of

DIVINE PRAYERS

and

SERVICES

of the

CATHOLIC ORTHODOX CHURCH

of

CHRIST

Book of

Divine

Prayers and Services

of the

Catholic Orthodox Church

of Christ

Comprising the most important of the Private and Public Prayers;
Services of the Dominical Feasts of the Distinguished Saints;
and of all Sundays of the Year; in the Order ordained
by the Holy Orthodox Church of Christ; to
which are appended an Index and a
Table for finding Easter, cover-
ing a Period of Twenty
Years, 1938 to
1 9 5 8

▼

Compiled and arranged by
THE REVEREND SERAPHIM NASSAR
the President of the Society

With the Permission and Approval of
HIS GRACE THE MOST REVEREND ANTONY BASHIR
Archbishop of New York and All North America

1938
THE BLACKSHAW PRESS, Inc.
New York, N. Y.

Preface and Invocation

PRAISED be God the absolute Being, whose greatness pervades all existence, great in himself, glorified in his creation, who made of religion a lighthouse for guidance, raising his saints as exemplars to those who would follow in their footsteps, now by their words of sound doctrine, and now by their blameless deeds. Praised be he whose abundant mercies have accepted prayer as a means of worship for his most holy glory, as a blessing to his servants, as nourishment for their souls, as a fountain of joy for their spirits, as a consolation to them in their sorrows, and as a light to lighten their hearts by day and by night.

I, Father Seraphim Nassar, son of George, son of Elias Nassar, Orthodox in doctrine, born in Marsine, having long realized the dire need of my Orthodox Christian brethren in the lands of their dispersion, and especially of their offspring for whom the English language has become the mother tongue, was moved by religious zeal and Christian love to undertake the translation into English of an unabridged prayer book, unlike the compendiums that are now in use, for these latter do not include such prayers and services as the Great Horologia, the Psalms, the Prophecies, the Epistles, the Gospels, the Oktoechos, the Menaion, the Triodion, the Pentecostarion, the service of the Holy Mass, and the Typicon, all of which are necessary for every Orthodox worshipper, especially chanters, lectors, and, of course, Priests.

After years of search and investigation I was successful, by God's help, in finding a capable person to fulfill my long cherished desire to bring this project to completion. This solemn undertaking was begun and finished in the town of Spring Valley, Illinois, in the United States of America, with the efforts and assistance of a group of God-fearing and devoted daughters of religion, who both in virtues and number represent the most essential of Christian graces —faith, hope, and charity. Thus I was enabled to complete this book according to the pattern I had laid down, so that it fulfills all the indispensable requirements of a full service book for use in Orthodox Churches.

To this volume I have added appendices explaining the true nature of the Church of Christ, founded by him, the attributes by which it is distinguished, its infallibility, the reason for its order of worship, with an exposition thereof. To this has been added the division of time, the number of prayers and notes on their authors, and the times of their inclusion in the Church services, especially those of the

v

service of the Divine Mass. For the convenience of the reader I have followed this appendix with a glossary of words and phrases which I left in the original Greek, with a table of contents and index. For further usefulness I added tables for the determination of Easter, after the Eastern Calendar, and the Western and Mosaic Passovers; the Epistle and Gospel selections, Tones, and the Eothina to be used each Sunday for a period of twenty years, with blank pages for the registration of marriages, births, baptisms, and deaths.

I have left the full exposition of the Divine Mass and other matters to the longer standard books dealing with these subjects. I have contented myself with the quotations and references which the reader will find in this book, taken from the writings of the Fathers and commentators, which, as I believe, are sufficient for the purpose of worship and the topics of the services.

Finally, I trust that this work of mine may receive the commendation and call forth the satisfaction of my superiors and the rest of my reverend brethren the Priests. I pray that they meet my weakness with their kindness; that they correct my errors with their gentle reprovals, pointing out my mistakes; and that they cover my shortcomings with their gracious indulgence; and that they encourage me with their prayers.

Receive thou, most merciful One, by thy great compassion and all-pervading bounty, the past and future efforts of thy handmaidens, the sisters of the Sisterhood of the Propagation of Divine Services and Religious Teachings in the United States—Mary, Elizabeth, and Sadie Abraham, referred to above — for the fulfillment of thy will, the strengthening of thy Church, and the glorification of thy Name. Sufficient unto me is thy mercy and the benefit accruing to the children of my Orthodox Church generally.

(Reverend) Seraphim Nassar
President of the Sisterhood.

The conclusion of the translation, comparison, correction, and revision of this work took place in my residence, 322 East Iowa Street, in the town of Spring Valley, Illinois, at the opening of the year 1938.

Petition

Submitted by Father Seraphim Nassar to his Grace, Archbishop
Antony Bashir, Seeking Permission for the Publication
of this Book.

*T*O the lordship of my venerable lord and master, the most wise,
the most noble, and the most learned Antony Bashir, Archbishop of New York and all North America, supreme in eloquence of mouth and pen. May the radiance of your years, like a
brilliant luminary long shine for the glory of the holy Church of
Christ.

Having kissed your holy hands and sought the beneficence of your
prayers and of your apostolic blessings, allow me to say that the best
act in this created world is the propagation of the worship of God
by which one proclaims the favour, goodness, and beneficence of the
Creator toward the creature.

Prayer is the most direct means whereby man can attain this sacred
end, since it comprises petition, praise, and thanksgiving for all the
favours which we have received through faith in the Son of God,
our only Saviour and Mediator.

Since most of the children of our Orthodox Church in these American countries are occupied with their worldly affairs, deserting their
Church, and turning away from the worship of their Creator, on
the pretext that they are ignorant of the language of their parents'
Church, religious zeal and Christian love have moved your son the
Priest, Seraphim Nassar, most unworthy sinner and captive to
iniquity, to translate the services of our Orthodox Church into the
English language, for their enlightenment, and to arouse them from
the slumber of their inadvertence, and to lead them to worship their
Creator.

I have called this book of mine The Divine Services of the Catholic
Orthodox Church of Christ and in it I have included all that the
Christian, clerical or lay, may need in his house or in the church.

Being an unworthy Priest, and knowing the duty of obedience
imposed on me toward the respected authority of the Church, I come
with this petition to supplicate your religious zeal, your Christian
love, and your apostolic blessing, to honour me with permission to
publish it, in order to universalize its benefits, and to crown my
efforts with success.

In conclusion, I kiss your holy hand again, and ask God to support
and establish your holy presidency.

Your suppliant and son,

Spring Valley, Illinois,   THE PRIEST, SERAPHIM NASSAR.
April 15, 1938.

THE MOST REVEREND ANTONY BASHIR
ARCHBISHOP OF NEW YORK AND ALL NORTH AMERICA

Imprimatur

*O*UR *beloved son in the Lord, the Reverend Seraphim Nassar, Pastor of St. George's Syrian Orthodox Church in Spring Valley, Illinois, is one in whom we have recognized religious zeal and true Christian love. He has spared no effort and has been tireless in the cause of the progress of the Holy Apostolic Catholic Orthodox Church of Christ, taking special interest in the younger generation of our holy Church who have been born and brought up in the United States, regardless of racial or linguistic origin.*

Among other things in evidence of this father's zeal for religion and Church, we may mention that some time ago he wrote a little novel based on the Annunciation to the Virgin Mary, which he called, The Daughter of David, *in which he sought to establish the Incarnation of the Word of God, and to prove that Christ is both God and Man. This novel was translated into English and favourably received by the various Orthodox communities and by the American people generally.*

At present, already translated and ready for publication when the opportunity offers, he has the following works:

1. Rays of Light on the Sacraments. *This is an exposition of the Seven Sacraments of the Church.*

2. Outline of Sacred History. *For the benefit of school children.*

3. Outline of Church History.

4. A Compendium of the Exposition of the Divine Mass.

5. *A more extended exposition of the Divine Mass.*

6. Exposition of the Creed, the Canon of Faith.

7. An Essay on the Sources of the Creed or Canon of Faith.

8. Exposition of the Lord's Prayer.

9. Exposition of the Church's Requirements for the Child from the Time He is Born until His Baptism.

10. *The first part of his book,* Proof of Morality and the Truth of the Faith. *This comprises some of his sermons and will be helpful to every Christian, particularly those of the younger generation among whom very few have a true understanding of Orthodoxy.*

Finally, he has finished his eleventh work, The Book of Divine Services of the Catholic Orthodox Church of Christ, *the manuscript of which is now in our hands, and which we have perused. We have*

ix

found it inclusive of all the services, rites, and prayers. It comprises in its pages, which exceed one thousand, the Great Horology, the Psalms, Prophecies, Epistles, Gospels, the Oktoechos, the Menaion, the Triodion, the Pentecostarion, as well as the service of the Divine Mass, and the Typicon. At the end of the book is an Appendix in which the reverend father explains the true meaning of the Church of Christ, established by God, its attributes, infallibility, purpose in ordaining the holy services, with an exposition of all that pertains thereto, and an explanation of the division of time in accordance with the number of services, and the times of their introduction into the Church, especially as regards the Divine Mass. The Appendix also contains an explanation of the Mass and of the words and phrases which have been left in the book in their original Greek forms. For further convenience the Appendix is followed by an Easter Table for the determination of the Jewish, or Mosaic Passover, the Eastern Orthodox Passover, and the Latin Passover. There is a section for the Epistles, another for the Gospels, a chapter on the Tones, and the Eothina for every Sunday of the year for a period of twenty years.

Having examined this book, unique in the English tongue, and having realized its benefit, and the growing urgency among our Orthodox people for it, especially the singers, readers, and venerable Priests, we have given our permission for its publication, prompted by our desire to see it widely distributed among our Church people, in order to propagate the spirit of piety and to confirm true religion through prayer and true worship.

ANTONY BASHIR,
Archbishop of New York and all North America.

METROPOLITE GERMANUS SHIHADAH

Dedication

To the spirit of my father in the Priesthood, the thrice blessed of memory, Metropolitan Germanus Shihadah; to that spirit without whose bountiful affluence towards me, manifested by my being the first to set the service of the Divine Mass into the English language, this door would not have been opened before me, nor would I have beheld that light which guided me in this way that I have taken, nor come to the end which I have now reached through the help of God.

For behold, while thou, O pure spirit, hast departed this existence, thou art still living in thine essence, through holy deeds, and through what thou hast left of beautiful memory, for the glory of God and the good of the Church.

Thy faithful son,
(Reverend) Seraphim Nassar.

Table of Contents

Table of Contents

Table of Contents

Table of Contents

III. HOLY PASSION WEEK FROM THE EVENING OF PALM SUNDAY TO GREAT SATURDAY

Table of Contents

Table of Contents

Table of Contents

FIRST SECTION

✠

PRAYER AFTER RISING UP FROM SLEEP

❡*When you arise from sleep, stand away from your bed, in reverence and fear of God; make the sign of the cross; and say:*

IN the Name of the Father, and of the Son, and of the Holy Spirit, one God. Amen.

Glory to thee our God, glory to thee.

O heavenly King, the Comforter, Spirit of truth, who art in all places and fillest all things; Treasury of good things, and Giver of life; come, take up thine abode in us, cleanse us from every stain, and save, good One, our souls.

Holy God, Holy Mighty, Holy Immortal One, have mercy upon us *(three times)*.

Glory to the Father, and to the Son, and to the Holy Spirit, now and ever, and unto ages of ages. Amen.

O all-holy Trinity, have mercy upon us; O Lord, forgive us our sins; O Master, pardon our transgressions. O holy One, visit and heal our infirmities for thy Name's sake. Lord, have mercy; Lord, have mercy; Lord, have mercy.

Glory to the Father *(complete)*.

OUR Father, who art in heaven, hallowed be thy Name; thy kingdom come; thy will be done, on earth as it is in heaven. Give us this day our daily bread. And forgive us our trespasses, as we forgive those who trespass against us. And lead us not into temptation, but deliver us from the evil one.

For thine is the kingdom, and the power, and the glory, O Father, Son, and Holy Spirit, now and ever, and unto ages of ages. Amen.

❡ *Then the following Trinitarian Troparia.*

AT our arising from sleep, we bow down before thee, O God, and cry out to thee, O mighty One, with the song of the angels, saying, Holy, Holy, Holy art thou, O God. For the sake of the Theotokos, have mercy upon us.

Glory to the Father, and to the Son, and to the Holy Spirit.

Thou hast gotten me up from my bed, and from my sleep. Lighten, O Lord, my mind and my heart; open my mouth to praise thee, O Holy Trinity, saying, Holy, Holy, Holy art thou, O God. For the sake of the Theotokos, have mercy upon us.

Now and ever, and unto ages of ages. Amen.

Suddenly the Judge shall come, and the deeds of each one of us shall be laid bare. Therefore, it behoveth us to cry with fear at midnight, saying, Holy, Holy, Holy art thou, O God. For the sake of the Theotokos, have mercy upon us.

❡ Lord, have mercy (*twelve times*) ; *and the following prayer.*

AT my rising from sleep I thank thee, O Holy Trinity, because of the abundance of thy goodness and long-suffering thou wast not wroth with me a sinner; nor let me perish by mine iniquities, but hast been gracious to me, sympathized with me after thine own manner, and raised me up, when I had fallen into despair, to hasten to praise thy power. Now lighten thou the eyes of my mind and open my mouth to meditate on thy words, to understand thy commandments, to do thy will, to sing to thee with confession of the heart, and to praise thine all-holy Name, O Father, Son, and Holy Spirit, now and ever, and unto ages of ages. Amen.

Another Prayer

GLORY to thee, Almighty King and God; for by thy philanthropic divine providence thou hast prepared me, an unworthy sinner, to rise from sleep and to gain entrance into thy holy house. Accept thou, Lord, the voice of my beseeching, as from thy holy intelligential powers. Be pleased that my song, issuing from impure lips, be offered to thee with a pure heart and with the spirit of humility, that I too may become a companion of the wise virgins, with the bright lamp of my soul, that I may glorify thee, Word of God, glorified in the Father and in the Holy Spirit. Amen.

SPECIAL MATIN PRAYERS

❡ Holy God, *and that which followeth; then recite the following Troparia.*

O LORD, save thy people and bless thine inheritance, granting our believing kings victory over the Barbarians, and, by the power of thy Cross, preserving thy commonwealth.

Glory to the Father, and to the Son, and to the Holy Spirit.

Do thou, who of thine own good will wast elevated upon the Cross, bestow thy bounties upon the new people which is called by thy Name, O Christ our God; make glad with thy might our believing kings, granting them victory over their adversaries. May thine aid be a panoply of peace, a trophy invincible.

Now and ever, and unto ages of ages. Amen.

O dread Champion, who cannot be put to confusion, despise not our petitions. O good one, all-lauded Theotokos, establish thou the way of those who hold the Orthodox Faith; save those whom thou hast called to rule over us; bestow upon them victory from heaven; for thou didst give birth unto God, O only blessed one.

Lord, have mercy *(twelve times)*.

Glory to God in the highest, and on earth peace and good will among men *(three times)*.

Lord, open thou my lips, and my mouth shall show forth thy praise *(two times)*.

¶ *Then the following Psalms.*

PSALM 3

WHY, O Lord, are they multiplied that afflict me? Many are they who rise up against me.

Many say to my soul: There is no salvation for him in his God.

But thou, O Lord, art my protector, my glory, and the lifter up of my head.

I have cried to the Lord with my voice: and he hath heard me from his holy hill.

I have slept and have taken my rest: and I have risen up, because the Lord hath protected me.

I will not fear thousands of the people, surrounding me: arise, O Lord; save me, O my God.

For thou hast struck all them who are my adversaries without cause: thou hast broken the teeth of sinners.

Salvation is of the Lord: and thy blessing is upon thy people.

PSALM 37

REBUKE me not, O Lord, in thy indignation; nor chastise me in thy wrath.

For thy arrows are fastened in me: and thy hand hath been strong upon me.

There is no health in my flesh, because of thy wrath: there is no peace for my bones, because of my sins.

For my iniquities are gone over my head: and as a heavy burden are become heavy upon me.

My sores are putrified and corrupted, because of my foolishness.

I am become miserable, and am bowed down even to the end: I walked sorrowful all the day long.

For my loins are filled with illusions; and there is no health in my flesh.

I am afflicted and humbled exceedingly: I roared with the groaning of my heart.

Lord, all my desire is before thee, and my groaning is not hidden from thee.

My heart is troubled, my strength hath left me, and the light of my eyes itself is not with me.

My friends and my neighbours have drawn near, and stood against me.

And they that were near me stood afar off:

And they that sought my soul used violence.

And they that sought evils to me spoke vain things, and studied deceits all the day long.

But I, as a deaf man, heard not: and as a dumb man not opening his mouth.

And I became as a man that heareth not: and that hath no reproofs in his mouth.

For in thee, O Lord, have I hoped: thou wilt hear me, O Lord my God.

For I said: Lest at any time my enemies rejoice over me: and whilst my feet are moved, they speak great things against me.

For I am ready for scourges: and my sorrow is continually before me.

For I will declare my iniquity: and I will think for my sin.

But my enemies live, and are stronger than I: and they that hate me wrongfully are multiplied.

They that render evil for good, have detracted me, because I followed goodness.

Forsake me not, O Lord my God: do not thou depart from me.

Attend unto my help, O Lord, the God of my salvation.

PSALM 62

O GOD, my God, to thee do I watch at the break of day.

For thee my soul hath thirsted; for thee my flesh, O how many ways.

In a desert land, and where there is no way, and no water: so in the sanctuary have I come before thee, to see thy power and thy glory.

For thy mercy is better than lives: thee my lips shall praise.

Thus will I bless thee all my life long: and in thy name I will lift up my hands.

Let my soul be filled as with marrow and fatness: and my mouth shall praise thee with joyful lips.

If I have remembered thee upon my bed, I will meditate on thee in the morning: because thou hast been my helper.

And I will rejoice under the covert of thy wings: my soul hath stuck close to thee: thy right hand hath received me.

But they have sought my soul in vain, they shall go into the lower parts of the earth:

They shall be delivered into the hands of the sword, they shall be the portions of foxes.

But the king shall rejoice in God, all they shall be praised that swear by him: because the mouth is stopped of them that speak wicked things.

Have I not remembered thee in my bed, and thought upon thee when I was waking, because thou hast been my helper, therefore under the shadow of thy wings will I rejoice, and my soul hangeth upon thee, thy right hand hath upholden me.

Glory to the Father, and to the Son, and to the Holy Spirit, now and ever, and unto ages of ages. Amen. Alleluia, Alleluia, Alleluia, glory to thee, O God. Lord, have mercy; Lord, have mercy; Lord, have mercy. Glory to the Father, and to the Son, and to the Holy Spirit, now and ever, and unto ages of ages. Amen.

PSALM 87

O LORD, the God of my salvation: I have cried in the day, and in the night before thee.

Let my prayer come in before thee: incline thy ear to my petition.

For my soul is filled with evils: and my life hath drawn nigh to hell.

I am counted among them that go down to the pit: I am become as a man without help, free among the dead.

Like the slain sleeping in the sepulchres whom thou rememberest no more: and they are cast off from thy hand.

They have laid me in the lower pit: in the dark places, and in the shadow of death.

Thy wrath is strong over me: and all thy waves thou hast brought in upon me.

Thou hast put away my acquaintance far from me: they have set me an abomination to themselves.

I was delivered up, and came not forth; my eyes languished through poverty.

All the day I cried to thee, O Lord: I stretched out my hands to thee.

Wilt thou shew wonders to the dead? or shall physicians raise to life, and give praise to thee?

Shall any one in the sepulchre declare thy mercy: and thy truth in destruction?

Shall thy wonders be known in the dark; and thy justice in the land of forgetfulness?

But I, O Lord, have cried to thee: and in the morning my prayer shall prevent thee.

Lord, why castest thou off my prayer: why turnest thou away thy face from me?

I am poor, and in labours from my youth: and being exalted have been humbled and troubled.

Thy wrath hath come upon me: and thy terrors have troubled me.

They have come round about me like water all the day: they have compassed me about together.

Friend and neighbour thou hast put far from me: and my acquaintance, because of misery.

O Lord God of my salvation I have cried day and night before thee: O let my prayer enter into thy presence, incline thine ear unto my calling.

Psalm 102

BLESS the Lord, O my soul: and let all that is within me bless his holy name.

Bless the Lord, O my soul, and never forget all he hath done for thee.

Who forgiveth all thy iniquities: who healeth all thy diseases.

Who redeemeth thy life from destruction: who crowneth thee with mercy and compassion.

Who satisfieth thy desire with good things: thy youth shall be renewed like the eagle's.

The Lord doeth mercies and judgment for all that suffer wrong.

He hath made his ways known to Moses: his wills to the children of Israel.

The Lord is compassionate and merciful: long-suffering and plenteous in mercy.

He will not always be angry: nor will he threaten for ever.

He hath not dealt with us according to our sins: nor rewarded us according to our iniquities.

For according to the height of the heaven above the earth: he hath strengthened his mercy towards them that fear him.

As far as the east is from the west, so far hath he removed our iniquities from us.

As a father hath compassion on his children, so hath the Lord compassion on them that fear him: for he knoweth our frame.

He remembereth that we are dust: man's days are as grass, as the flower of the field so shall he flourish.

For the spirit shall pass in him, and he shall not be: and he shall know his place no more.

But the mercy of the Lord is from eternity and unto eternity upon them that fear him:

And his justice unto children's children, to such as keep his covenant,

And are mindful of his commandments to do them.

The Lord hath prepared his throne in heaven: and his kingdom shall rule over all.

Bless the Lord, all ye his angels: you that are mighty in strength, and execute his word, hearkening to the voice of his orders.

Bless the Lord, all ye his hosts: you ministers of his that do his will.

Bless the Lord, all his works: in every place of his dominion, O my soul, bless thou the Lord.

PSALM 142

HEAR, O Lord, my prayer: give ear to my supplication in thy truth: hear me in thy justice.

And enter not into judgment with thy servant: for in thy sight no man living shall be justified.

For the enemy hath persecuted my soul: he hath brought down my life to the earth.

He hath made me to dwell in darkness as those that have been dead of old: and my spirit is in anguish within me: my heart within me is troubled.

I remembered the days of old, I meditated on all thy works: I meditated the works of thy hands.

I stretched forth my hands to thee: my soul is as earth without water unto thee.

Hear me speedily, O Lord: my spirit hath fainted away.

Turn not away thy face from me, lest I be like unto them that go down into the pit.

Cause me to hear thy mercy in the morning; for in thee have I hoped.

Make the way known to me, wherein I should walk: for I have lifted up my soul to thee.

Deliver me from my enemies, O Lord, to thee have I fled: teach me to do thy will, for thou art my God.

Thy good spirit shall lead me into the right land: for thy name's sake, O Lord, thou wilt quicken me in thy justice. Thou wilt bring my soul out of trouble: and in thy mercy thou wilt destroy my enemies.

And thou wilt cut off all them that afflict my soul
for I am thy servant.

Give ear to my supplications in thy truth: hear m
in thy justice.

And enter not into judgment with thy servant.

Thy good spirit shall lead me into the right land.

For thy name's sake, O Lord, for I am thy servant.

Glory to the Father (*complete*); Alleluia, Alleluia
Alleluia, glory to thee, O God (*three times*); our Go
and our Hope, glory to thee.

God the Lord hath appeared unto us. Blessed is h
that cometh in the Name of the Lord (*four times*).

❡ *Then the Troparion of the monthly Feast (see p. 26); or the fo
lowing daily Troparion with its Theotokion.*

TROPARIA, THEOTOKIA, AND KONTAKIA FOR WEEK-DAYS

On Sunday Evening and Monday Morning, in the Fourth Tone

O YE foremost of the heavenly hosts, we, thoug
unworthy, beseech you that by your petitions y
would encompass us with the shadow of your imma
terial glory, preserving us who kneel and cry ceas
lessly, Deliver us from oppressions since ye are th
princes of the ranks of dominions on high.

Theotokion

VERILY, Gabriel the archangel did offer his gree
ing and peace to her who was brought up in th
Temple of holiness of the saints, who is wrapped i
faith, wisdom, and blameless virginity, saying, Rejoic
O blessed one, rejoice, O glorified one, the Lord is wit
thee.

Kontakion to the Incorporals, in the Second Tone

O HEADS of the hosts of God, servants of the divir
glory, guides of human beings, and leaders of th

incorporals, intercede for that which benefiteth us, and seek for us the Great Mercy; for ye are the heads of the incorporeal hosts.

On Monday Evening and Tuesday Morning

Troparion to the Forerunner, in the Second Tone

THE memory of the righteous is in praise. And thou, Forerunner, the testimony of the Lord sufficeth thee; for in truth thou hast been revealed as nobler than all the Prophets, for having been considered worthy to baptize in running waters him who was preached. Therefore, thou didst strive for the truth happily. Thou didst proclaim to those in hades God appearing in the body, who taketh away the sin of the world, and who granteth us Great Mercy.

Theotokion

VERILY, through thee, O Theotokos of perpetual virginity, we have become partakers of thy divine Nature; for thou didst bear us an incarnate body; therefore, dutifully we all magnify thee with true worship.

Kontakion, in the Second Tone

O PROPHET of God and Forerunner of grace, we have found thy head in the earth as an all-pure rose. Wherefore, we seek from it healing at all times; for as of old thou ceasest not in the world to preach repentance.

On Tuesday and Thursday Evenings and Wednesday and Friday Mornings

Troparion, in the First Tone

O Lord, save thy people, etc. (p. 25).

Stauro-Theotokion

VERILY, we who are possessed of thine intercession, O pure one, who are delivered by thy pleadings from tribulations, and who are preserved through the Cross of thy Son at all times, do all magnify thee dutifully with true worship.

Kontakion, in the Fourth Tone

Do thou, who of thine own good will, etc. (p. 25).

ON WEDNESDAY EVENING AND THURSDAY MORNING

In the Third Tone

O holy Apostles, intercede with the merciful God to grant our souls forgiveness of sins.

Another, in the Fourth Tone

THY works of justice did show thee to thy congregation a canon of faith, the likeness of humility; wherefore, by humility thou didst achieve exaltation; and by meekness, riches. Intercede, therefore, with Christ to save our souls.

Theotokion

WE have verily known the Word of the Father— Christ our Lord, incarnate through thee, O virgin Theotokos, who alone art pure and blessed. Wherefore, we ceaselessly praise and magnify thee.

Kontakion, in the Second Tone

VERILY, O Lord, thou hast translated to bliss and the enjoyment of thy blessings, the two trustworthy preachers, theologians, and heads of thy Disciples; for thou didst accept their struggles and death as better than any sacrifice, O thou who alone knowest the secrets of our hearts.

Another Kontakion to St. Nicholas, in the Third Tone

THOU didst appear a Priest in Myra, O saint, for having fulfilled the Gospel of Christ, O righteous one; thou didst lay thyself down for thy people and rescued the innocent from death. Wherefore, thou wast sanctified as a great initiate of the grace of God.

ON FRIDAY EVENING AND SATURDAY MORNING

In the Second Tone

O YE Apostles, Martyrs, Prophets, hierarchs, saints, and righteous, who have fought the good fight and kept the faith, we beseech you, since ye have achieved favour with the Saviour, plead with him for our sake, for he is good, to save our souls.

Glory, to Those who have Passed Away

REMEMBER, Lord, thy servants; for thou art good. Forgive them all wherein they have erred in this life; for there is none without sin save thee, who art able to grant rest to the departed.

Now, to our Lady

O SAINT, Mother of the ineffable Light, in angelic praise do we honour thee, and in true worship do we magnify thee.

Kontakion, in the Eighth Tone

GIVE rest, O Christ, to the souls of thy servants who are with the saints, where there is no suffering nor sorrow, and no sighs, but immortal life.

Kontakion to the Martyrs, in the Eighth Tone

TO thee, O Lord and Author of all creation, the universe offereth as first-fruits of nature the divinity-bearing Martyrs. Wherefore, by their imploring, preserve thou thy Church in perfect safety, for the sake of the Theotokos, O most Merciful.

TROPARIA FOR SEVERAL SAINTS OF THE SAME RANK

❡*Note: To avoid repetition we have placed together below those Troparia which pertain to saints of the same rank, indicating each by a number with names of the saint monthly.*

1. *Troparion to a Martyred Saint, in the Fourth Tone*

THY Martyr, O Lord, by his struggle hath received from thee, our God, the imperishable crown; because, acquiring thy strength, he demolished usurpers and crushed the powerless might of Satan. Therefore, through his intercessions, O Christ God, save our souls.

2. *Troparion to a Martyred Saint, in the Fourth Tone*

THY Martyrs, O Lord, by their struggles have received from thee, our God, imperishable crowns; because, acquiring thy strength, they demolished usurpers and crushed the powerless might of Satan. Therefore, through their intercessions, O Christ God, save our souls.

3. *Or this, in the First Tone*

O LORD, by the sufferings of the saints, which they endured for thy sake, have compassion and heal all the sufferings of us who implore thee, who art alone the Lover of mankind.

4. *Troparion to a Woman Martyred Saint, in the Fourth Tone*

THY awe, O Jesus, doth cry unto thee with a loud voice, saying, My bride, I long for thee and in struggles seek thee. I am crucified and buried with thee in thy Baptism, and for thee I do suffer until I reign with thee. I die for thee that I may live in thee. Then as a sacrifice without blemish receive her who for thy sake was slain. Through her intercessions, therefore, since thou art merciful, save our souls.

5. *Troparion for a Martyred Priest, in the Fourth Tone*

THOU hast become like the Apostles in their states, a successor to their throne, finding indeed the intelligential ladder, O thou God-inspired. Therefore, thou hast followed the Word of God in righteousness, and striven unto blood for the Faith. O Martyr among Priests (N.   ), intercede with Christ God to save our souls.

6. *Troparion for a Righteous Saint, in the Fourth Tone*

THE barren wilderness thou didst make fertile with the streams of thy tears; and by thy deep sighing thou hast given fruit through thy struggles a hundred-fold. Accordingly, thou hast become a star for the universe, sparkling with miracles. Therefore, O righteous Father (N.   ), intercede with Christ God to save our souls.

7. *Or this, in the First Tone*

THOU didst appear making the wilderness thy home, an angel in the flesh, a doer of wonders; and by fasts, vigils, and prayers thou didst receive heavenly gifts. Therefore, thou dost heal the sick and the souls of those who hasten to thee, O God-mantled Father (N.   ). Glory to him who hath given thee power; glory to him who hath crowned thee; glory to him who through thee accomplished healing for all.

8. *Troparion to a Woman Righteous Saint, in the Eighth Tone*

THROUGH thee the divine likeness was securely preserved, O Mother (N.   ); for thou didst carry

the cross and followed Christ. By example and precept thou didst teach us to ignore the body because it
is perishable, and to attend to the concerns of the undy-
ing soul. Therefore, doth thy soul rejoice with the
angels.

9. Troparion to a Venerable Bishop, in the Fourth Tone

THY righteous acts have manifested thee to thy
flock as a model of faith, a reflection of humility,
and a teacher of abstinence, O Father Bishop (N.   ).
Therefore, through humility thou hast achieved exaltation, and through poverty, riches. Intercede thou
with Christ God to save our souls.

10. Or This, in the Eighth Tone

THOU hast shown thyself, O God-inspired (N.   ),
as a guide to the Orthodox Faith, a teacher of true
worship and purity, O star of the universe and companion of the Bishops, O wise one. Through thy light
thou hast enlightened all, O harp of the Spirit. Therefore, intercede with Christ God to save our souls.

11. Troparion to Venerable Bishops, in the Fourth Tone

O GOD of our fathers who doth always act toward
us in accordance with thy meekness, remove not
thy mercy from us, but by their intercessions guide our
lives in safety.

12. Troparion to an Apostle, in the Third Tone

O HOLY Apostle (N.   ), intercede with our merciful God to grant our souls forgiveness of sins.

¶If more than one Apostle, say, O holy Apostles, etc., with the
proper changes.

13. *Troparion to a Prophet, in the Second Tone*

VERILY, we celebrate the memory of thy Prophet (N.   ). Through him we implore thee, O Lord, save our souls.

¶ *Then say:*

IT is truly meet to bless the Theotokos who is ever blessed and all-blameless, the Mother of our God.

O thou who art more honourable than the cherubim, and beyond compare more glorious than the seraphim, who without corruption didst bear the Word of God, truly thou art the Theotokos, and thee do we magnify.

¶ *And immediately:*

THE LITTLE DOXOLOGY

THINE is the glory, our Lord and our God, and to thee do we address glory, O Father, Son, and Holy Spirit, now and ever, and unto ages of ages. Amen.

Glory to thee who hast shown us thy light. Glory to God in the highest.

Glory to God in the highest, and on earth peace, and good-will among men.

We praise thee, we bless thee, we worship thee, we glorify thee, we give thanks unto thee for the splendour of thy glory.

O Lord, O King, O heavenly God, Father Almighty, O Lord, O only-begotten Son Jesus Christ, and Holy Spirit.

O Lord God, O Lamb of God, O Son of the Father, that takest away the sins of the world, have mercy upon us, O thou that takest away the sins of the world.

Accept our prayers, O thou that sittest on the right hand of the Father, and have mercy upon us.

For thou only art holy, thou only art the Lord Jesus Christ, in the glory of God the Father.   Amen.

Every day will I bless thee and will praise thy Name for ever and ever.

O Lord, thou hast been our refuge from generation to generation. I said, Lord, have mercy upon me; heal my soul; for I have sinned against thee.

O Lord, I flee unto thee, teach me to do thy will; for thou art my God; for with thee is the Fountain of life, and in thy light we shall see light. Extend thy mercy unto those who know thee.

Vouchsafe, O Lord, to keep us this day without sin. Blessed art thou, O Lord God of our fathers, and praised and glorified is thy Name for ever. Amen.

Let thy mercy, O Lord, be upon us, as we have put our trust in thee. Blessed art thou, O Lord; teach me thy commandments. Blessed art thou, O Master; make me to understand thy statutes. Blessed art thou, O holy One; enlighten me with thy justice.

Thy mercy, O Lord, is everlasting; turn not away from the works of thy hands. To thee belongeth praise; laudation becometh thee; to thee glory is due; O Father, Son, and Holy Spirit, now and ever, and unto ages of ages. Amen.

Through the prayers of our Fathers, the saints, O Lord Jesus Christ our God, have mercy upon us. Amen.

PRAYERS AT TABLE
Prayer before Dinner

¶ Our Father, who art in heaven, *etc.* (*p. 23*); Glory to the Father (*complete*); Lord, have mercy (*three times*); *then the following prayer.*

BLESS, O Christ our Lord, the meat and drink of thy servants; for thou art holy, now and ever, and unto ages of ages.

Prayer after Dinner

BLESSED be God who is merciful to us, and provideth for us from our infancy, the Giver of good to all flesh; fill our hearts with joy and gladness, so that, as we earn our daily bread, we may increase in every good deed; through Jesus Christ our Lord, with whom and the Holy Spirit thou art worthy of glory, power, honour, and worship for, ever. Amen.

Glory to thee, O Lord; glory to thee, O holy One; glory to thee, O King; for thou hast granted us meats for pleasure: fill us also with the Spirit of thy holiness, that we may be found acceptable before thee and un-confounded when thou rewardest each one according to his own deeds.

Prayer before Supper

THE meek shall eat and be satisfied; they shall praise the Lord and those who seek him; their hearts shall live for ever.

Prayer after Supper

BLESSED be God who is merciful unto us and pro-videth for us from his abundant riches through his grace and love of mankind, now and always, and unto ages of ages. Amen.

PANAGIA

THIS is a Greek word which means *all-holy;* but it has come to be applied to a special piece of the bread of oblations cut in triangular shape, symbolizing the Holy Trinity. It is called Panagia because when the Priest lifts it up he calls for the aid of the all-holy Theotokos.

The service of lifting up the Panagia, as explained in the Big Book of Prayers (Horologion), originated, according to church tradition, in the time of the unde-filed Apostles. This is what church tradition has to say on the subject:

When our Lord and God Jesus Christ was preparing for his voluntary Passion and Death, he began to converse with his Disciples in his farewell discourse with them, as they sat at table for the Last Supper, at which he instituted the divine Sacrament of the Eucharist. Afterwards, when he rose from the dead, he appeared to his Disciples, and often blessed their tables and sat to eat with them. Thus he blessed the supper of the two Disciples who were going to Emmaus, and they recognized him when he took bread, blessed it, broke it, and gave them to eat (St. Lk. 24:13-31). On the same day Jesus appeared to the eleven Disciples and to those who were gathered in the Upper Room of Zion, and he asked them for food to eat. They gave him a piece of a broiled fish and a honeycomb. He took them and ate before them, then took that which was left and gave them to eat (St. Lk. 24:36-43). Likewise, Jesus appeared to his Disciples at the Lake of Tiberias. As they had worked hard all that night and had not been able to catch any fish, he commanded them to cast the net to the right side of the ship; and having cast it they caught a great quantity of fish. When they came to the beach they saw a stone with fish on it and bread. And Jesus came forward, took bread, and gave it to them, and he did likewise with the fish (St. Jno. 21:4-13).

The undefiled Apostles, therefore, in memory of the fact that Jesus before his voluntary Death and after it always blessed their tables and broke bread and ate with them, were accustomed to leave an empty space in the middle of the table where they placed a cushion. On this cushion they laid a piece of the bread they were eating for the Lord Jesus, as though he were present among them. When they had finished supper they would pray and give thanks, then take that piece of bread, and lift it high as they said, Glory to thee, our God, glory to thee. Glory to the Father, and to the Son, and to the Holy Spirit. Great is the Name of the Holy Trinity. The Lord is risen. These were the words they used from Easter to Ascension, and after Ascension they would say, Great is the Name of the Holy Trinity. O Lord Jesus Christ, help us. Thus did each Disciple wherever he happened to be, until they all came together at the falling asleep of the Lady Theotokos; for on the third day from her burial, when, as was their wont, they lifted up the piece of bread which is the Lord's, and were about to say, Great is the Name, behold, the virgin Theotokos, wrapped in a brilliant cloud and surrounded by radiant angels, appeared to them and said, Rejoice: I shall be with you unto the end of time.

The Disciples were greatly surprised at this wonderful appearance, and instead of saying, as they customarily did, O Lord Jesus Christ, they shouted spontaneously, O all-holy Theotokos, help us. Then they went to the tomb, and not finding her undefiled body there, they ascertained her resurrection from the dead on the third day after her burial.

This, therefore, according to tradition, is the origin of the *Lifting of the Panagia,* which is still carried out in all the monasteries of the holy mountain of Athos, and most of the monasteries of Russia, at the partaking of the dinner meal, after the Holy Mass.

This service was also performed, from time immemorial, in behalf of the health and safety of travellers by land or sea, as it is recorded in the Great Euchologia, and similarly as a service for health, safety, success, or deliverance from any sickness or affliction. On such occasions the Priest undertakes this service in the church, at the time of Matin Prayer, following the words, With songs of praise we do magnify the Theotokos and Mother of Light; or in the Divine Mass, after the Priest says, And especially for the all-holy, etc. At the conclusion of the prayer, the Priest delivers the lifted bread to those who offered the oblation. The service may be also carried out at home, when the Priest is invited to dinner, at which time he performs the

service of the Lifting of the Panagia after dinner
Here, however, instead of the Priest saying, O all-holy
Theotokos, help us, he says, O all-holy Theotokos, help
thy servant (or servants), mentioning the name or
names of those for whose benefit the service is per
formed.

The manner in which the service of the Panagia is
carried out is as follows:

After offering thanksgiving, and the recitation of the
Lord's Prayer, *Our Father, who art in heaven,* etc
for daily bread, they all get up from the table, and out
of one loaf of bread they take a triangular piece, sym
bolizing the Trinity and Oneness of the Holy Trinity
for both the three sides and the three angles indicat
the Trinity of the Holy Trinity, and each corner or
angle indicates its Oneness. Thus whichever way you
turn the piece of bread you find it with three angles
and this ends in a sharp point. This piece of bread
which the Fathers received by an unwritten apostolic
transmission, we offer unto the one God in the Trinity
in the name of the Theotokos, through whose divine
birthgiving we came to know the Holy Trinity, and the
one God in the Trinity.

It is placed in a special receptacle, and after the
Priest seals it with the sign of the cross, those present
light a lamp which they place in front of it. Then
after the usual saying of grace and dinner is over, one
of the Priests, chosen for this purpose, having first
sought permission of the brethren, lifts the piece of
bread, crying, Great is the Name, and the rest respond
Of the Holy Trinity. Then the Priest makes the sign
of the cross in the air with the bread, saying, O all-
holy Theotokos, help us. And all shout in unison
Through her intercessions, O God, have mercy upon
us and save us. Then immediately they sing to the
Theotokos, All generations bless thee, etc; Rejoice, O
Theotokos, Virgin Mary, full of grace, the Lord be
with thee, etc.; and It is meet, etc.

This piece of bread, therefore, because of the calling of the Name of the most Holy Trinity over it, and the making of the sign of the cross at the beginning of the service, and because through it we seek the aid of the Theotokos, is highly effective, in that it delivers us from all afflictions, fills us with blessings, and saves us at all times. And because of this, St. Simeon the Thessalonian proposed the performance of this service daily in all the churches, after the Ninth Ode in the Matin Prayer.

PRAYERS OF THE PARACLETICE

A Petition to the Theotokos, Sung at Every Catas-trophe and Affliction. Composed by Theostrictus, the Monk, or, according to some, Theophanius.

Priest. Blessed be God our God, always, now, and ever, and unto ages of ages.
Lector. Amen.

❡ *Then he repeateth Psalm 142.*

Hear, O Lord, my prayer, etc. (p. 31).
Choir. God the Lord hath appeared unto us. Blessed is he that cometh in the Name of the Lord *(four times).*

❡ *Then the following Troparia, in the Fourth Tone.*

TO the Theotokos let us, miserable, wretched sinners, hasten, and fall down before her in repentance from the depth of our soul. Succour us, O Lady, and have compassion on us. Hasten; for we have perished from the multitude of our sins. Turn not thy servants away in despair; for thou alone art a hope unto us.

❡ *Glory (repeated); and Now, in the Same Tone.*

O THEOTOKOS, we refrain not from talking of thy great deeds, though we are unworthy; for hadst thou not risen to intercede for us, who then would have delivered us from such tribulations and anxieties? Who would have kept us free until now? We shall not depart from thee, O Lady; for thou ever savest thy servants from divers tribulations.

❧ *The Lector reciteth Psalm 50 (p. 82); after which the Choir beginneth the following Canon, in the Eighth Tone and with each section of Troparia saith:*

O most holy Theotokos, save us.[1]

First Ode

VERILY, the people of Israel passed over the wet as on dry land, fleeing Egyptian misery; and they shouted, saying, Let us praise our Deliverer and God.

Sundry temptations have encompassed us, O Virgin. In thee do we seek refuge before seeking salvation. Therefore, O Mother of the Word, deliver us from our difficulties and oppressions.

The shocks of suffering, O Maiden, trouble us exceedingly, and our souls are filled with deep sorrow. Deliver us, therefore, into the tranquility of thy Son and God, O blameless one.

Since thou hast given birth, O Virgin to our God and Saviour, we beseech thee to deliver us from all mishaps; for in thee do we seek refuge, and towards thee do we stretch our soul and mind.

O thou alone, Theotokos, didst give birth to the good and righteous One; for thou art righteous. Make us who are sick in soul and body worthy of the divine covenant, and of providence from thee.

Third Ode

O LORD, Uplifter of the heavenly canopy and Builder of thy Church, establish thou me in thy love, O End of all desire, and Constancy of believers, O thou alone the Lover of mankind.

O virgin Theotokos, we have made thee an intercessor and protector of our lives. Direct us and lead us

---

[1] Save us through thine intercession with thy Son our God.

to thy haven, O thou cause of all good things, and the constancy of believers, O thou who art all-praised.

We beseech thee, O Virgin, to disperse in us all inward agitation, and every tempest of grief; for thou, O bride of God, didst give birth to Christ, the Essence of tranquility, O thou who alone art all-pure.

O thou who didst give birth to the Benefactor, the Cause of all good things, cause to spring forth for us all the riches of liberality and beneficence; for thou art capable of all that thou desirest, since thou didst give birth to Christ, mighty in power, O thou blessed of God.

We are visited, O Virgin, with pressing ills and distressing sufferings. Help us; for we know, O blameless one, that thou art a treasury of healing, never-failing and imperishable.

Deliver thy servants from tribulation, O Theotokos; for to thee, after God, we go for refuge, since thou art an impregnable fortress and an intercessor.

Turn with compassion, O all-praised Theotokos, to the wretchedness of our bodies, and heal the pains of our souls.

Deacon. Have mercy on us, O God, according to the multitude of thy tender mercies, we beseech thee. Answer, and have mercy.

Choir. Lord, have mercy (*three times*).

Deacon. Again we ask mercy, life, safety, health, and salvation for the servant of God (*here mention the name of him for whom petition is made*), to visit him, pardon him, and forgive him his sins.

Choir. Lord, have mercy (*twelve times*).

Priest. For thou art a merciful and philanthropic God, and to thee do we address glory, O Father, etc.

Choir. Amen.

❡ *And immediately the following Kathisma, in the Second Tone.*

O FERVID intercessor and unconquerable wall, O fount of mercies, and refuge of the world, to thee do we shout always, O Lady Theotokos. Lay hold on us, and deliver us from tribulations, O thou alone of swift intercession.

Fourth Ode

I HAVE heard, O Lord, of the mystery of thy dispensation, and have contemplated thy works, therefore have I glorified thy Godhead.

Soothe the agitation of our sufferings and calm the tempest of our sins, O thou bride of God, who didst give birth to the ordaining Lord.

O thou who didst give birth to the Compassionate, the Saviour of all who praise thee, grant us, we beseech thee, the depth of thy mercy.

Having enjoyed thy gifts, O all immaculate one, we who know that thou art the Theotokos sing to thee a song of praise.

Having possessed thee, O all-praised one, a hope and constancy, a wall of salvation unshaken, we are delivered by thee from trials.

Fifth Ode

ILLUMINATE us with thy commands, O Lord, and with thy high arm grant us thy peace, O Lover of mankind.

Fill our hearts, O pure one, with happiness, granting us, O thou who didst give birth to the Cause of happiness and joy, thine incorruptible joy.

O undefiled Theotokos, who didst give birth to eternal Redemption and Safety, surpassing all intelligence, deliver us from tribulation.

O thou who art a bride of God, who didst give birth to the divine Light before the ages, disperse the darkness, and grant us joy, thine incorruptible joy.

O pure one, heal the ills of our souls, preparing us for thy visitation, and grant us health through thine intercession.

Sixth Ode

BEFORE the Lord do I pour out mine invocation; and my sorrows before him do I tell; for my soul is filled with iniquities, and my life has drawn near to hades. With thee, therefore, do I plead, as Jonah, shouting, Raise me from corruption, O my God.

Beseech, O Virgin, thy Lord and Son, who by delivering himself to death saved our death-ridden and corrupt nature from death and corruption, that he may deliver me from the harm of evil enemies.

Thee do we know, O Virgin, as an intercessor for our lives, a sound protection, remover of diverse temptations, and repudiator of the devil's cunning wiles. We beseech thee always to deliver us from the corruption of our sufferings.

We have possessed thee, O Maiden, a wall of refuge, a full salvation for our souls, and a relief from our distresses. In thy light do we ever rejoice. Therefore, O Lady, deliver us now from tribulations and sufferings.

On a bed of ills are we now thrown, and there is no healing for our bodies. Wherefore, O thou who didst give birth to God, the Saviour of the world, and the Remover of ills, we beseech thee, O righteous one, to lift us from the corruption of ills.

Deliver thy servants from tribulations, O Theotokos; for we all, after God, seek refuge in thee, since thou art an impregnable fortress and an intercessor.

O pure one, who by a word didst give birth to the Word ineffably, plead with him; for thou hast the privilege of motherhood.

❡*And the Priest here repeateth the above, after the Third Ode. Then, after the Exclamation, the Choir singeth the following Kontakion, in the Second Tone.*

O UNDISPUTED intercessor of Christians, the unrejected mediatrix with the Creator, turn not away from the voice of our petitions who are sinners.

Come while there is time to us who cry to thee in faith, with assistance; for thou art good. Hasten to us with intercession, O Theotokos, who dost ever intercede for those who honour thee.

❧ *Then the First Antiphony of the Anabathmoi, in the Fourth Tone.*

FROM my youth many afflictions have fought against me. But thou, my Saviour, assist and save me (*two times*).

O ye haters of Zion, depart in shame from before the Lord; for ye shall be dry by fire as the grass.

Glory to the Father, and to the Son, and to the Holy Spirit.

By the Holy Spirit every soul liveth, and shall be purified, ascending, resplendent in the one Trinity, in an exalted and mysterious manner.

Now, and ever, and unto ages of ages. Amen.

By the Holy Spirit the streams and conduits of grace overflow, watering all creation with invigorating life.

❧ *And immediately the following Prokeimenon.*

I shall proclaim thy Name from generation to generation.

Stichos: Hearken, O daughter, and see, and incline thine ear; forget also thine own people and thy Father's house; and the king shall greatly desire thy beauty.

❧ *Then the Priest readeth the following.*

The Gospel: from St. Luke (1:39-56)

AND Mary arose in those days; and went into the hill country with haste into a city of Juda.

And entered into the house of Zacharias, and saluted Elisabeth.

And it came to pass, that, when Elisabeth heard the salutation of Mary, the babe leaped in her womb; and Elisabeth was filled with the Holy Ghost:

And she spake out with a loud voice, and said, Blessed art thou among women, and blessed is the fruit of thy womb.

And whence is this to me, that the mother of my Lord should come to me?

For, lo, as soon as the voice of thy salutation sounded in mine ears, the babe leaped in my womb for joy.

And blessed is she that believed: for there shall be a performance of those things which were told her from the Lord.

And Mary said, My soul doth magnify the Lord.

And my spirit hath rejoiced in God my Saviour.

For he hath regarded the low estate of his handmaiden: for, behold, from henceforth all generations shall call me blessed.

For he that is mighty hath done to me great things; and holy is his name.

And his mercy is on them that fear him from generation to generation.

He hath showed strength with his arm; he hath scattered the proud in the imagination of their hearts.

He hath put down the mighty from their seats, and exalted them of low degree.

He hath filled the hungry with good things; and the rich he hath sent empty away.

He hath received his servant Israel, being mindful of his mercy.

And he spake to our fathers, to Abraham, and to his seed for ever.

And Mary abode with her about three months, and returned to her own house.

Choir. Glory to thee, O Lord, glory to thee.

❡ *Then immediately is sung Glory, in the Second Tone.*

O FATHER, the Word, and the Spirit, the Trinity in Oneness, blot out the multitude of our sins and transgressions.

Now: Through the intercessions of the Theotokos and her entreaties, O merciful One, blot out our sins and transgressions.

Then: O merciful One, have mercy upon me, O God, according to thy great mercy. And according to the multitude of thy tender mercies blot out mine iniquity.

❡ *Then immediately, in the Sixth Tone.*

O MOST holy Lady, refer us not to human intercession, but receive our supplications, who are thy servants; for we are in distress and sorrow. We are unable to bear the darts of Satan. We are without shelter, and know not where to seek for refuge, being wretched and assailed on every side. We have no solace save in thee. Wherefore, O Lady of the world, O hope and intercession of believers, turn not away from our petitions, but perform that which profiteth us.

Verily, no one hasteneth to thee, and goeth away confounded, O pure virgin Theotokos, but seeketh grace and receiveth gifts in accordance with his petition.

O virgin Theotokos, thou art the solace of the distressed, the healer of the sick. Deliver thou therefore thy people and thy city, O safety of those who are attacked, O haven and calm of those encompassed by rain, who art alone the intercessor of believers.

Deacon. O God, save thy people, and bless thine inheritance. Visit thy world with mercy and compassion, and exalt the condition of the Orthodox Christians. Send upon us thy rich mercies through the intercessions of the most pure Theotokos of God, the ever-virgin Mary, and by the power of the precious and enlivening Cross, and through the petitions of the honoured and incorporeal heavenly powers, and through the beseechings of the honoured Prophet, the glorious Forerunner, John the Baptist, and of the honoured saints, of the all-praised Apostles, and of our fathers, the saints, of the teachers

of the world, the magnified chiefs of Priests, Basil the
Great, Gregory Theologus, John Chrysostom, of our
Father Saint Nicholas, the Archbishop of Myra, the
Thaumaturge, of the two righteous saints, grand-par-
ents of Christ God, Joachim and Anne, thy saint (N.
in whose name the day is observed), and of all thy
saints, we beseech thee, O Lord, abundant in mercies,
hear the prayers of us sinners, and have mercy upon us.

Choir. Lord, have mercy (*twelve times*).

Priest. By the mercy, compassion, and philanthropy
of thine only Son, with whom thine all-holy, the good
and life-giving Spirit, thou art blessed, now, etc.

Choir. Amen.

❡ *Then immediately begin singing the following.*

Seventh Ode

VERILY, when the youths from Judæa came to
Babylon of olden times, they trod the flames of the
furnace in the faith of the Trinity, singing, Blessed art
thou, God of our fathers.

When thou didst deign to institute our salvation, thou
didst dwell in the womb of the Virgin, whom thou
didst reveal as an intercessor for the world. Blessed
art thou, therefore, O God of our fathers.

Pray, O pure Mother, thy mercy-bound Son, to
whom thou didst give birth, to deliver from transgressions and impurities the souls of those who cry in faith,
Blessed art thou, God of our fathers.

A treasury of salvation, a fount of incorruption, a
fortified tower, a door of repentance, thou didst reveal
thy Mother to those who cry unto thee, Blessed art thou,
God of our Fathers.

O Theotokos, who didst give birth to Christ the Saviour, prepare us who hasten anxiously to the wing of
thy divine protection, for healing from the ills of body
and soul.

Eighth Ode

PRAISE the King of the heavens, whom the hosts of angels praise; exalt him yet more throughout the ages.

Turn not away, O virgin Maiden, from those who seek succour of thee, who praise and exalt thee throughout the ages.

Thou dost pour, O Virgin, thy healing abundantly on those who praise thee in faith, adding exaltation to thine ineffable birth-giving.

Thou dost heal, O Virgin, the ills of our souls and the pains of our bodies. Wherefore, do we glorify thee, O full of grace.

Thou dost drive away from us, O Virgin, the attacks of temptation, and the sources of passion. Wherefore, we praise thee throughout the ages.

Ninth Ode

WE, O immaculate Virgin, who have been saved through thee, do confess that thou art the Theotokos in truth, and magnify thee with the chorus of the incorporals.

Refuse not, O Virgin, the stream of our tears, O thou who didst give birth to Christ, who wiped from all faces every tear.

Fill, O Virgin, our hearts with joy, O thou who didst receive the fullness of joy, and remove from us the sorrow of sin.

Be thou, O Virgin, to those who seek refuge in thee, a haven, a protection, an unshakeable wall, a refuge, a shelter, and a joy.

Illuminate, O Virgin, with the rays of thy light those who proclaim in true worship that thou art the Theotokos. Put away from them the darkness of folly.

Having abased ourselves, O Virgin, in the home of wretchedness and ills, heal us, translating us from afflictions to health.

¶ Then, It is truly meet to bless, *etc.; and the following hymns, in the Eighth Tone.*

O THOU who art more exalted than the heavens, and more resplendent than the solar lamps, who hast delivered us from the curse, mistress of the world, thee in songs do we honour.

O thou who art full of grace, because of the multitude of our sins our bodies have sickened and our souls are weakened. To thee, therefore, do we come for refuge; O hope of the hopeless, help thou us.

Receive, O Lady, Mother of the Redeemer, the supplications of thine undeserving servants, that thou mayest mediate with him that was born of thee. O Lady, be thou a mediatrix for us.

We sing to thee with zeal and rejoicing a song of praise, O all-praised Theotokos. Plead with the Forerunner and all the saints, that they may be merciful unto us.

Let the lips of the liars be sealed, who worship not thy honoured icon, which was painted by the most pure Evangelist Luke, and by which we were converted.

O company of angels, O Forerunner of the Lord, the twelve Disciples, and all the saints, raise petitions with the Theotokos for our delivery and salvation.

Lector. Holy God, etc.

¶ Then after the Exclamation from the Priest, the following Troaria are sung in the Sixth Tone.

HAVE mercy upon us, O Lord, have mercy upon us; for, destitute of all defence, we sinners offer unto thee, O Master, this supplication, Have mercy upon us.

Glory

HAVE mercy upon us, O Lord; for in thee have we put our trust. Be not exceedingly wroth with us, nor remember our iniquities, but look upon us now again; for thou art compassionate, and deliver us from our enemies; for thou art our God and we are thy peo-

ple. We all are the work of thy hands, and we have
called upon thy Name.

Now

OPEN unto us the door of thy compassion, O blessed
Theotokos, that, as we hope in thee, we may not
fail in our petitions. May we be delivered through
thee from adversities; for through thee hath come the
salvation of the Christian race.

*❡ The Priest reciteth what followeth the Third Ode. And after the
Exclamation the Choir singeth the following Troparia, in the Second
Tone.*

O MOTHER of the high God, O righteous one,
defend all those who seek refuge in faith, in thy
dear shelter; for we sinners, bowed with the multitude
of iniquities, have no other constant mediator with God
in the time of tribulation and sorrow, save thee. Wherefore, we fall down before thee adoring. Deliver thy
servants from every tribulation.

Thou art the joy of all who are sad, the defender of
the oppressed, the nourishment of the wretched, the
consolation of strangers, staff of the blind, the visitation
of the sick, the shelter and succour of the defeated, the
help of orphans. Wherefore, O Mother of the high
God, O immaculate one, we beseech thee, hasten thou
to the deliverance of thy servants.

In the Eighth Tone

Receive the petitions of thy servants, O Lady, and
deliver us from every tribulation and sorrow.

In the Second Tone

All my hope I place in thee, O Theotokos. Keep me
under the wing of thy care.

❡ Then the Priest pronounceth the closing prayer.

NINTH HOUR

❡ *The Priest, standing before the Royal Door, maketh the sign of the cross three times, and saith in an audible voice:*

Blessed be God, our God, always, now, and ever, and unto ages of ages.

Choir. Amen.

Priest. Glory to thee, our God; glory to thee. O heavenly King, etc. (p. 23).

Lector. Holy God (*complete*, p. 23).

Priest. For thine is the kingdom, etc.

Lector. Amen. Lord, have mercy (*twelve times*). Glory to the Father (*complete*).

O come, let us worship and fall down to our King and God.

O come, let us worship and fall down to Christ our King and God.

O come, let us worship and fall down to Christ. He is our King and God (*with three reverences*).

❡ *And the following Psalms.*

PSALM 83

HOW lovely are thy tabernacles, O Lord of hosts! My soul longeth and fainteth for the courts of the Lord. My heart and my flesh have rejoiced in the living God.

For the sparrow hath found herself a house, and the turtle a nest for herself where she may lay her young ones: Thy altars, O Lord of hosts, my king and my God.

Blessed are they that dwell in thy house, O Lord: they shall praise thee for ever and ever.

Blessed is the man whose help is from thee: in his heart he hath disposed to ascend by steps, in the vale of tears, in the place which he hath set.

For the lawgiver shall give a blessing, they shall go from virtue to virtue: the God of gods shall be seen in Sion.

O Lord God of hosts, hear my prayer: give ear, O God of Jacob.

Behold, O God our protector: and look on the face of thy Christ.

For better is one day in thy courts above thousands.

I have chosen to be an abject in the house of my God, rather than to dwell in the tabernacles of sinners.

For God loveth mercy and truth: the Lord will give grace and glory.

He will not deprive of good things them that walk in innocence: O Lord of hosts, blessed is the man that trusteth in thee.

Psalm 84

LORD, thou hast blessed thy land: thou hast turned away the captivity of Jacob.

Thou hast forgiven the iniquity of thy people: thou hast covered all their sins.

Thou hast mitigated all thy anger: thou hast turned away from the wrath of thy indignation.

Convert us, O God our Saviour: and turn off thy anger from us.

Wilt thou be angry with us for ever: or wilt thou extend thy wrath from generation to generation?

Thou wilt turn, O God, and bring us to life: and thy people shall rejoice in thee.

Shew us, O Lord, thy mercy; and grant us thy salvation.

I will hear what the Lord God will speak in me: for he will speak peace unto his people:

And unto his saints; and unto them that are converted to the heart.

Surely his salvation is near to them that fear him: that glory may dwell in our land.

Mercy and truth have met each other: justice and peace have kissed.

Truth is sprung out of the earth: and justice hath looked down from heaven.

For the Lord will give goodness: and our earth shall yield her fruit.

Justice shall walk before him: and shall set his steps in the way.

PSALM 85

INCLINE thy ear, O Lord, and hear me: for I am needy and poor.

Preserve my soul, for I am holy: save thy servant, O my God, that trusteth in thee.

Have mercy on me, O Lord, for I have cried to thee all the day. Give joy to the soul of thy servant, for to thee, O Lord, I have lifted up my soul.

For thou, O Lord, art sweet and mild: and plenteous in mercy to all that call upon thee.

Give ear, O Lord, to my prayer: and attend to the voice of my petition.

I have called upon thee in the day of my trouble: because thou hast heard me.

There is none among the gods like unto thee, O Lord: and there is none according to thy works.

All the nations thou hast made shall come and adore before thee, O Lord: and they shall glorify thy name.

For thou art great and doest wonderful things: thou art God alone.

Conduct me, O Lord, in thy way, and I will walk in thy truth: let my heart rejoice that it may fear thy name.

I will praise thee, O Lord my God, with my whole heart, and I will glorify thy name for ever:

For thy mercy is great towards me: and thou hast delivered my soul out of the lower hell.

O God, the wicked are risen up against me, and the assembly of the mighty have sought my soul: and they have not set thee before their eyes.

And thou, O Lord, art a God of compassion, and merciful, patient, and of much mercy, and true.

O look upon me, and have mercy on me: give thy

command to thy servant, and save the son of thy hand
maid.

Shew me a token for good: that they who hate m
may see, and be confounded, because thou, O Lord, ha
helped me and hast comforted me.

Glory to the Father (*complete*).

Alleluia! Allelulia! Allelulia! Glory to thee,
God. Lord, have mercy (*three times*); Glory, etc.

¶ Then say the Troparion of the Saint of the day, if any (p. 36
otherwise the Troparion of the week (p. 32); then, Now, etc.

THOU, O good One, who for our sake wast bor
of a Virgin, and didst suffer crucifixion, and did
despoil death through thy Death, and as God did
reveal resurrection; despise not those whom thou ha
created with thine own hand; show forth thy love f
mankind, O merciful One; accept the intercession
thy Mother the Theotokos for us, and save thy despai
ing people, O our Saviour.

Forsake us not utterly, for thy holy Name's sake; an
destroy not thy covenant. Take not thy mercies fro
us, for the sake of Abraham beloved of thee, and f
the sake of Isaac thy servant, and of Israel thy holy on

Holy God, etc.

¶ Then the Kontakion of the Saint of the day (p. 36); or the week
Kontakion (p. 32); and immediately, Lord, have mercy (forty times
and the following Prayer.

O CHRIST our God, who art worshipped and glor
fied at all times at every hour both in heaven ar
on earth; who art long-suffering and plenteous in merc
and compassion; who lovest the just man and showe
mercy upon the sinner; and who callest all men
repentance through the promise of blessings to com
receive, O Lord, at this very hour our supplicatior
and direct our lives in the way of thy commandment
sanctify our souls: purify our bodies: set our min
aright: cleanse our thoughts: deliver us from all affli

tion, trouble, and distress; compass us about with thy holy angels, that, guided and guarded by thy hosts, we may attain unto the unity of the Faith, and to the knowledge of thine unapproachable glory; for thou art blessed unto ages of ages. Amen.

¶ Lord, have mercy *(three times)*; Glory to the Father *(complete)*; O thou who art more honourable, *etc.* *(p. 39)*; and, Bless, O Father, in the Name of the Lord.

Priest. God be merciful unto us and bless us, and cause his face to shine upon us, and be merciful unto us.

¶ *The Lector or Archpriest shall say the following Prayer of St. Basil.*

O MASTER, Lord Jesus Christ our God, who art patient with our sins, and who hast brought us even to the present hour, in the which, as thou didst hang upon the life-giving Tree thou didst make a way into paradise for the penitent thief, and by Death didst destroy death, cleanse us sinners, thine unworthy servants; for we have sinned and have dealt iniquitously, and we are not worthy to lift up our eyes and look upon the heights of heaven, inasmuch as we have departed from the path of thy righteousness, and have walked after the desires of our own hearts. But we implore thy boundless goodness. Spare us, O Lord, according to the multitude of thy mercies, and save us, for thy holy Name's sake; for our days have passed away in vanity. Wrest us from the hand of the adversary, and forgive us our sins, and mortify in us carnal imagination; that, putting off the old man, we may be clothed upon with the new man, and may live unto thee, our Master and Benefactor; that, following after thy commandments, we may attain unto rest eternal, where is the abode of all those who rejoice; for thou art in verity the true Joy and Exultation of those who love thee, O Christ our God, and unto thee we address glory, together with the Father, who is without beginning, and

thine all-holy, good, and life-giving Spirit, now and
ever, and unto ages of ages. Amen.

SPECIAL VESPER PRAYERS

❡ *If it is not a Sunday or a Feast Day, the daily Sunset Prayer is
restricted to* Holy God, *etc.* (*p. 23*); O come, let us worship, etc
(*three times*); *the Sunset Psalm 103,* Bless the Lord, O my soul, etc
(*below*); Glory to the Father (*complete*); Alleluia (*three times*)
Our God and our Hope, Glory to thee. *Then Psalms 140, 141, 129
and 116* (*pp.. 72-74*); *then,* Glory to the Father (*complete*); *and,* C
resplendent Light, *etc.* (*p. 74*); Vouchsafe, O Lord, *etc.* (*p. 76*); *and*
Holy God, *etc. Then the Troparion of the day with its Theotokion*
(*p. 32*); *and,* Through the prayers of our fathers, the saints, O Lord
Jesus Christ our God, have mercy upon us and save us. Amen.

THE GENERAL VESPER PRAYERS

❡ *The Priest, standing before the Holy Table and wearing the Stole
maketh the sign of the cross three times, and saith secretly,* O God
forgive me a sinner. *Then aloud:*

BLESSED be God, our God, always, now, and ever,
and unto ages of ages.

Lector. Amen. O come, let us worship and fall down
to our King and God.

O come, let us worship and fall down to Christ our
King and God.

O come, let us worship and fall down to Christ. He
is our King and God (*with three reverences*).

❡ *Then immediately the following Vesper Psalms.*

Psalm 103

BLESS the Lord, O my soul: O Lord my God, thou
art exceedingly great. Thou hast put on praise and
beauty: and art clothed with light as with a garment.

Who stretchest out the heaven like a pavilion: who
coverest the higher rooms thereof with water.

Who makest the clouds thy chariot: who walkest
upon the wings of the winds.

Who makest thy angels spirits: and thy ministers a
burning fire.

Who hast founded the earth upon its own bases: it
shall not be moved for ever and ever.

The deep like a garment is its clothing: above the
mountains shall the waters stand.

At thy rebuke they shall flee: at the voice of thy
thunder they shall fear.

The mountains ascend, and the plains descend into
the place which thou hast founded for them.

Thou hast set a bound which they shall not pass over;
neither shall they return to cover the earth.

Thou sendest forth springs in the vales: between the
midst of the hills the waters shall pass.

All the beasts of the field shall drink: the wild asses
shall expect in their thirst.

Over them the birds of the air shall dwell: from the
midst of the rocks they shall give forth their voices.

Thou waterest the hills from thy upper rooms: the
earth shall be filled with the fruit of thy works:

Bringing forth grass for cattle, and herb for the
service of men.

That thou mayest bring bread out of the earth: and
that wine may cheer the heart of man.

That he may make the face cheerful with oil: and
that bread may strengthen man's heart.

The trees of the field shall be filled, and the cedars
of Libanus which he hath planted: there the sparrows
shall make their nests.

The highest of them is the house of the heron. The
high hills are a refuge for the harts, the rock for the
urchins.

He hath made the moon for seasons: the sun knoweth
his going down.

Thou hast appointed darkness, and it is night: in it
shall all the beasts of the woods go about:

The young lions roaring after their prey, and seeking their meat from God.

The sun ariseth, and they are gathered together: and they shall lie down in their dens.

Man shall go forth to his work, and to his labour until the evening.

How great are thy works, O Lord! thou hast made all things in wisdom: The earth is filled with thy riches

So is this great sea, which stretcheth wide its arms there are creeping things without number:

Creatures little and great. There the ships shall go

This sea-dragon which thou hast formed to play therein. All expect of thee that thou give them food in season.

What thou givest to them they shall gather up: when thou openest thy hand, they shall all be filled with good

But if thou turnest away thy face, they shall be troubled: thou shalt take away their breath, and they shall fail, and shall return to their dust.

Thou shalt send forth thy spirit, and they shall be created: and thou shalt renew the face of the earth.

May the glory of the Lord endure for ever: the Lord shall rejoice in his works.

He looketh upon the earth, and maketh it tremble he toucheth the mountains, and they smoke.

I will sing to the Lord as long as I live: I will sing praise to my God while I have my being.

Let my speech be acceptable to him: but I will take delight in the Lord.

Let sinners be consumed out of the earth, and the unjust, so that they be no more: O my soul, bless thou the Lord.

The sun knoweth his going down. Thou hast appointed darkness, and it is night.

How great are thy works, O Lord! Thou hast made all things in wisdom.

Glory to the Father (*complete*). Alleluia! Alleluia

Alleluia! Glory to thee, O God (*three times*). O our God and our Hope, glory to thee.

¶*Then immediately the Deacon or Priest maketh the following Peace Petitions (Great Synapte), and the Choir chanteth after each,* Lord, have mercy.

IN peace let us pray to the Lord.

For the peace that is from above, and for the salvation of our souls, let us pray to the Lord.

For the peace of the whole world, the welfare of God's holy churches, and the union of them all, let us pray to the Lord.

For this holy house and for those who enter herein with faith, reverence, and godly fear, let us pray to the Lord.

For our Patriarch, our Archbishop (N.   ), for the honourable Presbytery, the Diaconate in Christ, all the Clergy, and the laity, let us pray to the Lord.

For our divinely protected kings of true worship, all of their palaces, and their armies, let us pray to the Lord.

For their help in war, and for the subjugation of every enemy and adversary beneath their feet, let us pray to the Lord.

For this holy city (*or monastery*), for every city and country, and for the faithful who dwell therein, let us pray to the Lord.

For good weather, for an abundance of the fruits of the earth, and for peaceful seasons, let us pray to the Lord.

For the sake of those that travel by sea and land, the sick, the suffering, and prisoners, and for their salvation, let us pray to the Lord.

For our deliverance from all affliction, wrath, anger, and depression, let us pray to the Lord.

Help, save, have mercy, and keep us, O God, by thy grace.

Remembering our all-holy, spotless, most highly blessed, and glorious Lady, the Theotokos, and ever-virgin Mary, and all the saints, let us commend ourselves, and each other, and all our life to Christ our God.

Choir. To thee, O Lord.

Priest. For all glory, honour, and worship are due to thee, O Father, etc.

Choir. Amen.

❡ *Then immediately the Lector readeth from the First Kathisma of the Psalms, as followeth.*

PSALM 1

BLESSED is the man who hath not walked in the counsel of the ungodly, nor stood in the way of sinners, nor sat in the chair of pestilence.

But his will is in the law of the Lord, and on his law he shall meditate day and night.

And he shall be like a tree which is planted near the running waters, which shall bring forth its fruit, in due season.

And his leaf shall not fall off: and all whatsoever he shall do shall prosper.

Not so the wicked, not so: but like the dust, which the wind driveth from the face of the earth.

Therefore the wicked shall not rise again in judgment: nor sinners in the council of the just.

For the Lord knoweth the way of the just: and the way of the wicked shall perish.

PSALM 2

WHY have the Gentiles raged, and the people devised vain things?

The kings of the earth stood up, and the princes met together, against the Lord, and against his Christ.

Let us break their bonds asunder: and let us cast away their yoke from us.

He that dwelleth in heaven shall laugh at them: and

the Lord shall deride them.

Then shall he speak to them in his anger, and trouble them in his rage.

But I am appointed king by him over Sion his holy mountain, preaching his commandment.

The Lord hath said to me: Thou art my son, this day have I begotten thee.

Ask of me, and I will give thee the Gentiles for thy inheritance, and the utmost parts of the earth for thy possession.

Thou shalt rule them with a rod of iron, and shalt break them in pieces like a potter's vessel.

And now, O ye kings, understand: receive instruction, you that judge the earth.

Serve ye the Lord with fear: and rejoice unto him with trembling.

Embrace discipline, lest at any time the Lord be angry, and you perish from the just way.

When his wrath shall be kindled in a short time, blessed are all they that trust in him.

PSALM 3

WHY, O Lord, are they multiplied that afflict me? many are they who rise up against me.

Many say to my soul: There is no salvation for him in his God.

But thou, O Lord, art my protector, my glory, and the lifter up of my head.

I have cried to the Lord with my voice: and he hath heard me from his holy hill.

I have slept and have taken my rest; and I have risen up, because the Lord hath protected me.

I will not fear thousands of the people, surrounding me. Arise, O Lord; save me O my God.

For thou hast struck all them who are my adversaries without cause. Thou hast broken the teeth of sinners.

Salvation is of the Lord, and thy blessing is upon thy people.

¶ Glory to the Father *(complete)*; Allelulia *(three times)*; Glory t
thee, O God; Lord, have mercy *(three times)*; *and* Glory to th
Father *(complete)*.

Psalm 4

WHEN I called upon him, the God of my justic
heard me. When I was in distress, thou hast en
larged me. Have mercy on me, and hear my prayer

O ye sons of men, how long will you be dull of heart
why do you love vanity, and seek after lying?

Know ye also that the Lord hath made his holy on
wonderful: the Lord will hear me when I shall cr
unto him.

Be ye angry, and sin not: the things you say in you
hearts, be sorry for them upon your beds.

Offer up the sacrifice of justice, and trust in the Lord
many say, Who sheweth us good things?

The light of thy countenance, O Lord, is signed upo
us: thou hast given gladness in my heart.

By the fruit of their corn, their wine, and oil, the
are multiplied.

In peace in the selfsame I will sleep and I will rest

For thou, O Lord, singularly hast settled me in hope

Psalm 5

GIVE ear, O Lord, to my words, understand my cry
Hearken to the voice of my prayer, O my Kin
and my God.

For to thee will I pray: O Lord, in the morning tho
shalt hear my voice.

In the morning I will stand before thee, and wil
see: because thou art not a God that willest iniquity.

Neither shall the wicked dwell near thee: nor shall
the unjust abide before thy eyes.

Thou hatest all the workers of iniquity: thou wil
destroy all that speak a lie.

The bloody and the deceitful man the Lord wil
abhor.

But as for me in the multitude of thy mercy,

I will come into thy house; I will worship towards thy holy temple, in thy fear.

Conduct me, O Lord, in thy justice: because of my enemies, direct my way in thy sight.

For there is no truth in their mouth: their heart is vain.

Their throat is an open sepulchre. They dealt deceitfully with their tongues; judge them, O God.

Let them fall from their devices: according to the multitude of their wickednesses cast them out: for they have provoked thee, O Lord.

But let all them be glad that hope in thee: they shall rejoice for ever, and thou shalt dwell in them.

And all they that love thy name shall glory in thee: For thou wilt bless the just.

O Lord, thou hast crowned us as with a shield of thy good will.

[Glory to the Father *(complete)*; Alleluia *(three times)*; Glory to thee, O God; Lord, have mercy *(three times); and* Glory to the father *(complete)*.

PSALM 6

O LORD, rebuke me not in thy indignation, nor chastise me in thy wrath.

Have mercy on me, O Lord, for I am weak: heal me, O Lord, for my bones are troubled.

And my soul is troubled exceedingly: but thou, O Lord, how long?

Turn to me, O Lord, and deliver my soul: O save me for thy mercy's sake.

For there is no one in death, that is mindful of thee: and who shall confess to thee in hell?

I have laboured in my groanings, every night I will wash my bed: I will water my couch with my tears.

My eye is troubled through indignation: I have grown old amongst all my enemies.

Depart from me, all ye workers of iniquity: for the Lord hath heard the voice of my weeping.

The Lord hath heard my supplication: the Lord hath received my prayer.

Let all my enemies be ashamed, and be very much troubled: let them be turned back, and be ashamed very speedily.

PSALM 7

O LORD my God, in thee have I put my trust: save me from all them that persecute me, and deliver me.

Lest at any time he seize upon my soul like a lion, while there is no one to redeem me, nor to save.

O Lord my God, if I have done this thing, if there be iniquity in my hands:

If I have rendered to them that repaid me evils, let me deservedly fall empty before my enemies.

Let the enemy pursue my soul, and take it, and tread down my life on the earth, and bring down my glory to the dust.

Rise up, O Lord, in thy anger: and be thou exalted in the borders of my enemies.

And arise, O Lord my God, in the precept which thou hast commanded: and a congregation of people shall surround thee.

And for their sakes return thou on high.

The Lord judgeth the people.

Judge me, O Lord, according to my justice, and according to my innocence in me.

The wickedness of sinners shall be brought to nought: and thou shalt direct the just: the searcher of hearts and reins is God.

Just is my help from the Lord: who saveth the upright of heart.

God is a just judge, strong and patient: is he angry every day?

Except you will be converted, he will brandish his sword: he hath bent his bow, and made it ready.

And in it he hath prepared the instruments of death, he hath made ready his arrows for them that burn.

Behold he hath been in labour with injustice; he hath conceived sorrow, and brought forth iniquity.

He hath opened a pit and dug it: and he is fallen into the hole he made.

His sorrow shall be turned on his own head: and his iniquity shall come down upon his crown.

I will give glory to the Lord according to his justice: and will sing to the name of the Lord the most high.

PSALM 8

O LORD our Lord, how admirable is thy name in the whole earth!

For thy magnificence is elevated above the heavens.

Out of the mouth of infants and of sucklings thou hast perfected praise, because of thy enemies, that thou mayest destroy the enemy and the avenger.

For I will behold thy heavens, the works of thy fingers: the moon and the stars which thou hast founded.

What is man that thou art mindful of him? or the son of man that thou visitest him?

Thou hast made him a little less than the angels, thou hast crowned him with glory and honour: and hast set him over the works of thy hands.

Thou hast subjected all things under his feet, all sheep and oxen: moreover the beasts also of the fields.

The birds of the air, and the fishes of the sea, that pass through the paths of the sea.

O Lord our Lord, how admirable is thy name in all the earth!

¶ Glory to the Father *(complete)*; Alleluia! Alleluia! Alleluia! Glory to thee, O God *(three times)*; O our God and our Hope, glory to thee.

Deacon. Again and again, etc.

Help, save, have mercy, and keep us, O God, by thy grace.

Remembering our all-holy, etc.

Priest. For thine is the might, and thine is the kingdom, power, and glory, O God, etc.

Right Choir. Amen.

❡ *The same Choir chanteth the following, in the Tone in use.*

PSALM 140

O LORD, to thee have I cried, hear me. Hear me,
O Lord. O Lord I have cried unto thee, hear me.
Receive the voice of my prayer when I call upon thee.
Hear me, O Lord.

Left Choir. Let my prayer be set forth in thy sight
as incense. And let the lifting up of my hands be an
evening sacrifice. Hear me, O Lord.

Set a watch, O Lord, before my mouth and a door
round about my lips.

Incline not my heart to evil words: to make excuses
in sins.

With men that work iniquity; and I will not communicate with the choicest of them.

The just man shall correct me in mercy, and shall
reprove me; but let not the oil of the sinner fatten my
head.

For my prayer also shall still be against the things
with which they are well pleased: their judges falling
upon the rock have been swallowed up.

They shall hear my words, for they have prevailed:
as when the thickness of the earth is broken up upon
the ground:

Our bones are scattered by the side of hell. But to
thee, O Lord, Lord, are my eyes: in thee have I put my
trust, take not away my soul.

Keep me from the snare, which they have laid for
me, and the gins of the workers of iniquity.

Let the wicked fall into their own nets whilst that I
withal escape.

PSALM 141

I CRIED unto the Lord with my voice; with my
voice unto the Lord did I make my supplication.

I poured out my complaint before him; I showed before him my trouble.

When my spirit was overwhelmed within me, then thou knewest my path. In the way wherein I walked have they privily laid a snare for me.

I looked on my right hand, and beheld, but there was no man that would know me: refuge failed me; no man cared for my soul.

I cried unto thee, O Lord: I said, Thou art my refuge and my portion in the land of the living.

Attend unto my cry; for I am brought very low:

Deliver me from my persecutors; for they are stronger than I.

Bring my soul out of prison, that I may praise thy name.

¶ *After this Stichos, chant ten Stichera.*

The righteous shall compass me about; for thou shalt deal bountifully with me.

PSALM 129

OUT of the depths have I cried unto thee, O Lord. Lord, hear my voice. *Eight Stichera.*

Let thine ears be attentive to the voice of my supplications.

If thou, Lord, shouldest mark iniquities, O Lord, who shall stand? But there is forgiveness with thee, that thou mayest be feared. *Six Stichera.*

I wait for the Lord, my soul doth wait, and in his word do I hope. My soul waiteth for the Lord.

More than they that watch for the morning: I say, more than they that watch for the morning.

Let Israel hope in the Lord. *Four Stichera.* For with the Lord there is mercy, and with him is plenteous redemption.

And he shall redeem Israel from all his iniquities.

PSALM 116

O PRAISE the Lord, all ye nations; praise him, all ye people. For his merciful kindness is great toward us; and the truth of the Lord endureth for ever.

❡ *Then are sung the Stichera of the evening, seven for the Resurrection, and three for the Saint of the Feast. Then, Glory for the Saint, and Now to our Lady, for the Resurrection.*

❡ *If Glory for the Saint be not sung, sing Glory and Now to our Lady for the Resurrection.*

❡ *After this, the Priest maketh the Eisodos with the censer, and then:*

Deacon. Wisdom! Let us stand.

Lector. O resplendent Light of the holy glory of the immortal Father, heavenly, holy, blessed Jesus Christ! In that we now are come unto the setting of the sun, and behold the light of evening, we praise the Father, Son, and Holy Spirit, God; for it is meet that at all times thou shouldest be praised by righteous voices, O Son of God, who bestowest life; for which cause all the world doth glorify thee.

Deacon.   Prokeimenon of the evening.

❡ *Then immediately the Choir chanteth the Prokeimenon of the present evening three times.*

Saturday, in the Sixth Tone

The Lord hath reigned, he is clothed with beauty.

Sunday, in the Eighth Tone

Behold now, bless ye the Lord, all ye servants of the Lord.

Monday, in the Fourth Tone

The Lord will hear me when I shall cry unto him.

Tuesday, in the First Tone

Thy mercy, O Lord, will follow me all the days of my life.

Wednesday, in the Fifth Tone

Save me, O God, by thy Name, and judge me in thy strength.

Thursday, in the Sixth Tone

My help is from the Lord, who made heaven and earth.

Friday, in the Seventh Tone

O God, thou art my defence. My God, thy mercy shall lead me.

❡ *Then are read the Prophecies, if any, after which the Deacon saith the following Petitions, as the Choir singeth,* Lord, have mercy, *once after the first and second, and three times after each of the rest.*

Deacon. Let us all say with all our soul and with all our mind:

O Lord Almighty, God of our fathers, we beseech thee, hear and have mercy.

Have mercy upon us, O God, after thy great mercy, we beseech thee, hear and have mercy.

Again, let us pray for all Orthodox Christians of true worship.

Again, let us pray for our Bishop (N.   ).

Again, let us pray for our brethren the Priests, Deacons, and monks, and all our brethren in Christ.

Again, let us pray for the blessed and ever-memorable founders of this holy house, and for all our fathers and brethren of the Orthodox who have fallen asleep and lie here and everywhere.

Again, let us pray for mercy, life, peace, health, salvation, shelter, forgiveness, and remission of sins, for God's servants, the Christian Orthodox of true worship who live and dwell in this city, and who gather in this holy church, for its trustees and its benefactors, for their visitation, forgiveness, and the remission of their sins.

Again, let us pray for those who bring the fruits of the earth to this holy and sacred church, and do good works therein, and for those who serve and sing in it, and for the people here present, awaiting the great and rich mercy that cometh from thee.

Priest. For thou art a merciful and philanthropic God, and to thee do we address glory, O Father, etc.

Choir. Amen.

Lector. Vouchsafe, O Lord, to keep us this evening without sin. Blessed art thou, O Lord God of our fathers, and praised and glorified is thy Name for ever. Amen.

Let thy mercy be upon us, O Lord, even as we have set our hope upon thee. Blessed art thou, O Lord, teach me thy commandments. Blessed art thou, O Master; make me to understand thy statutes. Blessed art thou, O holy One; enlighten me with thy justice.

Thy mercy, O Lord, is for ever; turn not away from the works of thy hands. To thee belongeth praise; laudation becometh thee; to thee glory is due; O Father, Son, and Holy Spirit, now, and ever, and unto ages of ages. Amen.

❡ *Then the Deacon immediately saith the following Petitions, as the Choir chanteth,* Lord have mercy, *after the first and second, and* Grant, O Lord *after each of the rest.*

Deacon. Let us finish our petitions of the evening to the Lord.

Help, save, have mercy, and keep us, O God, by thy grace.

That our whole evening may be perfect, holy, peaceful, and without sin, let us ask the Lord.

For the angel of peace, a faithful guide, a guardian of our souls and bodies, let us ask the Lord.

For the forgiveness and remission of our sins, let us ask the Lord.

For what is good and profitable for Christians, and for the peace of the world, let us ask the Lord.

That the rest of our life may be spent in peace and penitence, let us ask the Lord.

That the end of our life may be Christian, peaceful, without sorrow or shame, and that we may have a good response at the fearful judgment seat of Christ, let us ask the Lord.

Remembering our all-holy, spotless, most highly blessed, and glorious Lady, the Theotokos, and ever-virgin Mary, and all the saints, let us commend ourselves and each other and all our life to Christ our God.

Choir. To thee, O Lord.

Priest. For thou art a good God, and a Lover of mankind, and to thee, O Father, etc.

Choir. Amen.

Priest. Peace be unto you all.

Choir. And unto thy spirit also.

Deacon. Bow your heads unto the Lord.

Choir. To thee, O Lord.

Priest. Blessed and glorified be the might of thy kingdom, etc.

Choir. Amen.

❧ *And immediately sing the Aposticha of the Resurrection. Then, Glory of the Saint whose Feast is celebrated; and Now to our Lady, of the Resurrection. And if no Glory for the Saint be sung, then Glory and Now to our Lady, of the Resurrection. Then the Lector reciteth the following:*

NOW lettest thou thy servant depart, O Lord, according to thy word in peace. For mine eyes have seen thy salvation, which thou hast prepared before the face of all peoples. A light to the revelation of the Gentiles, and the glory of thy people Israel.

Then: Holy God, etc.

❧ *Then immediately shall be sung the Troparion of the Resurrection; then Glory, repeating the Troparion; and Now, singing the Theotokion; after which is said:*

Deacon. Wisdom!

Choir. Bless.

Priest. Christ our God who remaineth blessed always, etc.

Choir. Amen.

Lector. Strengthen, O God, our believing kings; yea, Lord, and multiply their years and sanctify their sovereignty. Preserve thou the Orthodox Faith, with this holy church (*or city*) for ever. Amen.

Priest. O most holy Theotokos, save us.

Lector. O thou who art more honourable than the cherubim, and beyond compare more glorious than the seraphim, who without corruption didst bear the Word of God; truly thou art the Theotokos, and thee do we magnify.

Priest. Glory to thee, O Christ, our God and our Hope, glory to thee.

Lector. Glory to the Father (*complete*) ; Lord, have mercy (*three times*). Bless, O Father, in the Name of the Lord.

¶*And the Priest saith:*

O CHRIST, our true God (*and if a Sunday evening, add, O thou who didst rise from the dead for our salvation*), by the intercessions of thy most underfiled and blameless Mother, by the enlivening power of the precious Cross, the petitions of the honourable, incorporeal powers, the precious Prophet and glorious Forerunner, the all-praised and honourable saints, the Apostles, the glorious martyred saints of good victory, our God-mantled fathers, and Saint (N.   ), the patron of this church, and those two righteous saints, the grandparents of Christ God, Joachim and Anne, and Saint (N.   ), whose memorial we celebrate today, and all thy saints, have mercy upon us and save us; for thou art the Lover of mankind.

Through the prayers of our fathers and saints, O Lord Jesus Christ our God, have mercy upon us.

Choir. Amen.

¶*Note: In the evening prayers of the Great Feasts and the Feasts of the Lord or of our Lady after the Sunset Psalm, the first three*

Psalms only, beginning with, Blessed is the man, etc., are recited. Then after the daily evening Prokeimenon, the Prophecies are read. And after, Lord, now lettest thou thy servant, the Troparion of the Feast is sung, if it is to the Lord or to our Lady; and if it is the Feast of a great saint, then this Troparion is sung two times, and at the third time is sung a Theotokion of the Resurrection, which is of the same Tone as that of the saint.

ALL NIGHT VIGIL PRAYERS

¶ *If the five loaves, known as Ighribniyyah, are present, then before the Aposticha of Evening Prayer, the Choir chanteth the Litiya of the Feast celebrated; and at its conclusion, the Priest cometh out through the Royal Door, preceded by the Deacon carrying the censer, to the middle of the church where the five loaves, with wheat, wine, and oil, are placed on a candle-lighted table. Then the Deacon delivereth the censer to the sexton, and lifteth the end of his girdle with his right hand, saying in a loud voice:*

Have mercy upon me, O God, according to the multitude of thy mercies. Of thee we ask; grant and have mercy.

Right Choir. Lord, have mercy (*three times*).

Deacon. And again we pray for our Bishop (N.   ) and all our brethren in Christ.

Left Choir. Lord, have mercy (*three times*).

Deacon. And again we ask for mercy, life, safety, sound health, and the salvation of the servants of God who offer this holy offering (*mentioning them by name*), and for all other Orthodox Christians of true worship, for their visitation, their forgiveness, and the remission of their sins.

Right Choir. Lord, have mercy (*three times*).

Deacon. And again we ask for the preservation of this holy church ,this city, and all other cities and towns, from famine, destruction, earthquakes, flood, fire, and the sword; from the surprise attacks of foreign tribes, civil wars, and sudden death. We pray that our good and philanthropic God, in pity, mercy, and compassion, turn away from us all destruction that riseth against us, deliver us from his just threat, and have mercy upon us.

❡ *Then the two Choirs chant alternately,* Lord, have mercy (*forty times, of ten times each*).

Deacon. And again we pray that the Lord God hear the voice of our supplication, though we be sinners, and have mercy upon us.

❡ *The two Choirs then chant,* Lord, have mercy (*three times*), *slowly, first one Choir then the other, and the third time, the two together.*

Priest. Grant to us, O God our Saviour, O Hope of all the earth and of those who are far at sea, thy kindness, O Lord, and be lenient towards our sins, and have mercy upon us; for thou art a compassionate and philanthropic God, and to thee do we address glory, O Father, etc.

Choir. Amen.
Priest. Peace be unto you all.
Choir. And unto thy spirit also.
Priest. Let us bow our heads to the Lord.
Choir. To thee, O Lord.
Priest. O most merciful Master, the Lord Jesus Christ our God, by the intercessions of our all-pure Lady, the everlastingly virgin Theotokos Mary, and by the might of thy precious enlivening Cross, and by the petitions of the incorporeal heavenly powers, of the honoured Prophet and glorious Forerunner John the Baptist, of the honourable saints, of all the all-praised Apostles, of the glorious saints, of the Martyrs of good victory, of our righteous, God-mantled fathers, of Saint (N.   ), Patron of this church, of Saint (N.   *whose celebration we observe today*), of the two righteous saints, grandparents of Christ, Joachim and Anne, and of the rest of thy saints, let our petitions be acceptable to thee; grant us the forgiveness of our sins; cover us with the shadow of thy wings; drive away all enemies and adversaries; and preserve our lives, O Lord; have

mercy upon us and upon thy world, and save our souls;
for thou art good and the Lover of mankind.

¶ *Then the Priest taketh the censer and censeth the five loaves from
the four sides, chanting the following Troparion.*

R EJOICE, O virgin Theotokos Mary, full of grace.
The Lord is with thee. Blessed art thou among
women, and blessed the fruit of thy womb; for thou
didst give birth to the Saviour of our souls.

¶ *As the Priest chanteth the above Troparion, the Deacon proceeds
around the table with him, keeping always opposite, with a candle
in his hand. And as the Priest cometh to the end of the Troparion,
the left Choir chanteth the conclusion.*

Deacon. Let us pray to the Lord.
Choir. Lord, have mercy.
Priest. O Lord Jesus Christ our God, who didst bless
the five loaves in the wilderness and therefrom didst
satisfy five thousand, bless thou also these loaves, and
this wheat, wine, and oil, and make them plentiful in
this city and in all the world. Sanctify the believers
who partake thereof in faith; for it is thou, O Christ
our God, who dost bless and sanctify all things; and to
thee do we address glory, together with thy Father who
hath no beginning, and thy most good and Holy Spirit,
the Giver of life, now, and always, etc.
Choir. Amen.

¶ *Then the Priest taketh one of the loaves, kisseth it, and breaketh
it slightly on each side in the form of a cross, as he chanteth the following Stichos, in the Seventh Tone.*

The rich have wanted, and suffered hunger: but they
that seek the Lord shall not be deprived of any good.

¶ *The above Stichos is repeated once by each of the two Choirs. Then
the Aposticha and the rest of the Vesper Prayers are chanted (p. 76).*

LITTLE COMPLINE

❡ *After* Blessed be God, our God, *etc.;* O heavenly King, *etc.;* Holy
God, *etc.;* For thine is the kingdom, *etc.;* Lord, have mercy (*twelve
times*)*; Glory and Now; and* O come, let us worship and fall down
to Christ our King and God (*three times*) :

PSALM 50

HAVE mercy upon me, O God, according to thy
great mercy.

And according to the multitude of thy tender mercies
blot out my iniquity.

Wash me yet more from my iniquity, and cleanse me
from my sin.

For I know my iniquity, and my sin is always before
me.

To thee only have I sinned, and have done evil before
thee: that thou mayest be justified in thy words, and
mayest overcome when thou art judged.

For behold I was conceived in iniquities; and in sins
did my mother conceive me.

For behold thou hast loved truth: the uncertain and
hidden things of thy wisdom thou hast made manifest
to me.

Thou shalt sprinkle me with hyssop, and I shall be
cleansed: thou shalt wash me, and I shall be made
whiter than snow.

To my hearing thou shalt give joy and gladness: and
the bones that have been humbled shall rejoice.

Turn away thy face from my sins, and blot out all
my iniquities.

Create a clean heart in me, O God: and renew a right
spirit within my bowels.

Cast me not away from thy face; and take not thy
holy spirit from me.

Restore unto me the joy of thy salvation, and strength-
en me with a perfect spirit.

I will teach the unjust thy ways: and the wicked shall
be converted to thee.

Deliver me from blood, O God, thou God of my
lvation: and my tongue shall extol thy justice.

O Lord, thou wilt open my lips: and my mouth shall
:clare thy praise.

For if thou hadst desired sacrifice, I would indeed
ive given it: with burnt offerings thou wilt not be
·lighted.

A sacrifice to God is an afflicted spirit: a contrite and
imbled heart, O God, thou wilt not despise.

Deal favourably, O Lord, in thy good will with Sion;
at the walls of Jerusalem may be built up.

Then shalt thou accept the sacrifice of justice, obla-
ins and whole burnt offerings: then shall they lay
ilves upon thy altar.

Psalm 69

) GOD, come to my assistance; O Lord, make haste
to help me.

Let them be confounded and ashamed that seek my
ul:

Let them be turned backward, and blush for shame
at desire evils to me:

Let them be presently turned away blushing for
iame that say to me: 'Tis well, 'tis well.

Let all that seek thee rejoice and be glad in thee; and
t such as love thy salvation say always: The Lord be
agnified.

But I am needy and poor; O God, help me.

Thou art my helper and my deliverer: O Lord, make
) delay.

Psalm 142

HEAR, O Lord, my prayer: give ear to my supplication in thy truth: hear me in thy justice.

And enter not into judgment with thy servant: for in
iy sight no man living shall be justified.

For the enemy hath persecuted my soul: he hath
rought down my life to the earth.

He hath made me to dwell in darkness as those th
have been dead of old: and my spirit is in angui
within me: my heart within me is troubled.

I remembered the days of old, I meditated upon t
works of thy hands.

I stretched forth my hands to thee: my soul is
earth without water unto thee.

Hear me speedily O Lord: my spirit hath faint
away.

Turn not away thy face from me, lest I be like un
them that go down into the pit.

Cause me to hear thy mercy in the morning; for
thee have I hoped.

Make the way known to me, wherein I should wal
for I have lifted up my soul to thee.

Deliver me from my enemies, O Lord, to thee have
fled: teach me to do thy will, for thou art my God.

Thy good spirit shall lead me into the right lan
For thy name's sake, O Lord, thou wilt quicken r
in thy justice.

Thou wilt bring my soul out of trouble: and in t
mercy thou wilt destroy my enemies.

And thou wilt cut off all them that afflict my sou
for I am thy servant.

Glory to God in the highest, and on earth peace, a
good will toward men.

We praise thee, we bless thee, we worship thee,
glorify thee, we give thanks unto thee for the splendo
of thy glory.

O Lord, O King, O heavenly God, Father Almight
O Lord, O only-begotten Son Jesus Christ, and t
Holy Spirit.

O Lord God, O Lamb of God, O Son of the Fath
that takest away the sins of the world, have mercy up
us, O thou that takest away the sins of the world.

Accept our prayers, O thou that sittest on the rig
hand of the Father, and have mercy upon us.

For thou only art holy, thou only art the Lord Jes

hrist, in the glory of God the Father. Amen.

Every day will I bless thee and will praise thy Name
r ever and ever.

O Lord, thou hast been our refuge from generation
generation. I said, Lord, have mercy upon me, heal
y soul; for I have sinned against thee.

O Lord, I flee unto thee, teach me to do thy will; for
ou art my God; for with thee is the Fountain of life,
d in thy light we shall see light.

Extend thy mercy unto them that know thee.

Vouchsafe, O Lord, to keep us this night without sin.
lessed art thou, O Lord God of our Fathers, and
aised and glorified is thy Name for ever. Amen.

Let thy mercy, O Lord, be upon us, as we have set
ir trust in thee. Blessed art thou, O Lord, teach me
y commandments. Blessed art thou, O Master, make
e to understand thy statutes. Blessed art thou, O
ly One, enlighten me with thy justice.

Thy mercy, O Lord, is for ever; turn not away from
e works of thy hands. To thee belongeth praise; lau-
tion becometh thee; to thee glory is due; O Father,
n, and Holy Spirit, now, and ever, and unto ages of
es. Amen.

BELIEVE in one God, the Father Almighty,
Maker of heaven and earth, and of all things visible
d invisible.

2. And in one Lord, Jesus Christ, and Son of God,
e only-begotten, begotten before all worlds: Light of
ght, very God of very God, begotten not made, con-
bstantial with the Father by whom all things were
ade.

3. Who for us men, and for our salvation, came
wn from heaven, and was incarnate of the Holy
irit and the Virgin Mary, and took on man:

4. And was crucified for us under Pontius Pilate,
d suffered, and was buried:

5. And the third day rose again according to the
criptures.

6. And ascended into heaven, and sitteth on the right
hand of the Father:

7. And he shall come again, with glory, to judge the
quick and the dead, whose kingdom shall have no end

8. And I believe in the Holy Spirit, the Lord, the
Giver of life, who proceedeth from the Father, who
together with the Father and the Son is worshipped and
glorified; who spake through the Prophets.

9. And in One, Holy, Catholic, and Apostolic
Church.

10. I acknowledge one Baptism for the remission
of sins.

11. I look for the resurrection of the dead,

12. And the life in the world to come. Amen.[1]

It is truly meet to bless the Theotokos, who is ever
blessed and all blameless, the Mother of our God.

O thou who art more honourable than the cherubim
and beyond compare more glorious than the seraphim
who without corruption didst bear the Word of God
truly thou art the Theotokos, and thee do we magnify

*⁋Then, Holy God, etc.; and if it be a Feast, say its Troparion
otherwise, the following Troparia.*

HAVE mercy upon us, O Lord, have mercy upon us
for, destitute of all defence, we sinners offer unto
thee, O Master, this supplication, Have mercy upon us

Glory

HAVE mercy upon us, O Lord; for in thee have we
put our trust. Be not exceedingly wroth with us
nor remember our iniquities, but look upon us now
again, for thou art compassionate, and deliver us from
our enemies; for thou art our God and we are thy peo
ple; we are all the work of thy hands, and we have
called upon thy Name.

---

[1] If you, O Christian, are prepared for the Holy Communion, read the
Canon of the Metalepsis, then finish the Little Compline.

Now

OPEN unto us the door of compassion, O blessed
Theotokos, that as we hope in thee we may not fail
in our petitions. May we be delivered through thee
from all adversities; for through thee hath come the
salvation of the Christian race.

❡ *Or these Troparia.*

O GOD of our fathers, who ever dealest with us
according to thy meekness, remove not thy mercy
from us; but by their intercessions direct our lives into
the way of peace.

Thy Church, arrayed in the blood of Martyrs in all
the world, as in purple and fine linen, crieth through
them unto thee. Pour thy compassion upon thy people;
give peace to thy fold, and to our souls the Great Mercy.

Glory

GIVE rest, O Christ, to the soul of thy servants with
thy saints, where there is no sickness, nor sorrow
nor sighing, but life immortal.

Now

THROUGH the intercession of all the saints and of
the Theotokos grant us thy peace and have mercy
upon us; for thou alone art compassionate.

Lord, have mercy (*forty times*).

❡ *Then the following prayer.*

O Christ our God, who art worshipped and glorified
at all times, etc. (p. 60).

Lord, have mercy (*three times*).

Glory to the Father (*complete*).

O thou who art more honourable than the cherubim,
etc. (p. 23). Bless, O Father, in the Name of the Lord.

Priest. God be merciful to us.

¶ *If there be no Priest, say,* Through the prayers of our Fathers, etc. *Then the following prayer to the most holy Theotokos.*

O SPOTLESS, undefiled, unstained, all-chaste, and pure Lady, blameless bride of God, who by thy glorious birth-giving hast united the Word of God with man and linked our fallen nature with heavenly beings, who art alone the hope of the hopeless, the helper of those attacked, the ready protection of those who hasten unto thee, and the refuge of all Christians; despise not me a sinner, wholly defiled by evil thoughts, words, and deeds, become by slothful will a servant of life's pleasures. But being Mother of God, the lover of mankind, have mercy, in compassion, upon me, thy sinful and prodigal servant. Accept this prayer which is offered to thee from my impure lips and, putting forth thy maternal favour with thy Son, our Lord and Master, beseech him to open unto me the wings of his love of mankind, his loving kindness and bounty. Beseech him to pass over my numberless transgressions, to lead me back to true repentance, and to make me a keeper of his commandments and a tried doer thereof. And as thou art gracious, compassionate, and tender-hearted, be thou ever present with me in this life as my advocate and helper, to turn aside the evil assaults of my adversaries, to guide me unto salvation, and at the departure of my wretched soul, encompass me, and drive from it all the dark forms of the evil ones; and in the dreadful Judgment Day deliver me from everlasting punishments and torments, revealing me as an inheritor of the unspeakable glory and an honour to thy Son, our God, all which I may obtain, O holy Theotokos my Lady, through thy mediation and help, by the grace and exceeding compassion of thine only begotten Son, our Lord God and Saviour Jesus Christ, to whom is due, with the eternal Father, and the all-holy, good, and life-giving Spirit, all honour, glory, and worship, now and always for ever and ever. Amen.

¶ *And the following Prayer to our Lord Jesus Christ.*

AND now as we lay us down to sleep, O Master, grant us repose both of body and of soul, and keep us from the dark sleep of sin and from the sensuous pleasure of the dark passions of the night. Still thou the assaults of passion; quench the fiery darts of the wicked one which are thrown insidiously at us; calm the commotions of our flesh and put away all earthly and material thoughts as we sleep. And grant us, O God, a watchful mind, chaste thoughts, a sober heart, and a gentle sleep, free from all the fantasies of Satan. And raise us up again at the hour of prayer, established in thy commandments and holding steadfast within ourselves the remembrance of thy judgments. Give us the words of thy glorification, all night long, that we may praise, bless, and glorify thy most honourable and magnificent Name, O Father, Son, and Holy Spirit, now and always and for ever and ever. Amen.

O most glorious one, O ever-virgin, O blessed Theotokos, commend our prayer to thy son, our God, and entreat him to save our souls through thee.

The Father is my hope; the Son is my refuge; the Holy Spirit is my shelter. O Holy Trinity, glory to thee.

All my hope I place in thee, O Theotokos; keep me under the wing of thy care.

¶ *Then the following Prayer to your Guardian Angel.*

O HOLY angel who accompanieth my wretched soul and lowly life, forsake me not, and depart not from me because of my extravagance and wickedness. Give not access to evil Satan to rule with his might this mortal body of mine, but hold me by my wretched, feeble hand, lead me in the path of salvation. Yea, O holy Guardian Angel of God, protector of my wretched soul and body, forgive me all wherewith I have heretofore saddened thee all the days of my life. And though this day I have sinned, be thou my shelter this night. Keep me from all the wiles

of the obstinate, that I may not anger God with any sin
Intercede with the Lord for me, that he may confirm
me in his fear, and reveal me a worthy servant of his
goodness. Amen.

❡ Glory to the Father (*complete*) ; Lord, have mercy (*three times*)
Bless, O Father, in the Name of the Lord, *and then the Priest closeth*
with the Benediction.

Priest. Through the prayers of our Fathers the saints
O Lord Jesus Christ our God, have mercy upon us and
save us. Amen.

CANON OF THE METALEPSIS, OR DIVINE
COMMUNION

❡ *When you are about to receive the divine Mysteries, after reading*
the Little Compline (p. 82) to the end of, I believe in one God, *etc.*
say contritely the following Canon.

First Ode, In the Second Tone

O COMPASSIONATE Lord, may thy holy Body
and thy precious Blood become the bread of everlasting life to me, and the healing of manifold diseases.
   Defiled as I am, O Christ, by unbecoming deeds, I
am not worthy of the communion of thy most pure Body
and divine Blood. Nevertheless, make thou me worthy
thereof.
   O thou most blessed bride of God, the good soil
which grew the untilled corn that saveth the world;
grant that partaking thereof I may be saved.

Third Ode

STABLISHING me on the rock of faith, thou hast
enlarged my mouth against mine enemies; for my
soul hath rejoiced to sing, There is none holy as the
Lord our God, nor any just save thee, O Lord.
   O Christ, Master, give me those tearful drops which
cleanse my heart's impurity, that, with a pure con-

science, I may approach with faith and fear the communion of thy divine gifts.

O thou Lover of mankind, may thy most pure Body and divine Blood be for the remission of my sins, for the communion of the Holy Spirit, for life everlasting, and for estrangement from passions and afflictions.

O thou most holy table of the bread of life, which, for mercy's sake, came from above and giveth new life unto the world; grant that I may now, unworthy as I am, taste thereof in fear and live thereby.

Fourth Ode

O MOST merciful One, when thou didst take flesh for our sake, thou wast willing to be slain as a lamb for the sins of men. Wherefore, I beseech thee, cleanse my sins also.

O Lord, heal the wounds of my soul and sanctify me wholly, and grant, O Master, that I, wretched man, may partake of thy divine and mystical supper.

O Lady, propitiate in my behalf him who was born of thee, and preserve me, thy supplicating servant, pure and undefiled, so that by receiving the supersensuous pearl I may be sanctified.

Fifth Ode

AS thou, O Christ, didst foretell, so let it be unto thine unprofitable servant, and abide in me, as thou didst promise; for lo! I eat thy divine Body and drink thy precious Blood.

O God and Word of God, may the live coal of thy Body be to the enlightenment of my darkness, and thy Blood to the cleansing of my defiled soul.

O Mary, Theotokos, thou honourable tabernacle of sweet ointment; make me, by thy prayers, a chosen vessel, that I may receive the sanctification of thy Son.

Sixth Ode

O SAVIOUR, sanctify my mind, my soul, my heart, and my body, and prepare me, O Lord, to approach uncondemned thy dread mysteries.

Grant that I may be rid of my passions, increase in thy grace, and be confirmed in my life by the communion of thy holy mysteries, O Christ.

O God, O holy Word of God, wholly sanctify me now approaching thy divine mysteries, through the supplications of thy holy Mother.

Kontakion

TURN not away from me wretched man, O Christ, Master, as I now receive thy dread mysteries, thy pure Body and thy precious Blood. Let not my partaking thereof be to my judgment, but to everlasting and immortal life.

Seventh Ode

O CHRIST, Fountain of blessings, may the communion of thine immortal mysteries now be to me light and life, freedom from passion, and for my progress and increase in divine virtues, that I may glorify thee who alone art good.

Grant that now approaching thine immortal and divine mysteries in trembling, longing, and piety, I may be delivered, O Lover of mankind, from passions and enemies, and from every affliction, distress, and sorrow, and vouchsafe that I may sing to thee. Blessed art thou, O Lord God of our Fathers.

O thou God-favoured one, who didst above comprehension bear the Saviour Christ, I, thine impure servant, desiring now to approach the most pure mysteries, pray thee, who art pure, cleanse me from all defilement of flesh and spirit.

Eighth Ode

O CHRIST God my Saviour, grant that I thy despairing servant may become now a partaker of thy heavenly dread and holy mysteries, and of thy divine and mystical Supper.

Seeking refuge in thy loving-kindness, O good Saviour, I cry unto thee with fear; abide in me, and let me also, as thou didst promise, abide in thee; for lo! trusting in thy mercy, I eat thy Body and I drink thy Blood.

I tremble in taking this fire lest I should be consumed as wax and grass. O fearful mystery! O the loving-kindness of God! How is it that I, an earthly creature, partake of the divine Body and Blood, and am made incorruptible?

Ninth Ode

O TASTE and see that the Lord is good, who for our sake was made like unto us of old, and once for all offered up himself as an offering to his Father, and is now forever slain, sanctifying the communicants.

O Master, let me be sanctified in body and soul; let me be enlightened and saved; and let me become thy dwelling through the communion of thy holy mysteries, having thee, O most merciful Benefactor, living in me, with the Father and the Spirit.

May thy Body and thy precious Blood, O Saviour, be as fire and light to me, consuming the substance of sin and burning the tares of my passions, and wholly enlightening me, that I may fall down, worshipping thy Divinity.

God took flesh from thy pure blood. Therefore, do all generations praise thee, O Lady, and the hosts of supersensuous powers glorify thee; for through thee they clearly behold him who ruleth all things endued with human nature.

¶ *And immediately,* It is truly meet to bless thee, *etc., and the rest of the Little Compline* (*p. 82*).

ON THE MORROW

❡*After the usual Matins, say* Holy God, *etc;* Lord, have mercy (*twelve times*); Glory to the Father (*complete*); O come let us worship, *etc.* (*three times*); *and then immediately:*

PSALM 22

THE Lord ruleth me: and I shall want nothing. He hath set me in a place of pasture.

He hath brought me up, on the water of refreshment: he hath converted my soul.

He hath led me on the paths of justice, for his own name's sake.

For though I should walk in the midst of the shadow of death, I will fear no evils, for thou art with me.

Thy rod and thy staff, they have comforted me.

Thou hast prepared a table before me, against them that afflict me.

Thou hast anointed my head with oil; and my chalice which inebriateth me, how goodly is it!

And thy mercy will follow me all the days of my life.

And that I may dwell in the house of the Lord unto length of days.

PSALM 23

THE earth is the Lord's and the fulness thereof: the world, and all they that dwell therein.

For he hath founded it upon the seas; and hath prepared it upon the rivers.

Who shall ascend into the mountain of the Lord: or who shall stand in his holy place?

The innocent in hands, and clean of heart, who hath not taken his soul in vain, nor sworn deceitfully to his neighbour.

He shall receive a blessing from the Lord, and mercy from God his Saviour.

This is the generation of them that seek him, of them that seek the face of the God of Jacob.

Lift up your gates, O ye princes, and be ye lifted up,

) eternal gates: and the King of Glory shall enter in.

Who is this King of Glory? the Lord who is strong
nd mighty: the Lord mighty in battle.

Lift up your gates, and the King of Glory shall enter
n.

Who is this King of Glory? the Lord of hosts, he is
he King of Glory.

PSALM 115

ᴵ HAVE believed, therefore have I spoken; but I
have been humbled exceedingly.

What shall I render to the Lord, for all the things
hat he hath rendered to me?

I will take the chalice of salvation; and I will call
ᵢpon the name of the Lord.

I will pay my vows to the Lord before all his people:
ᵣrecious in the sight of the Lord is the death of his
ᵢaints.

O Lord, for I am thy servant. I am thy servant, and
he son of thy handmaid.

Thou hast broken my bonds: I will sacrifice to thee
he sacrifice of praise, and I will call upon the name of
he Lord.

I will pay my vows to the Lord in the sight of all his
ᵣeople: in the courts of the house of the Lord, in the
ᵢidst of thee, O Jerusalem.

⟦Glory to the Father (*complete*); Alleluia (*three times*). Glory to
hee, O God; Lord, have mercy (*three times*). *And the following
Troparia, in the Eighth Tone:*

O LORD who wast born of the Virgin, turn away
from my transgressions and purify my heart, mak-
ng it a temple for thy most pure Body and precious
Blood, and cast me not away from thy presence, O thou
vho hast mercy without measure.

Glory

HOW shall I, unworthy, dare immodestly to partake
of thy holy Sacrament? If, with the worthy, I ven-

ture to approach thee, my garment will denounce me
for it is not a supper garment, and I shall call forth the
reproach and condemnation of my most sinful sou
Wherefore, cleanse, O Lord, the defilement of my sou
and save me, for thou art a lover of mankind.

Now

BECAUSE of the multitude of my transgressions,
come to thee, O pure Theotokos, asking for salva
tion. Visit thou mine ailing soul, and beseech thy So
and our God to grant me remission of the evils I hav
wrought, O thou blessed one.

❡*And on the Holy Great Thursday this Troparion is chanted.*

THE glorified Disciples, being illuminated, at th
evening washing, Judas, of evil worship, was stric
ken and darkened with the love of silver. And to law
less judges, O righteous Judge, he delivered and sur
rendered thee. Wherefore, O lover of wealth, behol
him who for its sake hanged himself, and ran awa
from the insatiable soul which ventured to that exten
against the Master. O thou whose goodness pervadet
all, glory to thee, O Lord.

❡ *Then,* Lord, have mercy *(forty times), and as many genuflexior
as thou wilt.*

HOW YOU SHOULD COME PREPARED TO
RECEIVE THE HOLY MYSTERIES

❡*If thou hast purposed, O man, to eat the Body of the Lord, ap
proach in fear lest thou be scorched; for it is fire: and, before drinkin
the Divine Blood unto communion, first reconcile thyself to them tha
have wronged thee, then venture to eat that mystical Food. Befor
partaking, however, of the fearful Sacrifice of the life-creating Boa
of the Lord, say in fear and reverence the following Prayers.*

First Prayer by Saint Basil the Great

O LORD Jesus Christ our God, Source of life an
immortality, Creator of all things visible and in

visible, Son coëternal with the everlasting Father, who out of thy great loving-kindness didst in the last days become incarnate and wast crucified for us ungrateful and thankless men, and hast renewed with thine own Blood our nature corrupted by sin, do thou thyself, immortal King, accept the repentance of thy sinful servant. Incline thine ear towards me and hearken unto my supplications; for I have sinned, O Lord, I have sinned against heaven and before thee, and I am not worthy to raise mine eyes to the height of thy glory. I have also angered thy goodness by transgressing thy commandments and by not obeying thine ordinances. But thou, O Lord, who art long-suffering and of great mercy, hast not given me over to perish in my sins, but always awaiteth my conversion; for thou hast said by thy Prophets, O thou Lover of mankind, that thou hast no pleasure in the death of a sinner, but rather that he should turn back and live. Thou willest not, O Lord, that the works of thy hands should be lost, neither hast thou pleasure in the perdition of men, but desirest that all should be saved and come to the knowledge of the truth. Therefore, even I unworthy of heaven, or yet of earth and of this temporal life, since I have submitted my whole self to sin and made myself a slave of pleasure, defiling thine image, but being still thy creature and thy handiwork, have not despaired of salvation, reprobate as I am; and, emboldened by thine immeasurable compassion, I come unto thee. Receive me then, even me, O man-loving Lord, as thou didst receive the adulteress, the thief, the publican, and the prodigal.

Take away the heavy load of my sins, O thou who takest away the sins of the world, who healest the infirmities of men, who callest unto thyself the weary and the burdened and givest them rest, who camest not to call the righteous but sinners to repentance. And do thou cleanse me from every defilement of the flesh and of the spirit, and teach me to perfect holiness in the

fear of thee, that, in the pure testimony of my conscience, receiving my portion of thy holy things, I may
be united with thy holy Body and precious Blood, and
have thee to dwell and remain within me, with the
Father and thy Holy Spirit. Yea, O Lord Jesus Christ
my God, grant that the communion of thy holy and life-
giving mysteries may not be to my condemnation; nor
let me be afflicted in soul and body by partaking thereof
unworthily; but grant me unto the last breath of my
life to partake uncondemned of my share of thy holy
things, looking to the fellowship of the Holy Spirit, to
provision for life eternal, and to a favourable answer at
thy terrible judgment-seat; that I, even I, may also become with thine elect a partaker of thine incorruptible
blessings, which thou hast prepared for those who love
thee, in whom, O Lord, thou art glorified to endless
ages. Amen.

Second Prayer by John Chrysostom

I KNOW, O Lord my God, that I am not worthy nor
sufficient that thou shouldest come under the roof
of my soul's habitation; for it is all deserted and in
ruins, and thou findest not in me where worthily to lay
thy head. But as from the height of thy glory thou
didst humble thyself for us, bear now also with my
humility; and as thou didst deign to lay thyself down
in a manger of dumb beasts, so deign now also to enter
into the manger of my dumb soul and defiled body;
and as thou didst not refuse to enter into the house of
Simon the leper and to sup there with sinners, so also
deign to enter the habitation of my humble soul, leprous and sinful; and as thou didst not reject the sinful
woman who approached and touched thee, so also have
pity on me, a sinner, coming to thee and touching thee;
and as thou didst not despise the mouth of that abominable impure one when he kissed thee, so also despise not
my more defiled mouth, unclean lips, and defiled tongue;
but may the live coal of thy most holy Body and pre-

ious Blood be for the sanctification, enlightenment,
and strengthening of my humble soul and body, for the
alleviation of the burden of my many sins, for my preservation from the very work of the devil, for victory
over my sinful and evil habits, for the mortification of
my passions, for the fulfillment of thy commandments,
or the increase of thy divine grace, and for the inheritance of thy kingdom; for it is not in lightness of heart,
O Christ my God, that I venture to approach thee, but
trusting in thine ineffable goodness, and in the fear,
lest being drawn far from thee, I become the prey of the
beast of the spirit. Therefore do I pray thee, O Lord,
who alone art holy, that thou wouldest sanctify my soul
and body, my heart, my reins and mind, and, renewing
me entirely, wouldest implant in my members the fear
of thee, and that thou let not thy sanctification be impugned by me. Be thou my help and guide, governing
my life in the ways of peace, and making me worthy
to obtain with thy saints a place at thy right hand;
through the prayers and supplications of thy most pure
Mother, of thine incorporeal ministers and undefiled
powers, and of all thy saints who from the ages have
found favour with thee. Amen.

Another Prayer, by Simeon the Neo-Theologian

O LORD, Jesus Christ, the Wisdom, Peace, and
Power of God, who alone art undefiled and imperishable, who for the compassion of thine ineffable
love to mankind didst take our entire nature from the
pure blood of the Virgin, the blood of her who in a
supernatural manner didst give thee birth by the de-
cent of the Holy Spirit and the pleasure of the eternal
Father, who, after the flesh which thou didst take, didst
accept the life-giving Passion of salvation, the Cross,
the nails, the spear, and death; deaden the soul-corrupting passions of my body, O thou who by thy Burial
didst lead captive the kingdom of hades. Bury under
good thoughts my evil counsels, O thou who by thy

life-giving, third-day Resurrection didst raise the fi
parent who had fallen, disperse from me the evil spiri
lift me, who slippeth in sin, placing before me the wa
of repentance, O thou who by thy glorious Ascensi
didst vouchsafe that the nature which thou hadst tak
should sit at the right hand of the Father, thereby e
nobling it, so prepare me that, by partaking of thy ho
mysteries, I may attain the favour of the saved. O th
who by the descent of the comforting Spirit didst ma
thy pure Disciples precious vessels, make me, too,
appear a vessel for his descent, O thou who art abc
to come to judge the universe with righteousness. Cc
sent, O my Maker and my Creator, that I too may w
come thee in the clouds with all thy saints, that I m
ceaselessly glorify thee, praising thee with thy Fath
who hath no beginning, and thy good, life-giving a
most Holy Spirit, now and forever and unto ages
ages. Amen.

Prayer, by St. John Damascene

I STAND before the gates of thy temple, O Lo
and yet my grievous thoughts forsake me not. F
thou, O Christ God, who didst justify the public;
hadst mercy on the Canaanitish woman, and didst op
the gates of paradise to the thief on the Cross, op
unto me the heart of thy most compassionate mercy, a
receive me coming unto thee and touching thee, li
the woman with the issue of blood, and like the sin
woman; for one touched but the hem of thy garme
and was healed, and the other embracing thy fe
received forgiveness of her sins. And lo! I, m
wretched, dare to partake of thy precious Body. O
me not be consumed, but receive me as thou receive
them, and enlighten my spiritual senses and destroy
my sinful inclinations. Hear me through the pray
of thy holy Mother and of thy heavenly hosts; for th
art blessed throughout all ages. Amen.

Prayer, by St. John Chrysostom

BELIEVE, O Lord, and confess that thou art verily Christ, the Son of the living God, who didst me into the world to save sinners, of whom I am the st. And I believe that this is thy most pure Body d this thy most pure Blood. I therefore pray thee, ve mercy upon me and forgive me my sins, voluntary involuntary, in word and in deed, committed in owledge or in ignorance; and vouchsafe me, to parke of thy most pure mysteries uncondemned, to the mission of sins, and to life eternal. Amen.

On approaching to communicate, say the following Stichoi of Saint neon, the Neo-Theologian.

BEHOLD, I approach the divine Communion!
My Creator, consume me not in the partaking of it;
For thou art a consuming Fire to the unworthy;
Purify me now from every stain.
Receive me today, O Son of God, a partaker of thy cramental Supper; for I shall not divulge thy mystery thine enemies, nor give thee a kiss like Judas. But ke the thief I shall confess to thee, Remember me, ord, in thy kingdom.

And again these Stichoi.

MAN, behold the divine Blood, and tremble;
For it is a fire consuming the unworthy.
The divine Body both deifieth and nourisheth me;
It deifieth the spirit, and strangely nourisheth the ind.

Also the following Troparia.

THOU hast enraptured me, O Christ, by thy longing and hast changed me by thy divine love. Conme my sins with thine immaterial fire, and enable me to be filled with thy bliss, that, rejoicing, I may magfy thy dual presence, O good One.

Into the brilliant company of thy saints how shall I
unworthy and sinful, enter? If I dare to enter into th
bridechamber, my garment will put me to shame, fo
it is not a wedding garment, and I shall be bound han
and foot and cast out by thine angels. Purify, Lord, m
polluted soul, and save me; for thou art a Lover o
mankind.

¶ *And the following Prayer.*

GRANT, O philanthropic Master, Lord Jesus Chris
my God, that I may not partake of this thy hol
Sacrament to my condemnation, because of mine un
worthiness, but to the purification and sanctification o
my soul and body, and as an earnest of thine everlastin
kingdom and life; for it is better for me to cleave unt
God, putting my hope of salvation in the Lord, Amen

¶ *Then,* Receive me today, O Son of God (*complete*).

PRAYERS OF THANKSGIVING AFTER DIVINE COMMUNION

Glory to thee, O God! Glory to thee, O God! Glor
to thee, O God!

¶ *Then the following Prayer of Thanksgiving.*

I THANK thee, O Lord my God, that thou hast no
rejected me, a sinner, but hast permitted me to be
come a partaker of thy Sacrament. I thank thee tha
thou hast enabled me, unworthy, to receive thy pur
and heavenly gifts. Wherefore, O philanthropic Lord
who didst die for us, and didst rise again, and hast be
stowed upon us these dread and life-giving mysterie
to the benefit and sanctification of our souls and bodies
grant that they may operate in me to the healing of m
soul and body, to the overthrow of every evil thing, t
the enlightenment of my heart, to the peace of my spir
itual faculties, to invincible faith, to sincere love, t
increase of wisdom, to the keeping of thy command
ments, to growth in grace, and to the inheritance of th

kingdom; that, preserved by them in thy sanctification, I may ever call to mind thy grace, and live not unto myself but unto thee, my Master and Benefactor. And thus when this life on earth shall have passed away in the hope of life eternal, may I attain unto everlasting rest where the hymn of those who glorify thee is unceasing, and the delight of those who behold the ineffable goodness of thy face is infinite; for thou art the true desire and inexpressible joy of those who love thee, O Christ our God, and all creation glorifieth thee to all eternity. Amen.

Another Prayer of Saint Basil the Great

O MASTER, Christ God, King of kings, and Creator of the universe, I thank thee for all the good things thou hast bestowed on me, but above all, for participation in thy pure and life-giving mysteries. I therefore pray thee, good and philanthropic Lord, keep me under thy shelter and in the shadow of thy wings, and grant me, in a pure conscience, to my latest breath, worthily to partake of thy holy Sacrament, to the remission of sins and to life eternal; for thou art the Bread of life, the source of sanctification, the Giver of all good; and to thee we ascribe all glory, with the Father and the Holy Spirit, now and ever, and unto ages of ages. Amen.

Prayer of Saint Simeon the Neo-Theologian in Verse

O THOU who of thine own good-will dost give unto me thy Body as food,
Thou who art a Fire consuming the unworthy;
Consume me not, O my Creator, consume me not,
But rather enter into my limbs, my joints, my inmost veins and heart.
And burn the tares of my transgressions.
Cleanse thou my soul, and sanctify my thoughts.
Strengthen my limbs, together with my bones.

Enlighten my five senses. Stablish me wholly in thy fear.

Ever cover me, preserve and protect me from all soul-corrupting words and deeds.

Make me chaste, purify and wash me, garnish me, instruct and enlighten me.

Show me to be a habitation of thy Spirit only, and in nowise again the dwelling-place of sin:

That becoming thy dwelling-place through communion; every evil and lustful being may flee from me as from fire.

I invoke, as supplicants for me, all the saints, the incorporeal powers, thy Forerunner, thy wise Apostles, and with them thy pure, most holy Mother.

Receive their prayers graciously, O my Christ, and render me, thy worshipper, a son of light.

For thou art the Sanctification and Delight of our souls, O God, and to thee, as is meet, we ascribe glory every day.

Another Prayer

MAY thy holy Body, O Lord Jesus Christ our God, be for eternal life unto me, and thy precious Blood for the remission of sins; and may this Eucharist be to me joy, health, and gladness; and at thy terrible Second Advent grant that I, a sinner, may stand at the right hand of thy glory; through the prayers of thy most pure Mother and of all thy saints. Amen.

Another Prayer to the Theotokos

O MOST holy Lady, Theotokos, light of my darkened soul, my hope, protection, refuge, comfort, and joy; I thank thee that thou hast enabled me, unworthy to be a partaker of the most pure Body and the most precious Blood of thy Son. Enlighten the eyes of my heart, thou who didst give birth to the Fountain of immortality; quicken thou me deadened by sin. O thou most tender and loving Mother of the merciful God, do thou have mercy upon me, and grant me a repentant and contrite heart with humility of mind. Recall my thoughts from wandering in places of captivity, and make me worthy to receive uncondemned, unto my last breath, the sanctification of thy most pure mysteries, to the healing of my soul and body. And give me tears of repentance and thanksgiving, that I may chant and praise thee all the days of my life; for thou art blessed and glorified to endless ages. Amen.

SECOND SECTION

✠

PRAYER SAID BY A CHRISTIAN ON ENTERING CHURCH

B UT as for me, in the multitude of thy mercies, I will come into thy house; I will worship towards thy holy temple in thy fear. Conduct me, O Lord, in thy justice: because of mine enemies direct my way in thy sight, that with clear conscience I may glorify the one Godhead, worshipped in three Persons. Father, Son, and Holy Spirit, for ever. Amen.

MIDNIGHT PRAYERS ON SUNDAYS

❡ *After* Blessed be God, *etc.;* O heavenly King, *etc.;* Holy God, *etc.;* For Thine is the kingdom, *etc.;* Lord, have mercy, (*twelve times*); Glory to the Father (*complete*); O come, let us worship, *etc.* (*three times*); and Psalm 50, Have mercy upon me, O God, *etc.* (*p. 82*), the Canon of the Triadikon[1] (*i.e. the Holy Trinity*), in the Oktoechos, in the Tone in use; chant immediately the following Trinitarians in the Sixth Tone.

I T is truly meet to praise the superdivine Trinity, the all-creating Father without beginning, the coëternal Word born of the Father before the ages without emanation, and the Holy Spirit proceeding from the timeless Father.

It is truly meet to glorify thee, O Word of God, before whom the cherubim shake and tremble, and whom the powers of heaven do glorify, the life-giving Christ risen from the tomb on the third day. Let us glorify him in fear.

---

[1] Composed by St. Metrophanes, Bishop of Smyrna (known in the 8th century).

Let us all with divine songs give fitting praise to the Father, Son, and divine Spirit, the three-personed Might, the one Kinghood, and the one Godhead.

When creation beheld thy Son, O pure Virgin, rising from the dead as befitteth a God, it was filled with ineffable joy, glorifying and honouring him.

❡ *Then say:* Holy God, *etc., and the Hypakoe in the Tone in use, and if it be a Feast Day and not a Sunday, sing the Litiva instead of the Canon of the Triadikon, and after it,* Holy God, *etc. Then the Troparion of the Feast, and at* Holy God, *the Priest enters the Sanctuary wearing the stole, and says,* For thine is the kingdom, *etc.; and while the Choir sings the Hypakoe or the Troparion, the Priest comes out wearing the Stole, and standeth in front of the Royal Door. When the Choir concludes, the Priest immediately saith the following Petitions.*

Have mercy upon us, O God, according to thy great mercy, we beseech thee. Hearken, and have mercy.

❡ *The Choir at each Petition chanteth alternately,* Lord, have mercy, (*three times*).

Again, let us pray for all pious and Orthodox Christians.

Again, we pray for our Father and Bishop (N.   ) and all our brethren in Christ.

And again, we ask mercy, life, safety, sound health, and the salvation of the servants of God and ever-memorable founders of this holy house; and those who pray therein (*its agents*), and its benefactors, for their visitation, and for their forgiveness, and the remission of their sins.

And again we ask for the preservation of this holy church, this city, and all other cities and towns, from famine, destruction, earthquake, flood, fire, and the sword; from the surprise attacks of foreign tribes, from civil wars, and sudden death. We pray that our good and philanthropic God in pity, mercy, and compassion turn away from us all desecration that riseth against us, deliver us from his just threat, and have mercy upon us.

❡ *Then the two Choirs chant alternately,* Lord, have mercy (*forty times of ten times each*).

Priest. And again we pray that the Lord God hear the voice of our supplication, who are sinners, and have mercy upon us.

Choir. Lord, have mercy (*three times*).

Priest. Grant, O God our Saviour, O Hope of all the earth and of those who are far at sea, to be kind to us, O Lord, and lenient towards our sins, and have mercy upon us; for thou art a compassionate and philanthropic God, and to thee do we address glory, O Father, etc.

Choir. Amen.

❡ *The Priest facing towards the East, saith:*

Glory to thee, O Christ God, our Hope, glory to thee.

Choir. Glory to the Father (*complete*) ; Lord, have mercy (*three times*). Bless.

Priest. O Christ our true God, (*who hath risen from the dead for our salvation*)[1] by the intercessions of thy holy, most pure and blameless Mother, and of our righteous, God-mantled Fathers, and of the two righteous holy grandparents of Christ, Joachim and Anne, and of all the saints, have mercy upon us and save us; for thou art good and the Lover of mankind.

❡ *Then he turneth to the people and saith:*

Forgive me, brethren.

❡ *And the Congregation replies:*

God forgive thee and us all.

❡ *Then the Priest turning to the Congregation and addressing them saith:*

For the peace of the world, let us pray.

❡ *And the Choir respondeth to this and each Petition,* Lord, have mercy.

---

[1] Said on Sundays.

For the Christians of true worship, the Orthodox.

For our kings of true worship, protected of God.

For the success and strength of the Christ-loving army.

For our Bishop (N.   ), and all our brethren in Christ.

For those of our parents and brothers who are absent from us.

For those who hate and those who love us.

For those who pity us and those who serve us.

For those who have requested us unworthy ones, to pray for them.

For the release of their captives and their safety.

For those who travel by sea, and those who travel by land.

For those bowed down with diseases and afflictions.

Let us pray also for an abundance of the fruits of the soil.

And for the souls of all the Christian Orthodox.

Let us beatify the kings of true worship.

And the Bishops of Orthodox opinion.

And those who built this holy temple.

And our parents, teachers, and all those departed of our Orthodox parents and brethren, lying in this place and every place.

Let us say for their sake, Lord, have mercy; Lord, have mercy; Lord, have mercy.

❡ *Then he turneth to the east and saith:*

Through the prayers of our Fathers the saints, O Lord Jesus Christ our God, have mercy upon us and save us.   Amen.

GENERAL MATIN PRAYERS ON SUNDAYS AND FEASTS

❡ *After* Blessed is God, *etc.;* O heavenly King, *etc.;* Holy God, *etc.; and the Troparia,* O Lord, save thy people, *etc.,* Do thou who, *etc.;* O dread Champion, *etc.* (*Look for Troparion on 25*).

Deacon. Have mercy upon us, O God, according to thy great mercy, we beseech thee; hearken and have mercy.

Choir. Lord, have mercy (*three times*).

Deacon. Again let us pray for all our God-preserved kings of true worship: and all their palaces and armies.

Choir. Lord, have mercy (*three times*).

Deacon. Again, let us pray for our Bishop (N.   ), and all our brethren in Christ.

Choir. Lord, have mercy (*three times*).

Deacon. Again, let us pray for our Orthodox Christians of true worship.

Choir. Lord, have mercy (*three times*).

Priest. For thou art a merciful and philanthropic God, and to thee we address glory, O Father, Son, etc.

Choir. Amen. Bless, Father, in the Name of the Lord.

Priest. Glory to the holy, consubstantial, life-giving, and undivided Trinity, now and ever, and unto ages of ages.

Choir. Amen.

¶ *The Lector immediately saith:*

Glory to God in the highest, and on earth peace, and good will among men (*three times*).

Lord, open thou my lips, and my mouth shall show forth thy praise (*two times*).

¶ *Then the Six Matin Psalms (p. 26). And after their completion by saying,* Glory to the Father (*complete*), Alleluia! Alleluia! Alleluia! Glory to thee, O God (*three times*); O our God and our Hope, glory to thee.

¶ *The Deacon saith the Great Synapte,* In peace, let us pray to the Lord, *etc. (p. 65).*

Priest. For all glory, honour, and worship are due to thee, O Father, etc.

Choir. Amen. God the Lord hath appeared unto us. Blessed is he that cometh in the Name of the Lord.

❡*Psalm 117: 26-27 (four times), with its following Stichoi, in the Tone as the Troparion of the Resurrection designates, or the Troparion of the Feast.*

O give thanks unto the Lord; call upon his Name.

All nations compassed me about, and in the Name of the Lord I have been revenged on them.

This is the Lord's doing.   It is marvelous in our eyes.

❡*If, however, it be a Sunday, the Troparion of the Resurrection is chanted (two times), or the Troparion of the Saint in whose honour the feast is celebrated, if it falleth on that Sunday, otherwise the Theotokion of the Tone; and immediately the Lector shall read the appointed selection of Psalms, and close by saying:*

Glory to the Father, etc. (*complete*); Alleluia! Alleluia! Alleluia! Glory to thee, O God (*three times*); O our God and our Hope, glory to thee.

❡*The Deacon then reciteth the Little Synapte,* Again and again, *etc.*

Priest. For thine is the might, and thine are the kingdom, power, and glory, O Father, etc.

Choir. Amen.

❡*And immediately the Choir chanteth or reciteth the Kathismata of the Resurrection. And after the Lector has read Psalm 118,* Blessed are they, *etc., the Choir singeth the following Benedictions in the Fifth Tone:*[1]

Blessed art thou, O Lord: teach me thy statutes.

THE company of the angels were amazed when they beheld thee numbered among the dead, O Saviour, yet destroying the power of death, and raising up Adam with thee and releasing us all from hades.

Blessed art thou, O Lord: teach me thy statutes.

Wherefore, O women Disciples, do ye mingle sweet-smelling spices with your tears of pity? The radiant angel within the sepulchre cried unto the ointment-

---

[1] That is, on a Sunday. But if it be a Feast of the Lord or our Lady, or a distinguished Saint, then after the Kathismata of the Feast, the Choir chanteth the first Antiphony of the Fourth Tone, *From my youth, etc.* (*p.* 50); the Prokeimenon and the rest of the Matin Gospel service of the Feast as designated in its proper place.

bearing women with joy; for the Saviour is risen from the tomb.

Blessed art thou, O Lord: teach me thy statutes.

Very early in the morning, did the ointment-bearing women run lamenting unto thy tomb; but the angel came toward them saying, The time for lamentation is past; weep not, but announce the Resurrection unto the Apostles.

Blessed art thou, O Lord: teach me thy statutes.

The ointment-bearing women mourned as, bearing ointments, they drew near to thy tomb, O Saviour. But the angel crying unto them with joy said, Why number ye the living among the dead? In that he is God, he is risen from the grave.

Glory

We worship the Father, and the Son, and the Holy Spirit, the Holy Trinity in one Essence, crying with the seraphim, Holy! Holy! Holy! art thou, O Lord.

Now

In that thou didst bear the Giver of life, O Virgin, thou didst redeem Adam from sin, and didst give to Eve joy in place of sadness; but he who was incarnate of thee, both God and Man, hath restored to life those who had fallen therefrom.

Alleluia! Alleluia! Alleluia! Glory to thee, O God (*three times*); O our God and our Hope, glory to thee.

❰ *The Deacon saith the Little Synapte.*

Priest. For thy Name is blessed, and thy kingdom glorified, O Father, etc.
Choir. Amen.

❰ *Then after chanting or reciting the Troparion of the Hypakoe and the Anabathmoi and the Prokeimenon, the Deacon saith:*

Let us pray to the Lord.
Choir. Lord, have mercy.

Priest. For thou art holy, our God, and in the saints doth dwell and abide, and unto thee do we address glory, O Father, etc.

Choir. Amen. Let everything that hath breath, praise the Lord (*three times*).

Deacon. And that we may be worthy to hear the holy Gospel of the Lord our God, we ask.

Choir. Lord, have mercy (*three times*).

Deacon. Wisdom! Let us stand, and hear the holy Gospel.

Priest. Peace be unto you all.

Choir. And unto thy spirit also.

Priest. A sacred chapter from Saint (N.   ) the Evangelist.

Choir. Glory to thee, O Lord, glory to thee.

Deacon. Let us hearken!

¶ *Then the Priest readeth the Matin Gospel, and at its conclusion, the Choir singeth:*

Glory to thee, O Lord, glory to thee.

IN that we have beheld the Resurrection of Christ, let us bow down before the Holy Lord Jesus, the only sinless One. Thy Cross do we adore, O Christ, and thy holy Resurrection we praise and glorify; for thou art our God, and we know none other beside thee; we call upon thy Name. O Come, all ye faithful, let us adore Christ's holy Resurrection. For lo! through the Cross is joy come into all the world. Ever blessing the Lord, let us sing his Resurrection; for in that he endured the Cross, he hath destroyed death by Death.

¶ *Then the Choir chanteth Psalm 50* (p 82.)[1] *and immediately in the Second Tone, Glory, and* Through the intercessions of the Apostles;[2] O merciful One, blot out the multitude of our transgressions.

---

[1] This if on a Sunday; otherwise, after reading the Matin Gospel of the Feast, Psalm 50 is recited by plain reading.

[2] If it be a Feast of the Lord or our Lady, then say, *Through the intercessions of the Theotokos;* and if it is a Feast of a celebrated Saint, then his name is substituted.

Now

Through the intercessions of the Theotokos and her prayers, O merciful God, blot out the multitude of our transgressions.

Then: O merciful One, have mercy upon me, O God, according to thy great mercy. And according to the multitude of thy tender mercies, blot out mine iniquity.

Jesus having risen from the grave as he foretold, hath given unto us life eternal and Great Mercy.[1]

Deacon. O God, save thy people, etc. (p. 52).

Choir. Lord, have mercy (*twelve times*).

Priest. By the mercy and compassion and philanthropy of the only Son with whom together with thy all-holy, good, and life-giving Spirit, thou art blessed, now, etc.

Choir. Amen.

❡ *Then the Lector beginneth by reciting the Canons, at the conclusion of which, the Choir chanteth the following Kathabasias, in the Fourth Tone.*[1]

1. Open my mouth and it shall be filled with the Spirit; and I shall declare a saying overflowing towards the Mother Queen. I shall shine forth, celebrating the season with rejoicing, and shall sing her wonders with gladness.

3. O Theotokos, since thou art a living fountain, bountifully overflowing, establish us who sing thy praises, who are gathered in a spiritual congregation. And in thy divine glory, prepare us for crowns of glory and honour.

---

[1] If not a Sunday, then instead of *Jesus having risen,* etc., the Idiomelons of the current Feast, designated in their proper places.

[2] The Katabasias beginning, *Open my mouth,* etc., are sung from All Saintᵣ Sunday to the 26th of July; and from the 22nd of September to the 20th of November, as well as on the Second, Fourth, and Fifth Sundays of the Great Fast, and the First and Fifth Saturdays thereof. The Katabasias of all the other Sundays and Feast Days of the year will be found in their indicated places, and in the Index.

4. Verily, Jesus the transcendentally Deified, who
tteth in glory on the throne of divinity, hath come on
bright cloud, saving in his incorruptible grasp those
ho cry unto him, Glory to thy power, O Christ.

5. O Virgin that knew no wedlock, the whole crea-
on hath been dazzled by thy divine glory; for thou
idst carry in thy womb the God of all, and conceived
ie Son not bound by time, granting salvation to all
iose who praise thee.

6. Come ye of divine minds, let us clap our hands,
:lebrating this most honourable Feast of the Theo-
)kos, and glorify God who was born of her.

7. The youths of godly minds worshipped not the
reature instead of the Creator, but trod the threat of
re bravely, singing joyfully, O exceeding of praise,
lessed art thou, Lord God of our Fathers.

Let us praise, bless, and worship the Lord.

8. The birth-giving of the Theotokos kept safe the
ure youths in the furnace, it having been so foreshad-
wed. But now that it hath actually been accomp-
shed, it moveth all the universe to sing aloud, Praise
ie Lord all his works, and exalt him yet more unto all
ges.

[*At the conclusion of the Eighth Ode, the Deacon cometh out, and
'anding before the Icon of our Lady in the Iconostasis, crieth, saying:*

The Theotokos, Mother of Light, in songs of praise
o we honour and magnify thee.

Choir. My soul doth magnify the Lord; and my
pirit hath rejoiced in God my Saviour.

O thou who art more honourable than the cherubim,
nd beyond compare more glorious than the seraphim;
vho without corruption didst bear the Word of God,
ruly, thou art the Theotokos, and thee do we magnify.

[*And immediately the following Stichoi, after each of which is re-
eated,* O thou who art more honourable, *etc.*

BECAUSE he hath regarded the humiliation of his
handmaid; for behold from henceforth all genera-
ions shall call me blessed.

Because he that is mighty, hath done great things
me; and holy is his Name; and his mercy is fr
generation to generation to them that fear him.

He hath shewed strength in his arm: he hath sc
tered the proud in the conceit of their heart.

He hath put down the mighty from their seat, a
hath exalted the humble. He hath filled the hung
with good things, and the rich hath he sent away emp

He hath received Israel his servant, being mind
of his mercy. As he spake to our Fathers, to Abraha
and to his seed forever.

❡ *Then immediately the Choir singeth the following Ninth Od
the Katabasias.*

The Ninth Ode—Hermos

LET all the earthly rejoice in the Spirit, carry
lamps. And the nature of the supersensuous, i
material ones celebrateth also the noble Feast of
Theotokos, shouting, Rejoice, O all-pure, all-bless
ever-virgin Theotokos.

Deacon. The Little Synapte, Again and again, c

Priest. For thee do all the powers of heaven pra
and to thee do they address glory, O Father, etc.

Choir. Amen. Holy is the Lord our God (*t
times*). Exalt ye the Lord our God and worship at
footstool; for he is holy.

❡ *Then sing the Exaposteilarion of the Resurrection and of the S
if a distinguished one, whose Feast may fall on this day; otherw
of our Lady. If not on a Sunday, then immediately after the Ex
mation of the Priest,* For thee do all the powers, *etc., the Exapo
larion of the Feast is sung; after which the Einos, in the Ton
use, is sung.*

LET everything that hath breath, praise the Lo
Praise ye the Lord from the heavens; praise ye h
in the highest; for to thee praise is due, O God.

Praise ye him, all his angels; praise ye him, all
hosts; for to thee praise is due, O God.

*f a Sunday, the Choir will sing the following eight Stichoi, the
r Stichera of the Resurrection, and four of the Saint, if it be the
st of a distinguished Saint, otherwise, the eight Stichera of the
urrection. And if not on a Sunday, then the Choir shall sing the
owing eight Stichoi on the Stichera of the Feast, if the latter are
it, or drop the last two if they are six, or drop the first one and
two, and couple the second and third, if they are four.*

Stichoi of the Einos

1. To execute upon them the judgment that is writ-
. This glory is to all his saints.

2. Praise ye the Lord in his sanctuary. Praise ye
n in the firmament of his power.

3. Praise ye him for his mighty acts. Praise ye him
:ording to the multitude of his greatness.

4. Praise him with sound of trumpet. Praise him
th psaltery and harp.

5. Praise him with timbrel and choir. Praise him
th strings and organs.

6. Praise him with high-sounding cymbals. Praise
n on cymbals of joy. Let everything which hath
eath, praise the Lord.

7. Arise, O Lord God, let thy hand be exalted. For-
t not the poor unto the end.

8. I will praise thee, O Lord, with my whole heart.
will relate all thy wonders.

*'f on a Dominical Feast or that of a great Saint, then is chanted
ory and Now of the Feast. But if on a Sunday, then the Glory
the Eothina and Now of the following to our Lady, in the Second
ne.*

THOU hast transcended all blessings, O virgin
Theotokos, for hades hath been spoiled by him
10 was incarnate of thee. Yea, Adam was recalled,
curse was abolished. Eve was delivered and death
1s caused to die, and we were made to live again.
herefore, with praise we cry, Blessed art thou, O
1rist our God, who hast thus shown thy pleasure;
ory to thee.

Then immediately, the following Great Doxology is sung.

THE GREAT DOXOLOGY

GLORY be to thee who hast shown us thy light.
Glory to God in the highest and on earth peace, and
good-will among men.

We praise thee, we bless thee, we worship thee, we
glorify thee, we give thanks unto thee for the splendour of thy glory.

O Lord, O King, O heavenly God, Father Almighty
O Lord, O only-begotten Son Jesus Christ, and Holy
Spirit.

O Lord God, O Lamb of God, O Son of the Father
that takest away the sins of the world, have mercy upon
us, O thou that takest away the sins of the world.

Accept our prayers, O thou that sittest on the righ
hand of the Father, and have mercy upon us.

For thou only art holy, thou only art the Lord Jesu
Christ, in the glory of God the Father. Amen.

Every day will I bless thee and will praise thy Name
for ever and ever.

Vouchsafe, O Lord, to keep us this day without sin

Blessed art thou, O Lord, God of our Fathers, and
praised and glorified is thy Name for ever. Amen.
our trust in thee.

Let thy mercy, O Lord, be upon us, as we have pu

Blessed art thou, O Lord, teach me thy statute
(*three times*).

O Lord thou hast been our refuge from generation
to generation. I said, Lord have mercy upon me, hea
my soul; for I have sinned against thee.

O Lord, I flee unto thee, teach me to do thy will
for thou art my God.

For with thee is the fountain of life, and in thy ligh
we shall see light.

Extend thy mercy unto them that know thee.

Holy God, Holy Mighty, Holy Immortal One, have
mercy upon us (*three times*).

Glory to the Father, and to the Son, and to the Holy
Spirit.

Now and ever and unto ages of ages. Amen.
Holy immortal One, have mercy upon us.

❡ *Then in a loud voice:*

Holy God, Holy Mighty, Holy Immortal One, have
mercy upon us.

❡ *If on a Feast, sing its Troparion, and if on a Sunday when Tones
1, 2, 3, or 4 are used, sing the following Troparion.*

TODAY hath salvation come into the world. Let
us sing praises unto him who rose again from the
grave, the Author of our life; for in that by Death he
hath destroyed death, he hath given unto us the victory
and Great Mercy.

❡ *If Tones 5, 6, 7, or 8, are used, sing the following Troparion.*

HAVING risen again from the tomb, and having
burst asunder the bonds of hades; thou didst unbind the condemnation of death, O Lord, redeeming
all men from the snares of the enemy. And having revealed thyself to thine Apostles, thou didst send them
forth to proclaim thee. And through them thou hast
granted thy peace unto the universe, O thou who
art alone all-merciful.

✠

The
Divine Liturgy of John Chrysostom
and Basil the Great[1]

❡ *At the singing of the Troparion at the Doxology, the Priest standeth before the Table and reciteth secretly,* O heavenly King, *etc.;*
Glory to God in the highest, and on earth peace, and goodwill among

---

[1] The Liturgy of John Chrysostom does not differ from that of Basil the
Great except in the prayers which the Priest repeats secretly. The latter is
performed ten times only throughout the year, i.e. on the Sundays of the Great
Fast (except Palm Sunday), on Great Thursday, Great Saturday, the Paramon
of the Nativity, the Paramon of the Epiphany, and on the day of the Feast
itself if either of these two Feasts fall on a Sunday or a Monday, and on the
Feast of Saint Basil the Great.

men (*three times*), *and* Lord, open thou my lips, and my mouth shall show forth thy praise (*two times*).

Deacon. Bless, Master.

❡ *The Priest lifteth the Gospel Book with both hands and maketh with it the sign of the cross over the Antimensium, saying:*

Blessed be the kingdom of the Father, and of the Son, and of the Holy Spirit, now, and ever, and unto ages of ages.

❡ *Then kissing the Gospel Book, he placeth it over the Antimensium.*

Choir. Amen.

❡ *Then the Deacon standeth, and, wearing his mitre, lifteth the end of his girdle with three fingers, and reciteth the Great Synapte (p. 65), the Choir responding to each Petition with, Lord, have mercy.*

Priest. For all glory, honour, and worship are due to thee, O Father, Son, and Holy Spirit, now and always and unto ages of ages.

Choir. Amen.

❡ *Then immediately they chant the following Psalm antiphonally.*

The First Antiphony (*Typica*)

PSALM 102

Right Choir. Bless the Lord, O my soul. Blessed art thou, O Lord.

Bless the Lord, O my soul; and let all that is within me bless his holy name.

Bless the Lord, O my soul, and never forget all he hath done for thee.

Who forgiveth all thy iniquities: who healeth all thy disease:

Who redeemeth thy life from destruction: who crowneth thee with mercy and compassion:

Who satisfieth thy desire with good things; thy youth shall be renewed like the eagle's.

The Lord doeth mercies and judgment for all that suffer wrong.

He hath made his ways known to Moses: his wills to
he children of Israel.

The Lord is compassionate and merciful: long-suf-
ering and plenteous in mercy.

He will not always be angry; nor will he threaten
orever.

He hath not dealt with us according to our sins: nor
ewarded us according to our iniquities.

For according to the height of the heaven above the
arth: he hath strengthened his mercy towards them
hat fear him.

As far as the east is from the west, so far hath he
emoved our iniquities from us.

As a father hath compassion on his children, so hath
he Lord compassion on them that fear him: for he
knoweth our frame.

He remembereth that we are dust: man's days are as
grass, as the flower of the field so shall he flourish.

For the spirit shall pass in him, and he shall not be:
and he shall know his place no more.

But the mercy of the Lord is from eternity and unto
eternity upon them that fear him:

And his justice unto children's children, to such as
keep his covenant,

And are mindful of his commandments to do them.

The Lord hath prepared his throne in heaven: and
his kingdom shall rule over all.

Bless the Lord, all ye his angels; you that are mighty
in strength, and execute his word, hearkening to the
voice of his orders.

Bless the Lord, all ye his hosts: you ministers of his
that do his will.

Bless the Lord, all his works: in every place of his
dominion, O my soul, bless thou the Lord.

Glory and Now

Bless the Lord, O my soul: and all that is within me,
bless his holy Name. Blessed art thou, O Lord.

❡ *Instead of the above, the following Antiphony may be used.*

Right Choir (Stichos). It is a good thing to give praise unto the Lord and to sing unto thy Name O most High.

Through the intercessions of the Theotokos, O Saviour, save us. (*Refrain.*)

Left Choir (Stichos). To proclaim thy mercy in the morning and thy truth at night. (*R.*)

Right Choir (Stichos). For our God is just and in him there is no oppression. (*R.*)

Left Choir. Glory. (*R.*)

Right Choir. Now. (*R.*)

❡ *The* Deacon. *The Little Synapte, Again, and again, etc.*

Priest. For thine is the might, and thine are the kingdom, and the power, and the glory, O Father, etc.

Choir. Amen.

❡ *And immediately the Choir sings the Second Antiphony.*

PSALM 145

Left Choir. Glory to the Father, and to the Son, and to the Holy Spirit.

Praise the Lord, O my soul, and in my life I will praise the Lord: I will sing to my God as long as I shall be.

Put not your trust in princes; in the children of men in whom there is no salvation.

His spirit shall go forth, and he shall return into his earth; in that day all their thoughts shall perish.

Blessed is he who hath the God of Jacob for his helper, whose hope is in the Lord his God: who made heaven and earth, the sea, and all things that are in them:

Who keepeth truth for ever: who executeth judgment for them that suffer wrong: who giveth food to the hungry.

The Lord looseth them that are fettered; the Lord enlighteneth the blind.

The Lord lifteth them that are cast down: the Lord loveth the just.

The Lord keepeth the strangers, he will support the fatherless and the widow: and the ways of the sinners he will destroy.

The Lord shall reign forever: thy God, O Sion, unto generation and generation.

Now

O ONLY-begotten Son and Word of God, who art immortal and who didst deign for our salvation to be incarnate of the holy Theotokos and ever-virgin Mary, and without transubstantiation wast made man, and also crucified, O Christ our God, and didst trample death by Death, being yet one of the holy Trinity, glorified together with the Father and the Holy Spirit, save us.

❧ *Instead of the above, the following Antiphony may be used on Sundays.*

Left Choir (Stichos). The Lord hath reigned: he is clothed with beauty. The Lord is clothed with strength and hath girded himself.

Save us, O Son of God, who didst rise from the dead, even us who sing unto thee, Alleluia. (*Refrain.*)

Right Choir (Stichos). For he hath established the world which shall not be moved. (*R.*)

Left Choir (Stichos). Holiness becometh thy house, O Lord, unto length of days. (*R.*)

Right Choir. Glory. (*R.*)

Left Choir. Now, O only-begotten Son, etc.

Deacon. The Little Synapte, Again and again, etc.

Priest. For thou art a good and philanthropic God, and to thee do we address glory, O Father, etc.

Right Choir. Amen.

❧ *After which the Choir beginneth the following Beatitudes.*

The Beatitudes (Makarizmoi)

Choir. In thy kingdom, remember me, O Lord, when thou comest into thy kingdom.

BLESSED are the poor in spirit; for theirs is the kingdom of heaven.

❡*Note: And at each of the Beatitudes from* Blessed are the merciful, *etc., is sung its designated piece in the Oktoechos, or of the third and sixth of the Canon of the current Feast.*

Blessed are they that mourn; for they shall be comforted.

Blessed are the meek; for they shall inherit the earth.

Blessed are they that hunger and thirst after righteousness; for they shall be filled.

Blessed are the merciful; for they shall obtain mercy.

Blessed are the pure in heart; for they shall see God.

Blessed are the peacemakers; for they shall be called the children of God.

Blessed are they that are persecuted for righteousness' sake; for theirs is the kingdom of heaven.

Blessed are ye when men shall revile you, and persecute you, and say all manner of evil against you falsely for my sake.

Rejoice and be glad, for great is your reward in heaven.

Glory and Now

❡*Instead of the Beatitudes, the Troparion of the Tone in use or that of the Feast in use is sung. Then followeth the Little Eisodos (entrance) with the Gospel, from the left door of the Sanctuary to the front of the Royal Door, as the Deacon crieth:*

Wisdom! Let us stand!

❡*If a Dominical Feast, the proper Eisodos thereof is sung, but on other Sundays, the Choir singeth:*

O come, let us worship and fall down to Christ. Save us, O Son of God, who didst rise, etc.

❡ *Then immediately chant the Troparion of the Resurrection or the Troparion of the Feast, and the Troparion of the Patron Saint of the church and the Hypakoe of the Tone, concluding with the Kontakion of the Feast., if it is a Dominical one, but on other Sundays the following Theotokion.*

O UNDISPUTED intercessor of Christians, the mediatrix unrejected by the Creator, turn not away from the voice of our petitions, though we be sinners. Come to us in time, who cry to thee in faith, with assistance; for thou art good.   Hasten to us with intercessions, O Theotokos, who dost ever intercede for those who honour thee.

Deacon.   Let us pray to the Lord.

Choir.   Lord, have mercy.

Priest.   For thou art holy, O our God, and unto thee do we address glory, O Father, etc.

Choir.   Amen.

❡ *And immediately the Choir singeth alternately (three times) the Trisagion, beginning with the right.*

Holy God!   Holy Mighty!   Holy Immortal One! Have mercy upon us.

Left Choir.   Glory.

Right Choir.   Now.

Left Choir.   Holy Immortal One!   Have mercy upon us.

Deacon (or Right Choir).   Dynamis!   (*Louder.*)[1]

---

[1] But if a Bishop be celebrating the Divine Mass, the following order is observed in singing the Trisagion:

Right Choir.   Holy God, etc.
Left Choir.   Holy God, etc.
From the Temple.   Holy God, etc.
Right Choir.   Holy God, etc.
From the Temple.   Holy God, etc.
Left Choir.   Glory.
Right Choir.   Now.
Left Choir.   Holy Immortal One!   Have mercy upon us.
From the Temple: The Trisagion is sung with a muffled voice, and after each, Holy, the Bishop, holding the Trikerion in his right and the Dikerion in his left hand, turns toward the worshippers and says in a loud voice, O Lord! O Lord! Look down from heaven and see, and visit this vineyard: and perfect the same which thy right hand planted (Psalm 79:15, 16).
Right Choir.   Holy God, etc.
Then the Right Choir closes with, Holy God, etc. for the seventh time, and

Right Choir. Holy God, etc.

Deacon. Let us hearken.

Priest. Peace be unto you all.

Lector. And unto thy spirit also.

¶*And immediately he saith the Prokeimenon of the Epistles.*

Deacon. Wisdom!

Lector. Section from the Epistle (*to the end*).

Deacon. Let us hearken.

¶*Then the Lector reciteth the Epistle, at the conclusion of which the Priest saith:*

Peace to thee that readeth, and to the whole congregation.

Lector. And unto thy spirit also.

Choir. Alleluia (*three times*).

Deacon. Peace be unto you all.

Choir. And unto thy spirit also.

Deacon. A Sacred Chapter from Saint (N.   ) the Evangelist.

Choir. Glory to thee, O Lord, glory to thee.

Deacon. Let us hearken!

¶*He readeth the Gospel, at the conclusion of which, the Choir singeth:*

Glory to thee, O Lord, glory to thee.

¶*Immediately the Deacon beginneth the Petitions of Supplication as the Choir singeth,* Lord, have mercy *once after the first and second, and three times after each of the rest.* (*p. 75*), Let us say with all our soul, *etc.*

Priest. For thou art a merciful and philanthropic God, and to thee do we address glory, etc.

---

the Deacon stands in the Royal Door and says, Lord save the believers, which is then sung alternately by the Right and Left Choirs.

Deacon. And hearken unto us.

Right Choir. And hearken unto us.

Then the Deacon, standing in the Royal Door and turning towards the congregation, recites the Theme (indicating the official title of the Bishop and extent of which comes the reading of the Epistles).

[When the Priest cometh to the words, O Father, *he maketh the
gn of the cross with the Gospel Book over the Antimensium, and
laceth the Gospel Book behind it.*

Choir. Amen.

Deacon. Catechumens, pray to the Lord.

Let us believers, pray for the Catechumens.

That the Lord may have mercy upon them.

That he may teach them the word of truth.

That he may reveal to them the Gospel of righteous-
ess.

That he may unite them to his Holy, Catholic, and
Apostolic Church.

Save, have mercy, help and keep them, O God, by
hy grace.

Catechumens, bow your heads to the Lord.

Choir. To thee, O Lord.

Priest. That they also, with us, may glorify thine
ll-honourable and magnificent Name, O Father, etc.

Choir. Amen.

Deacon. As many as are Catechumens, depart. Cate-
humens, depart.

As many as are Catechumens, depart. Let no Cate-
humens remain.

As many as are believers, remain.

Again and again, in peace let us pray to the Lord.

Choir. Lord, have mercy.

Deacon. Help, save, have mercy, and keep us, O
God, by thy grace.

Choir. Lord, have mercy.

Deacon. Wisdom!

Priest. For all glory, honour, and worship are due
to thee, O Father, etc.

Choir. Amen.

Deacon. Again and again, in peace, let us pray to
the Lord.

Choir. Lord, have mercy.

Deacon. Help, save, have mercy, and keep us, O
God, by thy grace.

Choir. Lord, have mercy.

Deacon. Wisdom!

Priest. That being preserved by thy might, we ma address to thee glory, O Father, etc.

Choir. Amen.

¶ *And immediately beginneth the singing of:*

The Cherubicon[1]

LET us who represent the cherubim mystically an who sing with them the thrice holy hymn to th life-giving Trinity, lay aside all worldly care, sinc we are about to receive the King of all (*pause*), su rounded invisibly by the angelic ranks, Alleluia! All luia! Alleluia!

Deacon. Let us finish our petitions to the Lord.

¶ *At each of the following Petitions the Choir respondeth,* Lord, hav mercy, *and when the Deacon saith,* Of the Lord, we ask, *the Cho respondeth,* Grant, O Lord.

FOR these noble oblations, here placed, let us pra to the Lord.

For this holy house, and those who enter therein wit faith, reverence, and godly fear, let us pray to the Lor

For our deliverence from all sorrow, wrath, afflic tions, and depression, let us pray to the Lord.

Help, save, have mercy, and keep us, O God, by th grace.

That our whole day may be perfect, holy, peacefu and without sin, let us ask the Lord. (*See rest on p. 76.*

Priest. For the compassion of thine only Son, wit

---

[1] As the Choir comes to the words, *King of all* in the Cherubicon, a ge eral pause follows as the Choir stops, and the Great Eisodos begins; t Deacon with the Priest holding the Sacramental Elements, emerge from t Left Door, preceded by candles, fans, the cross and censers, and standi before the Royal Door, preceded by candles, fans, the cross and censer and standing before the Royal Door, they turn towards the congregatio and mention in a loud voice the Kings of true worship, the Bishop, and t rest of the Orthodox people, saying, *May the Lord God remember you in his kingdom, always, now and forever and unto ages of ages,* Then th enter the Temple through the Royal Door, as the Choir resumes the singi of the Cherubicon.

whom, and with thy all-holy, good and life-giving
Spirit, thou art blessed, now, etc.

Choir. Amen.

Priest. Peace be unto you all.

Choir. And unto thy spirit also.

Deacon. Let us love one another, that in one united
purpose we may acknowledge and confess.

Choir. Father, Son, and Holy Spirit, the consubstantial and undivided Trinity.

Deacon. The Doors! The Doors! In wisdom let us
hearken.

Lector. I believe in One God, etc. (p. 85.)

Deacon. Let us stand upright, let us stand with fear,
let us hearken, to offer the holy Oblation in peace.

Choir. A favour of peace, a sacrifice of praise.

Priest. The grace of our Lord Jesus Christ, and the
love of God the Father, and the communion of the
Holy Spirit, be with you all.

Choir. And thy spirit also.

Priest. Let us lift up our hearts.

Choir. Our hearts are with the Lord.

Priest. Let us give thanks unto the Lord.

Choir. It is meet and right to worship the Father,
the Son, and the Holy Spirit, the consubstantial and
undivided Trinity.

Priest. Singing, shouting, proclaiming the triumphal
hymn, and saying,

Choir. Holy, Holy, Holy, Lord of Sabbaoth. Heaven
and earth are full of thy glory. Hosanna in the highest.
Blessed is he that cometh in the Name of the Lord.
Hosanna in the highest.

Priest. Take, eat; this is my Body, which is broken
for you for the remission of sins.

Choir. Amen.

Priest. Drink ye all of this; for this is my Blood of
the New Testament, which is shed for you and for
many, for the remission of sins.

Choir. Amen. Amen.

Priest. Of that which is thine, we offer thee thine own, for all things and of all.

Choir. Thee do we praise, thee do we bless; unto thee, O Lord, we give thanks, and of thee we make request O our God.[1]

Priest. Especially for the all-holy, pure, exceedingly blessed, and glorified, ever-virgin Mary, our Lady, the Theotokos.

Choir. It is truly meet to bless the Theotokos, who is ever-blessed, and all blameless, the Mother of our God.

O THOU who art more honourable than the cherubim, and beyond compare more glorious than the seraphim, who without corruption didst bear the Word of God, truly thou art the Theotokos, and thee do we magnify.

❡ *If the Liturgy of St. Basil the Great is being used the following hymn is sung in the Eighth Tone.*

IN thee rejoiceth all creation, O thou who art full of grace, the hierarchy of the angels, and all mankind, O consecrated temple and paradise endowed with speech, glory of virginity, of whom God, who is our God before the ages, was incarnate and became a little child.

❡ *Then in the Fifth Tone.*

FOR he made thy womb a throne, and thy belly did he make more spacious than the heavens. In thee doth all creation rejoice, O thou who art full of grace, and it glorifieth thee.

❡ *Then the following hymn, in the Second Tone.*

---

[1] At this particular moment, most august and important in all the service of the Divine Mass, the Celebrant falls on his knees and touches the ground with his forehead, as he beseeches God the Father to send his Holy Spirit on the fervantly exposed offerings, and to change the Bread and Wine into the Body and Blood of his Son, our Lord and God Jesus Christ. And in that very instant the Divine Mystery of Transubstantiation is accomplished.

LET us all laud Basil the Magnificent, that revealer of heavenly things, that initiate of Christ the Master, that brilliant star shining forth in Caesarea of Capadocia. Yea, it is meet for us all to honour him.

Priest. First, O Lord, remember our Bishop (N.). Vouchsafe him to thy holy churches safe and sound, honoured and of long years, handling aright thy word of truth.

Deacon. And all that are in the minds of those present here, those present all, men and women.

Choir. And all present, men and women.

Priest. And grant us, with one mouth, and one heart to glorify and praise thine all-honoured, most resplendent Name, O Father, etc.

Choir. Amen.

Priest. And may the mercies of the great God, and our Saviour Jesus Christ be with you all.

Choir. And with thy spirit also.

❡*And immediately the Deacon reciteth the following Petitions, after each of which the Choir chanteth,* Lord, have mercy; *and when the Deacon saith,* Of the Lord, we ask, *the Choir chanteth,* Grant, O Lord.

Deacon. Remembering all the saints, again and again in peace let us pray to the Lord.

For these precious offerings which have been offered and sanctified, let us pray to the Lord.

That our philanthropic God, receiving them at this holy, heavenly, and supersensuous Altar as a spiritual sweet odour, would send down to us in return the divine grace and gift of the Holy Spirit.

For our deliverance from all affliction, wrath, danger. and depression, let us pray to the Lord.

Help, save, have mercy, and keep us, O God, by thy grace.

That our whole day may be perfect, holy, peaceful, and without sin, let us ask the Lord.

For an angel of peace, a faithful guide, a guardian of our souls and bodies, let us ask the Lord.

For the forgiveness and remission of our sins, let us ask the Lord.

For what is good and profitable for Christians, and for the peace of the world, let us ask the Lord.

That the rest of our life may be spent in peace and penitence, let us ask the Lord.

That the end of our life may be Christian, peaceful, without sorrow or shame, and that we may have a good response at the fearful judgment seat of Christ, let us ask the Lord.

Praying for the unity of the Faith and the communion of the Holy Spirit, let us commend ourselves and each other, and all our life to Christ our God.

Choir. To thee, O Lord.

Priest. And vouchsafe us, O Master, that we may presume with privilege and without condemnation, to call upon thee, O heavenly God, as Father, and say

Lector. Our Father, who art in heaven, etc. (p. 23)

Priest. For thine is the kingdom, and the power, and the glory, O Father, etc.

Choir. Amen.

Priest. Peace be unto you all.

Choir. And unto thy spirit also.

Deacon. Bow your heads unto the Lord.

Choir. To thee, O Lord.

Priest. By the grace, compassion, and philanthropy of thine only Son with whom and with thy all-holy, the good and life-giving Spirit, thou art blessed, now, etc

Choir. Amen.

Deacon. Let us hearken.

Priest. The holy things for holy persons.

Choir. One Holy, one Lord, Jesus Christ, in the glory of God the Father. Amen.

❡ *Then immediately beginneth the singing of the Koinonikon (Communion Hymn).*

Praise ye the Lord from the heavens; praise ye him in the highest. Alleluia (*three times*).

❧ *And after the Koinonikon, the Royal Door is opened, as the Deacon, holding in his hands the Chalice, crieth:*

In godly fear, faith, and love, draw ye near.

❧ *Here the Communicants go forward to the Royal Door to receive the Communion, at which the Choir singeth the following Troparion.*

RECEIVE me today, O Son of God, a partaker of the sacramental Supper; for I shall not divulge thy mystery to thine enemies, nor give thee a kiss like Judas; but like the thief I shall confess to thee, Remember me, O Lord, in thy kingdom.

Choir. Blessed is he that cometh in the Name of the Lord. The Lord God hath appeared unto us (Psalm 117:26-27).

Priest. O Lord, save thy people, and bless thine inheritance.

Choir. We have seen the true light; and have received the heavenly Spirit. We have found the true Faith. Wherefore, let us worship the undivided Trinity; for he hath saved us.

Priest. At all times, now and ever, and unto ages of ages.

Choir. Amen. Let our mouths be filled with thy praise, O Lord, that we may sing of thy glory; for that thou hast made us worthy to partake of thy holy divine, immortal, and life-giving mysteries. Establish us in thy sanctification, that we may meditate upon thy righteousness all the day. Allelulia (*three times*).

Deacon. Let us stand up! Having partaken of the divine, holy, pure, immortal, heavenly, life-giving, and dread mysteries of Christ, let us thank the Lord worthily.

Right Choir. Lord, have mercy.

Deacon. Help, save, have mercy, and keep us, O God, by thy grace.

Left Choir. Lord, have mercy.

Deacon. Having asked that our whole day be perfect, holy, peaceful, and without sin, let us commend ourselves and each other and all our life to Christ our God.

Right Choir. To thee, O Lord.

Priest. For thou art our sanctification, and unto thee do we address glory, O Father, etc.

Choir. Amen.

Priest. Let us depart in Peace.

Choir. In the Name of the Lord.

Deacon. Let us pray to the Lord.

Right Choir. Lord, have mercy (*three times*). Bless.

❧ *And the Priest then exits by the Royal Door, and stands in front of the Lord's Icon and readeth the following prayer, known as* The Prayer from behind the Pulpit.

O LORD, who blesseth those who bless thee, and sanctifieth those who put their trust in thee, save thy people and bless thine inheritance. Preserve the fullness of thy Church. Sanctify those who love the beauty of thy house. Honour them in return with thy divine power and forsake not us who put our trust in thee. Give peace to the world, to thy churches, to thy Priest, to our kings, their armies, and to all thy people; for every good gift and every perfect blessing is from above, and cometh down from the Father of lights. And to thee, O Father, Son, and Holy Spirit, we ascribe all glory, thanksgiving and worship, now, and ever, and unto ages of ages.

Left Choir. Amen.

❧ *Then the two Choirs sing alternately:*

Blessed be the Name of the Lord from this time forth and for ever (*three times*).

❧ *The Priest here blesseth the worshippers, saying:*

May the blessing of the Lord and his mercy descend upon you by his divine grace and his love for mankind, now, etc.

Left Choir. Amen.

Priest. Glory to thee, O Christ our God, and our Hope, glory to thee.

Lector. Glory to the Father (*complete*). Lord, have mercy (*three times*), Bless, O Father, in the Name of the Lord.

❡ *Then the Priest standing in front of the Royal Door, facing the people, and carrying in his hands the precious cross, pronounceth the following closing Prayer.*

O THOU who didst rise from the dead, O Christ[1] our true God, by the intercessions of thy all-pure Mother, and of the glorified and most praiseworthy Apostles, and of our Father among the saints John Chrysostom (*or Basil the Great, or Gregory Theologus*) and Saint (N.) patron of the Church, and the two righteous saints, the grandparents of Christ God, Joachim and Anne, and (*the current*) saint, whose memory we celebrate today, and all the saints, have mercy upon us and save us; for thou art good and the Lover of mankind.

Through the prayers of our Fathers the saints,[2] O Lord, Jesus Christ our God, have mercy upon us and save us.

Choir. Amen.

❡ *Then the Priest distributeth the consecrated Bread to the congregation, saying to each one in turn:*

The blessing of the Lord be on thee.

❡ *And after the distribution, he says:*

By his grace and love of mankind, always, etc.

Troparion at the Kissing of the Lord's Icon

THY pure image do we adore, O good One, asking forgiveness of our sins, O Christ our God; for by

---

[1] This expression is used on Sundays throughout the year (and on the Feast of the Elevation of the Cross, even when it does not fall on a Sunday), except Palm Sunday and Whitsunday. On these two Sundays, on the Dominical Feast, and in Passion Week, special expressios are used as indicated in their proper places. As for the rest of the week days, this expression is omitted and the concluding prayer begins with, *O Christ our true Lord.* So also is the conclusion at Vespers, Matins, and with other Prayers.

[2] If a Bishop be present, *By the prayer of our master, Saint,* etc. is said.

thine own will thou didst ascend the Cross in the body
to save thy creatures from bondage to the enemy. Thou
hast verily filled all with joy, since thou didst come, O
our Saviour, to save the world.

Troparion at the Kissing of the Icon of the Theotokos

BEING a fountain of compassion, O Theotokos, make
me worthy of sympathy and pity. Look upon all
sinful people. Show forth thy wonted power, that
like Gabriel of old, the chief of the incorporeal hosts,
we may bid thee, Hail.

THIRD SECTION

Oktoechos or Book of Eight Tones

To which are appended the Matin Gospels, Exapos-teilarions, and the Eleven Eothinas of the Resurrection.

✛

FIRST TONE

1. SATURDAY VESPERS

The Stichera on O Lord, to thee have I cried

O HOLY Lord, accept our evening prayers. Grant us forgiveness of our sins; for thou alone art he who didst reveal the Resurrection in the world.

O ye peoples, encircle Zion and surround it; give ye glory therein to him who is risen from the dead; for he is our God who has delivered us from our sins.

Come, ye peoples, let us praise Christ and bow down to him, glorifying his Resurrection from the dead; for he is our God who delivered the world from the deception of the enemy.

Rejoice, O heaven, blow the horn, ye foundations of the earth, and cry, O mountains, with joy; for behold, Immanuel hath nailed our sins upon his Cross; and the Life-giver hath caused death to die, raising Adam; for he is the Lover of mankind.

Let us praise him who was willingly crucified in the flesh for our sake; who didst suffer, was buried, and who rose from the dead, saying, O Christ, confirm thy Church in sound doctrine and preserve our lives; for thou art good and the Lover of mankind.

Let us, though unworthy, stand by thy life-giving
tomb, O Christ our Lord, and let us offer glory to thine
ineffable compassion; for thou didst accept crucifixion
and death, O sinless One, that thou mightest grant resurrection to the world; for thou art good and the Lover
of mankind.

Let us praise the Word which had no beginning,
coëternal with the Father; who issued from the virginal
womb in an inexplicable way; who accepted willingly
crucifixion and death for our sakes, and arose in glory,
saying, Glory to thee, O life-giving Lord, the Saviour
of our souls.

Glory and Now to our Lady

LET us praise Mary the Virgin, the glory of the
whole world, branching from human seed and
mother of the Master, the heavenly gate, the praise of
the incorporals and the beauty of believers; for verily
she did appear as a paradise and tabernacle of Divinity.
She did tear down the middle wall of partition, the
intervening enmity, bringing safety instead thereof;
and did open the kingdom. Therefore, let us hold
fast to her; for she is the anchor of faith; and let
us accept the Lord, the child whom she bore, as our
helper. Be of good cheer now, O people of God, and
have faith; for he shall fight against our enemies; for
he is Almighty.

Aposicha

O CHRIST, by thy Passion we have been saved from
passion, and by thy Resurrection we have been
saved from corruption. O Lord, glory to thee.

Let creation rejoice and the heavens have joy; and
let the nations clap their hands together with gladness;
for Christ our Saviour did nail our sins upon his Cross;
and in causing death to die, did grant us life and did
raise the fallen Adam and all his descendants; for he is
the Lover of mankind.

O inscrutable Creator, the King of heaven and earth,
thou who for love of mankind didst accept crucifixion

willingly; verily, hades when it met thee below did
murmur; and the souls of the righteous when they
received thee did rejoice. And Adam, when he saw
thee beneath the earth did stand up and arise. How
wonderful it is that he who is the Life of all did taste
death, and that of his own will, for the lighting of the
world, which crieth out saying, O thou who didst rise
from the dead, O Lord, glory to thee.

Yea, the ointment-bearing women carried ointment
and hurried diligently, crying, and reached thy grave.
And when they could not find thy pure body, learning
from the angel the great and new happening, they did
tell the Disciples that the Lord had risen, granting the
world the Great Mercy.

Glory and Now to our Lady

BEHOLD the prophecy of Isaiah hath been fulfilled;
for while yet a Virgin thou hast given birth; and
thou hast remained after giving birth as thou wert
before; for he that is born of thee is God; therefore, he
renewed nature. Turn thou not away, therefore, O
Theotokos, from the supplications of thy servants, offered in thy temple. But since thou didst carry in thy
bosom the compassionate One, have compassion on
those who petition thee, and intercede for the salvation
of our souls.

Troparion for the Resurrection

THE stone being sealed by the Jews, and thy pure
body being guarded by the soldiers, thou didst rise
on the third day, O Saviour, granting life to the world.
Wherefore, the heavenly powers acclaimed thee, O
Giver of life, crying, Glory to thy Resurrection, O
Christ! Glory to thy kingdom! Glory to thy gracious
providence, O thou only Lover of mankind.

Theotokion

AS Gabriel cried unto thee, O Virgin, Hail! with that cry did the Lord of all become incarnate in thee, O holy ark, as spake the righteous David; and thou wast revealed as more spacious than the heavens, in that thou bore thy Creator. Wherefore, glory to him who abode in thee! Glory to him who came from thee! Glory to him who through thy birth-giving hath set us free!

2.   MATINS

First Kathisma

THE soldiers who kept watch over thy grave, O Saviour, became as dead from the shining of the appearing angel who told the good tidings of the Resurrection to the women. Thee, therefore, do we glorify, O Remover of corruption, and to thee do we bow, O thou who didst rise from the grave, O thou, our only Lord.

Glory: Thou wast nailed upon the cross willingly, O merciful One; and thou wast placed in a grave like one who is dead, O Giver of life, trampling the pride of death, O mighty One; for because of thee the gatekeepers of hades did tremble; and thou didst raise the dead with thee from eternity; for thou alone art the Lover of mankind.

Now: We have all known thee as Theotokos, and after giving birth thou didst appear truly virgin. We who eagerly seek refuge in thy goodness, have thus known thee; for we sinners have taken thee as intercessor, and in temptations have possessed thee as our salvation, O thou who alone art blameless.

Second Kathisma

VERILY did the women proceed to the grave early, where they beheld an angelic scene, and did tremble. And when the grave shone forth with life they were struck with astonishment. Wherefore, they returned to the Disciples and did preach the Resurrection, saying, Verily Christ hath invaded hades; for he alone is the powerful and mighty One; and he raised with him all those who were corrupt, and with the power of his Cross he removed the fear of condemnation.

Glory: Thou wast verily nailed upon the Cross, O Life of all; and wast numbered among the dead, O deathless Lord. Thou didst rise after three days, O Saviour, and didst raise Adam from corruption. Wherefore, the heavenly Powers shouted to thee, O Giver of life; Glory to thy Passion, O Christ, glory to thy Resurrection, glory to thy condescension, O thou alone the Lover of mankind.

Now: O Mary, the reverend abode of the Lord, lift us, who have fallen in the abyss of evil despair, trespasses, and sorrows; for thou didst give salvation to sinners. Thou art a helper and a strong intercessor, and dost save thy servants.

Hypakoe

THE repentance of the thief gained him paradise by stealth, and the sighing of the ointment-bearing women proclaimed the glad tidings that thou wast risen, O Christ, and hadst bestowed upon the world thy Great Mercy.

Anabathmoi — First Antiphony

O Lord, to thee in my sorrows do I cry. Hear thou my cry of pain.

Verily, the divine desire shall be without delay upon the people of the wilderness; for that they have come out of the vain world.

Glory and Now

VERILY, glory and honour become the Holy Spirit, as they become the Father and the Son. Wherefore, do we praise the Triune, One in might.

Second Antiphony

O GOD, since thou hast raised me to the hills of thy laws, shed brightly thy light of virtue upon me, that I may praise thee.

O Word, hold me fast with thy right hand; keep me and preserve me, lest the fire of sin consume me.

Glory and Now

VERILY, all creation together is regenerated by the Holy Spirit, and returns to its former being; for he is coömnipotent with the Father and the Word.

Third Antiphony

MY soul did rejoice with those who say, Let us go into the courts of the Lord. My heart was exceedingly glad.

Great fear shall be in the house of David, where the seats shall be set, and all tribes and tongues of the earth shall be judged.

Glory and Now

VERILY, it is meet to offer glory, might and power to the Holy Spirit as to the Father and to the Son; for the Trinity is one in substance, not in Person.

Prokeimenon: Now will I arise, saith the Lord.

Stichos: The words of the Lord are pure words.

Stichera of the Einos

O CHRIST, thy saving Passion do we praise; and thy Resurrection do we glorify.

O thou who didst submit to the Cross and didst abolish death, who didst arise from the dead, preserve our lives, O Lord, since thou alone art almighty.

O Christ, who as a Destroyer didst invade hades, and who didst raise man by thy Resurrection make us worthy to praise thee with pure hearts, and to glorify thee.

O Christ, we praise thee, glorifying thy condescension, which becometh God. O thou who wast born of a Virgin and wast yet inseparable from the bosom of the Father; who didst suffer like man, didst submit to the Cross willingly, didst arise from the tomb as from a chamber, that thou mightest save the world, glory to thee, O Lord.

When thou wast nailed upon the tree of the Cross, then was the power of the enemy put to death; then did creation tremble in fear of thee, by thy might hades was invaded, thou didst raise the dead from their graves, and thou didst open the gate of paradise to the thief. O Christ, our God, glory be to thee.

The honoured women did come hastening to the grave, with caution and wailing. And when they found the grave open and knew from the angels the story of the new and wonderful miracle, they did bring the good tidings to the Disciples that the Lord had risen, granting the world Great Mercy.

O Christ God, we do bow to the wound of thy divine Passion and to the lordly service which was fulfilled in Zion, coming at the end of times in thy divine Epiphany; for thou, O Sun of justice, didst shine on those who were sitting in darkness; thou didst lead them to the light which is never overtaken by eventide. O Lord, glory to thee.

O Jewish race, which loveth trouble, understand and comprehend. Where are they who went in unto Pilate? Let your guardian soldiers tell where the seals of the tomb are. Whither was the buried One moved from the grave? Whither was the priceless One sold? How was the Treasure stolen? Why do you deny the Resurrection of the Crucified, O wavering people, thus falling into error, O Jews who transgress the law? He hath verily risen, standing up, free among the dead, and hath granted great mercy to the world.

3. THE MASS

The Beatitudes

VERILY the enemy did expel Adam from paradise because he ate of the fruit. But Christ, by his Cross, admitted the thief in his place, when the latter cried, Remember me, O Lord, when thou comest into thy kingdom.

I do bow down to thy Passion; I glorify thy Resurrection; and, with Adam and the thief, cry with plaintive voice, Remember me, O Lord, when thou comest into thy kingdom.

Thou wast crucified, O sinless One, and willingly wast placed in a grave. But because thou art God, thou didst arise and with thee didst raise Adam, who cried, Remember me when thou comest into thy kingdom.

O Christ God, thou didst raise thy body on the third day after thy burial; and thou didst raise Adam and those who came from Adam, who cried, Remember us when thou comest into thy kingdom.

The ointment-bearers came in the early dawn to thy grave, O Christ God, wailing. And they found an angel sitting, attired in a white robe, who said to them, What seek ye? Verily, Christ hath risen. Wail ye therefore no more.

O Lord Saviour, thy Disciples went to the mount to which thou didst command them to go. And when they had knelt down, thou didst send them to the Gentiles to teach and to baptize them.

Glory: Let us worship the Father, let us glorify the Son, and let us all praise the all-holy Spirit, speaking out and saying, O Holy Trinity, save us all.

Now: O Christ, thy people doth offer supplication to thee and to thy Mother. By her pleadings, O good One, grant us thy compassion, that we may glorify thee, O thou who didst shine forth on us from the tomb.

SECOND TONE

1. SATURDAY VESPERS

The Stichera on O Lord, to thee have I cried

COME ye, let us worship him who was born of the
Father before all time, the Word of God, incarnate of the Virgin Mary; for he did submit to crucifixion by his own choice, was delivered to burial as he
himself willed, rose from the dead, and saved me, who
was lost.

Verily, Christ our Saviour nailed to his Cross the
handwriting of the decree, and did expunge it. And he
polished the might of death. Let us therefore adore
his third-day Resurrection.

Come, let us with the archangels praise the Resurrection of Christ; for he is the Redeemer and Saviour of
our souls, and he it is who will come with fearful magnificence and glorious might to judge the world which
he hath created.

O thou who wast crucified and wast buried, the angel
did proclaim thee, that thou art the Master, saying to
the women, Come ye and behold where the Lord was
laid; for he is risen as he said; for he is the Almighty
One, and therefore, do we worship thee, O thou who
alone art deathless; O Christ, Giver of life, have mercy
upon us.

With thy Cross thou didst abolish the curse of the
tree; with thy Death and Burial thou didst cause the
might of death to die; and with thy Resurrection thou
didst enlighten mankind. Wherefore, do we cry to
thee, O Christ our God, the Benefactor, glory to thee.

O Lord, verily, the gates of death were opened to thee
for fear of thee. And as the gate-keepers of hades saw
thee they did tremble; for thou didst break asunder its
brazen gates; didst crush its iron bars; didst bring us
out from the shadow and darkness of death; and didst
break our bonds asunder.

Come, let us all sing with our mouths a song of sa
vation. Let us kneel down in the house of the Lor(
saying, O thou who wast crucified on a Tree, who did:
rise from the dead, and who still remainest in the boso
of the Father, forgive us our sins.

Glory and Now to our Lady

O VIRGIN, verily, the shadow of the law hath bee
annulled by the coming of thy grace; for as th
bush was burning but not consumed, so didst thou gi\
birth while yet a Virgin. And instead of the pillar (
fire, the Sun of justice shone forth; and instead (
Moses, Christ the Saviour of our souls.

Aposticha

THY Resurrection, O Christ Saviour, hath illumine
the whole universe. Thou hast renewed thy crea
tion, O Lord Almighty. Glory to thee.

By the Tree, O Saviour, thou hast removed the curs
that was caused by a tree; and by thy Burial thou ha:
caused the might of death to die. Thou hast illumine
our race by thy Resurrection. Wherefore, do we shou
to thee, O Christ our Lord, Giver of life, glory to the

O Christ, when thou wast seen nailed upon the Cros:
thou didst invert the beauty of creation. Yet withal di
the soldiers show brutality when they pierced thy sid
with a spear. And the Hebrews comprehended not th
might of thine authority, seeking to seal thy tomb. Bu
thou who for the compassion of thy mercies didst accep
a tomb, and didst rise in three days, O Lord, glory t
thee.

O Christ God, O Giver of life, thou didst bear th
Passion willingly for the sake of the dead. Thou did:
descend into hades, for thou art mighty, and did:
snatch away from the hand of the proud one those wh
there awaited thy coming, bestowing paradise upo
them for an abode instead of hades. Wherefore, w

pplicate thee to give us who glorify thy third-day
esurrection forgiveness of sins, and the Great Mercy.

Glory and Now to our Lady

) WONDROUS event transcending all the ancient
miracles! For who ever hath heard of a mother
ving birth without man; and carrying in her arms
m who containeth all creation? Yet this is the will of
e born God. Cease not, therefore, O undefiled one
pray to him whom thou didst carry in thine arms as a
be, and with whom thou didst acquire motherly priv-
ge for us who honour thee, that he may have mercy
on us and save our souls.

Troparion of the Resurrection

HEN thou, O immortal Life, didst humble thyself unto death, then didst thou destroy death by
e brightness of thy Godhead; and when thou didst
ise the bowels of the earth, then all the heavenly
wers exclaimed, O Christ, thou art the Giver of life!
lory to thee, O our God!

Theotokion

XCEEDING glorious beyond the power of thought
are all thy mysteries, O Theotokos; for being sealed
purity and preserved in virginity, thou wast acknowl-
ged to be in very truth the Mother who didst bring
rth the true God. Wherefore, entreat him to save
r souls.

2. MATINS

First Kathisma

ERILY, the honourable Joseph did bring down thy
pure body from the Tree, wrapped it in fine linen,
d laid it in a new tomb. But thou didst rise in three
ys, O Lord, granting the world Great Mercy.

Glory: Verily, the angel did appear at the tomb, sa
ing to the ointment-bearing women, The ointment
worthy of the dead, but Christ hath been shown to
foreign to corruption. Rather cry ye instead, The Lo
is risen, granting the world Great Mercy.

Now: O virgin Theotokos, exceeding glorified, v
praise thee; for by the Cross of thy Son hades hath be
demolished and death hath been put to death. A
we did rise, after we were dead; and became worthy
life; and obtained the paradise of ancient bliss. Whe
fore, we glorify Christ in thankfulness; for he is o
dear God and alone abundant in mercies.

Second Kathisma

O LORD, since thou didst not prevent the seali
of the tombstone when thou didst arise, thou di
bestow on all the rock of fidelity. Glory to thee.

Glory: Verily, the assembly of thy Disciples rejoic
in unison with the ointment-bearing women. As f
us, we celebrate with them a common festival to t
honour and exaltation of thy Resurrection, exclaimi
to thee, O Lord, Lover of mankind, grant thy peop
through their supplications, Great Mercy.

Now: Thou hast transcended all blessings, O virg
Theotokos; for hades hath been spoiled by him w
was incarnate of thee. Yea, Adam was recalled; t
curse was abolished; Eve was delivered; death w
put to death; and we were made to live again. Whe
fore, in praise we cry, Blessed art thou, O Christ o
God, who hast thus shown thy pleasure. Glory to th

Hypakoe

THE women went to the tomb after thy Passion
anoint thy body, O Christ God, where they saw
vision of angels, and were astonished; for they hea
them crying with a loud voice, The Lord is risen a
hath granted the world Great Mercy.

Anabathmoi—First Antiphony

BEHOLD, O Saviour, toward heaven I raise the eyes
of my heart to thee.   Save me by thine illumination.
O Christ, have mercy upon us guilty men who trans-
ess against thee often and in every hour.   Give us
fore the end the means of a repentance acceptable to
ee.

Glory and Now

VERILY, sovereignty over creation, its sanctification,
and its motion are of the Holy Spirit; for he is God
nsubstantial with the Father and with the Word.

Second Antiphony

EXCEPT the Lord were in our midst, who could
have been kept safe from the man-destroying
emy?
Verily, my enemies roar like lions, O Saviour.   Deer not thy servant to their teeth.

Glory and Now

THE Holy Spirit is the Element of life and honour;
for as God he doth establish all creatures and pre-
rve them in the Father and the Son.

Third Antiphony

THEY who put their trust in the Lord are like the
holy mountain; for they are never shaken by the
acks of Belial.
They put not forth their hands to evil, who live the
vine life; for Christ God will not deliver his inherit-
ce to the evil ones.

Glory and Now

THE Holy Spirit is the Fount of all wisdom; for
from him cometh grace to the Apostles, the Martyrs

by him are crowned in their struggles, and the Prophet
in foreknowledge look to him.

Prokeimenon: Arise, O my Lord and God, in th
precept which thou hast commanded, and a congrega
tion of people shall surround thee.

Stichos: My Lord and my God, in thee have I pu
my trust.

Stichera of the Einos.

ALL creatures glorify thee, O Lord, with ever
breath; for by the Cross thou didst abolish deatl
that thou mightest manifest to the nations thy Resui
rection from the dead; for thou alone art the Lover c
mankind.

Answer, O Jews, how was it that the guardian so
diers lost the King whom they were guarding? Wh
was it that the stone could not retain the Book of life
Either must ye, therefore, deliver to us him that wa
buried, or worship with us him who is risen, shoutin;
Glory to thy bountiful mercies, our Saviour, glory t
thee.

Rejoice, O nations, and be glad; for the angel hat
sat on the stone of the grave, and given us the glad tic
ings, saying, Christ the Saviour of the world is rise
from the dead. He hath filled all with sweet scen
Rejoice, O ye nations, and be joyful.

O Lord God, verily, before thy Conception an ang
did come with peace to her who is full of grace. An
now an angel hath rolled the stone from the door c
thy tomb, made glorious by thy Resurrection. Th
first angel spake with signs of joy instead of sorrow
and the latter brought us the glad tidings of a Lor
who giveth life instead of death. Therefore, do w
shout to thee, O Benefactor of all, glory to thee, O Lor

Verily, the women did sprinkle spices with tears c
thy grave, and their mouths were filled with laught
when they said, The Lord is risen.

Let the nations and people, therefore, praise Chri
our God who did suffer crucifixion willingly for ou

kes, and did remain in hades three days. Let them
orship his Resurrection from the dead, by which all
ie ends of the earth were illuminated.

O Christ, thou wast crucified and buried as thou didst
ill; thou didst lead death captive, being God and
ord, who granteth the world life eternal and the Great
Mercy.

O transgressors of the law, when ye did seal the
one ye did in truth but magnify to us the miracle, as
ie guards know; especially since ye persuaded them
n the day of his Resurrection from the tomb, that they
iould say, While we slept the Disciples came and stole
im away; for who would steal a corpse, especially a
aked one? Verily, he arose by his own power (for he
: God), leaving his coffin in the grave. Come ye, there-
ore, O Jews, and see how he hath not broken the seals,
who hath trampled down death, giving to mankind life
ternal and Great Mercy.

3. THE MASS

The Beatitudes

WE come to thee, O Saviour, with the voice of the
thief, beseeching thee, Remember us in thy kingdom.

We offer to thee for the forgiveness of our sins thy
Cross which thou didst accept for our sake, O Lover
of mankind.

We worship, O Lord, thy Burial, and thy Resurrection, by both of which thou didst deliver the world from
corruption, O Lover of mankind.

Verily, death hath been swallowed up by death, O
Lord; and by thy Resurrection, O Saviour, thou didst
save the world.

When thou didst arise from the dead thou didst meet
the bearers of ointment; and thou didst command thy
Disciples to proclaim thy Resurrection.

They, O Christ, who slumber in darkness, when the
beheld thee, O Light in the abyss of hades, did veri
arise.

Glory: Let us glorify the Father, and worship th
Son, and praise together with faith the Holy Spirit.

Now: Rejoice, O throne of fiery figures. Rejoic
O bride without bridegroom. Rejoice, O Virgin, wh
didst give birth to God for mankind.

THIRD TONE

1. SATURDAY VESPERS

The Stichera on O Lord, to thee have I cried

O CHRIST Saviour, the might of death hath veri
broken down under thy Cross; and the deceit o
Diabolus hath ceased; and the race of man hath by fai
escaped and been saved. Wherefore, praise is offere
thee perpetually.

The whole creation, O Lord God, hath been lighte
by thy glorified Resurrection; and paradise hath bee
opened withal. Wherefore, all creatures laud thee an
offer thee praise perpetually.

I glorify the power of the Father, magnify the pow
of the Son, and praise the might of the Holy Spirit, or
Godhead, indivisible, uncreate, consubstantial Trinit
reigning through all eternity.

Thy glorified Cross, O Christ, do we worship, an
thy Resurrection do we praise and glorify; for by th
wounds we were all healed.

Let us praise the Saviour who was incarnate of th
Virgin; for he was crucified for our sake, and arose o
the third day, granting us Great Mercy.

Verily, Christ did descend to hades to bring good tic
ings to those therein, saying, Have faith now; for I hav
conquered; for I am the Resurrection, who, unlockin
the gates of death, shall set you free.

As we stand in thy holy house, we thine unworth
servants, offer thee evening praise from the depth
shouting, O Christ God, O thou who hast lighted th

world with thy third-day Resurrection, deliver thy people from the hands of thine enemies, O Lover of mankind.

Glory and Now to our Lady

O LADY of exceeding honour, how can we but wonder at thee giving birth to incarnate God? For
thou, O all-blameless, not knowing a man, didst give
birth in the flesh to a Son without father, who before
eternity was begotten of the Father without mother, the
property and essence of each substance remaining intact.
Wherefore, O virgin Mother, beseech him to save the
souls of those who assent and confess, with true belief,
that thou art the Theotokos.

Aposticha

O CHRIST, who didst darken the sun with thy Passion, and didst light all created things with the
light of thy Resurrection, and didst make them to rejoice, accept our evening praise, O Lover of mankind.

Verily, thy life-giving Resurrection hath lighted the
whole universe, renewing thy corrupt creation.

Wherefore, in that thou hast delivered us from the
curse of Adam, we shout to thee, O Lord Almighty,
glory to thee.

O changeless God, thou didst suffer in the changing
body, and when creation could not bear to behold thee
suspended on the Cross, it trembled with fear, and
sighed, praising thy long-suffering. Then, descending
to hades, thou didst arise on the third day, granting life
to the world and Great Mercy.

Thou didst suffer death, O Christ, that thou mightest
deliver our race from death. Thou didst rise from the
dead on the third day, and didst arouse with thee those
who know that thou art true God, verily illuminating
the world, O Lord. Wherefore, glory to thee.

Glory and Now to our Lady

THOU didst verily conceive by the Holy Spirit without human seed, at the pleasure of the Father the Son of God, begotten of the Father before eternity without mother. Thou didst give birth to him in the flesh coming of thee, for our sake, without father. Wherefore, cease not to intercede that he may deliver our souls from affliction.

Troparion for the Resurrection

LET the heavens rejoice and the earth be glad; for the Lord hath done a mighty act with his own arm. He hath trampled down death and become the First born from the dead. He hath delivered us from the depth of hades, granting the world the Great Mercy.

Theotokion

THEE, who are the mediatrix for the salvation of our race, we praise, O virgin Theotokos; for in the flesh assumed from thee, after that he had suffered the Passion of the Cross, thy Son and our God delivered us from corruption, because he is the Lover of mankind.

2. Matins

First Kathisma

CHRIST is risen from the dead, he who is the First fruits of them that slept, the First-born of creation and the Creator of all things created. He hath renewed by himself the nature of our corrupt race. Wherefore thou shalt reign no more, O death; for the Lord of all hath nullified thy power and dissolved it.

Glory: When thou didst taste death in the flesh, O Lord, thou didst check bitter death by thy Resurrection, and didst make man to prevail over it, restoring victory over the old curse. Wherefore, O Supporter and Champion of our life, glory to thee.

Now: Verily, Gabriel, overwhelmed by the splendour of thy virginity and the abundant brilliancy of thy purity, hailed thee, saying, O Theotokos! What dutiful praise shall I offer thee? Or what shall I call thee? I am overwhelmed with surprise and perplexity. But as I have been commanded, I shall hail thee, Rejoice, O full of grace.

Second Kathisma

BECAUSE of thine immutable Divinity, O Lord, and thy voluntary sufferings, hades was overwhelmed, and moaned within itself, saying, Verily, I am in dread fear of the Person of this incorruptible body; for I see the Unseen fighting me secretly, and behold those whom I have held shouting, Glory to thy Resurrection, O Christ.

Glory: Let us believers speak of divine things, of the secret of thine inscrutable Crucifixion, of thine ineffable Resurrection; for today have death and hades been led captive, and the race of man hath been invested with incorruption. Therefore, do we cry in gratitude, Glory to thy Resurrection, O Christ.

Now: Verliy, O Theotokos, the Incomprehensible and Boundless, consubstantial with the Father and the Spirit, hast thou held secretly in thy womb. And by thy birth-giving we have learned to glorify in the world the act of the one immiscible Trinity. Therefore, with gratitude we cry to thee, Rejoice, O thou that art full of grace.

Hypakoe

TO the ointment-bearing women the brilliant angel of sweet words, startling them, did say, Why seek ye the living One in the grave. He is verily risen, and hath emptied the tombs. Know ye, therefore, that the changeless One hath changed corruption to incorruption. And say ye to God, How dreadful are thy works; for thou has saved mankind!

Anabathmoi—First Antiphony

THOU didst verily deliver the captivity of Zion from Babylon, O Word. Likewise, draw thou me out of suffering into life.

They who sow in Timan with divine tears, shall reap with rejoicing the sheaves of eternal life.

Glory and Now

WITH the Holy Spirit every gift is good; for he doth shine forth together with the Father and the Son; and in him doth all creation live and move.

Second Antiphony

IF the Lord buildeth not the house of virtues, then vainly do we labour; but if he defend and protect our lives, none shall prevail against our city.

The saints are verily the hire of the fruit the womb. And they have not ceased to be thy sons, in the Spirit, O Christ, and thou art like a father.

Glory and Now

BY the Holy Spirit hath all holiness and wisdom been observed; for he is the Creator of all the essence of creation. Therefore, let us worship him; for he is God, as is the Father and the Word.

Third Antiphony

HAPPY are they who fear the Lord; for they walk in the way of his commandments, and eat of the fruits of universal life.

Rejoice with gladness, O chief Shepherd, as thou beholdest thy children's children around about thy table, offering branches of good deeds.

Glory and Now

VERILY, all the richness of honour is of the Holy Spirit. And of him too is grace and life for all creation. Wherefore, he is to be praised with the Father and the Word.

Prokeimenon: Say among the heathen that the Lord reigneth. The world also shall be so established that it shall not be moved.

Stichos: Praise the Lord with a new praise.

Stichera of the Einos

COME together, all ye people, and know the power of the dreadful secret; for Christ our Saviour, the eternal Word, hath been crucified for our sake, and was buried willingly, and hath risen from the dead to save all. To him let us bow down in worship.

The guards have published it abroad, O Lord, telling of all thy wonders. But the assembly of falsehood filled their right hands with bribes, thinking that thereby they might conceal thy Resurrection which the world doth glorify. Wherefore, have mercy upon us.

Verily, all creatures were filled with joy when they received the glad tidings of thy Resurrection; for Mary Magdalene, coming to thy grave, met an angel in a brilliant robe sitting on the stone, who said, Why seekest thou the living among the dead? He is not here, but is risen. As he said, he will go before you into Galilee.

O Master, Lover of mankind, with thy light do we behold light; for thou art risen from the dead, granting salvation to the race of man, that the whole creation may glorify thee alone, who art without sin. Have mercy upon us.

Verily, the ointment-bearing women, O Lord, did offer to thee their tears as a morning praise; for when they reached thy grave bearing exceeding sweet scent, hastening to seek thine incorruptible body, an angel,

sitting on the stone, spake to them, saying Why seek
ye the living among the dead? For verily, he hath
trodden down death and is risen, because he is God
granting to all Great Mercy.

Thou the brilliant angel on the life-giving tomb didst
say to the ointment-bearing women, Verily, the Sav
iour hath emptied the tombs, and hath led hades cap
tive, rising on the third day; for he alone is omnipoten
God.

On a Saturday, Mary Magdalene came seeking thee
in the grave. And when she found thee not, she wailed
crying with sighs, and said, Woe is me, O my Saviour
How hast thou been stolen, O King of all? And from
within the grave a pair of life-bearing angels cried ou
to her saying, Woman, why weepest thou? And she
answered, saying, I cry because they have removed my
Lord from the grave; and I know not where they have
taken him. But as she turned back and saw thee, she
cried, saying, My Lord and my God, glory to thee.

The Hebrews did close the tomb of life; but the
thief did open paradise with his tongue, as he cried
saying, O thou who for my sake hast been crucified
with me, hast hung on the tree of the Cross, and has
appeared to me sitting on the throne with the Father
thou art the Christ our God, Possessor of Great Mercy

3. THE MASS

The Beatitudes

VERILY, when Adam, the first ancestor, disobeyed
thy commandment, O Christ, thou didst exile him
from paradise. But when the thief confessed thee on
the Cross, O compassionate One, thou didst bring him
to dwell therein, because he cried out, Remember me
O Saviour, in thy kingdom.

O life-giving Lord, thou didst condemn us, because
we sinned against thee, with the curse of death. But
when thou didst suffer in thy blameless body, O Mas

r, thou didst bring to life the dead who cry out to
ıee, Remember us also in thy kingdom.

When thou didst rise from the dead, O Lord Saviour,
ıou didst raise us from suffering by thy Resurrection,
ıd didst abolish all the might of death. Wherefore,
e shout to thee in faith, Remember us also in thy king-
ɔm.

By thy three-day Burial, thou hast revived the dead
ho are in hades, and hast raised them with thee, since
ıou art God. And since thou art good, thou didst cause
ıcorruption to spring up for us who ever cry to thee
ı faith, Remember us also in thy kingdom.

Thou didst appear first to the ointment-bearing
omen, O Christ Saviour, when thou didst rise from
ıe dead, and shouted to them, Rejoice; and through
ıem thou didst proclaim thy Resurrection to thy be-
ɔved ones. And therefore we shout to thee in faith,
.emember us also in thy kingdom.

Verily, Moses, when he stretched out his hands on
ıe mountain, conquering Amalek, foreshadowed the
ʻross. As for us, having taken him in faith as a power-
ıl Weapon against demons, we shout together, Re-
ıember us also in thy kingdom.

Glory: Let us, O believers, praise the Father, the
on, and the Holy Spirit, one God and one Lord, as
ʻom one sun; for the Trinity is verily like the trinity
f light, and lighteth all those who cry to him, Remem-
er us also in thy kingdom.

Now: Rejoice, O gate of God, through whom the
ʻreator did pass incarnate, preserving thee sealed. Re-
ɔice, O bright cloud bearing Christ who is the divine
ʻain. Rejoice, O heavenly ladder and throne. Rejoice,
ɔ revered and fat mountain, never ending.

FOURTH TONE

1. SATURDAY VESPERS

The Stichera on O Lord, to Thee Have I Cried

WE worship untiringly thy quickening Cross,
Christ God, and glorify thy third-day Resurrection; for by it, O Almighty, thou hast renewed the corrupt nature of mankind, and made plain to us the ascent to heaven; for thou alone art good and the Lover
of mankind.

When thou wast willingly nailed upon the Cross, O
Saviour, thou solvedest the problem caused by the tree
of sin. And when thou didst descend into hades, thou
didst break the bonds of death, since thou art a mighty
God. Wherefore, we worship thy Resurrection from
the dead, shouting with joy, O Almighty Lord, glory
to thee.

Thou didst demolish by thy Death, O Lord, the gates
of hades; thou didst dissolve the realm of death; and
didst free the human race from corruption, granting
the world life and incorruptibility and Great Mercy.

Come, ye nations, let us praise the third-day Resurrection of the Saviour, by which we were delivered
from the unbreakable bonds of hades, and by which we
have all received life and incorruption, crying, O thou
who wast crucified, buried, and who didst rise, save us
by thy Resurrection, O thou only Lover of mankind.

Verily, the angels and men, O Saviour, praise thy
third-day Ressurrection, through which the ends of the
universe have been lighted, and by which thou hast redeemed from bondage to the enemy us who cry, saying,
O omnipotent Giver of life, save us by thy Resurrection, O Lover of mankind.

Thou hast demolished the brazen gates, O Christ
God, and hast shattered the bars, and hast raised the
fallen human race and made it to stand upright. Wherefore, do we shout to thee in unison, O thou rising from
the dead, O Lord, glory to thee.

Thy birth from the Father, O Lord, is eternal and timeless; and thine Incarnation from the Virgin is inexplicable and ineffable; and thy descent into hades is awe-inspiring to Satan and his angels; for thou didst trample down death and didst rise the third day, granting mankind incorruptibility and Great Mercy.

Glory and Now to our Lady

DAVID the Prophet who became through thee, O Theotokos, the grandparent of God, beforetime sang of thee in praise, and shouted to him who worked wonders through thee, saying, The queen did rise on thy right; for God hath shown thee to be a Mother bringing forth life, in that he was willing to appear incarnate from thee without father, renewing the creation of his likeness, corrupt with suffering, in order to find the sheep lost in the hills, and carry it on his shoulders, and offer it to the Father, and add it, through his will, to the heavenly hosts, and to save the whole world; for he is the reigning Christ, Possessor of rich and Great Mercy.

Aposticha

WHEN thou wast lifted up upon the Cross, O Lord, thou didst expunge our ancestral curse; and when thou didst descend to hades, thou didst free those who were bound from eternity, granting the human race incorruptibility. Wherefore, we offer praise, glorifying thy third-day Resurrection.

O thou who alone art mighty, when thou wast fastened upon a Tree, thou didst shake the whole earth; and when thou wast laid in the grave, thou didst raise those who lay in the graves, granting mankind life and incorruptibility. Wherefore, we offer praise, glorifying thy third-day Resurrection.

The law-transgressing people, O Christ, delivered thee to Pilate, who condemned thee to crucifixion. Thus the ingrate appeared before his Benefactor. But thou sufferedst burial willingly, and didst rise on the third day by thine own power; for thou art God, granting us endless and Great Mercy.

Verily, the women reached thy tomb seeking thee with tears. And when they found thee not, they shouted and wailed, saying, Woe to us, O our Saviour, King of all, how wast thou stolen? And what place containeth thy life-bearing body? And an angel answered them, saying, Weep not, but go preach that the Lord hath risen, granting us joy; for he alone is compassionate.

Glory and Now to our Lady

O THOU who art free from all blemish, hear the petitions of thy servants, removing from us the difficulties that rise against us, and delivering us from all sorrows; for thou alone art a safe and secure haven; and we have secured thee as an intercessor. Therefore, we who call upon thee shall never be put to shame. Hasten to fulfill the pleadings of those who cry to thee in faith, Rejoice, O Lady, the succour of all, O joy, protection, and salvation of our souls.

Troparion for the Resurrection

HAVING learned the joyful message of the Resurrection from the angel, the women Disciples cast from them their parental condemnation, and proudly broke the news to the Disciples, saying, Death hath been spoiled. Christ God is risen, granting the world Great Mercy.

Theotokion

THE mystery which was hidden from everlasting and was unknown of the angels, O Theotokos, was revealed through thee to those who dwell upon earth, in that God, having become incarnate in unconfused union, of his own good will, accepted the Cross for our sake; whereby he raised again the first created, and hath saved our souls from death.

2. Matins

First Kathisma

THE ointment-bearing women glanced into the entrance of the tomb; and, because they could not bear the brilliance of the angel, they trembled in astonishment, saying, Hath he been stolen who opened paradise to the thief? Or is he risen up who before his Passion did preach resurrection? Verily, Christ God hath risen, granting resurrection and life to those who are in hades.

Glory: Thou hast suffered crucifixion willingly, O Saviour, and mortal men placed in a new tomb thee who didst stablish the corners of the world with a word. Therefore, hath death the stranger been bound and taken captive, being defeated. And all those in hades, cried out through thy reviving Resurrection, Verily, Christ the Life-giver is risen; for he is everlastingly constant.

Now: Thy betrothed and guardian, O Theotokos, when he beheld thy supernatural Conception without seed, was amazed and perplexed. But he recalled to his mind the rain falling on the fleece of wool, and the bush burning with fire but not cosnumed, and he testified before the priests, crying, A Virgin giving birth, and after remaining virgin.

Second Kathisma

THOU didst rise from the tomb, O Christ Saviour our God, because thou art deathless; and thou didst raise with thee thy world by thy Resurrection, and didst crush the might of death, proclaiming resurrection to all. Wherefore, do we glorify thee, O thou who alone art merciful and the Lover of mankind.

Glory: Gabriel descended from his sublime height wrapped in a white robe, and came to the stone where the Rock of life was, and he shouted to the weeping women, saying, Cease your wailing and crying, and receive ye smiling joy, with comfort; for he whom ye seek weeping is verily risen. Wherefore, go and proclaim to the Apostles that the Lord is risen.

Now: All the ranks of the angels, O thou who art undefiled, have been dazzled by the secret of thy dreadful birth-giving; that the All-encompassing at a sign from him was encompassed in thy bosom as a babe, and that he who is before eternity received a temporal beginning, and that he who feedeth every living breath with his ineffable goodness was nourished with milk. Wherefore, did they glorify thee with praise; for thou art truly the Theotokos.

Hypakoe

THE ointment-bearing women hastened running to the Apostles and related to them the account of thy Resurrection, O Christ, saying, Thou hast risen because thou art God, granting the world Great Mercy.

Anabathmoi—First Antiphony

THE many sufferings from my youth combat me. But thou, O my Saviour, assist and save me.

O ye haters of Zion, depart in shame from before the Lord; for ye shall be dry by fire as the grass.

Glory and Now

BY the Holy Spirit every spirit shall live and shall be purified, ascending, and brilliant, through the one hidden and pure Trinity.

Second Antiphony

TO thee, O Lord, have I cried fervidly from the depth of my soul. Let thy divine ears listen to me.

All those who have placed their trust in the Lord
shall transcend all sorrows.

Glory and Now

VERILY, the Holy Spirit doth overflow with streams
and passages of grace, and doth water all creation
with refreshing life.

Third Antiphony

LET my heart rise to thee, O Word, and let not the
pleasures of the world enter in to me to vie with
the earthly life.

And as each of us hath surpassing love to his Mother,
the more should we love the Lord with utmost fervour.

Glory and Now

BY the Holy Spirit cometh the riches of divine knowledge, divine vision, and wisdom; for through him
the Word doth proclaim all the commandments of the
Father.

Prokeimenon: Arise, O God, help us and redeem us
for thy Name's sake.

Stichos: O God, with our own ears have we heard.

Stichera of the Einos

WE glorify thy Resurrection, O Lord Almighty, O
thou who sufferedst crucifixion and death and
didst rise from the dead.

Thou hast freed us, O Christ, from the first curse.
And by thy Death thou didst banish the insurgency of
Diabolus prevailing over our nature. And in thy Resurrection thou didst fill all with joy. Wherefore, we
cry to thee, O thou Lord, who didst rise from the dead;
glory to thee.

O Christ Saviour, who didst rise from the dead, lead
us by thy Cross to thy right hand, and save us from the
gins of the enemy. Stretch forth thine arm and raise

us who are fallen in sins; through the intercession o
thy saints, O Lord, the Lover of mankind.

O only Son of God, thou didst come to earth, bu
wast not separated from the Paternal bosom; and be
cause of thy love to mankind thou didst become un
changeable man. Thou didst suffer crucifixion an
death in the flesh, O thou who in thy Divinity suffereth
not. Thou didst rise from the dead, granting mankin
immortality; for thou alone art Almighty.

Thou didst purchase for us deathlessness, O Saviour
when thou didst accept death bodily. Thou didst dwel
in a grave to deliver us from hades, raising us with thee
for as man thou didst suffer, but since thou art God thou
didst arise. Therefore, do we shout, Glory to thee, C
Lord, Giver of life, who art alone the Lover of man
kind.

When thy Cross, O Saviour, was planted in Golgotha
the rocks were split asunder; and when thou wast placed
in a grave like the dead, the gate-keepers of hades wer
afraid; for thou didst abolish the might of death, an
in thy Resurrection thou didst bestow incorruptibility
on all the dead. Wherefore, O Lord, Giver of life
glory to thee.

The women, O Christ God, desired to behold thy
Resurrection. And Mary Magdalene went ahead o
them, and she found the stone rolled from the grave
and she saw the angel sitting thereon, who said, Why
seek ye the living among the dead? Verily, he hath
risen to save all creation; for he is God.

Say, O Jews, where is Jesus whom ye thought ye were
guarding? Where is he whom ye had thrown into the
grave, and sealed thereto the stone? Give us the dead
One, O deniers of life. Give us the buried One, o
else believe in the risen One. And if ye keep silen
about the Resurrection, the stone shall proclaim it, ever
that stone which was rolled away from the door of the
tomb. Albeit great is thy mercy, and great is the mys
tery of thy dispensation, O Saviour; glory to thee.

3. THE MASS

The Beatitudes

VERILY, Adam, because of a tree, became estranged from paradise. But the thief because of the tree of the Cross came to reside in paradise. The former, when he tasted of the fruit, disobeyed the command-ment of the Creator; and the latter, when he was cruci-fied with thee, confessed that thou art a God disguised, and cried, Remember me in thy kingdom.

O thou who didst ascend the Cross, and didst annul the power of death, and because thou art God didst ex-punge the handwriting of the decree against us, give us, O Lord, the repentance of the thief, O thou who art alone the Lover of mankind. We who do worship thee in faith, cry to thee, O Christ our God, remember us also in thy kingdom.

By the spear of the Cross, O Lord, thou didst tear in pieces the handwriting of the decree against us, and when thou wast numbered amongst the dead, thou didst bind the giant there, freeing us all from the bonds of hades by thy Resurrection, by which we are illumi-nated, who cry to thee, O Lover of mankind, remember us also in thy kingdom.

O thou who wast crucified and didst rise from the tomb after three days, since thou art mighty, and didst raise with thee Adam of the first creation, O Lord, who alone art deathless, make me worthy to return with all my heart to repentance, and to cry unto thee always with fervid faith, Remember me, O Saviour, in thy kingdom.

He who is free from sufferings became a suffering man for our sakes; and when he was nailed upon the Cross willingly, he did raise us with him. Wherefore, with the Cross do we glorify his Passion and his Resur-rection, through which he hath renewed our creation, and by which we are saved, crying, Remember us also in thy kingdom.

Let us pray, O believers, to him who is risen from the dead, who led captive the might of death, who appeared to the ointment-bearing women, saying to them, Rejoice, in that he can deliver our souls from corruption, who shout to him always with the voice of the grateful thief, Remember us also in thy kingdom.

Glory: Let us plead that we may be worthy, O believers, to glorify in unison, as it is proper to do, the Father, Son, and Holy Spirit, the one Trinity in three Persons, immovable, immiscible, single, indivisible, and unapproachable, through whom we are delivered from the fire of torment.

Now: O most Merciful, O Christ Lord, we offer thee for intercession thy Mother, truly virgin, who gave thee birth in the flesh without seed, and remained after birth-giving without corruption. Grant, therefore, forgiveness of sins to those who cry to thee at all times, Remember us also in thy kingdom.

FIFTH TONE

1. Saturday Vespers

The Stichera on O Lord, to thee have I cried

WITH thy noble Cross, O Christ, thou hast put the devil to shame, and with thy Resurrection thou hast annihilated the thorn of death. Thou hast saved us too from the gates of death. Wherefore, do we glorify thee, O only One.

The Bestower of resurrection to mankind was verily led like a lamb to slaughter. Therefore, the captains of hades were terrified by him, and its portals of agony were lifted; for Christ the King of glory hath entered it, saying to those in bonds, Come ye out! and to those in darkness, Be ye manifest!

The wonder is verily great; for the Creator of unseen creatures hath suffered in the flesh for his love of man-

...ind; and the deathless One hath risen up. Come ye, therefore, O tribes of the nations, let us bow to him in worship; for by his compassion have we been liberated from disobedience and have learned how to praise the one God in three Persons.

O Light that is not apprehended by eventide, we offer thee evening worship; for thou hast risen on the world at the completeness of time as in a mirror; and thou didst descend to hades and dissolved the darkness therein, revealing to the nations the light of the Resurrection. Wherefore, O Lord, Giver of light, glory to thee.

Let us praise with words of glorification Christ, the Element of our salvation; for by his rising from the dead he hath saved the world from falsehood, and the ranks of angels rejoiced; and the falsehood of demons hath vanished; and Adam rose up from the fall; and the authority of Diabolus was repudiated.

When the guardian soldiers were appointed by the transgressors of the law, they were instructed by them to conceal the Resurrection of Christ; for they said to them, Take ye silver and say, Behold when we were asleep the corpse was stolen from the tomb. But who hath ever seen or heard at any time that a corpse was stolen, especially if it were naked and embalmed, leaving its wrappings in the grave? Be ye not deceived, O Jews, but learn ye the sayings of the Prophets, and understand that this One in truth is the Saviour of the world, the omnipotent One.

O Lord, our Saviour, who didst lead hades captive and didst trample down death, and didst light the world with thy precious Cross, have mercy upon us.

Glory and Now to our Lady

THE sign of the virgin bride who knew not wedlock was at one time revealed in the Red Sea; for there Moses did cleave the waters, and there Gabriel was the minister of a miracle. At that time Israel

crossed the deep and their feet were not wet, and no
the Virgin hath given birth to Christ without seed. Th
sea remained uncrossed after the passing of Israel, an
the blameless one remained incorruptible after givin
birth to Immanuel. Therefore, O eternal God, wh
wast before eternity, and who didst appear as man, hav
mercy upon us.

Aposticha

O CHRIST Saviour, who didst become incarna
without leaving heaven, thee do we magnify wit
the voices of song; for thou didst accept the Cross an
death for the sake of our human race; for thou art th
Lord, the Lover of mankind. Thou didst demolish th
gates of hades, rising on the third day, and saving ou
souls.

Thy side being stabbed, O Giver of life, didst neve
theless overflow for all with springs of forgivenes
life, and salvation. And accepting death in the flesl
thou didst bestow on us deathlessness. And dwelling i
a tomb, thou didst free us and raise us in glory wit
thee, since thou art God. Wherefore, do we exclai
to thee, O Lord, Lover of mankind, glory to thee.

Wonderful is thy Crucifixion and thy descent
hades, O Lord, Lover of mankind; for thou didst lea
it captive, since thou art God, raising with thee in glo
those who of old had been chained. Thou didst ope
to them paradise and didst make them worthy to enjc
it. Grant us, therefore, forgiveness of sins, who glorif
thy third-day Resurrection, and prepare us for dwel
ings in paradise, since thou art compassionate.

O thou who, for our sake, didst submit to sufferinç
in the flesh, and who didst rise from the dead in thre
days, heal the sufferings of our bodies and lift us u
from our heavy sins, O Lover of mankind, and save u

Glory and Now to our Lady

O MOST reverend Virgin, O thou by means
whom my Saviour Christ the Lord did appear

those lying in darkness, he being the Sun of justice, wishing to light those whom he had made with his own hands after his likeness, thou art the temple, the gate, the palace and the thorne of the King. Wherefore, O all-praised one, thou hast attained with him maternal privilege; intercede ceaselessly for the salvation of our souls.

Troparion for the Resurrection

LET us believers praise and worship the Word, coëternal with the Father and the Spirit, born of the Virgin for our salvation; for he took pleasure in ascending the Cross in the flesh, to suffer death, and to raise the dead by his glorious Resurrection.

Theotokion

REJOICE! O uncrossed gate; rejoice O wall and protection of those who hasten to thee! Rejoice, O quiet haven who hast not known wedlock; O thou who hast given birth in the flesh to thy Creator and God, thou shalt continue to intercede for the sake of those who praise and worship thy birth-giving.

2. MATINS

First Kathisma

LET us laud the honoured Cross of the Lord; let us honour with song his holy Burial; let us glorify his divine Resurrection; for he hath raised the dead from the graves, since he is God, and hath led captive the might of death and the power of Diabolus, and hath shed light on those who are in hades.

Glory: Thou hast been called dead, O Lord, who hast caused death to die. And thou wast placed in a grave, O thou who hast emptied the grave. Above, the soldiers guarded the tomb, but below, thou didst raise the dead who were from eternity. Wherefore, O Lord Almighty, the Incomprehensible, glory to thee.

Now: Rejoice, O holy mountain whom the Lord crossed in passing. Rejoice, O respiring bush, unconsumed. Rejoice, O thou who alone art a bridge for the world towards God, transferring the dead to eternal life. Rejoice, O pure one, free of corruption, who didst give birth without wedlock to the Saviour of the world.

Second Kathisma

AFTER thy third-day Resurrection and the worship of the Disciples, O Lord, Peter cried to thee, The women made bold to thee, but I cowered fearing; the thief did speak of thy Divinity, and I denied thee ungratefully. Wouldest thou still, I wonder, call me Disciple, or make me a fisher of the deep? Nevertheless, O God, receive me, repentant, and save me.

Glory: The transgressors of the law, O merciful Lord, nailed thee between two thieves and stabbed thy side with a spear. And thou didst submit to burial, O thou who didst invade the gates of hades, and didst rise in three days. Wherefore, the women hastened to behold thee, and told the good tidings of thy Resurrection to the Apostles, O Saviour transcendent in height, and praised of angels. Wherefore, O blessed Lord, glory to thee.

Now: O Theotokos, transcendent in praise, O bride who hast not tried marriage, O thou who hast changed Eve's sorrow to joy, we worshipping believers give praise; for that thou didst lift us up from the first curse. And now intercede ceaselessly, O all-holy one, for our salvation.

Hypakoe

THE minds of the ointment-bearing women were dazzled by the angelic scene, and their souls with the divine Resurrection. Wherefore, they spake to the Apostles, saying, Declare in the nations the Resurrection of the Lord, who worketh wonders with you, who bestoweth on us the Great Mercy.

Anabathmoi—First Antiphony

O MY Lord, I sing to thee like David in my sorrow. Save my soul from the deceitful tongues.

Verily, the life of the dwellers in the wilderness is a very happy one; for by divine passion are they ever carried up.

Glory and Now

BY the Holy Spirit are all creations seen and unseen preserved, the control thereof being in himself who is without doubt one of the Trinity.

Second Antiphony

COME, my soul, let us ascend the mountain yonder, whence cometh thy help. O Christ, let thy raised right hand encompass me, preserving me from all evil deceits.

Glory and Now .

BY the Holy Spirit do we speak divinely, saying, Verily, thou art God, Life, Love, Light, and Mind. Thou art goodness. Thou dost reign for ages.

Third Antiphony

I HAVE been filled with great joy by those who say to me, Let us go into the courts of the Lord. Verily, I have offered a constant prayer.

In the house of David dread wonders take place; for there is a burning fire consuming every evil mind.

Glory and Now

VERILY, the Holy Spirit is the Element of life and its beginning; for through him doth every living thing breathe; as is the Father and the Word.

Prokeimenon: Arise, O my Lord and my God; for thou dost reign to the end of time.

Stichos: To thee do I confess, O my Lord, from my whole heart.

Stichera of the Einos

THE grave, O Lord, having been sealed by the transgressors of the law, thou didst emerge from within like as thou wast born of the Theotokos; for the incorporeal angels did not know how thou wert incarnate. Likewise the guardian soldiers were not aware when thou didst rise; for these two matters were concealed from all seekers. But the wonders appeared to those who worshipped the mystery in faith. Therefore, grant us who offer praise joy and Great Mercy.

O Lord, thou hast demolished the everlasting gates and broken asunder the chains. Thou didst rise from the tomb, leaving behind thy wrappings and ointments in the grave, in testimony of thy true three-day Burial, and didst go before into Galilee, O thou who wert kept in a cave. Great, therefore, are thy mercies, O ineffable Saviour; have mercy upon us.

The women did hasten to thy tomb to behold thee, O Lord, who didst suffer for us. And when they arrived, advancing, they saw an angel sitting on the stone rolled back from fear. And he shouted to them, saying, The Lord hath risen. Go and tell the Disciples that the Saviour of our souls is risen from the dead.

O Lord Saviour, thou didst enter unto thy Disciples, the doors being closed, as thou didst come out of the sealed tomb, showing the sufferings of the flesh which thou didst accept in long-suffering; for thou didst submit to pains patiently since thou art the seed of David. But since thou art the Son of God, thou didst liberate the world. Great therefore, are thy mercies, O incomprehensible Saviour. Have mercy upon us.

O Lord, King of ages and Creator of all, who didst accept crucifixion and burial in the body for our sakes, to deliver us all from hades, thou art our God, and beside thee we know no other.

O Lord God, who shall tell and who shall proclaim thy dazzling wonders? Or who shall declare thy dread mysteries? For thou wast incarnate for our sakes wil-ingly, manifesting the might of thy power. And by thy Cross thou didst open paradise to the thief, and by thy Death thou hast crushed the bars of hades, and by thy Resurrection thou hast enriched all creation. Therefore, O compassionate One, glory to thee.

Verily, the ointment-bearing women reached thy tomb very early seeking to anoint thee, O deathless Word. And when they were instructed by the words of the angel, they turned back with joy to tell the Apostles plainly that thou hadst risen, O Life of all, and hadst given the world forgiveness and Great Mercy.

The guards keeping watch over the God-bearing tomb said to the Jews, Woe to your vain counsel; for ye sought to keep the Boundless. Vainly have ye laboured; for ye thought that ye could hide the Resurrection of the Crucified, but ye only showed it in clearer manifestation. Woe to your council of false opinion! Why take ye counsel to hide what cannot be hidden? Better it were that ye hear of us and choose to believe in that which happened, which is, that an angel, resplendent like lightning, descended from heaven and rolled away the stone, and from fear of him we were encompassed by death. And to the ointment-bearing steadfast women he shouted saying, See ye not the death of the guards, the unsealing of the tomb, and the emptiness of hades? Why seek ye then as dead, him who abolished the victory of hades and crushed the thorn of death? Go ye in haste and tell the glad tidings of the Resurrection to the Apostles, and shout ye fearlessly, saying, In truth, the Lord, Possessor of Great Mercy, is risen.

3. The Mass

The Beatitudes

THE thief, O Christ, believed in thee while on the cross, affirming that thou art God. From the depth of his heart and with guilelessness he confessed thee, crying, Remember me, Lord, in thy kingdom.

Let us sing in unison to him who made life for our kind blossom by the tree of the Cross, effacing the curse resulting from the tree; for he is Saviour and Creator.

By thy death, O Christ, thou hast dissolved the power of death, raising with thee the dead from eternity who praise thee, O true God our Saviour.

The noble women, O Christ, did come to thy grave, seeking to anoint thee, O Giver of life. An angel did appear to them, shouting; The Lord is risen.

Between two condemned thieves, O Christ, thou wert crucified. One blasphemed thee falsely and was reproved justly; the other confessed thee and therefore dwelt in paradise.

The noble women went to the ranks of the Apostles and acclaimed, Christ hath risen, for he is the Master and Creator; let us worship him.

Glory: O indivisible Trinity, the all-creating Oneness, omnipotent, Father, Son, and Holy Spirit. Thee do we praise, O true God our Saviour.

Now: Rejoice, O living temple of God, O uncrossed door. Rejoice, O unconsumed throne of fiery figures, Rejoice, O Mother of Immanuel, Christ our God.

SIXTH TONE

1. SATURDAY VESPERS

The Stichera on O Lord, to thee have I cried

O CHRIST, Possessor of victory over hades, thou hast ascended the Cross that thou mightest raise with thee those who sit in darkness. O Free among the dead, overflowing with life from thine own light. O Almighty Saviour, have mercy upon us.

Today hath Christ trodden down death, and hath risen as he said. He hath given joy to the world, that we might all shout in praise, O Fountain of life, O unapproachable Light, and Almighty Saviour, have mercy upon us.

O Lord, who art in all creation, whither shall we sinners flee from thee? To heaven? For thou dwellest there; or to hades? For there thou art the Trampler over death, or to the depths of the sea? For there is thy hand, O Master. In thee, therefore, seek we refuge, and thee do we worship beseechingly; O thou who didst rise from the dead, have mercy upon us.

In thy Cross, O Christ, do we glory, and thy Resurrection do we praise and glorify; for thou art our God, and beside thee we know no other.

The Lord we bless always, and praise his Resurrection; for in submitting to crucifixion for our sakes, he hath shattered death by Death.

Glory to thy might, O Lord; for thou hast put a stop to the possessor of the might of death, and hast renewed us by thy Cross, bestowing on us life and incorruptibility.

Thy Burial, O Lord, hath torn and crushed the bonds of hades; and thy Resurrection from the dead did illuminate the world. Wherefore, O Lord, glory to thee.

Glory and Now to our Lady

WHO shall not beatify thee, most holy Virgin? Who shall not praise thy birth-giving, free of travailing and pain? For the only Son rising timelessly from the Father, himself did come incarnate from thee in an inexplicable way. He, who while God by nature, became for our sakes Man by nature, not divided into two persons, but known by two natures without mixture or confusion. To him, O noble and most blessed one, plead for the salvation of our souls.

Aposticha

THY Resurrection, O Christ our Saviour, the angels in heaven praise. Make us, who also are on earth, worthy to praise thee with a pure heart.

Thou hast demolished the brazen gates of hades and crushed its bars; for thou art an Almighty God, and didst raise fallen mankind. Wherefore, do we cry to thee in unison, O thou who didst rise from the dead, O Lord, glory to thee.

Christ God, when he wished to raise us from the old fall, was nailed on the Cross and placed in a grave. He it was whom the ointment-bearing women did seek, wailing with tears, and saying, Woe to us, Saviour of all, how didst thou consent to occupy a grave? And after thy lying therein willingly, how wast thou stolen? How wast thou removed? And what place screened thy life-bearing body? Yea, appear to us, O Lord, as thou didst promise us, and put a stop to the shedding of tears. And as they wailed, behold an angel shouted to them, saying, Cease wailing, and say to the Apostles that the Lord is risen, granting the world forgiveness and Great Mercy.

O Christ God, thou wast crucified as thou willed, Thou ledest death captive, and arose in glory on the third day, for thou art God, granting the world eternal life and Great Mercy.

Glory and Now to our Lady

O MOST pure one, when Christ the Lord, my Creator and Saviour, came forth from thy womb, putting me on, he did free Adam from the ancient curse. Wherefore, O most pure one, since thou art the Theotokos and a Virgin in truth, we shout to thee untiringly with the angels, saying, Rejoice, Lady, O thou who art the helper, the cover, and the salvation of our souls.

Troparion for the Resurrection

WHEN Mary stood at thy grave looking for thy sacred body, angelic powers shone above thy revered tomb, and the soldiers who were to keep guard became as dead men. Thou led hades captive and wast not tempted thereby. Thou didst meet the Virgin and

dst give life to the world; O thou that art risen from
e dead! O Lord, glory to thee.

Theotokion

THOU who didst call thy Mother blessed, of thine
own good will, and didst come to thy Passion, shin-
g radiantly upon the Cross, desiring to recall Adam,
d saying unto the angels, Rejoice with me; for I have
und the piece of silver which was lost. O our God,
ho with wisdom hast ordered all things, glory to thee.

2. MATINS

First Kathisma

WHEN the tomb was shown to be open and hades
wailing, Mary cried unto the cowering Apostles,
aying, Come out, ye labourers of the vineyard, and
roclaim the words of the Resurrection; for the Lord
risen, granting the world Great Mercy.

Glory: Mary Magdalene, O Lord, did stand by thy
omb and cry, weeping. And when she thought thou
vast the gardener, she said, Where hast thou hidden
he everlasting Life? Where hast thou placed him who
itteth on the cherubic throne? And when she saw the
uards who kept him, appearing from fear like dead,
he cried unto them, Give me my Lord; or else cry
vith me saying, O thou who wast numbered among the
lead, and who didst raise the dead, O Lord, glory to
hee.

Now: Verily, Gideon did picture thy Conception
foretime, and David interpreted thy birth-giving, O
Theotokos; for the Word did fall on thy womb as the
ain on the fleece, and so thou didst cause to branch
or us Christ our God, a Salvation to the world without
eed, O holy earth and full of grace.

Second Kathisma

VERILY, Life was placed in the grave, and seal
were applied to the stone. And the soldier
guarded Christ as they would a sleeping king. Bu
the Lord rose, smiting his enemies in an invisible way

Glory: Verily, Jonah did come before and made ;
sign of thy tomb; and Simeon did interpret thy divin
Resurrection, O deathless Lord; for thou didst descenc
into the grave as one who is dead, O thou who dids
invade the gates of hades, and didst rise free of corrup
tion for the salvation of the world, being the Master
O Christ our God, and didst light those who are ir
darkness.

Now: Pray, O virgin Theotokos, to thy son Chris
our God, who was willingly nailed upon the Cross anc
did rise from the dead, that he might save our souls.

Hypakoe

BY thy willing yet life-giving Death, O Christ, thou
hast crushed the gates of hades, because thou ar
God, and hast opened the old paradise; and having
risen from the dead, thou hast redeemed our life fron
corruption.

Anabathmoi—First Antiphony

TO the heavens do I lift mine eyes, O Word of God
Have mercy upon me that I may live by thee.

O Word, have mercy upon us who are despised, anc
make us good and chosen vessels.

Glory and Now

VERILY, in the Holy Spirit is the cause of salva
tion for all; for when he bloweth on one worthily
he doth raise him speedily from earthly things, dotf
wing him and cause him to grow, and doth rank hin
in the heavenly places.

Second Antiphony

WERE not the Lord in our midst it would not be possible for any of us to stand firm in his wrestling with the enemy; for only thereby do the victors attain the exaltation of victory.

Woe is me, how shall I escape the enemies while I am a lover of sin. Wherefore, deliver not my soul, O Lord, like a bird, to their teeth.

Glory and Now

VERILY, through the Holy Spirit is everyone made divine; and in him is pleasure, understanding, safety, and blessing; for he is equal to the Father and the Word together.

Third Antiphony

THEY who trust in the Lord are feared by their enemies and are wondered at by all; for their sight is very high.

The party of the righteous hath secured thee as its succour, O Saviour, and therefore shall not reach out its hands to iniquities.

Glory and Now

VERILY, the Holy Spirit hath might over all; for him do all the heavenly hosts worship, and every breath below.

Prokeimenon: O Lord, arouse thy strength, and come to our salvation.

Stichos: Hearken, O Shepherd of Israel.

Stichera of the Einos

THE Cross, O Lord, is life and resurrection to thy people, and in it we do trust. Wherefore, thee do we praise, O our risen Lord; have mercy upon us.

Thy Burial, O Master, hath opened paradise to man kind. Wherefore, as we escape corruption, we prai thee, O our risen God; have mercy upon us.

With the Father and the Spirit, let us praise Chri risen from the dead. Let us cry unto him, Thou a our life and resurrection. Have mercy upon us.

Thou hast risen from the tomb in three days, as was written, O Christ, and hast raised with thee ou ancestors. Wherefore, mankind doth glorify thee an praise thy Resurrection.

Great and fearful is the mystery of thy Resurrectio O Lord; for thou hast emerged from the grave like bridegroom from his chamber, annulling death b Death in order to free Adam. Wherefore, do the ange in heaven exchange glad tidings, and men on earth glo rify thy compassion toward us, O Lover of mankind.

O Jews, transgressors of the law, where are the sea and the silver which ye gave to the soldiers? Verily the Treasure hath not been stolen, but hath risen; for h is mighty. Be ye confounded, therefore, O deniers c Christ, the Lord of glory who suffered, was buried, an did rise from the dead. Him let us worship.

How were ye robbed of the buried One when th tomb was sealed, after having placed guards and sigr thereon? Behold, the King hath come out, the door being closed. Therefore, either show him as dead, o worship him with us as God, singing, Glory to th Cross and thy Resurrection, O Lord.

The ointment-bearing women, O Lord, came to th life-receiving grave, wailing and carrying ointmen seeking thy pure body to anoint it. Then they foun an angel wrapped with light and sitting on a stone; an he spake to them, saying, Why shed ye tears for On from whose side life overflowed to the world? Wh seek ye in the grave as dead One who is deathless? Mor proper for you that ye hasten to his Disciples to pro claim to them with joy his glorious Resurrection, glad dening the whole world, by which, O Saviour, sinc thou didst lighten us thereby, grant us forgiveness and the Great Mercy.

3. THE MASS

The Beatitudes

REMEMBER me, O God my Saviour, when thou comest into thy kingdom. Save me since thou alone art the Lover of mankind.

By the tree of the Cross thou didst save Adam deceived by the tree; and likewise the thief who cried, Remember me, Lord, in thy kingdom.

Thou didst demolish the gates of hades and its bars, O Giver of life, and didst raise all, O Saviour, who cry to thee, Glory to thy Resurrection.

Remember me, O thou who by thy Burial didst lead death captive, and by thy Resurrection didst fill all with joy; for thou art compassionate.

The ointment-bearing women came to thy grave and heard the angel saying, Christ God hath risen and lighted all creation.

Let us all in unison praise Christ who was nailed up on the tree of the Cross, and who saved the world from error.

Glory: We glorify the Father, Son, and Holy Spirit, saying, O Holy Trinity, save our souls.

Now: O thou who didst conceive in the completeness of time, in an ineffable manner, and didst give birth to thy Creator, O Virgin, save those who magnify thee.

SEVENTH TONE

1. SATURDAY VESPERS

The Stichera on O Lord, to thee have I cried

COME, let us rejoice in the Lord who crushed the sight of death and lighted mankind, crying to him with the incorporals, O Creator and our Saviour, glory to thee.

For our sakes, O Saviour, thou didst suffer crucifixion and burial. But thou didst cause death to die, for thou art God. Wherefore, do we worship thy third-day Resurrection, O Lord; glory to thee.

Verily, when the Apostles beheld the Resurrection of the Creator they were surprised, shouting in angelic praise, This is the honour of the Church, this is the richness of the kingdom. Wherefore, O thou who didst suffer for our sakes, O Lord, glory to thee.

Though thou wast arrested, O Christ, by the transgressors of the law, thou still remainest my God, and therefore I am not ashamed. And though thou wast lashed on thy back I shall not deny thee; or nailed upon the Cross, I shall not hide it; for in thy Resurrection do I glory; for thy death is my life, O Almighty One and Lover of mankind. O Lord, glory to thee.

Verily, Christ God did fulfill the Davidic prophecy; for he did manifest his wonders to his Disciples in Zion, when he revealed of himself, that he is praised and glorified always with the Father and the Holy Spirit. As for the beginning without body, for he is the Word, and for these last days he did appear in the body and died for our sakes as man, rising by his self-same power, for he is Lover of mankind.

Thou didst descend to hades, as thou didst will, O Christ, and didst lead death captive, since thou art God and Lord, and didst rise on the third day, raising Adam with thee from the bonds of hades and its corruption, who cried saying, Glory to thy Resurrection, O thou only Lover of mankind.

O Lord God, thou wast placed in a grave as one that slumbereth, and didst rise on the third day as one that is mighty and powerful, raising Adam with thee from the corruption of death; for thou art omnipotent.

Glory and Now to our Lady

O PURE Theotokos, thou wast known as a Mother in a supernatural way, and thou didst remain virgin in an indescribable and incomprehensible manner. Thus came about the wonder of thy birth-giving, ineffable for tongue, in that thy Conception appeared dazzling to the mind, and thy birth-giving incomprehensible; for where God willeth he overcometh the order of nature. Therefore, since we know thee as Theotokos, we beseech thee ceaselessly. Intercede then for the salvation of our souls.

Aposticha

THOU hast risen from the tomb, O Saviour of the world, and hast raised mankind with thy body, O Lord, glory to thee.

Come, let us worship him who rose from the dead and lightened all; for he hath liberated us from the oppression of hades by his third-day Resurrection, granting us life and the Great Mercy.

When thou didst descend to hades, O Christ, thou didst lead death captive and when thou didst rise on the third day, thou didst raise us with thee, glorifying thy almighty Resurrection, O Lord and Lover of mankind.

Thou didst appear awe-inspiring, O Lord, whereas thou wast placed in a grave like one that slumbereth, and didst rise in three days as a mighty one, and didst raise with thee Adam, crying, Glory to thy Resurrection, O thou alone the Lover of mankind.

Glory and Now to our Lady

WE earthly ones all, O Lady, seek refuge in thy protection, shouting to thee, O Theotokos, our hope, deliver us from our sins without number, and save our souls.

Troparion for the Resurrection

THOU didst shatter death by thy Cross; thou di
open paradise to the thief; thou didst turn t
mourning of the ointment-bearing women into joy, a
didst bid thine Apostles proclaim warning that th
hast risen, O Christ, granting the world Great Mer

Theotokion

IN that thou art the treasury of our resurrection,
all-praised one, lead thou forth from the pit a
deep of transgression those who set their hope in the
for thou hast saved those who were guilty of sin,
that thou didst give birth to our Salvation; O thou w
before birth-giving wast virgin and at birth-giving a
after birth-giving wast virgin still.

2. MATINS

First Kathisma

VERILY, Life was placed in a grave, and a seal w
placed on the stone, and the soldiers guarded Chr
as they would a slumbering king. The angels, the
fore, did glorify him; for he was a deathless God, a
the women cried, saying, The Lord hath risen, w
giveth the world Great Mercy.

Glory: O Lord Christ, thou hast led death capti
by thy three-day burial, and didst raise corrupt man
thy life-bearing Resurrection. Wherefore, glory to th
O thou alone the Lover of mankind.

Now: O virgin Theotokos, intercede untiringly
Christ God, who was crucified for our sakes, who r
and broke the might of death, to save our souls.

Second Kathisma

WHILE the tomb was sealed thou didst shine fo
from it, O Light. And while the doors we
closed, thou didst come to the Disciples, O Christ Go

the Resurrection of all, renewing in us, through them, an upright spirit, according to the greatness of thy mercy.

Glory: The women bearing ointment mixed with tears did hasten to thy grave. And when they saw the soldiers guarding thee, O King of all, they said to themselves, Who shall roll for us the stone? But the Messenger of the great counsel did rise, trampling down death. Wherefore, O Almighty One, O Lord, glory to thee.

Now: Rejoice, O virgin, full of grace, Theotokos, O haven of mankind and their intercessor; for from thee was incarnate the Saviour of the world; for thou alone art Mother and Virgin at the same time. Wherefore, intercede with Christ our God, that he grant safety to the universe, O ever-blessed and glorified one.

Hypakoe

O THOU that has taken our image and our likeness, and endured crucifixion in the flesh, save me by thy Resurrection, O Christ God, for thou art the Lover of Mankind.

Anabathmoi—First Antiphony

O SAVIOUR, who didst restore Zion from the captivity of error, deliver me from the bondage of sufferings and restore my life.

He that soweth sorrow in the south, fasting with tears, the same shall reap sheaves of reviving and ever-nourishing joys.

Glory and Now

IN the Holy Spirit is the fountain of divine treasures; for from him cometh wisdom, awe, and understanding. To him, therefore, be praise, glory, might, and honour.

Second Antiphony

IF the Lord buildeth not the house of the soul, then vainly do we labour; for without him no need in saying is ever complete.

Verily, the saints who are the hire of the fruit of thy womb, by the moving of the Spirit flourish the beliefs of fatherly adoption.

Glory and Now

BY the Holy Spirit was existence bestowed on all creation; for he is of the Godhead before existence, and he is the unapproachable Light, the God of all, and their life.

Third Antiphony

VERILY, they who fear the Lord are now for ever blessed; for they have found the way of life in the never-decaying glory.

O High Priest, as thou seest thy children's children like plants around thy table, rejoice and be happy, and offer them to Christ.

Glory and Now

BY the Holy Spirit is the abundance of gifts, the richness of glory, and depth of the great ordinances; for he is worshipful and coëternal in glory with the Father and the Son.

Prokeimenon: Arise, O Lord my God, and let thy hand be exalted. Forget not thy wretched ones to the end of time.

Stichos: To thee do I confess, O my Lord, from my whole heart.

Stichera of the Einos

CHRIST hath risen from the dead, loosening the bonds of death. Be of good cheer, and of great joy and, O heavens, praise the glory of God.

Seeing the Resurrection of Christ, let us worship the holy Lord Jesus, who alone is blameless of all error.

Verily, we cease not worshipping the Resurrection of Christ; for we are saved from our sins. Holy, therefore, is the Lord Jesus who did manifest the Resurrection.

With what shall we reward the Lord for all that he hath given us? For God, for our sakes, dwelt among men; and for corrupt nature the Word became flesh and lived among us. Yea, he hath done this, the Benefactor of ingrates, the Saviour of captives, the Sun of jutsice to those lying in darkness, the Passionless on the Cross, the Light in hades, the Life in death, the Resurrection of the fallen. Wherefore, do we cry to him, O our God, glory to thee.

O Lord, thou hast demolished the gates of hades, and by thy precious might thou hast abolished the power of death, and by thy divine and glorified Resurrection thou hast raised the dead lying in darkness from everlasting time; for thou art King of all and an almighty God.

Come, let us rejoice in the Lord, and be joyous in his Resurrection; for he hath raised the dead with him from the indissoluble bonds of hades. And, being God, he hath granted the world eternal life and the Great Mercy.

Verily, the resplendent angel sat on the stone of the life-receiving grave and proclaimed to the ointment-bearing women, The Lord hath risen as he foretold you. Tell, therefore, his Disciples that he will go before them to Galilee, he who granteth the world eternal life and the Great Mercy.

Why have ye rejected the Cornerstone, O ye Jews, transgressors of the law? For verily, the same is the stone which God hath placed in Zion, who in the wilderness poured forth water from the rock, and whose side poureth out for us deathlessness. He is the Stone that was cut out from the virginal mountain without

will of man, the Son of man, coming in the clouds of
heaven, to the Ancient of Days, as Daniel said, and his
kingdom shall last forever.

3. THE MASS

The Beatitudes

VERILY, the fruit which caused my death was pleasing and good to eat. But Christ is the Tree of life,
of whom if I eat, I shall not die. Albeit, I cry with the
thief, Remember me, O Lord, in thy kingdom.

When thou wast elevated on the Cross, O compassionate One, thou didst blot out the decree of Adam's
sins, written of old by hand, and didst save from error
the whole race of mankind. Wherefore, do we praise
thee, O Lord and Benefactor.

O compassionate Christ, thou didst nail our sins upon
the Cross, and by thy death thou didst cause death to
die, and didst raise the dead from the tombs. Wherefore, do we worship thy glorified Resurrection.

Verily, the serpent did inject her poison into the ears
of Eve. But Christ, by the tree of the Cross did pour
out to the world the sweetness of life. Wherefore, Lord,
remember me in thy kingdom.

Thou wast placed in the grave as dead, O Christ.
Life of all. Thou didst shatter the bars of hades and
didst rise in glory on the third day; for thou art mighty,
and thou didst enligthen all. Glory, therefore, to thy
Resurrection.

The Lord arose from the dead on the third day; and
he granted his peace to his Disciples, and blessed them,
and sent them, saying, Bring forth all to my kingdom.

Glory: Light is the Father; Light is the Son, the
Word; and Light the Holy Spirit. But the three are one
Light, one God in three Persons, one Nature and one
supremacy, indivisible and without confusion. And he
is eternal before the ages.

Now: O Theotokos, the virgin Mother, thou hast
~~en~~ birth in the flesh on earth to the Son, the Word
~~God~~, as he knoweth. Wherefore, we who have be-
~~co~~me divine through thee hail thee, O hope of Chris-
~~tia~~ns.

EIGHTH TONE

1. SATURDAY VESPERS

The Stichera on O Lord, to thee have I cried

~~E~~VENING praise and spoken worship do we offer
~~to~~ thee, O Christ; for thou didst consent to have mercy
on us by thy Resurrection.

O Lord, O Lord, cast us not from before thy face,
~~bu~~t consent to have mercy upon us by thy Resurrection.

Rejoice, O holy Zion, mother of the churches, the
~~ab~~ode of God; for thou didst first receive forgiveness
~~of~~ sins by his Resurrection.

Verily, the Word, born of the Father before the ages,
~~ha~~th himself been incarnate in the last times by his own
~~wi~~ll, of one who knowest not wedlock. He did suffer
~~cr~~ucifixion and death; and by his Resurrection he hath
~~sa~~ved man dead of old.

Let us glorify thy Resurrection from the dead, O
~~Ch~~rist, by which thou didst free the race of Adam from
~~th~~e usurpation of hades. And since thou art God, thou
~~ha~~st granted the world eternal life and the Great
~~M~~ercy.

Glory to thee, O Christ Saviour, only Son of God,
~~w~~ho wast nailed upon the Cross, and who didst rise
~~fr~~om the tomb on the third day.

Thee do we glorify, O Lord, O thou who, for our
~~sa~~kes, didst suffer crucifixion willingly; and thee do we
~~w~~orship, O almighty Saviour. Cast us not, therefore,
~~fr~~om before thy face, but give ear to us and save us by
~~th~~y Resurrection, O Lover of mankind.

Glory and Now to our Lady

VERILY, the King of heaven, for his love to ma
kind, did appear on earth; and with men did
deal; for he took unto himself a body from the pu
Virgin. And from her did he issue in the adopted bod
he being one Son, dual in Nature, not dual in Perso
Wherefore, do we confess, preaching the truth th
Christ our God is perfect God and perfect Man. Ther
fore, O Mother who hast no groom, beseech thou hi
to have mercy upon our souls.

Aposticha

THOU didst ascend the Cross, O Jesus, who did
descend from heaven. Thou didst come to deat
O Life that dieth not, and to those who are in darkne
O true Light, and to the fallen, O Resurrection of a
Wherefore, O our Light and Saviour, glory to thee.

Let us glorify Christ risen from the dead; for he d
take unto himself a soul and a body; and he separat
one from the other in the Passion, when his pure so
went down to hades which he led captive; and the ho
body saw no corruption in the grave, the body of t
Redeemer, Saviour of our souls.

With psalms and with songs of praise, O Christ,
we glorify thy Resurrection from the dead, by whi
thou didst deliver us from the rebellion of hades. A
since thou art God, thou didst grant us eternal life a
the Great Mercy.

O Lord of all, O incomprehensible One; O Mak
of heaven and earth, when thou didst suffer in thy Pa
sion on the Cross, thou didst pour out for me passio
lessness; and when thou didst submit to burial and di
rise in glory, thou didst raise Adam with thee by
mighty hand. Wherefore, glory to thy third-day Resu
rection by which thou didst grant us eternal life a
forgiveness of sins; for thou alone art compassiona

Glory and Now to our Lady

O VIRGIN without groom, blameless one, Mother of the high God; O thou who didst conceive in the flesh in an inexplicable way, receive the petitions of thy servants, O thou who bestowest on all the purification of sins; and in receiving our petitions beseech thou for the salvation of us all.

Troparion for the Resurrection

O COMPASSIONATE One, thou didst descend from the heights; thou didst submit to the three-day burial, that thou mightest deliver us from passion. Thou art our Life and our Resurrection, O Lord, glory to thee.

Theotokion

THOU who for our sake wast born of a Virgin, and didst suffer crucifixion, O good One, and didst despoil death through Death, and as God didst reveal resurrection; despise not those whom thou hast created with thine own hand; show forth thy love for mankind, O merciful One; accept the intercession of thy Mother, the Theotokos, for us; and save thy despairing people, O our Saviour.

2. MATINS

First Kathisma

THOU hast risen from the dead, O Life of all. And a resplendent angel shouted to the women, Dry your tears and proclaim to the Apostles, and cry out in praise, that Christ the Lord hath risen, he who hath been pleased to save mankind, since he is God.

Glory: Thou hast verily risen from the tomb; and thou didst command the righteous women to preach to the Apostles the Resurrection, as it was written. And as for Peter, he did hasten to the tomb; and when he saw the light in the grave he was dazzled with surprise.

Then he saw the linen clothes lying aside, where it was not possible to see them by night, and he believed, and cried out, Glory to thee, O Christ God; for thou has saved us all, O our Saviour, who still remainest in truth the Radiance of the Father.

Now: Let us glorify her who is the tabernacle and the heavenly gate, the most holy mountain, the shining cloud, the heavenly ladder, the paradise, endowed with speech, the deliverer of Eve, the precious and great treasure of the universe; for by her did salvation come to the world, and the forgiveness of ancient sins. Wherefore, do we cry to her, Intercede to thy Son and God to grant forgiveness of sins to those who bow in true worship to thy most holy birth-giving.

Second Kathisma

MEN did seal thy tomb, O Saviour, and the angels did roll the stone from off thy grave; and the women witnessed thy Resurrection from the dead. They proclaimed to thy Disciples in Zion that thou didst rise, O Life of all, and didst break asunder the bonds of death, O Lord, glory to thee.

Glory: Verily, when the women came with burial ointment they heard from the grave an angelic voice, saying, Cease your tears and receive joy instead of sorrow; and cry in praise that Christ the Lord is risen, who being God was pleased to save mankind.

Now: Verily, all creation rejoiceth in thee, O full of grace; the assemblies of angels and the races of men, O holy temple and paradise endowed with speech, the pride of virginity from whom God was incarnate and became a child, being yet our God before the ages; for he hath made thy receptacle a throne and thy womb more spacious than the heavens. Wherefore, O full of grace, the whole creation rejoiceth in thee and glorifieth thee.

Hypakoe

THE ointment-bearing women came to the tomb of the Life-giver, seeking among the dead the Lord who is not dead; and when they received the glad tidings from the angels they preached to the Apostles that the Lord hath risen, and granted the world the Great Mercy.

Anabathmoi—First Antiphony

FROM my youth the enemy hath tempted me and with temptations hath he beguiled me. But I, O Lord, trusting in thee, have rejected him in shame.

They who hate Zion shall become like grass before it is pulled up; for Christ shall cut down their necks with the scythe of torment.

Glory and Now

VERILY, in the Holy Spirit all shall live; for he is Light of Light, a great God. Let us, therefore, praise him with the Father and the Word.

Second Antiphony

YEA, let my humble heart be lighted by thy fear, lest it rise and fall from thee, O all-compassionate One.

He that trusteth in the Lord shall not fear when God shall judge all with tormenting fire.

Glory and Now

VERILY, by the Holy Spirit every divine one seeth and uttereth things to be, and performeth heavenly wonders; for he singeth to one God in three; for the Godhead, albeit of three Lights, is one in Leadership.

Third Antiphony

TO thee have I cried, O Lord, Listen and turn thy ear towards me when I shout. Purify me before thou raisest me from this place.

Verily, everyone shall return and disappear in his mother the earth, and shall be dissolved at once, to receive either honours or punishments as reward for what he hath done in his lifetime.

Glory and Now

VERILY, through the Holy Spirit one speaketh of the Godhead, the One, the Thrice-Holy; for from the Father, who is without beginning, the Son did proceed without time. And the Spirit, who is their equal in appearance and on the throne, hath shone from the Father likewise.

Fourth Antiphony

BEHOLD, how good and how beautiful for the brethren to live together; for of this did the Lord promise eternal life.

Verily, he who beautifieth the flowers of the field commandeth that no one take heed for his dress.

Glory and Now

VERILY, the Holy Spirit is the Cause of all, and containeth in himself the harmony of safety; for he is truly equal to the Father and the Son in substance.

Prokeimenon: The Lord shall reign for ever, thy God, O Zion, from generation to generation.

Stichos: Praise the Lord, O my soul.

Stichera of the Einos

THOUGH thou didst stand in judgment, O Lord, condemned by Pilate, thou didst not vacate thy throne, sitting with the Father. Thou didst arise from the dead, releasing the world from the bondage of the stranger; for thou art compassionate and the Lover of mankind.

Though, O Lord, the Jews placed thee in a grave like dead, the soldiers guarded thee as a slumbering

King; and as a Treasure of life, they sealed thee. But thou didst rise and grant incorruptibility to our souls.

Thou didst give us thy Cross, O Lord, as a weapon against Diabolus, who, unable to behold its power, doth fear and tremble; for it raiseth the dead and hath annulled death. Wherefore, do we worship thy Burial and Resurrection.

The angel proclaiming thy Resurrection, O Lord, did frighten the guards; but to the women he cried out, saying, Why seek ye the living among the dead? Verily, he hath risen, being God, and hath granted life to the universe.

Thou didst suffer by the Cross, O thou unsuffering through the Godhead, and didst accept burial for three days that thou mightest set us free from the bondage of the enemy and grant us life through thy Resurrection, O Christ, the Lover of mankind.

I do worship, glorify, and praise thy Resurrection from the tomb, O Christ, by which thou didst release us from the fast bonds of hades; for, being God, thou hast granted the world eternal life and the Great Mercy.

Verily, the transgressors of the law guarded thy life-receiving tomb, and didst seal it, placing guards. But thou, since thou art a deathless and almighty God, didst rise on the third day.

When thou didst pass through the gates of hades and didst demolish them, then its captive shouted, saying, Who is this who is judge not in the abyss of the earth, but who hath annulled the prison of death as though it were a tabernacle? For verily, I have received him as dead and have feared him as God. Wherefore, O almighty Saviour, have mercy upon us.

3. The Mass

The Beatitudes

REMEMBER us, O Christ, Saviour of the world, as thou didst remember the thief on the tree; and

make us worthy of thy heavenly kingdom, O thou who
art alone compassionate.

Hear, O Adam, and rejoice with Eve; for he who
of old stripped you naked and led you captive by de
ceit, hath vanished by the Cross of Christ.

Thou wast nailed upon the Cross of thine own voli
tion, O Saviour, and didst deliver Adam from the curse
of the tree, restoring him, since thou art compassionate
to his original form and to his abode in paradise.

Today hath Christ risen from the tomb, granting al
believers incorruption; and hath renewed the joy of the
ointment-bearing women after the Passion and the Res
urrection.

Rejoice, O women, the wise ointment-bearing one
who didst first see Christ rise and proclaimed to his
Disciples the recalling of the whole world.

Since, O Apostles, ye have been shown as the beloved
ones of Christ, ye shall become his companions in his
glory. Wherefore, intercede with him, since ye are
his Disciples, to make us to stand before him with
favour.

Glory: O Trinity without beginning, O indivisible
Essence, the Oneness coëqual in session, glory, and
honour, O Nature transcendent over every presidency
and sovereignty, save those who praise thee in faith.

Now: Rejoice, O spacious dwelling of God; rejoice
O tabernacle of the New Covenant, rejoice, O golden
jar, from which all were given the heavenly manna.

✠

The Eleven Matin Gospels of the Resurrection with the Exaposteilarions and the Eothinas[1] Pertaining Thereto

✝

THE FIRST GOSPEL: FROM ST. MATTHEW (28:16 TO END)

AT that time: The eleven disciples went into Galilee, unto the mountain where Jesus had appointed them.

And seeing him they adored: but some doubted.

And Jesus coming, spoke to them, saying: All power is given to me in heaven and in earth.

Going therefore, teach ye all the nations; baptizing them in the name of the Father, and of the Son, and of the Holy Spirit.

Teaching them to observe all things whatsoever I have commanded you; and, behold, I am with you all days, even to the consummation of the world. Amen.

First Exaposteilarion

LET us gather with the Disciples on the mount in Galilee to behold Christ in faith, saying, I have received the power of those on high and those below. And let us learn how to baptize all the nations in the Name of the Father, and of the Son, and of the Holy Spirit, and how he is present with his initiates to the end of the world as he promised.

And to our Lady

THOU didst rejoice with the Disciples, O virgin Theotokos; for thou didst behold Christ rising from the tomb on the third day as he said, who appeared to them teaching and declaring supreme things, and com-

---

1 The Eothinas are the composition of King Laon the Wise and the Exaposteilarions are the composition of his son, Constantine.

manding them to baptize in the Name of the Fathe
and of the Son, and of the Holy Spirit, and to believe i
his Resurrection and to glorify thee, O Maiden.

First Eothina—Glory, in the First Tone

VERILY, the Lord appeared to the Disciples goin
to the mountain for ascension from earthly things
and they worshipped him and learned from him th
power given to him in every place. And they were ser
to every place under heaven to preach his Resurrectio
from the dead, and his translation to heaven, to whon
he had promised, not lying, that he would be with then
forever; for he is Christ God and the Saviour of ou
souls.

THE SECOND GOSPEL: FROM ST. MARK (16:1-8)

AND when the Sabbath was past, Mary Magdalene
and Mary the mother of James, and Salom
brought sweet spices, that coming, they might anoin
Jesus.

And very early in the morning, the first day of th
week, they come to the sepulchre, the sun being nov
risen.

And they said one to another: Who shall roll us bacl
the stone from the door of the sepulchre?

And looking, they saw the stone rolled back. For i
was very great.

And entering into the sepulchre, they saw a young
man sitting on the right side, clothed with a white robe
and they were astonished.

Who saith to them: Be not affrighted; you seek Jesu
of Nazareth, who was crucified: he is risen, he is no
here, behold the place where they laid him.

But go, tell his disciples and Peter that he goeth be
fore you into Galilee; there you shall see him, as h
told you.

But they going out, fled from the sepulchre. For a
rembling and fear had seized them: and they said
nothing to any man; for they were afraid.

Second Exaposteilarion

VERILY, when the ointment-bearing women saw the
stone rolled, they rejoiced; for they saw a young
man sitting at the grave who said to them, Behold,
Christ hath risen, say to the Disciples with Peter to
hasten to the mountain; for there he shall appear to
you, O ye his beloved ones, as he foretold you.

To our Lady

BEFORE conceiving thee, O Christ, an angel hailed
the Virgin; and an angel also rolled the stone from
the grave. The former instead of sorrow proclaimed
signs of joy indescribable: and the latter instead of
death proclaimed to the women and thy beloved ones
thy Resurrection, magnifying thee, O Giver of life.

Second Eothina—Glory, in the Second Tone

THEY who were with Mary came and brought with
them ointments; and as they were at a loss how to
achieve their desire, they saw that the stone had been
rolled, and a divine young man removed all anxiety and
trouble from their souls by saying, The Lord Jesus hath
risen. Wherefore, they proclaimed to his Disciples,
that they should hasten to Galilee and behold him, risen
from the dead; for he is the Lord, the Giver of life.

THE THIRD GOSPEL: FROM ST. MARK (16:9 TO END)

AND Christ, rising early the first day of the week,
appeared first to Mary Magdalene, out of whom
he cast seven devils.

She went and told them that had been with him, who
were mourning and weeping.

And they hearing that he was alive, and had been seen by her, did not believe.

And after that, he appeared in another shape to two of them walking, as they were going into the country.

And they going told it to the rest: neither did they believe them.

At length he appeared to the eleven as they were at table: and he upbraided them with their incredulity and hardness of heart, because they did not believe them who had seen him after he was risen again.

And he said to them: Go ye into the whole world, and preach the gospel to every creature.

He that believeth and is baptized, shall be saved: but he that believeth not shall be condemned.

And these signs shall follow them that believe: In my name they shall cast out devils: they shall speak with new tongues.

They shall take up serpents; and if they shall drink any deadly thing, it shall not hurt them: they shall lay their hands upon the sick, and they shall recover.

And the Lord Jesus, after he had spoken to them, was taken up into heaven, and sitteth on the right hand of God.

But they going forth preached every where: the Lord working withal, and confirming the word with signs that followed.

Third Exaposteilarion

VERILY, Christ is risen. Let no one doubt, or be suspicious; for he appeared to Mary, and after that to those who went fishing. Then he appeared to his eleven initiates, as they were reclining, whom he sent to baptize. And he ascended to heaven whence he had descended, establishing his warning by a multitude of wonders.

To our Lady

O SUN that hast shone today from the tomb, as a groom from his chamber; who led hades captive and repudiated death. By the intercessions of thy

Mother, send us light to lighten our hearts and souls, a light to lead us all to walking in the way of the commandments and in paths of safety.

Third Eothina—Glory, in the Third Tone

VERILY, the Disciples were taunted for the hardness of their hearts because they doubted when Mary Magdalene proclaimed to them the fact of the Resurrection of the Saviour and his appearance to her. But, when they were armed with miracles and wonders, they were sent out to warn. As for thee, O Lord, thou didst ascend to thy Father, the Element of all light; and they preached in every place verifying their words with wonders and miracles. Wherefore, we who were enlightened by them glorify thy Resurrection from the dead, O Lover of mankind.

THE FOURTH GOSPEL: FROM ST. LUKE (24:1-12)

ON the first day of the week, very early in the morning, the women came to the sepulchre, bringing the spices which they had prepared, and certain others with them.

And they found the stone rolled back from the sepulchre.

And going in, they found not the body of the Lord Jesus.

And it came to pass, as they were astonished in their mind at this, behold, two men stood by them, in shining apparel.

And as they were afraid, and bowed down their countenance towards the ground, they said unto them: Why seek you the living with the dead?

He is not here, but is risen. Remember how he spoke unto you, when he was yet in Galilee,

Saying: The Son of man must be delivered into the hands of sinful men, and be crucified, and the third day rise again.

And they remembered his words.

And going back from the sepulchre, they told all these things to the eleven, and to all the rest.

And it was Mary Magdalene, and Joanna, and Mary of James, and the other women that were with them, who told these things to the apostles.

And these words seemed to them as idle tales; and they did not believe them.

But Peter rising up, ran to the sepulchre, and stooping down, he saw the linen cloths laid by themselves; and went away wondering in himself at that which was come to pass.

Fourth Exaposteilarion

LET us gleam, shining with virtues, and behold the man standing in brilliant clothes inside the grave, giving life to the ointment-bearing women with their faces downcast. Let us learn of the Resurrection of the Lord of heaven and hasten with Peter to the tomb and wonder at the great happening, waiting to behold Christ the Life.

To our Lady

O LORD, when thou didst shout, Rejoice, thou didst recompense thereby the sorrow of our ancestors who went before. And by thy Resurrection thou didst bring joy to the world. Wherefore, O Life-giver, by the one who gave thee birth, send us light to shine in our hearts, the light of thy compassion, that we may cry to thee, O Lover of mankind, incarnate God, glory to thy Resurrection.

Fourth Eothina—Glory, in the Fourth Tone

VERILY, the women came at early dawn to thy tomb, O Christ, but they found not thy body, precious to them. And as they were perplexed, behold there stood among them those who were in shining clothes who said to them, Why seek ye the living among the dead? He hath risen as he foretold. Why have

ve forgotten his words? And when they were assured
by their saying, they preached to the Disciples the
things seen. But their glad tidings were received with
ridicule; for they were still without understanding. But
Peter hastened to behold, and glorified thy wonders in
himself.

The Fifth Gospel: from St. Luke (24:12-35)

AT that time: Peter rising up, ran to the sepulchre,
and stooping down, he saw the linen cloths laid by
themselves, and went away wondering in himself at that
which was come to pass.

And behold, two of them went, the same day, to a
town which was sixty furlongs from Jerusalem, named
Emmaus.

And they talked together of all these things which
had happened.

And it came to pass, that while they talked and reasoned with themselves, Jesus himself also drawing near,
went with them.

But their eyes were held, that they should not know
him.

And he said to them: What are these discourses that
you hold one with another as you walk, and are sad?

And the one of them, whose name was Cleophas,
answering, said to him: Art thou only a stranger in
Jerusalem, and hast not known the things that have been
done there in these days?

To whom he said: What things? And they said:
Concerning Jesus of Nazareth, who was a prophet,
mighty in work and word before God and all the
people;

And how our chief priests and princes delivered him
to be condemned to death, and crucified him.

But we hoped, that it was he that should have redeemed Israel: and now besides all this, to day is the
third day since these things were done.

Yea and certain women also of our company affrighted us, who before it was light, were at the sepulchre.

And not finding his body, came saying, that they had
also seen a vision of angels, who say that he is alive.

And some of our people went to the sepulchre, and
found it so as the women had said, but him they found
not.

Then he said to them: O foolish, and slow of heart
to believe in all things which the prophets have spoken.

Ought not Christ to have suffered these things, and
so to enter into his glory?

And beginning at Moses and all the prophets, he ex-
pounded to them in all the scriptures, the things that
were concerning him.

And they drew nigh to the town, whither they were
going: and he made as though he would go farther.

But they constrained him; saying: Stay with us, because it is towards evening, and the day is now far
spent. And he went in with them.

And it came to pass, whilst he was at table with them,
he took bread, and blessed, and brake, and gave to them.

And their eyes were opened, and they knew him:
and he vanished out of their sight.

And they said one to the other: Was not our heart
burning within us, whilst he spoke in the way, and
opened to us the scriptures?

And rising up, the same hour, they went back to
Jerusalem: and they found the eleven gathered together, and those that were with them,

Saying: The Lord is risen indeed, and hath appeared
to Simon.

And they told what things were done in the way; and
how they knew him in the breaking of bread.

Fifth Exaposteilarion

VERILY, Christ who is the Way and the Life, after
his Resurrection from the dead, accompanied Luke
and Cleopas, who had recognized him at Emmaus, in

the breaking of the bread, whose hearts and souls were inflamed as he spake to them in the way, explaining to them from the books about all that he had suffered. Let us, therefore, shout with them crying, Verily, the Lord hath risen and appeared unto Peter.

To our Lady

I PRAISE thy countless mercy, my Creator; for thou didst empty thyself to put on the suffering nature of man, and save it. And whereas thou art God, thou didst consent for my sake to become like me from the pure Maiden of God, and to descend to hades, willing to save me by the intercession of thy Mother, O all-compassionate Lord.

Fifth Eothina—Glory, in the Fifth Tone

HOW wise are thy judgments, O Christ, in that thou didst grant Peter to understand thy Resurrection by the coffin wrappings alone; whereas Luke and Cleopas thou didst accompany conversing; and as thou didst so thou didst not reveal thyself to them, and thou wast taunted by them as though thou alone wert a stranger in Jerusalem, not knowing what had happened therein of late. But since thou ordainest all things in conformity with thy creation, thou didst explain to them what the Prophets had uttered concerning thee, and in the breaking of the bread they knew thee after their hearts were aflame for thy knowledge; and when they came together with the Disciples they proclaimed openly the Resurrection, by which have mercy upon us.

THE SIXTH GOSPEL: FROM ST. LUKE (24:36 TO END)

AT that time: Jesus after rising from the dead stood in the midst of his disciples and saith to them: Peace be unto you.

But they being troubled and frightened, supposed that they saw a spirit.

And he said to them: Why are you troubled, and why do thoughts arise in your hearts?

See my hands and feet, that it is I myself; handle, and see: for a spirit hath not flesh and bones, as you see me to have.

And when he had said this, he showed them his hands and feet.

But while they yet believed not, and wondered for joy, he said: Have you here any thing to eat?

And they offered him a piece of a broiled fish, and a honeycomb.

And when he had eaten before them, taking the remains, he gave to them.

And he said to them: These are the words which I spoke to you, while I was yet with you, that all things must needs be fulfilled, which are written in the law of Moses, and in the prophets, and in the psalms, concerning me.

Then he opened their understanding, that they might understand the scriptures.

And he said to them: Thus it is written, and thus it behoved Christ to suffer, and to rise again from the dead, the third day:

And that penance and remission of sins should be preached in his name, unto all nations, beginning at Jerusalem.

And you are witnesses of these things.

And I send the promise of my Father upon you: but stay you in the city, till you be endued with power from on high.

And he led them out as far as Bethania: and lifting up his hands, he blessed them.

And it came to pass, whilst he blessed them, he departed from them, and was carried up to heaven.

And they adoring went back into Jerusalem with great joy.

And they were always in the temple, praising and blessing God.

Sixth Exaposteilarion

WHEN thou didst rise from the grave, O Saviour, thou didst reveal thyself a Man by nature, as thou stood in the midst of the Disciples and ate with them and taught them the baptism of repentance. Then at once thou didst ascend to thy heavenly Father and promised to send them the Comforter. Wherefore, O most divine and incarnate God, glory to thy Resurrection.

To our Lady

THE Author of all creation and the God of all, O holy Virgin, took a carnal body from thy pure blood and renewed our nature, wholly corrupt, preserving thee after birth-giving as thou wast before it. Wherefore, we all praise thee in faith, exclaiming, Rejoice, O mistress of the world.

Sixth Eothina—Glory, in the Sixth Tone

SINCE thou art the true peace of God to man, O Christ, thou didst give thy peace to thy Disciples after thy Resurrection. Thou didst show them frightened when they thought that they were beholding a spirit. But thou didst remove the anxiety of their souls when thou didst show them thy hands and feet; and yet they were in doubt. But when thou didst take food with them, reminding them of thy preaching, thou didst open their minds to understand the books. And thou didst make with them the eternal covenant, blessed them, and rose, ascending into heaven. Wherefore, with them, do we worship thee, O Lord, glory be to thee.

THE SEVENTH GOSPEL: FROM ST. JOHN (20:1-10)

AND on the first day of the week, Mary Magdalene cometh early, when it was yet dark, unto the sepulchre; and she saw the stone taken away from the sepulchre.

She ran, therefore, and cometh to Simon Peter, and to the other disciple whom Jesus loved, and saith to them: They have taken away the Lord out of the sepulchre, and we know not where they have laid him.

Peter therefore went out, and that other disciple, and they came to the sepulchre.

And they both ran together, and that other disciple did outrun Peter, and came first to the sepulchre.

And when he stooped down, he saw the linen cloths lying; but yet he went not in.

Then cometh Simon Peter, following him, and went into the sepulchre, and saw the linen cloths lying,

And the napkin that had been about his head, not lying with the linen cloths, but apart, wrapped up into one place.

Then that other disciple also went in, who came first to the sepulchre: and he saw, and believed.

For as yet they knew not the scripture, that he must rise again from the dead.

The disciples therefore departed again to their home.

Seventh Exaposteilarion

WHEN Mary said, They have carried away my Lord, Simon Peter and the other Disciple, the initiate of Christ whom Jesus loved, hastened to the grave. And they both came and found the wrappings inside the tomb, and the turban which was on his head lying aside. Wherefore they remained till they truly beheld Christ.

To our Lady

O MOST merciful Christ, thou didst perform for my sake splendid wonders; for thou wast born of a virgin Maiden in an inexplicable manner, and didst consent to crucifixion and suffered death, rising in glory, and released our nature from death. Wherefore glory to thy glory, O Christ, glory to thy might.

Seventh Eothina—Glory, in the Seventh Tone

ƁEHOLD the dawn and rise of day; why hast thou
stood, O Mary, at the grave? And great darkness
ath covered thy mind, and thou asked him, Where
ath Jesus been placed? Yea, behold the Disciples who
astened to the tomb, how they surmised his Resurrec-
on from the coffin wrappings and the turban, and re-
iembered what was said about him in the books.
Vherefore, we who believed through them, praise thee
'ith them, O Christ, Giver of life.

THE EIGHTH GOSPEL: FROM ST. JOHN (20:11-18)

ᴀT that time: Mary was standing at the sepulchre
without, weeping. Now as she was weeping, she
ooped down, and looked into the sepulchre.

And she saw two angels in white, sitting, one at the
ead, and one at the feet, where the body of Jesus had
een laid.

They say to her: Woman, why weepest thou? She
ith to them: Because they have taken away my Lord;
nd I know not where they have laid him.

When she had thus said, she turned herself back,
nd saw Jesus standing; and she knew not that it was
esus.

Jesus saith to her: Woman, why weepest thou? whom
ekest thou? She, thinking that it was the gardener,
ith to him: Sir, if thou hast taken him hence, tell me
here thou hast laid him, and I will take him away.

Jesus saith to her: Mary. She turning, saith to him:
abboni (which is to say, Master).

Jesus saith to her: Do not touch me, for I am not yet
scended to my Father. But go to my brethren, and
y to them: I ascend to my Father and to your Father,
) my God and your God.

Mary Magdalene cometh, and telleth the disciples:
have seen the Lord, and these things he said to me.

Eighth Exaposteilarion

VERILY, when Mary saw two angels inside the grave she was taken by surprise. And when, she knowing not Christ, but thinking him the gardener, said to him, Sir, where hast thou placed the body of Jesus? she knew from his voice that he was the Saviour, and she obeyed him when he said, Touch me not; for I am going to my Father. Tell this to my brethren.

To our Lady

THOU hast given birth, O Maiden, to one of the Trinity in an inexplicable manner, dual in nature, dual in act, but one in Person. Wherefore, beseech him always for our sakes, who adore thee in faith, that we may escape the vexations of the enemy; for in thee do we now seek refuge, O Theotokos, our Lady.

Eighth Eothina—Glory, in the Eighth Tone

VERILY, the fervid tears of Mary were not shed in vain; for behold she hath been worthy to learn from the angels, and to look at thy face, O Jesus. But since she was a weak woman she was still thinking of earthly things. Therefore, was she put off from touching thee, O Christ. But she was sent to proclaim to thy Disciples, and to tell them the glad tidings and of the Ascension to the heavenly heritage. With her, therefore, make us worthy of thine appearance, O Lord.

The Ninth Gospel: from St. John (20:19 to End)

NOW when it was late that same day, the first of the week, and the doors were shut, where the disciples were gathered together, for fear of the Jews, Jesus came and stood in the midst, and said to them: Peace be to you.

And when he had said this, he showed them his hand and his side. The disciples therefore were glad, when they saw the Lord.

He said therefore to them again: Peace be to you. As the Father hath sent me, I also send you.

When he had said this, he breathed on them; and he said to them: Receive ye the Holy Ghost.

Whose sins you shall forgive, they are forgiven them; and whose sins you shall retain, they are retained.

Now Thomas, one of the twelve, who is called Didymus, was not with them when Jesus came.

The other disciples therefore said to him: We have seen the Lord. But he said to them: Except I shall see in his hands the print of the nails, and put my finger into the place of the nails, and put my hand into his side, I will not believe.

And after eight days again his disciples were within, and Thomas with them. Jesus cometh, the doors being shut, and stood in the midst, and said: Peace be to you.

Then he saith to Thomas: Put in thy finger hither, and see my hands; and bring hither thy hand, and put it into my side; and be not faithless, but believing.

Thomas answered, and said to him: My Lord, and my God.

Jesus saith to him: Because thou hast seen me, Thomas, thou hast believed: blessed are they that have not seen, and have believed.

Many other signs also did Jesus in the sight of his disciples, which are not written in this book.

But these are written, that you may believe that Jesus is the Christ, the Son of God: and that believing, you may have life in his name.

Ninth Exaposteilarion

WHEN thou didst enter while the doors were closed, O Lord, then thou didst fill thine Apostles with a holy spirit, breathing into them peace, and saying unto them, Loosen ye and bind ye sins. And after eight days thou didst show Thomas thy hands and thy side. With him, therefore, do we cry to thee, Thou art the Lord and God.

To our Lady

WHEN thou didst behold thy Son rising from the tomb after three days, O most holy bride of God thou didst put away all sorrow which thou hadst borne as Mother when thou beheld him suffering.

Ninth Eothina—Glory, in the Fifth Tone

IN the fullness of time, O Christ, thou didst appear among thy beloved ones on the eve of the sabbath and didst confirm to them a wonder through a wonder, namely thy Resurrection from the dead by thine entrance while the doors were closed. But thou didst fill the Disciples with joy, granting them a holy spirit, and didst bestow on them power to forgive sins. And as for Thomas, thou didst not permit him to drown in the depths of faithlessness. Wherefore, grant us the knowledge of the truth, and forgiveness of sins, O compassionate Lord.

THE TENTH GOSPEL: FROM ST. JOHN (21:1-14)

AT that time: Jesus showed himself again to his disciples at the sea of Tiberias. And he showed himself after this manner.

There were together Simon Peter, and Thomas, who is called Didymus, and Nathanael, who was of Cana of Galilee, and the sons of Zebedee, and two others of his disciples.

Simon Peter saith to them: I go a fishing. They say to him: We also come with thee. And they went forth, and entered into the ship: and that night they caught nothing.

But when the morning was come, Jesus stood on the shore: yet the disciples knew not that it was Jesus.

Jesus therefore said to them: Children, have you any meat? They answered him: No.

He saith to them: Cast the net on the right side of the ship, and you shall find. They cast therefore; and now they were not able to draw it, for the multitude of fishes.

That disciple therefore whom Jesus loved, said to Peter: It is the Lord. Simon Peter, when he heard that it was the Lord, girt his coat about him, (for he was naked,) and cast himself into the sea.

But the other disciples came in the ship, (for they were not far from the land, but as it were two hundred cubits,) dragging the net with fishes.

As soon then as they came to land, they saw hot coals lying, and a fish laid thereon, and bread.

Jesus saith to them: Bring hither of the fishes which you have now caught.

Simon Peter went up, and drew the net to land, full of great fishes, one hundred and fifty-three. And although there were so many, the net was not broken.

Jesus saith to them: Come, and dine. And none of them who were at meat, durst ask him: Who art thou? knowing that it was the Lord.

And Jesus cometh and taketh bread and giveth them, and fish in like manner.

This is now the third time that Jesus was manifested to his disciples, after he was risen from the dead.

Tenth Exaposteilarion

VERILY, the two sons of Zebedee with Peter and Nathaniel and two others and Thomas were fishing in the Lake of Tiberias, who by the command of Christ cast the net on the right side and drew out much fish. And when Peter knew him he came to him swimming. This, then, was a third appearance of the Lord, when he showed them bread and fish on the live coals.

To our Lady

PRAY for us, O Virgin, to the Lord who rose from the tomb on the third day, even for us Christians who praise and bless thee with zeal; for we have all taken thee as a refuge of salvation and as a mediatrix with him; for we are thy servants, O Theotokos, and thine inheritors, and we all await thy help.

Tenth Eothina—Glory, in the Sixth Tone

AFTER thy descent to hades, O Christ, and thy Resurrection from the dead, the Disciples sorrowed, as was fitting, grieving over thy removal. They returned to their occupations and attended to their nets and their ships; but there was no fishing whatsoever. But thou didst appear to them, and, since thou art Lord of all, thou didst command them to cast the nets on the right side. And at once the word became deed and they caught much fish and found a strange meal prepared for them on the ground. And thy Disciples at once partook thereof.

And now, make us worthy with them to enjoy it mentally, O Lord, Lover of mankind.

THE ELEVENTH GOSPEL: FROM ST. JOHN (21:14 TO END)

AT that time: Jesus showed himself to his disciples, after he was risen from the dead.

When therefore they had dined, Jesus saith to Simon Peter: Simon, son of John, lovest thou me more than these? He saith to him: Yea, Lord, thou knowest that I love thee. He saith to him: Feed my lambs.

He said to him again: Simon, son of John, lovest thou me? He saith to him: Yea, Lord, thou knowest that I love thee. He saith to him: Feed my lambs.

He said to him the third time: Simon, son of John, lovest thou me? Peter was grieved, because he had said to him the third time: Lovest thou me? And he said to him: Lord, thou knowest all things: thou knowest that I love thee. He said to him: Feed my sheep

Amen, amen, I say to thee, when thou wast younger thou didst gird thyself, and didst walk where thou wouldst. But when thou shalt be old, thou shalt stretch forth thy hands, and another shall gird thee, and lead thee whither thou wouldst not.

And this he said, signifying by what death he should glorify God. And when he had said this, he saith to him: Follow me.

Peter turning about, saw that disciple whom Jesus loved following, who also leaned on his breast at supper, and said: Lord, who is he that shall betray thee?

Him therefore when Peter had seen, he saith to Jesus: Lord, and what shall this man do?

Jesus saith to him: So I will have him to remain till I come, what is it to thee? follow thou me.

This saying therefore went abroad among the brethren, that that disciple should not die. And Jesus did not say to him: He should not die; but, So I will have him to remain till I come, what is it to thee?

This is that disciple who giveth testimony of these things, and hath written these things; and we know that his testimony is true.

But there are also many other things which Jesus did; which, if they were written every one, the world itself, I think, would not be able to contain the books that should be written.

Eleventh Exaposteilarion

WHEN the Lord, after his Resurrection, asked Peter thrice, Dost thou love me, he set him for a shepherd over his sheep. And when Peter saw the Disciple whom Jesus loved following him, he asked the Lord, And what is this? And the Lord said, If I will that he tarry until I come again, what is that to thee, O Peter my beloved.

To our Lady

WHAT a terrible mystery, what a dazzling wonder; for death hath been abolished completely by Death. Who, then, will not praise, and who will not glorify thy Resurrection, O Word, and the Theotokos who gave thee birth in the flesh and purity. Where-fore, by her pleadings, release us all from hades.

Eleventh Eothina—Glory, in the Eighth Tone

WHEN thou didst show thyself to the Disciples after thy Resurrection, O Saviour, thou didst appoint Simon to shepherd the sheep, for the renewal of love, asking him to tend the flock. And thou didst say to him, If thou lovest me, O Peter, feed my lambs, feed my sheep. But he at once inquired concerning the other Disciple, showing his exceeding love. Wherefore, by the intercession of both, O Christ, keep thy flock from corrupting wolves.

FOURTH SECTION

A Collection of Sunday Epistles and Gospels for the Whole Year

Being the chapters and portions of the Epistles and Gospels which are read in the Divine Liturgy on Sunday, from the Sunday of All Saints, known as the First Sunday after Pentecost, to the Sunday of the Pharisee and the Publican.

✠

¶ *The Epistles and Gospels on Feast Days, and the Sundays of the Triodion, and the Pentecostarion (the fifty Paschal Days), from the Sunday of the Pharisee and the Publican to that of Pentecost, may be found in their proper places.*

THE FIRST SUNDAY AFTER PENTECOST

[KNOWN AS ALL-SAINTS SUNDAY]

Prokeimenon, in the Fourth Tone

Marvelous is God in his saints.
Bless ye God in the congregations.

Section from the Epistle of St. Paul to the Hebrews (11:33 to end; 12:1-2)

YE brethren: All the saints by faith subdued kingdoms, wrought righteousness, obtained promises, stopped the mouths of lions.

Quenched the violence of fire, escaped the edge of the sword, out of weakness were made strong, waxed valiant in fight, turned to flight the armies of the aliens.

Women received their dead raised to life again: and others were tortured, not accepting deliverance; that they might obtain a better resurrection:

And others had trial of cruel mockings and scourg
ings, yea, moreover of bonds and imprisonment:

They were stoned, they were sawn asunder, wer
tempted, were slain with the sword: they wandered
about in sheepskins and goatskins; being destitute, af
flicted, tormented;

Of whom the world was not worthy: they wandered
in deserts, and in mountains, and in dens and caves o
the earth.

And these all, having obtained a good report through
faith, received not the promise:

God having provided some better thing for us, tha
they without us should not be made perfect.

Wherefore, seeing we also are compassed about with
so great a cloud of witnesses, let us lay aside ever
weight, and the sin which doth so easily beset us, an
let us run with patience the race that is set before us

Looking unto Jesus the author and finisher of ou
faith; who for the joy that was set before him endure
the cross, despising the shame, and is set down at th
right hand of the throne of God.

The Gospel: from St. Matthew (10:32-33; 37-38; 19:27 to end)

THE Lord saith to his disciples: Whosoever there
fore shall confess me before men, him will I con
fess also before my Father which is in heaven.

But whosoever shall deny me before men, him will
also deny before my Father which is in heaven.

He that loveth father or mother more than me is no
worthy of me: and he that loveth son or daughter mor
than me is not worthy of me.

And he that taketh not his cross, and followeth afte
me, is not worthy of me.

Then answered Peter and said unto him, Behold, w
have forsaken all, and followed thee; what shall w
have therefore?

And Jesus said unto them, Verily I say unto you, That ye which have followed me, in the regeneration when the Son of man shall sit in the throne of his glory, ye also shall sit upon twelve thrones, judging the twelve tribes of Israel.

And every one that hath forsaken houses, or brethren, or sisters, or father, or mother, or wife, or children, or lands, for my name's sake, shall receive a hundredfold, and shall inherit everlasting life.

But many that are first shall be last; and the last shall be first.

Second Sunday

Prokeimenon, in the First Tone

Let thy mercy, O Lord, be upon us.
Rejoice in the Lord, O ye just.

Section from the Epistle of St. Paul to the Romans (2:10-16)

YE brethren: Glory, honour, and peace to every man that worketh good, to the Jew first, and also to the Gentile:

For there is no respect of persons with God.

For as many as have sinned without law shall also perish without law; and as many as have sinned in the law shall be judged by the law;

(For not the hearers of the law are just before God, but the doers of the law shall be justified.

For when the Gentiles, which have not the law, do by nature the things contained in the law, these, having not the law, are a law unto themselves:

Which show the work of the law written in their hearts, their conscience also bearing witness, and their thoughts the mean while accusing or else excusing one another;)

In the day when God shall judge the secrets of men by Jesus Christ according to my gospel.

The Gospel: from St. Matthew (4:18-23)

AT that time: Jesus, walking by the sea of Galilee,
saw two brethren, Simon called Peter, and Andrew
his brother, casting a net into the sea; for they were
fishers.

And he saith unto them, Follow me, and I will make
you fishers of men.

And they straightway left their nets, and followed
him.

And going on from thence, he saw other two brethren, James the son of Zebedee, and John his brother, in
a ship with Zebedee their father, mending their nets;
and he called them.

And they immediately left the ship and their father,
and followed him.

And Jesus went about all Galilee, teaching in their
synagogues, and preaching the gospel of the kingdom,
and healing all manner of sickness and all manner of
disease among the people.

THIRD SUNDAY

Prokeimenon, in the Second Tone

The Lord is my strength and my praise.
The Lord chastising hath chastised me.

Section from the Epistle of St. Paul to the Roman
(5:1-10)

YE brethren: Therefore being justified by faith, we
have peace with God through our Lord Jesu
Christ:

By whom also we have access by faith into this grace
wherein we stand, and rejoice in hope of the glory o
God.

And not only so, but we glory in tribulations also
knowing that tribulation worketh patience;

And patience, experience; and experience, hope.

And hope maketh not ashamed; because the love of God is shed abroad in our hearts by the Holy Ghost which is given unto us.

For when we were yet without strength, in due time Christ died for the ungodly.

For scarcely for a righteous man will one die: yet peradventure for a good man some would even dare to die.

But God commendeth his love toward us, in that, while we were yet sinners, Christ died for us.

Much more then, being now justified by his blood, we shall be saved from wrath through him.

For if, when we were enemies, we were reconciled to God by the death of his Son; much more, being reconciled, we shall be saved by his life.

The Gospel: from St. Matthew (6:22-33)

THE Lord said: The light of the body is the eye: if therefore thine eye be single, thy whole body shall be full of light.

But if thine eye be evil, thy whole body shall be full of darkness. If therefore the light that is in thee be darkness, how great is that darkness!

No man can serve two masters: for either he will hate the one, and love the other; or else he will hold to the one, and despise the other. Ye cannot serve God and mammon.

Therefore I say unto you, Take no thought for your life, what ye shall eat, or what ye shall drink; nor yet for your body, what ye shall put on. Is not the life more than meat, and the body than raiment?

Behold the fowls of the air: for they sow not, neither do they reap, nor gather into barns; yet your heavenly Father feedeth them. Are ye not much better than they?

Which of you by taking thought can add one cubit unto his stature?

And why take ye thought for raiment? Consider the lilies of the field, how they grow; they toil not, neither do they spin:

And yet I say unto you, That even Solomon in all his glory was not arrayed like one of these.

Wherefore, if God so clothe the grass of the field, which to-day is, and to-morrow is cast into the oven, shall he not much more clothe you, O ye of little faith?

Therefore take no thought, saying, What shall we eat, or what shall we drink, or wherewithal shall we be clothed?

(For after all these things do the Gentiles seek) for your heavenly Father knoweth that ye have need of all these things.

But seek ye first the kingdom of God, and his righteousness; and all these things shall be added unto you.

FOURTH SUNDAY

Prokeimenon in the Third Tone

Sing praises to our God, sing praises.
O clap your hands all ye nations.

Section from the Epistle of Saint Paul to the Romans (6:18-end)

YE brethren: Being then made free from sin, ye became the servants of righteousness.

I speak after the manner of men because of the infirmity of your flesh: for as ye have yielded your members servants to uncleanness and to iniquity unto iniquity; even so now yield your members servants to righteousness unto holiness.

For when ye were the servants of sin, ye were free from righteousness.

What fruit had ye then in those things whereof ye are now ashamed? for the end of those things is death.

But now being made free from sin, and become servants to God, ye have your fruit unto holiness, and the end everlasting life.

For the wages of sin is death; but the gift of God is
ternal life through Jesus Christ our Lord.

The Gospel: from St. Matthew (8:5-13)

A T that time: When Jesus entered into Capernaum,
there came unto him a centurion, beseeching him,

And saying, Lord, my servant lieth at home sick of
ne palsy, grieviously tormented.

And Jesus saith unto him, I will come and heal him.

The centurion answered and said, Lord, I am not
vorthy that thou shouldest come under my roof: but
peak the word only, and my servant shall be healed.

For I am a man under authority, having soldiers
nder me: and I say to this man, Go, and he goeth;
nd to another, Come, and he cometh; and to my serv-
nt, Do this, and he doeth it.

When Jesus heard it, he marveled, and said to them
hat followed, Verily I say unto you, I have not found
o great faith, no, not in Israel.

And I say unto you, That many shall come from the
ast and west, and shall sit down with Abraham, and
saac, and Jacob, in the kingdom of heaven:

But the children of the kingdom shall be cast out
nto outer darkness: there shall be weeping and gnash-
ng of teeth.

And Jesus said unto the centurion, Go thy way; and
is thou hast believed, so be it done unto thee. And his
ervant was healed in the selfsame hour.

FIFTH SUNDAY

Prokeimenon, in the Fourth Tone

How great are thy works, O Lord!
Thou hast made all things in wisdom.
Bless the Lord, O my soul.

Section from the Epistle of St. Paul to the Romans
(10:1-10)

YE brethren: My heart's desire and prayer to Go
for Israel is, that they might be saved.

For I bear them record that they have a zeal of God
but not according to knowledge.

For they, being ignorant of God's righteousness, an
going about to establish their own righteousness, hav
not submitted themselves unto the righteousness of God

For Christ is the end of the law for righteousness t
every one that believeth.

For Moses describeth the righteousness which is o
the law, That the man which doeth those things shal
live by them.

But the righteousness which is of faith speaketh o
this wise, Say not in thy heart, Who shall ascend int
heaven? (that is, to bring Christ down from above:

Or, Who shall descend into the deep? (that is, t
bring up Christ again from the dead.) ·

But what saith it? The word is nigh thee, even i
thy mouth, and in thy heart: that is, the word of faitl
which we preach:

That if thou shalt confess with thy mouth the Lor
Jesus, and shalt believe in thine heart that God hat
raised him from the dead, thou shalt be saved.

For with the heart man believeth unto righteousness
and with the mouth confession is made unto salvatio

The Gospel: from St. Matthew (8:28-34; 9:1)

AT that time: When Jesus came to the country o
the Gergasenes, there met him two possessed wit
devils, coming out of the tombs, exceeding fierce, s
that no man might pass by that way.

And, behold, they cried out, saying, What have w
to do with thee, Jesus, thou Son of God? art thou con
hither to torment us before the time?

And there was a good way off from them a herd o
many swine feeding.

So the devils besought him, saying, If thou cast us out, suffer us to go away into the herd of swine.

And he said unto them, Go. And when they were come out, they went into the herd of swine: and, behold, the whole herd of swine ran violently down a steep place into the sea, and perished in the waters.

And they that kept them fled, and went their ways into the city, and told every thing, and what was befallen to the possessed of the devils.

And, behold, the whole city came out to meet Jesus: and when they saw him, they besought him that he would depart out of their coasts.

And he entered into a ship, and passed over, and came into his own city.

Sixth Sunday

Prokeimenon, in the Fifth Tone

Thou, O Lord, wilt preserve us: and keep us from this generation.

Save me, O Lord; for the godly man ceaseth.

Section from the Epistle of St. Paul to the Romans (12:6-14)

YE brethren: Having then gifts differing according to the grace that is given to us, whether prophecy, let us prophesy according to the proportion of faith:

Or ministry, let us wait on our ministering; or he that teacheth, on teaching;

Or he that exhorteth, on exhortation: he that giveth, let him do it with simplicity; he that ruleth, with diligence; he that showeth mercy, with cheerfulness.

Let love be without dissimulation. Abhor that which is evil; cleave to that which is good.

Be kindly affectioned one to another with brotherly love; in honour preferring one another;

Not slothful in business; fervent in spirit; serving the Lord;

Rejoicing in hope; patient in tribulation; continuing instant in prayer;

Distributing to the necessity of saints; given to hospitality.

Bless them which persecute you: bless, and curse not.

The Gospel: from St. Matthew (9:1-8)

AT that time: Jesus entered into a ship, and passed over, and came into his own city.

And, behold, they brought to him a man sick of the palsy, lying on a bed: and Jesus seeing their faith said unto the sick of the palsy; Son, be of good cheer, thy sins be forgiven thee.

And, behold, certain of the scribes said within themselves, This man blasphemeth.

And Jesus knowing their thoughts said, Wherefore think ye evil in your hearts?

For whether is easier, to say, Thy sins be forgiven thee; or to say, Arise, and walk?

But that ye may know that the Son of man hath power on earth to forgive sins, (then saith he to the sick of the palsy,) Arise, take up thy bed, and go unto thy house.

But when the multitudes saw it, they marveled, and glorified God, which had given such power unto men.

SEVENTH SUNDAY

Prokeimenon, in the Sixth Tone

Save, O Lord, thy people, and bless thine inheritance.

Unto thee will I cry, O Lord, O my God.

Section from the Epistle of St. Paul to the Romans (15:1-7)

YE brethren: We that are strong ought to bear the infirmities of the weak, and not to please ourselves.

Let every one of us please his neighbor for his good to edification.

For even Christ pleased not himself; but, as it is written, The reproaches of them that reproached thee fell on me.

For whatsoever things were written aforetime were written for our learning, that we through patience and comfort of the Scriptures might have hope.

Now the God of patience and consolation grant you to be likeminded one toward another according to Christ Jesus:

That ye may with one mind and one mouth glorify God, even the Father of our Lord Jesus Christ.

Wherefore receive ye one another, as Christ also received us, to the glory of God.

The Gospel: from St. Matthew (9:27-35)

AT that time: When Jesus departed thence, two blind men followed him, crying, and saying: Thou son of David, have mercy on us.

And when he was come into the house, the blind men came to him: and Jesus saith unto them, Believe ye that I am able to do this? They said unto him, Yea, Lord.

Then touched he their eyes, saying, According to your faith be it unto you.

And their eyes were opened; and Jesus straitly charged them, saying, See that no man know it.

But they, when they were departed, spread abroad his fame in all that country.

As they went out, behold, they brought to him a dumb man possessed with a devil.

And when the devil was cast out, the dumb spake: and the multitudes marveled, saying, It was never so seen in Israel.

But the Pharisees said, He casteth out devils through the prince of the devils.

And Jesus went about all the cities and villages, teaching in their synagogues, and preaching the gospel of the kingdom, and healing every sickness and every disease among the people.

EIGHTH SUNDAY

Prokeimenon, in the Seventh Tone

The Lord will give strength to his people.
Bring to the Lord, O ye children of God.

Section from the First Epistle of St. Paul to the Corinthians (1:10-17)

YE brethren: I beseech you, by the name of our Lord Jesus Christ, that ye all speak the same thing, and that there be no divisions among you; but that ye be perfectly joined together in the same mind and in the same judgment.

For it hath been declared unto me of you, my brethren, by them which are of the house of Chloe, that there are contentions among you.

Now this I say, that every one of you saith, I am of Paul; and I of Apollos; and I of Cephas; and I of Christ.

Is Christ divided? was Paul crucified for you? or were ye baptized in the name of Paul?

I thank God that I baptized none of you, but Crispus and Gaius;

Lest any should say that I had baptized in mine own name.

And I baptized also the household of Stephanas: besides, I know not whether I baptized any other.

For Christ sent me not to baptize, but to preach the gospel: not with wisdom of words, lest the cross of Christ should be made of none effect.

The Gospel: from St. Matthew (14:14-22)

AT that time: Jesus saw a great multitude, and was moved with compassion toward them, and he healed their sick.

And when it was evening, his disciples came to him, saying, This is a desert place, and the time is now past; send the multitude away, that they may go into the villages, and buy themselves victuals.

But Jesus said unto them, They need not depart; give ye them to eat.

And they say unto him, We have here but five loaves, and two fishes.

He said, Bring them hither to me.

And he commanded the multitude to sit down on the grass, and took the five loaves, and the two fishes, and looking up to heaven, he blessed, and brake, and gave the loaves to his disciples, and the disciples to the multitude.

And they did all eat, and were filled: and they took up of the fragments that remained twelve baskets full.

And they that had eaten were about five thousand men, beside women and children.

And straightway Jesus constrained his disciples to get into a ship, and to go before him unto the other side, while he sent the multitudes away.

NINTH SUNDAY

Prokeimenon, in the Eighth Tone

Vow ye, and pay to the Lord your God.
In Judah is God known.

Section from the First Epistle of St. Paul to the Corinthians (3:9-17)

YE brethren: We are labourers together with God: ye are God's husbandry, ye are God's building.

According to the grace of God which is given unto me, as a wise master-builder, I have laid the foundation, and another buildeth thereon. But let every man take heed how he buildeth thereupon.

For other foundation can no man lay than that is laid, which is Jesus Christ.

Now if any man build upon this foundation gold, silver, precious stones, wood, hay, stubble;

Every man's work shall be made manifest: for the day shall declare it, because it shall be revealed by fire; and the fire shall try every man's work of what sort it is.

If any man's work abide which he hath built thereupon, he shall receive a reward.

If any man's work shall be burned, he shall suffer loss: but he himself shall be saved; yet so as by fire

Know ye not that ye are the temple of God, and that the Spirit of God dwelleth in you?

If any man defile the temple of God, him shall God destroy; for the temple of God is holy, which temple ye are.

The Gospel: from St. Matthew (14:22-34)

AT that time: Jesus constrained his disciples to get into a ship, and to go before him unto the other side, while he sent the multitude away.

And when he had sent the multitudes away, he went up into a mountain apart to pray: and when the evening was come, he was there alone.

But the ship was now in the midst of the sea, tossed with waves: for the wind was contrary.

And in the fourth watch of the night Jesus went unto them, walking on the sea.

And when the disciples saw him walking on the sea, they were troubled, saying, It is a spirit; and they cried out for fear.

But straightway Jesus spake unto them, saying, Be of good cheer; it is I; be not afraid.

And Peter answered him and said, Lord, if it be thou, bid me come unto thee on the water.

And he said, Come. And when Peter was come down out of the ship, he walked on the water, to go to Jesus.

But when he saw the wind boisterous, he was afraid; and beginning to sink, he cried, saying, Lord, save me.

And immediately Jesus stretched forth his hand, and caught him, and said unto him, O thou of little faith, wherefore didst thou doubt?

And when they were come into the ship, the wind ceased.

Then they that were in the ship came and worshipped him, saying, Of a truth thou art the Son of God.

And when they were gone over, they came into the land of Gennesaret.

TENTH SUNDAY

Prokeimenon, in the First Tone

Let thy mercy, O Lord, be upon us.
Rejoice in the Lord, O ye just.

Section from the First Epistle of St. Paul to the Corinthians (4:9-16)

YE brethren: God hath set forth us the apostles last, as it were appointed to death, and we are made a spectacle unto the world, and to angels, and to men.

We are fools for Christ's sake, but ye are wise in Christ; we are weak, but ye are strong; ye are honourable, but we are despised.

Even unto this present hour we both hunger, and thirst, and are naked, and are buffeted, and have no certain dwelling place;

And labour, working with our own hands: being reviled, we bless; being persecuted, we suffer it:

Being defamed, we intreat: we are made as the filth of the world, and are the offscouring of all things unto this day.

I write not these things to shame you, but as my beloved sons I warn you.

For though ye have ten thousand instructors in Christ, yet have ye not many fathers: for in Christ Jesus I have begotten you through the gospel.

Wherefore I beseech you, be ye followers of me.

The Gospel: from St. Matthew (17:14-23)

AT that time: There came to Christ a certain man, kneeling down to him, and saying:

Lord, have mercy on my son; for he is epileptic, and sore vexed: for oft-times he falleth into the fire, and oft into the water.

And I brought him to thy disciples, and they could not cure him.

Then Jesus answered and said, O faithless and perverse generation, how long shall I be with you? how long shall I suffer you? bring him hither to me.

And Jesus rebuked the devil; and he departed out of him: and the child was cured from that very hour.

Then came the disciples to Jesus apart, and said, Why could not we cast him out?

And Jesus said unto them, Because of your unbelief: for verily I say unto you, If ye have faith as a grain of mustard seed, ye shall say unto this mountain, Remove hence to yonder place; and it shall remove: and nothing shall be impossible unto you.

Howbeit this kind goeth not out but by prayer and fasting.

And while they abode in Galilee, Jesus said unto them, The Son of man shall be betrayed into the hands of men:

And they shall kill him, and the third day he shall be raised again.

ELEVENTH SUNDAY

Prokeimenon, in the Second Tone

The Lord is my strength and my praise.
The Lord chastising hath chastised me.

Section from the First Epistle of St. Paul to the Corinthians (9:2-12)

YE brethren: The seal of mine apostleship are ye in the Lord.

Mine answer to them that do examine me is this: Have we not power to eat and to drink?

Have we not power to lead about a sister, a wife, as well as other apostles, and as the brethren of the Lord, and Cephas?

Or I only and Barnabas, have not we power to forbear working?

Who goeth a warfare any time at his own charges? who planteth a vineyard, and eateth not of the fruit thereof? or who feedeth a flock, and eateth not of the milk of the flock?

Say I these things as a man? or saith not the law the same also?

For it is written in the law of Moses, Thou shalt not muzzle the mouth of the ox that treadeth out the corn. Doth God take care for oxen?

Or saith he it altogether for our sakes? For our sakes, no doubt, this is written: that he that ploweth should plow in hope; and that he that thresheth in hope should be partaker of his hope.

If we have sown unto you spiritual things, is it a great thing if we shall reap your carnal things?

If others be partakers of this power over you, are not we rather? Nevertheless we have not used this power; but suffer all things, lest we should hinder the gospel of Christ.

The Gospel: from St. Matthew (18:23 to end)

THE Lord spake this parable: The kingdom of heaven is likened unto a certain king, which would take account of his servants.

And when he had begun to reckon, one was brought unto him, which owed him ten thousand talents.

But forasmuch as he had not to pay, his lord commanded him to be sold, and his wife, and children, and all that he had, and payment to be made.

The servant therefore fell down, and worshipped him, saying, Lord, have patience with me, and I will pay thee all.

Then the lord of that servant was moved with compassion, and loosed him, and forgave him the debt.

But the same servant went out, and found one of his fellow servants, which owed him a hundred pence: and he laid hands on him, and took him by the throat, saying, Pay me that thou owest.

And his fellow servant fell down at his feet, and besought him, saying, Have patience with me, and I will pay thee all.

And he would not: but went and cast him into prison, till he should pay the debt.

So when his fellow servants saw what was done, they were very sorry, and came and told unto their lord all that was done.

Then his lord, after that he had called him, said unto him, O thou wicked servant, I forgave thee all that debt, because thou desiredst me:

Shouldest not thou also have had compasison on thy fellow servant, even as I had pity on thee?

And his lord was wroth, and delivered him to the tormentors, till he should pay all that was due unto him.

So likewise shall my heavenly Father do also unto you, if ye from your hearts forgive not every one his brother their trespasses.

TWELFTH SUNDAY

Prokeimenon, in the Third Tone

Sing praises to our God, sing praises.
O clap your hands, all ye nations.

Section from the First Epistle of St. Paul to the Corinthians (15:1-11)

YE brethren: I declare unto you the gospel which I preached unto you, which also ye have received, and wherein ye stand:

By which also ye are saved, if ye keep in memory what I preached unto you, unless ye have believed in vain.

For I delivered unto you first of all that which I also received, how that Christ died for our sins according to the Scriptures;

And that he was buried, and that he rose again the third day according to the Scriptures:

And that he was seen of Cephas, then of the twelve:

After that, he was seen of above five hundred brethren at once; of whom the greater part remain unto this present, but some are fallen asleep.

After that, he was seen of James; then of all the apostles.

And last of all he was seen of me also, as of one born out of due time.

For I am the least of the apostles, that am not meet to be called an apostle, because I persecuted the church of God.

But by the grace of God I am what I am: and his grace which was bestowed upon me was not in vain; but I laboured more abundantly than they all: yet not I. but the grace of God which was with me.

Therefore whether it were I or they, so we preached, and so ye believed.

The Gospel: from St. Matthew (19:16-26)

AT that time: A young man came kneeling down to Jesus and said: Good Master what good thing shall I do, that I may have eternal life?

And he said unto him, Why callest thou me good? there is none good but one, that is, God: but if thou wilt enter into life, keep the commandments.

He saith unto him, Which? Jesus said, Thou shalt do no murder, Thou shalt not commit adultery, Thou shalt not steal, Thou shalt not bear false witness,

Honour thy father and thy mother: and, Thou shalt love thy neighbour as thyself.

The young man saith unto him, All these things have I kept from my youth up: what lack I yet?

Jesus said unto him, If thou wilt be perfect, go and sell that thou hast, and give to the poor, and thou shalt have treasure in heaven: and come and follow me.

But when the young man heard that saying, he went away sorrowful: for he had great possessions.

Then said Jesus unto his disciples, Verily I say unto you, That a rich man shall hardly enter into the kingdom of heaven.

And again I say unto you, It is easier for a camel to go through the eye of a needle, than for a rich man to enter into the kingdom of God.

When his disciples heard it, they were exceedingly amazed, saying, Who then can be saved?

But Jesus beheld them, and said unto them, With men this is impossible; but with God all things are possible.

THIRTEENTH SUNDAY

Prokeimenon, in the Fourth Tone

How great are thy works, O Lord! Thou hast made all things in wisdom.

Bless the Lord, O my soul.

Section from the First Epistle of St. Paul to the Corinthians (16:13 to end)

YE brethren: Watch ye, stand fast in the faith, do manfully, be strong.

Let all your things be done with charity.

I beseech you, brethren, (ye know the house of Stephanas, that it is the firstfruits of Achaia, and that they have addicted themselves to the ministry of the saints,)

That ye submit yourselves unto such, and to every one that helpeth with us, and laboureth.

I am glad of the coming of Stephanas and Fortunatus and Achaicus: for that which was lacking on your part they have supplied.

For they have refreshed my spirit and yours: therefore acknowledge ye them that are such.

The churches of Asia salute you. Aquila and Priscilla salute you much in the Lord, with the church that is in their house.

All the brethren greet you. Greet ye one another with a holy kiss.

The salutation of me Paul with mine own hand.

If any man love not the Lord Jesus Christ, let him be Anathema Maranatha.

The grace of our Lord Jesus Christ be with you.

My love be with you all in Christ Jesus. Amen.

The Gospel: from St. Matthew (21:33-42)

THE Lord spake this parable: There was a man a householder, who planted a vineyard, and made a hedge round about it, and dug a winepress in it, and built a tower, and let it out to husbandmen and went into a strange country.

And when the time of the fruit drew near, he sent his servants to the husbandmen, that they might receive the fruits of it.

And the husbandmen took his servants, and beat one, and killed another, and stoned another.

Again, he sent other servants more than the first: and they did unto them likewise.

But last of all he sent unto them his son, saying, They will reverence my son.

But when the husbandmen saw the son, they said among themselves, This is the heir; come, let us kill him, and let us seize on his inheritance.

And they caught him, and cast him out of the vineyard, and slew him.

When the lord therefore of the vineyard cometh, what will he do unto those husbandmen?

They say unto him, He will miserably destroy those wicked men, and will let out his vineyard unto other husbandmen, which shall render him the fruits in their seasons.

Jesus saith unto them, Did ye never read in the Scriptures, The stone which the builders rejected, the same is become the head of the corner: this is the Lord's doing, and it is marvellous in our eyes?

FOURTEENTH SUNDAY

Prokeimenon, in the Third Tone

Thou O Lord wilt preserve us and keep us from this generation.

Save me, O Lord, for the godly man ceaseth.

Section from the Second Epistle of St. Paul to the Corinthians (1:21 to end; 2:1-4)

YE brethren: He which stablisheth us with you in Christ, and hath anointed us, is God:

Who hath also sealed us, and given the earnest of the Spirit in our hearts.

Moreover I call God for a record upon my soul, that to spare you I came not as yet unto Corinth.

Not for that we have dominion over your faith, but are helpers of your joy: for by faith ye stand.

But I determined this with myself, that I would not come again to you in heaviness.

For if I make you sorry, who is he then that maketh me glad, but the same which is made sorry by me?

And I wrote this same unto you, lest when I came, I should have sorrow from them of whom I ought to rejoice; having confidence in you all, that my joy is the joy of you all.

For out of much affliction and anguish of heart I wrote unto you with many tears; not that ye should be grieved, but that ye might know the love which I have more abundantly unto you.

The Gospel: from St. Matthew (22:2-14)

THE Lord spake this parable: The kingdom of heaven is like unto a certain king, which made a marriage for his son.

And sent forth his servants to call them that were bidden to the wedding: and they would not come.

Again, he sent forth other servants, saying, Tell them which are bidden, Behold, I have prepared my dinner: my oxen and my fatlings are killed, and all things are ready: come unto the marriage.

But they made light of it, and went their ways, one to his farm, another to his merchandise:

And the remnant took his servants, and entreated them spitefully, and slew them.

But when the king heard thereof, he was wroth: and he sent forth his armies, and destroyed those murderers, and burned up their city.

Then saith he to his servants, The wedding is ready, but they which were bidden were not worthy.

Go ye therefore into the highways, and as many as ye shall find, bid to the marriage.

So those servants went out into the highways, and gathered together all as many as they found, both bad and good: and the wedding was furnished with guests.

And when the king came in to see the guests, he saw there a man which had not on a wedding garment:

And he saith unto him, Friend, how camest thou in hither not having a wedding garment? And he was speechless.

Then said the king to the servants, Bind him hand and foot, and take him away, and cast him into outer darkness; there shall be weeping and gnashing of teeth.

For many are called, but few are chosen.

FIFTEENTH SUNDAY

Prokeimenon, in the Sixth Tone

Save, O Lord, thy people, and bless thine inheritance
Unto thee I cry, O Lord, O my God.

Section from the Second Epistle of St. Paul to the Corinthians (4:6-15)

YE brethren: For God, who commanded the light to shine out of darkness, hath shined in our hearts, to give the light of the knowledge of the glory of God in the face of Jesus Christ.

But we have this treasure in earthen vessels, that th excellency of the power may be of God, and not of us

We are troubled on every side, yet not distressed; w are perplexed, but not in despair;

Persecuted, but not forsaken; cast down, but no destroyed;

Always bearing about in the body the dying of th Lord Jesus, that the life also of Jesus might be mad manifest in our body.

For we which live are always delivered unto deat for Jesus' sake, that the life also of Jesus might be mad manifest in our mortal flesh.

So then death worketh in us, but life in you.

We having the same spirit of faith, according as it written, I believed, and therefore have I spoken; w also believe, and therefore speak;

Knowing that he which raised up the Lord Jesus sha raise up us also by Jesus, and shall present us with yo

For all things are for your sakes, that the abunda grace might through the thanksgiving of many redoun to the glory of God.

The Gospel: from St. Matthew (22:35 to end)

AT that time: A certain lawyer came and ask Jesus, tempting him, saying:

Master, which is the great commandment in the law

Jesus said unto him, Thou shalt love the Lord thy God with all thy heart, and with all thy soul, and with all thy mind.

This is the first and great commandment.

And the second is like unto it, Thou shalt love thy neighbour as thyself.

On these two commandments hang all the law and the prophets.

While the Pharisees were gathered together, Jesus asked them,

Saying, What think ye of Christ? whose son is he? They say unto him, The son of David.

He saith unto them, How then doth David in spirit call him Lord, saying,

The Lord said unto my Lord, Sit thou on my right hand, till I make thine enemies thy footstool?

If David then call him Lord, how is he his son?

And no man was able to answer him a word, neither durst any man from that day forth ask him any more questions.

SIXTEENTH SUNDAY

Prokeimenon, in the Seventh Tone

The Lord will give strength to his peoples.
Bring to the Lord, O ye children of God.

Section from the Second Epistle of St. Paul to the Corinthians (6:1-10)

YE brethren: We then, as workers together with him, beseech you also that ye receive not the grace of God in vain.

(For he saith, I have heard thee in a time accepted, and in the day of salvation have I succoured thee: behold, now is the accepted time; behold, now is the day of salvation.)

Giving no offense in any thing, that the ministry be not blamed:

But in all things approving ourselves as the ministers of God, in much patience, in afflictions, in necessities, in distresses,

In stripes, in imprisonments, in tumults, in labours, in watchings, in fastings;

By pureness, by knowledge, by longsuffering, by kindness, by the Holy Ghost, by love unfeigned,

By the word of truth, by the power of God, by the armour of righteousness on the right hand and on the left,

By honour and dishonour, by evil report and good report: as deceivers, and yet true;

As unknown, and yet well known; as dying, and, behold, we live; as chastened, and not killed;

As sorrowful, yet always rejoicing; as poor, yet making many rich; as having nothing, and yet possessing all things.

The Gospel: from St. Matthew (25:14-30; St. Luke 8:8)

THE Lord spake this parable: A man travelling called his own servants, and delivered unto them his goods.

And unto one he gave five talents, to another two, and to another one; to every man according to his several ability; and straightway took his journey.

Then he that had received the five talents went and traded with the same, and made them other five talents.

And likewise he that had received two, he also gained other two.

But he that had received one went and digged in the earth, and hid his lord's money.

After a long time the lord of those servants cometh and reckoneth with them.

And so he that had received five talents came and brought other five talents, saying, Lord, thou deliveredst unto me five talents: behold, I have gained beside them five talents more.

His lord said unto him, Well done, thou good and faithful servant: thou hast been faithful over a few things, I will make thee ruler over many things: enter thou into the joy of thy lord.

He also that had received two talents came and said, Lord, thou deliveredst unto me two talents: behold, I have gained two other talents beside them.

His lord said unto him, Well done, good and faithful servant; thou hast been faithful over a few things, I will make thee ruler over many things: enter thou into the joy of thy lord.

Then he which had received the one talent came and said, Lord, I knew thee that thou art an hard man, reaping where thou hast not sown, and gathering where thou hast not strawed:

And I was afraid, and went and hid thy talent in the earth: lo, there thou hast that is thine.

His lord answered and said unto him, Thou wicked and slothful servant, thou knewest that I reap where I sowed not, and gather where I have not strawed:

Thou oughtest therefore to have put my money to the exchangers, and then at my coming I should have received mine own with usury.

Take therefore the talent from him, and give it unto him which hath ten talents.

For unto every one that hath shall be given, and he shall have abundance: but from him that hath not shall be taken away even that which he hath.

And cast ye the unprofitable servant into outer darkness: there shall be weeping and gnashing of teeth.

And when he had said these things, he cried, He that hath ears to hear, let him hear.

SEVENTEENTH SUNDAY

Prokeimenon, in the Eighth Tone

Vow ye and pay to the Lord your God.
In Judah is God known.

Section from the Second Epistle of St. Paul to the Corinthians (6:16 to end; 7:1)

YE brethren: Ye are the temple of the living God; as God hath said, I will dwell in them, and walk in them, and I will be their God, and they shall be my people.

Wherefore come out from among them, and be ye separate, saith the Lord, and touch not the unclean thing: and I will receive you,

And will be a Father unto you, and ye shall be my sons and daughters, saith the Lord Almighty.

Having therefore these promises, dearly beloved, let us cleanse ourselves from all filthiness of the flesh and spirit, perfecting holiness in the fear of God.

The Gospel: from St. Matthew (15:21-28)

AT that time: Jesus departed into the coasts of Tyre and Sidon.

And, behold, a woman of Canaan came out of the same coasts, and cried unto him, saying, Have mercy on me, O Lord, thou Son of David; my daughter is grievously vexed with a devil.

But he answered her not a word. And his disciples came and besought him, saying, Send her away; for she crieth after us.

But he answered and said, I am not sent but unto the lost sheep of the house of Israel.

Then came she and worshipped him, saying, Lord, help me.

But he answered and said, It is not meet to take the children's bread, and to cast it to dogs.

And she said, Truth, Lord: yet the dogs eat of the crumbs which fall from their masters' table.

Then Jesus answered and said unto her, O woman, great is thy faith: be it unto thee even as thou wilt. And her daughter was made whole from that very hour.

Sunday of the Fathers of Saints who Attended the Six Conventions of the World

From July 13th to 19th

Prokeimenon in the Eighth Tone

Blessed art thou, O Lord, the God of our Fathers.
For thou art just in all that thou hast done to us.

Section from the Epistle of St. Paul to his Disciple Titus (3:8 to end)

MY child Titus: This is a faithful saying and these things I will that thou affirm constantly, that they which have believed in God might be careful to maintain good works. These things are good and profitable unto men.

But avoid foolish questions, and genealogies, and contentions, and strivings about the law; for they are unprofitable and vain.

A man that is an heretic, after the first and second admonition, reject;

Knowing that he that is such is subverted, and sinneth, being condemned of himeslf.

When I shall send Artemas unto thee, or Tychicus, be diligent to come unto me to Nicopolis: for I have determined there to winter.

Bring Zenas the lawyer and Apollos on their journey diligently, that nothing be wanting unto them.

And let ours also learn to maintain good works for necessary uses, that they be not unfruitful.

All that are with me salute thee. Greet them that love us in the faith. Grace be with you all. Amen.

The Gospel: from St. Matthew (5:14-19)

THE Lord saith to his disciples: Ye are the light of the world. A city that is set on an hill cannot be hid.

Neither do men light a candle, and put it under a bushel, but on a candlestick; and it giveth light unto all that are in the house.

Let your light so shine before men, that they may see your good works, and glorify your Father which is in heaven.

Think not that I am come to destroy the law, or the prophets: I am not come to destroy, but to fulfil.

For verily I say unto you, Till heaven and earth pass, one jot or one tittle shall in no wise pass from the law, till all be fulfilled.

Whosoever therefore shall break one of these least commandments, and shall teach men so, he shall be called the least in the kingdom of heaven: but whosoever shall do and teach them, the same shall be called great in the kingdom of heaven.

THE SUNDAY BEFORE THE ELEVATION OF THE CROSS

From Sept. 7th to 13th

Prokeimenon, in the Sixth Tone

Save, O Lord, thy people and bless thine inheritance
Unto thee will I cry, O Lord, my God.

Section from the Epistle of St. Paul to the Galatian (6:11 to end)

YE brethren: See what a letter I have written unto you with mine own hand.

As many as desire to make a fair show in the flesh, they constrain you to be circumcised; only lest they should suffer persecution for the cross of Christ.

For neither they themselves who are circumcised keep the law; but desire to have you circumcised, that they may glory in your flesh.

But God forbid that I should glory, save in the cross of our Lord Jesus Christ, by whom the world is crucified unto me, and I unto the world.

For in Christ Jesus neither circumcision availeth any thing, nor uncircumcision, but a new creature.

And as many as walk according to this rule, peace be on them, and mercy, and upon the Israel of God.

From henceforth let no man trouble me: for I bear in my body the marks of the Lord Jesus.

Brethren, the grace of our Lord Jesus Christ be with your spirit. Amen.

The Gospel: from St. John (3:13-17)

THE Lord saith: No man hath ascended into heaven, but he that came down from heaven, even the Son of man which is in heaven.

And as Moses lifted up the serpent in the wilderness, even so must the Son of man be lifted up:

That whosoever believeth in him should not perish, but have eternal life.

For God so loved the world, that he gave his only begotten Son, that whosoever believeth in him should not perish, but have everlasting life.

For God sent not his Son into the world to condemn the world; but that the world through him might be saved.

THE SUNDAY AFTER THE ELEVATION OF THE CROSS

Sept. 15th to 21st

Prokeimenon, in the Eighth Tone

How great are thy works, O Lord, Thou hast made all things in wisdom.

Bless the Lord, O my soul.

Section from the Epistle of St. Paul to the Galatians (2:16-20)

YE brethren: Knowing that a man is not justified by the works of the law, but by the faith of Jesus Christ, even we have believed in Jesus Christ, that we might be justified by the faith of Christ, and not by the work of the law: for by the works of the law shall no flesh be justified.

But if, while we seek to be justified by Christ, we ourselves also are found sinners, is therefore Christ the minister of sin? God forbid.

For if I build again the things which I destroyed, I make myself a transgressor.

For I through the law am dead to the law, that I might live unto God.

I am crucified with Christ: nevertheless I live; yet not I, but Christ liveth in me: and the life which I now live in the flesh I live by the faith of the Son of God, who loved me, and gave himself for me.

The Gospel: from St. Mark (8:34 to end; 9:1)

THE Lord saith: Whosoever will come after me, let him deny himself, and take up his cross, and follow me.

For whosoever will save his life shall lose it; but whosoever shall lose his life for my sake and the gospel's, the same shall save it.

For what shall it profit a man, if he shall gain the whole world, and lose his own soul?

Or what shall a man give in exchange for his soul?

Whosoever therefore shall be ashamed of me and of my words, in this adulterous and sinful generation, of him also shall the Son of man be ashamed, when he cometh in the glory of his Father with the holy angels.

And he said unto them, Verily I say unto you, That there be some of them that stand here, which shall not taste of death, till they have seen the kingdom of God come with power.

EIGHTEENTH SUNDAY

Prokeimenon, in the First Tone

Let thy mercy, O Lord, be upon us.
Rejoice in the Lord, O ye just.

ection from the Second Epistle of St. Paul to the Corinthians (9:6-11)

E brethren: He which soweth sparingly shall reap also sparingly; and he which soweth bountifully all reap also bountifully.

Every man according as he purposeth in his heart, let him give; not grudgingly, or of necessity: for od loveth a cheerful giver.

And God is able to make all grace abound toward ou; that ye, always having all sufficiency in all things, ay abound to every good work:

(As it is written, He hath dispersed abroad; he ath given to the poor: his righteousness remaineth for ver.

Now he that ministereth seed to the sower both min- ter bread for your food, and multiply your seed sown, nd increase the fruits of your righteousness;)

Being enriched in every thing to all bountifulness, hich causeth through us thanksgiving to God.

The Gospel: from St. Luke (5:1-11)

T that time: As the Lord stood by the lake of Gene- saret, he saw two ships standing by the lake: but e fishermen were gone out of them, and were wash- g their nets.

And he entered into one of the ships, which was imon's, and prayed him that he would thrust out a ttle from the land. And he sat down, and taught the eople out of the ship.

Now when he had left speaking, he said unto Simon, aunch out into the deep, and let down your nets for draught.

And Simon answering said unto him, Master, we ave toiled all the night, and have taken nothing: nev- rtheless at thy word I will let down the net.

And when they had this done, they inclosed a great ultitude of fishes: and their net brake.

And they beckoned unto their partners, which we
in the other ship, that they should come and help the
And they came, and filled both the ships, so that th
began to sink.

When Simon Peter saw it, he fell down at Jes
knees, saying, Depart from me; for I am a sinful ma
O Lord.

For he was astonished, and all that were with hi
at the draught of the fishes which they had taken.

And so was also James, and John, the sons of Zel
dee, which were partners with Simon. And Jesus sa
unto Simon, Fear not; from henceforth thou shalt cat
men.

And when they had brought their ships to land, th
forsook all, and followed him.

Nineteenth Sunday

Prokeimenon, in the Second Tone

The Lord is my strength and my praise.
The Lord chastising hath chastised me.

*Section from the Second Epistle of St. Paul to the
Corinthians (11:31 to end; 12:1-9)*

YE brethren: The God and Father of our Lord Jes
    Christ which is blessed forevermore, knoweth tl
I lie not.

In Damascus the governor under Aretas the ki
kept the city of the Damascenes with a garrison, des
ous to apprehend me:

And through a window in a basket was I let do
by the wall, and escaped his hands.

It is not expedient for me doubtless to glory. I w
come to visions and revelations of the Lord.

I knew a man in Christ above fourteen years ag
(whether in the body, I cannot tell; or whether out
the body, I cannot tell: God knoweth;) such an o
caught up to the third heaven.

And I knew such a man, (whether in the body, or out of the body, I cannot tell: God knoweth;)

How that he was caught up into paradise, and heard unspeakable words, which it is not lawful for a man to utter.

Of such an one will I glory: yet of myself I will not glory, but in mine infirmities.

For though I would desire to glory, I shall not be a fool; for I will say the truth: but now I forbear, lest any man should think of me above that which he seeth me to be, or that he heareth of me.

And lest I should be exalted above measure through the abundance of the revelations, there was given to me a thorn in the flesh, the messenger of Satan to buffet me, lest I should be exalted above measure.

For this thing I besought the Lord thrice, that it might depart from me.

And he said unto me, My grace is sufficient for thee: for my strength is made perfect in weakness. Most gladly therefore will I rather glory in my infirmities, that the power of Christ may rest upon me.

The Gospel: from St. Luke (6:31-36)

THE Lord saith: As ye would that men should do to you, do ye also to them likewise.

For if ye love them which love you, what thank have ye? for sinners also love those that love them.

And if ye do good to them which do good to you, what thank have ye? for sinners also do even the same.

And if ye lend to them of whom ye hope to receive, what thank have ye? for sinners also lend to sinners, to receive as much again.

But love ye your enemies, and do good, and lend, hoping for nothing again; and your reward shall be great, and ye shall be the children of the Highest: for he is kind unto the unthankful and to the evil.

Be ye therefore merciful, as your Father also is merciful.

Twentieth Sunday

Prokeimenon, in the Third Tone

Sing praises to our God, sing praises.
O clap your hands, all ye nations.

Section from the Epistle of St. Paul to the Galatian (1:11-19)

YE brethren: I certify you, that the gospel which wa preached of me is not after man.

For I neither received it of man, neither was I taugh it, but by the revelation of Jesus Christ.

For ye have heard of my conversation in time pa in the Jews' religion, how that beyond measure I perse cuted the church of God and wasted it:

And profited in the Jews' religion above many m equals in mine own nation, being more exceeding zealous of the traditions of my fathers.

But when it pleased God, who separated me fror my mother's womb, and called me by his grace.

To reveal his Son in me, that I might preach hir among the heathen; immediately I conferred not wit flesh and blood:

Neither went I up to Jerusalem to them which wer apostles before me; but I went into Arabia, and re turned again unto Damascus.

Then after three years I went up to Jerusalem to se Peter, and abode with him fifteen days.

But other of the apostles saw I none, save James an the Lord's brother.

The Gospel: from St. Luke (7:11-16)

AT that time: Jesus was going into a city calle Nain, and many of his disciples went with him, an much people.

Now when he came nigh to the gate of the city, be hold, there was a dead man carried out, the only son o

his mother, and she was a widow: and much people of
the city was with her.

And when the Lord saw her, he had compassion on
her, and said unto her, Weep not.

And he came and touched the bier: and they that
bare him stood still. And he said, Young man, I say
unto thee, Arise.

And he that was dead sat up, and began to speak.
And he delivered him to his mother.

And there came a fear on all: and they glorified God,
saying, That a great prophet is risen up among us; and,
That God hath visited his people.

TWENTY-FIRST SUNDAY

Prokeimenon, in the Eighth Tone

How great are thy works, O Lord!
Thou hast made all things in wisdom.
Bless the Lord, O my soul.

Section from the Epistle of St. Paul to the Galatians (2:16-20)

YE brethren: Knowing that a man is not justified by
the works of the law, etc. (p. 249).

The Gospel: from St. Luke 8:5-15)

THE Lord spake this parable: A sower went out to
sow his seed: and as he sowed, some fell by the wayside; and it was trodden down, and the fowls of the air
devoured it.

And some fell upon a rock; and as soon as it was
sprung up, it withered away, because it lacked moisture.

And some fell among thorns; and the thorns sprang
up with it, and choked it. And other fell on good
ground, and sprang up, and bare fruit an hundredfold.

And his disciples asked him, saying, What might this
parable be? And he said, Unto you it is given to know
the mysteries of the kingdom of God: but to others in

parables; that seeing they might not see, and hearing they might not understand.

Now the parable is this: The seed is the word of God.

Those by the way side are they that hear; then cometh the devil, and taketh away the word out of their hearts, lest they should believe and be saved.

They on the rock are they, which, when they hear, receive the word with joy; and these have no root, which for a while believe, and in time of temptation fall away.

And that which fell among thorns are they, which, when they have heard, go forth, and are choked with cares and riches and pleasures of this life, and bring no fruit to perfection.

But that on the good ground are they, which in an honest and good heart, having heard the word, keep it, and bring forth fruit with patience. And when he had said these things, he cried, He that hath ears to hear, let him hear.

Twenty-second Sunday

Prokeimenon, in the Fifth Tone

Thou, O Lord, shalt preserve us and keep us from this generation.

Save me, O Lord, for the godly man ceaseth.

Section from the Epistle of St. Paul to the Galatians (6:11 to end)

YE brethren: See what a letter I have written unto you with mine own hand, etc. (p. 248).

The Gospel: from St. Luke (16:19 to end)

THE Lord saith: There was a certain rich man, which was clothed in purple and fine linen, and fared sumptuously every day:

And there was a certain beggar named Lazarus, which was laid at his gate, full of sores.

And desiring to be fed with the crumbs which fell from the rich man's table: moreover the dogs came and licked his sores.

And it came to pass, that the beggar died, and was carried by the angels into Abraham's bosom: the rich man also died, and was buried;

And in hell he lifted up his eyes, being in torments, and seeth Abraham afar off, and Lazarus in his bosom.

And he cried and said, Father Abraham, have mercy on me, and send Lazarus, that he may dip the tip of his finger in water, and cool my tongue; for I am tormented in this flame.

But Abraham said, Son, remember that thou in thy lifetime receivedst thy good things, and likewise Lazarus evil things: but now he is comforted, and thou art tormented.

And beside all this, between us and you there is a great gulf fixed: so that they which would pass from hence to you cannot; neither can they pass to us, that would come from thence.

Then he said, I pray thee therefore, father, that thou wouldest send him to my father's house:

For I have five brethren; that he may testify unto them, lest they also come into this place of torment.

Abraham saith unto him, They have Moses and the prophets; let them hear them.

And he said, Nay, father Abraham: but if one went unto them from the dead, they will repent.

And he said unto him, If they hear not Moses and the prophets, neither will they be persuaded, though one rose from the dead.

TWENTY-THIRD SUNDAY

Prokeimenon, in the Sixth Tone

Save, O Lord, thy people, and bless thine inheritance.
Unto thee will I cry, O Lord, my God.

Section from the Epistle of St. Paul to the Ephesian
(2:4-10)

YE brethren: God (who is rich in mercy) for hi
great love wherewith he loved us;

Even when we were dead in sins, hath quickened u
together with Christ, (by grace ye are saved;)

And hath raised us up together, and made us sit to
gether in heavenly places in Christ Jesus:

That in the ages to come he might show the exceed
ing riches of his grace, in his kindness toward us
through Christ Jesus.

For by grace are ye saved through faith; and that no
of yourselves: it is the gift of God:

Not of works, lest any man should boast.

For we are his workmanship, created in Christ Jesu
unto good works, which God hath before ordained tha
we should walk in them.

The Gospel: from St. Luke (8:27-39)

AT that time: Jesus came to the country of the Ger
gasenes, and there met him out of the city a certai
man which had devils long time, and ware not clothe
neither abode in any house, but in the tombs.

When he saw Jesus, he cried out, and fell down be
fore him, and with a loud voice said, What have I to d
with thee, Jesus, thou Son of God most high? I beseec
thee, torment me not.

(For he had commanded the unclean spirit to com
out of the man. For oftentimes it had caught him: an
he was kept bound with chains and in fetters; and h
brake the bands, and was driven of the devil into th
wilderness.)

And Jesus asked him, saying, What is thy name
And he said, Legion: because many devils were entere
into him.

And they besought him that he would not comman
them to go out into the deep.

And there was there a herd of many swine feeding on the mountain: and they besought him that he would suffer them to enter into them. And he suffered them.

Then went the devils out of the man, and entered into the swine: and the herd ran violently down a steep place into the lake, and were choked.

When they that fed them saw what was done, they fled, and went and told it in the city and in the country.

Then they went out to see what was done; and came to Jesus, and found the man, out of whom the devils were departed, sitting at the feet of Jesus, clothed, and in his right mind: and they were afraid.

They also which saw told them by what means he that was possessed of the devils was healed.

Then the whole multitude of the country of the Gadarenes round about besought him to depart from them; for they were taken with great fear: and he went up into the ship, and returned back again.

Now the man, out of whom the devils were departed, besought him that he might be with him: but Jesus sent him away, saying,

Return to thine own house, and show how great things God hath done unto thee. And he went his way, and published throughout the whole city how great things Jesus had done unto him.

TWENTY-FOURTH SUNDAY

Prokeimenon, in the Seventh Tone

The Lord will give strength to his people.
Bring to the Lord, O ye children of God.

Section from the Epistle of St. Paul to the Ephesians
(2:14 to end)

YE brethren: For Christ is our peace, who hath made both one, and hath broken down the middle wall of partition between us.

Having abolished in his flesh the enmity, even th
law of commandments contained in ordinances; for t
make in himself of twain one new man, so makin
peace;

And that he might reconcile both unto God in on
body by the cross, having slain the enmity thereby:

And came and preached peace to you which wer
afar off, and to them that were nigh.

For through him we both have access by one Spiri
unto the Father.

Now therefore ye are no more strangers and foreigr
ers, but fellow citizens with the saints, and of the house
hold of God;

And are built upon the foundation of the apostle
and prophets, Jesus Christ himself being the chic
corner stone;

In whom all the building fitly framed together grov
eth unto an holy temple in the Lord:

In whom ye also are builded together for an habita
tion of God through the Spirit.

The Gospel: from St. Luke (8:41 to end)

AT that time: There came a man to Jesus name
Jairus, and he was a ruler of the synagogue; an
he fell down at Jesus' feet, and besought him that h
would come into his house:

For he had one only daughter, about twelve years o
age, and she lay a dying. But as he went the peop
thronged him.

And a woman having an issue of blood twelve year
which had spent all her living upon physicians, neith
could be healed of any,

Came behind him, and touched the border of h
garment: and immediately her issue of blood stanche

And Jesus said, Who touched me? When all denie
Peter and they that were with him said, Master, th
multitude throng thee and press thee, and sayest tho
Who touched me?

And Jesus said, Somebody hath touched me: for I
·ceive that virtue is gone out of me.

And when the woman saw that she was not hid, she
ne trembling, and falling down before him, she
:lared unto him before all the people for what cause
· had touched him, and how she was healed imme-
tely.

And he said unto her, Daughter, be of good comfort:
/ faith hath made thee whole; go in peace.

While he yet spake, there cometh one from the ruler
the synagogue's house, saying to him, Thy daughter
dead; trouble not the Master.

But when Jesus heard it, he answered him, saying,
·ar not: believe only, and she shall be made whole.

And when he came into the house, he suffered no
an to go in, save Peter, and James, and John, and the
ther and the mother of the maiden.

And all wept, and bewailed her: but he said, Weep
·t; she is not dead, but sleepeth.

And they laughed him to scorn, knowing that she
as dead.

And he put them all out, and took her by the hand,
·d called, saying, Maid, arise.

And her spirit came again, and she arose straight-
ay: and he commanded to give her meat.

And her parents were astonished: but he charged
·em that they should tell no man what was done.

TWENTY-FIFTH SUNDAY

Prokeimenon, in the Third Tone

Vow ye, and pay to the Lord your God.
·In Judah is God known.

ection from the Epistle of St. Paul to the Ephesians
(4:1-7)

YE brethren: I therefore, the prisoner of the Lord,
beseech you that ye walk worthy of the vocation
·herewith ye are called;

With all lowliness and meekness, with long-suffering forbearing one another in love;

Endeavouring to keep the unity of the Spirit in th bond of peace.

There is one body, and one Spirit, even as ye ar called in one hope of your calling;

One Lord, one faith, one baptism,

One God and Father of all, who is above all, an through all, and in you all.

But unto every one of us is given grace according t the measure of the gift of Christ.

The Gospel: from St. Luke (10:25-37)

AT that time: A certain lawyer came and aske Jesus, tempting him, saying, Master, what shall do to inherit eternal life?

He said unto him, What is written in the law? how readest thou?

And he answering said, Thou shalt love the Lord th God with all thy heart, and with all thy soul, and with all thy strength, and with all thy mind; and thy neigh bour as thyself.

And he said unto him, Thou hast answered right this do, and thou shalt live.

But he, willing to justify himself, said unto Jesus And who is my neighbour?

And Jesus answering said, A certain man went down from Jerusalem to Jericho, and fell among thieves which stripped him of his raiment and wounded him and departed, leaving him half dead.

And by chance there came down a certain priest tha way; and when he saw him, he passed by on the othei side.

And likewise a Levite, when he was at the place came and looked on him, and passed by on the othei side.

But a certain Samaritan, as he journeyed, came where he was; and when he saw him, he had compassion on him,

And went to him, and bound up his wounds, pouring
oil and wine, and set him on his own beast, and
ought him to an inn, and took care of him.
And on the morrow when he departed, he took out
o pence, and gave them to the host, and said unto
m, Take care of him: and whatsoever thou spendest
ore, when I come again, I will repay thee.
Which now of these three, thinkest thou, was neigh-
ur unto him that fell among the thieves?
And he said, He that showed mercy on him.   Then
id Jesus unto him, Go, and do thou likewise.

TWENTY-SIXTH SUNDAY

Prokeimenon, in the First Tone

Let thy mercy, O Lord, be upon us.
Rejoice in the Lord, O ye just.

ection from the Epistle of St. Paul to the Ephesians (5:8-19)

E brethren: Walk as the children of light:
    (For the fruit of the Spirit is in all goodness and
ghteousness and truth;)
Proving what is acceptable unto the Lord.
And have no fellowship with the unfruitful works of
arkness, but rather reprove them.
For it is a shame even to speak of those things which
e done of them in secret.
But all things that are reproved are made manifest
y the light: for whatsoever doth make manifest is light.
Wherefore he saith, Awake thou that sleepest, and
rise from the dead, and Christ shall give thee light.
See then that ye walk circumspectly, not as fools,
ut as wise,
Redeeming the time, because the days are evil.
Wherefore be ye not unwise, but understanding what
he will of the Lord is.

And be not drunk with wine, wherein is excess; bu
be filled with the Spirit;

Speaking to yourselves in psalms and hymns an
spiritual songs, singing and making melody in you
heart to the Lord.

The Gospel: from St. Luke (12:16-21)

THE Lord spake this parable: The ground of a cer
tain rich man brought forth plentifully:

And he thought within himself, saying, What shal
I do, because I have no room where to bestow m
fruits?

And he said, This will I do: I will pull down m
barns, and build greater; and there will I bestow al
my fruits and my goods.

And I will say to my soul, Soul, thou hast much
goods laid up for many years; take thine ease, eat, drink
and be merry.

But God said unto him, Thou fool, this night thy
soul shall be required of thee: then whose shall those
things be, which thou hast provided?

So is he that layeth up treasure for himself, and is no
rich toward God. And when he had said these things
he cried, He that hath ears to hear, let him hear.

Twenty-seventh Sunday

Prokeimenon, in the Second Tone

The Lord is my strength and my praise.
The Lord chastising hath chastised me.

Section from the Epistle of St. Paul to the Ephesians (6:10-17)

YE brethren: Be strong in the Lord, and in the power
of his might.

Put on the whole armour of God, that ye may be able
to stand against the wiles of the devil.

For we wrestle not against flesh and blood, but against principalities, against powers, against the rulers of the darkness of this world, against spiritual wickedness in high places.

Wherefore take unto you the whole armour of God, that ye may be able to withstand in the evil day, and having done all, to stand.

Stand therefore, having your loins girt about with truth, and having on the breastplate of righteousness;

And your feet shod with the preparation of the gospel of peace;

Above all, taking the shield of faith, wherewith ye shall be able to quench all the fiery darts of the wicked.

And take the helmet of salvation, and the sword of the Spirit, which is the word of God.

The Gospel: from St. Luke (13:10-17)

AT that time: While Jesus was teaching in one of the synagogues on the sabbath, behold, there was a woman which had a spirit of infirmity eighteen years, and was bowed together, and could in no wise lift up herself.

And when Jesus saw her, he called her to him, and said unto her, Woman, thou art loosed from thine infirmity.

And he laid his hands on her: and immediately she was made straight, and glorified God.

And the ruler of the synagogue answered with indignation, because that Jesus had healed on the sabbath day, and said unto the people, There are six days in which men ought to work: in them therefore come and be healed, and not on the sabbath day.

The Lord then answered him, and said, Thou hypocrite, doth not each one of you on the sabbath loose his ox or his ass from the stall, and lead him away to watering?

And ought not this woman, being a daughter of Abraham, whom Satan hath bound, lo, these eighteen years, be loosed from this bond on the sabbath day?

And when he had said these things, all his adversaries were ashamed: and all the people rejoiced for all the glorious things that were done by him.

TWENTY-EIGHTH SUNDAY

Prokeimenon, in the Third Tone

Sing praises to our God, sing praises.
O clap your hands, all ye nations.

Section from the Epistle of St. Paul to the Colossians (1:12-18)

YE brethren: Give thanks unto the Father, which hath made us meet to be partakers of the inheritance of the saints in light;

Who hath delivered us from the power of darkness, and hath translated us into the kingdom of his dear Son:

In whom we have redemption through his blood, even the forgiveness of sins:

Who is the image of the invisible God, the firstborn of every creature:

For by him were all things created, that are in heaven, and that are in earth, visible and invisible, whether they be thrones, or dominions, or principalities, or powers: all things were created by him, and for him:

And he is before all things, and by him all things consist:

And he is the head of the body, the church: who is the beginning, the firstborn from the dead; that in all things he might have the preeminence.

The Gospel: from St. Luke (14:16-24)

THE Lord spake this parable: A certain man made a great supper, and bade many:

And sent his servant at supper time to say to them that were bidden, Come; for all things are now ready.

And they all with one consent began to make excuse. The first said unto him, I have bought a piece of ground, and I must needs go and see it: I pray thee have me excused.

And another said, I have bought five yoke of oxen, and I go to prove them: I pray thee have me excused.

And another said, I have married a wife, and therefore I cannot come.

So that servant came, and showed his lord these things. Then the master of the house being angry said to his servant, Go out quickly into the streets and lanes of the city, and bring in hither the poor, and the maimed, and the halt, and the blind.

And the servant said, Lord, it is done as thou hast commanded, and yet there is room.

And the lord said unto the servant, Go out into the highways and hedges, and compel them to come in, that my house may be filled.

For I say unto you, That none of those men which were bidden shall taste of my supper, for many are called, but few are chosen.

TWENTY-NINTH SUNDAY

Prokeimenon, in the Fourth Tone

How great are thy works, O Lord.
Thou hast made all things in wisdom.
Bless the Lord, O my soul.

Section from the Epistle of St. Paul to the Colossians (3:4-11)

YE brethren: When Christ, who is our life, shall appear, then shall we also appear with him in glory.

Mortify therefore your members which are upon the earth; fornication, uncleanness, inordinate affection, evil concupiscence, and covetousness, which is idolatry:

For which things' sake the wrath of God cometh on the children of disobedience:

In the which ye also walked sometime, when ye lived in them.

But now ye also put off all these; anger, wrath, malice, blasphemy, filthy communication out of your mouth.

Lie not one to another, seeing that ye have put off the old man with his deeds;

And have put on the new man, which is renewed in knowledge after the image of him that created him:

Where there is neither Greek nor Jew, circumcision nor uncircumcision, Barbarian, Scythian, bond nor free: but Christ is all, and in all.

The Gospel: from St. Luke (17:12-19)

AT that time: As Jesus was entering a certain village, there met him ten men that were lepers, which stood afar off;

And they lifted up their voices, and said, Jesus, Master, have mercy on us.

And when he saw them, he said unto them, Go show yourselves unto the priests. And it came to pass, that, as they went, they were cleansed.

And one of them, when he saw that he was healed, turned back, and with a loud voice glorified God,

And fell down on his face at his feet, giving him thanks: and he was a Samaritan.

And Jesus answering said, Were there not ten cleansed? but where are the nine?

There are not found that returned to give glory to God, save this stranger.

And he said unto him, Arise, go thy way: thy faith hath made thee whole.

THIRTIETH SUNDAY

Prokeimenon, in the Fifth Tone

Thou O Lord, shalt preserve us and keep us from this generation.

Save me, O Lord, for the godly man ceaseth.

Section from the Epistle of St. Paul to the Colossians (3:12-16)

YE brethren: Put ye on therefore, as the elect of God, holy and beloved, bowels of mercies, kindness, humbleness of mind, meekness, long-suffering:

Forbearing one another, and forgiving one another, if any man have a quarrel against any: even as Christ forgave you, so also do ye.

And above all these things put on charity, which is the bond of perfectness.

And let the peace of God rule in your hearts, to the which also ye are called in one body; and be ye thankful.

Let the word of Christ dwell in you richly in all wisdom; teaching and admonishing one another in psalms and hymns and spiritual songs, singing with grace in your hearts to the Lord.

The Gospel: from St. Luke (18:18-27)

AT that time: A certain ruler came and asked Jesus tempting him, saying, Good Master, what shall I do to inherit eternal life?

And Jesus said unto him, Why callest thou me good? none is good, save one, that is, God.

Thou knowest the commandments, Do not commit adultery, Do not kill, Do not steal, Do not bear false witness, Honour thy father and thy mother.

And he said, All these have I kept from my youth up.

Now when Jesus heard these things, he said unto him, Yet lackest thou one thing: sell all that thou hast, and distribute unto the poor, and thou shalt have treasure in heaven: and come, follow me.

And when he heard this, he was very sorrowful: for he was very rich.

And when Jesus saw that he was very sorrowful, he said, How hardly shall they that have riches enter into the kingdom of God!

For it is easier for a camel to go through a needle's eye, than for a rich man to enter into the kingdom of God!

And they that heard it said, Who then can be saved?

And he said, The things which are impossible with men are possible with God.

THIRTY-FIRST SUNDAY

Prokeimenon, in the Sixth Tone

Save, O Lord, thy people, and bless thine inheritance. Unto thee will I cry, O Lord, my God.

Section from the First Epistle of St. Paul to Timothy (1:15-17)

MY child Timothy: A faithful saying, and worthy of all acceptation, that Christ Jesus came into this world to save sinners; of whom I am chief.

Howbeit for this cause I obtained mercy, that in me first Jesus Christ might show forth all long-suffering, for a pattern to them which should hereafter believe on him to life everlasting.

Now unto the King eternal, immortal, invisible, the only wise God, be honour and glory for ever and ever. Amen.

The Gospel: from St. Luke (18:35 to end)

AT that time: When Jesus came nigh unto Jericho, a certain blind man sat by the wayside begging:

And hearing the multitude pass by, he asked what it meant.

And they told him, that Jesus of Nazareth passeth by.

And he cried, saying, Jesus, thou son of David, have mercy on me.

And they which went before rebuked him, that he should hold his peace: but he cried so much the more, Thou son of David, have mercy on me.

And Jesus stood, and commanded him to be brought unto him: and when he was come near, he asked him,

Saying, What wilt thou that I shall do unto thee?
And he said, Lord, that I may receive my sight.

And Jesus said unto him, Receive thy sight: thy faith
hath saved thee.

And immediately he received his sight, and followed
him, glorifying God: and all the people, when they saw
it, gave praise unto God.

THIRTY-SECOND SUNDAY

Prokeimenon, in the Seventh Tone

The Lord will give strength to his people.
Bring to the Lord, O ye children of God.

*Section from the First Epistle of St. Paul to Timothy
(4:9-15)*

MY son Timothy: A faithful saying and worthy of
all acceptation.

For therefore we both labour and suffer reproach,
because we trust in the living God, who is the Saviour
of all men, specially of those that believe.

These things command and teach.

Let no man despise thy youth; but be thou an example of the believers, in word, in conversation, in charity,
in spirit, in faith, in purity.

Till I come, give attendance to reading, to exhortation, to doctrine.

Neglect not the gift that is in thee, which was given
thee by prophecy, with the laying on of the hands of the
presbytery.

Meditate upon these things; give thyself wholly to
them; that thy profiting may appear to all.

The Gospel: from St. Luke (19:1-10)

AT that time: Jesus entered and passed through
Jericho.

And, behold, there was a man named Zacchæus, which was the chief among the publicans, and he was rich.

And he sought to see Jesus who he was; and could not for the press, because he was little of stature.

And he ran before, and climbed up into a sycamore tree to see him; for he was to pass that way.

And when Jesus came to the place, he looked up, and saw him, and said unto him, Zacchæus, make haste, and come down; for to-day I must abide at thy house.

And he made haste, and came down, and received him joyfully.

And when they saw it, they all murmured, saying, That he was gone to be guest with a man that is a sinner.

And Zacchæus stood, and said unto the Lord; Behold Lord, the half of my goods I give to the poor; and if I have taken any thing from any man by false accusation, I restore him fourfold.

And Jesus said unto him, This day is salvation come to this house, forsomuch as he also is a son of Abraham.

For the Son of man is come to seek and to save that which was lost.

THE SUNDAY OF THE FOREFATHERS

Dec. 11th to 17th

Prokeimenon, in the Eighth Tone

Blessed art thou, O Lord, the God of our Fathers. For thou art just in all that thou hast done to us!

Section from the Epistle of St. Paul to the Colossians

Ye brethren: When Christ, who is our life, shall appear, etc. (p. 267).

The Gospel: from St. Luke

The Lord spake this parable: A certain man made a great supper, etc. (p. 266).

THE SUNDAY BEFORE CHRISTMAS
[KNOWN AS THE SUNDAY OF THE GENEALOGY]

From Dec. 18th to 24th

Prokeimenon, in the Fourth Tone

Blessed art thou, O Lord, the God of our Fathers.
For thou art just in all that thou hast done to us.

*Section from the Epistle of St. Paul to the Hebrews
(11:9-10; 32 to end)*

YE brethren: By faith Abraham sojourned in the land of promise, as in a strange country, dwelling in tabernacles with Isaac and Jacob, the heirs with him of the same promise:

For he looked for a city which hath foundations, whose builder and maker is God.

And what shall I more say? for the time would fail me to tell of Gideon, and of Barak, and of Samson, and of Jephthae; of David also, and Samuel, and of the prophets:

Who through faith subdued kingdoms, wrought righteousness, obtained promises, stopped the mouths of lions,

Quenched the violence of fire, escaped the edge of the sword, out of weakness were made strong, waxed valiant in fight, turned to flight the armies of the aliens.

Women received their dead raised to life again: and others were tortured, not accepting deliverance; that they might obtain a better resurrection:

And others had trial of cruel mockings and scourgings, yea, moreover of bonds and imprisonment:

They were stoned, they were sawn asunder, were tempted, were slain with the sword: they wandered about in sheepskins and goatskins; being destitute, afflicted, tormented;

(Of whom the world was not worthy:) they wandered in deserts, and in mountains, and in dens and caves of the earth.

And these all, having obtained a good report throug faith, received not the promise:

God having provided some better thing for us, th they without us should not be made perfect.

The Gospel: from St. Matthew (1:1 to end)

THE book of the generation of Jesus Christ, the s of David, the son of Abraham.

Abraham begat Isaac; and Isaac begat Jacob; an Jacob begat Judas and his brethren;

And Judas begat Phares and Zara of Thamar; an Phares begat Esrom; and Esrom begat Aram;

And Aram begat Aminadab; and Aminadab beg Naasson; and Naasson begat Salmon;

And Salmon begat Booz of Rachab; and Booz beg Obed of Ruth; and Obed begat Jesse;

And Jesse begat David the king; and David the kin begat Solomon of her that had been the wife of Uria

And Solomon begat Roboam; and Roboam beg Abia; and Abia begat Asa;

And Asa begat Josaphat; and Josaphat begat Joran and Joram begat Ozias;

And Ozias begat Joatham; and Joatham beg Achaz; and Achaz begat Ezekias;

And Ezekias begat Manasses; and Manasses beg Amon; and Amon begat Josias;

And Josias begat Jechonias and his brethren, abo the time they were carried away to Babylon:

And after they were brought to Babylon, Jechoni begat Salathiel; and Salathiel begat Zorobabel;

And Zorobabel begat Abiud; and Abiud beg Eliakim; and Eliakim begat Azor;

And Azor begat Sadoc; and Sadoc begat Achin and Achim begat Eliud;

And Eliud begat Eleazar; and Eleazar begat Ma than; and Matthan begat Jacob;

And Jacob begat Joseph the husband of Mary, whom was born Jesus, who is called Christ.

So all the generations from Abraham to David are fourteen generations; and from David until the carrying away into Babylon are fourteen generations; and from the carrying away into Babylon unto Christ are fourteen generations.

Now the birth of Jesus Christ was on this wise: When as his mother Mary was espoused to Joseph, before they came together, she was found with child of the Holy Ghost.

Then Joseph her husband, being a just man, and not willing to make her a public example, was minded to put her away privily.

But while he thought on these things, behold, the angel of the Lord appeared unto him in a dream, saying, Joseph, thou son of David, fear not to take unto thee Mary thy wife: for that which is conceived in her is of the Holy Ghost.

And she shall bring forth a son, and thou shalt call his name Jesus: for he shall save his people from their sins.

Now all this was done, that it might be fulfilled which was spoken of the Lord by the prophet, saying,

Behold, a virgin shall be with child, and shall bring forth a son, and they shall call his name Emmanuel, which being interpreted is, God with us.

Then Joseph being raised from sleep did as the angel of the Lord had bidden him, and took unto him his wife:

And knew her not till she had brought forth her firstborn son: and he called his name Jesus.

THE SUNDAY AFTER CHRISTMAS

From Dec. 26th to 29th

Prokeimenon, in the Fourth Tone

Marvelous is God in his saints.
Bless ye God in the congregation.

Section from the Epistle of St. Paul to the Galatie

Ye brethren: I certify you, that the gospel, etc. 254).

The Gospel: from St. Matthew (2: 13 to end)

AND after the Magi were departed, the angel of t Lord appeareth to Joseph in a dream, sayin Arise, and take the young child and his mother, a flee into Egypt, and be thou there until I bring th word: for Herod will seek the young child to destr him.

When he arose, he took the young child and mother by night, and departed into Egypt:

And was there until the death of Herod: that it mig be fulfilled which was spoken of the Lord by prophet, saying, Out of Egypt have I called my se

Then Herod, when he saw that he was mocked of wise men, was exceeding wroth, and sent forth, a slew all the children that were in Bethlehem, and all the coasts thereof, from two years old and und according to the time which he had diligently inqui of the wise men.

Then was fulfilled that which was spoken by Jere the prophet, saying,

In Rama was there a voice heard, lamentation, a weeping, and great mourning, Rachel weeping for children, and would not be comforted, because th are not.

But when Herod was dead, behold, an angel of Lord appeareth in a dream to Joseph in Egypt,

Saying, Arise, and take the young child and mother, and go into the land of Israel: for they dead which sought the young child's life.

And he arose, and took the young child and mother, and came into the land of Israel.

But when he heard that Archelaus did reign Judæa in the room of his father Herod, he was afr to go thither: notwithstanding, being warned of God

dream, he turned aside into the parts of Galilee:
And he came and dwelt in a city called Nazareth:
at it might be fulfilled which was spoken by the
ophets, He shall be called a Nazarene.

SUNDAY BEFORE THE EPIPHANY

Dec. 30th to Jan. 5th

Prokeimenon, in the Sixth Tone

O Lord, save thy people, and bless thine inheritance.
Unto thee will I cry O Lord my God.

·ction from the Second Epistle of St. Paul to Timothy (4:5-8)

Y son Timothy: Watch thou in all things, endure
afflictions, do the work of an evangelist, make full
·oof of thy ministry.
For I am now ready to be offered, and the time of
y departure is at hand.
I have fought a good fight, I have finished my course,
have kept the faith:
Henceforth there is laid up for me a crown of right-
·usness, which the Lord, the righteous judge, shall
·ve me at that day: and not to me only, but unto all
·em also that love his appearing.

The Gospel: from St. Mark (1:1-8)

HE beginning of the gospel of Jesus Christ, the
Son of God.
As it is written in the prophets, Behold, I send my
·essenger before thy face, which shall prepare thy way
·fore thee.
The voice of one crying in the wilderness, Prepare
·e the way of the Lord, make his paths straight.
John did baptize in the wilderness, and preach the
·aptism of repentance for the remission of sins.

And there went out unto him all the land of Judæa, and they of Jerusalem, and were all baptized of him in the river of Jordan, confessing their sins.

And John was clothed with camel's hair, and with a girdle of a skin about his loins; and he did eat locusts and wild honey;

And preached, saying, There cometh one mightier than I after me, the latchet of whose shoes I am not worthy to stoop down and unloose.

I indeed have baptized you with water: but he shall baptize you with the Holy Ghost.

SUNDAY AFTER THE EPIPHANY

Jan. 7th to 13th

Prokeimenon, in the First Tone

Let thy mercy, O Lord, be upon us.
Rejoice in the Lord, O ye just.

Section from the Epistle of St. Paul to the Ephesians (4:7-13)

YE brethren: Unto every one of us is given grace according to the measure of the gift of Christ.

Wherefore he saith, When he ascended up on high, he led captivity captive, and gave gifts unto men.

(Now that he ascended, what is it but that he also descended first into the lower parts of the earth?

He that descended is the same also that ascended up far above all heavens, that he might fill all things.)

And he gave some, apostles; and some, prophets; and some, evangelists; and some, pastors and teachers;

For the perfecting of the saints, for the work of the ministry, for the edifying of the body of Christ:

Till we all come in the unity of the faith, and of the knowledge of the Son of God, unto a perfect man, unto the measure of the stature of the fullness of Christ:

The Gospel: from St. Matthew (4:12-17)

AT that time: When Jesus had heard that John was
cast into prison, he departed into Galilee;
And leaving Nazareth, he came and dwelt in Caper-
num, which is upon the seacoast, in the borders of
Zabulon and Nephthalim:
That it might be fulfilled which was spoken by Esaias
the prophet, saying,
The land of Zabulon, and the land of Nephthalim,
by the way of the sea, beyond Jordan, Galilee of the
Gentiles;
The people which sat in darkness saw great light;
and to them which sat in the region and shadow of
death light is sprung up.
From that time Jesus began to preach, and to say,
Repent: for the kingdom of heaven is at hand.

FIFTH SECTION
Menaion, or Monthly

Being a Book which Contains the Services of the Fixed Feasts, such as the Dominical Feasts, the Distin guished Saints, etc., as well as the Troparia and Kon tàkions of the Rest of the Saints throughout the Twelv Months of the Year.[1]

✠

1. SEPTEMBER

[Its days, 30; Hours of Day, 12; of Night, 12]

1.   The beginning of the Indiction, or the Ecclesias tical New Year; a plenary Memorial of the Theotoko in Miasena, and a Memorial of the Righteous Simeor the Stylite.

Troparion to the Indiction, in the Second Tone

O THOU Creator of the whole universe, who dids appoint times by thine own power, bless the crow of this year with thy goodness, O Lord.   Preserve i safety thy kings and thy city, by the intercessions o the Theotokos, and save us.

Troparion to the Theotokos, in the Seventh Tone

REJOICE, O virgin Theotokos, full of grace, C haven and intercessor for mankind; for from the was the Deliverer of the world incarnate; and tho alone art Mother and Virgin, blessed and glorifie always.   Intercede, therefore, with Christ God, to gran safety to all the universe.

---

1 For the Saints who have no Troparion or Kontakion, see p. 36.

Troparion to the Righteous, in the First Tone

FOR patience thou hast become a pillar, and the ancient fathers thou hast equalled and rivaled. Thou hast rivaled Job in sufferings, Joseph in temptations, and the life of the incorporals, while yet thou wast in the flesh. Therefore, O our righteous Father Simeon, intercede with Christ God to save our souls.

Kontakion for the Indiction, in the Fourth Tone

O GOD of all, verily transcendent in essence, Creator of the ages and their Master, bless the cycle of this year, saving by thy boundless mercy, O compassionate One, all those who worship only thee, O Master, and who cry unto thee in fear, saying, Grant to all, O Saviour, a fertile year.

Kontakion to the Righteous, in the Second Tone

TO sublime things thou didst aspire, seeking while yet among the earthly thou wast numbered, making of the pillar a fiery chariot, through which, O righteous one, thou didst commune with the angels. Cease not, therefore, to intercede with Christ for all our sakes.

The Epistle (1 Tim. 2:1-7) and The Gospel (St. Luke 4:16-22)

Koinonikon: Bless the crown of the year by thy goodness, O Lord. Alleluia.

2. John the Faster, Patriarch of Constantinople (9); and Mamas the Martyr (1).

.3. Anthimus the Martyr among Priests, Bishop of Nicomedia (5).

4. Moses the Prophet (13); and Babylas the Martyr among Priests, Bishop of Antioch (5).

5. Zacharias the Prophet, venerable Father of the Forerunner (13).

6. Memorial of the Miracle in Colossae by Archangel Michael (Troparion on Nov. 8).

7. Preparation for the Nativity of the Theotokos; Memorial of the Martyr Sozon (1).

Troparion for the Preparation, in the Fourth Tone

TODAY from the stem of Jesse and from the loins of David is born unto us Mary the divine Maiden. Wherefore, all creation rejoiceth and is rejuvenated; heaven and earth together are joyful. Wherefore, O ye tribes of the nations, praise her; for Joachim rejoiceth and Anne celebrateth, crying, The barren shall give birth to the Theotokos who nourisheth our life.

Kontakion, in the Third Tone

TODAY the virgin Theotokos, Mary, the fortified chamber of the heavenly groom, is born by the will of God of a barren woman, being prepared as a chariot for God the Word; for to this she had been foredestined, since she is the divine gate and the Mother of Life in truth.

8. THE NATIVITY OF OUR MOST HOLY LADY THE THEOTOKOS.

Typicon

⟨If the Nativity of our Lady falleth on a Sunday then at Vespers, four are sung for the Resurrection and six for the Feast of the Nativity; Glory and Now for the Feast; the Aposticha for the Resurrection; Glory and Now for the Feast; Troparion for the Resurrection (once); and for the Feast (two times). At Matins, the Troparia as at Vespers; The Kathisma for the Resurrection and for the Feast. The Benedictions of the Resurrection are omitted. The Anabathmoi for the Resurrection; the Prokeimenon and the Matin Gospel for the Feast; then; In that we have beheld the Resurrection, etc., and Psalm 50 (plain reading). And on O merciful One, have mercy, etc., the Idiomelon for the Feast; and instead of O thou who art more honourable, etc., sing the Ninth Ode. The Exaposteilarions for the Resurrection one, for the Feast two. In the Einos for the Resurrection four, and for the Feast four. Glory for the Feast; Now, Thou hast transcended, etc; then the Great Doxology; and Today hath salvation come into the world, etc. And in the Mass, the Second Antiphony, O thou who didst rise from the dead, etc. In the Eisodos, the Tro-

parion for the Resurrection; for the Feast; and for the Patron Saint of the church; the Kontakion for the Feast; The Epistle and Gospel for the Sunday before the Elevation of the Cross. And on Especially, the Ninth Hermos, Verily virginity, O Theotokos, *etc. The Koinonikon,* I will take the cup of salvation, etc.

1. VESPERS

❡*After the Sunset Psalm, recite,* Blessed is the man, *three Psalms only. Then on* O Lord, to thee have I cried, *the following Idiomelons are sung in the Sixth Tone.*

By Sergius The Jerusalemite

TODAY hath God who sitteth on noëtic thrones prepared himself a holy throne on earth. He who hath established the heavens in wisdom hath, by his love to mankind, made a living heaven; for from a barren stem he hath brought forth his Mother, a life-bearing branch. Thou God of wonders and Hope of the hopeless, O Lord, glory to thee.

This is the day of the Lord; wherefore, rejoice ye nations; for behold the chamber of Light, the scroll of the Word of life hath come forth from the womb; the gate facing the east hath been born. Wherefore, she awaiteth the entrance of the High Priest. And she alone admitted Christ into the universe for the salvation of our souls.

While famous barren women there were who bore fruit by the will of God, verily Mary hath surpassed, having been born in a strange manner from a barren mother, she herself gave birth in the flesh to the End of all, from a seedless womb in a transcendent manner. And she alone is the door of the only Son of God through which he passed and which he left closed, providing all with wisdom, as he himself knew, and brought salvation to all mankind.

By Stephen the Jerusalemite

TODAY the barren gates are opened, and there cometh forth the divine, the virginal gate. Today hath grace begun to give fruit, showing forth to the world the Theotokos, through whom the earthly and the heavenly beings unite for the salvation of our souls.

Today the glad tidings go forth to the world. Today sweet fragrance is wafted forth, foretelling the glad tidings of salvation; and the barrenness of our nature hath been united: for the barren one hath become a mother to the one who remained a Virgin after giving birth to the Creator; from whom cometh the God in nature, taking a foreign nature and working salvation in the flesh for the lost, Christ, the Lover of mankind, and the Deliverer of our souls.

Today Anne the barren giveth birth to the Maiden of God, forechosen from all generations as a dwelling-place for Christ God, King of all and Creator of all, for the fulfillment of his divine dispensation, through which the creation of us earthly beings was renewed, and we ourseves were renewed from corruption to life immortal.

❧ *Glory and Now; the First piece of the above Idiomelons, i.e.* Today hath God who sitteth, *etc; and after the daily Prokeimenon, the following Prophecies.*

First Reading: from Genesis (28:11-17)

AND when he was come to a certain place, and would rest in it after sunset, he took of the stones that lay there, and putting them under his head, slept in the same place.

And he saw in his sleep a ladder standing upon the earth, and the top thereof touching heaven: the angels also of God ascending and descending by it;

And the Lord leaning upon the ladder, saying to him: I am the Lord God of Abraham thy father, and the God of Isaac; the land, wherein thou sleepest, I will give to thee and to thy seed.

And thy seed shall be as the dust of the earth: thou shalt spread abroad to the west, and to the east, and to the north, and to the south: and in thee and thy seed all the tribes of the earth shall be blessed.

And I will be thy keeper whithersoever thou goest, and will bring thee back into this land: neither will I leave thee, till I shall have accomplished all that I have said.

And when Jacob awaked out of sleep, he said: Indeed the Lord is in this place, and I knew it not.

And trembling he said: How terrible is this place! This is no other but the house of God, and the gate of heaven.

Second Reading: from the Prophecy of Ezekiel the Prophet (43:27; 44:14)

AND the days being expired, on the eighth day and thenceforward the priests shall offer your holocausts upon the altar, and the peace offerings: and I will be pacified towards you, saith the Lord God.

And he brought me back to the way of the gate of the outward sanctuary, which looked towards the east: and it was shut.

And the Lord said to me: This gate shall be shut, it shall not be opened, and no man shall pass through it: because the Lord the God of Israel hath entered in by it, and it shall be shut

For the prince. The prince himself shall sit in it, to eat bread before the Lord: he shall enter in by the way of the porch of the gate, and shall go out by the same way.

And he brought me by the way of the north gate, in the sight of the house: and I saw, and behold, the glory of the Lord filled the house of the Lord: and I fell on my face.

Third Reading: from the Proverbs of Solomon the Wise (9:1-11)

WISDOM hath built herself a house, she hath hewn her out seven pillars.

She hath slain her victims, mingled her wine, and set forth her table.

She hath sent her maids to invite to the tower, and to the walls of the city:

Whosoever is a little one, let him come to me. And to the unwise she said:

Come, eat my bread, and drink the wine which I have mingled for you.

Forsake childishness, and live, and seek prudence for a pleasant life whereby to perfect understanding through knowledge.

He that teacheth a scorner, doth an injury to himself: and he that rebuketh a wicked man, getteth himself a blot; for reprimands are wounds to the wicked.

Rebuke not a scorner lest he hate thee. Rebuke a wise man, and he will love thee.

Give an occasion to a wise man, and wisdom shall be added to him. Teach a just man, and he shall make haste to receive it.

The fear of the Lord is the beginning of wisdom: and the knowledge of the holy is prudence.

For by me shall thy days be multiplied, and years of life shall be added to thee.

¶*And after the usual Petitions, the following Litiya, in the Eighth Tone.*

By Sergius

ON this our illustrious feast day, let us strike our spiritual harps; for today the Mother of Life, who is the renewal of the creation of Adam and the recall of Eve, the fountain of incorruption, the liberation from corruption, through whom we have been deified and delivered from death, is born of the seed of David, dispersing darkness. Wherefore, let us believers cry unto her joyfully with Gabriel, Hail, O full of grace. The Lord is with thee, bestowing on us through thee the Great Mercy.

¶*In the Aposticha, the following Idiomelons, in the Fourth Tone.*

By Germanus the Patriarch

THE joy of the whole world hath shone forth to us from the two righteous ones, Joachim and Anne

verily the all extolled Virgin, who because of her surpassing purity became a living temple of God, and
alone is known as truly Theotokos. Wherefore, by her
intercessions, O Christ God, send forth safety to the
world, and to our souls the Great Mercy.

Stichos: Hearken, O daughter and consider.

Today, O Virgin, thou hast been born a most noble
child from the righteous ones, Joachim and Anne, as
angels foretold, O paradise and throne of God, O vessel
of purity who went before and proclaimed joy unto all
the world, O cause of our life and annihilation of the
curse, and the bestowal of blessing. Wherefore, O
Maiden, called forth from God, seek, through thy
birth-giving, safety to our souls and Great Mercy.

Stichos: Unto thy face all the rich of the nations
pray.

Verily, Anne the barren, the fruitless, doth today clap
her hands with joy. Let the terrestrial ones enwrap
themselves with light, let the kings be happy and the
Priests rejoice with blessings; let the whole world celebrate; for behold the queen, the blameless bride of the
Father, hath sprouted from the stem of Jesse. Wherefore, thereafter, women do not bring forth children in
sorrow; for joy hath blossomed forth, and life shall
dwell in the world, and the offerings of Joachim shall
no more be rejected; for the wailing of Anne hath been
turned into joy, who saith, Rejoice with me, all ye
chosen of Israel; for the Lord hath given me the living
palace of his divine glory for universal joy and gladness, and for the salvation of our souls.

Glory and Now, in the Eighth Tone (By Sergius)

COME, all ye believers, let us hasten to the Virgin;
   for behold she who was forechosen a Mother to
our God before she was conceived in the womb, was of
the stem of Jesse. Yea, she who is the treasure of virginity, the budding rod of Aaron, the gospel of the

Prophets, and branch of Joachim and Anne the righteous ones, is now given birth. Verily, the world hath
been renewed by her. She is born, and the Church
shall be adorned in her splendour, who is the holy
temple and the vessel of the Godhead, the stay of
virginity and the kingly chamber, through whom the
strange mystery of the union of the two Natures of
Christ hath come about, whom we worship, praising
the blameless nativity of the Virgin.

Troparion, in the Fourth Tone (three times)

THY nativity, O Theotokos, hath proclaimed joy to
the whole universe; for from thee did shine forth
the Sun of justice, Christ our God, annulling the curse
and bestowing the blessing, abolishing death and granting us life everlasting.

2. MATINS

First Kathisma, in the Fourth Tone

SHOUT, O David, what God hath sworn to thee
Said he, All that he swore to me hath been fulfilled
for behold from the fruit of my belly hath he brought
forth the Virgin, of whom was born Christ the Creator
the new Adam, a King upon my throne, who reigneth
today; he is the unshaken kingdom, since the barren
one hath given birth to the Theotokos, nourisher of our
lives.

Second Kathisma, in the Same Tone

VERILY, Mary the Maiden of God, is born for us
today of the stem of Jesse and the loins of David
and all creation is renewed and deified. Wherefore
rejoice together, O heaven and earth; praise her, O ye
families of the Gentiles; for Joachim doth rejoice, and
Anne doth feast, crying out, The barren hath given
birth to the Theotokos, the nourisher of our lives.

Third Kathisma, in the Eighth Tone

LET heaven rejoice and the earth be glad: for the heaven of God hath been born on earth, she who is the bride of God after the promise; the barren one giveth suck to Mary the babe. And at her nativity Joachim rejoiceth, saying, Verily, a rod hath been born to me from which shall come forth the Flower from the stem of Jesse. Truly that is a strange wonder.

❡ *Then after the Anabathmoi,* From my youth, *etc. (p. 50), the following Prokeimenon.*

I shall call on thy Name from generation to generation. My heart is inditing of good matter.

❡ *Then the Matin Gospel,* And Mary arose *(p. 50); Psalm 50 (plain reading, p. 82); Glory,* Through the intercessions of the Theotokos, *etc; Now (repeated); then* O merciful One, have mercy upon me. O God, *etc; and the Idiomelon, in the Fourth Tone,* The Joy of the whole world, *etc. (p. 286); and the Katabasias of the Cross (p. 300). And instead of* O thou who art more honourable, *etc., sing the Ninth Ode, in the Eighth Tone.*

VERILY, virginity, O Theotokos, is impossible for a mother, as birth-giving is impossible for virgins. Yet in thee hath the dispensation of both been accomplished. Wherefore, all we families of the earth ceaselessly bless thee.

Thou hast achieved, O Theotokos, the promise of the birth-giving, as worthy of thy purity; for thou didst bestow on her who was fruitless a flourishing fruit from God. Wherefore, we nations of the earth ceaselessly bless thee.

Verily, O undefiled one, the prophecy of the crier hath been fulfilled; for he said, I shall raise the fallen tabernace of the noble David, which was foredesigned in thee, O thou in whom all the sod of humanity hath been renewed in form, a body unto God.

O Theotokos, as we adore thy swaddling clothes, we glorify him who gave fruit to the barren; who in a strange way opened an unproductive womb; for he doth what he willeth, since he is God ruling over all.

O Anne of divine mind, mother of the bride, thou hast produced from thy womb unexpectedly, after th promise, the flower of the plant of virginity, giving a fruit from God the goodness of purity. Wherefore, w all beatify thee, since thou art the origin of our life.

Glory: It is impossible for those who have not th law to glorify the eternal Trinity, Father, Son, an Holy Spirit, omnipotent and uncreate, in whom, an in the sign of whose might, the whole world is estab lished.

Now: In thy womb, O virgin Mother, thou dids hold one of the Trinity, Christ the King, whom a creation doth praise and before whom the celestia thrones do tremble. Wherefore, beseech him, O al revered one, to save our souls.

❡ *Then close with the Hermos of the Cross,* Thou art the mystic paradise, *etc.* (*p. 302*).

Exaposteilarions

O MAIDEN Mary, who didst give birth to God the unwedded bride, the whole universe rejoicet today at thy birth, through which thou didst undo th disgrace of thy parents' sad barrenness, and the fir curse of Eve at birth-giving.

Be renewed, O Adam, and be magnified, O Eve, an ye Prophets exchange glad tidings with the Apostle and the righteous ones; for there is universal joy in th world for angels and men, since today is born the Theo tokos from the righteous ones, Joachim and Anne.

❡ *Then in the Einos, sing the following Prosomia, in the First Ton*

O HOW strange, how wonderful, that the founda tion of life was born from a barren one, and grac hath begun to give fruit with splendour. Wherefore rejoice, Joachim, for having become a father to th Theotokos. Verily, there is none like thee of all earthl parents, O God-inspired one; for the tabernacle of God the most holy mountain, through thee was bestowed o us. (*Repeat.*)

O how strange, how wonderful, that the fruit of the barren one did shine by the direction of the Omnipotent, the Creator of all; he who in good and righteous steadfastness did loosen the barrenness of the world. Exchange glad tidings, therefore, ye mothers, with the Theotokos, Hail, O full of grace. The Lord is with thee, who granteth the world, through thee, the Great Mercy.

When the noble Anne was revealed a living pillar of purity, a shining vessel gleaming with grace, she did give birth to the true exemplar of virginity, the divine flower which is a gift to all virgins and lovers of virginity, who approveth openly the goodness of virginity, and granteth to all believers the Great Mercy.

¶ *Glory and Now, in the Sixth Tone,* This is the day of the Lord, *etc. (p. 283); then the Great Doxology; and the Troparion,* Thy nativity, O Theotokos, *etc. (p. 288).*

3. THE MASS
1.   Through the intercessions of the Theotokos, O Saviour, save.
2.   Save us, O Son of God, thou who art wonderful in thy saints, as we sing unto thee. Alleluia.
3.   Thy nativity, O Theotokos, etc.
Eisodikon: O come, let us worship and fall down to Christ. Save us, O Son of God, thou who art wonderful in thy saints, as we sing unto thee. Alleluia.

Kontakion, in the Fourth Tone

BY thy holy birth-giving, O pure one, Joachim and Anne were delivered from the reproach of barrenness; and Adam and Eve were delivered from the corruption of death; thy people do celebrate it, having been saved from the stain of iniquity, crying unto thee, The barren doth give birth to the Theotokos, who nourisheth our life.

The Epistle
My soul doth magnify the Lord. He hath regarded the humiliation of his handmaid.

Section from the Epistle of St. Paul to the Phillippian
(2:5-11)

YE brethren: Let this mind be in you, which was als
in Jesus Christ.

Who being in the form of God, thought it not robber
to be equal with God:

But emptied himself, taking upon him the form of
servant, and being made in the likeness of man: and i
habit found as a man,

He humbled himself, becoming obedient unto death
even to the death of the cross.

For which cause God also hath exalted him, and
given him a name which is above all names:

That at the name of Jesus every knee should bow, o
those that are in heaven, on earth, and under the earth

And that every tongue should confess that the Lor
Jesus Christ is in the glory of God the Father.

The Gospel: from St. Luke (10:38 to end; 11:27-28

AT that time: Jesus entered a certain town: and
certain woman named Martha, received him int
her house.

And she had a sister called Mary, who sitting also a
the Lord's feet, heard his word.

But Martha was busy about much serving. Who stoo
and said: Lord, hast thou no care that my sister hath
left me alone to serve? speak to her therefore, that sh
help me.

And the Lord answering, said to her: Martha
Martha, thou art careful, and art troubled about man
things:

But one thing is necessary. Mary hath chosen th
best part, which shall not be taken away from her.

And it came to pass, as he spoke these things, a cer
tain woman from the crowd, lifting up her voice, said
to him: Blessed is the womb that bore thee, and the pap
that gave thee suck.

But he said: Yea rather, blessed are they who hear the word of God, and keep it.

¶ *On Especially, the Hermos of the Ninth Ode,* Verily, virginity, O Theotokos, *etc. (p. 289).*

Koinonikon: I will take the cup of salvation and call upon the Name of the Lord. Alleluia (Psalm 116:13).

9. Joachim and Anne, Grandparents of Christ God; and the Martyr Severianus (1).

Troparion for the Grandparents of God, in the Second Tone

AS we celebrate the remembrance of thy righteous grandparents, through them we beseech thee, O Lord, to save our souls.

Kontakion, in the Second Tone

ANNE doth rejoice now that she is loosed from the bonds of her barrenness, as she nourisheth the most pure one, calling all to praise him who hath given the world her who alone is Mother, yet hath known no man.

10. Menodora, Metrodora, and Nymphodora, the Martyrs (8).

11. The Righteous Theodora of Alexandria (8).

12. Leave-taking of the Nativity of the Theotokos; Autonomus the Martyr among Priests (5).

13. Memorial of the Dedication of the Resurrection Temple; Preparation for the Feast of the Elevation of the Cross; Martyr among Priests, Cornelius the Centurion (5).

14. ELEVATION OF THE LIFE-GIVING CROSS (FAST DAY, ON WHICHEVER DAY IT FALLETH).

Typicon

¶ *If this day falleth on a Sunday, no part of the service of the Resurrection is chanted, but the whole service belongeth to the Feast of the Cross.*

1. Vespers

¶If it falleth on a Sunday evening, the whole First Kathisma of the Psalms is chanted; otherwise, after the Sunset Psalm, immediately on O Lord, to thee have I cried, sing the following six Prosomia, in the Sixth Tone.

THE Cross by its elevation calleth the whole creation to praise the pure Passion, the Passion of him who was elevated thereon; for having slain thereupon him who had slain us, he brought to life us who had been slain, and adorned us and made us worthy to dwell in the heavens, for the excess of his goodness; for he is compassionate. Whereupon, with rejoicing we exalt his Name and magnify his infinite condescension. (*Repeat.*)

Verily, Moses foreshadowed thee, O precious Cross, when he lifted up his hands and conquered the stubborn Amalek, O pride of believers and constancy of strivers, the adornment of the Apostles, the succour of the righteous, and the salvation of all the upright. Wherefore, creation, beholding thee elevated, rejoiceth and celebrateth, glorifying Christ, who through thee united the separables, in his infinite goodness. (*Repeat.*)

O most venerable Cross, surrounded in joy by the ranks of angels, by thine elevation today thou dost raise, by a divine sign, those who have been cast away by the deceit of food and carried headlong to death. Wherefore, we greet thee in faith with heart and lips, we receive sanctification, crying, Raise ye up Christ God, exceeding in goodness, and fall down to his divine footstool. (*Repeat.*)

Glory and Now, in the Second Tone

COME, all ye nations, let us adore the blessed Tree, through which everlasting justice hath come to pass; for he who by the tree did deceive the first Adam hath himself been deceived by the Cross; and he who like a robber confined the kingly creation, hath been cast down headlong with an amazing fall. And by the blood of God the venom of the serpent was washed away; and the curse was undone by the righteous sentence when the just One was condemned unjustly; for it is meet that the tree by the Tree be healed, and that by the Passion of the Passionless the passions of him who had been condemned by the tree should fall away. But glory to thy fearful dispensation towards us, O Christ, wherewith thou hast saved all, since thou art good and the Lover of mankind.

¶ *Then after the daily Prokeimenon, the following Prophecies are recited.*

First Reading: from Exodus (15:22 to end; and 16:1)

AND Moses brought Israel from the Red Sea, and they went forth into the wilderness of Sur: and they marched three days through the wilderness, and found no water.

And they came into Mara, and they could not drink the waters of Mara, because they were bitter: whereupon he gave a name also agreeable to the place, calling it Mara, that is bitterness.

And the people murmured against Moses, saying: What shall we drink?

But he cried to the Lord, and he shewed him a tree, which when he had cast into the waters, they were turned into sweetness. There he appointed him ordinances, and judgments, and there he proved him,

Saying: If thou wilt hear the voice of the Lord thy God, and do what is right before him, and obey his commandments, and keep all his precepts, none of the evils that I laid upon Egypt, will I bring upon thee: for I am the Lord thy healer.

And the children of Israel came into Elim, where there were twelve fountains of water, and seventy palm trees: and they encamped by the waters.

And they set forward from Elim, and all the multitude of the children of Israel came into the desert of Sin, which is between Elim and Sinai.

Second Reading: from the Proverbs of Solomon the Wise (3:11-18)

MY son, reject not the correction of the Lord: and do not faint when thou art chastised by him;

For whom the Lord loveth, he chastiseth: and as a father in the son he pleaseth himself.

Blessed is the man that findeth wisdom and is rich in prudence:

The purchasing thereof is better than the merchandise of silver, and her fruit than the chiefest and purest gold.

She is more precious than all riches: and all the things that are desired, are not to be compared with her

Length of days is in her right hand, and in her left hand riches and glory.

Her ways are beautiful ways, and all her paths are peaceable.

She is a tree of life to them that lay hold on her: and he that shall retain her is blessed.

Third Reading: from the Prophecy of Isaiah the Prophet (60:11-16)

THESE things saith the Lord, And thy gates shall shall be opened continually: they shall not be shut day nor night, that the strength of the Gentiles may be brought to thee, and their kings may be brought.

For the nation and the kingdom that will not serve thee, shall perish: and the Gentiles shall be wasted with desolation.

The glory of Libanus shall come to thee, the fir tree and the box tree, and the pine tree together, to beautify the place of my sanctuary: and I will glorify the place of my feet.

And the children of them that afflict thee, shall come bowing down to thee, and all that slandered thee shall worship the steps of thy feet, and shall call thee the city of the Lord, the Sion of the Holy One of Israel

Because thou wast forsaken, and hated, and there was none that passed through thee, I will make thee to be an everlasting glory, a joy unto generation and generation:

And thou shalt suck the milk of the Gentiles, and thou shalt be nursed with the breasts of kings: and thou shalt know that I am the Lord thy Saviour, and thy Redeemer, the mighty One of Jacob.

¶ *And after the usual Petitions, the following Litiya, in the Eighth Tone.*

WHEN Moses, O Christ, foreshadowed the effect of thy precious Cross, he defeated the stubborn Amalek in the wilderness of Sinai; for when he lifted his hands, making the sign of the cross, the people prevailed. But now things have attained their perfection in us. Today, as the Cross is elevated, evil spirits are driven away; today the whole creation is delivered from corruption; for by the Cross all gifts have shone forth upon us. Wherefore, we all kneel to thee, saying with joy, How great are thy works, O Lord, glory to thee.

¶ *In the Aposticha, the following Prosomia, in the Fifth Tone.*

Rejoice, O life-bearing Cross, invincible triumph of true worship; O gate of paradise, constancy of believers, and wall of the Church, through which corruption hath vanished and been abolished, and the power of death hath been swallowed, and we have ascended from earth to heaven. Thou art the unconquerable weapon, the adversary of Satan, since thou art the glory of the Martyrs and righteous ones, their adornment in truth, the haven of salvation, which granteth the world the Great Mercy.

Stichos: Raise ye the Lord our God, and fall down to his footstool.

Rejoice, O Cross of the Lord, by which the human race hath been absolved from the curse, which is the sign of true joy, the vanquisher of enemies through its elevation, thou most revered, our succour and the majesty of kings, the power of the righteous and the splendour of Priests, the sign of which delivereth from tribulation, O staff of power by which we are shepherds, weapon of safety surrounded by angels in fear, and glory of Christ who granteth the world the Great Mercy.

Stichos: As for God he is our King before the ages.

Rejoice, O Cross, thou guide of the blind and physician of the sick and resurrection of all the dead, which did raise us who had fallen in corruption, by which corruption hath been abolished and incorruption made to flourish, and we men have been deified, but Satan was completely crushed. Wherefore, today as we behold thee elevated in the hands of the High Priests, we exalt him who was elevated upon thee, and thee we adore, seeking that thou grant us the Great Mercy.

Glory and Now, in the Eighth Tone

O LORD, save thy people and bless thine inheritprecious Cross by which Moses, having foreshadowed the same in himself, did defeat Amalek, and David the singer, having shouted, commanded adoration to thy footstool, we praise thee who didst consent to be nailed thereon, crying unto thee with unworthy lips, O Lord, make us worthy, with the thief, of thy kingdom.

Troparion, in the First Tone (three times)

O LORD, save thy people and bless thine inheritance, granting our believing kings victory over the Barbarians, and by the power of thy Cross preserving thy commonwealth.

2. MATINS

❡ *On* God the Lord hath appeared unto us, *the Troparion is chanted three times, then the following Kathismata.*

First Kathisma, in the First Tone

WE adore the tree of thy Cross, O Lover of mankind; for thou wast nailed thereon, O life of all, and didst open paradise, thou Saviour of the thief, who,

aving confessed thee, became worthy of bliss, crying,
emember me, O Lord. Receive us, therefore, as thou
eceivedst him, as we cry to thee, We have all sinned.
y thy compassion, turn not away from us.

Second Kathisma, in the Sixth Tone

3Y the mere planting of thy Cross, O Christ, the
foundation of death did shake; for him whom hades
id swallow eagerly, it delivered up with trembling;
r verily, thou didst reveal to us thy salvation, O holy
ne. Wherefore, do we glorify thee, O Son of God.
Iave mercy upon us.

Third Kathisma, in the Third Tone

OSHUA the son of Nun, O my Saviour, in ancient
times did foreshadow thy Cross mystically as he
penly stretched forth his arms in the form of a cross,
nd the sun stood still until he destroyed the enemies
pposed to thee, O God. But now the sun hath grown
ark, since he hath seen thee upon the Cross abolishing
ie might of death and taking hades captive.

Then the Anabathmoi, From my youth, *etc. (p. 50); and the fol-
wing Prokeimenon.*

All the regions of the earth have seen the salvation
f our God.

Stichos: Sing unto the Lord a new song.

The Matin Gospel: from St. John (12:28-36)

THE Lord said: Father, glorify thy Name. A voice,
therefore, came from heaven. I have both glori-
ed it, and will glorify it again.

The multitude therefore that stood and heard, said
thundered. Others said: An angel spoke to him.

Jesus answered, and said: This voice came not be-
ause of me, but for your sakes.

Now is the judgment of the world: now shall the prince of this world be cast out.

And I, if I be lifted up from the earth, will draw all things to myself.

(Now this he said, signifying what death he should die.)

The multitude answered him: We have heard out of the law, that Christ abideth for ever; and how sayest thou: The Son of man must be lifted up? Who is this Son of man?

Jesus therefore said to them: Yet a little while, the light is among you. Walk whilst you have the light, that the darkness overtake you not. And he that walketh in darkness, knoweth not whither he goeth.

Whilst you have the light, believe in the light, that you may be the children of light.

❡ *Then immediately,* In that we have beheld the Resurrection of Christ, *etc.* (*p. 113*); *and Psalm 50* (*plain reading, p. 82*); *then Glory, in the Second Tone.*

O THOU tripartite Cross of Christ, thou art my secure protection. Sanctify me, therefore, by thy might, that with faith and longing I may adore and glorify thee.

❡ *Now* (*repeated*).

❡ *And on* O merciful One, have mercy upon me, O God, *etc., the following Idiomelon, in the Sixth Tone.*

O CROSS of Christ, O hope of Christians, and guide of the lost; O haven of the winter-locked; O victory in war and security of the universe; O physician of the sick and resurrection of the dead, have mercy upon us.

❡ *Then the following Katabasias of the Cross, in the Eighth Tone.*[1]

1. Verily, Moses having struck horizontally with his rod, cleaving the Red Sea and causing Israel to cross on foot, then having struck it transversely bringing it

---

[1] These Katabasias of the Cross are sung from August 1st to 13th and from August 24th to Sept. 21st.

together over Pharaoh and his chariots, did trace the
Cross, thus symbolizing that invincible weapon. Wherefore, do we praise Christ our God, for that he hath been
glorified.

3.   The rod is taken as a symbol of the mystery; for
by its budding, it designateth the Priest.   But now the
tree of the Cross hath blossomed forth with might and
steadfastness to the hitherto barren Church.

4.   I have heard, O Lord, of the mystery of thy dispensation, and have contemplated thy works.   Wherefore, have I glorified thy Godhead.

5.   O thou thrice-blessed Tree, whereon the Lord
Christ the King was stretched, and through which he
who was beguiled by the tree fell, having been beguiled
by thee, by the God that was nailed upon thee in the
flesh, who granteth safety to our souls.

6.   When Jonah in the belly of the whale did stretch
forth his hands in the form of a cross, he did foreshadow
clearly the Passion of salvation; and when he came out
on the third day, he did symbolize the world-transcending Resurrection of Christ, nailed upon thee in the flesh,
and illuminating the world by his third-day Resurrection.

7.   The mad command of the infidel tyrant hath shaken the nations, breathing forth threats and blasphemies
loathed of God.   But the three youths were not terrified by the bestial terror, nor the consuming fire; for
being together amidst the fire blown forth by a dewy
breeze, they were singing, O thou exceedingly praised,
blessed art thou, God of our fathers.

Let us praise, bless, and worship the Lord.

8.   O ye youths, equal in number to the Trinity, bless
the Father, the God Creator; praise the Word which
did condescend and turn the fire to a dewy breeze; and
exalt more and more the all-holy Spirit, who giveth life
to all for evermore.

❡ *Then instead of* O thou who art more honourable, *etc., the following Ninth Ode with its Hermos is sung in the Eighth Tone.*

9.   Thou art the mystical paradise, O Theotokos; for that thou, being untilled, didst bud forth Christ, by whom was planted on earth the life-giving tree of the Cross.   Wherefore, as we adore it being elevated, we magnify thee.

Let all the trees of the wood, planted from the beginning of time, rejoice; for their nature hath been sanctified by the stretching of Christ on the Tree.   Wherefore, now, we worship him, lifted up, and magnify him.

A noble horn hath been raised to those of divine mind, the Cross which is head of all, by which all the supersensuous horns of sinners are crushed.   Wherefore now, we adore it elevated, and magnify it.

Another Hermos

VERILY, death which befell the human race by eating from the tree, hath been abolished today by the Cross; for the curse of the first mother and all her descendents hath been undone by him who was born of the undefiled Theotokos, whom all the powers of heaven do magnify.

O Lord, that thou mightest not leave the bitterness of the tree abolished, thou didst remove it completely by the Cross.   Wherefore, in ancient times the tree made the waters of Marah sweet, anticipating the act of the Cross, whom all the powers of heaven do magnify.

O Lord, today by the Cross thou hast lifted up us who are immersed continually in the darkness of our first parent; for as nature fell aforetime into error perversely, the light of thy Cross did lead aright all us who believe, and we magnify it.

O Lord, that thou mightest make plain to the world the sign of thy Cross, adored since it is glorified of all, thou didst trace it in the sky, sparkling with shining light, an invincible and perfect weapon to the king. Wherefore, all the powers of the heavens do magnify it.

¶ *Then close with the two preceding Hermoses.*

Exaposteilarion, to be sung two times

THE Cross is the preserver of all the universe. The Cross is the comeliness of the Church. The Cross is the might of kings. The Cross is the steadfastness of believers. The Cross is the glory of the angels and the sting of Satan.

Another, to be sung only once

TODAY the Cross is elevated and the world sanctified; for thou who sitteth with the Father and the Holy Spirit, when thou didst stretch thy hands thereon, didst draw the whole world to thy knowledge. Make worthy, therefore, of thy divine glory those who rely on thee.

❧ *Then in the Einos, the following Prosomia are chanted in the Eighth Tone.*

HOW strangely wonderful that the life-bearing plant, the all-holy Cross, appeareth today lifted on high; and all quarters glorify it, and all evil spirits tremble thereat. O what a boon granted mankind! Wherefore, O Christ, save our souls; for thou alone art compassionate. (*Repeat.*)

How strangely wonderful that the Cross which bore the high One as a cluster of grapes full of life, appeareth today elevated from the earth, through which we were all drawn to God, and death was swallowed unto the end. O what a pure Tree through which we have received the non-mortifying food of Eden, glorifying Christ.

How strangely wonderful that the Cross appeared equalling heaven in length and breadth, sanctifying all things with divine grace, through which barbarian nations were conquered, and the scepters of kings were established! What a divine ladder over which we ascend to the heavens, raising with praises Christ the Lord.

Glory and Now, in the Sixth Tone

TODAY arriveth the Cross of the Lord, and believers receive it eagerly, acquiring therefrom healing
of soul and body and every sickness. Let us, therefore,
welcome it with joy and fear—with fear because of sin,
being unworthy; with joy because of the salvation
which Christ, who was nailed thereon and who possesseth the Great Mercy, granted to the world.

¶ *Then, the Great Doxology; and, as the Choir singeth,* Holy God,
*the Procession of the Precious Cross taketh place in the following
order: The minstering Priest approaching the altar, censeth the precious cross, then placeth it on his head in a tray filled with blossom-
ing twigs. Then emerging from the northern door of the Temple, preceded by taper carriers, fan carriers, and the Choir singing,* Holy
God, *the procession moveth to the center of the church, as the Deacon
censes the cross. Having reached the center, the Priest maketh the
circuit three times around a square table placed there for that purpose. Then turning eastward he crieth,* Wisdom! Let us attend!
*placing the precious cross on the table and censing it around in the
form of a cross, as he singeth the Troparion,* O Lord, save thy people,
*etc. (once); and each of the two Choirs sings it once. Then making
three reverences (on whatever day the Feast falleth), the Priest
holdeth the precious cross in his hand with the blossoms, in front of
the table, facing the east, and saith in a loud voice:*

Have mercy upon me, O God, according to the multitude of thy mercies. Of thee we ask; grant and have
mercy.

¶ *Then the two Choirs sing antiphonally, ten at a time, the first
hundred of* Lord, have mercy. *As the Choirs begin singing, the Priest
maketh the sign with the precious cross three times, prostrateth himself slowly till his head is within one span of touching the floor, then
he riseth slowly at the end of the first hundred. Then moving to the
right and looking northward, he saith:*

And also we ask for the sake of our kings of true worship, their victory, their preservation, their health, and
their salvation.

¶ *Then the Choir begins the second hundred of* Lord, have mercy,
*as the Priest repeateth the same acts as before. Then moving to the
eastern end of the table and looking westward, he saith:*

And also we pray for our Archbishop (N.   ) and
ll our brethren in Christ.

*The Choir then sings the third hundred, and the Priest repeateth
the previous acts. At the end the Priest moveth southward and look-
ng towards the north, saith:*

Also we pray for all the Orthodox Christians, for
heir health, their salvation, and the forgiveness of their
ins.

*The Choir then sings the fourth hundred, and the Priest repeateth
the same acts. Then the Priest returneth to the place whence he
tarted, in front of the table, turning eastward, as he saith:*

And also we pray for all those who serve, and those
who have served in this holy Church of Christ, for their
health, their salvation, and the forgiveness of their sins.

*The Choir sings the fifth hundred, as the Priest maketh the fifth
prostration. After its conclusion, the Priest lifteth the cross with the
blossoms, blessing the people by making the sign of the cross therewith, chanting:*

O thou who of thine own good will, upon the Cross
wast elevated, etc.

Then placing the cross on the table he singeth once:

Thy Cross, our Master, we adore, and thy holy Resurrection do we glorify.

This is repeated once by each of the two Choirs.

*The Priest kneels to the cross, followed by the congregation. After
this the Priest distributeth the twigs of blossoms among the people, as
the Choir singeth the following Idiomelon, in the Second Tone.*

COME, ye believers, let us adore the life-giving Tree,
whereon when Christ the King of glory stretched
his hands, he lifted us to the first bliss, us whom the
ancient enemy having led captive by desire drove away
from God. Come, ye believers, let us adore the Tree
through which we were made worthy to crush the heads
of invisible enemies. Come, all ye nations of the earth,
let us honour with songs of praise the Cross of the Lord,
crying, Peace be upon thee, O Cross, O perfection of

the redemption of fallen Adam; for in thee do our kin
of steadfast faith glory, since by thy might, they subj
gate the barbarian people mightily. Wherefore, as
Christians greet thee in fear, we glorify God nail
upon thee, saying, O Lord who wast crucified thereo
have mercy upon us, since thou art good and the Lov
of mankind.

❡*And at the conclusion of this, the following Troparion,* O Lo
save thy people, *etc.*

3. THE MASS

1. Through the intercessions of the Theotokos,
Saviour, save us.

2. Save us, O Son of God, who wast crucified in t
flesh, as we sing unto thee, Alleluia.

3. O Lord, save thy people, etc.

Eisodikon: Exalt ye the Lord our God, worship
his footstool; for he is holy. Save us, O Son of Go
who wast crucified in the flesh, as we sing unto th
Alleluia.

Kontakion

❡Do thou, who of thine own good will, *etc.* (*p. 25*); *and instead*
Holy God, *sing:*

Thy Cross, O Master, we adore, and thy holy Resu
rection we praise.

The Epistle

Exalt ye the Lord our God. The Lord hath reigne
let the people be angry.

Section from the First Epistle of St. Paul to the Cori
thians (1:18-24)

BRETHREN: The word of the cross to them inde
that perish is foolishness; but to them that a
saved, that is to us, it is the power of God.

For it is written, I will destroy the wisdom of t
wise, and the prudence of the prudent I will reject.

Where is the wise? where is the scribe? where is t
disputer of this world?

For seeing that in the wisdom of God the world by wisdom knew not God, it pleased God by the foolishness of our preaching to save them that believe.

For the Jews require a sign, and the Greeks seek after wisdom:

But we preach Christ crucified, unto the Jews indeed a stumblingblock, and unto the Gentiles foolishness;

But unto them which are called both Jews and Greeks, Christ the power of God, and the wisdom of God.

The Gospel: from St. John (19:6-35)

AT that time: All the chief priests and ancients of the people took counsel against Jesus, that they might put him to death.

And they came to Pilate, saying: Crucify him, crucify him. Pilate saith to them: Take ye him and crucify him: for I find no cause in him.

The Jews answered him: We have a law; and according to the law he ought to die, because he made himself the Son of God.

When Pilate therefore had heard this saying, he feared the more.

And he entered into the hall again, and he said to Jesus: Whence art thou? But Jesus gave him no answer.

Pilate therefore saith to him: Speakest thou not to me? knowest thou not that I have power to crucify thee, and I have power to release thee?

Jesus answered: Thou shouldst not have any power against me, unless it were given thee from above. Therefore, he that hath delivered me to thee, hath the greater sin.

And from henceforth Pilate sought to release him. But the Jews cried out, saying: If thou release this man, thou art not Cæsar's friend. For whosoever maketh himself a king, speaketh against Cæsar.

Now when Pilate had heard these words, he brought Jesus forth, and sat down in the judgment seat, in the place that is called Lithostrotos, and in Hebre Gabbatha.

And it was the parasceve of the pasch, about the six hour, and he saith to the Jews: Behold your king.

But they cried out: Away with him; away with hin crucify him. Pilate saith to them: Shall I crucify yo king? The chief priests answered: We have no king b Cæsar.

Then therefore he delivered him to them to be cru fied. And they took Jesus, and led him forth.

And bearing his cross, he went forth to that pla which is called Calvary, but in Hebrew Golgotha.

Where they crucified him, and with him two othe one on each side, and Jesus in the midst.

And Pilate wrote a title also, and he put it upon t cross. And the writing was: Jesus of Nazareth, t King of the Jews.

This title therefore many of the Jews did read: b cause the place where Jesus was crucified was nigh the city: and it was written in Hebrew, in Greek, ar in Latin.

Then the chief priests of the Jews said to Pilat Write not, The King of the Jews; but that he said, I a the King of the Jews.

Pilate answered: What I have written, I ha written.

The soldiers therefore, when they had crucified hir took his garments, (and they made four parts, to eve soldier a part,) and also his coat. Now the coat w without seam, woven from the top throughout.

They said then one to another: Let us not cut it, b let us cast lots for it, whose it shall be; that the scriptu might be fulfilled, saying: They have parted my ga ments among them, and upon my vesture they have ca lots. And the soldiers indeed did these things.

Now there stood by the cross of Jesus, his mothe and his mother's sister, Mary the wife of Cleophas, ar Mary Magdalen.

When Jesus therefore saw his mother and the disiple standing whom he loved, he saith to his mother: Woman, behold thy son.

After that, he saith to the disciple: Behold thy mother. And from that hour, the disciple took her to his own.

Afterwards, Jesus knowing that all things were now accomplished that the scripture might be fulfilled, said: I thirst.

Now there was a vessel set there full of vinegar. And they, putting a sponge full of vinegar about hyssop, put it to his mouth.

Jesus therefore, when he had taken the vinegar, said: It is consummated. And bowing his head, he gave up the spirit.

Then the Jews, (because it was the parasceve,) that the bodies might not remain upon the cross on the sabbath day, (for that was a great sabbath day,) besought Pilate that their legs might be broken, and that they might be taken away.

The soldiers therefore came; and they broke the legs of the first, and of the other that was crucified with him.

But after they were come to Jesus, when they saw that he was already dead, they did not break his legs.

But one of the soldiers with a spear opened his side, and immediately there came out blood and water.

And he that saw it, hath given testimony; and his testimony is true. And he knoweth that he saith true; that you also may believe.

¶ *And on Especially, the Hermos of the Ninth Ode,* Thou art the mystical paradise, *etc.*

Koinonikon: The light of thy countenance hath been impressed on us, O Lord. Alleluia.

¶ *And instead of* We have seen the true Light, *etc., sing the Troparion,* O Lord, save thy people, *etc.*

¶ *And the conclusion:* O thou who hast risen from the dead, O Christ, *etc.*

❡*Note: On the Sunday following the Feast of the Elevation of the Cross (Sept. 15-21), the Exaposteilarions of the Resurrection and of the Cross are sung together. And in the Einos, four for the Resurrection and four for the Cross; and in the Eisodos, with the Troparion of the Resurrection, the Troparion and Kontakion of the Cross.*

15. Nicetas, the Great Martyr (1).

16. Euphemia, the All-extolled Great Martyr.

17. Sophia, the Martyr, and her three Daughters, Pistis, Elpis, and Agape (4).

18. Eumenius, the Wonder-worker, Bishop of Gortyna (10).

19. Trophimus, the Martyr, and his Companions (2).

20. Eustathius, the Great Martyr, his Wife, and his two Children (2).

21. The Apostle Quadratus (12), Jonah the Prophet (13), and Leave-taking of the Feast of the Elevation.

22. Phocas, the Martyr, Bishop of Sinope (5).

23. Conception of the Prophet and Forerunner, John the Baptist.

Troparion, in the Fourth Tone

REJOICE, O barren one, who had not given birth; for behold thou hast conceived clearly the one who is the dawn of the Sun who was about to illuminate the whole universe, blighted with sightlessness. Shout in joy, O Zacharias, crying in favour, Verily, the one to be born is a Prophet of the High.

The Epistle (Gal. 4:22-27) and the Gospel: (St. Luke 1:5-25)

24. Thecla, the first Martyr and the equal of the Apostles (4).

The Epistle (2 Tim. 3:10-15), and the Gospel (St. Mt. 25:1-13)

25. Euphrosyne, the Righteous (8).

26. The Translation of John the Evangelical Apostle.

Troparion, in the Second Tone

) APOSTLE, speaker of divinity, the beloved of Christ God, hasten and deliver thy people power-s in argument; for he on whose bosom thou didst n accepteth thee as an intercessor. Beseech him, erefore, to disperse the cloud of the stubborn nations, ing for us safety and the Great Mercy.

27. Callistratus, the Martyr, and the forty-nine artyrs with him (2).

28. Chariton, the Righteous Confessor (6); and ruch the Prophet (13).

29. Cyriacus, the Righteous Pilgrim (7).

30. Gregory the Martyr, Bishop of Greater Ar-nia (5).

II OCTOBER

[Its Days, 31; hours of Day, 11; of Night, 13]

1. Ananias the Apostle (12); and Romanus the ghteous Chanter (8).

2. Cyprian the Martyr (5); and Justina the Martyr).

3. Dionysius the Martyr, the Areopagite (5).

4. Hierotheus the Bishop of Athens (10).

5. Charitine the Martyr (4).

6. Thomas the Apostle (12).

7. Sergius and Bacchus, the Martyrs (2).

8. Pelagia the Righteous (8).

9. James the Son of Alphaeus, the Apostle (12); d Andronicus the Righteous (7).

10. The two Martyrs, Euphlampius and Eulampia).

11. Philip the Apostle, one of the Seven Deacons 2); and Theophanes the Righteous Branded One 0).

SUNDAY OF THE HOLY FATHERS

rom the eleventh to the seventeenth of October, on whichever day nday falleth, shall be chanted the service of the Fathers of the enth Council convened for the second time in Nicea, in the year 7, against the Iconoclasts.

1. Vespers

On O Lord, to thee have I cried, *are chanted four for the Resur rection, in the Tone in use, and six for the Fathers, in the Six Tone.*

VERILY, the seven councils of the Fathers held at sundry times, were brought together under the canon and in good order by the Patriarch Germanus the New, inscribing and establishing their doctrine and offering themselves as intercessors with the Lord watchful for salvation, and shepherds with him of the fold.

The Book of the Law hath verily honoured the seventh day for the Hebrews, dispersed in the shadow and devoted thereto. But ye Fathers, by your partici pation in the Seven Councils, by the inspiration of God who in six days finished this universe and blessed the seventh day, have made it even more honourable by decreeing the bounds of faith.

Ye have given all, O thrice-blessed Fathers, to know the Trinity clearly by his works, he being the Cause of the creation of the world; for by your mystical speech having called first three Councils then four, ye have appeared as champions of the Orthodox word, proving that the Trinity is verily the Creator of the four ele ments and of the world.

It would have sufficed Elisha the Prophet to bend but once to instill life in the dead son of the servant but he kneeled and bent seven times. Thus in his fore vision did he prophesy your gathering wherewith ye revived the Incarnation of the Word of God, morti fying Arius and his co-workers.

In wisdom, O venerable Fathers, ye patched the ra ment of Christ, torn by barking dogs; for ye could not possibly bear to see his nakedness, like Shem and Japheth, who of old could not bear to see the nakedness of their father, thus confounding him who smote his own father, namely Arius, styled the fool, and those who followed his doctrines.

The Macedonians, the Nestorians, the followers of Ephtechnis, Dioscorus, Appolonarius, Sabelius, and Severus, having turned devouring wolves in lambs' skins, ye did expel from the Saviour's fold, ye who are true shepherds. Verily, ye did well, stripping the thrice-wretched ones naked; wherefore, we beatify you.

Glory, in the Sixth Tone

LET us extol today those mystical trumpets of the Spirit, namely the God-mantled Fathers, who, speaking of divine things, sang in the midst of the Church a hymn of unified tones, teaching that the Trinity is One, not differing in Substance or Godhead, refuting Arius and contending for Orthodoxy, who ever intercede with the Lord to have mercy on our souls.

¶Now, in the Tone in use; the Aposticha for the Resurrection; and Glory, in the Fourth Tone.

COME, ye assemblies of Orthodoxy, let us celebrate today in faith and true worship the anniversary of the God-mantled Fathers, who from the whole inhabited world came together in the splendid city of Nicea; for those in the sagacity of their pious minds did refute the impious belief which Arius the wretched had invented, banishing him by a decree of the Council from the universal Church, and instructing all to confess openly the Son of God, that he is consubstantial and coëternal with the Father before eternity, decreeing the same with precision and true worship in the Canon of Faith. Wherefore, following their divine doctrines in true faith, let us worship with the Father and the Son the most Holy Spirit, a Trinity consubstantial in one Godhead.

Now to our Lady

LEND ear, O all-blameless one, to the petitions of thy servants. Turn away from us evil uprisings and save us from all sorrows; for thou alone art our secure and safe refuge, and thee, O Lady, have we taken as our succour. Wherefore, we shall never be discomfited, who ask thee to hasten to those who beseech and hail thee in faith, saying, Rejoice, O Lady, the help of all, O joy, shelter, and salvation of our souls.

Troparion for the Resurrection, then for the Fathers, in the Eighth Tone

THOU, O Christ, art our God of exceeding praise who didst establish our holy Fathers as luminous stars upon earth, and through them didst guide us unto the true Faith, O most merciful One, glory to thee.

2. MATINS

The Exaposteilarions for the Resurrection and for the Fathers

O FATHERS of heavenly minds, assembled together in the Seventh Council, lift up your petitions constantly to the Trinity to save from every heresy and from eternal condemnation those who laud your divine gathering, that they may receive the kingdom of heaven.

By the intercessions of thy Mother and those of the Fathers, who were assembled in the Seven Councils, O Lord of exceeding goodness, establish thou thy Church, confirm the Faith, and make us all partners of the kingdom of heaven, when thou comest to earth to judge the whole creation.

❡ *And in the Einos, sing four for the Resurrection and four for the Fathers, in the Sixth Tone.*

HAVING indited the whole knowledge of the soul and considered it carefully in the Holy Spirit, the venerable, glorified, and all-blessed Fathers inscribed in divine writing the honourable and heavenly Canon, in which they clearly teach that the Word is coëternal and consubstantial with the Father, thus following unmistakably the teachings of the Apostles. (*Repeat.*)

When the blessed Christ-preachers received wholly ιe torch of the Holy Spirit, they spoke with divine in-ιition, with supernatural inspiration of few words and ιuch meaning, bringing to the front the evangelical ɔctrines and traditions of true worship, which, when ιey were clearly revealed to them from on high, they ere iluminated therewith, establishing the Faith they ad received from God.

Verily, the divine shepherds, being favoured ser-ιnts of God and all-honoured initiates of the divine reaching, having attained fully the experience of shep-erding, and having now most justly waxed wroth, in a ιdgment of truth, expelled from the perfection of the ʹhurch the devouring, destructive wolves, and stoned ιem with the sling-shot of the Spirit. Wherefore, they ʹll as unto death; for they were blighted with an incur-ble disease.

Glory, in the Eigth Tone

*W*HEN the rank of the holy Fathers flocked from the ends of the inhabited world, they believed in ιe Substance and one Nature of the Father, Son, and ƒoly Spirit, delivering plainly to the Church the mys-ʹry of discoursing in theology. Wherefore, in that we ιud them in faith, we beatify them, saying, What a ιvine army, ye God-inspired soldiers of the camp of ιe Lord, ye most brilliant luminaries in the supersensu-us firmament, ye impregnable towers of the mystical ion, ye scented flowers of paradise, the golden lights f the Word, the price and delight of the whole uni-erse, intercede ceaselessly for our souls.

Now: Thou hast transcended all blessings, etc.

3. THE MASS

[*The Typica and the Beatitudes. In the Eisodos, the Troparion r the Resurrection, the Fathers, and the Patron Saint of the church. ʹhen the Kontakion,* O undisputed intercessor of Christians, *etc. ɒ. 125); the Epistle and Gospel (p. 247).*

Koinonikon: The just shall be in everlasting remem
brance.   Alleluia.

12.   Probus, Tarachus, and Andronicus the Martyr
(2).

13.   Carpus, Papylus, Agathodorus, and Agathonice
the Martyrs (2).

14.   Nazarius, Gervasius, and Celsius, the Martyr
(2) ; and Cosmas the Poet (10).

15.   Lucian the Martyr among Priests (1).

16.   Longinus the Martyred Centurion (1).

17.   Andrew of Crisis (1) ; and Hosea the Prophe
(13).

18.   The Apostle Luke the Evangelist (12).

19.   Joel the Prophet (13), and Varus the Marty
(1).

20.   Artemius the Great Martyr (1), and Righteou
Gerasimus the New who died on the Island of Cephal
lenia in Greece in the year 1579 (1).

Troparion for the Righteous, in the First Tone

COME, let us believers laud the divine Gerasimu
newly revealed to us as a champion of the Ortho
dox, a God-mantled angel in the flesh and wonder
worker; for worthily did he receive of God the never
ending gift of healing, to heal the sick and to restore
to health the afflicted.   Wherefore, he overfloweth with
healing for those who honour him.

21.   Righteous Hilarion the Great (6).

22.   Abercius the Equal of the Apostles (9) ; and
the Seven Youths of Ephesus (2).

23.   James the Brother of the Lord and First Bishop
of Jerusalem.

Troparion, in the Fourth Tone

SINCE thou art a Disciple of the Lord, thou didst
receive the Gospel, O righteous one, and since thou
art a Martyr thou art never rejected, and since thou
art a brother of God, thou art privileged, and since thou

art a High Priest, it is thine to intercede. Wherefore, beseech thou Christ God to save our souls.

24. Arethas (al-Harith) the Martyr, and his Companions (3).

25. Marcianus and Martyrius the Martyrs (2).

26. THE GREAT AMONG THE MARTYRS, THE MYRRH-EXUDING DEMETRIUS: AND THE MEMORY OF THE GREAT EARTHQUAKE OF THE YEAR 741 IN CONSTANTINOPLE.

Typicon

❡ *If the Feast of St. Demetrius falleth on a Sunday then at Vespers, four are sung for the Resurrection and six for the Saint; Glory for the Saint and Now for the Resurrection, in the Tone in use; the Aposticha for the Resurrection; Glory for the Saint and Now for the Earthquake,* We implore thee, O all-holy Lady, *etc. (p. 319); the Troparion for the Resurrection, the Saint, and the Earthquake. And at Matins, the Troparia as at Vespers; the Kathismata for the Resurrection and the Saint. Then the Benedictions and the Anabathmoi, and the rest of the Matin Gospels, Service for the Resurrection. The Exaposteilarions for the Resurrection, the Saint, and our Lady; and in the Einos, four for the Resurrection and four for the Saint. Glory for the Saint, and Now,* Thou hast transcended, *etc. Then the Great Doxology; and* Today hath salvation come to the world, *etc. And in the Mass, the Epistle for the Saint and the Gospel for the Sunday. The Koinonikon,* Praise ye the Lord from the heavens, *etc.*

1. VESPERS

❡ *On* O Lord, to thee have I cried, *sing six Prosomia for the Saint, in the Eighth Tone.*

HOW strangely wondrous that today hath shone forth delight in heaven and on earth in memory of Demetrius the Martyr; for verily he is crowned with songs of praise from the angels and receiveth paeans from men. What a contender! Who fought the good fight, and through whom the deceitful enemy did fall, overcome for Christ.

How strangely wondrous that Demetrius doth ever shine in all quarters of the earth with rays of miracles more brilliant than the light of the sun, receiving light from the Light that is succeeded not by night, delight-

ing in the Light that setteth not, by whose illuminatio
the clouds of barbarism were cleared away, diseases di
persed, and the Satans vanquished.

How strangely wondrous that, when the thrice-bea
tified Demetrius was pierced for Christ's sake, he wa
ever manifest as a sword of double edge to his enemie
reaping therewith the haughtiness of his enemies, an
destroying the attacks of Satan. Wherefore, let u
acclaim him, saying, O Saint Demetrius, fold us i
thy protection, who celebrate thy ever-honoure
memory.

Thou hast become a tower of true worship, securel
founded on the rock of faith, uncloven by temptatior
and unshaken by tribulations; for when the waves o
atheism dashed against thee in a great torrent and ten
pest, they did not break down thine indomitable stead
fastness; for thou didst desire to be adorned with th
crown of martyrdom.

O fight-bearing Demetrius, having resembled in th
passion the enlivening Passion of Christ, thou didst re
ceive from him the gift of wonder-working. Wher
fore, thou dost save those who hasten to thee, savin
them from many tribulations; for thou art, O gloriou
one, well favoured by Christ, before whom thou stanc
est all the day, full of glory.

By the shedding of thy blood, O Demetrius, tho
didst come before the life-giving Christ, who shed h
own precious blood for thy sake, making thee a pa
taker in his glory and his kingdom, since thou did
prevail over the iniquitous one, annulling all his ev
wiles.

Glory, in the Sixth Tone

TODAY doth the general assembly of the fight-bea
ing one call us. Hasten ye, therefore, O feast-lov
ers, let us celebrate his memory in joy, saying, Hail
thee, who didst tear the robe of falsehood bravely, pu
ting on the Spirit. Hail to thee who didst annul th
spite of the law-transgressors by the power granted the

by God alone. Hail to thee, whose members were pierced, depicting in the spirit the blessed Passion of Christ. Wherefore, O Demetrius, the comeliness of strugglers, beseech him to save us from our invisible enemies, and to save our souls.

Now to our Lady, and, in the Same Tone, for the Earthquake

WE implore thee, O all-holy Lady, the help of the world and the hope of Christians, and seek of thee now, O good one, to plead with thy Son our Lord, O Theotokos, for us despairing sinners; for thou art able thus to do by using thy maternal privilege with him. Apprehend us, O undefiled one, apprehend us, mediate and save thy people from the pending threat. And for the compassion of thy mercies, turn not away those who praise thee.

¶*And after,* O resplendent Light, *etc., the Daily Prokeimenon, and the usual Petitions, the following Litiya in the Second Tone.*

By Germanus

CHRIST God, O wise Martyr Demetrius, did offer thy blameless soul unto abodes more sublime than earth; for thou didst become a contender for the Trinity, taking to the battlefield with fortitude adamantine as a diamond; and when thy pure side was pierced, O most venerable one, resembling him who was stretched on the Tree for the salvation of the whole world, thou didst receive the gift of miracle-working, granting mankind healing with bounty. Wherefore, as we celebrate today thy conveyance as is meet, we glorify the Lord who glorified thee.

¶*And in the Aposticha, the following three Idiomelons for the Earthquake, in the Second Tone.*

By Simeon

WHEN the earth trembled because of the fear ⸤
thy wrath, O Lord, the hills and mountains shoo⸤
Wherefore, as thou lookest down upon us with thi⸤
eye of compassion, be not indignant with us in th⸤
wrath, but have compassion on the creation of th⸤
hands, and deliver us from the fearful threat of eart⸤
quakes; for thou art good and the Lover of mankind.

Stichos: Thou hast moved the earth and thou ha⸤
troubled it.

Thou art awesome, O Lord; who can bear th⸤
just wrath? Who shall beseech thee, or who sha⸤
implore thee, O good One, on behalf of a despairi⸤
and sinful people? Verily, the heavenly myriads, th⸤
angels, principalities, powers, thrones, lords, the cher⸤
bim and seraphim, cry to thee for our sake, Holy! Hol⸤
Holy! art thou, O Lord. Turn not away, O good On⸤
from the works of thy hands; but by the compassion ⸤
thy mercies save a city threatened with danger.

Stichos: He looketh upon the earth, and maketh ⸤
tremble.

The people of Nineveh, because of their shortcon⸤
ings, heard of the threat of the earthquake. But ⸤
means of the sign of the whale, which made clear ⸤
them the Resurrection, they were called to repentan⸤
through Jonah. Wherefore, as thou didst hearken ⸤
them, hearken also to the cries of thy people, with th⸤
babes and beasts, and have compassion on us who a⸤
chastised. Pity us for the sake of thy third-day Resu⸤
rection, and have mercy upon us.

Glory to the Saint, in the Eighth Tone (by Anatoliu⸤

THY divine and blameless soul, O Demetrius ⸤
ever-constant memory, hath heavenly Jerusalem f⸤
its abode, whose walls were ordained by the hands ⸤
the invisible God. But thine all-honoured body, ha⸤
ing struggled exceedingly, hath on earth this renowne⸤

temple, a treasure-house of miracles that cannot be robbed, a healing for afflictions to which the afflicted flock and receive healing. Wherefore, O all-extolled one, preserve the city which doth magnify thee from the attacks of adversaries; for thou art favoured by Christ who did glorify thee.

Now to our Lady, in the Same Tone

O GROOMLESS Virgin and all-blameless, the Mother of the high God, who didst conceive God in the flesh in an inexplicable manner, receive thou the petitions of thy servants, who grantest to all purification of sins, and in accepting now our prayers, implore the salvation of us all.

Troparion to the Saint, in the Third Tone

VERILY, the inhabited world found thee a great succour in tribulations and a vanquisher of nations, O fight-bearing one. Wherefore, as thou didst demolish the arrogance of Lahosh, and on the battle-field didst hearten Nestor, beseech, O Saint, Christ God to grant us the Great Mercy. (*Repeat.*)

And for the Earthquake, in the Eighth Tone

O THOU who dost look upon the earth and make it tremble, deliver us from the fearful threat of earthquake, O Christ our God, and send upon us thy rich mercies by the intercessions of the Theotokos, thou only Lover of mankind.

2. MATINS

¶ *On* God the Lord hath appeared unto us, *etc., the Troparia as at Vespers. Then the following Kathismata.*

First Kathisma, in the Fourth Tone

THY memory, O glorious Martyr Demetrius, delighteth today the Church of Christ, and hath brought together all to extol thee in paeans, as is meet, since thou art a soldier in truth and a demolisher of thine enemies. Wherefore, by thine intercessions, O Godly-minded, deliver us from temptation.

Second Kathisma, in the Fifth Tone

WHEN the athlete of Christ bravely crushed by his undoubting faith the might of the usurpers, he did wrestle with the evil one in his struggle, and received the gift of miracles as a reward for his sufferings. Wherefore, he intercedeth for us with God to have mercy upon us.

Third Kathisma, in the Third Tone

O ALL-PITYING Martyr of the Lord, Demetrius, as we implore thee in faith, deliver us from the sundry oppressions which overtake us. Heal the wounds of our souls and bodies, and demolish the arrogance of our enemies, delivering, O Saint, our lives, that we may glorify thee.

❡ *Then after the Anabathmoi, From my youth, etc. (p. 50), sing the following Prokeimenon.*

Wonderful is God in his saints.

The Matin Gospel: from St. Luke (21:12-19)

THE Lord said to his disciples: Beware of men, for they will lay their hands on you, and persecute you, delivering you up to the synagogues and into prisons, dragging you before kings and governors, for my name's sake.

And it shall happen unto you for a testimony.

Lay it up therefore in your hearts, not to meditate before how you shall answer:

For I will give you a mouth and wisdom, which all your adversaries shall not be able to resist and gainsay.

And you shall be betrayed by your parents and brethren, and kinsmen and friends; and some of you they will put to death.

And you shall be hated by all men for my name's sake.

But a hair of your head shall not perish.

In your patience you shall possess your souls.

❡ *Then Psalm 50 (plain reading); Glory,* Through the intercessions of the fight-bearing, *etc; Now,* Through the intercessions of the Theotokos, *etc; and on* O merciful One, have mercy upon me, O God, *etc., sing the following Idiomelons, in the Second Tone.*

CHRIST God, O wise Martyr Demetrius, did offer thy blameless soul unto abodes more sublime than earth; for thou didst become a contender for the Trinity, taking to the battle-field with fortitude adamantine as a diamond; and when thy pure sude was pierced, O most venerable one, resembling hi mwho was stretched on the Tree for the salvation of the whole world, thou didst receive the gift of miracle-working, granting mankind healing with bounty. Wherefore, as we celebrate today thy conveyance as is meet, we glorify the Lord who glorified thee.

Katabasias: Open thou my mouth, etc.

Exaposteilarions

O MARTYR of Christ, Demetrius, as by divine grace thou didst crush aforetime the arrogance of Lahosh and the might of his chivalry, heartening in the battle-field the brave Nestor by the power of the Cross, also by thy petitions, O fight-bearing one, take thou my side always against satans and against soul-corrupting passions.

Cease not, O undefiled Virgin, to implore the Lord, incarnate from thy pure blood, for our sakes, that we thy servants may find grace and succour of good access in the day of tribulation, delivering the race of men by thy motherly intercession from the terrible threat of earthquake and from danger.

❡ *And in the Einos, the following Prosomia, in the Fifth Tone.*

HASTEN to us who beseech thee, O Martyr o
Christ, by thy pitying visitation. Deliver thos
who are in misery from the threatenings of usurpers and
from the vile folly of heretics, who persecute us like
naked captives ever driven from place to place, wan
dering in caves and mountains. Wherefore, O all-ex
tolled one, have compassion and grant us rest. Still the
tempest and put down the wrath that riseth against us
imploring God to grant the world the Great Mercy
(*Repeat.*)

Verily, thou hast been given unto us, O Demetrius, a
a fortified wall which feareth not the impacts of it
enemies, annulling the attacks of the Barbarians and al
the symptoms of disease. Wherefore, thou hast re
mained for thy city a firm pillar, an unshaken founda
tion, a keeper, a leader, and a contender therefor
Wherefore, since now it is encompassed by danger and
pressed hard by misery, by thine intercessions, O all
blessed one, save it, imploring Christ who granteth the
world the Great Mercy.

The rank of the fight-bearing ones, was revealed a
possessor of every virtue. Wherefore, according to
their worthiness, they have inherited the bliss and hap
piness of immortal life. And since thou, O Demetrius
worthy of praise, dost enjoy that life, exulting in thy
resemblance to Christ, and priding thyself that like him
thou wast pierced with a spear, therefore seek thou
ceaselessly, that we who honour thee, be delivered from
sufferings and severe hardships, beseeching him fer
vently who doth grant the world the Great Mercy.

Glory in the Fourth Tone

By Andrew the Jerusalemite

LET us honour the all-wise teacher, perfected among
the Martyrs, who by the spear did inherit the grace
of the saving side pierced by a spear, from which the
Saviour did cause to flow for us the waters of life and
incorruption, even Demetrius who finished his cours

f struggle by blood, sparkling with miracles unto all
he inhabited world, the emulator of the Master, the
over of the poor, the pitying leader of the people of
Thessalonica, and their champion in many severe hard-
hips.   Wherefore, as we celebrate his annual mem-
ry, we glorify Christ God who granteth through him
ealing to all.

Now to our Lady

O MOTHER of Christ God, who didst give birth to
the Creator of all, deliver thou us from our tribu-
ations, who cry to thee, Hail, O thou who alone art
he intercessor for our souls.

Then the Great Doxology, and the Troparion of the Saint.

3.   THE MASS

The Epistle: The just shall rejoice in the Lord.
Hearken, O Lord, to my voice.

Section from the Second Epistle of St. Paul to Timothy (2:1-10)

MY son Timohty: Be strong in the grace which is in
Christ Jesus.

And the things which thou hast heard of me by many
vitnesses, the same commend to faithful men, who shall
e fit to teach others also.

Labour as a good soldier of Christ Jesus.

No man, being a soldier to God, entangleth himself
vith secular business; that he may please him to whom
e hath engaged himself.

For he also that striveth for the mastery, is not
crowned, except he strive faithfully.

The husbandman, that laboureth, must first partake
of the fruits.

Understand what I say: for the Lord will give thee
n all things understanding.

Be mindful that the Lord Jesus Christ is risen agai
from the dead, of the seed of David, according to m
gospel.

Wherein I labour even unto bands, as an evildoer
but the word of God is not bound.

Therefore I endure all things for the sake of the elect
that they also may obtain the salvation, which is i
Christ Jesus with heavenly glory.

The Gospel: from St. John (15:17 to end; 16:1-2)

AND the Lord said to his disciples: These thing
I command you, that you love one another.

If the world hate you, know ye, that it hath hate
me before you.

If you had been of the world, the world would lov
its own: but because you are not of the world, but
have chosen you out of the world, therefore the worl
hateth you.

Remember my word that I said to you: The servan
is not greater than his master. If they have persecute
me, they will also persecute you: if they have kept m
word, they will keep yours also.

But all these things they will do to you for my name'
sake: because they know not him that sent me.

If I had not come, and spoken to them, they woul
not have sin; but now they have no excuse for their sin

He that hateth me, hateth my Father also.

If I had not done among them the works that no othe
man hath done, they would not have sin; but now the
have both seen and hated both me and my Father.

But that the word may be fulfilled which is writte
in their law: They hated me without cause.

But when the Paraclete cometh, whom I will sen
you from the Father, the Spirit of truth, who proceed
eth from the Father, he shall give testimony of me.

And you shall give testimony, because you are wit
me from the beginning.

Koinonikon: The just shall be in everlasting remembrance. Alleluia.

Kontakion of the Saint, in the Second Tone

VERILY, God, O Demetrius, who granted thee invincible power hath touched the Church with the live coal of thy blood streams, preserving the city unbreached; for it is established by thee.

27.   Nestor the Martyr (2).

28.   Terentius and Neonilea the Martyrs, and their seven children (2); and the Righteous Stephen the Sabbaite (1).

29.   Anastasia the Roman (4), and the Righteous Abraamius (8).

30.   Zenobius and Zenobia the Martyrs (2).

31.   Stachus, Apelles, Amplias, Urbanus, Narcíssus, and Aristobulus the Apostles (12).   Epimachus the Martyr (1).

III NOVEMBER

[Its days, 30; Hours of Day, 10; of Night, 14.]

1.   The Wonder-working and Unmercenary Saints, Cosmas and Damian.

Troparion, in the Third Tone

O YE silver-hating, wonder-working saints, visit our sicknesses.   Freely received ye, freely give unto us.

2.   Acindynus and his Companions the Martyrs (2).

3.   The Dedication of St. George's Temple in Lydia; Acepsimas, Joseph, and Aethelas the Martyrs (2).

4.   The two Martyrs Ioannicius the Great Righteous One (6); Nicander the Bishop, and Hermeus the Priest (5).

5.   Galaction and Episteme the Martyrs (2).

6.   Paul the Confessor, Archibishop of Constantinople (5).

7. The Thirty-three Martyrs of Melitene (2); Lazarus the Righteous Wonder-worker (6).

8. INCLUSIVE FEAST FOR THE ARCHANGELS MICHAEL, GABRIEL, RAPHAEL, AND THE REST OF THE INCORPORALS.

Typicon

⁋ *If this Feast falleth on a Sunday, then the order is the same as on the Feast of St. Demetrius on October twenty-sixth, to which refer.*

1. VESPERS

⁋ *On* O Lord, to thee have I cried, *etc., sing the following six Prosomia, in the Fourth Tone.*

AS thou hast been manifested standing all resplendent, before the triluminary Godhead, O Michael leader of hosts, thou dost shout rejoicing with the powers on high, Holy Father! Holy coëternal Word! Holy, Holy Spirit! one Glory and Sovereignty, one Nature, one Godhead, and one Power.

Thou art of fiery appearance and of wondrous beauty, O Archangel Michael, traversing the spaces with thine immortal nature, fulfilling the commands of the All-creator, and known as powerful by thy might. Verily, thou hast made thy temple a fount of healing, honoured by thy sanctified call.

O Lord the Word, who makest thine angels spirits, as it is written, and thy ministers flames of fire, thou hast manifested Michael, the prince of hosts among thy myriad archangels, as a leader submitting to thy commands, and raising his voice unto thy glory with the thrice-holy praise.

Verily, the Intelligence before the ages hath appointed thee, by divine partaking, a second light lighting the whole universe, and revealing to us the truly divine mystery, which is from eternity, namely that the Bodiless shall be incarnate in a virgin womb and become Man to save man.

Standing as thou dost before the throne of the tri-
uminary Trinity, O Gabriel, leader of hosts, and shin-
ng with the abundance of divine illumination emanat-
ng ceaselessly therefrom, deliver thou from the stark
larkness of passion those who joyfully stand in ranks
ɔn earth extolling thee. Delight them by illumination,
Ɔ intercessor for our souls.

Demolish, O Gabriel, leader of hosts the attacks of
ɪeretics, rising constantly against thy fold. Heal the
livision of thy Church; still the tempest of countless
emptations, and deliver from hardships and calamities
ɪhose who eagerly celebrate thy memory, who hasten to
ɪhe shadow of thy protection, O intercessor for our
ɪouls.

Glory, in the Sixth Tone

R EJOICE with us, all ye princes of the ranks of
angels; for your leader and our great champion,
ɪhe great prince of hosts, is today seen sanctified in a
ɪtrange manner in his noble temple. Wherefore, it is
ɪight and meet that we laud him, crying, Protect us
ɔy the shadow of thy wings, O Michael the great arch-
ɪngel.

Now to our Lady, in the Same Tone

R EJOICE with us, all ye ranks of virgins; for she
who is an intercessor and mediatrix, a great shelter
ɪnd refuge, doth on this day console the sorrowful with
ɪer divine and venerable providence. Wherefore, it is
ɪneet that we praise her, crying, Protect us, O pure
Lady and Theotokos, with thy divine intercessions.

¶And after the Daily Prokeimenon and the usual Petitions, the fol-
lowing Litiya, in the Fourth Tone.

T HE cherubim, O Christ God, praise thee with fiery
lips, and with immaterial mouths the ranks of archangels do glorify thee. Yea, Michael, the prince of the
hosts on high untiringly doth offer paeans to thy glory;

for he it is who illuminated us that we might form a brilliant assembly and sing wtih early lips, as is meet, the thrice-holy praise; for verily all have been filled with thy praise, and through it thou dost grant the world the Great **Mercy.**

❧ *And in the Aposticha, the following Prosomia in the First Tone.*

COME, ye who hold in the world an angelic celebration, let us raise our voices in praise unto God sitting on the throne of glory, Holy the heavenly Father! Holy the coëternal Word! Holy the most Holy Spirit!

Stichos: Who maketh his angels spirits.

O Michael, the leader of hosts, who beholdeth things indescribable, since thou art preferred with great privilege to the heavenly ones, and standeth in glory before the unapproachable throne, we beseech thee to save by thine intercessions us who endure the hardships of tribulations and temptations.

Stichos: Bless the Lord, O my soul.

As thou art clearly the foremost of the incorporeal angels, O Michael, the leader of hosts, the minister of the divine Light, a witness and initiate thereof, save us who honour thee annually in true worship, praising thy faith in the Trinity.

Glory and Now, in the Eighth Tone

SINCE thou art preferred in rank, and an archangel, O leader of hosts, deliver, O glorious one, from every oppression, sorrow, sickness, and from heavy sins, those who laud thee humbly, and implore thee. And since thou art immaterial, thou dost verily behold him who is without matter, gleaming in the unapproachable light, the light of the glory of the Lord, who for love of mankind took flesh from the Virgin for our sakes, when he willed to save mankind.

Troparion, in the Fourth Tone

O YE foremost of the heavenly hosts, we who are unworthy, beseech you that by your petitions ye encompass us with the shadow of your immaterial glory, preserving us who kneel and cry ceaselessly, Deliver us from oppressions, since ye are the princes of the ranks of dominions on high.

2. Matins

First Kathisma, in the Fourth Tone

O PRINCE of hosts, of the incorporeal ministers standing before God, gleaming with yonder illuminations, delight and sanctify those who laud thee in faith, delivering them from every persecution of the enemy, granting a life of peace to kings and to all regions.

Second Kathisma, in the Fourth Tone

THE cherubim and seraphim of many eyes, O most merciful Christ, and the hosts of ministering angels, with the presidencies, the thrones, the lords, the angels, the dominions, and the principalities, implore thee, our Creator, God, and Master, turn not away from the beseeching of a sinful people.

Third Kathisma, in the Eighth Tone

YE two leaders of the heavenly angels, foremost in dread, exalted on thrones of divine glory, Michael and Gabriel, princes of hosts and ministers of the Master with all incorporals, by your constant intercessions for the sake of the world, seek for us remission of sins, and that we may find mercy and grace in the Day of Judgment.

Glory and Now to our Lady, in the Eighth Tone

O BLESSED and pure one, favoured of God, beseech ceaselessly for our sakes, with the dominions on high, the archangels and the rest of the incorporals,

him who for the compassion of his mercies was born
of thee, to grant us before the end remission and forgiveness of our sins, and correction of our ways, that
we may find mercy.

❦ *Then after the Anabathmoi,* From my youth, *etc.* (*p. 50*), *the following Prokeimenon is sung.*

Who makest thy angels spirits: and thy ministers a
burning fire. Bless the Lord, O my soul, my Lord and
my God.

The Matin Gospel: from St. Matthew (18:10-20)

THE Lord said to his disciples: See that you despise
not one of these little ones: for I say to you, that
their angels in heaven always see the face of my Father
who is in heaven.

For the Son of man is come to save that which was
lost.

What think you? If a man have an hundred sheep,
and one of them should go astray: doth he not leave the
ninety-nine in the mountains, and go to seek that which
is gone astray?

And if it so be that he find it: Amen I say to you, he
rejoiceth more for that, than for the ninety-nine that
went not astray.

Even so it is not the will of your Father who is in
heaven, that one of these little ones should perish.

But if thy brother shall offend against thee, go and
rebuke him between thee and him alone. If he shall
hear thee, thou shalt gain thy brother.

And if he will not hear thee, take with thee one or
two more: that in the mouth of two or three witnesses
every word may stand.

And if he will not hear them: tell the church. And
if he will not hear the church, let him be to thee as the
heathen and publican.

Amen I say to you, whatsoever you shall bind upon earth, shall be bound also in heaven; and whatsoever you shall loose upon earth, shall be loosed also in heaven.

Again I say to you, that if two of you shall consent upon earth, concerning any thing whatsoever they shall ask, it shall be done to them by my Father who is in heaven.

For where there are two or three gathered together in my name, there am I in the midst of them.

❡ *Then Psalm 50* (*plain reading*)*; Glory,* Through the intercessions of the incorporals, O merciful One, *etc; Now,* Through the intercessions of the Theotokos, *etc; then* O merciful One, have mercy upon me, O God, *etc; and the following Idiomelons, in the Second Tone.*

By Arsenius

O DIVINE incorporals, intelligential essences, surrounding as ye do, the immaterial, incorporeal throne, ye do sing with fiery lips the Trisagion to God the King, Holy God, the Eternal Father, Holy Mighty, the Son coëternal with him. Holy Immortal One, the consubstantial Spirit, glorified with the Father and the Son.

❡ *The Katabasias,* Open my mouth, *etc; and at the end of the First Ode, say,* And I shall rejoice in her entrance 'with gladness. *In the Third Ode, instead of* In thy divine glory, *say,* And in thy solemn entrance; *in the fifth,* In thy solemn entrance; for thou didst go into the interior of the Temple as an all-pure temple, establishing with safety all those who praise thee. *And in the Ninth, instead of* For the festivity of the Theotokos, *say* For the entrance of the Theotokos.

Exaposteilarions

O DIVINE prince of hosts, verily God the Creator hath revealed thee a champion and a ruler over mankind, an honourable distributor. He hath honoured thee with glory in an ineffable manner, that thou mayest ceaselessly raise thy voice with the paeans of the Trisagion,

O Archangel Michael whose countenance is like lightning, gleaming in an ineffable manner with the illuminations of the Trinity, of exceeding divine brilliancy, thou dost traverse the whole creation like lightning, fulfilling the divine command, watching over, preserving, and sheltering those who joyfully laud thee.

O Michael, leader of the divine hosts, of exceeding glory, thou hast been appointed by God as leader of the dominions, powers, archangels, angels, thrones, and principalities. Wherefore, since thou dost stand before the unapproachable throne, shelter, watch, preserve, and save all those who celebrate thy memory in faith, O prince of the world.

❡*And in the Einos, the following Prokeimena, in the First Tone.*

A S thou art the head of the leaders of the heavenly hosts, a strong defender, a preserver and keeper of mankind on earth, we extol thee faithfully, O Archangel Michael, beseeching thee to deliver us from every destructive pain. *(Repeat.)*

Today doth the prince of the ranks of divine powers call the ranks of men to come together and celebrate in their divine gathering a feast of delight, singing together to God the thrice-holy praise.

As we in faith seek refuge under the shadow of thy divine wings, O divine Intelligence, may the Archangel Michael, preserve us and shelter us our life long, and at the hour of death, be present with us, and in compassion help us all.

Glory, in the Fifth Tone

W HEREVER thy grace casteth its shadow, O leader of the angels, Michael, the power of Satan is driven away; for falling Lucifer could not bear to stand before thy light. Wherefore, we petition thee to extinguish by thy mediation his fiery darts rising against us, delivering us from his doubts, O archangel worthy of laudation.

Now, in the Same Tone

O VIRGIN Theotokos, it is meet for us believers to bless thee and glorify thee, O unshaken city, impregnable wall, secure intercessor, and refuge of our souls.

3. THE MASS

¶ *The Troparion for the Archangels, and the Patron Saint of the church; the Kontakion,* The all-pure temple, *etc.* (*p. 349*).

The Epistle

Who makest thine angels spirits.
Bless the Lord, O my soul.

Section from the Epistle of St. Paul to the Hebrews
(2:2-10)

BRETHREN: For if the word, spoken by angels, be steadfast, and every transgression and disobedience received a just recompense of reward,

How shall we escape if we neglect so great a salvation? which having begun to be declared by the Lord, was confirmed unto us by them that heard him.

God also bearing them witness by signs, and wonders, and divers miracles, and distributions of the Holy Spirit, according to his own will.

For God hath not subjected unto angels the world to come, whereof we speak.

But one in a certain place hath testified, saying: What is man, that thou art mindful of him: or the son of man, that thou visitest him?

Thou hast made him a little lower than the angels: thou hast crowned him with glory and honour, and hast set him over the works of thy hands:

Thou hast subjected all things under his feet. For in that he hath subjected all things to him, he left nothing not subject to him. But now we see not as yet all things subject to him.

But we see Jesus, who was made a little lower than the angels, for the suffering of death, crowned with glory and honour: that, through the grace of God, he might taste death for all.

For it became him, for whom are all things, and by whom are all things, who had brought many children into glory, to perfect the author of their salvation, by his passion.

The Gospel: from St. Luke (10:16-21)

THE Lord said: He that heareth you, heareth me; and he that despiseth you despiseth me; and he that despiseth me, despiseth him that sent me.

And the seventy-two returned with joy, saying: Lord, the devils also are subject to us in thy name.

And he said to them: I saw Satan like lightning falling from heaven.

Behold, I have given you power to tread upon serpents and scorpions, and upon all the power of the enemy: and nothing shall hurt you.

But yet rejoice not in this, that spirits are subject unto you; but rejoice in this, that your names are written in heaven.

In that same hour, he rejoiced in the Holy Spirit, and said: I confess to thee, O Father, Lord of heaven and earth, because thou hast hidden these things from the wise and prudent, and hast revealed them to little ones. Yea, Father, for so it hath seemed good in thy sight.

Koinonikon: Who makest thine angels spirits; and thy ministers a burning fire.

Kontakion, in the Second Tone

O YE two princes of the hosts of God, ministers of the divine glory, guides of mankind, and leaders of the incorporals, ask for us that which becometh us and the Great Mercy, since ye are the princes of the hosts of the incorporals.

9.   Onesiphorus and Porphyrius the Martyrs (2) ; and the Righteous Woman Matrona (8).

10.   Olympas and his Companions the Apostles (12) ; Orestes the Martyr (1).

11.   Menas, Victor, and Vincent (2) ; The Righteous Theodore the Studite (10).

12.   John the Merciful, Archbishop of Alexandria (9) ; the Righteous Nilus (6).

13.   John Chrysostom, the Archbishop of Constantinople.

Troparion, in the Eighth Tone

GRACE hath shone forth from thy mouth like fire, illuminating the inhabited world. Thou hast treasured for the world the treasures of silver-hating and revealed to us the sublimity of humility. Wherefore, O educator, by thy words, O John the golden-mouthed, intercede with Christ God to save our souls.

Kontakion, in the Sixth Tone

THOU hast received from heaven the divine grace, O all-blessed John the golden-mouthed, teaching us all with thine own lips to worship one God in three Persons. Wherefore, it is meet for us to extol thee; for thou ceasest not to be a teacher explaining divine things.

The Epistle (Heb. 7:26-28; 8: 1-2) and the Gospel: from St. John (10:9-16)

14.   Philip the Apostle, one of the Twelve (12).

15.   Gorias, Samonas, and Abibus the Martyrs (2). On this day beginneth the noble Fast of the Nativity.

16.   The Evangelist, Matthew the Apostle (12).

17.   Gregory the Wonder-worker, the Bishop of Neo-Caesarea (10).

18.   Plato and Romanus the Martyrs (2).

19.   Obadiah the Prophet (13) ; Barlaam the Martyr (1).

20. The Preparation for the Presentation of our Lady in the Temple; Gregory of Decapolis, and Proclus the Archbishop of Constantinople (11).

Troparion for the Preparation of the Presentation, in the Fourth Tone

NOW doth Anne precede and bequeath unto all joy instead of sorrow, by giving forth the fruit, the only ever-virgin, whom she offereth in the Temple of the Lord, fulfilling her vow, being verily the temple of the Word, and an undefiled Mother.

Kontakion, in the Fourth Tone

TODAY the whole world is filled with gladness on the brilliant Feast of the Theotokos, raising its voice and saying, This is she who is the heavenly tabernacle.

21. THE FEAST OF THE PRESENTATION OF OUR LADY THE THEOTOKOS IN THE TEMPLE.

Typicon

❧*If this Feast falleth on a Sunday, see the order for our Lady's Nativity on September eighth, except the Epistle and Gospel of the Mass which are those of the Feast.*

1. VESPERS

❧*After the Sunset Psalm, say three Psalms only, begining with, Blessed is the man, etc; then on O Lord, to thee have I cried, sing six Prosomia, the following three of which are in the First Tone.*

LET us believers exchange glad tidings, singing to the Lord with psalms and songs of praise, honouring his holy tabernacle, the living ark who contained the uncontainable Word; for in a supernatural manner is she offered to God as a babe.

And Zachariah the great High Priest receiveth her rejoicing since she is God's abode.

Today the living temple of holy glory, the glory of Christ our God, who alone is blessed and undefiled, is presented in the Mosaic Temple, to live in its holy precincts. Wherefore, Joachim and Anne rejoice now with her in spirit, and the ranks of virgins praise the Lord with songs honouring his Mother.

Thou art the preaching of the Prophets, O virgin Theotokos, the glory of the Apostles and pride of the Martyrs, the renewal of the whole race of earthly ones. For through thee we are reconciled to God. Wherefore, we honour thy coming to the Temple of the Lord, shouting unto thee and hailing thee with the angel, O most honoured one; for we are saved by thine intercessions.

And three other Prosomia, in the Fourth Tone

VERILY, the blameless saint entereth by the Holy Spirit to dwell in the Holy of Holies and to be nourished by the angel, who in truth shall be a most holy temple for our holy God. He it is who by dwelling in her hath sanctified all creation and deified the perishing nature of man.

Today the young maidens come forth joyfully, carrying their lamps before the supersensuous torch, and in a noble manner take her into the Holy of Holies, going before and foretelling the ineffable Ray which shall shine forth from her, lighting in the spirit those who sit in the darkness of folly.

With joy the all-extolled Anne cried to Zachariah, saying, Receive thou her of whom the Prophets of God did preach in the Spirit, and take her into the holy Temple to be brought up in purity that she may become a divine throne to the Lord of all, a palace, a couch, and a shining abode.

Glory and Now, in the Eighth Tone

SINCE thou art sanctified, O Lary, bride of God, having proceeded after thy birth to the Temple, to be brought up in the Holy of Holies, verily, Gabriel was sent to thee with food. And all the heavens were amazed at beholding the Holy Spirit dwelling in thee. Wherefore, O pure and spotless Theotokos, glorified in heaven and upon earth, save our race.

¶ *Then after the Daily Prokeimenon, the following Prophecies.*

First Reading: from the Book of Exodus (40:1-5; 9-11; 16; 34-35)

AND the Lord spoke to Moses saying:
The first month, the first day of the month, thou shalt set up the tabernacle of the testimony.

And shalt put the ark in it, and shalt let down the veil before it:

And thou shalt bring in the table, and set upon it the things that are commanded according to the rite. The candlestick shall stand with its lamps,

And the altar of gold whereon the incense is burnt, before the ark of the testimony. Thou shalt put the hanging in the entry of the tabernacle,

And thou shalt take the oil of unction and anoint the tabernacle with its vessels that they may be sanctified:

The altar of holocaust and all its vessels:

The laver with its foot: thou shalt consecrate all with the oil of unction, that they be most holy.

And Moses reared it up, and placed the boards and the sockets and the bars, and set up the pillars,

If at any time the cloud removed from the tabernacle, the children of Israel went forward by their troops:

If it hung over, they remained in the same place.

Second Reading: 3 Kings (7:51 and 8:1-11)

AND Solomon finished all the work that he made in the house of the Lord, and brought in the things that David his father had dedicated, the silver and the gold, and the vessels, and laid them up in the treasures of the house of the Lord,

Then all the ancients of Israel with the princes of the tribes, and the heads of the families of the children of Israel were assembled to king Solomon in Jerusalem: that they might carry the ark of the covenant of the Lord out of the city of David, that is, out of Sion.

And all Israel assembled themselves to king Solomon on the festival day in the month of Ethanim, the same is the seventh month.

And all the ancients of Israel came, and the priests took up the ark,

And carried the ark of the Lord, and the tabernacle of the covenant, and all the vessels of the sanctuary, that were in the tabernacle: and the priests and the Levites carried them.

And king Solomon, and all the multitude of Israel, that were assembled unto him went with him before the ark, and they sacrificed sheep and oxen that could not be counted or numbered.

And the priests brought in the ark of the covenant of the Lord into its place, into the oracle of the temple, into the holy of holies under the wings of the cherubims.

For the cherubims spread forth their wings over the place of the ark, and covered the ark, and the staves thereof above.

And whereas the staves stood out, the ends of them were seen without in the sanctuary before the oracle, but were not seen farther out, and there they have been unto this day.

Now in the ark there was nothing else but the two tables of stone, which Moses put there at Horeb, when the Lord made a covenant with the children of Israel, when they came out of the land of Egypt.

And it came to pass, when the priests were come out of the sanctuary, that a cloud filled the house of the Lord.

And the priests could not stand to minister because of the cloud: for the glory of the Lord had filled the house of the Lord.

Third Reading: Ezekiel (43:27 and 44:1-4)

THESE things doth the Lord our Lord say: And the days being expired, on the eighth day and thenceforward, the priests shall offer your holocausts upon the Altar, and the peace offerings: and I will be pacified towards you, saith the Lord God.

And he brought me back to the way of the gate of the outward sanctuary, which looked towards the east, and it was shut.

And the Lord said to me: This gate shall be shut, it shall not be opened, and no man shall pass through it, because the Lord the God of Israel hath entered in by it, and it shall be shut

For the prince. The prince hmiself shall sit in it, to eat bread before the Lord: he shall enter in by the way of the porch of the gate, and shall go out by the same way.

. And he brought me by the way of the north gate, in the sight of the house: and I saw, and behold the glory of the Lord filled the house of the Lord.

℟*And after the usual Petitions, the following Litiya, in the Fifth Tone.*

By Laon

A JOYFUL day and an all-solemn feast hath broken forth, for she who before birth-giving was a Virgin and after birth-giving remained a Virgin, is presented today in the holy Temple. Wherefore, the old Zachariah, father of the Forerunner, rejoiceth and crieth with joy, Behold, she who is the hope of the sorrowful approacheth the Temple; for she is a saint, to be offered as a vow for the abode of the King of all. Let, therefore, Joachim the grandparent, and Anne be glad; for they have offered the blameless Lady as a heifer of three years. Wherefore, O ye mothers, rejoice, and ye virgins be joyful, and ye childless barren women exchange glad tidings; for the queen of all, pre-ordained, hath opened for us the kingdom of heaven, Rejoice, O ye nations, and be joyful.

❡*And in the Aposticha, the following Prosomia, in the Fifth Tone.*

VERILY, heaven and earth rejoice at beholding the supersensuous heaven, the only blameless Virgin, going forth to the divine abode to be brought up in a noble manner, of whom Zachariah cried in gladness, I open to thee the gate of the Temple, O gate of the Lord. Abide therein rejoicing; for I have known and do believe that the salvation of Israel shall come now openly, and from thee shall be born the Word of God who granteth the world the Great Mercy.

Stichos: And virgins shall come to the King.

Having openly enjoyed the divine grace, Anne, rejoicing, presenteth the pure ever-virgin one in the Temple, calling the maidens to present her, as they carry lamps, saying, Go forth, my daughter, to him who gave thee to me. Be thou to him a vow, an incense of sweet odour. Enter thou unto the veiled ones and learn the mysteries. Prepare thyself to become a delightful abode unto Jesus who granteth the world the Great Mercy.

Stichos: They shall come with gladness and rejoicing.

The all-holy Virgin, the temple that contained the Godhead, is placed in the Temple of God. And the maidens, going before her, carry lamps. Wherefore, her parents, the good husband and wife, Joachim and Anne, rejoice and exchange glad tidings; for they gave birth to the all-blameless one who gave birth to the Creator, who, as she resided in the heavenly abodes, fed by the angel's hand, was manifest as Mother of Christ, who granteth the world the Great Mercy.

Glory and Now, in the Sixth Tone

By Sergius the Jerusalemite

LET us, the assembly of believers, celebrate today spritualy in our gathering, and laud with true worship the virgin Maiden of God, the Theotokos, presented in the Temple of the Lord, forechosen from all generations for the abode of Christ, King of all. Wherefore, ye virgins, come forth, holding your lamps and honouring the solemn procession of the ever-virgin. And ye mothers, cast off all sorrow, and follow them, praising her who hath become a Theotokos, and a cause of joy to the world. Let us all, therefore, raise our voices with the angel, hailing the one who is full of grace, who ever intercedeth for our souls.

Troparion, in the Fourth Tone (three times)

TODAY the Virgin is the foreshadowing of the pleasure of God, and the beginning of the preaching of the salvation of mankind. Thou hast appeared in the Temple of God openly and hast gone before, preaching Christ to all. Let us shout with one thrilling voice, saying, Rejoice, O thou who art the fulfillment of the Creator's dispensation.

2. MATINS

First Kathisma, in the First Tone

VERILY, the fruit of Joachim and Anne the righteous, who nourished our lives, is offered to God in his holy Temple as a babe in the flesh, whom the noble Zachariah blessed. Wherefore, let us all bess her in faith; for she is the Mother of the Lord.

Second Kathisma, in the Fourth Tone

THOU wast consecrated to God before thou wast conceived. And since thou wast born on earth thou wast offered unto him, fulfilling purity by a promise.

And having been presented in purity from thy child-hood in the divine Temple with brilliant lamps, being thyself a divine temple in truth, thou wast revealed as a vessel of the unapproachable divine Light. Great, therefore, is thy procession in truth, O alone the ever-virgin bride of God.

Third Kathisma, in the Eighth Tone

LET David the writer of the Psalms rejoice; let Joa-chim and Anne exchange glad tidings; for from them hath appeared a holy-born child, Mary the light-bearing divine torch who, entering the Temple, was gladsome, and when the son of Barachia beheld her, he blessed her, lifting his voice with joy and crying, Rejoice, O miracle of the whole world.

❡ *Then the Anabathmoi,* From my youth, *etc.* (*p. 50*)*; and the following Prokeimenon.*

HEARKEN, O daughter, and see, and incline thine ear, and forget thy people and thy father's house. And the King shall greatly desire thy beauty.

Stichos: My heart overfloweth with a good word.

❡ *Then the Matin Gospel,* And Mary arose in those days *etc.* (*p. 50*)*; and Psalm 50 (plain reading); then Glory, in the Second Tone.*

TODAY the living temple, the temple of the great King, entereth into the Temple, to prepare a divine abode. Wherefore, O ye nations, rejoice.

Now (repeated)

❡ *Then,* O merciful One, have mercy upon me, O God, *etc; then the following Idiomelon is sung in the Fourth Tone.*

TODAY the God-containing temple, the Theotokos, shall be presented in the Temple of the Lord and be received by Zachariah. Today the Holy of Holies rejoiceth, and the ranks of angels celebrate mystically. Wherefore, today as we celebrate with them, we shout with Gabriel, Hail, O full of grace, the grace of the Lord who possesseth the Great Mercy is with thee.

¶ *Then the Katabasias of the Nativity,* Christ is born, glorify him, *etc. (p. 404); and instead of* O thou who art more honourable than the cherubim, *etc., sing the Ninth Ode with its Magnifications, in the Fourth Tone, as followeth.*

THE Angels beholding the entrance of the all-pure one were overtaken by surprise; how hath the Virgin entered into the Holy of Holies?

Since thou art a living temple of God, O Theotokos, no impure hand shall touch thee. But the lips of believers, let them ceaselessly laud thee, crying unto thee joyfully with the voice of the angels, Verily, O undefiled Virgin, thou art more exalted than all creatures.

The angels, beholding the entrance of the all-pure one, were overtaken by surprise: How hath she entered in a strange manner to the Holy of Holies?

Having attained the most resplendent, pure beauty of thy soul, O pure Theotokos, and the grace of God having been cast upon thee from heaven, thou shalt ever lighten with the eternal Light those who joyfully cry, O undefiled Virgin, verily, thou art more exalted than all creatures.

Let us, angels and men, honour the entrance of the Virgin; for she hath entered with glory into the Holy of Holies.

Thy miracles, O pure Theotokos, transcend words in sublimity; for I comprehend that thine is a body transcending description, not receptive to the flow of sin. Wherefore, I cry to thee gratefully, Thou O spotless Virgin, art verily more exalted than all creatures.

Rejoice with the saints, ye angels and ye virgins; exchange with each other glad tidings; for the Maiden of God hath entered into the Holy of Holies.

The Mosaic Law foretold thee by sign in a strange manner, O spotless one. Verily, thou art a tabernacle, a divine jar, a strange ark, a shelter, a rod, an everlasting temple, and a gate of God. Wherefore, it teacheth us to cry unto thee, O spotless Virgin, thou art verily more exalted than all creatures.

Another Canon, in the First Tone

MAGNIFY her, O my soul, who was presented in the Temple of the Lord, and was blessed by the hands of the priests.

Verily, the fruit of the promise did come forth from Joachim and Anne the righteous, namely Mary, the Maiden of God, who is presented as a child in the flesh, as an acceptable incense to the holy Temple, to live in the Sanctuary; for she is a saint.

Magnify her, O my soul, who was presented in the Temple of the Lord, and was blessed by the hands of the priests.

Let us praise her with songs who is a child by nature, and hath been manifest in a supernatural manner as Theotokos; for today she is offered to the Lord in the Mosaic Temple as a sweet incense and spiritual fruit to the righteous God.

Glory: Glorify, O my soul, the majesty of the triune Godhead, indivisible.

Let us glorify the inseparable Trinity, the three-personed Nature, the Glory indivisible, ceaselessly praised in heaven and on earth in one Godhead, bowing in true worship to the Father, Son, and Holy Spirit.

Now: Glorify, O my soul, her who is more honourable than the hosts on high.

O virgin Theotokos, pray for us, who faithfully seek refuge in thy compassion, who worship piously thy Son, the God of the world and its Lord, that he may deliver us from corruption and dangers, and from sundry temptations.

¶ *Then close with the Ninth Katabasia of the Nativity, with its Magnifications.*

Exaposteilarion (three times)

IN faith, let us extol Mary, the Maiden of God, whom the multitude of Prophets of old foretold, as being a jar, a rod, a tablet, and an unhewn mountain; for today doth she enter into the Holy of Holies to be brought up for the Lord.

¶ *And in the Einos, the following four Prosomia are sung in the First Tone.*

THE lamp-carrying virgins accompanied the ever-virgin one rejoicingly, truly prophesying in the spirit of the future; for the Theotokos, being the temple of God, was brought into the Temple from her child-hood in virginal glory.

The Theotokos, in truth, who is a holy promise and a very precious fruit, hath appeared unto the world as more exalted than all creatures. And being presented with true worship in the house of God, she fulfilleth the parental vow, preserved of the divine spirit.

Thou hast borne for the world, O Virgin, nourished by faith with heavenly bread in the Temple, the Bread of life, to whom thou wast formerly betrothed mystically by the Spirit; for thou a chosen temple, free of all blame, became a bride unto the Father.

Let the God-receiving Temple be opened, for Joachim hath taken her who is the temple of the King of all and his throne and placed her in glory therein, offering her as a Nazarite to the Lord who hath chosen her as a Mother to himself.

Glory and Now, in the Second Tone (By Laon)

TODAY the all-blameless Virgin is presented in the Temple for the abode of God, the King of all, the Nourisher of all our souls. Today the all-pure holiness doth enter into the Holy of Holies, as a three-year heifer. Wherefore, let us, like the angel, hail her, saying, Rejoice, O thou who alone art blessed among women.

❡ *The Great Doxology; the Troparion,* Today the Virgin is the foreshadowing, *etc.* (*p. 344*).

3. THE MASS

1. Through the intercessions of the Theotokos, O Saviour, save us.

2. Save us, O Son of God, thou who art wonderful in his saints, as we sing unto thee, Alleluia.

3. Today the Virgin who is the foreshadowing of the pleasure of God, etc.

Eisodikon: O come let us worship and fall down to Christ. Save us, O Son of God, who art wonderful in thy saints, as we sing to thee, Alleluia.

Kontakion, in the Fourth Tone

THE all-pure temple of the Saviour, the most precious bridal-chamber and Virgin, the treasure-house of the glory of God, today entered the Temple of the Lord, bringing with her the grace which is in the divine Spirit: whom also the angels of God do celebrate in song; for she is the heavenly tabernacle.

The Epistle: My soul doth magnify the Lord, for he hath regarded the humiliation of his handmaid.

Section from the Epistle of St. Paul to the Hebrews (9:1-7)

YE brethren: The former indeed had also justification of divine service, and a worldly sanctuary.

For there was a tabernacle made the first, wherein were the candlesticks, and the table, and the setting forth of loaves, which is called the holy.

And after the second veil, the tabernacle, which is called the holy of holies:

Having a golden censer, and the ark of the testament covered about on every part with gold, in which was a golden pot that had manna, and the rod of Aaron, that had blossomed, and the tables of the testament.

And over it were the cherubims of glory overshadowing the propitiatory: of which it is not needful to speak now particularly.

Now these things being thus ordered, into the first tabernacle the priests indeed always entered, accomplishing the offices of sacrifices.

But into the second, the high priest alone, once a year: not without blood, which he offereth for his own, and the people's ignorance.

The Gospel: from St. Luke

At that time: Jesus entered into a certain town, etc. (p. 292).

❡ *On Especially, the Hermos of the Ninth Ode with its Magnification, in the Fourth Tone, i.e.,* The angels, beholding the entrance of the all-pure one, *etc; and* 'Since thou art a living temple unto God, *etc. (p. 346).*

Koinonikon: I will take the cup of salvation, and call upon the Name of the Lord. Alleluia.

22. Philemon, Apphia, Archippus and Onesimus the Apostle (12); Cecilia the Martyr (4).

23. Gregory, Bishop of Agrigentum and Amphilochius, Bishop of Iconium (11).

24. Clement, Pope of Rome, and Peter, the Patriarch of Alexandria (11).

25. Catherine the Great Martyr, and Mercurius the Martyr (1); Leave-Taking of the Feast of our Lady's Presentation.

Troparion to St. Catherine, in the Fifth Tone

LET us extol the all-lauded bride of Christ, Catherine, the guardian of Sinai, who is our succour and our support; for by the power of the Spirit she silenced

brilliantly the nobility of liars. And now that she hath
been crowned as a Martyr, she seeketh for all the Great
Mercy.

Kontakion, in the Second Tone

FORM ye, O lovers of Martyrs, a solemn rank in a
divine manner, honouring Catherine the all-wise;
for she preached Christ on the battle-field, trampling
the serpent, ridiculing the knowledge of the eloquent.

*The Epistle for the Martyr: (Gal. 3:23 to end; 4:1-5);
and the Gospel: from St. Mark (5:24-34)*

26. Alypius the Stylite (see Sept. 1st for the Troparion of Simeon the Stylite (p. 385): Nikon the
Repentant (7).

27. James the Persian, the Great Martyr (1).

28. Stephen the Younger, the Righteous Martyr,
and Irenarchus the Martyr (2).

29. Paramonus and Philomenus the Martyrs (2).

30. Andrew the Apostle, the First called.

Troparion, in the Fourth Tone

SINCE thou wast first called among the Apostles, and
a brother of the head, implore, O Andrew, the Master of all to grant the inhabited world safety and our
souls the Great Mercy.

*The Epistle: (First Cor. 4:9-16) and the Gospel: from
St. John (1:35-51)*

IV DECEMBER

[Its Days, 31; Hours of Day, 9; of Night, 15]

1. Nahum the Prophet (13).

2. Habakkuk the Prophet (13).

3. Zephaniah the Prophet (13).

4. The Great Martyr Barbara, and the Righteous
John the Damascene (10).

Troparion to the Martyr, in the Fourth Tone

LET us honour the all-revered Saint Barbara; for she did demolish the gins of the adversary and escaped from them like a bird, by the help of the Cross as with a weapon.

Kontakion to the Righteous One, in the Fourth Tone

LET us praise with songs, O believers, the hymn-writer, the teacher of the Church, and its lamp, the revered John, contender against his enemies; for he did carry the weapon of the Cross of the Lord and therewith opposed all the error of the innovators; and inasmuch as he is a fervid intercessor with God, he granteth all the forgiveness of sins.

The Epistle: (Gal. 3:23; 4:1-5) and the Gospel: from St. Mark (5:24-34)

5. Sabas the Consecrated (6).

6. St. Nicholas the Wonder-Worker, Bishop of Myra in Lycia.

Typicon

¶*If this Feast falleth on a Sunday, then see the order of service as at the end of the Feast of Demetrius, on Oct. twenty-sixth.*

1. Vespers

¶*After the Sunset Psalm, recite three Psalms only, beginning with,* Blessed is the Man; *and the following eight Prosomia after the tune,* O Lord, to thee have I cried, *in the Second Tone.*

O SAINT Nicholas, Bishop of Christ, thou didst live after the sense in Myra, but didst truly appear as a sweet fragrance, having been anointed with supersensual ointment. Wherefore, thou dost scent those who everlastingly celebrate with faith and eagerness thy famous memory, delivering them, O father, from calamities, tribulations, and sorrows, by thine intercessions with the Lord (*Repeat*).

O Saint Nicholas, true servant of Christ, thou didst appear in truth a precious triumph to the faithful people in trials, as thy name implies; for, being called in every quarter, thou didst hasten warmly to the assistance of those who seek the shadow of thy protection. Wherefore, appearing to them in faith by day and by night, thou dost deliver them from trials and tribulations. (*Repeat.*)

Thou didst verily appear in a dream to Constantine the king with Ablabius, and having put them to fright thou didst address them, saying, Release at once from prison those in chains whom ye have arrested unjustly; for they are innocent of the law-defying murder; and if thou dost contradict me, O king, I shall call upon the Lord against thee. (*Repeat.*)

O glorious Saint Nicholas, the noble preacher of Christ, thou art a great and fervid helper of those in difficulties, of those who are on land, and of those who are at sea, all-compassionate, a precious intercessor for those who are far off and those who are near. Whereore, in our gathering we shout to thee to intercede with the Lord, that we be delivered from every tribulation. (*Repeat.*)

Glory, in the Sixth Tone

LET us come together, O feast-lovers, and praise in paeans the comeliness of Bishops, the pride of the fathers, and the fountain of miracles, the great helper of believers, saying, Rejoice, O watchman of the people of Myra, their revered leader and unshakeable pillar. Rejoice, O effulgent star, lighting the utmost corners of the world with miracles. Rejoice, O divine joy of the sorrowful, all-zealous champion of the oppressed. Wherefore, now, O all-beatified Nicholas, thou dost still intercede with Christ God on behalf of those who ever honour faithfully and eagerly thine all-festive and joyful memory.

Now, in the Same Tone

O CAVERN, make ready; for the ewe doth come bearing Christ in embryo; O manger receive him who by his word undid the bestial works of us earthly men. O shepherds watch and bear witness to the awesome wonder. And, O Magi, who come from Persia bring forth to the King gold, frankincense and myrrh for the Lord hath appeared from a virgin Mother whose Mother did bow to him as a servant, addressing him in her bosom, saying, How wast thou seeded in me and how didst thou grow in me, my God and my Deliverer?

¶ And after the Daily Prokeimenon, and usual Petitions, the following Litiya, in the Eighth Tone.

O FATHER Nicholas, righteous Bishop, the fruits of the virtue of thy courage have delighted the hearts of believers; for who could hear of thine unlimited condescension and wonder not at thy patience and cheerfulness towards the poor; thy compassion over the sorrowful? For thou didst teach all concerning God as is meet. Wherefore, now, having been crowned with an unfading crown, intercede for our souls.

¶ And in the Aposticha, the following Prosomia, in the Fifth Tone

REJOICE, O honoured head, a pure receptacle for virtues, a noble canon for the divine Priesthood the great shepherd and all-illuminating torch, the bearer of the sign of triumph, who breaketh his bread in compassion with beggars, listener to the petitions of the sick, all-responsive deliverer, watchman of salvation to all who celebrate in faith thy renowned memory Wherefore, all-beatified, beseech Christ to send us the Great Mercy.

Stichos: Precious in the sight of the Lord is the death of his saint.

Rejoice, O pure mind, O undefiled dwelling-place of the Trinity and pillar of the Church, steadfastness of

the faithful, and succour of the distressed; O star the
rays of whose good and accepted petitions ever disperse
the darkness of temptation and sorrow, calm haven of
those who are encompassed by the tempests of life, who
seeking refuge in thee are saved. Beseech thou, therefore, Christ to grant our souls the Great Mercy.

Stichos: Thy priests, O Lord, put on justice.

Rejoice, O thou who, filled with divine zeal, didst
deliver by thine awesome presence and by thine appearance in a dream, those who were awaiting the unjust
death through evil slander. O fountain in Myra, overflowing bountifully with spices, soul-satisfying, driving
away the stench of passions; O sword cutting down the
tares of error, winnower winnowing the straw teachings
of Arius, beseech thou Christ to send our souls the
Great Mercy.

Glory, in the Sixth Tone

O MAN of God, the faithful servant and attendant
of the Lord; O man of desires, the chosen vessel;
O pillar and foundation of the Church; O heir of the
kingdom, cease not thy crying to the Lord for our sakes.

Now, for the Preparation, in the Same Tone

O GROOMLESS Virgin, whence comest thou?
Who gave thee birth, and who is thy mother?
How carriest thou the Creator in thine arms? How
was thy womb unspoiled? Wherefore, O all-pure one,
we behold in thee great wonders, dread mysteries which
were fulfilled on earth. And we shall proceed to prepare for thee that which is meet from the cave of earth.
And the heavens we ask to give the stars. And the Magi
come from the ends of the east and the west to behold
the Salvation of mankind, a suckling babe.

Troparion, in the Fourth Tone

THY work of justice did show thee to thy congregation a canon of faith, the likeness of humility, a
teacher of abstinence, O Father, Bishop Nicholas.

Wherefore, by humility thou didst achieve exaltation, and by meekness, richness. Intercede, therefore, with Christ to save our souls.

2. MATINS

First Kathisma, in the First Tone

O WISE Nicholas, thou dost shine on earth with the rays of wonders. Thou dost move every tongue to glorify and praise him who did honour thee on earth. Therefore, beseech him to deliver from every difficulty those who faithfully and earnestly celebrate thy memory, O elect among the Fathers.

Second Kathisma, in the Fourth Tone

O RIGHTEOUS Father, the beatified, thou dost fight for believers, defending and guarding them and delivering them openly from every sorrow, O glory of Bishops and their pride.

Third Kathisma, in the Fourth Tone

THOU hast become, O Nicholas, an all-zealous defender of the Church of Christ, refuting with grace the blasphemous beliefs of heretics. Thou didst appear in all states a canon of Orthodoxy, interceding in behalf of all who follow thy divine teachings and counsels.

¶ *Then after the Anabathmoi, From my youth, etc (p. 50), sing the following Prokeimenon.*

Precious in the sight of the Lord is the death of his saint. What shall we render to the Lord for all the things that he hath rendered to us.

The Matin Gospel: from St. John (10:1-9)

SAID the Lord to those of the Jews who came unto him: I say unto you: he that entereth not by the door into the sheepfold, but climbeth up another way, the same is a thief and robber.

But he that entereth in by the door is the shepherd of
he sheep.

To him the porter openeth; and the sheep hear his
roice: and he calleth his own sheep by name, and leadeth them out.

And when he putteth forth his own sheep, he goeth
before them, and the sheep follow him: for they know
his voice.

But a stranger will they not follow, but will flee from
him; for they know not the voice of strangers.

This proverb spoke Jesus unto them; but they understood not what he spoke unto them.

Jesus therefore said to them again, I say unto you, I
am the door of the sheep.

All that ever came before me are thieves and robbers: but the sheep heard them not.

I am the door: by me if any man enter in, he shall
be saved, and shall go in and out, and shall find pastures.

*Then immediately Psalm 50, (plain reading); Glory, Through
he intercessions of Bishop Nicholas, O merciful One, etc; Now
Through the intercessions of the Theotokos, etc; O merciful One,
have mercy upon me, O God, etc; and the following Idiomelon, in
he Sixth Tone.*

WELL done, O good and faithful servant; well
done, O labourer in the field of Christ. Thou
didst bear the heat of the day; thou didst multiply the
talent delivered to thee; nor didst thou envy those who
came after thee. Wherefore, the gate of heaven was
opened to thee. Enter thou into the joy of thy Lord.
And intercede, O Saint Nicholas, for us.

Katabasias: Christ is born, glorify him, etc.

Exaposteilarions

LET us all extol Bishop Nicholas, the great head of
shepherds and leader of Myra; for he saved many
who were condemned to die unjustly, and appearing to
the king and Ablabius in a dream, refuted the unjust
decree.

O Bishop Nicholas, the Lord hath honoured thee greatly with wonders, in life and after death; for who calls on thy most holy Name, albeit in utmost faith, and is not granted his desire at once, finding in thee a warm defender?

O thou who didst give birth to Christ, Wisdom personified, Word of transcendent essence and Physician of all, heal, O Virgin, the bruises of my soul, and its chronic, bitter wounds, and remove from my heart unseemly thoughts.

❡*And in the Einos, the following Prosomia, in the First Tone.*

O THRICE-BEATIFIED Nicholas, having hovered about the blossoms of the Church like a bird from angelic nests, thou dost cry out always unto God for all of us who are in the straits of tribulations and temptations, delivering us by thine intercessions.

O God-mantled Father, thou hast made the comeliness of the priestly vestments shine with more splendour by practical virtues. Therefore, O minister of mysteries, thou dost perform for us miraculous wonders of everlasting memory, delivering us from difficulties.

O most noble Saint, having circled around the goodly things not vouchsafed to sight, thou didst comprehend that awesome glory, the glory of the saints. Wherefore, by thy heavenly sayings thou dost tell us of those deathless visions.

As thou didst stand in a dream, O Father, before the king of true worship, rescuing the prisoners from death, intercede thou ceaselessly that we who extol thee as is meet may now, through thy prayers, be delivered from trials, tribulations, and sufferings.

Glory, in the Fifth Tone

LET us blow the trumpets of praise. Let us be happy in the feast, rejoicing in the exchange of glad tidings on the day of the God-mantled one. Let kings and leaders hasten to extol him who appeared to the king in a dream in a terrible manner, convincing him to release the three generals arrested without cause. And let us shepherds and teachers come together and extol the shepherds, emulating the Good Shepherd in zeal. Let the sick extol the physician; those in tribulation, the rescuer; sinners, the intercessor; the poor, the treasure; the sorrowful, the comforter; travellers, the companion; and those at sea, the pilot; and let us all eulogize the great Bishop, who respondeth warmly everywhere, saying, O most holy Nicholas, apprehend us and rescue us from the present distress, and save thy congregation by thy pleadings.

Now to our Lady, in the Same Tone

LET us blow the trumpets of praise; for the queen of all, the virgin Mother, hath bent down from on high, whence looking, she crowneth with blessings those who extol her. Let kings and leaders hasten together with praises to the queen who gave birth to the King, who, because of his love to mankind, was pleased to release those who had been condemned to death, O ye shepherds and teachers, let us come together and praise the Mother exceeding pure, the Mother of the Good Shepherd, the light-house shining with gold, the cloud enwrapped with light, who is more spacious than the heavens, the living tabernacle, throne of the Master with the fiery likeness, the golden jar of manna, the sealed door of the Word, the refuge of all Christians, eulogizing her with God-inspired songs, saying, O palace of the Word, make us worthy, us wretched ones, of the kingdom of heaven; for through thee nothing is impossible.

℞ *Then the Great Doxology; and the Troparion of the Saint.*

3. THE MASS

℞ *Troparion for the Saint and the Patron Saint of the church; and the Preparatory Kontakion,* Today the Virgin cometh, *etc. (p. 365).*

The Epistle: Precious in the sight of the Lord is the death of his saint. What shall we render to the Lord?

Selection from the Epistle of St. Paul to the Hebrews
(13:17-21)

YE brethren: Obey your prelates, and be subject to
them. For they watch as being to render an account
of our souls; that they may do this with joy, and not
with grief. For this is not expedient for you.

Pray for us. For we trust we have a good conscience,
being willing to behave ourselves well in all things.

And I beseech you the more to do this, that I may
be restored to you the sooner.

And may the God of Peace, who brought again from
the dead the great pastor of the sheep, our Lord Jesus
Christ, in the blood of the everlasting testament.

Fit you in all goodness, that you may do his will;
doing in you that which is well pleasing in his sight,
through Jesus Christ, to whom is glory for ever and
ever. Amen.

The Gospel: from St. Luke (6:17-23)

AND it came to pass that Jesus stood in a plain place,
and the company of his disciples, and a very great
multitude of people from all Judæa and Jerusalem, and
the sea coast both of Tyre and Sidon.

Who were come to hear him, and to be healed of their
diseases. And they that were troubled with unclean
spirits, were cured.

And all the multitude sought to touch him, for virtue went out from him, and healed all.

And he, lifting up his eyes on his disciples, said:
Blessed are ye poor, for yours is the kingdom of God.

Blessed are ye that hunger now for you shall be filled.
Blessed are ye that weep, for you shall laugh.

Blessed shall you be when men shall hate you, and
when they shall separate you, and shall reproach you,
and cast out your name as evil, for the Son of Man's
sake.

Be glad in that day and rejoice; for behold, your reward is great in heaven. For according to these things did their fathers to the prophets.

Koinonikon: The just shall be in everlasting remembrance. Alleluia.

Kontakion to the Saint, in the Third Tone

THOU didst appear a priest in Myra, O saint, for having fulfilled the Gospel of Christ, O righteous one, thou didst lay down thy life for thy people, and rescued the innocent from death. Wherefore, thou wast sanctified, being a great initiate of the grace of God.

7. Ambrose, Bishop of Milan (9).

8. Patapius the Righteous (8).

9. The Conception of St. Anne, the Mother of the Theotokos.

Troparion, in the Fourth Tone

TODAY have the bonds of barrenness been loosened, God, having heard the prayers of Joachim and Anne, promised them openly that they should give birth, against hope, to the Maiden of God, from whom he, the infinite One was to be born, becoming man, commanding the angel to shout to her, Hail, O full of grace, the Lord be with thee.

Kontakion, in the Fourth Tone

TODAY the universe celebrateth the conception of Anne which is from God; for she hath given birth to her who gave birth to the Word, in an ineffable manner.

The Epistle: (Galatians 4:22-27) and the Gospel: from St. Luke (8:16-21)

10. Mena the sweet-voiced, Hermogenes, and Eugraphus the Martyrs (2).

11. Daniel the Righteous Stylite. (See Troparion of Simeon the Stylite on Sept. 1st, p. 281.)

SUNDAY OF THE HOLY FOREFATHERS

From December 11th-17th

❡*On* O Lord, to thee have I cried, *are sung six for the Resurrection and four for the Forefathers, in the Eighth Tone.*

A S we celebrate today the memory of the forefathers, let us, O believers, praise in faith Christ the Deliverer who magnified them among all nations; the Lord who doeth strange wonders; for he is precious and mighty, who showeth us through them a staff of strength. She is Mary the undefiled Maiden of God who alone knew no man, from whom proceeded Christ the Blossom, budding life for all, the everlasting Bliss and eternal Salvation.

O Master, who didst rescue the holy youths from fire and Daniel from the mouths of the lions, and didst bless Abraham, Isaac thy servant, and Jacob his son, O thou who wast willing to become, like us, of their seed, that thou mightest save our forefathers who fell of old, and to be crucified and buried in order to crush the bonds of death and raise the dead from eternity, we worship, O Christ, thine eternal kingdom.

The youths of God walking forth amidst the flame, rejoicing in the dew of the Spirit as though they were in a garden, did go before and foreshadow therein the mystery of the Trinity and the Incarnation of Christ. And in that they were wise men they quenched by faith the power of fire. And as for Daniel the righteous, he did appear closing the mouths of the lions. Wherefore, by their beseechings we plead with thee, O Saviour and Lover of mankind, to deliver us from the everlasting and unquenchable fire, and to make us worthy to receive thy heavenly kingdom.

Thy holy youths, O Christ, when they were in the furnace of fire, as though in dew, did go before and foreshadow mystically thy coming from the Virgin, which hath illuminated us without burning. And righteous Daniel, wonderful among Prophets, when he went before and explained plainly thy divine Second Coming, did shout, saying, And I saw the thrones placed, and the Judge sat, and the river of fire came before him. Wherefore, by their beseechings, O Master, deliver us.

Glory, in the Sixth Tone

LET us, O believers, extol today all the fathers before the law, Abraham the friend of God, Isaac born after the promise, Jacob with the twelve heads of the tribes, David the most meek, and Daniel the Prophet of desires, honouring with them the three youths who changed the furnace to a dewy place, asking forgiveness of Christ God, glorified in his saints.

Now to our Lady, in the Tone in Use

❡ *The Aposticha for the Resurrection.*

Glory, in the Third Tone

COME ye feast-lovers, let us extol with hymns the assembly of the forefathers, Adam the first father, Enoch, Noah, and Melchizedek, Abraham, Isaac, and Jacob; and those after the law—Moses, Aaron, Joshua, and Samuel; and with them Isaiah, Jeremiah, Ezekiel, Daniel, and the twelve Prophets, with Elijah and Elisha, and all the rest; and Zachariah, the Baptist, and those who preached Christ, the Life and Resurrection of our race.

❡ *Now, Theotokion of the Third Tone,* Thou didst verily conceive by the Holy Spirit, *etc.* (*p. 154*).

❡ *Troparion for the Resurrection; and Glory and Now for the forefathers, in the Fourth Tone.*

THOU hast justified by faith the ancient forefathers and through them thou hast gone before and betrothed unto thyself the Church of the Gentiles. Let the saints, therefore, take pride in glory; for from their seed sprouted forth a noble fruit, and she it was who gave birth to thee without seed. Wherefore, by their pleadings, O Christ God, save our souls.

2. MATINS

The Exaposteilarions for the Resurrection, then the Forefathers

LET us come together, O lovers of the Fathers, rejoicing in the memory of the Fathers, praising as is meet Abraham, Isaac, and Jacob from whom Christ was seen to come in the flesh for the abundance of his compassion.

Let us laud Adam and Abel, Seth and Enos, Enoch, Noah, Abraham, Isaac, and Jacob; Moses, Job, and Aaron; Eliezar, Joshua, Barak, Samson, Jephtæ, David, and Solomon.

❡*And in the Einos, sing four for the Resurrection and four for the Forefathers, in the Second Tone.*

LET us all celebrate the memory of the revered forefathers, extolling their lives by which they were made great. (*Repeat.*)

Verily, the youths did put down the power of fire sitting in the midst of the furnace and praising God the Almighty.

And Daniel the Prophet when he was locked in the den, living with the beasts, did appear safe, not harmed by their mischief.

Glory, in the Seventh Tone

COME, let us all celebrate the anniversary of their memory, the anniversary of the fathers before the law—Abraham and those with him. Let us honour meetly the tribe of Judah, and praise the youths who were in Babylon, who put down the flames of the furnace; for they foreshadowed the Trinity, and with them Daniel. And holding steadfastly the foresayings of the

Prophet, let us shout with a loud voice with Isaiah, saying, Behold the Virgin shall conceive in the womb and give birth to a son, Emmanuel, which being interpreted is, God with us.

❦ *Now,* Thou hast transcended, *etc; the Great Doxology; and the rest of the Sunday services.*

3. THE MASS

❦ *Troparion for the Resurrection, the Forefathers, and the Patron Saint of the church; and the Kontakion for the Preparation, in the Third Tone.*

TODAY the Virgin cometh to the cave to give birth in an ineffable manner to the Word before the ages. Rejoice, therefore, O universe, when thou hearest, and glorify with the angels and shepherds him who shall appear by his own will as a new babe, being God before the ages.

❦ *The Epistle.* Ye brethren: When Christ, who is our life (*p. 267*); *the Gospel,* The Lord spake this parable: A certain man made a great supper, *etc.* (*p. 266*).

❦ *On Especially, sing,* It is truly meet, *etc; and the Koinonikon,* Praise ye the Lord, *etc.*

Kontakion to the Forefathers, in the Second Tone

O THRICE beatified youths, ye worshipped not the idol made by hand. But when ye put on the incomprehensible armour of the Essence, ye were glorified in the strife of fire; for having stood in the midst of the unbearable flame, ye called upon God, saying, Hasten O compassionate One to our help, since thou art merciful; for thou art mighty to do what thou willest

12. Spiridion the Righteous Wonder-worker.

Troparion, in the First Tone

THOU didst appear as a contender for the first council and a wonder-worker, O our Father, God-mantled Spiridion. Therefore, thou didst converse with the dead woman in the tomb and didst convert a serpent into gold. And at thy chanting of the holy prayers the angels did accompany-thee in the service. O most pure one, glory be to him who glorified thee; glory be to him who crowned thee; glory be to him who worketh healing for all through thee.

Kontakion, in the Second Tone

O MOST honourable, when thou wast wounded by the love of Christ, elevating thy mind to the rays of the Spirit, thou who seekest refuge in God by actual observation found thy vocation, becoming a divine altar, and receiving for all divine illumination.

The Epistle: Ephesians (5:8-19) and the Gospel: from St. John (10:9-16)

13. Eustratius the Martyr and his Companions; and Lucy the Martyr (12).

14. Thyrsus the Martyr, and his Companions (2).

15. Eleutherius the Martyr, Bishop of Illyricum (5).

16. Haggai the Prophet (1); and Theophano the Queen (8).

17. Daniel the Prophet, and the three Youths, Ananias, Azarias, and Misael.

Troparion, in the Second Tone

GREAT are the accomplishments of faith; for the three holy youths rejoiced in the fountain of flames as thou at waters of rest. And the Prophet Daniel appeared a shepherd to the lions as though they were sheep. Wherefore, by their pleadings, O Christ God, have mercy upon us.

Kontakion to the Three Youths, in the Second Tone

O thrice-beatified youths, etc. (p. 365).

18. Sebastian the Martyr, and his Companions (2).

THE SUNDAY BEFORE CHRISTMAS, KNOWN AS THE SUNDAY OF GENEALOGY

From December 18th-24th

Typicon

¶ *If this Sunday falleth before the twentieth, then on* O Lord to thee have I cried, *six are chanted for the Resurrection and four for the Fathers. And if it falleth between the twentieth and the twenty-third, four are chanted for the Resurrection, three for the Preparation, and three to the Fathers. And if on the twenty-fourth, then four for the Fathers, and four for the Preparation. The following Glory and Now, according to the Tone in use. On the twenty-fourth,* O cavern make ready. *etc.* (*p. 354*).

1. VESPERS

Idiomelons of the Preparation, in the First Tone

LET us go before, O nations, and celebrate the Nativity of Christ. And lifting our minds to Bethlehem, let us ascend with our consciences, beholding with the thoughts of our hearts, the Virgin approaching, giving birth in the cave to the Lord of all, our God, whose stupendous wonders Joseph did behold, while at the time he thought he was beholding a man wrapped in swaddling clothes, but was assured from his works that he was the true God, granting our souls the Great Mercy.

Let us go before, O nations, and celebrate the Nativity of Christ; and lifting our minds to Bethlehem, let us ascend with our consciences and behold the great Mystery that is in the cave; for Eden hath verily been opened by the coming forth of God from the spotless Virgin, perfect in Divinity and perfect in Humanity. Wherefore, let us shout forth, Holy God, Eternal Father, Holy Mighty, the Incarnate Son, Holy Immortal One, the Comforting Spirit, O Holy Trinity, glory to thee.

Listen, O heaven, and give ear, O earth; for behold, the Son, the Word of the Father, cometh to be born of a Maiden that hath not known man. Wherefore, by the pleasure of him who gave him birth without passion, and by the assistance of the Holy Spirit, O Bethlehem, make ready, and, O Eden, open thou thy gates; for he who is, shall be that which hath not been; and the Maker of the entire creation shall become the Grantor of Great Mercy to the world.

¶*And to the Fathers; the three Prosomia,* As we celebrate today the memory of the Forefathers, *etc.;* O Master, who didst rescue the holy youths, *etc;* The youths of God walking forth in the midst, *etc.* (*p. 362*).

Glory, in the Sixth Tone

VERILY, Daniel, the man of desires, when he saw thee, O Lord, a Stone cut out without hands, did forecall thee a babe born without seed, O Word incarnate of the Virgin, the untransformed God, Saviour of our souls.

¶*In the Aposticha from the eighteenth-twenty-third, to the Tone of the Resurrection. And if the day falleth on the twenty-fourth, the following Prosomia, in the First Tone.*

O VIRGIN free of all blame, the breathing palace of God, thou hast held him whom the heavens hold not, to whom thou shalt give birth in a manner exceeding understanding; who humbled himself, becoming flesh, that he might make me worthy, and enrich me; who became poor by excess of the most bitter food.

Stichos: God shall come forth from Timan.

O long-suffering Christ, verily, because of thy compassion thou wast enrolled with the servants by order of Cæsar, that thou mightest come and grant liberty, life, and safety to thy thankless servants, who adore thy saving Nativity, O thou who comest to save our souls.

Stichos: Thy hearing I have heard, O Lord, and was afraid.

The all-holy and blameless one, when she apprehended the incomprehensible Nativity which reneweth the

orders of nature, shouted unto the Son, saying, My
greatly beloved Son, I am dazzled by this great mystery: that by thy might I shall still be a Virgin after thy
Birth, O thou who doest all things by thy will.

Glory, in the Eighth Tone

REJOICE, O honoured Prophets, who did organize
well the law of the Lord, and appeared as stable,
unshakeable pillars of faith; for verily, they became
mediators of the New Covenant of Christ. Wherefore,
having been translated to heaven, plead ye with him to
grant safety to the world and to save our souls.

Now, in the Same Tone

BEHOLD, the time of our salvation approacheth;
make thou ready, O cave; for it is time for the
Virgin to give birth: and thou, Bethlehem of Judah,
rejoice and be happy; for from thee shall shine forth
our Lord. Listen, O mountains and hills and the regions about Judah; for Christ cometh to save man
whom he did create; for he is the Lover of mankind.

¶ *Troparia on the eighteenth and nineteenth, for the Resurrection;
and* Great are the accomplishments of faith, *etc.* (*p. 366q; and* Exceeding glorious beond the power of thought, *etc.* (*p. 147*). *On the
twentieth-twenty-third, for the Resurrection; and* Great are the accomplishments of faith, *etc.; and the following Troparion for the
Preparation, in the Fourth Tone.*

MAKE ready, O Bethlehem; for Eden hath been
opened for all. Prepare, O Ephratha; for the
Tree of life hath blossomed forth in the cave from the
Virgin; for her belly did appear as a supersensual
paradise in which is planted the divine Plant, whereof
eating we shall live and not die as Adam. Verily,
Christ shall be born, raising the likeness that fell of old.

¶ *And on the twenty-fourth,* Great are the accomplishments, *etc;
and the following Troparion for the Resurrection, in the Fourth
Tone.*

A ND it came to pass that Mary was enrolled with
Joseph the old man, in Bethlehem, since she was
of the seed of David, and was great with the Lamb,
without seed. And when the time for delivery drew
near, and they had no place in the village, the cave did
appear to the queen as a delightful palace. Verily,
Christ shall be born, raising the likeness that fell of old.

2. MATINS

*❧On God the Lord hath appeared unto us, the Troparia as at Ves-
pers; the Kathismata for the Resurrection (this if the day falleth on
the eighteenth or nineteenth), and two for the Preparation; the Benedictions (unless it be the twenty-fourth, when they shall be omitted);
and the Anabathmoi and the Prokeimenon of the Tone; the Katabasias of the Nativity; the rest of the Order of the Matin Gospel of
the Resurrection; the Exaposteilarions for the Resurrection; the following two for the Fathers and the Preparation. (And on the eighteenth and nineteenth, instead of the last of these two, the Theotokion of the Tone.)*

V ERILY, the chiefs of the Patriarchs and the fathers
before the law did go before, gleaming with faith
like the stars, namely Abraham, Isaac, and Jacob; for
all the Prophets and righteous ones were illuminated by
them, since they were shining lamps, and by the rays
of their venerated prophecy illuminated the whole of
dark creation.

Rejoice, O Bethlehem, and thou, Ephratha, make
ready; for the Theotokos shall come to the cave and
the manger to give birth in an ineffable manner to God.
O what a terrible mystery, the mystery of him who
cometh before Abraham, Isaac, and Jacob, the Patriarchs, and all the Prophets; and mankind with the
angels shall celebrate his Nativity with divine rejoicing.

*❧And in the Einos, four for the Resurrection; for the Fathers the
following four Prosomia, in the Fifth Tone.*

I N truth raise thy voice, O Zion, divine city of God,
and preach the divine memory of the fathers, honouring with Abraham, Isaac, and Jacob him of everlasting memory. For lo! with Judah and Levi we mag-

nify Moses the great, and Aaron the wonderful; and with David we celebrate the memory of Joshua and Samuel, inviting all with divine songs and divine praise to the preparation of the Nativity of Christ, praying to receive his goodness; for he it is that granteth the world the Great Mercy. (*Repeat.*)

Come, O Elijah, who didst ascend of old the divine fiery chariot, and O Elisha of divine mind, and rejoice together with Ezekiel and Josiah. Yea, exchange glad tidings with them, O venerated rank of the twelve Prophets inspired of God, on the Nativity of the Saviour. And all ye righteous ones, sing hymns. And ye all-beatified youths who quench the flames of the furnace with the dew of the Spirit, pray for us, pleading with Christ to grant our souls the Great Mercy.

Verily, she hath appeared on earth, the Theotokos, who was proclaimed from the ages by the words of the Prophets, and whom the wise Patriarchs and the rank of righteous ones did foretell, with whom the comeliness of women, Sarah, Rebecca with glorious Anne, and Mary, the sister of Moses, shall exchange glad tidings; and with them shall rejoice the ends of the earth, and all creation; for God shall come to be born in the flesh and grant the world the Great Mercy.

Glory for the Fathers, in the Eighth Tone

VERILY, the collection of Mosaic teachings maketh plain the divine Nativity of Christ in the flesh to those to whom was preached the grace before the law, having transcended the law by faith. Wherefore, since the Nativity was the cause of salvation from corruption, they foretold thy Resurrection to the souls imprisoned in hades, O Lord, glory to thee.

¶*Now,* Thou hast transcended, *etc; the Great Doxology; and the Troparion,* Today hath salvation come, *etc.*

3. THE MASS

❡*In the Eisodos, the Troparion for the Resurrection, and to the Fathers,* Great are the accomplishments, *etc. (p. 366); and that of the Preparation of Vespers (unless it falleth on the eighteenth and nineteenth when the Troparion is omitted). Then the Troparion of the Patron Saint of the church; and the Kontakion,* Today the Virgin, *etc. (p. 365). Then the Epistle and Gospel of the Sunday preceding the Nativity (pp. 273-275). And on Especially,* It is meet, *etc., the Koinonikon,* Praise ye the Lord from the heavens. Alleluia.

19. Boniface the Martyr (1).

20. Preparation of the Nativity, and the God-mantled Ignatius (5).

❡*From this day to Jan. fourteenth, do not use the Oktoechos book.*

21. Juliana the Martyr (14).

22. Anastasia the Great Martyr, the Deliverer from Poison (4).

23. The Ten Martyrs of Crete (2).

24. Eugenia the Martyr (4); and the Day preceding the Nativity (Paramon).

25. THE NATIVITY OF OUR LORD GOD, AND SAVIOUR JESUS CHRIST IN THE FLESH.

1—ORDER OF THE GREAT HOURS FOR THE NATIVITY

❡*The Service of the Great Hours is celebrated on the morning of the Paramon of the Feast; and if it falleth on a Sunday or a Monday then the service of this Hour is celebrated on Friday morning.*

FIRST HOUR

❡*After,* Blessed be God, *etc., and* Holy God, *etc., and* O come, let us worship, *etc. (three times), recite the following three Psalms.*

PSALM 5

Give ear, O Lord, etc. (p. 68).

PSALM 44

MY heart hath uttered a good work: I speak my works to the king:

My tongue is the pen of a scrivener that writeth swiftly.

Thou art beautiful above the sons of men; grace is poured abroad in thy lips; therefore, hath God blessed thee for ever.

Gird thy sword upon thy thigh, O thou most mighty.

With thy comeliness and thy beauty set out, proceed prosperously, and reign.

Because of truth and meekness and justice: and thy right hand shall conduct thee wonderfully.

Thy arrows are sharp: under thee shall people fall, into the hearts of the king's enemies.

Thy throne, O God, is for ever and ever: the sceptre of thy kingdom is a scepter of uprightness.

Thou hast loved justice, and hated iniquity: therefore God, thy God, hath anointed thee with the oil of gladness above thy fellows.

Myrrh and stacte and cassia perfume thy garments, from the ivory houses out of which the daughters of kings have delighted thee in thy glory.

The queen stood on thy right hand, in gilded clothing; surrounded with variety.

Hearken, O daughter, and see, and incline thy ear: and forget thy people and thy father's house.

And the king shall greatly desire thy beauty, for he is the Lord thy God, and him they shall adore.

And the daughters of Tyre with gifts, yea, all the rich among the people, shall entreat thy countenance.

All the glory of the king's daughter is within in golden borders, clothed round about with varieties.

After her shall virgins be brought to the king: her neighbours shall be brought to thee.

They shall be brought with gladness and rejoicing: they shall be brought into the temple of the king.

Instead of thy fathers, sons are born to thee: thou shalt make them princes over all the earth.

They shall remember thy name throughout all generations.

Therefore shall people praise thee for ever; yea, for ever and ever.

PSALM 45

OUR God is our refuge and strength: a helper in troubles, which have found us exceedingly.

Therefore we will not fear, when the earth shall be troubled; and the mountains shall be removed into the heart of the sea.

Their waters roared and were troubled: the mountains were troubled with his strength.

The stream of the river maketh the city of God joyful: the most High hath sanctified his own tabernacle.

God is in the midst thereof, it shall not be moved: God will help it in the morning early.

Nations were troubled, and kingdoms were bowed down: he uttered his voice, the earth trembled.

The Lord of armies is with us: the God of Jacob is our protector.

Come and behold ye the works of the Lord: what wonders he hath done upon earth, making wars to cease even to the end of the earth.

He shall destroy the bow, and break the weapons: and the shield he shall burn in the fire.

Be still and see that I am God; I will be exalted among the nations, and I will be exalted in the earth.

The Lord of armies is with us: the God of Jacob is our protector.

℄ *Glory and Now;* Alleluia (*three times*); Glory to thee, O God; Lord have mercy (*three times*); *Glory; the Troparion,* And it came to pass that Mary was enrolled, *etc.* (*p. 370*); *and Now to our Lady.*

WHAT shall we call thee, O full of grace? Shall we call thee heaven because thou didst give rise to the Sun of righteousness? Or, shall we call thee paradise because thou didst bring forth the Flower of incorruption? Or a Virgin because thou didst remain without defilement? Or a pure Mother because thou didst carry in thy holy arms as a son the God of all? Therefore, plead with him that he may save our souls.

℄ *Then the following Idiomelons, in the Eighth Tone.*

PREPARE, O Bethlehem, and let the manger make ready and the cave receive; for truth hath come, and shadow hath passed. And God hath appeared to mankind from the Virgin, taking our likeness and deifying our nature. Wherefore, Adam and Eve are made new, crying, Goodwill hath appeared on earth to save our race.

Stichos: God cometh from Timan (*in the Third Tone*).

Now, hath come the time for the aforesaid prophecy mystically uttered to be fulfilled, namely, And thou Bethlehem in the land of Judah art not the least among princes, having gone before and prepared the cave; for out of thee shall come a Governor of nations, from the virgin Maiden incarnate, by whom I mean Christ God who shall govern his people, the new Israel. Let us, therefore, raise unto him magnification.

Glory and Now, in the Eighth Tone

THUS saith Joseph to the Virgin, What is this thing, O Mary, that I behold in thee. Verily, I am surprised and perplexed, and my mind is dazzled. Wherefore, henceforth from this moment be thou secluded in secret. What is this matter, O Mary, that I behold in thee? For thou hast given me instead of honour, disgrace; and instead of gladness, sorrow; and instead of being extolled, thou hast brought me blame. Therefore, I cannot bear the reproach of men, from the Temple of the Lord I took thee; from the priests I received thee as innocent of all blame. What then is this thing I behold?

¶ *And immediately the Prokeimenon of the Prophecy, in the Fourth Tone.*

The Lord hath said to me: Thou art my Son, this day have I begotten thee. Ask of me and I will give thee the Gentiles, for thine inheritance.

Selection from Micah the Prophet (5:2-4)

THESE things the Lord doth say: And thou, Bethlehem Ephrata, art a little one among the thousands of Judah: out of thee shall he come forth unto me that is to be the Ruler in Israel: and his going forth is from the beginning, from the days of eternity.

Therefore, will he give them up even till the time wherein she that travaileth shall bring forth: and the remnant of his brethren shall be converted to the children of Israel.

And he shall stand, and feed in the strength of the Lord, in the height of the name of the Lord his God: and they shall be converted, for now shall he be magnified even to the ends of the earth.

Selection from the Epistle of St. Paul to the Hebrews (1:1-12)

GOD, who at sundry times and in divers manners spoke in times past to the fathers by the prophets, last of all,

In these days hath spoken to us by his Son, whom he hath appointed heir of all things, by whom also he made the world.

Who being the brightness of his glory, and the figure of his substance, and upholding all things by the word of his power, making purgation of sins, sitteth on the right hand of the majesty on high.

Being made so much better than the angels, as he hath inherited a more excellent name than they.

For to which of the angels hath he said at any time: Thou art my Son, to-day have I begotten thee? And again, I will be to him a Father, and he shall be to me a Son?

And again, when he bringeth in the first begotten into the world, he saith: And let all the angels of God adore him.

And to the angels indeed he saith: He that maketh his angels spirits, and his ministers a flame of fire.

But to the Son: Thy throne, O God, is for ever and ever: a sceptre of justice is the sceptre of thy Kingdom.

Thou hast loved justice, and hated iniquity: therefore God, thy God, hath anointed thee with the oil of gladness above thy fellows.

And: Thou in the beginning, O Lord, didst found the earth: and the works of thy hands are the heavens.

They shall perish, but thou shalt continue: and they shall all grow old as a garment.

And as a vesture shalt thou change them, and they shall be changed: but thou art the selfsame: and thy years shall not fail.

The Gospel: from St. Matthew (1:18 to end)

NOW the generation of Christ was in this wise. When as his Mother Mary was espoused to Joseph, before they came together, she was found with child, of the Holy Spirit.

Whereupon Joseph her husband, being a just man, and not willing publicly to expose her, was minded to put her away privately.

But while he thought on these things, behold the angel of the Lord appeared to him in his sleep, saying: Joseph, son of David, fear not to take unto thee Mary thy wife, for that which is conceived in her, is of the Holy Spirit.

And she shall bring forth a son: and thou shalt call his name Jesus. For he shall save his people from their sins.

Now all this was done that it might be fulfilled which the Lord spoke by the prophet, saying:

Behold a virgin shall be with child, and bring forth a son, and they shall call his name Emmanuel, which being interpreted is, God with us.

And Joseph rising up from sleep, did as the angel of the Lord had commanded him, and took unto him his wife.

And he knew her not till she brought forth her first-born son: and he called his name Jesus.

⊄And after the Gospel, say:

ORDER my steps according to thy words: and let not every iniquity have dominion over me. Deliver me from the oppression of man; so will I keep thy precepts. Make thy face to shine upon thy servant; and teach me thy statutes. Let my mouth be filled with thy praise, O Lord, that I may praise thy glory all the day long for the greatness of thy splendour.

⊄Then, Holy God, etc; the Kontakion, Today the Virgin, etc. (p. 365); Lord have mercy (forty times); O Christ our God, etc. (p. 60); Lord, have mercy (three times); Glory and Now; and O thou who art more honourable, etc., and the Priest: God be merciful unto us, etc; and the following Prayer.

O CHRIST, true Light that lighteth and sanctifieth every man that cometh into the world, may the light of thy countenance be impressed on our faces, that we may see therewith the unapproachable Light. Order our steps after thy commandments, by the intercessions of thine all-pure Mother and all the saints. Amen.

THIRD HOUR

⊄After O come, let us worship, etc. (three times), recite the following Psalms.

PSALM 66

MAY God have mercy upon us, and bless us: may he cause the light of his countenance to shine upon us, and may he have mercy upon us.

That we may know thy way upon earth: thy salvation in all nations.

Let people confess to thee, O God: let all people give praise to thee.

Let the nations be glad and rejoice: for thou judgest the people with justice, and directest the nations upon earth.

Let the people, O God, confess to thee: let all the people give praise to thee: so the earth hath yielded her fruit.

May God our God bless us, may God bless us: and all the ends of the earth fear him.

PSALM 86

THE foundations thereof are in the holy mountains. The Lord loveth the gates of Sion above all the tabernacles of Jacob.

Glorious things are said of thee, O city of God.

I will be mindful of Rahab and of Babylon knowing me.

Behold the foreigners, and Tyre, and the people of the Ethiopians, these were there.

Shall not Sion say: This man and that man is born in her? and the Highest himself hath founded her.

The Lord shall tell in his writings of peoples and of princes, of them that have been in her.

The dwelling in thee is as it were of all rejoicing.

PSALM 50

Have mercy, on me, O God, according to thy great mercy, etc. (p. 82).

❡ *Glory and Now;* Alleluia *(three times);* Glory to thee, O God; Lord, have mercy *(three times); Glory: the Troparion,* And it came to pass that Mary was enrolled, *etc. (p. 370); and Now, to our Lady.*

THOU art the true vine, O Theotokos, bearing the Fruit of life. Thee do we implore. Wherefore, O Lady, intercede thou together with the Apostles and the saints, for the salvation of our souls.

❡ *Then these Idiomelons, in the Sixth Tone.*

THIS is our God, beside whom none other may be considered. He it was who was born of the Virgin and went about among men, the only Son, beheld as a man placed in a mean manger, the Lord of the house wrapped in swaddling clothes. And the star pointeth for the Magi to worship him; and we sing shouting, O Trinity, save our souls.

Stichos: Lord thy hearing have I heard *(in the Eighth Tone).*

When the supersensual hosts beheld thy mystery before thy Birth, O Lord, they were struck with surprise; for thou who didst adorn the heavens with stars wast pleased to become like a babe, and lie in a manger for beasts, O thou Almighty One in whose grasp are all the regions of the earth; for by thy dispensation thy compassion was made known, O Christ, and thy Great Mercy. Wherefore, glory to thee.

Glory and Now, in the Third Tone

TELL us, O Joseph, how it is that thou dost bring the Virgin whom thou didst receive from the holy places to Bethlehem great with child? And he replieth, saying, I have searched the Prophets, and it was revealed to me by the angel. Therefore, I am convinced that Mary shall give birth in an inexplicable manner to God, whom Magi from the east shall come to worship and to serve with precious gifts. Wherefore, O thou who wast incarnate for our sakes, glory to thee.

¶*And immediately the Prokeimenon of the Prophecy, in the Fourth Tone.*

For a child is born to us, and a son is given to us, and the government is upon his shoulders.

Reading: from the Prophecy of Jeremiah Baruch (3:36 to end; 4:1-4)

THIS is our God, and there shall no other be accounted of in comparison to him.

He found out all the way of knowledge, and gave it to Jacob his servant, and to Israel his beloved.

Afterwards he was seen upon earth, and conversed with men.

This is the book of the commandments of God, and the law, that is for ever: all they that keep it, shall come to life: but they that have forsaken it, to death.

Return, O Jacob, and take hold of it, walk in the way by its brightness, in the presence of the light thereof.

Give not thy honour to another, nor thy dignity to a strange nation.

We are happy, O Israel: because the things that are pleasing to God, are made known to us.

The Epistle of St. Paul to the Galatians (3:23 to end)

BRETHREN: But before the faith came, we were kept under the law, shut up unto that faith which was to be revealed.

Wherefore the law was our pedagogue in Christ, that we may be justified by faith.

But after the faith is come, we are no longer under a pedagogue.

For you are all the children of God by faith, in Christ Jesus.

For as many of you as have been baptized in Christ, have put on Christ.

There is neither Jew nor Greek: there is neither bond nor free; there is neither male nor female; for you are all one in Christ Jesus.

And if you be Christ's, then are you the seed of Abraham, heirs according to the promise.

The Gospel: from St. Luke (2:1-20)

AND it came to pass that in those days there went out a decree from Caesar Augustus, that the whole world should be enrolled.

This enrolling was first made by Cyrinius, the governor of Syria.

And all went to be enrolled, every one into his own city.

And Joseph also went up from Galilee, out of the city of Nazareth into Judea, to the city of David, which is called Bethlehem: because he was of the house and family of David,

To be enrolled with Mary his espoused wife, who was great with child.

And it came to pass, that when they were there, her days were accomplished, that she should be delivered.

And she brought forth her firstborn son, and wrapped him up in swaddling clothes, and laid him in a manger; because there was no room for them in the inn.

And there were in the same country shepherds watching, and keeping the night watches over their flock.

And behold an angel of the Lord stood by them, and the brightness of God shone round about them; and they feared with a great fear.

And the angel said to them: Fear not; for, behold, I bring you good tidings of great joy, that shall be to all the people:

For this day, is born to you a Saviour, who is Christ the Lord, in the city of David.

And this shall be a sign unto you. You shall find the infant wrapped in swaddling clothes, and laid in a manger.

And suddenly there was with the angel a multitude of the heavenly army, praising God, and saying:

Glory to God in the highest; and on earth peace to men of good will.

And it came to pass, after the angels departed from them into heaven, the shepherds said one to another: Let us go over to Bethlehem, and let us see this word that is come to pass, which the Lord hath showed to us.

And they came with haste; and they found Mary and Joseph, and the infant lying in the manger.

And seeing, they understood of the word that had been spoken to them concerning this child.

And all that heard, wondered; and at those things that were told them by the shepherds.

But Mary kept all these words, pondering them in her heart.

And the shepherds returned, glorifying and praising God, for all the things they had heard and seen, as it was told unto them.

❡ *And immediately say:*

Blessed is the Lord God. Blessed is the Lord day by day. May God order our salvation. Our God is a God of salvation.

❡ *Then, Holy God, etc; The Kontakion,* Today the Virgin, *etc.* (*p. 365*); Lord, have mercy (*forty times*); O Christ our God, *etc.* (*p. 60*); Lord, have mercy (*three times*); *Glory and Now; and* O thou who art more honourable, *etc; and the Priest:* God be merciful unto us, *etc; and the, following Prayer.*

O MASTER, God Almighty, and the Lord, the only Son Jesus Christ, and the Holy Spirit, the one Godhead and one Might, have mercy upon me, a sinner, and by the precepts which thou teachest, save me thine undeserving servant; for thou art blessed to ages of ages. Amen.

SIXTH HOUR

❡ *After* O come, let us worship, *etc.* (*three times*), *recite the following Psalms.*

PSALM 71

GIVE to the king thy judgment, O God; and to the king's son thy justice.

He shall judge the poor of the people, and he shall save the children of the poor: and he shall humble the oppressor.

And he shall continue with the sun, and before the moon, throughout all generations.

He shall come down like rain upon the fleece; and as showers falling gently upon the earth.

In his days shall justice spring up, and abundance of peace, till the moon be taken away.

And he shall rule from sea to sea, and from the river unto the ends of the earth.

Before him the Ethiopians shall fall down: and enemies shall lick the ground.

The kings of Tharsis and the islands shall offer presents: the kings of the Arabians and of Saba shall bring gifts.

And all kings of the earth shall adore him: all nations shall serve him.

For he shall deliver the poor from the mighty: and the needy that had no helper.

He shall spare the poor and needy: and he shall save the souls of the poor.

He shall redeem their souls from usuries and iniquity: and their names shall be honourable in his sight.

And he shall live and unto him shall be given of the gold of Arabia, for him they shall always adore: they shall bless him all the day.

And there shall be a firmament on the earth on the tops of mountains, above Libanus shall the fruit thereof be exalted: and they of the city shall flourish like the grass of the earth.

Let his name be blessed for evermore: his name continueth before the sun.

And in him shall all the tribes of the earth be blessed: all nations shall magnify him. Blessed be the Lord, the God of Israel, who alone doth wonderful things.

And blessed be the name of his majesty for ever: and the whole earth shall be filled with his majesty. So be it. So be it.

The praises of David, the son of Jesse, are ended.

Psalm 131

O LORD, remember David, and all his meekness.
How he swore to the Lord, he vowed a vow to the God of Jacob:

If I shall enter into the tabernacle of my house: if I shall go up into the bed wherein I lie.

If I shall give sleep to my eyes, or slumber to my eyelids.

Or rest to my temples: until I find out a place for the Lord, a tabernacle for the God of Jacob.

Behold we have heard of it in Ephrata: we have found it in the fields of the wood.

We will go into his tabernacle: we will adore in the place where his feet stood.

Arise, O Lord, into thy resting place: thou and the ark, which thou hast sanctified.

Let thy priests be clothed with justice: and let thy saints rejoice.

For thy servant David's sake, turn not away the face of thy anointed.

The Lord hath sworn truth to David, and he will not make it void: of the fruit of thy womb I will set upon thy throne.

If thy children will keep my covenant, and these my testimonies which I shall teach them.

Their children also for evermore shall sit upon thy throne.

For the Lord hath chosen Sion: he hath chosen it for his dwelling.

This is my rest for ever and ever: here will I dwell, for I have chosen it.

Blessing I will bless her widow: I will satisfy her poor with bread.

I will clothe her priests with salvation: and her saints shall rejoice with exceeding great joy.

There will I bring forth a horn to David: I have prepared a lamp for my anointed.

His enemies I will clothe with confusion: but upon him shall my sanctification flourish.

PSALM 90

HE that dwelleth in the aid of the most High shall abide under the protection of the God of Jacob.

He shall say to the Lord: Thou art my protector, and my refuge: my God, in him will I trust.

For he hath delivered me from the snare of the hunters: and from the sharp word.

He will overshadow thee with his shoulders: and under his wings thou shalt trust.

His truth shall compass thee with a shield: thou shalt not be afraid of the terror of the night.

Of the arrow that flieth in the day, of the business that walketh about in the dark: of invasion, or of the noonday devil.

A thousand shall fall at thy side, and ten thousand at thy right hand; but it shall not come night thee.

But thou shalt consider with thy eyes: and shalt see the reward of the wicked.

Because thou, O Lord, art my hope: thou hast made the most High thy refuge.

There shall no evil come to thee: nor shall the scourge come near thy dwelling.

For he hath given his angels charge over thee; to keep thee in all thy ways.

In their hands they shall bear thee up: lest thou dash thy foot against a stone.

Thou shalt walk upon the asp and the basilisk: and thou shalt trample under foot the lion and the dragon.

Because he hoped in me I will deliver him I will protect him because he hath known my name.

He shall cry to me, and I will hear him: I am with him in tribulation, I will deliver him, and I will glorify him.

I will fill him with length of days; and I will shew him my salvation.

¶ *Glory and Now; Alleluia (three times); Glory to thee, O God; Lord, have mercy (three times); Glory; and Troparion, And it came to pass that Mary was enrolled, etc. (p. 370); and Now, to our Lady.*

FOR verily, we have no favour for the multitude of our sins. Therefore, O virgin Theotokos, plead with him that was born of thee; for the pleadings of the Mother are very effective in seeking the favour of the

Master. Turn thou not away, therefore, from the pleadings of sinners, O most venerable one; for he who was willing to suffer for our sins is merciful and able to save us.

❡ *Then sing the following Idiomelons, in the First Tone.*

COME, ye believers, let us ascend in a divine manner and behold a divine condescension, revealed to us from on high, openly in Bethlehem. And having purified our minds by good conduct, let us offer virtues instead of frankinsence. Let us go before and prepare with faith entrances for the Nativity among the spiritual treasures, crying, Glory in the highest to God the One in Trinity, through whom good-will appeared among men to deliver Adam from the ancient curse; for he is the Lover of mankind.

Stichos: God cometh from Timan *(in the Fourth Tone)*.

Listen, O heaven, and give ear, O earth. Let the foundations shake, and let trembling fall on all below the earth; for God hath dwelt in a creation of flesh; and he who made creation with a precious hand is seen in the womb of a created one. O the depth of the riches and wisdom and knowledge of God! How unsearchable are his judgments, and his ways past finding out.

Glory and Now, in the Fifth Tone

COME, ye nations that have put on Christ, let us behold a wonder that overtaketh all minds with astonishment; and as we kneel down in true worship, let us give praise in faith; for the Maiden, having conceived, cometh today to Bethlehem, to give birth to the Lord. The ranks of angels hasten, and Joseph, seeing these things, shouted, crying, What is this strange mystery that hath befallen thee, O Virgin? And how shalt thou give birth, O heifer that hath not known wedlock?

❡ *And immediately the Prokeimenon of the Prophecy, in the Eighth Tone.*

From the womb before the morning star I bore thee.
Said the Lord to my Lord, Sit thou on my right hand.

Reading: from the Prophecy of Isaiah (7:10-16; 8:1-4, 9-10)

AND the Lord spoke again to Achaz saying:
    Ask thee a sign of the Lord thy God, either unto
the depth of hell, or unto the height above.

And Achaz said: I will not ask, and I will not tempt
the Lord.

And he said: Hear ye therefore, O house of David:
Is it a small thing for you to be grievous to men, that
you are grievous to my God also?

Therefore the Lord himself shall give you a sign.
Behold a virgin shall conceive, and bear a son, and his
name shall be called Emmanuel.

He shall eat butter and honey, that he may know to
refuse the evil, and to choose the good.

For before the child know to refuse the evil and to
choose the good, the land which thou abhorrest shall
be forsaken of the face of her two kings.

And the Lord said to me: Take thee a great book,
and write in it with a man's pen. Take away the spoils
with speed, quickly take the prey.

And I took unto me faithful witnesses, Urias the
priest, and Zacharias the son of Barachias.

And I went to the Prophetess, and she conceived, and
bore a son. And the Lord said to me: Call his name,
Hasten to take away the spoils: Make haste to take
away the prey.

For before the child know to call his father and his
mother, the strength of Damascus, and the spoils of
Samaria shall be taken away before the king of the
Assyrians.

Gather yourselves together, O ye people, and be overcome, and give ear, all ye lands afar off: strengthen
yourselves, and be overcome, gird yourselves, and be
overcome.

Take counsel together, and it shall be defeated: speak a word, and it shall not be done: because God is with us.

The Epistle of St. Paul to the Hebrews (1:10 to end, and 2:1-3)

THOU in the beginning, O Lord, didst found the earth: and the works of thy hands are the heavens.

They shall perish, but thou shalt continue; and they all shall grow old as a garment.

And as a vesture shalt thou change them, and they shall be changed: but thou art the self-same, and thy years shall not fail.

But to which of the angels said he at any time: Sit on my right hand, until I make thy enemies thy footstool?

Are they not all ministering spirits, sent to minister for them, who shall receive the inheritance of salvation.

Therefore, ought we more diligently to observe the things which we have heard, lest perhaps we should let them slip.

For if the word spoken by angels become steadfast, and every transgression and disobedience received a just recompense of reward;

How shall we escape, if we neglect so great a salvation? which having begun to be declared by the Lord, was confirmed unto us by them that heard him.

The Gospel: from St. Matthew (2:1-12)

WHEN Jesus therefore was born in Bethlehem of Judaea, in the days of King Herod, behold, there came Wise Men from the east to Jerusalem.

Saying: Where is he that is born king of the Jews? for we have seen his star in the East, and are come to adore him.

And king Herod hearing this, was troubled, and all Jerusalem with him.

And assembling together all the chief priests and the scribes of the people, he inquired of them where Christ should be born.

But they said to him: In Bethlehem of Juda. For so it is written by the prophet:

And thou Bethlehem in the land of Juda art not the least among the princes of Juda: for out of thee shall come forth the captain that shall rule my peope Israel.

Then Herod, privately calling the wise men, learned diligently of them the time of the star which appeared to them.

And sending them into Bethlehem, said: Go and diligently inquire after the child, and when you have found him, bring me word again, that I also may come and adore him.

Who having heard the king, went their way and behold the star which they had seen in the East, went before them, until it came and stood over where the child was.

And seeing the star they rejoiced with exceeding great joy.

And entering into the house, they found the child with Mary his Mother, and falling down, they adored him: and opening their treasures, they offered him gifts; gold, frankincense, and myrrh.

And having received an answer in sleep that they should not return to Herod, they went back another way into their country.

⁋ *And immediately say:*

Swiftly let thy compassion apprehend us, O Lord; for we are greatly impoverished. Help us, O God our Saviour, for thy Name's glory. Lord, deliver us and forgive us our sins for thy Name's sake.

⁋ *Then,* Holy God, *etc; The Kontakion,* Today the Virgin, *etc;* Lord, have mercy (*forty times*)*;* O Christ our God, *etc;* Lord, have mercy (*three times*)*; Glory and Now; and* O thou who art more honourable, *etc; and the Priest:* God be merciful unto us, *etc; and the following Prayer of Basil the Great.*

O GOD, Lord of powers, and Creator of all creatures, for the indescribable compassion of thy mercies thou didst send thine only Son Jesus Christ for the
salvation of our race; and by his Cross thou didst tear
up the decree of our sins; and through him didst shame
the principals and kings of darkness. Thou, Master,
Lover of mankind, accept from us sinners these petitions and pleadings of thanksgiving, and deliver us
from every dark and annihilating fall, from all those
who seek to do us wrong, and from enemies visible and
invisible. Nail the fear of thee in our bodies, and turn
not our hearts to evil speech or thoughts. Nay, by thy
longing, wound our souls that, beholding thee always,
and being guided by the light coming from thee, and
observing thee, O unapproachable eternal Light, we
may address to thee ceaselessly our thanksgiving and
confession, O Father without beginning, with thine only
Son, and thy most Holy Spirit, the Giver of life, now,
and always, and unto ages of ages. Amen.

NINTH HOUR

❡*After* O come, let us worship, *etc.* (*three times*), *say the following
Psalms.*

PSALM 109

THE Lord said to my Lord: Sit thou at my right
hand.

Until I make thy enemies thy footstool.

The Lord will send forth the sceptre of thy power
out of Sion: rule thou in the midst of thy enemies.

With thee is the principality in the day of thy
strength: in the brightness of the saints: from the womb
before the day star I begot thee.

The Lord hath sworn, and he will not repent: Thou
art a priest for ever according to the order of Melchisedech.

The Lord at thy right hand hath broken kings in the
day of his wrath.

He shall judge among nations, he shall fill ruins: he shall crush the heads in the land of many.

He shall drink of the torrent in the way: therefore, shall he lift up the head.

PSALM 110

I WILL praise thee, O Lord, with my whole heart, in the council of the just, and in the congregation.

Great are the works of the Lord: sought out according to all his wills.

His work is praise and magnificence: and his justice continueth for ever and ever.

He hath made a remembrance of his wonderful works, being a merciful and gracious Lord: he hath given food to them that fear him.

He will be mindful for ever of his covenant: he will show forth to his people the power of his works.

That he may give them the inheritance of the Gentiles: the works of his hands are truth and judgment.

All his commandments are faithful: confirmed for ever and ever, made in truth and equity.

He hath sent redemption to his people: he hath commanded his covenant for ever.

Holy and terrible is his Name: the fear of the Lord is the beginning of wisdom.

PSALM 85

Incline thine ear, O Lord, and hear me, etc. (p. 59).

¶ *Glory and Now; Alleluia (three times); Glory to thee, O God; Lord, have mercy (three times); Glory, and the Troparion, And it came to pass that Mary was enrolled, etc. (p. 370); Now; Theotokion, Thou, who for our sake wast, etc. (p. 193). Then the following Idiomelons, in the Seventh Tone.*

VERILY, Herod was overtaken by astonishment when he saw the piety of the Magi. And having been overridden with wrath, he began to inquire of them about the time. He robbed the mothers of their children and ruthlessly reaped the tender bodies of the babes. And the breasts dried up, and the springs of milk failed. Great then was the calamity. Wherefore, being gathered, O believers, in true worship, let us adore the Nativity of Christ.

Stichos: God cometh from Timan (*in the Second tone*).

As Joseph was going his way to Bethlehem pierced with sadness, thou didst cry unto him, O Virgin, saying, Why frownest thou and art troubled when thou seest me great with child, completely ignorant of the terrible mystery that is in me? Drive away from thee all dismay, comprehending the strange matter; for God, for his mercy's sake, hath descended to earth and hath now taken flesh in my womb, and thou shalt see him born, as it pleased him, and thou shalt be filled with joy, and worship him; for he is thy Creator, whom the angels praise ceaselessly and glorify, with the Father and the Holy Spirit.

Glory and Now, in the Sixth Tone[1]

TODAY is born of the Virgin him who holdest all creation in the hollow of his hand (*three times*). He whose essence is untouchable is wrapped in swaddling clothes as a babe. The God who from of old established the heavens lieth in a manger. He who showered the people with manna in the wilderness feedeth on milk from the breasts. And the bridegroom of the Church calleth the Magi. And the Son of the Virgin accepteth gifts from them. We worship thy Nativity, O Christ (*three times*).

¶ *Then immediately the Stichos of the Prophecy, in the Fourth Tone.*

And of the mother Zion, it shall be said, this and that man is born in her and the Highest himself hath founded her.

---

[1] This piece is chanted by the Reader in the middle of the church, repeating the first sentence three times, and also, We worship thy Nativity. O Christ, then it is sung by the two Choirs.

Reading: from the Prophecy of Isaiah (9:6-7)

FOR a child is born to us, and a son is given to us, and the government is upon his shoulders: and his name shall be called, Wonderful, Counsellor, God the Mighty, the Father of the world to come, the Prince of Peace.

His empire shall be multiplied, and there shall be no end of peace: He shall sit upon the throne of David, and upon his kingdom; to establish it and strengthen it with judgment and with justice, from henceforth and for ever: the zeal of the Lord of hosts will perform this.

The Epistle of St. Paul to the Hebrews (2:11 to end)

YE brethren: For both he that sanctifieth, and they who are sanctified, are all one, for which cause he is not ashamed to call them brethren, saying:

I will declare thy Name to my brethren; in the midst of the church will I praise thee.

And again: I will put my trust in him. And again: Behold I and my children, whom God hath given me.

Therefore because the children are partakers of flesh and blood, he also himself in like manner hath been partaker of the same: that through death, he might destroy him who had the empire of death, that is to say, the devil:

And might deliver them, who through the fear of death were all their lifetime subject to servitude.

For nowhere doth he take hold of the angels: but of the seed of Abraham he taketh hold.

Wherefore it behoved him in all things to be made like unto his brethren, that he might become a merciful and faithful high priest before God, that he might be a propitiation for the sins of the people.

For in that, wherein he himself hath suffered and been tempted, he is able to succour them also that are tempted.

The Gospel: from St. Matthew

And after the Magi were departed, etc. (p. 276).

And immediately say:

FORSAKE us not utterly, for thy holy Name's sake, and destroy not thy covenant. Take not thy mercies from us, for the sake of Abraham beloved of thee, and for the sake of Isaac thy servant, and of Israel thy holy one.

Then, Holy God, *etc; the Kontakion,* Today the Virgin, *etc. (p. 365); Lord,* have mercy *(forty times);* O Christ our God, *etc. (p. 60); Lord,* have mercy *(three times); Glory and Now, and O* you who art more honourable, *etc; and the Priest:* God be merciful unto us, *etc; and the following Prayer.*

O Master, Lord Jesus Christ our God, etc. (p. 61).

And immediately the Typica (Symbol) and Makarizmoi (Beatides) without intonation.

Bless the Lord, O my soul, etc. (p. 30).
Glory: Praise the Lord, O my soul, etc. (p. 122).
Now: O Only-begotten Son and Word of God, etc. (p. 123).
Then: In thy kingdom remember us, O Lord, etc. (p. 124).
Glory and Now: Remember us, O Lord, when thou comest into thy kingdom (*three times*).
The heavenly rank praiseth thee and saith, Holy, Holy, Holy, Lord of Sabaoth, heaven and earth are full of thy glory.
Stichos: Come ye before him and be lighted, and let not your faces be ashamed (*repeating,* The heavenly rank, *etc.*).
Glory: The rank of the holy angels and archangels, with all the heavenly powers praise thee, saying, Holy, Holy, Holy, Lord of Sabaoth, heaven and earth are full of thy glory.
Now: I believe in One God, etc. (p. 85).

PARDON, remit and forgive, O God, our intentiona
and unintentional falls, by word or deed, wittingl
or unwittingly, those by night and those by day, thos
of the mind or those of the senses, and forgive us all
for thou art good and the Lover of mankind.

❡ *Then:* Our Father who art in heaven, *etc; the Kontakion,* Toda
the Virgin, *etc.* (*p. 365*); Lord, have mercy (*twelve times*); Blesse
be the Name of the Lord from this time forth and for ever (*thre
times*); Glory and Now; and the Benediction. Then immediate
after the Benediction, Vespers with the Mass of Basil the Great tak
place (*unless Christmas falls on a Sunday or a Monday*).

2. GREAT VESPERS

❡ *After* Blessed be God, *etc., and the Sunset Psalm; on* O Lord,
thee have I cried, *chant the following six Idiomelons, in the Secon
Tone.*

By Germanus

COME, let us rejoice in the Lord, proclaiming th
present mystery; for he hath broken the middl
wall of partition, and the flaming spear shall turn abou
and the cherubim shall admit all to the tree of life. A
for me, I shall return to enjoy the bliss of paradise fror
which I was driven away before, by reason of iniquit
for the likeness of the Father, and the Person of h
eternity, which it is impossible to change hath taken th
likeness of a servant, coming from a Mother who ha
not known wedlock; free from transubstantiation, sinc
he remained as he was, true God, and took what had n
been, having become Man for his love of mankin
Wherefore, let us lift our voices unto him crying,
thou who wast born of the Virgin, O God, have merc
upon us. (*Repeat.*)

By Anatolius

WHEN the Lord Jesus was born of the holy Virgi
the whole creation was lighted, the shepher
keeping watch, the Magi worshipping, the angels prai

ng, and Herod trembling; for the God and Saviour of our souls hath appeared in the flesh. (*Repeat.*)

Thy kingdom, O Christ God, is a kingdom of all ages; and thy rule is from generation to generation; for thou who wast incarnate of the Holy Spirit and became Man from Mary the ever-virgin, hast caused light to shine on us by thy presence, O Christ God; O Light of Light, O Radiance of the Father, thou hast illuminated all creation; and every breath doth praise thee, O Likeness of the glory of the Father. Wherefore, O everlasting God, who art before eternity, who didst shine forth from the Virgin, O God, have mercy upon us.

What shall we render to thee, O Christ, for that thou didst appear on earth as a man for our sake? Verily, every individual of the creatures thou didst create shall offer thee thanksgiving. The angels shall tender thee praise; the heavens, the star; the Magi, gifts; the shepherds, wonder; the earth, the cave; the wilderness, the manger; and we men, a virgin Mother. Wherefore, O God before the ages, have mercy upon us.

Glory and Now, in the Second Tone (By Kassias)

WHEN Augustus became supreme ruler of earth, the multiplicity of rule among men ceased. And when thou becamest human from the spotless one, the worship of many heathen gods also ceased. Then the cities came under one worldly rule; and the nations believed in one divine supremacy. The nations were enrolled by an order of Caesar; but we believers were enrolled in the name of thy Divinity, O our incarnate God. Wherefore, great are thy mercies, glory to thee.

[*Then the Eisodos with the Gospel; and* O resplendent Light, *etc.* (*p. 74*); *and the following readings.*

First Reading: from Genesis (1:1-13)

IN the beginning God created heaven, and earth.

And the earth was void and empty, and darknes was upon the face of the deep; and the Spirit of God moved over the waters.

And God said: Be light made. And light was made And God saw the light that it was good; and he divided the light from the darkness.

And he called the light Day, and the darkness Night and there was evening and morning one day.

And God said: Let there be a firmament made amids the waters; and let it divide the waters from the waters

And God made a firmament, and divided the water that were under the firmament, from those that wer above the firmament, and it was so.

And God called the firmament, Heaven; and the eve ning and morning were the second day.

God also said: Let the waters that are under the heaven, be gathered together into one place: and le the dry land appear. And it was so done.

And God called the dry land, Earth; and the gath ering together of the waters, he called Seas. And Go saw that it was good.

And he said: Let the earth bring forth the green herb and such as may seed, and the fruit tree yielding afte its kind, which may have seed in itself upon the earth And it was so done.

And the earth brought forth the green herb, and such as yieldeth seed according to its kind, and the tre that beareth fruit, having seed each one according to it kind. And God saw that it was good.

And the evening and the morning were the third day

¶ Then the Right Choir singeth the following Troparion, in the Sixt Tone.

DISGUISED, O Saviour, thou wast born in a cave but heaven proclaimed thee to all, taking for it mouth a star. And it offered thee the Magi worship ping thee in faith. Wherefore, with them, have mercy upon us.

¶ *The last section of this Troparion, beginning,* And it offered thee the Magi, *etc. is repeated five times with the following Stichoi (Psalm 86).*

1. Whose foundation is in the holy mountains. The Lord loveth the gates of Zion more than all the dwellings of Jacob.
2. Glorious things are said of thee, O City of God. I will be mindful of Rahab and Babylon knowing me.
3. Behold strange nations, and Tyre and Ethiopia.
4. Those were born there. And of the mother Zion it shall be said, this man and that man is born in her, and the highest himself hath founded her.
5. The Lord shall tell in his writing of peoples and of princes of them that have been in her, the dwelling in thee is as it were of all rejoicing.

¶ *Then* Glory *and* Now, *repeating the whole Troparion; and immediately:*

Second Reading: from Isaiah the Prophet

For a child is born to us, etc. (p. 394).

¶ *Then the Left Choir chanteth the following Troparion, in the Sixth Tone.*

THOU hast shone forth from the Virgin, O Christ, supersensual Sun of justice. And a star pointed to thee, thou uncontainable One, who wast contained in a cave. And the Magi were led to thy worship. Wherefore, with them, we magnify thee, O thou Giver of life. Glory to thee.

¶ *The last paragraph,* And the Magi were led, *etc., is repeated five times with the following Stichoi (Psalm 92).*

1. The Lord hath reigned, he is clothed with beauty. The Lord is clothed with strength, and hath girded himself.
2. For he hath established the world, which shall not be moved. Thy throne is prepared from of old.

3. The floods have lifted up, O Lord; the floods have lifted up their voice. The floods have lifted up their waves, with the noise of many waters.

4. Wonderful are the surges of the sea. Wonderful is the Lord on high. Thy testimonies are become exceedingly credible.

5. Holiness becometh thine house, O Lord, unto length of days.

⁌ *Then, Glory and Now; and the whole Troparion is repeated; and immediately:*

Third Reading: from Isaiah the Prophet

And the Lord spake again to Achaz, saying, etc. (p. 388).

⁌ *Then immediately the Little Synapte; and the Proclamation,* For thou art Holy, *etc; and* Holy God, *then:*

The Epistle: from St. Paul to the Hebrews

God, who at sundry times and in divers manners, etc. (p. 376).

The Gospel: from St. Luke

And it came to pass that in those days there went a decree from Caesar Augustus, etc. (p. 381).

⁌ *The rest of the Divine Liturgy of Basil the Great (if chanting accompanies Vespers with the Hours).*

Koinonikon: Praise ye the Lord from the heavens.

⁌ *But if the Feast falls on a Sunday or a Monday, the Hours are chanted on Friday morning, and Great Vespers on Sunday evening. The Mass of Basil the Great being said on the day of the Feast. In this case at Great Vespers, after the Gospel, the Great Synapte,* Let us all say, *etc. (p. 75);* Vouchsafe, O Lord, *etc. (p. 76);* Let us finish our petitions, *etc. (p. 76); the Aposticha (p. 401); and* Lord, now lettest thou thy servant, *etc;* Holy God, *etc; and the Troparion of the Nativity,* Thy Nativity, O Christ our God, *etc. (p. 402). And in the Litiya, say, Glory and Now, in the Sixth Tone.*

By Germanus

TODAY all the angels exchange glad tidings and rejoice; and the entire creation exulteth for the Birth of the Lord Saviour in Bethlehem; for the error of the idols hath passed out completely, and Christ shall reign for ever.

❡ *And in the Aposticha, the following Idiomelons, in the Second Tone.*

By Germanus

TODAY hath come about a great and wonderful thing, in that a Virgin giveth birth, yet corruption hath not entered the womb; the Word is incarnate, yet is not separated from the Father; the angels give glory with the shepherds, and we lift our voices with them crying, Glory to God in the highest, and on earth peace.

Stichos: Said the Lord to my Lord; Sit thou at my right hand. *(In the Third Tone.)*

Today the Virgin doth give birth to the Creator of all; Eden offereth the cave; the star telleth to those in darkness of Christ the Sun; the Magi with presents worshipped him, enlightened by faith; and the shepherds beheld the wonder, the angels singing and saying, Glory to God in the Highest.

Stichos: From the womb, before the morning star, I begot thee.

WHEN the Lord Jesus was born in Bethlehem of Judæa, the Magi came from the east and worshipped him as incarnate God. Eagerly they opened their treasures and offered him precious gifts — pure gold for that he is King of the ages; frankincense in that he is God of all; and as dead for three days they offered myrrh to the deathless One. Wherefore, come, all ye nations, let us worship him who was born to save our souls.

Glory, in the Fourth Tone (By John of Damascus)

REJOICE, O Jerusalem, and celebrate all ye lovers of Zion; for the temporal bonds with which Adam was condemned have been loosened; paradise hath been opened for us, and the serpent hath been annihilated, having beheld now that the one deceived by her of old hath become a Mother to the Creator. Wherefore, O both the depth, the richness, the wisdom, and the knowledge of God, that the instrument of death which brought death to all flesh, hath become the first-fruit of salvation to all the world, because of the Theotokos; for the all-perfect God hath been born therefrom as a babe; and by his Birth he hath sealed her virginity; by his swaddling clothes he hath loosened the chains of our sins; and by his babyhood he hath healed the pains and sorrows of Eve. Let all creation, therefore, exchange glad tidings and rejoice; for Christ hath come to recall it and to save our souls.

Now, in the Same Tone (By Anatolius)

O CHRIST God, thou hast dwelt in a cave, and a manger did receive thee. The Magi with shepherds worshipped thee, thus fulfilling the preaching of the Prophets; and the angelic powers wondered, lifting their voices and saying, Glory to thy condescension, O thou only Lover of mankind.

Troparion, in the Fourth Tone (three times)

THY Nativity, O Christ our God, hath given rise to the light of knowledge in the world; for they that worshipped the stars did learn therefrom to worship thee, O Sun of justice, and to know that from the east of the Highest thou didst come O Lord, glory to thee.

3. Matins

¶ *On* God the Lord hath appeared to us, *sing the Troparion of the Feast (three times); then the following Kathismata, in the Fourth Tone.*

COME, ye believers, let us see where Christ was born. Let us follow the star whither it goeth with the Magi, kings of the east; for there angels praise him ceaselessly, and shepherds raise their voices in a worthy song of praise, saying, Glory in the highest to the One born today in a cave from the virgin Theotokos in Bethlehem of Judæa.

Why wonderest thou, O Mary; and why art thou astonished in thy inner self? And she respondeth, saying, Because I have given birth in time to a Son unbound by time; nor do I comprehend the manner of conception of him that is born. I have known no man; how then give I birth to a son? For who hath yet seen a birth without seed? But since God willeth, the order of nature is overcome, as it hath been written, Christ hath been born of the Virgin in Bethlehem of Judæa.

He that all containeth not, how was he contained in the womb? And he that is in the bosom of the Father, how shall he be carried in the arms of his Mother? Verily, all this hath been fulfilled as he himself knew and willed and was pleased to do; for he that is not carnal hath become incarnate by his own choice; and he that is, hath turned for our sakes to that which he was not, sharing our creation, yet inseparable from his essence. Verily, Christ hath been born with two Natures, desiring to perfect the heavenly world.

Prokeimenon, in the Fourth Tone

FROM the womb before the morning star I begot thee. The Lord hath sworn, and he shall not repent.

Stichos: Said the Lord to my Lord.

The Gospel: from St. Matthew

Now the generation of Jesus Christ was on this wise, etc. (p. 377, third paragraph).

¶ *And after the reading of Psalm 50, sing Glory, in the Second Tone.*

Today all creatures shall be filled with joy; for Christ hath been born of the Virgin.

¶*Now (Repeated); Today all creatures, etc; then* O merciful One, have mercy upon me, *etc; and sing the following Idiomelon, in the Sixth Tone.*

GLORY to God in the highest, and on earth be peace. Today doth Bethlehem receive him who sitteth with the Father for ever. Today the angels glorify, as worthy of God, the babe that is born, shouting, Glory to God in the highest, and on earth be peace, and good-will among men.

¶*Then sing the following Katabasias of the Nativity, in couples, in the First Tone.*[1]

Right Choir 1. Christ is born, glorify him. Christ hath come from the heavens, receive him. Christ is on earth, elevate him. Sing unto the Lord, all the earth; and ye nations, praise him with joy; for he hath been glorified.

Left Choir (Another). The Lord performed a miracle and saved the people when of old he turned the moist waves of the sea into dry land. And having been born now of a Virgin by his own choice, he hath trodden for us the way to heaven, being equal to the Father and to men in essence; therefore, do we glorify him.

Right Choir 3. Let us cry unto the Son, born of the Father before the ages without transubstantiation, Christ God who hath been incarnate in these last days of the Virgin, without seed, shouting, O thou who hath elevated our state, thou art holy, O Lord.

Left Choir (Another). Incline, O glorious Benefactor, to the praise of thy servants, abolishing the boasting of the proud adversary. And help us who sing to

---

[1] The First series of Katabasias, i.e. *Christ hath been born, glorify him,* etc. are chanted from November twenty-first to December twenty-fourth, the alternative ones from December twenty-sixth to the thirty-first; while on the twenty-fifth, the glorious Day of the Nativity itself, the two series are chanted together. The first of these series belongs to Cosmos, and the second to St. John of Damascus.

thee to overcome sin, and confirm us on the unshakeable foundation of faith.

Left Choir 4. O praised Christ, a stem hath come out of Jesse, and from it hast sprouted a Flower from a dense and shadowed mountain, O immaterial God, coming incarnate from the Virgin that hath not known man. Glory, therefore, to thy might, O Lord.

Right Choir (Another). The Prophet Habakuk of old foretold in song the re-creation of mankind; for he was worthy to behold that sign in an ineffable manner; for the Word did come forth as a new babe from the mountain of the Virgin, for the re-creation of the nations.

Right Choir 5. Since thou art the God of peace and the Father of mercies, O Lover of mankind, thou didst send to us the great Messenger of thy mind, granting us thy peace. Therefore, have we been led aright to the light of divine knowledge, glorifying thee as we come out of darkness.

Left Choir (Another). Grant forgiveness, O Christ, to us who have been in the darkness of our deeds of error since the night, who eagerly praise thee, since thou art our Benefactor; that thou mayest hasten to us and prepare for us a good way, wherein if we walk we shall find glory and honour.

Right Choir 6. The sea-monster did disgorge Jonah from its belly, as it received him safely like a fœtus. As for the Word, when he dwelt in the Virgin, taking from her a body, he was born, preserving her without corruption, and without transubstantiation, preserving his Mother without harm.

Left Choir (Another). Verily, Jonah when he was in the depth of the sea, begged to ascend to thee and to be rescued from the tempest. But as for me, having been pierced by the arrows of the tyrant, in thee I seek refuge, O evil-destroying Christ. Hasten thou to me and deliver me hastily from my negligence.

Right Choir 7. The youths having grown together in true worship, despising the command of the infidel, were not dismayed by the threat of fire; but were singing as they stood in the midst of the flames, Blessed art thou, God of our fathers.

Left Choir (Another). The youths having clung steadfastly to the love of the King of all, ridiculed the prating and blasphemy of the blaspheming usurper. And being filled with wrath, he delivered them to the terrible fire which did not harm them. Wherefore, they lifted their voices to the Master, saying, Blessed art thou unto all ages.

Let us praise, bless, and worship the Lord.

Left Choir 8. Verily, the dewy furnace did shadow the sign of the supernatural wonder; for it burned not the youths whom it received, as the fire of divinity also burned not the womb of the Virgin in which it dwelt. Wherefore, let us offer praise with song, saying, Let all creation praise the Lord, exalting him evermore, to the end of ages.

Right Choir (Another). The youths who were cast of old into the fire and remained unburned, were a sign of the womb of the Maiden who gave birth supernaturally while yet sealed. These two matters grace hath accomplished through one miracle, arousing the nations to praise.

¶*And immediately, instead of* O thou who art more honourable, *etc., the Ninth Ode of the two Canons is chanted with its Magnifications.*

Ninth Ode of the First Canon

MAGNIFY, O my soul, her who is more honourable and more exalted in glory than the heavenly hosts.

9. I behold a strange and wonderful mystery: the cave a heaven, the Virgin a cherubic throne, and the manger a noble place in which hath lain Christ the uncontained God. Let us, therefore, praise and magnify him.

Magnify, O my soul, the God born in flesh from the Virgin.

When the Magi saw a new and strange star appearing suddenly, moving in a wonderful way, and transcending the stars of heaven in brightness, they were guided by it to Christ, the King born on earth in Bethlehem, for our salvation.

Magnify, O my soul, the King born in a cave.

The Magi said, Where is the child King, the new born, whose star hath appeared? For we have verily come to worship him. And Herod, the contender against God, trembled, and began to roar in folly to kill Christ.

Magnify, O my soul, the God worshipped by the Magi.

Herod ascertained from the Magi about the time of the star by whose guidance they were led to Bethlehem to worship with presents Christ who guided them, and so they returned to their country, disregarding Herod, the evil murderer of babes, mocking him.

The Ninth Ode of the Other Canon

TODAY the Virgin giveth birth to the Lord inside the cave.

Verily, it is easier for us to endure silence since there is no dread danger therefrom for us. But because of our strong desire, O Virgin, and Mother of sameness, to indite well-balanced songs of praise, this becometh indeed onerous to us. Wherefore, grant us power to equal our natural inclination.

Glory: Magnify, O my soul, the might of the indivisible and three-personed Godhead.

O pure one, Mother of the Word that appeareth newly from thee, O closed door, verily, as we behold the dark shadowy symbols pass away, we glorify the light of the truth and bless thy womb as is meet.

Now: Glorify, O my soul, her who hath delivered us from the curse.

The Christ-pleasing people, O Virgin, having deserved to be granted its desire by the coming of God, doth seek now with tears thy help to worship the glory of his enlivening appearance wherein is the renewal of birth; for it is thou who dost distribute grace, O pure one.

❡ *Then conclude with the two Katabasias and their Magnifications,* I behold a strange and wonderful mystery, *etc.* (*p. 406*)*; and* Verily, it is easier, *etc.* (*p. 407*). *Or say with the second the following Magnification,* Magi with shepherds did come to worship Christ born in the city of Bethlehem.

Exaposteilarion (three times)

OUR Saviour hath visited us from on high, from the east of easts. Wherefore, we who are in darkness and shadows have found the truth; for the Lord hath been born of the Virgin.

❡ *Then in the Einos, the following four Idiomelons are sung, in the Fourth Tone.*

By Andrew the Jerusalemite

REJOICE, O righteous ones, and ye heavens be glad. Sing with joy, ye mountains, for the Nativity of Christ. The Virgin sitteth like the cherubim, holding in her bosom God the incarnate Word; the shepherds do glorify him who was born. The Magi offer presents to the Lord, and the angels give praise, saying, O Lord, hidden from comprehension, glory to thee.

The Father hath been pleased and satisfied; the Word hath become flesh; and the Virgin hath given birth to incarnate God. The star declaimeth, the Magi worship, the shepherds wonder, and creation rejoiceth.

O virgin Theotokos, O thou who hast given birth to the Saviour, thou hast revoked the ancient curse of Eve; for thou hast become a Mother according to the pleasure of God, carrying in thy bosom God the incarnate Word. Verily, the mystery is inscrutable; but we all glorify it with faith only, crying with thee and saying, O incomprehensible Lord, glory to thee.

Come, let us praise the Mother of the Saviour, who appeared a Virgin even after birth-giving, crying, Rejoice, O living city of God the King, in whom Christ having dwelt worked salvation. Wherefore, we with Gabriel do praise, and with the shepherds do glorify thee, crying, O Theotokos, intercede with him incarnate of thee to save us.

Glory, in the Sixth Tone (By Germanus)

WHEN it was time for thy presence on earth the the first enrollment of the world took place. Then it was that thou didst decide to enroll the names of men who believe in thy Nativity. Yea, that commandment did issue forth from Cæsar, since the everlastingness of thine eternal kingdom hath been renewed. Wherefore, we offer what is better than moneyed tax, namely Orthodox theological sayings; to thee, O God, Saviour of our souls.

Now, in the Second Tone (By John of Damascus)

TODAY Christ is born in Bethlehem of the Virgin Today the Beginningless doth begin, and the Word becometh incarnate. The powers of heaven rejoice, and earth is glad with mankind. The Magi do offer presents, and the shepherds with wonder declaim. As for us, we shout ceaselessly, crying, Glory to God in the highest, and on earth peace, good-will towards men.

❡ Then, the Great Doxology, concluded with the Troparion on the Nativity, Thy Nativity, O Christ. etc.

4. THE MASS

1. Through the intercessions of the Theotokos, O Saviour, save us.

2. Save us, O Son of God, O thou who wast born of the Virgin, even us who sing unto thee, Allelulia.

❡ Glory and Now, O only-begotten Son and Word of God, etc. (p. 123).

3. Thy Nativity, O Christ, our God, etc. (p. 402).

Eisodikon: From the womb before the morning star I begat thee. The Lord hath sworn, and he will not repent; thou art a Priest for ever according to the order of Melchisedek. Save us, O Son of God, O thou who wast born of the Virgin, even us who sing unto thee, Alleluia.

❡ *Then the Troparion,* Thy Nativity, O Christ our God, *etc.,* (*p. 402*); *and to the Patron Saint of the church; concluding with the following Kontakion of the Nativity, in the Third Tone.*

TODAY the Virgin giveth birth to the Transcendent in essence; the earth offereth the cave to the unapproachable One; the angels with the shepherds glorify him; and the Magi with the star travel on their way; for a new child hath been born for our sakes, God before the ages.

❡ *Then instead of* Holy God:

Ye who have been baptized into Christ, have put on Christ, Alleluia.

The Epistle: All those on earth worship thee and sing unto thee, Alleluia to God, O all the earth.

Selection from the Epistle of St. Paul to the Galatians (4:4-7)

YE brethren: But when the fullness of the time was come, God sent his Son, made of a woman, made under the law.

That he might redeem them who were under the law: that we might receive the adoption of sons.

And because you are sons, God hath sent the Spirit of his Son into your hearts, crying: Abba, Father.

Therefore, now he is not a servant, but a son. And if a son, an heir also through God.

The Gospel: from St. Matthew

When Jesus therefore, was born in Bethlehem, etc. (p. 389).

And on Especially, sing the Hermos of the Ninth Ode.

I behold a strange wonderful mystery, etc. *(with its Magnification, p. 406).*
Koinonikon: The Lord hath sent a redemption to his people, Alleluia.

And instead of We have seen the true Light, *etc., is sung,* Thy Nativity, O Christ our God, *etc.* (*p. 402*).

Benediction: O thou who wast born in a cave, and didst lie down in a manger for our salvation, etc.

SERVICE ON DAY FOLLOWING CHRISTMAS

1. VESPERS

The Stichology of the Psalms are not chanted, but immediately after singing, O Lord, to thee have I cried, *etc., proceed with the six stichoi and chant the six Idiomelons of the Feast,* Come, let us rejoice in the Lord, *etc.* (*p. 396*)*; then Glory and Now,* Glory to God in the highest, and on earth be peace, *etc.* (*p. 404*)*; then the Eisodos; and* O resplendent Light, *etc; and the Prokeimenon, in the Seventh Tone.*

What great god is like our God? Thou alone art God, Doer of miracles.

And in the Aposticha, the following Idiomelons, in the Eighth Tone.

By John of Damascus

TODAY hath been fulfilled a strange mystery; for nature hath been renewed and God hath become man. Yea, he hath remained as he has been, taking into himself what had not been, nor was he affected by any confusion or division.

Stichos: Said the Lord to my Lord.

O Lord, thou hast come to Bethlehem, thou hast dwelt in a cave, and hast lain down in a manger, O thou whose throne is in heaven. Thou didst condescend to the shepherds, O thou who art surrounded by the

hosts of angels, in order to save our race, since thou a
compassionate. Glory to thee.

Stichos: From the womb before the morning star,
begat thee, etc.

How shall I describe this great mystery? For t
Incorporeal hath become incarnate; the Word took un
himself the density of the flesh. The Unseen is seen, tl
Untouchable is touched, the Beginningless beginnet
and the Son of God becometh the Son of Man; ye
Jesus Christ himself who is the same yesterday, toda
and unto all ages.

Glory and Now, in the Eighth Tone

THE shepherds hastened to Bethlehem proclaimin
'thee, O true Shepherd, who sitteth on the cherubi
and lieth in a manger, taking the likeness of a child fc
our sakes. Wherefore, O Lord, glory to thee.

❡*And the Troparion,* Thy Nativity, O Christ our God, *etc.* (*thr
times*); *and the Benediction.*

2. MATINS

❡*The Troparion and the Kathismata for the Feast; and the Kat
basias of the Second Canon only. The Ninth Ode of the Feast wi
its Magnifications. The Exaposteilarion and Einos for the Feast; a*
Glory (*in the Einos*), *in the Sixth Tone.*

TODAY the invisible Nature doth unite with mar
kind from the Virgin. Today the boundless Essenc
is wrapped in swaddling clothes in Bethlehem. Toda
God doth guide the Magi by the star to worship, ind
cating beforehand his three-day Burial by the offerin;
of gold, frankincense, and myrrh. Wherefore, we sin
to him saying, O Christ God, who wast incarnate of th
Virgin, save our souls.

❡*Now, in the Second Tone,* Today Christ is born in Bethleher
etc. (*p. 409*); *then the Great Doxology and the Troparion,* Tl
Nativity, O Christ, *etc.*

3. The Mass

The whole order of the Nativity; The Epistle, Ye brethren: For th he that sanctifieth and they who are sanctified, *etc.* (*p. 394*); *he Gospel,* And after the Magi were departed, *etc.* (*p. 276*); *and on pecially,* Verily, it is easier, *etc.* (*p. 407*); *the Koinonikon for the east; and instead of* Having beheld the true Light, *etc., sing the roparion of the Feast.*

The Sunday After Christmas

Commemoration of Joseph the Bethrothed; David the Prophet and ing; and James the Brother of the Lord.

1. Vespers

On O Lord, to thee have I cried, *chant four for the Resurrection; ree for the Feast; and three for the saints of the following, in the irst Tone.*

COME, let us all extol David the king, the grandparent of God; for from him sprang out a stem, amely the Virgin, and from that did shine forth Christ ie Flower, renewing the creation of Adam and Eve rom corruption; for he is compassionate.

Verily, Joseph the betrothed, saw clearly in his old ge that the foresayings of the Prophets had been fullled openly; for he was given a strange earnest, receiv-ig inspiration from the angels, who cried, Glory to God; for he hath bestowed peace on earth.

Let us extol the brother of the Lord; for he is a Bishop, and he also radiated forth bravely in martyr-om. Wherefore, O Jesus our God, who was wrapped i swaddling clothes in the cave and manger, save hrough his petitions, all those who praise thee.

Glory, in the Sixth Tone

ET us celebrate the memory of David the Prophet-king of true worship, and with him James the Apostle, the first of Bishops; so that, being saved from rror by their teachings, we may glorify Christ who hone forth incarnate from the Virgin to save our souls.

❦ *Now to our Lady, in the Tone in use.*

❦ *The Aposticha of the Oktoechos; Glory, in the Sixth Tone.*

THY Nativity hath become a memorial for th
Priests, might and happiness for kings; and in
we take pride, saying, Our Father who art in heaven
hallowed be thy Name, O Lover of mankind.

Now, in the Same Tone

TODAY all the angels in heaven exchange glad tid
ings and rejoice; and the whole creation singet
with joy for the Lord Saviour born in Bethlehem; fo
the error of idols hath entirely disappeared, and Chris
reigneth unto all ages.

Troparion for the Resurrection, and Glory for the Saints, in the Second Tone

PROCLAIM, O Joseph, to David, the grandparen
of God, the amazing wonders; for thou hast seen
Virgin great with child; for with the shepherds thou
didst give glory, with the Magi thou didst worship
and by the angel it was revealed to thee. Wherefore
plead thou with Christ God to have our souls.

❦ *Now for the Feast,* Thy Nativity, O Christ, *etc.*

2. MATINS

❦ *On* God the Lord hath appeared unto us, *the Troparia as a Vesp
ers; the Kathismata for the Resurrection and the Feast; then th
Benedictions; the Anabathmoi of the Tone; the Prokeimenon; an
the rest of the Order of the Matin Gospel for the Resurrection; th
Katabasias of the Second Canon for the Feast; then sing,* O thou wh
art more honourable, *etc; and the Katabasia,* Verily, it is easier, *etc*

The Exaposteilarion for the Resurrection, and for the Saints

WITH James, the noble brother of the Lord, let u
extol David the grandsire of God, and the divine
Joseph, betrothed to the Theotokos; for they served th

divine Nativity of Christ in Bethlehem as befitteth God, singing praises thereto with the angels, the Magi, and the shepherds, since he is God and Lord.

Then for the Feast: Our Saviour hath visited us, etc. (p. 408).

❡*And in the Einos, four for the Resurrection and four for the Feast; Glory, in the Eighth Tone.*

By Anatolius

THE blood, fire, and pillars of smoke are the miracles of the earth which Joel foresow; for the blood is the Incarnation, the fire is the Divinity, and the pillars of smoke are the Holy Spirit which descended on the Virgin and scented the world. Wherefore, great is the mystery of thine Incarnation, O Lord, glory to thee.

❡*Now,* Thou hast transcended, *etc; then the Great Doxology; and the Troparion,* Today hath salvation, *etc. And in the Mass:*

The Epistle: Ye brethren: I certify you, that the Gospel, etc. (p. 254).

The Gospel: And after the Magi were departed, etc. (p. 276).

❡*And the rest of the Order of the Mass (p. 413).*

26. High Feast of the Theotokos[1]; Euthimius, Bishop (9).

27. Stephen, Archdeacon and the first of Martyrs.

Troparion, in the Fourth Tone

O FIRST of strivers among the Martyrs, thy head was crowned with a kingly crown, through the struggles that thou didst endure for the sake of Christ God; for thou didst reproach the folly of the Jews, and therefore, didst see thy Saviour on the right hand of the Father. Wherefore, to him continuously plead for our souls.

---

[1] See the complete service on the second day of the Nativity as above.

Kontakion, in the Fourth Tone

YESTERDAY the Lord came in the flesh; and to-day the servant hath departed in the flesh. Yesterday the King was born in the flesh; and today the servant is stoned for his sake, and for his sake did pass away, namely the divine Stephen, first of the Martyrs.

28. The Twenty Thousand Martyrs who were Burned in Nicomedia (3).

29. The Fourteen Thousand Children who were Killed by Herod (3); Marcellus the Righteous (8).

30. Anysia the Righteous Martyr (4).

31. Melamia the Righteous (8); Leave-taking to the Nativity, in which its whole service is sung.

V. JANUARY

[Its days, 31; Hours of Day, 10; of Night, 14.]

1. THE CIRCUMCISION OF OUR LORD JESUS CHRIST IN THE FLESH, AND THE MEMORIAL OF BASIL THE GREAT.

I. VESPERS

Typicon

❧ *If this Feast falleth on a Sunday, then the service of the Resurrection; the service of the Circumcision and the service of the Saints are chanted together.*

❧ *After the Sunset Psalm, recite three Psalms only, from* Blessed is the man; *and on* O Lord, to thee have I cried, *sing the Idiomelons of the Feast; three in the Eight Tone.*

WHEN the Saviour condescended for the sake of of mankind, he was willing to be wrapped in swaddling clothes, and he who was eight days old on the side of his Mother, and eternal on the side of his Father did not disdain the circumcision of the flesh. Wherefore, let us cry unto him, O believers, Thou art our God; have mercy upon us. (*Repeat.*)

The all-good God did not disdain to be circumcised by the circumcision of the flesh; but offered himself a Sign and an Exemplar of salvation to all, for the Maker of the law doth fulfill the precepts of the law, and the preaching of the Prophets concerning him. Wherefore, O thou who dost contain all in thy grasp, O thou who wast wrapped in swaddling clothes, O Lord, glory to thee

And to the Saint, three in the Fourth Tone

O THOU, whose name correspondeth to the name of the kingdom, when thou didst lead in thy kingly rank the holy people of Christ in wisdom and knowledge, O Father, then the King of kings and Lord of all, the Son united everlastingly with the Father, and co-eternal with him, did adorn thee with the crown of the kingdom. Wherefore, plead with him to save and illuminate our souls.

O thou who art adorned with the vestments of a Bishop, thou didst preach, O Basil, the Gospel of the kingdom gladly, and didst pour out for the Church the teachings of Orthodoxy, wherewith being lighted, we speak divinely and glorify the one Godhead, almighty Father, only Word of God, and divine Spirit, in three Persons, indivisible. Wherefore, implore him to save and enlighten our souls.

O thou who art in the ranks of the heavenly orders, O thou Father Basil who dwellest among them, emulating their way with the humility of thine all-resplendent way, verily, when thou wast in the flesh, thou didst dwell among men as one without the flesh. Wherefore, plead thou with Christ our God in behalf of us, who delight in thy God-inspired teachings, to save us from dangers and from the darkness of folly, and to lighten our souls.

Glory, in the Eighth Tone (By Anatolius)

O RIGHTEOUS one, thou didst become a lover of
wisdom, preferring the life with God to all possessions; and by thy contemplation of death thou didst
forsake wealth, as is meet; for by the hardships of
abstinence thou didst strip from thyself the passion of
the flesh; by thy study of divine law thou didst preserve
the rank of thy soul unsubjugated; and by richness of
virtue thou didst wholly subject the passion of the flesh
to the spirit. Wherefore, having disposed the flesh, the
world, and the chief of the world, standing before
Christ, seek thou for our souls the Great Mercy.

Now: When the Saviour condenscended for the sake
of mankind, etc. (p. 416).

❡ *Then the Eisodos,* O resplendent Light, *etc; the daily Prokeimenon; and the following Readings.*

First Reading: from Genesis (17:1-7; 9-14)

A ND the Lord appeared to Abram and said unto
him: I am the Almighty God: walk before me and
be perfect.

And I will make my covenant between me and thee:
and I will multiply thee exceedingly.

Abram fell flat on his face.

And God said to him: I am, and my covenant is with
thee, and thou shalt be a father of many nations.

Neither shall thy name be called any more Abram:
but thou shalt be called Abraham: because I have made
thee a father of many nations.

And I will make thee increase, exceedingly, and I
will make nations of thee, and kings shall come out of
thee.

And I will establish my covenant between me and
thee, and between thy seed after thee in their generations, by a perpetual covenant: to be a God to thee,
and to thy seed after thee.

Again God said to Abraham: And thou therefore shalt keep my covenant, and thy seed after thee in their generations.

This is my covenant which you shall observe, between me and you, and thy seed after thee: All the male kind of you shall be circumcised:

And you shall circumcise the flesh of your foreskin, that it may be for a sign of the covenant between me and you.

An infant of eight days old shall be circumcised among you, every man child in your generations: he that is born in the house, as well as the bought servant shall be circumcised, and whosoever is not of your stock:

And my covenant shall be in your flesh for a perpetual covenant.

The male, whose flesh of his foreskin shall not be circumcised, that soul shall be destroyed out of his people: because he hath broken my covenant.

Second Reading: from the Book of Proverbs (8:22-30)

THE Lord possessed me in the beginning of his ways, before he made any thing from the beginning.

I was set up from eternity, and of old before the earth was made.

The depths were not as yet, and I was already conceived, neither had the fountains of waters as yet sprung out:

The mountains with their huge bulk had not as yet been established: before the hills I was brought forth:

He had not yet made the earth, nor the rivers, nor the poles of the world.

When he prepared the heavens, I was present: when with a certain law and compass he enclosed the depths:

When he established the sky above, and poised the fountains of waters.

When he compassed the sea with its bounds, and set a law to the waters that they should not pass their limits: when he balanced the foundations of the earth;

I was with him forming all things: and was delighted every day, playing before him at all times.

Third Reading: from the Book of Wisdom

THE mouth of the righteous uttereth wisdom, and the lips of the wise direct blessings. The mouth of the wise contemplates wisdom, and the just shall deliver them from death. When the righteous man dieth, his hope shall not perish, for the righteous son is born unto life, and from his righteous deeds are reaped the fruits of justice. A light unto the righteous, shining for all time; and from the Lord they shall find grace and glory. The tongues of the wise excel in instruction, and in their hearts wisdom finds rest. The Lord loveth the righteous hearts, and they who are blameless in their ways are acceptable to him. The wisdom of the Lord lighteth the countenance of the understanding one; and they who desire it shall be apprehended by it before it is known. It is beholden without difficulty by those who love it, and he who riseth up early for it shall not tire. He who watcheth for it by night, soon will be without worry, for it goeth after those who seek it and seeketh them. In the highways it appeareth for them pleasantly. But no evil can overcome wisdom. Her have I loved, and have sought her out from my youth, and have desired to take her for my spouse, and I became a lover of her beauty.

She glorifieth her nobility by being conversant with God: yea and the Lord of all things hath loved her.

For it is she that teacheth the knowledge of God, and is the chooser of his works.

And if a man love justice: her labours have great virtues; for she teacheth temperance, and prudence, and justice, and fortitude, which are such things as men can have nothing more profitable in life.

And if a man desireth much knowledge: she knoweth things past, and judgeth of things to come: she knoweth the subtilties of speeches, and the solutions of arguments: she knoweth signs and wonders before they be done, and the events of times and ages.

I purposed therefore to take her to me to live with me: knowing that she will communicate to me of her good things, and will be a comfort in my cares and grief.

Thinking these things with myself, and pondering them in my heart, that to be allied to wisdom is immortality.

And that there is great delight in her friendship, and inexhaustible riches in the works of her hands, and in the exercise of conference with her, wisdom, and glory in the communication of her words: I went about seeking, that I might take her to myself.

As I knew that I could not otherwise be continent, except God gave it, and this also was a point of wisdom, to know whose gift it was: I went to the Lord, and besought him, and said with my whole heart:

God of my fathers, and Lord of mercy, who hast made all things with thy word,

And by thy wisdom hast appointed man, that he should have dominion over the creature that was made by thee,

That he should order the world according to equity and justice, and execute justice with an upright heart:

Give me wisdom, that sitteth by thy throne, and cast me not from among thy children:

For I am thy servant, and the son of thy handmaid.

Send her out of thy holy heaven, and from the throne of thy majesty, that she may be with me, and my labour with me, that I may know what is acceptable with thee:

For she knoweth and understandeth all things, and shall lead me soberly in my works, and shall perserve me by her power.

For the thoughts of mortal men are fearful; and our counsels uncertain.

❡*And in the Litiya, the following piece, in the Sixth Tone:*

By Phizandius

GRACE is poured upon thy lips, O righteous Father, and thou didst become a shepherd for the Church of Christ, teaching the sheep endowed with speech to believe in a consubstantial Trinity of one Godhead.

¶ *And in the Aposticha, the Idiomelons, in the First Tone.*

O WHAT a divine and noble bee of the Church of Christ, thou all-beatified Basil; for when thou didst arm thyself with the sting of divine passion, thou didst wound the blasphemies of God-transgressing heresies; and didst store in the souls of believers the sweetness of true worship. Wherefore, having now arrived at the resting-place of the everlasting divine pastures, remember us when thou standest before the consubtantial Trinity.

Stichos: My mouth shall speak wisdom.

By Basil the Anchorite

THOU hast acquired, our Father Basil, the virtues of all the saints; the humility of Moses, the zeal of Elijah, the confession of Peter, and the eloquence of John in theology. And like Paul thou dost still cry, Who is weak, and I am not weak? Who is offended, and I burn not? Wherefore, since thou dwellest with them, plead for the salvation of souls.

Stichos: The mouth of the just shall bring forth wisdom *(in the Second Tone).*

By John the Damascene

O BASIL, the revealer of noble things, having verily studied the nature of creatures and contemplated the unstability of all things, thou didst find but One who is stable, the Transcendent in essence, the Creator of all, to whom as thou didst the more incline, thou didst the more cast off desire of things transient. Wherefore, intercede for us that we may attain our divine desire.

Glory, in the Sixth Tone

O THOU all-beatified Basil, who didst receive the grace of wonders from heaven, who didst expose the errors of the heathen by thy doctrines thou art the glory of Chief Priests, their cornerstone, and examplar of the teachings of all the Fathers. Having, therefore, received favour with Christ, plead with him for the salvation of our souls.

Now: The all-good God did not disdain to be circumcised, etc. (p. 417).

Troparion for the Saint, in the First Tone

IN all the earth that received thy sayings, thy melody did resound, O righteous Father, through which thou didst go about and proclaim, as worthy of God, the nature of creatures, cultivating the character of mankind, O thou of kingly Priesthood, Basil. Wherefore, plead thou with Christ God to save our souls.

Glory: (Repeated).

Now: Another for the Feast, in the Same Tone

O MOST compassionate Lord, while yet God after thine essence, thou didst take human likeness without transubstantiation; and having fulfilled the law thou didst accept willingly cricumcision in the flesh, that thou mightest annul the shadowy signs and remove the veil of our passions. Glory to thy goodness, glory to thy compassion, glory to thine ineffable condescension, O Word.

2. MATINS

❡ *On* God the Lord hath appeared unto us, *the Troparion of the Saint* (two times) *and once to the Circumcision. Then the following Kathismata.*

First Kathisma, in the Fifth Tone

LET us extol Basil; for he is a royal adornment to the Church of Christ, an unpilfered treasury of doctrines, through whom we were instructed to worship a holy Trinity, united in Essence and divisible in Persons.

Glory and Now, in the First Tone

THE Maker of all and the Lord of the world who is in the highest with the Father and the Spirit is circumcised on earth as an eight-day old child. Verily, divine and wonderful are thy works; for thou wast circumcised for our sakes, O Lord, since thou art the Perfection of the law.

Second Kathisma, in the Eighth Tone

THOU didst pour out the mystic richness, the richness of the ineffable wisdom, in thy divine visions; thou didst store for all the waters of Orthodoxy, gladdening in a divine manner the hearts of believers, and drowning rightly the doctrines of the infidels. Wherefore, in both cases thou didst appear in the power of true worship, contending, undefeated, for the Trinity. Therefore, O Bishop Basil, intercede with Christ God to grant forgiveness of sins to those who eagerly celebrate thy holy memory.

Glory and Now, in the Fourth Tone

O LORD, since thou art the Deep of love to mankind, thou didst put on the likeness of a servant, and wast circumcised in the flesh, granting all mankind thy Great Mercy.

Third Kathisma, in the Eighth Tone

THOU didst refute by divine sayings the obscure heresies, drowning all the folly of Arius and preaching to mankind the Divinity of the Spirit; and by the lifting of thy hands thou didst kill thine enemies, exiling the worship of Sabellius wholly, and didst annul all the opinions of Nestorius. Wherefore, O Bishop Basil, intercede with Christ God to grant forgiveness of sins to those who eagerly celebrate thy memory.

Glory and Now, in the Same Tone

Verily, the Lord of all and their Creator, having taken flesh from thy holy womb, did reveal thee, O innocent of all blame, as a helper of mankind. Wherefore, in thee do we seek refuge, petitioning forgiveness of sins, and that we may escape everlasting punishment and all the harm of the wicked one, the ruler of this world.

Wherefore, do we cry unto thee, Intercede thou with thy Son and God to grant forgiveness of sins to those who worship in faith thine all-holy nativity.

¶ *Then the Anabathmoi,* From my youth, *etc.* (*p. 50*) ; *and this Prokeimenon.*

My mouth shall speak wisdom. Hear these things, all ye nations.

The Matin Gospel: from St. John (10:1-9)

THE Lord said to those of the Jews who came to him: Amen, Amen, I say to you: He that entereth not by the door into the sheep fold, but climbeth up another way, the same is a thief and a robber.

But he that entereth in by the door is the shepherd of the sheep.

To him the porter openeth; and the sheep hear his voice: and he calleth his own sheep by name, and leadeth them out.

And when he hath let out his own sheep, he goeth before them: and the sheep follow him, because they know his voice.

But a stranger they follow not, but fly from him, because they know not the voice of strangers.

This proverb Jesus spoke to them. But they understood not what he spoke to them.

Jesus therefore said to them again: Amen, amen, I say to you, I am the door of the sheep.

All others, as many as have come, are thieves and robbers: and the sheep heard them not.

I am the door. By me, if any man enter in, he shall be saved: and he shall go in, and go out, and shall find pastures.

❧ *And after Psalm 50, the Choir chanteth Glory,* By the intercessions of the Bishop, *etc; and Now,* By the intercessions of the Theotokos, *etc; then* O merciful One, have mercy upon me, O God, *etc; and the following Idiomelon, in the Sixth Tone.*

GRACE is poured upon thy lips, O righteous Father, and thou didst become a shepherd to the Church of Christ, teaching the sheep endowed with speech to believe in a consubstantial Trinity of one Godhead.

❧ *The Katabasias (in couples) of the Epiphany (Matins). And instead of* O thou who art more honourable, *etc., sing the following Ninth Ode, in the Second Tone (with its Magnifications).*

By Stephen

Magnify, O my soul, her who is more honourable, and more exalted in glory than the heavenly hosts.

O THOU blessed and all-pure one, in whose womb was incarnate in an effable manner, the God rising before the sun, coming to us in the flesh, thee, O Theotokos, do we magnify.

Magnify, O my soul, him who accepted circumcision on the eighth day.

Verily, Christ having passed all the bounds of human nature, was born of the Virgin in a supernatural manner and was circumcised in the flesh, fulfilling the law.

Today the Lord is circumcised in the flesh and his Name was called Jesus.

Come, let us celebrate in holiness the glorious naming of Christ; for he was called today Jesus, as worthy of God, and withal let us magnify the memory of the Bishop.

To the Saint, in the Same Tone

By John Damascene

Magnify, O my soul, Basil, the Great amongst
Bishops.

O Father Basil, thou didst follow in the life-bearing steps, the steps of Christ, faithful Head of shep-
erds for thou didst go forth and offer thyself to the
usurper, valiantly endangering thyself for the Church,
O most-beatified.

Magnify, O my soul, Basil the Great of Cæsarea.

Verily, the usurper, having seen the all-sanctified
assembly, the assembly of the Church of Christ, adorned
by the presidency of thy Priesthood, O wise one, was
confounded and fell down, utterly perishing, not being
able to bear the radiance of the spirit that was in thee,
O Basil.

Glory: Magnify, O my soul, the might of the three-
ersoned and indivisible Trinity.

Thou hast become worthy, O Basil, of the throne of
the Apostles, of the rank of the strivers for Christ, of
the paradise of the righteous, and of the assembly of
the Prophets; for thou wast an initiate of the Theo-
okos and a servant of the Trinity.

Now: Glorify, O my soul, the Maiden who delivered
us from the curse.

Verily, the Lord who alone roofed with waters his
high chambers, bridled the sea and dried up the waves,
and was incarnate of thee, O pure one, doth come down
from Bethlehem to the Jordan to be baptised in the
flesh.

Katabasia, Verily all tongues, *etc.* (*Matins of Epiphany*); *and* O
the wonders of thy superintelligent Nativity, *etc.* (*The same*).

Exaposteilarions

THOU hast circumcised, O wise Father Basil, the
uncircumcision of thyself with the love of philosophy; and by thy wonders thou didst appear to the

world like the sun, lighting the minds of believers
O thou of divine mind, O servant of the Trinity and
initiate of the Theotokos.

Verily, the Creator of ages who fulfilled the law i
circumcised in the flesh like an eight-day old child, i
wrapped in swaddling clothes like a man, and fed with
milk, he who is the All-controller through his bound
less might, since he is God, and the Maker of the law i
flesh.

❡*And in the Einos, the following four Prosomia are sung in the
Fifth Tone.*

VERILY, he who was begotten of the Father in an
inexplicable manner, free of division or change
since he is the Word and God of God, doth bear cir
cumcision in the flesh, remaining still unchanged i
his Divinity.   And he who is above the law hath sub
mitted to it, granting the blessing from on high
Wherefore, let us extol him, praising his condenscen
sion of transcendent goodness, and glorify him grate
fully, beseeching him to grant our souls the Grea
Mercy.

When thou didst become, O righteous one, th
adopted son of God by rebirth, that is divine Baptism
thou didst confess him who by nature and truth is th
Son before the ages, the Word of God, consubstanti
and coëternal with the Father.   And by the splendou
of thy sayings thou didst stop the open mouths of here
tics.   Wherefore, thou didst dwell in the celestial king
doms, reigning with him who is alone King by natur
Christ, who distributeth bountifully to the world th
Great Mercy.

O all-beatified Basil, the righteous, thou didst ste
within the heavenly temple, as pure chief of Priest
enwrapped by practice and theory in the two principl
of wisdom, as in a holy vestment.   And now that tho
art a Priest to the heavenly Altar, standing before Go
and celebrating the immaterial service, remember,

ll-compassionate one, those who celebrate thy noble
ll-revered memory, pleading with Christ who granteth
he Great Mercy.

Since thou art wholly consecrated to God, and in all
hy condition consecrated unto him from thy youth,
hou didst hide in the wisdom transcending wisdom,
nfolding the knowledge of creation, interpreting it
orilliantly, and conversing thereof in the ears wisely,
naking of instruction a proposition of divine knowl-
:dge. Wherefore, do we proclaim thee as theologian,
livine teacher, a radiance-bearing star of the Church,
oraising Christ who granteth the Great Mercy.

⁋ *Glory, in the Sixth Tone,* Grace is poured upon thy lips, *etc.*
(p. 426).

⁋ *Now, in the Eighth Tone,* When the Saviour condescended, *etc.*
(p. 416); the the Great Doxology; the Troparion of the Saint; and
he Benediction.

3. The Mass

1. By the intercessions of the Theotokos, O Saviour,
ave us.

2. Save us, O Son of God, who hath been circum-
:ised in the flesh, as we sing unto thee, Alleluia.

⁋ *Glory and Now,* O only-begotten Son, *etc. (p. 123).*

3. O Most Compassionate Lord, etc. *(i.e. Troparion*
of the Feast, p. 424).

Eisodikon: O come, let us worship and fall down
o Christ. Save us, O Son of God, who hast been cir-
:umcised in the flesh, as we sing unto thee, Alleluia.

⁋ *Then the Troparion for the Feast; for the Saint; and for the*
Patron Saint of the church.

The Kontakion of the Saint, in the Fourth Tone

THOU hast appeared as an unshaken pillar of the
Church, distributing to all mankind unrobbed authority, and sealing them with thy doctrines, O righteous Basil, who showeth heavenly things.

⁋ *Then conclude with the Kontakion of the Feast, in the Third Tone.*

THE Master of all endureth humiliation and is circumcised for the iniquities of mankind; for he is good, and granteth salvation to the world. And in the highest the High Priest of the Creator, clothed with light, the divine initiate of Christ, Basil, rejoiceth.

The Epistle

My mouth shall speak wisdom. Hear these things, all ye nations.

Section from the Epistle of St. Paul to the Colossians (2:8-12)

BRETHREN: Beware lest any man cheat you by philosophy, and vain deceit; according to the tradition of men, according to the elements of the world, and not according to Christ.

For in him dwelleth all the fulness of the Godhead corporeally;

And you are filled in him, who is the head of all principality and power:

In whom also you are circumcised with circumcision not made by hand, in the despoiling of the body of the flesh, but in the circumcision of Christ:

Buried with him in baptism, in whom also you are risen again by the faith of the operation of God, who hath raised him up from the dead.

The Gospel: from St. Luke (2:20-21; 40 to end)

AND it came to pass that the shepherds returned, glorifying and praising God, for the things they had heard and seen, as it was told unto them.

And after eight days were accomplished, that the child should be circumcised, his name was called Jesus, which was called by the angel, before he was conceived in the womb.

And the child grew, and waxed strong, full of wisdom; and the grace of God was in him.

And his parents went every year to Jerusalem, at the solemn day of the pasch,

And when he was twelve years od, they going up into Jerusalem, according to the custom of the feast,

And having fulfilled the days, when they returned, the child Jesus remained in Jerusalem; and his parents knew it not.

And thinking that he was in the company, they came a day's journey, and sought him among their kinsfolks and acquaintance.

And not finding him, they returned into Jerusalem, seeking him.

And it came to pass, that, after three days, they found him in the temple, sitting in the midst of the doctors, hearing them, and asking them questions.

And all that heard him were astonished at his wisdom and his answers.

And seeing him, they wondered. And his mother said to him: Son, why hast thou done so to us? behold thy father and I have sought thee sorrowing.

And he said to them: How is it that you sought me? did you not know, that I must be about my father's business?

And they understood not the word that he spoke unto them.

And he went down with them, and came to Nazareth, and was subject to them. And his mother kept all these words in her heart.

And Jesus advanced in wisdom, and age, and grace with God and men.

❧ *Then the rest of the Mass of Basil the Great. And after the Proclamation,* And may the mercies of the great God, *etc., chant the following Magnification for the Saint, in the Second Tone.*

LET us all extol the great Basil, revealer of heavenly things, initiate of the Master, the star shining from Cæsarea and the town of Capadocia, honouring and magnifying him.

Koinonikon: Praise ye the Lord from the heavens. Alleluia.

¶*And instead of* We have beheld the Light, *etc., say the Troparion of the Feast.* O most compassionate Lord, *etc.* (*p. 423*)*; The Benediction,* O thou who didst consent to be circumcised in the flesh on the eighth day for our salvation, *etc.*

2. Preparation for the Feast of the Epiphany; and Sylvester the Pope of Rome (9).
3. Malachi the Prophet (13); and Gordius the Martyr (1).
4. High Feast for the Seventy Apostles (12); and Theoctistus the Righteous (6).
5. Theopempus and Theonas the Martyrs (2); and Syncletice the Righteous (8).

¶*Note: The 5th of January is the Preparation Day (Paramon) of the divine Epiphany and shall be a fast day on whatever day it falls.*

Sunday Before the Epiphany

From January 2nd to 5th

1. Vespers

¶*On* O Lord, to thee have I cried, *sing six for the Resurrection; and four following to the Preparation, in the Fourth Tone.*

L ET us go before and shout songs in true worship to the Preparation of the Feast of the noble Baptism of our God; for, behold, he shall go in the flesh to his Forerunner as a Man, and ask for the baptism of salvation for the re-creation of all those enlightened in faith with purity, and of the partakers of the spirit. *(Repeat.)*

Verily, David did go before and write clearly that Christ should be revealed, and God appear and come before his servant seeking baptism. Be filled with joy, O River Jordan, and O ye earth, sea, hills, mountains, and hearts of men, rejoice now, receiving great light.

O all-powerful Lord, who art the River of peace, and the Valley of bliss, as it was written, how shall the courses of the river receive thee descending to it naked, O thou who didst mantle the heavens with clouds, and stripped naked all the evil of the adversary, and clothed mankind with incorruptibility.

Glory, in the Sixth Tone

THE true Christ cometh down towards the Jordan to be baptized of John, who saith to him, It is I who need to be baptized by thee, and thou comest to me? Verily, I who am grass dare not touch the fire. Wherefore, sanctify me, O Master by thy divine Epiphany.

⟨*Now for the Resurrection; the Aposticha for the Resurrection; Glory and Now (from Jan. second to fourth); the following is sung in the Eighth Tone.*

O JOHN the Baptizer, who didst know me, the Lamb, in the womb, serve me in the river with the angels. Stretch forth thy hand and touch my pure head. And when thou seest the mountains tremble and the Jordan turn back, then shout with them, saying, O thou who wast incarnate of the Virgin for our salvation, O Lord, glory to thee.

⟨*And if the day falleth on January fifth, then the following, in the Fifth Tone.*

VERILY, Christ our God cometh for baptism in the River Jordan, willing to cleanse us from our sins by his appearance; for he alone is good and the Lover of mankind.

⟨*Troparion for the Resurrection. And from Jan. second to fourth, the following Troparion for the Preparation, in the Fourth Tone.*

MAKE ready, O Zebulon, and prepare, O Nephtali, and thou, River Jordan, cease thy flow and receive with joy the Master coming to be baptized. And thou, Adam, rejoice with the first mother, and hide not yourselves as ye did of old in paradise; for having seen you naked, he appeared to clothe you with the first robe. Yea, Christ hath appeared desiring to renew the whole creation.

❡*And if the day falleth on Jan. fifth, then also the following Troparion, in the Fourth Tone.*

THE River Jordan receded of old by the mantle of Elisha when Elijah ascended to heaven; and the water was separated to this side and that, the wet element turning into a dry path for him, being truly a symbol of Baptism, by which we cross the path of transient age. Christ appeared in the Jordan to sanctify its waters.

2. MATINS

❡*The Troparia as at Vespers; the Kathismata for the Resurrection; and the Benedictions and the rest of the Order of the Matin Gospel for the Resurrection; the Katabasias for the ‹Epiphany; and sing, O thou who art more honourable, etc.*

The Exaposteilarion for the Resurrection; then for the Preparation

O THOU Lover of mankind, how shall the courses of the river receive thee, who didst create the rivers and the seas from nothing? Or how shall the Forerunner dare put his hand upon thy pure head, O Master? Wherefore, let us praise with trembling and sublimity thy humility, O Word.

❡*And in the Einos, four for the Resurrection; and four for the Preparation. But if the day falleth on January second to fourth, the following Prosomia are sung in the Sixth Tone.*

PROCEED, O angelic powers, advancing from Bethlehem to the courses of the Jordan. Go before, O John, forsaking the wilderness. Rejoice, O river, and prepare. Let all the earth rejoice; for Christ cometh to purify the sins of Adam; for he is compassionate.

Come, all ye nations of the earth, let us go out mysticaly from Bethlehem with pure lips and undefiled hearts and come with Christ to the Jordan to praise him now with gladness, saying with faith, Blessed art thou our God who cometh: glory to thee.

Verily, great and terrible is the mystery; for God hath emulated man, and the blameless One who knew no sin whatsoever, asketh today to be baptized of John in the Jordan River. Blessed, therefore, art thou, our pure God: glory to thee.

Verily, Christ that shineth from the Virgin, a Flower from David, hath come toward the courses of the Jordan River to wash in its waters the sins of our first sire. Be of good cheer, O Adam, and rejoice, O Eve, and let heaven be glad, and let us nations say, Blessed art thou, our God that cometh; glory to thee.

❡ *And if the day falleth on January fifth, the following Prosomia are sung in the Second Tone.*

BEHOLD, the King hath appeared; the Hope of Israel hath come. Rejoice, O nations; for the Light appeareth.

The divine Light hath been manifest in the flesh to those on earth; he hath appeared to those in darkness, and grace hath shone forth for all.

Serve, O Prophet, thou lamp for the Light, the dawn of the Sun, the righteous of the Bridegroom, the Forerunner of the Word.

❡ *Glory; the Eothina; and Now,* Thou hast transcended, *etc.* (*p. 117*). *Then the Great Doxology; and the Troparion,* Today hath salvation, *etc.* (*p. 119*).

3. The Mass

❡ *In the Eisodos, the Troparion for the Resurrection, the Preparation; and the Patron Saint of the church.*

Kontakion, in the Fourth Tone

TODAY hath the Lord appeared in the courses of the Jordan, crying to John and saying, Be not dismayed at my baptism; for I have verily come to save Adam the first to be created.

❧ *The Epistle and the Gospel for the Sunday before the Epiphany* (p. 277); *and on Especially,* It is truly meet, *etc; the Koinonikon,* Praise ye the Lord, *etc; and* We have seen the true Light, *etc.*

6. THE FEAST OF THE DIVINE EPIPHANY OF OUR LORD AND GOD JESUS CHRIST, OR HIS BAPTISM IN THE JORDAN.

1. THE ORDER OF THE GREAT HOURS

FIRST HOUR

❧ *After,* Blessed be God, *etc;* Holy God, *etc; and* O come, let us worship, *etc.* (three times), say the following three Psalms.

PSALM 5

Give ear, O Lord to my words, understand my cry, etc. (p. 68).

PSALM 22

The Lord ruleth me: and I shall want nothing, etc. (p. 94).

PSALM 26

THE Lord is my light and my salvation, whom I shall not fear.

The Lord is the protector of my life: of whom shall I be afraid?

Whilst the wicked draw near against me, to eat my flesh.

My enemies that trouble me, have themselves been weakened, and have fallen.

If armies in camp should stand together against me, my heart shall not fear.

If a battle should rise up against me, in this will I be confident.

One thing I have asked of the Lord, this will I seek after; that I may dwell in the house of the Lord all the days of my life.

That I may see the delight of the Lord, and may visit his temple.

For he hath hidden me in his tabernacle; in the day of evils, he hath protected me in the secret place of his tabernacle.

He hath exalted me upon a rock: and now he hath lifted up my head above my enemies.

I have gone round, and have offered up in his tabernacle a sacrifice of jubilation: I will sing, and recite a psalm to the Lord.

Hear, O Lord, my voice, with which I have cried to thee: have mercy on me and hear me.

My heart hath said to thee: My face hath sought thee: thy face, O Lord, will I still seek.

Turn not away thy face from me; decline not in thy wrath from thy servant.

Be thou my helper, forsake me not; do not thou despise me, O God my Saviour.

For my father and my mother have left me: but the Lord hath taken me up.

Set me, O Lord, a law in thy way, and guide me in the right path, because of my enemies.

Deliver me not over to the will of them that trouble me; for unjust witnesses have risen up against me; and iniquity hath lied to itself.

I believe to see the good things of the Lord in the land of the living.

Expect the Lord, do manfully, and let thy heart take courage, and wait thou for the Lord.

❡ *Glory and Now;* Alleluia (*three times*); Glory to thee, O God; *and* Lord, have mercy (*three times*); *then Glory; and the following Troparion,* The Jordan River receded, *etc.* (*p. 434*).

Now: What shall we call thee, O full of grace, etc. (p. 374).

❡ *Then the following Idiomelons in the Eighth Tone:*

TODAY the nature of water is sanctified, and the Jordan is cloven, and its waters shall be withheld from flowing; the Matser being shown washed therein.

Stichos: Therefore will I remember thee from the land of the Jordan.

Thou didst come to the river like a man, O Christ King. Thou dost hasten, O good One, to receive baptism as a servant at the hands of the Forerunner, for our sins, O Lover of mankind.

Glory and Now, in the Eighth Tone

TOWARD the voice in the wilderness, Prepare ye the way of the Lord thou didst come taking the likeness of a servant, seeking baptism, O thou who knowest no sin. The waters saw thee and were afraid, and the Forerunner trembled and cried, saying, How shall the Light seek to be lighted for the lamp? How shall the servant place his hand upon the Master? Wherefore, sanctify me and the waters, O Saviour, carrying the sin of the world.

Prokeimenon of the Prophecy, in the Fourth Tone

The voice of the Lord is upon many waters. I will love thee, O Lord, my strength.

Reading: from the Prophecy of Isaiah (35:1 to end)

THESE things, the Lord doth say: The Land that was desolate and impassable shall be glad; and the wilderness shall rejoice, and shall flourish like the lily.

It shall bud forth and blossom, and shall rejoice with joy and praise: the glory of Libanus is given to it: the beauty of Carmel, and Saron, they shall see the glory of the Lord, and the beauty of our God.

Strengthen ye the feeble hands, and confirm the weak knees.

Say to the fainthearted: Take courage, and fear not: behold your God will bring the revenge of recompense: God himself will come and will save you.

Then shall the eyes of the blind be opened, and the ears of the deaf shall be unstopped.

Then shall the lame man leap as a hart, and the tongue of the dumb shall be free: for waters are broken out in the desert, and streams in the wilderness.

And that which was dry land, shall become a pool, and the thirsty land springs of water. In the dens where dragons dwelt before, shall rise up the verdure of the reed and the bulrush.

And a path and a way shall be there, and it shall be called the holy way: the unclean shall not pass over it, and this shall be unto you a straight way, so that fools shall not err therein.

No lion shall be there, nor shall any mischievous beast go up by it, nor be found there: but they shall walk there that shall be delivered.

And the redeemed of the Lord shall return, and shall come into Sion with praise, and everlasting joy shall be upon their heads: they shall obtain joy and gladness, and sorrow and mourning shall flee away.

The Epistle: from the Acts of the Apostles (13:25-23)

AND it came to pass that when John was fulfilling his course he said: I am not he, whom you think me to be: but behold, there cometh one after me, whose shoes of his feet I am not worthy to loose.

Men, brethren, children of the stock of Abraham, and whosoever among you fear God, to you the word of this salvation is sent.

For they that inhabited Jerusalem, and the rulers thereof, not knowing him, nor the voices of the prophets, which are read every sabbath, judging him have fulfilled them.

And finding no cause of death in him, they desired of Pilate, that they might kill him.

And when they had fulfilled all things that were written of him, taking him down from the tree, they laid him in a sepulchre.

But God raised him up from the dead the third day:

Who was seen for many days, by them who came up with him from Galilee to Jerusalem, who to this present are his witnesses to the people.

And we declare unto you, that the promise wihch was made to our fathers,

This same God hath fulfilled to our children, raising up Jesus.

The Gospel: from St. Matthew (3:1-6)

AND in those days cometh John the Baptist preaching in the desert of Judæa.

And saying: Do penance: for the kingdom of heaven is at hand.

For this is he that was spoken of by Isaias the prophet, saying: A voice of one crying in the desert, Prepare ye the way of the Lord, make straight his paths.

And the same John had his garment of camel's hair, and a leathern girdle about his loins: and his meat was locusts and wild honey.

Then went out to him Jerusalem and all Judæa, and all the country about Jordan:

And were baptized by him in the Jordan, confessing their sins.

❡*And immediately,* Order my steps, *etc. (p. 378);* Holy God, *etc;* and the Kontakion, Today hath the Lord appeared, *etc. (p. 435).*
❡*The rest of the order as at end of the First Hour of the Nativity,* (*p. 378*).

THIRD HOUR

❡*After,* O come, let us worship, *etc. (three times), say the following Psalms.*

PSALM 28

BRING to the Lord, O ye children of God; bring to the Lord the offspring of rams.

Bring to the Lord glory and honour: bring to the Lord glory to his name: adore ye the Lord in his holy court.

The voice of the Lord is upon the waters; the God of majesty hath thundered, The Lord is upon many waters.

The voice of the Lord is in power; the voice of the Lord in magnificence.

The voice of the Lord breaketh the cedars: yea, the Lord shall break the cedars of Libanus.

And shall reduce them to pieces, as a calf of Libanus, and as the beloved son of unicorns.

The voice of the Lord divideth the flame of fire: The voice of the Lord shaketh the desert: and the Lord shall shake the desert of Cades.

The voice of the Lord prepareth the stags: and he will discover the thick woods: and in his temple all shall speak his glory.

The Lord maketh the flood to dwell: and the Lord shall sit king for ever.

The Lord will give strength to his people: the Lord will bless his people with peace.

Psalm 41

AS the hart panteth after the fountains of waters; so my soul panteth after thee, O God.

My soul hath thirsted after the strong living God; when shall I come and appear before the face of God?

My tears have been my bread day and night, whilst it is said to me daily: Where is thy God?

These things I remembered, and poured out my soul in me: for I shall go over into the place of the wonderful tabernacle, even to the house of God:

With the voice of joy and praise; the noise of one feasting.

Why art thou sad, O my soul? and why dost thou trouble me?

Hope in God, for I will still give praise to him: the salvation of my countenance, and my God.

My soul is troubled within myself: therefore will I remember thee from the land of Jordan and Hermoniim, from the little hill.

Deep calleth on deep, at the noise of thy flood-gates. All thy heights and thy billows have passed over me.

In the daytime the Lord hath commanded his mercy; and a canticle to him in the night.

With me is prayer to the God of my life. I will say to God: Thou art my support.

Why hast thou forgotten me? and why go I mourning, whilst my enemy afflicteth me?

Whilst my bones are broken, my enemies who trouble me have reproached me;

Whilst they say to me day by day: Where is thy God?

Why art thou cast down, O my soul? and why dost thou disquiet me?

Hope thou in God, for I will still give praise to him: the salvation of my countenance, and my God.

Psalm 50

Have mercy upon me, O God, according to thy great mercy, etc. (p. 82).

❡ *Glory and Now;* Alleluia (*three times*); Glory to thee, O God; Lord, have mercy (*three times*); *Glory,* The Jordan River, *etc.* (*p. 434*); *Now,* O thou art the true vine, *etc.* (*p. 379*).

❡ *Then sing the following Idiomelons, in the Eighth Tone.*

VERILY, the right hand of the Forerunner, Baptizer, and Prophet, exceeding all Prophets in honour, did tremble when he beheld thee, O Lamb of God that beareth the sins of the world. And being encompassed with fear shouted, saying, I dare not touch thy head, O Word. Sanctify thou me and enlighten me O compassionate One; for thou art the Life, the Light, and the Safety of the World.

Stichos: Therefore will I remember thee from the land of Jordan (*In the Fourth Tone*).

Our God the Trinity hath revealed himself to us today as free from division; for the Father uttered the clear testimony to his Son, and the Spirit descended from heaven in the likeness of a dove, and the son bowed his pure head to the Forerunner, and being baptized did save mankind from captivity, since he is the Lover of mankind.

Glory and Now, in the Fifth Tone

O LIFE-GIVING Lord, when thou didst come to the Jordan in the flesh, in the likeness of man, willing to be baptized to lighten us who have erred, delivering us from all the wiles of the dragon and his gins, since thou art compassionate, the Father testified of thee, and the divine Spirit did come to thee in the likeness of a dove. Dwell thou, therefore, in our souls, O Lover of mankind.

Prokeimenon of the Prophecy, in the Fourth Tone

The waters saw thee, O God. The voice of the Lord is upon the waters.

Reading: from the Prophecy of Isaiah (1:16-20)

THESE things the Lord doth say, Wash yourselves, be clean, take away the evil of your devices from my eyes: cease to do perversely.

Learn to do well: seek judgment, relieve the oppressed, judge for the fatherless, defend the widow.

And then come, and accuse me, saith the Lord: if your sins be as scarlet, they shall be made as white as snow: and if they be red as crimson, they shall be white as wool.

If you be willing, and will hearken to me, you shall eat the good things of the land.

But if you will not, and will provoke me to wrath: the sword shall devour you because the mouth of the Lord hath spoken it.

The Epistle: from the Acts of the Apostles (19:1-8)

AND it came to pass, while Apollos was at Corinth that Paul having passed through the upper coasts came to Ephesus and found certain disciples.

And he said to them: Have you received the Holy Spirit since ye believed? But they said to him: We have not so much as heard whether there be a Holy Spirit.

And he said: In what then were you baptized? Who said: In John's baptism.

Then Paul said: John baptized the people with the baptism of penance, saying: That they should believe in him who was to come after him, that is to say, in Jesus.

Having heard these things, they were baptized in the name of the Lord Jesus.

And when Paul had imposed his hands on them, the Holy Spirit came upon them, and they spoke with tongues and prophesied.

And all the men were about twelve.

And entering into the synagogue, he spoke boldly for the space of three months, disputing and exhorting concerning the kingdom of God.

The Gospel: from St. Mark

The beginning of the Gospel of Jesus Christ, etc. (p. 277).

¶*And immediately,* Blessed is the Lord God, *etc. (p. 383);* Holy God, *etc., and what followeth; the Kontakion,* Today hath the Lord appeared, *etc. (p. 435); and the rest of the Order as at the end of the Third Hour of the Nativity (p. 383).*

SIXTH HOUR

¶*After* O come, let us worship, *etc. (three times), recite the following Psalms.*

PSALM 73

O GOD, why hast thou cast us off unto the end? why is thy wrath enkindled against the sheep of thy pasture?

Remember thy congregation, which thou hast possessed from the beginning.

The sceptre of thy inheritance which thou hast redeemed: mount Sion in which thou hast dwelt.

Lift up thy hands against their pride unto the end; see what things the enemy hath done wickedly in the sanctuary.

And they that hate thee have made their boasts, in the midst of thy solemnity.

They have set up their ensigns for signs, and they knew not both in the going out and on the highest top.

As with axes in a wood of trees, they have cut down at once the gates thereof, with axe and hatchet they have brought it down.

They have set fire to thy sanctuary: they have defiled the dwelling place of thy name on the earth.

They said in their heart, the whole kindred of them together: Let us abolish all the festival days of God from the land.

Our signs we have not seen, there is now no prophet: and he will know us no more.

How long, O God, shall the enemy reproach: is the adversary to provoke thy name for ever?

Why dost thou turn away thy hand: and thy right hand out of the midst of thy bosom for ever?

But God is our king before ages: he hath wrought salvation in the midst of the earth.

Thou by thy strength didst make the sea firm: thou didst crush the heads of the dragons in the waters.

Thou hast broken the heads of the dragon: thou hast given him to be meat for the people of the Ethiopians.

Thou hast broken up the fountains and the torrents: thou hast dried up the Ethan rivers.

Thine is the day, and thine is the night: thou hast made the morning light and the sun.

Thou hast made all the borders of the earth: the summer and the spring were formed by thee.

Remember this, the enemy hath reproached the Lord: and a foolish people hath provoked thy name.

Deliver not up to beasts the souls that confess to thee: and forget not to the end the souls of thy poor.

Have regard to thy covenant: for they that are the obscure of the earth have been filled with dwellings of iniquity.

Let not the humble be turned away with confusion: the poor and needy shall praise thy name.

Arise, O God, judge thy own cause: remember thy reproaches with which the foolish man hath reproached thee all the day.

Forget not the voices of thy enemies: the pride of them that hate thee ascendeth continually.

PSALM 76

I CRIED to the Lord with my voice; to God with my voice; and he gave ear to me.

In the day of my trouble I sought God, with my hands lifted up to him in the night, and I was not deceived.

My soul refused to be comforted: I remembered God, and was delighted, and was exercised, and my spirit swooned away.

My eyes prevented the watches: I was troubled, and I spoke not.

I thought upon the days of old: and I had in my mind the eternal years.

And I meditated in the night with my own heart: and I was exercised and I swept my spirit.

Will God then cast off for ever? or will he never be more favourable again?

Or will he cut off his mercy for ever, from generation to generation?

Or will God forget to shew mercy? or will he in his anger shut up his mercies?

And I said, Now have I begun: this is the change of the right hand of the most High.

I remembered the works of the Lord: for I will be mindful of thy wonders from the beginning.

And I will meditate on all thy works: and will be employed in thy inventions.

Thy way, O God, is in the holy place: who is the great God like our God? Thou art the God that doest wonders.

Thou hast made thy power known among the nations: with thy arm thou hast redeemed thy people the children of Jacob and of Joseph.

The waters saw thee, O God, the waters saw thee: and they were afraid, and the depths were troubled.

Great was the noise of the waters: the clouds sent out a sound.

For thy arrows pass: the voice of thy thunder in a wheel.

Thy lightnings enlightened the world: the earth shook and trembled.

Thy way is in the sea, and thy paths in many waters: and thy footsteps shall not be known.

Thou hast conducted thy people like sheep, by the hand of Moses and Aaron.

PSALM 90

He that dwelleth in the aid of the most High, etc. (p. 385).

❡*Glory and Now;* Alleluia (*three times*); Glory to thee, O God; Lord, have mercy (*three times*); *then Glory,* The Jordan River, *etc.* (*p. 434*). *Now,* For verily we have no favour, *etc.* (*p. 386*).

❡*Then the following Idiomelons, in the Eighth Tone.*

THUS saith the Lord to John, Come, O Prophet, and baptize me, who have created thee, the Illuminator and Purifier of all by grace. Touch my divine head and falter not, O Prophet. Let be now; for I have come to fulfill all justice. Be not doubtful, therefore, at all; for verily, I have come to destroy Archon of darkness, the Contender, who hideth in the waters, now rescuing the world from his traps, and granting eternal life, since I am the Lover of mankind.

Stichos: Therefore will I remember thee from the land of Jordan *(in the Sixth Tone)*.

Today it is time for the prophecy of the Psalms to take effect; for it saith that the sea beheld and ran away; and Jordan turned back from the face of the Lord, from the face of the God of Jacob, who cometh to accept baptism from a servant, so that having been washed from abominable idolatry, our souls may be illuminated by him.

Glory and Now, in the Fifth Tone

WHY are thy waters troubled, O Jordan, and why turnest thou backward, not proceeding forward according to thy natural flow? It shall answer, saying, I cannot bear a consuming fire. Therefore, do I marvel and tremble at thy exceeding condescension; for I am not accustomed to wash the Pure; I have not learned to purify the sinless One; but to purify impure vessels; for Christ who baptized in me doth teach me to burn the thorns of sins. And John, the voice of the Word, doth testify with me, crying, Behold the Lamb of God who beareth the sin of the world. Let us believers therefore cry unto him, saying, O God that hath appeared for our salvation, glory to thee.

Prokeimenon of the Prophecy, in the Eighth Tone

The voice of the Lord is upon the waters. Bring to the Lord, O ye children of God.

Reading: from the Prophecy of Isaiah (12:3 to end)

THESE things the Lord doth say: You shall draw waters with joy out of the Saviour's fountains:

And you shall say in that day: Praise ye the Lord, and call upon his name: make his works known among the people: remember that his name is high.

Sing ye to the Lord, for he hath done great things: show this forth in all the earth.

Rejoice, and praise, O thou habitation of Sion: for great is he that is in the midst of thee, the Holy One of Israel.

The Epistle: from St. Paul to the Romans (6:3-11)

BRETHREN, know you not that all we, who are baptized in Christ Jesus, are baptized into his death?

For we are buried together with him by baptism into death; that as Christ is risen from the dead by the glory of the Father, so we also may walk in newness of life.

For if we have been planted together in the likeness of his death, we shall be also in the likeness of his resurrection.

Knowing this, that our old man is crucified with him, that the body of sin may be destroyed, to the end that we may serve sin no longer.

For he that is dead is justified from sin.

Now if we be dead with Christ, we believe that we shall live also together with Christ:

Knowing that Christ rising again from the dead, dieth now no more, death shall no more have dominion over him.

For in that he died to sin, he died once; but in that he liveth, he liveth unto God.

So do you also reckon, that you are dead to sin, but alive unto God, in Christ Jesus our Lord.

The Gospel: from St. Mark (1:9-11)

AND it came to pass in those days, Jesus came from Nazareth of Galilee, and was baptized by John in the Jordan.

And forthwith coming up out of the water, he saw the heavens opened, and the Spirit as a dove descending, and remaining on him.

And there came a voice from heaven: Thou art my beloved Son; in thee I am well pleased.

❡*And immediately;* Swiftly let thy compassion apprehend us, *etc.* (*p. 390*); Holy God, *and what followeth; the Kontakion,* Today hath the Lord appeared, *etc. (p. 435); and the rest of the Order as at the end of the Sixth Hour of the Nativity (p. 390).*

Ninth Hour

❡*After* O come, let us worship, *etc. (three times), say the following Psalms.*

Psalm 92

THE Lord, hath reigned, he is clothed with beauty: the Lord is clothed with strength, and hath girded himself.

For he hath established the world which shall not be moved.

Thy throne is prepared from of old: thou art from everlasting.

The floods have lifted up, O Lord: the floods have lifted up their voice.

The floods have lifted up their waves, with the noise of many waters.

Wonderful are the surges of the sea: wonderful is the Lord on high.

Thy testimonies are become exceedingly credible: holiness becometh thy house, O Lord, unto length of days.

Psalm 113

WHEN Israel went out of Egypt, the house of Jacob from a barbarous people:

Judea was made this sanctuary, Israel his dominion.

The sea saw and fled: Jordan was turned back.

The mountains skipped like rams, and the hills like the lambs of the flock.

What ailed thee, O thou sea, that thou didst flee: and thou, O Jordan, that thou wast turned back?

Ye mountains, that ye skipped like rams, and ye hills, like lambs of the flock?

At the presence of the Lord the earth was moved, at the presence of the God of Jacob:

Who turned the rock into pools of water, and the stony hill into fountains of waters.

Not to us, O Lord, not to us; but to thy name give glory.

For thy mercy, and for thy truth's sake: lest the Gentiles should say: Where is their God?

But our God is in heaven: he hath done all things whatsoever he would.

The idols of the Gentiles are silver and gold, the works of the hands of men.

They have mouths and speak not: they have eyes and see not.

They have ears and hear not: they have noses and smell not.

They have hands and feel not: they have feet and walk not: neither shall they cry out through their throat.

Let them that make them become like unto them: and all such as trust in them.

The house of Israel hath hoped in the Lord: he is their helper and protector.

The house of Aaron hath hoped in the Lord: he is their helper and their protector.

They that fear the Lord have hoped in the Lord: he is their helper and their protector.

The Lord hath been mindful of us, and hath blessed us.

He hath blessed the house of Israel: he hath blessed the house of Aaron.

He hath blessed all that fear the Lord, both little and great.

May the Lord add blessings upon you: upon you, and upon your children.

Blessed be you of the Lord, who made heaven and earth.

The heaven of heaven is the Lord's: but the earth he has given to the children of men.

The dead shall not praise thee, O Lord: nor any of them that go down to hell.

But we that live bless the Lord: from this time now and for ever.

PSALM 85

Incline thy ear, O Lord, and hear me, etc. (p. 59).

⟨And after Glory and Now, Alleluia *(three times);* Lord, have mercy *(three times); Glory,* The Jordan River, etc. *(p. 434); and Now,* Thou who for our sake wast born of a Virgin, etc. *(p. 193).*

⟨And the following Idiomelons, in the Seventh Tone.

IT is an astonishing thing how the Maker of heaven and earth is seen naked in the river, accepting like a servant baptism from a servant for our salvation. Therefore, the ranks of the angels were astonished in fear and rejoicing. With them therefore, we worship thee. Save us, O Lord.

Stichos: Therefore, I will remember thee from the land of Jordan *(in the Second Tone).*

Verily, the Forerunner, seeing the Lord of glory coming towards him, cried, saying, Behold the Redeemer of the world cometh from corruption. Behold he rescueth us from sorrow. Behold he who granteth forgiveness of sins hath come to the earth from a pure Virgin, of his own mercy. Wherefore, he maketh us sons of God instead of servants; and instead of darkness he illuminateth mankind with the water of his divine baptism. Let us, therefore, glorify him in unison with the Father and the Holy Spirit.

Glory and Now, in the Fifth Tone

THY hand which touched the head of the Master, free of corruption *(three times),* the same with which thou didst point him to us by the pointing of the finger, raise thou it to him for our sakes, O Forerunner;

for thou hast attained great favour, since it was testified of thee by him that thou art the greatest of all the
Prophets. And thine eyes also, which did behold the
all-holy Spirit descending in the likeness of a dove,
raise to him, O Baptizer, gaining mercy for us. Come,
thou, and stand with us (*three times*), concluding our
praise and beginning the celebration of the Feast.

❡*And immediately the Reading of the Prophecy, in the Third Tone.*

The Lord is my Light and my Salvation. The Lord
is the protector of my life.

Reading: from the Prophecy of Isaiah (49:815)

THUS saith the Lord: In an acceptable time I have
heard thee, and in the day of salvation I have
helped thee; and I have preserved thee, and given thee
to be a covenant of the people, that thou mightest raise
up the earth and possess the inheritances that were
destroyed.

That thou mightest say to them that are bound:
Come forth: and to them that are in darkness: Show
yourselves. They shall feed in the ways, and their
pastures shall be in every plain.

They shall not hunger, nor thirst, neither shall the
heat nor the sun strike them: for he that is merciful to
them, shall be their shepherd, and at the fountains of
waters he shall give them drink.

And I will make all my mountains a way, and my
paths shall be exalted.

Behold these shall come from afar, and behold these
from the north and from the sea, and these from the
south country.

Give praise, O ye heavens, and rejoice, O earth, ye
mountains, give praise with jubilation: because the
Lord hath comforted his people, and will have mercy
on his poor ones.

And Sion said: The Lord hath forsaken me, and the
Lord hath forgotten me.

Can a woman forget her infant, so as not to have pity on the son of her womb? and if she should forget, yet will not I forget thee.

The Epistle: from St. Paul to Titus (2:11 to end; 3:4-7)

MY son Titus: The grace of God our Saviour hath appeared to all men;

Instructing us, that, denying ungodliness and worldly desires, we should live soberly, and justly, and godly in this world,

Looking for the blessed hope and coming of the glory of the great God and our Saviour Jesus Christ.

Who gave himself for us, that he might redeem us from all iniquity, and might cleanse to himself a people acceptable, a pursuer of good works.

These things speak, and exhort and rebuke with all authority. Let no man despise thee.

But when the goodness and kindness of God our Saviour appeared:

Not by the works of justice, which we have done, but according to his mercy, he saved us, by the laver of regeneration, and renovation of the Holy Spirit;

Whom he hath poured forth upon us abundantly, through Jesus Christ our Saviour:

That, being justified by his grace, we may be heirs, according to hope of life everlasting.

The Gospel: from St. Luke (3:1-18)

NOW in the fifteenth year of the reign of Tiberius Cæsar, Pontius Pilate being governor of Judæa and Herod being tetrarch of Galilee, and Philip his brother tetrarch of Itruræa and the country of Trachonitis, and Lysanias tetrarch of Abilene.

Under the high priests Annas and Caiphas; the word of the Lord was made unto John, the son of Zachary, in the desert.

And he came into all the country about the Jordan, preaching the baptism of penance for the remission of sins;

As it was written in the book of the sayings of Isaias the prophet: A voice of one crying in the wilderness: Prepare ye the way of the Lord, make straight his paths.

Every valley shall be filled; and every mountain and hill shall be brought low; and the crooked shall be made straight; and the rough ways plain;

And all flesh shall see the salvation of God.

He said therefore to the multitudes that went forth to be baptized by him: Ye offspring of vipers, who hath showed you to flee from the wrath to come?

Bring forth therefore fruits worthy of penance; and do not begin to say, We have Abraham for our father. For I say unto you, that God is able of these stones to raise up children to Abraham.

For now the axe is laid to the root of the trees. Every tree therefore that bringeth not forth good fruit, shall be cut down and cast into the fire.

And the people asked him, saying: What then shall we do?

And he answering, said to them: He that hath two coats, let him give to him that hath none; and he that hath meat, let him do in like manner.

And the publicans also came to be baptized, and said to him: Master, what shall we do?

But he said to them: Do nothing more than that which is appointed you.

And the soldiers also asked him, saying: And what shall we do? And he said to them: Do violence to no man; neither calumniate any man; and be content with your pay.

And as the people were of opinion, and all were thinking in their hearts of John, that perhaps he might be the Christ;

John answered, saying unto all: I indeed baptize you with water; but there shall come one mightier than

I, the latchet of whose shoes I am not worthy to loose: he shall baptize you with the Holy Spirit, and with fire:

Whose fan is in his hand, and he will purge his floor, and will gather the wheat into his barn; but the chaff he will burn with unquenchable fire.

And many other things exhorting, did he preach to the people.

❡ *And immediately,* Forsake us not utterly, *etc. (p. 395);* Holy God, *and what followeth; the Kontakion,* Today hath the Lord appeared, *etc. (p. 435); and the rest of the Order as at the end of the Ninth Hour of the Nativity (p. 395).*

❡ *And immediately the Typica and Makarizmoi as on p. 395, with out intonation; and the Kontakion,* Today hath the Lord appeared, *etc. (p. 435).*

❡ Lord, have mercy *(twelve times); and* Blessed be the Name of the Lord from this time forth and for ever *(three times); Glory and Now; and the Benediction.*

❡ *And immediately after the Benediction, Vespers take place, with the Mass of Basil the Great (unless the Epiphany falleth on a Sunday or a Monday).*

2. GREAT VESPERS

❡ *On* O Lord, to thee have I cried, *sing the following six Idiomelons, in the Second Tone.*

By John the Damascene

WHEN the Forerunner saw him who is our Illumination, who doth illuminate every man, coming to be baptized, his soul rejoiced, and his hand trembled. Then, pointing to him he said to the people, Behold the Rescuer of Israel, who delivereth us from corruption. Wherefore, O Christ our God, who art sinless; glory to thee. *(Repeat.)*

The hosts of the angels trembled when they beheld our Redeemer being baptized by a servant, and testified to by the presence of the Spirit, while a heavenly voice from the Father cried, saying, Verily, this One on whom the Forerunner placeth his hands, is my beloved Son in whom I am well pleased. Wherefore, O Christ our God, glory to thee. *(Repeat.)*

The courses of the Jordan received thee, O Fountain; and the Comforter descended in the likeness of a dove. Yea, he who bowed the heavens, boweth his own head; and the clay crieth unto the potter, saying, How dost thou command me to do what is more exalted than my station? It is I who need to be baptized by thee. Wherefore, O Christ God, who art sinless, glory to thee.

When thou didst choose to save lost man, thou didst not disdain to put on the likeness of a servant; for it was meet for thee, O Lord God, to accept what is ours for our sakes; for when thou wast baptized in the flesh, O Redeemer, thou didst make us worthy of forgiveness. Wherefore, we cry to thee, O Christ our benevolent God, glory to thee.

Glory and Now, in the Second Tone (By Phizandius)

THOU didst bow thy head to the Forerunner, thereby crushing the heads of the dragons. And having stood in the streams, thou didst illuminate the whole creation. Wherefore, let it glorify thee, O Saviour, thou Illumination of our souls.

¶*Then the Eisodos with the Gospel; and* O resplendent Light, *etc; and the following Readings.*

First Reading: from Genesis

In the beginning God created heaven and earth, etc. (p. 398).

¶*And at its conclusion, the Choir singeth the following Troparion, in the Fifth Tone.*

THOU didst appear in the world, O Creator of the world, to lighten them that sit in darkness. Wherefore, O Lover of mankind, glory to thee.

¶*And the Choir repeateth (four times),* To lighten them that sit, *etc., with the following Stichoi.*

1. May God have mercy upon us and bless us; may he cause the light of his countenance to shine upon us.

2. That we may know thy way upon earth; thy salvation in all nations.

3. Let the people, O God, confess to thee; let all the people give praise to thee; the earth hath yielded her fruit.

4. May God, our God, bless us; may God bless us; and all the ends of the earth fear him.

❡ *Then Glory and Now, chanting the Troparion completely.*

Second Reading: from the Fourth Book of Kings (2:6-14)

AND Elias said to Eliseus: Stay here, because the Lord hath sent me as far as the Jordan. And he said: As the Lord liveth, and as thy soul liveth, I will not leave thee. And they two went on together.

And fifty men of the sons of the prophets followed them, and stood in sight at a distance: but they two stood by the Jordan.

And Elias took his mantle and folded it together, and struck the waters, and they were divided hither and thither, and they both passed over on dry land.

And when they were gone over, Elias said to Eliseus: Ask what thou wilt have me to do for thee, before I be taken away from thee. And Eliseus said: I beseech thee that in me may be thy double spirit.

And he answered: Thou hast asked a hard thing: nevertheless if thou see me when I am taken from thee, thou shalt have what thou hast asked: but if thou see me not, thou shalt not have it.

And as they went on, walking and talking together, behold a fiery chariot, and fiery horses parted them both asunder: and Elias went up by a whirlwind into heaven.

And Eliseus saw him, and cried: My father, my father, the chariot of Israel, and the driver thereof. And he saw him no more: and he took hold of his own garments, and rent them in two pieces.

And he took up the mantle of Elias, that fell from him: and going back, he stood upon the bank of the Jordan,

And he struck the waters with the mantle of Elias, that had fallen from him, and they were divided, hither and thither, and Eliseus passed over.

❦And at the conclusion; the Choir chanteth the following Troparion, in the Sixth Tone.

THOU didst appear, O our Saviour, to sinners and tax-gatherers out of the multitude of thy mercy; for where else would thy light shine but to those who sit in darkness? Wherefore, glory to thee.

❦Repeat (four times) from For where else would thy light, etc., with the following Stichoi.

1. The Lord hath reigned, he is clothed with beauty.
2. The floods have lifted up, O Lord; the floods have lifted up their voice.
3. Wonderful are the surges of the sea; wonderful is the Lord on high.
4. Holiness becometh thy house, O Lord, unto length of days,

❦Then Glory and Now, chanting the Troparion completely, and immediately:

Third Reading: from the Fourth Book of Kings (2:19-22)

AND the men of the city of Jericho said to Eliseus: Behold the situation of this city is very good, as my lord seest: but the waters are very bad, and the ground barren.

And he said: Bring me a new vessel, and put salt into it. And when they had brought it,

He went out to the spring of the waters, and cast the salt into it, and said: Thus saith the Lord: I have healed these waters, and there shall be no more in them death or barrenness.

And the waters were healed unto this day, according to the word of Eliseus, which he spoke.

❡ *Then the Little Synapte, and the Proclamation from the Priest,* For thou art holy, our God, *etc;* Holy God.

The Epistle: The Lord is my Light and my Salvation. The Lord is the Protector of my life.

Section from the First Epistle of St. Paul to the People of Corinth (9:19 to end)

BRETHREN: Whereas I was free as to all, I made myself the servant of all, that I might gain the more,

And I became to the Jews, a Jew, that I might gain the Jews:

To them that are under the law, as if I were under the law, (whereas myself was not under the law,) that I might gain them that were without the law. To them that were without the law, as if I were without the law, (whereas I was not without the law of God, but was in the law of Christ,) that I might gain them that were without the law.

To the weak I became weak, that I might gain the weak. I became all things to all men, that I might save all.

And I do all things for the gospel's sake: that I may be made partaker thereof.

Know you not that they that run in the race, all run indeed, but one receiveth the prize? So run that you may obtain.

And every one that striveth for the mastery, refraineth himself from all things: and they may receive a corruptible crown; but we an incorruptible one.

I therefore so run, not as at an uncertainty: I so fight, not as one beating the air:

But I chastise my body, and bring it into subjection: lest perhaps, when I have preached to others, I myself should become a castaway.

The Gospel: from St. Luke

Now in the fifteenth year, etc. (p. 454).

⁅*And the rest of the Divine Liturgy of Basil the Great (if the chanting of Vespers falleth with the Hours).*

Koinonikon: Praise ye the Lord from the heavens. Alleluia.

3. THE GREAT SERVICE FOR THE SANCTIFICATION OF THE WATER

⁅*At the end of the Liturgy, the Priest cometh out to the water-basin, preceded by the lamp-bearers and the incense-bearer, while the Choir singeth the following Idiomelons, in the Eighth Tone.*

By Sophronius the Jerusalemite Patriarch

THE voice of the Lord upon the waters crieth, saying, Come ye all and take the spirit of wisdom, the spirit of understanding, the spirit of the fear of God, by the appearance of Christ.

Today the nature of water is sanctified, and the Jordan is cloven, and its waters shall be held from flowing, the Master being shown washed therein.

Thou didst come to the river like a man, O Christ King. Thou dost hasten, O good One, to receive baptism as a servant at the hands of the Forerunner, for our sins, O Lover of mankind.

Glory and Now, in the Eighth Tone

Toward the voice crying, etc. (p. 438).

⁅*Then immediately recite the following Readings.*

First Reading: from the Prophecy of Isaiah

These things, the Lord doth say: The Land that was desolate and impassable shall be glad, etc. (p. 438).

Second Reading: from the Prophecy of Isaiah
(55:1 to end)

THESE things the Lord doth say: All that thirst, come to the waters: and you that have no money, make haste, buy and eat: come ye, buy wine and milk without money, and without any price.

Why do you spend money for that which is not bread, and your labour for that which doth not satisfy you? Hearken diligently to me, and eat that which is good, and your soul shall be delighted in fatness.

Incline your ear and come to me: hear and your soul shall live, and I will make an everlasting covenant with you, the faithful mercies of David.

Behold I have given him for a witness to the people, for a leader and a master to the Gentiles.

Behold thou shalt call a nation, which thou knewest not: and the nations that knew not thee shall run to thee, because of the Lord thy God, and for the Holy One of Israel, for he hath glorified thee.

Seek ye the Lord, while he may be found: call upon him, while he is near.

Let the wicked forsake his way, and the unjust man his thoughts, and let him return to the Lord, and he will have mercy on him, and to our God: for he is bountiful to forgive.

For my thoughts are not your thoughts: nor your ways my ways, saith the Lord.

For as the heavens are exalted above the earth, so are my ways exalted above your ways, and my thoughts above your thoughts.

And as the rain and the snow come down from heaven, and return no more thither, but soak the earth, and water it, and make it to spring, and give seed to the sower, and bread to the eater:

So shall my word be, which shall go forth from my mouth: it shall not return to me void, but it shall do whatsoever I please, and shall prosper in the things for which I sent it.

For you shall go out with joy, and be led forth with peace: the mountains and the hills shall sing praise before you, and all the trees of the country shall clap their hands.

Instead of the shrub, shall come up the fir tree, and instead of the nettle, shall come up the myrtle tree: and the Lord shall be named for an everlasting sign, that shall not be taken away.

Third Reading: from the Prophecy of Isaiah

These things the Lord doth say: You shall draw waters, etc. (p. 448).

The Epistle: The Lord is my Light and my Salvation. The Lord is the Protector of my life.

Section of the First Epistle of St. Paul to the People of Corinth (10:1-4)

BRETHREN : For I would not have you ignorant, brethren, that our fathers were all under the cloud, and all passed through the sea.

And all in Moses were baptized, in the cloud, and in the sea:

And did all eat the same spiritual food,

And all drank the same spiritual drink; (and they drank of the spiritual rock that followed them, and the rock was Christ.)

The Gospel: from St. Mark

And it came to pass, in those days Jesus came, etc. (p. 449).

⁋ *Then immediately the Deacon saith the Great Synapte (p. 65); and after saying,* For the sake of those that travel by sea, *add the following Petitions, at the end of each of which the Deacon saith,* Let us pray to the Lord, *while the Choir saith,* Lord, have mercy.

THAT this water be sanctified by the power, act, and descent of the Holy Spirit,

That in this water may be planted the action of purification which belongeth to the Trinity transcendent in essence,

That it may be granted the grace of redemption and the blessing of the Jordan,

That we may be lighted by the light of knowledge and true worship, by the descent of the Holy Spirit,

That this water may become a gift for sanctification, redemption for sins, for the healing of soul and body, and for every meet benefit,

That this water may be beneficial for eternal life,

That it may drive away all the cunning devices of our enemies, visible and invisibe,

For those who drink therefrom and take home for the sanctification of their homes,

That it may be for those who drink and receive therefrom in faith, a purification for their souls and bodies,

That we may be worthy to be filled with sanctification, as we receive of these waters, by the appearance of the Holy Spirit, in an invisible manner,

That the Lord answer the voice of our beseeching, even of us who are sinners, and have mercy upon us.

❡ *The Deacon completeth the Petitions of the Great Synapte, saying,* For our deliverance from all affliction, *etc. (p. 65), as the Priest repeateth privately the following Prayer.*

O LORD Jesus Christ the only Son, who remaineth in the bosom of the Father, true God, Fountain of life and immortality, Light of Light, O thou who comest into the world to light it, lighten our minds by thy Holy Spirit and accept us as we offer thee magnification and gratitude for thy great and wonderful works which are from eternity, and for thy dispensation of salvation in these last days, in which thou didst put on our weak, poor creation, condescending, O King of all, even to become Man. And thou didst consent also to be baptized at the hand of a servant, that by the sanctification of the nature of water, O sinless One, thou mightest prepare for us a way for the renewal of birth by water and the Spirit, restoring us to our first freedom. Wherefore, as we celebrate the memory of this divine mystery, we beseech thee O Lover of mankind, to sprinkle us, thine unworthy servants, according to thy divine promise, with purifying water, and the gift of thy compassion. May the prayers of us sinners over this water be wholly acceptable to thy goodness, that thou mayest grant through it thy blessing to us and to all thy believing people, to the glory of thy holy adored Name; for thou art worthy of all glory, honour, and worship, with the Father who hath no beginning, and the good all-holy Spirit that worketh life, now and for ever and unto ages of ages. Amen.

❡ *And as he saith silently,* Amen, *at the same time that the Deacon hath finished the recitation of the Petitions, the Priest beginneth with the following Prayer, in a loud voice.*

By Sophronius the Jerusalemite Patriarch

O TRINITY, transcendent in essence, in goodness, and in Divinity, the Almighty who watcheth over all, invisible and incomprehensible, O Creator of intelligent essences, natures endowed with speech, the Goodness of utter, unapproachable Light, that lighteth every man that cometh into the world, lighten me also, thine unworthy servant. Illuminate the eyes of my mind that I may venture to praise thy countless benevolences and thy might. Let my beseeching on behalf of this people be wholy acceptable, so that my sins may not prevent the descent here of thy Holy Spirit; that I may be allowed to cry to thee without condemnation, and say, We glorify thee, O Master, Lover of mankind, the Almighty King before eternity. We glorify thee, O Creator and Author of all; we glorify thee, O only Son, who art without father on the side of thy Mother, and without mother on the side of thy Father; for in the previous feast we beheld thee a babe, and in this feast we behold thee perfect, O our perfect God, appearing from the Perfect; for today we have reached the time of the Feast; and the rank of saints gathers with us, and the angels celebrate with men. Today the grace of the

Holy Spirit hath descended on the waters in the likeness of a dove. Today hath shone the Sun that setteth not, and the world is lighted by the light of the Lord. Today the moon shineth with the world in its radiating beams. Today the shining stars adorn the universe with the splendour of their radiance. Today the clouds from heaven moisten mankind with showers of justice. Today the Uncreate accepteth of his own will the laying on of hands by his own creation. Today the Prophet and Forerunner draweth nigh to the Master, and halteth with trembling when he witnesseth the condescension of God towards us. Today the waters of the Jordan are changed to healing by the presence of the Lord. Today the whole universe is watered by mystical streams. Today the sins of mankind are blotted out by the waters of the Jordan. Today hath paradise been opened to mankind, and the Sun of righteousness hath shone for us. Today the bitter water is changed at the hands of Moses to sweetness by the presence of the Lord. Today are we delivered from the ancient mourning, and like a new Israel we have been saved. Today we have escaped from darkness, and by the light of the knowledge of God we have been illuminated. Today the darkness of the world vanisheth with the appearance of our God. Today the whole creation is lighted from on high. Today is error annulled, and the coming of the Lord prepareth for us a way of salvation. Today the celestials celebrate with the terrestrials, and the terrestrials commune with the celestials. Today the assembly of noble and great-voiced Orthodoxy rejoiceth. Today the Lord cometh to baptism to elevate mankind above. Today the Unbowable boweth to his servant to deliver us from slavery. Today we have bought the kingdom of heaven, for the kingdom of heaven hath no end.

Today the land and the sea have divided between them the joy of the world, and the world hath been filled with rejoicing. The waters saw thee, O God, the waters saw thee; they were afraid. Jordan turned back when it beheld the fire of the Godhead coming down and descending upon it in the flesh. Jordan turned back at beholding the Holy Spirit descending in the likeness of a dove and hovering over thee. Jordan turned back when it saw the Invisible visible, the Creator incarnate, and the Master in the likeness of a servant. Jordan turned back and the mountains shouted with joy at beholding God in the flesh. And the clouds gave voice, wondering at him that cometh, who is Light of Light, true God of true God, drowning in the Jordan the death of sin, the thorn of error, and bond of hades, granting the world the baptism of salvation. So also I, thine unworthy sinning servant, as I proclaim thy great wonders, am encompassed by fear, crying reverently unto thee, and saying,

¶*And at once he saith in a louder voice:*

G REAT art thou, O Lord, and wonderful are thy works, and no word doeth justice to the praise of thy wonders (*three times*); for by thy will thou didst bring out all things from nonexistence to existence; and by thy might thou dost control creation, and by thy providence thou dost govern the world. Thou it is who didst organize creation from four elements, and crowned the cycle of the year with four seasons. Before thee tremble supersensual powers; thee the sun praiseth, the moon worshippeth, the stars submit to thee, the light obeyeth, the tempests tremble, the springs worship thee. Thou didst spread out the heaven like a tent; thou didst establish the earth on the waters. Thou didst surround the sea with sand. Thou didst pour out the air for breathing. Thee do the angelic hosts serve; thee the ranks of the archangels do worship, the many-eyed cherubim, the six-winged seraphim, as they stand in thy presence and fly about thee, hiding with fear from thine unapproachable glory; for while remaining a boundless God, beginningless and ineffable, thou didst come to earth, taking the likeness of a servant, and became like men. By the feeling of thy compassion, O

Master, thou couldest not bear to see mankind defeated by Satan, but didst come and save us; for to thee do we attribute grace, and preach mercy, and conceal not benevolence. The sons of our nature thou didst free; the virginal womb by thy Nativity thou didst sanctify. Therefore, all creation hath praised thee in thine appearance; for thou our God didst appear on earth, and among men thou didst walk. The courses of the Jordan thou didst sanctify, having sent unto it from heaven thine all-holy Spirit, and didst crush the heads of the dragons nestling therein. Wherefore, thou King and Lover of mankind, be present now by the descent of thy Holy Spirit and sanctify this water *(three times)*. And grant it the grace of redemption and the blessing of the Jordan. Make it a fount of incorruptibility, a gift for sanctification, a redemption for sins, an elixir for maladies, a destroyer of Satans, unapproachable by the adversary powers and full of angelic powers; so that to all who drink therefrom and receive thereof it may be for the sanctification of their souls and bodies, for the healing of sufferings, for the sanctification of homes, and for every befitting benefit; for thou art our God who with water and the Spirit renewed our nature made old by sin. Thou art our God who didst drown sin in the water at the time of Noah. Thou art our God who in the sea deliveredst the Hebrews from the bondage of Pharoah at the hands of Moses. Thou art our God who didst cleave the rock in the wilderness, so that the waters gushed out and the valleys overflowed, thus satisfying thy thirsty people. Thou art our God who with fire and water deliveredst Israel from the error of Baal at the hands of Elisha. Wherefore, O Master, sanctify this water by thy Holy Spirit *(three times)*. Grant to all who touch it and who are anointed by it and who receive thereof, sanctification, blessing, cleansing, and health. Save, O Lord, thy servants, our believing kings *(three times)*. Keep them under thy shadow in peace. Subdue under their feet every enemy and adversary. Grant to them the means of salvation, and eternal Life. Remember, Lord, our Bishop (N.) and all Priests, servants of God, and all the priestly hierachy, and the people standing about us, and our brethren who absent themselves for praiseworthy reasons. Have mercy on them and us acocrding to thy loving-kindness, that thy all-holy Name may be glorified by the elements, by the angels, by men, and by visible and invisibe creatures, with the Father and Holy Spirit, now and for ever, and unto ages of ages. Amen.

Then: Peace be unto you all.

Choir. And unto thy Spirit also.

Priest. Bow your heads unto the Lord.

Choir. To thee, O Lord.

¶*And the Priest saith the following Prayer privately.*

INCLINE thine ear, O Lord, and hear us. O thou who didst sanctify water when thou didst consent to be baptized in the Jordan, bless us all, who by the bowing of our heads have signified our bondage, and make us worthy to be filled with thy sanctification, by the receiving of this water and its sprinkling. Let it be to us, O Lord, for health of soul and body.

¶*And this Proclamation.*

FOR thou art the sanctification of our souls and bodies, and to thee we address glory, thanks, and worship, with the Father who hath no beginning and the all-holy Spirit, the God and Author of life, now and for ever and unto ages of ages. Amen.

¶*And then immediately the Priest blesseth the water in the form of a cross, and immerseth the precious cross up and down, holding it straight, as he singeth the following Troparion (three times), in the First Tone.*

BY thy baptism, O Lord, in the River Jordan, worship to the Trinity hath made its appearance; for the voice of the Lord did come forth to thee with the testimony, naming thee beloved Son; and the Spirit in the likeness of a dove, confirming the truth of the word. Wherefore, O thou who didst appear and lighted the world, O Christ, glory to thee.

❡ *Then he sprinkleth the holy water on all the people, as the Choir singeth the following Idiomelon, in the Sixth Tone.*

L ET us praise, O believers, the great dispensation of God, that worketh for us; for he who alone is pure and spotless, having become Man because of our fall, purifieth us in the Jordan, sanctifying me and the waters and crushing the heads of the dragons in the water. Let us, therefore, O brethren, draw water with gladness, for those who draw it in faith shall be granted in an invisible manner the grace of the Spirit, by the presence of Christ God, the Saviour of our souls.

❡ *Note: If the Feast falleth on a Sunday or a Monday, the Hours are chanted on Friday. But the sanctification of the water taketh place on the morning of the Paramon, after Mass. And Great Vespers are said on Saturday (if the Feast be on a Sunday), or on a Sunday evening (if the Feast be on a Monday). But the Liturgy of Basil the Great is said on the day of the Feast. At Great Vespers, after the Gospel, the order of Evening Prayer taketh place as usual. And in the Litiya, say, Glory and Now, in Eighth Tone.*

By John the Damascene

O LORD, when thou didst fulfill what thou hadst designed from the ages, thou didst take servants from all creation for thy mystery; from the angels, Gabriel; from mankind, the Virgin; from the heavens, the stars; and from the waters, the Jordan, with which thou didst blot out the iniquity of the world. O our Saviour, glory to thee.

❡ *And in the Aposticha, the following Idiomelons are sung in the Second Tone.*

By Anatolius

O CHRIST God, when John saw thee advancing to him in the Jordan, he cried, saying, How hast thou come to thy servant, O thou spotless Lord? In whose

Name shall I baptize thee? In the Name of the Father? For thou dost bear it in thee. In the Name of the Son? For thou art the incarnate One? In the Name of the Holy Spirit? For thou hast known how to grant him to believers by the mouth? Wherefore, O God manifest, have mercy upon us.

Stichos: The sea saw and fled.

The waters beheld thee, O God, the waters beheld thee and feared; for verily, the cherubim dare not gaze upon thy glory, nor the seraphim stare at thee; but they stand in fear; for of them are some that bear, and some that glorify thy might. Wherefore, with them, O compassionate One, we proclaim thy praise, saying, O manifest God, have mercy upon us.

Stichos: What ailed thee, O thou sea, that thou didst flee?

Today the Maker of heaven and earth cometh in the flesh to the Jordan seeking baptism, though he is sinless, to purify the world from the error of the adversary: and the Lord of all is baptized by a servant, granting mankind cleansing by water. Wherefore, let us cry unto him, saying, O our appearing God: glory to thee.

Glory and Now, in the Eighth Tone (By Theophano)

VERILY, the shining lamp, born of a barren woman, when he saw the Sun radiant from the Virgin, seeking baptism in the Jordan, cried out to him in fear and joy, saying, Sanctify thou me, O Master, by thy divine Epiphany.

❦*And the Troparion,* By thy baptism, O Lord, in the River Jordan, *etc. (three times, p. 469); and the Benediction.*

4. MATINS

❦*On* God the Lord hath appeared unto us, *the Troparion of the Feast (three times); then the following Kathismata.*

First Kathisma, in the Third Tone

O CHRIST Saviour, by thine appearance in the Jordan, and by thy baptism of the Forerunner, it was testified of thee that thou art a beloved Son. Wherefore, thou didst appear coëternal with the Father, and the Holy Spirit descended upon thee, by whom being lighted we cry, saying, Glory to God in three Persons.

Second Kathisma, in the Fourth Tone

O JORDAN River, why wast thou astonished at beholding the Invisible naked? And he answereth, saying, I beheld him and trembled; for how shall I not tremble and fear, when the angels trembled at sight of him, heaven was astounded, earth was encompassed by trepidation, and the sea was bashful, with all things visible and invisible; for Christ hath appeared in the Jordan to bless the waters.

Third Kathisma, in the Fourth Tone

O CHRIST our God, thou hast sanctified the courses of the Jordan, crushed the might of sin, bowed thyself under the hand of the Forerunner, and saved mankind from error. Wherefore, we plead with thee to save thy world.

¶ *Then the Anabathmoi,* From my youth, *etc. (p. 50), and the following Prokeimenon.*

The sea saw and fled: Jordan turned back.

The Matin Gospel: from St. Mark

And it came to pass in those days Jesus came etc. (p. 449).

¶ *And Psalms 50 (p. 82). Then, Glory, in the Second Tone.*

Let all the universe rejoice; for Christ hath appeared in the Jordan.

¶ *And Now (repeated); and after* O merciful One, have mercy upon me, O God, *etc., the following Idiomelon, in the Sixth Tone.*

GOD the Word appeared in the flesh to mankind. He stood up to be baptized in the Jordan, and the Forerunner addressed him saying, How shall I stretch out my hand and touch the head of the Controller of all creation? Verily, thou camest as a child from Mary; I have known thee as eternal God walking the earth, O Christ, who art praised by the seraphim. And I, thy servant, have not learned to baptize the Master. Wherefore, O ineffable Lord, glory to thee.

¶ *Then sing the following Antiphonal Katabasias of the Epiphany in couples, in the Second Tone.*[1]

The first set by Kyr Cozma and the second by John the Damascene

Right Choir. 1. The Lord mighty in wars uncovered the bottom of the sea, and drew his own to dry land; and with it he submerged his adversaries; for he hath been glorified.

Left Choir. Another. Verily, Israel passed the tempest of the tumultuous sea, having appeared to him again as dry land. But the tri-speared Egyptians were lost wholly by the darkness of the deep, as a graveyard swept by waters, by the power of the precious right hand of the Master.

Right Choir. 3. The Lord that granteth power to our kings, and who raiseth those born of his anointed ones, was born of the Virgin, and cometh to baptism. Wherefore, let us believers shout, There is none holy like our God, and there is none just except thee, O Lord.

Left Choir. Another. O ye who were delivered from the ancient snares, since the tusks of devouring lions had been crushed. Wherefore, let us rejoice and open

---

[1] The Katabasias of the Epiphany are sung antiphonally from January first to sixth; and from the seventh to the fourteenth the second set of Katabasias, beginning with, Verily, Israel etc. singly.

wide our mouths, inditing to the Word sayings of praise for his benefactions granted to us; for he is pleased thereby.

Left Choir. He of whom thou didst say, O Lord, that he is a voice crying in the wilderness, heard thy voice when thou didst thunder on the many waters, testifying to thy Son. And having been filled wholly by the presence of the Spirit, he shouted, saying, Thou art Christ, the Wisdom of God and his Power.

Right Choir. Another. The Prophet having been cleansed by the fire of mystical vision, praising the renewal of mankind, sang with a great voice, moved by the Spirit, revealing the ineffable Incarnation, the Incarnation of the Word, by which the might of the mighty hath been crushed.

Right Choir. 5. Verily Jesus, the Originator of life, cometh to unravel the fall of Adam, the first of creation; and he who needeth not purification, since he is God, granteth to the fallen one purification in the Jordan. And as he abolisheth in him the enmity, he thereby granteth safety transcending all intelligence.

Left Choir. Another. We who have been washed by the purification of the Spirit from the dark, mire-defiled venom of the enemy, have come upon a new way, not misleading, but leading to a bliss unapproachable except by those who have been reconciled to God.

Right Choir. 6. Verily the voice of the Word, the lamp of the Light, the mystical star and Forerunner of the Sun, doth cry out in the wilderness, saying to all the people, Repent and be purified; for Christ hath come to deliver the world from corruption.

Left Choir. Another. Him whom the Father had caused to overflow from the belly, in his all-blissful voice he proclaimed beloved, saying, Yea, this is my Son consubstantial with me; the Radiance of my light hath been born of mankind. And he himself is my living Word and Man at the same time, for his own dispensation.

Right Choir. 7. The youths of true worship when they were cast in the furnace of fire, were kept from harm by the gentle dewy breeze and by the descent of the divine angel. Wherefore, when they were moistened by the flames, they sang with gratitude, shouting, Blessed art thou, O Lord, transcending praise, the God of our fathers.

Left Choir. Another. Verily, he who quenched the flaming fire of the furnace containing the youths of true worship, hath burned the heads of dragons in the courses of water; and by the dew of the Spirit hath cleansed the abysmal darkness resulting from sin.

Let us praise, bless, and worship the Lord.

Left Choir. 8. Verily, the furnace of Babylon revealed a strange secret when it overflowed with dew. But Jordan was about to receive in its courses the immaterial Fire, and was to contain the Creator baptized in the flesh, whom the nations bless and exalt yet more unto the end of ages.

Right Choir. Another. The prince of darkness sigheth to himself because creation hath been freed, and those who were of old in darkness have become sons of the Light. Wherefore, all the nations of the Gentiles that before had been wretched, now ceaselessly bless Christ the Cause.

❡*And immediately, instead of* O *thou who art more honourable, etc., the Ninth Ode of the two Canons is sung with its Magnifications.*

Magnify, O my soul, her who is more honourable, and more exalted than the heavenly hosts.

Right Choir. 9. Verily, all tongues are at a loss to praise thee properly; and every mind, even though transcending the world, is distracted in thy praise, O Theotokos. But because thou art good, accept our faith, having known our divine longing. Wherefore, since thou art the aider of Christians, we do magnify thee.

Magnify, O my soul, him who came to be baptized in the Jordan.

Come, O David, in the spirit, and sing, saying to those who seek the light, Come ye now to God in faith, and shine. This poor man Adam cried when he fell, and the Lord heard him, coming to the courses of the Jordan and renewing him who had been overtaken by corruption.

Magnify, O my soul, him who received baptism from the Forerunner.

Verily, Isaiah crieth, saying, Wash ye, make ye clean; put away the evil of your doings from before the eyes of the Lord; and ye that thirst come to the living water; for Christ overfloweth with renovating water for those who hasten to him in faith. He baptizeth them with the Spirit to immortal life.

Magnify, O my soul, him of whom the fatherly voice testified.

Let us be preserved, O believers, in grace and by the seal; for, as the Jews escaped of old from destruction by smearing their thresholds with blood, thus shall this divine cleansing be for us the cleansing of rebirth, a way wherein we shall see the never-setting light of the Trinity.

The Ninth Ode of the Other Canon

Today the Master bendeth his neck to the hand of the Forerunner.

O the wonder of thy superintelligent Nativity, thou all-pure bride, the blessed Mother to whom having received therefrom perfect salvation, we indite a fitting song, offering as a gift the song of gratitude.

Glory: Magnify, O my soul, the might of the three-personed and indivisible Trinity.

Having known the outward things which appeared to Moses in the bush, let us come and behold the wonders taking place with strange signs; for as that was perserved, so the Virgin was preserved when she conceived Fire, giving birth to the light-bearing Benefactor. And so was it with the courses of the Jordan when they received him.

Now: Magnify, O my soul, the Maiden who delivered us from the curse.

O eternal King, when thou didst cleanse the substance of mankind in pure streams, and anointed it, perfecting it by the communion of the Spirit, and betraying the power of darkness that had possessed it, thou didst translate it to life immortal.

❡ *Then conclude with the two Katabasias with their Magnifications, as above.*

Exaposteilarion (three times)

VERILY, the Saviour, who is Grace and Truth, hath appeared in the courses of the Jordan and lighted those who lie in darkness and the shadow of death; for he hath come, and the unapproachable Light hath appeared.

❡ *Then in the Einos are sung the following six Idiomelons, in the First Tone.*

By Patriarch Germanus

CHRIST our God who is Light of Light, God manifest, hath shone forth to the world. Let us, O nations, worship him. (*Repeat.*)

How shall we servants fittingly honour thee, O Christ Master; for by water thou didst renew us all.

When thou wast baptized in the Jordan, O our Saviour, thou didst sanctify the courses by the laying of thy servant's hand upon thee, healing the sufferings of the world. Wherefore, great is the mystery of thy dispensation. O Lord, Lover of mankind, glory to thee.

The true Light hath appeared, granting illumination to all. And Christ transcending all purity is baptized with us, charging the water with sanctity for the puri-

fication of souls. Verily, the thing apparent is earthly,
but its significance transcendeth the heavens; for by
washing salvation is attained, by water the Spirit, and
by immersion ascent to God. Wherefore, great are
thy works, O Lord, glory to thee.

He that encompasseth the heavens with clouds putteth on today the courses of the Jordan; and he that
lifteth the sin of the world, cleanseth and purifieth me.
Yea, the Spirit hath testified of him from on high that
he is the only Son of the Father on high. Let us, therefore, shout to him, crying, O thou who didst appear
and save us. Glory to thee.

Glory, in the Sixth Tone (By Anatolius)

O SAVIOUR, who putteth on light like a robe, thou
hast put on the waters of the Jordan, bowing thy
head to the Forerunner, O thou who measurest the
heaven with a span, that thou mayest restore the world
from error and save our souls.

Now, in the Sixth Tone (By Anatolius)

TODAY Christ cometh to the Jordan to be baptized.
Today John toucheth the head of the Master. The
powers of heaven were astonished at beholding the
strange mystery. The sea saw and fled; Jordan, beholding, turned back. But we who were lighted shout,
saying, Glory to God who was manifest on earth and
lighted the world.

❡ *The the Great Doxology; and conclude with the Troparion,* By
thy baptism, O Lord, *etc.* (*p. 469*)*; and the Benediction.*[1]

5. THE MASS

1. By the intercessions of the Theotokos, O Saviour,
save us.

---

[1] After the Benediction of the Matin services, the rite of the Great Sanctification of the Water is held as above. But it has become customary to hold
it after the Service of the Mass, to preserve quiet and silence during the
Divine Liturgy.

2. Save us, O Son of God, O thou who wast baptized of John in the Jordan, as we sing unto thee, Alleluia.

❡ *Then Glory and Now, and* O only-begotten Son and Word of God, *etc.*

3. By thy Baptism, O Lord, in the River Jordan, etc.

Eisodikon: Blessed is he that cometh in the Name of the Lord. God the Lord hath appeared unto us. Save us, O Son of God, O thou who wast baptized of John in the Jordan, as we sing unto thee, Alleluia.

❡ *The Troparion,* By thy baptism, O Lord, *etc; then the following Kontakion, in the Fourth Tone.*

TODAY thou hast appeared to the universe, O Lord, and thy light hath been shed upon us, who praise thee with knowledge, saying, Thou hast come and appeared, O unapproachable Light.

❡ *Then instead of* Holy God, *sing:*

Ye who have been baptized into Christ have put on Christ, Alleluia.

The Epistle: Blessed is he that cometh in the Name of the Lord. Confess to the Lord, for he is good.

Section from Epistle of St. Paul to Titus

My son Titus: The grace of God, our Saviour, hath appeared, etc. (p. 454).

The Gospel: from St. Matthew (3:13 to end)

AND it came to pass in those days that Jesus came from Galilee to the Jordan, unto John, to be baptized by him.

But John stayed him, saying: I ought to be baptized by thee, and comest thou to me?

And Jesus answering, said to him: Suffer it to be so now. For so it becometh us to fulfill all justice. Then he suffered him.

And Jesus being baptized, forthwith came out of the water: and lo, the heavens were opened to him: and he saw the Spirit of God descending as a dove, and coming upon him.

And behold a voice from heaven, saying: This is my beloved Son, in whom I am well pleased.

❧*And on Especially, the Ninth Ode of the first Canon,* Verily, all tongues, *etc.* (*p. 475*), *with its Magnification.*

Koinonikon: The grace of God our Saviour hath appeared to all men. Alleluia.

❧*And instead of* We have seen the true Light, *etc. say,* By thy baptism, O Lord, in the River Jordan, *etc.*

Benediction: O thou who didst consent to be baptized of John in the Jordan for our salvation, etc.

7. A HIGH MEMORIAL FOR THE GLORIOUS PROPHET, JOHN THE FORERUNNER AND BAPTIZER.

1. VESPERS

❧*On* O Lord, to thee have I cried, *chant three for Vespers of the Epiphany, and the following three Prosomia, in the First Tone.*

O ALL-EXTOLLED Forerunner of Christ, O God-inspired Baptizer, as we beatify thee in true worship, we glorify Christ who bowed his head to thee in the Jordan, sanctifying the nature of man. Wherefore, him do thou implore to grant to our souls safety and the Great Mercy.

Thou hast come before and beheld, O John, the wise Forerunner, the ineffable glory of the Father from on high, and the Son in the waters. And thou didst see the Spirit descending on him in the likeness of a dove, purifying and lighting the ends of the earth. Wherefore, as we proclaim thee a heavenly initiate of the Trinity, we honour thy divine Feast.

When thou wast confirmed, O Forerunner and Baptizer, by the divine grace of Christ, thou didst show us the Lamb that taketh away all the sins of the world, joining to him gladly two Disciples. Wherefore, implore thou him to grant our souls safety and the Great Mercy.

Glory, in the Sixth Tone

O THOU lamp in the flesh, O Forerunner of Christ, the branch of the barren, and friend of the Virgin-born. O thou who didst worship him leaping in the womb, and didst baptize him in the waters of the Jordan, we implore thee, O Prophet, to interecede with him to deliver us from impending tempests.

Now: God the Word appeared in the flesh, etc. (p. 473).

¶ *Then the Eisodos; O* resplendent Light, *etc; and the Prokeimenon, in the Seventh Tone.*

Our God is in heaven and on earth. Whatever the Lord pleased, that hath he done.

¶ *In the Aposticha, the following Prosomia, in the Fourth Tone.*

WHEN John the Forerunner saw thee advancing toward him, O Master, he was overtaken by surprise, and shouted as a grateful servant, saying, What is this condescension, O Saviour, and what is this humility with which thou hast encompassed thyself, O thou who by the richness of thy goodness didst raise humble man, by putting him on; for thou art compassionate?

Stichos: The sea saw and fled.

The Saviour of all answered the Forerunner, saying, Advance thou towards me and perform the terrible mystery which I fulfill today, and fear not; for I who appear now in nature, am baptized like a man in the waters of the Jordan in which thou seest me present. But verily, I renew Adam bruised by sin.

Stichos: What ailed thee, O thou sea, that thou didst flee?

John replied, saying, Who of the earthly ones hath ever seen the Sun being bathed, and he that encompasseth the heavens with clouds completely naked, the Creator of springs and rivers descending into the waters? Verily, I am astonished at thine ineffable dispensation, O Master. Tax not thou thy servant with such terrible ceremonies.

Glory, in the Fourth Tone

SINCE thou art a lover of the Spirit, O Forerunner, and a God-proclaiming swallow of grace, thou hast clearly proclaimed to mankind the dispensation of the King rising with shining splendour from the undefiled one for the recall of mankind, putting away the arrogance of vicious character, straightening the hearts of those who are baptized with repentance, for the reception of everlasting life, O thou beatified and inspired of God.

Now, in the Same Tone

COME, let us emulate the wise virgins! Come, let us welcome the manifest Master; for he hath advanced towards John like a bridegroom. The Jordan, seeing thee, stood in awe, and John shouted, saying, I dare not take hold of the deathless head. And the Spirit descended in the likeness of a dove to sanctify the waters, while a voice from heaven was heard shouting, This is my Son that cometh into the world to save mankind. Wherefore, O Lord, glory to thee.

Troparion for the Feast; and for the Forerunner, in the Second Tone

The memory of the righteous is in praise, etc. (*See August 29, Vespers.*)

¶ *Then for the Feast.*

2. MATINS

¶ *The Katabasias are for the Second Canon only. And instead of O thou who art more honourable, etc., sing the Ninth Ode with its Magnifications. Katabasia, O the wonders of thy superintelligent Nativity, etc. with its Magnifications (p. 476).*

¶ *The Exaposteilarion for the Feast, and the following.*

THE Master did forecall thee a Prophet, O thou who art more exalted than the law foretold; thou didst see him in the flesh; and having baptized him thou didst appear nobler than them all.

¶*And in the Einos, the Idiomelons of the Feast are sung in the First Tone.*

Glory, in the Sixth Tone

THOU hast come from the suffering of barrenness, O Baptizer, an angel and a dweller in the wilderness from the age of swaddling clothes, appearing as the seal of all the Prophets; for he whom they beheld in sundry manners, foretelling him by symbols, thou wast worthy to baptize in the Jordan. And thou didst hear from heaven a fatherly voice testifying to his Sonship; and thou didst see the Spirit in the likeness of a dove attracting the voice of the One baptized. Wherefore, O thou who art greater than all the Prophets, cease not to intercede for our sakes, who celebrate thy memorial in faith.

Now: Today Christ cometh to the Jordan, etc. (p. 478).

¶*Then the Great Doxology, and;* By thy baptism, O Lord, *etc.* (*p. 469*).

3. THE MASS

¶*The Antiphonies and the Eisodikon for the Feast; the Troparion,* By thy baptism, *etc;* The memory of the righteous is in praise, *etc; and the Kontakion,* Today thou hast appeared to the universe, *etc.* (*p. 479*). *And instead of* Holy God *sing,* Ye who have been baptized, *etc.*

The Epistle: from the Acts of the Apostles

And it came to pass, that while Appollos, etc. (p. 444).

The Gospel: from St. John (1:29-34)

AND it came to pass that John saw Jesus coming to him, and he saith: Behold the Lamb of God, behold him who taketh away the sin of the world.

This is he, of whom I said: After me there cometh a man, who is preferred before me: because he was before me.

And I knew him not, but that he may be made manifest in Israel, therefore am I come baptizing with water.

And John gave testimony, saying: I saw the Spirit coming down, as a dove from heaven, and he remained upon him.

And I knew him not; but he who sent me to baptize with water, said to me: He upon whom thou shalt see the Spirit descending, and remaining upon him, he it is that baptizeth with the Holy Spirit.

And I saw, and I gave testimony, that this is the Son of God.

❡*And on Especially,* Today doth John baptize the Master in the courses of the Jordan, *etc., and* O the wonder of thy superintelligent Nativity, *etc. (p. 476).*

Koinonikon: The just shall be in everlasting remembrance. Alleluia.

8. Dominica, the Righteous (8); and George the Khozibite (7).

9. Polyeuctus the Martyr (1).

10. Gregory, Bishop of Nyssa (9); and Domitianus, Bishop of Malta (10).

11. Theodosius (Gift of God), Head of Monastries (6).

12. Tatania the Martyr (2).

13. Hermilus and Stratonicus the Martyrs (2).

14. The Fathers Killed in Sinai and Rhaitho (11); and Leave-Taking of the Epiphany, in which the Whole Service of the Feast is Sung.

15. Paul of Thebes (7); and John the Hut Dweller (6).

16. Adoration of the Precious Chain of St. Peter.

17. The Righteous Anthony the Great, the God-mantled.

Troparion, in the Fourth Tone

THOU didst become like the zealous Elijah in his condition, and followed John the Baptist in his upright ways, becoming a dweller in the wilderness and an establisher of the universe by thy prayer, O Father Anthony. Wherefore, intercede thou with Christ God to save our souls.

Kontakion, in the Second Tone

WHEN thou didst put away worldly troubles, thou didst spend thy life in quietude and silence, becoming in all ways like John the Baptist, O all-righteous One. Wherefore, with him we honour thee, O father of fathers, Anthony.

The Epistle: (Hebrews 13:17-21), and the Gospel: from St. Luke (6:17-23)

18. Athanasius and Cyril, Patriarchs of Alexandria.

Troparion, in the Sixth Tone

WITH work of Orthodoxy, ye shone forth and extinguished wicked opinion, becoming triumphant and clothed with victory. And having enriched all with true worship, and adorned the Church with great adornment, ye worthily found Christ God, granting to all, through your prayer, the Great Mercy.

Kontakion, in the Fourth Tone

O YE two great High Priests of the Church, brave strivers for true worship through Christ, guard all who sing, Save, O compassionate One, all who honour thee in faith.

The Epistle: (Hebrews 13:7-16) and the Gospel: from St. Matthew (5:14-19)

19. Macarius the Egyptian (7); Arsenius, Bishop of Corcyra (9); and Mark Bishop of Ephesus (10).

20. Euthymius the Great, the God-mantled Righteous One (6).
21. Maximus the Confessor (10); and Neophytus the Martyr (1).
22. Timothy the Apostle (12); and Anastasius the Persian (1).
23. Clement, Bishop of Angora (5); and Agathangelus the Martyr (1).
24. Xenia the Righteous One (8).
25. Gregory the Theologian, Archbishop of Constantinople.

Troparion, in the First Tone

THE pastoral psalter of thy discourse in theology triumphed over the trumpets of orators and overcame it; for having sought the depth of the Spirit, there was vouchsafed to thee also excellence of speech, O Father Gregory. Wherefore, intercede thou with Christ God to save our souls.

Kontakion, in the Third Tone

THOU hast loosened by thy tongue, discoursing in theology, the entanglements of orators, adorning the Church with the robe of Orthodoxy, spun from on high. And having clothed thyself therewith, she crieth with us, thy children, saying, Peace be unto thee, O father of sublime intelligence, discoursing in theology.

The Epistle: (Hebrews 7:26-28; 8:1-2) and the Gospel: from St. John (10:9-16)

26. Xenophon the Righteous and his Companions (11).
27. Translation of the Body of John Chrysostom. (See November 13).
28. Ephraim Syrus (6).
29. Translating the Remains of the God-mantled Ignatius (5).

30. The Three Bishops, Basil the Great, Gregory the Theologian, and John Chrysostom, Styled
the Three Satellites.

Typicon

¶ *If this Feast fall on a Sunday, see the same Order as that of St.
Demetrius, on October twenty-sixth. And if that Sunday happens
to be one of the Triodion Sundays, the Service of the Saints is sung
along with those of the Triodion and the Resurrection.*

1. Vespers

¶ *After the Sunset Psalm, say three Psalms only, beginning with*
Blessed is the man, *and on* O Lord, to thee have I cried, *sing the
following six Prosomia, in the Fourth Tone.*

LET us honour, as is befitting, those instruments of
grace, those zithers of the Spirit and preaching
trumpets of good tone; those thunders from on high
breaking with fearful things; those renowned, proclaiming to the ends of the earth the glory of God,
namely, Basil and Gregory with John, the three satellites preaching the great Trinity. (*Repeat.*)

Let them be honoured, defenders of the Trinity, exemplars of true worship, the three apostles after the
Twelve; the river overflowing with the living water
from Eden, watering the face of the earth with its divine life-overflowing courses, the great elements organizing the faith like creation. (*Repeat.*)

The Prophet spake, saying, There is no speech nor
language where their voice is not heard; for in all the
earth and sea, the words of the wise divines, teachers
of creation, have been broadcast. Wherefore, the regions are well organized by their divine laws, and are
united in one Orthodox opinion.

Let us who follow in the steps of their doctrines
praise with the voice of song, those instruments of the
Spirit, those trumpets of the truth, those orators of

words, imploring them, since they attained favour with the Lord, to seek for the universe firm peace for ever, and for us all forgiveness.

Glory, in the Sixth Tone

Let us extol today those mystical trumpets of the Spirit, etc. (p. 313).

Now: Who shall not beatify thee, etc. (p. 177).

❡ *Then the Eisodos,* O resplendent Light, *etc.; the daily Prokeimenon.*

❡ *In the Litiya, Glory, in the Sixth Tone.*

By Linilus Xanthropolus

COME, ye feast-lovers, let us come together and extol with eulogy those sons, the Bishops of Christ, the pride of the Fathers, towers of faith, and teachers of believers, and their guards, saying, Rejoice, O Basil the Wise, star of the Church and its unshakeable pillar. Rejoice, O heavenly intelligence, Gregory the Theologian, the great High Priest. Rejoice, O John of golden words, Chrysostom, fervid preacher of repentance. Wherefore, O thrice-blessed Fathers, cease not to intercede with Christ always for those who celebrate in faith and longing your all-noble divine Feast.

Now to our Lady, in the Same Tone

COME, ye feast lovers, let us come together and extol in eulogizing songs the comeliness of virgins, the gladness of intelligences, and the Theotokos who alone is the impregnable wall of believers, saying, Rejoice, O pure virgin Mother, the golden lighthouse and heavenly gate. Rejoice, O tabernacle of sanctification, all-pure one who contained God in her womb. Rejoice, O thou who art beyond measure more exalted than all

the heavenly hosts.   Wherefore, O spouseless Lady
Mother, thou shalt yet protect thy servants who ever
praise thee faithfully and eagerly, and who worship thy
seedless birth-giving.

❡*And in the Aposticha, the following Prosomia in the Fifth Tone.*

By Linilus Xanthopolus

R EJOICE, O trinity of high priests, those great towers of the Church, and pillars of true worship, O
steadfastness of believers, and downfall of heretics; ye
who pastured the people of Christ in divine doctrine,
and taught them varied virtues, O honourable preachers
of grace, who went before and laid down rules for
Christian perfection, celestial guides, the entrances to
paradise.   Wherefore, seek ye of Christ to send to our
souls the Great Mercy.

Rejoice trinity of High Priests, terrestrial angels
ascending to heaven, who are the salvation of the world,
the joy of mankind, and teachers of the universe, O
defenders of the word, those proficient physicians for
illness of spirit and body, those ever-flowing rivers of
the Spirit, ye who watered with your sayings the whole
face of the earth.   Wherefore, O ye speakers in theology, divine golden-worded pillars, seek ye of Christ
to send to our souls the Great Mercy.

Rejoice, O trinity of High Priests, sun of the earthly
firmament, rays and lamps lighted by the three-sunned
Dawn, and the restoration of sight to those in darkness;
O beatified fragrant blossoms of paradise, Basil the
Wise, the Theologian, and those golden-mouthed treasures of the Spirit, tablets traced by God, and breasts
overflowing with the milk of salvation.   Wherefore, O
ye who are the delight of wisdom, implore Christ to
grant our souls the Great Mercy.

Glory, in the Fifth Tone

L ET us blow the trumpets of sons, and rejoice in
feasting, exchanging glad tidings in the feast of
our most celebrated teachers.   Let kings and princes

hasten to extol in songs of praise those High Priests;
for they overflow in three rivers of doctrine exceeding
great, free-flowing, and for ever reviving the spirit.
Let us shepherds and teachers come together and extol
those three, faithful to the noble mysteries of the venerable Trinity. And let all lovers of wisdom extol those
wise ones; and Priests, those shepherds; sinners, those
intercessors; the poor, those enrichers; the sorrowful,
those comforters; travellers, those companions; and
those at sea, those captains; and let us all extol those
divine High Priests, who respond fervently everywhere, saying, O all-holy teachers, hasten to save us
who believe from the stumblings of time, and to our
rescue from Godly punishments.

Now to Our Lady, in the Same Tone

Let us blow the trumpets of praise for the queen of
all, etc. (p. 358).

Troparion, in the First Tone (two times)

LET us all come together and honour with songs of
praise those three great stars of the three-sunned
Trinity, who illuminated the universe with rays of divine doctrines; those rivers of wisdom flowing with
honey, who watered the whole universe with streams
of divine knowledge, Basil the Great, Gregory the
Theologian, and glorious John the golden-tongued; for
they shall intercede with the Trinity for our sakes, who
love their sayings.

Another, in the Fourth Tone

BEING like the Apostles in their states, and teachers
of the universe, intercede to the Lord of all to
grant safety to the universe, and to our souls the Great
Mercy.

2. MATINS

¶ On God the Lord hath appeared unto us, the Troparia as at
Vespers. Then the following Kathismata, in the Fourth Tone.

O FATHERS, stars of transcendent splendour, set by God as judges over the Church of Christ, ye have illuminated the world with your teachings, abolishing the heresies of all those of evil opinion, and quenching the blazing agitation of blasphemers. Wherefore, being High Priests of Christ, intercede for our salvation.

Ye approach the meadows of books like bees, gathering well the flowers of virtue. Ye set before all believers the honey of your teachings as a banquet. Wherefore, every individual being sweetened thereby shouteth with joy, Watch over us, who praise you, even after death, O blessed ones.

Let us glorify today those wise teachers of the universe, who glorified God on earth with their deeds and with their words; for they are concerned in our salvation.

❡ *Then the Anabathmoi,* From my youth, *etc.* (*p. 50*); *and the following Prokeimenon.*

Thy priests, O Lord, put on justice. My mouth shall speak wisdom.

The Matin Gospel: from St. John (10:9-16)

THE Lord said: I am the door. By me, if any man enter in, he shall be saved; and he shall go in, and go out, and shall find pastures.

The thief cometh not, but for to steal, and to kill, and to destroy. I am come that they may have life, and may have it more abundantly.

I am the good shepherd. The good shepherd giveth his life for his sheep.

But the hireling, and he that is not the shepherd, whose own the sheep are not, seeth the wolf coming, and leaveth the sheep, and flieth: and the wolf catcheth, and scattereth the sheep:

And the hireling flieth, because he is a hireling: and he hath no care for the sheep.

I am the good shepherd; and I know mine, and mine know me.

As the Father knoweth me, and I know the Father: and I lay down my life for my sheep.

And other sheep I have, that are not of this fold: them also I must bring, and they shall hear my voice, and there shall be one fold and one shepherd.

❡ *And Psalm 50; Glory, By the intercessions of those teachers, etc; and Now, By the intercessions of the Theotokos, etc. Then on O merciful One, have mercy upon me, O god, etc., the following Ideomelon, in the Sixth Tone.*

GRACE is poured upon thy lips, O righteous Fathers, and ye have become shepherds of the Church of Christ, teaching the sheep endowed with speech to believe in a consubstantial Trinity of one Godhead.

❡ *The Katabasias for the Feast of Entrance (See February second, p. 502).*

Exaposteilarions

LET us all now extol those vessels of light, those radiant lightening bolts, Basil the Great, Gregory the Theologian, and John Chrysostom.

O one Trinity, Father, Son, and Holy Spirit, by the intercessions of Basil, Gregory, John, and the pure Theotokos, separate me not from thy glory.

❡ *And in the Einos, the following four Prosomia, in the Second Tone.*

WITH what crowns of praise shall we crown those teachers, separated in body, united in spirit; leaders of the God-mantled ones, servants of the Trinity and equal to it in number; stars illuminating the universe, and pillars of the Church, who being victorious, have been crowned with crowns of glory by Christ our King and God who possesseth the Great Mercy?

With what beautiful songs shall we clothe those God-mantled ones, who are heavenly initiates, preachers of Orthodoxy, and heads of those who discourse in theology? Basil the great revealer of divine things, Gregory the divine Theologian, and the venerable, golden-tongued John, have been worthily glorified by God the Trinity, Possessor of the Great Mercy.

With what panegyrics shall we praise those High Priests, equal to the Apostles in grace, ranking with them in honour and gifts, abolishers of infidelity, saviours and guides by word and deed, shepherds resembling Christ in faith, earthly angels, celestial humans, who were honoured by Christ, the Lord of glory and Possessor of the Great Mercy?

With what crowns of praise shall we crown the golden-worded, with Basil and Gregory, those Spirit-revering vessels and steadfast contenders for the faith, pillars of the Church, confirmation of believers, and comforters to all sinners, springs overflowing with water, from which as we drink, our souls are refreshed, seeking forgiveness of iniquities and the Great Mercy?

Glory, in the Second Tone

TODAY the souls of terrestials hold aloof from earthly things. Today they become celestial in remembrance of the saints; for the gates of heaven are lifted and the things of the Master are revealed unto us. Words preach his sayings, and tongues sing his wonders. As for us, we shout to the Saviour, saying, Glory to thee, O Christ God; for through them, safety hath been attained by believers.

Now, in the Same Tone

TODAY Christ is presented in the Temple as a child; today he cometh under the law who gave the law to Moses. Wherefore, the hosts of angels were astonished when they beheld the Container of all creation borne in the arms of an old man. As for Simeon, he was filled with reverence and joy, and cried out saying, Now, O Saviour, lettest thou me depart from this temporal life to the end immortal; for I have beheld and rejoiced.

¶ *Then the Great Doxology; the Troparion; and the Benediction.*

3. THE MASS

❡ *Troparia for the Feast and the Patron Saint of the church; and the following Kontakion, in the Second Tone.*

THOU didst translate to thy rest and the enjoyment of thy goods, those pure ones who preached and discoursed in divine things, those chiefs of teachers; for thou didst accept their works and hardships above any burnt offering, O thou who alone dost glorify thy saints.

❡ *Then conclude with the Kontakion of the Feast of Entrance,* Thou, O Christ God, who by thy birth, *etc.* (*p. 508*).

The Epistle: Their sound hath gone forth into all the earth. The heavens show forth the glory of God.

Section from the Epistle of St. Paul to the Hebrews

Ye brethren: Obey your prelates, and be subject to them, etc. (p. 360).

The Gospel: from St. Matthew

The Lord saith to his disciples: Ye are the light of the world, etc. (p. 247).

❡ *And on Especially,* It is truly meet, *etc.* (*p. 130*).

Koinonikon: Their sound hath gone forth into all the earth.

31. Cyrus and John the Unmercenary.

The Troparion: O ye silver-hating, etc. (p. 327).

VI. FEBRUARY

[Its Days, 28, and if Leap Year, 29; Hours of Day, 11; of Night, 13.]

1. Preparation for the Feast of the Presentation; and Tryphon the Martyr (1).

2. THE PRESENTATION OF OUR LORD JESUS CHRIST IN THE TEMPLE.

Typicon

❡*If this Feast falleth on a Sunday, its service is chanted with that of the Resurrection, as explained at the end of the Nativity of our Lady on September eighth. And if that Sunday happeneth to be one of the Triodion Sundays, then its service is chanted with those of the Resurrection and the Triodion.*

1. VESPERS

❡*After* O Lord, to thee have I cried, *the following six Idiomelons are sung in the First Tone.*

By Patriarch Germanus

SAY, O Simeon, whom carriest thou in the Temple in thine arms with rejoicing?   Towards whom dost thou cry, shouting, Now I have been let to depart; for I have beheld my Saviour.   This is he born of the Virgin.   This is the Word, God of God, who was incarnate for our sakes, and saved man.   Him let us worship.   (*Repeat.*)

Receive, O Simeon, him whom Moses foresaw on Sinai below the clouds laying down the law, becoming a child, and obeying the law.   He it is who uttereth the law.   He it is who was symbolized by the Prophets, who hath become incarnate for our sakes and saved man. Him let us worship.   (*Repeat.*)

Come, let us also welcome Christ and receive him with divine songs of praise, whose salvation Simeon saw, of whom David speaketh.   He it is who spake through the Prophets, who is incarnate for our sakes, and speaketh in the law. Him let us worship. (*Repeat.*)

Glory and Now, in the Sixth Tone (By John of Damascus)

TODAY let the gate of heaven be opened; for the Word of the Father who is without beginning, having taken a beginning in time, not separating from his Godhead, is offered by his own will, by a virgin Mother as a child forty days old in the Mosaic Temple;

and the priest, his servant, receiveth him in his arms, crying with joy, Now lettest thou me depart, for mine eyes have beheld thy salvation. Wherefore, O thou who didst come into the world to save mankind, O Lord, glory to thee.

❡ *Then the Eisodos; and* O resplendent Light, *etc; the daily Prokeimenon; and the following Readings.*

First Reading

AND the Lord spoke to Moses, in the same day the Lord brought forth the children of Israel, saying: Sanctify unto me every first-born that openeth the womb amongst the children of Israel.

And Moses went forth and gathered all the people and said to them: Remember this day in which you came forth out of Egypt, and out of the house of bondage, for with a strong hand hath the Lord brought you forth out of this place. Thou shalt keep this observance.

And when the Lord shall have brought thee into the land of the Chanaanite, as he swore to thee and thy fathers, thou shalt set apart all that openeth the womb of the male sex for the Lord. And when thy son shall ask thee tomorrow, saying: What is this? Thou shalt answer him: With a strong hand did the Lord bring us forth out of the land of Egypt, out of the house of bondage. For when Pharao was hardened, and would not let us go, the Lord slew every first-born in the land of Egypt, from the first-born of man to the first-born of beasts: therefore, I sacrifice to the Lord all that openeth the womb of the male sex, and all the first-born of my sons I redeem.

And it shall be as a sign in thy hand, and as a thing hung between thy eyes.

For in this wise saith the Lord Almighty: Thou shalt give me the first-born of thy sons, and every infant male born to thee shall be circumcised on the eighth day.

She shall remain three and thirty days and shall touch no holy thing, neither shall she enter into the sanctuary, until the days of her purification be fulfilled.

And when the days of her purification are expired, she shall bring to the door of the tabernacle of the testimony, a lamb of a year old for a holocaust, and a young pigeon or a turtle dove for sin, and shall deliver them to the priest or instead of this, she shall bring to the Lord, a pair of turtle doves, or pair of young pigeons. And the priest shall pray for her, and so she shall be cleansed. For as a gift they were given me by the children of Israel.

I have taken them instead of the first-born that open every womb in Israel.

For all the first-born of the children of Israel, both of men and of beasts, are mine. From the day that I slew every first-born in the land of Egypt, have I sanctified them to myself.

Second Reading: from Isaiah (6:1-12)

IN the year that king Oxias died, I saw the Lord sitting upon a throne high and elevated: and his train filled the temple.

Upon it stood the seraphims: the one had six wings, and the other had six wings: with two they covered his face, and with two they covered his feet, and with two they flew.

And they cried one to another, and said: Holy, holy, holy, the Lord God of hosts, all the earth is full of his glory.

And the lintels of the doors were moved at the voice of him that cried, and the house was filled with smoke.

And I said: Woe is me, because I have held my peace; because I am a man of unclean lips, and I dwell in the midst of a people that hath unclean lips, and I have seen with my eyes the King the Lord of hosts.

And one of the seraphims flew to me, and in his hand was a live coal, which he had taken with the tongs off the altar.

And he touched my mouth, and said: Behold this hath touched thy lips, and thy iniquities shall be taken away, and thy sin shall be cleansed.

And I heard the voice of the Lord, saying: Whom shall I send? and who shall go for us? And I said: Lo, here am I, send me.

And he said: Go, and thou shalt say to this people: Hearing, hear, and understand not: and see the vision, and know it not.

Blind the heart of this people, and make their ears heavy, and shut their eyes: lest they see with their eyes, and hear with their ears, and understand with their heart, and be converted and I heal them.

And I said: How long, O Lord? And he said: Until the cities be wasted without inhabitant, and the houses without man, and the land shall be left desolate.

And the Lord shall remove men far away, and she shall be multiplied that was left in the midst of the earth.

Third Reading: from Isaiah

BEHOLD the Lord will ascend upon a swift cloud, and will enter into Egypt, and the idols of Egypt shall be moved at his presence, and the heart of Egypt shall melt in the midst thereof.

And the spirit of Egypt shall be broken in the bowels thereof, and I will cast down their counsel.

And I will deliver Egypt into the hand of cruel masters, and a strong king shall rule over them, saith the Lord the God of hosts.

The Egyptians shall drink water from the shore of the sea, and the river shall be wasted and dry.

Where are now thy wise men? Let them tell thee, and show what the Lord of hosts hath purposed upon Egypt.

In that day Egypt shall be like unto women, and they shall be amazed, and afraid, because of the moving of the hand of the Lord of hosts, which he shall move over it.

In that day there shall be an altar of the Lord in the midst of the land of Egypt, and a monument of the Lord at the borders thereof;

It shall be for a sign, and for a testimony to the Lord of hosts in the land of Egypt. For they shall cry to the Lord because of the oppressor, and he shall send them a Saviour and a defender to deliver them.

And the Lord shall be known by Egypt, and the Egyptians shall know the Lord in that day, and shall worship him with sacrifices and offerings: and they shall make vows to the Lord, and perform them.

¶*And after the usual Petitions, the following Litiya, in the Fifth Tone.*

By Andrew the Cretan

SEARCH the books, as Christ our God said in the Gospels; for there we shall see him born and wrapped in swaddling clothes, a suckling babe feeding on milk; accepting circumcision, borne in the arms of Simeon, and appearing to the world, not in fancy or imagination, but in truth. Wherefore, let us shout to him, saying, O God before eternity, glory to thee.

¶*And in the Aposticha, the following Idiomelons, in the Seventh Tone.*

By Cosmos the Anchorite

ADORN thy chamber, O Zion, and receive Christ the King. Welcome Mary the heavenly gate; for she hath appeared as a cherubic throne; she carrieth the King of glory. Verily, the Virgin is a cloud of light carrying in her body the Son who is before the morning star, whom Simeon carrying in his arms, proclaimed to the nations as the Lord of life and death, and the Saviour of our souls.

Stichos: Now lettest thou thy servant depart, O Lord, in peace.

He that riseth from the Father before eternity, and
in these last days from a Virgin's womb, hath been carried to the Temple by his spouseless Mother; and him
who laid down the law in the Mount of Sinai, she offereth to the righteous old priest, to whom it was revealed that he should behold the Lord Christ obeying
the ceremonies of the law. And when Simeon received
him in his arms, he rejoiced, crying. This is God coëternal with the Father, and the Deliverer of our souls.

Stichos: A light to the revelation of the Gentiles.

Him that rideth in the chariots of the cherubim, and
is praised with the songs of the seraphim, the Theotokos
carried in her arms, incarnate of her who knew no
spouse. And she delivered him who gave the law, fulfilling the order of the law, into the hands of the old
priest, who, having carried Life sought deliverance
from life, saying, Now lettest thou me depart, O Master, that I may tell Adam that I beheld as babe the
immutable God, who is before eternity, and the Saviour
of the world.

Glory and Now, in the Eighth Tone (By Andrew the Cretan)

HE that rideth on the cherubim, who is praised by
the seraphim, today is offered acording to the law
in the divine Temple, lying in the arms of an old man,
and receives from Joseph offerings becoming God, two
pairs of turtle doves, the undefiled Church and the people chosen anew from the Gentiles, and two pairs of
pigeons, since he is the Head of the Old and New
Covenants. But Simeon, having received the meaning
of revelation which was made unto him, blessed the
Virgin Mary, the Theotokos, foretelling and pointing
to the sufferings of him who was born of her, seeking
deliverance from him and crying, Now letest thou me
depart, O Master, as thou wentest before and promisedst
me; for I have beheld thee, O Light before eternity,
the Lord and Saviour of the Christian people.

The Troparion, in the First Tone (three times)

REJOICE, O virgin Theotokos, full of grace; for from thee arose the Sun of justice, Christ our God, lighting those who are in darkness. Rejoice and be glad, O righteous old man, carrying in thine arms the Deliverer of our souls, who granteth us resurrection.

2. MATINS

❡*After* God the Lord hath appeared unto us, *the Troparion (three times); and the following Kathismata.*

First Kathisma, in the First Tone

LET the ranks of angels be astonished with wonder, and let us men raise our voices in praise, as we behold the ineffable condescension, the condescension of God; for he before whom the powers of heaven tremble is carried today in the arms of an old man, and he alone is the Lover of mankind.

Second Kathisma, in the First Tone

HE that is with the Father on the holy throne, came down to earth, was born of the Virgin, becoming a babe, is unbounded in time, and Simeon, having carried him in his arms, shouted with joy, saying. Now lettest thou thy servant, O compassionate One, depart; for thou hast gladdened him.

Third Kathisma, in the Fourth Tone

VERILY, the Ancient of Days becometh a babe for my sake; and the all-pure God shareth in the impure to save me in the flesh which he took from the Virgin. And Simeon, having been made confidant to these mysteries, knew him as God appearing in the flesh. Wherefore, he kissed him; for he is Life; and the old man cried with joy saying, Lettest thou me depart; for I have beheld thee, O Life of all.

❡*Then the Anabathmoi,* From my youth, *etc. (p. 50); and the following Prokeimenon.*

I shall proclaim thy Name from generation to generation. My heart overfloweth with a good word.

The Matin Gospel: from St. Luke (2:25-32)

IN those days: There was a man in Jerusalem named Simeon, and this man was just and devout, waiting for the consolation of Israel; and the Holy Spirit was in him.

And he had received an answer from the Holy Spirit, that he should not see death, before he had seen the Christ of the Lord.

And he came by the Spirit into the Temple. And when his parents brought in the child Jesus, to do for him according to the custom of the law,

He also took him into his arms, and blessed God, and said:

Now thou dost dismiss thy servant, O Lord, according to thy word in peace:

Because my eyes have seen thy salvation,

Which thou hast prepared before the face of all peoples:

A light to the revelation of the Gentiles, and the glory of thy people Israel.

❡ *Then Psalm 50 (plain reading); Glory,* By the intercessions of the Theotokos, *etc.; Now (repeat); then,* O merciful One, have mercy upon me, O God, *etc.; and the Idiomelon, in the Sixth Tone,* Today let the gate of heaven be opened, *etc. (p. 495).*

Katabasias of the Presentation, in the Third Tone
By Cosmos the Anchorite[1]

1. The sun of old passed over the depth of the tempest begetting dry land; for the water dried up on both sides like a wall for the people to pass through its depth, singing songs well pleasing to God, and shouting, Let us praise the Lord; for by glory he hath been glorified.

---

[1] These Katabasias of the Feast of the Presentation are sung from January first to February ninth.

3. O Lord, the Confirmation of those who put their trust in thee, confirm thy Church which thou hast bought with thy precious blood.

4. Thy virtue, O Christ, hath covered the heavens; for when the tabernacle of thy holiness came, thy Mother, free of corruption, and thou didst appear in the Temple of thy glory borne in arms as a babe, the whole creation was filled with thy praise.

5. When Isaiah saw God symbolically on a high altar, surrounded by the angels of glory, he lifted his voice, crying, Woe is me, wretched man; for I have foreseen God incarnate, the Light not apprehended by night, and the Lord of peace.

6. When the old man saw with his own eyes the Salvation that was revealed to the nations, he cried to thee, saying, O Christ, thou art my God, coming from the presence of God.

7. Thee do we praise, O Word of God, who moistened in the fire the God-speaking youths, and dwelt in an incorruptable Virgin, singing in true worship, Blessed art thou, God of our Fathers.

Let us praise, bless, and worship the Lord.

8. The youths striving for true worship, standing in the midst of unbearable fire and not hurt at all by the flames, sang a song of divine praise, saying, Bless the Lord, all his works, exalt him still more to the end of ages.

¶ *Then sing the following Magnifications.*

O VIRGIN Mother Thou,
The Mystery fulfilling
Transcending human minds,
With heavenly hosts attending.

Simeon the Prophet held
Upon his arms the God,
The Law Creator who
Reigneth in heaven, the Lord.

And having willed it thus
To save man from his fate,
God from a Virgin's womb,
Came sharing our state.

Thy praise, O Virgin pure,
Floweth on every tongue;
For thy first-born the Christ,
Thou art extolled by song.

Lift up your eyes to him,
Ye princes of all lands!
Behold the Lord Christ borne
On Glorious Simeon's hands!

Our earth at the sight of thee
Doth shake for fear, O God.
Transcending all mankind,
How can one hand thee hold?

Simeon did verily stay,
Alive thy face to see;
Then cried: Now lettest thou
My soul depart to thee!

The mystic ember held,
By tongues of old, It's said
Is Christ borne in the womb,
O precious first-born maid.

By thy own firm, clear will
A body thou didst take;
And on the Fortieth day
A visit to the temple make.

When from his heaven above,
The Lord to earth did come;
Simeon his servant true,
Rejoicing did welcome.

Ninth Ode

Be thou a light, My God,
To my vision and my mind;
With Paeans that I may
Praise thee among mankind.

Let us magnify, O believers, the first-born Son, the
eternal Word of the Father, First-born of a Mother who
knew no man; for we have beheld in the shadow of the
law and the Scriptures a sign, that every first-born male
that openeth the womb is called holy to God.

To the Temple Mary came,
Offering her first-born child,
Where glorious Simeon stood
With open arms and wide.

Let us magnify, O believers, let us magnify, etc.

My God of thee I seek;
Lettest thou me depart.
The Myst'ry to me now clear,
I will prepare to start.

Of old they offered a pair of turtle doves and a pair
of pigeons. But instead of them the divine old man
and Anna the pure prophetess were offered to him who
was born of the Virgin, who was offered in the Temple,
who is the Son of God. Wherefore, they served him
magnifying.

He whom the angels serve,
With trembling and with fear;
Lo, he is on our earth,
And him doth Simeon bear.

Of old they offered, etc.

Glory: O One who didst appear
In Trinity exalting.
Keep them who hope in thee
Of thy redemption granting.

Verily, Simeon cried, saying, Thou hast granted me, O Christ, the delight of thy salvation. Wherefore, receive thou thy servant lying in darkness, a divine proclaimer and new initiate of grace, magnifying thee with praise.

Now: Keep thou, Theotokos
Them who thy succour seek;
Preserve them from life's harms,
Thy servants true and meek.

Verily, Anna the pure prophetess and righteous old woman, confessed God as is meet, thanking the Master openly in the Temple, proclaiming the Theotokos and magnifying her before all present.

❡ *Then repeat the Hermos of the Ninth Ode,* Let us magnify, O believers, *etc., with its Magnifications.*

Exaposteilarion

WHEN the old man came in the spirit to the Temple he received the Lord of the law in his arms, crying, Free me now from the bounds of the body in peace according to thy word; for I have beheld with mine eyes the revelation of the Gentiles and the salvation of Israel.

❡ *And in the Einos, the following four Prosomia, in the Fourth Tone.*

VERILY, the Lover of mankind is offered today in the Temple, fulfilling the written law. And Simeon receiveth him in his weak arms, crying, Now lettest thou me depart to the bliss beyond; for I have beheld thee today mantled in mortal flesh, O thou who rulest life and art Lord of death. (*Repeat.*)

O Lord, Sun of justice, thou hast appeared as a light for the revelation of the Gentiles, sitting on a bright cloud, fulfilling the shadowy law and revealing the beginning of the new grace. Wherefore, when Simeon beheld thee he lifted his voice, crying, Lettest thou me depart from corruption; for I have today beheld thee.

Thou wast incarnate as thou wast pleased to be, being carried in the arms of the ever-virgin, without being separated from thy Godhead in the bosom of the Father; and wast delivered into the hands of Simeon, the God-receiver, O thou who holdest all creation in thy hand. Wherefore, he shouted with joy, crying, Now lettest thou me, thy servant, depart in peace; for I have beheld thee, O Master.

Glory and Now, in the Sixth Tone (by Germanus)

O CHRIST God, who willed today to lie in the hands of the old man as thou didst ride in the chariot of the cherubim, deliver us from the woe of passions, reclaim us who praise thee, and save our souls.

¶ *Then the Great Doxology; the Troparion; and the Benediction.*

3. THE MASS

1. By the intercessions of the Theotokos, O Saviour, save us.

2. Save us, O Son of God, who wast borne in the arms of Simeon the righteous, as we sing unto thee, Alleluia.

Glory and Now: O only-begotten Son and Word of God, etc. (p. 123).

3. Rejoice, O virgin Theotokos, etc. (p. 501).

Eisodikon: The Lord hath made known his salvation; he hath revealed his justice in the sight of the Gentiles. Save us, O Son of God, who wast borne in the arms of Simeon the righteous, as we sing unto thee, Alleluia.

❡ *Then the Troparion of the Feast; and of the Patron Saint of the church; and conclude with the following Kontakion, in the First Tone.*

THOU, O Christ God, who by thy Birth, didst sanctify the Virgin's womb, and, as is meet, didst bless Simeon's arms, and didst also come to save us; preserve thy fold in wars, and confirm them whom thou didst love; for thou alone art the Lover of mankind.

The Epistle: My soul doth magnify the Lord. For he hath regarded the humiliation of his handmaid.

Section from the Epistle of St. Paul to the Hebrews (7:7-17)

AND without all contradiction, that which is less, is blessed by the better.

And here indeed, men that die, receive tithes: but there he hath witness, that he liveth.

And (as it may be said) even Levi who received tithes, paid tithes in Abraham:

For he was yet in the loins of his father, when Melchisedech met him.

If then perfection was by the Levitical priesthood, (for under it the people received the law,) what further need was there that another priest should rise according to the order of Melchisedech, and not be called according to the order of Aaron?

For the priesthood being translated, it is necessary that a translation also be made of the law.

For he, of whom these things are spoken, is of another tribe, of which no one attended on the altar.

For it is evident that our Lord sprung out of Juda: in which tribe Moses spoke nothing concerning priests.

And it is yet far more evident: if according to the similitude of Melchisedech there ariseth another priest,

Who is made not according to the law of a carnal commandment, but according to the power of an indissoluble life:

For he testifieth: Thou art a priest for ever, according to the order of Melchisedech.

The Gospel: from St. Luke (2:22-40)

IN those days; his parents carried the child Jesus to Jerusalem, to present him to the Lord.

As it is written in the law of the Lord: Every male opening the womb shall be called holy to the Lord:

And to offer a sacrifice, according as it is written in the law of the Lord, a pair of turtledoves, or two young pigeons:

And behold there was a man in Jerusalem named Simeon, and this man was just and devout, waiting for the consolation of Israel: and the Holy Spirit was in him.

And he had received an answer from the Holy Spirit, that he should not see death, before he had seen the Christ of the Lord.

And he came by the Spirit into the temple. And when his parents brought in the child Jesus, to do for him according to the custom of the law,

He also took him into his arms, and blessed God, and said:

Now thou dost dismiss thy servant, O Lord, according to thy word in peace;

Because my eyes have seen thy salvation,

Which thou hast prepared before the face of all peoples:

A light to the revelation of the Gentiles, and the glory of thy people Israel.

And his father and mother were wondering at those things which were spoken concerning him.

And Simeon blessed them, and said to Mary his mother: Behold this child is set for the fall, and for the resurrection of many in Israel, and for a sign which shall be contradicted;

And thy own soul a sword shall pierce that out of many hearts, thought may be revealed.

And there was one Anna, a prophetess, the daughter of Phanuel, of the tribe of Aser; she was far advanced in years, and had lived with her husband seven years from her virginity.

And she was a widow until fourscore and four years; who departed not from the temple, by fasting and prayers serving night and day.

Now she, at the same hour, coming in, confessed to the Lord; and spoke of him to all that looked for the redemption of Israel.

And after they had performed all things according to the law of the Lord, they returned into Galilee, to their city Nazareth.

And the child grew, and waxed strong, full of wisdom; and the grace of God was in him.

¶*And on Especially, the Hermos of the Ninth Ode, with the last Magnification,* Keep thou, Theotokos, *etc. (p. 506).*

Koinonikon: I will take the cup of salvation, and call upon the Name of the Lord. Alleluia.

And: We have seen the true Light, etc.

And the Benediction: O thou who consented to be borne in the arms of Simeon the righteous for our salvation, etc.

3. Simeon the God-Receiver and Anna the Prophetess (Troparion and Kontakion of the Feast, pp. 501 and 508).

4. Isidore of Pelusium (8).

5. Agatha the Martyr (4).

6. Bukolus, Bishop of Smyrna (9); Photius, the Patriarch of Constantinople (10); and Julian the Martyr of Homs.

Troparion to the Martyr, in the Third Tone

O SAINT, clothed in strife, and the healing physician Julian, intercede with our merciful God to grant forgiveness of sins to our souls.

7. Parthenius, the Bishop of Lampsacus (10); and Luke the Righteous (11).

8. Theodore the General (1); and Zechariah the Prophet (13).

9. Nicephorus the Martyr (1); and Leave-taking of the Feast of Presentation, in which the whole service of the Feast is sung.

10. Charalampes the Martyr among Priests (5).

11. Blasius the Martyr among Priests (5); and Theodora Augusta (8).

12. Meletius the Archbishop of Antioch (9).

13. Martinianus the Righteous (6).

14. Auxentius the Righteous (7).

15. Onesimus the Apostle (12).

16. Pamphilus the Martyr, and his Companions (2).

17. Theodore the Recruit of Tyre, the great Martyr.

Troparion: Great are the accomplishments, etc. (*See Sec. 6, First Sunday of the Great Fast*).

18. Leo the Pope of Rome (9).

19. Archipus the Apostle (12).

20. Leo, Bishop of Catania (20).

21. Timothy of Symbole (7); and Eustathius Bishop of Antioch (11).

22. Finding of the Relics of the Saints that were in Eugenius (2).

23. Polycarp, Bishop of Smyrna (5).

24. First and Second Finding of the Venerable Head of John the Forerunner.

Troparion, in the Fourth Tone

VERILY, from the earth rose the head of the Forerunner, bequeathing to believers incorruptible rays of healing, gathering the crowds of angels from above and calling below the races of mankind to address their voices in unison in glory to Christ God.

Kontakion, in the Second Tone

O PROPHET of God and Forerunner of grace, we have found thy head in the earth as an all-pure rose. Wherefore, we seek from it healing at all times; for, as of old, thou ceasest not into the world to preach repentance.

The Epistle: (2 Corinthians 4:6-14)

Ye brethren: For God, who commanded the light to shine out of darkness, etc. (p. 242).

The Gospel : from St. Luke (7:17-30)

25. Tarasius the Archbishop of Constantinople (9).
26. Porphyrius Bishop of Gaza (9).
27. Procopius of Banias the Confessor (7).
28. Basil the Confessor (7).
29. Cassian the Righteous Roman (6).

VII. MARCH ·

[Its Days, 31; Hours of Day, 12; of Night, 12]

1. Eudocia the Righteous Martyr (8).
2. Hesychius the Martyr (1).
3. Eutropius the Martyr, and his Companions (2).
4. Gerasimus the Righteous who was in the Country of the Jordan (7).
5. Conton the Martyr (1).
6. The Forty-two Martyrs of Amorium (2).
7. The Martyr among Priests Ephraim, and his Companions, the Bishops of Cherson (11).
8. Theophylact the Bishop of Nicomedia (10).
9. The Forty who were Martyred in the City of Sebaste (3).

The Epistle: (Hebrews 12:1-10)

AND therefore we also having so great a cloud of witnesses over our head, laying aside every weight and sin which surrounds us, let us run by patience to the fight proposed to us:

Looking on Jesus, the author and finisher of faith, who having joy set before him, endured the cross, despising the shame, and now sitteth on the right hand of the throne of God.

For think diligently upon him that endured such opposition from sinners against himself; that you be not wearied, fainting in your minds.

For you have not yet resisted unto blood, striving against sin:

And you have forgotten the consolation, which speaketh to you, as unto children, saying: My son, neglect not the discipline of the Lord; neither be thou wearied whilst thou art rebuked by him.

For whom the Lord loveth, he chastiseth; and he scourgeth every son whom he receiveth.

Persevere under discipline. God dealeth with you as with his sons; for what son is there, whom the father doth not correct?

But if you be without chastisement, whereof all are made partakers, then are you bastards, and not sons.

Moreover we have had fathers of our flesh, for instructors, and we reverenced them: shall we not much more obey the Father of spirits, and live?

And they indeed for a few days, according to their own pleasure, instructed us: but he, for our profit, that we might receive his sanctification.

The Gospel: from St. Matthew (20:1-16)

THE kingdom of heaven is like to an householder, who went out early in the morning to hire labourers in his vineyard.

And having agreed with the labourers for a penny a day, he sent them into his vineyard.

And going out about the third hour, he saw others standing in the market place idle.

And he said to them: Go you also into my vineyard, and I will give you what shall be just.

And they went their way. And again he went out about the sixth and the ninth hour, and did in like manner.

But about the eleventh hour he went out and found others standing, and he saith to them: Why stand you here all the day idle?

They say to him: Because no man hath hired us. He saith to them: Go you also into my vineyard.

And when evening was come, the lord of the vineyard saith to his steward: Call the labourers and pay them their hire, beginning from the last even to the first.

When therefore they were come, that came about the eleventh hour, they received every man a penny.

But when the first also came, they thought that they should receive more: and they also received every man a penny.

And receiving it they murmured against the master of the house,

Saying: These last have worked but one hour, and thou hast made them equal to us, that have borne the burden of the day and the heats.

But he answering said to one of them: Friend, I do thee no wrong: didst thou not agree with me for a penny?

Take what is thine, and go thy way: I will also give to this last even as to thee.

Or, is it not lawful for me to do what I will? is thy eye evil, because I am good?

So shall the last be first, and the first last. For many are called, but few chosen.

10. Quadratus the Martyr, and his Companions (2).

11. Sophronius the Damascene, Archbishop of Jerusalem (9).

12. Theophanes the Confessor (6).

13. The Translation of the Relics of Nicephorus, the Archbishop of Constantinople (9).

14. Benedict the Righteous (6).

15. Agapius, and his Seven Companions the Martyrs (2).

16. Sabinus the Martyr (1); Christodulus (7).

17. Alexius the Man of God (7).

18. Cyril the Archbishop of Jerusalem (9).

19. Chrysanthus and Darias the Martyrs (2).

20. The Fathers Martyred in the Monastery of St. Sabas (3).

21. James the Righteous Confessor (6).

22. The Martyr among Priests, Basil, Bishop of Angora (5).

23. Nikon the Righteous, and his One Hundred and Ninety-nine Disciples (2).

24. Preparation for the Feast of the Annunciation.

Troparion, in the Fourth Tone

TODAY is the prelude of joy for the whole world. Let us, therefore, go forward and celebrate with gladness; for behold, Gabriel cometh bringing glad tidings to the Virgin, crying to her with fear and wonder, saying, Hail, O full of grace. The grace of the Lord is with thee.

Kontakion, in the Same Tone

BY the descent of the most Holy Spirit and with the voice of the archangel, O Theotokos, and with the recall of Adam, thou didst conceive him who is equal to the Father in Session and Essence.

25. THE ANNUNCIATION OF THE THEOTOKOS, THE EVER-VIRGIN MARY.

¶*If the Feast of the Annunciation falleth on any day of the Great Fast, its service is chanted as here. And on Sundays of the Great Fast its service is chanted along with that of the Resurrection and the Triodion. And if it falleth on Great Friday or Great Saturday, then it is transferred to the Day of Glorious Easter.*

1. VESPERS

¶*After the Sunset Psalm, omit* Blessed is the man, *and immediately on* O Lord, to thee have I cried, *sing the following six Prosomia, in the Sixth Tone.*

VERILY, Gabriel did come to thee, disclosing the purpose which was before the ages, hailing thee and saying, Rejoice, O unseeded land! Rejoice, O unburning bush! Rejoice, O depth inaccessible to vision! Rejoice, O bridge leading to the heavens! Rejoice, O lofty ladder whom Jacob did behold! Rejoice, O jar of divine manna! Rejoice, O dissolution of the curse! Rejoice, O recall of Adam! The Lord is with thee. (*Repeat.*)

And the blameless Maiden, replied to the captain of hosts, Verily, thou dost appear to me as a man. Wherefore, then, dost thou utter superhuman things, saying that God shall be with me and dwell in my womb? Tell me, how am I, then, to become a spacious place of sanctification for him, who rideth on the cherubim? Mislead me not with deceit; for I have known no pleasure, and have not approached wedlock. How, then shall I give birth to a son? (*Repeat.*)

Then the incorporeal one cried unto her, saying, Whensoever God willeth, the order of nature is overcome, and that which is superhuman is accomplished. Wherefore, O all-pure and holy one, believe thou my true words. But she cried, saying, Let it be unto me as thou sayest, and I will give birth to the Incorporeal, who shall take a body from me, that by his union therewith he may raise man to the first rank, since he alone is mighty. (*Repeat.*)

Glory and Now, in the Sixth Tone (by John of Damascus)

FROM heaven the archangel Gabriel was sent to announce the Conception to the Virgin. He went to Nazareth thinking within himself and wondering greatly, how it is that he who is in the highest and incomprehensible shall be born of a Virgin. He whose throne is heaven, and earth his footstool, how shall he be contained in a woman's womb? How was he pleased to be incarnate of her by a word only, he whom the six-winged ones and those of many eyes cannot gaze upon? Yea, he who cometh is the Word of God. Why then do I hesitate, and not address the Maiden, saying, Hail, O full of grace, the grace of the Lord is with thee? Hail, O spotless Virgin! Hail, O groomless bride! Hail, O Mother of life; blessed is the fruit of thy womb?

❧*And after the Eisodos, and O resplendent Light, etc., and the daily Prokeimenon, read the Prophecies (which see in the Feast of our Lady's Nativity, pp. 284-286).*

❧*And after the usual Petitions, sing the following Litiya, in the Second Tone.*

By Cozma the Anchorite

TODAY doth Gabriel make announcement to her who is full of grace, saying, Hail, O groomless and unwedded Maiden. Let not my strange appearance dazzle thee, nor be dismayed at me; for I am the archangel. Verily, the serpent did deceive Eve of old, and now I bring thee glad tidings of joy. Thou shalt remain without corruption, and shalt give birth to the Lord, O pure one.

❧*And in the Aposticha, the following Idiomelons, in the Fourth Tone.*

IN the sixth month the archangel was sent to a pure Virgin. And as he opened his mouth to her with, Peace, he announced to her that from her should come the Redeemer. And having accepted the greeting with faith, she conceived thee, O God before eternity, who wast pleased, in an inexplicable manner, to become incarnate for the salvation of our souls.

Stichos: From day to day, show forth the salvation of our Lord.

The Theotokos heard a language she did not understand; for the archangel uttered to her the words of the Annunciation. And having accepted the greeting with faith, she conceived thee, O God before eternity.

Wherefore, we lift our voice to thee in joy, saying, O God who wast incarnate without transubstantiation, grant the world safety and our souls the Great Mercy.

Stichos: Sing unto the Lord a new canticle.

Behold, now is our recall made manifest; for God is united with mankind in an ineffable manner. And at the voice of the archangel error hath vanished; for the Virgin hath received joy and earthly things have become heavenly, and the world is freed from the ancient curse. Wherefore, let creation rejoice; let it raise its voice with praise, O Lord, our Creator and Redeemer, glory to thee.

Glory and Now, in the Fourth Tone (by Andrew the Jerusalemite)

TODAY is the Annunciation, the virginal celebration; for terrestrials shall unite with celestials, Adam being renewed and Eve freed of the first sorrow. And the tabernacle who is of our own substance hath become a temple for God, by deification of the clay derived from her. What mystery, the incomprehensible quality of the condescension, and the ineffable manner of the Conception! An angel ministering the wonder, and the virgin womb receiving the Son. The Holy Spirit is sent, and on high the Father is well pleased. The reconciliation was effected by the universal will, through which and by which having been saved, let us with Gabriel sing unto the Virgin, Hail, O full of grace. The Lord is with thee, from whom Christ our Lord God and Saviour did take our nature and join it to himself. Wherefore, implore thou him to save our souls.

The Troparion, in the Fourth Tone (three times)

TODAY is the beginning of our salvation, and the manifestation of the mystery from the ages; for the Son of God becometh the Son of the Virgin, and Gabriel proclaimeth grace. Wherefore, do we shout

with him to the Theotokos, Hail, O full of grace.   The
Lord is with thee.

❡ *Then the Benediction.*

2. MATINS

❡ *On* God the Lord hath appeared unto us, *sing the Troparion three
times; then the following Kathismata.*

First Kathisma, in the First Tone

THE great leader of the immaterial hosts hath come
to the city of Nazareth announcing to thee, O pure
one, the Lord, King of the ages, and saying unto thee,
Hail, O blessed Mary, thou incomprehensible and inexplicable wonder, and the reclaimer of mankind.

Second Kathisma, in the Third Tone

TODAY the whole Creation rejoiceth; for the archangel hath cried unto thee, Hail, O blessed one,
spotless, pure, and all-blameless.   Today the haughtiness of the serpent vanisheth, as the bond of the curse
of the first father is undone.   Wherefore, with all things
we cry unto thee, saying, Hail O full of grace.

Third Kathisma, in the Fourth Tone

VERILY, Gabriel lifteth his voice to thee in greeting, O pure one, since thou carriest in thy womb
God before the ages, by whose Word he did establish
the ends of the earth.   And Mary replied, saying, I have
not known man.   How then shall I give birth to a
son?   For who hath ever seen a birth without seed? The
angel explained to the virgin Theotokos, saying, The
Holy Spirit shall come upon thee, and the power of
the Highest shall overshadow thee.

Fourth Kathisma, in the Same Tone

VERILY, Gabriel was sent unto the spotless Virgin, announcing to her the ineffable joy, that she should conceive without seed, and that no corruption should touch her, crying, Behold, thou shalt give birth to a Son who is before the ages, who shall deliver his people from their sins, and he who sent me to hail thee testifieth, saying, Hail, thou who art blessed; for thou shalt give birth, being yet a Virgin, and after birth thou shalt remain a Virgin.

❧ *Then the Anabathmoi,* From my youth, *etc.* (*p. 50*)*; and the following Prokeimenon.*

From day to day show forth the salvation of our God. Sing unto the Lord a new canticle.

The Matin Gospel: from St. Luke

And Mary arose in those days, etc. (p. 50).

❧ *And Psalm 50* (*plain reading*)*; then Glory,* By the intercessions of the Theotokos, *etc; and Now* (*repeated*).

❧ *And on* O merciful One, have mercy upon me, O God, *etc., sing the following Idiomelon, in the Second Tone.*

TODAY doth Gabriel announce to her who is full of grace, Hail, O groomless and unwedded Maiden. Let not my strange appearance dazzle thee, nor be dismayed at me; for I am the archangel. Verily, the serpent did deceive Eve of old, and now I bring thee glad tidings of joy. Thou shalt remain without corruption, and shalt give birth to the Lord, O pure one.

❧ *The Katabasias,* Open my mouth, *etc; and instead of the Fourth sing the following.*

THE transcendently divine Jesus, sitting in glory on the throne of the Godhead, hath come on a bright cloud, saving with the clasp of his incorruptible hands those who cry unto him, Glory to thy might, O Christ.

❧ *And instead of the Sixth, the following.*

IN the belly of the whale, Jonah the Prophet foreshadowed the three-day Burial, lifting his voice and
imploring, Deliver me from corruption, O Jesus, King
of the powers.

❡*And instead of the Eighth, the following.*

HEARKEN, O Maiden, virgin and pure, that
Gabriel may tell the eternal will of the Highest.
Make thee ready to receive God; for the Uncontainable shall, through thee, mingle with mankind. Wherefore, rejoicing, I cry, Bless the Lord, all his works.

❡*Then sing the Ninth Ode, repeating the following Magnification
on each of its Troparia.*

Receive, O earth, the glad tidings of great joy, and
ye heavens, praise the glory of God.

THE Theotokos, being the living tabernacle of God,
shall never be touched by an unclean hand. But
the lips of believers shall sing unto her ceaselessly with
the voice of angels, crying joyfully, Hail, O full of
grace. The Lord is with thee.

Thou hast transcended the bounds of nature, O
Maiden, having conceived God in an ineffable manner;
for being of a perishable nature, thou wast exempted in
thy birth-giving from that which pertaineth to mothers.
Wherefore, as is meet, thou dost hear, Hail, O full of
grace, The Lord is with thee.

How dost thou overflow with milk, O undefiled Virgin? Verily, thou hast appeared as a strange manifestation, unutterable by human tongue, transcending nature and the bounds of the laws of birth. Wherefore,
thou dost hear, as is meet, Hail, O full of grace. The
Lord is with thee.

The God-inspired Scriptures, O Mother of the Highest, have spoken of thee mystically; for Jacob when he
saw the ladder of old, which was a foresign of thee,
cried, saying, This is the ascent of God. Wherefore,
as is meet, thou dost hear, Hail, O full of grace. The
Lord is with thee.

The bush and the fire did reveal to God-beholding Moses a wonderful miracle. And seeking the fulfillment thereof with the passing of time, he cried, saying, I shall behold her who is a spotless Maiden, who shall be addressed with rejoicing as the Theotokos, Hail, O full of grace. The Lord is with thee.

Verily, Daniel called thee a supersensuous mountain, and Isaiah the Mother of God. Gideon saw thee as a fleece. David called thee a sanctuary, and another a door. But Gabriel cried unto thee, saying, Hail, O full of grace. The Lord is with thee.

❡ *Then conclude with the Ninth Ode with its Magnification.*

Exaposteilarions

THE Leader of the heavenly hosts was sent from Almighty God to an undefiled Virgin to announce to her the strange and ineffable wonder that God as Man shall, without seed, become a child from her, restoring the whole creation of mankind. Wherefore, ye nations, receive the glad tidings of the re-creation of the whole world.

Rejoice, O Theotokos, O deliverance of Adam from the curse! Rejoice, chaste Theotokos! Rejoice, O living bush! Rejoice, O lamp! Rejoice, O throne! Rejoice, O ladder and door! Rejoice, O divine chariot! Rejoice, O bright cloud! Rejoice, O temple, O most-gilded jar! Rejoice, O mountain! Rejoice, O tabernacle and table! Hail to thee, O deliverer of Eve!

❡ *And in the Einos, sing the following four Prosomia, in the First Tone.*

FROM the arches on high did Gabriel descend coming towards Nazareth. He came to the Virgin Mary, lifting his voice to her and saying, Hail; for thou shalt conceive a Son older than Adam, to the Maker and Creator of the ages, who delivereth those who cry to thee, O undefiled one, Hail!

From heaven did Gabriel come, bringing the Annunciation to the Virgin, and crying unto her, Hail; for thou dost carry in thy womb him who shall be contained in thee, the Uncontainable in space. Thou shalt be revealed as carrying him who shineth forth from the Father, before the morning star.

The Word, coëternal with the Father before eternity, was not separated from the celestials. But he descended, through his exceeding compassion, to those who are below, taking pity on our stumbling and fall, and putting on the humility of Adam, taking on a strange likeness.

The transubstantial Word, appearing eternally from his Father, and in time from his Mother, taketh on the likeness of a servant, becoming flesh, without separation from the Godhead and renewing the creation of Adam in the womb of her who conceived him without seed.

Glory and Now, in the Second Tone (by Theophanis)

TODAY is disclosed the mystery before the ages; and the Son of God shall become the Son of Man, that by his adoption of the lowest he may grant me the highest. Of old Adam failed to become a God as he desired, so God became Man that Adam might become a God. Wherefore, let creation rejoice, and nature exchange greetings, for the archangel did stand reverently before the Virgin and offered her joy instead of sorrow. Wherefore, O our God, who by thy compassion became man, glory be to thee.

⁋ *Then the Great Doxology; and the Troparion,* Today is the beginning of our salvation, *etc.* (*p. 518*).

3. THE MASS

1. By the intercessions of the Theotokos, O Saviour, save us.

2. Save us, O Son of God, who wast incarnate for our sake, as we sing unto thee, Alleluia.

⁋ *Glory and Now,* O Only-begotten Son, *etc.*

3. Today is the beginning of our salvation, etc.

Eisodikon: From day to day show forth the salvation of our God. Save us, O Son of God, who wast incarnate for our sakes, as we sing unto thee, Alleluia.

❡ *Then the Troparion; and the following Kontakion, in the Eighth Tone.*

VERILY, I, thy city, O Theotokos, inscribe to thee the banners of conquest, O defending soldier, and offer thee thanks as a deliverer from tribulations. And since thine is the unconquerable might, deliver me from sundry oppressions, that I may cry unto thee, Rejoice, O groomless bride.

The Epistle: My soul doth magnify the Lord. For he hath regarded the humiliation of his handmaid.

Section from the Epistle of St. Paul to the Hebrews

Ye brethren: For both he that sanctifieth and they who are sanctified, etc. (p. 394).

The Gospel: from St. Luke (1:24-38)

AND in those days, his wife Elisabeth conceived, and hid herself five months, saying:

Thus hath the Lord dealt with me in the days wherein he looked on me, to take away my reproach among men.

And in the sixth month the angel Gabriel was sent from God unto a city of Galilee, named Nazareth,

To a virgin espoused to a man whose name was Joseph, of the house of David; and the virgin's name was Mary.

And the angel came in with her, and said, Hail, thou that art highly favoured, the Lord is with thee: blessed art thou among women.

And when she saw him, she was troubled at his saying, and cast in her mind what manner of salutation this should be.

And the angel said unto her, Fear not, Mary: for thou hast found favour with God.

And, behold, thou shalt conceive in thy womb, and bring forth a son, and shalt call his name Jesus.

He shall be great, and shall be called the Son of the Highest; and the Lord God shall give unto him the throne of his father David:

And he shall reign over the house of Jacob for ever; and of his kingdom there shall be no end.

Then said Mary unto the angel, How shall this be, seeing I know not a man?

And the angel answered and said unto her, The Holy Spirit shall come upon thee, and the power of the Highest shall overshadow thee: therefore also that holy thing which shall be born of thee shall be called the Son of God.

And, behold, thy cousin Elisabeth, she hath also conceived a son in her old age; and this is the sixth month with her, who was called barren.

For with God nothing shall be impossible.

And Mary said, Behold the handmaid of the Lord; be it unto me according to thy word. And the angel departed from her.

❡ *And the rest of the Liturgy of John Chrysostom, and the Especially, the Hermos of the Ninth, with its Magnification.*

Koinonikon: The Lord hath chosen Zion: he hath chosen it for his dwelling. Alleluia.

❡ *Then,* We have seen the true Light, *etc; and the Benediction.*

26. A Plenary Memorial for Gabriel the Archangel (*See the Troparion on November eighth*).

27. Matrona the Righteous, who is of Thessalonica (8).

28. New Hilarion the Righteous (6).

29. Mark the Righteous Bishop of Arethusa (10); Cyril the Deacon and Martyr, and his Companions (2).

30. John the Righteous, Author of the Climacus (the Ladder of Virtues) (6).

31. Hypatius, Bishop of Gangara (5).

VIII. APRIL

[Its Days, 30; Hours of Day, 13; of Night, 11]

1. Mary the Righteous, the Egyptian (8).

2. Titus the Righteous, the Wonder-Worker (6).

3. Nicetas, Head of the Monastery of Medicium; and Joseph the Hymnographer (6).

4. George the Righteous of Malium (7).

5. Claudius and Diodorus, and the Martyrs with them (2).

6. Eutychius, the Archbishop of Constantinople (10).

7. Calliopius the Martyr (1); George, the Bishop of Mytilene (10).

8. Herodion, and his Companions of the Seventy Apostles (12).

9. Eupsychius the Martyr of Cæsarea (1).

10. Terentius and Pompeius, and their Companions (2).

11. Antipas Bishop of Pergamus (5).

12. Basil the Confessor, Bishop of Parium (10).

13. Martin the Confessor, Pope of Rome (10).

14. Aristarchus, Pudens, and Trophimus who are of the Seventy (12).

15. Crescens the Martyr (1).

16. Agape, Irene, and Chionia the Virgin Martyrs (4).

17. The Martyr among Priests Simeon, Martyred in Persia (5).

18. John the Righteous, Disciple of Gregory of Panias (6).

19. The Martyr among Priests Paphnutius (5).

20. Theodore the Righteous of Trichinos (5).

21. The Martyr among Priests Januarius (5).

22. Theodore the Righteous of Syceum (8).

23. THE GREAT SAINT AMONG MARTYRS, THE VICTORY-CLAD GEORGE.

Typicon

¶*If this Feast falleth on Great Saturday or Easter Sunday, then its service is transferred to Easter Monday, and is chanted with the Easter Service.*

1. VESPERS

¶*On* O Lord, to thee have I cried, *sing the following six Prosomia, in the Fourth Tone.*

O FIGHT-BEARING George, since thou art brave among the Martyrs, we gather today to extol thee; for thou didst finish thy course and keep the Faith, receiving from God the crown of victory. Wherefore, implore thou him to deliver from corruption and tribulations those who celebrate in faith thy ever-solemn memory.

Thou didst go forward to the fight, O George, with steadfast energy, confident like a lion, ignoring the body, since it shall pass away, and concerning thyself wisely with the incorruptible spirit. Wherefore, wast thou refined with all kinds of sufferings, as gold of seven-fold purity.

Thou didst suffer with the Saviour, O great and glorious Martyr George, resembling him by thy voluntary death. Wherefore, thou dost reign with him mantled in the purple of thine own blood and adorned with the crown of thy struggles, exulting in the crown of victory to unending ages.

Thou wast fortified with the shield of faith, the helmet of grace, and the spear of the Cross, O brave George, becoming indefeasable against thine enemies. And being a divine hero, thou hast vanquished the ranks of Satans and dost abide with the angels; and, since thou dost watch over believers, thou dost sanctify and save them when they call upon thee.

We know thee, O victory-mantled George, as a brilliantly shining star, as the radiant sun in the firmament, as a pearl of great price, a dazzling precious stone, a son of the day, and a valiant one among the Martyrs.

Guard me, O all-blessed George, coming to my help as I travel by sea, or walk on land, or sleep by night. Save me as I awake, and guide me to do the Lord's will, that I may find forgiveness in the Day of Judgment for what I have done in life, seeking refuge under the wing of thy protection.

Glory, in the Sixth Tone

THOU hast walked according to thy name, O George the soldier; for, in carrying the cross of Christ on thy shoulder, thou didst plough the earth, made barren by the errors of Satan; and having uprooted the thorns of heathen worship thou didst plant the vine of Orthodox faith. Wherefore, thou dost bud healing to believers in all the inhabited world, and having become a faithful husbandman of the Trinity, we beseech thee to intercede for the safety of the world and the salvation of our souls.

❧*And Now for the Pentecost Week in which the Feast falleth. Then the Eisodos; and* O *resplendent Light, etc.; and the daily Prokeimenon. And after the usual Petitions, sing the following Litiya, in the Second Tone.*

By John of Damascus

VERILY, Solomon did cry out, Let the eyelids of men gaze straight; for he foretold that whosoever shall look straight shall have mercy from Christ God. Readily didst thou hearken to this, O most-contending George, following the teachings of Christ. And when thou wast delivered to the evil ones thou didst refuse unflinchingly the sacrifices of error, because they are impure; and thy body, which thou didst offer for the sake of the Creator's love, was severed member by member. But the deceitful enemy was wholly wounded when, seeing thee wearing the crown and exulting, he was confounded. Wherefore, as thou abidest with thy Master and the powers on high, intercede, O champion of Christ, for the salvation of our souls.

❧*In the Aposticha, the following Prosomia, in the Fourth Tone.*

THE nations praise with psalms and songs thine
ever-memorable feast, O George; for it hath shone
forth resplendent and clothed with light, adorned with
glory and grace. Wherefore, the myriads of angels
and Martyrs with the Apostles applaud the trophies of
thy struggles, O Martyr, praising Christ our God, the
Saviour, who glorified thee. Implore thou him, therefore, to illuminate and save our souls.

Stichos: The just shall flourish like a palm tree.

Thou hast become a shield-bearer for Christ, being
found by those who sought thee not. Thou wast consumed by fire for the sake of Christ, disdaining the soul-
corrupting error of false gods. Then didst thou cry
out to the law-transgressors, saying, I am enlisting as a
soldier of Christ, my King. Neither beasts, therefore,
nor wheels, nor fire, nor sword can separate me from the
love of Christ our God. Wherefore, implore thou him
to illuminate and save our souls.

Stichos: The Lord hath made his saints a wonder.

O crown-wearing George, thou didst make light of
many instruments, varigated torments, and horrible cutting tools, finishing the course of martyrdom in true
worship. Wherefore, with the flowers of paeans we
crown thy most resplendent memory, greeting thy venerable members in faith. And as thou standest, light-
mantled, before the throne of Christ our God, beseech
thou him to illuminate and save our souls.

Glory, in the Fourth Tone

LET us, brethren, extol spiritually that supersensuous intelligence of diamond firmness, the ever-
memorable Martyr George who, having enthusiasti-
cally declared for Christ, by dangers and sufferings
hardened and exercised his perishable body, after nature, which was melted away by various torments.
Albeit, love conquered nature and persuaded the lover
to reach, through death, to the Beloved, Christ God the
Saviour of our souls.

❡ *And Now, for the week.*

Troparion for the Week and the Saint, in the Fourth Tone

SINCE thou art a liberator and deliverer of captives, a help and succour of the poor and needy, a healing physician of the sick, a contender and fighter for kings, O great among Martyrs, the victory-clad George; intercede with Christ God for the salvation of our souls.

2. MATINS

❡ *On* God the Lord hath appeared unto us, *the Troparia as at Vespers; the Kathismata of the Week; and the following ones for the Saint.*

First Kathisma, in the First Tone

BEHOLD, the Spring of grace hath flourished, and for all hath risen the Resurrection of Christ: and with them doth shine forth the all-adored day, light-mantled, the day of the Martyr George. Wherefore, let us altogether joyfully celebrate it, wrapped with splendour in a divine manner.

Second Kathisma, in the Third Tone

O VICTORY-CLAD and all-blessed George, when thou didst fervently seek Christ, thou didst bravely demolish the chambers of error; and in the battle-field thou didst confess Christ. Wherefore, O glorious Martyr, implore Christ God to grant us the Great Mercy.

Third Kathisma, in the Fourth Tone

THOU didst diligently sow the seeds of divine commandments, O glorious Martyr, distributing thy whole wealth piously to the poor, gaining in its place Christ's glory. Wherefore, thou didst hasten towards unceasing struggles and sufferings confidently. And when thou didst become a partaker with the Passionless in his Passion and Resurrection, thou enjoyedst his kingdom, imploring him now for our sakes.

❡ *Then the Anabathmoi,* From my youth, *etc. (p. 50); and the following Prokeimenon.*

The just shall flourish like the palm tree planted in the house of the Lord.

The Matin Gospel: from St. Luke

The Lord said to his disciples, etc. (p. 322).

❡ *And* In that we have beheld the Resurrection of Christ, *etc. (p. 113); and Psalm 50 (plain reading); Glory,* By the intercessions of the victory-clad, *etc; Now* By the intercessions of the Theotokos, *etc; then, on* O merciful One, have mercy upon me, O God, *etc., the followiwng Idiomelon, in the Sixth Tone.*

TODAY the whole universe is illuminated by the rays of the fight-bearing one; and the Church of Christ, adorned with flowers, crieth unto thee, O George, saying, O minister of Christ and all-fervid helper, cease not to intercede with the Lord for our sake.

❡ *The Katabasias for Easter. Then sing,* O thou who art more honourable than the cherubim, *etc; Katabasia,* The angel spake to her that is full of grace, *etc. (See Sec. 7, Easter Day, following Ninth Ode and Magnifications).*

Exaposteilarion

A JOYFUL spring hath risen for us, the divine and radiant Resurrection of the Master, translating us from earth to a heavenly passover. And therewith doth radiate the light-giving memorial of the all-honoured Martyr George. Wherefore, let us celebrate it with rejoicing, that we may become worthy of the divine grace from Christ the Saviour.

❡ *Then for the Week.*

❡ *And in the Einos, sing the following four Prosomia for the Saint, in the Second Tone.*

COME, let us all, celebrating the all-joyful and all-festal Feast of the glorious Resurrection, celebrate also the joyful anniversary of the Martyr George, and crown him with vernal flowers, for he is unconquerable, that, by his beseechings, we may attain liberation from sins and sorrows.

To him who granted thee the perfection of life, O all-blessed George, thou didst offer thyself wholly as a breathing, living burnt-offering, a pure and well-accepted sacrifice. Wherefore, thou hast become a fervid intercessor, O Martyr, delivering from oppressions those who extol thee and call on thee in faith.

When thou didst diligently till the seed of the Word, sown in thy pure self, O blessed one, thou didst cultivate it with hardships and struggles; and wisely having treasured it in the heavenly garner, thou didst find the immortal bliss, wherein thou dost now delight, By thine intercessions with God, preserve those who extol thee in faith.

O struggle-bearing Martyr of Christ, save by thine intercessions those who are in various tribulations, delivering them from all oppressions, and putting away from them evil, soul-corrupting dismay, seeking for us grace and mercy, that, being delivered by thine intercessions, we may all honour in joy thy solemn struggles.

Glory, in the Fifth Tone

SPRING hath shone forth; come, let us be glad; the Resurrection of Christ hath occurred; come, let us rejoice; for the memorial of the struggle-bearing one hath appeared unto those who believe. Wherefore, O feast-lovers, let us celebrate it mystically; for this one, being a good soldier, did prevail over the usurpers and disappoint them, becoming an emulator of Christ in his Passion, not pitying his earthly vessel. Rather did he leave it naked as brass, rewarding it with torments. Wherefore, let us lift our voices to him, crying, O struggle-bearer, plead for the salvation of our souls.

¶ *And Now, for the Week. Then the Great Doxology; and the Troparion for the Saint.*

3. THE MASS

❡ *The Antiphony and the Eisodikon for Easter; the Troparia as at Vespers; the Kontakion for Easter,* Though thou, O deathless One, didst descend into the grave, *etc. (See Sec. 7, Easter Day, Matins, following Sixth Ode).*

The Epistle: The just shall rejoice in the Lord. Hear, O God, my voice.

Section from the Acts of the Holy Apostles (12:1-11)

AND at the same time, Herod the king stretched forth his hands, to afflict some of the church.

And he killed James, the brother of John, with the sword.

And seeing that it pleased the Jews, he proceeded to take up Peter also. Now it was in the days of the Asymes.

And when he had apprehended him, he cast him into prison, delivering him to four files of soldiers to be kept, intending, after the pasch, to bring him forth to the people.

Peter therefore was kept in prison. But prayer was made without ceasing by the church unto God for him.

And when Herod would have brought him forth, the same night Peter was sleeping between two soldiers, bound with two chains: and the keepers before the door kept the prison.

And behold an angel of the Lord stood by him: and a light shined in the room: and he striking Peter on the side, raised him up, saying: Arise quickly. And the chains fell off from his hands.

And the angel said to him: Gird thyself and put on thy sandals. And he did so. And he said to him: Cast thy garment about thee, and follow me.

And going out, he followed him, and he knew not that it was true which was done by the angel: but thought he saw a vision.

And passing through the first and the second ward, they came to the iron gate that leadeth to the city, which of itself opened to them. And going out, they passed on through one street: and immediately the angel departed from him.

And Peter coming to himself, said: Now I know in very deed, that the Lord hath sent his angel, and hath delivered me out of the hand of Herod, and from all the expectation of the people of the Jews.

The Gospel: from St. John

And the Lord said to his disciples: These things I command you, etc. (p. 326).

❡*And on Especially,* It is truly meet, *etc.*

Koinonikon: The just shall be in everlastng remembrance. Alleluia.

❡*And instead of,* We have seen the true Light, *etc.,* Christ is risen, *etc.*

Kontakion for the Saint, in the Fourth Tone

THOU hast been tilled by God, becoming an honoured and pious husbandman. The sheaves of virtue thou hast gathered unto thyself, O George; for having sowed with tears thou didst reap with joy; and didst struggle unto blood, attaining Christ. Wherefore, by thine intercessions, O Saint, thou dost grant to all remission of sins.

24. Elizabeth the Righteous Wonder-Worker (8).

25. Mark the Evangelical Apostle (12).

26. The Martyr among Priests, Basil, Bishop of Amasia (5).

27. The Martyr among Priests, Simeon, the Kinsman of the Lord, and Bishop of Jerusalem (5).

28. The Nine Martyrs of Cyzicus (2).

29. The two Apostles, Jason and Sosipater (12).

30. James the Apostle, Brother of John the Evangelist (12).

IX. MAY

[Number of Days, 31; Hours of the Day, 14;
of Night, 10]

1. Jeremiah the Prophet (13).

2. Translation of the Body of Athanasius the Great (10).

3. Timothy and Maura the Martyrs (2).

4. Pelagia the Martyr (4).

5. Irene, the Great among Martyrs (4).

6. Job of Many Contests (3).

7. Anniversary of the Sign of the Cross which Appeared in the Sky in Jerusalem.
❧ *Troparion,* O Lord, save thy people, *etc.* (*p. 298*).

8. John the Evangelical Apostle.
❧ *Troparion,* O Apostle speaker of divinity, *etc.* (*p. 311*).
Arsenius the Great (6).

9. Isaiah the Prophet (13); Christopher the Martyr (1).

10. The Apostle Simon the Zealot (12).

11. Renewal of Constantinople; and the Martyr among Priests Mucius (5).

12. Epiphanius Bishop of Cyprus; and Germanus the Archbishop of Constantinople (11).

13. Glyceria the Martyr (4).

14. Isidore who was Martyred in Chios (1).

15. Pachomius the Great (6); Achillius the Archbishop of Larissa the Wonder-Worker (9).

16. The Righteous Theodore, the Sanctified (7).

17. The Apostles Andronicus and Junia, of the Seventy (12).

18. Peter, Dionysius, Christina, Andrew, and Paul, the Martyrs (2).

19. Patricius the Martyr, Bishop of Prusa, and his Companions (2).

20. Thalelaius the Martyr (1).

21. The Great among Kings, Constantine, and Helen, the Equal of the Apostles.

1. Vespers

❡ Read three Psalms only, from Blessed is the man. *And on* O Lord, to thee have I cried, *chant the six Prosomia, three for the Pentecost Week in which the Feast falleth; and the following three for the two Saints, in the Fourth Tone.*

THOU hast granted our king thy precious cross as a dear weapon with which he reigned over the earth in justice, radiating true worship, and, by thy compassion, becoming worthy of the kingdom of heaven. Wherefore, with him, we glorify thy philanthropic dispensation, O Almighty Jesus, Saviour of our souls.

Thou hast granted thy pious servant, O Lover of mankind, the wisdom of Solomon, the meekness of David, and the Orthodoxy of the Apostles; since thou art King of kings and Lord of all lords. Wherefore, we glorify thy philanthropic dispensation, O Almighty Jesus, Saviour of our souls.

By thy might, O ever-memorable king, thou wast the first to subjugate the purple to Christ willingly; for thou hast made him known as God and King of all, a Benefactor of all, the Vanquisher of every leadership, and the Superior of every sovereign. Henceforth, O Christ-lover, Jesus Christ, the Lover of mankind, the Saviour of our souls, hath prepared for thee the kingdom.

Glory, in the Second Tone

O CONSTANTINE, the dear and magnified king, thou receivedst from God the richness of good gifts, whereby thou didst radiate in goodness; for having been illuminated through Baptism with the rays of the most Holy Spirit, at the hands of Sylvester the Priest, thou didst appear unvanquished among kings, offering the inhabited world to thy Creator as a dower, as well as the God-loving reigning city. Wherefore, since thou hast attained favour, thou dost still beseech Christ God to grant to all those who celebrate thy memorial the forgiveness of sins and the Great Mercy.

⁋And Now to Pentecost. And if the day falleth on the Fast of the Apostles, then sing Now for our Lady, in the Second Tone, O Virgin, verily the shadow, etc. (p. 146).

⁋Then after the Eisodos, and O resplendent Light, etc., the daily Prokeimenon, and the usual Petitions, sing the following Litiya, in the Second Tone.

TODAY hath the memorial of the pious Constantine shone for us like outpouring spice; for having longed for Christ he despised idols, erecting on earth a temple to the One who was crucified for our sakes. Wherefore, he attained the crown of hope in the heavens.

⁋And in the Aposticha, the following Prosomia, in the Second Tone.

THOU hast received from Christ, O Constantine, the first of Christian kings, the sceptre of kingship, because his saving likeness appeared to thee hidden in the earth. Wherefore, by it, O blessed one, thou didst subjugate all other nations under the feet of the faithful, adopting the life-giving Cross as an unconquerable weapon, and through it thou didst draw near to our God.

Stichos: I have exalted one chosen out of my people.

Verily, blessed is the womb and sanctified the belly which bore thee, O King Constantine, crowned by God, beloved of the world, joy of Christians, glory of believers, the richness of orphans and widows and their champion, the shelter of the humble and weak, the steadfastness of the sorrowful, and the deliverance of captives in truth.

Stichos: Therefore, God, thy God, hath anointed thee.

Verily, Helen, mother of the all-sweet branch, infatuated by longing for and love of Christ, hath come hastening to holy Zion, to the holy place where our

Saviour, by his own will, was crucified to save us. And, having lifted the Cross, she cried with joy, Glory to thee who hast granted me what I had hoped for.

Glory, in the Eighth Tone

LIKE a brilliant ray, like the evening star, thou wast drawn away from faithlessness to faith in the Godhead, and wast privileged to sanctify a people and a city. And, having beheld the sign of the Cross in heaven, thou didst hear thence that with it thou shouldest conquer thine enemies. Wherefore, thou didst receive the knowledge of the Spirit and wast anointed a priest and king, establishing with mercy the Church of God, O father of Orthodox kings, whose font doth well forth with healing. Intercede thou, O Constantine, the equal of the Apostles, for the sake of our souls.

¶*And Now for the Pentecost Week in which the Feast falleth. And if it falleth in the Fast of the Apostles, then sing Now to our Lady, in the Eighth Tone,* O Virgin without groom, *etc.* (*p. 193*).

Troparion for the Week: and for the Saint, in the Eighth Tone

CONSTANTINE, who is thine apostle among kings, O Lord, having beheld with his own eyes the sign of thy cross in heaven, and like Paul having accepted thy call not from man, entrusted the reigning city to thy hands, delivering it with safety for all time by the intercessions of the Theotokos, O thou who art alone the Lover of mankind.

¶*And if the day falleth in the Fast of the Apostles, then the Troparion for the Saint; and the Theotokion of the Oktochos, in the Same Tone.*

2. MATINS

¶*On* God the Lord hath appeared unto us, *the Troparion (three times); and the following Kathismata.*

First Kathisma, in the Third Tone

BY thine attributes thou hast become a new David, having received the prize from on high, the oil of anointment on thy head; for the Lord the Word, transcendent in essence, hath anointed thee with the Spirit. Wherefore, thou didst receive the royal sceptre, O wise and glorious one, seeking for us the Great Mercy.

Second Kathisma, in the First Tone

BY thine attribute of piety, O Constantine, the pride of pious kings, thou didst emulate Elijah in zeal, calling together the assembly of the God-mantled Fathers, through whom thou didst establish those luminaries of Orthodoxy, to believe in the equality of the Word with the Father in substance, and with the Spirit in rank.

Third Kathisma, in the Fourth Tone

THY memorial of good repute, O God-inspired Constantine, hath appeared unto us, illuminating the ends of the earth with the light of divine knowledge; for thou didst appear of true worship among kings, keeping the laws of the heavenly King. Wherefore, by thy beseechings deliver us from temptations.

❡ *Then the Anabathmoi. From my youth, etc. (p. 50), and the Prokeimenon.*

I HAVE exalted one chosen out of my people. I have found David my servant; and anointed him with the oil of my holiness. Therefore, God thy God, hath anointed thee, with the oil of gladness.

The Matin Gospel: from St. John

The Lord said: I am the door, etc. (p. 491).

❡ *Then Psalm 50 (plain reading); Glory, By the intercessions of the two crowned by God, etc; Now, By the intercessions of the Theotokos, etc.; then, on O merciful One, have mercy upon me, O God, etc., the following Idiomelon, in the Second Tone.*

Today hath the memorial of the pious Constantine, etc. (p. 537).

❡ *The Katabasias for the Pentecost Week in which falleth this Feast. And if it falleth on the Fast of the Apostles, then the Katabasias of our Lady,* Open my mouth, *etc. (p. 114).*

❡ *The Exaposteilation of the Feast (if there be any), and the following for the Saint.*

THE great Constantine with his mother received not the majesty of kingship from mankind, but from divine grace; for, having beheld the sign of the cross radiating from heaven, he vanquished therewith the obstinate, removing the error of idolatry, and confirming in the world the Orthodox Faith.

❡ *And in the Einos, the following Prosomia, in the Eighth Tone.*

REJOICE, O all-wise Constantine, the fount of Orthodoxy, which ever watereth the whole universe with its reviving waters! Rejoice, O stem from which did sprout the fruit that nourisheth the Church of Christ! Rejoice, O glorious one, the pride of all quarters of the earth! Rejoice O first of Christian kings! Hail, O gladness of believers.

The King of creation, O all-wise ones, having foreseen the goodness of thy heart's submission, caught thee supersensuously, being formerly in the control of bestiality, enlightening thy mind with the knowledge of true worship, and revealing thee to the world, as a light-radiating sun, sending forth the rays of thy divine works, O glorious one.

And thou, all-extolled and most wise Helen, like a choice land didst receive the commandments of God, sprouting the fruits of virtuous deeds, nourishing our hearts with the example of thy conduct. Wherefore, we celebrate the day of thy memorial in feasting and joy.

Thou hast anointed thy partakers, Constantine and Helen, O Christ, with the oil of rejoicing in a strange manner; for they hated error and desired thy heavenly kingdom and thy coveted beauty; and foreordained them by thy inspiration, O Word, to reign over the earth with true worship.

Glory, in the Eighth Tone

THE King of kings and their God, who adorneth the worthy with rich gifts, hath caught thee, O Constantine, with the sign of the cross, as he did the ever-memorable Paul, saying, By this thou shalt conquer. And having sought him with thy godly-minded mother and found him according to thy desire, thou didst persuade them. Wherefore, with her, beseech thou him who alone is the Lover of mankind, in behalf of the Orthodox kings and Christ-loving soldiers and all those who celebrate thy memorial in faith, to deliver them from every oppression.

❡*And Now for the Feast. And if it falleth in the Fast of the Apostles, then the following, in the same Tone.*

Receive the petitions of thy servants, O Lady, and deliver us from every tribulation and sorrow.

❡*Then the Great Doxology, and the Benediction.*

3. THE MASS

❡*In the Eisodos, the Troparia for the Feast (if any); for the Saint; and for the Patron of the church. Then the following Kontakion for the Saint, in the Third Tone.*

TODAY Constantine and his mother Helen reveal to us the Cross, the all-revered Tree, which is confusion to all the Jews and a weapon to believing kings against the obstinate ones; for verily, it hath appeared to us as a great sign, terrible in war.

❡*Then conclude with the Kontakion of the Feast (if any); otherwise with the usual Kontakion,* O undisputed intercessor of Christians, *etc. (p. 125).*

The Epistle: Their sound hath gone forth into all the earth. The heavens show forth the glory of God.

Section from the Acts of the Pure Apostles
(26:1, 12-20)

AT that time: Agrippa said to Paul: Thou art permitted to speak for thyself. Then Paul, stretching forth his hand, began to make his answer.

When I was going to Damascus, with authority and permission of the chief priests,

At midday, O king, I saw in the way a light from heaven above the brightness of the sun, shining round about me, and them that were in company with me.

And when we were all fallen down on the ground, I heard a voice speaking to me in the Hebrew tongue: Saul, Saul, why persecutest thou me? It is hard for thee to kick against the goad.

And I said: Who art thou, Lord? And the Lord answered: I am Jesus whom thou persecutest.

But rise up, and stand upon thy feet: for to this end have I appeared to thee, that I may make thee a minister, and a witness of those things which thou hast seen, and of those things wherein I will appear to thee.

Delivering thee from the people, and from the nations, unto which now I send thee:

To open their eyes, that they may be converted from darkness to light, and from the power of Satan to God, that they may receive forgiveness of sins, and a lot among the saints, by the faith that is in me.

Whereupon, O king Agrippa, I was not incredulous to the heavenly vision:

But to them first that are at Damascus, and at Jerusalem, and unto all the country of Judea, and to the Gentiles did I preach, that they should do penance, and turn to God, doing works worthy of penance.

The Gospel: from St. John

Said the Lord to those of the Jews who came unto him, etc. (p. 356).

Koinonikon: The just shall be in everlasting remembrance. Alleluia.

22. Basil the Martyr (1).

23. Michael the Confessor, Bishop of Synnada (9).

24. Simeon the Righteous, who was in the Wonderful Mountain (7).

25. Third Discovery of the Honoured Head of the Forerunner.

❡ *The Troparion, Kontakion, Epistle, and Gospel as on February twenty-fourth.*

26. The Apostle Carpus, one of the Seventy (12).

27. The Martyr among Priests, Alladius (5).

28. Eutyches the Martyr, Bishop of Melitene (5).

29. Theodosia the Martyr (4).

30. Isaacus the Righteous, Head of the Monastery of Dalmaton (7).

31. Hermius the Martyr (1).

X. JUNE

[Number of Days, 30; Hours of Day, 15; of Night, 9]

1. Justin the Philosopher and Martyr (1).

2. Nicephorus the Confessor, Archbishop of Constantinople (9).

3. Lucillianus the Martyr (1).

4. Metrophanes the Archbishop of Constantinople (9).

5. Dorotheus the Martyr, Bishop of Tyre (5).

6. New Hilarion, Head of the Monastery of the Dalmatians (7).

7. Theodore the Martyr, Bishop of Angora (5).

8. Translation of the Relics of Theodore the General (1).

9. Cyril the Archbishop of Alexandria (10).

10. Alexander and Antonia the Martyrs (2).

11. Bartholomew and Barnabas the Apostles (12).

12. Onuphrius and Peter who were in the Mount of Athos (11).

13. Acylina the Martyr (4).

14. Elisha the Prophet (13); Methodius the Confessor, Archbishop of Constantinople (9).

15. Amos the Prophet (13).

16. Tychon the Bishop of Amathus in Cyprus (9).

17. Isaurus and his Companions; and Manuel, Sabel, and Ismael the Martyrs (2).

18. Leontius the Martyr (1).

19. Jude the Apostle, Brother of the Lord, and Writer of the General Epistle (12).

20. Methodius the Martyr, Bishop of Patara (5).

21. Julian of Tarsus the Martyr (1).

22. Eusebius the Martyr, Bishop of Samosata (5).

23. Agrippina the Martyr (4).

24. The Nativity of the Forerunner John the Baptist.

Troparion, in the Fourth Tone

WE who eagerly honour thee are unable, O Prophet, Foreruner of the presence of Christ, to extol thee as it is meet to do; for by thy noble and solemn nativity the barrenness of thy mother was undone, and the tongue of thy father was loosened, and to the world was proclaimed the Incarnation of the Son of God.

Kontakion, in the Third Tone

SHE who formerly was barren giveth birth today to the Forerunner of Christ, who is the perfection of the prophecies; for in the Jordan he laid his hand on him whom the Prophet foretold, thus revealing him as a Prophet proclaiming the Word of God and going before him.

The Epistle: Ye brethren: Now our salvation, etc. p. 641.

The Gospel: from St. Luke (1:1-25; 57-68; 76; 80)

FORASMUCH as many have taken in hand to set forth in order a narration of the things that have been accomplished among us;

According as they have delivered them unto us, who from the beginning were eyewitnesses and ministers of the word:

It seemed good to me also, having diligently attained to all things from the beginning, to write to thee in order, most excellent Theophilus,

That thou mayest know the verity of those words in which thou hast been instructed.

There was in the days of Herod, the king of Judea, a certain priest named Zachary, of the course of Abia; and his wife was of the daughters of Aaron, and her name Elizabeth.

And they were both just before God, walking in all the commandments and justifications of the Lord without blame.

And they had no son, for that Elizabeth was barren, and they both were well advanced in years.

And it came to pass, when he executed the priestly function in the order of his course before God,

According to the custom of the priestly office, it was his lot to offer incense, going into the temple of the Lord.

And all the multitude of the people was praying without, at the hour of incense.

And there appeared to him an angel of the Lord, standing on the right side of the altar of incense.

And Zachary seeing him, was troubled, and fear fell upon him.

But the angel said to him: Fear not, Zachary, for thy prayer is heard; and thy wife Elizabeth shall bear thee a son, and thou shalt call his name John:

And thou shalt have joy and gladness, and many shall rejoice in his nativity.

For he shall be great before the Lord; and shall drink no wine nor strong drink: and he shall be filled with the Holy Ghost, even from his mother's womb.

And he shall convert many of the children of Israel to the Lord their God.

And he shall go before him in the spirit and power of Elias; that he may turn the hearts of the fathers unto the children, and the incredulous to the wisdom of the just, to prepare unto the Lord a perfect people.

And Zachary said to the angel: Whereby shall I know this? for I am an old man, and my wife is advanced in years.

And the angel answering, said to him: I am Gabriel, who stand before God; and am sent to speak to thee, and to bring thee these good tidings.

And behold, thou shalt be dumb, and shalt not be able to speak until the day wherein these things shall come to pass, because thou hast not believed my words, which shall be fulfilled in their time.

And the people were waiting for Zachary; and they wondered that he tarried so long in the temple.

And when he came out, he could not speak to them: and they understood that he had seen a vision in the temple. And he made signs to them, and remained dumb.

And it came to pass, after the days of his office were accomplished, he departed to his own house.

And after those days, Elizabeth his wife conceived, and hid herself five months, saying:

Thus hath the Lord dealt with me in the days wherein he hath had regard to take away my reproach among men.

And when Elizabeth's full time of being delivered was come, and she brought forth a son.

And her neighbours and kinsfolks heard that the Lord had showed his great mercy towards her, and they congratulated with her.

And it came to pass, that on the eighth day they came to circumcise the child, and they called him by his father's name Zachary.

And his mother answering, said: Not so; but he shall be called John.

And they said to her: There is none of thy kindred that is called by this name.

And they made signs to his father, how he would have him called.

And demanding a writing table, he wrote, saying: John is his name. And they all wondered.

And immediately his mouth was opened, and his tongue loosed, and he spoke, blessing God.

And fear came upon all their neighbours; and all these things were noised abroad over all the hill country of Judea.

And all they that had heard them laid them up in their heart, saying: What an one, think ye, shall this child be? For the hand of the Lord was with him.

And Zachary his father was filled with the Holy Spirit; and he prophesied, saying:

Blessed be the Lord God of Israel; because he hath visited and wrought the redemption of his people:

And thou, child, shalt be called the prophet of the Highest: for thou shalt go before the face of the Lord to prepare his ways:

And the child grew, and was strengthened in spirit; and was in the deserts until the day of his manifestation to Israel.

25. Febronia the Righteous Martyr (4).

26. David the Righteous who was in Thessalonica (8).

27. Samson the Righteous, Host of the Strangers (6).

28. Translation of the Relics of Saints Cyrus and John the Unmercenary.

❧ *Troparion,* O ye two silver-hating, *etc.* (*p. 327*).

29. THE GLORIOUS SAINTS AND HEADS OF THE APOSTLES, PETER AND PAUL.

Typicon

❧ *If the Feast falleth on a Sunday, then follow the order of the Feast of St. Demetrius on October twenty-sixth.*

1. VESPERS

❧ *After reciting three Psalms beginning with* Blessed is the man, *etc. sing on* O Lord, to thee have I cried, *the following three Prosomia, in the Second Tone:*

WITH what crowns of paeans shall we crown Peter and Paul, separated in the body, united in the spirit, the one foremost among the proclaimers of God, the other because he laboured more than the others? These two were crowned with the crowns of incorruptible glory, as is truly meet, by Christ our God who possesseth the Great Mercy. (*Repeat.*)

With what delightful songs of praise shall we extol Peter and Paul, those two wings of divine knowledge, flying in the four quarters of the earth and ascending unto heaven, those two hands of the gospel of grace, those two feet of the preaching of the truth, those two rivers of wisdom, those two horns of the Cross through which Christ, who possesseth the Great Mercy, did demolish the haughtiness of devils? (*Repeat.*)

With what spiritual panegyrics shall we laud Peter and Paul, the undulled edges of the drawn sword of the Spirit, slaughtering infidelity, the open adornment of Rome, and the bliss of the whole world, the God-inscribed tablets of the New Covenant, known in Zion, according to their call by Christ who possesseth the Great Mercy? (*Repeat.*)

Glory, in the Fourth Tone

CHRIST, by enquiring three times, Peter, lovest thou me? did make right the three denials. Wherefore, Simon cried unto the Lord who knoweth all secrets, saying, Thou knowest all things; thou knowest that I love thee. After this the Saviour said unto him; Feed my sheep, feed my ewes, feed my sheep which I have fashioned for salvation with my own blood. Beseech thou him, therefore, O Apostle blessed of God, to grant us the Great Mercy.

¶*Now,* David, the Prophet, *etc.* (*p. 161*)*; and* O resplendent Light *etc. And after the daily Prokeimenon and the usual Petitions, sing the following Litiya, in the Fifth Tone.*

THE wisdom of God and the Word of the Father coëternal with him hath verily foretold you, O all-extolled Apostles, in his Gospel, that ye are the two vines of good fertility who bore in your branches the ripe, delightful cluster whereof as we believers eat, we feel the pleasure-giving taste. Wherefore, O Peter, the rock of faith, and Paul, the pride of the universe, strengthen the flock which became yours through your teachings.

¶*And in the Aposticha, the following Idiomelon, in the First Tone.*

O GLORIOUS Apostle Paul, who can describe thy bondage and tribulations in the cities; or expatiate on the struggles and hardships which thou didst encounter in the preaching of Christ, that thou mightest win all and present the Church to Christ? Wherefore, O Apostle Paul, teacher of the churches, plead thou that she may preserve thy good confession unto her last breath.

Stichos: Their sound hath gone forth into all the earth.

O glorious Apostle, who can describe thy bondage and sorrows in the cities; the tribulations, hardships, watchings, and painful misfortunes, through hunger and thirst, through cold, nakedness, barrel, beatings with rods, stoning, crossing of wildernesses, and drowning in the bottom of the sea? Thou hast become a spectacle to angels and men, bearing all with the help of Christ who established thee. Wherefore, we, who celebrate thy memorial in faith, beseech thee to intercede for the salvation of our souls.

Stichos: The heavens show forth the glory of God.

Let us extol Peter and Paul, the two great luminaries of the Church; for they did shine forth in the firmament of faith, transcending the sun in brilliancy; by the rays of whose preaching they led forth the Gentiles from ignorance into divine knowledge. Wherefore, one of them was nailed upon the Cross, making his way unto heaven where he received the keys of the kingdom from Christ himself; and the other was beheaded with the sword, and was carried to the Saviour, being blessed as is meet; both declaring that Israel laid hand against the Lord unjustly. By their petitions, therefore, O Christ our God, demolish our enemies and establish the Orthodox Faith; for thou art the Lover of mankind.

Glory, in the Sixth Tone

TODAY hath shone forth to the ends of the earth a delightful Feast by the all-solemn memorial, the memorial of the all-wise Apostles, the heads of the Apostles, Peter and Paul. Wherefore, let Rome receive the glad tidings rejoicing, and let us, brethren, feast this all-solemn day, crying unto them, Rejoice, O Peter the Apostle and the especial friend of the Teacher Christ our God. Rejoice, O truly beloved Paul, preacher of the Faith and teacher of the universe. And because of your privilege, O sanctified pair, beseech Christ God to save our souls.

Now, to our Lady

THOU art the true vine, O Theotokos, bearing the Fruit of life. Thee do we implore. Wherefore, O Lady, intercede thou, together with the Apostles and saints, for the salvation of our souls.

Troparion, in the Fourth Tone

O FOREMOST in the ranks of Apostles, and teachers of the world, intercede with the Master of all to grant safety to the world and to our souls the Great Mercy. (*Repeat.*)

¶*And Now; The Theotokion for the Resurrection, in the Fourth Tone.*

3. MATINS

¶*On* God the Lord hath appeared unto us, *the Troparion as at Vespers; then the following Kathismata, in the Eighth Tone.*

HAVING abandoned the fishing grounds thou didst receive from the Father himself the revelation of the Word's Incarnation, and as one who is privileged thou didst cry to all, saying unto thy Creator, I have known thee as Son of God, consubstantial with him. Wherefore, thou wast truly revealed as the rock of faith, as is meet, and a trustee of the keys of grace. Intercede, therefore, O Apostle Peter with Christ God to grant forgiveness of iniquities to those who eagerly celebrate thy memorial.

From heaven, from Christ God, thou didst receive the call, thus appearing as the preacher of light, illuminating all with the teachings of grace; for having impugned the worship of the written law, thou didst cause to rise the knowledge of the Spirit for believers. Therefore, worthily thou didst ascend to the third heaven and attained paradise. Wherefore, O Apostle Paul, intercede with Christ God to grant forgiveness of iniquities to those who eagerly celebrate thy holy memorial.

Let us extol those two great luminaries of exceeding radiance, the all-wise Peter and Paul, who have been manifested as heads of the Disciples, radiating with the fire of the divine Spirit, and burning up the darkness of error, thus attaining worthily their abode in the kingdom on high, being equal in grace and rank. Wherefore, we cry unto them, saying, O Apostles of Christ God, seek forgiveness of iniquities for those who eagerly celebrate your holy memorial.

¶ *Then the Anabathmoi, From my youth, etc. (p. 50), and the following Prokeimenon.*

Their sound hath gone forth into all the earth. The heavens show forth the glory of God.

¶ *Then the Eleventh Gospel of the Eothina (p. 216), and Psalm 50 (plain reading). Then Glory, By the intercessions of the Apostles, etc; and Now, By the intercessions of the Theotokos, etc; and on O merciful One, have mercy upon me, O God, etc., sing the following, in the Second Tone.*

O PETER, head of the honoured Apostles and rock of the Faith, and O wonderful Paul, orator and star of the holy churches, as ye stand before the divine throne, intercede with Christ for our sake.

❡ *The Katabasias,* Open thou my mouth, *etc; and sing,* O thou who art more honourable, *etc.*

Exaposteilarions

COME, let us all extol the Apostles Peter and Paul, those divine heads of the Apostles, luminaries of the universe and preachers of the Faith, those two trumpets declaring things divine and revealing doctrines, those two pillars of the Church, and refuters of error.

The great and amazing mystery of thy birth-giving, O virgin Theotokos, favoured of God, was preached by the Prophets, taught by the Apostles, and confessed by Martyrs. Yea, it is praised by the angels and worshipped by men.

❡ *And in the Einos, the following Prosomia, in the Fourth Tone.*

WHEN the Saviour asked the rank of the twelve Disciples, Who do men say that I am? Then Peter, the forechosen of the Disciples and recipient of grace from heaven, proclaimed thee clearly, speaking of thy Godhead, and saying, Thou art Christ the Son of the living God. Wherefore, it is meet to beatify him, since he received the revelation from above and the gift to bind and loosen sins.

O thou who wast called from above and not from man, when the earthly darkness covered the eyes of thy body, revealing the dismay of infidelity, then the heavenly light gleamed forth in thy mind's eye, revealing the splendour of true worship. Wherefore, thou didst know Christ our God, who bringeth out light from darkness. Plead thou with him to lighten and save our souls.

Worthily thou wast called the rock, on which the Lord established the unshakeable Faith of the Church, making thee the head shepherd of the sheep endowed with speech. And then, since thou art good, he appointed thee keeper of the keys of the heavenly gates, to open unto those who hasten thither with faith. Wherefore, thou wast counted worthy to be crucified as thy Master was crucified. Plead thou with him to lighten and save our souls.

O preacher of Christ and proud bearer of his cross, thou didst sincerely prefer to all things the greatly desired divine love, since it linketh its lovers to the Beloved. Then thou wast called a captive of Christ, choosing the disasters of temptations, considering them sweeter than all bliss. Thus thou wast worthy of the precious dissolution, attaining thy Master. Wherefore, plead thou with him to lighten and save our souls.

Glory, in the Sixth Tone

VERILY, the all-solemn Feast of the two Apostles hath arrived, bringing us salvation. Wherefore, let us mystically exult, crying unto them, Rejoice, O ye who have become luminaries to those in darkness, two rays of the Sun! Rejoice, O Peter and Paul, adamant pillars of the divine doctrines, ye friends of Christ and two honoured vessels! Be ye present among us in an invisible manner, and grant immaterial gifts to those who extol your feast with paeans.

¶ *And Now,* Thou art the true vine. O Theotokos *etc.* (*p. 550*); *then the Great Doxology, and the Troparion of the Feast.*

3. THE MASS

¶ *The Troparion for the two Saints, and the Patron Saint of the church; and the following Kontakion, in the Second Tone.*

VERILY, O Lord, thou hast translated to bliss and the enjoyment of thy blessings, those two trustworthy preachers, theologians, and heads of thy Disciples; for thou didst accept their struggles and death as better than any sacrifice, O thou who alone dost know the secrets of the hearts.

The Epistle: Their sound hath gone forth into all the earth. The heavens show forth the glory of God.

Section from the Second Epistle of St. Paul to the Corinthians (11:21 to end; 12:6-9)

YE brethren: Whatever any man dare (I speak foolishly), I dare also.

They are Hebrews: so am I. They are Israelites: so am I. They are the seed of Abraham: so am I.

They are the ministers of Christ (I speak as one less wise): I am more; in many more labours, in prisons more frequently, in stripes above measure, in deaths often.

Of the Jews five times did I receive forty stripes, save one.

Thrice was I beaten with rods, once I was stoned, thrice I suffered shipwreck, a night and a day I was in the depth of the sea.

In journeying often, in perils of waters, in perils of robbers, in perils from my own nation, in perils from the Gentiles, in perils in the city, in perils in the wilderness, in perils in the sea, in perils from false brethren.

In labour and painfulness, in much watchings, in hunger and thirst, in fastings often, in cold and nakedness.

Besides those things which are without: my daily instance, the solicitude for all the churches.

Who is weak, and I am not weak? Who is scandalized, and I am not on fire?

If I must needs glory, I will glory of the things that concern my infirmity.

The God and Father of our Lord Jesus Christ, who is blessed for ever, knoweth that I lie not.

At Damascus, the governor of the nation under Aretas the king, guarded the city of the Damascenes, to apprehend me.

And through a window in a basket was I let down by the wall, and so escaped his hands.

For though I should have a mind to glory, I shall not be foolish; for I will say the truth. But I forbear, lest any man should think of me above that which he seeth in me, or any thing he heareth from me.

And lest the greatness of the revelations should exalt me, there was given me a sting of my flesh, an angel of Satan, to buffet me.

For which thing thrice I besought the Lord, that it might depart from me.

And he said to me: My grace is sufficient for thee: for power is made perfect in infirmity. Gladly, therefore, will I glory in my infirmities, that the power of Christ may dwell in me.

The Gospel: from St. Matthew (16:13-19)

A T that time: When Jesus came into the quarters of Cæsarea Philippi: and he asked his disciples, saying: Whom do men say that the Son of man is?

But they said: Some John the Baptist, and other some Elias, and others Jeremias, or one of the prophets.

Jesus saith to them: But whom do you say that I am?

Simon Peter answered and said: Thou art Christ, the Son of the living God.

And Jesus answering, said to him: Blessed art thou, Simon Bar-Jona: because flesh and blood hath not revealed it to thee, but my Father who is in heaven.

And I say to thee: That thou art Peter; and upon this rock I will build my church, and the gates of hell shall not prevail against it.

And I will give to thee the keys of the kingdom of heaven. And whatsoever thou shalt bind upon earth, it shall be bound also in heaven: and whatsoever thou shalt loose on earth, it shall be loosed also in heaven.

Koinonikon: Their sound hath gone forth into all the earth. Alleluia.

30. A Plenary Feast for the Twelve Apostles (12).

Kontakion, in the Second Tone

CHRIST the Rock doth openly glorify the rock of faith, forechosen from the Disciples, with Paul and the whole rank of the Twelve, and as we celebrate today their memorial, we glorify him who glorified them.

The Epistle: First Corinthians (4:9-16)
The Gospel: from St. Matthew (9:36-38; 10:1-8)

AND seeing the multitude, he had compassion on them; because they were distressed, and lying like sheep that have no shepherd.

Then he saith to his disciples, The harvest indeed is great, but the labourers are few.

Pray ye, therefore, the Lord of the harvest, that he send forth labourers into his harvest.

And having called his twelve disciples together, he gave them power over unclean spirits, to cast them out, and to heal all manner of diseases, and all manner of infirmities.

And the names of the twelve apostles are these: The first, Simon who is called Peter, and Andrew his brother,

James the son of Zebedee, and John his brother, Philip and Bartholomew, Thomas and Matthew the publican, and James the son of Alpheus, and Thaddeus,

Simon the Cananean, and Judas Iscariot, who also betrayed him.

These twelve Jesus sent: commanding them, saying: Go ye not into the way of the Gentiles, and into the city of the Samaritans enter ye not.

But go ye rather to the lost sheep of the house of Israel.

And going, preach, saying: The kingdom of heaven is at hand.

Heal the sick, raise the dead, cleanse the lepers, cast out devils: freely have you received, freely give.

Koinonikon: Their sound hath gone forth into all the earth.

XI. JULY

[Number of Days, 31; Hours of Day, 14; of Night, 10]

1. The Unmercenary and Wonder-Working Saints, Cosmas and Damian.
Troparion: O ye two silver-hating, etc. (p. 327).
2. Placing of the Robe of the Theotokos in Blachornas.

Troparion, in the Eighth Tone

THOU hast bestowed upon thy city, O ever-virgin Theotokos and shelter of mankind, the robe and the belt of thy pure body, as a secure mantle, which by thy seedless birth-giving have remained without corruption; for by thee are nature and time regenerated. Wherefore, we implore thee to grant thy city safety, and our souls the Great Mercy.

3. Hyacinthus the Martyr (1); Anatolius the Archbishop of Constantinople (9).
4. Andrew the Jerusalemite, Bishop of Crete, and Composer of the Great Canon (9).
5. Athanasius the Righteous who was in Athos (7); Lampadus the Wonder-Worker (6).
6. Sisoes the Great Righteous (7).
7. Thomas the Righteous who was in Maleum (6); Cyriace the Great Martyr (4).
8. Procopius the Great Martyr (1).
9. Pancratius the Martyr, Bishop of Tauromenias (5).
10. The Forty-five who were Martyred in Nicopolis of Armenia (2).
11. Euphemia the Great Martyr (4).
12. Proclus and Hilarius the Martyrs (2).
13. A Plenary Memorial for Gabriel the Archangel (*See November 8th*); Stephen the Righteous of the Monastery of Sabas (10).

SUNDAY OF THE HOLY FATHERS
ASSEMBLED IN THE FIRST SIX ECUMENICAL COUNCILS

From July 13th-19th

1. VESPERS

¶ *On* O Lord, to thee have I cried, *sing six for the Resurrection, in the Tone in use; and four for the Fathers, in the Sixth Tone.*

O PHILANTHROPIC Word, boundless and indescribable, having become incarnate for our sake, the solemn Assembly of the wise Fathers proclaimed thee, that thou art perfect God and perfect Man, complete, dual of Nature and acts, and dual also of Will, and that thou thyself art one in Person. Wherefore, having known thee as one God with the Father and the Spirit we worship thee in faith, blessing them.

O glorified ones, verily ye did refute Pyrrhus Sergius, Honorius, Ephtechis, Dioscorus, with Nestor the ugly, saving the flock of Christ from the fall of either side, proclaiming Christ aloud as dual in Nature and one in Person, manifest in acts alone. Him, therefore, we worhsip with the Father and the Spirit, perfect God and perfect Man, and honour you with glory.

Those God-mantled blessed ones, assembled together, wisely declared that the divine act, the act of him who humbled himself in our flesh, and his divine Will are uncreate, ascribing createdness to the human act and human will to escape the confusion of his Nature and the division of his Person. Wherefore, we believers honour them in annual feasts, glorifying in unison Christ who glorified them.

Those God-mantled Fathers have proclaimed today in concert that the uncreated Trinity is one God and one Lord, explaining to all the agreement of the simplicity of the one Nature through participation of the will, and the simplicity of the deed, and defining all as without beginning and without end. Wherefore, we glorify them, as being like to the Apostles and teaching their Gospel to all.

Glory: Let us today extol those mystical trumpets of the Spirit, etc. (p. 313).

❡ *Now, in the Tone in use.*

❡ *The Aposticha for the Resurrection; and Glory for the Fathers, in the Third Tone.*

YE have become, O holy Fathers, conscientious keepers of the apostolic traditions; for, having believed in the consubstantiality of the holy Trinity with Orthodox opinion, ye did refute the blasphemy of Arius in council. Then, after rebuking Macedonies the combatter against the Spirit, ye destroyed Nestor, Ephtechis, Dioscorus, Sabbalius, Severus, the headless one. Wherefore, we implore you to seek for us deliverance from their error, and that our life be kept blameless in faith from every pollution.

❡ *Now to our Lady, in the Tone in use; the Troparion for Resurrection and the Fathers (p. 314).*

2. MATINS

❡ *On God the Lord hath appeared unto us, the Troparia as at Vespers; and the rest of the Order for Sundays. The Katabasias Open my mouth, etc. and O thou who are more honourable, etc. The Exaposteilarion for the Resurrection; and the following two for the Fathers and for our Lady.*

BY celebrating today the memorial of the divine Fathers, O all-compassionate Lord, we implore thee, through their petitions to deliver thy people from the harm from all heretics, making us all worthy to glorify the Father, the Word, and the all-holy Spirit.

O all-blameless one, thou didst give birth in an ineffable manner to God in two Natures, two Wills and one Person, who humbled himself by his own will unto crucifixion, granting us the richness of the Godhead by his Resurrection from the dead.

❡ *Then the Einos as on p. 314. The Epistle and the Gospel, as on p. 247.*

Koinonikon: Praise ye the Lord from the heavens. Alleluia.

14. Aquila the Apostle (12) ; Joseph, the Bishop of Thessalonica (9).

15. Cerycus, and Julietta the Martyr (2).

16. The Martyr among Priests, Athenogenes (5).

17. Marina the Great Martyr (4).

18. Aemilianus the Martyr (1).

19. Macrina the Sister of Basil the Great (8) ; Dius the Righteous (7).

20. THE GLORIOUS PROPHET ELIJAH THE TISHBITE.

Typicon

¶*If this Feast falleth on a Sunday, then observe the Order of the Feast of St. Demetrius on October 26th.*

1. VESPERS

¶*After reciting three Psalms beginning with* Blessed is the man, *etc. sing on* O Lord, to thee have I cried, *the following three Prosomia, in the First Tone.*

O ALL-COMPASSIONATE Word, who didst translate Elijah the Tishbite from the earth in a fiery chariot; by his beseeching save us, who glorify thee in faith and who celebrate his divine and noble memorial in gladness. (*Repeat.*)

Not in the earthquakes, but in the still, small voice, O Elijah blessed of God, didst thou behold the presence of God, illuminating thee of old. Thus didst thou ascend to heaven, mounting a chariot of four horses in a strange manner, becoming wonderful, O God-inspired One. (*Repeat.*)

Fired by divine zeal, O all-wise Elijah, thou didst slaughter the priests of confusion with the edge of the sword; and by thy tongue thou didst bind the heaven that it might not rain on earth. And having bestowed thy mantle on Elisha, thou didst fill him with double divine grace. (*Repeat.*)

Glory, in the Sixth Tone (By Eukandioa)

COME, ye assembly of the Orthodox, let us assemble together in the all-solemn Temple, the Temple of those two God-inspired Prophets. Let us sing a paean of harmonious tones, glorifying Christ our God who honoured them. Let us raise our voices in rejoicing and joy, saying, Rejoice, O earthly angel and heavenly man, Elijah of great name! Rejoice, O thou who didst receive double grace from God, O all-revered Elisha! Rejoice, O ye two fervid supports, ye two champions and two physicians of the souls and bodies of the Christ-loving people. Deliver from every obstacle and from divers tribulations and oppressions those who celebrate in faith thine all-adored feast.

¶ *And Now for our Lady,* Who shall not beatify thee, (*p. 177*).

¶ *Then after the Eisodos, the daily Prokeimenon, and usual Petitions, sing the following Litiya, in the Fourth Tone.*

THOU didst mount a fiery chariot, and wast translated to a brilliant city, O Elijah the Tishbite, having repulsed the prophets of confusion. Wherefore, as thou didst bind the heaven by thy word, loosen our iniquities by thine intercessions before the Lord, to save our souls.

¶ *And in the Aposticha the following Prosomia, in the Fourth Tone.*

HE who was sanctified before he was conceived, that angelic of body and fiery of intelligence, that heavenly man and forerunner of the Second Coming of Christ, the glorious Elijah, pillar of the Prophets and their cornerstone, hath called together in spirit the feast-lovers to celebrate his divine Feast. Wherefore, by his intercessions, O Christ our God, preserve thy people unharmed from all the sundry harms of the deceitful.

Stichos: Touch ye not my anointed and do no evil to my prophets.

When Elijah of celestial mind saw that all the people of Israel had departed from the Lord God and were led to the worship of idols, he was stirred with zeal, holding back the clouds, burning the earth and closing the heavens with a single word, saying, Not a drop shall be on the earth except by my mouth. This is he who is feasted now, who bestoweth on those who celebrate his feast in faith, ineffable grace.

Stichos: Thou art a priest for ever according to the order of Melchisedech.

Thou didst cleave the courses of Jordan, O Elijah the observer of ineffable mysteries. Thou didst turn the deceit of idols into ashes, by the lightning of thy divine sayings. Thou didst rebuke the king when he disobeyed the law, killed the priests of iniquity, and burned their sacrifice with prayer. Wherefore, now, the fires of thine intercessions extinguished the flames of passions and live coals of sorrows of thy people.

Glory, in the Sixth Tone

O CHRIST-PROCLAIMING Prophet, thou art inseparable from the throne of greatness, and everpresent at the side of every one in sickness. Wherefore, O thou minister of the Highest, who blessest the universe and art glorified in every quarter, seek forgiveness for our souls.

❡*And Now to our Lady,* Thou art the true vine, O Theotokos, *etc.* (*p. 550*).

Troparion, in the Fourth Tone

O ANGELIC of body, pillar of the Prophets and their corner-stone, the forerunner of the Second Coming of Christ, the venerable and glorious Elijah, thou didst send grace from on high to Elisha to dispel sicknesses and to purify lepers. Wherefore, he ever overfloweth with healing to those who honour him.

❡*Then Glory and Now to our Lady; and the Benediction.*

2. MATINS

❡ *On* God the Lord hath appeared unto us, *the Troparia as at Vespers. Then the following Kathismata.*

First Kathisma, in the First Tone

O BLESSED one who beholdeth God, we proclaim thee in unison as an all-radiant luminary, ascending in a fiery chariot, an angel in the body, burning with divine zeal, uprooting infidelity and rebuking those who turn away from the law, the head of the Prophets. Wherefore, visit us with thy watchings.

Second Kathisma, in the Same Tone

BY sublimity of virtue thou wast drawn near to God, having passed on earth a heavenly life. And when thou didst attain the life of grace, O blessed one, thou didst raise a dead young man by thy breath. Verily, thou ceasest not until now to be incorruptible, above death, O God-inspired Elijah.

Third Kathisma, in the Eighth Tone

IN paeans of praise let all us believers extol Elijah the Tishbite, that fount of miracles and comeliness of the Prophets; for he still remaineth immortal in his body, confirming, though dead, the Resurrection of the dead. Whrefore, having attained privilege with God, he bestoweth healing, and granteth the requests of those who cry unto him in faith, saying, Intercede, O Prophet, with Christ, to grant forgiveness of sins to those who eagerly celebrate thy holy memorial.

❡ *Then the Anabathmoi,* From my youth, *etc. (p. 50); and the following Prokeimenon.*

Thou art a priest for ever according to the order of Melchisedech. Touch ye not mine anointed; and do no evil to my prophets.

The Matin Gospel: from St. Matthew

At that time, when Jesus came, etc. (p. 555).

❡*And Psalm 50 (plain reading); Glory,* By the intercessions of thy Prophet, *etc; Now,* By the intercessions of the Theotokos, *etc; then on* O merciful One, have mercy upon me, O God, *etc., the following Idiomelon, in the Sixth Tone.*

O Christ-proclaiming Prophet, etc. (p. 562).
Katabasias: Open my mouth, etc.

Exaposteilarion

THE light of the four-horsed fiery chariot, O Elijah, sent thee ascending into heaven without burning thee at all, O thou who by thine earthly tongue didst draw down fire, drying up the rains.

O virgin Theotokos, who gave birth to the Light, by thine intercessions implore thy Son to have compassion on me who depend on thy venerable help, and to save me from eternal darkness.

❡*And in the Einos, sing the following four Prosomia, in the Eighth Tone.*

WHEN thou wast united to God by virtue and good conduct, O wonderful Prophet, thou wast given authority by him, thus organizing creation in accordance with thine opinion, closing the doors of rain by thy will and bringing down fire from above to burn the infidels. Wherefore, implore thou salvation for our souls. (*Repeat.*)

When thou waxed in the zeal of the Lord, thou didst fiercely rebuke the law-transgressing kings, slaughtered with enthusiasm the priests of confusion, and kindled a miraculous fire in the waters. Thou didst secure fire without tilling, and didst cleave with thy mantle the waters of the Jordan. Wherefore, implore thou the salvation of our souls.

Manifesting on earth a truly heavenly life, O Prophet, thou wast enriched in thyself by the spiritual life. By thy breath thou didst raise a dead person, remaining more sublime than death, and ascending in a fiery chariot on high. Wherefore, implore thou the salvation of our souls.

Glory, in the Eighth Tone

LET us believers honour with laudation the heads of the Prophets, those two all-radiant luminaries of the universe, Elijah and Elisha. Let us lift our voices unto Christ with rejoicing, saying, By the intercessions of thy two Prophets, O compassinate Lord, grant thy people forgiveness of sins and the Great Mercy.

Now, in the Same Tone

Receive the petitions of thy servants, O Lady, and deliver us from every tribulation and sorrow.

❧ *Then the Great Doxology and the Benediction.*

3. THE MASS

❧ *In the Eisodos, the Troparia for the Prophet and for the Patron Saint of the church; and the following Kontakion, in the Second Tone.*

O PROPHET, who foresaw the great acts of God, Elijah of great name, who with a word didst stop the flow of the rain, intercede thou for our sake with him who alone is the Lover of mankind.

❧ *Then close with the usual Kontakion,* O undisputed intercessor of Christians, *etc.* (*p. 125*).

The Epistle: Thou art a priest for ever according to the order of Melchisedech. Said the Lord to my Lord, Sit thou at my right hand.

Section from the Catholic Epistle of St. James (5:10 to end)

YE brethren: Take for an example of suffering evil, of labour and patience, the prophets, who spoke in the name of the Lord.

Behold, we account them blessed who have endured. You have heard of the patience of Job, and you have seen the end of the Lord, that the Lord is merciful and compassionate.

But above all things, my brethren, swear not, neither by heaven, nor by the earth, nor by any other oath. But let your speech be, yea, yea: no, no: that you fall not under judgment.

Is any of you sad? Let him pray. Is he cheerful in mind? Let him sing Psalms.

Is any man sick among you? Let him bring in the priests of the church, and let them pray over him, anointing him with oil in the name of the Lord.

And the prayer of faith shall save the sick man: and the Lord shall raise him up: and if he be in sins, they shall be forgiven him.

Confess therefore your sins one to another: and pray one for another, that you may be saved. For the continual prayer of a just man availeth much.

Elias was a man passible like unto us: and with prayer he prayed that it might not rain upon the earth, and it rained not for three years and six months.

And he prayed again: and the heaven gave rain, and the earth brought forth her fruit.

My brethren, if any of you shall err from the truth, and one convert him:

He must know that he who causeth a sinner to be converted from the error of his way, shall save his soul from death, and shall cover a multitude of sins.

The Gospel: from St. Luke (4:22-26; 28-30)

A T that time: People wondered at the words of grace that proceeded from his mouth, and they said: Is not this the son of Joseph?

And he said to them: Doubtless you will say to me this similitude: Physician, heal thyself: as great things as we have heard done in Capharnaum, do also here in thine own country.

And he said: Amen I say to you, that no prophet is accepted in his own country.

In truth I say to you, there were many widows in the days of Elias in Israel, when heaven was shut up three years and six months, when there was a great famine throughout all the earth.

And to none of them was Elias sent, but to Sarepta of Sidon, to a widow woman.

And all they in the synagogue, hearing these things, were filled with anger.

And they rose up and thrust him out of the city; and they brought him to the brow of the hill, whereon their city was built, that they might cast him down headlong.

But he passing through the midst of them, went his way.

Koinonikon: Rejoice, O just ones in the Lord. Alleluia.

21. Simeon who Feigned Idiocy for Christ's Sake; and John his Companion (11).

22. Mary Magdalene, the Ointment-Bearer and Equal of the Apostles.

Troparion, in the First Tone

THOU didst follow Christ who was born of the Virgin for our sakes, O Mary Magdalene, keeping his precepts and statutes. Wherefore, as we celebrate today thy holy memorial, we receive, through thy prayers, forgiveness of sins.

23. The Martyr among Priests, Phocas (5); Ezekiel the Prophet (13).

24. Christina the Great Martyr (4).

25. The Falling Asleep of Anne the Mother of Theotokos.

Troparion, in the Fourth Tone

O GODLY-minded Anne, thou didst give birth to the Theotokos, the spotless Mother of Life. Wherefore, thou hast been translated now in gladness to thy heavenly end, which is the abode of all who rejoice, seeking forgiveness of sins for those who eagerly honour thee, O ever-blessed one.

26. Prisca the Righteous Martyr (8); the Martyr among Priests, Hermolaus (5).

27. Pantaleon the Great Martyr and Healer.

Troparion, in the Third Tone

O STRUGGLE-BEARING and healing physician Pantaleon, intercede with the merciful God to bestow on our souls the forgiveness of sins.

Kontakion, in the Fifth Tone

SINCE thou art like unto the merciful One, and a Martyr of Christ, thou hast received from him the grace of healing. Wherefore, by thy petitions, heal the diseases of our souls, and put away the doubts of the adversary from those who cry ceaselessly, Save us, O Lord.

The Epistle and the Gospel of St. Demetrius (pp. 325-326)

28. Prochorus, Nicanor, Timon and Parmenas the Apostles (12).

29. Callinicus the Martyr (1); Theodote the Martyr (4).

30. Silas, Silvanus, Crescens, and Andronicus of the Seventy (12).

31. Eudocimus the Righteous (8).

XII. AUGUST

[Its Days, 31; Hours of Day, 13; of Night, 11]

1. Procession of the Cross; The seven Maccabean Youths, their Mother Salome, and their Teacher Eleazar (3).

Troparion: O Lord, save thy people, etc. (p. 298).

¶ *And this day beginneth the Fast of the Falling-asleep of the Virgin.*

2. The Translation of the Bones of Stephen, first among Martyrs and Archdeacon.

Troparion: O first of strivers, etc. (p. 415).

❡*Note: From this day to the fourteenth of the same month, every day after Vespers, the service of the Paracletice is chanted as found on p. 45*

3. The Martyrs Isaacius, Dalmatius, and Faustus (11).

4. The Seven youths of Ephesus (2).

5. The Martyr Eusigenius (1); and the Preparation for the Feast of the Transfiguration.

Troparion for the Preparation, in the Fourth Tone

LET us, O believers, come forth and welcome the Transfiguration of Christ, joyfully celebrating the Preparation of the Feast and declaring aloud, Verily, the day of divine rejoicing hath arrived and shed forth the radiance of his Godhead.

Kontakion, in the Same Tone

TODAY doth the whole of human nature glitter in the divine Transfiguration, in a divine manner, shouting with joy, Christ is transfigured, Saviour of all.

6. THE TRANSFIGURATION OF OUR LORD GOD AND SAVIOUR JESUS CHRIST.

Typicon

❡*If this falleth on a Sunday, no part of the Resurrection is chanted, but the whole service belongeth to this Feast.*

1. VESPERS

❡*Do not recite the Psalm,* Blessed is the man, *etc; but immediately after the Sunset Psalm and the Petitions for Peace, the following six Idiomelons, in the Fourth Tone, are chanted on* O Lord, to thee have I cried.

By Cozma the Anchorite

WHEN thou wast transfigured before thy Crucifixion, O Lord, the mount resembled heaven, and a cloud spread out like a canopy, and the Father bore witness unto thee. And there were present Peter with James and John, since they were to be with thee at thy Betrayal; so that seeing thy wonders they might not be dismayed at thy sufferings. Make us, therefore, to worship the same in peace for thy great mercy. (*Repeat.*)

Before thy Crucifixon, O Lord, thou didst take thy Disciples to a high mountain and wast transfigured before them, illumining them with rays of might; being desirous to manifest to them the light of the Resurrection, on the one side through thy love of mankind, and on the other through thy might. Wherefore, make us worthy thereof, O God, in peace; for thou art good and the Lover of mankind. (*Repeat.*)

When thou wast transfigured, O Saviour, on a high mountain, in the presence of thy chief Disciples, thou didst shine forth in glory, symbolizing that they who are recognized for the sublimity of virtue, shall also be made worthy of divine glory. As for Moses and Elijah, when they conversed with Christ they made manifest that he was the Lord of the quick and the dead, and that he was the God who spake of old in the law and the Prophets, the same to whom the voice of the Father did bear witness from a radiant cloud, saying, Him do ye hear; for he it is who by the Cross hath taken captive hades and hath bestowed life eternal to the dead.

Yea, the mountain which was thick with smoke of old hath become now honourable and holy; for that thy feet did rest on it, O Lord, for the mystery hidden before the ages, thy Transfiguration before Peter, James, and John hath made manifest. And they, not being able to bear the radiance of thy face and the splendour of thy raiment, did fall down on their faces kneeling, and being overcome with astonishment, wondered at the sight of Moses and Elijah conferring with

thee on things that were to befall thee, while a voice
from the Father bore witness, saying, This is my beloved Son in whom I am well pleased, hear him who
giveth to the world the Great Mercy.

Glory and Now, in the Sixth Tone (By Anatolius)

WHEN thou didst prefigure thy Resurrection, O
Christ God, thou didst take thy three Disciples,
Peter, James, and John, and with them didst ascend
Mount Tabor. And at thy Transfiguraton, O Saviour,
Mount Tabor was covered with light. As for thy Disci-
ples, they threw themselves on the ground, unable to
bear the sight of thy figure that may not be looked upon,
O Word. And the angels did minister in fear and awe,
while the heavens were affrighted and the earth trem-
bled when they beheld on earth the Lord of Glory.

¶ *Then the Eisodos, and* O resplendent Light, *etc.; the daily Pro-
keimenons; and the following Readings.*

First Reading: from Exodus (24:12 to end)

AND the Lord said unto Moses: Come up to me into
the mount, and be there: and I will give thee tables
of stone, and a law, and the commandments which I
have written; that thou mayest teach them.

And Moses rose up, and his minister Joshua; and
Moses went up into the mount of God.

And he said unto the elders, Tarry ye here for us,
until we come again unto you: and, behold, Aaron and
Hur are with you: if any man have any matters to do,
let him come unto them.

And Moses went up into the mount, and a cloud covered the mount.

And the glory of the Lord abode upon mount Sinai,
and the cloud covered it six days: and the seventh day
he called unto Moses out of the midst of the cloud.

And the sight of the glory of the Lord was like devouring fire on the top of the mount in the eyes of the
children of Israel.

And Moses went into the midst of the cloud, and got him up into the mount: and Moses was in the mount forty days and forty nights.

Second Reading: from Exodus (33:11 to end;
34:4-6, 8)

AND the Lord spake unto Moses face to face, as a man speaketh unto his friend. And he turned again into the camp: but his servant Joshua, the son of Nun, a young man, departed not out of the tabernacle.

And Moses said unto the Lord, See, thou sayest unto me, Bring up this people: and thou hast not let me know whom thou wilt send with me. Yet thou hast said, I know thee by name, and thou hast also found grace in my sight.

Now therefore, I pray thee, if I have found grace in thy sight, show me now thy way, that I may know thee, that I may find grace in thy sight: and consider that this nation is thy people.

And he said, My presence shall go with thee, and I will give thee rest.

And he said unto him, If thy presence go not with me, carry us not up hence.

For wherein shall it be known here that I and thy people have found grace in thy sight? is it not in that thou goest with us? So shall we be separated, I and thy people, from all the people that are upon the face of the earth.

And the Lord said unto Moses, I will do this thing also that thou hast spoken: for thou hast found grace in my sight, and I know thee by name.

And he said, I beseech thee, show me thy glory.

And he said, I will make all my goodness pass before thee, and I will proclaim the name of the Lord before thee; and will be gracious to whom I will be gracious, and will show mercy on whom I will show mercy.

And he said, Thou canst not see my face: for there shall no man see me, and live.

And the Lord said, Behold, there is a place by me, and thou shalt stand upon a rock:

And it shall come to pass, while my glory passeth by, that I will put thee in a cleft of the rock, and will cover thee with my hand while I pass by:

And I will take away mine hand, and thou shalt see my back parts; but my face shall not be seen.

And Moses rose up early in the morning, and went up unto mount Sinai, as the Lord had commanded him, and took in his hand the two tables of stone.

And the Lord descended in the cloud, and stood with him there, and proclaimed the name of the Lord.

And the Lord passed by before him, and proclaimed, The Lord, the Lord God, merciful and gracious, long-suffering, and abundant in goodness and truth,

And Moses made haste, and bowed his head toward the earth, and worshipped the Lord.

Third Reading: from 3 Kings (19:3-16)

AT that time, Elijah arose, and came to Beersheba, which belongeth to Judah, and left his servant there.

But he himself went a day's journey into the wilderness, and came and sat down.

And slept under a juniper tree, behold, then an angel touched him, and said unto him, Arise and eat.

And he looked, and, behold, here was a cake baken on the coals, and a cruse of water at his head. And he did eat and drink, and laid him down again.

And the angel of the Lord came again the second time, and touched him, and said, Arise and eat; because the journey is too great for thee.

And he arose, and did eat and drink, and went in the strength of that meat forty days and forty nights unto Horeb the mount of God.

And he came thither unto a cave, and lodged there; and, behold, the word of the Lord came to him, and he said unto him, What doest thou here, Elijah?

And he said, I have been very jealous for the Lord God of hosts: for the children of Israel have forsaken thy covenant, thrown down thine altars, and slain thy prophets with the sword; and I, even I only, am left; and they seek my life, to take it away.

And he said, Go forth, and stand upon the mount before the Lord. And, behold, the Lord passed by, and a great and strong wind rent the mountains, and brake in pieces the rocks before the Lord; but the Lord was not in the wind; and after the wind an earthquake; but the Lord was not in the earthquake:

And after the earthquake a fire; but the Lord was not in the fire: and after the fire a still small voice.

And it was so, when Elijah heard it, that he wrapped his face in his mantle, and went out, and stood in the entering in of the cave.

And the Lord said unto him, Go, return on thy way to the wilderness of Damascus; and anoint Elisha the son of Shaphat prophet instead of thyself.

❡*And after the usual Petitions, the following Litiya is chanted in the Fifth Tone.*

COME, let us go up to the mount of the Lord, and to the house of our God, to behold the glory of his Transfiguration, the glory as of an only Son of the Father, receiving light from his light. And ascending by the Spirit, we praise through the ages the consubstantial Trinity.

❡*And in the Aposticha, the following Idiomelons are chanted in the First Tone.*

VERILY, he who spoke to Moses by symbols on Mount Sinai of old, saying, I am who I am, hath manifested himself today on Mount Tabor to his Disciples, showing in himself the beauty of the element of the first image, by taking unto himself human substance. And he raised as witness for this grace, Moses and Elijah, making them partakers in his joy and precursors of the Gospel of emancipation through the Cross and the Resurrection of salvation.

Stichos: Thine are the heavens, and thine is the earth.
Verily, David, God's sire, when he foresaw in the
spirit thy coming to men in the flesh, O only Son, called
creation from afar to rejoice, shouting prophetically,
Tabor and Hermon shall rejoice in thy Name; for it is
on this mount thou didst ascend with thy Disciples, O
Saviour, and by thy Transfiguration didst cause the
dark nature of Adam to flourish, restoring its element
to glory and splendour. Wherefore, O All-creator, we
cry out rejoicing, Glory to thee.

Stichos: Tabor and Hermon shall rejoice in thy
Name.

The pre-called Disciples, O Christ, without beginning, when they beheld on the mount of Transfiguration
the unbearable radiance of thy light, and thine unapproachable Godhead, were overpowered by a divine
dazzlement. And when they were illumined by the
light of the radiant cloud, they heard the voice of the
Father confirming the mystery of thine Incarnation;
for thou verily remainest one, even after the Incarnation, thou only Son and Saviour of mankind.

Glory and Now, in the Sixth Tone

TODAY hast thou manifested on Mount Tabor, O
Lord, the glory of thy divine image to the chosen
of thy Disciples, Peter, James, and John; for when
they saw thy garments glistening as light, and thy face
surpassing the sun in splendour, and they could no more
bear to behold thine unbearable radiance, they fell to
the ground, utterly unable to gaze upon it; and they
heard a voice from on high testifying and saying, This
is my beloved Son, who cometh into the world to save
man.

Troparion, in the Seventh Tone (three times)

WHEN, O Christ our God, thou wast transfigured
on the mountain, thou didst reveal thy glory to
thy Disciples in proportion as they could bear it. Let

thine everlasting light also enlighten us sinners, through the intercessions of the Theotokos, O thou Bestower of light, glory to thee.

2. Matins

¶ *On* God the Lord hath appeared unto us, *the Troparion* (*three times*); *and the following Kathismata.*

First Kathisma, in the Fourth Tone

THOU hast been transfigured, O Saviour, on Mount Tabor, indicating the transformation of mankind which shall take place at thy dreadful Second Coming. Moses and Elijah did converse with thee. But thy Disciples, whom thou didst call, when they beheld thy glory, O Master, were dazzled by thy brightness. Wherefore, O thou who didst at that time cause thy light to shine on them, lighten our souls.

Second Kathisma, in the Same Tone

THOU has been transfigured, O Jesus, on Mount Tabor, and a brilliant cloud spread out itself like a tabernacle, covering the Apostles of thy glory. They looked to the ground, unable to behold the unapproachable splendour of the glory of thy countenance, O Christ, Saviour and God without beginning. Therefore, O thou who didst cause thy light to shine on them, lighten our souls.

Third Kathisma, in the Same Tone.

O THOU who didst ascend the mount with thy Disciples, and didst shine in the glory of the Father, Moses and Elijah were present with thee; for the law and the Prophets do serve thee since thou art God. And the Father designated for thee natural prophetship, calling thee Son. Wherefore, do we praise him, with thee, and with the Holy Spirit.

¶ *Then the Anabathmoi,* From my youth, *etc.* (*50*), *and the Prokeimenon.*

Tabor and Hermon shall rejoice in thy Name. Thine are the heavens, and thine is the earth.

The Matin Gospel: from St. Luke (9:28-36)

AT that time: Jesus took Peter and John and James, and went up into the mountain to pray.

And as he prayed, the fashion of his countenance was altered, and his raiment was white and glistering.

And, behold, there talked with him two men, which were Moses and Elias:

Who appeared in glory, and spake of his decease which he should accomplish at Jerusalem.

But Peter and they that were with him were heavy with sleep: and when they were awake, they saw his glory, and the two men that stood with him.

And it came to pass, as they departed from him, Peter said unto Jesus, Master, it is good for us to be here: and let us make three tabernacles; one for thee, and one for Moses, and one for Elias: not knowing what he said.

While he thus spake, there came a cloud, and overshadowed them: and they feared as they entered into the cloud.

And there came a voice out of the cloud, saying, This is my beloved Son: hear him.

And when the voice was past, Jesus was found alone. And they kept it close, and told no man in those days any of those things which they had seen.

❡ *Then Psalm 50 (plain reading) Glory,* By the intercession of the Apostles, *etc.; Now,* By the intercessions of the Theotokos, *etc.*

❡ *Then on* O merciful One, have mercy upon me, O God, *the following Idiomelon, the Second Tone.*

O THOU holy One who hast sanctified the whole universe by thy light, thou hast been transfigured on a high mountain, and hast shown thy Disciples thy might and that thou shalt deliver the world from transgression. Wherefore, do we cry out to thee, O compassionate Lord, save our souls.

¶*Note: The following Hermoses are chanted as Katabasias from July twenty-seventh to thirty-first, in the Fourth Tone.*

1. The hosts of Israel, having passed the Red Sea and watery deep with feet unmoist, and having seen the three-speared riders of the enemy drowned beneath the waters, sang aloud with joy, Let us praise our God; for he hath been glorified.

2. The bows of the mighty are become weak; and the weak ones are girded with strength. Therefore, hath my heart been made steadfast in the Lord.

4. O Christ, I have heard of thy glorious providence, and that thou wast born of a Virgin to deliver those who are in error, who cry out to thee, Glory to thy might, O Lord.

5. O Christ, Creator, who didst separate light from primeval darkness, that thy works might praise thee in the light, guide thou our feet in thy light.

6. In my sorrow I cried unto the Lord, and the God of my salvation hath heard me.

7. Verily, the Abrahamite youths did tread of old the flames of the furnace in Babylon, singing in praise, Blessed art thou, God of our fathers.

8. When the youths in Babylon were kindled by divine zeal they trampled bravely upon the flames and the threats of the violator. And when they were cast into the midst of the fire, being watered with dew, they sang, Bless the Lord, all his works.

¶*But in the present Feast, sing the Katabasias of the Cross (p. 300), and instead of O thou who art more honourable, etc., the following Ninth Ode is sung in the Fourth Tone.*

9. Thy birth-giving, O Theotokos, has been shown free of corruption; for God did come forth from thy womb putting on flesh; and on earth he did appear, and walked among men. Wherefore, thee do we all magnify.

Verily, the Disciples when they were instantly illuminated by the effulgence of created light, looked at one another with fright, falling on their faces to the ground, and worshipped thee, O Master of all.

And the cloud, for the confirmation of the miracle, gave forth a voice from a God-moved reverberation; for the Father of light did shout to the Disciples, saying, This is my beloved Son: hear ye him.

The servants of the Word, beholding new and wondrous things, and hearing the fatherly voice on Tabor, cried out rejoicing, This is our Saviour, the Element of the ancient covenant.

O Word, untransformed Son, O true image of the Being on high, and his unshaken Seal, his Wisdom, Arm, right Hand, and Power, thee do we praise with the Father and Holy Spirit.

⁋Also the following Ninth Ode, in the Eighth Tone.

ALL ears were alarmed at the ineffable condescension of God; how the high One condescended willingly even unto the flesh and became man from the virginal womb. Therefore, we believers do magnify the undefiled Theotokos.

That thou mightest, O Christ, make clear thine ineffable second descent, how the high God appeareth standing among the gods, thou didst shine forth upon the Apostles and Moses with Elijah on Tabor, in an ineffable manner. Wherefore, we all magnify thee.

Come, all ye nations and hearken to me, as we ascend the heavenly holy mountain. Let us stand in an immaterial manner in the living city of God, beholding with spiritual eye the immaterial Godhead, the Godhead of the Father and the Holy Spirit, shining forth in the unique Son.

Thou hast infatuated me by thy longing, O Christ, and hast transformed me by thy divine Passion. Burn thou, therefore, my sins by an immaterial fire, and make me worthy to be filled with thy bliss, so that, rejoicing in both, I may magnify thy presence, O good One.

❡ *And conclude with the Ninth Katabasia of the Cross,* Thou art the mystical paradise, O Theotokos, *etc.* (*302*).

O THOU Word, untransformable Light, the Light of the unborn Father, by thy light which hath shown today on Tabor, we have seen the Father's light and the Spirit's light, lighting the whole creation.

❡ *And in the Einos, the following four Prosomia, in the Fourth Tone.*

BEFORE thy precious Crucifixion and thy Passion, O Master, thou didst take those whom thou didst choose of thy pure Disciples, and with them didst ascend Mount Tabor, desiring to show them thy glory. And when they beheld thee transfigured and shining forth with a splendour greater than the sun's, they fell down dazzled by thy might, crying out to thee, O Christ, thou art the Light without time, the Radiance of the Father, though seen by thy will an untransformable body. (*Repeat.*)

O thou who before the ages art God the Word, O thou clothed with light like a garment, thou wast transfigured before thy Disciples, O Master, and didst shine forth surpassing the sun. Verily, Moses and Elijah did stand before thee, clearly showing that thou art Lord of the quick and the dead, glorifying thine ineffable providence, thy mercy, and thy great condescension wherewith thou didst save the lost world.

Verily, thou wast born of the cloud of the Virgin, O Lord, and hast become flesh and wast transfigured on Mount Tabor. Then a bright cloud did surround thee, and the voice of the Father did manifest thee openly, in the presence of the Disciples, as a beloved Son, since thou art consubstantial with him and equal in rank. Therefore, Peter was astonished, saying, It is good for us to be here, not knowing what he saith, O Benefactor and abundant of mercy.

Glory and Now, in the Eighth Tone

VERILY Christ took Peter, James, and John to a high mountain alone. And he was transfigured before them, his countenance shining as the sun, and his clothes became white as light. Moses and Elijah appeared and conversed with him, and a bright cloud covered them. Then behold, a voice from the cloud said, This is my beloved Son in whom I am well pleased; hear him.

❡ *Then the Great Doxology; the Troparion of the Feast; and the Benediction.*

3. THE MASS

1. By the intercessions of the Theotokos, O Saviour, save us.

2. Save us, O Son of God, thou who wast transfigured on Mount Tabor, as we sing unto thee. Alleluia.

Glory and Now, O only-begotten Son, etc.

3. When, O Christ our God, thou wast transfigured, etc.

Eisodikon: For with thee is the Fountain of life, and in thy light we shall see light. Save us, O Son of God, who wast transfigured on Mount Tabor, as we sing unto thee, Alleluia.

❡ *Then the Troparion of the Feast; the Troparion of the Patron Saint of the church; and conclude with the following.*

Kontakion, in the Seventh Tone

THOU wast transfigured on the mount, and thy Disciples, in so far as they were able, beheld thy glory, O Christ our God: so that, when they should see thee crucified, they would remember that thy suffering was voluntary, and could declare to all the world that thou art truly the effulgent Splendour of the Father.

Epistle: How great are thy works, O Lord. Thou hast made all things in wisdom. Bless the Lord, O my soul.

Section from the Second Epistle of St. Peter (1:10-19)

YE brethren: Labour the more, that by good works you may make sure your calling and election: for doing these things, you shall not sin at any time.

For so an entrance shall be ministered to you abundantly into the everlasting kingdom of our Lord and Saviour Jesus Christ.

For which cause I will begin to put you always in remembrance of these things: though indeed you know them, and are confirmed in the present truth.

But I think it meet as long as I am in this tabernacle, to stir you up by putting you in remembrance.

Being assured that the laying away of this my tabernacle is at hand, according as our Lord Jesus Christ also hath signified to me.

And I will endeavour, that you frequently have after my decease, whereby you may keep a memory of these things.

For we have not by following artificial fables, made known to you the power, and presence of our Lord Jesus Christ; but we were eyewitnesses of his greatness.

For he received from God the Father, honour and glory: this voice coming down to him from the excellent glory: This is my beloved Son, in whom I am well pleased; hear ye him.

And this voice we heard brought from heaven, when we were with him in the holy mount.

And we have the more firm prophetical word: whereunto you do well to attend, as to a light that shineth in a dark place, until the day dawn, and the day star arise in your hearts.

The Gospel: from St. Matthew (17:1-9)

AT that time: Jesus taketh Peter, James, and John his brother, and bringeth them up into a high Mountain apart.

And was transfigured before them: and his face did shine as the sun, and his raiment was white as the light.

And behold, there appeared unto them Moses and Elias talking with him.

Then answered Peter, and said unto Jesus, Lord, it is good for us to be here: if thou wilt, let us make here three tabernacles; one for thee, and one for Moses, and one for Elias.

While he yet spake, behold, a bright cloud over-shadowed them: and behold a voice out of the cloud, which said, This is my beloved Son, in whom I am well pleased; hear ye him.

And when the disciples heard it, they fell on their face, and were sore afraid.

And Jesus came and touched them, and said, Arise, and be not afraid.

And when they had lifted up their eyes, they saw no man, save Jesus only.

And as they came down from the mountain, Jesus charged them, saying, Tell the vision to no man, until the Son of man be risen again from the dead.

And on Especially, sing the following Hymn, in the Eighth Tone.

NOW hath been heard that which had never been heard before; for the Son, who is from the Virgin without father, hath been testified to in glory by the voice of the Father; for he himself is God and Man together unto the end of ages.

Koinonikon: We shall walk, O Lord, in the light of thy countenance for ever. Alleluia.

And instead of We have seen the true Light, *etc., the Troparion of the Feast.*

Benediction: O thou who wast transfigured in glory on Mount Tabor before thy Disciples, the holy Apostles, etc.

7. The Righteous Martyr Domitius (1).

8. Aemilianus the Confessor, Bishop of Cyzicus (10).

9. The Apostle Matthias (12).

10. Archdeacon Lawrence the Martyr (1).

11. Deacon Euplus the Martyr (1).
12. Photius and Anicetus the Martyrs (2).
13. Maximus the Righteous Confessor (1); and Leave-Taking of the Feast of Transfiguration.
14. Micah the Prophet (13); and the Preparation for the Feast of the Falling-asleep of the Theotokos.

Troparion for the Preparation, in the Fourth Tone

COME forward, O ye people, and receive the glad tidings, clapping your hands together. Gather together today anxiously and joyfully, and shout ye all in joy; for the Theotokos is about to rise in glory from the earth to the heavens. Let us ever glorify her with praises; for she is the Theotokos.

Kontakion, in the Same Tone

TODAY the universe, rejoicing mystically in thy glorious memorial, O Theotokos, doth go before crying and shouting with joy, Hail, O Virgin, pride of Christians!

15. THE FALLING ASLEEP OF OUR LADY, THE MOST HOLY THEOTOKOS.

Typicon

¶*If this Feast falleth on a Sunday, see the Order set forth in the Nativity of our Lady, on Sept. eighth, excepting the Epistle and Gospel, which are those of the Feast.*

1. VESPERS

¶*After reading the three Psalms beginning with* Blessed is the man, *sing on* O Lord, to thee have I cried, *the following Prosomia, in the First Tone.*

O MARVELOUS wonder! The Fount of life hath been laid in the grave, and the tomb hath become a ladder leading to heaven. Rejoice, O Gethsemane, the holy chamber of the Theotokos. And let us believers, shout to her with Gabriel the chief of angels, saying,

Hail, O full of grace. The Lord is with thee, granting the world, through thee, the Great Mercy. (*Repeat.*)

How strange are thy mysteries, undefiled Virgin; for thou didst appear as a throne to the high One, and today art thou translated from earth to heaven. Verily, thy glory is a true splendour shining forth with the rays of divine gifts. Ascend, therefore, O ye virgins, with the King's Mother, shouting, Hail, O full of grace. The Lord is with thee, granting, through thee, to the world the Great Mercy. (*Repeat.*)

Verily, the fearful dominions, thrones, presidencies, the lords, powers, cherubim, and seraphim, glorify thy falling asleep. The terrestrials too, adorned with thy glory, rejoice; and kings, with archangels and angels, sing shouting, Hail, O full of grace. The Lord is with thee, granting, through thee, to the world, the Great Mercy. (*Repeat.*)

Glory and Now, in the Eight Tones

First Tone. Verily, the God-mantled Apostles were caught up on all sides, ascending the clouds by a divine sign.

Fifth Tone. And they came up to thy most pure, life-originating resting-place to kiss it reverently.

Second Tone. As for the most sublime heavenly powers, they came with their own chief.

Sixth Tone. To escort, enwrapped in awe, thy all-honoured, God-receiving body, they went before in a superearthly manner, shouting invisibly to the heavenly ranks, Behold the queen of all, the divine Maiden, has come.

Third Tone. Lift up the gates and receive superearthly-wise the Mother of everlasting Light.

Seventh Tone. For through her hath salvation come to the whole human race. And she is the one on whom it is impossible to gaze, and whom we can never honour sufficiently.

Fourth Tone. For the honour through which she became sublime transcendeth all understanding.

Eighth Tone. Wherefore, O undefiled Theotokos, everlasting with thy life-bearing Son, intercede with him unceasingly that he may preserve and save thy new people from every hostile assault; for we have taken thee unto us as our helper.

Then in the First Tone. Therefore, do we magnify thee with voices of joy unto all ages.

¶ *Then the Eisodos, and* O resplendent Light, *etc.; the daily Prokeimenon; and the Readings pertaining to Sept. eighth (p. 284).*

¶ *And in the Litiya, the following piece. in the Fifth Tone.*

COME, ye feast-lovers; come, let us form one rank; come, let us crown the Church with songs on the falling asleep of the ark of God; for today doth heaven open its bosom to receive her who gave birth to the One whom all cannot contain. And earth doth adorn itself in blessing and splendour, restoring the fount of life. And the angels fall into line with the Apostles, gazing in awe on her who gave birth to the Element of life, moving from life to life. Let us all adore her, entreating, and saying, Forget not, O Lady, those who share thy humanity, who celebrate in faith thy most holy falling asleep.

¶ *And in the Aposticha, the following Idiomelons are sung in the Fourth Tone.*

COME, ye people, let us praise the all-holy, undefiled Virgin, from whom did issue incarnate, in an ineffable manner, the Word of the Father, crying, and saying, Blessed art thou among women, and blessed is thy womb which did contain Christ. Placing thy soul between his holy hands, intercede thou with him, O undefiled one, to save our souls.

Stichos: Arise, O Lord, into thy resting place: thou and the ark which thou hast sanctified.

O most holy and undefiled Virgin, the multitudes of angels in heaven and men on earth do bless thine all-honoured falling-asleep; for thou didst become a Mother to Christ God, the Creator of all. Thee do we supplicate that thou mayest continue interceding with him for our sakes, who place our hope, after God, on thee, O all-praised, unwedded Theotokos.

Stichos: The Lord hath sworn in truth unto David: he will not turn from it.

Let us, O peoples, sing to Christ God today with the song of David who saith, The virgins that follow her shall be brought before the king, with gladness and rejoicing; for she who is of the seed of David, through whom we have been deified, hath been translated at the hands of her Son and Master with surpassing glory. Wherefore, save us who do confess that thou art the Theotokos from every tribulation, and deliver our souls from danger.

Glory and Now, in the Fourth Tone

WHEN thou wast translated to him who was born of thee in an inexplicable way, O virgin Theotokos, there were present James, the brother of the Lord and first of the Chief Priests, and Peter, the honoured head and leader of theologians, with the rest of the divine rank of Apostles, clearly uttering divine words, praising the amazing divine mystery, the mystery of the dispensation of Christ God, and with joy preparing thy body which was the God-receiving originator of life, O most glorified one, while the most holy and honoured angels looked from one high, struck with astonishment and surprise, and saying one to another; Lift ye your gates and receive ye the mother of the Maker of heaven and earth. Let us laud with songs of praise her sanctified, noble body which contained the Lord, invisible to us. Therefore we, too, celebrate thy memory, O all-praised one crying; Exalt the state of Christians and save our souls.

Troparion, in the First Tone (three times)

IN thy birth-giving, O Theotokos, thou didst keep and preserve virginity; and in thy falling-asleep thou hast not forsaken the world; for living thou wast translated, being the Mother of Life. Wherefore, by thine intercessions, deliver our souls from death.

2. MATINS

¶ *On* God the Lord hath appeared to us, *the Troparion* (*three times*); *and the following Kathismata.*

First Kathisma, in the Fourth Tone

CALL out, O David. What is this present feast? He said; Verily she whom I praised in the Psalms as daughter, Maiden of God and Virgin, hath been translated by Christ, who was born of her without seed, to yonder abodes. Wherefore, mothers, daughters, and brides of Christ shout in joy, Rejoice, O thou who hast been translated to the heavenly kingdom.

Second Kathisma, in the First Tone

VERILY, the most honoured rank of the wise Apostles came together in a miraculous way to prepare with glorification thine undefiled body, thou all-praised Theotokos. And with them the multitudes of angels sang, praising thy solemn assumption, which we celebrate in faith.

Third Kathisma, in the Third Tone

AS for thy birth-giving, it was with a seedless conception; and as for thy falling-asleep, it was death without corruption. Lo, a wonder was joined to another wonder, doubly wonderous; for how can the unwedded give suck to a babe and yet remain undefiled? Or how is the Theotokos prepared with ointments as one who is dead? Wherefore, with the angels do we cry to thee, Hail, O full of grace.

¶ *Then the Anabathmoi,* From my youth, *etc.* (*p.* 50); *and the following Prokeimenon.*

I shall proclaim thy Name from generation to generation. Hearken, O daughter, and see.

The Gospel

And Mary arose in those days, etc. (p. 50).

❡*And Psalm 50 (plain reading); then Glory, By the intercessions of the Theotokos, etc. and Now (repeated); and on O merciful One, have mercy upon me, O God, etc. the following Idiomelons, in the Sixth Tone.*

WHEN the assumption of thine undefiled body was being prepared, the Apostles gazed on thy bed, viewing thee with trembling. Some contemplated thy body and were dazzled, but Peter cried out to thee in tears, saying, I see thee clearly, O Virgin, stretched out, O life of all, and am astonished. O thou undefiled one, in whom the bliss of future life dwelt, beseech thy Son and God to preserve thy city unimpaired.

❡*Then the following Hermoses of the First Canon are sung in place of the Katabasias, in the First Tone.*

By Cozma the Anchorite

1. Thy noble solemn memorial, O Virgin, adorned with divine glory, hath brought all believers together in rejoicing as Miriam did of old, coming forward with timbrels and dances, singing to thine only Son; for in glory hath he been glorified.

3. O Christ, Wisdom of God and his creating and almighty Power, establish thy Church without guile, and unshaken; for thou alone art holy, O thou who dwellest among the holy.

4. The sayings of the Prophets, O Christ, and their symbols explained clearly thine Incarnation of the Virgin; and the brilliance of thy lightning doth send forth light to the Gentiles, and the deep calleth out to thee shouting with joy, Glory to thy might, O Lover of mankind.

5. Verily, I proclaim, O Christ, the divine goodness of thine ineffable virtues; for thou didst rise from eternal glory as a ray, coëternal in thy Person, and wast incarnate in the Virgin's womb, bringing forth a sun to those who are in darkness and error.

6. Verily, the fire in the vitals of the deep-born whale was a symbol of thy three-day Burial, of which Jonah was an exemplar; for having escaped without hurt when he was swallowed, he shouted, saying, I will sacrifice unto thee with the voice of thanksgiving, O Lord.

7. Verily, the divine passion did defeat the bestial wrath and fire, moistening the fire, and with inspired works issuing forth from the three-voiced song of the righteous ones, scorning wrath, opposing the musical instruments, as they sang in the midst of the flames, shouting, Blessed art thou, O glorified One, the God of our Fathers.

8. Verily, the angel of the Almighty God did reveal the flames moistening the three righteous youths and burning the infidels. And he made the Theotokos a fountain for the Element of life, Destroyer of death, and overflowing with life to those who sing, We who are saved praise the Creator alone, ever exalting him to the end of ages.

¶*And instead of* O thou who art more honourable, *etc., the Ninth Ode of the Canons with the two following Magnifications.*

The Ninth Ode of the First Canon, in the First Tone

Magnification: All generations bless thee, O thou only Theotokos.

9. In thee, O spotless Virgin, the laws of nature were suspended; for thy virginity was preserved in thy child-bearing, and Life is joined with death. Thou, O Theotokos, didst remain a Virgin after child-birth, and after death art still alive and dost ever deliver thy heritage.

The angelic powers were dazzled when they beheld in Zion their own Master holding in his hands a feminine soul; for he addressed as befitting a son the one who immaculately gave him birth saying, Come, thou pure one, and be glorified with thy Son and God.

Verily, the ranks of the Apostles did bury thy God-bearing body, beholding it reverently, and shouting with melodious tunes, saying, O Theotokos, since thou departest to the heavenly abodes to thy son, thou shalt ever save thine inheritance.

The Ninth Ode of the Other Canon, in the Fourth Tone (By John of Damascus)

Verily, the angels, when they beheld the falling-asleep of the all-pure Virgin, were taken by surprise that she ascendeth from the earth to the highest.

LET the multitude of earthly ones rejoice in the spirit, carrying lamps; and let the nature of the incorporeal intellects feast, celebrating the noble assumption of the Theotokos, crying aloud, Rejoice, O undefiled, most blessed and ever-virgin Theotokos.

Come, let us rejoice in Zion, the divine and fertile hill of the living God, beholding the Theotokos; for Christ hath translated her to the most worthy and divine abode, in the Holy of Holies; for she is his Mother.

Come, ye believers, let us approach the tomb of the Theotokos, kissing it with our lips, hearts, eyes, and brow, touching it meekly, receiving from the ever-flowing fount precious gifts of healing.

O Mother of the living God, accept from us our farewell praise, and cover us with thy light-giving divine grace, granting victory to the king and peace to thy Christ-loving people; and to us who sing to thee, forgiveness and the salvation of our souls.

❡ *Then conclude with the Ninth Katabasia,* In thee, O spotless Virgin, *etc.* (p. 590).

Exaposteilarion, in the Third Tone (three times)

O APOSTLES gather ye from the regions to this town of Gethsemane and lay away my body. And thou, my Son and God, receive my soul.

❡ *And in the Einos, the following Prosomia, in the Fourth Tone,*

O THOU most holy Virgin, who knew not wedlock, the heavens rejoice in thy glorious falling-asleep, the hosts of angels are glad, and the whole earth crieth out in joy, singing to thee the funeral song, O Mother of the Lord of all, thou who hast delivered human kind from its ancestral condemnation.

The first-called of the Apostles did hasten from the regions by divine sign to lay thee away. And when they saw thee ascending from earth to heaven they shouted to thee in the tone of Gabriel, saying with joy, Hail, O chariot of the whole Godhead. Hail, O thou whose birth-giving alone didst unite the earthly with the heavenly ones.

O bride of God, the virgin Mother, who didst give birth to Life, thou hast removed, by thy solemn falling-asleep, to immortal life, surrounded by angels, presidencies, Apostles, Prophets, and the rest of creation. As for thy blameless soul, thy Son did take it up into his pure hands.

Glory and Now, in the Sixth Tone

VERILY, the clouds, O Theotokos, Mother of Life, at thy death-free falling-asleep, caught up the Apostles into the sky; and after they were all dispersed throughout the world gathered them into one rank beside thy pure body, which, when they had reverently laid it away, they sang with the tone of Gabriel, saying, Rejoice, O full of grace, the groomless virgin Mother, the Lord be with thee. With them, therefore, beseech thou him, for he is thy Son and our God, to save our souls.

❡*Then the Great Doxology; the Troparion of the Feast; and the Benediction.*

3. THE MASS

1. By the intercessions of the Theotokos, O Saviour, save us.

2. Save us, O Son of God, thou who art wonderful in his saints, as we sing unto thee, Alleluia.

❦ *Then* Glory *and* Now, *O only-begotten Son and Word of God, etc.*

3. In thy birth-giving, O Theotokos, thou didst keep and preserve virginity, etc.

❦ *In the Eisodos, the Troparion of the Feast, and to the Patron of the church; then conclude with the following Kontakion, in the Second Tone.*

VERILY, the Theotokos, who is ever watchful in intercessions, who is never rejected, neither tomb nor death could control. But being the Mother of Life, he who dwelt in her ever-virgin womb did translate her to life.

The Epistle

My soul doth magnify the Lord. Because he hath regarded the humiliation of his handmaid.

Section from the Epistle of St. Paul to the Phillipians

Ye brethren: Let this mind be in you, etc. (p. 292).

The Gospel: from St. Luke

At that time: Jesus entered into a certain town, etc. (p. 292).

❦ *And on Especially, the Hermos of the Ninth Ode with its Magnifications,* All generations bless thee, *etc., and* In thee, O spotless Virgin, *etc. (p. 590).*

Koinonikon: I will take the cup of salvation and call upon the Name of the Lord, Alleluia.

❦ *Then* We have seen the true Light, *etc., and the Benediction.*

16. Diomedes the Martyr (1); and the Translation of the Portrait of Christ, Not Made by Hands and Known as the Venerable Kerchief, from the City of Raha (Urfa) to Constantinople.

Troparion, in the Second Tone

THY pure image do we venerate, O good One, asking forgiveness of our sins, O Christ our God; for by thine own will thou didst ascend the Cross in thy body, to save thy creatures from the bondage of the enemy. Thou hast verily filled all with joy, since thou didst come, O our Saviour, to save the world.

17. Myron the Martyr (1).

18. Florus and Laurus the Martyrs (2).

19. Andrew the Martyr, General of the Army and his Companions (2).

20. The Prophet Samuel (13).

21. The Apostle Thaddaeus (12); and Passa the Martyr and her Three Children (2).

22. Agathonicus the Martyr (1).

23. Lupus the Martyr (1); and Leave-Taking of the Falling-asleep of our Lady.

24. Eutyches Martyr among Priests (1).

25. Return of the Body of Bartholomew the Apostle (12); and Memorial of Titus the Apostle (12).

26. Adrian and Natalia the Martyrs (2).

27. Poemen the Righteous (6).

28. Moses the Abyssinian the Righteous (7).

29. BEHEADING OF THE GLORIOUS FORERUNNER, JOHN THE BAPTIST.

¶ *A Fast on whichver day it falleth.*

1. VESPERS

¶ *After reciting three Psalms, beginning with,* Blessed is the man, *sing on* O Lord, to thee have I cried, *the following Idiomelons, in the Sixth Tone.*

By John of Damascus

AS the birthday of the impudent Herod was being kept, the object of the termagant dancer's oath was achieved; for the head of the Forerunner was cut off and offered on a charger, as food for those reclining. What a loathsome banquet, replete with wickedness and horrible murder. As for us, we bless the Baptizer, honouring him as is meet; for he is the greatest born of women. (*Repeat.*)

Verily, the disciple of the all-evil Satan did dance and remove thy head, O Forerunner, as a hire. What a bloody banquet; and would that thou hadst not made that vow, O iniquitous Herod, offspring of a lie. And since thou didst make the vow, would that thou hadst not carried it out; for it were better to have foresworn thyself and receive life, than remaining true to thine oath to have cut off the head of the Forerunner. As for us, let us bless the Baptizer, honouring him as is meet; for he is the greatest born of women. (*Repeat.*)

It was not worthy of thee, O Herod, to condemn to death, because of a satanic passion, him who reproached thee for thine adultery, and the folly of thy feminine propensity. Nay, it was not worthy of thee to err and deliver his all-honoured head to a transgressing woman for the sake of a vow made to a dancer. Woe to thee, how didst thou dare accomplish such murder! And how was it that this adulterous dancer was not consumed by fire in the midst of the banquet as she carried the head on a charger? As for us, let us bless the Baptizer, honouring him as is meet; for he is the greatest born of women.

Yea, again Herodias hath lost her self-control; again she is perturbed! What deceiving dance, and what intoxication with cunning! For the Forerunner's head was cut off, and Herod is troubled. Wherefore, O Lord, by the intercessions of thy Forerunner, grant peace to our souls.

¶ *Glory,* As the birthday, *etc.* (*p. 594*)

¶ *Now to our Lady,* Who shall not beatify, *etc.* (*p. 177*).

¶ *And after the Eisodos and* O resplendent Light, *etc., and the daily Prokeimenon, and the usual Petitions, sing the following Litiya, in the Fifth Tone.*

By John of Damascus

WHEN Herod wished to free himself from the rebuke of his iniquitious acts, he delivered unjustly thy head, O Forerunner, to a transgressing woman. Nor did this wretched one realize that offering it in a charger was ignominy for him. Wherefore, since thou art a practical teacher of purity, and a saving guide to repentance, O Baptizer, implore thou Christ, to deliver us from the humiliation of passions.

❡*And in the Aposticha, the following Idiomelons are chanted in the Second Tone.*

O JOHN the Baptizer and preacher of repentance, thou didst sanctify the earth when thy head was cut off; for thou didst make plain to believers the law of God, abolishing disobedience to the law. Wherefore, since thou standest by the throne of Christ, the heavenly King, beseech him to have mercy on our souls.

Stichos: The just shall flourish like the palm-tree.

O most holy John, thy head was cut off for the law of the Lord; for in blameless privilege thou didst reproach the infidel king when he disobeyed the law. Wherefore, do the hosts of angels wonder at thee, and the ranks of Apostles and Martyrs praise thee. And we, too, honour thy yearly memorial, O most noble one, glorifying the holy Trinity which hath crowned thee, O blessed Forerunner.

Stichos: The just shall rejoice in the Lord.

Verily, the Prophet of Prophets, he who became greater than the Prophets, sanctified from his mother's womb for the service of the Lord, today had his head cut off by an evil king. And the maiden who danced insolently, he rebuked openly before his beheading and after it, thus shaming the procession of sin. Wherefore, we shout, O John the Baptizer, having acquired favour, beseech ceaselessly for our souls.

Glory, in the Eighth Tone

THOU didst rebuke kings, O Forerunner of the Saviour, that they might not act contrary to the law. But the frolicking of an iniquitous woman won over Herod to cut off thy head. Therefore, is thy name praised from the place of rising to the place of setting of the sun. And since thou hast favour with the Lord, beseech him ceaselessly for the salvation of our souls.

And Now, to our Lady

O GROOMLESS Virgin, who didst conceive God in an inexplicable manner, accept the petitions of thy servants, O all-blameless Mother of the high God, giving to them all purification from guilt, as thou receivest our petitions, implore the salvation of us all.

Troparion, in the Second Tone (two times)

THE memory of the righteous is in praise. And thee, Forerunner, the testimony of the Lord sufficeth; for in truth thou hast been revealed as nobler than all the Prophets, for having been considered worthy to baptize in the running waters him who was preached. Therefore, thou didst strive for the truth happily. Thou didst proclaim to those in hades God appearing in the body, the Lifter up of the sin of the world, who granteth us the Great Mercy.

❡ And to our Lady in the Same Tone.

2. MATINS

❡ On God the Lord hath appeared unto us, the same Troparion as at Vespers. Then the following Kathismata.

First Kathisma, in the Fifth Tone

LET us gather together, O believers, and praise in unison him who was the mediator between law and grace; for he did come before and preach to us repentance, and having boldly and openly exposed Herod, his head was cut off. And now, being among the angels, he intercedeth with Christ for our salvation.

Second Kathisma, in the Same Tone

LET us praise with songs John the Forerunner and baptizer of Christ, who did appear to us as a Prophet from the womb, of a barren woman, a star brightening the universe and a contender clad in victory; for that he intercedeth with the Lord to have mercy on our souls.

Third Kathisma, In the Eighth Tone

O THOU of everlasting memory, thou didst rise from the barren pair chosen of God, loosening the ties of thy father's tongue, and didst show forth the splendour-bearing sun shining forth, preaching the Creator to the people in the wilderness, the Lamb of God who taketh away the sins of the world. And then, when thou didst rebuke the king in zeal, thy glorious head was cut off. Wherefore, O all-praised John, implore Christ God to grant forgiveness of sins to those who eagerly celebrate thy holy memory.

¶ *Then the Anabathmoi, From my youth, etc., (p. 50), and the following Prokeimenon.*

PRECIOUS in the sight of the Lord is the death of his saint. What shall we render to the Lord, for all the things that he hath rendered to us.

The Matin Gospel: from St. Matthew (14:1-13)

AT that time: Herod the tetrarch heard the fame of Jesus.

And he said to his servants: This is John the Baptist: he is risen from the dead, and therefore mighty works shew forth themselves in him.

For Herod had apprehended John and bound him, and put him into prison, because of Herodias, his brother's wife.

For John said to him: It is not lawful for thee to have her.

And having a mind to put him to death, he feared the people: because they esteemed him as a prophet.

But on Herod's birthday, the daughter of Herodias danced before them: and pleased Herod.

Whereupon he promised with an oath, to give her whatsoever she would ask of him.

But she being instructed before by her mother, said: Give me here in a dish the head of John the Baptist.

And the king was struck sad: yet because of his oath, and for them that sat with him at table, he commanded it to be given.

And he sent, and beheaded John in the prison.

And his head was brought in a dish: and it was given to the damsel, and she brought it to her mother.

And his disciples came and took the body, and buried it, and came and told Jesus.

Which when Jesus had heard, he retired from thence by a boat, into a desert place apart, and the multitudes having heard of it, followed him on foot out of the cities.

❡*And Psalm 50 (plain reading); Glory,* Through the intercessions of the Forerunner, *etc; Now,* Through the intercessions of the The-otokos, *etc. Then, on* O merciful One, have mercy upon me, O God, *etc., the following Idiomelon, in the Second Tone.*

O John the Baptizer and preacher of repentance, etc. (p. 596).

❡*Katabasias for the Cross.*

Exaposteilarions

LET us crown with songs of praise the Forerunner, known to be greater than the Prophets, and become foremost of the Apostles; for his head was cut off for the law of the Lord.

The adulterous Herod cut thy head off deceitfully, O Baptizer of the Lord and sower of purity; for he could not cut completely the reproach of thy tongue.

O thou undefiled Maid, by whose divine birth-giving thou hast removed the curse from the world, save thy fold which beseecheth thee in faith, and deliver it by thine intercessions from sundry dangers.

¶ *And in the Einos, chant the following three Prosomia, in the Eighth Tone.*

HOW strange a wonder! The noble head, respected of angels and reproaching the law-transgressing tongue, a dancing, adulterous maid did carry and offer to her immoral mother. Ah! for thy surpassing forbearance, O Christ, Lover of mankind, through it save our souls; for thou alone art compassionate. (*Repeat.*)

Ah! for the seduction of Herod, who, disgracing God by his disobedience of the law, pretended deceitfully and cunningly to keep his oath, adding murder to adultery, and affecting a frown. Ah! for thy surpassing compassion, Christ Lord. Through it deliver our souls; for thou alone art compassionate.

What an astonishing thing, surpassing the mind, that the seal of the Prophets and the earthly angel was offered as a prize for an immoral dance. And the tongue constantly speaking of God precedeth and is sent to preach Christ to those who are in hades. Ah! for thy surpassing providence, Christ Master. Through it save our souls; for thou alone art compassionate.

Glory, in the Sixth Tone

Yea, again Heriodias hath lost her self-control, etc. (p. 595).

Now: Thou art the true vine, etc. (p. 550).

¶ *Then the Great Doxology; the Troparion of the Feast; and the Benediction.*

3. THE MASS

⟨In the Eisodos, the Troparion for the Forerunner and the Patron Saint of the church; and the following Kontakion, in the Fifth Tone.

THE beheading of the glorious Forerunner was by divine providence, that the coming of the Saviour might be preached to those in hades. Let, Herodias, therefore, mourn, she who sought unlawful murder; for she hath not affected the law of God, nor hath she sought eternal life, preferring the worldly one.

The Epistle: The just shall rejoice in the Lord. Hear, O God, my voice.

Section from the Acts of the Holy and Pure Apostles (13:25-33)

IN those days, when John fulfilled his course, he said: I am not he, whom you think me to be; but behold, there cometh one after me, whose shoes of his feet I am not worthy to loose.

Men, brethren, children of the stock of Abraham, and whosoever among you fear God, to you the word of this salvation is sent.

For they that inhabited Jerusalem, and the rulers thereof, not knowing him, nor the voices of the prophets, which are read every sabbath, judging him have fulfilled them.

And finding no cause of death in him, they desired of Pilate, that they might kill him.

And when they had fulfilled all things that were written of him, taking him down from the tree, they laid him in a sepulchre.

But God raised him up from the dead the third day.

Who was seen for many days, by them who went up with him from Galilee to Jerusalem, who to this present are his witnesses to the people.

And we declare unto you, that the promise which was made to our fathers,

This same God hath fulfilled to our children, raising up Jesus.

The Gospel: from St. Mark (6:14-30)

And others said: It is Elias. But others said: It is a prophet, as one of the prophets.

Which Herod hearing, said: John whom I beheaded, he is risen again from the dead.

For Herod himself had sent and apprehended John, and bound him in prison for the sake of Herodias the wife of Philip his brother, because he had married her.

For John said to Herod: It is not lawful for thee to have thy brother's wife.

Now Herodias laid snares for him: and was desirous to put him to death, and could not.

For Herod feared John, knowing him to be a just and holy man: and kept him, and when he heard him, did many things: and he heard him willingly.

And when a convenient day was come, Herod made a supper for his birthday, for the princes, and tribunes, and chief men of Galilee.

And when the daughter of the same Herodias had come in, and had danced, and pleased Herod, and them that were at table with him, the king said to the damsel: Ask of me what thou wilt, and I will give it thee.

And he swore to her: Whatsoever thou shalt ask I will give thee, though it be the half of my kingdom.

Who when she was gone out, said to her mother, What shall I ask? But she said: The head of John the Baptist.

And when she was come in immediately with haste to the king, she asked, saying: I will that forthwith thou give me in a dish, the head of John the Baptist.

And the king was struck sad. Yet because of his oath, and because of them that were with him at table, he would not displease her:

But sending an executioner, he commanded that his head should be brought in a dish.

And he beheaded him in the prison, and brought his head in a dish: and gave it to the damsel, and the damsel gave it to her mother.

Which his disciples hearing, came, and took his body, and laid it in a tomb.

And the apostles coming together unto Jesus, related to him all things that they had done and taught.

A T that time: King Herod (for his name was made manifest) heard of Jesus, and said, John the Baptist is risen again from the dead; and therefore mighty works show forth themselves in him.

Koinonikon: The just shall be in everlasting remembrance. Alleluia.

30. Alexander, John, and New Paul, the Patriarchs of Constantinople (11).

31. Placing of the Girdle of the Theotokos.

Troparion: Thou hast bestowed upon thy city, etc. (p. 557).

SIXTH SECTION
Triodion

A Trihymnal Book, consisting of Services for the Movable Feasts from the Sunday of the Pharisee and the Publican to the Great Saturday of Passion Week.

✠

I. FROM THE SUNDAY OF THE PHARISEE AND THE PUBLICAN TO CHEESE FARE SUNDAY

SUNDAY OF THE PHARISEE AND THE PUBLICAN

¶ *During this week it is permitted to eat meat.*

1. VESPERS

¶ *On* O Lord, to thee have I cried, *seven for the Resurrection, in the Tone in use; and three for the following Triodion, in the First Tone.*

LET us not pray, brethren, Pharisee-like; for he who exalteth himself shall be abased. Wherefore, let us humble ourselves before God, crying by means of fasting, with the voice of the publican, saying, God forgive us sinners. (*Repeat.*)

When the Pharisee went down with empty glory, and the publican bowed himself in repentance, they came to thee alone, O Master. But the one through boasting lost his reward, and the other by his silence deserved gifts. Wherefore, by those sighs confirm me, O Christ God, since thou art the Lover of mankind.

Glory, in the Eighth Tone

ALMIGHTY Lord, I have known how effective are
tears; for they snatched Hezekiah from the doors
of death, and saved the sinning woman from her chronic
iniquities. And as for the publican they justified him
more than the Pharisee. Wherefore, I implore thee to
number me among them, and have mercy upon me.

¶*And Now to our Lady, in the Tone in use; the Aposticha for the
Resurrection; and Glory, in the Fifth Tone.*

Mine eyes being weighed down because of mine iniquities, I am unable to gaze at the horizon of heaven.
But thou, O Saviour, accept me penitent as the publican.

¶*And Now to our Lady, in the Same Tone. Then the Troparion for
the Resurrection and our Lady; and the Benediction.*

2. MATINS

¶*On* God the Lord hath appeared unto us *the Troparia; Kathismata; Blessings (Eulogetaria); Anabathmoi for the Resurrection;
and the Katabasias for the Presentation. And if the Leave-Taking of
the Presentation is past, the following Katabasias are sung in the
Sixth Tone.*

1. When Israel walked on foot at the bottom of the
sea as on dry land, and beheld Pharaoh the persecutor
drowned, they shouted, Let us praise our God; for he
hath triumphed.

3. There is none holy like thee, O Lord my God,
who didst exalt the horn of those who believe in thee,
O good One, and established them on the rock of thy
confession.

4. The venerable Church raiseth her voice in song,
as is meet to God, celebrating to the Lord with a pure
conscience. Christ is my might, my Lord, and my God.

5. O good One, lighten with thy divine light the
souls of those who come to thee early and eagerly that
they may know thee, O Word of God, the true God,
who callest us from the darkness of iniquities.

6. O most merciful One, when I saw the sea of this life agitated with the tumult of temptations, I hastened to thy quiet haven, crying, Raise my life from corruption.

7. Verily, the angel made the furnace overflow with dew for the righteous youth, burning the Chaldeans by the command of God, and constraining the usurper to shout, crying, Blessed art thou, God of our fathers.

8. Thou didst spring forth from the flames as dew for those righteous ones, and with water thou didst consume the sacrifice of the righteous one; for thou doest all things by thy mere will. Wherefore, we exalt thee still more to the end of ages.

9. Verily, the God whom no man can see, nor the ranks of angels dare look upon, through thee, O pure one, was seen among men as incarnate Word. Wherefore, with the heavenly hosts, we magnify him, and thee do we bless.

❡*And after the Gospel of the Eothina, and* In that we have beheld the Resurrection of Christ, *etc., and Psalm 50, sing in the Eighth Tone:*

Glory to the Father, and to the Son, and to the Holy Spirit.

OPEN to me the doors of repentance, O Life-giver; for my soul goeth early to the temple of thy holiness, coming in the temple of my body, wholly polluted. But because thou art compassionate, purify me by the compassion of thy mercies.

Now and ever, and unto ages of ages. Amen.

Prepare for me the ways of salvation, O Theotokos; for I have profaned myself with coarse sins, and consumed my whole life with procrastination. But by thine intercessions purify thou me from all abomination.

❡*And on,* O merciful One, have mercy on me, O God, *etc., the following Idiomelon, in the Sixth Tone.*

IF I think upon the multitude of my evil deeds, I tremble for the terrible Day of Judgment. But, trusting the compassion of thy mercy, I shout to thee like David, Have mercy upon me, O God, according to thy Great Mercy.[1]

❧ *Then sing, O thou who art more honourable than the cherubim, etc; and after that the Exaposteilarions for the following for the Triodion.*

LET us run away from the evil vaunting of the Pharisee, and learn the true humility of the publican, that we may ascend crying to God with him, Forgive us thy servants, O Christ Saviour, who wast born of the Virgin and willingly bore the Cross for our sakes, and with him raised the world by his divine might.

O all-praised Theotokos, the Author of creation and the God of all hath taken a human body from thine undefiled belly, wholly renewing my rotting nature, leaving thee after birth as thou hadst been. Wherefore, we all praise thee in faith, shouting, Rejoice, O glory of the world.

❧ *And in the Einos, five for the Resurrection; and three for the following Triodion, in the Third Tone.*

HAVING known, O my soul, the difference between the Pharisee and the publican, loathe thou the tone of that braggart, and emulate this one's prayer of true reverence, crying, God be merciful to me, a sinner, and forgive me. (*Repeat.*)

Let us eschew, O believers, the boastful tone of the Pharisee, and emulate the prayer of the publican in true reverence. Let us not be exalted in our own thoughts, but humble ourselves and cry contritely, God forgive us our sins.

---

[1] These three reverential Troparia are sung every Sunday, from the Sunday of the Pharisee and the Publican to the Fifth Sunday of the Great Fast, or Lent.

Glory, in the Sixth Tone

O LORD, thou didst reproach the Pharisee when he justified himself, boasting of his deeds; and justified the publican when he approached humbly, seeking forgiveness with sighs; for thou dost not draw near to arrogrant thoughts, nor turn away contrite hearts. Wherefore, we also kneel before thee meekly, O thou who didst suffer for our sakes. Grant us forgiveness and the Great Mercy.

❧ *And Now,* Thou hast transcended, *etc; then the Great Doxology; and the Troparion,* Today hath salvation come into the world, *etc; and the Benediction.*

3. THE MASS

❧ *The Typica and the Makarizmoi of the Tone. And after the Eisodos, the Troparion for the Resurrection and the Patron of the church. And if the Leave-Taking of the Feast of Presentation is past, then chant the following Kontakion, in the Fourth Tone.*

L ET us run away from the words of the boastful Pharisee, and learn the humility of the publican, crying with sighs to the Saviour, Have mercy upon us, O thou alone of true reconciliation.

The Epistle: Vow, and pay unto the Lord your God. In Judah is God known.

Section from the Second Epistle of St. Paul to his Disciple Timothy (3:10-15)

M Y child Timothy: Thou hast fully known my doctrine, manner of life, purpose, faith, long-suffering, charity, patience.

Persecutions, afflictions, which came unto me at Antioch, at Iconium, at Lystra; what persecutions I endured: but out of them all the Lord delivered me.

Yea, and all that will live godly in Christ Jesus shall suffer persecution.

But evil men and seducers shall wax worse and worse, deceiving and being deceived.

But continue thou in the things which thou hast learned and hast been assured of, knowing of whom thou hast learned them.

And that from a child thou hast known the holy scriptures, which are able to make thee wise unto salvation through faith which is in Christ Jesus.

The Gospel: from St. Luke (18:10-14)

THE Lord saith, This is a parable: Two men went up into the temple to pray; the one a Pharisee, and the other a publican.

The Pharisee stood and prayed thus with himself, God, I thank thee, that I am not as other men are, extortioners, unjust, adulterers, or even as this publican.

I fast twice in the week, I give tithes of all that I possess.

And the publican, standing afar off, would not lift up so much as his eyes unto heaven, but smote upon his breast, saying, God be merciful to me a sinner.

I tell you, this man went down to his house justified rather than the other: for every one that exalteth himself shall be abased; and he that humbleth himself shall be exalted.

¶ *And the rest of the Liturgy of John Chrysostom.*

¶ *Note: The same order is observed on the following three Sundays, i.e., the Sunday of the Prodigal Son, the Sunday of Meat Fare, and Sunday of Cheese Fare.*

SYNAXARION

ON THIS DAY WE COMMEMORATE THE PARABLE OF THE PHARISEE AND THE PUBLICAN, WHICH OCCURS IN THE HOLY GOSPEL.

STICHOS

IF YOU RESEMBLE THE PHARISEE, RUN FAR AWAY FROM THE TEMPLE; FOR INSIDE IS CHRIST BEFORE WHOM ONLY THE HUMBLE ARE ACCEPTABLE.

Stichos for the Triodion

O Creator of Everything Heavenly or Earthly, Receive Thou from the Angels a Trinitarian Song, and from Us Men a Noble and Reverent Triodion.

THE Pharisees were an old and famous sect among the Jews. Being wicked hypocrites, the Pharisees hid their vices while hypocritically simulating every virtue, doing all their work to be seen by men (St. Matt. 23:5). Thus people imagined them to be virtuous, as they themselves were separated from the people, as their name implies, pretending holiness and piety in their daily life. The publicans, on the other hand, were tax-farmers. And, since in the course of collecting taxes they were moved by avarice and greed to oppress the people, they were considered sinners and oppressors. In the parable he told, Christ used a Pharisee who was regarded by public opinion as virtuous, and a publican who was regarded as a sinner, thus teaching us the harm that comes from pride and the good that comes from humility.

The divine Fathers, realizing that after three weeks we shall enter the field of Quadragesima and of the spiritual contests of virtues, and that humility is the most efficient weapon for winning virtue, as pride is the greatest obstacle thereto, saw fit to consider the above mentioned weeks as a prelude to participation in those contests. And for this reason they called this week *prophonisimon*, meaning a *herald*, as though it preceded and proclaimed the approach of the time of fasting. They also decreed that the parable of the Pharisee and the Publican be read during this week, intending thereby to teach us not to pride ourselves in self-satisfaction, nor boast and exaggerate as the proud Pharisee, but rather take him as an example proving to us that the smoke of pride and the rottenness of boasting drive away the grace of the Holy Spirit, stripping man of every virtue and throwing him into the abyss of hell; also that we beseech God with awed hearts, imitating the humility of the publican through which man is justified and by which he may ascend to sublime heights however low he has fallen in sin.

Through the intercession of the wonder-working saints, O Christ our God, have mercy upon us and save us. Amen.

Koinonikon: Praise ye the Lord from the heavens: praise ye him in the highest. Alleluia. *(three times.)*

SUNDAY OF THE PRODIGAL SON

¶ *On* O Lord, *to thee have I cried, seven of the Resurrection; and the following three for the Triodion, in the First Tone.*

I HAVE been entrusted with a verdant and faultless region, but I planted evil in its soil and reaped its ears with the scythe of laziness. And I gathered my deeds into sheaves but placed them not on the threshing-floor of repentance. Wherefore, I ask thee, O divine Husbandman, to winnow the straw of my deeds with the breeze of thy compassionate love; and fill my soul with the wheat of forgiveness. Store me in thy heavenly garners and save me. *(Repeat.)*

Our way, O brethren, is to know the power of this mystery; for when the prodigal son ran away from sin, hastening to that fatherly refuge, his all-good father welcomed him and kissed him, granting him signs of glory. He celebrated the mystical joy to the celestial ones when he killed the fatted calf, that we might conduct ourselves becomingly towards the Sacrificer, the Father and Lover of mankind, and to the sacrificed One, the glorious Saviour of our souls.

Glory, in the Second Tone

OF what goodly things have I, wretched one, denied myself. And from what sovereignty have I, luckless one, fallen. I have squandered the riches that were given to me, and transgressed the commandment. Woe to thee, wretched soul, when thou shalt be condemned to eternal fire. Wherefore, before the end, cry to Christ God, God receive me as the prodigal son, and have mercy upon me.

¶ *The Aposticha of the Resurrection; and Glory, in the Sixth Tone.*

HAVING squandered the riches of the fatherly gift, I, wretched one, grazed with the dumb beasts. I desired their food and hungered; for I had not enough. Wherefore, I shall return to the compassionate Father, crying with tears, Receive me as one of thy servants, as I kneel to thy love to mankind, and save me.

2. Matins

Katabasias, in the Second Tone

1. O my soul, take up the Son of Moses and cry out, saying, A help and a refuge hath he become to me for salvation. This is my God, and I will glorify him.

3. O God, Husbandman of benevolences and Planter of good things, make my barren mind fruitful, for the compassion of thy mercies.

4. When the Prophet foresaw thy Nativity from the Virgin, he proclaimed, crying, I have heard thy hearing and feared; for, O Christ, thou didst come from Teman, from a holy and shadowy mountain.

5. When night passed, day broke, and light shone upon the world. Wherefore, the ranks of angels praise thee, O Christ God, and glorify thee.

6. I am encompassed in the deep of sins, O Saviour, and drowned in the tempest of this life. But as thou raised Jonah from the belly of the whale, so draw me out of passion, and save me.

7. Verily, the youths emulated the cherubim, exchanging glad tidings in the furnace, crying, Blessed art thou, O God; for in justice and truth thou broughtest all this upon us for our sins, O thou who art exceedingly praised and glorified unto the end of all ages.

8. Bless him who of old traced for Moses the wonder of the Virgin, in the bush in the Mount of Sinai. Praise him and exalt him yet more unto all ages.

9. Who of the terrestrials ever heard or beheld such a thing! A Virgin found with child in the womb, who gave birth to a child without travail? This then is the wonder which hath been fulfilled in thee; and, O undefiled Mary, the Theotokos, we magnify thee.

❡ *The Exaposteilarions for the Resurrection; and the following for the Triodion.*

THE riches of the grace which thou, O Saviour, didst give me, I spent vainly, wretched one, when I set out on a hapless journey. Living in extravagance with devils, I squandered it in an evil way. But having returned, receive me, O compassionate Father, as the prodigal son, and save me.

I have destroyed thy riches, O Lord, wretched one, squandering it, and submitted myself to evil devils. Wherefore, O most compassionate Saviour, have compassion on me, purify me, polluted one, and restore to me the first robe of thy kingdom.

❡ *And in the Einos, five for the Resurrection; and the following three for the Triodion, in the Second Tone.*

I OFFER thee, Lord, the voice of the prodigal son, crying, I have sinned in thy sight, O good One, and squandered the fortune of thy gifts. Albeit, receive me repentant, O Saviour, and save me.

In the Fourth Tone

I TOO have come, O compassionate One, like the prodigal son, I who spent all my life-time in estrangement, and squandered the riches which thou gavest me, O Father. Wherefore, receive me, O God, repentant, and have mercy upon me.

In the Eighth Tone

WHEN in extravagance I spent and squandered the fortune of fatherly riches, I became a wanderer, living in the country of the wicked. And unable longer to bear their company, I shall return to thee, O compassionate Father, crying, I have sinned against heaven, and therefore thee, and am no more worthy to be called a son of thine: make me as one of thy hired servants, O God, and have mercy upon me.

Glory, in the Sixth Tone

O GOOD Father, I have withdrawn from thee. Do not forsake me nor cast me out from thy kingdom. The most evil enemy hath stripped me naked and robbed me of my fortune; and I have wasted the gifts of the soul in riotous living. Wherefore, I will rise and return to thee, crying, Make me as one of thy hired servants, O thou who for my sake didst stretch thy pure hands on the Cross to snatch me from the wicked beast and clothe me with the first robe, since thou alone art most compassionate.

3. THE MASS

¶*After the Eisodos, chant the following Kontakion, in the Third Tone.*

WHEN I disobeyed in ignorance thy fatherly glory, I wasted in iniquities the riches that thou gavest me. Wherefore, I cry to thee with the voice of the prodigal son, saying, I have sinned before thee, O compassionate Father, receive me repentant, and make me as one of thy hired servants.

The Epistle: Let thy mercy, O Lord, be upon us. Rejoice in the Lord, O ye just.

Section from the First Epistle of St. Paul to the Corinthians (6:12 to end)

YE brethren: All things are lawful unto me, but all things are not expedient: all things are lawful for me, but I will not be brought under the power of any.

Meats for the belly, and the belly for meats: but God shall destroy both it and them. Now the body is not for fornication, but for the Lord; and the Lord for the body.

And God hath both raised up the Lord, and will also raise up us by his own power.

Know ye not that your bodies are the members of Christ? shall I then take the members of Christ, and make them the members of an harlot? God forbid.

What! know ye not that he which is joined to an harlot is one body? for two, saith he, shall be one flesh.

But he that is joined unto the Lord is one spirit.

Flee fornication. Every sin that a man doeth is without the body; but he that committeth fornication sinneth against his own body.

What! know ye not that your body is the temple of the Holy Spirit which is in you, which ye have of God, and ye are not your own?

For ye are bought with a price: therefore glorify God in your body, and in your spirit, which are God's.

The Gospel: from St. Luke (15:11 to end)

THE Lord saith, This is a parable: A certain man had two sons:

And the younger of them said to his father, Father, give me the portion of goods that falleth to me. And he divided unto them his living.

And not many days after the younger son gathered all together, and took his journey into a far country, and there wasted his substance with riotous living.

And when he had spent all, there arose a mighty famine in that land; and he began to be in want.

And he went and joined himself to a citizen of that country; and he sent him into his fields to feed swine.

And he would fain have filled his belly with the husks that the swine did eat; and no man gave unto him.

And when he came to himself, he said, How many hired servants of my father's have bread enough and to spare, and I perish with hunger!

I will arise and go to my father, and will say unto him, Father, I have sinned against heaven, and before thee,

And am no more worthy to be called thy son: make me as one of thy hired servants.

And he arose, and came to his father. But when he was yet a great way off, his father saw him, and had compassion, and ran, and fell on his neck, and kissed him.

And the son said unto him, Father, I have sinned against heaven, and in thy sight, and am no more worthy to be called thy son.

But the father said to his servants, Bring forth the best robe, and put it on him; and put a ring on his hand, and shoes on his feet:

And bring hither the fatted calf, and kill it; and let us eat, and be merry:

For this my son was dead, and is alive again; he was lost, and is found. And they began to be merry.

Now his elder son was in the field: and as he came and drew nigh to the house, he heard music and dancing.

And he called one of the servants, and asked what these things meant.

And he said unto him, Thy brother is come; and thy father hath killed the fatted calf, because he hath received him safe and sound.

And he was angry, and would not go in: therefore came his father out, and entreated him.

And he answering said to his father, Lo, these many years do I serve thee, neither transgressed I at any time

thy commandment; and yet thou never gavest me a kid,
that I might make merry with my friends:

But as soon as this thy son was come, which hath
devoured thy living with harlots, thou hast killed for
him the fatted calf.

And he said unto him, Son, thou art ever with me,
and all that I have is thine.

It was meet that we should make merry, and be glad:
for this thy brother was dead, and is alive again; and
was lost, and is found.

SYNAXARION

ON THIS DAY WE COMMEMORATE THE PARABLE OF
THE PRODIGAL SON, WHICH OCCURS IN THE NOBLE
GOSPEL AND WHICH OUR DEIFIED FATHERS RE-INSTI-
TUTED IN THE TRIODION.

STICHOS

O THOU WHO ART LIKE ME, A PRODIGAL, COME FOR-
WARD WITH CONFIDENCE AND TRANQUILITY; FOR UNTO
ALL HAS BEEN OPENED THE DOOR OF DIVINE MERCY.

IN the gospel parable read on this day, the Saviour
illustrated three things: the condition of the sinner,
the canon of repentance, and the knowledge of God's
compassion. The divine Fathers prescribed its reading
on this day, following the reading of the Parable of the
Pharisee and the Publican (on the previous Sunday)
for our instruction; for in the person of the prodigal
son we view the wretched condition in which we are so
long as we are wallowing in sin, remote from God and
his undefiled Sacraments. Finally, we become aware
of ourselves and awaken, hastening our return to him
through repentance, even in these days of holy fasting.

The holy Fathers had another purpose. Because
some people commit grave sins and iniquities, persisting therein for a long time, they are overtaken by despair, thinking that they have no more hope of forgiveness. In this way they fall deeper and deeper in their

sinful acts, even committing worse ones. The holy Fathers, realizing this, intended to remove the evil of despair from their hearts, encouraging them and reviving their energies for deeds of virtue. Thus they decreed the reading of this parable in the days preceding the fast, illustrating thereby the compassion of our most righteous God, and that no sin may overcome his kindness and his inclination for the love of mankind, however great the sin may be.

Through thine ineffable love to mankind, therefore, O Christ our God, have mercy upon us. Amen.

Koinonikon: Praise ye the Lord from the heavens, etc.

SATURDAY OF MEAT FARE—FOR THE DEAD

On which is held a Requiem for all who have fallen asleep of our Orthodox Fathers and brothers from all time, and therefore this Saturday is called the Saturday of the Dead.

1. VESPERS

¶*On* O Lord, to thee have I cried, *the following Prosomia, in the Eighth Tone.*

AS we believers fulfill today the memorial of all those who have fallen asleep, from all time, who lived in true worship, each by name, let us praise the Lord and Saviour, praying to him with supplication, that they give good answer in the hour of judgment to our God himself, who is about to judge the earth, and come to stand at his right hand in joy, in the company of the righteous, in the shining inheritance of the saints, and be deserving of his heavenly kingdom. (*Repeat.*)

O Saviour, who didst buy us men with thy blood, and delivered us by thy Death from bitter death, and granted us by thy Resurrection life everlasting, grant rest, O Lord, to all who slumber in true worship who died, whether in the wilderness or in cities, whether on land or sea, or anywhere, to kings, Priests, Bishops, ascetics, and laymen, of every stature and of every race, and make them worthy of thy heavenly kingdom. (*Repeat.*)

O Christ, by thy Resurrection from the dead, death no more ruleth over them that slumber in true worship. Wherefore, we beseech thee ceaselessly that we may rest in thy tabernacles in the bosom of Abraham, even thy servants who have worshipped thee in purity from the days of Adam until now, with our fathers, brothers, relatives, and friends, and every man that hath passed through this life in faith, in sundry manners, and make us worthy of thy heavenly kingdom. (*Repeat.*)

Glory and Now, in the Eighth Tone

I WAIL and moan when I think of death, and see our beauty, created after the likeness of God, laid in the grave, without form, honour, or comeliness. O what wonder, this mystery which is befalling us. How have we been delivered to corruption? And how hath death been joined to us? Verily, it is at the command of God, as it is written, who granteth those who are translated, rest and repose.

¶*And instead of the daily Prokeimenon, sing, in the Eighth Tone, Alleluia (three times), with the following Stichoi.*

1. Blessed are they whom thou has chosen and taken to thee, O Lord.

2. And their mention is from generation to generation.

¶*In the Aposticha, the following Prosomia, in the Sixth Tone.*

O CHRIST, of incomprehensible compassion toward us, and a never failing Fountain of goodness, O most merciful Master, to those who have passed to thee to dwell in the land of the living, in thy beloved and chosen dwelling-places, which grant them for an eternal possession for ever; for thou didst shed thy blood for all, and freed the world with an enlivening price.

Stichos: Blessed are they whom thou hast chosen and taken to thee, O Lord.

Thou didst suffer death willingly, O Christ, bringing forth life, granting the faithful eternal bliss. Therefore, at this time prepare for it those who slumber in the hope of resurrection, forgiving them their trespasses through thy bounty; for thou alone art sinless, and thou alone art good and the Lover of mankind, that through all thy Name may be praised, and we the saved, glorify thy love to mankind.

Stichos: And their mention is from generation to generation.

O Christ, since we know that thou rulest the living and encompassest the dead with thy divine authority, we implore thee to grant rest to thy believing servants who have passed to thee, O sole Benefactor, with thine elect, in a place of rest, giving them repose in the splendour of thy holiness; for thou art the Willer of mercies, and the Saviour of those whom thou didst create in thy likeness, O alone most merciful.

Glory and Now, in the Sixth Tone

THE beginning of the creation of my stature was by thy creating command; for when thou willedst to perfect me, thou didst make me an animal composed of two natures, visible and invisible. As for my body, thou didst create it from the earth, and as for my soul, thou didst grant me thy divine enlivening breath. Wherefore, O Christ, grant rest to thy servants in the city of the living, in the dwelling-places of the righteous.

Troparion, in the Eighth Tone

O ONLY Creator, who directest all in the depth of the wisdom of thy love to mankind, and rewardest all according to their worth, grant rest, O Lord, to the souls of thy servants; for in thee have they placed their hope, O God our Author and Creator.

Glory: For in thee have they placed their hope, O our Creator, and Author, and God.

Now: We have verily accepted thee, O groomless Theotokos, as a wall and haven and a well-accepted intercessor with God whom thou barest, and as a salvation of the faithful.

2. MATINS

❡*Instead of* God the Lord hath us, *sing, Alleluia, in the Eighth Tone, (four times); and the Troparia as at Vespers. And after the Psalm,* Blessed are they, *etc, the following Kathismata, in the Fifth Tone.*

GRANT rest to thy servants, O our Saviour, with the righteous, and that they may abide in thy dwelling-places, as it is written. Turn away, O good One, from all the iniquities committed by them, voluntarily and involuntarily, knowingly and unknowingly, Lover of mankind.

Glory and Now: O Christ, who didst rise to the world from the Virgin, make us, through her petitions, sons of the light, and have mercy upon us.

❡*Then the Priest maketh mention of all those of our fathers and brothers who have fallen asleep. Then the Choir singeth the following Benedictions of the dead, in the Fifth Tone, and to each one respondeth,* Blessed art thou, O Lord; teach me thy statutes.

THE rank of the saints have found the Fount of life and the Gate of paradise. O that I too may find the way through repentance, I the lost sheep. Wherefore, O Saviour, call me and save me.

O saintly Martyrs, who proclaimed the Lamb of God, and were slaughtered like sheep, passing on to everlasting life, cease not to seek of him that he grant us forgiveness of crimes and iniquities.

O all ye who are in the world, who have walked the narrow and sad way, ye who have carried the cross like a yoke and followed me in faith, come, and enjoy what I have prepared for you of heavenly rewards and crowns.

I am the likeness of thine ineffable glory, even though I bear the marks of iniquity. Wherefore, O Master, have mercy upon thy creature and purify me by thy compassion. Grant me the beloved homeland, and make me also a dweller in paradise.

O thou who from ancient times didst create me from nothingness, and honoured me with thy likeness, and though I transgressed thy commandment didst return me to the earth from which I had been taken, restore me also to that likeness, that I may contemplate its pristine beauty.

Grant rest, O Lord, to thy servants, and array them in paradise, where the ranks of the saints and the righteous ones shine like stars. There, O God, grant rest to thy slumbering servants, who turn away from all their iniquities.

Glory to the Trinity

LET us praise in true worship the one Trinity of three-fold splendour, crying, Holy art thou, O Father without beginning, and Son coëternal with thee and the divine Spirit. Light us, who worship thee in faith, and snatch us from the eternal fire.

Now—Theotokion

REJOICE, O undefiled one, who didst bear God in the flesh for the salvation of all, through whom mankind found salvation. O that through thee we may find paradise, blessed and pure Theotokos.

Alleluia! Alleluia! Alleluia! Glory to thee, O God, etc. (*three times*).[1]

---

[1] In each Synapte of Vespers, the Priest thus makes mention of all those who have fallen asleep of our Orthodox forefathers, fathers, and brothers who have passed away in the hope of everlasting life.

Katabasias, in the Sixth Tone: When Israel, etc. (p. 605).

Exaposteilarions

O THOU who rulest the living and the dead, since thou art God, grant rest to thy servants in the dwelling-places of thine elect; for though they have sinned, O Saviour, they have not been separated from thee.

Grant rest to thy servants, O Lord, in the city of the living, where there is cessation of pain, sorrow, and sighing. And in that thou art the Lover of mankind, forgive them all wherein they have sinned in this life; for thou alone art sinless and merciful and Lord of the living and the dead.

¶*And in the Einos, the following Prosomia, in the Eighth Tone.*

COME, all ye brethren, before our end, let us look at our clay, contemplating the weakness of our nature and our humiliation; let us behold the result of our fate and the instruments of our bodily vessels; that man is dust and food for worms, perishable and transient; that our bones are dry and entirely without the breath of life. Come, let us bow down and observe our graves. Where is our glory and honour? Where is our comeliness of figure? Where is our eloquent tongue? Where are the eyebrows, where the eyes? All is shadow and dust. Wherefore, O Saviour, pity us all. (*Repeat.*)

Verily, Christ rose to deliver Adam, the first creation, from his bonds, undoing the power of hades. Wherefore, all ye dead, have faith that death hath passed away, and hades hath been led captive therewith. Yea, Christ who hath been crucified and is risen, doth reign. He it is who granteth us incorruptibility of the body. He it is who raiseth us and granteth us resurrection, preparing us also for yonder glory in bliss and rejoicing; us who in fervid faith have placed our trust in him. (*Repeat.*)

Glory and Now, in the Second Tone

EVERY man fadeth like a flower, and like a dream passeth away and perisheth, when the trumpet calleth. Wherefore, all who slumber rise, as though in an earthquake, to welcome thee, O Christ God. Then, O Master, array the souls of thy servants whom thou hast removed from us in the dwelling-places of thy saints for ever.

❡ *And immediately, the Little Doxology.*

Thine is the glory, our Lord and our God, etc. (p. 39).

❡ *Then the Priest saith,* Let us finish our morning petitions to the Lord, *etc. (p. 76).*

❡ *Then in the Aposticha of the Einos, the following Prosomia, in the Eighth Tone.*

O MASTER, as King thou ordainedst for me deliverance and freedom, when thy fingers were dyed with blood, and thou wast stained by the dye of thy red blood. Wherefore, now we desire of thee in faith to number among the first-born those who have passed away from us and make them worthy to receive the joy of the righteous, O thou who art alone compassionate.

Stichos: Blessed are they whom thou hast chosen and taken to thee, O Lord.

O Lover of mankind, thou hast become a High Priest like a man. And when thou was slaughtered like a lamb thou didst offer thyself an offering to the Father, rescuing man from corruption. Wherefore, array the departed ones in the city of the living, where the rivers of bliss flow abundantly, and where thine everlasting springs overflow.

Stichos: And their mention is from generation to generation.

With the incomprehensible depth of thy wisdom thou dost limit life, and advancing, thou dost behold death, transporting thy servants to another life. Therefore, array those whom thou didst take away at the waters of rest in the splendour of thy holy ones, where the voice of praise and rejoicing is heard forevermore.

Glory and Now, in the Sixth Tone

VERILY, the taste of the tree brought pain to Adam; for the serpent injected in him its deadly poison, through which death did enter and swallow all mankind. Albeit, when the Master came he destroyed the dragon, granting us rest. Wherefore, let us cry out to him, Have pity, O Saviour, on those whom thou hast removed hence, and grant them rest with thine elect.

Reader. Good it is to confess to the Lord, and to sing praises unto thy Name, O most High, to show forth thy loving kindness in the morning, and thy faith every night.

❡ *And immediately,* Holy God, *etc; the Troparion,* O only Creator, who directest all, *etc. (p. 620); and the Benediction.*

3. THE MASS

The Epistle: Their souls shall dwell among good things. Unto thee will I cry, O Lord.

Section from the First Epistle of St. Paul to the Thessalonians (4:12-16)

YE brethren: We will not have you ignorant, concerning them that are asleep, that you be not sorrowful, even as others who have no hope.

For if we believe that Jesus died, and rose again; even so them who have slept through Jesus, will God bring with him.

For this we say unto you in the word of the Lord, that we who are alive, who remain unto the coming of the Lord, shall not prevent them who have slept.

For the Lord himself shall come down from heaven with commandment, and with the voice of an archangel, and with the trumpet of God: and the dead who are in Christ, shall rise first.

Then we who are alive, who are left, shall be taken up together with them in the clouds to meet Christ, into the air, and so shall we be always with the Lord.

The Gospel: from St. John (5:24-30)

THE Lord said to the Jews which came unto him: Verily, verily, I say unto you, that he who heareth my word, and believeth him that sent me, hath life everlasting; and cometh not into judgment, but is passed from death to life.

Amen, amen I say unto you, that the hour cometh, and now is, when the dead shall hear the voice of the Son of God, and they that hear shall live.

For as the Father hath life in himself, so he hath given to the Son also to have life in himself:

And he hath given him power to do judgment, because he is the Son of man.

Wonder not at this; for the hour cometh, wherein all that are in the graves shall hear the voice of the Son of God.

And they that have done good things, shall come forth unto the resurrection of life; but they that have done evil, unto the resurrection of judgment.

I cannot of myself do any thing. As I hear, so I judge: and my judgment is just; because I seek not my own will, but the will of him that sent me.

SYNAXARION

ON THIS DAY THE DIVINE FATHERS ORDAINED A MEMORIAL FOR ALL THOSE WHO HAVE FALLEN ASLEEP SINCE THE AGES IN TRUE WORSHIP AND IN HOPE OF EVERLASTING LIFE.

STICHOS

REMEMBER NOT CONCERNING THE DEAD THEIR TRANSGRESSIONS, O TIMELESS WORD: SHOW NOT THY GOOD EMOTIONS AND COMPASSION AS INACTIVE.

ON this day we celebrate a memorial to all those of our fathers, brothers, and sisters of true worship who have fallen asleep from time immemorial; for the Church of Christ hath received from the Command-ments of the Apostles themselves (Command 42, Book 8) the custom of holding funeral Masses on the third, the ninth, the fortieth, etc. And since many have died at sea, in the mountains, or in the wilderness, or, be-cause of their poverty, have died without the prescribed Masses, the divine Fathers, moved by their zeal and their love of mankind, instituted a universal funeral Mass on this day for the souls of all the faithful of true worship, who have died from time immemorial, to include therein all those who did not for any reason receive special Masses.

Further, as we shall celebrate the anniversary of the Second Appearance of Christ on the Day of Resurrec-tion, those slumbering, not having yet been judged, nor having received full recompense, as the Holy Scrip-tures make clear. (Acts 17:31; 2 St. Peter 2:9; and Heb. 11: 39, 40), the Church doubtless performs this funeral Mass today at a fitting time for the souls of those who have fallen asleep, remembering them, and petitioning God to have compassion on the sinners. This she does in her great confidence in God's infinite mercy. There is a third reason why the holy Fathers instituted this Mass, namely, that, in remembering all the dead generally, it will remind us also of death, at an appro-priate time, arousing us to remorse and repentance.

Grant repose, O Master Christ, to the souls of those who have preceded us in slumber, in the dwelling-places of the righteous, and have mercy upon us; for thou alone art deathless. Amen.

Koinonikon: Blessed are they whom thou hast chosen and taken to thee, O Lord. And their mention is from generation to generation.

The Sunday of Meat Fare

1. Vespers

❡ *On* O Lord, to thee have I cried, *etc., sing six for the Resurrection, in the Tone in use; and the following four for the Triodion, in the Sixth Tone.*

WHEN thou art about to come to execute just judgment, O thou just Ruler, and sittest upon the throne of thy glory, the river of fire flowing before thine altar dazzling all, and the powers of heaven stand before thee in fear, and men are being judged with tribulation, each according to his deeds, then, O Christ, have pity on us, and make worthy of those who are saved, us who beseech thee in faith; for thou art compassionate.

Verily, the books shall be opened, and the works of men shall be revealed before the terrible throne; and the vale of mourning shall echo with horrible gnashing, at beholding all sinners vainly mourning being sent to eternal punishment, according to thy just sentence. Wherefore, we implore thee, O good and compassionate One, pity us who praise thee, O thou alone most merciful.

The trumpets shall blow, and the graves shall be empty, and all mankind shall rise trembling. They who have done good shall rejoice with joy, expecting their reward; and those who have done evil shall tremble greatly, moaning and shaking, as they are sent to suffering, separated from the elect. Wherefore, O Lord of glory, be compassionate toward us, and make us worthy to be of those who love thee; for thou art good.

Verily, I wail and moan when I recall eternity, the utmost darkness and Tartarus, the painful worms, the gnashing of teeth, and the unceasing pain which is theirs who commit unnumbered sins, and with evil intent have enraged thee, O good One, of whom I, most wretched man, am one, and the first among them. Wherefore, O Judge, save me by thy mercy; for thou art compassionate.

Glory, in the Eighth Tone

WHEN the thrones are placed, and the books are opened, and God sitteth for judgment, O what a fearful sight, as the angels stand in fright, and the river of fire floweth by! What then shall we do, we men who have come under condemnation by reason of the multitude of our sins? And as we hear him call the blessed of his Father to his kingdom, and send the sinners to punishment, who will bear that terrible verdict? Wherefore, O Saviour and Lover of mankind, alone King of the ages, hasten to me before the end with repentance, and have mercy upon me.

The Aposticha for the Resurrection, and Glory, in the Eighth Tone

WOE to thee, O darkened soul! For how long wilt thou not cease from evil doing? How long wilt thou lie down in idleness? Why thinkest thou not on the fearful hour of death? And why tremblest thou not at all at the terrible Altar of the Saviour? What, perchance, shalt thou reply or what reason give, when thy deeds shall rise to reproach thee, and thy works condemn and confute thee? Wherefore, O my soul, the time is at hand, hasten in faith before it is too late, and cry, I have sinned against thee, O Lord, I have sinned; but I know thy compassion, O Good Shepherd, Lover of mankind. Forbid me not, therefore, to stand at thy right hand, for the multitude of thy mercies.

❧ *Now, to our Lady, to the Oktoechos.*

2. MATINS

Katabasias, in the Sixth Tone

1. A help and a refuge hath salvation become to me. This is my God, therefore will I glorify him; the God of my Fathers, therefore will I exalt him; for in glory hath he been glorified.

3. O Lord, confirm my unstable heart on the rock of thy commandments; for thou alone art holy and Lord.

4. The Prophet heard of thy coming, O Lord, and that thou wast about to be born of the Virgin and appear to men; and he was dismayed, crying, Thy hearing have I heard and feared. Glory to thy power, O Lord.

5. In the night I rise up early beseeching thee, O Lover of mankind. Lighten me and guide me to thy commandments. Teach me, O Saviour, to do thy will.

6. With my whole heart I cried to the compassionate God, and he heard me from the nether hades, bringing my life out of corruption.

7. We have sinned, and done iniquity and injustice before thee. We have not kept nor done thy commandments. But deliver us not unto the end, O God of our Fathers.

8. Praise, O creation, with every breath, and bless him whom the hosts of heaven do glorify, and whom the cherubim and seraphim dread. Exalt him yet more unto all the ages.

9. Verily, the Nativity is ineffable; for the Conception was without seed and without corruption, of a spouseless Mother; for the Nativity of God hath renewed nature. Wherefore, with steadfast faith, all generations magnify thee; for thou art the Mother of our God.

❦ *Exaposteilarions for the Resurrection; and the following for the Triodion.*

AS I remember the terrible Day of Judgment, and thy dark, ineffable glory, I tremble altogether and dread, O Lord, crying to thee in fear, O Christ God, deliver me, luckless man, from all punishments, when thou comest to earth in glory to judge all creatures; and make me worthy to sit at thy right hand, O Master.

Lo, the Day of the Almighty Lord cometh, who shall bear the fear of its presence? For it is a day of wrath and a burning furnace, on which the Judge sitteth for judgment, to recompense each according to his works.

As I think of the hour of account, and the coming of the Lord, Lover of mankind, I tremble altogether, and therefore cry with grief, O my just Ruler, alone most merciful, receive me repentant, by the intercessions of the Theotokos.

¶ *And in the Einos, five for the Ressurrection, and three for the Triodion, in the Sixth Tone.*

I PICTURE that day and that hour, when we shall stand naked and condemned before the just Judge. Then the trumpet shall blow with great shouting, and the foundations of the earth shall shake, and the dead shall rise from their graves, and all become of one stature, and the secret thoughts of all stand revealed before thee. And they who repented not in their lifetime shall wail and mourn, and shall proceed to the nethermost fire. But the righteous shall enter the heavenly chamber with joy and rejoicing.

What a terrible hour, and what a fearful day, when the Judge sitteth on the terrible throne, and the books shall be opened, and deeds rebuked, and the secret things of darkness revealed, and the angels go out to gather all the nations! Come and hear, ye kings and princes, ye slaves and free, ye sinners and righteous, the rich and the poor; for he that is about to judge the whole universe shall come. Who then shall be able to stand before his face, when the angels shall rise before him reproaching the deeds, thoughts, and opinions that came forth in the night and in the day. What a terrible hour then! Wherefore, O soul, beware, before the end, and cry out, God, save me again; for thou alone art compassionate.

Verily, Daniel the Prophet when he became the man of desires, and saw the power of God, cried thus, The judgment seat was set, and the books were opened. See, therefore, O my soul. Dost thou fast? Deal not treacherously with thy neighbour. Wilt thou eschew food?

Judge not thy brother, lest thou be sent to the fire and be burned up like wax; that without hindrance Christ shall bring thee with him into his kingdom.

Glory, in the First Tone

LET us go before, O brethren, and cleanse ourselves for the queen of virtues; for behold she hath come bringing to us a fortune of good deeds, quenching the uprisings of passion and reconciling the wicked to the Master. Let us welcome her, therefore, shouting to Christ God, O thou who rose from the dead, keep us uncondemned, who glorify thee, O thou who alone art sinless.

3. THE MASS

❧*After the Eisodos, Kontakion in the First Tone.*

WHEN thou comest, O God, to earth with glory, and all creatures tremble before thee, and the river of fire floweth before the Altar, and the books are opened and sins revealed, deliver me then from that unquenchable fire, and make me worthy to stand at thy right hand, O righteous Judge.

The Epistle: Prokeimenon, in the Second Tone

The Lord is my strength and my praise.
The Lord chastising hath chastised me:
But he hath not delivered me over to death.

Section from the First Epistle of St. Paul to the Corinthians (8:8 to end; 9:1-2)

YE brethren: Meat commendeth us not to God: for neither, if we eat, are we the better; neither, if we eat not, are we the worse.

But take heed lest by any means this liberty of yours become a stumbling block to them that are weak.

For if any man see thee which hast knowledge sit at meat in the idol's temple, shall not the conscience of him which is weak be emboldened to eat those things which are offered to idols;

And through thy knowledge shall the weak brother perish, for whom Christ died?

But when ye sin so against the brethren, and wound their weak conscience, ye sin against Christ.

Wherefore, if meat make my brother to offend, I will eat no flesh while the world standeth, lest I make my brother to offend.

Am I not an apostle? am I not free? have I not seen Jesus Christ our Lord? are not ye my work in the Lord? If I be not an apostle unto others, yet doubtless I am to you: for the seal of mine apostleship are ye in the Lord.

The Gospel: from St. Matthew (25:31 to end)

THE Lord saith: When the Son of man shall come in his glory, and all the holy angels with him, then shall he sit upon the throne of his glory:

And before him shall be gathered all nations: and he shall separate them one from another, as a shepherd divideth his sheep from the goats:

And he shall set the sheep on his right hand, but the goats on the left.

Then shall the King say unto them on his right hand, Come, ye blessed of my Father, inherit the kingdom prepared for you from the foundation of the world:

For I was an hungered, and ye gave me meat: I was thirsty, and ye gave me drink: I was a stranger, and ye took me in:

Naked, and ye clothed me: I was sick, and ye visited me: I was in prison, and ye came unto me.

Then shall the righteous answer him, saying, Lord, when saw we thee an hungered, and fed thee? or thirsty, and gave thee drink?

When saw we thee a stranger, and took thee in? or naked, and clothed thee?

Or when saw we thee sick, or in prison, and came unto thee?

And the King shall answer and say unto them, Verily I say unto you, Inasmuch as ye have done it unto one of the least of these my brethren, ye have done it unto me.

Then shall he say also unto them on the left hand, Depart from me, ye cursed, into everlasting fire, prepared for the devil and his angels:

For I was an hungered, and ye gave me no meat: I was thirsty, and ye gave me no drink:

I was a stranger, and ye took me not in: naked, and ye clothed me not: sick, and in prison, and ye visited me not.

Then shall they also answer him, saying, Lord, when saw we thee an hungered, or athirst, or a stranger, or naked, or sick, or in prison, and did not minister unto thee?

Then shall he answer them, saying, Verily I say unto you, Inasmuch as ye did it not to one of the least of these, ye did it not to me.

And these shall go away into everlasting punishment: but the righteous into life eternal.

SYNAXARION

ON THIS DAY WE COMMEMORATE THE SECOND COMING OF OUR LORD JESUS CHRIST THE RIGHTEOUS JUDGE.

STICHOS

WHEN THOU SITTEST TO JUDGE THE EARTH, O JUST AND RIGHTEOUS JUDGE, MAKE ME, TOO, WORTHY OF THE VOICE THAT SAITH, COME YE.

THE two parables above mentioned, especially the Parable of the Prodigal Son, illustrate to us God's ineffable goodness and his great love for mankind. And so lest some who are lazy should loiter and spend the time appropriate to their salvation in the pursuit of sin, and be suddenly overtaken by death, the divine Fathers decree that on this day the remembrance of the

Second Appearance of Christ, which shows no favours may be celebrated, intending thereby to remind them that, as God is good and loving to mankind, he is also a very righteous Judge who recompenses each according to his deeds.

The purpose of the holy Fathers, therefore, was to awaken us from the inadvertency of slothfulness by reminding us of that terrible day and by arousing our energy to the work of virtue, by urging us to compassion, mercy, and the love of one another. And since on the following Sunday falls the Carnival of Cheese, there is held the anniversary of the expulsion of Adam from the paradise of bliss which marks the beginning of our present life. Hence the Feast that falls on this day is the last of the Feasts; for in truth on it end all our affairs and the world itself.

Wherefore, by the abundance of thine ineffable compassion, O Christ God, make us worthy of thine illustrious voice and number us among those who stand at thy right hand.

Koinonikon: Praise ye the Lord from the heavens, etc.

¶*Note: From the Monday following the Sunday of Meat Fare until the Sunday of Cheese Fare, the eating of meat is forbidden; but cheese, milk, etc. are allowed, even on Wednesday and Friday.*

SATURDAY OF CHEESE FARE

On which is celebrated the memory of all our righteous God-mantled Fathers who shone forth in the ascetic life.

Troparion, in the Fourth Tone

O GOD of our Fathers, who ever dealest with us according to thy meekness, remove not thy mercy from us; but by their intercessions direct our lives into the way of peace.

Theotokion, in the Same Tone

O HOLY Mother of the ineffable Light, in angelic praise do we honour thee; and in true worship do we magnify thee.

Kontakion, in the Eighth Tone

THOU didst delight, O Lord, the company of the God-mantled, who lighted the universe, preaching true worship, and abolishing infidelity and lies. Wherefore, by their intercessions, preserve in perfect security all those who glorify and magnify thee, that they may sing to thee. Alleluia.

SYNAXARION

ON THIS DAY WE COMMEMORATE ALL THE SAINTS MEN AND WOMEN, WHO DID SHINE FORTH IN THE ASCETIC LIFE.

STICHOS

I WILL OFFER THESE WORDS AS PERPETUAL OBLATIONS FOR EVER.

UNTO THE SOULS OF THE RIGHTEOUS WHOSE REMEMBRANCE REMAINS UNTO THE END OF DAYS.

ON this day we make remembrance for all our God-mantled Fathers glittering with asceticism.

For the divine Fathers, having instructed us and chastised us (as we said formerly of the preceding feasts), and having prepared us gradually to enter the field of spiritual combat; saw fit to remind us of those who have lived a righteous life, acceptable unto God, men and women alike, that through their example we might wax in the work of virtue, in power, and in courage, bridling our passions and our sufferings; for as veteran and experienced leaders, when their armies are ready for war and lined against the armies of the enemy, arouse their soldiers' courage by reminding them of renowned heroes and their splendid deeds, in addition to speaking words of zeal which strengthen their hearts and make them attack the enemy with valour with steadfast steps, so also did the divine Fathers deal with us. Thus they decreed that on this day there shall be a remembrance and a Feast of all the saints who pleased God, vanquishing passion and sufferings by great tribulations and hardships, that we may follow in their steps as far as possible, bravely striving against sufferings and concentrating our attention on the accomplishment of divers virtues, putting their lives before our eyes and acting as though they were men like us, who have the same nature as we.

Wherefore, through the intercession of all the righteous, O Christ our God, have mercy upon us. Amen.

SUNDAY OF CHEESE FARE

1. VESPERS

❧ *On,* O Lord, to thee have I cried, *etc., six for the Resurrection, and four for the Triodion, in the Sixth Tone.*

VERILY, the Lord, my Creator, took dust from the earth and with life-giving breath gave me a soul and revived me, honouring me and setting me in the earth as chief of all things visible, to live like the angels. But deceiving Satan, using the serpent as an instrument, deceived me through eating, and separated me from the glory of God, delivering me by nether death to the earth. But since thou art Lord and compassionate, recall thou me.

Lord, when I disobeyed thy divine command at the counsel of the adversary, I, wretched one, was stripped of my God-woven robe. And now I have put on the mantle of skin and fig-leaves, and have been condemned to eat in sweat the bread of hardship. The earth was cursed to bring forth thorns and husks for me. Albeit, O thou who in the last days wast incarnate from the Virgin, recall me and make me to enter the paradise of bliss.

O most honoured paradise, comeliness transcendent in splendour, the dwelling-place perfected by God, unending joy and enjoyment, the glory of the righteous, the joy of the Prophets, and the dwelling-place of the saints, beseech the Creator of all, by the tune of the rustling of thy leaves, to open for me the gates which I closed by sin, and that I be worthy to partake of the tree of life and joy, which I enjoyed in thee of old.

Woe is me! Verily, Adam by disobedience was exiled from paradise and driven from bliss, having been deceived by the words of the woman; and he sat opposite Eden naked and wailing. Let us all, therefore, be careful how we receive the season of fasting, obeying the traditions of the Gospels, that, becoming thereby acceptable to Christ, we may once more attain to paradise.

Glory, in the Sixth Tone

VERILY, Adam sat opposite paradise bewailing his nakedness and crying, Woe is me, the robbed one. who hearkened to the evil deception, and was driven away from glory. Woe is me, who through simplicity of heart became naked, and am now perplexed. Wherefore, O paradise, I shall no more attain thy bliss, nor behold my Lord, my God, and my Creator; for I shall return to the earth from which I was taken, and I shall cry to thee, O compassionate One, have mercy upon me who am fallen.

The Aposticha for the Resurrection, and Glory, in the Sixth Tone

VERILY, Adam for eating was driven from paradise. Wherefore, he sat opposite thereto, wailing and mourning in a pitiful voice, saying, Woe is me; what hath befallen me, wretched man? I transgressed one commandment of my Lord and was denied all kinds of good things. Wherefore, O most holy paradise, which for me wast planted, and for the sake of Eve wast closed, implore him who made thee, that I may contemplate the flowers of thy gardens. Therefore, the Saviour cried out to him, saying, I desire not the loss of my creation, but that it be saved, and come to the knowledge of the truth; for he that cometh to me, I shall not cast out.

2. Matins

Katabasias: When Israel walked, etc. (*p. 605*).

❡ *The Exaposteilarion for the Resurrection, and the following for the Triodion.*

WOE is me, wretched one; for I have transgressed thy commandment, and have been stripped of thy glory, and, therefore, was filled with confusion and cast out of paradise, O compassionate One. Wherefore, O merciful One, have mercy upon me, who was justly denied thy good things.

O Lord, we were estranged before from paradise, because of eating from the tree. Therefore, lead us into it again by thy Cross and by thy Passion, my Saviour and my God. Fortify us therein that we may fulfill our fast with becoming purity, and worship thy divine Resurrection and passover of salvation, by the intercessions of thy Mother.

❡ *And in the Einos, four for the Resurrection, and four for the Triodion, in the Fifth Tone.*

VERILY, Adam cried moaning, and said, Woe is me; for the serpent and the woman drew me away from divine favour; and the taste of the tree hath estranged me from paradise. Woe is me; I cannot bear the disgrace, I who was formerly king over all earthly creatures. Behold, I am now captive because of a counsel aside from the law. And I, who was for a time robed with the glory of immortality, have become like one dead, wrapped in the rags of death, in a pitiful manner. Woe is me; whom shall I make my helper in wailing? But thou, Lover of mankind, mantled in compassion, who didst create me from the earth, recall and save me from the bondage of the enemy. (*Repeat.*)

When Adam received of the food, as a transgressor was he driven from paradise. But Moses, purifying the pupils of his eyes with fasting, was made worthy to behold God. Wherefore, ye who long to dwell in paradise, come, let us keep far from unprofitable food; and ye who desire to see God, come, let us fast the four Mosaic tens. And by perseverance and sincerity in prayer we shall put down the passions of the soul and remove the wiles of the flesh, ascending lightly towards the celestial way, where the ranks of angels praise the indivisible Trinity with unceasing voices, to behold the transcending comeliness of the Master. Therefore, O life-giving Son of God, make us who trust in thee, worthy there to exchange glad tidings with the hosts of angels; by the intercessions of the passion of thy Mother, O Christ, and of the Apostles, Martyrs, and all the saints. (*Repeat.*)

Glory, in the Sixth Tone

THE time cometh which is the beginning of spiritual struggles and triumph over Satan. And the complete armour of abstinence is the beauty of the angels and in favour with God; for thereby Moses communed with God, and received in an invisible manner a voice in his ear. Wherefore, O Lord, prepare us thereby to worship thy holy Passion and Resurrection, since thou art the Lover of mankind.

Now: Thou hast transcended, etc. (p. 117).

3. THE MASS

❧*After the Eisodos, the following Kontakion, in the Sixth Tone.*

O THOU who guidest to wisdom, and givest understanding and intelligence, the Instructor of the ignorant, and Helper of the poor, strengthen my heart and grant it understanding, O Master. Give me word,

O Word of the Father; for behold, I shall not refrain my lips from crying to thee, O merciful One, have mercy upon me who am fallen.

The Epistle: Prokeimenon, in the Third Tone

Sing praises to our God, sing ye: sing praises to our king, sing ye.
O clap your hands, all ye nations.

Section from the Epistle of St. Paul to the Romans (13:11 to end; 14:1-4)

YE brethren: Now our salvation is nearer than when we believed.

The night is far spent, the day is at hand: Let us therefore cast off the works of darkness, and let us put on the armour of light.

Let us walk honestly, as in the day; not in rioting and drunkenness, not in chambering and wantonness, not in strife and envying:

But put ye on the Lord Jesus Christ, and make not provision for the flesh, to fulfil the lusts thereof.

Him that is weak in the faith receive ye, but not to doubtful disputations.

For one believeth that he may eat all things: another, who is weak, eateth herbs.

Let not him that eateth despise him that eateth not; and let not him which eateth not judge him that eateth: for God hath received him.

Who art thou that judgest another man's servant? to his own master he standeth or falleth. Yea, he shall be holden up: for God is able to make him stand.

The Gospel: from St. Matthew (6:14-21)

THE Lord saith: If ye forgive men their trespasses, your heavenly Father will also forgive you;

But if ye forgive not men their trespasses, neither will your Father forgive your trespasses.

Moreover when ye fast, be not, as the hypocrites, of a sad countenance: for they disfigure their faces, that they may appear unto men to fast. Verily I say unto you, They have their reward.

But thou, when thou fastest, anoint thine head, and wash thy face;

That thou appear not unto men to fast, but unto thy Father which is in secret: and thy Father which seeth in secret shall reward thee openly.

Lay not up for yourselves treasures upon earth, where moth and rust doth corrupt, and where thieves break through and steal:

But lay up for yourselves treasures in heaven, where neither moth nor rust doth corrupt, and where thieves do not break through nor steal:

For where your treasure is, there will your heart be also.

SYNAXARION

ON THIS DAY WE COMMEMORATE THE EXPULSION OF ADAM OF THE FIRST CREATION FROM THE PARADISE OF BLISS.

STICHOS

LET THE WORLD MOURN WITH THE LEADERS OF THE HUMAN RACE AND LET IT BITTERLY BEWAIL:

FOR HAVING FALLEN THROUGH THE SWEET REPAST, THE HUMAN RACE FELL STUMBLING WITH THEM.

THE divine Fathers set the anniversary of the exile of Adam from the paradise of bliss on this day, at the entrance of the holy Quadragesima fast, to show us by deed as well as word how great is the benefit that accrues to man from fasting; and, on the contrary, how great the harm that comes from destructive gluttony and from disobediece to the divine commandments. They also wished to explain to us that the first commandment given men was the commandment of fasting, which, since our first created ancestors disobeyed, not only did they not become gods, as they had imagined they would, but lost the life of happiness and bliss which they enjoyed, falling into the pit of corruption and death, and transmitting these to the whole human race, along with all the many iniquities and tribulations that followed therefrom. The divine Fathers thought to place all these things before our eyes, that, seeing them, and remembering the cause of our fall, and what befell us because of the gluttony of our first two ancestors, and their disobedience, we might strive to return to that ancient glory and primeval happiness by means of fasting and obedience to all the divine commandments.

Wherefore, through thine ineffable compassion, O Christ our Lord, make us worthy of the paradise of bliss, and have mercy upon us, O thou who art alone the Lover of mankind. Amen.

Koinonikon: Praise ye the Lord from the heavens, etc.

Sunday Evening of Cheese Fare[1]

❡ *On* O Lord, to thee have I cried, *etc., the following Prosomia for the Triodion, in the Second Tone.*

L ET us all hasten to the subjugation of the flesh by abstinence, as we approach the divine battle-field, the battle-field of blameless fasting. Let us pray the Lord, our Saviour, in tears and prayers, turning away completely from sin, and crying, We have sinned against thee, O Christ the King. Save us, therefore, as of old thou didst save the people of Ninevah; and make us partakers of thy heavenly kingdom, O compassionate One.

If I were to imagine all my sins deserving all punishment, I would despair of myself, O Lord Saviour; for by them have I disobeyed thy noble commandment, wasting my life in extravagance. Wherefore, I be-

---

1 The Order of the Vesper services for the Sunday Evening of Cheese Fare, is observed complete on every Sunday evening during Lent.

seech thee to purify me with thy showers of forgiveness, and lighten me with fasting and supplication; for
thou alone art compassionate; and reject me not, O all-
bountiful and of transcendent goodness.

Let us begin the season of fasting with rejoicing,
giving ourselves to spiritual strife, purifying soul and
body, fasting from passions, as we fast from foods, far-
ing on the virtues of the Spirit, which, if we continue
to long for, we shall all be worthy to behold the most
solemn Passion of Christ, and the holy passover, rejoicing with spiritual joy.

¶ *Glory and Now to our Lady; and after* O *resplendent Light, etc.,
the following Prokeimenon, in the Eighth Tone.*

Turn not away thy face from thy servant; for I am
in trouble: hear me speedily. Attend to my soul, and
deliver it.
Stichos: Thy salvation, O God, hath set me up. The
poor see and rejoice.

¶ *And in the Aposticha, the following Idiomelons, in the Fourth
Tone.*

THY grace hath risen, O Lord, the illumination of
our souls hath shone forth. Lo, now is the acceptable time; the season of repentance hath come. Let us
cast down the works of darkness, and put on the works
of light, that we may pass the great tempest of fasting
and reach the summit of the third-day Resurrection of
our Lord and Saviour Jesus Christ, the Saviour of our
souls. (*Repeat.*)

O Christ God, glorified in the mention of thy saints,
send us, through their beseechings, the Great Mercy.

Glory and Now, in the Fourth Tone

THE ranks of angels praise thee, O most holy Theotokos; for thou didst bear God who for ever is with
the Father and the Holy Spirit, by whose will the ranks
of angels arose from nothing. Wherefore, beseech him

to save and lighten the souls of those who praise thee in Orthodoxy, O most pure one.

¶ *And after,* Holy God, *the following Troparia.*

REJOICE, O virgin Theotokos, Mary full of grace; the Lord is with thee. Blessed art thou among women, and blessed the fruit of thy womb; for thou didst give birth to the Saviour of our souls.

O Baptizer of Christ, remember our congregation, that we may escape from our iniquities; for to thee was given grace to intercede for us.

Glory: O pure Apostles, and all ye saints, pray for our sakes, that we escape tribulations and sorrows; for we have taken you as fervid intercessors with the Saviour.

Now: We have taken refuge under the wing of thy compassion, O Theotokos. Turn not away from our beseechings in tribulation, but save us from distress, O thou who alone art pure and blessed.

¶ *And after* Lord, have mercy *(forty times), the Priest saith:*

Christ our God who remaineth blessed always, now and for ever, and unto the ages of ages.

Lector. O heavenly King, support our believing kings; confirm their faith; guide the nations; give peace to the world; and preserve well this holy church. Grant repose to our departed fathers and brothers, in the dwelling-places of the righteous. Receive us in repentance and confession; for thou art good and the Lover of mankind.

¶ *Then make the three great reverences, responding to each with a part of the following prayer of St. Iphram the Syrian.*

O LORD and Master of my life, deliver me from the spirit of indolence, meddling, ambition, and vain talk.

But bestow thou upon me thy servant the spirit of chastity, meekness of mind, patience, and love.

Yea, King and God, grant that I may know my sins and my faults, and not judge my brother; for thou art blessed for ever. Amen.

❧ *Then the Choir singeth the following Troparion, in the Second Tone.*

O RIGHTEOUS one, Mother of the most high God, defend all those who take refuge in faith in thy precious protection; for we sinners, bowed by the multitude of sins, have no other constant intercessor with God in tribulations and sorrows, save thee. Wherefore, we bow to thee, adoring. Save thou thy servants from every distress.

Then: Through the prayers of our Fathers the saints, O Lord Jesus Christ our God, have mercy upon us.
Choir. Amen.

II. THE HOLY QUADRAGESIMA, OR LENTEN FAST[1]

[FROM MONDAY AFTER THE SUNDAY OF CHEESE FARE TO THE EVENING OF PALM-SUNDAY]

❧ *Special services are held during this Holy Fast, namely: (1) Great Compline (or Slumber Prayer); (2) the Mass of the Presanctified Gifts; (3) the Great Canon; and (4) the Praise of the Akathiston (in which it is not permissible to sit). The Grand Canon (abbreviated), and the Praise of the Akathiston (in full) will be given in their proper places, the first on Wednesday evening of the Fifth Week, and the latter on Friday evening of the same Week. Great Compline and the Mass of the Presantified Gifts are given below.*

GREAT COMPLINE

❧ *Great Compline is recited during the period of the Great Fast, on the evening of Monday, Tuesday, Wednesday, and Thursday, until Great Tuesday.*

---

[1] The period of this Fast is exactly forty days from the Monday after Cheese Fare to the Friday preceding Lazarus Saturday. The last week, however, which is called Passion Week, is a special Fast to the honour of the Passion of our Lord and God Jesus Christ.

❡ *After* Blessed be God, *etc;* O heavenly King, *etc;* Holy God, *etc;*
Lord, have mercy *(two times); and* O come, let us worship, *etc.*
(three times with three reverences) begin thus:

PSALM 4

When I called upon him, etc. (p. 68).

PSALM 6

O Lord, rebuke me not in thy indignation, etc. (p.
69).

PSALM 12

HOW long wilt thou forget me, O Lord? for ever?
how long wilt thou hide thy face from me?

How long shall I take counsel in my soul, having
sorrow in my heart daily? how long shall mine enemy
be exalted over me?

Consider and hear me, O Lord my God: lighten mine
eyes, lest I sleep the sleep of death;

Lest mine enemy say, I have prevailed against him;
and those that trouble me rejoice when I am moved.

But I have trusted in thy mercy; my heart shall rejoice in thy salvation.

I will sing unto the Lord, because he hath dealt
bountifully with me.

Consider and hear me, O Lord my God: lighten
mine eyes, lest I sleep the sleep of death;

Lest mine enemy say, I have prevailed against him.

❡ *Glory and Now:* Alleluia *(three times); (three reverences);*
Lord, have mercy, *etc. (three times); and Glory and Now.*

PSALM 24

UNTO thee, O Lord, do I lift up my soul.
O my God, I trust in thee: let me not be ashamed,
let not mine enemies triumph over me.

Yea, let none that wait on thee be ashamed which
transgress without cause.

Show me thy ways, O Lord; teach me thy paths.

Lead me in thy truth, and teach me: for thou art the God of my salvation; on thee do I wait all the day.

Remember, O Lord, thy tender mercies and thy lovingkindnesses; for they have been ever of old.

Remember not the sins of my youth, nor my transgressions: according to thy mercy remember thou me for thy goodness' sake, O Lord.

Good and upright is the Lord: therefore will he teach sinners in the way.

The meek will he guide in judgment: and the meek will he teach his way.

All the paths of the Lord are mercy and truth unto such as keep his covenant and his testimonies.

For thy name's sake, O Lord, pardon mine iniquity; for it is great.

What man is he that feareth the Lord? him shall he teach in the way that he shall choose.

His soul shall dwell at ease; and his seed shall inherit the earth.

The secret of the Lord is with them that fear him; and he will show them his covenant.

Mine eyes are ever toward the Lord; for he shall pluck my feet out of the net.

Turn thee unto me, and have mercy upon me; for I am desolate and afflicted.

The troubles of my heart are enlarged: O bring thou me out of my distresses.

Look upon mine affliction and my pain; and forgive all my sins.

Consider mine enemies; for they are many; and they hate me with cruel hatred.

O keep my soul, and deliver me: let me not be ashamed; for I put my trust in thee.

Let integrity and uprightness preserve me; for I wait on thee.

Redeem Israel, O God, out of all his troubles.

PSALM 30

IN thee, O Lord, do I put my trust; let me never be ashamed: deliver me in thy righteousness.

Bow down thine ear to me; deliver me speedily: be thou my strong rock, for a house of defense to save me.

For thou art my rock and my fortress; therefore for thy name's sake lead me, and guide me.

Pull me out of the net that they have laid privily for me: for thou art my strength.

Into thine hand I commit my spirit: thou hast redeemed me, O Lord God of truth.

I have hated them that regard lying vanities: but I trust in the Lord.

I will be glad and rejoice in thy mercy: for thou hast considered my trouble; for thou hast known my soul in adversities;

And hast not shut me up into the hand of the enemy: thou hast set my feet in a large room.

Have mercy upon me, O Lord, for I am in trouble: mine eye is consumed with grief, yea, my soul and my belly.

For my life is spent with grief, and my years with sighing: my strength faileth because of mine iniquity, and my bones are consumed.

I was a reproach among all mine enemies, but especially among my neighbors, and a fear to mine acquaintance: they that did see me without, fled from me.

I am forgotten as a dead man out of mind: I am like a broken vessel.

For I have heard the slander of many: fear was on every side: while they took counsel together against me, they devised to take away my life.

But I trusted in thee, O Lord: I said, Thou art my God.

My times are in thy hand: deliver me from the hand of mine enemies, and from them that persecute me.

Make thy face to shine upon thy servant: save me for thy mercies' sake.

Let me not be ashamed, O Lord; for I have called upon thee: let the wicked be ashamed, and let them be silent in the grave.

Let the lying lips be put to silence; which speak grievous things proudly and contemptuously against the righteous.

Oh how great is thy goodness, which thou hast laid up for them that fear thee; which thou hast wrought for them that trust in thee before the sons of men!

Thou shalt hide them in the secret of thy presence from the pride of man: thou shalt keep them secretly in a pavilion from the strife of tongues.

Blessed be the Lord: for he hath showed me his marvelous kindness in a strong city.

For I said in my haste, I am cut off from before thine eyes: nevertheless thou heardest the voice of my supplications when I cried unto thee.

O love the Lord, all ye his saints: for the Lord preserveth the faithful, and plentifully rewardeth the proud doer.

Be of good courage, and he shall strengthen your heart, all ye that hope in the Lord.

PSALM 90

He that dwelleth in the aid of the Most High, etc. (p. 385).

¶ *Glory and Now;* Alleluia (*three times*); Lord, have mercy, (*three times*); *Glory and Now. Then the following Stichoi are sung alternately by both choirs, slowly and loudly, repeating at the end of each Stichos,* For God is with us. *The Right Choir starts this.*

WITH us is God, understand ye nations and flee. For God is with us.

Hear ye to the uttermost ends of the earth. For God is with us.

Ye mighty ones, be overthrown. For God is with us.

For even if ye rise again ye shall be overthrown. For God is with us.

And every counsel ye take, the Lord shall destroy. For God is with us.

And every word ye utter shall not abide in you. For God is with us.

For your terror we shall not fear, nor be moved thereby. For God is with us.

And the Lord our God, him we will sanctify; and he shall be our Fear. For God is with us.

And as I put my trust in him, he shall be my Sanctification. For God is with us.

On him I will set my hope, and by him shall I be saved. For God is with us.

Lo, I and the children whom God hath given me. For God is with us.

The people that walk in darkness, have seen a great light. For God is with us.

And ye that dwell in the land of the shadow of death, on you shall light shine. For God is with us.

For unto us a Son is born, unto us a child is given. For God is with us.

And the government shall be upon his shoulders. For God is with us.

And of his peace there shall be no end. For God is with us.

And his name shall be the Messenger of the Great Opinion. For God is with us.

Wonderful, Counsellor. For God is with us.

The Mighty God, Prince of peace. For God is with us.

The Father of the world to come. For God is with us.

Glory: For God is with us.

Now: For God is with us.

Then the Right Choir. God is with us, understand ye nations and flee.

Left Choir. For God is with us.

❡ *And immediately, the following Troparia.*

HAVING passed this day, I thank thee, Lord; and ask thee to grant me, Saviour, to spend this evening and the rest of the night without sin; and to save me.

Glory: Having passed this day, I glorify thee, Master; and ask thee, O Saviour, to grant me this evening and the rest of the night without doubts, and to save me.

Now: Having passed this day, I praise thee, holy One; and seek of thee, Saviour, to grant me to be unassailed this evening, and the rest of the night, and to save me.

❡ *Then the Choir sing alternately, the Left Choir beginning:*

THE incorporeal nature of the cherubim glorifieth thee in unsilenced praise.

And the seraphim, those six-winged beasts, exalt thee in unceasing voices.

And all the hosts of angels praise thee with thrice-holy Alleluia.

For before all thou art still, O Father; and hast with thee thy Son, who, like thee, is without beginning.

And as thou bearest the Spirit of life, equal to thee in honour, thou dost make manifest the indivisible Trinity.

O Virgin, the most holy Theotokos; and ye eye-witnesses of the Word and his ministers,

O all ye ranks of the Prophets and Martyrs, since yours is the life immortal,

Intercede ceaselessly for all; for we are all in distress,

That, escaping the error of the evil one, we may cry unto thee with the praises of the angels, saying,

Holy! Holy! Holy! O thrice-sanctified Lord. Have mercy upon us and save us. Amen.

❡ *Then immediately in hushed voice;* I believe in One God, *etc.* (p. 85); *and the following Stichoi, the first of which is sung three times and the rest twice, except the last one which is sung only once, the Left Choir beginning.*

O LADY, most holy Theotokos, intercede for us sinners.

O all ye powers of the heavenly angels, and holy archangels, intercede for us sinners.

O John, the holy Prophet, the Forerunner and Baptizer of our Lord Jesus Christ, intercede for us sinners.

O honoured saints, Apostles, Prophets, Martyrs, and all saints, intercede for us sinners.

O righteous Fathers, God-mantled shepherds and teachers of the universe, intercede for us sinners.

O divine, life-giving, unconquerable, and incomprehensible power of the Cross, forsake not us sinners.

O God, forgive us sinners, and have mercy upon us.

❡ *Then* Holy God, *etc; and the following Troparia, in the Second Tone.*

LIGHTEN mine eyes, O Christ God, lest I sleep unto death; lest my enemy say, I have prevailed over him.

Glory: O God, be a Defender of my soul; for I walk in the midst of many snares. Rescue me therefrom and save me, O good One, since thou art the Lover of mankind.

Now: For verily, we have no favour, for the multitude of our sins. Therefore, O virgin Theotokos, plead thou with him that was born of thee; for the pleadings of the Mother are indeed effective in seeking the favour of the Master. Turn thou not away therefore from the pleadings of sinners, O most venerable one; for he who was willing to suffer for our sins is merciful and able to save us.

Other Troparia chanted from day to day, in the Eighth Tone

THOU knowest, O my Lord, the wakefulness of mine invisible enemies; and the weakness of my wretched body thou hast learned, O my Creator. Wherefore, I entrust my soul to thy hands. Cover me with the wings of thy goodness, lest I sleep unto death. Lighten my inner eyes with the delight of thy divine sayings, and wake me at a time proper for thy glorification, since thou art good and the Lover of mankind.

Stichos: Look thou upon me and have mercy on me.

Thy judgment, O Lord, is verily terrible, when the angels shall be standing, men assembled, the books opened, works uncovered, and thoughts searched. What judgment then will be mine, who am enmeshed in sins? Who shall extinguish the flames of fire for me? Who shall lighten my darkness if thou have not mercy upon me, O Lord, since thou art the Lover of mankind?

Glory: Give me tears, O God, as thou gavest the sinful woman of old. Make me always worthy to wash thy feet which delivered me from the way of error, to offer thee fragrant ointment, a pure life bought with repentance, that I, too, may hear thy good voice, Thy faith hath saved thee. Depart in peace.

Now: Having possessed, O Theotokos, unforsaking confidence in thee, whereby I am saved; and having attained thy help, O most pure one, whence I fear not, I shall pursue mine enemies and drive them away, taking along thy refuge as a breastplate, and crying to thy all-powerful help. Save me, therefore, O Lady, by thine intercession, and wake me from dark sleep to thy glorification; by the might of the Son of God, incarnate of thee.

❡ *Then,* Lord, have mercy *(forty times); Glory and Now,* O thou who art more honourable, *etc; and the Priest saith:* Through the prayers of our Fathers, *etc; and the following Prayer.*

By Basil the Great

LORD, Lord, who hast delivered us from every arrow that flieth by day, save us from every creature that walketh in darkness, and accept the lifting up of our hands as an evening offering. Prepare us to pass the span of night blameless and untempted by evils. Deliver us from every trouble and dismay that cometh to us from Satans. Grant our souls reverence, and our minds diligence to search thy just and terrible judgment. Pierce our bodies with fear, and mortify our members that are on earth that in the stillness of the night me may be lighted by the contemplation of thy precepts. Drive from us every evil imagination and harmful passion, and raise us in time of prayer, established in the Faith and prospering in thy commandments, by the pleasure and goodness of thine only Son, who art blessed with him, and with thy good and most Holy Spirit, the Life-giver, now and always, and unto ages of ages. Amen.

❡ *Then,* O come, let us worship, *etc.* (*three times with three reverences*).

PSALM 50

Have mercy upon me, O God, etc. (p. 82).

PSALM 101

HEAR my prayer, O Lord, and let my cry come unto thee.

Hide not thy face from me in the day when I am in trouble; incline thine ear unto me: in the day when I call answer me speedily.

For my days are consumed like smoke, and my bones are burned as a hearth.

My heart is smitten, and withered like grass; so that I forget to eat my bread.

By reason of the voice of my groaning my bones cleave to my skin.

I am like a pelican of the wilderness: I am like an owl of the desert.

I watch, and am as a sparrow alone upon the housetop.

Mine enemies reproach me all the day; and they that are mad against me are sworn against me.

For I have eaten ashes like bread, and mingled my drink with weeping,

Because of thine indignation and thy wrath: for thou hast lifted me up, and cast me down.

My days are like a shadow that declineth; and I am withered like grass.

But thou, O Lord, shalt endure for ever; and thy remembrance unto all generations.

Thou shalt arise, and have mercy upon Zion: for the time to favour her, yea, the set time, is come.

For thy servants take pleasure in her stones, and favour the dust thereof.

So the heathen shall fear the name of the Lord, and all the kings of the earth thy glory.

When the Lord shall build up Zion, he shall appear in his glory.

He will regard the prayer of the destitute, and not despise their prayer.

This shall be written for the generation to come: and the people which shall be created shall praise the Lord.

For he hath looked down from the height of his sanctuary; from heaven did the Lord behold the earth;

To hear the groaning of the prisoner; to loose those that are appointed to death;

To declare the name of the Lord in Zion, and his praise in Jerusalem;

When the people are gathered together, and the kingdoms, to serve the Lord.

He weakened my strength in the way; he shortened my days.

I said, O my God, take me not away in the midst of my days: thy years are throughout all generations.

Of old hast thou laid the foundation of the earth: and the heavens are the work of thy hands.

They shall perish, but thou shalt endure: yea, all of them shall wax old like a garment; as a vesture shalt thou change them, and they shall be changed:

But thou art the same, and thy years shall have no end.

The children of thy servants shall continue, and their seed shall be established before thee.

The Prayer of Manasseh, King of Judah

O MIGHTY Lord, thou God of our fathers, of Abraham, Isaac, Jacob, and of their righteous seed; who hast made heaven and earth with all the array thereof; who hast bound the sea by the word of thy command; who hast shut up the deep and sealed it by thy terrible and glorious Name; whom all things fear, yea and before whose power they tremble; for the majesty of thy glory cannot be borne and the anger of thy threatening toward sinners is intolerable; and yet thy merciful promise is immeasurable and unsearchable; for thou art the Lord most high, of great compassion, long-suffering, abundant in mercy, and repentest of the evils against me.

Thou, O Lord, according to thy great goodness, hast promised repentance and forgiveness to them that have sinned against thee; and of thine infinite mercies hast appointed repentance unto sinners, that they may be saved.

Thou, therefore, O Lord of hosts, hast not appointed repentance to the just, to Abraham, to Isaac, and to Jacob, who have not sinned against thee; but thou hast appointed repentance unto me who am a sinner; for my sins are more in number than the sands of the sea. My transgressions, O Lord, are multiplied, my transgressions are multiplied, and I am not worthy to behold and look unto the height of heaven for the multitude of mine iniquities.

I am bowed down with many iron bands, so that I cannot lift up my head by reason of my sins, neither have I any respite; for I have provoked thy wrath and done that which is evil before thee; I did not thy will, neither kept I thy commandments; I have set up abominations and multiplied detestable things.

Now, therefore, I bow the knee of my heart, beseeching thee for grace. I have sinned, O Lord, I have sinned, and I acknowledge mine iniquities: but I humbly beseech thee, forgive me, O Lord, forgive me, and destroy me not with mine iniquities. Be not angry with me for ever, by reserving my evils for me; neither condemn me to the lower parts of the earth; for thou, O Lord, art the God of them that repent; and in me wilt thou show all thy goodness; for thou will save me that am unworthy, according to thy great mercy. And I will praise thee henceforth all the days of my life; for all the host of heaven doth sing thy praise, and thine is the glory for ever and ever. Amen.

❡ *Then.* O Holy God, *etc; and the following Troparia, in the Sixth Tone.*

HAVE mercy upon us, O Lord, have mercy upon us; for, destitute of all defence, we sinners offer unto thee, O Master, this supplication, Have mercy upon us.

Glory: Have mercy upon us, O Lord; for in thee have we put our trust. Be not exceedingly wroth with us, nor remember our iniquities; but look upon us now again; for thou art compassionate, and deliver us from our enemies; for thou art our God and we are thy people. We are all the work of thy hands, and we have called upon thy Name.

Now: Open unto us the door of compassion, O blessed Theotokos, that as we hope in thee we may not fail in our petitions. May we be delivered, through thee, from all adversities; for through thee hath come the salvation of the Christian race.

❡ *Then,* Lord, have mercy *(forty times); Glory and Now,* O thou who art more honourable, *and the following Prayer of St. Mardarius.*[1]

O ALMIGHTY Master, God, Father, and the Lord, thine only Son Jesus Christ, and the Holy Spirit, one Godhead and one Power, have mercy upon me a sinner; and by judgments known to thee save me, thine unworthy servant; for thou art blessed unto ages of ages. Amen.

---

[1] If it is the first week of the Great Fast, then here, after the Little Doxology, is sung the Great Canon (which see on the Thursday of the Fifth Week.)

¶ *Then,* O come, let us worship, *etc.* (*three times with three reverences*).

PSALM 69

O God, come to my assistance, O Lord, etc. (p. 83).

PSALM 142

Hear, O Lord, my prayer, etc. (p. 83).
Glory to God in the highest, etc. (p. 84).

¶ *Then* Holy God *and what followeth; and the following Troparion with its Stichoi, in the Sixth Tone.*

O LORD of hosts, be with us; for we have none other help in times of sorrow but thee.   O Lord of hosts, have mercy upon us.

Praise ye the Lord, in his sanctuary.   Praise ye him in the firmament of his power.

Praise ye him for his mighty acts.   Praise ye him. according to the multitude of his greatness.

Praise him with sound of trumpet.   Praise him with psaltery and harp.

Praise him with timbrel and choir.   Praise him with strings and organs.

Praise him with high-sounding cymbals.   Praise him on cymbals of joy.   Let everything which hath breath, praise the Lord.

Then the Right Choir.   Praise ye the Lord in his sanctuary.

Left Choir.   Praise ye him in the firmament of his power.

Then both Choirs together.   O Lord of hosts, be with us, etc.

Glory: Were not thy saints our intercessors, O Lord, and thy goodness pitying us, how could we have dared to praise thee, O Saviour, whom the angels bless ceaselessly?   Wherefore, O thou who knowest the secret things of the heart, pity our souls.

Now: Greatly have mine iniquities multiplied, O Theotokos. Wherefore, I take refuge in thee, O pure one, seeking salvation. Visit my weak soul, and intercede with thy Son our God to give me forgiveness of the sins I have committed, O thou who alone art blessed.

O all-holy Theotokos, forsake me not in the years of my life, O intercessor for mankind; but help me and have mercy upon me.

All my hope I place in thee, O Theotokos; keep me under the wings of thy care.

¶ Then, Lord, have mercy *(forty times);* O Christ our God, who art worshipped, *etc. (p. 60);* Lord, have mercy *(three times); Glory and Now,* O thou who art more honourable, *etc; and* Bless, O Father, in the Name of the Lord.

Priest: God be merciful unto us and bless us, and cause his face to shine upon us, and be merciful unto us.

¶ Then we make three reverences, saying at each reverence part of the Prayer, O Lord and Master of my life, *etc. (p. 645); then twelve little reverences, and one great, with the last part of the Prayer. Then,* Holy God, *etc;* Lord, have mercy *(twelve times). Then all the prayers at the end of Little Compline, starting with,* O spotless, undefiled, unstained, *etc. (pp. 88-89). Then Glory and Now; and* Lord, have mercy *(three times); and the Priest saith:* Peace be unto you all. Bow your heads unto the Lord. *And as the congregation bow, the Priest immediately saith:*

O most merciful Master, etc. (p. 80).

¶And immediately the following Petitions.

For the peace of the world; let us pray, *and what followeth* (pp. 108-109).

¶ Then the following Prayer.

FORGIVE, Lord, those who hate us and those who oppress us. Act kindly toward those who themselves act kindly, and grant our brethren and all those who belong to us all the means of salvation and of eternal life. Visit those who are in sickness, and grant them healing. Direct those who are at sea; be with those who are on land; and assist our kings in war. Grant those who serve us and are merciful to us forgiveness of sins; and upon those who have asked us to pray for them, have mercy according to thy great mercy. Remember, Lord, those of our fathers and brothers who have preceded us in slumber. Grant them repose where the light of thy countenance shineth. Remember, Lord, those who offer fruits and perform deeds of kindness in thy holy churches, and grant them all the means of salvation and of eternal life. Remember us also, thy sinful, wretched and unworthy servants, and lead us in the way of thy commandments, by the intercessions of thy most holy Mother, our ever-virgin Lady, the Theotokos Mary, and of all thy saints; for thou art blessed unto the ages of ages. Amen.

¶ *Then as all kiss the hand of the Priest, the Choir singeth on Monday and Wednesday evenings the following Troparion, in the Second Tone.*

O righteous One, etc. (p. 646).

¶ *And on the evening of Tuesday and Thursday the Stauro-Theotokion, in the First Tone.*

WHEN the Virgin beheld thee unjustly sacrificed, O Christ, she wailed, crying unto thee, My most sweet child, how didst thou so unjustly? And how wast thou suspended on a Tree, O thou who didst suspend the whole earth on the waters? Wherefore, I beg thee not to leave me alone, thy Mother and servant, O most merciful Benefactor.

Priest. Through the prayers of our Fathers the saints, O Lord Jesus Christ our God, have mercy upon us. Amen.

ORDER OF THE LITURGY OF THE PROEGIASMENA GIFTS (PRESANCTIFIED GIFTS)

¶ *On Wednesday and Friday mornings of each week of the Great Fast; on Thursday of the Great Canon; and on Monday, Tuesday, and Wednesday of Passion Week, and on any day on which falleth the memorial day of St. Charalampias, and the first and second Find-*

ings of the precious head of the Forerunner; and the Forty Martyr Saints, except Saturday and Sunday, celebrate the Liturgy of the Presanctified Gifts, i.e. the Divine Mass which has been already consecrated, according to the following Order.

❡ *After the Priest saith,* Blessed be the kingdom of the Father, *etc., and the recitation of the Sunset Psalm, recite the first three Kathismata from Friday Matins from Psalm 19 and those which follow,* In my trouble I cried to the Lord, *etc; and on* O Lord, to thee have I cried, *the Idiomelon of the day is sung twice, then the pieces of the Triodion or the Martyr pieces of the Tone, and for the Saint whose Feast is celebrated, if any. Glory for the Saint, and Now for our Lady. Then the Eisodos, and* O resplendent Light, *etc; the Prokeimenon; and the First Reading (from Genesis). And at its conclusion the Reader turneth to the Priest in the Temple and saith,* Command, O master. *At this the Royal Door is opened and the Priest cometh out holding candle and censer, and crieth out:*

Wisdom! Let us stand. The light of Christ shineth for all.

❡ *Then the Second Reading (from the Proverbs of Solomon) is read, and at its conclusion is sung,* Let my prayer be set forth, *etc., with its Stichoi, as followeth.*

L ET my prayer be set forth in thy sight as incense. And let the lifting up of my hands be an evening sacrifice.

Right. O Lord, to thee have I cried, hear me. Let my prayer be set forth, etc.

Left. Set a watch, O Lord, before my mouth, and a door round about my lips. Let my prayer be set forth, etc.

Incline not my heart to evil words, to make excuses for sins. Let my prayer be set forth, etc.

Glory and Now: Let my prayer be set forth, etc.

❡ *Then repeat;* Let my prayer be set forth, *etc; and at its end the Deacon saith,* Let us all say with all our soul, *etc. (p. 75); as well as the Petitions of the Catechumens, as in the service of the Divine Liturgy (p. 127). And from Wednesday of the middle of the Fast, after the Priest saith,* That they also with us, may glorify, *etc. (p. 127) are said the Petitions of the Catechumens, with the following additions.*

Deacon. All ye Catechumens, depart! Ye Catechumens depart: All ye that approach for illumination, depart! Ye that come for illumination, pray, let us pray to the Lord.

O believers, for the sake of the brethren, ready for the holy illumination, and for their salvation, let us pray to the Lord.

That the Lord confirm them and strengthen them, let us pray to the Lord.

Enlighten them with the light of knowledge and true worship, let us pray to the Lord.

And prepare them at the proper time for the bath of rebirth, the forgiveness of sins, and the robe of incorruptibility, let us pray to the Lord.

To renew their birth by water and the Spirit, let us pray to the Lord.

To grant them the perfection of faith, let us pray to the Lord.

To number them in his holy and chosen fold, let us pray to the Lord.

Save, have mercy, help, and keep, and have mercy upon him, O Lord, by thy grace.

O ye who come for illumination, bow your heads to the Lord.

Priest. For thou art our illumination, and to thee do we address glory, O Father, etc.

Deacon. All ye who approach for illumination, come out! All ye who approach for illumination, come out! All ye catechumens come out! Let no one of the catechumens remain. But all ye believers. Again and again in peace let us pray to the Lord.

Help, save, and have mercy, and keep us, O God by thy grace. Wisdom!

Priest. For all glory, honour, and worship are due to thee, O Father, etc.

Deacon. Again and again, in peace, let us pray to the Lord, Help, save, etc.

Priest. In accordance with the gift of thy Christ, with whom thou art blessed and with thy most holy and

life-giving Spirit, now and ever, and unto the ages of
ages.

❡ *Then the following Cherubicon is sung.*

BEHOLD now the heavenly powers serve with us in
an invisible manner; for behold the King of glory
passeth by. Behold the mystical Sacrifice goeth out in
perfect procession. Let us come forward in faith and
longing that we may become partakers of eternal life.
Alleluia.

❡ *And when the Choir cometh to the word* by, *the Priest, carrying
the Presanctified Gifts, issueth from the Left Door of the Temple
and entereth very slowly and silently through the Royal Door, as
the Choir concludeth the Cherubicon, after which:*

Deacon. Let us finish our petitions of the evening to
the Lord.

For these precious Offerings, which have been offered and presanctified, etc. (pp. 131-132).

❡ *And after the Priest saith,* By the grace, compassion, *etc. (p. 132),
the Deacon saith,* Let us hearken, *and the Priest saith:*

The holy Things presanctified are for the holy.

❡ *Then the following Koinonikon is sung.*

O taste and see that the Lord is good. Alleluia.

❡ *And after exposition of the holy Offerings, the Choir singeth in
the Second Tone:*

I will bless the Lord at all times; his praise shall be
always in my mouth. The heavenly bread and the cup
of life, taste ye and see ye that the Lord is good, Alleluia. Alleluia. Alleluia. Alleluia.

Deacon. Let us stand up! Having partaken, etc. (p.
133).

❡ *And after the Deacon has said,* Let us pray to the Lord, *the Priest,
standing outside the Royal Door, saith the following Prayer.*

ALMIGHTY God who in wisdom didst make all
creation; O thou who for thine ineffable providence and the greatness of thy goodness, didst bring

us these most solemn days, for the purification of our souls and bodies by abstinence from passion, and for hope of resurrection; O thou who didst give thy servant Moses the tablets written by thee, because of his forty days fast; grant us too, O good One, that we may fight the good fight, finish the course of the fast, and keep the Faith intact, bruising the heads of the invisible dragons, appearing victorious over sin, and arriving at the worship of the holy Resurrection without condemnation; for thy most honoured and exalted Name is blessed and glorified, O Father, Son, and Holy Spirit, now and ever, and unto the ages of ages.   Amen.

Then: Let the Name of the Lord be blessed, etc.

¶ *And the Benediction.*

ORDER OF THE PRAYER OF THE LAUDATIONS FOR THE THEOTOKOS

¶ *On Friday evening of the First Week, Little Compline is recited up to* It is truly meet, *etc. when the Canon of the Akathiston is sung,* Open my mouth, *etc. (complete). And at the end of the Ninth Ode of the Canon, the Choir singeth slowly the Kontakion,* Verily, I am thy servant, *etc., and the Priest, coming out of the Temple, standeth before the Icon of our Lady and reciteth the first six stanzas from the Laudation of the Akathiston. At the completion of the stanzas, the Choir repeateth the chanting of* Verily, I am thy servant, *etc. Then,* Holy God, *etc., and the rest of Little Compline (which see, complete, in service for Saturday of the Fifth Week).*

¶ *The same order is observed on Fridays of the Second, Third, and Fourth Weeks of the holy Quadragesima Fast, except that during the Second Week the Priest reciteth the next six stanzas of the Akathiston; during the Third Week, the six stanzas following these; during the Fourth Week, the last six stanzas; while during the Fifth Week, he repeateth the recitation of the whole twenty-four stanzas.*

THE FIRST SATURDAY OF THE GREAT FAST

On which is celebrated the Memorial of the Boiled Wheat Miracle which happened to the great among Martyrs, Theodore of Tyre.

Troparion, in the Second Tone

GREAT are the accomplishments of faith; for the martyred Saint Theodore rejoiced in the fount of flames as though in the waters of rest; for being burned by fire, he was offered as delicious bread to the Trinity. Wherefore, by his pleadings, O Christ God, save our souls.

Glory and Now to our Lady, in the Same Tone

Exceeding glorious beyond the power of thought, etc. (p. 147).

Kontakion, in the Eighth Tone

THOU didst take the faith of Christ to thy heart in place of a shield, treading down the power of the obstinate, O most striving one, and wast crowned with the heavenly crown for ever; for thou art unconquerable.

SYNAXARION

ON THIS DAY, THE SATURDAY OF THE FIRST WEEK OF THE GREAT FAST, WE CELEBRATE THE SPLENDID MIRACLE WHICH WAS PERFORMED BY THE GLORIOUS AMONG MARTYRS, THEODORE OF TYRE, THROUGH THE BOILED WHEAT.

STICHOS

BY THE EATING OF BOILED WHEAT THEODORE HAS ANNEXED THE CITY OF THE TYRIANS, ANNULING THE STRATAGEM OF THE UNCLEAN FOOD, AND VOIDING THE CUNNING OF THE HEATHEN.

IN which we fulfill the remembrance of the miracle of boiled wheat which the great among Martyrs, Theodore of Tyre worked.

Julian the Apostate, having learned that Christians usually purify themselves in the first week of the holy

Quadragesima, which, therefore, is called the Week of
the Purification (*Kathara*), wished to force them to
pollute themselves particularly during that week. Secretly he commanded that food made unclean with the
blood of sacrifices to idols be exposed everywhere in
the markets. However, Theodore the Martyr, following a revelation of God, appeared to Aphdoxius, Archbishop of Constantinople, and revealed to him the situation. He commanded him to call the faithful together at once on Monday morning and forbid them to
eat of those foods, commanding them to subsist instead
on boiled wheat which is easy to prepare. In this way
the despotic king's purpose was annulled, and the people of true worship were kept pure throughout the week
of purification. They raised thanks to the Martyr on
that day, celebrating his remembrance with boiled
wheat in that year, the 362nd of Christ. Afterwards
the Church decreed that remembrance of him be made
each year on the day corresponding to that day, in his
honour and for the glorification of God.

Wherefore, through his intercessions, O God, have
mercy upon us and save us. Amen.

❡ *The Feast of this saint falls on February seventeenth.*

THE FIRST SUNDAY OF THE FAST

*Which is known as the Sunday of Orthodoxy, for
thereon is celebrated the Memorial of the Holy Icons.*

1. VESPERS

❡ *On* O Lord, to thee have I cried, *six for the Resurrection; and
the following four for the Triodion, in the Sixth Tone.*

O LORD incomprehensible, and shining eternally
before the morning star, from the belly of the immaterial and incorporeal Father, the Prophets, inspired
by thy Spirit, foretold that thou shouldest become a
child incarnate from her who knoweth no wedlock, taking thy place among men, and visible to those who are

on earth. Wherefore, O compassionate One, by their pleadings make worthy of thine illumination us who praise thine ineffable and glorious Resurrection.

Verily, the God-proclaiming Prophets, when they preached thee by their words, and honoured thee by their deeds, bore the fruits of unending life; for, having refused adamantly to worship creation apart from thee, O Master and Creator, they renounced the world evangelically, emulating thy Passion which they had prophesied. Wherefore, by their pleadings prepare us to pass blamelessly over the battle-field of abstinence, O thou who alone art most merciful.

Though infinite in thy divine Nature, O Master, thou didst condescend to be incarnate in these last days, and become finite; for by putting on the body thou didst also put on all its properties. Wherefore, we draw the likeness of thine image and embrace it in consideration of its prototype, ascending towards thy love and drinking therefrom the grace of healing, following the divine traditions of the Apostles.

Verily, the Church of Christ hath taken on a most honoured adornment, the noble sanctified Icons pertaining to Christ the Saviour, the Theotokos, and all the saints, elevated in joy and gladness, wherein she rejoiceth in grace, refuting the crowds of heretics, glorifying with gladness her philanthropic God, who patiently bore his voluntary sufferings for her sake.

Glory, in the Second Tone

THE grace of truth hath shone, and the things which were fore-shadowed of old have now been fulfilled openly; for behold, the Church hath put on the incarnate likeness of Christ, a world-transcending adornment, in accordance with the foresign of the tabernacle of the Covenant, that, keeping the Icon of him whom we worship and revere, we may not go astray. Let those, therefore, who believe not thus be robed with confusion; for our kneeling in true worship (not deifying the

Icon) of the Incarnate is a glory to us. Let us, therefore, embrace it, O believers, crying, Save, O God, thy
people and bless thine inheritance.

❡*And Now to our Lady, in the Tone in use; the Aposticha for the
Resurrection; and Glory, in the Second Tone.*

O YE who have passed from evil doctrine to true
worship, who are illumined with the light of
knowledge, let us clap our hands, as in the Psalms, offering God grateful praise. Let us bow in adoration to the
Icon of Christ, the Icon of the most Pure, the pictures
of all the saints drawn on the walls, tablets, and holy
vessels, refuting the lie of the evil-opinioned; for the
adoration of the picture, Basil saith, is transmitted to
its prototype, imploring thee, O Christ God, by the
intercessions of thy pure Mother and all the saints, to
grant us the Great Mercy.

❡*And Now to our Lady, in the Second Tone; the Troparia for the
Resurrection; then for the Feast, in the Second Tone,* Thy
pure image do we adore, *etc. (p. 594).*

❡*Then the Theotokion, in the Second Tone; and the Benediction.*

2. MATINS

Katabasias, in the Fourth Tone

1. Old Israel having passed through the depth of
the Red Sea on unmoistened feet, defeated the power
of Amalek in the wilderness, by the hands of Moses
stretched in the form of a cross.

3. Thy Church, O Christ, rejoiceth in thee, crying
unto thee, Thou, Lord, art my strength, my stay, and
my refuge.

4. When the Church saw thee elevated on the Cross,
O Sun of justice, she stood in her array, shouting to
thee as is meet, Glory to thy power, O Lord.

5. Thou, my Lord, didst come as Light to the world,
a holy Light, turning those who praise thee away from
abysmal folly.

6. The Church haileth thee, O Lord, crying, I will sacrifice to thee with the voice of praise, purified from the vileness of Satan by the blood which dripped from thy side, because of thy compassion.

7. The Abrahamite youths in the furnace in the land of Persia burned with the fervour of true worship more than with the fire, crying, Blessed art thou in the temple of thy holiness, O Lord.

8. When Daniel stretched his hands in the pit, he closed the mouths of the devouring lions; and the youths, lovers of true worship, when they girded themselves with virtue, quenched the power of fire, crying, Bless the Lord, all ye his works.

9. An unhewn Stone, O Virgin, opposite thy mountain was cut, but not by hand, even Christ, who brought together the separated natures. Wherefore, we rejoice gladly, and glorify thee, O Theotokos.

❡ *Then the Exaposteilarions for the Resurrection; and the following for the Triodion.*

EXCHANGE glad tidings and clap your hands together, hailing one another joyfully and crying, How wonderful and how strange are thy works, O Christ. Who dare speak of thy great works, thou who didst accomplish our accord and unity in one Church.

Verily, the fierce spears of the heretics and the mention of them have been destroyed resoundingly; for seeing, O most pure One, thy temple adorned in splendour with the graces of venerable Icons, we are all filled with joy and gladness.

❡ *And in the Einos, five for the Resurrection; and the following three for the Triodion, in the Fourth Tone.*

THY Church, O Lover of mankind, rejoiceth in thee, O thou her Bridegroom and her Creator, who by thy will, as becoming God, didst rescue her from the worship of idols, and joined her to thee by thy precious blood, enjoying the elevation of the noble Icons. Wherefore, she praiseth thee in faith, glorifying thee in joy.

We hang the likeness of thy body and embrace it in consideration of its Source, making plain the mystery of thy dispensation, O Lord, Lover of mankind; for thou didst not appear unto us in delusion or imagination, as claim the followers of Mani, those contenders against God, but in truth and in nature of the body by which we ascend to thy divine longing and love.

Today hath appeared, a day full of joy, because the splendour of true doctrine shineth forth brilliantly, and the Church of Christ now sparkleth, adorned by the elevation of the Icons of the saints and their illustrating pictures, and believers attain there a unity rewarded of God.

Glory, in the Sixth Tone

MOSES received the law in a period of abstinence and led his people: and Elijah, when he fasted, closed the heavens. As for the Abrahamite youths, they vanquished by fasting the transgressing usurper. Wherefore, through the same, O Saviour, prepare us to meet thy Resurrection, shouting, Holy God! Holy Mighty! Holy Immortal One, have mercy upon us.

❡*And Now,* Thou hast transcended, *etc; the Great Doxology.*

3. THE MASS

❡*The Troparia for the Resurrection, the Sunday, and the Patron Saint of the church; then the Kontakion,* Verily, I am thy servant, *etc.*

The Epistle: Prokeimenon, in the Fourth Tone

Blessed art thou, O Lord, the God of our Fathers. *Stichos:* For thou art just in all that thou hast done to us.

Section from the Epistle of St. Paul to the Hebrews (11:24-26; 32 to end)

YE brethren: By faith Moses, when he was come to years, refused to be called the son of Pharaoh's daughter.

Choosing rather to suffer affliction with the people of God, than to enjoy the pleasures of sin for a season;

Esteeming the reproach of Christ greater riches than the treasures in Egypt: for he had respect unto the recompense of the reward.

And what shall I more say? for the time would fail me to tell of Gideon, and of Barak, and of Samson, and of Jephthæ; of David also, and Samuel, and of the prophets:

Who through faith subdued kingdoms, wrought righteousness, obtained promises, stopped the mouths of lions,

Quenched the violence of fire, escaped the edge of the sword, out of weakness were made strong, waxed valiant in fight, turned to flight the armies of the aliens.

Women received their dead raised to life again: and others were tortured, not accepting deliverance; that they might obtain a better resurrection:

And others had trial of cruel mockings and scourgings, yea, moreover of bonds and imprisonment:

They were stoned, they were sawn asunder, were tempted, were slain with the sword: they wandered about in sheepskins and goatskins; being destitute, afflicted, tormented;

(Of whom the world was not worthy:) they wandered in deserts, and in mountains, and in dens and caves of the earth.

And these all, having obtained a good report through faith, received not the promise:

God having provided some better thing for us, that they without us should not be made perfect.

The Gospel: from St. John (1:43 to end)

AT that time: Jesus went forth into Galilee, and findeth Philip, and saith unto him: Follow me.

Now Philip was of Bethsaida, the city of Andrew and Peter.

Philip findeth Nathanael, and saith unto him, We have found him, of whom Moses in the law, and the prophets, did write, Jesus of Nazareth, the son of Joseph.

And Nathanael said unto him, Can there any good thing come out of Nazareth? Philip saith unto him, Come and see.

Jesus saw Nathanael coming to him, and saith of him, Behold an Israelite indeed, in whom is no guile!

Nathanael saith unto him, Whence knowest thou me? Jesus answered and said unto him, Before that Philip called thee, when thou wast under the fig tree, I saw thee.

Nathanael answered and saith unto him, Rabbi, thou art the Son of God; thou art the King of Israel.

Jesus answered and said unto him, Because I said unto thee, I saw thee under the fig tree, believest thou? thou shalt see greater things than these.

And he saith unto him, Verily, verily, I say unto you, Hereafter ye shall see heaven open, and the angels of God ascending and descending upon the Son of man.

¶ *And the rest of the Liturgy of St. Basil the Great.*

Synaxarion

On This Day, the First Sunday of the Fast, We Commemorate the Hanging of the Venerable and Holy Icons; Which was Performed by the Ever-Memorable Kings of Constantinople, Michael and his Mother Theodora, in the Days of the Saint and Confessor Methodius.

Stichos

When i behold the Icons unseemly put away, i bow down, as it is meet to do, and rejoice.

On which we fulfill the remembrance of the hanging of the honoured icons.

THE persecution of the iconomachal kings of false worship, the first of whom was Leon Severus and the last of whom was Theophilus, the spouse of St. Theodora (*see February eleventh*) suppressed the Church of Christ and disturbed her rest for more than one hundred years. But Theodora, the queen of happy memory, after her husband's death, restored and established the Orthodox doctrine in the year 842; for she first kissed the Icon of the Theotokos before Patriarch Methodius (*see June fourteenth*) and many of the righteous people and confessors, calling out in a loud and clear voice, if any kneel not to them and kiss them anxiously in sign of veneration to their original elements (not the kneeling and kissing of worship, but considering them as icons representing their original elements, not as gods), then let him be anathema. Then she besought God asking of him forgiveness for her husband, praying and fasting continually for the whole first week of the Great Fast. Then on the following Sunday, having offered the prescribed prayers and petitions, along with her son, the Emperor Michael, and with all the clergy and the people, she hung the holy Icons, adorning therewith the Church of Christ as formerly. In remembrance, therefore, of this holy act, all we Orthodox celebrate this glorious and brilliant day as the Sunday of Orthodoxy.

Wherefore, O uncreated likeness of the Father, through the intercession of thy two confessing saints, have mercy upon us. Amen.

Koinonikon: Praise ye the Lord from heaven, etc.

THE EVENING OF THE FIRST SUNDAY OF THE FAST

❧*On* O Lord, to thee have I cried, *the following Prosomia, in the Fourth Tone.*

GRANT me reverence, estrangement from evil, and perfect discipline, who am now drowned in the passions of the flesh, estranged from thee, and entirely without hope, O my God, King of all. Save me, thy prodigal son, by the bounty of thy goodness, O Jesus the Almighty, the Saviour of our souls.

When Moses the wonderful was purified by fasting, he beheld the beloved One. Wherefore, emulate him, my humble soul, and hasten to be purified of evils on the day of abstinence, that the Lord may bestow forgiveness on thee, and that thou mayest behold him; for he is the Almighty, the good Lord, and the Lover of mankind.

Let us, O brethren, begin the second week of the Fast, fulfilling it day by day with rejoicing, making unto ourselves, like Elijah the Tishbite, a fiery chariot of the great cardinal virtues, elevating our minds by subduing our passions, arming ourselves with purity, to chase away and vanquish the enemy.

¶ *Glory and Now to our Lady; and after* O resplendent Light, *etc., the following Prokeimenon, in the Eighth Tone.*

Thou hast given an inheritance, O Lord, to them that fear thy Name.

Stichos: From the ends of the earth I cried unto thee. I shall be protected under the covert of thy wings.

¶ *In the Aposticha, the following Idiomelons, in the Eighth Tone.*

Come, let us purify our souls with alms and mercy to the poor, not blowing the trumpet, nor making public what we accomplish in charity, lest the left hand know what the right hand doeth, and vainglory do away with the fruit of alms. Let us, however, plead secretly with him who knoweth our secrets, crying, Father, forgive us our mistakes; for thou art the Lover of mankind. (*Repeat.*)

¶ *And the following Martyricon.*

EVERY place ye sanctify, O Martyrs of the Lord, and every sickness ye heal. Wherefore, now, intercede with him, asking him to deliver our souls from the traps and snares of the enemy.

Glory and Now, Theotokion, in the Same Tone

THE celestials do praise thee, O full of grace, the spouseless Mother. We glorify thine inapprehensible birth-giving. Wherefore, O Theotokos, intercede for the salvation of our souls.

❧ *The rest of the service as on the Evening of Cheese Fare Sunday (p. 645).*

THE SECOND SUNDAY OF THE FAST

Wherein is sung the Service of Saint Gregory Palamas, Bishop of Thessalonica.

1. VESPERS

❧ *On* O Lord, to thee have I cried, *the Stichera for the Resurrection.*

Glory, in the Sixth Tone

O THRICE-BLESSED, righteous, and most holy Father, the good shepherd and Disciple of Christ, the chief of shepherds, seek now, O thou who didst also give himself for the sheep, O God-mantled Father Gregory, that by thine intercessions we may be granted the Great Mercy.

❧ *The Aposticha for the Resurrection.*

Glory, in the Eighth Tone

THY tongue, awakened unto doctrines, hath sounded in the hearing of our hearts, rousing the souls of the tardy; and thy God-speaking words have become a ladder transporting those on earth to God. Wherefore, O Gregory, wonder of Thessalonica, cease not to intercede with Christ God to illuminate with his divine light those who honour thee.

Troparion to the Saint, in the Eighth Tone

O STAR of Orthodoxy, support of the Church and its teacher, O comeliness of ascetics, and incontestable champion of those who speak in theology, Gregory the wonder-worker, the pride of Thessalonica and preacher of grace, implore thou constantly for the salvation of our souls.

2. MATINS

¶ *Katabasias.* Open my mouth, *etc.* (*p. 114*); *and Exaposteilarion for the Resurrection; and the following for the Tridion.*

REJOICE, O pride of the Fathers and mouth-piece of those who speak in theology, O dwelling-place of calm and house of wisdom, leader of teachers, and sea of intellect. Rejoice, O instrument of work, O end of vision, and healer of human illness. Rejoice, O Father, treasure of the Spirit, alive and dead.

O Lady, queen of all, embrace us in our sorrows. Be present on the Last Day, the day of tribulation, lest Satan, hades, and destruction overrule us. Make us all stand upright before the terrible tribune of thy Son, without offense, by thine intercessions, O Lady Theotokos.

¶ *And in the Einos, five for the Resurrection; and three for the Triodion, in the First Tone.*

THOU didst live in the world a blessed life. Wherefore, thou dost rejoice now with the congregations of the blessed, and dwellest in the land of the meet, as one who is meek, O Bishop Gregory, enriched by God with the grace of miracles, which thou dost grant to those who honour thee.

Planting the doctrines of Orthodoxy, uprooting the thistles of wicked opinion, O blessed one, and growing well the plant of faith with the rain of thy sayings, thou didst offer to God, like a good farmer, ears a hundred fold.

The ranks of angels and assemblies of men wondered at the splendour of thy blameless life, O blessed one; for by thine own choice thou didst reveal thyself as a firm striver, an ascetic, a worthy Bishop, a deserving minister of God, and a chosen friend.

Glory, in the Sixth Tone

THOU didst shine forth, O Christ, a Light to those who dwell in the darkness of sin, in the season of abstinence. Show us, therefore, the glorious day of thy Passion, that we may cry to thee aloud, Arise, O God, and have mercy upon us.

Now: Thou hast transcended, etc.

3. THE MASS

❡ *Troparia for the Resurrection for Saint Gregory, and for the Patron Saint of the church; and the Kontakion,* Verily, I am thy servant, *etc.*

The Epistle: Prokeimenon, in the Fifth Tone

O Lord, thou wilt preserve us and keep us from this generation.

Stichos: Save me, O Lord; for the godly man ceaseth.

Section from the Epistle of St. Paul to the Hebrews (1:10 to end; 2:1-3)

Thou, in the beginning, O Lord, didst found the earth, etc. (p. 389).

The Gospel: from St. Mark (2:1-12)

AT that time: Jesus entered into Capernaum after some days; and it was noised that he was in the house.

And straightway many were gathered together, insomuch that there was no room to receive them, no, not so much as about the door: and he preached the word unto them.

And they come unto him, bringing one sick of the palsy, which was borne of four.

And when they could not come nigh unto him for the press, they uncovered the roof where he was: and when they had broken it up, they let down the bed wherein the sick of the palsy lay.

When Jesus saw their faith, he said unto the sick of the palsy, Son, thy sins be forgiven thee.

But there were certain of the scribes sitting there, and reasoning in their hearts,

Why doth this man thus speak blasphemies? who can forgive sins but God only?

And immediately when Jesus perceived in his spirit that they so reasoned within themselves, he said unto them, Why reason ye these things in your hearts?

Whether is it easier to say to the sick of the palsy, Thy sins be forgiven thee; or to say, Arise, and take up thy bed, and walk?

But that ye may know that the Son of man hath power on earth to forgive sins, (he saith to the sick of the palsy,)

I say unto thee, Arise, and take up thy bed, and go thy way into thine house.

And immediately he arose, took up the bed, and went forth before them all; insomuch that they were all amazed, and glorified God, saying, We never saw it on this fashion.

¶ *And the rest of the Liturgy of Basil the Great.*

SYNAXARION

ON THIS DAY, THE SECOND SUNDAY OF THE GREAT FAST, WE CELEBRATE THE MEMORY OF OUR HOLY FATHER ST. GREGORY, ARCHBISHOP OF THESSALONICA, WHO IS KNOWN AS PALAMAS.

STICHOS

VERILY, THE GREAT PREACHER OF THE WONDROUS AND BRILLIANT LIGHT HAS BEEN LED NOW BY THE FOUNT OF SPLENDOUR UNTO THE UNSETTING LIGHT.

ON his day we chant the service of our Father the glorious among saints, Gregory Palamas, the Archbishop of Thessalonica.

This divine Father was born in Asia and was brought up from infancy in the royal palace of Constantinople, where he acquired his religious and secular education. When he reached the age of youth he left the palace and gave himself up to asceticism in the holy mount of Athos and in the monastery that is in Berœa. Then he moved to the city of Thessalonica where he resided for a time seeking cure from the diseases that he contracted because of his asceticism and piety. He also attended the two Councils held in Constantinople, the one in 1341 against Barlaam the Calabrian and the other in 1347 against Acyndinus who held Barlaam's doctrine, striving valiantly and defending the Eastern Orthodox doctrines of Christ. In 1349 he was elevated to be Archbishop of Thessalonica, tending its people in an apostolic fashion for a period of thirteen years, resting in the Lord at the age of 63, having written several books. His venerable bones rest in the Archbishopric of Thessalonica to this day. As for the songs chanted in the service of his Feast, they were composed by Patriarch Philotheus in 1368, the year in which the celebration of his Feast was renewed on this day.

Wherefore, O God, by his intercessions have mercy upon us and save us. Amen.

Koinonikon: Praise ye the Lord from the heavens, etc.

Evening of the Second Sunday of the Fast

¶ *On* O Lord, to thee have I cried, *the following Prosomia, in the Eighth Tone.*

I HAVE committed against thee countless sins, and expect unnumbered punishments—the gnashing of teeth, inconsolable weeping, the fire of hell, the darkness and Tartarus. Wherefore, O righteous Judge, grant me tears wherewith I may find forgiveness of sins and delivery from mine iniquities, that fasting, I may cry to thee, Have compassion on me, O Christ Lord, for thy great and rich mercy.

Seek me, O Word, who am lost in the hills of evil iniquities, who call to thee, and who for the multitude of my evil traits have been put far away from thee. Revive me also, dead, and purify me with fasting and constant weeping and crying to thee, O Christ Lord, have compassion on me, for thy rich and Great Mercy.

Having begun, O believers, the third week of the Fast, let us praise the venerable Trinity, passing the rest with gladness and joy, emaciating the passions of the flesh. Let us cull from our souls divine flowers, plaiting therewith crowns for the day that is lord of days, that, all being crowned, we may praise Christ as triumphant.

❡ *Then Glory and Now, to our Lady; and after* O resplendent Light, *etc., the Prokeimenon,* Turn not away thy face, *etc., with its Stichoi (p. 644).*

❡ *In the Aposticha, the following Idiomelon, in the Eighth Tone.*

I WRETCHED man, did reject with inconstant mind, fatherly restraints, living in the thoughts of bestial sins, and wasting all my life in extravagance. And when I was in need of heart-strengthening food, I was feeding on the delight that fatteneth but for a while. Wherefore, O good One, shut not against me the wings of thy love for mankind, but open them and receive me as the prodigal son, and save me. (*Repeat.*)

❡ *Then the Martyricon and Theotokion as on the Evening of the First Sunday of the Fast (pp. 675-676); and the rest of the service as on the Evening of Cheese Fare Sunday. (p. 645).*

THIRD SUNDAY OF THE FAST

In which we celebrate the Adoration of the Precious Cross

1. VESPERS

❡ *On* O Lord, to thee have I cried, *etc. six for the Resurrection; and the following four for the Cross, in the Fifth Tone.*

O CROSS of the Lord to which the world aspireth, let the light-giving flashes of thy grace raise the hearts of those who honour thee and welcome thee with divine love, O thou through whom the dismay of tears hath passed away, and by whom we have been saved from the snares of death and translated into joy imperishable, reveal to us the splendour of thy comeliness, granting the prizes of abstinence to thy servants who ask in faith for thy rich succour and the Great Mercy.

Rejoice, O life-bearing Cross, O bright paradise of the Church, O Tree of incorruption, thou who didst bring forth for us the enjoyment of glory everlasting, through whom the hosts of devils are driven out, the ranks of angels rejoice together, and the congregations of believers celebrate, O unconquerable weapon and impregnable foundation, the triumph of kings and the pride of Priests, grant us to apprehend the Passion of Christ and his Resurrection.

Rejoice, O life-bearing Cross, the unconquerable triumph of true worship, O door of paradise, the confirmation of believers, the wall of the Church, through which corruption hath disappeared and perished, and the power of death was swallowed, and we ascend from earth to heaven, thou incontestable weapon and adversary of Satans; for thou art the glory of Martyrs and their adornment in truth, the haven of salvation that granteth to the world the Great Mercy.

Come, ye first created couple who fell from the heavenly rank through man-destroying envy, because of a bitter delight resulting from the taste of the olden tree. Behold, here cometh in truth the most revered Tree. Hasten to kiss it, shouting to it in faith, Thou art our helper, O most revered Cross, of whose fruit when we partook we attained incorruption and received securely the first Eden and the Great Mercy.

Glory, in the Third Tone

O CHRIST our God, who didst accept crucifixion willingly for the general resurrection of mankind; and by the red of the Cross didst dye thy fingers with blood; and with a crimson dye didst compassionately ordain for us forgiveness with kingly authority; forsake us not in our danger of estrangement from thee, but have compassion, O thou who alone art long-suffering, on thy harrassed people. Arise, and fight them who fight us; for thou art Almighty.

℣ *And Now, the Theotokion of the Oktoechos.*

℣ *The Aposticha for the Resurrection.*

Glory and Now, in the Fourth Tone

O LORD, who didst support in war the all-humble David, subjecting the stranger to him, fight with our believing king; repulse our enemies with the weapon of the Cross, and reveal to us thine ancient mercies, O compassionate One; that they may know of a truth that thou art God; that by our trust in thee we may vanquish them; and that by the wonted intercessions of thy Mother, thou mayest grant us the Great Mercy.

℣ *Troparion for the Resurrection; and for the Cross, in the First Tone,* O Lord, *save thy people, etc. (p. 298); and the Theotokion, in the First Tone.*

2. MATINS

Katabasias, in the First Tone

1. Of old the divine Moses foreshadowed thy Cross, passing Israel across the Red Sea when he struck the moist element with his rod, singing to thee, O Christ God, a song of exodus.

3. O Christ Master, establish me by thy Cross on the rock of faith, lest my heart be shaken by the impacts of the arrogant enemy; for thou alone art holy.

4. When the greater luminary beheld thee suspended on the Cross, O mighty One, he trembled and, drawing in his rays, hid them. And the whole of creation praised thy long-suffering; for the earth was filled with thy praise.

5. To thee, O Saviour of the world, do we travel early, praising thee, having found safety in thy Cross, through which thou didst renew mankind and led us to the never-setting light.

6. Jonah the Prophet foreshadowed thy divine Cross, when he stretched out his hands in the belly of the whale, and sprang out, saved from the beast by thy might, O Word.

7. He who delivered the three youths from the flames came to earth, taking a body, and was nailed to the Cross, freely granting us salvation, he who alone is blessed, transcendent in glory, the God of our Fathers.

8. When Daniel, the great among Prophets, was thrown of old into the den of lions, and stretched out his hands in the shape of a cross, he escaped from their ravening without hurt, blessing Christ God unto all ages.

9. O virgin Mother, truly the birth-giver of God, who didst conceive without seed Christ our God, elevated in the flesh on the Cross, these happenings all we believers now magnify, as is meet.

¶ *Exaposteilarion for the Resurrection; then the following for the Cross.*

SEEING today the precious Cross of Christ laid down, let us adore it in faith, rejoicing, and embrace it with longing, imploring the Lord who on it was willingly crucified, to make us worthy to adore the precious Cross, and to reach the Day of Resurrection free of all condemnation.

O most pure one, in true worship we now adore the Tree on which thy Son stretched out his pure hands, nailed thereto. Wherefore, grant us safety, and arrival at the adoration of the all-revered Passion of salvation, and the all-brilliant Easter Day that giveth joy to the world.

¶And in the Einos, four for the Resurrection; and the following, four for the Cross, in the Fourth Tone.

LET us rejoice with melodies and magnify with praises the precious Cross, embracing it and crying to it, O all-revered Cross, sanctify our souls and bodies by thy power, and keep us who adore thee in true worship safe from the sundry harms of adversaries. (*Repeat.*)

Come ye, and take to drink of the unfailing waters from the rivers of the bliss of the Cross, beholding prone before us the holy Tree, the fountain of gifts, watered with blood and water, flowing from the Lord of all, who was elevated thereon by his own will, and therewith elevated mankind.

Thou art, O all-revered Cross, the pillar of the Church, the confirmation of kings, the pride of ascetics, and their salvation. Wherefore, we adore thee, and seek illumination from thee with our hearts and souls by the divine grace of him who was stretched on thee, who demolished the power of the deceiver and abolished the curse.

Glory, in the Eighth Tone

THE Lord of all taught us by a proverb to run away from the haughtiness of the evil Pharisees; and instructed all not to exalt themselves in their opinions from duty, having himself become a Symbol and an Exemplar, emptying himself unto the Cross and death. Wherefore, with the publican, let us offer him thanks, saying, O thou who didst suffer for our sakes and remained an unsuffering God, deliver us from sufferings and save our souls.

¶And Now, Thou hast transcended, etc; then the Great Doxology, and its conclusion, i.e., when you sing, Holy God, the Priest standeth before the Holy place and censeth the precious cross. Then he taketh it up on a tray strewn with flowers and placeth it on his head and

cometh out from the northern door of the holy Temple, preceded by lamps and censers, coming to the middle of the church where a table is placed. He circleth around it three times, then turneth towards the east and crieth out, saying, Wisdom! Let us attend, *and placeth the precious cross on the table, censing it in the form of the cross, singing,* O Lord, save thy people, *etc.* (once) *; and each of the Choirs* (once). *Then the Clergy bow to the precious cross, while the Priest and the Choir sing,* Thy Cross, our Master, we adore, and thy holy Resurrection we glorify. *Then the congregation bow as the Choir singeth the Idiomelon,* Come, ye believers, let us adore the life-giving Tree, *etc.* (p. 305) *; and at its conclusion is sung the Troparion,* O Lord, save thy people, *etc.*

3. THE MASS

❧ *The Troparia for the Resurrection, the Cross, and the Patron Saint of the church. Then the Kontakion,* Verily, I am thy servant, *etc; and instead of* Holy God *is sung,* Thy Cross, our Master, we adore, and thy holy Resurrection we glorify.

The Epistle: Prokeimenon in the Sixth Tone

Save, O Lord, thy people, and bless thine inheritance. Unto thee will I cry, O Lord, O my God.

Section from the Epistle of St. Paul to the Hebrews (4:14 to end; 5:1-6)

YE brethren: Having therefore a great high priest, that hath passed into the heavens, Jesus the Son of God; let us hold fast our confession.

For we have not an high priest which cannot be touched with the feeling of our infirmities; but was in all points tempted like as we are, yet without sin.

Let us therefore come boldly unto the throne of grace, that we may obtain mercy; and find grace to help in time of need.

For every high priest taken from among men is ordained for men in things pertaining to God, that he may offer both gifts and sacrifices for sins:

Who can have compassion on the ignorant, and on them that are out of the way; for that he himself also is compassed with infirmity.

And by reason hereof he ought, as for the people, so also for himself, to offer for sins.

And no man taketh this honour unto himself, but he that is called of God, as was Aaron.

So also Christ glorified not himself to be made a high priest; but he that said unto him, Thou art my Son, to-day have I begotten thee.

As he saith also in another place, Thou art a priest for ever after the order of Melchisedec.

The Gospel: from St. Mark (8:34 to end; 9:1)

THE Lord saith: Whosoever will come after me, let him deny himself, and take up his cross, and follow me.

For whosoever will save his life shall lose it; but whosoever shall lose his life for my sake and the gospel's, the same shall save it.

For what shall it profit a man, if he shall gain the whole world, and lose his own soul?

Or what shall a man give in exchange for his soul?

Whosoever therefore shall be ashamed of me and of my words in this adulterous and sinful generation, of him also shall the Son of man be ashamed, when he cometh in the glory of his Father with the holy angels.

And he said unto them, Verily I say unto you, That there be some of them that stand here, which shall not taste of death, till they have seen the kingdom of God come with power.

¶*And the rest of the Liturgy of St. Basil the Great.*

SYNAXARION

ON THIS DAY, THE THIRD SUNDAY OF THE FAST, WE CELEBRATE THE PRECIOUS CROSS.

STICHOS

LET ALL THE UNIVERSE OFFER ADORATION TO THE CROSS, THROUGH WHICH IT HATH LEARNED TO WORSHIP THEE, O WORSHIPPED ONE.

O N which we feast for the life-giving and precious Cross.

Every hard and strenuous work is accomplished with great difficulty, which appears especially in the middle of such work; for the effort expended in this perform- ance brings with it fatigue which makes the accomplish- ment of the rest very hard. Having, therefore, arrived with God's grace, at the middle of the Fast, and being undoubtedly overcome by fatigue and increasing diffi- culties, our compassionate mother, the holy Church of Christ, thought fit to reveal to us the holy Cross as the joy of the world, power of the faithful, bulwark of the pious, hope of sinners, a sure foundation, and a secure help. And having kissed it piously, we shall receive grace and power which will help us to carry on the struggles of the divine Fast.

Wherefore, through its power, O Christ God, pro- tect us against the harm of the deceitful one, and make us worthy to traverse safely the battle-ground of Quad- ragesima, and to adore thy divine Passion and thy life- giving Resurrection; and have mercy upon us; for thou alone art the Lover of mankind.

Koinonikon: The light of thy countenance hath been impressed on us, O Lord, Alleluia.

❡*And instead of* We have seen the true Light, *etc., sing the Tro- parion,* O Lord, *save thy people,* etc; *and the Benediction.*

EVENING OF THE THIRD SUNDAY OF THE FAST

❡*On* O Lord, *to thee have I cried, the following Prosomia, in the Eighth Tone.*

O LORD, who willingly didst stretch out thy hands on the Cross, prepare us to adore it with reverent hearts, shining forth well with fastings, beseechings, ab- stinence, and charity; for thou art good and the Lover of mankind.

O most compassionate Lord, blot out the multitude of my sins by the multitude of thy mercies. Make me worthy to behold thy Cross and to embrace it with a pure soul in this week of abstinence; for thou art the Lover of mankind.

What a great wonder to behold the Tree on which Christ was crucified in the flesh, with the world adoring it and being lighted therewith, crying, O the power of the Cross, which when Satans behold they are burned, and by its sign it is revealed consuming them with flames. Wherefore, I bless thee, O pure Tree, honour and adore thee with fear, glorifying God who granted me through thee unending life.

❡ *Glory and Now to our Lady. And after* O resplendent Light, *etc., the Prokeimenon,* Thou hast given an inheritance, *etc., with its Stichoi* (*p. 675*).

❡ *In the Aposticha, the Idiomelon, in the Eighth Tone.*

BECAUSE of my evil deeds, I, wretched man, dare not gaze with mine eyes on heaven. But like the publican, sighing, I cry to thee, God, forgive me, a sinner, and deliver me from pharisaic hypocrisy; for thou alone art compassionate. (*Repeat.*)

❡ *Then the Martyrikon and Theotokion as on the First Sunday evening of the Fast; and the rest of the service as on the Evening of Cheese Fare Sunday.*

FOURTH SUNDAY OF THE FAST

Memorial of our righteous Father John, Author of the Ladder of Virtues.

1. VESPERS

❡ *On* O Lord, to thee have I cried, *the Stichera for the Resurrection; then Glory, in the Fifth Tone.*

O RIGHTEOUS Father, thou heardest the voice of the Gospel and forsook the world, riches, and glory, counting them as naught. Wherefore, thou didst cry unto all, Love God, and ye will find eternal favour. Put nothing above his love, that when he cometh in his glory ye may find rest with all the saints. Wherefore, by their intercessions, O Christ God, preserve and save our souls.

❡*Aposticha for the Resurrection; Glory, in the Second Tone.*

LET us honour John, that pride of ascetics, that angel on earth, that man of God in heaven, that adornment of the world, and that bliss of virtues and good deeds; for, planted in the house of God, he flourished with justice; and, like a cedar tree in the wilderness, he caused the flock of Christ to grow, those sheep endowed with speech, in righteousness and justice.

❡*Troparion for the Resurrection, and the Saint, in the Eighth Tone,* The barren wilderness, *etc.* (*p. 37*).

2. MATINS

❡*The Katabasias,* Open my mouth, *etc.* (*p. 114*); *the Exaposteilarion for the Resurrection; and the following for the Triodion.*

O RIGHTEOUS John of perpetual memory, thou didst turn aside from worldly luxury because it is loathsome; and, emaciating thy body with abstinence, thou didst renew the power of thy soul, and enriched it with heavenly glory. Wherefore, thou ceasest not to intercede for our sakes.

❡*And in the Einos, the Stichera for the Resurrection; Glory, in the First Tone.*

COME, let us labour in the mystical field, working therein fruits of repentance. Let us not spend ourselves in food and drink, but reap virtues with fasting and prayer; for these doth the Master of labour accept, and for them he giveth us the pence through which he redeemeth our souls from the debt of sin; for he alone is most compassionate.

3. THE MASS

❡*The Troparion for the Resurrection, to the Righteous John, and the Patron Saint of the church; the Kontakion,* Verily, I am thy servant, *etc.*

The Epistle: Prokeimenon in the Seventh Tone

The Lord will give strength to his people. The Lord will bless his people with peace.

Section from the Epistle of St. Paul to the Hebrews (6:13 to end)

YE brethren: When God made promise to Abraham, because he could swear by no greater, he sware by himself.

Saying, Surely blessing I will bless thee, and multiplying I will multiply thee.

And so, after he had patiently endured, he obtained the promise.

For men verily swear by the greater: and an oath for confirmation is to them an end of all strife.

Wherein God, willing more abundantly to show unto the heirs of promise the immutability of his counsel, confirmed it by an oath:

That by two immutable things in which it was impossible for God to lie, we might have a strong consolation, who have fled for refuge to lay hold upon the hope set before us:

Which hope we have as an anchor of the soul, both sure and steadfast, and which entereth into that within the veil;

Whither the forerunner is for us entered, even Jesus, made an high priest for ever after the order of Melchisedec.

The Gospel: from St. Mark (9:16-30)

AT that time: One of the multitude came forth to Jesus, bowing down and saying unto him: Master, I have brought unto thee my son, which hath a dumb spirit:

And wheresoever he taketh him, he teareth him; and he foameth, and gnasheth with his teeth, and pineth away: and I spake to thy disciples that they should cast him out; and they could not.

He answereth him, and saith, O faithless generation, how long shall I be with you? how long shall I suffer you? bring him unto me.

And they brought him unto him: and when he saw him, straightway the spirit tare him; and he fell on the ground, and wallowed foaming.

And he asked his father, How long is it ago since this came unto him? And he said, Of a child.

And ofttimes it hath cast him into the fire, and into the waters, to destroy him: but if thou canst do any thing, have compassion on us, and help us.

Jesus said unto him, If thou canst believe, all things are possible to him that believeth.

And straightway the father of the child cried out, and said with tears, Lord, I believe; help thou mine unbelief.

When Jesus saw that the people came running together, he rebuked the foul spirit, saying unto him, Thou dumb and deaf spirit, I charge thee, come out of him, and enter no more into him.

And the spirit cried, and rent him sore, and came out of him: and he was as one dead; insomuch that many said, He is dead.

But Jesus took him by the hand, and lifted him up; and he arose.

And when he was come into the house, his disciples asked him privately, Why could not we cast him out?

And he said unto them, This kind can come forth by nothing, but by prayer and fasting.

And they departed thence, and passed through Galilee; and he would not that any man should know it.

For he taught his disciples, and said unto them, The Son of man is delivered into the hands of men, and they shall kill him; and after that he is killed, he shall rise the third day.

¶ *And the rest of the Liturgy of St. Basil the Great.*

SYNAXARION
ON THIS DAY, THE FOURTH SUNDAY OF THE FAST, WE CELEBRATE THE MEMORY OF OUR FATHER JOHN, THE AUTHOR OF THE LADDER.

STICHOS

VERILY, JOHN WHO, WHILE LIVING WAS YET DEAD IN THE BODY, EVEN THOUGH HE MAY APPEAR NOW AS DEAD AND BREATHLESS, HE LIVETH FOR EVER, HAVING LEFT HIS BOOK THROUGH WHICH HE ASCENDED ON HIGH, CLEARLY REVEALING IN IT THE WAY OF HEAVENLY ASCENT FOR EVERYONE.

IN which we chant the service of our righteous Father John, author of *The Ladder of Virtues.*

The anniversary of this Father actually takes place on the thirtieth of the month of March, in which the annals of his life were compiled. The celebration of his Feast on this day, however, probably arose from the custom prevalent in the honourable monasteries of starting holy Quadragesima with the reading of his book of sermons known as *The Ladder of Virtues.*

Koinonikon: Praise ye the Lord from the heavens, etc.

EVENING OF THE FOURTH SUNDAY OF THE FAST

❧ *On* O Lord, to thee have I cried, *the following Prosomia, in the Third Tone.*

LET us, O believers, in this season of abstinence exert every effort, that we may attain great glory and escape the fire of hades, by the mercy of God, the great King.

Having passed half the period of this holy Fast, let manifest clearly the beginning of divine glory. Let us fervently hasten to the achievement of good conduct, that we may receive the never-ending bliss.

Having passed half the distance of this holy Fast, let us strive with steadfastness unto its end, rejoicing. Let us anoint ourselves with the oil of charity, that we may be worthy to adore the noble Passion of Christ our God, and arrive at his august and holy Resurrection.

¶ *Glory and Now to our Lady. And after* O resplendent Light, *etc.* *the Prokeimenon,* Turn not away thy face, *etc.* (*p. 644*).

¶ *In the Aposticha, the following Idiomelons, in the Sixth Tone.*

THE Saviour who planted the vineyard and called the labourers verily is near. Come, therefore, O strivers in the Fast, let us receive our hire; for the Giver is rich and merciful. And even if we laboured little we receive the Great Mercy.

When Adam fell among the robbers of thought, he was robbed of his mind, his soul was wounded, and he himself was cast out naked without any help. Neither did the priest who is before the law listen to him, nor the Levite who came after the law have compassion on him, except thou, O God who cometh not from Samaria but from the Theotokos. Wherefore, Lord, glory be to thee.

Thy Martyrs, O Lord, have never denied thee nor turned aside from thy commandments at any time. Wherefore, by their intercessions have mercy upon us.

¶ *Glory and Now to our Lady, in the Same Tone.*

LET us give, O believers, angelic praise to the heavenly chamber, the truly sealed door, crying, Rejoice, O Lady, who for us didst rouse Christ God, and raise up the Life-giver and Saviour of all. Demolish thou, therefore, with thine own hands, O undefiled one, our giant enemies, the heretics, O hope of Christians.

¶ *And the rest of the service as at the end of the Evening of Cheese* *Fare Sunday.* (*p. 645*).

THURSDAY OF THE FIFTH WEEK OF THE FAST
SERVICE OF THE GREAT CANON

¶ *This service is chanted usually on Wednesday evening. Here only* *a compendium of the Canon is given, as followeth.*

¶ *Note: At each piece we should make three reverences, as we say,* Have mercy upon me, O God, have mercy upon me.

First Ode, in the Sixth Tone—Hermos

A HELP and a refuge hath salvation become to me. This is my God, therefore, I will glorify him; the God of my Fathers, therefore, will I exalt him; for in glory hath he been glorified.

Where, O Christ, shall I begin to mourn the deeds of my miserable life-time? And what beginning shall I make to the present mourning? But since thou art compassionate, grant me forgiveness of sins.

Come, O wretched soul, with thy body, and confess before the Creator of all. Refrain from thy former bestiality, and offer to God tears with repentance.

I have emulated in iniquity Adam the first creation, and found myself stripped naked of God and of eternal kingship and bliss because of my sins.

Woe is me, O wretched soul, why didst thou resemble the first Eve? Because thou didst cast an evil look and boldly tasted the forbidden food.

Glory: O transubstantial Trinity, worshipped in unity, lift from me the heavy shackles of sin, and grant me (for thou art compassionate) tears of reverence.

Now: O Theotokos, hope and intercessor of those who praise thee, lift from me the shackles of sin. And since thou art an undefiled Lady, receive me repentant.

Second Ode—Hermos

Hearken, O heaven, and I will speak; and I will praise Christ who was offered in the flesh from the Virgin.

Hearken, O heaven, and I will speak. Give ear, O earth, to the voice of a penitent who praiseth God.

Turn to me with thy merciful sight and save me, my God and my Saviour, and accept my most fervid confession.

I have sinned more than all people. I alone have sinned against thee. But as God, have compassion on thy work, O Saviour.

I have painted the ugliness of my passions with the surging love of pleasure, marring the comeliness of my mind.

Glory: I praise thee, God of all, the One in three Persons, the Father, Son and Holy Spirit.

Now: O pure Theotokos, alone all-praised, plead constantly for our salvation.

Third Ode—Hermos

ESTABLISH thy Church, O Christ, on the unshakeable rock of thy commandments.

The Lord, O my soul, in the beginning, rained fire from above and burned the land of the Sodomites.

Escape, O my soul, to the mount, like Lot. Run ahead to Zoar and be saved.

Run, O my soul, from the blaze. Run from the flame of Sodom, and escape from the destruction of the godly fire.

Unto thee have I sinned. I alone have sinned more than all. Forget me not, O Christ Saviour.

Glory: O Trinity, the one God, save us from error, temptation, and tribulation.

Now: Rejoice, O God-receiving belly. Rejoice, O throne of the Lord. Rejoice, O Mother of our life.

Fourth Ode—Hermos

THE prophet heard of thy coming, O Lord, and that thou wast about to be born of the Virgin and appear to men, and he was dismayed, crying, Thy hearing have I heard, and I feared. Glory to thy power, O Lord.

O Righteous Judge and Lover of mankind, forsake not thy works, and turn not away from thy creation, even though I alone have sinned as man, exceeding all men. But since thou art Lord of all, thou hast power to forgive sins.

Thy end hath come, and thy departure draweth near; nor hast thou shown concern or prepared. Life passeth away, arise. The Judge is near at the doors. The time of life passeth like a dream and like flowers. Why are we troubled in vain?

Arise, my soul, and review thy deeds which have proceeded from thee. Scrutinize them closely, and shed the rain of thy tears, declaring openly to Christ thy thoughts and deeds, that thou mayest be justified.

There hath never been a sin in the world, O Saviour, no deed of iniquity, that I have not committed, sinning in thought, word, and intention; in plan, determination, and action, as no one else hath done.

Glory: I speak of thy Godhead, that thou art indivisible, in Persons immiscible; that the one triune Divinity is coëqual in kingship and rank. I hail thee with the great three-fold song of praise with which thou art praised above.

Now: Thou didst give birth being a Virgin, and remained in both states unwed by nature. The Begotten renewed the law of nature, and the womb gave birth without travailing; for when God willeth, he overcometh the law of nature; for he doeth what he willeth.

Fifth Ode—Hermos

IN the night I rise up early, beseeching thee, O Lover of mankind. Lighten me and guide me in thy commandments. Teach me, O Saviour, to do thy will.

I have passed all my life in darkness; for the night of sin hath brought me darkness and dense fog. But since thou art the Saviour, make me manifest as a son of the day.

I, wretched man, have rivalled Reuben, forming an opinion transgressing the law and the high God. I have defiled my bed, as he defiled his father's bed.

O Christ king, to thee I confess. I have sinned against thee, and erred, having sold the fruit of purity and chastity as the brothers of Joseph of old sold him.

His soul was bartered by his brothers, and that sweet lad was delivered into bondage, an example of the Lord. Thou, O soul, wast sold in thine entirety to thine evil deeds.

Glory: Thee we glorify, O one God, Trinity. Holy! Holy! Holy art thou, the Father, Son, and Holy Spirit, simple and single Essence worshipped everlastingly.

Now: O Mother Virgin, who hath not known wedlock, from thee God, Creator of all the ages, did put on my creation, uniting in himself human nature.

Sixth Ode—Hermos

WITH my whole heart I cried unto the compassionate God, and he heard me from the nether hades, bringing my life out of corruption.

To thee I offer with purity, with the tears of mine eyes, with sighs from the depth, and with shouting of the heart, Against thee have I sinned, O God. Forgive thou me.

Thou didst revolt against thy Lord, O my soul, as did Dathan and Abiram. Wherefore, lest the hades of earth open and swallow thee, cry from the nether hades; Pity thou me.

Thou hast become like Ephraim, O my soul, like a runaway calf. Deliver thy life, winged with action, intelligence and vision, like a deer, from the noose.

The hand of Moses, O my soul, did demonstrate how God can whiten thy leprous conduct and purify it. Be not dismayed at thyself, though afflicted with leprosy.

Glory: The Father, Son, and Divine Spirit saith, I am a simple, indivisible Trinity, varied in Countenance, and One in united Nature.

Now: Thy womb, O Theotokos, hath borne us a God, formed like us. Wherefore, since he is Creator of all, implore him that we be justified by thine intercessions.

❡ *Then slowly sing the following Kontakion, in the Sixth Tone.*

MY SOUL, O my soul, arise. How long wouldest thou sleep? Thine end draweth near, and thou art about to be disturbed. Awake, therefore, that Christ may have compassion on thee, God present in every place and filling all.

SYNAXARION

ON THIS DAY, WHICH IS THE THURSDAY OF THE FIFTH WEEK OF THE FAST, WE SING ACCORDING TO THE OLD TRADITION, THE ORDER OF THE GREAT CANON.

STICHOS

VERILY, JESUS, I WILL NOW SING UNTO THEE THE GREAT CANON; GRANT THOU ME TEARS OF CONTRITION AND AWE.

IN which we chant the Service of the Great Canon. This reverential Canon, which is called Great, not only because of the large number of Troparia used therein as compared with other Canons, but also because of the sublime symbolical allusions it contains and pious references, was composed after this Tone, and perfected by Andrew, the Archbishop of Crete (See July fourth) who included in it quotations from the Old and New Testaments of the Holy Bible. In this Canon the author urges all souls to imitate good deeds and to shun evil ones, and to return to God through repentance.

Wherefore, through the intercessions of St. Andrew, have mercy upon us, and save us. Amen.

Seventh Ode—Hermos

WE have sinned, and done iniquity and injustice before thee. We have not kept nor done what thou didst command us. But deliver us not unto the end, O God of our Fathers.

I have erred and sinned and transgressed thy commandment; for I have gone too far in my sins, and

brought on ulcerous wounds. But since thou art compassionate, have mercy upon me, O God of our Fathers.

To thee I confess the secrets of my heart, O my Judge.
Look down upon my humility, behold my sorrow and
listen now to my complaints. And since thou art compassionate, have mercy upon me, O God of our Fathers.

When Saul lost for a time his father's asses, he found
a kingdom, and came to be called a king without intent.
But see that thou prefer not unwittingly thy bestial desires to the kingdom of Christ.

O my soul, David, the father of God, sinned doubly,
having been pierced with the arrow of adultery, and
stabbed with the spear of murderous crime. Thou art
yet laid low with a sickness more onerous to the stir-
rings of thine energy.

Glory: O thou simple and indivisible Trinity, holy
Unity, consubstantial, triune God, praised as light and
as lights, holy One and Three. Praise thou, my soul,
and glorify the God of all, who is Life and lives.

Now: We praise thee, O Theotokos, bless thee, and
adore thee; for thou didst bear One of the Trinity, indivisible as Son and God, opening the heavens to us
earthly men.

Eighth Ode—Hermos

PRAISE, O creation, with every breath, and bless
him whom the hosts of heaven do glorify, and whom
the cherubim and seraphim dread. Exalt him yet more
unto all the ages.

I have erred, O Saviour; have mercy upon me.
Awaken my mind to thy return, receive me and have
compassion on me, as I cry to thee, Against thee only
have I sinned and done evil. Have mercy upon me,
and save me.

Elijah who rode in the chariot, having alighted on
the chariot of virtues for a time, was exalted above
earthly things. Contemplate, then, O my soul, his ascension.

And Elisha, having for a time received Elijah's mantle, received from the Lord double grace. But thou, O my soul, hast not shared this grace because of thy wastefulness.

The flow of the Jordan ceased on either side by Elijah's mantle in the hands of Elisha. But thou, O my soul, hast not shared this grace because of thy wastefulness.

We bless the Father, Son, and Holy Spirit.

O eternal Father, and Son coëternal with him, and the comforting Spirit, upright and good; O Father of God the Word; O Word of the eternal Father; O living, creating Spirit, one Trinity, have mercy upon me.

Now: The supersensual purple of Immanuel, O undefiled one, which is the flesh, was woven in thy womb, inwardly, as of the dye of a royal robe. Wherefore, since thou art in truth the Theotokos, we honour thee.

Ninth Ode—Hermos

VERILY, the Nativity, is ineffable; for the Conception was without seed and without the corruption of a spouseless Mother; for the Nativity of God hath renewed nature. Wherefore, with steadfast faith all generations magnify thee; for thou art the Mother of our God.

Lo! the mind is wounded and the body is weak; the spirit is ill and speech is powerless; life hath been mortified and the end is at the door. What, then, shalt thou do, wretched soul, when the Judge cometh to examine thine affairs?

I have adduced to thee, O my soul, how the world spoken of by Moses, and every canonical book therefrom, chronicleth to thee all the just and the unjust. But thou didst not resemble the former, but rather emulated the latter, having erred against God.

The law hath become weak, the Gospel hath been abolished, and every book hath been neglected by thee.

The Prophets have tired, and the speech of every one that is righteous. But thy wounds have multiplied, O my soul, where there is no physician to heal thee.

I have produced for thee all the examples of the New Book to guide thee to reverence. Emulate, then, the righteous, and avoid the sinful. Beseech Christ with prayers, fastings, purity, and reverence.

O righteous Mary the Egyptian, intercede for us.

O righteous Mother, implore the Creator for us who honour thee; that we may escape the distresses and sorrows that surround us; that being saved from temptations we may ceaselessly magnify the Lord who hath magnified thee.

O Saint of God, Andrew, intercede for us.

O venerable Andrew, the thrice-blessed Father, shepherd of Crete, cease not to plead for us who praise thee, that we may be delivered from every abomination, sorrow, and corruption, and be saved from iniquities; for we honour thy memory in faith.

Glory: Let us glorify the Father, exalt the Son, and worship in faith the divine Spirit, the indivisible Trinity, one in Substance; for he is Light, and enlightens life, and lives, enlivening and lighting the ends of the earth.

Now: O Pure Theotokos, preserve thy city; for by thee it reigneth in faith, by thee it is established, by thee it conquereth, by thee it repulseth every distress, leadeth captive its attackers, and protecteth those who submit to it.

SATURDAY OF THE FIFTH WEEK OF THE FAST

Service of Laudation of the Akathiston (in which no sitting is permitted) for the Theotokos

⁋ *On Friday evening Little Compline is recited up to* It is truly meet, *etc. Then sing twice slowly, and once quickly the following Troparion, in the Eighth Tone.*

THE bodiless having learned what he was commanded to do secretly, hastened towards the house of Joseph, saying to her who knew no wedlock, Behold, he to whose descent the heavens did bow, shall be altogether held in thee without transubstantiation. As I behold him in thy womb, taking the likeness of a servant, I become amazed, crying to thee, Hail, O bride, who hath no bridegroom.

❡ *Then the stanzas for our Lady are chanted, and at each stanza, the following Canon is sung.*

First Stanza

1. The archangel was sent from heaven to say to the Theotokos, Rejoice. And when he saw thee, O Lord, incarnate with unincarnate voice, he was amazed, and stood, crying unto her, Rejoice, O recall of fallen Adam. Rejoice, O deliverer of Eve from weeping and mourning. Rejoice, O height inaccessible to the eyes of angels. Rejoice; for thou hast become a throne for the King. Rejoice; for thou carriest the Almighty. Rejoice, O star revealing the Sun. Rejoice, O belly of the divine Incarnation. Rejoice, O thou in whom creation is renewed. Rejoice, O thou in whom the Creator hath become a babe. Rejoice, O bride without bridegroom.

2. When the saintly one saw herself in utmost purity, she boldly said to Gabriel, Thy strange voice appeareth to me hard of acceptance; for how speakest thou of birthgiving without seed, crying, Alleluia.

3. The Virgin sought to know the unknowable, and she cried unto the servant, Tell me, how is it possible for a son to be born from a pure womb? And that one answered her with fear, crying thus, Rejoice, O keeper of the mystery of ineffable opinion. Rejoice, O faith of those who need silence. Rejoice, O preface of the miracles of Christ. Rejoice, O head of his commandments. Rejoice, O heavenly ladder on which God descended. Rejoice, O bridge transporting those on

earth to heaven. Rejoice, O wonder of the angel, greatly renowned. Rejoice, O wound of demons, much mourned. Rejoice, O thou who didst bear the ineffable Light. Rejoice, O thou who informed no one how. Rejoice, O thou who dost exceed the knowledge of the wise. Rejoice, O thou who dost illuminate the minds of the faithful. Rejoice, O bride without bridegroom.

4. The power of the most High overshadowed, at the Conception, her who had had no experience of marriage, revealing her fruitful womb as a delectable field for all those who desire to reap salvation, as they sing, Allelulia.

5. With the God-bearing belly, Mary hastened towards Elizabeth. And at once when that one's babe heard the salutation, he rejoiced; and with running as though with praises, he cried aloud to the Theotokos, Rejoice, O vine of a branch that fadeth not. Rejoice, O holder of an incorruptible Fruit. Rejoice, O husbandry of the Husbandman who loveth mankind. Rejoice, O thou who didst cause to grow the Planter of our life. Rejoice, O fruitful field, fertile with compassions. Rejoice, O table carrying the Treasure of forgiveness. Rejoice, because thou didst grow the meadows of bliss. Rejoice, because thou preparest the Haven of souls. Rejoice, O acceptable fragrance of intercession. Rejoice, O forgiveness of all the world. Rejoice, O good-will of God among the dead. Rejoice, O thou who art their favour before him. Rejoice, O bride without bridegroom.

6. When Joseph the chaste saw thee, unwed, O blameless one, he was perplexed and amazed because of his troubled thoughts, thinking that thou hadst committed infidelity. But when he knew that thy Conception was from the Holy Spirit, he cried, Alleluia.

¶ *Then sing the following Canon; and with the First and Second Troparia, say,* O most holy Theotokos, save us.

First Ode, in the Fourth Tone—Hermos

OPEN my mouth and it shall be filled with the Spirit; and I shall declare a saying overflowing upon the Mother Queen. I shall show forth, celebrating the season with rejoicing, and shall sing her wonders with gladness.

When the great archangel saw, O pure one, that thou art a living scroll of Christ, sealed with the Spirit, he shouted unto thee, saying, Rejoice, O dwelling-place of joy and pleasure; O thou in whom the curse of the first mother is undone.

Rejoice, O virgin bride of God. Rejoice, O reformation of Adam and his correction. Rejoice, O thou who didst cause hades to die. Rejoice, O all-blameless one. Rejoice, O palace of the only King. Rejoice, O fiery throne of the Almighty.

Glory: Hail, O thou who alone didst sprout the fadeless Rose. Rejoice, O thou who didst bear the fragrant Apple for the nostrils of the King of all. Rejoice, O thou who knew no wedlock. Hail, O salvation of the world.

Now: Rejoice, O treasure of purity. Rejoice, O thou through whom we rose from our fall. Rejoice, O Lady, thou lily delicate to smell, perfuming the faithful, a sweet-scented incense, and ointment of great price.

Third Ode-Hermos

O THEOTOKOS, since thou art the living fountain, bountifully overflowing, establish us who sing thy praises, who are gathered in a spiritual congregation. And in thy divine glory prepare us for crowns of glory and honour.

Rejoice, O Lady, who didst clearly sprout the divine Ear, like an untilled field. Rejoice, O living table that hath held the Bread of life. Rejoice, O unfailing fountain of the living Water.

Hail, O heifer, who bore for the faithful the blameless Calf. Rejoice, O ewe who gave birth to the Lamb of God who beareth the sins of the whole world. Rejoice, O fervid forgiveness.

Glory: Rejoice, O brilliant morn, who alone didst bear for us Christ the Sun. Hail, O dwelling-place of Light. Rejoice, O remover of darkness, abolisher of the abysmal gloom of demons.

Now: Rejoice, O only door through which the Word alone did pass. Rejoice, O thou who didst demolish by thy birth-giving the gates of hades and its bolts. Rejoice, O divine entrance of the saved. Hail, O all-praised Lady.

❡ *Then chant the Kontakion,* Verily, I am thy servant, *etc., alternately, slowly, and with intonation.*

Second Part

7. The shepherds heard the angels praise the presence of Christ in the flesh. They hastened as unto a shepherd, and they beheld him as a blameless lamb grazing on Mary's bosom; and they praised her, saying, Rejoice, O Mother of the Lamb and the Shepherd. Rejoice, O fold of the sheep endowed with speech. Rejoice, O vengeance of invisible enemies. Rejoice, O key of the doors of heaven. Rejoice for the things of earth; rejoice with those of heaven. Rejoice; for the earthly things exchange glad tidings with the heavenly. Rejoice, O unsilenced mouth of the Apostles. Rejoice, O unconquerable might of strivers. Rejoice, O firm foundation of faith. Rejoice, O brilliant token of grace. Rejoice, O thou through whom hades hath been denuded. Rejoice, O thou through whom we have put on glory. Rejoice, O bride without bridegroom.

8. When the Magi saw a star guided by God, they followed its light as a lamp, searching with it for the mighty King. And when they approached the Unapproachable, rejoicing, they shouted, Alleluia.

9. When the Chaldean youths saw in the hands of the Virgin him who created man with his own hands, and knew that he was the Master, albeit he had taken on the likeness of a servant, they hastened with presents to the service of the blessed One, shouting, Rejoice, O Mother of the never-setting Star. Rejoice, O mystical dawn of the Day. Rejoice, O thou who didst quench the furnace of error. Rejoice, O lighthouse of the initiates of the Trinity. Rejoice, O thou who expelled the inhuman usurper from his chieftancy. Rejoice, O thou who didst reveal mankind loving Christ. Rejoice, O thou who didst save us from the doctrines of the Barbarians. Rejoice, O thou who didst rescue us from the slough of works. Rejoice, O thou who didst stop the worship of fire. Rejoice, O rescuer from the fire of suffering. Rejoice, O guide of the faithful to chastity. Rejoice, O delight of all generations. Rejoice, O bride without bridegroom.

10. When the Magi became God-mantled preachers, they returned to Babylon, having fulfilled thine inspiration and preached unto all that thou art Christ, neglecting Herod as one who prateth, not knowing how to sing, Alleluia.

11. When thou didst cause the Light of truth to rise in Egypt, thou didst expel the darkness of error; for its idols, unable to stand against thy might, O Saviour, fell and rolled down. And they who were saved from their worship shouted to the Theotokos, saying, Rejoice, O source of humanity. Rejoice, O downfall of Satans. Rejoice, O thou who didst tread down the error of deceit. Rejoice, O thou who didst betray the deceit of idols. Rejoice, O sea that drowned the supersensuous Pharaoh. Rejoice, O rock that satisfied the thirsty for life. Rejoice, O pillar of fire guiding those who are in darkness. Rejoice, O shelter of the world, more spacious than the clouds. Rejoice, O nourishment in place of manna. Rejoice, O servant of holy bliss. Rejoice, O land of promise. Rejoice, O thou who flowest with milk and honey. Rejoice, O bride without bridegroom.

12. When Simeon was about to depart from this present life, deceiving age, thou wast delivered to him as a babe. But thou wast known of him as perfect God besides. Wherefore, he was dazzled by thine ineffable wisdom, crying, Alleluia.

Fourth Ode—Hermos

VERILY, Jesus the transcendentally Deified, who sitteth in glory on the throne of Divinity, hath come on a bright cloud, saving in his unbreakable grasp, those who cry to him, Glory to thy power, O Christ.

We raise our voices to thee in faith, O all-praised one, saying, Hail, O fat mountain, fermented by the Spirit. Rejoice, O lighthouse, the manna-carrying jar, sweetening the sense of those of true worship.

Hail, O undefiled Lady, O forgiveness of the world. Rejoice, O ladder that bringeth up all from the earth by grace. Rejoice, O bridge that truly leadeth all who praise thee from death unto life.

Rejoice, O pure one, who art more exalted than the heavens. Rejoice, O thou who didst carry in thy womb without effort the Foundation of the earth. Hail, O murex that hath dyed with her own blood a purple robe for the King of powers.

Glory: Peace be upon thee, O Lady, who bore him who layeth down the law, who remitteth the sins of all freely. Rejoice, O incomprehensible depth, ineffable height. Rejoice, O thou who knowest no wedlock, through whom we have been deified.

Now: Thee do we praise, O Virgin, who didst plait for the world a crown not braided by hand, crying to thee, Rejoice. O fortress, wall, confirmation, and noble refuge for all.

Fifth Ode—Hermos

O VIRGIN that knew no wedlock, the whole creation hath been dazzled by thy divine glory; for thou didst carry in thy womb the God of all, and bore the Son not bound by time, granting salvation to all those who praise thee.

Rejoice, O all-blameless one, who didst bear the Way of life, and saved the world from the flood of sin. Hail, O bride of God. Rejoice, O terrible hearing, O dread speech. Hail, O dwelling-place of the Master of creation.

Hail, O pure one, O power of humanity and its steadfastness, the holy place of glory, the death of hades and the all-brilliant chamber. Rejoice, O rejoicing of the angels. Peace be upon thee, O help of those who seek thee in faith.

Rejoice, O Lady, the chariot of fiery likeness for the Word, O living paradise, holding in its midst the Lord, the Tree of life, whose sweetness reviveth those who have fallen into corruption, if they partake of him in faith.

Glory: We who have been confirmed by thy power, shout to thee in faith, saying, Rejoice, O city of the King of all, of whom were sung the songs of praise, meet to be heard plainly, the mountain not cut out. Hail, O utterly fathomless depth.

Now: Hail, O pure one, the spacious dwelling-place of the Word, the shell that produced the divine Pearl. Rejoice, O Theotokos, the ultimate miracle which reconciled with God all those who constantly bless thee.

Sixth Ode—Hermos

COME, ye of divine minds, let us clap our hands, celebrating this most honourable Feast of the Theotokos, and glorify God who was begotten in her.

Rejoice, O immaculate chamber of the Word, the cause of the deification of all, O most pure one, the proclamation of the Prophets. Hail, O comeliness of the Apostles and their adornment.

From thee dripped the dew that extinguished the flame of polytheism. Wherefore, we shout to thee, saying, Rejoice, O Virgin, the dewy fleece which Gideon foresaw of old.

Glory: Behold, we hail thee with salutation. Be thou a haven and a refuge, unto us who are swallowed completely by the sea of sorrows, the doubts and stumblings of the adversary.

Now: O cause of joy, be gracious unto our minds that we may cry to thee, Rejoice, O unburning bush, the all-brilliant cloud which ever overshadoweth the faithful.

❡ *Then the Choir beginneth to sing the Kontakion,* Verily, I am thy servant, *etc.*

Third Part

13. When the Creator appeared he revealed us, through himself, as a new creation, having branched from a seedless belly, preserving it as it had been without corruption: so that, having seen this miracle, we may praise her, saying, Rejoice, O flower of incorruptibility. Rejoice, O crown of abstinence. Rejoice, O thou who dost give rise to the Sign of resurrection. Rejoice, O thou who dost reveal the conduct of angels. Rejoice, O tree of delectable fruit nourishing the faithful. Rejoice, O plant of shady leaves in whom many find shade. Rejoice, O thou who didst bear the Guide of the erring. Rejoice, O thou who gave birth to the Deliverer of captives. Rejoice, O intercessor with the righteous Judge. Rejoice, O forgiveness of sins to the many. Rejoice, O robe of favour to the naked. Rejoice, O love of every overcoming longing. Rejoice, O bride without bridegroom.

14. Having beheld a strange Birth, let us be estranged from the world, and transport our minds to the heavens; for the most high God for this purpose appeared on earth as a meek Man, desiring to attract on high those who cry unto him, Alleluia.

15. The boundless Word was altogether with the earthly ones, but was not absent at all from the heavenly ones, which was a divine condescension, not a special translation. And his Birth was from a Maiden chosen

of God, who listened to this saying, Rejoice, O city of
God whom no place holdeth. Rejoice, O door of the
honoured mystery. Rejoice, O hearing perplexing to
the infidels. Rejoice, O pride of the faithful, not marred
by confusion. Rejoice, O most holy chariot of him
who rideth on the cherubim. Rejoice, most beautiful
dwelling-place of him who is on the seraphim. Rejoice,
O unifier of all antitheses into one state. Rejoice, thou
who didst make common ground of virginity and travailing. Rejoice, O thou through whom iniquity was
loosened. Rejoice, O thou through whom paradise
was opened. Rejoice, O key of the kingdom of Christ.
Rejoice, O hope of eternal goods. Rejoice, O bride
without bridegroom.

16. The angelic nature was wholly surprised at the
great act of thine Incarnation; at beholding the Unapproachable (in that he is God) becoming Man ap-
proachable by all, walking among us, and hearing from
all, Alleluia.

17. Behold, the eloquent with wide speech have become in thy comprehension like fish without voice; for
they are at a loss what to say in explanation of how thou
wast able to give birth yet remain a Virgin. But we
wonder at the mystery, and hail thee in faith, saying,
Rejoice, O vessel of the wisdom of God. Rejoice, O
chest of his dispensation. Rejoice, O thou who madest
the philosophers appear as without philosophy. Rejoice, O thou who didst expose the teachers of dialectics
as being those who have nothing to say. Rejoice; for
those who were astute in arguing about thee were
proven fools. Rejoice, because through thee the in-
ventors of myths faded away. Rejoice, because thou
didst tear apart the subtilities of the Athenians. Rejoice; for thou didst discomfit the nets of the fishermen. Rejoice, O thou who dost extricate us from the
depths of ignorance. Rejoice, O thou who dost illuminate many with knowledge. Rejoice, O ship for those

who prefer salvation. Rejoice, O haven of those who swim in life. Rejoice, O bride without bridegroom.

18. When the Adorner of all wished to save the world, he went to it called by himself. And still being God and a Shepherd, he appeared to us a Man like unto us, calling the like by the like. And being God, he heareth our cry, Alleluia.

SYNAXARION

On this Day Which is the Saturday of the Fifth Week of the Fast, We Celebrate the Praise of our Most Holy Lady, the Ever-virgin Mary, during Which it is not Permitted to Sit.

STICHOS

The city in thanksgiving and watchfulness doth praise her who upholdeth and constantly watcheth in war-time, giving the victory.

In which we chant the praise of the most holy Theotokos, and throughout which it is not permitted to sit.

. In the year 620 of Christ, the Persians from the east and the Arians, a tribe of the Scythians from the west, attacked the imperial city of Constantinople with great armies to besiege and occupy it. King Heracles was then absent, and the invaders filled the sea, particularly the Gulf of Constantinople (which is known to the Turks as *Iwan Serai Qabusi*) with their ships, and the land with their infantry, cavalry, and military machines, making ready to attack. With valour and perseverance the inhabitants held back the enemy, but being greatly outnumbered and unable to cope with such a great force, they surrendered to despair, and all hope of delivery was gone. Then they sought refuge in the Theotokos, asking succour and protection. Suddenly, a violent tempest broke out in which the ships of the enemy were wrecked, sinking with all on board. The waves flung the bodies of the drowned Barbarians in front of the Church of the Theotokos in the suburb of Blachernae (See July second). When the people saw this, they gained courage, went out, and expelled the remaining soldiers, who fled in fear. In the evening, the people gathered in the Church of the Theotokos, and spent the whole night, standing, thanking her and praising her with the cantons of the Canon known as Akathiston, during which it is not permitted to sit. In remembrance of this miracle, through which the faithful were saved, we celebrate this day, glorifying and honouring the Mother of our Lord and God.

As for the twenty-four verses which belong to this Canon, and which we recite especially on this day, some assign them to Sergius, who was Patriarch of Constantinople at that time; and some to George of Pisidia, who was custodian of manuscripts in that great church, in the same period. A poem of his has come down to us with the title, *On the Barbarians' Attack, and Their Failure, which is an Account of the War that Occurred before the Walls of Constantinople, between the Arians and its People.*

Wherefore, through the intercessions of thy combatting Mother who fighteth not, O Christ God, deliver us from all afflictions that encompass us, and have mercy upon us; for thou alone art the Lover of mankind.

Seventh Ode—Hermos

THE youths of godly minds worshipped not the creature for the Creator, but trod the threat of fire bravely, singing joyfully, O thou of exceeding praise, blessed art thou, Lord God of our fathers.

To thee we lift our voices with songs of praise, saying, Rejoice, O supersensual chariot of the Sun, O truthful vine that gave fruit to the ripe cluster, dripping with wine that rejoiceth the souls of those who glorify thee in faith.

Rejoice, O bride of God who bore the Healer of mankind. Rejoice, O mystical rod that budded the fadeless Flower. Rejoice, O thou through whom we are filled with joy, and inherit life.

The tongues of eloquent orators fall short in their ineptitude to discourse of thy praises; for thou hast transcended the seraphim by giving birth to Christ the King. Wherefore, implore him to deliver from all harm those who praise thee in faith.

Glory: The ends of the earth praise thee, O pure one, blessing thee and crying unto thee, Rejoice, O scroll on which the Word was inscribed by God's finger. Wherefore, O Theotokos, implore him to write down thy servants in the Book of Life.

Now: We thy servants implore thee, O pure Theotokos, and our hearts bow to thee. Wherefore, turn thine ear to us and save us who are drowned in sorrows. Keep thy city from all the surprises of the enemy.

Eighth Ode—Hermos

THE birth-giving of the Theotokos kept the pure youths in the furnace safe, this having been so foreshadowed. But now that it hath actually been accomplished, it moveth all the universe to sing aloud, Praise the Lord, all ye his works, and exalt him more and more unto all the ages.

Thou didst receive the Word in thy womb, O pure one, didst bear the Almighty, and nourished him with milk, and, by a sign from him, the universe also: to whom we sing, hailing, Praise the Lord, all ye his works, and exalt him more and more unto all the ages.

Verily, Moses, O holy Virgin free of corruption, did comprehend in the bush the mystery of thy great birth-giving. And the youths went before and foreshadowed it with all clearness by standing in the midst of the fire and not being burned. Wherefore, we praise thee unto all the ages.

O Maiden, dwelling-place of Light, we who have been denuded by the old deceit have put on by thy birth-giving the robe of incorruption; and we who sit in the darkness of downfalling have seen the Light. Wherefore, we praise thee unto the end of ages.

Glory: The dead by thee are brought to life, O Virgin; for thou bore the life of one Person; and those who are afflicted in their speech become eloquent, lepers are purified, diseases are driven away, and all the spirits in the sky are vanquished, defeated by thee, O salvation of mankind.

Now: Rejoice, O all-blessed pure one, who gave birth to Salvation for the world, O thou through whom we have ascended from earth on high. Rejoice, O shelter, confirmation, wall, and refuge of those who sing, Praise the Lord, all his works and exalt him more and more unto the ages.

Ninth Ode—Hermos

LET all the earthly rejoice in the Spirit, carrying their lamps. And the nature of the supersensuous, immaterial ones celebrateth also the noble Feast of the Theotokos, shouting, Rejoice, O all-pure, all-blessed, ever-virgin Theotokos.

Deliver us, O Maiden, from temptation, barbaric captivity, and from every calamity that cometh to us sinful men; that we believers, who have become partakers of everlasting joy, may hail thee.

Thou hast appeared unto us, O pure one, an illumination and a confirmation. Wherefore, we shout to thee, saying, Rejoice, O star that setteth not, bringing to the world the great Sun. Hail, thou who didst open the closed Eden. Rejoice, O fiery pillar, leading the earthly into the heavenly life.

Let us stand with reverence in the house of our God, and cry, saying, Hail, O Mary, mistress of the world; Hail, O Mary, our Lady. Rejoice, thou who alone art beautiful among women and without blame. Hail, O vessel that received the never-failing ointment that was poured on thee.

Glory: Hail, O dove that gave birth to the compassionate One. Rejoice, thou of perpetual virginity. Rejoice, O pride of all the righteous, the crown of strivers. Rejoice, O divine beauty of all the upright. Hail, O salvation of us who believe.

Now: Have pity, O God, on thine inheritance; and overlook now all our sins, since there is one who pleadeth with thee, she who gave thee birth on earth without seed, when, by the multitude of thy mercies, thou willed to be in the likeness of a stranger, O Christ.

❡ *Then the Choir singeth the Kontakion,* Verily, I am thy servant, *etc.*

Fourth Part

19. Thou art, O virgin Theotokos, a wall to virgins, and to all who hasten unto thee; for the Author of heaven and earth made thee, O pure one, and dwelt in thy womb, teaching all to cry thus unto thee, Rejoice, O column of virginity. Rejoice, O door of salvation. Rejoice, O element of the recall of mental creation. Rejoice, O bestower of divine beneficence. Rejoice; for thou hast re-created those whose conception was unseemly. Rejoice; for thou hast preached to those who are robbed of minds. Rejoice, O annuller of the corrupter of minds. Rejoice, O Mother of the Sower of purity. Rejoice, O chamber of matrimony without seed. Rejoice, thou who didst reconcile the faithful to the Lord. Rejoice, O good instructress of virgins. Rejoice, O thou who adornest the souls of the righteous with the adornment of thy wedding. Rejoice, O bride without bridegroom.

20. All praise falleth short, O holy King, when it stretcheth toward the bounds of thy bountiful compassion; in that, if we offer thee praises equalling the sands

in number, we would have accomplished nothing comparable to what thou hast given us, who shout unto thee, Alleluia.

21. We behold the holy Virgin as a lamp containing the Light, appearing unto those in darkness, having kindled the immaterial Light. Wherefore, she leadeth all to divine knowledge, and lighteth the mind with brilliancy. Let her, therefore, thus he praised aloud, Rejoice, O rays of the supersensuous Sun. Rejoice, O dart of the unsetting Sun. Rejoice, O lightning illuminating our souls. Rejoice, O thou who, as thunder, astoundeth thine enemies. Rejoice; for thou sheddest a Light of great brilliancy. Rejoice; for thou followest the river of swift current. Rejoice, who didst represent the sign of the pool. Rejoice, thou who didst remove the abomination of sin. Rejoice, O bath that cleanseth the intent. Rejoice, O cup in which happiness is mixed. Rejoice, O fragrance of Christ. Rejoice, O life of the mystical banquet. Rejoice, O bride without bridegroom. ·

22. When the Remitter of the debts of all mankind wished to bestow his grace of the remission of the old debts, he came of himself to those who had been driven away from his grace, tearing up the handwriting of ordinances, hearing thus from all, Allelulia.

23. Since thou art a living temple, O Theotokos, we all praise thee, singing to thy birth-giving; for God, who holdeth all in his hand, dwelt in thy belly, sanctifying and glorifying thee, and teaching all to hail thee thus, Rejoice, O saint greater than all saints. Rejoice, O ark gilded with the Holy Spirit. Rejoice, O endless treasure of Life. Rejoice, O honoured crown for the kings of true worship. Rejoice, O venerable pride of pious Priests. Rejoice, O unshakable tower of the Church. Rejoice, O indestructible wall of the kingdom. Rejoice, thou through whom victory is achieved. Rejoice, thou through whom the enemy falleth. Rejoice, O healing of my body. Rejoice, O salvation of my soul. Rejoice, O bride without bridegroom.

24. O all-praised, O Mother that gave birth to the Word, more holy than all the saints, accept this praise and deliver all from all afflictions. Save from the impending punishment all those who cry to thee, Allelulia.

❡ *Then repeat the first Stanza,* The archangel, *etc. (p. 703).*

❡ *Then,* Holy God, *etc;* Verily, I am thy servant, *etc. (plain reading); and the rest of Little Compline.*

2. MATINS

❡ *On* God the Lord hath appeared unto us, *etc., the Troparion,* The bodiless having learned, *etc. (three times, p. 703); then the Canon of the Theotokos; and the Katabasias,* Open my mouth, *etc.*

Exaposteilarion

VERILY, the mystery before the ages hath been made known today; for the Word God hath by his compassion become Son to the Virgin Mary; with Gabriel preaching glad tidings of joy. Wherefore, let us all shout together, Rejoice, O Mother of the Lord.

❡ *And in the Einos, the following Prosomia, in the Fourth Tone.*

THE hidden mystery, hidden from the angels, was entrusted to Gabriel the chief of angels, who comes to thee now, who art alone without defilement, the beautiful dove and recall of our race, hailing thee and saying, Rejoice, O all-holy one, and be ready; for by my words thou shalt receive in thy womb the Word of God. (*Repeat.*)

A brilliant palace hath been prepared for thee, O Master, the womb of the pure Maiden of God. Hasten, therefore, descend thou to it, having compassion on envy-ridden creation, confined in the bondage of the wicked, devoid of its first beauty, and awaiting the condescension of thy salvation.

The archangel Gabriel came to thee openly, O innocent of all blame, and hailed thee, saying, Rejoice, O remover of the curse and lifter up of the fallen. Rejoice, thou who alone became chosen unto God. Rejoice, O living cloud of the Sun. Receive thou the Uncontainable, who willeth to dwell in thy womb.

Glory and Now, in the Fourth Tone

THE Theotokos heard an ambiguous language; for the archangel uttered to her words of glad tidings. But when she accepted the salutation in faith, she conceived thee, O God before the ages. Wherefore, we joyfully cry unto thee, O God, who wast incarnate from her without mutability, grant peace to the world and to our souls the Great Mercy.

❡ *Then the Great Doxology; and the Troparion,* Verily, the bodiless having learned, *etc.*

3. THE MASS

❡ *The Troparion,* Verily, the bodiless having learned, *etc; and the Kontakion,* Verily, I am thy servant, *etc.*

The Epistle: Ye brethren: The former indeed had also justifications, etc. (p. 349).

The Gospel: And Mary arose in those days, etc. (p. 50).

❡ *And on Especially, the Hermos of the Ninth Ode,* Let all the earthly, *etc.* (*p. 715*).

Koinonikon: I will take the cup of salvation, and call upon the Name of the Lord.

THE FIFTH SUNDAY OF THE FAST

Memory of our Righteous Mother, Mary the Egyptian

1. VESPERS

❡ *On* O Lord, to thee have I cried, *the Stichera of the Resurrection; then Glory, in the Fourth Tone.*

THE power of thy Cross, O Christ, hath done wonders; for she who had been a harlot strove in the ascetic way. Whereupon she cast away the weakness of nature, and bravely contended against Satan. Then, having achieved the prize of victory, she doth intercede for our souls.

¶ *Now to our Lady for the Oktoechos.*

¶ *The Aposticha for the Resurrection; Glory, in the Second Tone.*

THOU didst sever with the sword of abstinence the snares of the soul and the passion of the body, O righteous one. And by the silence of asceticism thou didst choke the sins of thought. And by the stream of thy tears thou didst water the whole wilderness, bringing forth for us the fruits of repentance. Wherefore, we celebrate thy memory.

¶ *Now to our Lady for the Octoechos, in the Same Tone.*

Troparion for the Resurrection and for the Righteous One, in the Eighth Tone

Through thee the divine likeness, etc. (p. 37).

2. MATINS

Katabasias, Open my mouth, *etc. (p. 114); the Exaposteilarion for the Resurrection; and the following for the Righteous One.*

HAVING taken thee, O righteous Mary, as an exemplar of repentance, implore thou Christ to grant the same to us in this period of the Fast; that in faith and longing we may praise thee with songs.

O virgin Mother of the Lord, in that thou art the sweetness of the angels, the consolation of the sorrowful, and the intercessor for Christians; help me and rescue me from eternal punishment.

¶ *And in the Einos, the Stichera for the Resurrection; Glory, in the First Tone.*

THE kingdom of God is not meat and drink, but righteousness and asceticism with holiness. Wherefore, the rich do not enter it, but they who place their treasures in the hands of the poor. This doth the Prophet David teach, saying, The righteous man is he that doeth mercy all the day long; who delighteth in the Lord; and, walking in his light, stumbleth not. All this was written for our instruction, that we should fast and do good; and the Lord grant us heavenly things in place of earthly.

¶ *Now,* Thou hast transcended, *etc.*

3. The Mass

¶ *The Troparia for the Resurrection, the Righteous One, and the Patron Saint of the church; the Kontakion,* Verily, I am thy servant, *etc. And if the Feast of the Annunciation is past, then say,* O undisputed intercessor of Christians, *etc. (p. 125).*

The Epistle: Vow and pay unto the Lord your God. In Judah is God known.

Section from the Epistle of St. Paul to the Hebrews (9:11-14)

YE brethren: When Christ came an high priest of good things to come, by a greater and more perfect tabernacle, not made with hands, that is to say, not of this creation:

Neither by the blood of goats and calves, but by his own blood he entered in once into the holy place, having obtained eternal redemption for us.

For if the blood of bulls and of goats, and the ashes of an heifer sprinkling the unclean, sanctifieth to the purifying of the flesh;

How much more shall the blood of Christ, who through the eternal Spirit offered himself without spot to God, purge your conscience from dead works to serve the living God?

The Gospel: from St. Mark (10:32-45)

AT that time: Jesus took the twelve disciples and began to tell them what things should happen unto him,

Saying, Behold, we go up to Jerusalem; and the Son
of man shall be delivered unto the chief priests, and
unto the scribes; and they shall condemn him to death,
and shall deliver him to the Gentiles:

And they shall mock him, and shall scourge him, and
shall spit upon him, and shall kill him; and the third
day he shall rise again.

And James and John, the sons of Zebedee, come unto
him, saying, Master, we would that thou shouldest do
for us whatsover we shall desire.

And he said unto them, What would ye that I should
do for you?

They said unto him, Grant unto us that we may sit,
one on thy right hand, and the other on thy left hand,
in thy glory.

But Jesus said unto them, Ye know not what ye ask:
can ye drink of the cup that I drink of? and be baptized with the baptism that I am baptized with?

And they said unto him, We can. And Jesus said unto
them, Ye shall indeed drink of the cup that I drink of;
and with the baptism that I am baptized withal shall
ye be baptized:

But to sit on my right hand and on my left hand is
not mine to give; but it shall be given to them for whom
it is prepared.

And when the ten heard it, they began to be much
displeased with James and John.

But Jesus called them to him, and saith unto them,
Ye know that they which are accounted to rule over
the Gentiles exercise lordship over them; and their
great ones exercise authority upon them.

But so shall it not be among you: but whosoever will
be great among you, shall be your minister:

And whosoever of you will be the chiefest, shall be
servant of all.

For even the Son of man came not to be ministered
unto, but to minister, and to give his life a ransom for
many.

¶ *And the rest of the Liturgy of St. Basil the Great.*

SYNAXARION

ON THIS DAY, THE FIFTH SUNDAY OF THE FAST, IT
WAS ORDAINED THAT WE CELEBRATE THE MEMORY OF
OUR RIGHTEOUS MOTHER, MARY THE EGYPTIAN.

STICHOS

VERILY, THE SOUL DID RISE OF OLD FROM MARY, AND
BLOOD DID FLOW FROM HER BODY.

SHELTER, O EARTH, WHAT REMAINETH OF HER DEAD
AND BLEACHED BONES.

ON which we chant the service of our Mother
Miriam the Egyptian.

The anniversary of this pious soul falls on the first of
April, when the annals of her life were compiled. But
remembrance of her is also made on this day, as the
end of holy Quadragesima approaches, to arouse the
energy of the slothful, and to urge sinners to repentance,
imitating her example.

Wherefore, through her intercessions with God, have
mercy upon us and save us. Amen.

Koinonikon: Praise the Lord in the heavens, etc.

EVENING OF THE FIFTH SUNDAY OF THE FAST

¶ *On* O Lord, to thee have I cried, *the following Prosomia, in the
First Tone.*

O CHRIST the Rich, thou hast assumed poverty
and enriched the human race with illumination
and immortality. Therefore, enrich me, a poor man
impoverished by the pleasures of life, with virtues. Establish me with Lazarus the poor, and deliver me from
the punishments of the rich and from hades that is
prepared for me.

I have become rich with evil in a miserable way. I
have loved luxury, exploited the pleasures of life, and
have come under the condemnation of the fire of hades.
I have slighted my mind, and am famished and cast

down like Lazarus before the gates of divine deeds.
Wherefore, have compassion on me, O Lord Master.

Let us believers begin with diligence the sixth week
of the solemn Fast. Let us sing songs of offering for
Palm Sunday, to the Lord coming in glory to Jerusalem, to cause death to die by his divine power. Wherefore, let us make ready the banners of victory, in true
worship, and the branches of virtues, shouting, Hosanna
to the Creator of all.

❡ *Glory and Now to our Lady, and after,* O resplendent Light, *etc.,*
the Prokeimenon, Thou hast given an inhertance, *etc., with its Sti-*
choi (*p. 675*).

❡ *And in the Aposticha, the following Idiomelons, in the First Tone.*

WONDERFUL is the purpose of the compassionate
Saviour towards us; for possessing the knowledge
of future things as present, he made known the story
of the Rich Man and Lazarus. Let us contemplate the
end of both. As for the one, let us run away from his
cruelty and hatred of men. As for the other, let us emulate his endurance and long-suffering; that, delighting
with him in the bosom of Abraham, we may shout, saying, O Lord, righteous Judge, glory be to thee. (*Repeat.*)

O Lord, by the intercessions of all the saints and of the
Theotokos, grant us thy peace and have mercy upon
us, since thou alone art compassionate.

Glory and Now to our Lady, in the Same Tone

O DELIGHT of the heavenly hosts, O pure virgin
Theotokos, and precious champion of men on
earth, save us who take refuge in thee; for in thee, after
God, have we placed our hope.

❡ *And the rest of the service as at the end of Vespers on Cheese*
Fare Sunday (*p. 645*).

SATURDAY OF LAZARUS THE RIGHTEOUS SAINT

1. MATINS

❡ *On* God the Lord hath appeared unto us, *the following Troparion, in the First Tone (three times).*

O CHRIST God, when thou didst raise Lazarus from the dead, before thy Passion, thou didst confirm the universal resurrection. Wherefore, we, like babes, carry the insignia of triumph and victory, and cry to thee, O Vanquisher of death, Hosanna in the highest. Blessed is he that cometh in the Name of the Lord.

Kathisma, in the First Tone

O CHRIST God, thou didst have compassion on the tears of Mary and Martha. And, commanding that the stone be rolled away from the tomb, thou didst call the dead and raise him, O Life-giver, confirming thereby the resurrection of the world. Glory, therefore, to thy might, O Saviour. Glory to thy power. Glory to thee, O thou who didst indite all things by a word.

❡ *Glory and Now (repeated).*

❡ *Then the Benediction of the Resurrection (p. 111). The Matin Gospel is not read, but instead,* In that we have beheld the Resurrection of Christ, *etc. (p. 113); and Psalm 50. Then the Katabasias* Verily, the people of Israel, *etc. (p. 46); and instead of* O thou who art more honourable that the cherubim, *etc., sing the following Ninth Ode, in the Eighth Tone.*

L ET us glorify and honour, O ye people, the pure Theotokos, who bore within her without burning the divine Fire. Let us magnify her with unceasing songs of praise.

When the nations saw one dead four days walking about erectly, they were dazzled with wonder and shouted to the Rescuer, Thee, O God, with songs of praise do we magnify.

When thou wentest before, O my Saviour, and verified thy glorious Resurrection, thou didst deliver Lazarus from hades, having been dead four days. Wherefore, with songs of praise do we magnify thee.

¶ *Then sing,* Holy is the Lord our God (*three times*); *and the fol* *lowing Exaposteilarions.*

BY thy word, O Word of God, Lazarus came to life a second time. But the nations honour thee with branches, O mighty One; for by thy Death thou shalt abolish hades to the end.

Christ hath taken thee captive, O death, by Lazarus. Where then is thy victory, O hades? Behold the weeping of Bethany hath turned upon thee. And we all offer him branches of victory and triumph.

¶ *In the Einos, the following eight Idiomelons, in the First Tone.*

O LONG-SUFFERING Christ, since thou art the Life of mankind and its Resurrection, thou didst come to the tomb of Lazarus, verifying for us thy two Substances; and that thou didst come from a pure Virgin, God and Man; for as Man thou didst enquire, Where was he buried? and as God, thou didst raise the four-day dead by a divine gesture.

Thou didst raise from hades Lazarus dead four days, O Christ, and before thine own Death thou didst shake the might of death. And through one friend thou didst foretell the delivery of all mankind from corruption. Wherefore, we worship thine almighty power, crying, Blessed art thou, our Saviour; have mercy upon us.

Verily, Mary and Martha said to the Saviour, Lord hadst thou been here Lazarus would not have died. But Christ, the Resurrection of those who slumber, raised him, after four days, from the dead. Wherefore, all ye believers, let us worship him that cometh in glory to save our souls.

Wishing to grant thy Disciples signs of thy Godhead, O Christ, thou didst humble thyself before the crowds, desiring to hide it. Wherefore, since thou art God and hadst foreknowledge, thou didst foretell the death of Lazarus to the Apostles. But when thou didst come to Bethany in the presence of the people, thou didst ignore the tomb of thy friend, asking, as a Man, to know where it was. But he whom thou didst raise after four days, declared thy divine might. Wherefore, O Almighty God, glory to thee.

Thou didst raise thy friend after four days, O Christ, and wiped the tears of Mary and Martha, making plain to all that thou art he who fillest all with thy divine might, and with a will of divine authority, O thou to whom the cherubim cry ceaselessly, Hosanna in the highest. Blessed art thou who art still God over all. Glory to thee.

Martha said to Mary, The Teacher cometh and he calleth thee; come. But she hastened to where the Lord stood, and seeing him, she fell down and worshipped him, kissing his pure feet, and cried, saying, Lord, if thou hadst been here, my brother had not died.

Thou didst raise Lazarus in Bethany after four days, O Lord; for by thy mere coming to the tomb, thy voice became life to the dead. Hades sighed and fearfully loosed him. Wherefore, great is the wonder, O Lord of great mercy. Glory to thee.

As thou saidst to Martha, O Lord, I am the Resurrection, thou didst fulfill the word by the deed, calling Lazarus from hades. Likewise, I implore thee, O Lover of mankind, to raise me, dead in passion; for thou art compassionate and merciful.

Glory, in the Second Tone

TODAY hath been fulfilled a great and strange wonder; for Christ invoked a man dead four days, and raised him from the tomb, calling him, Beloved. Let us, therefore, glorify him; for he is greatly to be praised; that, by the intercessions of Lazarus the righteous, he may save our souls.

¶ *And Now,* Thou hast transcended, *etc; then the Great Doxology; and* Today hath salvation come into the world, *etc; and the Benediction.*

2. The Mass

Eisodikon: Come, let us worship and fall down to Christ. Save us, O Son of God, who didst rise from the dead, us who sing unto thee, Alleluia.

❧*Troparion,* O Christ God, when thou didst raise Lazarus, *etc.,* (*p. 725*); *and the folowing Kontakion, in the Second Tone.*

CHRIST, who is the Truth and Joy of all, the Light, the Life, and the Resurrection of the world, hath appeared in his goodness to those on earth, and become a Sign of resurrection, granting all divine forgiveness.

❧*And instead of* Holy God, *sing,* Ye who have been baptized into Christ, have put on Christ; Alleluia.

The Epistle: The Lord is my light and my salvation. The Lord is the Protector of my life.

Section from the Epistle of St. Paul to the Hebrews (12:28 to end; 13:1-8)

YE brethren: If we receive a kingdom which cannot be moved, let us have grace, whereby we may serve God acceptably with reverence and godly fear:

For our God is a consuming fire.

Let brotherly love continue.

Be not forgetful to entertain strangers: for thereby some have entertained angels unawares.

Remember them that are in bonds, as bound with them; and them which suffer adversity, as being yourselves also in the body.

Marriage is honourable in all, and the bed undefiled: but whoremongers and adulterers God will judge.

Let your conversation be without covetousness; and be content with such things as ye have: for he hath said, I will never leave thee, nor forsake thee.

So that we may boldly say, The Lord is my helper, and I will not fear what man shall do unto me.

Remember them which have the rule over you, who have spoken unto you the word of God: whose faith follow, considering the end of their conversation.

Jesus Christ the same yesterday, and to-day, and for ever.

The Gospel: from St. John (11:1-45)

AT that time: A certain man was sick, named Lazarus, of Bethany, the town of Mary and her sister Martha.

(It was that Mary which anointed the Lord with ointment, and wiped his feet with her hair, whose brother Lazarus was sick.)

Therefore his sisters sent unto him, saying, Lord, behold, he whom thou lovest is sick.

When Jesus heard that, he said, This sickness is not unto death, but for the glory of God, that the Son of God might be glorified thereby.

Now Jesus loved Martha, and her sister, and Lazarus.

When he had heard therefore that he was sick, he abode two days still in the same place where he was.

Then after that saith he to his disciples, Let us go into Judæa again.

His disciples say unto him, Master, the Jews of late sought to stone thee; and goest thou thither again?

Jesus answered, Are there not twelve hours in the day? If any man walk in the day, he stumbleth not, because he seeth the light of this world.

But if a man walk in the night, he stumbleth, because there is no light in him.

These things said he: and after that he said unto them, Our friend Lazarus sleepeth; but I go, that I may awake him out of sleep.

Then said his disciples, Lord, if he sleep, he shall do well.

Howbeit Jesus spake of his death: but they thought that he had spoken of taking of rest in sleep.

Then said Jesus unto them plainly, Lazarus is dead.

And I am glad for your sakes that I was not there, to the intent ye may believe; nevertheless let us go unto him.

Then said Thomas, which is called Didymus, unto his fellow disciples, Let us also go, that we may die with him.

Then when Jesus came, he found that he had lain in the grave four days already.

Now Bethany was nigh unto Jerusalem, about fifteen furlongs off:

And many of the Jews came to Martha and Mary, to comfort them concerning their brother.

Then Martha, as soon as she heard that Jesus was coming, went and met him: but Mary sat still in the house.

Then said Martha unto Jesus, Lord, if thou hadst been here, my brother had not died.

But I know, that even now, whatsoever thou wilt ask of God, God will give it thee.

Jesus saith unto her, Thy brother shall rise again.

Martha saith unto him, I know that he shall rise again in the resurrection at the last day.

Jesus said unto her, I am the resurrection, and the life: he that believeth in me, though he were dead, yet shall he live:

And whosoever liveth and believeth in me shall never die. Believest thou this?

She saith unto him, Yea, Lord: I believe that thou art the Christ, the Son of God, which should come into the world.

And when she had so said, she went her way, and called Mary her sister secretly, saying, The Master is come, and calleth for thee.

As soon as she heard that, she arose quickly, and came unto him.

Now Jesus was not yet come into the town, but was in that place where Martha met him.

The Jews then which were with her in the house, and comforted her, when they saw Mary, that she rose up hastily and went out, followed her, saying, She goeth unto the grave to weep there.

Then when Mary was come where Jesus was, and saw him, she fell down at his feet, saying unto him, Lord, if thou hadst been here, my brother had not died.

When Jesus therefore saw her weeping, and the Jews also weeping which came with her, he groaned in the spirit, and was troubled,

And said, Where have ye laid him? They say unto him, Lord, come and see.

Jesus wept.

Then said the Jews, Behold how he loved him!

And some of them said, Could not this man, which opened the eyes of the blind, have caused that even this man should not have died?

Jesus therefore again groaning in himself cometh to the grave. It was a cave, and a stone lay upon it.

Jesus said, Take ye away the stone. Martha, the sister of him that was dead, saith unto him, Lord, by this time he stinketh: for he hath been dead four days.

Jesus saith unto her, Said I not unto thee, that, if thou wouldest believe, thou shouldest see the glory of God?

Then they took away the stone from the place where the dead was laid. And Jesus lifted up his eyes, and said, Father, I thank thee that thou hast heard me.

And I knew that thou hearest me always: but because of the people which stand by I said it, that they may believe that thou hast sent me.

And when he thus had spoken, he cried with a loud voice, Lazarus, come forth.

And he that was dead came forth, bound hand and foot with graveclothes; and his face was bound about with a napkin. Jesus saith unto them, Loose him, and let him go.

Then many of the Jews which came to Mary, and had seen the things which Jesus did, believed on him.

¶ *And the rest of the Liturgy of John Chrysostom. And on Especially sing the following Hermos, in the Eighth Tone.*

COME, ye people, let us honour with glorifications the undefiled Theotokos, who bore in her womb the divine Fire and was not consumed; and with ceaseless praises let us glorify her.

SYNAXARION

ON THIS DAY, WHICH IS THE SATURDAY BEFORE PALM SUNDAY, WE CELEBRATE THE FOURTH-DAY RISING FROM THE DEAD OF ST. LAZARUS, THE RIGHTEOUS FRIEND OF CHRIST.

STICHOS

THY WAILING FOR THY FRIEND, O JESUS, WAS THE ATTRIBUTE OF MORTAL HUMANITY AND THY BRINGING HIM BACK TO LIFE IS THE ACT OF A DIVINE AND SUBLIME POWER.

LAZARUS was beloved of Jesus, as also were his two sisters, Martha and Mary, who were frequent hosts of Jesus, and who served him much (St. Luke 10:38-40 and St. John 12: 2 and 3). They were of the town of Bethany in Judæa, in the shadow of the Mount of Olives on the eastern side, at a distance of two Roman miles from Jerusalem. A few days before the Passion of salvation, Lazarus took sick. And while Jesus was still in Galilee, Lazarus' sister told Jesus of his sickness. Jesus remained purposely in Galilee two days until Lazarus died. Then he said to his Disciples, Let us go to Judæa, that I may awaken our beloved Lazarus who has fallen asleep, meaning thereby the deep sleep of death. And when he reached Bethany, four days after the burial of Lazarus, he comforted his sister, and having groaned in spirit at the death of his beloved friend, he asked where they had put him. He wept, and, having come to the tomb, he commanded that the stone be removed. Then he lifted up his eyes and thanked God the Father, and cried with a loud voice, Lazarus, come forth. And the dead came out wrapped in grave-clothes. And Jesus said to those standing by, Loose him and let him go (St. John 11). In remembrance, there-fore, of this supernatural miracle, we celebrate this day.

It is related in ancient accounts that Lazarus was thirty years old when Jesus raised him, and that he lived thereafter thirty years longer, and died in Cyprus in the year 63 of Christ. It is also said that near the city of Citium lies a tomb on which there is the follow-ing legend, *Lazarus of four days, beloved of Christ.* In 890, Leo the Wise removed his bones to Constanti-nople. Doubtless it was then that the duets chanted at Vespers of his festival were composed. They begin, If thou wishest, O Lord, to see the tomb of Lazarus, etc.

Wherefore, through the intercessions of thy friend, O Christ God, have mercy upon us. Amen.

Koinonikon: Out of the mouths of infants and of sucklings thou hast perfected praise.

❡*And instead of* We have seen the true Light, *etc., sing the Tro-parion,* O Christ God, when thou didst raise Lazarus, *etc.* (*p. 725*).

Benediction: O thou who by the raising of Lazarus from the dead didst confirm universal resurrection, O Christ our true God, etc.

PALM SUNDAY

1. VESPERS

❡*On* O Lord, to thee have I cried, *the following five Idiomelons, in the Sixth Tone, repeating each.*

TODAY hath the grace of the Holy Spirit brought us together; and we all lift thy Cross as we say, Blessed is he that cometh in the Name of the Lord. Hosanna in the highest.

The Word of God the Father, the Son who is coëter-nal with him, whose throne is heaven and whose foot-stool is the earth, hath today humbled himself, coming

to Bethany on a dumb ass. Wherefore, the Hebrew
lads praised him, carrying in their hands branches, and
crying, Blessed is he that cometh, King of Israel.

Let us also, the new Israel, come together today, the
Church of the Gentiles, to shout with the Prophet
Zachariah, Rejoice greatly, O daughter of Zion; shout,
O daughter of Jerusalem; behold thy King cometh unto
thee: he is meek and having salvation, and riding upon
an ass, and upon a colt the foal of an ass. Wherefore,
like babes, feast thou, carrying branches in thy hands,
and praise him, singing, Hosanna in the highest. Blessed
is he that cometh, King of Israel.

O good Christ, when thou didst foreshadow for us
thine exalted Resurrection, thou didst raise from the
tomb by thine own command thy breathless friend Lazarus, who had been dead for four days, and had become
decomposed. Thou didst mount symbolically upon an
ass, as one borne upon a chariot, thus indicating the
Gentiles. Wherefore, beloved Israel did offer thee
praise from the mouths of innocent babes and sucklings,
having beheld thee, O Saviour, entering into the holy
city six days before the Passover.

Before the six days of the Passover, Jesus came to
Bethany, and his Disciples came to him and said, O
Lord, where wouldest thou that we prepare for thee to
eat the Passover? And he sent them, saying, Go to the
town that lieth before you, and ye shall find a man carrying a jar of water. Follow him, and say to the Lord
of the house, The Master saith, I shall eat the Passover
with my Disciples.

¶ *Glory and Now; The first Idiomelon,* Today hath the grace of the
Holy Spirit, *etc; then the Eisodos; and after,* O resplendent Light,
etc., and the daily Prokeimenon, the following Readings.

First Reading: from the Book of Genesis
(49:1-2; 8-12)

JACOB called unto his sons, and said: Gather yourselves together, that I may tell you that which shall
befall you in the last days.

Gather yourselves together, and hear, ye sons of Jacob; and hearken unto Israel your father.

Judah, thou art he whom thy brethren shall praise: thy hand shall be in the neck of thine enemies; thy father's children shall bow down before thee.

Judah is a lion's whelp: from the prey, my son, thou art gone up: he stooped down, he couched as a lion, and as an old lion; who shall rouse him up?

The sceptre shall not depart from Judah, nor a lawgiver from between his feet, until Shiloh come; and unto him shall the gathering of the people be.

Binding his foal unto the vine, and his ass's colt unto the choice vine; he washed his garments in wine, and his clothes in the blood of grapes:

His eyes shall be red with wine, and his teeth white with milk.

*Second Reading: from the Prophecy of Zephaniah
the Prophet (3:14-19)*

THESE sayings the Lord doth say: Sing, O daughter of Zion; shout, O Israel; be glad and rejoice with all the heart, O daughter of Jerusalem.

The Lord hath taken away thy judgments, he hath cast out thine enemy: the King of Israel, even the Lord, is in the midst of thee: thou shalt not see evil any more.

In that day it shall be said to Jerusalem, Fear thou not: and to Zion, Let not thine hands be slack.

The Lord thy God in the midst of thee is mighty; he will save, he will rejoice over thee with joy; he will rest in his love, he will joy over thee with singing.

I will gather them that are sorrowful for the solemn assembly, who are of thee, to whom the reproach of it was a burden.

Behold, at that time I will undo all that afflict thee: and I will save her that halteth, and gather her that was driven out; and I will get them praise and fame in every land.

Third Reading: from the Prophecy of Zachariah the Prophet (9:9-15)

THESE sayings the Lord doth say: Rejoice greatly, O daughter of Zion; shout, O daughter of Jerusalem: behold, thy King cometh unto thee: he is just, and having salvation; lowly, and riding upon an ass and upon a colt the foal of an ass.

And I will cut off the chariot from Ephraim, and the horse from Jerusalem, and the battle bow shall be cut off: and he shall speak peace unto the heathen: and his dominion shall be from sea even to sea, and from the river even to the ends of the earth.

As for thee also, by the blood of thy covenant I have sent forth thy prisoners out of the pit wherein is no water.

Turn you to the stronghold, ye prisoners of hope: even to-day do I declare that I will render double unto thee;

When I have bent Judah for me, filled the bow with Ephraim, and raised up thy sons, O Zion against thy sons, O Greece, and made thee as the sword of a mighty man.

And the Lord shall be seen over them, and his arrow shall go forth as the lightning: and the Lord God shall blow the trumpet, and shall go with whirlwinds of the south.

The Lord of hosts shall defend them.

¶ *And in the Litiya, Glory and Now, in the Third Tone.*

SIX days before the Passover, Jesus came to Bethany to call Lazarus, who had been dead for four days, and to preach beforehand of the Resurrection. And the two women, Mary and Martha, the sisters of Lazarus, met him crying, Lord, if thou hadst been here our brother had not died. Then he said unto them, Have I not told you that whosoever believeth in me, though he die he shall live again? Show me where ye have laid him. And the All-creator cried out to him, Lazarus, come forth.

❧ *In the Aposticha, the following Idiomelons, in the Eighth Tone.*

R EJOICE and be happy, O city of Zion. Be joyful and glad, O Church of God; for behold, thy King is come sitting upon a colt and praised by youth. Hosanna in the highest. Blessed art thou who art possessed of bountiful mercies: have mercy upon us.

Stichos: Out of the mouths of infants and of sucklings thou hast perfected praise.

Today hath the Saviour come to Jerusalem to fulfill the Scriptures; and all did take in their hands branches of palm trees. And they spread their clothes for him, knowing that it was he, our Lord, to whom the cherubim unceasingly call out, Hosanna in the highest. Blessed art thou who art possessed of bountiful mercies; have mercy upon us.

Stichos: O Lord, our Lord, how admirable is thy Name in all the earth!

O thou who ridest upon the cherubim, and who art praised by the seraphim, thou didst ride upon a colt, O holy, Davidič One. And the youths were praising thee as befitteth God. And the Jews did blaspheme against thee wickedly. Thy sitting on an ass foreshadowed the transformation of the bolting of the Gentiles from infidelity to faith. Glory to thee O Christ, who alone art merciful and the Lover of mankind.

❧ *Glory and Now, in the Sixth Tone;* Today hath the grace of the Holy Spirit, *etc.* (*p. 733*).

❧ *The Troparion,* O Christ God, when thou didst raise Lazarus, *etc.* (*two times*) (*p. 725*).

❧ *Then the following, in the Fourth Tone.*

O CHRIST God, when we were buried with thee in Baptism, we became deserving of thy Resurrection to immortal life. Wherefore, we praise thee, crying, Hosanna in the highest, blessed is he that cometh in the Name of the Lord.

2. MATINS

❡ *The Troparia as at Vespers; then the following Kathismata, in the Fourth Tone.*

LET us come with branches to praise Christ the Master in faith like babes, purifying our souls supersensuously, and crying to him with a loud voice, Blessed art thou O Saviour, thou who didst come into the world, and didst become a new, spiritual Adam. As thou didst consent to rescue Adam from the first curse, and didst prepare all things for the best, O thou Word, Lover of mankind, glory to thee.

O Lord, thou didst raise Lazarus from the tomb after four days, and thou didst teach all to shout to thee with palm leaves and branches, Blessed art thou that comest.

O Christ Saviour, thou didst shed tears in secret over thy friend Lazarus lying dead. Thou didst raise him from the dead, thereby declaring thy pity in love to mankind. And when the multitude of little children knew of thy presence they went out today carrying in their hands branches and crying to thee, Hosanna, blessed art thou who didst come to save the world.

❡ *Then the Anabathmoi,* From my youth, *etc. (p. 50); and the following Prokeimenon.*

Out of the mouths of infants and of sucklings thou hast perfected praise. O Lord, our Lord, how admirable is thy name in all the earth.

The Matin Gospel: from St. Matthew
(21:1-11; 15-17)

AT that time: When Jesus drew nigh unto Jerusalem, and was come to Bethphage, unto the Mount of Olives, then sent Jesus two disciples,

Saying unto them, Go into the village over against you, and straightway ye shall find an ass tied, and a colt with her: loose them, and bring them unto me.

And if any man say aught unto you, ye shall say, The Lord hath need of them; and straightway he will send them.

All this was done, that it might be fulfilled which was spoken by the prophet, saying,

Tell ye the daughter of Sion, Behold, thy King cometh unto thee, meek, and sitting upon an ass, and a colt the foal of an ass.

And the disciples went, and did as Jesus commanded them,

And brought the ass, and the colt, and put on them their clothes, and they set him thereon.

And a very great multitude spread their garments in the way; others cut down branches from the trees, and strewed them in the way.

And the multitudes that went before, and that followed, cried, saying, Hosanna to the Son of David: Blessed is he that cometh in the name of the Lord; Hosanna in the highest.

And when he was come into Jerusalem, all the city was moved, saying, Who is this?

And the people said, This is Jesus the prophet of Nazareth of Galilee.

And when the chief priests and scribes saw the wonderful things that he did, and the children crying in the temple, and saying Hosanna to the son of David; they were sore displeased.

And he said unto him, Hearest thou what these say? And Jesus saith unto them, Yea; have ye never read, Out of the mouth of babes and sucklings thou hast perfected praise?

And he left them, and went out of the city into Bethany; and he lodged there.

❡ *Then immediately, Psalm 50, (p. 82); and on Glory and Now, sing the following, in the Second Tone.*

Today Christ entereth the Holy City, sitting on an ass to loosen the barren bestiality of the Gentiles, long in an evil state.

❡ *And on* O merciful One, have mercy upon me, *etc; is sung,* Today hath the grace of the Holy Spirit, *etc.* (*p. 733*).

Then the following Katabasias, in the Fourth Tone

1. Verily, the springs of the deep appeared dry, and the foundations of the tumultuous sea were uncovered; for thou didst rebuke the tempest with a sign, and thou didst save thy chosen people singing to thee, O Lord, a triumphant song.

3. Verily, at thy command the children of Israel drank from a hard, cloven rock. As for the rock, it is thou, O Christ, the Life by which the Church gaineth strength, crying, Hosanna, blessed art thou that comest.

4. Verily, Christ our Lord clearly cometh and delayeth not; from a thick and shadowy mountain, from a Virgin who giveth birth without knowing man, as was told by the Prophet of old. Wherefore, we all shout together, Glory be to thy power, O Lord.

5. O thou bringer of good tidings to Zion, ascend the mountain; and O thou watchman of Jerusalem, raise thy voice with strength. Glorious things have been spoken of thee, O city of God. Peace to Israel, and salvation to the Gentiles.

6. Verily, the souls of the righteous have shouted with joy, saying, Now a new covenant hath been given the world, let the people be renewed with the drops of divine blood.

7. O thou who didst preserve the Abrahamite youths safe from fire, and didst kill the Chaldeans who preyed unjustly upon the innocent, O most praised Lord, blessed art thou, God of our fathers.

8. Rejoice, O Jerusalem, and feast O lovers of Zion; for the Lord of power, who ruleth for ever, hath come.

Let the earth be solemn before his face, and let it shout,
Praise the Lord all ye his works.

⊄ *Then instead of* O thou who art more honourable, *etc., sing:*

The Ninth Ode—Hermos

9. God the Lord hath appeared unto us; let us celebrate the Feast, and let us rejoice and magnify Christ;
and with palms and branches let us raise our voices
unto him with praise, saying, Blessed is he that cometh
in the Name of the Lord our Saviour.

Why did ye tremble, O ye Gentiles? And ye priests
and scribes, why did ye rant in falsehood, saying, Who
is this to whom the youths with palms and branches
shout, Blessed is he that cometh in the Name of the
Lord our Saviour?

He is the God whom no one may equal. He hath
devised every just way, and hath bestowd it on beloved
Israel, after he appeared, and walked with the people.
Blessed, therefore, is he that cometh in the Name of the
Lord our Saviour.

O rebellious ones! Why have ye placed stumbling-
blocks in our ways? Your feet are fast to shed the
blood of the Master, but he shall rise to save those who
cry unto him, Blessed is he that cometh in the Name of
the Lord our Saviour.

⊄*Instead of the Exaposteilarion, chant* (*three times*) Holy is the
Lord our God, *etc. Then the Bishop or Priest reciteth the Palm
Prayer.*

⊄*And in the Einos, sing the following Idiomelons, in the Fourth
Tone.*

O LORD, great multitudes spread their garments in
the way, and others cut down branches from the
trees and carried them; and those that went before and
those that followed cried, Hosanna to the Son of David,
thou who hast come and wilt yet come, in the Name of
the Lord.

O Lord, when thou wast about to enter the Holy
City, the Gentiles did carry tree branches, praising thee,
O Lord of all; for in seeing thee mounted on the colt

they saw thee as sitting on the cherubim, and therefore shouted thus, Hosanna in the highest blessed art thou who comest, and wilt yet come, in the Name of the Lord.

Go ye out, O people! Go ye out, O Gentiles, and see today the King of heaven sitting on a humble ass as on a sublime throne, coming to Jerusalem. And ye corrupt and unbelieving generation of Jews, come ye out and see him whom Isaiah saw coming in the body for our sakes. How he would take unto himself the new Zion as a pure bride, and cast out the confounded council. And the young, innocent, and unpolluted, have come out together, praising as it were an incorrupt and immaculate marriage. With them let us cry out with the praise of angels, Hosanna in the highest to whom belongeth the Great Mercy.

O Christ God, when before thy voluntary sufferings thou didst explain to all the confirmation of universal resurrection; thou didst raise Lazarus in Bethany by thine exalted might, after he had been dead for four days. And to the blind thou didst give sight; for thou art the Giver of light, O Saviour. Thou didst also enter the city with thy Disciples, sitting on an ass, fulfilling the preaching of the Prophets, as though riding upon the cherubim, and the Hebrew youths received thee with palms and branches. Wherefore, we also carry olive branches and palms, crying out to thee in gratitude, Hosanna in the highest, blessed is he that cometh in the Name of the Lord.

❡ *Glory and Now, in the Sixth Tone,* Before the six days of Passover, *etc.* (*p. 734*). *Then the Great Doxology; and the Troparion,* O Christ God, when we were buried, *etc.* (*p. 737*)*; and the Benediction.*

3. The Mass

1. Through the intercessions of the Theotokos, O Saviour, save us.

2. Save us, O Son of God, who didst sit upon the foal of an ass, as we sing unto thee, Alleluia.

❡ *Glory and Now,* O only-begotten Son, *etc.*

3. O Christ God, when thou didst raise Lazarus, etc.

Eisodikon: Blessed is he that cometh in the Name of the Lord. The Lord God hath appeared unto us. Save us, O Son of God, who didst sit upon the foal of an ass, as we sing unto thee, Alleluia.

❡ *Then the Troparion for Lazarus and for Palm Sunday; and conclude with the following Kontakion, in the Sixth Tone.*

UPBORNE upon the heavenly throne, and seated upon the earthly foal, O Christ our God, receive the praises of angels and the hymns of men, exclaiming before thee, Blessed is he that cometh to restore Adam.

The Epistle: Blessed is he that cometh in the Name of the Lord. Confess to the Lord; for he is good.

Section from the Epistle of St. Paul to the Philippians (4:4-9)

YE brethren: Rejoice in the Lord always; again, I say, rejoice.

Let your modesty be known to all men. The Lord is nigh.

Be nothing solicitous; but in every thing, by prayer and supplication, with thanksgiving, let your petitions be made known to God.

And the peace of God, which surpasseth all understanding, keep your hearts and minds in Christ Jesus.

For the rest, brethren, whatsoever things are true, whatsoever modest, whatsoever just, whatsoever holy, whatsoever lovely, whatsoever of good fame, if there be any virtue, if any praise of discipline, think on these things.

The things which you have both learned, and received, and heard, and seen in me, these do ye, and the God of peace shall be with you.

The Gospel: from St. John (12:1-18)

JESUS, six days before the pasch, came to Bethania, where Lazarus had been dead, whom Jesus raised to life.

And they made him a supper there: and Martha served: but Lazarus was one of them that were at table with him.

Mary therefore took a pound of ointment of right spikenard, of great price, and anointed the feet of Jesus, and wiped his feet with her hair; and the house was filled with the odour of the ointment.

Then one of his disciples, Judas Iscariot, he that was about to betray him, said:

Why was not this ointment sold for three hundred pence, and given to the poor?

Now he said this, not because he cared for the poor; but because he was a thief, and having the purse, carried the things that were put therein.

Jesus therefore said: Let her alone, that she may keep it against the day of my burial.

For the poor you have always with you; but me you have not always.

A great multitude therefore of the Jews knew that he was there; and they came, not for Jesus' sake only, but that they might see Lazarus, whom he had raised from the dead.

But the chief priests thought to kill Lazarus also:

Because many of the Jews, by reason of him, went away, and believed in Jesus.

And on the next day, a great multitude that was come to the festival day, when they had heard that Jesus was coming to Jerusalem,

Took branches of palm trees, and went forth to meet him, and cried: Hosanna, blessed is he that cometh in the name of the Lord, the king of Israel.

And Jesus found a young ass, and sat upon it, as it is written:

Fear not, daughter of Sion: behold, thy king cometh, sitting on an ass's colt.

These things his disciples did not know at the first; but when Jesus was glorified, then they remembered that these things were written of him, and that they had done these things to him.

The multitude therefore gave testimony, which was with him, when he called Lazarus out of the grave, and raised him from the dead.

For which reason also the people came to meet him, because they heard that he had done this miracle.

❡*And the rest of the Liturgy of St. John Chrysostom.*

❡*On Especially, the Ninth Hermos,* God the Lord hath appeared unto us, let us, *etc.* (*p. 741*).

SYNAXARION

ON THIS DAY, WHICH IS PALM SUNDAY, WE CELEBRATE THE GLORIOUS AND BRILLIANT FEAST OF THE ENTRANCE OF OUR LORD JESUS CHRIST INTO JERUSALEM.

STICHOS

HE SITTETH ON AN ASS, WHO DID STRETCH OUT THE EARTH'S POLE BY HIS DIVINE WORD, SEEKING TO DELIVER MANKIND FROM BESTIALITY.

JESUS came to Bethany on a Sunday falling on the eighteenth of March, before the Mosaic Passover of six days. On the following day he sent two of his Disciples, who brought him an ass on which he sat to enter the city. And when the great multitude heard that Jesus was coming to Jerusalem, they immediately took palm branches in their hands and went out to meet him. Some even spread their clothes in the road which he was about to traverse, and some cut down branches from the trees and strewed the road therewith. And those who went before him, and those who followed, even the children, were all crying, Hosanna, blessed is he that cometh in the Name of the Lord, King of Israel! (St. John 12:13). Therefore, we celebrate on this festal and brilliant day the entrance of our Lord into Jerusalem.

The branches of palm trees were a symbol of Christ's victory over Satan and death. And the meaning of *Hosanna* is, *We pray thee save,* or, *Therefore, save.* And the ass's colt, which was still an untamed animal, and impure according to the law, and Christ's sitting thereon, symbolize the former savagry and impurity of the Gentiles, and their subsequent taming and obedience to the holy law of the Gospel.

Wherefore, through thine indescribable mercy, O Christ, grant us to overcome our beastly passions, and make us worthy to behold thy brilliant triumph over death, and thine illustrious and life-giving Resurrection; and have mercy upon us. Amen.

Koinonikon: Blessed is he that cometh in the Name of the Lord.

❡*And instead of* We have seen the true Light, *etc., the following Troparion is sung,* O Christ God, when thou didst raise Lazarus, *etc.*

The Benediction: O thou who wast willing to sit on a colt, the foal of an ass, for our salvation, O Christ, etc.

EVENING OF PALM SUNDAY

❡*On* O Lord, to thee have I cried, *etc., sing, in the Eighth Tone, the Idiomelons,* Rejoice and be happy, *etc, and the two pieces following it, and repeat them* (*p.* 737); Glory *and* Now: O thou who ridest upon the cherubim, *etc.* (*p.* 737); *then the Eisodos; and* O resplendent Light, *etc; and the Prokeimenon,* Behold now, bless ye the Lord, all ye servants of the Lord; *and in the Aposticha, the following Idiomelons.*

In the Second Tone

LET us hasten, O believers, moving from one divine festival to another; from palms and branches to the fulfillment of the august and saving sufferings of Christ. Let us watch him, bearing his sufferings voluntarily for our sake; and let us sing unto him with worthy praise, crying, O Fountain of mercy, O Haven of salvation, O Lord, glory to thee.

In the Third Tone

VERILY, it is fearful and terrible to fall into the hands of the living God. Behold the Judge of the thoughts and imaginations of our hearts. Let no one enter to make trial of our blameless faith. But let us come forward to Christ in meekness and in fear, that we may receive mercy and find grace for help in proper season.

In the Seventh Tone

O WICKED and depraved society, which hath not kept faith with her husband. Why keepest thou a covenant which thou hast not inherited? Why pridest thou thyself in the Father when thou hast denied the Son? Hast thou not accepted the Prophets who told of the Son? Be thou, therefore, ashamed even of thine own children, crying thus, Hosanna to the Son of David, blessed is he that cometh in the Name of the Lord.

Glory: Let us hasten, O believers, etc. (p. 746).

Now: Verily, it is fearful and terrible to fall into the hands of the living God, (above).

¶*And after,* Holy God, *etc., the* Troparia; Rejoice, *O virgin Theotokos,* Mary, *etc., as at the end of Vespers of Cheese Fare (p. 645).*

The Benediction: O thou who didst come to voluntary sufferings for our salvation, etc.

¶*This Benediction is repeated every day from the evening of Palm Sunday to Great Wednesday, the last Mass of the Proegiasmena, i.e. Presanctified Gifts.*

III. HOLY PASSION WEEK

From the evening of Palm Sunday to Great Saturday

EVENING OF PALM SUNDAY

¶*The Matin Prayer, known as the Bridegroom Prayer, is chanted.*

¶*After the Benediction at Vespers of Palm Sunday, the Priest saith immediately,* Blessed be God, *etc; then,* Glory to thee, our God, glory *to thee, O heavenly King, etc; Holy God, etc; Lord, have mercy (twelve times); O come, let us worship, etc. (threee times); and the following two Psalms, with little intonation, during which the Priest burneth incense.*

PSALM 19

MAY the Lord hear thee in the day of tribulation: may the name of the God of Jacob protect thee.

May he send thee help from the sanctuary: and defend thee out of Sion.

May he be mindful of all thy sacrifices: and may thy whole burnt offering be made fat.

May he give thee according to thy own heart; and confirm all thy counsels.

We will rejoice in thy salvation; and in the name of our God we shall be exalted.

The Lord fulfill all thy petitions: now have I known that the Lord hath saved his anointed.

He will hear him from his holy heaven: the salvation of his right hand is in powers.

Some trust in chariots, and some in horses: but we will call upon the name of the Lord our God.

They are bound, and have fallen, but we are risen, and are set upright.

O Lord, save the king: and hear us in the day that we shall call upon thee.

PSALM 20

IN thy strength, O Lord, the king shall joy; and in thy salvation he shall rejoice exceedingly.

Thou hast given him his heart's desire: and hast not withholden from him the will of his lips.

For thou hast prevented him with blessings of sweetness: thou hast set on his head a crown of precious stones.

He asked life of thee: and thou hast given him length of days for ever and ever.

His glory is great in thy salvation: glory and great beauty shalt thou lay upon him.

For thou shalt give him to be a blessing for ever and ever: thou shalt make him joyful in gladness with thy countenance.

For the king hopeth in the Lord: and through the mercy of the most High he shall not be moved.

Let thy hand be found by all thy enemies: let thy right hand find out all them that hate thee.

Thou shalt make them as an oven of fire, in the time of thy anger: the Lord shall trouble them in his wrath, and fire shall devour them.

Their fruit shalt thou destroy from the earth: and their seed from among the children of men.

For they have intended evils against thee: they have devised counsels which they have not been able to establish.

For thou shalt make them turn their back: in thy remnants thou shalt prepare their face.

Be thou exalted, O Lord, in thy own strength: we will sing and praise thy power.

¶ *And after the six Matin Psalms (pp. 26-32), sing slowly and with intonation,* Allelulia *(four times), in the Eighth Tone. Then sing slowly twice, and once briefly, the following Troparion.*

BEHOLD, the Bridegroom cometh at midnight, and blessed is the servant whom he shall find awake. But he whom he shall find neglectful, is verily unworthy. Behold, therefore, my soul, beware, lest thou fallest into deep slumber, and the door of the kingdom be closed against thee, and thou be delivered to death. But be thou wakeful, crying, Holy! Holy! Holy! art thou, O God. Through the intercessions of the incorporals, have mercy upon us.

¶ *On the evening of Great Monday say,* Through the intercessions of the Forerunner, *etc; and on Great Tuesday,* By the power of thy Cross, *etc; and at its repetition the third time, say* For the sake of the Theotokos.

¶ *Then sing the following Kathismata, in the First Tone.*

VERILY, on this present day shall be revealed to the world the solemn Passion as a saving light; for Christ of his own goodness shall come to suffer. And he who holdeth all in the hollow of his hand consenteth to be suspended on a Tree to save man.

O thou unseen Judge, how wast thou seen in the flesh, and how camest thou to be killed in the body by transgressors of the law, judging our case by thy Passion? Wherefore, we address to thee praise and magnification, O Word, and in unison we offer glory to thy power.

¶ *And the following, in the Eighth Tone.*

VERILY, this present day ushereth in with splendour the Passion of the Lord. Come, therefore, O feast lovers, let us welcome it with songs; for the Creator cometh to accept crucifixion, examination, lashes, and to be condemned by Pilate, smitten on his face by a servant, and to bear all things to save man. Wherefore, we cry unto him; O Christ God, Lover of mankind, grant forgiveness of sins to them who in faith worship thy pure Passion. (*Repeat.*)

¶ *And immediately the Priest shall say,* And that we may be worthy, etc.

The Gospel: from St. Matthew (21:18-43)

AT that time: As the Lord returns to the city, he hungered.

And seeing a fig tree by the way side, he came to it, and found nothing thereon, but leaves only; and he saith unto it, Let there be no fruit from thee henceforward for ever. And immediately the fig tree withered away.

And when the disciples saw it, they marvelled, saying, How did the fig tree immediately wither away?

And Jesus answered and said unto them, Verily I say unto you, If ye have faith, and doubt not, ye shall not only do what is done to the fig tree, but even if ye shall say unto this mountain, Be thou taken up and cast into the sea, it shall be done.

And all things, whatsoever ye shall ask in prayer, believing, ye shall receive.

And when he was come to the temple, the chief priests and the elders of the people come unto him as he was teaching, and said; By what authority doest thou these things? And Jesus answered and said unto them, I also will ask you one question, which if ye tell me, I likewise will tell you by what authority I do these things.

The baptism of John, whence was it? from heaven or from men? And they reasoned with themselves, saying, If we shall say, From heaven, he will say unto us, Why then did ye not believe him?

But if we will say, From men: we fear the multitude; for all hold John as a prophet.

And they answered Jesus, and said; We know not. He also said unto them; Neither tell I you by what authority I do these things.

But what think ye? A man had two sons: and he came to the first, and said, Son, go work today in the vineyard.

And he answered and said, I will not: but afterward he repented himself, and went.

And he came to the second, and said likewise. And he answered and said, I go, sir: and went not.

Which of the two did the will of his father? They say, The first. Jesus said unto them, Verily I say unto you, that the publicans and the harlots go into the kingdom of God before you.

For John came unto you in the way of righteousness, and ye believed him not: but the publicans and harlots believed him: and ye, when ye saw it, did not even repent yourselves afterward, that ye might believe him.

Hear another parable: There was a man that was an householder, who planted a vineyard, and set a hedge about it, and digged a winepress in it, and built a tower, and let it out to husbandmen and went into another country.

And when the season of the fruits drew near, he sent his servants to the husbandmen, to receive his fruits.

And the husbandmen took his servants, and beat one, and killed another, and stoned another.

Again, he sent other servants more than the first and they did unto them in like manner.

But afterward he sent unto them his son, saying, They will reverence my son.

But the husbandmen, when they saw the son, said among themselves, This is the heir; come, let us kill him, and take his inheritance.

And they took him and cast him forth out of the vineyard, and killed him.

When therefore the lord of the vineyard shall come, what will he do unto those husbandmen?

They say unto him; He will miserably destroy those miserable men, and will let out the vineyard unto other husbandmen, who shall render him the fruits in their seasons.

Jesus saith unto them; Did ye never read in the scriptures.

> The stone which the builders rejected,
> The same was made the head of the corner;
> This was from the Lord.
> And it is marvellous in our eyes.

Therefore say I unto you, the kingdom of God shall be taken from you, and given to a nation bringing forth the fruits thereof.

¶ *Then Psalm 50 (p. 82); the Little Synapte; and the following Canon, the Hermos being sung after the Ode as a Katabasia.*

First Ode, in the Second Tone—Hermos

LET us praise the Lord by whose divine command the tumultuous, uncharted sea was dried up, and who led the children of Israel through it; for in glory he hath been glorified.

Verily, the ineffable condescension of the Word of God, even Christ, who is himself God and Man, was not accounted robbery, he being God and taking the likeness of a servant, as he revealed to his Disciples; for in glory he hath been glorified.

Yea, I the Creator, rich in Godhead, came myself to serve poor Adam, whose likeness I took willingly, and to give myself as a Redemption for him, who am without suffering as to my Godhead.

Then the Little Synapte; and the following Kontakion, in the Eighth Tone.

JACOB wailed the loss of Joseph while that brave youth was sitting in a chariot like an honoured king; for at that time, not having enslaved himself to the pleasures of Egypt, he was glorified instead by God, who looketh into the hearts of men, and who granteth them incorruptible crowns.

Oikos: Let us add wailing to wailing, shedding tears, and mourning with Jacob for chaste Joseph of perpetual memory, who was enslaved in the flesh. But his soul he preserved free, and he was lord over all Egypt; for God granteth his servants incorruptible crowns.

SYNAXARION

GREAT HOLY MONDAY

ON this day begins the anniversary of the holy Passion of the Saviour, he of whom Joseph of exceeding beauty is taken as the earliest symbol; for this Joseph was the eleventh of the sons of Jacob, and because his father loved him exceedingly, his brothers envied him and threw him into a pit. Then they took him out and sold him to strangers, who sold him in Egypt. He was slandered for his chastity, and was thrown into prison. But finally he was taken out of prison, and he attained a high rank, and received honours worthy of kings, becoming governor of the whole of Egypt, whose people he supported. Thus he symbolized in himself the Passion of our Lord Jesus Christ and his consequent great glory (Gen. 40:41).

To the remembrance of Joseph is added the story of the fig tree which the Lord cursed on this day (corresponding at that time to the nineteenth of the month of March) because of its barrenness, so that it dried up. The fig tree was a symbol of the Council of the Jews which did not show the necessary fruits of virtue and righteousness, so that Christ stripped it of every spiritual grace (St. Mt. 21:18-20).

Wherefore, by the intercessions of all-comely Joseph, O Christ, have mercy upon us.

Eighth Ode—Hermos

VERILY, the fire fed with measureless matter, fled trembling from the agreement of the pure youths and from their bodies free of corruption. And its ever rising flames having subsided, they shouted, crying, Praise the Lord, all his works; exalt him more and more unto the ages.

As the Saviour went to his Passion, he said to his beloved, If ye keep my commandments then all will know that ye are my Disciples. Be at peace one with another and with all, and be of humble mind that ye may be exalted. Know that I am the Lord, and praise and exalt me more and more unto the ages.

Let it be contrariwise with you to the order of the Gentiles, in their lordship over their kind; for such are not of mine, and their absolute purpose is to ursurp rule. Wherefore, whosoever willeth among you to be first, let him be last of all. And know that I am the Lord, and praise and exalt me more and more unto the ages.

❡*Deacon: the Little Synapte; then,* To the Theotokos, Mother of Light, *etc; and the Ninth Ode is chanted while the Deacon is censing.*

Ninth Ode—Hermos

O CHRIST our Creator, thou hast magnified thy Mother, the Theotokos, from whom thou didst put on the body, like unto ours in passion, delivering us from our ignorance. Wherefore, we bless her through all generations, and thee we magnify.

O Wisdom of all, thou didst make announcement to thy Disciples, saying, Put away all the filth of passion, and take unto yourselves a steadfast mind, worthy of the divine kingdom wherein ye shall be glorified and shall shine more brightly than the sun.

Thus, O Lord, thou didst say to thy Disciples, Look unto me, and be not exalted in your own minds, but die with the humble. Drink the cup that I drink; for ye shall be glorified with me in my Father's kingdom.

Exaposteilarion, in the Third Tone (three times)

VERILY, I behold thy chamber adorned, and I possess no robe to enter thereinto. Delight thou in the robe of my soul, O thou who granteth light, and save me.

⁋ *And in the Einos, hold four Stichoi, and chant the following Idiomelons, and repeat them.*

In the First Tone

WHEN the Lord was coming to his voluntary Passion, he said to the Disciples on the way, Behold, we go up to Jerusalem, and the Son of Man shall be delivered as it was written of him. Wherefore, let us, O brethren, accompany him with spotless consciences and be crucified with him, and with him kill the pleasures of life, that we may live with him and hear him say, I am not ascending to the earthly Jerusalem to suffer, but to my Father and your Father, to my God and your God, that I may draw you with me to the Jerusalem above in the kingdom of heaven. (*Repeat.*)

In the Fifth Tone

O BELIEVERS, having arrived at the saving Passion of Christ, let us praise his ineffable long-suffering, that by his compassion he may raise us who are dead in sin; for he is good and the Lover of mankind. (*Repeat.*)

Glory and Now, in the Fifth Tone

WHEN thou wast going to thy Passion, thou didst take thy Disciples aside to confirm them, saying, How is it ye do not remember the words that I spake to you before; that no Prophet is killed except in Jerusalem, as it is written? And now the time hath come concerning which I told you; for behold, I shall be delivered to ridicule at the hands of sinners, who shall nail me upon the Cross, deliver me to the tomb, and account me dead and abandoned. But be of good cheer; for I will rise the third day, for the joy of the faithful, and for their eternal life.

¶ *Then,* Thine is the Glory, our Lord and our God, *etc.* (*p. 39*); *and after this,* Let us finish our petitions, *etc.* (*p. 76*); *and the Proclamation.*

¶ *In the Aposticha, the following Idiomelons, in the Fifth Tone.*

THE Mother of the sons of Zebedee, O Lord, being unequal to the mystery of thine ineffable dispensation, begged thee to grant her two sons the honours of a temporal kingdom. But instead, thou didst promise thy beloved that they should drink the cup of death, the cup which thou didst say thou wouldest drink before them for the purification of sins. Wherefore, we cry unto thee, O Salvation of our souls, glory be to thee.

Stichos: We are filled in the morning with thy mercy.

Thou taughtest thy Disciples, O Lord, to think on that which is more perfect, and didst tell them not to imitate the Gentiles in lordship over the lowly, saying, Let not that be among you, my Disciples; for I have become poor of my own will. And the first among you, let him be servant of all; the ruler as one who is ruled;

and the foremost as the hindmost; for I have come to serve poor Adam and to give myself a Redemption for the many who cry, Glory to thee.

Stichos: And let the brightness of the Lord our God be upon us.

In the Eighth Tone

LET us, O brethren, be awed at the rebuking of the fig tree which dried up for lack of fruit. Let us offer fruits worthy of repentance to Christ who granteth us the Great Mercy.

Glory and Now, in the Same Tone

THE dragon verily found the Egyptian Eve a second time, and hastened to trip up Joseph with words of flattery. But he left his robe and ran away from sin, not being ashamed of nakedness, as the first creatures before their disobedience. Wherefore, by his intercessions, O Christ, have mercy upon us.

¶ *Then say,* It is a good thing to confess to the Lord, and to sing to thy Name, O most High, to show forth thy mercy in the morning, and thy truth every night; Holy God, *etc; the Kontakion,* Jacob wailed the loss of Joseph, *etc.* (*p. 753*); Lord, have mercy (*twelve times*); *and the Prayer of Ephram the Syrian,* O Lord and Master of my life, *etc.* (*p. 645*), *with three great reverences.*

The Benediction: O thou who didst come to thy voluntary Passion for our salvation, etc.

THE MORNING OF GREAT MONDAY

¶ *The Liturgy of the Proegiasmena taketh place.*

¶ *After the Sunset Psalm and the usual Stichology,* In my trouble I cried unto the Lord, *etc., on* O Lord, to thee have I cried, *sing for ten Stichera the Idiomelons of the Einos and Aposticha that are in the preceding Bridegroom Service.*

The Gospel: from St. Matthew (24:3-35)

AT that time: As Jesus sat upon the Mount of Olives the disciples came to him privately, saying: Tell us when shall these things be? and what shall be the sign of thy coming, and of the consummation of the world?

And Jesus answering, said to them: Take heed that no man seduce you:

For many will come in my name saying, I am Christ: and they will seduce many.

And you shall hear of wars and rumours of wars. See that ye be not troubled. For these things must come to pass, but the end is not yet.

For nation shall rise against nation, and kingdom against kingdom; and there shall be pestilences, and famines, and earthquakes in places:

Now all these are the beginnings of sorrows.

Then shall they deliver you up to be afflicted, and shall put you to death: and you shall be hated by all nations for my name's sake.

And then shall many be scandalized: and shall betray one another: and shall hate one another.

And many false prophets shall rise, and shall seduce many.

And because iniquity hath abounded, the charity of many shall grow cold.

But he that shall persevere to the end, he shall be saved.

And this gospel of the kingdom, shall be preached in the whole world, for a testimony to all nations, and then shall the consummation come.

When therefore you shall see the abomination of desolation, which was spoken of by Daniel the prophet, standing in the holy place: he that readeth let him understand.

Then they that are in Judea, let them flee to the mountains:

And he that is on the house-top, let him not come down to take any thing out of his house:

And he that is in the field, let him not go back to take his coat.

And woe to them that are with child, and that give suck in those days.

But pray that your flight be not in the winter, or on the sabbath.

For there shall be then great tribulation, such as hath not been from the beginning of the world until now, neither shall be.

And unless those days had been shortened, no flesh should be saved: but for the sake of the elect those days shall be shortened.

Then if any man shall say to you: Lo here is Christ, or there, do not believe him.

For there shall arise false Christs and false prophets, and shall show great signs and wonders, insomuch as to deceive (if possible) even the elect.

Behold I have told it to you, beforehand.

If therefore they shall say to you: Behold he is in the desert, go ye not out: Behold he is in the closets, believe it not.

For as lightning cometh out of the east, and appeareth even into the west: so shall also the coming of the Son of man be.

Wheresoever the body shall be, there shall the eagles also be gathered together.

And immediately after the tribulation of those days, the sun shall be darkened and the moon shall not give her light, and the stars shall fall from heaven, and the powers of heaven shall be moved:

And then shall appear the sign of the Son of man in heaven: and then shall all tribes of the earth mourn: and they shall see the Son of man coming in the clouds of heaven with much power and majesty.

And he shall send his angels with a trumpet, and a great voice: and they shall gather together his elect from the four winds, from the farthest parts of the heavens to the utmost bounds of them.

And from the fig tree learn a parable: When the branch thereof is now tender, and the leaves come forth, you know that summer is nigh.

So you also, when you shall see all these things, know ye that it is nigh, even at the doors.

Amen I say to you, that this generation shall not pass, till all these things be done.

Heaven and earth shall pass, but my words shall not pass.

❡ *And the rest of the service from the Liturgy of the Proegiasmena.*

EVENING OF GREAT MONDAY

❡ *After Great Compline, the Bridegroom Service taketh place, after the Order for the evening of Palm Sunday (p. 747); and after, Behold the Bridegroom, etc. (p. 749), chant the following Kathismata, in the Fourth Tone.*

LET us admire and love the Bridegroom, brethren, preparing our lamps to shine with virtues and the Orthodox Faith, that, like the wise virgins of the Lord, we may be ready to enter with him to the wedding; for the Bridegroom, being God, granteth to all an incorruptible crown.

The priests and scribes, O Christ, through great envy, brought against thee a Council deviating from the law, moving Judas to the Betrayal. Wherefore, he went out with audacity and spake to those law-transgressing people, saying, What will ye give me, and I will deliver him into your hands? Wherefore, O Lord, save our souls from his condemnation.

❡ *And the following, in the Eighth Tone (repeated).*

JUDAS that evil enemy, was moved by a silver-loving mind. He planned by conspiracy, the Betrayal of the Master, and fell from the light, accepting darkness. And having bargained for the sale, he sold the priceless One. Wherefore, that wretched man found hanging and horrible death a reward of his deed. Save us, therefore, O Christ, from his company, and grant forgiveness of sins to those who eagerly celebrate thy pure Passion.

The Gospel: from St. Matthew
(22:15 to end; 23:1 to end)

AT that time: The Pharisees took counsel how they might entangle Christ in his talk.

And they sent out unto him their disciples with the Herodians, saying, Master, we know that thou art true, and teachest the way of God in truth, neither carest thou for any man: for thou regardest not the person of men.

Tell us therefore, What thinkest thou? Is it lawful to give tribute unto Cæsar, or not?

But Jesus perceived their wickedness, and said, Why tempt ye me, ye hypocrites?

Show me the tribute money. And they brought unto him a penny.

And he saith unto them, Whose is this image and superscription?

They say unto him, Cæsar's. Then saith he unto them, Render therefore unto Cæsar the things which are Cæsar's; and unto God the things that are God's.

When they had heard these words, they marveled, and left him, and went their way.

The same day came to him the Sadducees, which say that there is no resurrection, and asked him,

Saying, Master, Moses said, If a man die, having no children, his brother shall marry his wife, and raise up seed unto his brother.

Now there were with us seven brethren: and the first, when he had married a wife, deceased, and having no issue, left his wife unto his brother:

Likewise the second also, and the third, unto the seventh.

And last of all the woman died also.

Therefore in the resurrection, whose wife shall she be of the seven? for they all had her.

Jesus answered and said unto them, Ye do err, not knowing the Scriptures, nor the power of God.

For in the resurrection they neither marry, nor are given in marriage, but are as the angels of God in heaven.

But as touching the resurrection of the dead, have ye not read that which was spoken unto you by God, saying,

I am the God of Abraham, and the God of Isaac, and the God of Jacob? God is not the God of the dead, but of the living.

And when the multitude heard this, they were astonished at his doctrine.

But when the Pharisees had heard that he had put the Sadducees to silence, they were gathered together.

Then one of them, which was a lawyer, asked him a question, tempting him, and saying,

Master, which is the great commandment in the law?

Jesus said unto him, Thou shalt love the Lord thy God with all thy heart, and with all thy soul, and with all thy mind.

This is the first and great commandment.

And the second is like unto it, Thou shalt love thy neighbour as thyself.

On these two commandments hang all the law and the prophets.

While the Pharisees were gathered together, Jesus asked them,

Saying, What think ye of Christ? whose son is he? They say unto him, The son of David.

He saith unto them, How then doth David in spirit call him Lord, saying,

The Lord said unto my Lord, Sit thou on my right hand, till I make thine enemies thy footstool?

If David then call him Lord, how is he his son?

And no man was able to answer him a word, neither durst any man from that day forth ask him any more questions.

Then spake Jesus to the multitude, and to his disciples,

Saying, The scribes and the Pharisees sit in Moses' seat:

All therefore whatsoever they bid you observe, that observe and do; but do not ye after their works: for they say, and do not.

For they bind heavy burdens and grievous to be borne, and lay them on men's shoulders; but they themselves will not move them with one of their fingers.

But all their works they do for to be seen of men: they make broad their phylacteries, and enlarge the borders of their garments,

And love the uppermost rooms at feasts, and the chief seats in the synagogues,

And greetings in the markets, and to be called of men, Rabbi, Rabbi.

But be not ye called Rabbi: for one is your Master, even Christ; and all ye are brethren.

And call no man your father upon the earth: for one is your Father, which is in heaven.

Neither be ye called masters: for one is your Master, even Christ.

But he that is greatest among you shall be your servant.

And whosoever shall exalt himself shall be abased; and he that shall humble himself shall be exalted.

But woe unto you, scribes and Pharisees, hypocrites! for ye shut up the kingdom of heaven against men: for ye neither go in yourselves, neither suffer ye them that are entering to go in.

Woe unto you, scribes and Pharisees, hypocrites! for ye devour widows' houses, and for a pretense make long prayer: therefore ye shall receive the greater damnation.

Woe unto you scribes and Pharisees, hypocrites! for ye compass sea and land to make one proselyte; and when he is made, ye make him twofold more the child of hell than yourselves.

Woe unto you, ye blind guides, which say, Whosoever shall swear by the temple, it is nothing; but whosoever shall swear by the gold of the temple, he is a debtor!

Ye fools and blind: for whether is greater, the gold, or the temple that sanctifieth the gold?

And, Whosoever shall swear by the altar, it is nothing; but whosoever sweareth by the gift that is upon it, he is guilty.

Ye fools and blind: for whether is greater, the gift, or the altar that sanctifieth the gift?

Whoso therefore shall swear by the altar, sweareth by it, and by all things thereon.

And whoso shall swear by the temple, sweareth by it, and by him that dwelleth therein.

And he that shall swear by heaven, sweareth by the throne of God, and by him that sitteth thereon.

Woe unto you, scribes and Pharisees, hypocrites! for ye pay tithe of mint and anise and cummin, and have omitted the weightier matters of the law, judgment, mercy, and faith: these ought ye to have done, and not to leave the other undone.

Ye blind guides, which strain at a gnat, and swallow a camel.

Woe unto you, scribes and Pharisees, hypocrites! for ye make clean the outside of the cup and of the platter, but within they are full of extortion and excess.

Thou blind Pharisees, cleanse first that which is within the cup and platter, that the outside of them may be clean also.

Woe unto you, scribes and Pharisees, hypocrites! for ye are like unto whited sepulchres, which indeed appear beautiful outwardly, but are within full of dead men's bones, and of all uncleanness.

Even so ye also outwardly appear righteous unto men, but within ye are full of hypocrisy and iniquity.

Woe unto you, scribes and Pharisees, hypocrites! because ye build the tombs of the prophets, and garnish the sepulchres of the righteous,

And say, If we had been in the days of our fathers, we would not have been partakers with them in the blood of the prophets.

Wherefore ye be witnesses unto yourselves, that ye are the children of them which killed the prophets.

Fill ye up then the measure of your fathers.

Ye serpents, ye generation of vipers, how can ye escape the damnation of hell?

Wherefore, behold, I send unto you prophets, and wise men, and scribes: and some of them ye shall kill and crucify; and some of them shall ye scourge in your synagogues, and persecute them from city to city:

That upon you may come all the righteous blood shed upon the earth, from the blood of righteous Abel unto the blood of Zacharias son of Barachias, whom ye slew between the temple and the altar.

Verily I say unto you, All these things shall come upon this generation.

O Jerusalem, Jerusalem, thou that killest the prophets, and stonest them which are sent unto thee, how often would I have gathered thy children together, even as a hen gathereth her chickens under her wings, and ye would not!

Behold, your house is left unto you desolate.

For I say unto you, Ye shall not see me henceforth, till ye shall say, Blessed is he that cometh in the name of the Lord.

¶ *Then Psalm 50 (p. 82); the Little Synapte; and the Kontakion, in the Second Tone.*

O WRETCHED soul, think of thy last hours. Be dismayed at the rebuking of the fig tree. Act, and double the talent given to thee with a fatigue-loving purpose. Awake, watching and crying out, lest we remain outside the chamber of Christ.

Oikos: O wretched soul, why art thou indifferent, and why dost thou vainly imagine unavailing ventures? Why dost thou direct thine energies to things passing? For it is the last hour; and we are about to be separated from what is here. Wherefore, while still thou hast time, listen, and cry, I have sinned, O Christ my Saviour; despise me not like the barren fig tree. But since thou art compassionate, have mercy upon me, who cry to thee in fear, lest I remain outside the chamber of Christ.

GREAT HOLY TUESDAY

SYNAXARION

ON this day we make remembrance of the Parable of the Ten Virgins which Jesus spake along with others as he was coming to the Passion. It teaches us not to rest as though safe in virginity, but to guard it whenever possible, and not to desist from any virtues and good deeds, especially deeds of mercy, which make the lamp of virginity shine brilliantly. It teaches us also to be ready for our end, not knowing when our hour is coming, as the wise virgins were ready to meet the bride, lest death overtake us and close the door of the heavenly chamber in our face, and we hear the terrible judgment which the foolish virgins heard, Verily, verily, I know you not (St. Mt. 25:1-13).

Wherefore, O Christ the Bridegroom, number us with the wise virgins and have mercy upon us. Amen.

The Eighth Ode, in the Second Tone—Hermos

VERILY, the three upright youths yielded not to the command of the usurper when they were thrown into the furnace, but confessed God, singing, Bless the Lord, all his works.

Let us cast indifference away from us, and with sparkling lamps and songs of praise let us welcome Christ the Bridegroom who dieth not, crying, Bless the Lord, all his works.

Let there be sufficient of the oil of mercy in our vessels, lest we make the time of receiving prizes a time of bargaining; and let us sing, Bless the Lord, all his works.

O ye who have received the talent from God, double it with the help of Christ, who granteth equal grace, as ye sing, Bless the Lord, all his works.

❡*Deacon: The Little Synapte; then,* To the Theotokos, *etc.*

The Ninth Ode—Hermos

O ALL-HOLY Virgin, who didst contain in thy womb the uncontainable God, and bore joy to the world, thee do we praise.

Thou didst say to thy Disciples, O good One, Watch; for ye know not the hour in which the Lord cometh to reward everyone.

In thy terrible Second Coming, O Master, establish me with the sheep on thy right hand, overlooking the multitude of my sins.

❡*The Exaposteilarion,* Verily, I behold thy chamber, *etc.* (*p. 755*).

❡*In the Einos, sing the following Idiomelons.*

In the First Tone

UNTO the splendour of thy saints, how shall I, unworthy, enter? For if I shall dare to enter with them into the chamber, my raiment will reproach me; for they are not wedding garments; and I shall be thrown down and bound by the angels. Cleanse, Lord, therefore, the stain of my soul and save me; for thou art the Lover of Mankind. *(Repeat.)*

In the Second Tone

O CHRIST the Groom, I who negligently slept and, like the foolish virgins, procrastinated in the time of work, was not in possession of a lamp of virtues. But, O Master, close not against me the wings of thy compassion. Drive away dark sleep from me, waken me, and bring me into thy chamber with the wise virgins, where is the song of the undefiled feasters and of those who cry ceaselessly, Glory be to thee, O Lord. *(Repeat.)*

Glory and Now, in the Fourth Tone

HAVING heard of the judgment of him who buried the talent, O my soul, hide not the word of God, but proclaim his wonders, that thou mayest double the gift, and enter into the joy of thy Lord.

¶*In the Aposticha, the following Idiomelons, in the Sixth Tone.*

COME, ye believers, let us work diligently for the Master; for he distributeth wealth to his servants. Let each of us according to his ability, double the gift of grace. Let one be adorned with wisdom according to good deeds, another accomplish a splendid service; let one preach to the unillumined in word and faith, another distribute wealth to the poor; for thus shall we double the loan, as faithful agents of the grace, and be worthy of the Master's joy. Wherefore, O Christ God, prepare us for it, since thou art the Lover of mankind.

Stichos: We are filled in the morning with thy mercy.

When thou comest in glory with the angelic hosts, O Jesus, and sittest on the throne of judgment, separate me not from the ways of thy right hand; for thou knowest that the ways of the left are crooked. And destroy me not, hardened sinner, with the goats, but number me with the sheep on thy right hand, and save me; for thou art the Lover of mankind.

Stichos: And let the brightness of the Lord our God be upon us.

O Bridegroom, brilliant in thy beauty above all mankind, who didst call us to the spiritual banquet of thy chamber, cast away from me the likeness of the rags of iniquity, by participation in thy Passion, and adorn me with the robe of thy beauty. Distinguish me as a brilliant guest in thy kingdom; for thou art compassionate.

Glory and Now, in the Seventh Tone

BEHOLD, the Master entrusteth thee with a talent, O my soul. Wherefore, receive thou the gift with fear. Lend to the giver and console the poor. Obtain the Lord as a Friend, that thou mayest stand on his right hand when he cometh in glory, and that thou mayest hear that blessed voice, Enter, O Servant, into the joy of thy Lord. Prepare me, a prodigal, for it. O Saviour, for the multitude of thy mercies.

❡ *And the rest of the Order as at the end of the Bridegroom Prayer on the Evening of Palm Sunday (p. 757).*

MORNING OF GREAT TUESDAY

❡ *The Mass of the Presanctified Gifts taketh place in accordance with the preceding Order on the Morning of Great Monday (p. 757), where on* O Lord, to thee have I cried, *etc., are sung the Idiomelons of the Einos, and the Aposticha occuring in Vespers of the Bridegroom Service on the preceding day (p. 760). And after* Let my prayer be set forth, *etc. read:*

The Gospel: from St. Matthew
(24:36 to end; 25:1 to end; 26:1-2)

THE Lord saith to his disciples: That day and hour no one knoweth, not the angels of heaven, but the Father alone.

And as in the days of Noe, so shall also the coming of the Son of man be.

For as in the days before the flood, they were eating and drinking, marrying and giving in marriage, even till that day in which Noe entered into the ark,

And they knew not till the flood came, and took them all away; so also shall the coming of the Son of man be.

Then two shall be in the field: one shall be taken, and one shall be left.

Two women shall be grinding at the mill: one shall be taken, and one shall be left.

Watch ye therefore, because you know not what hour your Lord will come.

But this know ye, that if the goodman of the house knew at what hour the thief would come, he would certainly watch, and would not suffer his house to be broken open.

Wherefore be you also ready, because at what hour you know not the Son of man will come.

Who, thinkest thou, is a faithful and wise servant, whom his lord hath appointed over his family, to give them meat in season.

Blessed is that servant, whom when his lord shall come he shall find so doing.

Amen I say to you, he shall place him over all his goods.

But if that evil servant shall say in his heart: My lord is long a coming:

And shall begin to strike his fellow servants, and shall eat and drink with drunkards:

The lord of that servant shall come in a day that he hoped not, and at an hour that he knoweth not:

And shall separate him, and appoint his portion with the hypocrites. There shall be weeping and gnashing of teeth.

Then shall the kingdom of heaven be like to ten virgins, who taking their lamps went out to meet the bridegroom and the bride.

And five of them were foolish, and five wise.

But the five foolish, having taken their lamps, did not take oil with them.

But the wise took oil in their vessels with the lamps.

And the bridegroom tarrying, they all slumbered and slept.

And at midnight there was a cry made: Behold the bridegroom cometh, go ye forth to meet him.

Then all those virgins arose and trimmed their lamps.

And the foolish said to the wise: Give us of your oil, for our lamps are gone out.

The wise answered, saying: Lest perhaps there be not enough for us and for you, go ye rather to them that sell, and buy for yourselves.

Now whilst they went to buy, the bridegroom came: and they that were ready, went in with him to the marriage, and the door was shut.

But at last came also the other virgins, saying: Lord, Lord, open to us.

But he answering said: Amen I say to you, I know you not.

Watch ye therefore, because you know not the day nor the hour the Son of man will come. Then the Lord saith this parable: A man travelling called his servants, and delivered unto them his goods;

And to one he gave five talents, and to another two, and to another one, to every one according to his proper ability: and immediately he took his journey.

And he that had received the five talents, went his way, and traded with the same, and gained other five.

And in like manner he that had received the two, gained other two.

But he that had received the one, going his way digged into the earth, and hid his lord's money.

But after a long time the lord of those servants came, and reckoned with them.

And he that had received the five talents coming, brought other five talents, saying: Lord, thou didst deliver to me five talents, behold I have gained other five over and above.

His lord said to him: Well done, good and faithful servant: because thou hast been faithful over a few things, I will place thee over many things: enter thou into the joy of thy lord.

And he also that had received the two talents came and said: Lord, thou deliveredst two talents to me: behold I have gained other two.

His lord said to him: Well done, good and faithful servant: because thou hast been faithful over a few things, I will place thee over many things: enter thou into the joy of thy lord.

But he that had received the one talent, came and said: Lord, I know that thou art a hard man; thou reapest where thou hast not sown, and gatherest where thou hast not strewed.

And being afraid I went and hid thy talent in the earth: behold here thou hast which is thine.

And his lord answering, said to him: Wicked and slothful servant, thou knewest that I reap where I sow not, and gather where I have not strewed:

Thou oughtest therefore to have committed my money to the bankers, and at my coming I should have received my own with usury.

Take ye away therefore the talent from him, and give it him that hath ten talents.

For to every one that hath shall be given, and he shall abound: but from him that hath not, that also which he seemeth to have shall be taken away.

And the unprofitable servant cast ye out into the exterior darkness. There shall be weeping and gnashing of teeth.

And when the Son of man shall come in his majesty, and all the angels with him, then shall he sit upon the seat of his majesty:

And all nations shall be gathered together before him, and he shall separate them one from another, as the shepherd separateth the sheep from the goats:

And he shall set the sheep on his right hand, but the goats on his left.

Then shall the king say to them that shall be on his right hand: Come, ye blessed of my Father, possess you the kingdom prepared for you from the foundation of the world.

For I was hungry, and you gave me to eat; I was thirsty, and you gave me to drink; I was a stranger, and you took me in:

Naked, and you covered me: sick, and you visited me: I was in prison, and you came to me.

Then shall the just answer him, saying: Lord, when did we see thee hungry, and fed thee; thirsty, and gave thee drink?

And when did we see thee a stranger, and took thee in? or naked, and covered thee?

Or when did we see thee sick or in prison, and came to thee?

And the king answering, shall say to them: Amen I say to you, as long as you did it to one of these my least brethren, you did it to me.

Then he shall say to them also that shall be on his left hand: Depart from me, you cursed, into everlasting fire which was prepared for the devil and his angels.

For I was hungry, and you gave me not to eat: I was thirsty, and you gave me not to drink.

I was a stranger, and you took me not in: naked, and you covered me not: sick and in prison, and you did not visit me.

Then they also shall answer him, saying: Lord, when did we see thee hungry, or thirsty, or a stranger, or naked, or sick, or in prison, and did not minister to thee?

Then he shall answer them, saying: Amen I say to you, as long as you did it not to one of these least, neither did you do it to me.

And these shall go into everlasting punishment: but the just, into life everlasting.

And it came to pass, when Jesus had ended all these words, he said to his disciples:

You know that after two days shall be the pasch, and the son of man shall be delivered up to be crucified.

❧*And the rest of the Liturgy of the Proegiasmena.*

EVENING OF GREAT TUESDAY

❧*After Great Compline, sing the Bridegroom Service after the preceding Order. And after* Behold, the Bridegroom, *etc., the following Kathismata.*

In the Third Tone

THE adulterous woman, O Christ, approaching thee and pouring on thy feet ointment with tears, was delivered by thy command from the rottenness of iniquity. But thine ingrate Disciple, who was fully possessed of thy grace, rejected it, and wallowed in the mire, selling thee with the love of silver. Wherefore, glory be to thy compassion, O Lover of mankind.

In the Fourth Tone

THE deceitful Judas, because of his passion for silver, O Lord, Treasury of life, plotted thy betrayal with deceit. Wherefore, he ran madly to the law-transgressing Jews and said to them, What will ye give me, and I will surrender him to you to crucify?

In the First Tone

THE adulterous woman, O compassionate One, cried to thee moaning; and with the hair of her head wiped thy feet passionately, deeply sighing, as she said, Put me not away, O my God, and reject me not. But accept me repentant and save me; for thou alone art the Lover of mankind. *(Repeat.)*

The Gospel: from St. John (12:17 to end)

AT that time: The people that was with Jesus when he called Lazarus out of his grave, and raised him from the dead, bare record.

For this cause the people also met him, for that they heard that he had done this miracle.

The Pharisees therefore said among themselves, Perceive ye how ye prevail nothing? behold, the world is gone after him.

And there were certain Greeks among them that came up to worship at the feast:

The same came therefore to Philip, which was of Bethsaida of Galilee, and desired him, saying, Sir, we would see Jesus.

Philip cometh and telleth Andrew: and again Andrew and Philip tell Jesus.

And Jesus answered them, saying, The hour is come, that the Son of man should be glorified.

Verily, verily, I say unto you, Except a corn of wheat fall into the ground and die, it abideth alone: but if it die, it bringeth forth much fruit.

He that loveth his life shall lose it; and he that hateth his life in this world shall keep it unto life eternal.

If any man serve me, let him follow me; and where I am, there shall also my servant be: if any man serve me, him will my Father honour.

Now is my soul troubled; and what shall I say? Father, save me from this hour: but for this cause came I unto this hour.

Father, glorify thy name. Then came there a voice from heaven, saying, I have both glorified it, and will glorify it again.

The people therefore that stood by, and heard it, said that it thundered: others said, An angel spake to him.

Jesus answered and said, This voice came not because of me, but for your sakes.

Now is the judgment of this world: now shall the prince of this world be cast out.

And I, if I be lifted up from the earth, will draw all men unto me.

This he said, signifying what death he should die.

The people answered him, We have heard out of the law that Christ abideth for ever: and how sayest thou, The Son of man must be lifted up? who is this Son of man?

Then Jesus said unto them, Yet a little while is the light with you. Walk while ye have the light, lest darkness come upon you: for he that walketh in darkness knoweth not whither he goeth.

While ye have light, believe in the light, that ye may be the children of light. These things spake Jesus, and departed, and did hide himself from them.

But though he had done so many miracles before them, yet they believed not on him:

That the saying of Esaias the prophet might be fulfilled, which he spake, Lord, who hath believed our report? and to whom hath the arm of the Lord been revealed?

Therefore they could not believe, because that Esaias said again,

He hath blinded their eyes, and hardened their heart; that they should not see with their eyes, nor understand with their hearts, and be converted, and I should heal them.

These things said Esaias, when he saw his glory, and spake of him.

Nevertheless among the chief rulers also many believed on him; but because of the Pharisees they did not confess him, lest they should be put out of the synagogue:

For they loved the praise of men more than the praise of God.

Jesus cried and said, He that believeth on me, believeth not on me, but on him that sent me.

And he that seeth me seeth him that sent me.

I am come a light into the world, that whosoever believeth on me should not abide in darkness.

And if any man hear my words, and believe not, I judge him not: for I came not to judge the world, but to save the world.

He that rejecteth me, and receiveth not my words, hath one that judgeth him: the word that I have spoken, the same shall judge him in the last day.

For I have not spoken of myself; but the Father which sent me, he gave me a command, what I should say, and what I should speak.

And I know that his commandment is life everlasting: whatsoever I speak therefore, even as the Father said unto me, so I speak.

❧ *Then Psalm 50; the Little Synapte; and the following Canon, in the Second Tone.*

Third Ode—Hermos

THOU hast established me upon the rock of faith, and hast enlarged my mouth over mine enemies; for my soul rejoiceth in her own singing. There is none holy as the Lord, and there is none righteous beside thee, O Lord.

Verily, the law-deviating Council is false, and hath met with an evil mind, to show thee guilty, O Christ the Rescuer, to whom we sing, Thou art our God, and there is none holy beside thee, O Lord.

Verily, the wicked, law-transgressing Council, since their souls are wicked and God-contending, conspired to kill Christ the Righteous as one lacking goodness. Wherefore, to him we sing, Thou art our God, and there is none holy beside thee, O Lord.

Kontakion, in the Fourth Tone

I HAVE sinned against thee, O good One, more than the adulterous woman, and have not even offered thee a flood of tears. But silently and calmly I kneel asking, kissing thy pure feet with longing, that thou mayest grant me, O Saviour, since thou art the Master, remission of my sins, who cry, Deliver me from the mire of my deeds.

Oikos: The shameless woman of old suddenly appeared chaste, despising her horrible deeds of sin and the pleasures of the body, contemplating her great shame and the condemnation of punishment which the adulterous and insolent, of whom I am first, endure. I tremble thereat; yet I who am ignorant am confirmed in my evil habits. But the adulterous woman trembled with fear, and hastened to her Rescuer, crying, O Lover of mankind, rescue me from the mire of my deeds.

GREAT HOLY WEDNESDAY
SYNAXARION

THE more accurate and exacting of the commentators on the four Gospels say that two women anointed the Lord, one long before his Passion, and one a few days before. One of these was a harlot, while the other was a chaste, virtuous woman. On this day the Church commemorates this act of piety and righteousness which proceeded from the harlot, contrasting it with the treachery of Judas and his Betrayal of Christ. Both of these acts fell on Wednesday, corresponding to the twenty-first of March, two days before the Mosaic passover, as it appears from the course of the account of St. Matthew the Evangelist.

The above mentioned harlot anointed the head and feet of Jesus with spikenard, and wiped them with the hair of her head. The precious ointment was worth three hundred dinars, or about fifteen pieces of Venetian gold. When the Disciples saw this they stumbled, especially Judas, the money-lover, and were angry because of the wasting of such an amount of ointment. Jesus rebuked them, lest the woman be embarrassed. Judas was wroth, and went to the high priests, where they were gathered in the house of Caiphas, taking counsel against Jesus, and agreed with them to deliver the Master for thirty pieces of silver. From that time Judas sought an opportunity to deliver him (St. Mt. 26:2-16). Because of this the fast of Wednesday was instituted from the days of the apostolic age itself.

Wherefore, O Christ God, anointed with the supersensuous ointment, deliver us from suffering, and have mercy upon us.

Eighth Ode—Hermos

VERILY, the furnace of old was heated sevenfold by the usurper's command, and in it the youths were not burned, but they trod at the command of the king, shouting, Praise the Lord, all his works; exalt him more and more unto the ages.

The adulterous woman, O Christ, poured precious ointment on thy divine, terrible, lordly head. She held thy pure feet with her defiled hands and cried, Bless the Lord, all his works, and exalt him more and more unto the ages.

She who was under the guilt of iniquity, washed the feet of the Creator with her tears, and wiped them with her hair. Wherefore, she was not disappointed of salvation, in spite of the sins she had committed during her life, but shouted, Praise the Lord, all his works; exalt him more and more unto the ages.

Thou hast accomplished redemption for her who, with pent emotions of salvation and fountains of tears, in which, confessing she had been washed, was of grateful mind, not being ashamed, but crying, Praise the Lord, all his works, and exalt him more and more unto the ages.

❡*Deacon: The Little Synapte. Then,* To the Theotokos, *etc.*

Ninth Ode—Hermos

COME, let us magnify with undefiled souls and pure lips that immaculate, most spotless one, Immanuel's Mother, whom we offer as an intercessor to him who was born of her, saying, Pity our souls, O Christ God, and save us.

The evil Judas appeared disloyal and wickedly zealous, having consented to sell the Gift worthy of God, through whom the debts of sin were undone, adulterating the God-beloved grace. Wherefore, O Christ God, have pity on our souls and save us.

Verily, Judas went to the law-transgressing chiefs and said to them, What will ye give me to deliver to you the Christ whom ye seek, exchanging his adoption for gold. Wherefore, O Christ God, have pity on our souls and save us.

Ah for thy vicious love of silver, thou traitor! which made thee forget that the whole world doth not equal one soul, as thou didst learn; for burning with dismay, thou didst hang thyself, O betrayer. But, O Christ God, have pity on our souls and save us.

❡ *The Exaposteilarion,* Verily, I behold thy chamber, *etc.* (*p. 755*).

❡ *In the Einos, the following Idiomelons, in the First Tone.*

WHEN the adulteress knew thee as God, O Son of the Virgin, she shouted with tears, imploring, having committed deeds demanding tears, and said, Loose my debt as I have loosed my braids. Love thou her who is justly hated, that I may make a vow to thee with the publicans, O Benefactor and Lover of mankind.

When the adulteress mixed her tears with ointment of great price and poured it over thy pure feet, kissing them, immediately thou didst justify her. Wherefore, grant us forgiveness, O thou who didst suffer for us, and save us.

When the sinful woman was offering her spice, the Disciple was bargaining with the transgressors of the law. The one rejoiced in pouring out the spice of great price, while the other hastened to sell the priceless One. The one knew the Lord, the other was separated from the Lord. She was freed and Judas became a slave to the enemy. Indifference is evil, and repentance is great, which last grant us, O Saviour, who didst suffer for us, and save us.

Ah for the wretchedness of Judas! For, seeing the adulteress kiss the traces of his feet, he was thinking with deceit of the kiss of betrayal. She loosed her braids, and he was bound with wrath, offering instead of spice, rotted evil; for envy knoweth not how to honour the seemly. Woe to the wretchedness of Judas, and from it, O God, save our souls.

Glory, in the Second Tone

THE sinful woman hastened to the spicer to buy of him spice of great price, wherewith to anoint the Benefactor, crying to him, Give me spice with which I may anoint him who hath remitted all my sins.

Now, in the Sixth Tone

VERILY, she who was deep in sin, found thee a Haven of salvation. She poured on thee spice with tears, and cried to thee, saying, Look upon me, O thou who dost accept the repentance of sinners, and save me, Master, from the tempests of sin, for the richness of thy mercies.

❦ *In the Aposticha, the Idiomelons, in the Sixth Tone.*

TODAY hath Christ come to the house of the Pharisee; and a sinful woman approached and rolled at his feet, crying, Look at her who is drowned in sin, who is despondent because of her deeds, and who is not rejected by thy goodness. Grant me, Lord, forgiveness of iniquity, and save me.

Stichos: We are filled in the morning with thy mercy.

O Saviour, the adulteress stretched forth her hair to thee, and Judas stretched forth his hands to the transgressors of the law; she to gain forgiveness, and he to take silver. Wherefore, we cry to thee, O thou who wast sold and didst free us, O Lord, glory be to thee.

Stichos: Look upon thy servants and upon their works; and direct their children.

An unclean woman, spattered with mud, came shedding tears at thy feet, O Saviour, forewarning of the Passion, and crying, How shall I gaze at thee, O Master; for thou hast come to save the adulteress. Raise me who am dead from the depths, O thou who didst raise Lazarus from the tomb after four days, and accept me, wretched one, and save me.

Stichos: And let the brightness of the Lord our God be upon us.

She who was despondent because of her conduct, and whose character was known, came to thee carrying spice and crying, Cast me not away, an adulteress, O thou who wast born of the Virgin, and turn not away from my tears, O Joy of the angels. But accept me, Lord, whom thou didst not put away because of sin, for thy great mercy.

Glory and Now, in the Eighth Tone

THE woman who fell into many sins, O Lord, having perceived thy Divinity, received the rank of ointment-bearer, offering thee spices before thy Burial, wailing and crying, Woe is me; for the love of adultery and sin hath given me a dark and lightless night. Accept the fountains of my tears, O thou who draweth the waters of the sea by the clouds; incline to the sighing of my heart, O thou who didst bend the heavens by thine inapprehensible condescension. I will kiss thy pure feet and wipe them with my tresses, thy feet whose tread when it fell on the ears of Eve in paradise, dismayed her so that she hid herself for fear. Who then shall examine the multitude of my sins, and the depth of thy judgments? Wherefore, O my Saviour, and the Deliverer of my soul, turn not away from thy handmaiden, O thou of countless mercy.

¶*And the rest of the Order as at end of the Bridegroom Prayer on the Evening of Palm Sunday. (p. 757).*

MORNING OF GREAT WEDNESDAY

¶*The Liturgy of the Proegiasmena as in preceding Order; and on* O Lord, to thee have I cried, *etc., sing the Idiomelons of the Einos and Aposticha which are in the Bridegroom Service, from the preceding day; and* Let my prayer be set forth, *etc.*

The Gospel: from St. Matthew (26:6-16)

WHEN Jesus was in Bethania, in the house of Simon the leper,

There came to him a woman having an alabaster box of precious ointment, and poured it on his head as he was at table.

And the disciples seeing it, had indignation, saying: To what purpose is this waste?

For this might have been sold for much, and given to the poor.

And Jesus knowing it, said to them: Why do you trouble this woman? for she hath wrought a good work upon me.

For the poor you have always with you: but me you have not always.

For she in pouring this ointment upon my body, hath done it for my burial.

Amen I say unto you, wheresoever this gospel shall be preached in the whole world, that also which she hath done, shall be told for a memory of her.

Then went one of the twelve, who was called Judas Iscariot, to the chief priests.

And said to them: What will you give me, and I will deliver him unto you? But they appointed him thirty pieces of silver.

And from thenceforth he sought opportunity to betray him.

¶ *Then the rest of the Liturgy of the Proegiasmena.*

EVENING OF GREAT WEDNESDAY

¶ *Recite Little Compline. Then the faithful who are ready to receive the holy Sacrament on the following morning, come to the tribune of confession, one by one. It is also customary on this night to hold the Service of the Holy Oil.*

THE MORNING OF GREAT THURSDAY

¶ *After the six Matin Psalms, and the singing of* Alleluia, *chant the following Troparion, in the Eighth Tone (three times).*

THE glorified Disciples, being illuminated at the evening washing, Judas, of evil worship, was stricken and darkened with the love of silver. And to lawless judges, O righteous Judge, he delivered and surrendered thee. Wherefore, O lover of wealth, behold him who for its sake hanged himself, and flee that insatiable soul which ventured thus far against the Master. O thou whose goodness pervadeth all, glory to thee, O Lord.

The Gospel: from St. Luke (22:1-39)

AT that time: The feast of unleavened bread, which is called the pasch, was at hand.

And the chief priests and the scribes sought how they might put Jesus to death: but they feared the people.

And Satan entered into Judas, who was surnamed Iscariot, one of the twelve.

And he went, and discoursed with the chief priests and the magistrates, how he might betray him to them.

And they were glad, and covenanted to give him money.

And he promised. And he sought opportunity to betray him in the absence of the multitude.

And the day of the unleavened bread came, on which it was necessary that the pasch should be killed.

And he sent Peter and John, saying: Go, and prepare for us the pasch, that we may eat.

But they said: Where wilt thou that we prepare?

And he said to them: Behold, as you go into the city, there shall meet you a man carrying a pitcher of water: follow him into the house where he entereth in.

And you shall say to the goodman of the house: The master saith to thee, Where is the guest chamber, where I may eat the pasch with my disciples?

And he will shew you a large dining room, furnished; and there prepare.

And they going, found as he had said to them, and made ready the pasch.

And when the hour was come, he sat down, and the twelve apostles with him.

And he said to them: With desire I have desired to eat this pasch with you, before I suffer.

For I say to you, that from this time I will not eat it, till it be fulfilled in the kingdom of God.

And having taken the chalice, he gave thanks, and said: Take, and divide it among you:

For I say to you, that I will not drink of the fruit of the vine, till the kingdom of God come.

And taking bread, he gave thanks, and brake; and gave to them, saying: This is my body, which is given for you. Do this for a commemoration of me.

In like manner the chalice also, after he had supped, saying: This is the chalice, the new testament in my blood, which shall be shed for you.

But yet behold, the hand of him that betrayeth me is with me on the table.

And the Son of man indeed goeth, according to that which is determined: but yet, woe to that man by whom he shall be betrayed.

And they began to inquire among themselves, which of them it was that should do this thing.

And there was also a strife amongst them, which of them should seem to be the greater.

And he said to them: The kings of the Gentiles lord it over them; and they that have power over them, are called beneficent.

But you not so: but he that is the greater among you, let him become as the younger; and he that is the leader, as he that serveth.

For which is greater, he that sitteth at table, or he that serveth? Is not he that sitteth at table? But I am in the midst of you, as he that serveth:

And you are they who have continued with me in my temptations:

And I dispose to you, as my Father hath disposed to me, a kingdom;

That you may eat and drink at my table, in my kingdom: and may sit upon thrones, judging the twelve tribes of Israel.

And the Lord said: Simon, Simon, behold Satan hath desired to have you, that he may sift you as wheat:

But I have prayed for thee, that thy faith fail not: and thou, being once converted, confirm thy brethren.

Who said to him: Lord, I am ready to go with thee, both into prison, and to death.

And he said: I say to thee, Peter, the cock shall not crow this day, till thou thrice deniest that thou knowest me. And he said to them:

When I sent you without purse, and scrip, and shoes, did you want any thing?

But they said: Nothing. Then said he unto them: But now he that hath a purse, let him take it, and likewise a scrip; and he that hath not, let him sell his coat, and buy a sword.

For I say to you, that this that is written must yet be fulfilled in me: And with the wicked was he reckoned. For the things concerning me have an end.

But they said: Lord, behold here are two swords. And he said to them, It is enough.

And going out, he went, according to his custom, to the mount of Olives. And his disciples also followed him.

❧ *Then Psalm 50; the Little Synapte; and the Hermoses of the following Canon, in the Second Tone.*

1. Verily, the Red Sea was cleft by the rod, and the tumultuous depth dried up, becoming at once a path for those without weapons and a grave to those heavily armed. Wherefore, Israel sang an acceptable song of praise to God, saying, Christ our God in glory hath been glorified.

3. O God, Creator and Lord of all, the truly Passionless, thou hast humbled thyself, uniting the creature to thyself. And since thou art the Passover, thou didst offer thyself to those for whom thou wast about to die, saying, Eat ye my Body, and be established in the Faith.

4. The Prophet, O Christ, who foresaw thine ineffable mystery, cried, O compassionate and good Father, thou hast accomplished profound and strong love, having sent thine only Son, a Sin-offering to the world.

5. Bound with the bonds of love, and throwing themselves on Christ who ruleth all, the Disciples, with beautiful, washed feet, proclaimed peace to all.

6. The uppermost abyss of sins encompassing me, and unable to bear its great tumult, like Jonah I cry unto thee, Master, lead me forth from corruption.

Kontakion, in the Second Tone

JUDAS the deceitful servant, when he stretched his hand privily and took bread, did therewith take the price of him who made man with his own hands, thus remaining reprobate.

Oikos: Let us all draw near in fear to the mystical table, and with pure souls receive the bread. Let us stay with the Master and behold how he washeth the feet of his Disciples and wipeth them with a towel. Let us follow the example of what we behold, submitting one to another, and washing one another's feet; for Christ himself did so command his Disciples, having thus spoken to them. But Judas, the deceitful and treacherous servant, heard not, and remained reprobate.

GREAT HOLY THURSDAY

SYNAXARION

ON the evening of this day, corresponding at that time to the twenty-second of the month of March, on the eve of the Feast of Unleavened Bread, or the eve of the Mosaic Passover, Jesus ate the Supper in the city of Jerusalem with his twelve Disciples, and on it he blessed Bread and Wine, thus instituting the Sacrament of the Eucharist. He also washed the feet of the Disciples, giving them a great example of humility, and said openly that one of them was about to betray and surrender him. Then he pointed out his betrayer, who was Judas, by giving him the sop dipped in the liquid that was in the dish. And when Judas suddenly departed, Jesus delivered to his Disciples the sublime last teachings contained in the first of the evangical chapters known as the Passion Gospels, and which are recited on the evening of this day. After that, Jesus went to the Mount of Olives and began to sorrow and grieve. Then he drew apart from the Disciples, knelt, and prayed fervently till his sweat fell like drops of blood on the earth. He had not finished with that prayer and strife before Judas appeared with armed soldiers, and with a great multitude of people. And Judas greeted Jesus the Master and kissed him with a false kiss and thus delivered him up.

And when the soldiers and the servants of the Jews had laid hands on Jesus, they bound him and went with him to Ananias and Caiphas, the high priests, and the Disciples were dispersed, except Peter who was more zealous than the rest and who followed him, with John, to the house of the high priest. But Peter finally denied that he was one of his Disciples. Then Jesus was brought before the wicked, unjust Council where he was examined and asked about his Disciples and teachings, and where he was asked to swear by God whether he were truly Christ. And when he explained the truth he was condemned to die, as though he had deserved this for blasphemy. His face was spit upon, he was smitten, and ridiculed in sundry ways all that night until the next morning.

Wherefore, by thine ineffable compassion, O Christ our God, have mercy upon us. Amen.

7. The youths in Babylon despaired not because of the fire of the furnace. But when they were cast into the midst of the flames, they were moistened with dew, singing, Blessed art thou, O Lord God of our fathers.

8. The blessed youths endangered themselves in Babylon for their fathers' laws, refusing the ignorant and foolish commands of him who considered himself king. And being united in the fire that consumed them not, they sang a seemly song to him who helped them, shouting, Praise the Lord, all his works; exalt him more and more unto the ages.

9. Come, ye believers, let us enjoy the banquet of the Lord, an immortal table, in the upper chamber, receiving with uplifted minds exalted words from the Word whom we magnify.

❡ *The Exaposteilarion,* Verily, I behold thy chamber, *etc.* (*p. 755*).

❡ *And in the Einos, chant the following Idiomelons, in the Second Tone.*

THE Council of the Jews cometh together to deliver to Pilate the Author and Creator of all. Woe to their iniquity and infidelity! For him that cometh to judge the living and the dead they prepare for judgment; the Healer of sufferings they make ready for suffering, Wherefore, O long-suffering Lord, great is thy mercy, glory to thee.

The law-transgressing Judas, O Lord, who dipped his hand with thee in the plate at supper, hath put forth his hand with iniquity to take silver; and he who calculated the price of the spice, did not shrink from selling thee, O priceless One. And he who put forth his feet for the Master to wash, deceitfully kissed him to deliver him to law-breakers. Verily, he hath been cast away with his thirty pieces of silver, without beholding thy third-day Resurrection, through which, have mercy upon us.

Judas the traitor, being deceitful, betrayed the Saviour Lord with a lying kiss; and he sold the Master of all like a slave to the transgressors of the law. But the Lamb of God followed like a sheep to the slaughter, who is the only Son of the most merciful Father.

Judas, that deceitful and cunning slave, assassinator of the righteous One, hath been revealed through his works; for he followed the Master, and concealed within himself the Betrayal. He would say to himself, I will surrender this One and gain the accumulated wealth. He sought to sell the spice and maliciously hold Jesus. He offered a kiss and surrendered Christ who, like a sheep, followed to slaughter, who is alone compassionate and the Lover of mankind.

Glory and Now, in the Second Tone

VERILY, the Lamb whom Isaiah preached cometh to voluntary slaughter, offering his back to scourges, and his cheeks to be slapped. Even his face he turned not from the shame of spitting, as he was condemned to die a horrible death. Yea, and the sinless One endureth all willingly that he may grant to all resurrection from the dead.

❧ *Then,* Thine is the glory, our Lord and our God, *etc.* (*p. 39*); *in the Aposticha, the following Idiomelons, in the Eighth Tone.*

TODAY hath the wicked Council convened and falsely conspired against him, to deliver the Innocent to Pilate to die. Today Judas setteth up for himself the gallows of wealth, and loseth both the temporal and the divine life. Today Caiphas prophesieth unwittingly, saying, It is better that one die for the people; for he came to suffer for our sins, that he may deliver us from the bondage of the enemy, since he is good and the Lover of mankind.

Stichos: He who ate my bread, hath greatly supplanted me.

Today Judas hath hidden the veil of the love of the poor, and uncovered the likeness of greed, not caring for the poor. No longer he selleth the spice of the sinful woman, but the heavenly Spice, and through it he stealeth the silver and cometh to the law-transgressing Jews and saith to them, What will you give me, and I will deliver him to you? Wherefore, woe to the traitor's love of silver; for he hath lowered the price of the sale, and bargained over him that is sold, after the manner of traders; nor did he ask a high price. Nay, like a runaway slave he sold him; for it is the custom of robbers not to regard the price of precious things; and the Disciple cast holy things to the dogs; for the rabies of the love of money hath made him howl madly against his Master. Let us, therefore, flee this temptation, crying, O long-suffering Lord, glory to thee.

Stichos: He went out and spake to the multitude.

Thy way, O law-breaking Judas, is full of deceit; for because of thine infatuation thou didst gain the contempt of humanity; for if thou wert a lover of wealth, why didst thou become a Disciple to him who taught

poverty? And if thou didst love the priceless One, why
didst thou sell and deliver him to the violation of the
oppressor? Wherefore, O sun, dread, and O earth, sigh
and cry with trembling. O long-suffering Lord, glory
to thee.

Stichos: They determined an unjust word against
me.

Let no one, O believers, remain uninitiated in the
Lord's Supper; let no one at all approach the table, like
Judas, with deceit; for he received a mouthful, and
turned around an assassin of the Bread. In appearance,
verily, he was a Disciple; but in truth he was a murderer. With the Jews he was happy, but with the Disciples he made his abode. He loved with hatred, and
with a kiss he sold God who bought us from the curse,
the Saviour of our souls.

¶ *Glory,* Thy way, O law-breaking Judas, *etc.* (*p 790*).

Now, in the Fifth Tone

THOU didst confide in thy Disciples, O Lord, and
taught them, saying, Behold, my beloved, let no
fear separate you from me; for though I suffer, it is
for the sake of the world. Doubt me not, therefore;
for I came not to be served, but to serve and give myself
a Redemption for the world. If, therefore, ye are my
beloved, imitate me, And he among you who wisheth
to be first, let him be last; and the master be like the
servant. Abide in me, that ye may bear fruit; for I am
the Vine of life.

¶ *Then,* It is a good thing to confess to the Lord, *etc.. Holy God,
etc; and the following hymn.*

O Lord, who wast smitten for the sake of mankind,
and wast not wroth, deliver our lives from corruption,
and save us.

¶ *And immediately the Priest saith,* Blessed be the kingdom, *etc; O
come, let us worship, etc. (three times); and the Sunset Psalm. And
on O Lord, to thee have I cried, etc., chant the Idiomelons of the
Einos (p. 789), with the repetition of the first.*

Glory and Now, in the Sixth Tone

IN truth Judas is son of the vipers who ate the manna in the wilderness, and murmured against the Nourisher; for those ingrates, while food was still in their mouths, murmured against God. Similarly, this wicked one of false worship, while the heavenly Bread was still in his mouth, conspired to deliver the Saviour. O what insatiate purpose! What beastly boldness! For he sold the Nourisher and delivered to death the Master who loved him. Verily, this violater of the law is a son of those others, and with them became an inheritor of destruction. Wherefore, O Lord, deliver our souls from such inhumanity, who art alone of ineffable long-suffering.

❡ *Then the Eisodos with the Gospel; and* O resplendent Light, *etc. (p. 74); and the Readings. And after the Little Synapte, and the Proclamation from the Priest,* For thou art holy, our God, *etc., sing the Trisagion i.e.,* Holy God, *etc.*

The Epistle: The rulers set themselves together. Why do the Gentiles tremble?

Section from the First Epistle of St. Paul to the Corinthians (11:23-32)

YE brethren: I have received of the Lord that which also I delivered unto you, that the Lord Jesus, the same night in which he was betrayed, took bread.

And giving thanks, broke, and said: Take ye, and eat: this is my body, which shall be delivered for you: this do for the commemoration of me.

In like manner also the chalice, after he had supped, saying: This chalice is the new testament in my blood: this do ye, as often as you shall drink, for the commemoration of me.

For as often as you shall eat this bread, and drink the chalice, you shall shew the death of the Lord, until he come.

Therefore whosoever shall eat this bread, or drink the chalice of the Lord unworthily, shall be guilty of the body and of the blood of the Lord.

But let a man prove himself: and so let him eat of that bread, and drink of the chalice.

For he that eateth and drinketh unworthily, eateth and drinketh judgment to himself, not discerning the body of the Lord.

Therefore are there many infirm and weak among you, and many sleep.

But if we would judge ourselves, we should not be judged.

But whilst we are judged, we are chastised by the Lord, that we be not condemned with this world.

The Gospel: from St. Matthew (26:2-20); St. John (13:3-17); St. Matthew (26:21-39); St. Luke (22:43-44); St. Matthew (26:40 to end; 27:1-2)

THE Lord saith to his disciples: You know that after two days shall be pasch, and the Son of man shall be delivered up to be crucified:

Then were gathered together the chief priests and ancients of the people into the court of the high priest, who was called Caiphas:

And they consulted together, that by subtility they might apprehend Jesus, and put him to death.

But they said: Not on the festival day, lest perhaps there should be a tumult among the people.

And when Jesus was in Bethania, in the house of Simon the leper,

There came to him a woman having an alabaster box of precious ointment, and poured it on his head as he was at table.

And the disciples seeing it, had indignation, saying: To what purpose is this waste?

For this might have been sold for much, and given to the poor.

And Jesus knowing it, said to them: Why do you trouble this woman? for she hath wrought a good work upon me.

For the poor you have always with you: but me you have not always.

For she in pouring this ointment upon my body, hath done it for my burial.

Amen I say to you, wheresoever this gospel shall be preached in the whole world, that also which she hath done, shall be told for a memory of her.

Then went one of the twelve, who was called Judas Iscariot, to the chief priests,

And said to them: What will you give me, and I will deliver him unto you? But they appointed him thirty pieces of silver.

And from thenceforth he sought opportunity to betray him.

And on the first day of the Azymes, the disciples came to Jesus, saying: Where wilt thou that we prepare for thee to eat the pasch?

But Jesus said: Go ye into the city to a certain man, and say to him: The master saith, My time is near at hand, with thee I make the pasch with my disciples.

And the disciples did as Jesus appointed to them, and they prepared the pasch.

But when it was evening, he sat down with his twelve disciples.

Knowing that the Father had given him all things into his hands, and that he came from God, and goeth to God;

He riseth from supper, and layeth aside his garments, and having taken a towel, girded himself.

After that, he putteth water into a basin, and began to wash the feet of the disciples, and to wipe them with the towel wherewith he was girded.

He cometh therefore to Simon Peter. And Peter saith to him: Lord, dost thou wash my feet?

Jesus answered, and said to him: What I do thou knowest not now; but thou shalt know hereafter.

Peter saith to him: Thou shalt never wash my feet. Jesus answered him: If I wash thee not, thou shalt have no part with me.

Simon Peter saith to him: Lord, not only my feet, but also my hands and my head.

Jesus saith to him: He that is washed, needeth not but to wash his feet, but is clean wholly. And you are clean, but not all.

For he knew who he was that would betray him; therefore he said: You are not all clean.

Then after he had washed their feet, and taken his garments, being set down again, he said to them: Know you what I have done to you?

You call me Master, and Lord; and you say well, for so I am.

If then I being your Lord and Master, have washed your feet; you also ought to wash one another's feet.

For I have given you an example, that as I have done to you, so you do also.

Amen, amen I say to you: The servant is not greater than his lord; neither is the apostle greater than he that sent him.

If you know these things, you shall be blessed if you do them.

And whilst they were eating, he said: Amen I say to you, that one of you is about to betray me.

And they being very much troubled, began every one to say: Is it I, Lord?

But he answering, said: He that dippeth his hand with me in the dish, he shall betray me.

The Son of man indeed goeth, as it is written of him: but woe to that man by whom the Son of man shall be betrayed: it were better for him, if that man had not been born.

And Judas that betrayed him, answering, said: Is it I, Rabbi? He saith to him: Thou hast said it.

And whilst they were at supper, Jesus took bread, and blessed, and broke: and gave to his disciples, and said: Take ye, and eat. This is my body.

And taking the chalice, he gave thanks, and gave to them, saying: Drink ye all of this.

For this is my blood of the new testament, which shall be shed for many unto remission of sins.

And I say to you, I will not drink from henceforth of this fruit of the vine, until that day when I shall drink it with you new in the kingdom of my Father.

And a hymn said, they went out unto mount Olivet.

Then Jesus saith to them: All you shall be scandalized in me this night. For it is written: I will strike the shepherd, and the sheep of the flock shall be dispersed.

But after I shall be risen again, I will go before you into Galilee.

And Peter answering, said to him: Although all shall be scandalized in thee, I will never be scandalized.

Jesus said to him: Amen I say to thee, that in this night before the cock crow, thou wilt deny me thrice.

Peter saith to him: Yea, though I should die with thee, I will not deny thee. And in like manner said all the disciples.

Then Jesus came with them into a country place which is called Gethsemani; and he said to his disciples: Sit you here, till I go yonder and pray.

And taking with him Peter and the two sons of Zebedee, he began to grow sorrowful and to be sad.

Then he saith to them: My soul is sorrowful even unto death: stay you here, and watch with me.

And going a little further, he fell upon his face, praying, and saying: My Father, if it be possible, let this chalice pass from me. Nevertheless not as I will, but as thou wilt.

And there appeared to him an angel from heaven, strengthening him. And being in an agony, he prayed the longer.

And his sweat became as drops of blood, trickling down upon the ground.

Then he ariseth from praying and cometh to his disciples, and findeth them asleep, and he saith to Peter: What? Could you not watch one hour with me?

Watch ye, and pray that ye enter not into temptation. The spirit indeed is willing, but the flesh weak.

Again the second time, he went and prayed, saying: My Father, if this chalice may not pass away, but I must drink it, thy will be done.

And he cometh again, and findeth them sleeping: for their eyes were heavy.

And leaving them, he went again: and he prayed the third time, saying the selfsame word.

Then he cometh to his disciples, and saith to them: Sleep ye now and take your rest; behold the hour is at hand, and the Son of man shall be betrayed into the hands of sinners.

Rise, let us go: behold he is at hand that will betray me.

As he yet spoke, behold Judas, one of the twelve, came, and with him a great multitude with swords and clubs, sent from the chief priests and the ancients of the people.

And he that betrayed him, gave them a sign, saying: Whomsoever I shall kiss, that is he, hold him fast.

And forthwith coming to Jesus, he said: Hail Rabbi. And he kissed him.

And Jesus said to him: Friend, whereto art thou come? Then they came up, and laid hands on Jesus, and held him.

And behold one of them that were with Jesus, stretching forth his hand, drew out his sword: and striking the servant of the high priest, cut off his ear.

Then Jesus saith to him: Put up again thy sword into its place: for all that take the sword shall perish with the sword.

Thinkest thou that I cannot ask my Father, and he will give me presently more than twelve legions of angels?

How then shall the scriptures be fulfilled, that so it must be done?

In that same hour Jesus said to the multitudes: You are come out as it were to a robber with swords and clubs to apprehend me. I sat daily with you, teaching in the temple, and you laid not hands on me.

Now all this was done, that the scriptures of the prophets might be fulfilled. Then the disciples all leaving him, fled.

But they holding Jesus led him to Caiphas the high priest, where the scribes and the ancients were assembled.

And Peter followed him afar off, even to the court of the high priest. And going in, he sat with the servants, that he might see the end.

And the chief priests and the whole council sought false witness against Jesus, that they might put him to death:

And they found not, whereas many false witnesses had come in. And last of all there came two false witnesses:

And they said: This man said, I am able to destroy the temple of God, and after three days to rebuild it.

And the high priest rising up, said to him: Answerest thou nothing to the things which these witness against thee?

But Jesus held his peace. And the high priest said to him: I adjure thee by the living God, that thou tell us if thou be the Christ the Son of God.

Jesus saith to him: Thou hast said it. Nevertheless I say to you, hereafter you shall see the Son of man sitting on the right hand of the power of God, and coming in the clouds of heaven.

Then the high priest rent his garments, saying: He hath blasphemed; what further need have we of witnesses? Behold, now you have heard the blasphemy:

What think you? But they answering, said: He is guilty of death.

Then did they spit in his face, and buffeted him: and others struck his face with the palms of their hands,

Saying: Prophesy unto us, O Christ, who is he that struck thee?

But Peter sat without in the court: and there came to him a servant maid, saying: Thou also wast with Jesus the Galilean.

But he denied before them all, saying: I know not what thou sayest.

And as he went out of the gate, another maid saw him, and she saith to them that were there: This man also was with Jesus of Nazareth.

And again he denied with an oath: I know not the man.

And after a little while they came that stood by, and said to Peter: Surely thou also art one of them; for even thy speech doth discover thee.

Then he began to curse and to swear that he knew not the man. And immediately the cock crew.

And Peter remembered the word of Jesus which he had said: Before the cock crow, thou wilt deny me thrice. And going forth, he wept bitterly.

And when morning was come, all the chief priests and ancients of the people took counsel against Jesus, that they might put him to death.

And they brought him bound, and delivered him to Pontius Pilate the governor.

❡ *And the rest of the Divine Liturgy of Basil the Great.*

❡ *And instead of the Cherubicon and the Koinonikon, and also instead of* We have seen the true Light, *etc., the following Troparion, in the Sixth Tone.*

R ECEIVE me today, O Son of God, as a partaker of thy sacramental Supper; for I shall not divulge thy mystery to thine enemies, nor give thee a kiss like Judas. But like the thief, I shall confess thee. Remember me, Lord, in thy kingdom.

Benediction: O thou who because of thine exceeding goodness didst reveal humility as a virtuous way when thou didst wash the feet of thy Disciples; and didst condescend to crucifixion and burial for our sakes, etc.

THE EVENING OF GREAT THURSDAY

SERVICE OF THE HOLY PASSION GOSPELS

❡*After the six Matin Psalms sing* Alleluia *(four times); and the* Troparion, The glorified Disciples, *etc. (three times p. 783); and immediately the Priest saith,* And that we may be worthy; *etc; and reciteth:*

The First Gospel[1]: from St. John (13:31 to end; 14:1 to end; 15:1 to end; 16:1 to end; 17:1 to end; 18:1)

THE Lord saith to his Disciples: Now is the Son of man glorified in him, and God is glorified in him.

If God be glorified in him, God shall also glorify him in himself, and shall straightway glorify him.

Little children, yet a little while I am with you. Ye shall seek me; and as I said unto the Jews, Whither I go, ye cannot come; so now I say to you.

A new commandment I give unto you, That ye love one another; as I have loved you, that ye also love one another.

By this shall all men know that ye are my disciples, if ye have love one to another.

Simon Peter said unto him, Lord, whither goest thou?

Jesus answered him, Whither I go, thou canst not follow me now; but thou shalt follow me afterward.

Peter said unto him, Lord, why cannot I follow thee now? I will lay down my life for thy sake.

Jesus answered him, Wilt thou lay down thy life for my sake? Verily, verily, I say unto thee, The cock shall not crow, till thou hast denied me thrice.

Let not your heart be troubled: ye believe in God, believe also in me.

---

[1] Note that at the beginning and the end of each of the Passion Gospels, instead of, Glory to thee, O Lord, glory to thee, the Choir shall sing, *Glory be to thy long-suffering, O Lord.*

In my Father's house are many mansions: if it were not so, I would have told you. I go to prepare a place for you.

And if I go and prepare a place for you, I will come again, and receive you unto myself; that where I am, there ye may be also.

And whither I go ye know, and the way ye know.

Thomas saith unto him, Lord, we know not whither thou goest; and how can we know the way?

Jesus saith unto him, I am the way, the truth, and the life: no man cometh unto the Father, but by me.

If ye had known me, ye should have known my Father also: and from henceforth ye know him, and have seen him.

Philip saith unto him, Lord, show us the Father, and it is enough for us.

Jesus saith unto him, Have I been so long time with you, and yet hast thou not known me, Philip? he that hath seen me hath seen the Father; and how sayest thou then, Show us the Father?

Believest thou not that I am in the Father, and the Father in me? the words that I speak unto you I speak not of myself: but the Father that dwelleth in me, he doeth the works.

Believe me that I am in the Father, and the Father in me: or else believe me for the very works' sake.

Verily, verily, I say unto you, He that believeth on me, the works that I do shall he do also; and greater works than these shall he do; because I go unto my Father.

And whatsoever ye shall ask in my name, that will I do, that the Father may be glorified in the Son.

If ye shall ask any thing in my name, I will do it.

If ye love me, keep my commandments.

And I will pray the Father, and he shall give you another Comforter, that he may abide with you for ever;

Even the Spirit of truth; whom the world cannot receive, because it seeth him not, neither knoweth him:

but ye know him; for he dwelleth with you, and shall be in you.

I will not leave you comfortless: I will come to you.

Yet a little while, and the world seeth me no more; but ye see me: because I live, ye shall live also.

At that day ye shall know that I am in my Father, and ye in me, and I in you.

He that hath my commandments, and keepeth them, he it is that loveth me: and he that loveth me shall be loved of my Father, and I will love him, and will manifest myself to him.

Judas saith unto him, not Iscariot, Lord, how is it that thou wilt manifest thyself unto us, and not unto the world?

Jesus answered and said unto him, If a man love me, he will keep my words: and my Father will love him, and we will come unto him, and make our abode with him.

He that loveth me not keepeth not my sayings: and the word which ye hear is not mine, but the Father's which sent me.

These things have I spoken unto you, being yet present with you.

But the Comforter, which is the Holy Spirit, whom the Father will send in my name, he shall teach you all things, and bring all things to your remembrance, whatsoever I have said unto you.

Peace I leave with you, my peace I give unto you: not as the world giveth, give I unto you. Let not your heart be troubled, neither let it be afraid.

Ye have heard how I said unto you, I go away, and come again unto you. If ye loved me, ye would rejoice, because I said, I go unto the Father: for my Father is greater than I.

And now I have told you before it come to pass, that, when it is come to pass, ye might believe.

Hereafter I will not talk much with you: for the prince of this world cometh, and hath nothing in me.

But that the world may know that I love the Father; and as the Father gave me commandment, even so I do. Arise, let us go hence.

I am the true vine, and my Father is the husbandman.

Every branch in me that beareth not fruit he taketh away: and every branch that beareth fruit, he purgeth it, that it may bring forth more fruit.

Now ye are clean through the word which I have spoken unto you.

Abide in me, and I in you. As the branch cannot bear fruit of itself, except it abide in the vine; no more can ye, except ye abide in me.

I am the vine, ye are the branches. He that abideth in me, and I in him, the same bringeth forth much fruit; for without me ye can do nothing.

If a man abide not in me, he is cast forth as a branch, and is withered; and men gather them, and cast them into the fire, and they are burned.

If ye abide in me, and my words abide in you, ye shall ask what ye will and it shall be done unto you.

Herein is my Father glorified, that ye bear much fruit; so shall ye be my disciples.

As the Father hath loved me, so have I loved you: continue ye in my love.

If ye keep my commandments, ye shall abide in my love; even as I have kept my Father's commandments, and abide in his love.

These things have I spoken unto you, that my joy might remain in you, and that your joy might be full.

This is my commandment, That ye love one another, as I have loved you.

Greater love hath no man than this, that a man lay down his life for his friends.

Ye are my friends, if ye do whatsoever I command you.

Henceforth I call you not servants; for the servant knoweth not what his lord doeth: but I have called you friends; for all things that I have heard of my Father I have made known unto you.

Ye have not chosen me, but I have chosen you, and ordained you, that ye should go and bring forth fruit, and that your fruit should remain; that whatsoever ye shall ask of the Father in my name, he may give it you.

These things I command you, that ye love one another.

If the world hate you, ye know that it hated me before it hated you.

If ye were of the world, the world would love his own; but because ye are not of the world, but I have chosen you out of the world, therefore the world hateth you.

Remember the word that I said unto you, The servant is not greater than his lord. If they have persecuted me, they will also persecute you; if they have kept my saying, they will keep yours also.

But all these things will they do unto you for my name's sake, because they know not him that sent me.

If I had not come and spoken unto them, they had not had sin; but now they have no cloak for their sin.

He that hateth me, hateth my Father also.

If I had not done among them the works which none other man did, they had not had sin: but now have they both seen and hated both me and my Father.

But this cometh to pass, that the word might be fulfilled that is written in their law, They hated me without a cause. But when the Comforter is come, whom I will send unto you from the Father, even the Spirit of truth, which proceedeth from the Father, he shall testify of me:

And ye also shall bear witness, because ye have been with me from the beginning.

These things have I spoken unto you, that ye should not be offended.

They shall put you out of the synagogues: yea, the time cometh, that whosoever killeth you will think that he doeth God service.

And these things will they do unto you, because they have not known the Father, nor me.

But these things have I told you, that when the time shall come, ye may remember that I told you of them. And these things I said not unto you at the beginning, because I was with you.

But now I go my way to him that sent me; and none of you asketh me, Whither goest thou?

But because I have said these things unto you, sorrow hath filled your heart.

Nevertheless I told you the truth; It is expedient for you that I go away: for if I go not away, the Comforter will not come unto you; but if I depart, I will send him unto you.

And when he is come, he will reprove the world of sin, and of righteousness, and of judgment:

Of sin, becasue they believe not on me;

Of righteousness, because I go to my Father, and ye see me no more;

Of judgment, because the prince of this world is judged.

I have yet many things to say unto you, but ye cannot bear them now.

Howbeit when he, the Spirit of truth, is come, he will guide you into all truth: for he shall not speak of himself; but whatsoever he shall hear, that shall he speak: and he will show you things to come.

He shall glorify me: for he shall receive of mine, and shall show it unto you.

All things that the Father hath are mine: therefore said I, that he shall take of mine, and shall show it unto you.

A little while, and ye shall not see me: and again, a little while, and ye shall see me, because I go to the Father.

Then said some of his disciples among themselves, What is this that he saith unto us, A little while, and ye shall not see me: and again, a little while, and ye shall see me: and, Because I go to the Father?

They said therefore, What is this that he saith, A little while? we cannot tell what he saith.

Now Jesus knew that they were desirous to ask him, and said unto them, Do ye inquire among yourselves of that I said, A little while, and ye shall not see me: and again, a little while, and ye shall see me?

Verily, verily, I say unto you, That ye shall weep and lament, but the world shall rejoice; and ye shall be sorrowful, but your sorrow shall be turned into joy.

A woman when she is in travail hath sorrow, because her hour is come: but as soon as she is delivered of the child, she remembereth no more the anguish, for joy that a man is born into the world.

And ye now therefore have sorrow: but I will see you again, and your heart shall rejoice, and your joy no man taketh from you.

And in that day ye shall ask me nothing. Verily, verily, I say unto you, Whatsoever ye shall ask the Father in my name, he will give it you.

Hitherto have ye asked nothing in my name: ask, and ye shall receive, that your joy may be full.

These things have I spoken unto you in proverbs: but the time cometh, when I shall no more speak unto you in proverbs, but I shall show you plainly of the Father.

At that day ye shall ask in my name: and I say not unto you, that I will pray the Father for you:

For the Father himself loveth you, because ye have loved me, and have believed that I came out from God.

I came forth from the Father, and am come into the world: again, I leave the world, and go to the Father.

His disciples said unto him, Lo, now speakest thou plainly, and speakest no proverb.

Now are we sure that thou knowest all things, and needest not that any man should ask thee: by this we believe that thou camest forth from God.

Jesus answered them, Do ye now believe?

Behold, the hour cometh, yea, is now come, that ye shall be scattered, every man to his own, and shall leave me alone: and yet I am not alone, because the Father is with me.

These things I have spoken unto you, that in me ye might have peace. In the world ye shall have tribulation: but be of good cheer, I have overcome the world.

These words spake Jesus, and lifted up his eyes to heaven, and said, Father, the hour is come; glorify thy Son, that thy Son also may glorify thee:

As thou hast given him power over all flesh, that he should give eternal life to as many as thou hast given him.

And this is life eternal, that they might know thee the only true God, and Jesus Christ, whom thou hast sent.

I have glorified thee on the earth: I have finished the work which thou gavest me to do.

And now, O Father, glorify thou me with thine own self with the glory which I had with thee before the world was.

I have manifested thy name unto the men which thou gavest me out of the world: thine they were, and thou gavest them me; and they have kept thy word.

Now they have known that all things whatsoever thou hast given me are of thee.

For I have given unto them the words which thou gavest me; and they have received them, and have known surely that I came out from thee, and they have believed that thou didst send me.

I pray for them: I pray not for the world, but for them which thou hast given me; for they are thine.

And all mine are thine, and thine are mine; and I am glorified in them.

And now I am no more in the world, but these are in the world, and I come to thee. Holy Father, keep through thine own name those whom thou hast given me, that they may be one, as we are.

While I was with them in the world, I kept them in thy name: those that thou gavest me I have kept, and none of them is lost, but the son of perdition; that the Scripture might be fulfilled.

And now come I to thee; and these things I speak in the world, that they might have my joy fulfilled in themselves.

I have given them thy word; and the world hath hated them, because they are not of the world, even as I am not of the world.

I pray not that thou shouldest take them out of the world, but that thou shouldest keep them from the evil.

They are not of the world, even as I am not of the world.

Sanctify them through thy truth: thy word is truth.

As thou hast sent me into the world, even so have I also sent them into the world.

And for their sakes I sanctify myself, that they also might be sanctified through the truth.

Neither pray I for these alone, but for them also which shall believe on me through their word;

That they all may be one; as thou, Father, art in me, and I in thee, that they also may be one in us: that the world may believe that thou hast sent me.

And the glory which thou gavest me I have given them; that they may be one, even as we are one:

I in them, and thou in me, that they may be made perfect in one; and that the world may know that thou hast sent me, and hast loved them, as thou hast loved me.

Father, I will that they also, whom thou hast given me, be with me where I am; that they may behold my glory, which thou hast given me: for thou lovedst me before the foundation of the world.

O righteous Father, the world hath not known thee: but I have known thee, and these have known that thou hast sent me.

And I have declared unto them thy name, and will declare it; that the love wherewith thou hast loved me may be in them, and I in them.

When Jesus had spoken these words, he went forth with his disciples over the brook Cedron, where was a garden, into the which he entered, and his disciples.

⟪ Then sing the following Antiphonies.

First Antiphony, in the Eighth Tone

THE rulers of the nations took counsel against the
Lord and against his Anointed.

Words contrary to the law they contrived against me.
Wherefore, Lord, O Lord, forsake me not.

Let us direct our senses undefiled towards Christ;
and as his lovers let us sacrifice ourselves for him, nor
be choked, like Judas, with worldly anxieties. Let us,
contrariwise, cry in our chambers, O Father who art
in heaven, deliver us from evil.

Glory and Now: Thou, who knewest not wedlock,
hast given birth while still a Virgin, and didst remain a
Virgin. Wherefore, O Mary, the Theotokos, the
Mother without groom, beseech Christ our God to
save us.

Second Antiphony, in the Sixth Tone

TOWARDS the law-transgressing Scribes Judas
hastened, saying, What will you give me, and I will
deliver him to you. Invisibly thou hast stood, O Christ,
among the conspirators, being plotted against. Wherefore, thou who knowest the contents of our hearts, have
pity on our souls.

Let us serve the Lord with mercy, like Mary at Supper. And let us not be possessed of the love of silver,
like Judas; that we may be always with Christ.

Glory and Now: Cease not, O Virgin, to implore
him whom thou didst bear ineffably, that he may save
from tribulations those who take refuge in thee; for he
is the Lover of mankind.

Third Antiphony, in the Second Tone

THE Hebrew youths, O Lord, for the resurrection
of Lazarus, hailed thee, saying, Hosanna, O Lover
of mankind! But law-breaking Judas refused to understand.

Thou didst foretell it at thy Supper, O Christ God, and saidst to thy Disciples, Verily, one of you shall betray me. But law-breaking Judas refused to understand.

When John asked thee, O Lord, who shall betray thee, thou didst point him out to him by means of the bread. But the law-breaking Judas refused to understand.

The Jews sought thy death with thirty pieces of silver and a kiss of deceit. But the law-breaking Judas refused to understand.

At the washing of thy Disciples, O Christ God, thou didst urge them saying, As ye have seen, so do ye. But the law-breaking Judas refused to understand.

Thou didst tell thy Disciples, O God, Watch and pray, lest ye be tempted. But the law-breaking Judas refused to understand.

Glory and Now: Deliver thy servants from tribulation, O Theotokos; for we all, after God, seek refuge in thee, since thou art an impregnable fortress and an intercessor.

Kathisma, in the Seventh Tone

WHEN thou didst help thy Disciples at the Supper and knewest the intent to betray, thou didst reproach Judas for it, knowing the while that he was incorrigible; but preferring to make all know that thou wast betrayed of thine own will, that thou mightest snatch the world from the stranger. Wherefore, O long-suffering One, glory be to thee.

The Second Gospel: from St. John (18:1-28)

AT that time: Jesus went forth with his disciples over the brook Cedron, where was a garden into the which he entered, and his disciples.

And Judas also, which betrayed him, knew the place: for Jesus ofttimes resorted thither with his disciples.

Judas then, having received a band of men and officers from the chief priests and Pharisees, cometh thither with lanterns and torches and weapons.

Jesus therefore, knowing all things that should come upon him, went forth, and said unto them, Whom seek ye?

They answered him, Jesus of Nazareth. Jesus saith unto them, I am he. And Judas also, which betrayed him, stood with them.

As soon then as he had said unto them, I am he, they went backward, and fell to the ground.

Then asked he them again, Whom seek ye? And they said, Jesus of Nazareth.

Jesus answered, I have told you that I am he: if therefore ye seek me, let these go their way:

That the saying might be fulfilled, which he spake, Of them which thou gavest me have I lost none.

Then Simon Peter having a sword drew it, and smote the high priest's servant, and cut off his right ear. The servant's name was Malchus.

Then said Jesus unto Peter, Put up thy sword into the sheath: the cup which my Father hath given me, shall I not drink it?

Then the band and the captain and officers of the Jews took Jesus, and bound him,

And led him away to Annas first; for he was father-in-law to Caiaphas, which was the high priest that same year.

Now Caiaphas was he, which gave counsel to the Jews, that it was expedient that one man should die for the people.

And Simon Peter followed Jesus, and so did another disciple: that disciple was known unto the high priest, and went in with Jesus into the palace of the high priest.

But Peter stood at the door without. Then went out that other disciple, which was known unto the high priest, and spake unto her that kept the door, and brought in Peter.

Then saith the damsel that kept the door unto Peter, Art not thou also one of this man's disciples? He saith, I am not.

And the servants and officers stood there, who had made a fire of coals, for it was cold; and they warmed themselves: and Peter stood with them, and warmed himself.

The high priest then asked Jesus of his disciples, and of his doctrine.

Jesus answered him, I spake openly to the world; I ever taught in the synagogue, and in the temple, whither the Jews always resort; and in secret have I said nothing.

Why askest thou me? ask them which heard me, what I have said unto them: behold, they know what I said.

And when he had thus spoken, one of the officers which stood by struck Jesus with the palm of his hand, saying, Answerest thou the high priest so?

Jesus answered him, If I have spoken evil, bear witness of the evil: but if well, why smitest thou me?

Now Annas had sent him bound unto Caiphas the high priest.

And Simon Peter stood and warmed himself. They said therefore unto him, Art not thou also one of his disciples? He denied it, and said, I am not.

One of the servants of the high priest, being his kinsman whose ear Peter cut off, saith, Did not I see thee in the garden with him?

Peter then denied again; and immediately the cock crew.

Then led they Jesus from Caiphas unto the hall of judgment: and it was early; and they themselves went not into the judgment hall, lest they should be defiled; but that they might eat the passover.

Fourth Antiphony, in the Fifth Tone

TODAY Judas leaveth the Master and followeth after Satan. He, darkened one, was blinded by the suffering of the love of silver, and fell from the light;

for how can he see who sold the Star for thirty pieces of silver. But he who suffered for our sake hath shone forth upon us. Wherefore, let us hail him, saying, O thou who didst suffer in pity for mankind, glory be to thee.

Today doth Judas adulterate the worship of God, and becometh estranged from the Gift. He was a Disciple, and became a betrayer. He covered deceit with the semblance of friendship, and preferred thirty pieces of silver to the love of the Master, becoming a guide to the Council of law-transgressors. But having Christ as our Salvation, let us glorify him.

O brethren, let us take possession of brotherly love, as brethren of Christ, not mercilessness towards our neighbours, lest we be condemned as that merciless servant for the sake of money; nor repent, like Judas, when such repentance availeth us not.

Glory and Now: Glorious things have been spoken of thee everywhere, O Mary, Theotokos, who didst give birth in the flesh without wedlock to the Creator of all, O all-praised.

Fifth Antiphony, in the Sixth Tone

THE Disciple bargained over the price of the Master, selling the Lord for thirty pieces of silver. And with a deceitful kiss he delivered him to those who are without law to kill him.

Today the Creator of heaven and earth said to his Disciples, The hour draweth near, and Judas my betrayer approacheth. Wherefore, let no one deny me when he seeth me on the Cross between two thieves; for as Man I shall suffer and save those who believe in me; for I am the Lover of mankind.

Glory and Now: O thou who, in the last days, didst conceive ineffably, and didst give birth to thy Creator, save, O Virgin, those who magnify thee.

Sixth Antiphony, in the Seventh Tone

TODAY Judas watcheth the night to deliver the eternal Lord, the Saviour of the World, who satisfied the multitudes with five loaves. Today that lawless one denieth his Master. A Disciple he was, yet delivered the Master, selling for silver him who fed man with manna.

Today the Jews nail on the Cross him who did cleave the sea with a rod, and made them to pass through the wilderness. Today they pierce with a spear the side of him who scourged Egypt with curses for their sake; and will give him bitterness to drink who rained down manna for their nourishment.

When thou camest to thy suffering, willingly, O Lord, thou didst cry out to thy Disciples: If ye cannot watch with me one hour, why then promised ye that ye would die for me? Rather see ye how Judas sleepeth not, but hasteneth to deliver me to those who disobey the law. Arise and pray, and let no one deny me when he seeth me on the Cross. Wherefore, O longsuffering One, glory be to thee.

Glory and Now: Rejoice, O Theotokos, who didst hold in thy womb him whom the heavens hold not. Rejoice, O Virgin, whom the Prophets preached, from whom Immanuel shone forth upon us. Rejoice, O Mother of Christ God.

Kathisma, in the Seventh Tone

WHAT caused thee, O Judas, to betray the Saviour? Did he set thee aside from the Disciples? Did he deny thee the gift of healing? Did he take supper with the others and send thee away from the table? Did he wash the feet of the rest and pass thee by? Of how much goodness hast thou become forgetful? Yea, thine unpraiseworthy mind hath been exposed. But his incalculable long-suffering and his great mercies are proclaimed with praise.

The Third Gospel: from St. Matthew (26:57 to end)

AT that time: The soldiers had laid hold on Jesus and led him away to Caiphas the high priest, where the Scribes and the elders were assembled.

But Peter followed him afar off unto the high priest's palace, and went in, and sat with the servants, to see the end.

Now the chief priests, and elders and all the council, sought false witness against Jesus, to put him to death;

But found none: yea, though many false witnesses came, yet found they none. At the last came two false witnesses,

And said, This fellow said, I am able to destroy the temple of God, and to build it in three days.

And the high priest arose, and said unto him, Answerest thou nothing? what is it which these witness against thee?

But Jesus held his peace. And the high priest answered and said unto him, I adjure thee by the living God, that thou tell us whether thou be the Christ, the Son of God.

Jesus saith unto him, Thou hast said: nevertheless I say unto you, Hereafter shall ye see the Son of man sitting on the right hand of power, and coming in the clouds of heaven.

Then the high priest rent his clothes, saying, He hath spoken blasphemy; what further need have we of witnesses? behold, now ye have heard his blasphemy.

What think ye? They answered and said, He is guilty of death.

Then did they spit in his face, and buffeted him; and others smote him with the palms of their hands,

Saying, Prophesy unto us, thou Christ, Who is he that smote thee?

Now Peter sat without in the palace: and a damsel came unto him, saying, Thou also wast with Jesus of Galilee.

But he denied before them all, saying, I know not what thou sayest.

And when he was gone out into the porch, another maid saw him, and said unto them that were there, This fellow was also with Jesus of Nazareth.

And again he denied with an oath, I do not know the man.

And after a while came unto him they that stood by, and said to Peter, Surely thou also art one of them; for thy speech betrayeth thee.

Then began he to curse and to swear, saying, I know not the man. And immediately the cock crew.

And Peter remembered the word of Jesus, which said unto him, Before the cock crow, thou shalt deny me thrice. And he went out, and wept bitterly.

Seventh Antiphony, in the Eighth Tone

WITH patience and forbearance thou didst cry out, O Lord, to the law-violators who laid hold upon thee, saying, If ye have stricken the Shepherd and dispersed my Disciples, those twelve sheep, I am able to bring more than twelve ranks of angels. But suffer ye long that that may be fulfilled which I have revealed to you through my Prophets of mysteries and hidden things. Wherefore, Lord, glory be to thee.

Three times did Peter deny. And perceiving immediately what was told him, he offered thee tears of repentance, saying, God, forgive me and save me.

Glory and Now: Let us praise the holy Virgin; for she is a door of salvation, a delightful paradise, and a cloud unto the eternal Light; and let us all hail her, saying, Rejoice!

Eighth Antiphony, in the Second Tone

SAY ye, O transgressors of the law, what heard ye from our Saviour? Is it not that he appointed a law and the teachings of the Prophets? How then did ye think to deliver to Pilate the Word, God of God, and the Deliverer of our souls.

They who benefited always by thy gifts, O Christ, were crying, Let him be crucified. And the killers of the righteous sought to free an evil-doer in place of the Benefactor. But thou wast silent, enduring their arrogance, wishing to suffer and to save us, since thou art the Lover of mankind.

Glory and Now: For verily, we have no favour, for the multitude of our sins. Therefore, O virgin Theotokos, plead with him who was born of thee; for the pleadings of the Mother are greatly effective in winning the favour of the Master. Turn thou not away, therefore, from the pleadings of sinners, O most venerable; for he who was willing to suffer for our sins is merciful and able to save us.

Ninth Antiphony, in the Third Tone

VERILY, they set the thirty pieces of silver, the price of him that was valued, whom they of the children of Israel did value. Watch ye and pray, lest ye enter into temptation; for the spirit is ready, but the flesh is weak. Wherefore, watch ye.

They gave me gall in my meat; and in my thirst they gave me vinegar to drink. But thou, O Lord, raise me, that I may reward them.

Glory and Now: We who are of the Gentiles praise thee, O undefiled Theotokos; for thou didst bear Christ our God, who through thee delivered mankind from the curse.

Kathisma, in the Second Tone

WOEFUL is it that Judas, who had been thy Disciple, plotted thy Betrayal in thy very presence. He supped with thee in deceit, that unrighteous assassin; then went to the priests, saying, What will ye give me to deliver unto you him who loosed the law and profaned the sabbath? Wherefore, O Lord, glory be to thy long-suffering.

The Fourth Gospel: from St. John (18:28 to end;
19:1-16)

AT that time: They led Jesus from Caiphas to the governor's hall. And it was morning; and they went not into the hall, that they might not be defiled, but that they might eat the pasch.

Pilate then went out unto them, and said, What accusation bring ye against this man?

They answered and said unto him, If he were not a malefactor, we would not have delivered him up unto thee.

Then said Pilate unto them, Take ye him, and judge him according to your law. The Jews therefore said unto him, It is not lawful for us to put any man to death:

That the saying of Jesus might be fulfilled, which he spake, signifying what death he should die.

Then Pilate entered into the judgment hall again, and called Jesus, and said unto him, Art thou the King of the Jews?

Jesus answered him, Sayest thou this thing of thyself, or did others tell it thee of me?

Pilate answered, Am I a Jew? Thine own nation and the chief priests have delivered thee unto me: what hast thou done?

Jesus answered, My kingdom is not of this world: if my kingdom were of this world, then would my servants fight, that I should not be delivered to the Jews: but now is my kingdom not from hence.

Pilate therefore said unto him, Art thou a king then? Jesus answered, Thou sayest that I am a king. To this end was I born, and for this cause came I into the world, that I should bear witness unto the truth. Every one that is of the truth heareth my voice.

Pilate saith unto him, What is truth? And when he had said this, he went out again unto the Jews, and saith unto them, I find in him no fault at all.

But ye have a custom, that I should release unto you one at the passover: will ye therefore that I release unto you the King of the Jews?

Then cried they all again, saying, Not this man, but Barabbas. Now Barabbas was a robber.

Then Pilate therefore took Jesus, and scourged him.

And the soldiers platted a crown of thorns, and put it on his head, and they put on him a purple robe,

And said, Hail, King of the Jews! and they smote him with their hands.

Pilate therefore went forth again, and saith unto them, Behold, I bring him forth to you, that ye may know that I find no fault in him.

Then came Jesus forth, wearing the crown of thorns, and the purple robe. And Pilate saith unto them, Behold the man!

When the chief priests therefore and officers saw him, they cried out, saying, Crucify him, crucify him. Pilate saith unto them, Take ye him, and crucify him: for I find no fault in him.

The Jews answered him, We have a law, and by our law he ought to die, because he made himself the Son of God.

When Pilate therefore heard that saying, he was the more afraid;

And went again into the judgment hall, and saith unto Jesus, Whence art thou? But Jesus gave him no answer.

Then saith Pilate unto him, Speakest thou not unto me? knowest thou not that I have power to crucify thee, and have power to release thee?

Jesus answered, Thou couldest have no power at all against me, except it were given thee from above: therefore he that delivered me unto thee hath the greater sin.

And from thenceforth Pilate sought to release him: but the Jews cried out, saying, If thou let this man go, thou art not Cæsar's friend: whosoever maketh himself a king speaketh against Cæsar.

When Pilate therefore heard that saying, he brought Jesus forth, and sat down in the judgment seat in a place that is called the Pavement, but in the Hebrew, Gabbatha.

And it was the preparation of the passover, and about the sixth hour: and he saith unto the Jews, Behold your King!

But they cried out, Away with him, away with him, crucify him. Pilate saith unto them, Shall I crucify your King? The chief priests answered, We have no king but Cæsar.

Then delivered he him therefore unto them to be crucified.

Tenth Antiphony, in the Sixth Tone

HE that putteth on light like a robe standeth naked in his trial, accepting a blow on his cheek from the hands that he created. And the Lord of glory was nailed to the Cross by that law-transgressing people. Then was the veil of the Temple rent, and the sun was darkened, unable to see humiliated the God before whom all tremble. Wherefore, let us worship him.

Verily, the Disciple denied, like an ingrate; and the thief cried out, saying, Remember me, Lord, in thy kingdom.

Glory and Now: O thou who didst will to receive from the Virgin a body, for thy servants' sake, grant peace to the world, that we may glorify thee in unison, O Lord and Lover of mankind.

Eleventh Antiphony, in the Sixth Tone

IN place of the good things that thou didst for the Hebrew people, O Christ, they condemned thee to be crucified, giving thee vinegar and gall to drink. But thou, Lord, render to them according to their deeds; for they understood not thy condescension.

The Hebrew people, O Christ, was not satisfied to deliver thee up. But whilst so doing they shook their heads, heaping upon thee ridicule and reproach. But thou, O Lord, reward them according to their deeds; for they ridiculed thee falsely.

Neither the earth in its quaking, the rocks when they were split, the veil of the Temple, nor the rising from the dead could convince the Jews. But thou, O Lord, reward them according to their deeds; for they ridiculed thee falsely.

Glory and Now: Verily, we have known that from thee God was incarnate, O virgin Theotokos, O thou who alone art undefiled, and alone blessed. Wherefore, we ceaselessly praise and magnify thee.

Twelfth Antiphony, in the Eighth Tone

THUS saith the Lord to the Jews, My people, what have I done unto thee; and wherewith have I harmed thee? Thy blind have I lighted; thy lepers have I cleansed, and the man on his couch have I raised.

O my people, what have I done unto thee, and wherewith hast thou rewarded me? Instead of manna, gall; and in place of water, vinegar; and instead of loving me, thou didst nail me to the Cross. I can endure no more. I will call the Gentiles, and they shall glorify me with the Father, and the Spirit. And I will grant them everlasting life.

Today the veil of the Temple is rent as a reproach to those transgressors of the law; and the sun hideth its rays at seeing the Master crucified.

Ye Jews and Pharisees who lay down the law for Israel, verily, the assembly of the Disciples cry out to you, Behold the Temple which ye destroyed! Behold the Lamb whom ye crucified! Ye delivered him to the grave, but he arose by his own power. Do not err, O Jews; for it is he who saved you in the sea and nourished you in the wilderness. He is the Life, the Light, and the Peace of the world.

Glory and Now: Hail, O gate of the King of glory, through which the Highest alone did enter, preserving thee sealed for our salvation.

Kathisma, in the Eighth Tone

WHEN thou stoodest before Caiphas, O God of judgment, and wast delivered to Pilate, the heavenly powers trembled for fear. Then wast thou lifted up upon a Tree between two thieves, and numbered among the wicked, O innocent One, to save man. Wherefore, O long-suffering Lord, glory to thee.

The Fifth Gospel: from St. Matthew (27:3-32)

AT that time: Judas, which had betrayed him, when he saw that he was condemned, repented himself, and brought again the thirty pieces of silver to the chief priests and elders,

Saying, I have sinned in that I have betrayed the innocent blood. And they said, What is that to us? see thou to that.

And he cast down the pieces of silver in the temple, and departed, and went and hanged himself.

And the chief priests took the silver pieces, and said, It is not lawful for to put them into the treasury, because it is the price of blood.

And they took counsel, and bought with them the potter's field, to bury strangers in.

Wherefore that field was called, the field of blood, unto this day.

Then was fulfilled that which was spoken by Jeremy the prophet, saying, And they took the thirty pieces of silver, the price of him that was valued, whom they of the children of Israel did value;

And gave them for the potter's field, as the Lord appointed me.

And Jesus stood before the governor: and the governor asked him, saying, Art thou the King of the Jews? And Jesus said unto him, Thou sayest.

And when he was accused of the chief priests and elders, he answered nothing.

Then said Pilate unto him, Hearest thou not how many things they witness against thee?

And he answered him to never a word; insomuch that the governor marveled greatly.

Now at that feast the governor was wont to release unto the people a prisoner, whom they would.

And they had then a notable prisoner, called Barabbas.

Therefore when they were gathered together, Pilate said unto them, Whom will ye that I release unto you? Barabbas, or Jesus which is called Christ?

For he knew that for envy they had delivered him.

When he was set down on the judgment seat, his wife sent unto him, saying, Have thou nothing to do with that just man: for I have suffered many things this day in a dream because of him.

But the chief priests and elders persuaded the multitude that they should ask Barabbas, and destroy Jesus.

The governor answered and said unto them, Whether of the twain will ye that I release unto you? They said, Barabbas.

Pilate saith unto them, What shall I do then with Jesus which is called Christ? They all say unto him, Let him be crucified.

And the governor said, Why, what evil hath he done? But they cried out the more, saying, Let him be crucified.

When Pilate saw that he could prevail nothing, but that rather a tumult was made, he took water, and washed his hands before the multitude, saying, I am innocent of the blood of this just person: see ye to it.

Then answered all the people, and said, His blood be on us, and on our children.

Then released he Barabbas unto them: and when he had scourged Jesus, he delivered him to be crucified.

Then the soldiers of the governor took Jesus into the common hall, and gathered unto him the whole band of soldiers.

And they stripped him, and put on him a scarlet robe.

And when they had platted a crown of thorns, they put it upon his head, and a reed in his right hand: and they bowed the knee before him, and mocked him, saying, Hail, King of the Jews!

And they spit upon him, and took the reed, and smote him on the head.

And after that they had mocked him, they took the robe off from him, and put his own raiment on him, and led him away to crucify him.

And as they came out, they found a man of Cyrene, Simon by name: him they compelled to bear his cross.

Thirteenth Antiphony, in the Sixth Tone

THE Jewish rabble, O Lord, sought from Pilate to crucify thee; and though finding no cause against thee, it freed Barabbas who was under guilt. But thee, O righteous One, they did condemn, becoming heirs to the cruel crime of murder. But thou, O Lord, give them their reward: for they conspired against thee in vain.

Christ, who is the power of God and the wisdom of God, before whom all tremble and whom all dread, and whom every tongue praiseth, verily, the priests smote, and gave him gall to drink. He consented to undergo all kinds of suffering, desiring to save us from our iniquities with his blood; for he is the Lover of mankind.

Glory and Now: O Theotokos, who by a word didst give birth to the Creator himself ineffably, implore him to save our souls.

Fourteenth Antiphony, in the Eighth Tone

O LORD, who didst take as companion the thief who had polluted his hands with blood, number us too with him, since thou art good and the Lover of mankind.

The thief, still on his cross, uttered a little song. Whereupon he found great faith and was saved by a single glance. First, he opened the doors of paradise, and then he entered in. O thou who didst accept his repentance, O Lord, glory be to thee.

Glory and Now: Hail, thou who didst receive from the angel the Joy of the world. Rejoice, thou who didst give birth to thy Lord and Creator. Hail, thou who wast considered worthy to become Mother to Christ God.

Fifteenth Antiphony, in the Sixth Tone

❧ *The first Stanza of the following Antiphony is sung alternately, each clause separately.*[1]

TODAY he is suspended on a Tree who suspended the earth over the waters (*three times*).

A crown of thorns was placed on the head of the King of angels.

He who wore a false purple robe covered the heavens with clouds.

He was smitten who, in the Jordan, delivered Adam.

The Groom of the Church was fastened with nails, and the Son of the Virgin was pierced with a spear.

Thy sufferings we adore, O Christ (*three times*).

Make us to behold thy glorious Resurrection.

We shall not feast like the Jews; for our Passover, Christ God, hath been slain for our sake.

But let us purify ourselves of every defilement, and with purity beseech him, saying, Rise, Lord, and save us; for thou art the Lover of mankind.

---

[1] It has been the custom, since the middle of the past century, in Greek churches, and particularly Syrian, for the Arch-priest to carry the crucifix, and, after circling the holy Altar, to come out through the left door, and to carry it in procession in the church, as he sings, *Today is suspended on a Tree*, etc., in the intonation of the Gospel reading. Then he plants the crucifix in a marble base, placed in the middle of the church for that purpose. Then making an adoration to the crucifix, and kissing it, the Priest returns to the Temple, while the congregation, one by one, come forward and kiss the crucifix, as the Choir sing antiphonally the same piece.

There is no mention of this custom in the ancient Triodions and Typicons, but it was formally ordained in the days of Sophronius, the Patriarch of Constantinople, in the year 1864.

Thy Cross, O Lord, is life and resurrection for thy people; and therein is our trust. And thee, our God, who wast crucified, do we praise. Have mercy upon us.

Glory and Now: She who gave thee birth, O Christ, seeing thee on the Cross, shouted, saying, What strange mystery do I behold, O my Son? How hast thou died elevated in the body on a Tree, O thou who givest and grantest life?

Kathisma, in the Fourth Tone

THOU didst redeem us, our Saviour, from the curse of the law with thy precious blood, when thou wast nailed to the Cross and pierced with a spear, bearing deathlessness for mankind. Glory to thee.

The Sixth Gospel: from St. Mark (15:16-32)

AT that time: The soldiers led Jesus away into the hall, called Prætorium; and they call together the whole band.

And they clothed him with purple, and platted a crown of thorns, and put it about his head,

And began to salute him, Hail, King of the Jews!

And they smote him on the head with a reed, and did spit upon him, and bowing their knees worshipped him.

And when they had mocked him, they took off the purple from him, and put his own clothes on him, and led him out to crucify him.

And they compel one Simon a Cyrenian, who passed by, coming out of the country, the father of Alexander and Rufus, to bear his cross.

And they bring him unto the place Golgotha, which is, being interpreted, The place of a skull.

And they gave him to drink wine mingled with myrrh: but he received it not.

And when they had crucified him, they parted his garments, casting lots upon them, what every man should take.

And it was the third hour, and they crucified him.

And the superscription of his accusation was written over, The King of the Jews.

And with him they crucify two thieves; the one on his right hand, and the other on his left.

And the Scripture was fulfilled, which saith, And he was numbered with the transgressors.

And they that passed by railed on him, wagging their heads, and saying, Ah, thou that destroyest the temple, and buildest it in three days,

Save thyself, and come down from the cross.

Likewise also the chief priests mocking said among themselves with the scribes, He saved others; himself he cannot save.

Let Christ the King of Israel descend now from the cross, that we may see and believe.

❡ *Then sing the Makarizmoi, on Eight Stichoi, in the Fourth Tone.*

In thy kingdom, remember us, O Lord, when thou comest into thy kingdom.

Blessed are the poor in spirit; for theirs is the kingdom of heaven.

Blessed are they that mourn; for they shall be comforted.

Blessed are the meek; for they shall inherit the earth.

BECAUSE of a tree, Adam was estranged from paradise; and the thief because of the tree of the Cross abode in paradise; for the former in tasting, disobeyed the commandment of the Creator; but the latter, who was crucified with thee, confessed, admitting to thee that thou art a hidden God. Wherefore, O Saviour, remember him and us in thy kingdom.

Blessed are they that hunger and thirst after righteousness; for they shall be filled.

The law-transgressors verily did buy the Ordainer of the law from a Disciple. And as a law-breaker they brought him before Pilate, crying out that he who gave them manna in the wilderness be crucified. But we, emulating the righteous thief, cry out in faith, Remember him and us, O Saviour, in thy kingdom.

Blessed are the merciful; for they shall obtain mercy.

The assembly of the Jews, that wicked, God-attacking nation, madly cried to Pilate, saying, Crucify Christ the innocent; pleading that Barabbas be rather released. But we cry in the voice of the grateful thief, Remember him and us, O Saviour, in thy kingdom.

Blessed are the pure in heart; for they shall see God.

Thy life-bearing side, O Christ, overfloweth like a spring from Eden, watering thy Church as a paradise endowed with speech; and thence divideth the glad tidings into four Gospels, as into four heads, watering the world, gladdening creation, and teaching the Gentiles to adore thy kingdom in faith.

Blessed are the peacemakers; for they shall be called the children of God.

Thou wast crucified, O Christ, for my sake, that thou mightest pour forth salvation for me. And thy side was pierced with a spear, that it might cause rivers of life to flow for me. Thou wast fastened with the nails; and so realizing the depth of thy Passion and the height of thy might, I will cry unto thee, Glory to thy Passion and to thy Crucifixion, O life-giving Saviour.

Blessed are they which are persecuted for righteousness' sake; for theirs is the kingdom of heaven.

The whole creation, O Christ, beholding thy Crucifixion, trembled; the foundations of the earth were shaken for dread of thy might; the two luminaries went into hiding; the veil of the Temple was rent; the mountains quaked; and the rocks burst asunder, as the believing thief cried with us unto thee, Saviour, remember me.

Blessed are ye when men shall revile you, and persecute you, and say all manner of evil against you falsely for my sake.

Thou hast torn with the spear, O Lord, the handwriting of ordinances that were against us, and thou wast numbered among the dead, binding there the usurper, and delivering all from the bonds of death by thy Resurrection, by which we have been enlightened. Wherefore, we cry to thee, O Lover of mankind, to remember us in thy kingdom.

Rejoice and be glad, for great is your reward in heaven.

O Lord, who wast elevated on the Cross, and who, being God, loosed the bonds of death and blotted out the handwriting of ordinances against us, grant us and the thief his repentance, O thou who art alone the Lover of mankind, us who worship thee in faith, O Christ our God, and who cry to thee, Remember him and us in thy kingdom.

Glory: Come, all ye believers, let us with one mind beseech, glorifying as is meet, the Father, Son, and Holy Spirit, the one Godhead in three Persons, permanent without confusion, simple, indivisible, and unapproachable, through whom we escape the fire of punishment.

Now: We offer thee for intercession, O most merciful Christ Lord, thy Mother, the true Virgin, who without seed, gave thee birth in the body and remained without corruption after her birth-giving, that thou mightest forgive the transgressions of those who cry to thee constantly, Remember him and us, O Saviour, in thy kingdom.

Prokeimenon, in the Fourth Tone

They parted my garments among them, and upon my vesture did they cast lots. My God, my God, behold, why hast thou forsaken me?

The Seventh Gospel: from St. Matthew (27:3354)

AT that time: The soldiers brought Jesus unto a place called Golgotha, that is to say, a place of a skull.

They gave him vinegar to drink mingled with gall: and when he had tasted thereof, he would not drink.

And they crucified him, and parted his garments, casting lots: that it might be fulfilled which was spoken by the prophet, They parted my garments among them, and upon my vesture did they cast lots.

And sitting down they watched him there;

And set up over his head his accusation written, This is Jesus the King of the Jews.

Then were there two thieves crucified with him; one on the right hand, and another on the left.

And they that passed by reviled him, wagging their heads,

And saying, Thou that destroyest the temple, and buildest it in three days, save thyself. If thou be the Son of God, come down from the cross.

Likewise also the chief priests mocking him, with the scribes and elders, said,

He saved others; himself he cannot save. If he be the King of Israel, let him now come down from the cross, and we will believe him.

He trusted in God; let him deliver him now, if he will have him: for he said, I am the Son of God.

The thieves also, which were crucified with him, cast the same in his teeth.

Now from the sixth hour there was darkness over all the land unto the ninth hour.

And about the ninth hour Jesus cried with a loud voice, saying, Eli, Eli, lamasabachthani? that is to say, My God, my God, why hast thou forsaken me?

Some of them that stood there, when they heard that, said, This man calleth for Elias.

And straightway one of them ran, and took a sponge, and filled it with vinegar, and put it on a reed, and gave him to drink.

The rest said, Let be, let us see whether Elias will come to save him.

Jesus, when he had cried again with a loud voice, yielded up the ghost.

And, behold, the veil of the temple was rent in twain from top to the bottom; and the earth did quake, and the rocks rent;

And the graves were opened; and many bodies of the saints which slept arose,

And came out of the graves after his resurrection, and went into the holy city, and appeared unto many.

Now when the centurion, and they that were with him, watching Jesus, saw the earthquake, and those things that were done, they feared greatly, saying, Truly this was the Son of God.

¶ *Then read Psalm 50 (p. 82); and immediately:*

The Eighth Gospel: from St. Luke (23:32-49)

AT that time: There were also two other, malefactors, led with him to be put to death.

And when they were come to the place, which is called Calvary, there they crucified him, and the malefactors, one on the right hand, and the other on the left.

Then said Jesus, Father, forgive them; for they know not what they do. And they parted his raiment, and cast lots.

And the people stood beholding. And the rulers also with them derided him, saying, He saved others; let him save himself, if he be Christ, the chosen of God.

And the soldiers also mocked him, coming to him, and offering him vinegar,

And saying, If thou be the King of the Jews, save thyself.

And a superscription also was written over him in letters of Greek, and Latin, and Hebrew, This is the King of the Jews.

And one of the malefactors which were hanged railed on him, saying, If thou be the Christ, save thyself and us.

But the other answering rebuked him, saying, Dost not thou fear God, seeing thou art in the same condemnation?

And we indeed justly; for we receive the due reward of our deeds: but this man hath done nothing amiss.

And he said unto Jesus, Lord, remember me when thou comest into thy kingdom.

And Jesus said unto him, Verily I say unto thee, To-day shalt thou be with me in paradise.

And it was about the sixth hour, and there was a darkness over all the earth until the ninth hour.

And the sun was darkened, and the veil of the temple was rent in the midst.

And when Jesus had cried with a loud voice, he said, Father, into thy hands I commend my spirit: and having said thus, he gave up the ghost.

Now when the centurion saw what was done, he glorified God, saying, Certainly this was a righteous man.

And all the people that came together to that sight, beholding the things which were done, smote their breasts, and returned.

And all his acquaintance, and the women that followed him from Galilee, stood afar off, beholding these things.

❧ *Then the Canon, in the Sixth Tone.*

Fifth Ode

EARLY will I seek thee, O Word of God, who of thy compassion didst empty thyself, being led even unto suffering without transubstantiation and without suffering, for the sake of the fallen. Wherefore, grant me safety, O Lover of mankind.

Thy servants, O Christ, when thou hadst washed their feet, and they had now become purified by sharing thy dread mystery, ascended with us from Zion to the great Mount of Olives, praising thee, O Lover of mankind.

Thou didst say, Behold, my beloved, be not troubled; for now my hour hath come in the which I shall be laid hold on, and be killed at the hands of the lawless wick-

ed; and ye shall all be dispersed and leave me alone.
But I shall bring you together to preach me; for I am
the Lover of mankind.

Kontakion, in the Eighth Tone

COME, let us all praise him who was crucified for
our sakes, to whom Mary, having beheld him upon
the Tree said, Though thou hast endured crucifixion
willingly, thou art still my Son and my God.

Oikos: Having beheld her Lamb being led to
slaughter, Mary, the ewe, followed him in the company
of other women, troubled, and crying thus, Where goest
thou, my Son? And why hastenest thou to finish this
course? Is there, perchance, another wedding in Cana
to which thou hastenest now to change the water for
them into wine? Shall I go with thee, or shall I rather
tarry? Give me word, O Word, nor pass me in silence,
O thou who didst keep me undefiled; for thou art still
my Son and my God.

SYNAXARION

ON this great and holy Friday we celebrate the holy,
dread, and saving Passion of our Lord God and
Saviour Jesus Christ, the spittings, blows, and scourges;
the curses, cheers, and the wearing of the purple; the
rod, sponge, and vinegar; the nails, the spear, and especially the Cross and death; which he received willingly for our sakes. We celebrate also the confession
of salvation which the grateful thief made on the cross
with him.

Stichoi of the Cross

THOU art a living God, albeit thou wast elevated on
a Tree and wast made to die.

O thou naked Dead, Word of the living God, begotten of the Father.

Another for the Grateful Thief

THE thief hath opened the closed gates of Eden by a sign from thy might.

When using as a key this saying, Remember me, Lord, in thy kingdom.

At the dawn of day on a Friday that fell on the twenty-third of March, Jesus, bound by Caiphas, was sent to Pontius Pilate, the governor of Judæa, who investigated him carefully. And finding no fault with him he twice confessed his innocence. Nevertheless, he condemned him to death to please the Jews. And the Lord of all, having been scourged, like a runaway slave, was delivered to be crucified. The soldiers then took him, stripped him and put on a scarlet robe. They put on his head a crown of thorns, and in his right hand a reed instead of a sceptre. And they began to kneel before him mockingly, and spat upon him, and smote him, and struck him on the head. Then they put on him his clothes, made him carry the Cross and took him to Golgotha, the place for the execution of his sentence, and there they crucified him, about the third hour of the day, between two thieves. Those who passed by blasphemed against him, and the high priests mocked him. Then the soldiers gave him to drink vinegar mixed with wormwood. And in the ninth hour Jesus, the Lamb of God, who took away the sins of the world (St. Jn. 1:29), cried with a loud voice, It is finished, and gave up the ghost, at the very hour in which the Lamb of the Mosaic Passover was being slaughtered, which the Jews had been commanded to sacrifice every year as a symbol of him 1642 years previously. The moon on that night was full (Ex. 12).

And when mute creation looked upon the Master's Death it grieved, trembling and fearful. Then after the Maker of all creation gave up the ghost his side was pierced, and from it flowed blood and water. Then Joseph of Arimathea came at the setting of the sun, and with him was Nicodemus, both of whom were secretly

Disciples of Jesus, and took down his body from the Cross, wound it with linens and spices and laid him in a new sepulchre, and over its door they rolled a great stone.

In memory, therefore, of this fearful redemptive Passion of our Lord Jesus Christ, we celebrate today; and at that time it was delivered to us by an apostolic commandment to fast every Friday.

Wherefore, O Christ God, by thy boundless compassion for our sakes, have mercy upon us. Amen.

Eighth Ode

THE divine youths exposed the God-contending pillar of wickedness; and the assembly of the wicked, roaring at Christ, conspired falsely, studying how to kill him who holdeth life in his grasp, whom all creation doth bless, glorifying me unto all ages.

Thou didst say to thy Disciples, O Christ, Drive away sleep from your eyelids; watch in prayer lest ye fall; and especially thou, Simon; for the haughty suffereth greater trial. Know thou me, O Peter, whom all creation doth bless, glorifying me unto all ages.

Verily, Peter cried, saying, No evil words, O Master, shall come out of my lips, but, as one of true loyalty, I will die with thee, even though all deny thee; for flesh and blood hath not revealed thee unto me, but the Father whom all creation blesseth, glorifying him unto all ages.

And the Lord said, Thou dost not comprehend, O man, the depth of the divine wisdom and knowledge; thou hast not fathomed my decrees; for since thou art flesh, vaunt not boastfully; for thou shalt deny me thrice, whom all creation doth bless, glorifying unto all ages.

O Simon Peter, said the Lord, Thou shalt presently deny what thou hast been convinced of, as it hath been said; for a maiden shall suddenly appear and frighten thee. Then thou shalt weep bitterly, but thou shalt find me forgiving, whom all creation doth bless, glorifying unto all ages.

Ninth Ode

O THOU who art more honourable than the cherubim, and beyond compare more glorious than the seraphim, who without corruption didst bear the Word of God; truly, thou art the Theotokos, and thee do we magnify.

The corrupting soldiers, despised of God, and the band of God-killing wicked hastened to thee, O Christ, and led thee away as an unrighteous one, thou Creator of all whom we magnify.

The impious, for their ignorance of the law and their false study of the sayings of the Prophets, have unjustly led thee like a sheep to slaughter, O Lord of all, whom we magnify.

The priests with the scribes, wounded by the evil of their utter envy, delivered Life to the Gentiles to be killed; thee, O natural Source of life, whom we magnify.

They have surrounded thee like many dogs, O King, and smitten thee on the cheeks, questioning thee and bearing false witness against thee; and thou hast borne it all, delivering all.

Exaposteilarion, in the Third Tone (three times)

Thou made the thief worthy of paradise on the same day, O Lord. Wherefore, illuminate me too by the tree of thy Cross and save me.

The Ninth Gospel: from St. John (19:25-37)

AT that time: There stood by the Cross of Jesus his mother and his mother's sister Mary the wife of Cleophas, and Mary Magdalene.

When Jesus therefore saw his mother, and the disciple standing by, whom he loved, he saith unto his mother, Woman, behold thy son!

Then saith he to the disciple, Behold thy mother! And from that hour that disciple took her unto his own home.

After this, Jesus knowing that all things were now accomplished, that the Scripture might be fulfilled, saith, I thirst.

Now there was set a vessel full of vinegar: and they filled a sponge with vinegar, and put it upon hyssop, and put it to his mouth.

When Jesus therefore had received the vinegar, he said, It is finished: and he bowed his head, and gave up the ghost.

The Jews therefore, because it was the preparation, that the bodies should not remain upon the cross on the sabbath day, (for that sabbath day was a high day,) besought Pilate that their legs might be broken, and that they might be taken away.

Then came the soldiers, and brake the legs of the first, and of the other which was crucified with him.

But when they came to Jesus, and saw that he was dead already, they brake not his legs:

But one of the soldiers with a spear pierced his side, and forthwith came there out blood and water.

And he that saw it bare record, and his record is true; and he knoweth that he saith true, that ye might believe.

For these things were done, that the Scripture should be fulfilled, A bone of him shall not be broken.

And again another Scripture saith, They shall look on him whom they pierced.

❡*In the Einos, sing the following four Idiomelons, in the Third Tone.*

MY first-born, Israel, hath done double evil, having forsaken me, the Fountain of the water of life, and hewed him a broken cistern, crucifying me on a Tree, seeking Barabbas and releasing him. Wherefore, heaven was amazed at this, and the sun hid its rays. And thou, O Israel, refrained not, but delivered me unto death. O holy Father, forgive them; for they know not what they have done. *(Repeat.)*

Every member of thy holy body, O Saviour, hath endured humiliation for our sakes; the head with thorns, the face with spitting, the cheeks with blows, the mouth with the taste of vinegar mixed with gall, the ears with blasphemies replete with infidelity, the back with scourges, the hand with the rod, and the extension of the whole body with the Cross, the extremities with nails, and the side with the spear. Wherefore, O thou who didst suffer for us and deliveredst us from suffering, condescending to us for thy love of mankind, and raised us, O thou Almighty, have mercy upon us.

The whole creation, O Christ, beholding thee crucified, trembled; and the foundations of the earth shook for dread of thy might; for by thine elevation today the Hebrew race perished, and the veil of the Temple was rent in twain, the graves were opened, and the dead rose from their tombs, as the centurion, beholding this miracle, was frightened. As for thy Mother, she stood by wailing and moaning as mothers do, saying, How shall I not wail, and smite my breast as I see thee naked and elevated on a Tree, as one condemned? Wherefore, O thou who wast crucified, buried, and rose from the dead, O Lord, glory to thee.

Glory, in the Sixth Tone

THEY have taken off my clothes from me and clothed me with a scarlet robe, and placed on my head a crown of thorns, delivering into my right hand a rod wherewith I may crush them like pottery.

Now, in the Same Tone

I HAVE delivered my back to scourges, and my face I have not turned away from spitting. Before the tribune of Pilate I stood, and the Cross I endured for the salvation of the world.

The Tenth Gospel: from St. Mark (15:43 to end)

AT that time: Joseph of Arimathea, and honourable counsellors who were also awaiting the kingdom of God, came, and went in boldly unto Pilate, and craved the body of Jesus.

And Pilate marvelled if he were already dead: and calling unto him the centurion, he asked him whether he had been any while dead.

And when he knew it of the centurion, he gave the body to Joseph.

And he bought fine linen, and took him down, and wrapped him in the linen, and laid him in a sepulchre which was hewn out of a rock, and rolled a stone unto the door of the sepulchre.

And Mary Magdalene and Mary the mother of Joses beheld where he was laid.

Then: Thine is the glory, our Lord and our God, etc. (p. 39).

❡*And the Priest saith the Petitions,* Let us finish our petitions of the evening to the Lord, *etc. with the petitions following thereon (p. 76). And after the Proclamation,* For thou art the God of mercy and salvation, our God, and to thee do we address glory, *etc., immediately read:*

The Eleventh Gospel: from St. John (19:38 to end)

AT that time: Joseph of Arimathea, (being a disciple of Jesus, but secretly for the fear of the Jews) besought Pilate that he might take away the body of Jesus. And Pilate gave him leave. He came therefore, and took the body of Jesus!

And there came also Nicodemus, which at the first came to Jesus by night, and brought a mixture of myrrh and aloes, about a hundred pound weight.

Then took they the body of Jesus, and wound it in linen clothes with the spices, as the manner of the Jews is to bury.

Now in the place where he was crucified there was a garden: and in the garden a new sepulchre, wherein was never man yet laid.

There laid they Jesus therefore because of the Jews' preparation day; for the sepulchre was nigh at hand.

❡ *Then in the Aposticha, sing the following Idiomelons.*

In the First Tone

THE whole creation, O Christ, hath been transfigured by fear at beholding thee suspended on the Cross. The sun was darkened, the foundations of the earth were troubled, and everything suffered with the Creator of all. Wherefore, O thou who didst endure this willingly for us, O Lord, glory be to thee.

In the Second Tone

Stichos: They parted my garments among them, and upon my vesture did they cast lots.

Why doth the law-transgressing people of false worship meditate in falsehood? Why was he condemned to death who is the Life of all? What great wonder that the Creator of the world hath been delivered into the hands of the wicked; and the Lover of mankind hath been elevated on a Tree to deliver those who are bound in hades, who cry, O long-suffering Father, glory to thee.

Stichos: In my food they gave me gall, and in my thirst did they give me vinegar to drink.

Today the blameless Virgin hath seen thee, O Word, suspended on the Cross, and her heart was wounded with mourning from parental emotions. She sighed disconsolately from the depth of her soul; she pulled her hair and cheeks bitterly; she smote her breast. crying with copious tears, Woe is me, O my divine Son! Woe is me, O Light of the world! Now hast thou disappeared before mine eyes, O Lamb of God. Then the incorporeal hosts were engulfed with trembling, crying, O incomprehensible Lord, glory to thee.

Stichos: As for God, he is our King before the ages. He hath worked salvation in the midst of the earth.

O Christ, God of all creation and its Maker, she who without seed gave thee birth, seeing thee suspended on a Tree, cried bitterly, Whither hath the beauty of thy countenance disappeared, O my Son? I cannot endure the sight of thine unjust Crucifixion. Arise soon, that I may behold thy third-day Resurrection from the dead.

Glory, in the Eighth Tone

AT thine elevation upon the Cross, O Lord, fear and consternation fell on creation. Albeit thou didst restrain the ground from swallowing up thy crucifiers. And thou didst command hades to deliver up its captives for the restoration of the order of humanity; for thou didst come to grant them life, not death. Wherefore, O Judge of the quick and the dead, O Lover of mankind, glory to thee.

Now, in the Same Tone

NOW the pen of judgment is dipped by the unrighteous judges, sentence is passed on Jesus, and he is condemned to crucifixion!

Now doth creation travail at beholding the Lord on the Tree. But, O thou who didst suffer in the nature of the flesh for my sake, O good Lord, glory to thee.

The Twelfth Gospel: from St. Matthew (27:62 to end)

ON the next day, which followed the day of preparation, the chief priests and the Pharisees came together to Pilate,

Saying: Sir, we have remembered, that that seducer said, while he was yet alive: After three days I will rise again.

Command therefore the sepulchre to be guarded until the third day: lest perhaps his disciples come and steal him away, and say to the people: He is risen from the dead; and the last error shall be worse than the first.

Pilate saith to them: You have a guard; go, guard it as you know.

And they departing, made the sepulchre sure, sealing the stone, and setting guards.

❡ *Then,* It is a good thing to confess to the Lord, *etc.* (*p. 757*); *the Troparion,* Thou didst redeem us, our Saviour, from Curse of the law, *etc.* (*p. 826*); *and the Petitions,* Let us all say with our souls *etc.* (*p. 75*).

Benediction: O thou who didst endure spitting, scourges, reviling, and death for the salvation of the world, O Christ our God, etc.

The Morning of Great Friday
Service of the Hours
First Hour

❡ *After* Blessed be God; O heavenly King, *etc;* Holy God, *etc;* Lord, have mercy (*twelve times*); *and* O come, let us worship, *etc.* (*three times*), *say the following Psalms:*

Psalm 5

Give ear, O Lord, to my words, etc. (p. 68).

Psalm 2

Why have the Gentiles raged, etc. (p. 66).

Psalm 21

O GOD, my God, look upon me: why hast thou forsaken me?
Far from my salvation are the words of my sins.

O my God, I shall cry by day, and thou wilt not hear: and by night, and it shall not be reputed as folly in me.

But thou dwellest in the holy place, the praise of Israel.

In thee have our fathers hoped: they have hoped, and thou hast delivered them.

They cried to thee, and they were saved: they trusted in thee, and were not confounded.

But I am a worm, and no man: the reproach of men, and the outcast of the people.

All they that saw me have laughed me to scorn: they have spoken with the lips, and wagged the head.

He hoped in the Lord, let him deliver him: let him save him seeing he delighteth in him.

For thou art he that hast drawn me out of the womb: my hope from the breasts of my mother. I was cast upon thee from the womb.

From my mother's womb thou art my God, depart not from me.

For tribulation is very near: for there is none to help me.

Many calves have surrounded me: fat bulls have besieged me.

They have opened their mouths against me, as a lion ravening and roaring.

I am poured out like water; and all my bones are scattered.

My heart is becoming like wax melting in the midst of my bowels.

My strength is dried up like a potsherd, and my tongue hath cleaved to my jaws: and thou hast brought me down into the dust of death.

For many dogs have encompassed me: the council of the malignant hath besieged me.

They have dug my hands and feet. They have numbered all my bones.

And they have looked and stared upon me. They parted my garments amongst them: and upon my vesture they cast lots.

But thou, O Lord, remove not thy help to a distance from me: look towards my defence.

Deliver, O God, my soul from the sword: my only one from the hand of the dog.

Save me from the lion's mouth; and my lowness from the horns of the unicorns.

I will declare thy name to my brethren: in the midst of the church will I praise thee.

Ye that fear the Lord, praise him: all ye the seed of Jacob, glorify him.

Let all the seed of Israel fear him: because he hath not slighted nor despised the supplication of the poor man.

Neither hath he turned away his face from me: and when I cried to him he heard me.

With thee is my praise in a great church: I will pay my vows in the sight of them that fear him.

The poor shall eat and shall be filled: and they shall praise the Lord that seek him: their hearts shall live for ever and ever.

All the ends of the earth shall remember, and shall be converted to the Lord:

And all the kindreds of the Gentiles shall adore in his sight.

For the kingdom is the Lord's; and he shall have dominion over the nations.

All the fat ones of the earth have eaten and have adored: all they that go down to the earth shall fall before him.

And to him my soul shall live: and my seed shall serve him.

There shall be declared to the Lord a generation to come: and the heavens shall shew forth his justice to a people that shall be born which the Lord hath made.

❡ *Glory and Now;* Alleluia (*three times*); Lord, have mercy (*three times*); Glory; *and the following.*

Troparion, in the First Tone

BY thy Cross, O Christ, the usurper hath been destroyed, and the power of the adversary hath been trodden down; for it was not an angel or man, but thou who didst save us. Glory to thee.

Now: What shall we call thee, O full of Grace, etc. (p. 374).

❡ *Then sing the following Idiomelons, in the Eighth Tone.*

TODAY the veil of the Temple is rent in reproach of the law-transgressors; and the sun hath hidden its rays at beholding the Lord crucified.

Stichos: Why do the heathen rage, and the people imagine a vain thing?

Like a sheep thou hast been led to slaughter, O Christ King; and like a guileless lamb, O King of all, thou wast nailed on the Cross by law-transgressing men for our sins, O Lover of mankind.

Glory and Now: With patience and forbearance, etc. (p. 816).

❡ *Then the Prokeimenon of the Prophecy, in the Fourth Tone.*

He went out and spoke to the multitudes: Blessed is he that understandeth concerning the needy and the poor.

Reading: from the Prophecy of Zachariah the Prophet (11:10-13)

THESE sayings the Lord doth say: So I shall take my rod that was called Beauty, and cut it asunder to make void my covenant, which I had made with all people.

And it was made void in that day: and so the poor of the flock that keep for me, understand that it is the word of the Lord.

And I said to them: If it be good in your eyes, bring hither my wages: and if not, be quiet. And they weighed for my wages thirty pieces of silver,

And the Lord said to me: Cast it to the statuary, a handsome price, that I was prized at by them. And I took the thirty pieces of silver, and I cast them into the house of the Lord to the statuary, according to what the Lord intimated.

The Epistle: Section from the Epistle of St. Paul to the Galatians (6:14 to end)

YE brethren: But far be it from me to glory, save in the cross of our Lord Jesus Christ, through which the world hath been crucified unto me, and I unto the world.

For in Christ Jesus neither circumcision availeth any thing, nor uncircumcision, but a new creature.

And whosoever shall follow this rule, peace on them, and mercy, and upon the Israel of God.

From henceforth let no man be troublesome to me; for I bear the marks of the Lord Jesus in my body.

The grace of our Lord Jesus Christ be with your spirit, brethren. Amen.

The Gospel: from St. Matthew (27:1-56)

AT that time: When morning was come, all the chief priests and ancients of the people took counsel against Jesus, that they might put him to death.

And they brought him bound, and delivered him to Pontius Pilate the governor.

Then Judas, who betrayed him, seeing that he was condemned, repenting himself, brought back the thirty pieces of silver to the chief priests and ancients, saying: I have sinned in betraying innocent blood. But they said: What is that to us? Look thou to it.

And casting down the pieces of silver in the temple, he departed: and went and hanged himself with an halter.

But the chief priest having taken the pieces of silver, said: It is not lawful to put them into the corbona, because it is the price of blood.

And after they had consulted together, they bought with them the potter's field, to be a burying place for strangers.

For this cause that field was called Haceldama, that is, the field of blood, even to this day.

Then was fulfilled that which was spoken by Jeremias the prophet, saying: And they took the thirty pieces of silver, the price of him that was valued, whom they prized of the children of Israel.

And they gave them unto the potter's field, as the Lord appointed to me.

And Jesus stood before the governor, and the governor asked him, saying: Art thou the king of the Jews? Jesus saith to him: Thou sayest it.

And when he was accused by the chief priests and ancients, he answered nothing.

Then Pilate saith to him: Dost not thou hear how great testimonies they allege against thee?

And he answered him to never a word; so that the governor wondered exceedingly.

Now upon the solemn day the governor was accustomed to release to the people one prisoner, whom they would.

And he had then a notorious prisoner, that was called Barabbas.

They therefore being gathered together, Pilate said: Whom will you that I release to you, Barabbas, or Jesus that is called Christ?

For he knew that for envy they had delivered him.

And as he was sitting in the place of judgment, his wife sent to him, saying: Have thou nothing to do with that just man; for I have suffered many things this day in a dream because of him.

But the chief priests and ancients persuaded the people, that they should ask Barabbas, and take Jesus away.

And the governor answering, said to them: Whether will you of the two to be released unto you? But they said, Barabbas.

Pilate saith to them: What shall I do then with Jesus that is called Christ? They say all: Let him be crucified.

The governor said to them: Why, what evil hath he done? But they cried out the more, saying: Let him be crucified.

And Pilate seeing that he prevailed nothing, but that rather a tumult was made; taking water washed his hands before the people, saying: I am innocent of the blood of this just man; look you to it.

And the whole people answering, said: His blood be upon us and upon our children.

Then he released to them Barabbas, and having scourged Jesus, delivered him unto them to be crucified.

Then the soldiers of the governor taking Jesus into the hall, gathered together unto him the whole band;

And stripping him, they put a scarlet cloak about him.

And platting a crown of thorns, they put it upon his head, and a reed in his right hand. And bowing the knee before him, they mocked him, saying: Hail king of the Jews.

And spitting upon him, they took the reed, and struck his head.

And after they had mocked him, they took off the cloak from him, and put on him his own garments, and led him away to crucify him.

And going out, they found a man of Cyrene, named Simon: him they forced to take up his cross.

And they came to the place that is called Golgotha, which is the place of Calvary.

And they gave him wine to drink mingled with gall. And when he had tasted, he would not drink.

And after they had crucified him, they divided his garments, casting lots; that it might be fulfilled which was spoken by the prophet, saying: They divided my garments among them; and upon my vesture they cast lots.

And they sat and watched him,

And they put over his head his cause written: This is Jesus the King of the Jews.

Then were crucified with him two thieves: one on the right hand, and one on the left.

And they that passed by, blasphemed him, wagging their heads,

And saying: Vah, thou that destroyest the temple of God, and in three days dost rebuild it: save thy own self: if thou be the Son of God, come down from the cross.

In like manner also the chief priests, with the scribes and ancients, mocking, said:

He saved others; himself he cannot save. If he be the king of Israel, let him now come down from the cross, and we will believe him.

He trusted in God; let him now deliver him if he will have him; for he said: I am the Son of God.

And the selfsame thing the thieves also, that were crucified with him, reproached him with.

Now from the sixth hour there was darkness over the whole earth, until the ninth hour.

And about the ninth hour Jesus cried with a loud voice, saying: Eli, Eli, lamma sabacthani? that is, My God, my God, why hast thou forsaken me?

And some that stood there and heard, said: This man calleth Elias.

And immediately one of them running took a sponge, and filled it with vinegar; and put it on a reed, and gave him to drink.

And the others said: Let be, let us see whether Elias will come to deliver him.

And Jesus again crying with a loud voice, yielded up the ghost.

And behold the veil of the temple was rent in two from the top even to the bottom, and the earth quaked, and the rocks were rent.

And the graves were opened: and many bodies of the saints that had slept arose,

And coming out of the tombs after his resurrection, came into the holy city, and appeared to many.

Now the centurion and they that were with him watching Jesus, having seen the earthquake, and the things that were done, were sore afraid, saying: Indeed this was the Son of God.

And there were there many women afar off, who had followed Jesus from Galilee, ministering unto him:

Among whom was Mary Magdalen, and Mary the mother of James and Joseph, and the mother of the sons of Zebedee.

⁋*And immediately,* Order my steps, *etc.* (*p. 378*); *and,* Holy God, *etc.*

The Kontakion, in the Eighth Tone

COME, let us all praise him who was crucified for our sakes; for him did Mary behold on the Tree, and she said, Even though thou hast endured crucifixion willingly, thou art still my Son and my God.

⁋*Then,* Lord, have mercy (*forty times*); O Christ our God, *etc.* (*p. 60*); Lord, have mercy (*three times*); *Glory and Now,* O thou who art more honourable, *etc., while the Priest saith,* God be merciful unto us, *etc; and the Prayer,* O Christ, true Light, *etc.* (*p. 378*).

THIRD HOUR

⁋*After* O come, let us worship, *etc.* (*three times*), *the following Psalms.*

PSALM 34

JUDGE thou, O Lord, them that wrong me: overthrow them that fight against me.

Take hold of arms and shield: and rise up to help me.

Bring out the sword, and shut up the way against them that persecute me: say to my soul: I am thy salvation.

Let them be confounded and ashamed that seek after my soul.

Let them be turned back and be confounded that devise evil against me.

Let them become as dust before the wind: and let the angel of the Lord straiten them.

Let their way become dark and slippery; and let the angel of the Lord pursue them.

For without cause they have hidden their net for me unto destruction: without cause they have upbraided my soul.

Let the snare which he knoweth not come upon him: and let the net which he hath hidden catch him: and into that very snare let them fall.

But my soul shall rejoice in the Lord; and shall be delighted in his salvation.

All my bones shall say: Lord, who is like to thee?

Who deliverest the poor from the hand of them that are stronger than he; the needy and the poor from them that strip him.

Unjust witnesses rising up have asked me things I knew not.

They repaid me evil for good: to the depriving me of my soul.

But as for me, when they were troublesome to me, I was clothed with haircloth.

I humbled my soul with fasting; and my prayer shall be turned into my bosom.

As a neighbour and as an own brother, so did I please: as one mourning and sorrowful so was I humbled.

But they rejoiced against me, and came together: scourges were gathered together upon me, and I knew not.

They were separated, and repented not: they tempted me, they scoffed at me with scorn: they gnashed upon me with their teeth.

Lord, when wilt thou look upon me? rescue thou my soul from their malice: my only one from the lions.

I will give thanks to thee in a great church; I will praise thee in a strong people.

Let not them that are my enemies wrongfully rejoice over me: who have hated me without cause, and wink with the eyes.

For they spoke indeed peaceably to me; and speaking in the anger of the earth they devised guile.

And they opened their mouth wide against me; they said: Well done, well done, our eyes have seen it.

Thou hast seen, O Lord, be not thou silent: O Lord, depart not from me.

Arise, and be attentive to my judgment: to my cause, my God, and my Lord.

Judge me, O Lord my God according to thy justice, and let them not rejoice over me.

Let them not say in their hearts: It is well, it is well to our mind: neither let them say: We have swallowed him up.

Let them blush: and be ashamed together, who rejoice at my evils.

Let them be clothed with confusion and shame, who speak great things against me.

Let them rejoice and be glad, who are well pleased with my justice, and let them say always: The Lord be magnified, who delights in the peace of his servant.

And my tongue shall meditate thy justice, thy praise all the day long.

PSALM 108

O GOD, be not thou silent in my praise: for the mouth of the wicked and the mouth of the deceitful man is opened against me.

They have spoken against me with deceitful tongues, and they have compassed me about with words of hatred; and have fought against me without cause.

Instead of making me a return of love, they detracted me; but I gave myself to prayer.

And they repaid me evil for good: and hatred for my love.

Set thou the sinner over him: and may the devil stand at his right hand.

When he is judged, may he go out condemned; and may his prayer be turned to sin.

May his days be few; and his bishopric let another take.

May his children be fatherless, and his wife a widow.

Let his children be carried about vagabonds, and beg; let them be cast out of their dwellings.

May the usurer search all his substance: and let strangers plunder his labours.

May there be none to help him: nor none to pity his fatherless offspring.

May his posterity be cut off; in one generation may his name be blotted out.

May the iniquity of his fathers be remembered in the sight of the Lord: and let not the sin of his mother be blotted out.

May they be before the Lord continually, and let the memory of them perish from the earth: because he remembered not to shew mercy,

But persecuted the poor man and the beggar; and the broken in heart, to put him to death.

And he loved cursing, and it shall come unto him: and he would not have blessing, and it shall be far from him.

And he put on cursing, like a garment: and it went in like water into his entrails, and like oil in his bones.

May it be unto him like a garment which covereth him; and like a girdle with which he is girded continually.

This is the work of them who detract me before the Lord: and who speak evils against my soul.

But thou, O Lord, do with me for thy name's sake: because thy mercy is sweet.

Do thou deliver me, for I am poor and needy, and my heart is troubled within me.

I am taken away like the shadow when it declineth, and I am shaken off as locusts.

My knees are weakened through fasting: and my flesh is changed for oil.

And I am become a reproach to them: they saw me and they shaked their heads.

Help me, O Lord my God; save me according to thy mercy.

And let them know that this is thy hand, and that thou, O Lord, hast done it.

They will curse and thou wilt bless: let them that rise up against me be confounded: but thy servant shall rejoice.

Let them that detract me be clothed with shame: and let them be covered with their confusion as with a double cloak.

I will give great thanks to the Lord with my mouth: and in the midst of many I will praise him.

Because he hath stood at the right hand of the poor, to save my soul from persecutors.

❡*Psalm 50 (p. 82); Glory and Now,* Alleluia *(three times);* Lord, have mercy *(three times); Glory, Troparion, in the Sixth Tone.*

THE Jews, O Lord, condemned thee to death, thou Life of all: and they whom thou didst cause to cross the Red Sea nailed thee on a Cross. They to whom thou gavest honey from the rock to eat, offered thee gall. Albeit, thou didst endure it willingly in order to deliver us from bondage to the enemy. O Christ our God, glory to thee.

Now: Thou art the true vine, O Theotokos, etc. (p. 379).

❡*Then chant the following Idiomelons, in the Eighth Tone.*

Stichos: Give ear, O Lord, to my words. Understand my cry.

FOR fear of the Jews, O Lord, Peter, thy friend and neighbour, denied thee, mourning thus, Turn not away from my tears; for I said that I would keep faith but did not, O compassionate One. Wherefore, receive thou thus our repentance, and have mercy upon us.

Stichos: Hearken to the voice of my prayer, O my King and my God.

At thy venerable Cross, O Lord, when the soldiers were mocking thee, the hosts of angels were dazzled; for thou didst wear the crown of slander, thou who didst adorn the earth with flowers. Thou didst wear the robe of revilement, O thou who didst clothe the firmament with clouds. In this dispensation, therefore, was known thy compassion, O Christ of great mercy, Glory to thee.

Glory and Now, in the Fifth Tone

WHEN thou wast led to the Cross, O Lord, thou didst say, For what act do ye wish, O Jews, to crucify me? Is it because I have strengthened your cripples? Is it because I raised your dead as from sleep, healed the woman with an issue of blood, and showed mercy upon the Canaanitish woman? For what act, O ye Jews, desire ye my death? But ye shall behold him whom ye have pierced, O law-transgressors, and know that he is Christ.

❡ *Then the Prokeimenon of the Prophecy, in the Fourth Tone.*

Verily, I am ready to be scourged. O Lord, rebuke me not in thy wrath.

Reading: from the Prophecy of Isaiah (50:4 to end)

THE Lord hath given me a learned tongue, that I should know how to uphold by word him that is weary: he wakeneth in the morning, in the morning he wakeneth my ear, that I may hear him as a master.

The Lord God hath opened my ear, and I do not resist: I have not gone back.

I have given my body to the strikers, and my cheeks to them that plucked them: I have not turned away my face from them that rebuked me, and spit upon me.

The Lord God is my helper, therefore am I not confounded: therefore have I set my face as a most hard rock, and I know that I shall not be confounded.

He is near that justifieth me, who will contend with me? let us stand together, who is my adversary? let him come near to me.

Behold the Lord God is my helper: who is he that shall condemn me? Lo, they shall all be destroyed as a garment, the moth shall eat them up.

Who is there among you that feareth the Lord, that heareth the voice of his servant, that hath walked in darkness, and hath no light? let him hope in the name of the Lord, and lean upon his God.

Behold all you that kindle a fire, encompassed with flames, walk in the light of your fire, and in the flames which you have kindled: this is done to you by my hand, you shall sleep in sorrows.

Section from the Epistle of St. Paul to the Romans (5:6-10)

YE brethren: For Christ, when as yet we were weak, according to the time, died for the ungodly.

For scarce for a just man will one die; yet perhaps for a good man some one would dare to die.

But God commendeth his charity towards us; because when as yet we were sinners, according to the time,

Christ died for us; much more therefore, being now justified by his blood, shall we be saved from wrath through him.

For if, when we were enemies, we were reconciled to God by the death of his Son; much more, being reconciled, shall we be saved by his life.

The Gospel: from St. Mark (15:16-41)

AT that time: The soldiers led Christ away into the court of the palace, and they called together the whole band:

And they clothe him with purple, and platting a crown of thorns, they put it upon him.

And they began to salute him: Hail, king of the Jews.

And they struck his head with a reed: and they did spit on him. And bowing their knees, they adored him.

And after they had mocked him, they took off the purple from him, and put his own garments on him, and they led him out to crucify him.

And they forced one Simon a Cyrenian who passed by, coming out of the country, the father of Alexander and of Rufus, to take up his cross.

And they bring him into the place called Golgotha, which being interpreted is, The place of Calvary.

And they gave him to drink wine mingled with myrrh; but he took it not.

And crucifying him, they divided his garments, casting lots upon them, what every man should take.

And it was the third hour, and they crucified him.

And the inscription of his cause was written over: The King of the Jews.

And with him they crucify two thieves; the one on his right hand, and the other on his left.

And the scripture was fulfilled, which saith: And with the wicked he was reputed.

And they that passed by blasphemed him, wagging their heads, and saying: Vah, thou that destroyest the temple of God, and in three days buildest it up again; Save thyself, coming down from the cross.

In like manner also the chief priests mocking, said with the scribes one to another: He saved others; himself he cannot save.

Let Christ the king of Israel come down now from the cross, that we may see and believe. And they that were crucified with him reviled him.

And when the sixth hour was come, there was darkness over the whole earth until the ninth hour.

And at the ninth hour, Jesus cried out with a loud voice, saying: Eloi, Eloi, lamma sabacthani? Which is, being interpreted, My God, my God, why hast thou forsaken me?

And some of the standers by hearing, said: Behold he calleth Elias.

And one running and filling a sponge with vinegar, and putting it upon a reed, gave him to drink, saying: Stay, let us see if Elias come to take him down.

And Jesus having cried out with a loud voice, gave up the ghost.

And the veil of the temple was rent in two, from the top to the bottom.

And the centurion who stood over against him, seeing that crying out in this manner he had given up the ghost, said: Indeed this man was the son of God.

And there were also women looking on afar off: among whom was Mary Magdalen, and Mary the mother of James the less and of Joseph, and Salome:

Who also when he was in Galilee followed him, and ministered to him, and many other women that came up with him to Jerusalem.

¶*And then immediately,* Blessed is the Lord God, *etc.* (*p. 383*); Holy God, *etc; and the Kontakion,* Come, let us all, *etc.* (*p. 833*); *and the rest of the Order as in the First Hour. Then the Prayer,* O Master, God Almighty, *etc.* (*p. 383*).

SIXTH HOUR

¶*After* O come, let us worship, *etc.* (*three times*). *the following Psalms.*

PSALM 53

SAVE me, O God, by thy name, and judge me in thy strength.

O God, hear my prayer: give ear to the words of my mouth.

For strangers have risen up against me; and the mighty have sought after my soul: and they have not set God before their eyes.

For behold God is my helper: and the Lord is the protector of my soul.

Turn back the evils upon my enemies; and cut them off in thy truth.

I will freely sacrifice to thee, and will give praise, O God, to thy name: because it is good:

For thou hast delivered me out of all trouble: and my eye hath looked down upon my enemies.

PSALM 139

DELIVER me, O Lord, from the evil man: rescue me from the unjust man.

Who have devised iniquities in their hearts: all the day long they designed battles.

They have sharpened their tongues like a serpent: the venom of asps is under their lips.

Keep me, O Lord, from the hand of the wicked: and from unjust men deliver me.

Who have proposed to supplant my steps: the proud have hidden a net for me.

And they have stretched out cords for a snare: they have laid for me a stumblingblock by the wayside.

I said to the Lord: Thou art my God: hear, O Lord, the voice of my supplication.

O Lord, Lord, the strength of my salvation: thou hast overshadowed my head in the day of battle.

Give me not up, O Lord, from my desire to the wicked: they have plotted against me; do not thou forsake me, lest they should triumph.

The head of them compassing me about: the labour of their lips shall overwhelm them.

Burning coals shall fall upon them; thou wilt cast them down into the fire: in miseries they shall not be able to stand.

A man full of tongue shall not be established in the earth: evil shall catch the unjust man unto destruction.

I know that the Lord will do justice to the needy, and will revenge the poor.

But as for the just, they shall give glory to thy name: and the upright shall dwell with thy countenance.

PSALM 90
(p. 385)

¶ *Glory and Now;* Alleluia (*three times*); Lord, have mercy (*three times*).

Glory, Troparion, in the Second Tone

A SALVATION thou produced in the midst of the earth, O Christ our God, when thou didst stretch out thy pure hands upon the Cross, calling together all the nations, who cry to thee, O Lord, glory to thee.

¶*Now,* For verily, we have no favour, *etc. (p. 386); then the following Idiomelons, in the Eighth Tone.*

Thus saith the Lord to the Jews, etc. (p. 821).

Stichos: In my food they gave me gall, and in my thirst they gave me vinegar to drink.

Ye Jews and Pharisees, etc. (p. 821).

Glory and Now, in the Fifth Tone

O YE nations which have put on Christ, come ye, let us see what it is that Judas the betrayer counselled with the law-transgressing priests against our Saviour. Today have they placed the deathless Word under punishment of death. They have delivered him to Pilate, and crucified him in the place of Golgotha. And as our Saviour was suffering, he cried, saying, Father, forgive them this sin, that the Gentiles may know my Resurrection from the dead.

¶*Then the Prokeimenon of the Prophecy, in the Fourth Tone.*

O Lord, our Lord, how admirable is thy Name in the whole earth.

Stichos: For thy magnificence is elevated above the heavens.

Reading: from the Prophecy of Isaiah the Prophet (52:13 to end; 53:1 to end; 54:1)

THESE sayings the Lord doth say: Behold my servant shall understand; he shall be exalted, and extolled, and shall be exceeding high.

As many have been astonished at thee, so shall his visage be inglorious among men, and his form among the sons of men.

He shall sprinkle many nations, kings shall shut their mouth at him: for they to whom it was not told of him, have seen: and they that heard not, have beheld.

Who hath believed our report? and to whom is the arm of the Lord revealed?

And he shall grow up as a tender plant before him, and as a root out of a thirsty ground: there is no beauty in him, nor comeliness; and we have seen him, and there was no sightliness, that we should be desirous of him:

Despised, and the most abject of men, a man of sorrows, and acquainted with infirmity: and his look was as it were hidden and despised, whereupon we esteemed him not.

Surely he hath borne our infirmities and carried our sorrows: and we have thought him as it were a leper, and as one struck by God and afflicted.

But he was wounded for our iniquities, he was bruised for our sins: the chastisement of our peace was upon him, and by his bruises we are healed.

All we like sheep have gone astray, every one hath turned aside into his own way: and the Lord hath laid on him the iniquity of us all.

He was offered because it was his own will, and he opened not his mouth: he shall be led as a sheep to the slaughter, and shall be dumb as a lamb before his shearer, and he shall not open his mouth.

He was taken away from distress, and from judgment: who shall declare his generation? Because he is cut off out of the land of the living: for the wickedness of my people have I struck him.

And he shall give the ungodly for his burial, and the rich for his death: because he hath done no iniquity, neither was there deceit in his mouth.

And the Lord was pleased to bruise him in infirmity: if he shall lay down his life for sin, he shall see a long-lived seed, and the will of the Lord shall be prosperous in his hand.

Because his soul hath laboured, he shall see and be filled: by his knowledge shall this my just servant justify many, and he shall bear their iniquities.

Therefore will I distribute to him very many, and he shall divide the spoils of the strong, because he hath delivered his soul unto death, and was reputed with the wicked: and he hath borne the sins of many, and hath prayed for the transgressors.

Give praise, O thou barren, that bearest not: sing forth praise, and make a joyful noise, thou that didst not travail with child: for many are the children of the desolate, more than of her that hath a husband, saith the Lord.

The Epistle: from St. Paul to the Hebrews

Ye brethren: For both he that sanctifieth, and they who are sanctified, are all one, etc. (p. 394).

The Gospel: from St. Luke

At that time: There were also two other, malefactors, led with him to be put to death, etc. (p. 831).

¶*And immediately,* Swiftly let thy compassion apprehend us, *etc* (*p. 390*); Holy God, *etc; and the Kontakion,* Come, let us all, *etc.* (*p. 833*); *the rest of the Order as in the First Hour* (*p. 842*); *and the Prayer,* O God, Lord of powers, *etc.* (*p. 391*).

NINTH HOUR

¶*After,* O come, let us worship, (*three times*), *the following Psalms.*

PSALM 68

SAVE me, O God; for the waters are come in even unto my soul.

I stick fast in the mire of the deep: and there is no sure standing.

I am come into the depth of the sea: and a tempest hath overwhelmed me.

I have laboured with crying; my jaws are become hoarse: my eyes have failed, whilst I hope in my God.

They are multiplied above the hairs of my head, who hate me without cause. My enemies are grown strong who have wrongfully persecuted me: then did I pay that which I took not away.

O God, thou knowest my foolishness; and my offences are not hidden from thee:

Let not them be ashamed for me, who look for thee O Lord, the Lord of hosts.

Let them not be confounded on my account, who seek thee, O God of Israel.

Because for thy sake I have borne reproach, shame hath covered my face.

I am become a stranger to my brethren, and an alien to the sons of my mother.

For the zeal of thy house hath eaten me up: and the reproaches of them that reproached thee are fallen upon me.

And I covered my soul in fasting: and it was made a reproach to me.

And I made haircloth my garment: and I became a byword to them.

They that sat in the gate spoke against me: and they that drank wine made me their song.

But as for me, my prayer is to thee, O Lord; for the time of thy good pleasure, O God. In the multitude of thy mercy hear me, in the truth of thy salvation.

Draw me out of the mire, that I may not stick fast: deliver me from them that hate me, and out of the deep waters.

Let not the tempest of water drown me, nor the deep swallow me up: and let not the pit shut her mouth upon me.

Hear me, O Lord, for thy mercy is kind; look upon me according to the multitude of thy tender mercies.

And turn not away thy face from thy servant: for I am in trouble, hear me speedily.

Attend to my soul, and deliver it: save me because of my enemies.

Thou knowest my reproach, and my confusion and my shame.

In thy sight are all they that afflict me; my heart hath expected reproach and misery.

And I looked for one that would grieve together with me, but there was none: and for one that would comfort me, and I found none.

And they gave me gall for my food, and in my thirst they gave me vinegar to drink.

Let their table become as a snare before them, and a recompense, and a stumblingblock.

Let their eyes be darkened that they see not; and their back bend thou down always.

Pour out thy indignation upon them: and let thy wrathful anger take hold of them.

Let their habitation be made desolate: and let there be none to dwell in their tabernacles.

Because they have persecuted him whom thou hast smitten; and they have added to the grief of my wounds.

Add thou iniquity upon their iniquity: and let them not come into thy justice.

Let them be blotted out of the book of the living and with the just let them not be written.

But I am poor and sorrowful: thy salvation, O God, hath set me up.

I will praise the name of God with a canticle; and I will magnify him with praise.

And it shall please God better than a young calf, that bringeth forth horns and hoofs.

Let the poor see and rejoice: seek ye God, and your soul shall live.

For the Lord hath heard the poor; and hath not despised his prisoners.

Let the heavens and the earth praise him; the sea, and every thing that creepeth therein.

For God will save Sion, and the cities of Juda shall be built up.

And they shall dwell there, and acquire it by inheritance.

And the seed of his servants shall possess it; and they that love his name shall dwell therein.

Psalm 69
(p. 83)

Psalm 85
(p. 59)

❡ *Glory and Now;* Alleluia *(three times);* Lord have mercy *(three times); Glory, Troparion, in the Eighth Tone.*

WHEN the thief beheld the Origin of life suspended on the Cross, he said, Were not he who is crucified with us incarnate God, the sun would not have hidden his rays, nor the earth quaked with trembling. But thou who endurest all, remember me, Lord, when thou comest into thy kingdom.

❡ *Now,* Thou who for our sake wast born of a Virgin, *etc. (p. 193); then the following Idiomelons, in the Seventh Tone.*

A WONDER to behold, how the Maker of heaven and earth was suspended on the Cross; how the sun was darkened and the day changed into night; and how the earth gave up the bodies of the dead from their graves. Wherefore, with them, we worship thee. Save thou us.

In the Second Tone

Stichos: They parted my garments among them and upon my vesture did they cast lots.

When the lawless nailed thee upon the Cross, O Lord of glory, thou didst cry unto them, Wherein have I caused you sorrow? Wherein have I angered you? And who before me delivered you from sorrow? And now wherewith do ye reward me?

Instead of goodness, evil; for the pillar of fire, ye nailed me on the Cross; for the clouds, ye dug me a grave; instead of water, ye gave me vinegar to drink. I will henceforth call the Gentiles, and they shall glorify me with the Father and Holy Spirit.

Glory and Now, in the Sixth Tone

❡ *This is first read by the Reader from the middle of the church in a reverent, high voice, then sung alternately by the two Choirs, sentence by sentence.*

Today he is suspended on a Tree, etc. (p. 825).

Prokeimenon of the Prophecy, in the Sixth Tone

The fool hath said in his heart: There is no God. There is none that doeth good, no, not one.

Reading: from the Prophecy of Jeremiah the Prophet (11:18 to end; 12:1-5, 9-10, 14-15)

BUT thou, O Lord, hast shown me, and I have known: then thou showedst me their doings.

And I was as a meek lamb, that is carried to be a victim: and I knew not that they had devised counsels against me, saying: Let us put wood on his bread, and cut him off from the land of the living, and let his name be remembered no more.

But thou, O Lord of Sabaoth, who judgest justly, and triest the reins and the hearts, let me see thy revenge on them: for to thee have I revealed my cause.

Therefore thus saith the Lord to the men of Anathoth, who seek thy life, and say: Thou shalt not prophesy in the name of the Lord, and thou shalt not die in our hands.

Therefore thus saith the Lord of hosts: behold I will visit upon them: their young men shall die by the sword, their sons and their daughters shall die by famine.

And there shall be no remains of them: for I will bring in evil upon the men of Anathoth, the year of their visitation.

Thou indeed, O Lord, art just, if I plead with thee, but yet I will speak what is just to thee: Why doth the way of the wicked prosper: why is it well with all them that transgress, and do wickedly?

Thou hast planted them, and they have taken root; they prosper and bring forth fruit: thou art near in their mouth, and far from their reins.

And thou, O Lord, hast known me, thou hast seen me, and proved my heart with thee: gather them together as sheep for a sacrifice, and prepare them for the day of slaughter.

How long shall the land mourn, and the herb of every field wither for the wickedness of them that dwell therein? The beasts and the birds are consumed: because they have said: He shall not see our last end.

If thou hast been wearied with running with footmen, how canst thou contend with horses? and if thou hast been secure in a land of peace, what wilt thou do in the swelling of the Jordan?

Is my inheritance to me as a speckled bird? is it as a bird dyed throughout? come ye, assemble yourselves, all ye beasts of the earth, make haste to devour.

Many pastors have destroyed my vineyard, they have trodden my portion under foot: they have changed my delightful portion into a desolate wilderness.

They have laid it waste, and it hath mourned for me. With desolation is all the land made desolate.

Thus saith the Lord against all my wicked neighbours, that touch the inheritance that I have shared out to my people Israel: Behold I will pluck them out of their land, and I will pluck the house of Juda out of the midst of them.

And when I shall have plucked them out, I will return, and have mercy on them: and I will bring them back, every man to his inheritance, and every man into his land.

The Epistle: Section from the Epistle of St. Paul to the Hebrews (10:19-31)

YE brethren: Having therefore, confidence in the entering into the holies by the blood of Christ;

A new and living way which he hath dedicated for us through the veil, that is to say, his flesh.

And a high priest over the house of God:

Let us draw near with a true heart in fulness of faith, having our hearts sprinkled from an evil conscience, and our bodies washed with clean water.

Let us hold fast the confession of our hope without wavering (for he is faithful that hath promised).

And let us consider one another, to provoke unto charity and to good works:

Not forsaking our assembly, as some are accustomed; but comforting one another, and so much the more as you see the day approaching.

For if we sin wilfully after having the knowledge of the truth, there is now left no sacrifice for sins,

But a certain dreadful expectation of judgment, and the rage of a fire which shall consume the adversaries.

A man making void the law of Moses, dieth without any mercy under two or three witnesses:

How much more, do you think he deserveth worse punishments, who hath trodden under foot the Son of God, and hath esteemed the blood of the testament unclean, by which he was sanctified, and hath offered an affront to the Spirit of grace?

For we know him that hath said: Vengeance belongeth to me, and I will repay. And again: The Lord shall judge his people.

It is a fearful thing to fall into the hands of the living God.

The Gospel: from St. John (19:23-37)

AT that time: When they had crucified Jesus, they took his garments, (and they made four parts, to every soldier a part,) and also his coat. Now the coat was without seam, woven from the top throughout.

They said then one to another: Let us not cut it, but let us cast lots for it, whose it shall be: that the scripture might be fulfilled, saying: They have parted my garments among them, and upon my vesture they have cast lots. And the soldiers indeed did these things.

Now there stood by the cross of Jesus, his mother, and his mother's sister, Mary of Cleophas, and Mary Magdalen.

When Jesus therefore had seen his mother and the disciple standing whom he loved, he saith to his mother: Woman, behold thy son.

After that, he saith to the disciple: Behold thy mother. And from that hour, the disciple took her to his own.

Afterwards, Jesus knowing that all things were now accomplished, that the scripture might be fulfilled, said: I thirst.

Now there was a vessel set there, full of vinegar. And they, putting a sponge full of vinegar about hyssop, put it to his mouth.

When Jesus, therefore, had taken the vinegar, he said: It is consummated. And bowing his head, he gave up the ghost.

Then the Jews, (because it was the parasceve,) that the bodies should not remain upon the cross on the sabbath day, (for that was a great sabbath day,) besought Pilate that their legs might be broken, and that they might be taken away.

The soldiers therefore came; and they broke the legs of the first, and of the other that was crucified with him.

But after they were come to Jesus, when they saw that he was already dead, they did not break his legs.

But one of the soldiers with a spear opened his side, and immediately there came out blood and water.

And he that saw it, hath given testimony and his testimony is true. And he knoweth that he saith true; that you also may believe.

For these things were done, that the Scripture might be fulfilled; You shall not break a bone of him.

And again another scripture saith: They shall look on him whom they pierced.

¶ *Then immediately,* Forsake us not utterly, *etc.* (*p. 395*); Holy God, *etc;* and the *Kontakion,* Come, let us all, *etc.* (*p. 856*); *and the rest of the Order as in the First Hour; and the Prayer,* O Master, Lord Jesus Christ our God, *etc.* (*p. 61*); *then the Makarizmoi,* In thy kingdom remember us, O Lord, *etc.* (*p. 124*); *and the Kontakion,* Come, let us all, *etc; and the Benediction as at the end of the service, of the Passion Gospel* (*p. 842*).

❡*Note: Know that this day, i.e., the Great and Holy Friday, is the only day on which the service of the Holy Mass is not celebrated.*

GREAT FRIDAY AT EVENTIDE

VESPERS

❡*After the Sunset Psalm, on* O Lord, to thee have I cried, *etc., take six Stichoi; sing the four Idiomelons, which are,* The whole creation, *etc.* (*repeated*); *and the three following it.* (*p. 840*). *Then the following Idiomelons, in the Sixth Tone.*

TODAY the Lord of creation standeth before Pilate, and the Creator of all is delivered up to crucifixion, offered as a lamb, of his own will. He is fastened with nails, pierced with a spear, and a sponge is brought near to him who rained manna. The Redeemer of the world is smitten on his cheek; and the Redeemer of all is ridiculed by his own servants. What love the Master showed to mankind! For he prayed his Father on behalf of his crucifiers, saying, Remit them this sin; for the transgressors of the law know not what they unjustly do.

Glory, in the Sixth Tone

OH, how the assembly of the law-transgressors condemn to death the King of creation, not being ashamed nor abashed by his benevolences, of which he had assured them formerly, calling them to their remembrance, saying, My people, what have I done to thee? Have I not showered Judaism with wonders? Have I not raised the dead by only a word? Have I not healed every sickness and every weakness? With what, then, hast thou rewarded me? And why forgetest thou me? For healing, thou hast inflicted wounds upon me; and for raising the dead, thou dost cause me, the Benevolent, to die suspended upon a Tree as an evil-doer; the Giver of the law, as a law-transgressor; and the King of all, as one who is condemned. Wherefore, O long-suffering Lord, glory to thee.

Now, in the Same Tone

TODAY is beheld the working of a dread and strange mystery; for he who is inapprehensible is laid hold of; and he who released Adam is chained. He who trieth the hearts and reins is tried falsely; and he who looketh into the depths is locked in prison. He before whom the heavenly powers stand trembling standeth before Pilate. The Creator is smitten by the hand of his creatures; the Judge of the living and the dead is condemned to death on a Tree; and the Destroyer of hades is enfolded in a grave. Wherefore, O thou who didst of thy compassion bear all these things, saving all from the curse, O long-suffering Lord, glory to thee.

❡ *Then the Eisodos with the Gospel; and* O resplendent Light, *etc; then immediately:*

THE FIRST READING

They parted my garments among them, and upon my vesture, did they cast lots.

My God, my God, look upon me. Why hast thou forsaken me?

Reading: from the Book of Exodus (33:11 to end)

AND the Lord spoke unto Moses face to face, as a man speaketh unto his friend. And he turned again into the camp; but his servant Joshua, the son of Nun, a young man, departed not out of the tabernacle.

And Moses said unto the Lord, See thou sayest unto me, Bring up this people: and thou hast not let me know whom thou wilt send with me. Yet thou hast said, I know thee by name, and thou hast also found grace in my sight.

Now therefore, I pray thee, if I have found grace in thy sight, show me now thy way, that I may know thee, that I may find grace in thy sight: and consider that this nation is thy people.

And he said, My presence shall go with thee, and I will give thee rest.

And he said unto him, If thy presence go not with me, carry us not up hence.

For wherein shall it be known here that I and thy people have found grace in thy sight? is it not in that thou goest with us? So shall we be separated, I and thy people, from all the people that are upon the face of the earth.

And the Lord said unto Moses, I will do this thing also that thou hast spoken: for thou hast found grace in my sight, and I know thee by name.

And he said, I beseech thee, show me thy glory.

And he said, I will make all my goodness pass before thee, and I will proclaim the name of the Lord before thee; and will be gracious to whom I will be gracious, and will show mercy on whom I will show mercy.

And he said, Thou canst not see my face: for there shall no man see me, and live.

And the Lord said, Behold, there is a place by me, and thou shalt stand upon a rock:

And it shall come to pass, while my glory passeth by, that I will put thee in a cleft of the rock, and will cover thee with my hand while I pass by:

And I will take away mine hand, and thou shalt see my back parts; but my face shall not be seen.

THE SECOND READING

Judge thou, O Lord, them that wrong me.
They repaid me evil for good.

Reading: from the Book of Job the Righteous
(42:12 to end)

SO the Lord blessed the latter end of Job more than
his beginning: for he had fourteen thousand sheep,
and six thousand camels, and a thousand yoke of oxen,
and a thousand she asses.

He had also seven sons and three daughters.

And he called the name of the first, Jemima; and the
name of the second, Kezia; and the name of the third,
Kerenhappuch.

And in all the land under the firmament of heaven
were no women found so fair as the daughters of Job:
and their father gave them inheritance among their
brethren.

And after the affliction lived Job a hundred and forty
years and saw his sons, and his sons' sons, even four
generations.

So Job died, being old and full of days. The same
dwelt in Hauran, on the borders of Edom and Arabia.
And he was called Yobab, and he took unto himself a
wife, an Arabian woman, and she bore him a son called
Hannoun. And Job's father was Zerah, the son of
Esau, making him the fifth in descent from Abraham.
And it was also written that he will rise with those
whom our Lord shall raise.[1]

THE THIRD READING

From the Prophecy of Isaiah the Prophet

These sayings the Lord doth say: Behold, my servant
shall understand, etc. (p. 860).

The Epistle

They have laid me in the lower pits in the dark
places.

O Lord, the God of my salvation: I have cried in the
day, and in the night before thee.

---

[1] This paragraph is from the Syriac Version.

Section from the First Epistle of St. Paul to the
Corinthians (1:18 to end; 2:1-2)

YE brethren: For the preaching of the cross is to them that perish foolishness; but unto us which are saved it is the power of God.

For it is written, I will destroy the wisdom of the wise, and will bring to nothing the understanding of the prudent.

Where is the wise? Where is the scribe? Where is the disputer of this world? Hath not God made foolish the wisdom of this world?

For after that in the wisdom of God the world by wisdom knew not God, it pleased God by the foolishness of preaching to save them that believe.

For the Jews require a sign, and the Greeks seek after wisdom:

But we preach Christ crucified, unto the Jews a stumblingblock, and unto the Greeks foolishness;

But unto them which are called, both Jews and Greeks, Christ the power of God, and the wisdom of God.

Because the foolishness of God is wiser than men; and the weakness of God is stronger than men.

For ye see your calling, brethren, how that not many wise men after the flesh, not many mighty, not many noble, are called:

But God hath chosen the foolish things of the world to confound the wise; and God hath chosen the weak things of the world to confound the things which are mighty;

And base things of the world, and things which are despised, hath God chosen, yea, and things which are not, to bring to nought things that are:

That no flesh should glory in his presence.

But of him are ye in Christ Jesus, who of God is made unto us wisdom, and righteousness, and sanctification, and redemption:

That, according as it is written, He that glorieth, let him glory in the Lord.

And I, brethren, when I came to you, came not with excellency of speech or of wisdom, declaring unto you the testimony of God.

For I determined not to know any thing among you, save Jesus Christ, and him crucified.

The Gospel: from St. Matthew (27:1-38; St. Luke 23:39-43; St. Matthew 27:39-54; St. John 19:31-37; St. Matthew 27:55-61).

A T that time: All the chief priests and elders of the people took counsel against Jesus to put him to death;

And when they had bound him, they led him away, and delivered him to Pontius Pilate the governor.

Then Judas, which had betrayed him, when he saw that he was condemned, repented himself, and brought again the thirty pieces of silver to the chief priests and elders,

Saying, I have sinned in that I have betrayed the innocent blood. And they said, What is that to us? See thou to that.

And he cast down the pieces of silver in the temple, and departed, and went and hanged himself with a halter.

And the chief priests took the silver pieces, and said, It is not lawful for to put them into the treasury, because it is the price of blood.

And they took counsel, and bought with them the potter's field, to bury strangers in.

Wherefore that field was called, the field of blood, unto this day.

Then was fulfilled that which was spoken by Jeremy the prophet, saying, And they took the thirty pieces of silver, the price of him that was valued, whom they of the children of Israel did value;

And gave them for the potter's field, as the Lord appointed me.

And Jesus stood before the governor: and the governor asked him, saying, Art thou the King of the Jews? And Jesus said unto him, Thou sayest.

And when he was accused of the chief priests and elders, he answered nothing.

Then said Pilate unto him, Hearest thou not how many things they witness against thee?

And he answered him to never a word; insomuch that the governor marvelled greatly.

Now at that feast the governor was wont to release unto the people a prisoner, whom they would.

And they had then a notable prisoner, called Barabbas.

Therefore when they were gathered together, Pilate said unto them, Whom will ye that I release unto you? Barabbas, or Jesus which is called Christ?

For he knew that for envy they had delivered him.

When he was set down on the judgment seat, his wife sent unto him, saying, Have thou nothing to do with that just man: for I have suffered many things this day in a dream because of him.

But the chief priests and elders persuaded the multitude that they should ask Barabbas, and destroy Jesus.

The governor answered and said unto them, Whether of the twain will ye that I release unto you? They said, Barabbas.

Pilate saith unto them, What shall I do then with Jesus which is called Christ? They all say unto him, Let him be crucified.

And the governor said, Why, what evil hath he done? But they cried out the more, saying, Let him be crucified.

When Pilate saw that he could prevail nothing, but that rather a tumult was made, he took water, and washed his hands before the multitude, saying, I am innocent of the blood of this just person: see ye to it.

Then answered all the people, and said, His blood be on us, and on our children.

Then released he Barabbas unto them: and when he had scourged Jesus, he delivered him to be crucified.

Then the soldiers of the governor took Jesus into the common hall, and gathered unto him the whole band of soldiers.

And they stripped him, and put on him a scarlet robe.

And when they had platted a crown of thorns, they put it upon his head, and a reed in his right hand: and they bowed the knee before him, and mocked him, saying, Hail, King of the Jews!

And they spit upon him, and took the reed, and smote him on the head.

And after that they had mocked him, they took the robe off from him, and put his own raiment on him, and led him away to crucify him.

And as they came out, they found a man of Cyrene, Simon by name: him they compelled to bear his cross.

And when they were come unto a place called Golgotha, that is to say, a place of a skull,

They gave him vinegar to drink mingled with gall: and when he had tasted thereof, he would not drink.

And they crucified him, and parted his garments, casting lots: that it might be fulfilled which was spoken by the prophet, They parted my garments among them, and upon my vesture did they cast lots.

And sitting down they watched him there;

And set up over his head his accusation written, This is Jesus the King of the Jews.

Then were there two thieves crucified with him; one on the right hand, and another on the left.

And one of the malefactors which were hanged railed on him, saying, If thou be Christ, save thyself and us.

But the other answering rebuked him, saying, Dost not thou fear God, seeing thou art in the same condemnation?

And we indeed justly; for we receive the due reward of our deeds: but this man hath done nothing amiss.

And he said unto Jesus, Lord, remember me when thou comest into thy kingdom.

And Jesus said unto him, Verily I say unto thee, To day shalt thou be with me in paradise.

And they that passed by reviled him, wagging their heads,

And saying, Thou that destroyest the temple, and buildest it in three days, save thyself. If thou be the Son of God, come down from the cross.

Likewise also the chief priests mocking him, with the scribes and elders, said,

He saved others; himself he cannot save. If he be the King of Israel, let him now come down from the cross, and we will believe him.

He trusted in God; let him deliver him now, if he will have him: for he said, I am the Son of God.

The thieves also, which were crucified with him, cast the same in his teeth.

Now from the sixth hour there was darkness over all the land unto the ninth hour.

And, about the ninth hour Jesus cried with a loud voice, saying, Eli, Eli, lama sabachthani? that is to say, My God, my God, why hast thou forsaken me?

Some of them that stood there, when they heard that said, This man calleth for Elias.

And straightway one of them ran, and took a sponge, and filled it with vinegar, and put it on a reed, and gave him to drink.

The rest said, Let be, let us see whether Elias will come to save him.

Jesus, when he had cried again with a loud voice, yielded up the ghost.

And, behold, the veil of the temple was rent in twain from the top to the bottom; and the earth did quake, and the rocks rent;

And the graves were opened; and many bodies of the saints which slept arose,

And came out of the graves after his resurrection, and went into the holy city, and appeared unto many.

Now when the centurion. and they that were with him, watching Jesus, saw the earthquake, and those things that were done, they feared greatly, saying, Truly this was the Son of God.

Then the Jews, (because it was the parasceve), that the bodies should not remain upon the cross on the sabbath day, (for that was a great sabbath day) besought Pilate that their legs might be broken, and that they might be taken away.

The soldiers therefore came: and they broke the legs of the first, and of the other that was crucified with him.

But after they were come to Jesus, and saw that he was already dead, they did not break his legs.

But one of the soldiers with a spear opened his side: and immediately there came out blood and water.

And he that saw it, hath given testimony; and his testimony is true. And he knoweth that he saith true; that you also may believe.

For these things were done, that the Scripture might be fulfilled: You shall not break a bone of him.

And again another Scripture saith: They shall look on him whom they pierced.

And many women were there beholding afar off, which followed Jesus from Galilee, ministering unto him:

Among which was Mary Magdalene, and Mary the mother of James and Joseph, and the mother of Zebedee's children.

When the even was come, there came a rich man of Arimathea, named Joseph, who also himself was Jesus' disciple:

He went to Pilate, and begged the body of Jesus. Then Pilate commanded the body to be delivered.

And when Joseph had taken the body, he wrapped it in a clean linen cloth,

And laid it in his own new tomb, which he had hewn out in the rock; and he rolled a great stone to the door of the sepulchre, and departed.

And there was Mary Magdalene, and the other Mary, sitting over against the sepulchre.

¶ *Then the Petitions,* Let us all say with all our soul, *etc;* Vouchsafe, O Lord, *etc; and* Let us finish our evening Petitions, *etc. (pp. 76-77); and after the Proclamation, the Choirs proceed to the Northern Gate of the Temple and begin with the singing of the Aposticha, while the Priest, assisted by one or more Priests (when possible), take hold of the Epitaphion and raise it over their heads, the senior Priest among them holding the Gospel Book in one of his hands. And after the Procession from behind the holy Altar, they come out from the Northern Door, preceded by the Priests, the lamp, and cross bearers, the fanners, and the censers, proceeding in the interior of the church till they come to the center, where the bier is stationed, adorned with flowers. They circle around it three times, then place the Epitaphion over the bier, and the Gospel Book over the Epitaphion. And after making the genuflexion in order, and kissing the Epitaphion, the Procession returneth to the Temple, as the Choirs finish singing the following Aposticha, in the Second Tone, with, Glory and Now.*

O CHRIST, Life of all, when Joseph of Ramah brought thee down dead from the Cross, he laid thee in balms and linen, hastening anxiously to kiss thy lips and bury thy pure body free of corruption. But he was reverent with fear as he cried to thee with joy, Glory be to thy condescension, O Lover of mankind.

Stichos: The Lord hath reigned; he is clothed with beauty.

Hades, made ridiculous at seeing thee, O Deliverer of all, placed in a new tomb for the sake of all, trembled with fear. Its locks were shattered; its doors broken; the tombs were opened; and the dead awoke. Then Adam cried to thee with joy and gratitude, Glory to thy condescension, O Lover of mankind.

Stichos: For he hath established the world which shall not be moved.

O Christ, who in thy divine Nature art boundless and infinite, when thou wast enclosed in the grave by thine own will after the flesh, thou didst close the chambers of death and hades, and didst demolish all its kingdoms. Then thou preparedst this Saturday for thy glory, thine illumination, and thy divine blessing.

Stichos: Holiness becometh thy house, O Lord, unto length of days.

The angelic hosts, O Christ, beholding those lawless ones victimize thee as a criminal, and seeing the tombstone sealed by the hands of those who pierced thy side, were frightened at thine ineffable long-suffering. But, rejoicing at our salvation, they cried unto thee, Glory be to thy condescension, O Lover of mankind.

Glory and Now, in the Fifth Tone

O THOU who puttest on light like a robe, when Joseph, with Nicodemus, brought thee down from the Tree and beheld thee dead, naked, and unburied, he mourned outwardly and grieviously, crying to thee with sighs, and saying, Woe is me, sweet Jesus, whom but a while ago, when the sun beheld suspended upon the Cross, it was shrouded in darkness, the earth quaked with fear, and the veil of the Temple was rent asunder. Albeit, I see that thou willingly enduredst death for my sake. How then shall I array thee, my God? How shall I wrap thee with linen? Or what dirges shall I chant for thy funeral? Wherefore, O compassionate Lord, I magnify thy Passion, and praise thy Burial with thy Resurrection, crying, Lord, glory to thee.

❡*And after* Now lettest thou thy servant, *etc;* (*p.* 77)*; Holy God, etc., the following two Troparia, in the Second Tone.*

THE pious Joseph, having brought down thy pure body from the Tree, wrapped it in pure linen, embalmed it with ointment, arrayed it, and laid it in a new tomb.

Verily, the angel came to the tomb and said to the ointment-bearing women, The ointment is meet for the dead, but Christ hath been shown to be remote from corruption.

❡*And the Benediction as in the Service of the Passion Gospels* (*p.* 842).

The Night of Great Friday

The Matin Service of Great Saturday

❡ *This service is chanted either on Friday night or at early dawn of Saturday.*

❡ *After* Blessed be God, *etc; the Troparia and the six Matin Psalms (p. 26), sing,* God the Lord hath appeared unto us, *etc., in the Second Tone. Then the Troparion,* The pious Joseph having brought down, *etc. (p. 881);* Glory, When thou, O immortal Life, *etc. (p. 147); and* Now, Verily the angel came to the tomb, *etc. (see above); then the Little Synapte; and the Exclamation,* For thou art the King of peace, O Christ our God, *etc; then chant the following Kathismata, in the First Tone.*

VERILY, Joseph requested of Pilate the precious body, which he wrapped in fine linen, after embalming it with divine spices, and placed it in a new grave. Wherefore, the ointment-bearing women rose up early, crying, Reveal to us, O Christ, thy Resurrection, as thou hast foresaid.

Glory and Now: The ranks of the angels were dazzled at beholding him who sitteth in the bosom of the Father placed in a grave like one dead. How could the immortal One at whom the myriads of angels gaze, glorifying, be with the dead in hades, being the Lord Creator?

❡ *Then Psalm 50; and immediately sing the following Canon, in the Sixth Tone, using the Hermoses as Katabasias.*

First Ode—Hermos [1]

THE children of those who were saved, hid under ground the God who made the persecuting giant of old to disappear in the waves of the sea. As for us, however, let us praise the Lord as did the youths; for in glory hath he been glorified.

O Lord my God, I shall praise thy Burial with funeral dirges, and indite unto thee paeans, O thou through

---

[1] Here the Clergy take the Kyron and enter the Sanctuary to put on their vestments.

whose Burial the entrance of life hath opened for me;
and who by Death caused death and hades to die.

Verily, the super-terrestial, and those below the earth,
beholding thee on thy throne on high and in the grave
below, were amazed, trembling at thy Death; for thou
O Element of life, wast seen to be dead in a manner
transcending the mind.

To the depths of the earth thou descendest to fill all
with thy glory; for my person that is in Adam was not
hidden from thee; and when thou wast buried thou
didst renew me, who was corrupt, O Lover of mankind.

Third Ode—Hermos [1]

VERILY, creation, having beheld thee suspended
on Golgotha, O thou who didst suspend the whole
earth on the waters without hinges, was overtaken with
great surprise, crying aloud, There is none holy save
thee, O Lord.

Thou hast revealed, O Master, numerous sights as
signs of thy Burial. But now thou hast revealed thy
hidden things as God and Man to those who are in
hades also, who shouted, saying, There is none holy save
thou, O Lord.

Thou hast stretched forth thy hands, O Saviour, and
gathered the things dispersed of old; and by thy Burial
in the linen and the grave thou hast loosed the captives,
who shout, There is none holy save thee, O Lord.

A grave and seals contained thee by thy will, O Uncontainable; for by deeds, O Lover of mankind, thou
hast made thy power known by a divine act to those
who sing, There is none holy save thee, O Lord.

Deacon: The Little Synapte.

Kathisma, in the First Tone

THE soldiers who watched thy tomb, O Saviour,
became like dead men from the lightning of the

---

[1] Here the Deacons come out with the Trikerions and the Dikerions and
stand before the Patriarch or the Archbishop.

appearing angel who proclaimed thy Resurrection to the women. Wherefore, thee do we glorify, O Remover of corruption, and to thee do we kneel, O thou who didst rise from the grave, alone our God.

Fourth Ode—Hermos [1]

VERILY, Habakuk, O good One, foresaw thy divine condescension even to the Cross; and was dazzled as he cried, Thou abolishedst the prestige of the mighty, when thou didst appear in hades, since thou art Almighty.

Thou hast blessed, O Saviour, this seventh day, which thou hadst blessed at the beginning with rest from work; for thou hast brought out everything, renewing it and restoring it to its former state, thus keeping the sabbath.

Thy soul, by the power of the best, hath vanquished the body, O Word, breaking the bonds of hades and death together by thy might.

Hades in welcoming thee, O Word, murmured at beholding a deified Man marked with wounds, who is yet Almighty. Wherefore, at that terrible sight it shouted in fear.

Fifth Ode—Hermos

WHEN Isaiah, O Christ, saw thy light, that setteth not, the light of thy divine appearance coming to us in pity, he rose up early, crying, The dead shall rise, and they who are in the tombs shall awake, and all those on the earth shall rejoice.

When thou becamest earthly, O Creator, thou didst renew those who are earthly. And the linen and the grave explained thy hidden mystery, O Word; for the honourable Joseph, of sound belief, fulfilled thy Father's plan, through whom thou hast renewed me by the might of his greatness.

---

[1] Here the Patriarch (or the Archbishop) enters the Sanctuary to put on his vestments.

Thou hast transported the dead by Death, and the corrupt by Burial; for as becometh God thou hast made the body which thou didst create incorrupt and deathless; for thy body, O Master, did not see corruption, and thy soul in a strange manner was not left in hades.

Thou didst come from a Virgin who knew no travail. Thy side, O my Creator, was pierced with a spear, by which thou didst accomplish the re-creation of Eve, having thyself become Adam. Supernaturally thou didst fall into a sleep that renewed nature, raising life from sleep and corruption; for thou art Almighty.

Sixth Ode—Hermos

VERILY, Jonah the Prophet was caught but not held in the belly of the whale. But being a sign of thee, O thou who didst suffer and wast delivered to burial, he came out of the whale as out of a chamber, and cried unto the watchmen, In vain do ye watch, O watchmen; for ye have neglected mercy.

Thou wast killed, O Word, but wast not separated from the body which thou didst share with us; for even though thy temple were dissolved at the time of the Passion, the Person of thy Divinity and Humanity is one only; and in both thou art still a single Son, the Word of God, God and Man.

The fall of Adam resulted in the Death of a Man, not God; for though the substance of thine earthly body suffered, thy Divinity hath remained passionless, transforming the corrupt to incorruptibility. And by thy Resurrection thou hast uncovered the incorrupt fountain of life.

Verily, hades ruled the race of man, but not for ever; for thou, O mighty One, when thou wast placed in the grave didst demolish the locks of death with the palm of thy hand, O Element of life, proclaiming to those sitting yonder from the ages a true salvation, having become, O Saviour, the First-born of the dead.

Deacon: The Little Synapte.

Kontakion, in the Second Tone

HE who closed the depth of the sea is beheld wrapped in linen and embalmed with myrrh; the deathless one placed in a tomb like one who is dead. The women came to embalm him, weeping bitterly and crying: Behold the Sabbath transcendent in blessings in which Christ hath slept and shall rise on the third day.

Oikos

VERILY, the Almighty hath been elevated upon the Cross, and the whole creation mourned, seeing him suspended naked upon a Tree. The sun hid his rays, and the stars gave not their light; the earth quaked with great fright, and the sea ran away; the rocks were spilt asunder, and many graves were opened, and the bodies of holy men arose. Hades sighed below, but the Jews were planning slanders against the Resurrection of Christ; and the women shouted, crying, Behold the sabbath transcendent in blessings on which Christ hath slept, to rise on the third day.

GREAT HOLY SATURDAY

SYNAXARION

ON the Great Holy Saturday, we celebrate the Burial of the divine body, and the descent of our Lord and Saviour Jesus Christ to hades, through which he restored our kind from corruption and transplanted it to eternal life.

On the following day, which was Saturday, and which fell on the twenty-fourth of March, the enemies of God, the high priests and Pharisees, came to Pilate and asked him to seal the tomb until the third day, lest the Disciples come at night, as they claimed, and steal the buried body, and then preach among the people, proclaiming the truth of the Resurrection, which that deceiver had foretold when he was alive, and the last error should be worse than the first. Thus they obtained permission to seal the tomb, and so they went and sealed it and placed a guard upon it from among the soldiers who were guarding the city (St. Mat. 27: 62-66).

Wherefore, by thine ineffable condescension, O Christ our God, have mercy upon us. Amen.

Seventh Ode—Hermos

AN ineffable wonder! He who saved the righteous youths from the fire of the furnace, hath been placed in the grave, a breathless corpse, for our salvation and deliverance, who sing, Blessed art thou, O delivering God.

Verily, hades was pierced and destroyed by the divine fire when it received in its heart him who was pierced in his side with a spear for our salvation, who sing, Blessed art thou, O delivering God.

The tomb is happy, having become divine when it received within it the Treasure of life, the Creator, as one who slumbereth for our salvation, who sing, Blessed art thou, O delivering God.

The Life of all was willing to lie in a grave, in accordance with the law of the dead, making it appear as the fountain of the resurrection of our salvation, who sing, Blessed art thou, O delivering God.

The Godhead of Christ was one without separation in hades, in the tomb, in Eden, and with the Father and the Spirit, for our salvation, who sing, Blessed art thou, O delivering God.

Eighth Ode—Hermos

BE thou amazed, O heaven, and let the foundations of the earth quake; for behold, he who dwelleth in the highest hath been accounted among the dead, and hath been Guest in a humble tomb. Wherefore, O ye youths, bless him. Praise him, ye Priests; and ye nations, exalt him more and more unto all the ages.

The pure Temple hath been destroyed, then rising, he raised with him the fallen tabernacle; for the second Adam who dwelleth in the highest hath descended unto the first Adam in the uttermost chambers of hades. Wherefore, ye youths, bless him. Praise him, ye Priests; and ye nations, exalt him more and more unto all the ages.

The courage of the Disciples hath come to its end. But Joseph of Ramah hath shown great valour; for beholding the God of all dead and naked, he sought him and arrayed him, shouting, O ye youths, bless him. Praise him ye Priests; and ye nations, exalt him more and more unto the end of ages.

O what dazzling wonders! O what endless goodness! O what ineffable endurance! For he that dwelleth in the highest is sealed up under the earth by his own will. God is slandered as a misleader. Wherefore, O ye youths, bless him. Praise him, ye priests, and ye nations, exalt him yet more and more to the end of ages.

❧ *Deacon: After the Little Synapte,* The Theotokos, Mother of Light, thee in songs of praise, do we honour magnifying.

❧ *Here candles are distributed to the Congregation.*

Ninth Ode—Hermos

MOURN not for me, Mother, as thou beholdest me in the grave; for I thy Son, whom thou didst conceive in thy womb without seed, shall rise and shall be glorified. And being God, I will ceaselessly exalt and ennoble those who in faith and longing magnify thee.

My eternal Son, I escaped sufferings at thy strange Birth and was supernaturally blessed. And now, beholding thee, O my Son, dead and breathless, I am pierced with the spear of bitter sorrow. But arise thou, that I may be magnified by thee.

The earth, O my Mother, hath hidden me by mine own will. And the gate-keepers of hades trembled at beholding me clothed with a robe spattered with revenge; for I being God, have vanquished mine enemies with the Cross, and I will rise again and magnify thee.

Let all creation rejoice, and all the earthly be glad; for hades and the enemy have been spoiled. Let the women meet me with spices; for I redeem Adam and all their descendants, and will rise on the third day.

And at the completion of the Ninth Ode, the Patriarch (or Archbishop), preceded by all the Clergy, fully vested, exit and go to where the Bier is, decorated with flowers, on which is the Epitaphion. The Priests and the Choir stand on both sides of it, and the Patriarch (or Archbishop) stand before it, with the Deacons on either side of him, and starts chanting the first of the Eulogies to follow, which are divided into three parts, and he censeth the Bier on its four sides. Then he censeth the Congregation, with the two Deacons preceding him, carrying the Trikerions and the Dikerion. As for the Archbishops, they stand in their proper places and chant the first part of the Eulogies until the Patriarch (or Archbishop) returns, and stands at his chair.

First Part, in the Fifth Tone

1. O Christ the Life, thou wast placed in a tomb, and the hosts of angels were dazzled, glorifying thy condescension.

2. O Life, how liest thou dead? How dwellest thou in a tomb? Albeit thou didst unbind the power of death, and raised the dead from hades.

3. Thee do we magnify, O Jesus King. We honour thy Passion and thy Burial, through which thou hast delivered us from corruption.

4. O Jesus, King of all, who settest the measures of the earth, today thou dwellest in a small tomb, raising the dead from their tombs.

5. O Jesus my Christ, King of all, what camest thou to seek in hades? Was it to deliver therefrom the race of man?

6. The Master of all creation is seen to be dead and placed in a new tomb, he who emptied the tomb of the dead.

7. O Christ the Life, thou hast been placed in a tomb. By thy Death thou hast abolished death, sprouting life to the world.

8. Thou hast been accounted a sinner among evil-doers, to justify us all, O Christ, from the evil of the ancient heel tripper.

9. He who is more beautiful than all men, appeareth as dead without form, he who beautified the nature of all.

10. How doth hades endure thy presence, O Saviour, and not be crushed and darkened at once, not become gloomy from the lightning of the rays of thy light.

11. O sweet Jesus, my Light and my Salvation, how wast thou hidden in a dark tomb? O what an indescribable and ineffable endurance.

12. Intelligent nature, and the ranks of the incorporals were dazzled at the mystery of thine indescribable and incomprehensible Burial, O Christ.

13. O what strange wonders! O what wonderful matters! For he that giveth breath is carried away breathless, prepared for his funeral with Joseph's hands.

14. Though hidden in a tomb, O Christ, thou wast not separated from the fatherly bosom. Verily, it is a strange matter, exceedingly wonderful.

15. It was known, O Jesus, by all creation that thou wast in truth the King of heaven and earth, even though thou wast enclosed in a narrow tomb.

16. When thou wast placed in a tomb, O Christ Creator, the foundations of hades quaked, and the graves of men were opened.

17. He who holdeth the earth hath died in the flesh. He was held by the earth to deliver the dead from the hold of hades.

18. O my Life and my Saviour, thou ascended from corruption when thou wast dead, walking among the dead, and crushing the bars of hades.

19. Now is the body of God hidden under the earth, like a light under a bushel, driving away the darkness that is in hades.

20. The choirs of the supersensuous angels, hasten now with thee, that with Joseph and Nicodemus they may bury thee in a small tomb, O thou who art uncontainable.

21. By thine own choice thou didst die, and wast buried beneath the earth. Wherefore, thou didst revive me, dead in bitter iniquity, O Jesus overflowing with life.

22. All creation was changed at thy Passion, O Word; for all suffered with thee, knowing that thou art Almighty.

23. When devouring hades engulfed the Rock of life, it released from their graves the dead whom it had swallowed from the ages.

24. In a new tomb thou wast placed, O Christ, renewing the nature of mankind, when thou didst rise from the dead as God.

25. Thou didst descend into the earth to save Adam; and not finding him there, O Master, thou didst descend to hades seeking him.

26. The whole earth quaked with fear, O Word, and the sun hid its rays, when thy great light was covered inside the earth.

27. Thou didst willingly die like man, O Saviour. And being God, thou didst raise the dead from their tombs and from the abyss of sin.

28. The pure one, O Jesus, shed tears over thee. She cried, mourning with the agony of mothers, How shall I lay thee away, O my Son?

29. In the bosom of the earth thou didst disappear like a grain of wheat, giving out most flourishing ears, when thou didst raise the descendants of Adam.

30. Like the disappearing sun, thou wast hidden under the earth. Thou wast screened by the night of death. Albeit, arise, O Saviour, with greater splendour.

31. As the moon screeneth the sun's disc, so did a tomb screen thee, when thou wast eclipsed, crying in the flesh.

32. Christ the Life, tasting death, released mankind from death, and now granteth life to all.

33. Adam, formerly dead in the flesh, thou didst raise to life by thy Death, O Saviour, when thou didst appear in the flesh as the new Adam.

34. The ranks of the supersensible beholding thee O Saviour, lying dead for our sake, were dazzled, covering themselves with their wings.

35. From upon the Tree Joseph brought thee down dead, placing thee now in a tomb, O Word. Albeit arise, and as God save all.

36. O Saviour, Joy of the angels, thou hast become now the cause of their sorrow, as they behold thee dead in the flesh, and breathless.

37. When thou wast elevated on the Tree thou didst elevate the living; and when thou wast buried under the ground thou didst raise those who were placed underneath.

38. Like a lion thou didst lie down, O Saviour; and like a lion's cub thou didst rise up, casting off from thee the old age of the flesh.

39. O thou who didst take from Adam a rib and therewith make Eve, thy side was pierced with a spear and from it sprang forth the fountain of purification.

40. The Lamb of old was slain secretly, but by thy Death in the presence of all the people, O meek One thou didst, O Saviour, purify all creatures.

41. Who can describe this terrible and strange happening? For he who reigneth over creation today accepteth sufferings, and died for our sake.

42. The angels were puzzled and dazzled, shouting How is the Treasure of life seen dead? How is God enclosed in a tomb?

43. From thy pierced side, O Saviour, thou hast dripped life on Eve, who expelled me from life, reviving me with her.

44. When thou wast outstretched upon the Tree, O Jesus, thou didst gather in all men; and when thy life-flowing side was pierced, thou didst gush forth pardon and forgiveness for all.

45. The honourable Joseph, trembling, wrapped thee about, O Saviour. With reverence and decorum he laid thee away as one dead, being dazzled by the dread sight of thee.

46. Willingly thou didst descend under the ground as dead, raising therefrom the fallen, O Jesus, and translating them from earth to the heavens.

47. And though seen as dead, thou art yet alive, raising the fallen from the dead, and translating them from earth to the heavens.

48. And though seen dead, thou art yet alive. Wherefore, thou didst restore life to the dead, and didst cause to die him who brought me death.

49. O what joy! Oh what abounding delight, wherewith thou didst fill those who are in hades, when thou didst rise as a light in its dark abyss.

50. I worship thy Passion and praise thy Burial. I magnify thy might, O Lover of mankind, through which thou hast delivered me from corrupting passion.

51. They brandished the spear over thee, O Christ. But the spear of the mighty one was snatched away; and the spear of Eden was vanquished.

52. When Eve beheld her Lamb slain, she was wounded, and wailing, moving the herd to lamentation.

53. Though thou wast buried in a tomb, O Saviour, and didst descend to hades, thou didst strip it, O Christ, emptying the graves.

54. Under the ground, willingly, thou didst descend, restoring the life of dead humanity, and rising therewith in Fatherly glory.

55. When one of the Trinity for our sake suffered in the flesh and censured death, the sun feared and the earth quaked.

56. The progeny of Judah, as from a bitter spring, placed Jesus in a pit, he who fed them and nourished them with manna.

57. The Judge stood before Pilate the judge, and like a condemned man he was condemned to an unjust death, death on the Tree.

58. O obstinate Israel, O murderous people, why did ye release Barabbas, delivering up the Saviour to crucifixion?

59. O thou who didst fashion Adam from the earth with thine own hand, thou didst become Man in Nature for his sake, and of thine own choice wast crucified willingly.

60. Thou didst obey thy Father, O God the Word, descending to the nethermost of bitter hades and raising mankind therefrom.

61. Thy virgin Mother mourned, sighing, Woe is me, O Light of the world! Woe is me, mine Illumination, O most desirable Jesus!

62. O envious and bloody people, be ashamed at least of the linen, when Christ rose victorious!

63. Come, O thou vile, murderous Disciple, explain to me the reason of thy wickedness, wherein thou didst deliver Christ.

64. O foolish traitor, utterly corrupt and blind, in hypocrisy thou didst appear as a lover of men, selling the spice for a price.

65. O cursed Satan, what price that thou possessest can equal the price of the honours of the spice of heaven? But thou didst find madness and greed.

66. If thou wast a lover of the poor, and regretted the spice that was poured out for the forgiveness of a soul, how dost thou sell the Light and Illumination for silver?

67. O God the Word, O my Joy and my Pleasure, how shall I endure thy three-day Burial? For my vitals are torn, as those of mothers.

68. The virgin Mother, the Bride of God, cried, Who will give me water of tears, that I may weep for sweet Jesus.

69. O all ye mountains and hills, and all ye gatherings of men, mourn, weep, and lament with me, the Mother of your God.

70. The Virgin cried, moaning and sighing, When shall I see thee, O Saviour and eternal Light, O Pleasure of my heart and its Happiness?

71. Though thou art the adamant Rock, thou didst accept death, and didst gush forth the rivers of life, O my Saviour; for thou art the Fountain of life.

72. From thy side, as from a single spring, there flowed forth a double river, from which we drank, and which overflowed with life imperishable.

73. Thou appeared in the tomb as dead, O Word, by thine own will. But thou art alive, and shalt raise humanity by thy Resurrection, as thou didst say, O my Saviour.

74. *Glory:* We praise thee, O Word, God of creation, with thy Father and Holy Spirit, and we glorify thy divine Burial.

75. *Now:* We bless thee, O undefiled Theotokos. In faith we honour the three-day Burial of thy Son our God.

¶ *Then the First Troparion is repeated.*

O Christ the Life, thou wast placed in a tomb, and the hosts of angels were dazzled, glorifying thy condescension.

¶ *Then the Little Synapte; and the Exclamation by the Priest (If neither Patriarch or Archbishop be present).*

For thy Name hath been blessed, and thy kingdom glorified, O Father, etc.

¶ *And as the Priest is censing, begin the singing of the Second Part.*

Second Part, also in the Fifth Tone

1. It is meet to magnify thee, O Life-giver, who didst stretch forth thy hands upon the Cross, crushing the might of the enemy.

2. It is meet to magnify thee, O Creator of all; for by thy Passion we all have gained passionlessness, and escaped corruption.

3. When thou didst disappear bodily in the tomb, O Christ, Saviour and unsetting Sun, the earth trembled and the sun disappeared.

4. Thou hast slumbered in the tomb, O Christ, a nature-reviving slumber, arousing the human race from the slumber of sin.

5. She who is undefiled said, Alone among women have I borne thee without pain. And now I suffer unbearable passion, my Son, in thy Passion.

6. The seraphim trembled, O Saviour, at beholding thee in the highest with the Father, indivisible, and on earth below stretched out dead.

7. The veil of the Temple, O Word, was rent at thy Crucifixion; and the stars hid their rays, when thou wast hidden, O Sun, under the earth.

8. He who in the beginning stablished the globe with but a gesture, as breathless man disappeared underground. Wherefore, be alarmed, O heaven, at this sight.

9. Thou didst disappear underground, thou who didst fashion man with thy hands, to raise the assemblies of men from the fall by thine almighty power.

10. Come, let us sing divine dirges to the Death of Christ, that like the ointment-bearing women of old, we may with them hear the rejoicing.

11. To thee, O Word, who art in truth the unceasing Spice, the women came with spices as to one dead, O living One.

12. When thou wast buried, O Christ, thou didst demolish the kingdoms of hades. Death was made to

die and cease by Death, and mankind was delivered from corruption.

13. The Wisdom of God, gushing out rivers of life, having been hidden and screened in a tomb, revived those who were in the chambers of hades.

14. Lament me not by grieving, O Mother, because I willingly accepted death in the flesh that I might renew the bruised nature of mankind.

15. Thou hast disappeared, screened under death, O Star of righteousness, raising the dead as from sleep, driving completely away the darkness of hades.

16. The two-natured Grain of Wheat, hath been sown today in tears in the bosom of the earth. But it shall bring joy to the world when it groweth.

17. Adam was frightened at God's walking in paradise. But now he shall rejoice at his coming to hades; for he shall rise after that he had fallen.

18. When thou wast placed bodily in the tomb, O Christ, thy Mother offered thee tears, crying, Arise, my Son, as thou foresaidst.

19. Reverently Joseph veiled thee in a new tomb, O Saviour, singing to thee lamentations, mixed with weeping and mourning, worthy of God.

20. Seeing thee fastened with nails on the Cross, O Word, thy Mother's soul was transfixed by the nails of sorrow and hurled down by its shafts.

21. Seeing thee quaffing the bitter drink, O thou Sweetness of all, thy Mother moistened her cheeks with bitter tears.

22. She who is undefiled, O Word, cried, I am wounded, and my vitals are torn, at seeing thee unjustly slain.

23. Joseph, O Word of God, cried, trembling, How shall I close thy lips, and thy sweet eyes? How shall I lay thee down as becometh the dead?

24. Joseph and Nicodemus now indite lamentations at the funeral of the dead Christ; and with them the ranks of the seraphim.

25. At thy hiding beneath the ground, O Sun of righteousness, the moon, thy Móther, was eclipsed by sorrow at no longer seeing thee.

26. O Life-giver, hades, seeing thee spoiling his riches, and raising those dead before the ages, was frightened, O Saviour.

27. The Sun shineth in splendour after the night, O Word. But thou shineth after death by thy Resurrection, beaming forth and coming out as from a chamber.

28. When the earth received thee in its folds, O Creator, it was overcome trembling at thee, O Saviour, arousing the dead with its shock.

29. In spices Joseph and Nicodemus now lay thee, O Christ, in a strange manner, shouting, Be alarmed, all the earth.

30. When thou wast set, O Author of light, the sun set with thee. Creation was overcome with trembling, giving warning that thou art Creator of all.

31. A hewn stone may screen the corner-stone; and a dead man in the tomb eclipseth God as one who is dead. Wherefore, be dismayed O earth.

32. She who is undefiled was crying with tears, Behold thy Mother and the Disciple whom thou didst love. Grant me a song, O most Sweet.

33. Since thou art alone the Bestower of life, O Word of God, thou didst not cause the Jews to die when thou wast stretched upon the Cross, but thou didst even raise their dead.

34. At thy Passion there was no appearance of beauty left to thee. And when thou didst rise, thou didst shine in splendour, O Word, adorning humanity with divine rays.

35. Thou didst disappear underground, O Star that setteth not. And as the sun could not bear to part with thee, he was darkened at the noon of the day.

36. The sun and moon together were darkened, O my Saviour; for like two loyal slaves they wrapped themselves with the dark garments of mourning.

37. The centurion knew thee as God though thou wast dead. And Joseph trembling cried, How shall I touch thee with my hands, O my God.

38. When Adam slumbered, death was brought forth from his side. But thou, O Word of God, when thou didst slumber, thou didst gush out from thy side life for the world.

39. When thou didst slumber, O righteous One, thou broughtest the dead to life. And when thou, awakening, didst rise, thou didst raise those who had slumbered from the beginning of time.

40. Thou wast lifted up from the earth, gushing out for me the wine of salvation, O thou life-flowing Vine, Wherefore, I glorify thy Passion and Crucifixion.

41. How did the chiefs of the supersensible choirs, O my Saviour, behold thee naked, condemned, and stained, yet conquering the audacity of thy crucifiers?

42. O ye Hebrews, most cruel and haughty race of the Jews, verily, ye did know of the rebuilding of the Temple. Wherefore then, did ye condemn Christ to death?

43. The Adorner of all, who spangled the heavens with stars and wonderfully ornamented the earth, put on the robe of ridicule.

44. When thy side, O Word of God, was wounded, phoenix-like thou didst revive thy dead children, pouring forth enlivening rivers for them.

45. Of old Joshua stopped the sun in his attack against strangers. But thou didst hide it when thou didst vanquish the prince of darkness.

46. Thou didst consent, O Christ, to become Man, and descend to hades, O compassionate One, without separation from the Fatherly bosom.

47. He was suspended on the Tree who suspended the earth on the waters. He hung thereon as one without breath, unable to bear the quaking of death.

48. Woe is me, O my Son, cried she who knew no wedlock. Him whom I hoped to see king, I behold now condemned to die on the Cross.

49. When Gabriel descended upon me, verily, he told me, saying, that the kingdom of my Son Jesus shall be sure and everlasting.

50. Alas, the old prophecy of Simeon hath been fulfilled; for thy spear, O Immanuel, hath pierced through my heart.

51. Be ye confounded, O Jews whom the Bestower of life did raise even from the dead, whom ye killed out of envy.

52. The sun, O Christ, was darkened in its light at beholding thee, O unbeholden Light, hidden breathless in a tomb.

53. O God, the eternal Word beyond description, thy pure Mother, beholding thee in a tomb, wept bitterly.

54. Thy Mother, free of corruption, O Christ, beholding thy Death, cried bitterly, Linger not, O Life, among the dead.

55. When cruel hades beheld thee, O Sun of glory, it trembled greatly because of thee, O immortal One, delivering its captives forthwith.

56. Thou wast seen, O Saviour, as a dread and great Sight; for the Cause of life endured death, desiring to revive all by his Death.

57. When thy side was pierced, O Master, and thy hands were nailed, thou didst heal the wound that came from thy side, and the excessiveness of the hands of our forefathers.

58. Everyone mourned in the house for Rachel's son. But for the Virgin's Son the ranks of the Disciples mourned with his Mother.

59. Christ the Lord who fashioned man with his own hands, who shattered the tusks of the beast of prey, was smitten by hands on the cheek.

60. Now, O Christ, all we who believe praise thy Crucifixion and Burial; for by thy Burial we were delivered from death.

61. *Glory:* O eternal God, and Word coëternal with him and the Spirit, confirm the kings' scepters against their enemies; for thou art righteous.

62. *Now:* O pure and undefiled, who didst give birth to Life, end thou the dissensions of the Church, and envelope her with peace; for thou art righteous.

❧ *Then repeat the First Troparion.*

It is meet to magnify thee, O Life-giver, who didst stretch forth thy hands upon the Cross, crushing the might of the enemy.

❧ *Then the Little Synapte; and the Exclamation by the Priest as formerly.*

For thou art holy, O our God who sittest on the throne of glory of the cherubim, and to thee do we address glory, etc.

❧ *And as the Priest burneth the incense, begin the singing of the Third Part.*

Third Part, in the Third Tone

1. All generations offer praise to thy Burial, O my Christ.

2. He of Ramah brought thee down from the Tree and laid thee in a tomb.

3. The ointment-bearing women, O my Christ, anxiously offered thee spices.

4. Come, all ye creatures, let us offer our lamentations to the Creator.

5. Let us, with the ointment-bearing women anxiously anoint the living as one who is dead.

6. O blessed Joseph, lay away the body of the Lord, the Life-giver.

7. Verily, they who were fed with manna, behold, they have raised their heel against the Benefactor.

8. They who were fed with manna, behold, they have brought to the Lord vinegar and gall.

9. O what ignorance! The killing of Christ by the killers of the Prophets.

10. The Christ initiate, being an ignorant servant, delivered the sea of wisdom.

11. The treacherous Judas, having sold the Deliverer, became captive.

12. A wide pit is the mouth of the sinful Jews, as Solomon saith.

13. The wicked, crooked ways of the Jews have gins and snares.

14. Joseph with Nicodemus provided for the Creator as befits the dead.

15. Thy might we glorify, O Reviver and Saviour, Abolisher of hades.

16. She who is undefiled saw thee stretched out, O Word, and she mourned like a mother.

17. O my clear Springtime, my sweet Child, whither hath thy comeliness disappeared.

18. When thou didst die, O Word, thy pure Mother was moved to mourning.

19. Women with ointment came to anoint Christ, even divine ointment.

20. Thou, my God, didst cause death to die by the might of thy Godhead.

21. The oppressor was oppressed, but the oppressed escaped by thy wisdom, O my God.

22. The betrayer hath tumbled into the pit of corruption and the abyss of hades.

23. The ways of Judas, wretched fool, are gins and snares.

24. Thy crucifiers have perished, O Word of God, the Son, the King of all.

25. The men of blood have all perished in the pit of corruption.

26. My God and Fashioner, the Son of God the King, how didst thou accept the Passion.

27. The heifer mourned, beholding the Calf elevated on a Tree.

28. Joseph with Nicodemus prepared the life-bearing body.

29. Verily, the Maiden, pierced in her vitals, did lament with warm tears.

30. O Light of mine eyes, my sweet Child, how art thou screened in a tomb?

31. Mourn not, my Mother; for I suffer to deliver Adam and Eve.

32. I glorify, O my Son, thy uttermost compassion, through which thou dost suffer.

33. Vinegar and gall didst thou taste, O compassionate One, dissolving the ancient taste.

34. On a Tree wast thou nailed, O thou who of old didst shade thy people with a pillar of cloud.

35. To thy tomb, O Saviour, the ointment-bearing women did come with ointment.

36. Arise, O compassionate One, and raise us with thee from the depths of hades.

37. Thy sorrowful Mother cried with tears, Arise, O Life-giver.

38. Hasten, arise, O Word, and loose the sorrow of her who in undefilement did give thee birth.

39. The heavenly powers, when they beheld thee, trembled with fear.

40. Grant us remission of sin, as with longing and fear we honour thy Passion.

41. A dread and strange sight, O Word, that the earth doth hide thee.

42. A Joseph, O Saviour, fled with thee before, and now another doth bury thee.

43. Thy pure Mother, O Saviour, in thy death lamented thee with mourning.

44. All minds were frightened, O Maker of creation, at thy strange Burial.

45. The ointment-bearing women to thy tomb did come, pouring out their ointment at early dawn.

❡ *Here the Priest or Bishop (if one be present) taketh a bottle of rose water and sprinkleth it over the Bier and those present.*

46. By thy Resurrection grant peace to the Church, and to thy people salvation.

47. *Glory:* O my God, the Trinity, the Father, Son, and the Spirit, have mercy upon the world.

48. *Now:* Prepare thy servants, O chaste Virgin, to behold the Resurrection of thy Son.

❡ *Then the First Troparion is repeated.*

All generations offer praise to thy burial, O my Christ.

❡ *Then the Little Synapte; and the Exclamation by the Priest as formerly,* For thou art the King of peace, O Christ our God, and to thee do we address glory, *etc.*

❡ *Then immediately sing the Benedictions, in the Fifth Tone (p. 111); Then the Little Synapte; and the Exclamation by the Priest,* For thee do all the powers of heaven praise, and to thee do they address glory, O Father, *etc. Then the Exaposteilarion, in the Second Tone,* Holy is the Lord our God *(three times); And in the Einos, sing the following Idiomelons with their Stichoi, in the Second Tone.*

TODAY he who holdeth creation on the hollow of his hand is contained in a tomb; and he who covereth the heavens with virtue is covered by a stone. Life slumbereth, hades is alarmed, and Adam is delivered from his bonds. Wherefore, glory be to the dispensation through which thou hast fulfilled all, thy most holy Resurrection from the dead granting us rest and everlasting sabbath.

What is this sight which we behold? What is this present rest? For the King of the ages, having fulfilled the mystery of dispensation by the Passion, hath rested, keeping the sabbath in the tomb, granting us a new sabbath. Wherefore, let us hail him, Arise, O God, and Judge of the earth; for thou dost reign for evermore, O thou who possesseth the countless and Great Mercy.

Come ye, let us behold our Life placed in a tomb to give life to those who are placed in tombs. Come, let us today behold him sleeping who springeth from Judah, shouting to him prophetically, Thou hast crouched and lain down like a lion. Who shall arouse thee, O King? But arise by thine own power, thou who didst deliver thyself by thine own choice for our sake. O Lord, glory to thee.

Verily, Joseph sought the body of Jesus and placed it in his new tomb; for it is fitting that he come out of the tomb; as out of a chamber. Wherefore, thou who didst crush the might of death, and opened the gates of paradise for mankind, glory to thee.

Glory, in the Sixth Tone

THE great Moses foreshadowed this day mystically by his saying, And God blessed the seventh day; for this is the day of quiet and rest, on which the only Son of God rested from all his works, keeping sabbath in the body (by means of the mystery of the dispensation taking effect in death) returning through Resurrection to what he had been, and granting us eternal life; for he alone is good and the Lover of mankind.

¶*And Now,* Thou hast transcended, *etc; and the Great Doxology (p. 118), and at its conclusion the Priests make a procession around the church with the Gospel Book and the Epitaphion (the funeral picture) raised over their heads, as the congregation follow them; and the Choirs sing in the Sixth Tone:*

Holy God, Holy Mighty, Holy Immortal One. Have mercy upon us.

Or the following Troparion, in the Fifth Tone

WHEN he saw that the sun had hidden its rays, and the veil of the Temple was rent at the death of the Saviour, Joseph, approaching Pilate, pleaded with him, crying out and saying, Give thou me this Stranger who from his youth has wandered like a stranger. Give me this Stranger whom his kinsmen killed in hatred like a stranger. Give me this Stranger at whom I wonder, beholding him as a Guest of death. Give me this Stranger who knoweth how to take in the poor and strangers. Give me this Stranger whom the Jews in envy estranged from the world. Give me this Stranger that I may bury him in a tomb, who being a Stranger hath no place whereon to lay his head. Give me this Stranger, to whom his Mother, beholding him dead, cried, My Son and my vitals be wounded, and my heart burn, as I behold thee dead, yet trusting in thy Resurrection, I magnify thee. In these words the honourable Joseph pleaded with Pilate, took the Saviour's body, and with fear wrapped it in linen and balm. In a tomb he placed thee, O thou who grantest to all everlasting life and the Great Mercy.

¶ *When all the Congregation have returned into the church, and the Priests enter the Temple, the Proto-priest exclaimeth, saying,* Let us hearken! Peace be unto you all. Wisdom! *And immediately the Choir sings the Troparion,* The pious Joseph, *etc. (once p. 881), as the Priests go three times around the holy Altar with the Epitaphion, placing it over the Altar where it remaineth to the Leave-taking of Easter. Then immediately the Reader readeth the following Prophecy.*

Reading: from the Prophecy of Ezekiel the Prophet (37:1-14)

THE hand of the Lord was upon me, and brought me forth in the spirit of the Lord: and set me down in the midst of a plain that was full of bones.

And he led me about through them on every side: now they were very many upon the face of the plain, and they were exceeding dry.

And he said to me: Son of man, dost thou think these bones shall live? And I answered: O Lord God, thou knowest.

And he said to me: Prophesy concerning these bones; and say to them: Ye dry bones, hear the word of the Lord.

Thus saith the Lord God to these bones: Behold, I will send spirit into you, and you shall live.

And I will lay sinews upon you, and will cause flesh to grow over you, and will cover you with skin: and I will give you spirit and you shall live, and you shall know that I am the Lord.

And I prophesied as he had commanded me: and as I prophesied there was a noise, and behold a commotion: and the bones came together, each one to its joint.

And I saw, and behold the sinews, and the flesh came up upon them: and the skin was stretched out over them, but there was no spirit in them.

And he said to me: Prophesy to the spirit, prophesy, O son of man, and say to the spirit: Thus saith the Lord God: Come, spirit, from the four winds, and blow upon these slain, and let them live again.

And I prophesied as he had commanded me: and the spirit came into them, and they lived: and they stood up upon their feet, an exceeding great army.

And he said to me: Son of man: All these bones are the house of Israel: they say: Our bones are dried up, and our hope is lost, and we are cut off.

Therefore prophesy, and say to them: Thus saith the Lord God: Behold I will open your graves, and will bring you out of your sepulchres, O my people: and will bring you into the land of Israel.

And you shall know that I am the Lord, when I shall have opened your sepulchres, and shall have brought you out of your graves, O my people:

And shall have put my spirit in you, and you shall live, and I shall make you rest upon your own land: and you shall know that I the Lord have spoken, and done it, saith the Lord God:

The Epistle: Arise, O Lord, let thy hand be exalted. I will give praise to thee, O Lord, with my whole heart.

Section from the First Epistle of St. Paul to the Corinthians (5:6-8); Galatians (3:13-14)

YE brethren: A little leaven corrupteth the whole lump?

Purge out the old leaven, that you may be a new paste, as you are unleavened. For Christ our pasch is sacrificed.

Therefore let us feast, not with the old leaven, nor with the leaven of malice and wickedness; but with the unleavened bread of sincerity and truth.

Christ hath redeemed us from the curse of the law, being made a curse for us: for it is written: Cursed is every one that hangeth on a tree:

That the blessing of Abraham might come on the Gentiles through Christ Jesus: that we may receive the promise of the Spirit by faith.

The Gospel: from St. Matthew

On the next day, which followed, etc. (p. 841).

❧ *Then the Petitions,* Let us all say, *etc;* Let us finish our petitions, *etc. (pp. 76-77); and the rest of the Matin Service as usual.*

Benediction: O thou who for our sakes, and for our salvation, didst accept in the flesh the dread Passion, the enlivening Crucifixion and voluntary Burial, O Christ, etc.

THE MORNING OF GREAT SATURDAY

VESPERS AND MASS

❧ *After* Blessed be the kingdom of the Father, *etc., recite the Sunset Psalm. And on* O Lord, to the have I cried, *etc. chant the first three Stichera of the Resurrection, in the First Tone (p. 137); and the first piece of the Aposticha of the same Tone,* O Christ, by thy Passion, *etc. (p. 138); and the following Idiomelons, in the Eighth Tone.*

TODAY hath hades sighed, crying, It were better for me that I had not received the Begotten of Mary; for when he approached me, he loosed my power and crushed my gates of brass, arousing the souls which I had possessed, he being God. Wherefore, glory be to thy Crucifixion and to thy Resurrection, O Lord *(Repeat.)*

Today hath hades sighed, crying, My power hath vanished, because I received a dead Man as one of the dead, but could not hold him completely. Rather, I lost with him those who were under my reign. From the beginning of time I have held control over the dead. But this One raised all. Wherefore, glory be to thy Crucifixion and to thy Resurrection, O Lord.

Today hath hades sighed, crying, My power hath been swallowed up; for the Shepherd, crucified, hath raised Adam; and those whom I had possessed I lost. Those whom I had swallowed by my might, I have given up completely; for the Crucified hath emptied the graves, and the might of death hath vanished. Wherefore, glory to thy Cross, O Lord, and to thy Resurrection.

Glory, in the Sixth Tone

The great Moses foreshadowed, etc. (p. 905).

Now, in the First Tone

Let us praise Mary the Virgin, etc (p. 138).

❧ *Then the Eisodos with the Gospel; and* O resplendent Light, *etc; and immediately the following Prophecies.*

First Reading: from the Book of Genesis

In the beginning God created the heaven, etc. (p. 398).

Second Reading: from the Book of Exodus (12:1-11)

AND the Lord said to Moses and Aaron in the land of Egypt:

This month shall be to you the beginning of months: it shall be the first in the months of the year.

Speak ye to the whole assembly of the children of Israel, and say to them: On the tenth day of this month let every man take a lamb by their families and houses.

But if the number be less than may suffice to eat the lamb, he shall take unto him his neighbour that joineth to his house, according to the number of souls which may be enough to eat the lamb.

And it shall be a lamb without blemish, a male, of one year: according to which rite also you shall take a kid.

And you shall keep it until the fourteenth day of this month: and the whole multitude of the children of Israel shall sacrifice it in the evening.

And they shall take of the blood thereof, and put it upon both the side posts, and on the upper door posts of the houses, wherein they shall eat it.

And they shall eat the flesh that night roasted at the fire, and unleavened bread with wild lettuce.

You shall not eat thereof any thing raw, nor boiled in water, but only roasted at the fire: you shall eat the head with the feet and entrails thereof.

Neither shall there remain any thing of it until morning. If there be any thing left, you shall burn it with fire.

And thus you shall eat it: you shall gird your reins, and you shall have shoes on your feet, holding staves in your hands, and you shall eat in haste: for it is the Phase (that is the Passage) of the Lord.

Third Reading: from the Prophecy of Daniel the Prophet (3:1-88)

IN the eighteenth year, King Nabuchodonosor made a statue of gold, of sixty cubits high, and six cubits broad, and he set it up in the plain of Dura of the province of Babylon.

Then Nabuchodonosor the king sent to call together the nobles, the magistrates, and the judges, the captains, the rulers, and governors, and all the chief men of the provinces, to come to the dedication of the statue which king Nabuchodonosor had set up.

Then the nobles, the magistrates, and the judges, the captains, and rulers, and the great men that were placed in authority, and all the princes of the provinces, were gathered together to come to the dedication of the statue, which king Nabuchodonosor had set up. And they stood before the statue which king Nabuchodonosor had set up.

Then a herald cried with a strong voice: To you it is commanded, O nations, tribes, and languages:

That in the hour that you shall hear the sound of the trumpet, and of the flute, and of the harp, of the sackbut, and of the psaltery, and of the symphony, and of all kind of music; ye fall down and adore the golden statue which king Nabuchodonosor hath set up.

But if any man shall not fall down and adore, he shall the same hour be cast into a furnace of burning fire.

Upon this therefore, at the time when all the people heard the sound of the trumpet, the flute, and the harp, of the sackbut, and the psaltery, of the symphony, and of all kind of music: all the nations, tribes, and languages fell down and adored the golden statue which king Nabuchodonosor had set up.

And presently at that very time some Chaldeans came and accused the Jews,

And said to king Nabuchodonosor: O king, live for ever:

Thou, O king, hast made a decree that every man that shall hear the sound of the trumpet, the flute, and the harp, of the sackbut, and the psaltery, of the symphony, and of all kind of music, shall prostrate himself, and adore the golden statue:

And that if any man shall not fall down and adore, he should be cast into a furnace of burning fire.

Now there are certain Jews whom thou hast set over the works of the province of Babylon, Sidrach, Misach, and Abednago: these men, O king, have slighted thy decree: they worship not thy gods, nor do they adore the golden statue which thou hast set up.

Then Nabuchodonosor in fury, and in wrath, commanded that Sidrach, Misach, and Abednago should be brought: who immediately were brought before the king.

And Nabuchodonosor the king spoke to them, and said: Is it true, O Sidrach, Misach, and Abednago, that you do not worship my gods, nor adore the golden statue that I have set up?

Now therefore if you be ready at what hour soever you shall hear the sound of the trumpet, flute, harp, sackbut, and psaltery, and symphony, and of all kinds of music, prostrate yourselves, and adore the statue which I have made: but if you do not adore, you shall be cast the same hour into the furnace of burning fire: and who is the God that shall deliver you out of my hand?

Sidrach, Misach, and Adbednago answered and said to king Nabuchodonosor: We have no occasion to answer thee concerning this matter.

For behold our God, whom we worship, is able to save us from the furnace of burning fire, and to deliver us out of thy hands, O king.

But if he will not, be it known to thee, O king, that we will not worship thy gods, nor adore the golden statue which thou hast set up.

Then was Nabuchodonosor filled with fury: and the countenance of his face was changed against Sidrach, Misach, and Abednago, and he commanded that the furnace should be heated seven times more than it had been accustomed to be heated.

And he commanded the strongest men that were in his army, to bind the feet of Sidrach, Misach, and Abednago, and to cast them into the furnace of burning fire.

And immediately these men were bound and were cast into the furnace of burning fire, with their coats, and their caps, and their shoes, and their garments.

For the king's commandment was urgent, and the furnace was heated exceedingly. And the flame of the fires slew those men that had cast in Sidrach, Misach, and Abednago.

But these three men, that is, Sidrach, Misach, and Abednago, fell down bound in the midst of the furnace of burning fire.

And they walked in the midst of the flame, praising God and blessing the Lord.

Then Azarias standing up prayed in this manner, and opening his mouth in the midst of the fire, he said:

Blessed art thou, O Lord, the God of our fathers, and thy name is worthy of praise, and glorious for ever:

For thou art just in all that thou hast done to us, and all thy works are true, and thy ways right, and all thy judgments true.

For thou hast executed true judgments in all the things that thou hast brought upon us, and upon Jerusalem the holy city of our fathers: for acording to truth and judgment, thou hast brought all these things upon us for our sins.

For we have sinned, and committed iniquity, departing from thee: and we have trespassed in all things:

And we have not hearkened to thy commandments, nor have we observed nor done as thou hadst commanded us, that it might go well with us.

Wherefore all that thou hast brought upon us, and every thing that thou hast done to us, thou hast done in true judgment:

And thou hast delivered us into the hands of our enemies that are unjust, and most wicked, and prevaricators, and to a king unjust, and most wicked beyond all kings that are upon the earth.

And now we cannot open our mouths: we are become a shame and reproach to thy servants, and to them that worship thee.

Deliver us not up for ever, we beseech thee, for thy name's sake, and abolish not thy convenant.

And take not away thy mercy from us for the sake of Abraham thy beloved, and Isaac thy servant, and Israel thy holy one:

To whom thou hast spoken, promising that thou wouldest multiply their seed as the stars of heaven, and as the sand that is on the sea shore.

For we, O Lord, are diminished more than any nation, and are brought low in all the earth this day for our sins.

Neither is there at this time prince, or leader, or prophet, or holocaust, or sacrifice, or oblation, or incense, or place of firstfruits before thee,

That we may find thy mercy: nevertheless in a contrite heart and humble spirit let us be accepted.

As in holocausts of rams, and bullocks, and as in thousands of fat lambs: so let our sacrifice be made in thy sight this day, that it may please thee: for there is no confusion to them that trust in thee.

And now we follow thee with all our heart, and we fear thee, and seek thy face.

Put us not to confusion, but deal with us according to thy meekness, and according to the multitude of thy mercies.

And deliver us according to thy wonderful works, and give glory to thy name, O Lord:

And let all them be confounded that shew evils to thy servants, let them be confounded in all thy might, and let their strength be broken.

And let them know that thou art the Lord, the only God, and glorious over all the world.

Now the king's servants that had cast them in, ceased not to heat the furnace with brimstone, and tow, and pitch, and dry sticks,

And the flame mounted up above the furnace nine and forty cubits:

And it broke forth, and burnt such of the Chaldeans as it found near the furnace,

But the angel of the Lord went down with Azarias and his companions into the furnace: and he drove the flame of the fire out of the furnace,

And made the midst of the furnace like the blowing of a wind bringing dew, and the fire touched them not at all, nor troubled them, nor did them any harm.

Then these three as with one mouth praised, and glorified, and blessed God in the furnace, saying:

(*Here the congregation kneels.*)

Blessed art thou, O Lord the God of our fathers: and worthy to be praised, and glorified, and exalted above all for ever: and blessed is the holy name of thy glory: and worthy to be praised, and exalted above all in all ages.

Blessed art thou in the firmament of heaven: and exceedingly to be praised, and exceeding glorious for ever.

Blessed art thou on the throne of thy kingdom, and exceedingly to be praised, and exalted above all for ever.

Blessed art thou, that beholdest the depths, and sittest upon the cherubims: and worthy to be praised and exalted above all for ever.

Blessed art thou in the firmament of heaven: and worthy of praise, and glorious for ever.

¶ *Then standing, sing the following song of praise, in the Sixth Tone. The first verse is repeated with every one of the Stichoi following it.*

PRAISE the Lord, and exalt him more and more unto all the ages.

O all ye works of the Lord, bless ye the Lord: praise and exalt him above all for ever.

O ye angels of the Lord, and the heavens of the Lord, bless ye the Lord.

O ye waters that be above the heaven, and all the powers of the Lord, bless ye the Lord.

O ye sun and moon, and O ye stars of heaven, bless ye the Lord.

O ye light and darkness, and night and day, bless ye the Lord.

O every shower and dew, and O all ye winds, bless ye the Lord.

O ye fire and heat, and, O ye winter and summer, bless ye the Lord.

O ye dews and storms of snow, and, O ye ice and cold, bless ye the Lord.

O ye frost and snow, lightning and clouds, bless ye the Lord.

O let the earth, mountains, and little hills, and, O all ye things that grow on the earth, bless ye the Lord.

O ye fountains, seas and rivers, whales, and all that move in the waters, bless ye the Lord.

O ye fowls of the air, beasts, and cattle, bless ye the Lord.

O ye children of men, and, O Israel, bless ye the Lord.

O ye priests of the Lord, and ye servants of the Lord, bless ye the Lord.

O ye spirits and souls of the righteous, and ye holy and humble men of heart, bless ye the Lord.

O Ananias, Azarias, and Misael, bless ye the Lord.

O ye Apostles, Prophets, and Martyrs of the Lord, bless ye the Lord.

Let us bless the Father, Son, and Holy Spirit.

We praise the Lord and exalt him more and more unto all the ages.

Let us praise, bless, and worship the Lord.

We praise the Lord and glorify him unto all the ages.

¶ *Then the little Synapte; and after the Exclamation,* For thou art holy, O our God, and unto thee do we address glory, O Father, *etc. the Choir singeth:*

Ye who have been baptized into Christ, have put on Christ. Alleluia.

The Epistle: Let all the earth adore thee, and sing to thee. Shout with joy to God, all the earth.

Section from the Epistle of St. Paul to the Romans (6:3-11)

YE brethren: As many of us as were baptized into Jesus Christ were baptized into his death.

For we are buried together with him by baptism into death; that as Christ is risen from the dead by the glory of the Father, so we also may walk in newness of life.

For if we have been planted together in the likeness of his death, we shall be also in the likeness of his resurrection.

Knowing this, that our old man is crucified with him, that the body of sin may be destroyed, to the end that we may serve sin no longer.

For he that is dead is justified from sin.

Now if we be dead with Christ, we believe that we shall live also together with Christ:

Knowing that Christ rising again from the dead, dieth now no more, death shall no more have dominion over him.

For in that he died to sin, he died once; but in that he liveth, he liveth unto God:

So do you also reckon, that you are dead to sin, but alive unto God, in Christ Jesus our Lord.

❡*Do not sing* Alleluia; *but immediately sing (seven times) the following Stichos, in the Seventh Tone, with its Stichoi, (as the Priest streweth bay leaves in the Temple and the church, as a sign of triumph and victory over death).*

Arise, O God, judge thou the earth; for thou shalt inherit among all the nations.

1. God hath stood in the congregation of gods, and being in the midst of them he judgeth gods.

2. How long will you judge unjustly: and accept the persons of the wicked?

3. Judge the needy and fatherless. Do justice to the humble and the poor.

4. Rescue the poor; and deliver the needy out of the hand of the sinner.

5. They have not known nor understood; they walk on in darkness. All the foundations of the earth shall be moved.

6. I have said: You are gods and all sons of the most High. But you, like men, shall die: and shall fall like one of the princes.

The Gospel: from St. Matthew (28:1 to end)

AND now in the end of the sabbath, when it began to dawn towards the first day of the week, came Mary Magdalen and the other Mary to see the sepulchre.

And behold there was a great earthquake. For an angel of the Lord descended from heaven, and coming rolled back the stone, and sat upon it.

And his countenance was as lightning, and his raiment as snow.

And for fear of him, the guards were struck with terror, and became as dead men.

And the angel answering, said to the women: Fear not you; for I know that you seek Jesus who was crucified.

He is not here, for he is risen, as he said. Come, and see the place where the Lord was laid.

And going quickly, tell ye his disciples that he is risen: and, behold, he will go before you into Galilee: there you shall see him. Lo, I have foretold it to you.

And they went out quickly from the sepulchre with fear and great joy, running to tell his disciples.

And behold Jesus met them, saying: All hail. But they came up and took hold of his feet, and adored him.

Then Jesus said to them: Fear not. Go, tell my brethren that they go into Galilee, there they shall see me.

Who when they were departed, behold some of the guards came into the city, and told the chief priests all things that had been done.

And they being assembled together with the ancients, taking counsel, gave a great sum of money to the soldiers,

Saying: Say you, His disciples came by night, and stole him away when we were asleep.

And if the governor shall hear of this, we will persuade him, and secure you.

So they taking the money, did as they were taught: and this word was spread abroad among the Jews even unto this day.

And the eleven disciples went into Galilee, unto the mountain where Jesus had appointed them.

And seeing him they adored: but some doubted.

And Jesus coming, spoke to them, saying: All power is given to me in heaven and in earth.

Going therefore, teach ye all nations: baptizing them in the name of the Father, and the Son, and of the Holy Spirit.

Teaching them to observe all things whatsoever I have commanded you: and behold I am with you all days, even to the consummation of the world.

¶And the rest of the Liturgy of St. Basil the Great. And instead of the Cherubicon, chant the following Troparion, in the Fifth Tone.

LET all mortal flesh keep silence and in fear and trembling stand, pondering nothing earthly minded. For the King of kings and the Lord of lords cometh forth to the faithful. Before him go the ranks of angels, with all the principalities and powers; the cherubim full of eyes and the six-winged seraphim covering their faces and chanting their Hymn, Alleluia, Alleluia, Alleluia.

Koinonikon: And the Lord was awaked as one out of sleep, and arose as one delivered to us. Alleluia.

¶And instead of We have seen the true Light, etc., sing:

Remember us merciful One as thou didst remember the thief in the kingdom of heaven.

Benediction: O Christ, our true God, by the intercessions of thy pure Mother, etc.

SEVENTH SECTION

Pentecostarion, or Book of Fifties

Being the Book which Includes the Services of the other Revolving Feasts, from the Sunday of Holy Easter to the Feast of All Saints, after the Epiphany.

✠

SUNDAY OF THE GREAT AND HOLY EASTER

1. MATINS

With the procession known as the Rush Procession

¶*A little before midnight, the Priest giveth the blessing, saying,* Glory to thee, our God, glory to thee; *and,* O heavenly King, *etc; and,* Holy God, *etc; and,* Lord, have mercy (*twelve times*); Glory and Now, *and* O come, let us worship, *etc.* (*three times*); *and Psalm 50. Then the Canon,* The children of them who were saved, *etc* (*pp. 882-883*). *The Kathisma in the Fourth Ode is not sung. And after the Ninth Ode of the Canon, is recited from inside the Sanctuary,* Holy God, *etc; and the Troparion,* When thou didst descend, *etc.* (*p. 185*); *then the Petitions and Benediction.*

¶*Then the High Priest, or Proto-priest appeareth at the Royal Door, in full vestments, carrying a lighted candle, from which those in the church light their candles as he and the Choir sing:*

COME ye, take light from the Light that is never overtaken by night. Come, glorify the Christ, risen from the dead.

¶*After this, the Procession, known as the* Rush, *begins. All the Clergy then come out of the Sanctuary, singing the following Troparion, in the Sixth Tone.*

To thy Resurrection, O Christ, our Saviour, the Angels in heaven sing. Make us also who are on earth, worthy to glorify thee with pure hearts.

⁋When they come to the appointed place, the Deacon crieth out, And that we may be worthy, *etc. Then the High Priest, or the Proto-priest, readeth the Second Eothina Gospel (p. 200), at the conclusion of which the Proto-priest crieth in a loud voice:*

Glory to the holy, consubstantial, life-giving and undivided Trinity, now, and ever, and unto ages of ages.[1]

⁋And immediately, sing in the Fifth Tone.

Christ is risen from the dead; by Death hath he trodden death, and upon those in tombs, hath he bestowed life.

⁋This is sung three times by the Priest, and six times by the Choir, with the following Stichoi.

1. Let God arise, and let his enemies be scattered: and let them who hate him flee from before his face.

2. As smoke vanisheth, so let them vanish away: as wax melteth before the fire.

3. So do sinners perish from before the face of God; and the righteous do rejoice.

4. This is the day which the Lord hath made; let us be glad and rejoice therein.

5. Glory be to the Father, and to the Son, and to the Holy Spirit.

6. Now and ever, and unto ages of ages, Amen.

⁋Then the Priest singeth in a loud voice, Christ is risen from the dead; by Death hath he trodden death, *and the Choir concludeth,* And upon those in the tombs, hath he bestowed life. *Then the Deacon saith the Great Synapte, i.e.,* In peace, let us pray to the Lord, *etc. (p. 65); and after the Priest's Exclamation,* For all glory, honour, and worship are due to thee, *etc. they enter the church singing the following Canon, in the First Tone (by John of Damascus).*

First Ode

TODAY is the Day of Resurrection! O nations, let us shine forth; for the Passover is the Passover of the Lord, in that Christ did make us pass from death to

---

[1] This piece is said instead of *Blessed be God,* etc. in the Matin and Vesper services on every day of the New Week.

life, and from earth to heaven, who now sing the song of victory and triumph.

Let us cleanse our senses that we may behold Christ shining like lightning with the unapproachable light of Resurrection, that we may hear him say openly, Rejoice! while we sing to him the hymn of victory and triumph.

Let the heavens rejoice, and the earth be glad, as is meet; and let the whole world, visible and invisible, feast; for Christ hath risen to everlasting joy.

Then: Christ is risen, etc. (*three times*).

Verily, Jesus is risen from the tomb, as he had foretold, and hath bestowed life eternal upon us, and great mercy (*once*).

❡ *Then the Little Synapte; and the Exclamation,* For thine is the might and thine are the kingdom, and the power, and the glory, O Father, *etc.*

Third Ode

COME, let us drink a new drink, not wondrously produced from a barren rock, but from the fount of incorruption, that hath come to us with the overflowing of Christ from the tomb, in whom we are strengthened.

Verily, all creatures have been filled with light, the heaven and the earth, and all that is below the earth. Let all creation, therefore, celebrate the Resurrection of Christ, in which it is strengthened.

O Christ Saviour, we were but yesterday buried with thee, and we shall rise with thee in thy Resurrection. We were but yesterday crucified with thee: glorify us with thee in thy kingdom.

❡ *Then,* Christ is risen, *etc.* (*three times*)*;* Verily, Jesus is risen, *etc.* (*once*). *Then the Little Synapte; and the Exclamation,* For thou art holy, our God, and unto thee do we address glory, *etc.*

The Hypakoe, in the Fourth Tone

THEY who were with Mary came before the dawn, found the stone rolled away from the sepulchre, and heard the angels say unto them, Why seek ye him as man with the dead, who dwells in light eternal?

Behold the grave wrappings; make haste and declare to the world that the Lord is risen, and hath caused death to die; for he is the Son of God, the Saviour of mankind.

Fourth Ode

UPON the divine watchtower let the God-spoken Habakuk stand and show us the angel attired in light, saying openly, Today is salvation to the world; for Christ is risen, Almighty as he is.

Verily, Christ hath been revealed as our Passover; for that he was a male opening a virginal womb; and for that he was Nourishment he was called a Lamb; and for that he is immaculate he was called blameless; and for that he is very God, he is called perfect.

Christ who is the crown of the year, blessed by us, hath been sacrificed for us of his free will, like a year-ling lamb, a cleansing Passover. Then on us the Sun of righteousness from the tomb did shine, brilliant, resplendent.

Before the symbolical ark, David, God's forefather, did leap and dance. Let us, therefore, the holy people, seeing the fulfillment of those symbols, rejoice with divine rejoicing; for Christ the Almighty is risen.

❡ *Then,* Christ is risen, *etc.* (*three times*); Verily, Jesus is risen, *etc.* (*once*); *the Little Synapte, and the Exclamation,* For thou art a good and philanthropic God, *etc.*

Fifth Ode

LET us rise early at morn, at the break of dawn, and let us instead of fragrant ointment bring pure praise to the Master. Let us behold Christ who is the Son of righteousness bringing life unto all.

O Christ, they who in hades' bonds are chained, seeing thy boundless lovingkindness, hastened with blithe feet, celebrating an eternal passover.

Let us, lamps in hand, come forth to meet Christ risen from the tomb, as we would a bridegroom. Let us celebrate in the feast-loving ranks the saving Passover of our God.

❡ *Then,* Christ is risen, *etc.* (*three times*); Verily, Jesus is risen, *etc.* (*once*); For thy Name hath been sanctified and glorified, *etc.*

Sixth Ode

O CHRIST, into the deepest abyss of earth thou didst descend, and didst break the unyielding everlasting bars which held men prisoner; and on the third day thou didst rise from the tomb as Jonah from the whale.

O Christ, thou who didst not break the locks of virginity in thy birth, didst rise from the tomb, keeping its seals intact, and didst open to us the gates of paradise.

O my Saviour, O thou living and unsacrificed offering, as thou art God, thou didst of thy free will offer thyself an offering to the Father. And when thou didst rise from the tomb, thou didst raise Adam and all his race with thee.

❡ *Then,* Christ is risen, *etc.* (*three times*); Verily, Jesus is risen, *etc.* (*once*); *the Little Synapte; and the Exclamation,* For thou art the King of peace and the Saviour of our souls, *etc.*

Kontakion, in the Eighth Tone

THOUGH thou, O deathless One, didst descend into the grave, thou didst destroy the power of hell and, as Victor, thou didst rise again, O Christ our God. Thou didst greet the ointment-bearing women, saying, Rejoice! Thou didst bestow peace upon thy Disciples, and resurrection upon those that are fallen.

Oikos

TO the Sun before the sun, as it set for a time in the grave, the ointment-bearing maidens came at dawn, seeking him as they would the day. And they shouted one to another, Come, let us, O friends, anoint with spices the life-bearing body, now buried; the body that raiseth fallen Adam, lying in the sepulchre. Come, let us hasten, as did the Magi, and fall down in worship; let us offer of our spices like unto their offerings, to him who is no longer wrapped in swaddling clothes, but in finest linen. Let us lament; let us weep; and let us cry, Master, arise, O thou who dost grant resurrection to the fallen.

THE GREAT AND HOLY EASTER SUNDAY

SYNAXARION

ON the Holy and Great Sunday of the Passover we celebrate the life-giving Resurrection of our Lord and God and Saviour Jesus Christ; for Christ alone did descend with condescension to fight hades; and he ascended, bringing the abundant spoils of victory which he had snatched.

Mary the Magdalene and the rest of the women (see Sunday of the Ointment-Bearing Women) who were present at the Saviour's Burial on Friday evening, returned that very day from Golgotha to the city and prepared ointment and spices, that they might come later and anoint the body of Jesus. They rested the next day, Saturday, in fulfillment of the commandment. And on the following day, which was Sunday and which the Evangelists call the first day of the week, which fell on the twenty-fifth of March, or thirty-six hours after the Death of life-giving Jesus, the women came to the sepulchre with their prepared ointments. And as they were pondering the difficulty of rolling the stone from the gate of the sepulchre, a great earthquake took place, an angel of the Lord came down, whose ap-

pearance was like lightning and his clothes like snow,
and rolled away the stone and sat thereon. The guards
trembled with fear, became like dead, and fled. But
the women entered the sepulchre and found not Jesus.
But they found two other angels in the form of men
dressed in white raiment who proclaimed to them the
Resurrection of the Saviour, commanding them to hasten and give the good news to the Disciples. In the
meantime Peter and John, who had received the report
from Mary the Magdalene (see July twenty-second),
hastened and entered the tomb and found there only the
linen clothes. They returned with great joy to the city,
and began to preach the supernatural Resurrection of
Christ, having seen him alive in truth five times that
very day.

For this joyful Resurrection we therefore celebrate
today, kissing one another in Christ with the brotherly
kiss, illustrating thereby the dissolution of the enmity
that was between us and God, and our reconciliation
through Christ. This Feast was called Passover from
the Jewish name; for Christ by his Passion and Resurrection translated us from the curse of Adam and the
bondage of Satan to the ancient liberty and bliss. As
for the day of the week, which is called in Hebrew, the
first day, being dedicated to our Lord for his glorification and magnification, it is called in Greek *Kuriake,*
or the Lord's Day. The Disciples transferred to it the
dignity of the sabbath after the law of the Old Testament, and prescribed that it be a holiday and a day of
rest.

To him be glory and power for ever and ever. Amen.

¶*And immediately after* In that we have beheld the Resurrection of
Christ, *etc. (three times p. 113); and,* Verily Jesus is risen, *etc.*

Seventh Ode

HE who did save the children from the furnace,
when he became Man, suffered like unto a mortal,
and with his sufferings invested the mortal with the

beauty of incorruption, who is the God of our fathers. To him alone be blessing and glory.

O Christ, the Godly-wise women with their minds did hasten with the ointment after thee. And he whom they sought, mourning him as dead, they now worshipped with joy, the living God. And to the Disciples they told the glad news of thy mystical Passover.

We celebrate the death of death, the destruction of hades, the first fruit of another and endless life. And as we leap with joy, we praise the Cause of these good gifts, the God of our fathers. Blessed and glorified be he alone.

In truth, how noble is this radiant and all-festal night of salvation; for it precedeth the proclamation of the light-bearing day of Resurrection, in which the timeless Light did shine forth bodily from the grave.

❡ *Then* Christ is risen, *etc.* (*three times*); Verily, Jesus is risen, *etc.* (*once*); *the Little Synapte; and the Exclamation,* May the might of thy kingdom be blessed and glorified, *etc.*

Eighth Ode

VERILY, this day, which is called holy, is the first day among sabbaths, their king and lord. It is the feast of feasts, the season of seasons, in which we bless Christ for evermore.

Come, let us on this famous day of Resurrection participate in the kingdom of Christ, and in the new fruit of the Vine which is for divine rejoicing. Praise him; for he is God for evermore.

O Zion, lift up thine eyes round about and see. For lo! these thy children have followed thee as God-lighted stars, from the west and from the north, from the sea and from the east, blessing the Christ in thee for evermore.

O Father Almighty, the Word, and the Spirit, one Nature in three Persons, God transcendent in Godhead and Essence, in thee have we been baptized, and thee do we bless for evermore.

¶ *Then,* Christ is risen, *etc.* (*three times*); *and* Verily, Jesus is risen, *etc.* (*once*)*; the Little Synapte; the Exclamation,* For thy Name hath been blessed, O Father, *etc. Then the Deacon crieth,* The Theotokos, Mother of Light, thee in songs of praise do we honour, magnifying. *Then the Choir singeth:*

Ninth Ode

SHINE, shine, O new Jerusalem; for the glory of the Lord hath risen upon thee. Rejoice and exult now, O Zion, and thou, O pure one, Theotokos, rejoice at the Resurrection of thy Son.

And how noble! O how dear! O how sweet is thy voice, O Christ; for thou hast verily made us a true promise, that thou shalt be with us to the end of time; a promise to which we believers hold, an anchor for our hopes, as we sing rejoicing.

O Christ, the perfect, most exalted Passover, O Wisdom of God, his Word and his Power, grant us that we may partake of thee more perfectly in thy kingdom's day, which setteth not.

¶ *Note: The above Troparia are sung twice each, with the following Magnifications.*

Magnify, O my soul, him who died of his own free will, and was buried, and did rise from the tomb on the third day.

Magnify, O my soul, the life-giving Christ, who is risen from the tomb on the third day.

Verily, Christ is a new Passover, a living Sacrifice, the Lamb of God who beareth the sin of the world.

Today doth all creation rejoice and is glad; for Christ is risen, and hades he hath despoiled.

Glory: Magnify, O my soul, the might of the indivisible and three-personed Godhead.

Now: Rejoice, O Virgin, rejoice; rejoice, O blessed one; rejoice, O glorified one; for thy Son is risen from the tomb on the third day.

¶ *Then conclude with the following Magnification.*

The angel spake to her that is full of grace, saying, O pure Virgin, rejoice; and I say also, Rejoice; for thy Son is risen from the tomb on the third day.

❡ *And immediately,* Shine, shine, *etc., followed by* Christ is risen, *etc.* *(three times); and* Verily, Jesus is risen, *etc. (once); the Little Synapte, and the Exclamation,* For thee do all the powers of heaven praise, *etc. And immediately:*

Exaposteilarion, in the Second Tone (three times)

WHEN thou didst fall asleep in the body as mortal, O thou who art Lord and King, thou didst abolish death. And on the third day thou didst surely rise, verily raising Adam from corruption, O thou incorruptible Passover, O Salvation of the world.

❡ *In the Einos, sing four Stichera of the Resurrection in the First Tone (p. 142); and the following Stichera of Easter with their Stichoi, in the Fifth Tone.*

LET God arise, and let his enemies be scattered; and let them who hate him flee from before his face.

Today Christ, our saving Passover, hath been revealed unto us a noble Passover; the Passover new and holy; the mystical Passover; the Passover all august; the blameless Passover; the great Passover; the Passover of the faithful; the Passover which openeth unto us the gates of paradise; the Passover which sanctifieth all the faithful.

As smoke vanisheth so let them vanish away; and like as wax melteth before the fire.

O come from the vision, ye women, heralds of good tidings, and say ye unto Zion, Receive from us the glad tidings of the joy of the Resurrection of Christ. Rejoice, O Jerusalem, and leap for joy, in that thou beholdest Christ the King like a bridegroom come forth from the grave.

So do sinners perish from before the face of God; and the righteous rejoicce.

When the ointment-bearing women stood, very early in the morning, before the tomb of the Life-giver, they found an angel sitting upon the stone. And he cried out unto them, saying, Why seek ye the Living among the dead? Why mourn ye the Incorruptible amidst corruption? Go, proclaim the glad tidings to his Disciples.

This is the day which the Lord hath made; let us rejoice and be glad therein.

The joyful Passover, the Passover of the Lord, the Passover all majestic hath shone upon us! The Passover in which we embrace one another with joy! Oh what a Passover, delivering from sorrow! For today from the tomb, as from a chamber Christ shone, and hath filled the women with joy, saying, Proclaim the glad tidings to the Apostles.

Glory and Now, in the Fifth Tone

TODAY is the Day of Resurrection! Let us shine with the Feast! Let us embrace one another. Let us say, Brethren! And because of the Resurrection, let us forgive all things to those who hate us, and in this wise, exclaim, Christ is risen from the dead; by his Death hath he trodden down death, and on those in the tombs hath he bestowed life.

❡ *Then* Christ is risen, *etc.* (*three times*).

❡*Note: In singing,* Today is the Day of Resurrection, *etc., the High Priest or the Proto-priest appeareth, standing in front of the Royal Door, holding the holy Gospel Book. Then all the Clergy and congregation come forward to kiss the Book and shake hands with the Priest. The congregation gathered, then shake hands one with another, One saith* Christ is risen, *while the other answereth,* He is risen indeed, *And so concludeth the Matin Service.*

2. THE MASS

❡*After* Blessed be the kingdom of the Father *etc. is sung,* Christ is risen, *etc. with its Stichoi, as in the beginning of Matins. And after the Great Synapte, the Choir singeth the following Antiphonies.*

1. Through the intercessions of the Theotokos, Saviour, save us.

Shout with joy to God, all the earth.

Sing ye a psalm to his Name; give glory to his praise.

Say unto God: How terrible are thy works.

Let all the earth adore thee, and sing to thee: Let it sing a psalm to thy Name, O most High.

Glory and Now: Through the intercessions of the Theotokos, etc.

2. O Son of God who didst rise from the dead, save us who sing unto thee, Alleluia.

May God have mercy upon us, and bless us.

May he cause the Light of his countenance to shine upon us, and may he have mercy upon us.

That we may know thy way upon the earth; thy salvation in all nations.

Let the people confess to thee, O God: let all people give praise to thee.

Glory: Save us, O Son of God, etc.

Now: O only-begotten Son and Word of God, etc.

3. Christ is risen, etc. (*with its Stichoi*).

Eisodikon: In the gathering places bless ye God the Lord from the springs of Israel. O Son of God, who didst rise from the dead, save us, who sing unto thee. Alleluia.

¶ *Then immediately,* Christ is risen, *etc. (three times); the Hypakoe,* They who were with Mary, *etc.* (*p. 923*)*; and the Kontakion,* Though thou, O deathless One didst descend, *etc.* (*p. 924*). *And instead of* Holy God, *sing:*

Ye who have been baptized into Christ, have put on Christ. Alleluia.[1]

The Epistle: This is the day which the Lord hath made; let us rejoice and be glad therein.

---

[1] This verse is sung throughout Passover Week.

Section from the Acts of the Saintly and Pure Apostles (1:1-8)

THE former treatise I have made, O Theophilus, of all things which Jesus began to do and to teach.

Until the day on which, giving commandments by the Holy Spirit to the apostles whom he had chosen, he was taken up:

To whom also he shewed himself alive after his passion, by many proofs; for forty days appearing to them, and speaking of the kingdom of God.

And eating together with them, he commanded them, that they should not depart from Jerusalem, but should wait for the promise of the Father, which you have heard (saith he) by my mouth.

For John indeed baptized with water: but you shall be baptized with the Holy Spirit, not many days hence.

They, therefore, who were come together, asked him, saying: Lord, wilt thou at this time restore again the kingdom to Israel?

But he said to them: It is not for you to know the times or moments, which the Father hath put in his own power.

But you shall receive the power of the Holy Spirit coming upon you, and you shall be witnesses unto me in Jerusalem, and in all Iudea, and Samaria, and even to the uttermost part of the earth.

The Gospel: from St. John (1:1-17)

IN the beginning was the Word, and the Word was with God, and the Word was God.

The same was in the beginning with God.

All things were made by him: and without him was made nothing that was made.

In him was life, and the life was the light of men.

And the light shineth in darkness, and the darkness did not comprehend it.

There was a man sent from God, whose name was John.

This man came for a witness, to give testimony of the light, that all men might believe through him.

He was not the light, but was to give testimony of the light.

That was the true light, which enlighteneth every man that cometh into this world.

He was in the world, and the world was made by him, and the world knew him not.

He came unto his own, and his own received him not.

But as many as received him, he gave them power to be made the sons of God, to them that believe in his name.

Who are born, not of blood, nor of the will of the flesh, nor of the will of man, but of God.

And the Word was made flesh, and dwelt among us, (and we saw his glory, the glory as it were of the only begotten of the Father,) full of grace and truth.

John beareth witness of him, and crieth out, saying: This was he of whom I spoke: He that shall come after me, is preferred before me: because he was before me.

And of his fulness we all have received, and grace for grace.

For the law was given by Moses; grace and truth came by Jesus Christ.

¶*And the rest of the Divine Liturgy of St. John Chrysostom. And on Especially, the Hermos of the Ninth Ode is sung, with its Magnification,* The angel did speak, *etc., and* Shine, *etc.*

Koinonikon: Receive ye the Body of Christ, and taste ye him that is found deathless.

¶*And instead of* We have seen the true Light, *etc, and* Blessed be the Name of the Lord, *etc. sing,* Christ is risen, *etc. And after the Benediction Prayer is said,* Christ is risen, *etc. (three times). then the Priest delivereth the following Sermon.*

SERMON OF ST. JOHN CHRYSOSTOM, ARCHBISHOP

OF CONSTANTINOPLE

Deacon: Bless, O Master.

Priest: Whosoever is a devout lover of God, let him enjoy this beautiful bright Festival. And whosoever is a grateful servant, let him rejoice and enter into the joy of his Lord. And if any be weary with fasting, let him now receive his penny. If any have toiled from the first hour, let him receive his due reward. If any have come after the third hour, let him with gratitude join in the Feast. And he that arrived after the sixth hour, let him not doubt; for he too shall sustain no loss. And if any have delayed to the ninth hour, let him not hesitate, but let him come too. And he that hath arrived only at the eleventh hour, let him not be afraid by reason of his delay; for the Lord is gracious and receiveth the last even as the first. He giveth rest to him that cometh at the eleventh hour, as well as to him that hath toiled from the first. Yea, to this one he giveth and upon that one he bestoweth. He accepteth works as he greeteth the endeavour. The deed he honoureth and the intention he commendeth.

Let all then enter into the joy of our Lord. Ye first and last receiving alike your reward; ye rich and poor, rejoice together. Ye sober and ye slothful, celebrate the day. Ye that have kept the fast and ye that have not, rejoice today; for the Table is richly laden. Fare ye royally on it. The calf is a fatted one. Let no one go away hungry. Partake ye all of the cup of faith. Enjoy ye all the riches of his goodness. Let no one grieve at his poverty; for the universal kingdom hath been revealed. Let no one mourn that he hath fallen again and again; for forgiveness hath risen from the grave. Let no one fear death; for the Death of our Saviour hath set us free. He hath destroyed it by enduring it. He spoiled hades when he descended thereto. He vexed it even as it tasted of his flesh. Isaiah foretold this when he cried, Thou, O hell, hast been vexed by encountering him below. It is vexed; for it is even done away with. It is vexed; for it is made a mockery. It is vexed; for it is destroyed. It is vexed; for it is annihilated. It is vexed; for it is now made captive. It took a body, and, lo! it discovered God. It took earth, and, behold, it encountered heaven. It took what it saw, and was overcome by what it did not see. O death, where is thy sting? O hades, where is thy victory? Christ is risen and thou art annihilated. Christ is risen, and the evil ones are cast down. Christ is risen, and the angels rejoice. Christ is risen, and life is liberated. Christ is risen, and the tomb is emptied of the dead; for Christ, having risen from the dead, is become the first-fruits of those that have fallen asleep. To him be glory and power for ever and ever. Amen.

¶ *And immediately the Troparion of the Saint,* Grace hath shone forth *etc.* (*p. 337*); *and after the Benediction,* O thou who didst rise from the dead, O Christ our true God, *etc., the Priest calleth out to the people,* Christ is risen, (*three times*); *and the people respond* Verily, he is risen (*each time*). *Then the Priest finally saith,* Let us adore his third-day Resurrection. Amen.

3. Prayers of Compline of Easter

¶ *These are said instead of the Midnight Prayer, Prayers of the Hours, and Compline Prayer, during the entire New Week, in the following order.*

Priest: Blessed be God, our God, etc.

Reader: Christ is risen, etc. (*three times*).

In that we have beheld the Resurrection of Christ, etc. (p. 113).

They who were with Mary did come before the dawn, etc. (p. 923).

Though thou, O deathless One, didst descend, etc. (p. 924).

IN the grave with the body, but in hades with the soul, in that thou art God; in paradise with the thief, and on the throne with the Father and the Spirit, wast thou, O Christ, filling all things, O infinite One.

Glory: Thy sepulchre, O Christ, the fountain of our Resurrection, hath been revealed as life-bearing, more radiant than paradise and fairer than any royal palace.

Now: Rejoice, O thou hallowed, divine abode of the most High! For through thee, O Theotokos, was joy given unto those who cry aloud to thee, Blessed art thou among women, O Lady all-undefiled.

❧ *Then,* Lord, have mercy, *(forty times); Glory and Now,* O thou who art more honourable than the cherubim, *etc;* Bless, O Father, in the Name of the Lord.

Priest: By the prayers of our fathers the saints, etc.

❧ *This arrangement to be said three times instead of the Midnight Prayer, Prayer of the Hours, and Compline in which we say:*

Prayer of Basil the Great

Blessed art thou, Almighty Master, who illuminatest the day, etc. (Sec. 7, Vespers of Pentecost Sunday).

❧ *Then,* Christ is risen, *etc; and the Benediction.*

4. VESPER PRAYER ON EASTER SUNDAY

❧ *About the third hour in the afternoon, the Priest standeth before the Holy Altar in vestments, and holding the censer in his hand, with which he maketh the sign of the cross, saying,* Glory to the Holy Consubstantial, *etc., he singeth,* Christ is risen, *etc. (three times), from the Sanctuary, and the Choir (six times) with the Stichoi. And after the Sunset Psalm, and the Great Synapte, sing on* O Lord, to thee have I cried, *the first six Stichera of the Oktoechos of the Second Tone. (p. 145).*

Glory, in the Second Tone

Come, let us all sing, etc. (p. 146).

Now: O Virgin, verily, the shadow of the law, etc. (p. 146).

❧ *Then the Eisodos with the Gospel,* O resplendent Light, *etc; and the following Prokeimenon, in the Seventh Tone.*

Who is so great a God as our God? Thou alone art the God that doest wonders.

❮ *Then the Priest saith,* And that we may be worthy, *etc., followed by the reading of the Gospel in several languages.*

The Gospel: from St. John (20:19-25)

1. Now when it was late that same day, the first of the week, and the doors were shut, where the disciples were gathered together, for fear of the Jews, Jesus came and stood in the midst, and said to them: Peace be to you.

2. And when he had said this, he showed them his hands and his side, The disciples therefore were glad when they saw the Lord.

3. He said therefore to them again: Peace be to you. As the Father hath sent me, I also send you.

When he had said this, he breathed on them; and he said to them: Receive ye the Holy Ghost.

Whose sins you shall forgive, they are forgiven them; and whose sins you shall retain, they are retained.

4. Now Thomas, one of the twelve, who is called Didymus, was not with them when Jesus came.

The other disciples therefore said to him: We have seen the Lord.

5. But he said to them: Except I shall see in his hands the print of the nails, and put my finger into the place of the nails, and put my hand into his side, I will not believe.

❮ *Then the Petitions,* Let us all say, *etc;* Vouchsafe, O Lord, *etc; and* Let us finish our evening petitions, *etc. (pp. 76-77) And after the Exclamation, sing the first Sticheron from the Aposticha of the Second Tone,* Thy Resurrection, O Christ, *etc. (p. 146); and the Easter Stichera with their Stichoi (p. 929). Glory and Now,* Today is the day of Resurrection, *etc;* Christ is risen, *etc. and the Benediction.*

THE NEW WEEK

❮ *The characteristics of the New Week, which falleth between Easter Sunday and the night of the Saturday preceding Thomas Sunday, are, first: The Service of Easter itself is observed therein, both Vespers and Matins, with the difference that the Stichera of the Resurrection Tones are sung in it consecutively, i.e., the Second Tone for Monday, the Third Tone for Tuesday, etc. Second: The three Doors of the Temple, the Northern, Southern, and Royal Doors, are kept open until Saturday evening, when they are closed. This is to indicate that Christ by his Resurrection from the dead hath opened for us the doors of the kingdom of heaven. Third: It is permitted to eat meat on all days of this week, which is considered as one continuous day of rejoicing. But during the remaining weeks to Pentecost Sunday, it is permitted to eat fish on Wednesday and Friday.*

FRIDAY OF THE NEW WEEK

On which is chanted the Service of the Life-Receiving Fountain of the Theotokos

SYNAXARION

OUTSIDE the city of Constantinople, in the suburb known as the Seven Towers, there was a very beautiful church called after the name of the exalted Theotokos. It was built in the middle of the fifth century by King Leo Thrax, who was also styled Makelles (or Butcher). The church was situated near a spring of water which accomplished many miracles at various times, healing diseases by the grace of the Theotokos. Hence it was called Life-Giving. The Church of Christ, therefore, celebrates today the consecration of this church, which, after the fall of the empire, was pulled down by edict, and the stones from its ruins were used in building the mosque named after Sultan Bayazid. There remained in the place of the beautiful old church only a small, mean, subterranean one covered by debris, to which one descended by twenty-five steps, and lighted faintly by lamps in the ceiling. The spring of holy water was close to the church on its western side, surrounded by an iron railing, through which one could see a few fish swimming. This condition remained till the year 1821, when the church was completely demolished, and the spring sank into the ground and disappeared without a trace.

However, in the resplendent days of Sultan Mahmoud when his Ottoman subjects were accorded religious freedom, the Orthodox sought permission to build at least the little church. On the twenty-seventh of July, 1833, work began on the construction of the Small Spring Church, which was restored, more beautiful than ever, then, when a second sultanic permission was received, a very beautiful and large church was built on the foundations of the first. The construction began on the fourteenth of September of the year 1833, and it was finished on the thirteenth of December, 1834. And on the second of February, Patriarch Costandios II of Constantinople, with twelve archbishops, consecrated the church with a great ecclesiastical celebration, which was witnessed by a great crowd of Christians, for the glorification of the Theotokos, and the pride of the Orthodox Church.

By the intercession of thy pure Mother, O Christ our God, have mercy upon us. Amen.

Kontakion, in the Eighth Tone

O THOU favoured of God, thou dost confer on me ineffably from thine ever-sprniging fountain the healing of thy grace. Wherefore, having, in an incomprehensible manner, given birth to the Word, I beseech thee to moisten me with the dew of thy grace, that I may cry unto thee, Rejoice, O water of Salvation!

❧*Note: From Easter Sunday to the Sunday of Pentecost, the Troparion,* O heavenly King, *etc. is not sung. And from Easter Sunday to its Leave-taking, instead of* Holy God, *etc;* O come, let us worship and fall down, *etc., in Matins, the Hours, and Vespers; and,* We have seen the true Light, *etc; in the Mass, say,* Christ is risen, *etc.*

NEW SUNDAY, OR THOMAS SUNDAY

❧*On this Sunday nothing pertaining to the Resurrection is sung, but all for the Feast.*

1. VESPERS

❧*After the Priest's blessing, say,* Christ is risen, *etc. (three times); then the Sunset Psalm, and the First Kathisma of the Psalms; and on* O Lord, to thee have I cried, *etc., take the Stichoi and chant the following Stichera, in the First Tone.*

INTO the gathering of the Disciples while the doors were shut, thou didst suddenly enter, O Jesus our Almighty God. And standing in their midst, thou didst grant them peace, and filled them with a holy spirit, commanding them to tarry and not depart from Jerusalem until they were vested with power from above. Wherefore, O our Light, Resurrection, and Peace, we cry unto thee, glory to thee. (*Repeat.*)

Eight days after thy Resurrection, O Lord, thou didst appear to thy Disciples in the place where they were gathered, and cried unto them, Peace unto you, showing thy hands and pure side to the doubting Disciple. Having, therefore, believed, he shouted unto thee, My Lord and my God, glory to thee. (*Repeat.*)

O good Christ, when thou enteredst unto thy Disciples, the doors being shut, Thomas, who was called Didymus, was not with them. Wherefore, he doubted what was told him. Albeit, thou didst not deem him unworthy for his lack of faith, rather assuring him of faith, by showing him thy pure side, and the wounds in thy hands and feet. Therefore, having sought and beheld, he confessed that thou art an unabstract God, and an unsimple Man, crying, My Lord and my God, glory to thee. (*Repeat.*)

The Disciples, being doubtful, the Saviour, after eight days, came to where they were gathered and granted them peace. Then he cried unto Thomas, Come, O Apostle, and probe the two palms which were pierced by the nails. O the delicacy of the beautiful unbelief of Thomas, as coming with the heart of an unbeliever to knowledge, he called out with fear, My Lord and my God, glory to thee. (*Repeat.*)

In the Second Tone

AFTER thy Resurrection, O Lord, thou didst stand in the midst of thy Disciples, as they were gathered together, the doors being shut, and bestowed peace on them. As for Thomas, having been convinced by beholding thy hands and side, he confessed that thou art Lord, God, and Saviour of those who put their trust in thee, O Lover of mankind.

Verily, Jesus approached the Disciples, the doors being shut, and granted them safety and the passing away of fear. Then he pointed to Thomas and said, Why believest thou not in my Resurrection from the dead? Reach hither thy hand and thrust it into my side. See and know; for thy lack of faith shall teach every one my Passion and Resurrection, and they shall all shout with thee, My Lord and my God, glory to thee.

Glory and Now, in the Sixth Tone

THOU didst come to thy Disciples, O Christ, the doors being shut, but through design thou didst not find Thomas with them; for he said, I will not believe until I behold the Master, view the side from which blood and water issued for baptism, observe the wound through which he healed man from the great wound, and see that he is not a ghost, but of body and bones. Wherefore, O thou who didst tread down death and convinced Thomas, O Lord, glory to thee.

¶And in the Aposticha, the following Stichera, in the Fourth Tone.

WHAT miraculous wonder, that lack of faith became conviction of faith; for Thomas exclaimed, Unless I see, I will not believe. Wherefore, when he searched the side he spoke of the Godhead of the Incarnate, who is Son of God, and knew that he verily did suffer in the flesh, and thus cried proclaiming the Risen God, shouting in a loud voice, My Lord and my God, glory to thee.

Stichos: Praise the Lord, O Jerusalem, Praise thy God, O Zion.

What miraculous wonder, that grass should touch fire and be safe; for Thomas cast his hand into the fire of the side of Jesus Christ God, and was not consumed

by touching him. Verily, the obstinate soul turned
with fervour to true faith, and he shouted from the
depth of his spirit, Thou art my Master and my God
who didst rise from the dead. Glory to thee.

Stichos: Because he hath strengthened the bolts of
thy gates, he hath blessed thy children within thee.

What miraculous wonder! John did lean against
the World's bosom, yet Thomas was made worthy to
probe his side. Albeit, that one drew therefrom the
depth of theology and dread dispensation; this one
was privileged to announce to us openly, and reveal
the mystery of his Resurrection, crying, My Lord and
my God, glory to thee.

Glory and Now, in the Fifth Tone

HOW great is the multitude of thine infinite compassion, O Lover of mankind; for because of thy
long-suffering thou wast struck by the Jews, wast examined by an Apostle, and deeply probed by those
who denied thee. How wast thou incarnated? How
wast thou crucified, O thou who hast not possessed sin?
Albeit, make us understand, as Thomas, that we may
call out to thee, My Lord and my God, glory to thee.

Troparion, in the Seventh Tone (three times)

WHILE the tomb was sealed, thou didst shine forth
from it, O Light. While the doors were closed,
thou didst come in to thy Disciples, O Christ God,
Resurrection of all, renewing in us through them an
upright spirit, according to the greatness of thy mercy.

2. MATINS

Kathismata, in the First Tone

AS the Disciples were gathered in the upper chamber of Zion, for fear of the Jews, thou didst enter
unto them, O good One. Thou didst stand in their
midst, the doors being shut, and filled them with joy

when thou didst show them the wounds of thy hands and unpolluted side, saying unto the doubting Disciple, Reach out thy hand, examine, probe, that I am he who suffered for thy sake.

Thou didst stand in the midst of the Disciples, the doors being shut, O Christ, Life of all, and showed them thy side, hands, and feet together, a prelude to belief in thy Resurrection from the tomb. But Thomas happened not to be there. Therefore, spake he, saying If I see not with mine own eyes, I will not be convinced by your words.

When the Lord rose from the tomb and appeared ineffably to the Disciples, he said, Having seen, O Thomas, my side and the prints of the nails why believest thou not in my Resurrection? But Didymus, being convinced, called out to the Creator, saying, Thou art verily my Lord and my God.

¶ *Then the Anabathmoi,* From my youth, *etc. (p. 50); and the following Prokeimenon.*

Praise thy Lord, O Jerusalem, Praise thy God, O Zion. Because he hath strengthened the bolts of thy gates, he hath blessed thy children within thee.

¶ *Then the First Gospel of the Eothina.*

¶ *The Katabasias for Easter; and instead of* O thou who art more honourable, *etc., sing the Ninth Ode, in the First Tone.*

O most radiant lamp, the Theotokos, the immeasurable honour, which is more exalted than all creatures, with praises do we magnify thee.

On thy all-radiant day, most resplendent with the light of grace, O Christ, in which thou didst appear in the comeliness of beauty to thy Disciples, with praises do we magnify thee.

O thou whose side was probed and touched with the earthly palm, not burned by the fire of thine immaterial Divinity, with praises do we magnify thee.

O Christ, who didst rise from the tomb, being God, though we have not beheld thee, yet have we with eager hearts believed in thee, and with songs of praise do we magnify thee.

❡ *Then the Hermos of the Ninth Ode from the Easter Canon with its Magnification, i.e.* The angel did speak, *etc; and,* Shine, *etc.*

Exaposteilarions

BE not faithless, O Thomas, to me who was wounded for thy sake. And having probed my wounds with thy hands, be of one mind with the Disciples, and proclaim I am a living God. (*Repeat.*)

Today the fragrance of spring is shed forth, and the new creation shall rejoice. Today the locks shall be lifted from the doors with the faithlessness of the beloved Thomas, as he shouteth out, Thou art my Lord and my God.

❡ *In the Einos, four Prosomia for Thomas, in the First Tone.*

AS thou didst not break the seals of the tomb at thy dread Resurrection, O life-giving Christ, so didst thou enter unto thy glorious Apostles, the doors being shut, and made them glad. And at once thou didst bestow on them an upright spirit, for thy countless mercies. (*Repeat.*)

When thou appeared among thy Disciples, O Lord, Thomas, who is called Didymus, was not there. Therefore, he doubted the fact of thy Resurrection, and unto those who had seen thee he cried, saying, Except I thrust my hand into his side, in the prints of the nails, I will not believe that he is risen.

Verily, Christ called unto Thomas, saying, Probe as thou wilt; thrust in thy hand and know me, that I have earthly flesh, bones, and body. Be not doubtful, but believe as the rest. But that one shouted, crying, Glory to thy Resurrection, O thou who art my Lord and my God.

Glory and Now, in the Sixth Tone

EIGHT days after thy Resurrection, O Jesus, King, the Word, and only Son of the Father, thou didst appear to thy Disciples, the doors being shut, granting them thy peace. And to the Disciple who believed not thou didst show the marks, saying, Reach out and probe my hands, feet, and incorruptible side. But he, being convinced, cried out unto thee, saying, My Lord and my God, glory to thee.

3. THE MASS

¶ *The Antiphonies and Eisodikon for the Passover; the Troparion for Thomas; and the following Kontakion, in the Eighth Tone.*

WITH his anxiously searching right hand, O Christ God, Thomas did probe thy life-giving side; for when thou didst enter, the doors being shut, he shouted with the rest of the Disciples, crying, Thou art my Lord and my God.

¶ *Then conclude with the Kontakion,* Though thou. O deathless One, *etc. (p. 924)*.

The Epistle: Great God is our Lord and of great power. Praise ye the Lord; for he is good.

Section from the Acts of the Saintly and Pure Apostles (5:12-20)

IN those days: By the hands of the apostles were many signs and wonders wrought among the people; (and they were all with one accord in Solomon's porch).

And of the rest durst no man join himself unto them; but the people magnified them.

And the multitude of men and women who believed in the Lord, was now increased:

Insomuch that they brought forth the sick into the streets, and laid them on beds and couches, that when Peter came, his shadow at the least, might overshadow any of them, and they might be delivered from their infirmities.

And there came also together to Jerusalem a multitude out of the neighbouring cities, bringing sick persons, and such as were troubled with unclean spirits; who were all healed.

Then the high priest rising up, and all they that were with him, (which is the heresy of the Sadducees,) were filled with envy.

And they laid hands on the apostles, and put them in the common prison.

But an angel of the Lord by night opening the doors of the prison, and leading them out, said

Go, stand and speak in the temple to the people all the words of this life.

The Gospel: from St. John

Now when it was late that same day, etc. (p. 212).

¶ And on, Especially, the Hermos of the Ninth Ode of the Canon of Thomas, O most radiant lamp, etc. (p. 943).

SYNAXARION

AS the Disciples were gathered together on the Sunday following the Resurrection, in a room with the doors closed, Jesus entered miraculously, and, standing in their midst, greeted them in his usual way, saying, Peace be unto you: and he showed them his hands, feet, and side. Then, taking some broiled fish and honey, he ate before them, and thus assured them of his Resurrection. But Thomas, who was not then with the Disciples, believed not their testimony concerning Christ's Resurrection, but said positively, Unless I see the print of the nails in his hands and of the spear in his side I will not believe. Eight days after, on the day corresponding to this one, as the Disciples were gathered together, and Thomas with them, Jesus came, while the doors were locked, as at the first time. He stood in their midst and said, Peace be unto you. Then to Thomas, Reach hither thy hand, and thrust it into my side; and be not faithless, but believing.

And when Thomas beheld the Master's hands and side, he cried out in faith, My Lord and my God, thus clearly illustrating the two Natures of Christ, the human and the divine. *(St. Luke 24:36-43 and St. John 20:19-28.)*

Koinonikon: Praise the Lord, O Jerusalem. Praise thy God, O Zion.

❡*And instead of* We have seen the true Light, *etc., sing* Christ is risen, *etc. until the Feast of the Ascension.*

SUNDAY OF THE OINTMENT-BEARERS

❡*On* O Lord, to thee have I cried, *the Stichera of the Resurrection of the Second Tone; and the following three for the Ointment-bearers in the Same Tone.*

EARLY, at dawn, the ointment-bearing women arose, and carrying ointments, came to the Lord's tomb. And not attaining their desire, the pious women pondered the removal of the stone, addressing one another and saying, Where are the seals of the grave? Where are Pilate's watchmen and the security of his great care? And lo, an angel, radiant as lightning, proclaimed to them that of which they were ignorant, addressing them and saying, Why, wailing, seek ye the Living who produceth life for mankind? Christ our God hath risen from the dead, since he is Almighty, bestowing on all, life, incorruptibility, illumination, and the Great Mercy.

Why mingle ye tears with the ointment, O women Disciples? Behold, the stone hath been rolled away, and the sepulchre is empty. Behold corruption trodden under of Life, the seals bearing clear witness, the guards of the rebellious fast asleep, the dead saved by the body of God, and hades mourning. Hasten ye with joy, and tell the Disciples that Christ, who is First-born of the dead, who caused death to die, shall go before you into Galilee.

The ointment-bearers, O Christ, rose up early and hastened to thy tomb, seeking to anoint with oils thine incorruptible body. But when the glad tidings were brought to them by the words of the angel, with signs of joy they proclaimed to the Apostles that the Element of our salvation had risen, leading death captive, and granting the world life eternal and the Great Mercy.

Glory, in the Sixth Tone

THE ointment-bearing women, O Saviour, came to thy tomb; and when they beheld the seals, not finding thy body, they hurried anxiously, wailing and saying, Who hath stolen our Hope? Who hath taken away a naked, embalmed corpse, the only consolation to his Mother? Woe! how hath the dead-reviving One died? And how was he buried who spoiled hades? But arise thou, by thine own power after three days, as thou didst say, and save our souls.

¶*And Now,* O Virgin, verily, the shadow of the law, *etc.* (*p.146*).

¶*And in the Aposticha, the First Sticheron of the Second Tone for the Resurrection,* Thy Resurrection, O Christ Savior, *etc.* (*p. 146*), *the Paschals* (*p. 929*). *Glory,* O thou who puttest on Light like a robe, *etc.* (*p. 881*); *and Now,* Today is the Day of Resurrection, *etc.* (*p. 930*). *Then the Troparia, in the Second Tone.*

When thou, O immortal life, etc. (p. 147).

THE pious Joseph, having brought down thy pure body from the Tree, wrapped it in fine linen, embalmed it with ointment, provided for it, and laid it in a new tomb. But thou didst verily rise, after three days, O Lord, granting the world the Great Mercy.

Verily, the angel came to the tomb and said to the ointment-bearing women, The ointment is meet for the dead, but Christ is shown to be remote from corruption. But cry ye, The Lord is risen, granting the world the Great Mercy.

2. MATINS

❡ *The Kathismata, Blessings, Hypakoe, Anabathmoi, and Prokei-*
menon for the Resurrection, in the Second Tone; the Fourth Gospel
of the Eothina; the Katabasias for the Resurrection; and instead of
O *thou who art more honourable, etc., sing the Ninth Ode for Easter,*
Shine, *etc., and what followeth it.*

❡ *The Exaposteilarion for Easter, and the following.*

HEAR the voice of gladness, O women; for I have trodden down rebellious hades, and raised the world from corruption. Wherefore, hasten ye and proclaim the glad tidings to my beloved; for I desire that joy shall break forth thence upon my creation, whence first came forth sorrow.

❡ *And in the Einos, the first four Stichera of the Second Tone (p.*
150); then the Paschals (p. 929); Glory; the Second Eothina;
They who were with Mary, *etc. (p. 201); and* Now, Today is the
Day of Resurrection, *etc. (p. 930).*

❡ *In the Mass, the Antiphonies and Eisodikon for Easter; then the*
Troparion for the Resurrection, When thou, O immortal Life, *etc;*
(p. 147) and The pious Joseph, *etc; and* Verily, the angel, *etc. (p.*
948); and the following Kontakion, in the Fourth Tone.

WHEN thou didst speak to the ointment-bearing women with joy, thou didst end the wailing of Eve the first mother, by thy Resurrection, commanding thy Disciples to proclaim that the Saviour is risen from the tomb.

❡ *Then conclude with the Kontakion of Easter,* Though thou, O
deathless One, *etc. (p. 924).*

The Epistle: The Lord is my strength and praise.
The Lord chastising hath chastised me.

Section from the Acts of the Saintly and Pure Apostles (6:1-7)

IN those days, the number of the disciples increasing, there arose a murmuring of the Greeks against the Hebrews, for that their widows were neglected in the daily ministrations.

Then the twelve calling together the multitude of the disciples, said: It is not reason that we should leave the word of God, and serve tables.

Wherefore, brethren, look ye out among you seven men of good reputation, full of the Holy Spirit and wisdom, whom we may appoint over this business.

But we will give ourselves continually to prayer, and to the ministry of the word.

And the saying was liked by all the multitude. And they chose Stephen, a man full of faith, and of the Holy Spirit, and Philip, and Prochorus, and Nicanor, and Timon, and Parmenas, and Nicolas, a proselyte of Antioch.

These they set before the apostles; and they praying, imposed hands upon them.

And the word of the Lord increased; and the number of the disciples was multiplied in Jerusalem exceedingly: a great multitude also of the priests obeyed the faith.

The Gospel: from St. Mark (15:43 to end; 16:1-8)

AT that time: Joseph of Arimathea, a noble counsellor, who was also himself looking for the kingdom of God, came and went in boldly to Pilate, and begged the body of Jesus.

But Pilate wondered that he should be already dead, and sending for the centurion, he asked him if he were already dead.

And when he had understood it by the centurion, he gave the body to Joseph.

And Joseph, buying fine linen, and taking him down, wrapped him up in the fine linen, and laid him in a sepulchre which was hewed out of a rock. And he rolled a stone to the door of the sepulchre.

And Mary Magdalen, and Mary the mother of Joses, beheld where he was laid.

And when the sabbath was past, Mary Magdalen, and Mary the mother of James, and Salome, brought sweet spices, that coming they might anoint Jesus.

And very early in the morning, the first day of the week, they came to the sepulchre, the sun being now risen.

And they said one to another: Who shall roll us back the stone from the door of the sepulchre?

And looking, they saw the stone rolled back. For it was very great.

And entering into the sepulchre, they saw a young man sitting on the right side, clothed with a white robe: and they were astonished.

Who saith to them; Be not affrighted; you seek Jesus of Nazareth, who was crucified: he is risen, he is not here, behold the place where they laid him.

But go, tell his disciples and Peter that he goeth before you into Galilee; there you shall see him, as he told you.

But they going out, fled from the sepulchre. For a trembling and fear had seized them: and they said nothing to any man; for they were afraid

¶*And on Especially,* The angel spake, *etc.* (*p. 929*); *and* Shine, *etc.* (*p. 928*).

SYNAXARION

AT the beginning of the year 32 Jesus frequently came to Galilee, preaching and performing miracles. Many women then left their homes and followed him, ministering unto him out of their own means, even when he was on the Cross and in the sepulchre. Finally, they went with ointment, which they had prepared to anoint his body (see Easter Sunday). And from this they were called ointment-bearing women. We know the names of only seven of these. They are those named Mary the Magdalene (see July twenty-second), Mary the mother of James and Joses, the wife of Cleophas, Joanna the wife of Chuza, Herod Antipas' steward, Salome the mother of the sons of Zebedee, and Susanna (St. Mt. 27:56; St. Lk. 8:2-3; and St. Jn. 19:25), and Mary and Martha, the sisters of Lazarus. As for the rest, the Evangelists are silent concerning their names.

Along with these we celebrate also in honour of Joseph and Nicodemus, who were two Disciples of Christ, secretly at the beginning. It is probable that Nicodemus was a Jerusalemite, one of the leaders of the Jews, of the sect of Pharisees, versed in the law and the Holy Scriptures. Early in the preaching of salvation, Nicodemus believed in Christ, having come to him at night (St. Jn. 3:1-21). And at his Burial also he came carrying a mixture of myrrh and aloes, a hundred menas in weight, or a hundred pounds, for the purpose of scenting and embalming, and as a gesture of reverence and love to the divine Master. Joseph, on the other hand, was a rich and noble man of the city of Ramah, or Arimathea, and one of the Privy Council of Jerusalem. At the death of Jesus he ventured to approach Pilate and ask for the undefiled body of Christ, and he and Nicodemus accompanied it to the sepulchre and buried it there. It was said that the garden where Jesus was buried was one of the possessions of Joseph, and that he had prepared therein a tomb for himself, hewed in the rock. As time did not permit the digging out of another tomb and preparing it, he placed the body of Jesus in his own tomb. That seems to be the meaning of Matthew the Evangelist when he says, And laid it in his own tomb, which he had hewn out in the rock. (St. Mt. 27:60).

¶ *The Koinonikon of Easter,* Christ is risen, *etc; and the Benediction.*

The Sunday of the Paralytic

1. Vespers

¶ *On O Lord, to thee have I cried, seven Stichera for the Resurrection, in the Third Tone; and the following three for the Paralytic, in the First Tone.*

O CHRIST God, the Compassionate, who by thy pure palm didst create man, thou didst come to heal the sick. By thy word thou didst make the paralytic to stand in the sheep's pool of blood. Upon the son of the Canaanitish woman thou didst have mercy, and the request of the centurion thou didst not deny. Wherefore, we cry unto thee, O Almighty Lord, glory to thee. (*Repeat.*)

The paralytic, who was like unto a dead man unburied, having seen thee, O Lord, cried out, Have mercy upon me; for my bed hath become my grave. Of what use is my life? I have no need for the sheep's pool; for there is none to put me into the pool. Albeit, I come to thee, O Fountain of all healing, that, with all I may cry unto thee, Lord Almighty, glory be to thee.

Glory, in the Fifth Tone

JESUS went up to Jerusalem, to the sheep's pool which in Hebrew was called Bethesda, having five porches. And there lay a great multitude of the sick; for the angel of the Lord went down at certain seasons and moved the water, granting healing to those who approached in faith. And the Lord saw there a man with a chronic disease, and he said unto him, Wilt thou be made whole? And the sick man replied, I have no man, when the water is moved, to put me into the pool. I have wasted my money on physicians and received no help from any one. But the physician of soul and body said unto him, Take up thy bed and walk, proclaiming through the regions my might and the greatness of my mercy.

❡*And Now for the Resurrection, in the Third Tone,* O Lady of exceeding honour, *etc.* (*p. 153*).

❡*And in the Aposticha, the first Sticheron of the Third Tone. Then the Paschals.*

Glory, in the Eighth Tone

IN Solomon's porch many sick were lying. But in the midst of the Feast Christ found there a paralytic who had been impotent for thirty-eight years. To him he called out in a lordly tone, Wilt thou be whole? And the infirm replied, Lord, I have no man, when the water is moved, to put me into the pool. And the Lord said unto him, Take up thy bed. Behold thou hast become whole, sin not again. Wherefore, O Lord, by the intercessions of the Theotokos, send us thy Great Mercy.

And Now. Today is the day of Resurrection, *etc; the Troparion and Theotokion of the Third Tone (p. 154).*

2. MATINS

The Fifth Gospel of the Eothina; and the Katabasias for Easter.

The Exaposteilarion for Easter: then the following:

THE all-compassionate and philanthropic Lord, standing by the sheep's pool to heal infirmities, found a man who had been lying there for many years. And he called out to him, saying, Take up thy bed and go in the straight way.

In the Einos, the first four Stichera of the Third Tone; then the Paschals.

Glory, in the Eighth Tone

THE paralytic was not healed by the pool; but the word renewed him; nor was he hindered by his infirmity of many years; for the effect of thy voice was seen to be sharper than the infirmity. Wherefore, he cast down his heavy burden and carried the weight of his bed, a testimony to the abundance of thy compassion. Glory to thee.

And Now, Today is the day of Resurrection, *etc.*

And in the Mass, the Antiphonies and the Eisodikon for Easter. Troparion of the Third Tone, and for the Patron Saint of the church; and the following Kontakion, in the Third Tone.

Arouse, O Lord, with thy divine providence my soul, sorely paralytic with divers sins and unseemly deeds, as thou didst raise the paralytic of old, that being saved, I may cry, saying, Glory to thy might, O compassionate Christ.

❰ *Then conclude with the Kontakion of the Passover,* Though thou, O deathless One, *etc.* (*p. 924*).

The Epistle: Sing praises to our God.   Sing ye praises to our king, sing ye.
O clap your hands all ye nations.   ·

Section from the Acts of the Saintly and Pure Apostles (9:32-42)

IN those days: As Peter passed throughout all quarters, he came down also to the saints which dwelt at Lydda.

And he found there a certain man named Eneas, who had kept his bed for eight years, who was ill of the palsy.

And Peter said to him: Eneas, the Lord Jesus Christ healeth thee: arise, and make thy bed. And immediately he arose.

And all that dwelt at Lydda and Saron, saw him: who were converted to the Lord.

And in Joppe there was a certain disciple named Tabitha, which by interpretation is called Dorcas. This woman was full of good works and almsdeeds which she did.

And it came to pass in those days that she was sick, and died. Whom when they had washed, they laid her in an upper chamber.

And forasmuch as Lydda was nigh to Joppe, the disciples hearing that Peter was there, sent unto him two men, desiring him that he would not be slack to come unto them.

And Peter rising up, went with them. And when he was come, they brought him into the upper chamber. And all the widows stood about him weeping, and shewing him the coats and garments which Dorcas made them.

And they all being put forth, Peter kneeling down prayed, and turning to the body, he said: Tabitha, arise. And she opened her eyes; and seeing Peter she sat up.

And giving her his hand, he lifted her up. And when he had called the saints and the widows, he presented her alive.

And it was made known throughout all Joppe; and many believed in the Lord.

The Gospel: from St. John 5:1-15)

AT that time: Jesus went up to Jerusalem.

Now there is at Jerusalem a pond, called Probatica, which in Hebrew is named Bethsaida, having five porches.

In these lay a great multitude of sick, of blind, of lame, of withered; waiting for the moving of the water.

And an angel of the Lord descended at certain times into the pond; and the water was moved. And he that went down first into the pond after the motion of the water, was made whole, of whatsoever infirmity he lay under.

And there was a certain man there, that had been eight and thirty years under his infirmity.

Him when Jesus had seen lying, and knew that he had been now a long time, he saith to him: Wilt thou be made whole?

The infirm man answered him: Sir, I have no man when the water is troubled, to put me into the pond. For whilst I am coming, another goeth down before me.

Jesus saith to him: Arise, take up thy bed, and walk.

And immediately the man was made whole: and he took up his bed, and walked. And it was the sabbath that day.

The Jews therefore said to him that was healed: It is the sabbath; it is not lawful for thee to take up thy bed.

He answered them: He that made me whole, he said to me, Take up thy bed, and walk.

They asked him therefore: Who is that man who said to thee, Take up thy bed, and walk?

But he who was healed, knew not who it was; for Jesus went aside from the multitude standing in the place.

Afterwards, Jesus findeth him in the temple, and saith to him: Behold thou art made whole: sin no more, lest some worse thing happen to thee.

The man went his way, and told the Jews, that it was Jesus who had made him whole.

¶*And on Especially sing,* The angel spake *etc; then the following instead of* Shine, *etc.*

WE believers in unison bless thee, O Virgin, crying, Rejoice, O gate of the Lord. Rejoice, O living city. Rejoice, O thou from whom did rise upon us from the dead the Light of Resurrection, he who was born of thee.

SYNAXARION

NEAR one of the gates of Jerusalem, known as the Sheep Gate, there was a pool also known as the Sheep Pool, because they brought there sacrificial beasts and washed their insides therein. The gate was likely called by that name because it was near the pool. Or the gate might have been called so because through it passed sheep and other beasts acceptable for sacrifice The pool itself, it seems, was pentagonal in shape, having five porches, with corresponding arches, under which a multitude of people, afflicted with various diseases, sat awaiting the troubling of the waters; for an angel of the Lord used to come down and trouble the water, and whoever first stepped in after the troubling of the water was healed of whatever disease he had.

There sat the impotent man, whose story is told us in the Gospel section read on this day, and who had

had an infirmity thirty and eight years. When Jesus
saw him he said unto him, Wilt thou be made whole?
The impotent man, who was undoubtedly a poor man
and a stranger, replied in a meek voice, I have no man,
when the water is troubled, to put me into the pool.
And Jesus said to him, Rise, take up thy bed, and walk.
Immediately the man was healed, and he carried his
bed and walked before all the people, going to his
home happy and pleased. According to accurate
scholars, Jesus healed this man in Easter of the year
32 when he went up to Jerusalem for the Feast and
remained there, teaching, and performing miracles.
Unquestionably, too, he healed him on the sabbath, as
we are told by John the Evangelist (St. John 5:1-19).

❧ *The Koinonikon for Easter; and* Christ is risen, *etc; and the Benediction.*

THE WEDNESDAY OF MID-PENTECOST

Troparion, in the Eighth Tone

IN the midst of this Feast, O Saviour, give thou my
thirsty soul to drink of the waters of true worship;
for thou didst call out to all, saying, Whosoever is
thirsty, let him come to me and drink. Wherefore, O
Christ our God, Fountain of life, glory to thee.

Kontakion, in the Fourth Tone

IN the midst of the Mosaic Feast thou didst say to
those present, O Christ God, Master and Maker of
all, Come ye, and receive the water of immortality.
Wherefore, we kneel to thee, crying out in faith, saying, Grant us thy mercy and compassion; for thou art
the Fountain of life.

The Epistle: Acts (14:6-18) and The Gospel: from St. John (7:14-31)

SYNAXARION

AFTER Jesus performed the miracle of healing the impotent man, the Jews, and especially the Pharisees and Scribes, were moved with envy to persecute him. They sought to kill him on the pretense that he did not keep the sabbath, performing miracles thereon instead. From there Jesus went to Galilee, and in the midst of the Feast of Tabernacles he went up again to Jerusalem, where he taught. The Jews wondered at the wisdom of his words, saying, How does this man know the Scriptures when he is not educated? But he rebuked them at first for their lack of faith and their disobedience of the law. Then he proved to them from the law that they were seeking to kill him unjustly on the flimsy accusation that he scorned the law by healing the paralytic man on the sabbath.

As there is a clear connection between what Jesus spoke in the midst of the above-mentioned feast and the story of the paralytic which was recited on the previous Sunday, and since we have reached the middle of the period between the Passover and Pentecost, the Church set this feast after the Sunday known as the Sunday of the Impotent Man, to be a bond between the two great Feasts, calling it Mid-Pentecost, applying to it literally the Gospel section which begins, And when the feast had drawn to its middle, although its context refers to the Feast of Tabernacles (St. John 7).

The Jews had three big feasts, namely, the Passover, Pentecost, and the Feast of Tabernacles. They celebrated the Passover on the fifteenth of March, being the first month in their year, commemorating the command that was given to eat the lamb on its eve, and to smear the doors of their homes with its blood, as it commemorates their delivery from bondage to the Egyptians, the death which passed over their first-born and their crossing of the Red Sea. It is also called the Feast of Unleavened Bread because in it they eat unleavened bread for seven days. Pentecost was celebrated by the Jews on the fiftieth day after the Passover, commemorating their arrival from Egypt at Mount Sinai, their reception of the law from God, and their entrance into the land of promise, when they ate bread, after the manna, which they had eaten until the forty years had ceased. For this reason they used to offer God on this feast two loaves of the purest of the new wheat. Thirdly, the Feast of Tabernacles was celebrated by them on the seven days between September fifteenth and twenty-second, when they sat under tents and tree branches in memory of their ancestors who lived in tents and tabernacles for forty years in the wilderness (Exodus 12:19 and Lev. 23).

Koinonikon: The Lord saith, He that eateth my flesh, and drinketh my blood abideth in me, and I in him.

THE SUNDAY OF THE SAMARITAN WOMAN

1. VESPERS

¶ *On* O Lord, to thee have I cried, *sing four for the Resurrection in the Fourth Tone; and the following three for Mid-Pentecost, in the Fourth Tone.*

THE middle of those days which begin with the saving Resurrection and end with the divine Feast of Pentecost hath come. Verily it shineth forth, being possessed of illumination from both and uniting both, and hath appeared manifesting the honour of the Lord's Ascension and radiating therewith.

Verily, Zion heard and was glad; for it hath received the glad tidings of Christ's Resurrection. Her believing children also rejoiced at beholding it. Yea, it shall wash away, cleansing with the Spirit, the stain of

Christ's murder, making ready with joy and feasting for the delightful Mid-Feast, for the sake of both of them.

The rich overflowing of the divine Spirit over all, as it hath been written, hath drawn near; for the deferment of the clear promise that lieth not, given by Christ to his Disciples after his Death, Burial, and Resurrection, giveth promise of the appearance of the Comforter.

In the First Tone

AT the sixth hour thou didst come to the well, O Fountain of wonder, to ensnare the fruit of Eve; for that one, at the very same hour, had been driven from paradise by the serpent's temptation. Then the Samaritan woman came to draw water, and when thou didst see her, O Saviour, thou didst say to her, Give me water to drink, and I will fill thee with everlasting water. And that chaste woman hastened at once to the city and said to the crowds, Come and see Christ the Lord, the Saviour of our souls.

In the Second Tone

WHEN the compassionate Lord came to the well, the Samaritan woman asked him, saying, Give me the water of faith, O Giver of life, that I may take the water of baptism for delight and for salvation; O Lord, glory to thee.

In the Same Tone

VERILY, the Son, the Word of the Father, equal to him in eternity and beginninglessness, the Fountain of wonders, came to the spring, where a woman of Samaria came to draw water. And when the Saviour saw her he said unto her, Give me water to drink, and go call thy husband. But she, addressing him as Man and not as God, wished to withhold herself from him, say-

ing, I have no husband. And the Master replied, Thou
hast said the truth, that thou hast no husband; for thou
hast had five husbands, and he whom thou now hast is
not thy husband. And she, bewildered by these words,
went to the city and shouted to the crowds, saying, Come
and behold Christ who granteth the world the Great
Mercy.

Glory, in the Sixth Tone

AT Jacob's well Jesus met the Samaritan woman. He
who screened the earth with clouds, asked water of
her. What wonder, that he who rideth on the cherubim
converseth with an adulterous woman. He asked water
who suspended the earth on the waters. He seeketh water who caused the springs of water and their lakes to
overflow. Yea, that he may draw to him the truth en-
snared by the contending enemy, and give her water to
drink who was inflamed with ugly vices; for he alone is
compassionate and the Lover of mankind.

❡*And now for the Resurrection, in the Fourth Tone,* David the Prophet who became through thee, O Theotokos, *etc. (p. 161).*

❡*In the Aposticha, the first Sticheron of the Fourth Tone; and the
Paschals.*

Glory, in the Eighth Tone

WHEN by thine ineffable dispensation thou didst
appear on earth, O Christ, the Samaritan woman,
hearing thy philanthropic words, left off drawing water
at the well and hastened, saying to those in the city,
Come and behold the Knower of hearts: perchance he
may be the expected Christ whose is the Great Mercy.

❡*And Now,* Today is the Day of Resurrection, *etc; The Troparion
for the Resurrection of the Fourth Tone; and for Mid-Pentecost,* In
the midst of this Feast, *etc. (p. 958).*

2. MATINS

❧ *The Seventh Gospel of the Eothina and the Katabasias for Easter.*

❧ *The Exaposteilarions for Easter and the following two for the Samaritan woman and for Mid-Pentecost.*

O ALMIGHTY Saviour, who didst pour forth water for the Hebrews from a solid rock, thou didst come to the Land of Samaria, and addressed a woman, seeking of her water to drink, whom thou didst attract to faith in thee, and who hath now attained life in the heavens everlastingly.

Thou didst come to the Temple in the midst of the Feast and cried out, He who is athirst, let him come to me and drink of the water of everlasting life, through which ye may all be kept in the grace of bliss and life never ending.

❧ *And in the Einos, the first four Stichera of the Fourth Tone (p. 165); and the Paschals.*

Glory, in the Sixth Tone

O UR Saviour Jesus, the Element of life, came to the Spring of Jacob, the head of the patriarchs, and was about to drink water at the hand of a Samaritan woman. But she intercepted him by telling him that the Jews had no dealings with the Samaritans. Albeit, the wise Creator turned her by the sweetness of his words rather to seek of him the water of everlasting life, which, when she received, she proclaimed to all, saying, Come and see the Knower of secrets, God who hath appeared in the flesh to save mankind.

❧ *And Now,* Today is the Day of Resurrection, *etc.*

❧ *And in the Mass, the Antiphonies and the Eisodikon for Easter; the Troparia for the Resurrection of the Fourth Tone and for Mid-Pentecost,* In the midst of the Feast, *etc; and for the Patron Saint of the church; and the following Kontakion, in the Eighth Tone.*

The Samaritan woman of everlasting memory, coming to the well in faith, beheld thee, O Water of wisdom, from which, having abundantly drunk, she inherited the kingdom on high for ever.

❡ *And conclude with the Kontakion of the Passover,* When thou, O immortal one, *etc.*

The Epistle: How great are thy works, O Lord! Thou hast made all things in wisdom. Bless the Lord, O my soul.

Section from the Acts of the Saintly and Pure Apostles (11:19 to end)

IN those days: When the disciples had been dispersed by the persecution that arose on occasion of Stephen, went about as far as Phenice and Cyprus and Antioch, speaking the word to none, but to the Jews only.

But some of them were men of Cyprus and Cyrene, who, when they were entered into Antioch, spoke also to the Greeks, preaching the Lord Jesus.

And the hand of the Lord was with them: and a great number believing, were converted to the Lord.

And the tidings came to the ears of the church that was at Jerusalem, touching these things: and they sent Barnabas as far as Antioch.

Who, when he was come, and had seen the grace of God, rejoiced: and he exhorted them all with purpose of heart to continue in the Lord.

For he was a good man, and full of the Holy Ghost and of faith. And a great multitude was added to the Lord.

And Barnabas went to Tarsus to seek Saul: whom, when he had found, he brought to Antioch.

And they conversed there in the church a whole year; and they taught a great multitude, so that at Antioch the disciples were first named Christians.

And in these days there came prophets from Jerusalem to Antioch:

And one of them named Agabus, rising up, signified by the Spirit, that there should be a great famine over the whole world, which came to pass under Claudius.

And the disciples, every man according to his ability, purposed to send relief to the brethren who dwelt in Judea:

Which also they did, sending it to the ancients, by the hands of Barnabas and Saul.

The Gospel: from St. John (4:5-42)

AT that time: As Christ cometh to a city of Samaria, which is called Sichar, near the land which Jacob gave to his son Joseph.

Now Jacob's well was there. Jesus therefore being wearied with his journey, sat thus on the well. It was about the sixth hour.

There cometh a woman of Samaria, to draw water. Jesus saith to her: Give me to drink.

For his disciples were gone into the city to buy meats.

Then that Samaritan woman saith to him: How dost thou, being a Jew, ask of me to drink, who am a Samaritan woman? For the Jews do not communicate with the Samaritans.

Jesus answered, and said to her: If thou didst know the gift of God, and who he is that saith to thee, Give me to drink; thou perhaps wouldst have asked of him, and he would have given thee living water.

The woman saith to him: Sir, thou hast nothing wherein to draw, and the well is deep; from whence then hast thou living water?

Art thou greater than our father Jacob, who gave us the well, and drank thereof himself, and his chidlren, and his cattle?

Jesus answered, and said to her: Whosoever drinketh of this water, shall thirst again; but he that shall drink of the water that I will give him, shall not thirst for ever:

But the water that I will give him, shall become in him a fountain of water, springing up into life everlasting.

The woman saith to him: Sir, give me this water, that I may not thirst, nor come hither to draw.

Jesus saith to her: Go, call thy husband, and come hither.

The woman answered, and said: I have no husband. Jesus said to her: Thou hast said well, I have no husband:

For thou hast had five husbands: and he whom thou now hast, is not thy husband. This thou hast said truly.

The woman saith to him: Sir, I perceive that thou art a prophet.

Our fathers adored on this mountain, and you say, that at Jerusalem is the place where men must adore.

Jesus saith to her: Woman, believe me, that the hour cometh, when you shall neither on this mountain, nor in Jerusalem, adore the Father.

You adore that which you know not: we adore that which we know; for salvation is of the Jews.

But the hour cometh, and now is, when the true adorers shall adore the Father in spirit and in truth. For the Father also seeketh such to adore him.

God is a spirit; and they that adore him, must adore him in spirit and in truth.

The woman saith to him: I know that the Messias cometh (who is called Christ); therefore, when he is come, he will tell us all things.

Jesus saith to her: I am he, who am speaking with thee.

And immediately his disciples came; and they wondered that he talked with the woman. Yet no man said: What seekest thou? or, why talkest thou with her?

The woman therefore left her waterpot, and went her way into the city, and saith to the men there:

Come, and see a man who has told me all things whatsoever I have done. Is not he the Christ?

They went therefore out of the city, and came unto him.

In the mean time the disciples prayed him, saying: Rabbi, eat.

But he said to them: I have meat to eat, which you know not.

The disciples therefore said one to another: Hath any man brought him to eat?

Jesus saith to them: My meat is to do the will of him that sent me, that I may perfect his work.

Do not you say, There are yet four months, and then the harvest cometh? Behold, I say to you, lift up your eyes, and see the countries; for they are white already to harvest.

And he that reapeth receiveth wages, and gathereth fruit unto life everlasting: that both he that soweth, and he that reapeth, may rejoice together.

For in this is the saying true: That it is one man that soweth, and it is another that reapeth.

I have sent you to reap that in which you did not labour: others have laboured, and you have entered into their labours.

Now of that city many of the Samaritans believed in him, for the word of the woman giving testimony: He told me all things whatsoever I have done.

So when the Samaritans were come to him, they desired that he would tarry there. And he abode there two days.

And many more believed in him because of his own word.

And they said to the woman: We now believe, not for thy saying: for we ourselves have heard him, and know that this is indeed the Saviour of the world.

❡ *On Especially,* The angel spake, *etc., then the following instead of* Shine, *etc.*

REJOICE and be glad, O gate of the divine Light; for Jesus who disappeared in the tomb hath risen with greater radiance than the sun, illuminating all believers, O Lady favoured of God.

SYNAXARION

THE city of Shechem was one of the most ancient cities in the land of promise. It was built at the foot of Mount Gerizim, east of Jericho, where the sons of Israel of old recited their blessings (Deut. 11:29). In the neighbourhood of this city Jacob, as he was returning from Mesopotamia, bought a village, which was called at the time of Christ, Jacob's Well, or Jacob's Spring. And when Jacob died in Egypt, he left this as a special inheritance to Joseph (Gen. 33:19 and 48:22). As for the above-mentioned city, it became the capital of the ten tribes of Israel, before the city of Samaria was built. And because the people of Israel there indulged in the worship of idols, the rest of the Jews, who stood fast in piety and true worship, ridiculed the others, and according to some, called their city *Sukhar,* which means drunkenness; and from it comes the word *sokhara,* which means intoxicating drinks.

To this city came Jesus about midday. And being tired from travel and the heat, he sat down at the above-mentioned well. A little after, the woman whose story is told in today's lesson, came to draw water, and there followed a long conversation between her and Jesus, in which she heard something about her own secrets, and she believed in him, and through her believed many of the Samaritans of her home town (St. John 4:5-42).

We may also note that Shalmaneser, king of the Assyrians, took captive the ten tribes of Israel in the year 721 before Christ, transporting them as a whole to Babylon and Media. Then he brought together various peoples from Babylon and Media and sent them to Samaria. These people were idol-worshippers, who learned the worship of the Jews, believing in God the Creator but also preserving the worship of idols. They accepted of the Holy Bible only the five books of Moses, contemptuously rejecting the rest, and considering themselves the true descendants of Abraham and Jacob. Those Judaized idol worshippers the Jews called

Samaritans, because they were strangers and Gentiles.
They did not mingle with them, as appears from the
words of the Samaritan woman to Jesus that, The Jews
have no dealings with the Samaritans (St. John 4:9).
From this the name Samaritan in the Gospel accounts
assumes the meaning of degradation.

¶ *The Koinonikon for Easter,* Christ is risen, *etc; and the Benediction.*

The Sunday of the Blind Man

1. Vespers

¶ *On* O Lord, to thee have I cried, *sing seven for the Resurrection
of the Fifth Tone; and the following three for the Blind Man, in
the Second Tone.*

TO himself did the blind man think and say, Is it, I
wonder, for the sin of my parents that I was born
without eyes? Have I become an example because of the
faithlessness of the Gentiles? I cease not from asking,
When is the night, when is the day? My feet have no
more strength from the impact of the stones; for I have
never seen the sun shining, nor have I seen my Creator
in any form whatever. Albeit, I beseech thee, O Christ,
God, to look upon me and have mercy upon me. (*Repeat.*)

Passing through the Temple, Jesus saw a man blind
from his birth. He had compassion on him and put
clay on his eyes, then said to him, Go to the pool of Siloam
and wash. And as he washed his sight was restored,
and he declared the glorification of God. But
his relatives said unto him, Who opened thine eyes
whom none that see could heal? And he answered them,
crying, A man called Jesus. He told me to go and wash
in the pool of Siloam, and now I see. He is in truth
Christ the Messiah, of whom Moses wrote in the law.
He is the Saviour of our souls.

Glory, in the Fifth Tone

PASSING by, O Lord, thou didst find a man blind from birth. The Disciples, in surprise, asked thee, Teacher, who did sin, this man or his parents that he was born blind? But thou, O Saviour, answered them, saying, Neither hath this man sinned, nor his parents: but that the works of God should be made manifest in him. I must work the works of him that sent me, which none else can work. And as thou saidst that, thou didst spit on the ground, and make clay thereof, and anoint his eyes. And thou didst say unto him, Go, wash in the pool of Siloam. And when he washed, he began to shout unto thee, Lord, I believe. And he worshipped thee. Wherefore, we, too, cry out to thee, Have mercy upon us.

¶ *And Now for the Resurrection of the Fifth Tone,* The sign of the Virgin bride, *etc.* (*p. 169*).

¶ *And in the Aposticha the first Sticheron of the Fifth Tone,* O Christ Saviour, *etc.* (*p. 170*) *then the Paschals.*

Glory, in the Eighth Tone

O CHRIST God, supersensuous Sun of justice, O thou, who by thy pure touch, didst lighten the eyes of him who was born lightless from his mother's womb, lighten thou our souls' eyes, and reveal us as sons of the day, that we may cry out to thee in faith, Bountiful is thy compassion toward us, O Lover of mankind, glory to thee.

¶ *And Now,* Today is the Day of Resurrection, *etc; the Troparion and Theotokion of the Fifth Tone* (*p. 171*).

2. MATINS

¶ *The Eighth Gospel of the Eothina; and the following Katabasias, in the Fifth Tone.*

1. Let us praise our God and only Saviour, who led his people in the sea with feet unmoistened, and

drowned Pharaoh and all his soldiers; for he is glorified.

3. Strengthen my mind by the power of thy Cross, O Christ, that I may praise and glorify thy saving Ascension.

4. Hearing have I heard, O Lord, of the might of thy Cross, through which paradise was thrown open. Wherefore, I cried, Glory to thy might, O Lord.

5. Early in the morning we come unto thee, O Lord, Save us; for thou art our God, and beside thee we know no other.

6. The depth hath encompassed me, O Lord, and the whale hath become my tomb. But I cried unto thee and thou didst save me by thy right hand, O Lover of mankind.

7. O thou who didst save the youths praising thee from the midst of the consuming fire, blessed art thou, O God of our fathers.

8. Praise, O Priests, God the Son, begotten of the Father before the ages, who, in these last days, was incarnate from a virgin Mother. Exalt him more and more, O nations, unto the end of time.

9. In unison we believers do magnify thee, because thou didst give birth in time to the Word not bound by time; and in manner trancending every mind and utterance, thou became the Theotokos.

❡ *The Exaposteilarion for Easter; and the following two for the Blind Man.*

LIGHTEN, O Lord, my supersensuous eyes, made blind by the gloom of sin. Anoint them, O compassionate One, with humility; wash them with the tears of repentance.

Our Saviour, passing by, found a sightless man. Spitting on the ground, he made clay and anointed him therewith, sending him to Siloam to wash. And when he washed he saw thy light again, O Christ.

❡ *In the Einos, the first four Stichera of the Fifth Tone (p. 174); then the Paschals.*

Glory, in the Eighth Tone

WHO shall declare thy might, O Christ? And who shall number the multitude of thy wonders? For as thou wast doubly seen in thy goodness on earth, so didst thou doubly grant healing to the sick; for not only didst thou heal the bodily eyes of the man born blind from the womb, but the eyes of his soul also. Wherefore, he confessed that thou art a hidden God, granting all the Great Mercy.

¶*And Now,* Today is the Day of Resurrection, *etc.*

¶*In the Mass, the Antiphonies and the Eisodikon for Easter; the Troparion for the Resurrection of the Fifth Tone, (p. 171); and for the Patron Saint of the church; and the following Kontakion, in the Fourth Tone.*

TO thee I come, O Christ, blinded in my soul's eyes, like the man blind from his birth, crying unto thee in repentance, Thou art the Light of transcendent radiance to those who who are in darkness.

¶*Then conclude with the Kontakion of Easter,* Though thou O deathless One, *etc. (p. 924).*

The Epistle: Thou, O Lord shalt preserve us, and keep us from this generation.

Save me, O Lord; for the godly man ceaseth.

Section from the Acts of the Saintly and Pure Apostles
(16:16-34)

IN those days, as we the disciples went to prayer: A certain girl, having a pythonical spirit, met us, who brought to her masters much gain by divining.

This same following Paul and us, cried out, saying: These men are the servants of the most high God, who preach unto you the way of salvation.

And this she did many days. But Paul being grieved, turned, and said to the spirit: I command thee, in the name of Jesus Christ, to go out from her. And he went out the same hour.

But her masters, seeing that the hope of their gain was gone, apprehending Paul and Silas, brought them into the marketplace to the rulers.

And presenting them to the magistrates, they said: These men disturb our city, being Jews;

And preach a fashion which it is not lawful for us to receive nor observe, being Romans.

And the people ran together against them; and the magistrates rending off their clothes, commanded them to be beaten with rods.

And when they had laid many stripes upon them they cast them into prison, charging the gaoler to keep them diligently.

Who having received such a charge, thrust them into the inner prison, and made their feet fast in the stocks.

And at midnight, Paul and Silas praying, praised God. And they that were in prison, heard them.

And suddenly there was a great earthquake, so that the foundations of the prison were shaken. And immediately all the doors were opened, and the bands of all were loosed.

And the keeper of the prison, awaking out of his sleep, and seeing the doors of the prison open, drawing his sword, would have killed himself, supposing that the prisoners had been fled.

But Paul cried with a loud voice, saying: Do thyself no harm, for we all are here.

Then calling for a light, he went in and trembling, fell down at the feet of Paul and Silas.

And bringing them out, he said: Masters, what must I do, that I may be saved?

But they said: Believe in the Lord Jesus, and thou shalt be saved, and thy house.

And they preached the word of the Lord to him and to all that were in his house.

And he, taking them the same hour of the night, washed their stripes, and himself was baptized, and all his house immediately.

And when he had brought them into his own house, he laid the table for them, and rejoiced with all his house, believing God.

The Gospel: from St. John (9:1-38)

AT that time: When Jesus passed by, he saw a man, who was blind from his birth:

And his disciples asked him: Rabbi, who hath sinned, this man, or his parents, that he should be born blind?

Jesus answered: Neither hath this man sinned, nor his parents; but that the works of God should be made manifest in him.

I must work the works of him that sent me, whilst it is day: the night cometh, when no man can work.

As long as I am in the world, I am the light of the world.

When he had said these things, he spat on the ground, and made clay of the spittle, and spread the clay upon his eyes,

And said to him: Go, wash in the pool of Siloe, which is interpreted, Sent. He went therefore, and washed, and he came seeing.

The neighbours therefore, and they who had seen him before that he was a beggar, said: Is not this he that sat and begged? Some said: This is he.

But others said: No, but he is like him. But he said: I am he.

They said therefore to him: How were thy eyes opened?

He answered: That man that is called Jesus made clay, and anointed my eyes, and said to me: Go to the pool of Siloe, and wash. And I went, I washed, and I see.

And they said to him: Where is he? He said: I know not.

They bring him that had been blind to the Pharisees.

Now it was the sabbath, when Jesus made the clay, and opened his eyes.

Again therefore the Pharisees asked him, how he had received his sight. But he said to them: He put clay upon my eyes, and I washed, and I see.

Some therefore of the Pharisees said: This man is not of God, who keepeth not the sabbath. But others said: How can a man that is a sinner do such miracles? And there was a division among them.

They say therefore to the blind man again: What sayest thou of him that hath opened thy eyes? And he said: He is a prophet.

The Jews then did not believe concerning him, that he had been blind, and had received his sight, until they called the parents of him that had received his sight,

And asked them, saying: Is this your son, who you say was born blind? How then doth he now see?

His parents answered them, and said: We know that this is our son, and that he was born blind:

But how he now seeth, we know not; or who hath opened his eyes, we know not: ask himself: he is of age, let him speak for himself.

These things his parents said, because they feared the Jews: for the Jews had already agreed among themselves, that if any man should confess him to be Christ, he should be put out of the synagogue.

Therefore did his parents say: He is of age, ask himself.

They therefore called the man again that had been blind, and said to him: Give glory to God. We know that this man is a sinner.

He said therefore to them: If he be a sinner, I know not: one thing I know, that whereas I was blind, now I see.

They said then to him: What did he to thee? How did he open thy eyes?

He answered them: I have told you already, and you have heard: why would you hear it again? will you also become his disciples?

They reviled him therefore, and said: Be thou his disciple; but we are the disciples of Moses.

We know that God spoke to Moses: but as to this man, we know not from whence he is.

The man answered, and said to them: Why, herein is a wonderful thing, that you know not from whence he is, and he hath opened my eyes.

Now we know that God doth not hear sinners: but if a man be a server of God, and doeth his will, him he heareth.

From the beginning of the world it hath not been heard, that any man hath opened the eyes of one born blind.

Unless this man were of God, he could not do any thing.

They answered, and said to him: Thou wast wholly born in sins, and dost thou teach us? And they cast him out.

Jesus heard that they had cast him out: and when he had found him, he said to him: Dost thou believe in the Son of God?

He answered, and said: Who is he, Lord, that I may believe in him?

And Jesus said to him: Thou hast both seen him; and it is he that talketh with thee.

And he said: I believe, Lord. And falling down, he adored him.

¶ *On Especially,* The angel spake, *etc;* (*p.929*) ; *and* Shine, *etc.* (*p. 928*) ; *and the Benediction.*

SYNAXARION

WHILE Jesus was leaving the Temple on a sabbath he met on the way this young blind man, whose story is told in the Gospel section read on this day. The young man was blind from his mother's womb, of age, and incurable after every human effort. When Jesus saw him, he spit on the ground, and making clay of the spittle, anointed the eyes of the man, and said to him, Go, wash in the Pool of Siloam (which is by interpretation, Sent). This pool was a famous spring of water in Jerusalem, because it was used so often by the people, and it flowed around the city walls from the eastern side and emptied into the Pool of Siloam.

Jesus did not send the blind man to that pool to wash his eyes that had been anointed with the clay, because the water had any special property to heal blind men's eyes, but to test the faith and obedience of him who was sent, and also to give the miracle greater fame, that it might become known of all people beyond doubt. The blind man believed the words of Jesus and obeyed his command. He washed and returned whole and seeing, not blind as he had been. As the Gospel section read on this day (St. John 9:1-38) tells the story of the blind man in detail, especially making clear his confession of the Name of his Healer, in his answer to the questioners, how he preached him before the Pharisees, and how finally he was expelled with curses by the enemies of truth because he explained the truth, and because of his confession, we need not expand it here.

❡ *The Koinonikon for Easter,* Christ is risen, *etc; and the Benediction.*

THE WEDNESDAY BEFORE ASCENSION

In which Easter is taken leave of, and through which its entire service is sung

ASCENSION THURSDAY

1. VESPERS

❡ *After the Sunset Psalm, sing on* O Lord, to thee have I cried, *the following six Idiomelons, in the Sixth Tone.*

THE Lord ascended to the heavens to send the Comforter into the world. Wherefore, the heavens made ready his throne, and the clouds his mount. The angels wonder as they see a man more exalted than they. The Father receiveth into his bosom him who is eternally with him. The Holy Spirit commandeth all the angels, Lift your heads, O princes, and all ye nations, clap your hands; for Christ hath ascended whither he was before. (*Repeat.*)

The cherubim were surprised, O Lord, at thine Ascension, when they beheld him who sitteth on them ascending upon the clouds. Wherefore, we praise thee; for thy mercy is true, glory to thee.

Having beheld thine Ascension on the holy mountains, O Christ, the Splendour of the Father's glory, we praise the likeness of thy radiant appearance. We worship thy Passion and honour thy Resurrection, glorifying thy glorious Ascension. Have mercy upon us.

When the Apostles saw thee ascending in the clouds, life-giving Christ, they frowned deeply, and mourned with tears, saying, Leave us not orphans, O Master, thy servants whom thou didst love in thy mercy; for thou art compassionate. But send us thy most Holy Spirit as thou didst promise to illumine our souls.

When thou didst fulfill the mystery of thy dispensation, O Lord, thou didst take thy Disciples and ascend the Mount of Olives, passing through the firmament of heaven. Wherefore, O thou who becamest humble for my sake, and who didst ascend to the place from which thou couldest not be separated, send down thy most Holy Spirit to illumine our souls.

Glory and Now, in the Same Tone

FROM the Fatherly bosom thou wast inseparable, O sweet Jesus, and on earth thou didst behave like a man. Today hast thou ascended in glory from the Mount of Olives; and by thy pity thou didst raise our fallen nature and seat it with the Father. Wherefore, the ranks of the incorporeal celestials were amazed and overtaken by surprise. They trembled from wonder and magnified thy love to mankind. With them we terrestrials also glorify thy condescension to us, and thine Ascension from us, imploring and saying, O thou who didst fill thy Disciples and thy Mother the Theotokos with immeasurable joy by thine Ascension, make us worthy by their beseechings of the joy of thy chosen ones, for the sake of thy Great Mercy.

¶ *Then the Eisodos; and,* O resplendent Light, *etc; the daily Prokeimenon; and the following readings.*

First Reading: from the Prophecy of Isaiah the Prophet (2:2-3)

THESE sayings the Lord doth say: In the last days the mountain of the house of the Lord shall be prepared on the top of mountains, and it shall be exalted above the hills, and all nations shall flow unto it.

And many people shall go, and say: Come and let us go up to the mountain of the Lord, and to the house of the God of Jacob, and he will teach us his ways, and we will walk in his paths.

Second Reading: from the Prophecy of Isaiah (62:10 to end; 63:1-3; 7-9)

THESE sayings the Lord doth say: Go through, go through the gates, prepare the way for the people, make the road plain, pick out the stones, and lift up the standard to the people.

Behold the Lord hath made it to be heard in the ends of the earth, tell the daughter of Sion: Behold thy Saviour cometh: behold his reward is with him, and his work before him.

And they shall call them, The holy people, the redeemed of the Lord. But thou shalt be called: A city sought after, and not forsaken.

Who is this that cometh from Edom, with dyed garments from Bosra, this beautiful one in his robe, walking in the greatness of his strength. I, that speak justice, and am a defender to save.

Why then is thy apparel red, and thy garments like theirs that tread in the winepress?

I have trodden the winepress alone, and of the Gentiles there is not a man with me: I have trampled on them in my indignation, and have trodden them down in my wrath, and their blood is sprinkled upon my garments, and I have stained all my apparel.

I will remember the tender mercies of the Lord, the praise of the Lord for all the things that the Lord hath bestowed upon us, and for the multitude of his good things to the house of Israel, which he hath given them according to his kindness, and according to the multitude of his mercies.

And he said: Surely they are my people, children that will not deny: so he became their saviour.

In all their affliction he was not troubled, and the angel of his presence saved them: in his love, and in his mercy he redeemed them, and he carried them and lifted them up all the days of old.

Third Reading: from the Prophecy of Zecharia the Prophet (14:1; 4; 8-11)

THESE sayings the Lord doth say: The days of the Lord shall come; his feet shall stand in that day upon the mount of Olives, which is over against Jerusalem toward the East.

And it shall come to pass in that day, that living waters shall go out from Jerusalem: half of them to the east sea, and half of them to the last sea: they shall be in summer and in winter.

And the Lord shall be king over all the earth: in that day there shall be one Lord, and his name shall be one.

And all the land shall return even to the desert, from the hill to Remmon to the south of Jerusalem: and she shall be exalted, and shall dwell in her own place, from the gate of Benjamin even to the place of the former gate, and even to the gate of the corners: and from the tower of Hananeel even to the king's wine presses.

And people shall dwell in it, and there shall be no more an anathema: but Jerusalem shall sit secure.

¶ *And in the Litiya, the following piece, in the Fourth Tone.*

WHEN thou didst fulfill the mystery hidden from the generations since the ages, since thou art good, O Lord, thou didst come with thy Disciples to the Mount of Olives, and with thee was thy Mother, O Maker and Creator of all; for she, who more than all suffered maternally at thy Passion, should likewise enjoy more than all the joy of thy humanity's honouring, O Master, which having also attained by thine Ascension to the heavens, we glorify exceedingly thy mercies upon us.

¶ *And in the Aposticha, the following Idiomelons, in the Second Tone.*

THOU wast born as thou didst will, O our God; thou didst appear of thine own choice, and suffer in the flesh. Thou didst rise from the dead, and didst tread down death, ascending in glory, O thou who fulfillest all, and didst send us the divine Spirit, that we may praise thy Godhead, glorifying.

Stichos: O clap your hands, all ye nations.

The powers, beholding thine Ascension from the Mount of Olives, O Christ, shouted one to another, saying, Who is this? And it was said to them, He is the mighty and precious One. He is the mighty in battles. He is in truth the King of glory. Wherefore, are his clothes red? Because he cometh from Bosor, which is the flesh. But thou, being God, didst sit at the right hand of majesty and didst send us the Holy Spirit that he may guide us and save our souls.

Stichos: God is ascended with jubilee.

Thou didst ascend in glory from the Mount of Olives, O Christ God, at thy Disciples' side, and didst sit down at the right hand of the Father, O thou who dost fill all with thy Godhead, sending to them thy Holy Spirit, the Illuminator, Strengthener, and Sanctifier of our souls.

Glory and Now, in the Sixth Tone

GOD hath ascended with the voice of rejoicing, the Lord with the voice of, the trumpet, to raise the fallen likeness of Adam, and send the comforting Spirit to sanctify our souls.

Troparion, in the Fourth Tone (three times)

THOU hast ascended in glory, O Christ our God, and gladdened thy Disciples with the promise of the Holy Spirit, having become confident of the blessing. Verily, thou art the Son of God, and Deliverer of the world.

2. MATINS

Kathismata, in the First Tone

AS the angels, O Saviour, wondered at thy strange elevation, and the Disciples were amazed at thy dread rising, thou didst ascend in glory, being God, and the gates were lifted up for thee. Wherefore, the heavenly powers were surprised, shouting, Glory to thy condescension, O Saviour, glory to thy reign, glory to thine Ascension, O thou who art alone the Lover of mankind.

In the Third Tone

THE eternal Word before all the ages, who took a human nature and deified it in a mystical way, today doth rise ascending. Wherefore, the angels came forth to show him to the Disciples going to heaven in great glory. And they worshipped him, saying, Glory to the ascending God.

In the Fifth Tone

THOU didst descend from the heavens, O Christ, towards the earthly ones, and with thee, being God, didst raise the likeness of Adam, cast into the vaults of hades, lifting it with thine Ascension to the heavens and making it equal in rank to thy Father's throne; for thou art merciful and the Lover of mankind.

❧ *Then the Anabathmoi,* From my youth, *etc.* (*p. 50*)*; and the following Prokeimenon.*

God hath ascended with the voice of rejoicing, the Lord with the voice of the trumpet. O clap your hands, all ye nations.

❧ *Then the Third Gospel of the Eothina* (*p. 201*)*; and* In that we have beheld the Resurrection of Christ, *etc.* (*p. 113*)*; Psalm 50* (*plain, p. 82*)*; Glory,* Through the intercessions of the Apostles, *etc; and Now,* Through the intercessions of the Theotokos, *etc; and on* O merciful One, have mercy on me, O God, *the following Idiomelon, in the Sixth Tone.*

TODAY the Powers above, beholding our nature in the heavens, were perplexed, being surprised at the manner of its strange Ascension, and said one to another, Who is this that cometh? And when they saw that it was their own Master, they were commanded to lift the heavenly gates. Wherefore, with them we ceaselessly praise thee, O thou who didst come thence in the flesh, as thou art the Judge of all, and Almighty God.

❧ *Then the following Katabasias, in the Fourth Tone.*

1. The heavy of tongue, screened by the divine clouds, proclaimed the God-inscribed law; for he shook the dust from the eye of intelligence, beholding the Being and attaining the knowledge of the Spirit, singing divine songs of praise.

3. Hannah the Prophetess of old, drawn near with contrite spirit to the mighty God of intelligences, by her prayer alone undid the bonds of the barren one's womb, and the hard rebuke of her with children.

4. O Word, King of kings, who alone came forth from the only uncaused Father, since thou art the Benefactor, thou didst send the Holy Spirit, truly equal to thee in might, to the Disciples, who glorify thy power, O Lord.

5. O children of the Church, of illuminated likeness, receive ye the dew of the fire-breathing Spirit, which is a purification and an absolution from crimes; for the law hath now gone forth out of Zion in the shape of tongues of fire, being the grace of the Holy Spirit.

6. Thou hast shone for us from the Virgin, O Christ Master, as forgiveness and salvation to extricate from corruption fallen Adam and all his descendants, as thou didst extricate Jonah from the belly of the wild beast.

7. The unison of instrumental music called people in trembling to the worship of the lifeless image made of gold. But the light-bearing grace of the Comforter doth move the faithful to cry out, O eternal Trinity, equal in power, thou alone art ever blessed.

8. The tri-radiant sign of divine headship moistened the flames with dew and loosened the bonds; for he is the Benefactor, Saviour, and Creator of all. Wherefore, the entire creation, with the youths, doth praise him and bless him only.

9. Rejoice, O Queen, pride of virgins and mothers; for every eloquent and capable mouth doth fall short of extolling thee worthily, and every mind is dazzled at understanding the manner of thy birth-giving. Wherefore, in unison do we glorify thee.

¶ *And instead of* O thou who art more honourable, *etc., the Ninth Ode, and on each piece chant the following Magnificat.*

The angels, beholding the Ascension of the Master, were bewildered. How did he ascend in glory from the earth to the highest?

WHAT incomprehensible gifts! What terrible mystery! For he who reigneth over all hath risen from earth to heaven, and sent the Holy Spirit to his Disciples, lighting their minds and revealing them as afire with grace.

To the ranks of the Disciples the Lord did say, Tarry ye in Jerusalem and I will send you another Comforter who is equal to the Father and to me in the throne and

in honour, to me whom ye behold ascending and mounting a radiant cloud.

In a manifestation of great glory he who humbled
himself in the flesh hath risen above the heavens; and
our fallen nature hath been honoured by sitting with
the Father. Wherefore, let us all feast and clap our
hands together, singing in unison the songs of rejoicing.

He who hath risen radiating Light from Light, O all-
blameless one, hath risen from thee, undoing all the
darkness of infidelity, and lighting those who lie in the
night of darkness. Wherefore, as a debt of everlasting
duty, we beatify thee unto all ages.

¶ *Then conclude with the Hermos,* Rejoice, O queen, *etc. (p. 984).*

Exaposteilarion, in the Second Tone (three times)

WHEN the Disciples beheld thee, O Christ, ascending unto the Father and sitting down beside him,
the angels raced, shouting, Lift ye the gates, lift ye; for
the King hath ascended unto the glory of his Nature's
light.

¶ *And in the Einos, chant the following four Prosomia, in the First
Tone.*

LET us who are in the world feast angelically and
praise God who sitteth on the throne of his glory,
crying, Holy is the heavenly Father, Holy the coëternal
Word, Holy the most Holy Spirit. *(Repeat.)*

The foremost of the angels, O Saviour, beholding thy
strange Ascension, were bewildered, as they consulted
one with another, saying, What sight is this? For he who
is seen in the likeness of man, yet being God, doth ascend in the flesh above the heavens.

When the Galileans beheld thee, O Word, ascending
in the flesh from the Mount of Olives, they heard angels shouting unto them, Why stand ye gazing up?
This same shall so come in the flesh, in the manner that
ye have seen him.

❡ *Glory and Now,* Thou wast born as thou didst will, *etc.* (*p. 981*); then the Great Doxology; the Troparion (*p. 982*); and the Bene-diction.

3. THE MASS

Eisodikon: God hath ascended in songs of rejoicing, the Lord with the voice of the trumpet. Save us, O Son of God, who didst rise from us in glory to the heavens, as we sing unto thee, Alleluia.

❡ *The Troparion for the Feast and the Patron Saint of the church; then conclude with the following Kontakion, in the Sixth Tone.*

WHEN thou didst fulfill thy dispensation for our sakes, uniting the terrestrials with the celestials, thou didst ascend in glory, O Christ our God, insep-arable in space, but constant without separation, and crying unto thy beloved, I am with you, and no one shall be against you.

The Epistle: Be thou exalted, O God above the heavens. My heart is ready, O God.

Section from the Acts of the Saintly and Pure Apostles (1:1-12)

THE former treatise I made, O Theophilus, of all things which Jesus began to do and to teach,

Until the day on which, giving commandments by the Holy Ghost to the apostles whom he had chosen, he was taken up.

To whom also he showed himself alive after his pas-sion, by many proofs, for forty days appearing to them, and speaking of the kingdom of God.

And eating together with them, he commanded them, that they should not depart from Jerusalem, but should wait for the promise of the Father, which you have heard (saith he) by my mouth.

For John indeed baptized with water, but you shall be baptized with the Holy Ghost, not many days hence.

They therefore, who were come together, asked him, saying: Lord, wilt thou at this time restore again the kingdom to Israel?

But he said to them: It is not for you to know the times or moments, which the Father hath put in his own power.

But you shall receive the power of the Holy Ghost coming upon you, and you shall be witnesses unto me in Jerusalem, and in all Judea, and Samaria, and even to the uttermost part of the earth.

And when he had said these things, while they looked on, he was raised up: and a cloud received him out of their sight.

And while they were beholding him going up to heaven, behold two men stood by them in white garments.

Who also said: Ye men of Galilee, why stand you looking up to heaven? This Jesus who is taken up from you into heaven, shall so come, as you have seen him going into heaven.

Then they returned to Jerusalem from the mount that is called Olivet, which is nigh Jerusalem, within a sabbath day's journey.

The Gospel: The Sixth Gospel of the Eothina (p. 207).

❡*And on, Especially,* In unison we believers do magnify thee, *etc.* (*p. 971*).

SYNAXARION

AFTER his Resurrection Jesus remained on earth forty days, appearing at intervals to his Disciples in various places. He ate, drank, and conversed with them, thus verifying and assuring his Resurrection. On this day, corresponding to the fortieth day from the Passover, falling then on the third of May, he appeared to them in Jerusalem. He first conversed with them on various topics; then he gave them his last commandment, to go forth and preach in his Name to all the

nations, beginning with Jerusalem. At the same time
he told them not to depart from Jerusalem, but to remain there a while until they were clothed with power
from on high by the descent of the Holy Spirit upon
them.

Having said this, he led them to the Mount of Olives.
Then he lifted up his hands and blessed them. And as
he was speaking to them with words of fatherly blessing, he was parted from them and ascended into heaven,
being received by a shining cloud, indicating his divine
majesty. He sat on it as on a royal chariot and began
to ascend to heaven, gradually disappearing from the
sight of the Disciples as they gazed at him. And as they
stood thus two angels in brilliant white robes appeared
to them in the form of men and said to them, Ye men
of Galilee, why stand ye gazing up into heaven? This
same Jesus, which is taken up from you into heaven,
shall so come in like manner as ye have seen him go into
heaven. In these words, therefore, is fulfilled and de-
fined the doctrine concerning the Son of God and his
Word, in the Confession of Faith. And thus after our
Lord Jesus Christ fulfilled all his great dispensation
for us, He ascended in glory into heaven, and sat on
the right hand of God the Father. As for his undefiled
Disciples, they returned to Jerusalem from the Mount
of Olives, rejoicing in the promise of the coming of the
Holy Spirit (St. Lk. 24:46-52 and Acts 1:1-12).

It may be explained that the Mount of Olives was at
such a distance from Jerusalem as would permit the
Jews to walk to it on the sabbath; hence, it is said that
it was a sabbath day's journey. Incomanius (in his
commentary on Acts) explained that the distance must
have been one mile, or two thousand cubits, as Origen
also says in the Fifth of his Stromata. They deduce
this from the fact that the tents of the Israelites of old
in the wilderness were about that distance from the cu-
pola of the holy tabernacle of the covenant, to which
they walked on the sabbath for the worship of God.

Koinonikon: God hath ascended in songs of rejoicing, the Lord with the voice of the trumpet.

❡*And instead of* We *have seen the true Light, etc., the Troparion,* Thou didst ascend in glory, *etc. (p. 981).*

Benediction: O thou who didst rise from us in glory to the heavens, and didst sit on the right hand of God the Father, etc.

SUNDAY OF THE HOLY FATHERS

Gathered in the First Council of the City of Nicea

1. VESPERS

❡*On* O Lord, to thee have I cried, *three for the Resurrection of the Sixth Tone, and three for the Ascension, in the Same Tone (see the first three pieces for Vespers of the Ascension, p. 977); and the following four for the Fathers, in the Same Tone.*

OF the Father before the morning star thou wast begotten from the belly without mother before all the ages, even though Arius did believe thee to be created, not God, classing thee in ignorance and impudence with creatures, storing up for himself the element of eternal fire. Yet the Nicean Council proclaimed thee, preaching that thou art, O Lord, Son of God, equal to the Father in the throne, and to the Spirit also.

When thou wast asked, O Saviour, Who rent thy raiment? Thou didst reply that it was Arius, who divided the headship of the Trinity, united in honour, into parts; for this same denied that thou art one of the most Holy Trinity. He it was who taught the transgressing Nestorius not to say that the Virgin is the Theotokos. But the Nicean Council warned openly that thou art Son of God, equal in the throne to the Father, and to the Spirit also.

Pretending blindness that he might not see the light, Arius toppled into the pit of sin, and his bowels were torn by a divine hook that he might give up his whole substance. In a repulsive manner his soul came out, and he became another Judas by his own purpose and character, but the Nicean Council proclaimed openly that thou art Son of God, equal in the throne to the Father, and to the Spirit also.

The foolish Arius divided the headship of the most HolyTrinity into three different and unequal substances. Wherefore, the God-mantled Fathers, having, like Elijah the Tishbite, come together with energy, and burning with zeal, did cut with the sword of the Spirit him who is marked with confusion because of his blaspheming belief, being prompted by the directing Spirit.

¶ *Glory, in the Sixth Tone,* Let us extol today those mystical trumpets of the Spirit, *etc.* (*p. 313*); *and Now to our Lady, in the Same Tone,* Who shall not beatify thee, *etc.* (*p. 177*).

¶ *The Aposticha for the Resurrection, in the Sixth Tone, Glory for the Fathers in the Fourth Tone,* Come, ye assemblies of Orthodoxy, *etc.* (*p. 313*); *and Now for the Ascension, in the Fourth Tone,* When thou didst fulfill, *etc.* (*p. 981*).

¶ *The Troparia for the Resurrection, in the Sixth Tone,* When Mary stood at thy grave, *etc.* (*p. 178*); *for the Fathers, in the Eighth Tone,* Thou, O Christ, art our God, (*p. 314*); *and for the Ascension, in the Fourth Tone,* Thou didst ascend in glory, *etc.* (*p. 981*).

2. MATINS

¶ *The Tenth Gospel of the Eothina* (*p. 214*); *the Katabasias for the Ascension,* The heavy of tongue, *etc.* (*p. 983*); O thou who art more honourable, *etc., the Exaposteilarions for the Fathers,* By celebrating today, *etc.* (. *559*); *and for the Ascension,* When the Disciples beheld thee, *etc.* (*p. 985*); *and in the Einos, four for the Resurrection of the Sixth Tone, and four for the Fathers,* Having indited the whole knowledge, *etc.* (*p. 314*); *Glory for the Fathers,* When the rank of the holy Fathers, *etc.* (*p. 315*); *and Now,* Thou hast transcended, *etc.* (*p. 117*); *The Great Doxology;* Today hath salvation, *etc.* (*p. 119*); *and the Benediction.*

3. THE MASS

¶ *The Antiphonies of the Ascension, in the Second Tone, on which say,* O thou who didst rise from the dead, *etc.*

¶ *In the Eisodos, the Troparia for the Resurrection,* When Mary stood at thy grave, *etc.* (*p. 178*); *for the Ascension,* Thou didst ascend in glory, *etc. (p. 981); for the Fathers,* Thou O Christ, *etc. (p. 314); and the Kontakion for the Ascension,* When thou didst fulfill, *etc. (p. 986).*

The Epistle: Blessed art thou, O Lord, the God of our Fathers; for thou art just in all that thou hast done toward us.

Section from the Acts of the Saintly and Pure Apostles (20:16-18; 28-36)

IN those days: Paul had determined to sail by Ephesus, lest he should be stayed any time in Asia. For he hasted, if it were possible for him, to keep the day of Pentecost at Jerusalem.

And sending from Miletus to Ephesus, he called the ancients of the church.

And when they were come to him, and were together, he said to them:

Take heed to yourselves, and to the whole flock, wherein the Holy Ghost hath placed you bishops, to rule the church of God, which he hath purchased with his own blood.

I know that, after my departure, ravening wolves will enter in among you, not sparing the flock.

And of your own selves shall arise men speaking perverse things, to draw away disciples after them.

Therefore watch, keeping in memory, that for three years I ceased not, with tears to admonish every one of you night and day.

And now I commend you to God, and to the word of his grace, who is able to build up, and to give an inheritance among all the sanctified.

I have not coveted any man's silver, gold, or apparel, as

You yourselves know: for such things as were needful for me and them that are with me, these hands have furnished.

I have showed you all things, how that so labouring you ought to support the weak, and to remember the word of the Lord Jesus, how he said: It is a more blessed thing to give rather than to receive.

And when he had said these things, kneeling down, he prayed with them all.

The Gospel: from St. John (17:1-13)

AT that time: Jesus lifting up his eyes to heaven, he said: Father, the hour is come, glorify thy Son, that thy Son may glorify thee.

As thou hast given him power over all flesh, that he may give eternal life to all whom thou hast given him.

Now this is eternal life: That they may know thee, the only true God, and Jesus Christ, whom thou hast sent.

I have glorified thee on the earth; I have finished the work which thou gavest me to do.

And now glorify thou me, O Father, with thyself, with the glory which I had, before the world was, with thee.

I have manifested thy name to the men whom thou hast given me out of the world. Thine they were, and to me thou gavest them; and they have kept thy word.

Now they have known, that all things which thou hast given me, are from thee:

Because the words which thou gavest me, I have given to them; and they have received them, and have known in very deed that I came out from thee, and they have believed that thou didst send me.

I pray for them: I pray not for the world, but for them whom thou hast given me: because they are thine:

And all my things are thine, and thine are mine; and I am glorified in them.

And now I am not in the world, and these are in the world, and I come to thee. Holy Father, keep them in thy name whom thou hast given me; that they may be one, as we also are.

While I was with them, I kept them in thy name. (Those whom thou gavest me have I kept; and none of them is lost, but the son of perdition, that the scripture may be fulfilled.

And now I come to thee; and these things I speak in the world, that they may have my joy filled in themselves.

❡ *On Especially, sing* It is truly meet, *etc.*

SYNAXARION

O N which is chanted the service of the three hundred and eighteen divines who were gathered in the First Ecumenical Council held in the city of Nicea.

Arius, the notorious heretic, was a native of Libya, and was first ordained archpriest of Alexandria. Following this, in the year 315, he began to blaspheme against the Son of God and his Word, saying that he was not God consubstantial with the Father, but that he was created, a stranger to the Substance of the Father and his glory. He troubled the faithful of Alexandria with his horrible blasphemy, and it was then that Cyril, the Archbishop of Alexandria, tried to restrain him with his counsels. Failing in this, Cyril was forced in 321 to call a local council and to cut him off and excommunicate him. But that blasphemer did not stop, nor wished to desist from sowing the seeds of his tares, by propagating that destructive, venemous heresy. And thus the poison of his error crept into many, reaching distant places, disturbing the Church of Christ, and causing it great harm.

And when Constantine the Great, the first of the Christian kings, coëqual with the Apostles, saw this, he was moved by divine zeal, and held an ecumenical council in the city of Nicea in Bithynia, which was the first of the ecumenical councils. To this came the Bishops and teachers of the Church of Christ from every land and proclaimed all, as by one mouth, the equality of the Son of God, and his Word, with the Father, in Substance, and that he was very God of very God, laying down the noble Confession of Faith (the Creed) to where it says, And in the Holy Spirit (for the completion of the Creed was written by the Second Ecumenical Council). As for Arius the atheist of evil doctrine, and those who agreed with him, they were excommunicated and cut off from the body of the Church.

And since the Church regards those divine Fathers as preachers of the faith next to the divinity-speaking Apostles, and confesses to the same, it decreed that their memory be celebrated each year on this Sunday, for the glorification of God and his praise, and to honour and praise those Fathers for the establishment of the Orthodox Faith.

Koinonikon: Praise ye the Lord from the heavens. The just shall be in everlasting remembrance. Alleluia.

¶*And instead of* We have seen the true Light, *etc., sing the Troparion,* Thou didst ascend in glory, *etc. (p. 981); and the Benediction.*

FRIDAY BEFORE PENTECOST

Leave-Taking of the Ascension in Which the Whole Service of the Ascension is Sung

SATURDAY BEFORE PENTECOST

[KNOWN AS THE SATURDAY OF THE DEAD]

¶*On this day sing the service designated for the Saturday of Meat Carnival, (pp. 618-637).*

SUNDAY OF PENTECOST (*Whitsunday*)

¶*Throughout the Week of Pentecost it is permitted to eat meat.*

1. VESPERS

¶*On* O Lord, to thee have I cried, *sing the following Stichera.*

In the First Tone

LO, we celebrate the Feast of Pentecost, the presence of the Spirit, the fulfillment of the promise and the completion of hope. How wonderful is this mystery; for it is great and most solemn. Wherefore, we cry unto thee, O Lord and Creator of all, glory to thee. (*Repeat.*)

Thou hast renewed for thy Disciples, O Christ, a different kind of tongues, that they might therewith proclaim that thou art the immortal Word and God who granteth our souls the Great Mercy.

The Holy Spirit provideth all; overfloweth with prophecy; fulfilleth the Priesthood; and hath taught wisdom to the illiterate. He hath revealed the fishermen as theologians. He bringeth together all the laws of the Church. Wherefore, O Comforter, equal to the Father in Substance and the throne, glory to thee.

In the Second Tone

WE have seen the true Light; we have received the Holy Spirit; we have found the true Faith. Wherefore, let us worship the indivisible Trinity; for he hath saved us. (*Repeat.*)

By the Prophets thou didst tell us the way of salvation, O our Saviour, and by the grace of thy Spirit. Thou art God from the beginning; and for time to come, and unto the ages, verily, thou art our God.

In thy dwelling-places I offer praise, O Saviour of the world, and by the bending of the knees I worship thine unconquerable might. In the evening, on the morrow, at midnight, and at all times, I bless thee, O Lord.

As we believers bend, O Lord, in thy dwelling-places, the knees of the soul and the body together, we praise thee, O Father without beginning, the Son equally without beginning, and the most Holy Spirit coëternal with thee, the Illuminator and Sanctifier of our souls.

Let us praise the consubstantial Trinity, the Father and the Son with the Holy Spirit; for thus did all the Prophets preach, and the Apostles with the Martyrs too.

Glory and Now, in the Eighth Tone

COME ye nations, let us worship the three-personed Godhead, a Son in the Father, with a Holy Spirit; for the Father timelessly hath begotten the Son, equal to him in eternity and the throne; and the Holy Spirit was in the Father, glorified with the Son, one Might, one Substance, one Godhead, which we all worship, saying, Holy God who created everything through the Son with the help of the Holy Spirit; Holy Mighty, in whom we knew the Father, and through whom the Holy Spirit came to the world; Holy Immortal One, the comforting Spirit, proceeding from the Father and resting in the Son; O Holy Trinity, glory to thee.

❡ *Then after the Eisodos and O resplendent Light, etc., and the daily Prokeimenon, recite the following Readings.*

First Reading: from the Book of Numbers (11:16-17; 24-29)

AND the Lord said to Moses: Gather unto me seventy men of the ancients of Israel, whom thou knowest to be ancients and masters of the people: and thou shalt bring them to the door of the tabernacle of the covenant, and shalt make them stand there with thee.

That I may come down and speak with thee: and I will take of thy spirit, and will give to them, that they may bear with thee the burden of the people, and thou mayest not be burdened alone.

Moses therefore came, and told the people the words of the Lord, and assembled seventy men of the ancients of Israel, and made them to stand about the tabernacle.

And the Lord came down in a cloud, and spoke to him, taking away of the spirit that was in Moses, and

giving to the seventy men. And when the spirit had
rested on them they prophesied, nor did they cease afterwards.

Now there remained in the camp two of the men, of
whom one was called Eldad, and the other Medad,
upon whom the spirit rested; for they also had been
enrolled, but were not gone forth to the tabernacle.

And when they prophesied in the camp, there ran a
young man, and told Moses, saying: Eldad and Medad
prophesy in the camp.

Forthwith Josue the son of Nun, the minister of
Moses, and chosen out of many, said: My lord Moses
forbid them.

But he said: Why hast thou emulation for me? O
that all the people might prophesy, and that the Lord
would give them his spirit!

Second Reading: from the Prophecy of Joel
(2:23 to end)

THESE sayings our Lord doth say: O children of
Sion, rejoice, and be joyful in the Lord your God:
because he hath given you a teacher of justice and he
will make the early and the latter rain to come down to
you as in the beginning.

And the floors shall be filled with wheat, and the
presses shall overflow with wine and oil.

And I will restore to you the ears which the locust,
and the bruchus, and the mildew, and the palmerworm
have eaten; my great host which I sent upon you.

And you shall eat in plenty, and shall be filled: and
you shall praise the name of the Lord your God, who
hath done wonders with you, and my people shall not
be confounded for ever.

And you shall know that I am in the midst of Israel:
and I am the Lord your God, and there is none besides:
and my people shall not be confounded for ever.

And it shall come to pass after this, that I will pour
out my spirit upon all flesh: and your sons and your

daughters shall prophesy: your old men shall dream dreams, and your young men shall see visions.

Moreover upon my servants and handmaids in those days I will pour forth my spirit.

And I will shew wonders in heaven; and in earth blood, and fire, and vapour of smoke.

The sun shall be turned into darkness, and the moon into blood: before the great and dreadful day of the Lord doth come.

And it shall come to pass, that every one that shall call upon the name of the Lord shall be saved.

Third Reading: from the Prophecy of Ezekiel the Prophet (36:24-28)

THESE sayings our Lord doth say: I will take you from among the Gentiles, and will gather you together out of all the countries, and will bring you into your own land.

And I will pour upon you clean water, and you shall be cleansed from all your filthiness, and I will cleanse you from all your idols.

And I will give you a new heart, and put a new spirit within you: and I will take away the stony heart out of your flesh, and will give you a heart of flesh.

And I will put my spirit in the midst of you: and I will cause you to walk in my commandments, and to keep my judgments, and do them.

And you shall dwell in the land which I gave to your fathers, and you shall be my people, and I will be your God.

❧ *And in the Litiya, sing the following piece, in the Eighth Tone.*

WHEN thou didst send thy Spirit, O Lord, the Apostles, being seated, the sons of the Hebrews took note, and were astonished; for they heard them speak in strange tongues, according as the Spirit bestowed on them; for they were illiterate. They philosophized, driving the Gentiles to the Faith, as they preached of things divine. Wherefore, we cry to thee, O thou who wast revealed on earth and didst save us from error, glory to thee, O Lord.

¶And in the Aposticha, the following Stichera, in the Sixth Tone.

BEING ignorant of the power of thy most Holy Spirit who came to thine Apostles, the Gentiles imagined that the gift of tongues was drunkenness. But we who are confirmed by them cry ceaselessly, beseeching, Thy Holy Spirit take not from us, O Lover of mankind.

Stichos: Create in me a new heart, O God; and renew a right spirit within my bowels.

The coming of the Holy Spirit, O Lord, and his encompassing of thy Disciples, revealed them as speaking with other tongues, hence the miraculous wonder. As for the unbelievers, they thought it drunkenness, and the believers, a cause of salvation to them. Wherefore, we beseech thee to make us ready for his illumination, O Lover of mankind.

Stichos: Cast me not away from thy face, and take not thy Holy Spirit from me.

O heavenly King, the Comforter, Spirit of Truth, who art in all places, and fillest all things, Treasury of good things, and Giver of life, come, and take up thine abode in us, and cleanse us from every stain; and save, O good One, our souls.

Glory and Now, in the Eighth Tone

OF old there was confusion of tongues because of the boldness of the tower-builders. But those tongues have not uttered wisdom for the glory of divine knowledge. There God condemned the infidels to punishment, and here with the Spirit Christ illuminated the fishermen. At that time the confusion of tongues was designed for vengeance, and now the unison of tongues hath been renewed for the salvation of our souls.

Troparion, in the Eighth Tone (three times)

BLESSED art thou, O Christ our God, who hast revealed the fishermen as most wise, having sent upon them the Holy Spirit, and through them thou hast fished the universe, O Lover of mankind, glory to thee.

2. MATINS

❡ *On* God the Lord hath appeared unto us, *sing the Troparion; then the following Kathismata.*

First Kathisma, in the Fourth Tone

LET us, O believers, celebrate with joy the last Feast, which is also the last of the Feast—Pentecost—which is the end and fulfillment of the preördained promise; for then did come down the fire of the Comforter upon the earth in the likeness of tongues, lighting the Disciples and revealing them plainly as initiates of heavenly things. Verily, the light of the Comforter hath come and lighted the world.

Second Kathisma, in the Same Tone

THE spring of the Spirit hath come to those on earth, dividing supersensuously into fire-bearing rivers, moistening the Apostles and illuminating them. The fire hath become to them a dewy cloud, lighting, and raining flames upon them, from whom we received grace by the fire and the water. Verily, the fire of the Comforter hath come and lighted the world.

Third Kathisma, in the Eighth Tone

AFTER thy rising from the tomb, O Christ, and thy divine ascent to the celestial heights, thou didst send thy glory, O compassionate One, to thy Godhead-seeing Disciples, renewing in them a right spirit.

Wherefore, like a musical harp, they proclaimed their words unto all mystically, through the instrument of thy dispensation.

❡ *Then the Anabathmoi, From my youth, etc. (p. 50); and the following Prokeimenon.*

Thy good spirit, shall lead me into the right land. Hear, O Lord, my prayer.

❡ *The Ninth Eothina Gospel (p. 212); and do not say* In that we have beheld the Resurrection of Christ, *etc., but immediately Psalm 50; then Glory,* Through the intercessions of the Apostles, *etc; and Now,* Through the intercessions of the Theotokos, *etc. And on* O merciful One, have mercy upon me, O God, *etc., the Idiomelon, in the Sixth Tone,* O heavenly King, *etc. (p. 999); then the dual Katabasias, i.e. the Katabasias of the Ascension,* The heavy of tongue *etc. (p. 983); with the following Katabasias, in the Seventh Tone.*

1. Let us praise him who overwhelmed Pharaoh and his chariots in the sea; who crusheth wars with a mighty hand; for he hath been glorified.

3. Thou didst call unto thy Disciples, O Christ, saying, Stay ye in Jerusalem till ye be endued with power from on high, and I will send you another Comforter like me, who is my Spirit and the Spirit of the Father, and in him ye shall be strengthened.

4. When the Prophet perceived thy coming in the last days, O Christ, he lifted his voice crying, I have heard, O Lord, the hearing of thy might; for thou didst verily come to save all thine anointed ones.

5. The Spirit of salvation, O Lord, who for fear of thee was conceived in the belly of the Prophets and wast begotten on earth, hath created the hearts of the Apostles pure, being renewed in the faithful; for thy commands are light and peace.

6. My soul hath been stirred with the agitation of worldly concerns. Yea, I am drowned therein, from the sins that accompany me, and cast to the soul-corrupting beast. Wherefore, like Jonah, I cry unto thee, O Christ, lift me out of the mortifying depth.

7. The righteous youths who were thrown into the furnace of fire, changed the flames into dew when they lifted their voices in songs of praise, crying thus, Blessed art thou, O Lord God of our fathers.

8. The unconsumed bush which mingled with fire in Sinai made God known to the heavy-tongued and hoarse-voiced Moses. In like manner, God's zeal manifested the three youths as unconsumed by fire, but praising thus, Praise the Lord, all his works, and exalt him more and more unto the ages.

¶*And instead of* O thou who art more honourable, *etc. sing the following Ninth Ode of the Pentecost Canon, in the Seventh Tone.*

9. O Mother that hath known no man, thou didst conceive, not experiencing corruption, lending a body to the Word, the Creator of all, becoming a receptacle to thine insupportable Creator, a dwelling-place to thine incomprehensible Maker. Wherefore, O virgin Theotokos, thee do we magnify.

Of old the fire-breathing, zealous Elijah did mount with joy the all-flaming chariot. Wherefore, this sign did explain the rising of the gentle breeze illuminating the Apostles from on High, through which they were lighted, making known to all the Trinity.

Strange things contrary to the law of nature are now heard; for by the one voice, which the Disciples received in divers kinds, through the grace of the Spirit, all the nations, tribes, and tongues heard the great things of God, and received the knowledge of the Trinity.

¶*And the following, in the Fourth Tone.*

REJOICE, O Queen, pride of virgins and mothers; for every eloquent and capable mouth doth fall short of extolling thee worthily, and every mind is dazzled at the understanding of the manner of thy birth-giving. Wherefore, in unison do we glorify thee.

Let us worthily praise the Maiden who revived nature, who alone did screen the Word in her womb, the same who healed the weakness of mankind, sat on the right hand of the Father, and sent the grace of the Spirit.

We on whom the grace coming from God did blow, have become luminous and bright, changed in a resplendent manner of exceeding beauty, comprehending the indivisible equi-potent, tri-luminous, wise Essence. Wherefore, let us glorify him.

❡ *Then conclude with the two Hermoses,* O Mother that hath known no man, *etc., and* Rejoice, O Queen, *etc.*

Exaposteilarions, in the Third Tone

ALL-HOLY Spirit, issuing from the Father and coming through the Son upon the illiterate Disciples, save and sanctify all those who know thee as God. (*Repeat.*)

Light is the Father; and Light the Son; Light is the Holy Spirit descending upon the Apostles in fiery tongues, through which the whole universe was illuminated to worship the holy Trinity.

❡*In the Einos, sing the following three Idiomelons, in the Fourth Tone (to be repeated).*

TODAY all the nations in the city of David beheld wonders, when the Holy Spirit descended in fiery tongues, as the God-inspired Luke spake; for he said, The Disciples of Christ being gathered together, there was a sound as of a mighty wind, and it filled the whole house where they were sitting. And they began to speak strange doctrines and strange teachings with divers tongues, to the holy Trinity. (*Repeat.*)

The Holy Spirit hath ever been, is and ever shall be; for he is wholly without beginning and without end. Yet he is in covenant with the Father and the Son, counted as Life and Life-giver, Light and Light-giver, good by nature and a Fountain of goodness, through whom the Father is known and the Son glorified. And by all it is understood that one power, one rank, one worship are of the Holy Trinity. (*Repeat.*)

Light, Life, and a living supersensuous Fountain is the Holy Spirit, good, upright, supersensuous Spirit of understanding, presiding, and purifying offenses, God and deifying, Fire projecting from Fire, speaking, active, Distributor of gifts, through whom all the Prophets, the Apostles of God, and the Martyrs are crowned, a strange Report, a strange sight, a Fire divided for the distribution of gifts. (*Repeat.*)

❡*Glory and Now,* O heavenly King, *etc.* (*p. 999*)*; then the Great Doxology; the Troparion of the Feast* (*p. 1000*)*; and the Benediction.*

3. THE MASS

Eisodikon: Be thou exalted, O Lord, in thine own strength. We will sing and praise thy power. Save us, O good Comforter, as we sing to thee. Alleluia.

❡*Then the Troparion of the Feast; the Troparion of the Patron Saint of the church; and conclude with the following Kontakion, in the Eighth Tone.*

When the high One descended, confusing tongues, he divided the nations. And when he distributed the fiery tongues he called all to one unity. Wherefore, in unison we glorify the most Holy Spirit.

❡*And instead of* Holy God, *etc., sing,* Ye who have been baptized into Christ, have put on Christ. Alleluia.

The Epistle: Their sound hath gone forth into all the earth. And their words unto the ends of the world.

Section from the Acts of the Saintly and Pure Apostles
(2:1-11)

AND when the days of the Pentecost were accomplished, they were all together in one place;

And suddenly there came a sound from heaven, as of

a mighty wind coming, and it filled the whole house where they were sitting.

And there appeared to them parted tongues as it were of fire, and it sat upon every one of them:

And they were all filled with the Holy Ghost, and they began to speak with divers tongues, according as the Holy Ghost gave them to speak.

Now there were dwelling at Jerusalem, Jews, devout men, out of every nation under heaven.

And when this was noised abroad, the multitude came together, and were confounded in mind, because that every man heard them speak in his own tongue.

And they were all amazed, and wondered, saying: Behold, are not all these that speak, Galileans?

And how have we heard, every man our own tongue wherein we were born?

Parthians, and Medes, and Elamites, and inhabitants of Mesopotamia, Judea, and Cappadocia, Pontus and Asia.

Phrygia, and Pamphylia, Egypt, and the parts of Libya about Cyrene, and strangers of Rome,

Jews also, and proselytes, Cretes, and Arabians: we have heard them speak in our own tongues the wonderful works of God.

The Gospel: from St. John (7:37-52; 8:12)

AND on the last, and great day of the festivity, Jesus stood and cried, saying: If any man thirst, let him come to me and drink.

He that believeth in me, as the scripture saith, Out of his belly shall flow rivers of living water.

Now this he said of the Spirit which they should receive, who believed in him: for as yet the Spirit was not given, because Jesus was not yet glorified.

Of that multitude therefore, when they had heard these words of his, some said: This is the prophet indeed.

Others said: This is the Christ. But some said: Doth the Christ come out of Galilee?

Doth not the scripture say: That Christ cometh of the seed of David, and from Bethlehem the town where David was?

So there arose a dissension among the people because of him.

And some of them would have apprehended him: but no man laid hands upon him.

The ministers therefore came to the chief priests and the Pharisees. And they said to them: Why have you not brought him?

The ministers answered: Never did man speak like this man.

The Pharisees therefore answered them: Are you also seduced?

Hath any one of the rulers believed in him, or of the Pharisees?

But this multitude, that knoweth not the law, are accursed.

Nicodemus said to them, (he that came to him by night, who was one of them:)

Doth our law judge any man, unless it first hear him, and know what he doeth?

They answered, and said to him: Art thou also a Galilean? Search the scriptures, and see, that out of Galilee a prophet riseth not.

Again therefore, Jesus spoke to them, saying: I am the light of the world: he that followeth me, walketh not in darkness, but shall have the light of life.

¶ *And on Especially sing,* O Mother that hath known no man, *etc.* (*p. 1002*).

SYNAXARION

AFTER the Saviour's ascent to heaven the eleven Apostles, the rest of the Disciples, the pious women who were accustomed to follow him from the beginning, his most holy Mother the Virgin Mary, and his brothers returned from the Mount of Olives to Jerusalem. Altogether they were about one hundred and twenty souls. When they had entered the house in which they lived, they went up to the upper room to await the coming of the Holy Spirit, according to the promise of their divine Master, continuing in prayer and supplication. About that time the election fell on Matthias who was counted among the eleven Apostles (see August ninth).

On a corresponding Sunday, which is the tenth day after the Ascension, and the fiftieth after the Passover, falling then on the thirteenth of May, about the third hour of the day, there came a sound from heaven as of a rushing mighty wind, and it filled all the house where the Apostles were sitting. And immediately there appeared to them cloven tongues like as of fire, and sat upon the head of each of them. And all those who were there were filled with the Holy Spirit, and they began to speak, not with the tongues of their ancestors, but with other tongues with which the Holy Spirit supplied them as He inspired them.

And by divine provision, there were gathered in Jerusalem for the feast great multitudes from about eighteen different nations and tongues, such as Parthians, Medes, Elamites, and others, who were all Jews by race and religion, but, because they had been born and brought up in various places among strange nations, they were dispersed from ancient times, and each was called after the place of his birth. When these heard the sound from heaven, descending to where the Disciples of Christ were gathered, they all hastened thither to find out what had happened. And as each heard the Apostles speaking in his own language, they were all amazed and marvelled, saying one to another, Behold, are not all these which speak Galileans? And how hear we every man in our own tongue, wherein we were born?

And there were others (perhaps the blind Scribes and Pharisees), who, because of their great wickedness and folly, mocked the miracle, saying that the Apostles were drunk.

Then Peter, standing with the Eleven, lifted up his voice and spake before the multitude, explaining that what had happened was not due to intoxication, but to the fulfillment of God's promise, speaking to Joel, which says, And it shall come to pass in the last days, I will pour of my spirit upon all flesh: and your sons and your daughters shall prophesy, etc. (Acts 2:2-28). Then he preached Jesus the Nazarene, explaining with many proofs that he was Christ the Lord whom the Jews crucified and whom God raised from the dead.

Many then were touched in their hearts because of his words, and, accepting them, were baptized. And on that day there were added to the faithful about three thousand souls. (Acts 1:12 to 2:41).

This then is the object of the present Feast, namely, the coming of the Holy Spirit into the world, the fulfillment of the promise of Jesus Christ, and the completion of the undefiled Disciples' hope. It is the sequel and the conclusion of the Feasts of the great mystery of the divine Incarnation. On the day corresponding to this day of salvation, the day of Pentecost, the Saviour's Apostles, who were formerly simple fishermen and illiterate, were suddenly instructed by the advent of the Holy Spirit, becoming possessed of the greatest wisdom and speaking plainly of heavenly doctrines. They became preachers of truth and teachers to the whole world. From that day they began the work of their great mission, the wonderful and delectable first-fruit of which was the conversion of three thousand souls on that very same day.

Some hold that the above mentioned upper room, which the Jews used to consider a place of worship and prayer, since it was designated for that purpose, was the same upper room in which the Saviour delivered the divine Sacrament of the Eucharist. But others hold that it was in the house of John the Evangelist.

Still others think it was in the house of Mary the mother of John, who was known as John Mark (Acts 12:12), where afterwards a church was built and named the Upper Church of the Apostles (see the sixteenth Sermon of Cyril of Jerusalem). Again, there are others who say that it was one of the many upper rooms in the outer court of the Temple, which were open to people who were gathered in the Temple, and prepared for those who cared to enter them. They cite as proof of their claim the words of St. Luke, And they were continually in the Temple, praising and blessing God (St. Lk. 24:53). It may also be noted here that the name of Mary the Theotokos is mentioned at this point for the last time in the New Testament.

Koinonikon: Thy good Spirit shall lead me into the right land.

¶*And instead of* We have seen the true Light, *etc. sing the Troparion,* Blessed art thou, *etc.* (*p. 1000*).

Benediction: O thou who from heaven didst send the most Holy Spirit in the shape of fiery tongues upon thy holy Disciples, etc.

SERVICE OF VESPERS

[KNOWN AS THE KNEELING SERVICE]

¶*At the conclusion of the Divine Mass, the Priest saith;* Blessed be God, *etc; and after the Sunset Psalm, the Deacon saith the following Synapte.*

IN peace, let us pray to the Lord.

For the peace that is from above, and for the salvation of our souls . . .

For the peace of the whole world, the welfare of God's holy churches and the union of them all . . .

For this people standing and expecting the grace of the Holy Spirit . . .

For those who bend their hearts and their knees before the Lord . . .

That the Lord may strengthen us unto the attainment of a good and acceptable end . . .

That he may send upon us his abundant mercy . . .

That he may accept the bending of our knees as incense before him . . .

For those who are in need of help from God . . .

For our deliverance from all affliction, wrath, danger, and depression . . .

Help, save, have mercy, and keep us, O God, by thy grace.

Remembering our all-holy, spotless, most highly blessed and glorious, etc.

Exclamation: For all glory, honour, and worship are due to thee, O Father, etc.

❧ *Then on* O Lord, to thee have I cried, *sing the Idiomelons of the Einos (p. 1003), and repeat; Glory and Now, in the Sixth Tone,* O heavenly King, etc. *(p. 999).*

❧ *Then the Eisodos; and* O resplendent Light, *etc; and the following Prokeimenon, in the Seventh Tone.*

Who is the great God like our God? Thou art alone the God that doest wonders.

Deacon: Again and again, with the bending of the knees, we pray to the Lord.

❧ *Here the congregation kneel as the Priest repeateth the following Prayer in a loud voice.*

O PURE and blameless Lord, who art without beginning, invisible and incomprehensible, unsearchable, unchangeable, immeasurable, and unbounded, who art without evil and alone immortal, who dwellest in the unapproachable light, Maker of heaven and earth and the seas and all that was created therein, who grantest to all their petitions before asking, to thee we pray and of thee we ask, O philanthropic Master, the Father of our Lord and God and Saviour Jesus Christ, who for us men and for our salvation came down from heaven and was incarnate of the Holy Spirit and of the ever-virgin Mary, the noble Theotokos; who first did teach by word, and at last manifested in deed; who, having borne the saving Passion, granted us thine unworthy, sinful, and miserable servants, a command and example that we should offer our supplication with bending of the neck and the knees for our sins and the ignorances of the people. Wherefore, O most merciful and philanthropic Lord, hear us on whatever day we call upon thee, and especially on this day of Pentecost, whereon, after our Lord Jesus Christ had ascended into heaven and sat on thy right hand, O God and Father, he sent down the Holy Spirit to his Disciples, the holy Apostles, who alighted on each of them and filled them all with his inexhaustible and divine grace; and they did speak in strange tongues, prophesying thy great deeds. Hear us who beseech thee, and remember us, wretched and condemned. Restore us from the captivity of our souls, whose intercessor with thee is thine own lovingkindness. Accept us who kneel down before thee and cry out unto thee, We have sinned against thee, and upon thee were we thrown even from our mother's womb. Thou art our God, but having passed our days in vanity we have been stripped of thine aid, and have been deprived of every defence. Yet do we trust in thy compassion and cry unto thee, Remember not the sins of our youth and ignorance; cleanse us of our secret sins. Reject us not in our old age, and forsake us not at the dissolution of our strength. And before we return to the earth, prepare us to return to thee. With bountiful pity hearken thou unto us. Over against our iniquities set thy compassion, and against our transgressions the abyss of thy lovingkindness. Look down from the height of thy holiness upon thy people who stand and await from thee abundant mercy. Visit us with thy goodness and deliver us from the possession of Diabolus, and preserve our life with thy holy and solemn laws. Commit thy people unto a faithful and guardian angel. Gather us all unto thy kingdom, and grant remission of sins to those who put their trust in thee, and forgive us and them our sins. Purify us by the operation of thy Holy Spirit, and remove from us the wiles of the adversary.

❡ *And then immediately:*

BLESSED art thou, Almighty Master, who illuminatest the day with the light of the sun and delightest the night with the glow of fire; who hast made us worthy to spend the whole day and draw near to the beginning of the night; hear our petitions and those of all the people. Forgive us all our sins, both voluntary and involuntary, and accept our evening beseechings. Send down the multitude of thy mercies and compassion upon thine inheritance. Encompass us with thy holy angels. Arm us with the armour of thy justice. Hedge us in with thy righteousness. Keep us by thy power, and deliver us from every oppression and from every conspiracy of the obstinate one. Grant us that this evening and the approaching night and all the days of our life may be perfect, holy, peaceful, sinless, without doubt and vain imaginings, by the intercessions of holy Theotokos and all the saints who have done thy will from the beginning of time.

Deacon. Help, save, have mercy, and raise us, O God, and keep up by thy grace.

Remembering our all-holy, spotless, etc.

Priest. For of thee, O Christ our God, are mercy and salvation; and to thee, with thy Father who is without beginning and thy good life-giving most Holy Spirit, we address glory, now, etc.

❡ *Then the Deacon saith the Ektene,* Let us all say, *etc.* (*p. 75*); *and after the Exclamation of the Priest,* For thou art a merciful God, *etc., the Deacon saith:*

Again and again, with the bending of the knees, let us pray to the Lord.

❡ *And the Priest repeateth the following Prayer.*

O LORD Jesus Christ our God, who bestowest thy safety on mankind, and who, while yet in this world, didst grant us believers the gift of the all-holy

Spirit, an inheritance that shall never be taken away from us; who on this day didst direct and send this grace openly upon thy Disciples, the Apostles; who didst place in their mouths and upon their lips tongues of fire, through which we, together with all mankind, have received the knowledge of God by the hearing of the ear, each in his own tongue, and have been illuminated by the light of the Spirit, being emancipated from error as from darkness; and by the distribution of the material tongues of fire and their supernatural effect; we have become Disciples to thee by believing in thee; and having been enlightened, discoursed on thy Godhead; for thou, with the Father and the Holy Spirit, art one Godhead, one Power, and one Authority. Wherefore, O Splendour of the Father, the Likeness of his Essence, his immutable and unchangeable Nature, thou art the Fountain of salvation and grace. Open my lips, sinner that I am, and teach me how and for whom I should pray; for thou dost know the multitude of my sins, but thine unbounded compassion doth overcome the enormity thereof. Behold, I come and stand before thee in fear and dismay, casting my soul's despair into the depth of thy mercy. Ordain my life, O thou who ordainest the whole creation by thine unutterable Word, and by the power of thine ineffable wisdom, O tranquil Haven to those who are caught in the rages of winter, and make known to me the way in which I should walk. Grant to my thoughts the spirit of thy wisdom, and bestow upon mine ignorance the spirit of thine understanding. Overshadow my acts with the spirit of thy fear; a right spirit create thou within me, and by thy sovereign Spirit strengthen thou mine unstable mind, that I may be worthy each day to do thy commandments, being guided by thy righteous Spirit into that which is profitable, ever mindful of thy glorified Coming that searcheth our life's deeds. Let me not be led astray by the corrupting pleasure of this world, but strengthen me to delight in the treasures to come. For thou, O Master, didst say that, whatever ye ask in my Name ye shall receive from God the Father, coëternal with thee. Wherefore, I a sinner, implore thy goodness for the coming of thy Holy Spirit. Grant thou my request for salvation: yea, good Lord, who grantest all riches and benevolence; for thou art he who grantest us more than we ask, the merciful and pitying, who hast become a Partaker with us in the flesh without sin. Thou art he who, for his love to mankind, dost have compassion on those who bend the knee to thee, having become an offering for our sins. Grant, Lord, thy compassion to thy people, and incline thine ear to us from the heaven of thy holiness; sanctify them by the saving might of thy right hand, shield them with the shelter of thy wings, and turn not away from the works of thy hands. Against thee only have we sinned, yet thee only have we worshipped. A strange God we have not learned to worship, nor did we lift our hands to another God. Pardon our iniquities, O Master, and accept our beseechings with the bending of the knees. Extend to us all a helping hand, and accept our whole prayer as acceptable incense rising before thy most righteous kingdom.

¶ *Then immediately this Prayer by St. Basil the Great.*

LORD, Lord, thou who hast delivered us from every arrow that flieth by day, save us from everything that walketh in darkness, and accept the lifting up of our hands as an evening offering. Prepare us to pass the distance of night blameless and untempted by evils. Deliver us from Satan. Grant our souls reverence, and our thoughts concern to search thy just, terrible, judgment. Pierce our bodies with thy fear, and mortify our members that are on earth, that in the stillness of the night we may be lighted by the contemplation of thy precepts. Drive from us every evil imagining and harmful passion, and raise us in time of prayer, established in the Faith, and prospering in thy commandments.

Deacon. Help, save, have mercy, and raise us, O God, and keep us by thy grace.

Remembering our All-Holy, etc.

Priest. Through the pleasure and grace of thine only Son, with whom thou art blessed, and with thy most holy, righteous, and life-giving Spirit, now, etc.

¶ *And after* Vouchsafe, O Lord, *etc.,* (*p. 76*) *the Deacon saith:*

Again and again, with the bending of the knee, let us pray to the Lord.

¶ *And the Priest saith the following Prayer.*

O CHRIST our God, the ever-flowing spring, life-giving, illuminating, creative Power, coëternal with the Father, who for us men dost fulfill thy whole dispensation in a manner transcending beauty; didst tear apart the indestructible bonds of death, break asunder the bolts of hades, and tread down the multitude of evil spirits, offering thyself a blameless Sacrifice and offering us thy pure, spotless, and sinless body: who, for this ineffable and dread service, didst grant us life everlasting, O thou who didst descend into hades, and demolish the eternal bars, revealing an ascent to those who are in the lower abode; who with the bait of divine wisdom didst entice the dragon, the head of subtle evil, binding him in Tartarus with abysmal bonds, unquenchable fire, and outer darkness; through thine infinite power, O Wisdom of the Father, thou of great Name who dost manifest thyself a great Helper to those who are in distress; a luminous Light to those who sit in darkness and the shadow of death; thou art the Lord of everlasting glory, the beloved Son of the most high Father, eternal Light from eternal Light, thou Son of justice; hear thou us who beseech thee, and give rest to the souls of fathers, brethren, and the rest of our kinsmen in the flesh, and those who are of the fold of faith who have fallen asleep, and for whom we celebrate now this memorial; for in thee is all might, and in thy hands are the ends of the earth, O Almighty Master, God of our fathers, Lord of mercy and Creator of all the races of men, the living and the dead, and of all human nature, composed and decomposed. O thou in whose hands are life and death, disposal here on earth, and translation yonder; who settest the years for the living and appointest the time for the dead; who bringest down to hades and raisest to bliss; who bindest with weakness and loosest with power; who disposest the future as is meet; who workest life through hope of resurrection to those who are smitten with the arrows of death; thou art the Master of all, our God and our Saviour, O hope of all the ends of the earth and of those who are away on the seas, O thou who on this last and great day of salvation, the day of the Feast of Pentecost, hast revealed to us the mystery of the holy Trinity, consubstantial and coëternal, indivisible and immiscible, who didst overflow upon thine undefiled Apostles with thy Holy Spirit, life-giving in his descent and in his presence, in the likeness of tongues of fire, revealing them as proclaimers of the true Faith, making of them true confessors and preachers of the word of God, who makest us worthy that our propitiatory prayers be accepted on this all-perfect day of salvation for those who are imprisoned in hades, who grantest us great hope that unto the dead, held in the bondage of grief, thou shalt send rest and consolation from thy presence. Hear us, disconsolate and wretched, who beseech thee, and give rest unto the souls who have fallen asleep, and make them to repose in a resplendent place, a place of verdure and rest, where there is no sorrow of any kind, nor suffering nor sighs. Array their souls in the tabernacles of the righteous, and make them worthy of peace and repose; for it is not the dead who praise thee, O Lord, nor do those who are in hades venture to offer unto thee confession, but we, the living, do bless thee and supplicate thee, O Lord, who offer unto thee prayers of supplication, petitions, and sacrifices for their soul's sake.

¶ *And immediately:*

O GREAT eternal God, holy and loving toward mankind, who dost make us worthy to stand at this hour before thine unapproachable glory, praising and glorifying thy wonders, forgive us, unworthy sinners, and grant us grace that from a humble and contrite heart we may offer thee the thrice-holy glorification, and gratitude for thy great gifts which thou workedst and dost still work through us at all times. Remember, Lord, our weakness, and destroy us not in our iniquities; but in accordance with our humility show unto us thy great mercy, that being delivered from the darkness of sin, we may walk in the day of justice, equipped with the armour of light, and freed from all the evil attacks of the wicked one, glorifying thee in all things, as those who are favoured, O only true God and Lover of mankind; for thine is in truth, O Master and Creator of all, the great Mystery, the temporary dissolution of thy creatures, and their restoration thereafter unto eternal repose. In all things we acknowledge thy favour, at our entrance into this world and at our going out therefrom, O thou who by thine unfailing promises didst hold out to us the hope of everlasting life, resurrection, and life unapprehended by corruption, which shall be ours to enjoy at thy Second Coming; for thou art the Beginning of our resurrection, the unswayed Judge of our life's work, the Lover of mankind, the rewarding Lord and Master, who hast become a partaker with us of flesh and blood, through which thou didst suffer the temptation of our sufferings willingly, out of thine exceeding condescension and compassion; and having been tempted through thy sufferings, thou didst become of thyself a Warner and a Helper for us who are tempted, guiding us into passionlessness. Wherefore, O Master, accept our prayers and supplications, and grant repose to each of our fathers, mothers, brothers, sisters, children, blood relatives, and kinsfolk, and all those who have fallen asleep in the hope of resurrection and life everlasting. Array their souls and their names in the Book of Life; in the bosoms of Abraham, Isaac, and Jacob; in the land of the living, the kingdom of heaven, and the paradise of bliss, guiding them all into thy holy dwelling-places by thy radiant angels, and raise their bodies on the day that thou hast appointed, according to thine unfailing holy promises; for there is no death, O Lord, to thy departing servants who migrate from the body and come unto thee, O God, but a translating from things sorrowful to things pleasant and benign, to repose and joy. And if they have sinned aught against thee, forgive them, and be thou compassionate unto them and us; for there is none without stain before thee, even though his life be but a day, save thou alone, Jesus Christ our God, who didst appear on earth without sin, and through whom we all trust to attain mercy and the remission of sins. Wherefore, O righteous and philanthropic God, remit, pardon, and forgive our sins and theirs; overlook both our voluntary and involuntary offenses, which we have committed either willfully or through ignorance, by the outward senses or in secret, whether by word, deed, or thought, or in any of our states and moods. As for those who have preceded us, grant them emancipation and repose, even to all thy people, and bless us who are still living, and grant us a righteous and peaceful end. Open to us the wings of thy compassion, mercy, and love to mankind; and in thy dreadful presence make us worthy of thy kingdom.

Then

O THOU most exalted God, who alone dost possess immortality, who dwellest in the unapproachable light, who in wisdom didst bring into being all creation, who didst separate between the light and the darkness,

setting the sun to rule the day, and the moon and stars
to rule the night, who on this day didst vouchsafe to
us sinners, to apprehend thy countenance by confession,
lifting to thee our evening prayer; thou, O philanthropic
God, set our prayers like incense before thee, and receive them as a sweet odour. Grant that this evening
and the approaching night may be peaceful and serene
for us. Clothe us with the armour of light, and deliver
us from nightly fears and from everything that walketh
in darkness. Vouchsafe that the slumber which thou
didst grant us for rest from our weakness be also free
from every satanic phantom. Yea, O Master, who pro-
videst good things for all, grant that, lying solemnly in
our beds, we may recall at night thy most holy Name;
and being illumined by the contemplation of thy precepts, we may wake up with a soul anxious to glorify
thy goodness, offering to thy compassion petitions and
supplications for our sins, and for those of all thy people. Wherefore, by the intercessions of the holy Theotokos visit us with mercy.

Deacon. Help, save, and have mercy, and raise us,
O God, and keep us by thy grace.

Remembering our all-holy, etc.

Priest. For thou art the Repose of our souls and
bodies, and to thee we address glory, etc.

❡ *Then the Deacon saith,* Let us finish our evening Petitions, *etc;*
and what followeth (*p. 76*).

❡ *And in the Aposticha, the following Idiomelons, in the Third Tone.*

VERILY, the tongues have become manifest wonders to all; for the Jews, of whom cometh Christ
after the flesh, were divided by lack of faith. They fell
from the divine grace and the divine light which we,
the Gentiles, have attained, who are established by the
sayings of the Disciples, giving utterance to the glory
of God, the All-benefactor, with whom we bend our
hearts as well as our knees, and worship the Holy Spirit
in faith, being strengthened by the Saviour of our souls.

Stichos: Create a clean heart in me, O God.

Now the comforting Spirit hath been poured on all flesh; for, starting with the rank of the Apostles, he extended grace through the communion of believers, certifying his effective presence by the distribution of tongues to the Disciples in fiery likeness for the praise of God and his glory. Wherefore, being supersensuously illumined with them and confirmed in the steadfast Faith, we beseech the Holy Spirit to save our souls.

Stichos: Cast me not away from thy face.

The Apostles of Christ have put on might and power from above; for the Comforter hath renewed them, and in them renewed the knowledge of the new mysteries which they proclaimd to us in tones and resounding words, teaching us to worship the all-bountiful God of simple, eternal Nature of three Persons. Wherefore, being illumined by their teachings, let us worship the Father, Son, and Holy Spirit, beseeching them to save our souls.

Glory and Now, in the Eighth Tone

Come, ye nations, let us worship the three-personed Godhead, etc. (p. 996).

❡ *Then:* Now lettest thou thy servant, *etc.* (*p. 77*); Holy God. *etc;* *and the Troparion,* Blessed art thou, O Christ, our God, *etc.* (*three times p. 1000*); *and the Priest concludeth the Prayer with the following.*

O THOU who didst empty thyself in the Fatherly bosom, condescending to take upon thyself our human nature wholly and to deify it, thereafter ascending into heaven and sitting on the right hand of the Father, whence thou didst send the eternally divine Holy Spirit, equal to thee and to thy Father in substance, might, glory, honour, and eternity, to thy holy and pure Apostles, being illumined by him, and through him illuminating the whole universe. Wherefore, O Christ our true God, by the intercessions of thine all-pure and all-blameless Mother, and the exalted all praised, God-preaching, Spirit-mantled, holy Apostles and all the saints, have mercy upon us and save us for thy goodness' sake. Amen.

MONDAY OF THE HOLY SPIRIT

❡ *The Katabasias,* The heavy of tongue, *etc.* (*p. 983*); *the Exapostei-larions of Pentecost* (*p. 1003*); *in the Einos, the first three Stichera of Vespers of Pentecost* (*p. 995*); *Glory and Now,* Of old there was confusion of tongues, *etc.* (*p. 999*); *and the rest of the Liturgy as in the Feast of Pentecost.*

❡ *And on, Especially, sing the Hermos,* Rejoice, O Queen, *etc.* (*p. 1002*); *and* We have seen the true Light, *etc; and the Benediction.*

SATURDAY AFTER PENTECOST

On which falleth the Leave-taking of Pentecost, and the whole Service of that Feast is chanted thereon.

ALL SAINTS SUNDAY

1. VESPERS

❡ *On* O Lord, to thee have I cried, *sing Six for the Resurrection, in the Eighth Tone; and the following four for All Saints.*

THE Spirit-proclaiming Disciples of the Saviour, having become, through faithfulness, instruments of the Spirit, and being scattered to the ends of the earth, sowed in steadfastness of opinion the solemn warning, and from their divine husbandry blossomed forth unto grace the army of Martyrs, who inscribed the signs of the noble passions by sundry kinds of tortures, scourgings, and fire. Verily, as favoured ones, they plead for our souls.

The venerable Martyrs, fired by the Lord's love, despised the fire; and being consumed as divine live coals, they burned, through Christ, the dried grass of the arrogance of error; bridled the mouths of beasts with

their own befitting supplications; and, being beheaded,
they themselves beheaded all the hosts of the enemy.
Yea, having dauntlessly shed their blood, they watered
the firm Church with faith.

Verily, the heroic Martyrs having wrestled with
beasts, were torn by their claws. They were cut up
with swords, their arms were dislocated, and their members writhed with the pain of arrow wounds. They
were consumed with material fire, dismembered and
prodded with lances. All this they bore magnanimous-
ly when they foresaw their approaching end, the un-
withering crowns, and the glory of Christ, whom, as
favoured ones, they implore for our souls.

Dutifully and with songs of praise let us extol the
noble assembly of the Apostles, Martyrs, Godly-minded Priests, and noble women who fought with faith
in all the ends of the earth; for, being earthly, they
united with the heavenly ones; and by their passions
attained passionlessness by the grace of Christ. And
lo, as constant luminaries they illuminate us, and as
favoured ones, plead for our souls.

Glory, in the Sixth Tone

YE are the pillars of the Church and the fulfillment
of the Gospel, O divine ranks of Martyrs. In deeds
ye have fulfilled the sayings of the Saviour; for through
you the gates of hades, opened against the Church, have
been closed; and your shed blood dried up the liba-
tions of the idols. And having nourished the perfection of believers through your slaughter, ye dazzled
the incorporals, standing before Christ wearing your
crowns. Wherefore, intercede ye ceaselessly with him
for our souls.

❡ *And Now to our Lady, in the Eighth Tone;* Verily, the King of
heaven for his love, *etc. (p. 192); in the Aposticha, the Stichera for
the Resurrection, in the Eighth Tone (p. 192); Glory, in the Sixth
Tone.*

COME, ye believers, let us today stand in rank and celebrate with true worship; let us exalt with glorifications the memorial of all-honoured, all-revered saints, shouting, Rejoice, O glorious Apostles, Prophets, Martyrs, and Bishops! Rejoice, O company of the righteous and just! Rejoice, O rank of honoured women! Supplicate ye Christ to grant the king victory over the Barbarians, and our souls the Great Mercy.

¶*And Now, the Theotokion of the Fourth Tone,* The mystery which (*p. 162*); *the Troparion for the Resurrection, in the Eighth Tone,* O compassionate One, *etc.* (*p. 193*); *and Glory for the Saints, in the Fourth Tone.*

THY Church, O Christ God, hath regaled herself in the blood of thy Martyrs throughout all the world, as in porphyry and purple. Through them she lifteth her voice, crying, Turn with thy compassion to thy people, and grant peace to thy city, and to our souls the Great Mercy.

¶*And Now, the Theotokion of the Fourth Tone,* The mystery which was hidden, *etc.* (*p. 162*).

2. MATINS

¶*The Kathismata, Blessings, Anabathmoi, and Prokeimenon for the Resurrection of the Eighth Tone; the first Matin Gospel; and the rest as usual. The Katabasias,* Open my mouth, *etc.* (*p. 114*); *then sing,* O thou who art more honourable, *etc; the Exaposteilarion for the Resurrection, and the following for the Saints.*

AS a duty let us crown with songs of praise the Forerunner, with the Apostles, Prophets, Martyrs, Bishops, righteous ones, ascetics, martyred Priests, and God-loving women, with all the God-fearing, and the myriad of angels, beseeching, through their petitions, that we may attain by their glory, glory from the presence of Christ the Saviour.

¶*And in the Einos, five for the Resurrection of the Eighth Tone; and the following three for the Saints, in the Fourth Tone.*

VERILY, the Lord hath made his Saints on earth a wonder, in that they accept his stigmata, and his Passion in the flesh, adorning themselves therewith. Plainly they regaled themselves with his divine benevolences, whom we extol as unfading flowers and fixed stars of the Church, voluntary, bloody sacrifices.

Stichos: The just cried, and the Lord heard them.

Let us extol with divine songs of praise the assembly of the Apostles, Prophets, righteous ones, teachers, and Martyrs among Priests, yea, all the God-fearing, and the ranks of holy women who strove and eagerly lived the ascetic life, and the myriads of holy ones; for they have become inheritors of the kingdom on high, and dwellers in paradise.

Stichos: Marvelous is God in his Saints.

Let us extol the Martyrs who made earth like unto heaven with excellent virtues, who emulated the death of Christ which brought about deathlessness, who walked in the narrow way and cured the sufferings of mankind with the medicine of grace, who bravely strove with united effort throughout the whole world.

¶ *Glory, the First Eothina, in the First Tone,* Verily, the Lord appeared to the Disciples, *(p. 200); Now,* Thou hast transcended, *etc. (p. 117); the Great Doxology; and* Having risen again from the tomb, *etc. (p. 119).*

3. THE MASS

¶ *The Antiphonies and Makarizimoi of the Eighth Tone for the Resurrection. And after the Eisodos, the Troparion for the Resurrection, All Saints, and the Patron Saint of the church.*

Kontakion, in the Eighth Tone

TO thee, O Lord and Author of all creation, the universe offereth as first-fruits of nature the divinity-bearing Martyrs. Wherefore, by their implorings

preserve thou thy Church in perfect safety, for the sake
of the Theotokos, O most Merciful.

❡ *The Epistle and Gospel for the First Sunday after Pentecost, known
as All-Saints Sunday (p. 219). And on Especially, sing, It is truly*
meet, *etc.*

SYNAXARION

DAVID the Prophet and king who revered the beloved of God and respected them because of his
great piety, said, How precious are thy beloved unto
me, O God (Ps. 138:17). And the divine Apostle,
having recounted the deeds of the saints and reviewed
their memory that they might serve as examples for us
in their patience, their perseverance in persecutions,
their virtues, their contempt for sin, and their turning
away from worldly things, said, Wherefore, seeing we
also are compassed about with so great a cloud of witnesses, let us lay aside every weight, and the sin that doth
so easily beset us, and let us run with patience the race
that is set before us (Heb. 12:1).

In pursuance, therefore, of the teachings of the divine
Scriptures and apostolic traditions, we also, a people of
piety and of true worship, honour the beloved saints of
God, respecting them as keepers of God's commandments, shining examples of virtue, and benefactors of
human nature. We honour every one of the known
saints on a special day of the year, as may be discovered
from the famous list of saints. But since their number
has increased many-fold at various times, still increases,
and will increase continually to the end of the world,
and since the names of many of them have escaped us,
the Church designates one day in the year on which
is celebrated the memory of all the saints, which is this
day, on which we piously beatify and honour all the
righteous, the Prophets, the Martyrs, Confessors,
Bishops, teachers, and pious ones, all those who were
counted and are counted among those who spent their
lives in piety and true worship, glorifying God with their

deeds, whether men or women, known or unknown, and on this day we also honour the hosts of angels, and especially our Lady the ever-virgin Theotokos, putting their lives before our eyes as an example and a model of virtue, petitioning them to intercede with God for us, that his grace and his boundless mercy be with us all. Amen.

Koinonikon: Praise ye the Lord from the heavens. Rejoice in the Lord, O ye just: Praise becometh the upright. Alleluia.

EIGHTH SECTION
Appendices

✠

THE CHURCH

The word *Ekklesia, Church* from which the English word *ecclesiastical* is derived, comes from the Greek word *kalein,* to call, combined with the Greek prefix *ek,* meaning to call out. In its general sense it meant a crowd of people called together at one place for some purpose. In this sense the ancient Greeks used it to signify public gatherings. In the more restricted sense it means two things: the congregation of the faithful, wherever found in all parts of the world; of those found in one diocese, or one city, as in Isidore of Pelusum, where he says of the Church that, "It is the multitude of the saints, embraced by Orthodox faith and good conduct." [1] And said St. Eubius in a more extensive sense, "It is the people who believe in Christ." It also means the place or house where the grave multitude of the faithful meet, discharging their obligations of religion and worship to God. The first connotation, which is the true one, is the one we shall employ here. The second is a figurative sense, applying the name of the place to those who occupy it, as in the Holy Bible.[2] But the conclusive and definite meaning of the word is, "The multitude of those who admit and confess faith in Christ, an Orthodox and single faith, united in communion in particular Sacraments, governed by spiritual, canonical pastors, with Christ Himself as their Head."

---

[1] Book 2 Epistle 246.   [2] 1 Ki. 8:11 and 20 and 27-30.

Divisions of the Church

The Church is divided into the "Teaching Church," consisting of pastors, teachers, and their assistants, whom Eusebius calls the "rank of the saints," and the "Learning Church," consisting of the faithful who live under the management of those spiritual pastors, and whom Eusebius calls "rank of the submitting." [1] There is another division, into the "Church Militant," and the "Church Triumphant." The first is the totality of the striving faithful on this earth, and the latter is the rank of the glorified faithful in heaven, as St. Macarius the Great said (First Discourse).

We may here state the distinguishing signs of the true Church, which is in truth the Body of Christ.

Marks of the True Church

The signs and attributes which the true Orthodox Church of Christ possesses and takes pride in are those plainly and explicitly recorded in the Holy Bible and in the Confession of Faith, which was partly of the authorship of the First Ecumenical Council of Nicea, and partly that of the Second Ecumenical Council held in Constantinople. These Marks are four: Unity, Holiness, Catholicity (universality), and Apostolicity. Said the Confession, "And in One, Catholic, Holy, and Apostolic Church." Let us examine each separately.

Unity

By the Unity of the Church we understand that all the faithful, scattered over all the face of the earth, from one body or entity, or Orthodox opinion, confessing one faith, pressing towards one aim unto salvation. Hence the Church must have two things before that oneness is realized. The first is the agreement and unity of Orthodox doctrine; the second is the brotherhood of the faithful everywhere and their unity, as one

---

[1] Evangelical Proof (Cap. 17:2).

body, especially of the honoured pastors, preserving outwardly the canonically instituted rules of deserving submission and homage, and inwardly united by the unity of faith. The center of this unity is Christ, the head of the Church. The Holy Scriptures declare plainly this unity of faith, where it is written, "Endeavouring to keep the unity of the Spirit in the bond of peace. There is one body, and one Spirit, even as ye are called in one hope of your calling. One Lord, one faith, one baptism, one God and Father of all, who is above all, and through all, and in you all." [1] And again, "For as the body is one, and hath many members, and all the members of that one body, being many, are one body, so also is Christ. For by one Spirit are we all baptized into one body, whether we be Jews or Gentiles, whether we be bond or free; and have been all made to drink into one Spirit." [2]

The Holy Fathers are equally explicit and clear. Thus St. Clement of Alexandria says, "The Church is one, true, of ancient verity, in which are counted those of upright intentions. And since God is one and the Lord is one, the inestimable thing is praised by its singleness, because it resembles the one principle. And since the Church belongs to One, She is naturally One, even if all heresies should rise against her to break her up. She is, as we say of her, one ancient Church, Catholic in her nature, and from the point of view of belief, origin, and sublimity." [3]

And in his 149th Discourse, of his bound Discourses, St. Chrysostom says, "In the cities and villages are numerous churches. But the Church is one; for the Christ who is present in them all is one, perfect, and indivisible." And in the First Discourse of his Commentary on First Corinthians, he also says, "The Church is God's united and one, not only in Corinth but in all the inhabited earth. Separation cannot be understood from the name Ecclesia, for it is a name

---

1 Eph. 4:3-6.   2 1 Cor. 12:12-13.   3 1 Stromata 7, p. 765.

for unity and brotherhood." And again in the Second Discourse of his Commentary on Second Corinthians he says, "We must all seek shelter in the Church, because she is one home for us all, and behave as it is proper for us to do; for we are one body, since Baptism is one, the Table is one, the Fountain is one, the creation is one, and the Father is one."

Of similar import are the words in the letter of Theodorite, Bishop of Cyr, to King Constantine the Great, "God willed it and there was his One and Catholic Church. True, her branches have spread to many places, but she lives and grows by one Spirit, according to the divine will."[1]

And Epiphanius, Archbishop of Cyprus, speaking of the thirty-first hersey, said, "Though the Church be scattered all over the earth, to the furthermost parts, she keeps the glad tidings diligently as though dwelling in one house. Thus the churches in Germany did not believe in anything different, nor were they taught anything different, neither the churches that are in Kurgia, in Cilicia (northern Thrace), in the lands of the rising sun, or those in Egypt, or in Libya, or the churches founded at the extreme parts of the inhabited world. But in every place the gospel of salvation shines forth by its ownself as the God-created sun illuminates the whole world, yet being one himself."

"All they whose hope is in Christ," said Basil the Great, "are one people; and the Christians today are one Church, though called after many countries."[2] And Theophlactus, commenting on the first chapter of the First Epistle to the Corinthians, also said, "All the faithful are one Church, wherever they are, and wherever they happen to be."

And the sainted Martyr Cyprian, who lived in the middle of the third century, said, in a special Epistle he wrote on the unity of the Church, "He who cannot call the Church his mother, cannot make God his

---

[1] Church History, First Division, No. 9. [2] 1 Epistle 293.

Father. And if it could not be possible for one outside Noah's ark to survive, it could not be possible for one outside the Church's gates to be saved."

And the beatified Augustine, in his discussion of the unity of the Church, (Cap 19) says, "He for whom Christ is not head, cannot attain salvation for himself, and eternal life. Nor can one make Christ his head unless he joins the body of Christ, which is the Church."

Now since the Church is one, and that oneness consists primarily and universally of perfect agreement in Orthodox doctrines, it necessarily follows that all those who do not conform to those Orthodox doctrines, whether by addition or omission, or by any innovation of their own, thus changing the truth, are outside this one Holy Church, as one may also ascertain from a review of the sixth and seventh canons of the Second Ecumenical Council, and the first canon of St. Basil the Great.

Catholicity

The word *Catholicity* comes from the Greek *katholo,* a compound word consisting of *kata* a Greek preposition of many meanings, and the Greek noun *holos,* meaning whole. It is an adverbial word signifying universality, and from it the word *katholikos* is derived, as also the feminine, *katholike.* Thus the term *Katholike Ekklesia,* means universal, or unrestricted Church.

The Christian Church, therefore, was called *Catholic* because, first, she was not intended to be confined to one place, time, or nation; and, secondly, because she comprises and embraces wholly all the correct teaching, propagated in all parts of the inhabited world, through transmission from the Apostles, and preserved at all times and by all peoples as received by her and as taught to her children for salvation. She is also in agreement on doctrine, rites, and church polity, without dissension.

In the first meaning the Christian Church differs from the Jewish, in that God's law in the Old Covenant was restricted to the Jewish people. The Church of God was exclusively confined to that nation. And because the worship of the true God, the offering of sacrifices, and the other Jewish rites, or worship, were restricted to Jerusalem, and hence the Church of God was limited in space to that place, and because the Jewish Church was restricted in time, too, ending with the coming of Christ, the Saviour Jesus Christ (may his Name be worshipped) came and gave us a Catholic Church, not confined in place as at Jerusalem, nor restricted in time, as to the period before his coming, nor the property of one nation, as the Jewish.

In confirmation of this the glorified Master said, by the mouth of his Prophet Isaiah, "And it shall come to pass in the last days, that the mountain of the Lord's house shall be established in the top of the mountains, and shall be exalted above the hills; and all nations shall flow unto it. And many people shall go and say; Come ye, and let us go up to the mountain of the Lord, to the house of God of Jacob; and he will teach us of his ways." [1] And again in his Prophet Malachi, "For, from the rising of the sun even unto the going down of the same, my name shall be great among the Gentiles; and in every place incense shall be offered unto my name, and a pure offering." [2] And he himself (may he be praised and glorified) said plainly to his Disciples, "Go ye therefore and teach all nations. Go ye into all the world, and preach the Gospel to every creature." [3] And again he said, "But ye shall receive power, after that the Holy Spirit is come upon you: and ye shall be witnesses unto me both in Jerusalem, and in all Judæa, and in Samaria, and unto the uttermost part of the earth." [4] This is explained further by his beloved Disciple in the Book of Revelation, speaking by the mouth of the elders, "Thou art worthy to take the book, and to open the seals thereof: for thou wast slain, and hast redeemed us to God by thy blood out of every kin-

---

[1] Is. 2:2-3.   [2] Mal. 1:11.   [3] St. Matt. 28:19; St. Mark.16:15.   [4] Acts 1:8

dred, and tongue, and people and nation."[1] Also,
"After this I beheld, and lo, a great multitude, which
no man could number, of all nations, and kindreds, and
people, and tongues, stood before the throne."[2]

In this sense St. Cyril of Jerusalem wrote, "She (the
Church) is called Catholic because of her existence
throughout the inhabited world."[3] Similarly St. Athanasius the Great, "The Church is called Catholic
because she is spread throughout all the world."[4] And
Theophlactus, commenting on the twelfth chapter of
the First Epistle to the Corinthians, "The Catholic
Church is the one found in all the inhabited world,
whose body is the churches of the various climes, and
whose head is Christ."

So much for the catholicity of space. But the Church
is Catholic in more than that sense. In the temporal
sense the Catholicity of the Church indicates her existence from the time she was founded to our own days,
and that there was no time, and there will be no time,
in which the Church was not and shall not be. This
we may ascertain from the words of the Saviour himself to his Disciples, "Lo, I am with you always even
unto the end of the world."[5]

She is also Catholic in consideration of her teaching
all the Orthodox doctrines, in a satisfactory and thor-
ough way. Thus St. Cyril of Jerusalem, in his sermon
quoted above, says, "The Church is called Catholic
because she teaches all the doctrines which mankind
needs to know, about things visible and invisible, about
things heavenly and earthly, and, in general, without
omitting anything."

Again she is called Catholic in consideration of her
purpose, which is to attract to her all nations and subject to her, for true worship, all mankind, of whatever
race or station, to heal all sorts of sins, and to teach all
virtues which consist of deeds and words. And this,

---

[1] Rev. 5:9. [2] Rev. 7:9. [3] Didactic Sermons, 18. [4] Vol. II, p. 202;
[5] St. Mt. 28:20; 1 Cor. 11:26.

too, St. Cyril refers to in his sermon (Cap. 23) where he says, "The Church is called Catholic because of her subjugation to true religion of all mankind, the leaders and the led, the learned and the illiterate; and because she treats and cures every sort of sin, committed by the soul or body, and contains within herself every conceivable thought of virtue, in word and deed, and all the various spiritual gifts."

In this and the preceding quotation, this venerable Father among saints, and divinely-minded teacher of theology comprehended all the attributes of Catholicity in the Church—her extension in the inhabited world, in the north, south, east, and west; and her inclusion of every race, tongue, and kindred, as the Apostle says, "There is neither Greek nor Jew, circumcision nor uncircumcision, Barbarian, Scythian, bond nor free: but Christ is all, and in all.[1]

Secondly, comprising all the true teachings of salvation and Orthodox doctrines. And this descripton is the original and essential one by which the Church is called Catholic; for it is an attribute belonging intrinsically to her, potentially and actually, impossible of separation from her; for there has been no time when the Church has not held the true teaching or maintained it.

However, the description of the Church as extending through the whole inhabited world, and her subjection of all mankind, is a potative one; for it is not otherwise rightful for any of the Christian churches to claim catholicity, since to the present day there is no church nor any that has subjected the whole human race, leaders and led, learned and illiterate. Said the beatified of everlasting memory, St. Macarius, Bishop of Moscow, in his book on *Orthodox Theology,* "It is not necessary for the Church to embrace actually all the inhabited world and all mankind to be called Catholic; for it was not possible for the Church to spread

---

[1] Col. 3:11; 1 Cor. 12:13.

except gradually, as she is still spreading and as she has for eighteen centuries. The Church may even be delimited by heresies and innovations, or by the persecutions of her enemies, yet be said to have been and still to be Catholic in her purpose. . . . And from this it becomes evident why the holy Fathers called the Church in the age of the Apostles, and generally in the first three centuries, Catholic, when she was incomparably smaller than she is now, indicating thereby her tendency or inclination to catholicity."

Is the application of the attribute of Catholicity to the Church of Christ, however, sufficient to indicate the meaning of truth? I say, No. For all the churches that call on the Name of Christ throughout the world claim thereby to be Catholic; for they all differ from the Jewish Church, being unrestricted in themselves, in any particular place, time, or nation. How then shall we distinguish the truth of this claim? We reply, to know one truly Catholic Church we simply go to the original and true definition of catholicity by which the holy Canons and the Confession of Faith called the Church Catholic, or universal. According to this, the Church is called Catholic because her teachings and commandments are complete and all-inclusive, comprising all that is necessary for salvation, laid down and approved by the holy Apostles and the noble Ecumenical Councils, and kept in one form by all her Christian sons in all parts of the inhabited world, not merely by some of her individual members or organizations.

The true Catholic Church, therefore, is the firm canonical and legal Church, comprising the Apostolic teaching, sound in all its parts and at all times, without fault or discord in the sacred doctrines, Christian customs, and church organization just as she received these from the holy Apostles and the holy Ecumenical Councils. And therefore, as the Church is distinguished by the first attribute, non-restriction, from the restricted Jewish Church, so by the second, that is by her inclusiveness and preservation of the universal teaching of doctrine, church doctrines, and unimpaired Apostlic traditions, she is distinguished from heretics, innovators, and schismatics, who have deviated from sound teaching. She is therefore not spurious, claiming unity when in truth she is separated into many divisions, and differs in her organization, her customs, and her doctrines withal.

If one of these divisions usurps to itself the title of Catholicity, claiming this as its truthful title either because of the large number of its followers or because it is spread in numerous places, the true Church does not vouchsafe it this right, believing such a division to be faulty in Orthodoxy, and because the Catholicity of the Church consists briefly in Orthodoxy. For this cause the holy Fathers did not stop at describing the Church as One, Catholic, and Holy, but added Apostolic. Hence every church that is not Apostolic, Orthodox, is not Catholic.

It is therefore proper to conclude this discussion with the words of St. Athanasius the Great, in his Epistle against those who consider truth in a matter only in proportion to the great number who follow it, "The multitude who claim the truth without sound reasons are more able to intimidate than to convince."

Holiness

The third distinguishing mark of the Church of Christ is Holiness, of which St. Paul says, "As Christ also loved the Church and gave himself for it; that he might sanctify and cleanse it with the washing of the water by the word, that he might present it to himself a glorious church not having spot, or wrinkle, or any such thing; but that it should be holy and without blemish." [1]

---

[1] Eph. 5:25-27.

She is Holy, first because of her origin; for God himself, the Fountain of holiness, is her Foundation and Help. Secondly, in view of her means, her teachings and her holy Sacraments, through which she is preserved and perfected for the sanctification of her faithful. Thirdly, in view of her purpose or aim; for her members are called unto holiness and required to press forward to it. Should one ask, "How can the Church be holy when there are many members in her who are unholy, yea, sinners and defiled by all kinds of evils and vices?" We reply, as we previously said, that the Church is considered holy in view of her origin, means, and purpose. The purpose or aim of the Church, therefore, is to sanctify, purify, and save all members that belong to her. It does not mar this holy purpose, nor defile the Holiness of the Church, if some of her members wallow in the pollutions of this age, robed in adultery, and putting off the robes of divine grace and holiness. Howbeit, the Church never despairs of healing these, her ill members, nor has she ceased to care for them, steadying their steps towards repentance by counsels, reproofs, and canon which she imposes on them to bring them unto the sanctification of soul and body.

This we learn from the acts of the Apostles and the ancient Church. Thus the Apostles used to establish and strengthen all the faithful for the preservation of goodly virtues and pure conduct. They did not consider the wicked and those of ill repute as altogether outside the Church. On the contrary, they employed various means and methods for reforming them, this being one of their main cares, as the Apostle John said in his first general Epistle. "My little children, these things write I unto you, that ye sin not. And if any man sin, we have an advocate with the Father, Jesus Christ the righteous."[1] And also in the same Epistle, "If we say that we have no sin, we deceive ourselves, and the truth is not in us."[2] And in the Gospels the Church is lik-

---

[1] 1 St. Jn. 2:1. [2] 1 St. Jn. 1:8.

ened to a field in which the wheat and tares grow together, and to a net that is cast into the sea and is filled with all kinds of fish. It is not strange, therefore, to find in the Church the sheep and the goats, the wicked servant and good servant, the wise virgins and the foolish virgins. It is for God to discriminate between them. And lastly, we say the Church here on earth resembles the threshing-floor on which wheat is mixed with the chaff, and the just God will purge his floor and gather the wheat into his garners on the last day, but the chaff He will burn with unquenchable fire.[1] And for what reason did the Son of God bow the heavens and come down to earth? Was it not to save sinners? For if the Church embraced only the holy, why was it founded? For whom is sanctification, and for whom was instituted the Sacrament of Penance, and the other Sacraments? For whom came salvation? The true Church, therefore, is one as Christ said which calls sinners not the righteous to repentance. As for the sinners who repent not, sometimes by the divine authority granted the pastors of the Church, and sometimes by an invisible act of God, they are cut off from the body of the Church as dead members, and in this way the Church continues to be holy.

Apostolicity

The fourth distinguishing sign of the Orthodox Church is Apostolicity, meaning that it is built on the foundation of the Apostles, as the Apostle Paul said in his Epistle to the people of Ephesus, "And are built upon the foundation of the apostles and prophets, Jesus Christ himself being the chief corner stone."[2]

This Apostolicity consists, first, of the teaching of the faith, provided such teaching is kept as preached and taught by the holy Apostles, without defect in statement or measure; secondly, in the canonical ordination

---

[1] St. Mt. 3:12. [2] Eph. 2:20.

of pastors for the Church, as successors of the Apostles, and the continuity of the chain of their succession after them.

These four marks are possessed only by the Orthodox Church. For this reason she is the only ark patterned by God which saves, which brings the faithful to eternal bliss, and without her there is no salvation. She is ONE because all the multitudes of the faithful Orthodox, of whatever tribe, and in whatever place found, confess by one Orthodox confession the noble doctrines of faith, and worship one God in true worship, being one body only.

She is HOLY because from the time she was instituted she grew in a holy way, preserving and completing the holy Sacraments to sanctify the faithful.

She is CATHOLIC because she embraces all the faithful in all parts of the inhabited world from the time she was founded to the end of time, teaching the doctrines of salvation in a general way, without exception, and managing the affairs of her own members as much as possible.

She is APOSTOLIC because she has preserved the doctrines of faith safe and sound to the utmost, without defect, as she received them from the holy Apostles, changing nothing and inventing nothing, however slight.

In conclusion, in true Catholicity it is not expansion in space, or greatness of number only, that are looked for, but the Catholicity of space must be identical with Catholicity of doctrine, the divine teaching in general, being perfect and complete, recalling here what the great St. Athanasius said, "The multitude who claim the truth without sound reason are more able to intimidate than to convince."

The True Church

This Apostolic, Orthodox, and Catholic Church, is the Orthodox Church in truth, the Eastern Church in name, which embraces all true Christians, in the north and the south, in the east and the west, and which gathers into her bosom many nations from all parts of the world. She is in truth Apostolic because she took her beginning from the Lord Jesus Christ and his undefiled Apostles, as we said before, who founded her and established her not only in her entirety, but in her parts also, as in Jerusalem, Antioch, Alexandria, Constantinople, and other places. These apostolic sees (cathedras) have remained firm, and the chain of their pastors is in successive continuity, having been founded by the Lord and his Apostles. She is organized in accordance with the wish of her founder, Jesus Christ, and his holy Apostles. She knows one Head, not a mortal man, temporal by nature, subject at every moment to error and mistake, and residing in this city or that metropolis. Rather, she recognizes the One and true Head, the invisible and incarnate God, Saviour of the world, Jesus Christ, who is alone infallible. She has also true pastors, coming in an unbroken succession from the Apostles. Her Ministry is divided into three Orders or degrees. Every local church has its own Bishop, and all her Bishops recognize and submit equally to the ultimate authority of the Ecumenical Councils. The teaching of faith, and true worship is uninterrupted in her, and the rites of her services and Sacraments are complete and perfect, being founded on original canons, set forth from ancient times, and confirmed by those who have the right to confirm. She is in truth a Church because all the attributes of a Church belong to her, such as Holiness, Unity, Catholicity, etc. Her teaching is holy because it corresponds to God's words and pure transmission of the Fathers, ancient, Orthodox, free of all falsification and alteration, of any addition or omission. Nor does she hold anything that is contrary thereto, of heresy or innovation of the human mind. She is sufficient to the nourishment of the faithful, and to cause to grow in them all that is necessary for salvation, and required for godliness. Her Sacraments and fulfillments are also holy, because in spirit and in fact they are in the most appropriate form, worthy to grant the faithful sanctification by grace, to cause to grow in them the feeling of piety, elevating their minds and souls to the heavens, in accordance with her purpose. She is too pure to mingle with anything that is false, dense, worldly, or unseemly. She is holy in her pastorate; for this pastorate is spiritual, based on apostolic and paternal canons and commandments, and also removed from worldly things and all that has a tendency to be immersed in temporal authority. She is holy in her children, because she has brought a countless multitude into possession of the triumphant Church in all periods of time. These are the cloud of witnesses of countless number, the ranks of High Priests, the mass of godly people and confessors, and the rest of the righteous in whom the great wonders of God have appeared, and who in every age are soldiers of the Lord of hosts, who receive the crown of victory after triumph. She is also One since she does not side with the spirit of every teaching; for, while embracing many tongues and many nations, her faith is one, her Sacraments, services, doctrines, and canons are one, her Ministry is one, and her Head is one, Jesus Christ, and her pastors are united in the one bond of love, keeping "The unity of the Spirit in the bond of peace." [1] This quality makes her remote from any stigma of hatred, and to be ceaseless in prayer and supplication for the unity of all churches. And while she works to her utmost for this unity, she does not approve at all of the use of force and persecution, or of deceitful societies for its attainment. On the contrary, she calls men to it by counsel and teaching, meekness and the proof of the Spirit. Above all this, she embraces in her bosom many nations, as we said before, guarding the definitions of the Apostolic, Ecumenical Councils and the truth and perfection of the noble and holy Confession of Faith.

---

[1] Eph. 4:3.

*On the Infallability of the Christian Church and Her
Ecumenical Councils*

This Catholic, Holy, and Apostolic Church, being
the body of Christ and one in relation to her one Head,[1]
and consisting of the totality of believers in the Son of
God, Jesus Christ, both leaders and led, pastors and
congregation, teachers and disciples, is built by Christ
God Himself, who stands in her midst to the end of
time, and who is always found in her among those who
come together in his Name.[2] She is led by the Holy
Spirit who ever guides her into all the truth, and abides
with her for ever, according to his truthful promise,
"And I will pray the Father, and he shall give you another Comforter, that he may abide with you for ever.
. . . He shall teach you all things, and bring all things
to your remembrance, whatsoever I have said unto you
. . . and he will guide you into all truth."[3] She is also
confirmed by God the Father by his sanctification of
her through his truth.[4] She being "The pillar and
ground of the truth,"[5] established firmly for ever on her
foundation Christ, and the truth of faith in him, preserving his Gospel and teachings and preaching them
in all the inhabited world, according to his divine command, "Go ye into all the world and preach the Gospel
to every creature . . . teaching them to observe all things
whatsoever I have commanded you: and lo, I am with
you always even unto the end of the world",[6] they
having rightly divided the word of truth,[7] it follows
that she is infallible from all error and falsehood, especially in her Ecumenical Councils; for it is necessary
that the attribute of truth, hence infallibility, hence, salvation, go always with her religious and moral teachings, this being connected with man's true worship, his
salvation, and hence his union with God.

---

[1] Eph 1:22-23; 4:5; 5:22-23; and Col. 1:8. [2] St. Mt. 18:20. [3] St. Jn.
14:16, 26, and 16:13. [4] St. Jn. 17:17. [5] 1 Tim. 3:15. [6] St. Mk. 16:15;
St. Mt. 28:20. [7] 2 Tim. 2:15.

If it is possible to admit error, falsehood, and lies as pertaining to the Holy Church of Christ, in her determination of doctrines, religious teachings, rules, and canons, it is possible to admit this even in the case of the Holy Scriptures which contain the truths inspired by God for the guidance of mankind.

This can never be. The Prophets who wrote the Holy Scriptures, spoke of God as their title implies; for the word *Prophet* signifies *speaking for God* (from the Greek *pro* and *phanae*), since the Prophets spoke of God, his purposes, and his will.

If this be the case, how is it possible to admit error and falsehood in the Prophets of God and his Apostles, when we are commanded by God himself to follow them, obey them, and believe what they told us of him (may he be glorified). Would we not be, in that case, as those following, obeying, and believing erroneous, false, and lying men?

Or, how could God who commanded us to beware lying, falsehood, and error consent to our following persons who are subject to these things? How could God the Undefiled use such vessels for his Holy Spirit? Further, what will be their position who hold God above all blame and deficiency, yet ascribe to his servants, who are the image of his perfection, what is beneath his dignity? For this reason we have said that we cannot consider the Church except as above error, infallible in her faith, her sayings, her teachings, her decrees, and her rules, free of lying, deceit, intellectual hypocrisy, error, falsehood, and baseness in her canons.

The teaching of the Holy Bible on the infallibility of the Church in her Ecumenical Councils was known to all the venerable Fathers of the Church and to her honourable teachers from ancient times to the present day. It was recognized by the Ecumenical Councils themselves as the Seventh Ecumencial Council in its first canon regarding the previous six councils, where it says, and its saying is true and free of every defect,

"The divine canons are an example unto the clergy that may follow in their way, and thus we accept them all gladly, singing with David, the revealer of divinities, to the Lord and saying, 'I have rejoiced in the way of thy testimonies, as much as in all riches."[1] And also, "The righteousness of thy testimonies is everlasting: give me understanding, and I shall live."[2] If therefore, these prophetic words thus reveal to us that we should keep God's testimonies and live by them for ever, it is evident that they remain firm and unshaken, and Moses the beholder of God, also says that we cannot add unto them nor diminish aught from them.[3] And the Apostle Peter, filled with pride in them, cries out, "Which things the angels desire to look into."[4] And again St. Paul says, "But though we, or an angel from heaven, preach any other gospel unto you than that which we have preached unto you, let him be accursed."[5] These things, therefore, being known unto us in this manner, let us concern ourselves with them, as one finding many treasures. Let us serenely receive these divine canons and keep their contents with unshaken confidence, in accordance with what was set forth by those trumpets of the Holy Spirit, the all-praised Apostles, and was decreed by the six holy Ecumenical and local Councils, which were held for delivering such commandments, and in accordance with what was determined by our holy Fathers, who were all illuminated by the very same Spirit, laying down what is fitting.

And likewise the Patriarchs of the East, in their Epistle to the Holy Russian Synod, "We admit and confess, without the least doubt, this firm truth, namely that the universal (Catholic) Church cannot err and deviate from the truth; or be deceived and thus reveal lies instead of truth; for the all-holy Spirit who worketh always in those who serve in faith, whether

---

[1] Ps. 119:14.   [2] Ps. 119:43.   [3] Dt. 4:2; 12:32.   [4] 1 St. Pe. 1:12.
[5] Gal. 1:8.

they be church Fathers or Teachers, preserves her safe from every error and deviation."[1]

WHAT PRAYER IS AND ITS ACKNOWLEDG-MENT

This Church of the Son of God, sanctified by his Father's truth and administered by his Holy Spirit, acting in accordance with what he revealed in his precious Book, was led to him and guided by his commandments by conviction of the conscience that what he revealed to his servants is God's religion, his true law, and the way of salvation leading to him, decreed the necessity of prayer, which is only the rising of the soul to God, union with him mentally, and communicating with him spiritually.

This prayer is always either a supplication, by which one seeks to draw near to God; a petition for forgiveness; thanks for his grace; a deliverance from some adversity; a performance of the religious duty of worship; or glorification for miracles; as in the words of the Son of Sirach the Wise, "And he hath given men skill, that he might be honoured in his marvelous works."[2]

The Effect of Prayer and Its Purpose

And as there is no spiritual life without prayer, God made it compulsory for man, linking it with appointed and successive times, that its succession may make for the permanency of obedience and supplication to him, as in his saying, "Watch and pray."[3] And like what the Apostle said, "Pray without ceasing."[4] Thus with the continuity of our prayers and supplications our obedience will continue, and with continuity of our obedience, our awe of him and our desire for him will continue; and with the continuity of our awe and desre will continue the goodness of God's creatures and the purity of conduct leading unto him.

---

[1] Cap. 12. [2] Sirach 28:6. [3] St. Mt. 26:41. [4] 1 Thes. 5:17.

By prayer, therefore, we discharge our debt to the Creator,[1] receiving in exchange absolution of our sins,[2] deliverance from distresses and calamities,[3] with the healing of our bodies and the salvation of our souls, as in the Holy Bible, "My son, in thy sickness be not negligent: but pray unto the Lord, and he will make thee whole."[4] And also, "Is any among you afflicted? Let him pray. . . . And the prayer of faith shall save the sick, and the Lord shall raise him up: And if he have committed sins, they shall be forgiven him."[5]

If we are not healed at once of our ills, we shall be granted by God's favour the power and help to bear our ills patiently, however long they endure. And if the sickness is incurable, then through God's mercies, we obtain suitable time for repentance and for sufficient preparation to face death with an easy conscience. In this there is enough consolation for our souls at the end of our lives, after which we may stand with great favour before our righteous Judge, having fulfilled what he commanded us to do, enjoying thereafter that to which the intent of prayer and the effectiveness of worship lead, which is union with God who is exalted and praised, as it is said, "Whatsoever ye shall ask in prayer, believing, ye shall receive."[6] As it was with that thief on the cross, who uttered that passionate prayer in the last moment of his life, saying, "Lord, remember me when thou comest into thy kingdom," the Saviour answering him and saying, "Today shalt thou be with me in paradise."[7]

THE FOUNDING OF THE CHURCH AND BY WHOM IT WAS FOUNDED

By this we mean the true Church of the Word of God, his only Son, which he founded at the time of his

---

[1] Ps. 42:8. [2] Numbers 21:7. [3] Acts 10:2, 4. [4] Sirach 38:9. [5] St. Ja. 5:13, 15. [6] St. Mt. 21:22. [7] St. Lk. 23:42, 43.

Incarnation for the salvation of mankind; for God, in his abundant mercy and surpassing love, not wishing that the work of salvation cease with his Ascension into heaven, instituted a rank of persons to work with him, after his departing bodily from this world. This is af-affirmed by the God-mantled Ignatius in his Epistle to gether with God, ye are God's husbandry, ye are God's building."[1] In this way, then, was salvation to pervade all peoples at all times, as he himself said, "Go ye therefore, and teach all nations . . . teaching them to observe all things whatsoever I have commanded you. And lo, I am with you always even unto the end of the world."[2] And again, "Then Jesus said to them again, Peace be unto you, as my Father hath sent me, even so, send I you."[3]

Ritual Books

In accordance with this command, therefore, and with this divine economy, the undefiled Apostles and their followers after them walked, teaching men the way of salvation and true belief. In addition also to the moral teachings and the beliefs which pertain to salvation, and in compliance with God's revelation in his previous book, the Old and the New Testaments, they introduced special prayers applying to every occasion or sickness. In this way were the church ordinances also formed and recorded in ritual books as they were called. These ritual books consist of services, such as the divine service of the Mass by the Apostle James, and that of Saints Basil, John, and Gregory, the baptisimal service and the services for the rest of the Sacraments; of offices, such as the Midnight Office, Matins, the Canonical Hours, the Makarizmoi, Vespers, the Slumber Prayer (Compline), the Paracletice, and others; of useful eulogies and hymns of praise, such as the praise of the Theotokos, and the eulogies of the saints in the Horologium, the Menaion, and others; of

---

[1] 1 Cor. 1:9.   [2] St. Mt. 28:19, 20.   [3] St. Jn. 20:21.

the accounts and acts of the saints; of divine teachings from the Gospel, the Epistles, the Old Testament, such as the Prophets, etc; of hymns of praise unto God for his benevolences; of petitions and supplications to God for his power and benignancy in times of distress and hardship, and of other similar topics, sometimes intertwined with religious doctrines, sometimes consisting of religious doctrines alone, and sometimes separate.

The Nature of Hymns, Eulogies, Ritual, and Service in Prayer

For further elucidation, it may be said here that church hymns and eulogies are not of the nature of doctrinal or canonical definitions. They are rather the outpourings of righteous or pietistic feelings which move the listeners to piety and righteousness, and to the imitation of God's chosen ones. They arouse in those who hear them the same spirit of piety that was in the eulogized saints, bringing out great admiration and reverence for virtue, that thereby we may come to love it and hold fast to it, following the example of those who thereby pleased God, for which he had chosen them, yea even adopted them as his sons.

If, therefore, we find that the eulogist, in praising one of the Apostles, Fathers, teachers, or saints, of whatever rank, has gone too far, his act should not be regarded as wrong, but merely as excessive reverence, in which the aim is the benefit of the listeners. Equally, the eulogy should not be taken as a recording of history, the promulgation of a rule, the statement of a doctrine, or the designation of office or rank. Rather, the eulogizer's aim and purpose is the exaltation of the eulogized, the depicting of his attributes, and the glorification of his virtues. And this latter the eulogist does for two reasons—first, to express his feelings towards the eulogized, and secondly, for the instruction of the listeners in the virtues and attributes of the eulogized, thus making them objects of emulation by those listeners. And what

is said of church eulogies may be said also of the sermons, discourses, and teachings.

Rites, or rituals, on the other hand, are the orders
and classification of religious celebrations, while the
service is the actual performance of religious worship,
in accordance with a set order and embodied especially
in a book for the arrangement of the services and known
as the

Typicon

which signifies *order* or *arrangement*. The Typicon
gives the order of church rites for all the services, special prayers, and church celebrations for the whole year.

The Object of Ceremonies and Rites Displayed in Prayer

We have already seen the object which the Church
had in instituting its doctrines and moral teachings, the
prayers, the order of celebrations, rites and festivities,
the eulogies, which most likely appeared in the eighth,
ninth, and tenth centuries, and after that time, and the
service of the Divine Mass. All these the Church ordained well and with respect to the dignity of their
respective subjects, lest there be any confusion in the
subjects of worship and in its holy rites. But
there is another object. It is to give us sensible proofs,
pointing to the true Orthodox doctrines which are invisible, as the revealer of the divine Sacraments said,
"God reveals to us spiritual things under the guise of
corporeal things." And thus God leads us through
these to his divine perfection, and finally, to eternal
unity with him.

On the Sublimity of Religion and how People Differ in its Reception

The Christian religion received its perfection from
its beginning, because it is not a human invention, but

an act of God, which he wrought without ambiguity for the salvation of mankind. Whence we say that no succession of time, even unto the end of ages can bring forth anything for the cultivation of character and the regulation of the life of mankind, that can be better, more sublime, or more beneficial than what Christ God taught his Apostles, and the Apostles taught those who succeeded them.

However, this teaching, so sublime, showed different effects, according to the differences in the condition of those who received it, and according to the measure of grace with which God accompanied it.

The true Israelites, having been taught from the traditions of their ancestors and from the study of the Holy Scriptures, and having been brought up from infancy in the knowledge of God and the keeping of the law, showed themselves capable of carrying out all the perfection of this teaching, as soon as this perfection was revealed to them. They understood what that salvation was which the Messiah was about to offer them, and what his kingdom was going to be like. But for the Gentiles it was difficult to be led to that perfection;[1] for up to the time of its revelation they had lived without God and without law,[2] being guided by habit to their idols, like beasts, wallowing in every iniquity. And it was this which made the Apostles refrain from being too severe with the faithful among the Gentiles.[3]

That from Jerusalem Alone must the Worship, Services, and Commandments of Religion be sought

Since holy Jerusalem is the place where the Christian religion came down, then from its Christians, the undefiled Apostles and their successors, must we seek the true teachings of religion, its church orders and regulations, and the services of its divine worship, as we are doing now.

---

[1] 1 Cor. 12:2. [2] Eph. 2:12. [3] Acts 15:19.

Christian Worship

Christian worship differs in its nature both from Jewish and from heathen worship, all of which consisted of outward rites and appearances. But in Christianity the essential element is the worship of God in spirit and in truth, as the Saviour himself taught.[1]

For this reason there were introduced into the divine service, as early as the time of the Apostles, the reading of the Holy Scriptures, with their interpretation, the Psalms, prayers, and hymns, with the fulfillment of the Sacrament of the Eucharist, as in the Holy Book, where it is written, "And they continued steadfastly in the apostles' doctrine and fellowship, and in the breaking of the bread and in prayers".[2]

Places of Worship

Since it is permitted in the Christian religion to worship God not only in Jerusalem, as the Jews did, but everywhere, the Apostles held their worship wherever they found themselves, whether in the Temple at Jerusalem, or in private houses. It was customary for most homes in ancient times to have a special part set aside for worship, in which Christians came together for prayers and the celebration of the Sacraments, as stated in the Holy Bible itself, "And they, continuing daily with one accord in the temple, and breaking bread from house to house." From this it appears that they persevered in the teaching of the Apostles, by listening to what they taught them orally,[3] whether in public or in private homes.[4]

Breaking of Bread and the Agape

The breaking of bread, which is mentioned often in the Gospels, indicated, from the context, the Eucharist

[1] St. Jn. 4:23, 24.　[2] Acts 2:42.　[3] St. Mt. 18:20-21; St. Lk. 10:16; 12:3; St. Jn. 5:29; 15:5, 6, and 17; 11:21; 1 Cor. 11:2.　[4] Acts 20:20.

(or Sacrament of Holy Communion), and because the
Apostles were not wholly free to minister this Sacrament at its proper times, and in accordance with their
own wishes and direction, they used to minister it in
homes, while outwardly they fulfilled the Mosaic law,
offering sacrifices,[1] which it was unlawful to do except
in Jerusalem. Thus, since they celebrated the Euchar-
istic Sacrament in homes, and sometimes in the wilderness, mountains, and caves, accompanied by their wives
and children, and since they could not perform the sacrifices and the partaking of food together, there arose
among them the tradition of holding a banquet which
they called *Agape* (which took place after the breaking
of bread) or *Love Feast,* which took the place of quiet
sacrifice. In these agapes, celebrated with *joy and simplicity* of heart, the worshippers brought various foods
from their homes to the church, exchanging them one
with another.[2] The Apostles refer to these agapes re-
provingly when evil practices crept into them.[3]

In the year 70 of the Christian era, when Jerusalem
was destroyed by Titus the Roman, and when the walls
of the city and the Temple had fallen, the Christians
fled from the city, being warned of God. Then they
returned from the city of Bala beyond the Jordan in
which they sought refuge from God's vengeance, in
accordance with the Saviour's command.[4] And on the
ruins of old Jerusalem, the kingdom of David and the
seat of the kings of Judah, they built a new and spiritual
Jerusalem, the kingdom of Christ, the Son of David
from the seed of Judah. Then it was that the shadow
disappeared, the symbol vanished, the requirements of
the law, the offering of sacrifices and the fulfillment of
rites ceased, and the Jewish religion was completely
abolished. In its place there arose the truth, which
consisted of the saving sacrifice of redemeption, the
establishment of the Christian religion, and the fulfill-

---

[1] St. Jn. 11:56; Acts 21:20-26; 24:11-14.   [2] Acts 2:46.   [3] 1 Cor. 11:20-
24 and 34.   [4] St. Mt. 24:2, 15-16.

ment of the agape which had replaced the Mosaic sacrifices. This era, or the destruction of Jerusalem, was called by the Fathers, "The glorious burial of the councils." [1]

The offerings and sacrifices of the Old Testament were not able in themselves to purify the consciences of those who offered them, but were only for the benefit of the body. Nor was it possible for those who offered these sacrifices to be justified in their sins and iniquities because of any virtue in the sacrifices themselves, but because of the faith in the coming Christ of those who sacrificed, and because of the love which accompanied these acts. To make this plain, the Apostles performed the statutes of the law and the offering of sacrifice in the spirit of love and unity for the service of the body. Then to point out that these statutes and that worship were temporal, and that Christ by his coming had instituted something better, having offered himself a Sacrifice unto the purification of souls and the salvation of the world, they coupled the two sacrifices and the fulfillment of the rites of worship until such time as one was abolished. Thus they held the agape which consisted of eating and drinking, signifying thereby the unity of Christians generally in the one love, as the Jews participated in their outward rites for the benefit of the body.[2]

Panagia

(See its Service p. 41.)

THE HOLY BIBLE

Faith in Christ presupposes proclamation of him (evangel), which can mean only the conforming of the prophecies of the Old Testament to him who is proclaimed. To fulfill their work of proclamation of Christ the Apostles first started with the translation of

---

[1] Ephcostinus 19th Epistle. [2] Heb. 9:9-15; 1 Cor. 11:19-22; 23 etc.

the Old Testament, citing the prophecies therein to show that the proclaimed One is verily the Christ who cometh for the salvation of the world. That was done first orally, as their Master prompted them, and before they wrote the Gospels. The first day they undertook this was after their return from his Ascension. Then, ten days after, on the Festival of Pentecost, they began their preaching. On the first day they undertook their Apostolic office about three thousand believed in Christ.[1] They continued preaching and spreading the word of salvation in Jerusalem and its environs, until Saint Matthew wrote his Gospel about the year 38 A.D. And about the year 45 A.D. they scattered throughout the world, preaching him, according to their Master's commandment,[2] except St. John, who could not leave Jerusalem till after the death of the Theotokos in 48 A.D., thus keeping the commandment of his Master.

The translation of the Holy Bible, its reading and interpretation, constituted the most important part of the Apostles' preaching: as the reading of a part of the Gospels and Epistles was to them the most essential part of the rites of worship. In the second and third centuries the written sections and readings were specified, instead of being left to the discretion of the leading Priest. Thus each day was assigned its sections of the Epistles, Gospels, and other books. In these two centuries also teaching replaced interpretation, since the book had been translated into the languages of those who had been Christianized, into Syriac in the East and into Latin in the West.

THE APOSTLE, THE ELDER, AND WHAT IS MEANT BY THE EXPRESSION, "AT HIS DISCRETION"

The Apostolic age was distinguished by many things not found in any other age; for it so happened that the

---

[1] Acts 2:41. [2] St. Mt. 28:19; St. Mk. 16:15.

spiritual services were predominantly in the hands of the Apostles. But when the number of the faithful increased, and by their dispersion the faith spread to many parts, it was not possible for them to perform these services at one time in several places. To facilitate the propagation of the word of salvation they sought the help of distinguished persons among the faithful, both men and women. From this arose two ranks, one for administration and teaching, which consisted of prophets, missionaries, pastors, and teachers;[1] and the other for the reception of the seeds of faith and its cultivation in constructive service. The first was called clergy, and the other was called laity. This distinction, however, did not separate between the faithful, but both clergy and laity together constituted the one Church of Christ. They were in perfect unity; for it was not the aim of the first to preside, but to benefit; and it was not the aim of the other to revolt, but to assist.

Now an Apostle's authority was not restricted to the one church which he had founded, nor to the one congregation which had accepted the faith at his hands. His work and authority, indeed, prevaded the whole universe, since it was his in all its totality, as he was for the whole universe, in accordance with the divine teaching directed to each of them alike, without exception, as he said, "Go ye into all the world, and preach the Gospel to every creature.[2]

Accordingly, when the Apostles appointed ecclesiastical ranks in the Church, they travelled throughout the universe establishing churches on the pillar of their calling, visiting Christians wherever they happened to be. And wherever an Apostle was found they vacated for him the first place, and thus he would lead in counsel, administration, teaching, interpretation, preaching, the fulfillment of the Sacraments, and the conducting of worship. In short everything was left to him. From this arose the expression, "At the discretion of the eld-

---

[1] 1 Cor. 12:29-30; Eph. 4:11.　　[2] St. Mark 16:15.

er," or, "Then the elder saith", whether the elder happened to be a Patriarch among Bishops, a Bishop among Priests, an abbot among monks, or an elderly person who leads the laity in prayer when there are no clergy. It also follows from what has preceded that the churches founded by the Apostles are first in order among all churches, being the mothers from which were born the rest of the churches. The organization of these churches is the pattern for all organization, and the true seat of authority for the true teaching of the Gospel, for ruling on true doctrines, and they are examples for the order of Church rites. This is all so because these churches received the Gospel and the true faith in Christ from the Apostles and from the traditions which they deposited in these churches, as is affirmed by the God-mantled Ignatius in his Epistle to the Ephesians, in that he "urged the congregation of the faithful to preserve the apostolic traditions, to be united as members of one body whose head is Christ, to observe faithfully their holy meetings, open for all, communing in the offering of prayers and offerings, showing good obedience to the Bishops and Priests, in accordance with the ordination which Christ himself ordained, and that those who do not obey the Bishop and unite with him and with one another, nor meet in the public prayers under his leadership, are hence cast outside the Church and denied the heavenly bread." [1]

DIVISION OF TIME AND SPECIFICATION OF THE HOURS OF PRAYER

Moses, the Prophet and great lawgiver at the command of God, ordained the rites of worship for his people Israel. He instituted festivals for them, and designated times of prayer, that, with the beauty of those rites and publicly recited prayers, he might lead them to worship and reverence their Creator. Besides cultivating them and teaching them, these ceremonies

---

[1] St. Lk. 10:16.

had the effect of bringing them together as one tribe and one league. From time to time they also provided rest for their bodies, felicity of life, and an opportunity for thanksgiving for what God had bestowed upon them of his abundant favours. All this was carried out in accordance with the Mosaic law which was read to them and explained while the religious ceremonies and festivities were going on.

Moses commanded them to be strict in their performance of those precepts which he had enacted for them in his law. And in accordance with God's command, they carried out all the precepts, rites, worship, acts of piety, sacrifices, offerings, and festivities, which acted as reminders, and through which they gave thanks to God who had established these things for their sakes.

In order to set definite times for the performance of those prayers, and that worship, which were going on day and night in the Ark of the Covenant and in the Temple, they computed their day from sunset to sunset, i.e., into two divisions, day and night, as was mentioned in Genesis, "And it was evening and it was morning, one day".[1] Likewise, Moses commanded them, "From even unto even, shall ye celebrate your sabbath."[2] And since this was exhausting to them, they afterwards divided the day into six unequal watches. The first of these was called the dawn;[3] the second, morn, which was at the rise of the sun from the horizon;[4] the third, the course of the day, which began about nine a.m.: the fourth, noon;[5] the fifth, the cool of day, so called because in eastern countries a breeze blew every day between afternoon and nightfall;[6] and the sixth, nightfall, which was from suset to dusk, when darkness covers the face of the earth.

They observed this division of time till the time of Christ, when they followed the Roman method divid-

---

[1] Gen, 1:5. [2] Lev. 23:32. [3] Job 3:9;24:17. [4] Gen. 19:15.
[5] Gen. 43:16. [6] Gen. 3:8.

ing the night into four watches. The first of these began at sunset and continued three hours, and was known
as evening;[1] the second ended at midnight, and hence
was called midnight;[2] the third continued from midnight until the third hour after midnight, and was
known as cockcrowing;[3] and the fourth ended at sunrise, and was known as dawn.[4]

In like manner they divided the day into four periods,
each consisting of three hours. The first, which was
called the first hour, began at sunrise and continued
three hours; the second was called the third hour, after
sunrise till noon; the third was known as the sixth
hour, beginning at noon and ending at the third hour
in the afternoon; and the fourth was known as the ninth
hour, which continued through the rest of the afternoon
till sunset, so that the last hour in these divisions, which
Ozone called *trihorae* (consisting of three hours) co-
incided with the twelfth hour of the day. The third,
sixth, and ninth hours are mentioned as times of prayer.[5]

Number of Prayers and How the Prayers of the Hours Began

From this followed the courses of service, which accompanied the hours of prayer, in accordance with the
shifts in the lots of the worshippers, the psalmists, and
those who performed the tasks of worship, and the rest
of the services, and from which came the names of the
services of the canonical hours, and the number of these
services. The Prophet David refers to them when he
says, "Seven times a day do I praise thee because of thy
righteous judgments." The names and order of these
times of prayer are, Vespers, Compline, Midnight
Prayer, Matins, Prime, Terce, Sext, and lastly None.
The Prophet David mentioned them separately when
he said, "Evening and morning, and at noon, will I

---

[1] St. Mk. 11:19.　[2] St. Mat. 25:6.　[3] St. Mk. 13:35,　[4] St. Lk. 12:35-39.
[5] Dan. 6:10, 13; Ac. 2:15; 3; 1; 10:3,9.

pray, and cry aloud: and he shall hear my voice."[1] And of the Slumber Prayer (or Compline) he said, "All the night make I my bed to swim: I water my couch with my tears",[2] and, "That which ye say in your hearts, ye shall repent in your beds."[3] And of the Midnight Prayer he said, "At midnight will I rise to give thanks unto thee because of thy righteous judgments."[4] And of the Morning Prayer or Matins, he said, "When I remember thee upon my bed, and meditate on thee in the night watches."[5] Again of the Prayer of the First Hour, or Prime, he said, "My voice shalt thou hear in the morning, O Lord; in the morning will I direct my prayer unto thee, and will look up."[6] The venerable Clement also mentioned these prayers under the twenty-fourth caption of his *Canons of the Saints.*

Following the example of the church of the Old Testament, the Christian Church adopted the times of prayer from the Israelites, including in them references to events taken from Christian history. The arrangement of the Offices in these prayers was followed with strict observance in reference to the Master's Passion, and they were fulfilled at seven different times. Hence The Midnight Prayer commemorates that night on which Christ the Master was delivered to the Jews, who came with lamps and sticks; Matins commemorates that dawn when Christ was mocked and ridiculed; the Prayer of the First Hour, or Prime, commemorates his delivery to the Gentiles. In the third and sixth hours he was condemned to death and crucified; while in the ninth he gave up the ghost. Vespers commemorates the descent of his body from the Cross, and Compline commemorates his Burial, as we shall see.

Prayer of the Ninth Hour, or None, and its Explanation

The Prayer of the Ninth Hour is said before the

---

[1] Ps 55:17.   [2] Ps. 6:6.   [3] Ps. 4:5.   [4] Ps. 118:62.   [5] Ps. 62:6.   [6] Ps. 5:3.

Vesper Prayer because it is the concluding office of
the ecclesiastical day. This the Church received from
the Apostolic Saints, setting it aside for the memory of
the Death of Christ, our Lord and God, who tasted
death in the flesh in the ninth hour of the day, that
therewith he might bestow upon us mercy, truth, grace,
glory, and dwelling in the Lord's mansions, with reference to the fruits of justification which the faithful received from the ancestral sin, and to our reconciliation
with divine justice and our deliverance from hades. As
it also refers to the sign of the precious cross, which
assists the faithful and frightens their enemies, visible
and invisible, reminding us also of the Saviour's Death
on the Cross. All this is referred to in the Psalms of the
Ninth Hour Prayer,[1] along with the Troparia, Kontakions, and the prayer beginning, "O Master and Lord
Jesus Christ", etc.

Explanation of Vespers, or Sunset Prayer

Saint Clement received from his teacher, Saint Peter
the Apostle, all the doctrines of faith, the rites of worship, their noble offices and services and their holy prayers. Hence he commands us, saying, "The offerings
and services must not be fulfilled as they come, but in
order, and at set times and hours." Likewise the Council of Laodicea (Eski-Shahr) which was held in the
year 367, says in its eighteenth canon, "The prayers recited at the Ninth Hour and at evening must always
be the same in order that the human mind which is
subject to passion and enamoured by the seductions of
its conflicting imaginations, and which goes after its
endless inclinations, may not overrule the everlasting
and ever true ordinances of God."

Beginning of the Day
Further Explanation of the Vesper Prayer

As we saw previously, the day's beginning was computed from the evening, as it is said in the Holy Book,

---

[1] Ps. 83:1, 4, 10-12; 84:2, 3, 11; 85:3, 17.

"And it was even and it was morn, one day." [1] Hence the Church considers the beginning of her day the Evening or Vesper Prayer, in memory of the beginning of the day on which God started the Creation of the visible world.

And in commemoration of the events of the six days of creation, the Church adopted the one hundred and third Psalm, which begins, "Bless the Lord, O my soul," and which refers clearly and plainly to all the events of creation, from the creation of light to the creation of man, with symbols clearly indicating the symbolized events.

Similarly in the service of this Prayer, the Holy of Holies symbolizes the interior of paradise; the Temple (where the congregation stand) symbolizes the outside of paradise; the removal of the curtain from the Royal Door, or opening it, symbolizes our forefathers within paradise while the doors were open; the closing of the curtain of the Royal Door, symbolizes the closing of the gates of paradise after our forefathers were expelled therefrom; the Priest standing bareheaded, in front of the Royal Door, and repeating the reverential prayer of the Sunset Psalm, symbolizes the expulsion of our forefathers from paradise and their standing in front of its gates outside; the repetition of the Peace Petitions and the Kathisma of the Psalms, symbolizes their asking for reconciliation and forgiveness of God, and their petition to return to paradise. The fact that the Prayer consists solely of beseechings and supplications, with the repetition of the Peace Petitions, devoid of sacrifices, signifies that our forefathers' prayer was likewise, and that the Vesper Prayer is a substitute for the evening sacrifice in the Old Covenant. [2] Hence we chant the Psalm, "Lord, I cry unto thee; make haste unto me; give ear unto my voice, when I cry unto thee. Let my prayer be set forth before thee as incense; and the lifting up of my hands as the evening sacrifice,"

---

[1] Gen. 1:5.   [2] Ez. 9:5.

and the rest of the Vesper Psalms.[1] Furthermore, the appearance of the Priest, who has been hidden within the throne, and his coming out in the procession (Eisodos) from the northern door of the Holy of Holies, which faces the Altar, refers to the fulfillment of God's promise to our forefathers, of the One who should be born and should bruise the serpent's head,[2] namely, the God born in Bethlehem, according to the prophecy of the Prophet Micah,[3] who hath appeared unto the world in the flesh having been hidden in his Divinity from their eyes. The incense burner and the Gospels in the Priest's hand, as he comes out from the sanctuary signify that God accepted Adam's repentance as a scent of sweet odour, and to the grace of the most Holy Spirit which was bestowed on Adam and the whole world through the annunciation of the Gospel of the only Son of God. The lighted candle in front of the Priest, while carrying the Gospels, and his standing in front of the open Royal Door, and his shouting, "Wisdom! Let us stand up", signify that the flame of that spear with which the angel prevented our forefathers from entering paradise[4] has been quenched by the preaching of the Baptist who preceded Christ and preached of him, that he was the Light, the Holy Place, and the Entrance into heaven,[5] and to the fact that this has been ours through Orthodox faith in the one God of three Persons, the Father, Son, and Holy Spirit. Hence after the Priest enters to the throne, we chant or recite the trinitarian evening hymn of thanksgiving, "O resplendent Light, unto the holiness of the Father's glory . . ." which embraces all that has been mentioned heretofore concerning the divine promise of the Saviour's coming, his being God's Wisdom and his brilliant Light. Said St. Basil the Great concerning this thanksgiving hymn (under Caption twenty-nine of his Mimar sermon) on the Holy Spirit, "Our forefathers thought it

---

[1] Ps. 140, 141, 142, 116.　[2] Gen. 3:15.　[3] Mi. 5:2.　[4] Gen. 3:24,
[5] St. Jno. 1:4-9, 15, 23, 29, 31.

proper not to accept the gift of evening light in silence, but to offer thanksgiving as soon as it appeared. We do not know and cannot say who of the Fathers originated these words of evening thanksgiving, but only that the congregation from ancient times recited them, nor did they consider it blasphemy for one to say (instead), "We praise the Father, Son, and Holy Spirit, God." And those who believe that this hymn belongs to Athenogenes, and that he left it as a talisman or farewell speech to those who were with him as he was being led to martyrdom, to the fire that was prepared for him, will realize what faith the Martyrs had in the Holy Spirit.

The Prokeimenon, and the Rest of the Explanation of the Vesper Prayer

In order that we may refer to the faith of the fathers of the Old Covenant in the coming Saviour we may say after the foregoing, *Prokeimenon,* which means, that which had been stated before by the Prophets, the prophecies and symbols with which God was preparing the world to receive the Saviour. Hence, we say after the Prokeimenon a verse of the Psalms, or recite the Readings on the evenings of festivals. As for the Prokeimenon which follows the Anabathmoi, it means, *Introduction,* and signifies a new stanza or new tune for new hymns. While the Prokeimenon of the Epistles indicates that the Apostles who preached of Christ in the New Covenant were preceded by the Prophets who foretold His coming in the New Testament.

The Greater Ektene, or Petitions

This term means *supplication,* or fervent prayer that comes out of the heart, as its opening words imply, "Let us all say with all our souls and with all our mind", etc. St. Basil the Great also called it *The Protracted Petition,* and likewise St. Methodius calls it, *The Protracted*

Imploration, which signifies that it was a lengthy prayer. However, it was so designated not only because of its length and its pervading and numerous petitions, but because it is read loudly, with intonation and with eagerness and utmost attention; for in it we petition God for mercy, life, safety, health, and salvation for all the people of the world, of all ranks, in their life on earth. And to each petition the congregation chants thrice, "Lord, have mercy." Then we ask God that he keep our nights without sin, overshadow us with his mercy, lead us to his commandments, make us to understand his statutes, and lighten our paths with the decrees of his justice. This is explained in the petition, "Prepare us, O Lord, to be preserved this evening without sin," etc., as well as from the several evening petitions which begin, "Let us continue our petitions to the Lord," and what follow them, in which we ask God Almighty to make us ready to finish our evening prayer, remembering thereby the setting of our life's sun. And in it also we ask God to grant us all that is good and godly in our worldly life, in preparation for our end. To all these petitions we respond, "Grant, O Lord." Then we revert to where we started, recalling our two ancestors and their sin, which came down to us, confessing our sins, before God, which are the consequence of our ancestors' sin, beseeching him for forgiveness and salvation for our faith in him as the Saviour who has come, having also saved our two ancestors with the rest of the patriarchs of the Old Testament, who likewise believed in him as the coming Saviour.

Stichera, Stichos, and Aposticha

We also sing hymns which we call *Stichera* and which means the Hymns preceded by a Stichos, or a corresponding verse of the Psalms. Or for further elucidation, we may call such a hymn the *Sticherous Hymn,* in view of the Stichos or verse which precedes it. *Apos-*

ticha means that which follows the Stichos, as the Evening Prayer also reminds us of the bringing down of the Saviour's body and its burial at evening.

And in order that we may point to the end of the Old Testament time, and the substitution of the New Testament in its place by the coming of the Saviour, we end our Evening Prayer, which comprises all the events of the Old Testament as we explained above, with the Prayer of Simeon the Elder, which is the last of the prophecies about Christ and which comprises both the truth and the symbol; for the symbol is Simeon himself, the last of the Old Testament fathers, and the truth is Jesus Christ, whom Simeon, having borne in his arms and having known by the Spirit that he was the Lord of the living and of the dead, addressed saying, "Lord, now lettest thou thy servant depart in peace, according to thy word; for mine eyes have seen thy salvation, which thou hast prepared before all people; a light to lighten the Gentiles, and a glory to thy people Israel." [1] Whereupon we respond with, *Holy God,* and what follows it, as we make the sign of the cross on our foreheads. Then we sing the Troparion of Absolution, and conclude the Prayer.

Trisagion, or Holy God

In the days of St. Proclus who succeeded his Master Chrysostom in the Archbishopric of Constantinople, in the reign of Theodosius the younger, in the year 434, the people were making a procession in the streets of Constantinople, supplicating God because of a divine threat. Suddenly a little boy by the name of Acacius, was snatched to heaven. And having been restored to the people, he was heard to sing what he had learned from the angels in heaven: "Holy God, Holy Mighty, Holy Immortal One, have mercy upon us." And in this fashion the divine threat ceased.

---

[1] St. Lk. 2:29-32.

This *Trisagion,* or *Thrice-holy Song,* was included
in the Acts if the Fourth Ecumenical Council, which
was held in Chalcedon in the year 451, to put an end
to the schism of the deluded Peter the Fuller. From
that time its use in churches was ordained. The account
of the beatified Acacius is mentioned by John the Sa-
baite to his friend St. John the Ladderite, and the latter included it in his famous work, *The Ladder of
Virtues.*

The Sign of the Cross

St. Meletius ascended the throne of the Patriarchate
of Antioch by consent of the Orthodox and Arian Bishops. Because of the confidence of the Council in him,
they all, including King Constantius, agreed in writing
to accept the saint's interpretation of the verse in Solomon the Wise which says, "The Lord hath created me",
which, in the opinion of the Arians, referred to the creation of the Son. The saint said that Adam begat Seth,
and that the meaning of the word *created* in this verse
is to give birth, not to create in the usual sense. Those
who were present were greatly rejoiced, and asked him
for further proof. Then he raised three fingers of his
right hand, the thumb, the index, and the middle finger,
and bent the other two, as he said, "These three fingers
are a symbol of the Trinity." Then bending the index
and middle fingers and leaving the thumb raised, he
added, "And as these fingers now are one, so also the
Substance is one." The Arians were greatly enraged
at hearing this, accusing St. Meletius of harbouring the
heresy of Sabellius, Bishop of Pentapolis. Conspiring
with the king's viceroy, they caused him to be exiled
to his native city, Sebaste.

It was St. Meletius who established the custom of
making the sign of the cross, which derives from Ignatius the Martyr, Partiarch of Antioch. This sign is made
by the faithful by drawing the shape of the cross on
their bodies, holding the first three fingers of the right

hand together, as it is prastised to this day in the Orthodox Church throughout the world. It may also be mentioned in passing that the Jews, on the feast of Purim,
used to erect crosses over their houses, commemorating
the crucifixion of Haman, but they were later pro-
hibited from doing so.

Alleluia

This word is Hebrew and means, "God hath appeared; praise ye him and glorify him"; for *Al* stands
for God who hath outwardly come, while *El* means
God. And since this expression signifies the coming
of God the Word, the Church ordained that it be chanted between the reading of the Epistle and the Gospels,
as well as on days of jubilation, as in the Antiphonies
of the Dominical Feasts, when we say, "Save us . . .
that we may sing unto thee, Alleluia." And this is
sung in all churches in the original Hebrew because
John in his revelation thus heard it from the beatified
angels.[1]

Bless, O Father, in the Name of God

We read in the Holy Scriptures, "And the Lord
spake unto Moses, saying: Speak unto Aaron and unto
his sons, saying, On this wise ye shall bless the children
of Israel, saying unto them, the Lord bless thee, and
keep thee; the Lord make his face shine upon thee, and
be gracious unto thee: the Lord lift up his countenance
upon thee, and give thee peace. And they shall put
my name upon the children of Israel; and I will bless
them." [2] We gather the same from David the Prophet
where he says, "God be merciful to us, and bless us; and
cause his face to shine upon us.[3] Following, therefore,
this divine instruction, concerning the manner in which
the Bishop or Priest should bless the people, the holy
Church ordained this expression, "Bless, O Father, in

---

[1] Rev. 19.   [2] Nu. 6:22 to end.   [3] Ps. 66:1.

the Name of the Lord", calling for the blessing of the congregation in the divine Name. And when the Priest hears this from the Choir or Lector (reader), he responds by saying, "Through the prayers of our Fathers the saints, O Lord Jesus Christ our God, have mercy upon us and save us." Or he may repeat the verse, "God be merciful unto us," etc. And at the final Benediction of the Prayer the Priest, facing the congregation and making the sign of the cross with the fingers of his hand, says, "The blessing and the mercy of God descend upon you", etc.

Apolytikion, or Conclusion of the Prayer and Benediction (Dismissal)

The customary command for dismissal (Benediction) from the presence of majesty is given either in a sign or in plain words. Similarly in the Church, the congregation cannot leave it until they are absolved finally from the bondage of religious duties, except in an emergency. Then it is that the worshippers are allowed to depart from the divine presence, where their spirits have been communing with their Lord, visibly in the body and invisibly in the spirit.

This command for dismissal is called in Greek, *Apolytikion,* which means loosening or absolution. It consists of a hymn or troparion, so named because it is sung, especially after the petition of Simeon the Righteous who, having beheld Christ and known by the Spirit that he was the Lord of the living and the dead and that it was he who had bound him in life to the body, cried out, "Lord, now lettest thy servant depart in peace," etc. This is then followed by, "Holy God", etc. and the Troparion, while the Priest says, "Glory to thee, our God, glory to thee", and the rest of what is ordained in the lesser Dismissal in Evening Prayer. But the Major Dismissal in the Divine Liturgy begins after the Priest has pronounced the words, "Let us go out in peace, of thee we pray," followed by the prayer, "O Lord who blessest those who bless thee," to the end of the Dismissal, as in the service of the Mass.

This is all in accordance with what the Saviour told his Disciples at the conclusion of the Eucharist, "Rise, let us be going." [1] In the same way James, the Lord's brother, at the end of his Mass Service, says, "Let us depart in the peace of Christ." While St. Clement says, "Depart in peace."

Pyramon

This means stopping at what preceded, before resumption of what follows. It also signifies rising from the slumber of inattention and apathy before resuming the journey to God.

For the holy Church, in propitiation for the apathy which overtakes her children during the days of fasting, awakens them from their slumber and straightens their path to God on this day which she has called *Pyramon* (which means a stop, preparation, standing, or yesterday). On it the faithful prepare by absolute fasting and by desisting from all worldly affairs, being engaged in continuous prayer for the observance of the following feast day. This prayer is also called *Hours,* because it exhausts almost all the hours of the day, and at the conclusion of it was formerly held the service of the Mass. And to the present day the Divine Liturgy is fulfilled on the day of Pyramon at Vespers. It was customary for the Byzantine kings to be present at the services throughout the hours, and hence they were also called by some of the ancient church writers, *The Royal Hours.*

Compline Prayer

The Compline Prayer, or bedtime prayer, is of two kinds, Great Compline and Little Compline. Great Compline, in turn has three parts. The first of these

---

[1] St. Mt. 26:46.

begins with the words of the Priest, "Blessed be God", etc., to the end of the Prayer of St. Basil the Great, "Lord, Lord, who hast delivered us from every arrow that flieth by day . . ." In this part the worshipper before he falls to sleep contemplates the thoughts, words, and deeds which he has committed during the day, as it is written by the Prophet David, "Commune with your own heart upon your bed, and be still"; and, "All the night make I my bed to swim: I water my couch with my tears." [1]

The second part begins with, "Let us bow down", thrice, and the Fiftieth Psalm and what follows it, ending with the Prayer of St. Mordarius, "Master, God, and Almighty Father", thus indicating man's surrender to divine Providence, as when the Prophet David says, "Unto thee, O Lord, do I lift up my soul"; and, "Into thy hand I commit my spirit." [2]

The third part begins with, "Let us bow down", thrice, and the Sixty-ninth Psalm, "Make haste, O God, to deliver me", and what follows it, to the end of the prayer, "Forgive, O Lord, those who hate us . . .", thus petitioning God not to let us fall into the slumber of sin, to raise us from sleep safe and sound, walking in the way of his commandments, as it is said in the Psalm, "Lighten mine eyes, lest I sleep the sleep of death. Look upon mine affliction and my pain; and forgive all my sins." [3]

Great Compline in general reminds us of the setting of our life's sun on this earth, and that sleep is temporary death and an example of eternal death. It reminds us that Christ at such a time was in hades saving the righteous and the saints who were expecting his presence. Our rising from sleep in the morning, and the succession of days and nights also afford us a perceptible proof of our belief in the resurrection of the dead and of the life to come. From this Great Com-

---

[1] Ps. 4:4; 6:6.   [2] Ps. 24:1; 30:5.   [3] Ps. 12:3; 24:18.

pline, which is repeated on the days of the Great Fast, the Church produced Little Compline, to be repeated before we go to sleep, from which we might never rise, seeking God's forgiveness of our shortcomings, and petitioning his pardon, mercy, and pleasure, showing thereby our remorse and repentance. For the fulfillment of these three objects Little Compline adopted from the first part of Great Compline the Creed of Faith; from the second, the Fiftieth Psalm; and almost the whole of the third part.

Midnight Prayer, Sometimes Called the Prayer of Watching, or Agrypinia, or the Prayer of the Five Loaves: and how Singing by the Choir Alternately was Introduced

Christian teachings enjoin us, "To pray always";[1] but in order that the people may attain at least their daily nutrition of prayer, the Apostles designated set prayers at the third, sixth, and ninth hours. Afterwards they added the Midnight Prayer. The introduction of this Prayer goes back to the times of the Apostles themselves. When Herod the king found that the killing of James, the brother of John, was pleasing to the Jews, he laid hands on Peter also, whom he planned to present to them after the Passover. And while Peter was chained between two soldiers in prison, the Church was praying ceaselessly for him. And while the faithful were thus engaged, Peter knocked at the door where they were gathered; for an angel of the Lord had delivered him. In the same manner the Apostles Paul and Silas, having been beaten almost to death and thrust into prison, were praying and praising God at midnight. Suddenly there was a great earthquake which shook the foundation of the prison and set the Apostles free.[2]

On the strength of these two events, which establish the efficacy of prayer and piety, the Church instituted

---

[1] St. Lk. 18:1.   [2] Acts 12:1-17; 16:23-30.

the Midnight Prayer, in imitation of the Apostles. From that time there grew the custom of meeting at night for prayer.[1] And sometimes the faithful spent the whole night worshipping God, as in the Pyramon of Easter. In the fourth century Vespers were joined to the night prayer in the monasteries, and the two were then called the Prayer of Watching, or the Prayer of the Five Loaves, and in Greek, *Agrypinia*. This prayer, or service, was held on Sundays and feast days and other nights according to the Abbot's wish, as we find in the Typicon, the Great Euchologia, and the Apostolic Regulations. This custom is also mentioned by most of the church Fathers and teachers, among them John Chrysostom, who says, "Go into the temple and see the poor standing there from midnight until the morn, and listen to the services of the holy watches which join the day to the night." In another place he says, "I rejoice at your zeal towards your Mother, the Church, and because you stand without rest throughout the night prayer, offering articulate glorification to the Creator." [2]

In Milan, Italy, the Midnight Prayer took rise in the days of St. Ambrose, when it was feared that King Valentinian II sought his exile. The faithful then gathered in the church and remained there several days and nights, singing hymns and Psalms, and keeping watch all the time with a resolute determination to guard their saintly Bishop, ready to bear any hardship rather than allow him to be led out of his house. In order that the congregation might not tire at night, the saint ordered that the two choirs should chant alternately, as the Eastern Church had done for generations before. In this way the Midnight Prayer gradually be-

---

[1] Histories of Paronius. 51:68, etc.

[2] St. Chrysostom, in the Twenty-fifth Sermon on the Book of Acts, Cap. 14, and the Epistle to the Romans; Clement of Alexandria, in Pedagogue II:9; Tertullian, in his Discourse to his Wife; Cyprian, On Prayer; Augustine, Sermon 42; and Ambrose, On Virginity, Book 3.

came universal, as also the chanting of the two choirs in all the western churches.

Divisions of the Midnight Prayer

There are three Midnight Prayers instituted by the holy Church: the daily one, the one held at midnight on sabbaths, and the one held on Sundays, also at midnight. Each has its own service, and its own reference to appropriate events of the New Testament.

The Daily Midnight Prayer

This prayer the Orthodox Church instituted in remembrance of the Second Coming of the Lord, which, according to the Gospels, will take place at night suddenly.[1] It was likened by God to the wedding in which the ten virgins went out at midnight to welcome the groom.[2]

In order to arouse our interest and to prepare us for the Lord's reception and for meeting him face to face on that dreadful day, the Church urges us first to bless God by saying, "Blessed be God, our God", etc.[3] From this we proceed to commune with his Holy Spirit, the Source of all goodness, who fills the whole universe. We entreat him to dwell in us and cleanse us of our impurities, and to save us from ourselves, as we say, "O heavenly King and Comforter", etc. And while we are thus carried up in our communion with the good and comforting Spirit, we lift up our voices in the Trisagion, or thrice-holy song, saying, "Holy God, Holy Mighty, Holy Immortal One, have mercy upon us", following the example of the seraphic angels who praise God constantly, saying, "Holy, Holy, Holy, Lord of hosts", referring thus to the Trinity in the repetition of the word, Holy, and the Unity in Substance by saying, "Lord of hosts."

---

[1] St. Mt. 24:42.   [2] St. Mt. 25:1-13.   [3] 1 Cor. 1:3; 2 Cor. 1:1.

Glory to the Father, Lord, Have Mercy, and Amen

And since it is this most Holy Spirit who speaks through his Church and directs it, he has led us to the necessity of seeking God's mercy, by which we have our being, live, escape evil, and grow in goodness; through whom we were chosen, called, and justified. Finally, it is through God's mercy that we are about to be glorified by union with him. It is therefore meet that we offer glorification to the most Holy Trinity by saying, "Glory to God, and to the Son, and to the Holy Spirit", etc. This, too, is taken from the Apostle where he says, "For of him, and through him, and unto him, are all things. To him be the glory for ever. Amen."[1] To this we join our petition for God's mercy, as we say, "Lord, have mercy."

This last expression finds frequent use in our holy Church; for in its relation to worship, it is in itself the best prayer that a creature could think of to offer to God, asking thereby his mercy and forgiveness. Often we repeat it hundreds of times, as in the Feast of the Elevation of the Cross, simply to petition God's mercy through which he had raised us after we were fallen. At other times we employ it to seek God's blessings, and still at other times to glorify him thereby, or to seek forgiveness for the sins we have committed throughout the twelve hours of the day. At times also we use it as a propitiation for the days of the year, which fall a little short of four hundred. This brief petition goes back to the days of the Apostles, when they instituted the Divine Liturgy, as we gather from the commentaries of St. Jerome and St. Cyprian.[2] Similarly, the word *Amen,* which is also taken from the Apostle, where he says, "Else if thou bless with the spirit, how shall he that filleth the place of the unlearned say Amen at thy giving of thanks?"[3]

---

[1] Ro. 11:36. [2] See discussion on singing (pp. 1070-1083).
[3] 1 Cor. 14:16.

Now, since the seeking of God's mercy and forgiveness necessitates penitence and repentance, the Church decreed the recital of the Fiftieth Psalm. And in order that she may lead us to purity of heart, cleanliness of conduct, and to seek refuge in righteousness and the keeping of God's commandments, she ordained also the recitation of the 118th Psalm, "Blessed are they that are perfect in the way". This is followed by confession of our true Orthodox Faith by reciting the Creed, which was compiled in the First and Second Councils from the teachings of the Scriptures, and which begins, "I believe in one God". Then come the Troparia of the Midnight Prayer, "Behold, the bridegroom cometh at midnight", "Be alert, O my soul, on that fearful day, and watch", and "Thou art a secure wall and pillar of our salvation, O virgin Theotokos".

Then we supplicate God with the prayer, "O thou who at all times, and at each hour", that God may have mercy on us and make the end of our faith union with him and the enjoyment of his glory, in accordance with the saying of the Apostle; for the Apostle taught that whereas faith shall be done away with when it shall have been fulfilled through union with him in whom we believe, and whereas hope shall cease when we shall have attained the glory that is hoped for, love hath no end, as there is no end to unity with God the Beloved. Thus we see that because in love there is no separation between man, who is promised everlasting unity, and his Beloved, who is God, it achieves the distinction of being the best and greatest of all virtues; for, while all other virtues are temporal in nature, love is eternal. Likewise, our knowledge of God's glory shall come to an end, because it stops in this life with parables, hyperboles, and enigmas, viewing it in the mirror of faith and the Scriptures. But there, face to face as we are known of him, our clear knowledge of him shall take its place. And thus we understand the passage in the aforesaid prayer wherein we beg that we may "arrive at the unity of faith with thee, and to the knowledge of thine unapproachable glory." [1]

Then we beseech God by reciting the 120th Psalm, "I will lift up mine eyes unto the mountains"; and the 133rd Psalm, "Behold, bless ye Jehovah all ye servants of Jehovah", that he will protect us and preserve us from all evil. Then, returning to our Vespers, we lift up our hands to God and ask his blessing. After this we ask his mercy for those who have fallen asleep, in a prayer which begins, "Remember, good Lord", "O thou who directest all with thy sublime wisdom", "Give rest, O Christ", "All generations bless thee, O Virgin", etc., and the prayer, "Remember, Lord, those who slumber", etc. The Midnight Prayer is then concluded with the little prayers, "O glorious and blessed one", "The Father is my trust", "In thee have I placed all my trust", followed by the supplicatory petitions for all the living and all who have fallen asleep of the Orthodox of true worship. After this the Elder says, "Through the prayers of our Fathers, the saints", etc., thus concluding the Prayer.

Midnight Prayer on Sabbaths

The sabbath is a feast day pertaining to the church of the Old Testament. To remind us, however, of the signs, symbols, and rites which relate to that day, the Church of Christ designated another prayer especially for the sabbath. This differs from the ordinary Midnight Prayer in the following ways: Instead of the 118th Psalm, six Psalms are substituted, from the Sixty-fourth to the Sixty-ninth inclusive, containing prophecies of the Second Coming of Christ, bringing awe to sinners and the wicked, and joy to the righteous and just. Secondly, instead of the Troparion, "Behold the bridegroom cometh at midnight", etc., is sung the Troparion, "Open our lips", etc., "We are on earth", etc.,

[1] 1 Tim. 6:16.

"Thou hast gotten me up from my bed". Thirdly, after the prayer, "We bless thee, O most high God",[1] we substitute the prayer, "Verily, do I magnify thee", etc.[2] In all this the Church calls us to imitate the holy angels who ceaselessly praise God.

Midnight Prayer for Sundays

As for the Midnight Prayer on Sundays, it was ordained by the Church to remind us of the glorious Resurrection of Christ, which took place at midnight. Hence, instead of the prayers for the dead and the Psalms, the Triodion (or song of three tones) is sung; and, instead of the Creed, the Tridion beginning, "It is truly meet", etc.; and for the Troparia, the Hypakoe is sung. Through these changes the Church leads us to the praise of the most Holy Trinity, and to the glorification of him who did rise from the grave on the third day, Christ God who giveth life to all by his holy Resurrection.

Matin Prayers[3]

The most appropriate time for the contemplation of the great deeds and mysteries of God, when one is moved to praise and to sing unto him, is at dawn, when one rises from sleep. It is then that the mind is at its fullest power, having received its sufficiency of rest, as the Psalmist says, "My heart is ready, O God, my heart is ready: I will sing, yea, I will sing praises. Awake up, my glory, awake, psaltery and harp: I myself will awake right early." [4]

Thus the Prophet David indicated that his praise of the divine Majesty was not merely by word of mouth; but also by the awakening of his spirit, by the singing

---

[1] By St. Madarius. [2] By St. Eustratius.

[3] Matins are the prayers said at dawn, which, according to the old divisions of time, was also divided into the false dawn, or thither dawn, and the true or hither dawn, which precedes the rise of day.

[4] Ps. 56:7-8.

of his heart, by the rejoicing of his heart as by a musical instrument, which, by way of repetition and antiphony, he mentions as the psaltery and the harp.

The Prophet refers here first to the praise which results from the agitation of the spirit from above downward by mentioning the psaltery, which likewise is played beginning with its upper part downward, then to the raising of the voice in rejoicing from below upward, thus including the two dawns, the upper dawn and the lower dawn or morn. In the same way the Church ordained the service of Matins, beginning from above downward, i.e., beginning by blessing God the Creator, the Almighty and majestic, and with the seraphic song of praise, offering him glory and praying for his mercy. Then, having descended to the offering of the necessary worship to him after his Incarnation on earth, we ascend, praying God for the earthly king and his support, in accordance with the Apostle's command that "Supplications, prayers, intercessions, thanksgivings, be made for all men; for kings and all that are in high places". "For there is no power but of God; and the powers that be are ordained of God."[1] All this appears in the saying of the Priest, "Blessed be God", etc., followed by the choir's "Holy God," and "Lord, have mercy" (*twelve times*), "Come, let us bow down" (*three times*), and the Nineteenth Psalm, "Jehovah answer thee in the day of trouble", etc., the Twentieth Psalm, "The king shall joy in thy strength, O Jehovah", etc. This is then followed by the Troparia, "O Lord, save thy people", etc., "O dread Champion", etc., and the petitions, "Have mercy upon us, O God", etc., and what follows it, with which we conclude the prelude of the Matin service for kings and men in authority, and proceed to the Matin Prayer, as the choir addresses the Priest, saying, "Bless, O Father, in the Name of the Lord." Then the Priest opens the prayer referring to the appearance of the Saviour on earth, whom the an-

---

[1] 1 Tim. 2:1-4; Ro. 13:1.

gels proclaimed when he was born at night, thus indicating that before the Saviour's Nativity we were in
darkness, contrary to the light of faith with which we
were lightened after his appearance on earth in the
flesh. This is all understood from the words of the
Priest, "Glory to the holy, consubstantial", etc., and the
choir's respond, "Glory to God in the highest", etc.

After this we recite the six Matin Psalms in which
we show our readiness to accept faith in him. And thus
after we give expression through those Psalms to the
acknowledgment of our sins, confess them, and ask their
forgiveness, and deliverance from our enemies who
compass us about, we are then conscious of the mercies
of God who suffered his Son to be sent to us, that he
might reconcile us to the Father. This reconciliation,
pervading every race and rank in the world, is indicated in the Great Synapte in which we say, "In peace
let us pray to the Lord. For the peace that is from
above and for the salvation of our souls, let us pray to
the Lord," etc.

The Great and Little Synaptes

In the first book of his Epistle, Isador of Pelusium
says, "We must not only secure peace among ourselves,
but also inseparable unity with our Lord and Master."
Similarly he says in that Epistle, "O Lord our God,
who didst grant us peace and understanding one with
another, grant us safety for our unity with thee, insep-
arably, that we may attain thee as peace through thy
Holy Spirit; and that we may be established in thee,
inseparable from thy love." Again St. John Chrysostom, contemplating the Great Synapte, wrote in the
sixth book of his work on the Priesthood, "What do I
say, that the Priest prays for a city, town, or village?
Nay, he makes petition for the whole universe, praying
the Lord to forgive all those who beseech him."

---

1 By St. Madarius.

These petitions are called in Greek *The Great Synapte,* meaning collection, because so many of these petitions are brought together and recited at one time. They are also called *peace-petitions,* because each one begins with a petition for peace. Sometimes it is also called the *Great Preaching.* The term *Great* is used to distinguish it from the *Little Synapte,* which opens its petitions with the expression, "Again and again in peace, let us pray to the Lord."

After offering our thanks to God who gave us rest with our night's sleep and aroused us early [1] to perform our duty of praise and glorification for his goodness, he having made us worthy to behold our Saviour, born in Bethlehem, and to realize that he is Christ the Saviour who cometh as light and guidance to the world, and that we have been illumined by the light of his knowledge. Hence, at the conclusion of the peace-petitions, we sing at once the prophetic passage which demonstrates visibly the coming up of the true Sun of righteousness, by beholding the light of day which we shall have reached at that time. Then we say, "God the Lord hath appeared unto us." [2] As we say this we light the lamps, pointing thereby by the visible and sensible light to the invisible light of our faith in the invisible Godhead of incarnate God. This prayer, as well as Vespers, is also called the *Prayer of Lamps.* This is taken from the custom of the Old Testament when the priests used to enter the Temple every morning to offer incense and put out the lights, then return in the evening and light them. And as in ancient times the lighting of the lamps was a reminder of the improvement of their condition, and an expression of their hearts' rejoicing and gladness, so the Apostles also, as they persisted in prayers and the breaking of bread, employed lighted lamps frequently. [3]

---

[1] At this point we have reached the time indicated by the word "early" of early morn, having finished the Midnight and Matin Prayers, and hence this prayer is also called, *The Early Prayer.*
[2] Ps. 117:26-27. [3] Acts 20:7-8.

Troparion

Then to give expression to our faith, and our respect to virtue and the virtuous, we sing a hymn which we call *Troparion,* set to a special tone, and made for a special occasion or person, from which the attributes of the subject of the song are brought to view. Thus, if the Troparion is for the Resurrection, that event is described for us and its sequence made clear. If it is for a dominical feast, we learn from it the event to which it refers; and if it is for a saint, we learn from it the saint's great faith and the sanctity of his life. And because of its appropriate and descriptive nature the Troparion is also called *movable hymn.* The music of the Troparion is composed after one of the eight tones of the Resurrection. The Troparion is followed by a recital of the Stichologia of the Psalms and the Kathismata.

However, before we come to the discussion of the Psalms, the Stichologia and the Kathismata, we will say a word about the tones and hymns, with the mention of some of the musical composers and the authors of those hymns.

Tones, Composers, and Hymn Writers

When the soul is moved by the force of love, there are born therein motives of joy. And when love takes its effect, these motives or reactions take their course in the body, clarifying the blood, bringing contentment to the heart, and reviving the whole soul. The vital parts of the body are then moved with joy and happiness, and this appears in the effect as voices of gladness, and shoutings of joy as praises and hymns of thanksgiving to the Creator, as happened with David the Prophet; for when David was aroused by the joy that comes from the effect of the love of divine things, he began to dance, to shout, and to sing songs of praise before the Ark of the Covenant.[1]

---

[1] 2 Samuel 6:14, 15; 1 Chron. 16:4, 7.

In the same way John the Evangelist tells us in his Revelation about this joy which manifests itself in the lifting of the voice and in singing in unison, in which the heavenly powers and the souls of the saints in heaven join at the Lamb's wedding; for we read, "And a voice came forth from the throne, saying, 'Give praise to our God, all ye servants, ye that fear him, the small and the great! And I heard as it were the voice of a great multitude, and the voice of many waters, and the voice of mighty thunders, saying, Alleluia: for the Lord our God, the Almighty, reigneth. Let us rejoice and be exceeding glad, and let us give the glory unto him: for the marriage of the Lamb is come."[1]

It is obvious from this that what affects the soul, and and what the spirit yearns to, by the effect of love, joy, and rejoicing, is natural unto it as a living, rational being. It also indicates that the propensity for merriment is a vestige of speech, which the soul, failing to express in measured words by the tongue, gives expression to by rhythm. The melodious consonance of the voice, sometimes imitating the voices of doves or other birds, and measured in accordance with time, volume, modality, frequency of trilling, emphasis, repetition, etc., is accordingly called singing, when in the form of poetry; and chanting, when in the form of prose.

The church Fathers, especially those who were musicians, realized the importance of music in the church services. They knew its effect on the soul, the mental pleasure it gives, the ecstacy, the joy, the elevation from earthly things, the unity with the ranks of the angels, and the acknowledgment of the Creator's Godhead. To proclaim God's benevolence in songs of thanksgiving and praise, the holy Fathers began composing spiritual songs and hymns, thus leading the faithful to God, and away from the defilements of worldly and heathen songs, and from heresy.

---

[1] Rev. 19:5-7.

Among those who thus set about to counteract the popular songs of their day were Ephram the Syriac, the Three Luminaries, Ambrose of Milan, Anatolius of Constantinople, author of the Stichoi for Sundays and Holidays, who died in 458, Romanus the Melodious, author of most of the Kontakions and the type of song known as the Oikos, who died in 510; Gregory Dialogus, who introduced modern tunes into the western church, and who died in 604; and Sophronius of Jerusalem, who died in 641.

Singing, and the Appearance of the Two Choirs

When it was first introduced, singing in the church was by the whole congregation, as we gather from St. Cyprian in his book on Prayer, where he says that when the Priest called out, "Let us lift up our hearts," the congregation responded, "Our hearts are with the Lord." Similarly St. Jerome, who was a pupil of Gregory Theologus, in his Epistle to the People of Galatia says, "Often when the congregation of a church responded with an 'Amen' or 'Lord, have mercy', you could hear a rumbling like that of thunder."

But to avoid confusion and noise in a sacred place, the Fathers of the Council of Laodicea, which was held in 364, ordained that only Priests participate in the chanting and singing, assisted by the choirs singing antiphonally.[1]

In the eighth chapter of his sixth book, Isocrates mentions that the author of this rite, as well as the complete service, was the great among martyrs, Ignatius.

Then when St. John of Damascus came, he found that the natural voices are eight in number, which he called a scale, ascending and descending with the voice into octaves. From this scale he adopted eight tones, which he called the principal tones. He was not satisfied with this, however, elaborating on each tone and

---

[1] See explanation on p. 1072.

creating several tunes. In this he was followed by succeeding musicians until the number of tunes ran into hundreds. St. John of Damascus died in 760. Along with his friend and companion, St. Cosma of Jerusalem, he enriched the Church with hundreds of spiritual songs and hymns.

Prosomion and Idiomelon

Among the tunes introduced by the Church is one called *Prosomion,* which means a Troparion sung after the rhythm of an original Troparion. The Greek word means *resemblance,* and the tune of the Prosomion is according to musical beats. An Idiomelon, on the other hand, is a Troparion which has its own tune, and is sung in a long drawn out fashion.

The Psalms, and their Use in the Church

The Book of Psalms is a collection of poems, songs, hymns, and paeans, written by God's inspiration. It is the most important of the Holy Scriptures among the Hebrews, an inexhaustible treasure of divine praise for all the ages.

The Hebrews divided the Psalms into five parts: the first from the first Psalm to the forty-first; the second from the forty-second to the seventy-second; the third from the seventy-third to the eighty-ninth; the fourth from the nintieth to the one hundred and seventh; and the fifth part from the hundred and eighth to the hundred and fiftieth. This corresponded, according to them, to the five external senses of man and the five internal forces, and in the recital of these Psalms the senses and forces are blessed and sanctified.

The Bible informs us that the Prophet David appointed two hundred and eighty-eight men, whom he divided into twenty-four lots, presided over by twenty-four men consisting of Asaph, Heman, Jeduthun, and their sons. Each lot consisted of twelve men to sing, praise, and sanctify God in the Tabernacle, and later in the Temple of Jerusalem.[1] Some of the Psalms were individual in nature, and some composed for the congregation, suiting the whole body of worshippers, and sung in unison by them. The Prophet David set tunes to the Psalms in order that they might be delectable to the senses, bringing contentment to the soul, and drawing it away from carnal songs to the service of the Creator and the doing of his pleasure. Thus the body is attracted to the tune while the mind is attracted to the meaning of the Psalm. The Psalms, therefore, with their tunes, each fitting the other, are like a medicine which one mixes for a sick man until he regains his health, after which he goes about his duties.

For this reason the Psalms were used in the Church from the days of the Apostles, who adopted them and were accustomed to them from the old Covenant. The Church persisted in the use of the Psalms, winning the faithful to them;[2] for in the Psalms were found in compact form things that were scattered throughout the rest of the divine books—commandments, prohibitions, interpretations, sermons, warnings, and information about creatures that lead to the Creator. Withal they are consolation to the sorrowful, courage to the persecuted, an aid to the afflicted, a bridle to the wicked, a humbling of the strong, and a stimulation to patience in times of distress. They prophesy of Christ the Master and his entire dispensation. In truth, the Psalms are like a paradise full of fruitful trees. And besides using them in their prayers, the faithful were commanded by the Apostles to use them also in their conversation one with another.[3]

Stichologia, the Kathisma, and the Divisions of the Psalms

The Christians who came after the Apostles were very fond of the Psalms. They divided them into twen-

---

[1] 1 Chr. 25.   [2] Eph. 5:19.   [3] Col. 3:16.

ty parts, each part consisting usually of six or seven Psalms, which they called *stichologia*, meaning a certain number or collection of Psalms. Then they distributed these stichologias into seven divisions, after the seven Matins of the week thus: For Sunday Vespers, one: for Matins of Monday, Tuesday, Wednesday, Thursday, and Friday, three each; and for Saturday Matins, two. Each stichologia in turn was divided into three stages of a few Psalms each, followed by "Glory"; [1] after which we ask God's mercy, and resume the recitation of the Psalms. At the end of the third stage we sing a hymn which we call *Kathisma* (*pl. Kathismata*) which means *sitting,* because it is permissible for the congregation to sit while it is sung, and to take a little rest.

This division of the Psalms is very old, going back to a time before the Council of Laodicea (ad Lycum, called *Eski Hissar* by the Turks, and meaning *the Old Castle*) which was held in the year 364; for in the seventeenth canon of that Council we are told that "The Psalms should not be read continuously in the churches, but between one Psalm and another there should be inserted some reading."

Anabathmoi

When the Hebrews were released from their captivity in Babylon, they returned to Jerusalem, ascending, because Jerusalem was higher than Babylon. And as they ascended they sang Psalms which Symmachus and Theodotion called *Ascension* Hymns, and which the Seventy, who translated the Old Testament, called *Praise Songs of the Ascension.* These Psalms, which were sung in praise of God, were fifteen in number, beginning with the One Hundred and Nineteenth Psalm. They sang these Psalms at the various stations where they rested, and hence they were also called *Resting Psalms.*

---

[1] Since the recitation of *Glory* comes alternately from the two choirs it is also called *Antiphony.*

When the Israelites had reached Jerusalem and had built the Temple, which was of great length, width, and height, the priests used to sing these Psalms as they ascended the steps of the Temple to the Holy of Holies, reciting a Psalm at each step until they reached the highest step. For this reason those Psalms were variously known as *Steps, Stations,* or *Ascents.*

As for us Christians, we have a heavenly Jerusalem to which we are about to ascend from the land of our sojourn on this earth, according to our Saviour's promise.[1] Following the Church of the Old Testament, the Orthodox Church arranged little hymns which she called *Anabathmoi,* signifying thereby the New Jerusalem to which we shall ascend through the mercies of our Saviour and the power of our Hope. And as the service then enters a new stage we announce this by saying, "Prokeimenon".[2]

Kontakion and Oikos

In order that the Church may glorify God in brief expressions and similarly praise his saints, God's grace called his saint Romanus, Deacon of the Church of Beirut, to this task. It is related that this saint, who was very fond of monastic life, went to Constantinople and stayed in the Monastery of Cyrus, dedicated to the Virgin Mary. So great was his piety and religious zeal that he used to go from his cell to the Church of the Ever-virgin in Flashrines and spend the whole night in prayer. This he did especially on the days of dominical feasts, persisting in singing and prayers in the church. On one of these occasions, on the night of the Nativity, as he was in that church, he was overtaken by fatigue and slept. In his sleep the Virgin Mary appeared to him in a dream. She approached him, holding in her hand a scroll, and said, "Open your mouth and eat this grace that I am about to give you." The

---

[1] St. Jn. 14:2-3. [2] See p. 1063.

saint opened his mouth and swallowed the scroll. And when he awoke and realized what the dream meant he went up into the pulpit, as one who had been carried away by ecstacy to the seventh heaven from the effect of the dream, and began to chant a song which the Church has called *Kontakion,* meaning *abbreviation,* or *the abbreviated song.*

So surprised were the people at the sweet voice with which the saint sang this song that it was obvious to them that what they were hearing was nothing less than a tune given to him as a gift from heaven. And because of the sweetness of his voice he was called Melodus (or Melodious). St. Romanus was thus the first to compose the Kontakion, beginning with the Kontakion of Christmas. Subsequently he composed the rest of the Kontakions for the dominical feasts, for the all-holy Virgin, and for all the saints, altogether over a thousand Kontakions, many of which the Church has adopted in her services all the year round. St. Romanus died in the year 510.

The Oikos also, like the Kontakion, is a condensed form of hymn. The Greek word means *house,* signifying that the Oikos contained all the essentials of a household. Similarly the Oikos of the church service comprised in brief indications of the saint or the feast.

Canon and Ode

The Canon, as used in the church service, signifies several hymns which are divided into nine divisions, symbolizing, as Zonares said in his commentary on church hymns, the nine ranks of the angels.

These divisions are called Odes, an Ode being a song of praise, taken from the songs of praise of the Prophets and prophetesses of the Old Testament. An exception is the Ninth Ode which is taken from the contents of the sayings of the Theotokos and of Zacharias the parent of John the Forerunner.

Further, the Second Ode is omitted throughout the year, and is used only in the Great Fast, being in its contents a rebuke of the Jewish people for their iniquities. For this reason it is sung in the Great Fast to warn sinners, and to induce them to reform their conduct and purify their consciences.

Katabasia and Hermos

The holy Church in order to represent the descent of the Word of God, his Nativity, and his Ascension, composed songs which she called *Katabasias,* meaning *descent* or *songs of descension,* which are nine in number corresponding to the nine principal Odes.

In the days of St. Cosma, the great composer and singer of his time, while sitting in his usual seat in the choir, he came down to the middle of the church, and in his angelic voice sang a song which he had composed on the Nativity of Christ, "Christ is born, glorify him; Christ has come from the heavens, receive him; Christ is on earth, arise ye." And when he came to the last word he went back and ascended to his seat.

In this way the saint symbolized the descent of the Word of God from his heaven, by his own descent from his seat to the middle of the church. And again he symbolized Christ's ascent by his own ascent to his seat in the choir, as he said, "Arise ye." As in a sermon St. Cosma taught us how to elevate ourselves spiritually from things earthly and to receive Christ in the spirit whence he came.

The meaning of the Katabasias was also carried out by the Church when the Bishop descended from his cell to the church, singing the first Katabasia, and later as he ascends his throne in the church. If however, the Bishop is in his throne before he sings the first Katabasia, he descends one step as he sings it; and when he says, "Arise ye", he goes back to his place. The singer, too, in the absence of the Bishop, descends from his seat as he sings the first Katabasia, and returns to it when he comes to the end of the song.

The Katabasias being poetical compositions set to special tunes, are also called *Hermoses,* which means *key,* or *measure,* thus called because they represent the keys to the Odes that follow them.

Magnifications and Theotokion

The holy Church ordained that the Ninth Ode should be a hymn of praise to the Theotokos, and called it *Magnification (Magnificat)* because it starts with the words, "My soul doth magnify the Lord." This Ode is sung in almost all the canons. The Church made this Ode, which is the last of the hymns, also the last of the hymns of the Old Testament, signifying thereby the Virgin's unity with her Son, who is the fulfillment of the law and the Prophets; for since the Virgin sang this while bearing Christ, it is meet that she be glorified and magnified at the same time with her Son with these Magnifications. The Church also ordained that after each verse of the Magnifications the hymn, *"O thou who art more honourable,"* etc., be sung, referring to the immeasurable glory and ineffable station which she attained by the unity with her of the Word of God and because of his assumption of a body from her undefiled blood, and her giving of birth to the Salvation of the world.

For the same reason and purpose the Church also arranged hymns which she called *Theotokions,* meaning songs to the Theotokos, which always follow the hymns addressed to her Son. The Theotokions thus signify the unity of the Theotokos with Christ through her motherhood, and his unity with her through his sonship.

Akathiston

The Greek word means *not permitted to sit,* and is applied to a paean for the Theotokos in which the congregation is not permitted to sit.[1]

Paracletice

Or *Paracletike,* pertaining to Paraclesis. This latter word has two distinct meanings, the first is *consolation,* from which the Holy Spirit was called Paraclete, or Consoler, and the second is *Supplication,* or *Petition.* From the latter meaning we derive the two canons the Great and the Little Paracletice, which are supplicatory hymns to the Theotokos.[2]

Oktoechos

A Greek word meaning *eight tones,* which idiomatically began to be applied to the collection of hymnal canons composed by St. John of Damascus.

Photagogikon—Exaposteilarion and Hypakoe

Having reached in our Matin service the time of the dawn when the sun is about to appear, we chant a hymn which is called *Photagogikon,* which means *illuminator,* because we recite it always after the canon and at the appearance of the light of day. And in this hymn we petition God to send us his divine light for the illumination of our minds and the sanctification of our souls.

On Sundays and feast days, however, we sing instead of it the Exaposteilarion, which means *dispatching,* and refers to the dispatching by Christ after his Resurrection of the ointment-bearing women, and to the dispatching of the Disciples to preach to the world and to warn it. The Exaposteilarion is the composition of King Constantine the Porphrogint (born in Porphry) who reigned in the year 912 and died in 959.

---

[1] See Fifth Week of the Fast.   [2] p. 32.

But Emperor Leo the Wise, who preceded the above-mentioned Constantine and who reigned in 886 and died in 912, having observed behind the physical phenomenon of the rise of the sun its spiritual significance —the obedience of the women in the mission on which Christ had sent them—composed a song which he called *Hypakoe,* meaning *obedience;* for in it there is reference to the obedience shown by the ointment-bearing women, and more especially to the Theotokos, who is the second Eve, as they were going to the tomb of the Life-giver, who is the second Adam. And having beheld him in the garden, the women submitted in obedience to him, in expiation of the disobedience of our first forefathers.

For in that Eve disobeyed God's commandment and because of her we were expelled from paradise, so those women, and particularly the Theotokos, when they beheld Christ and offered him their obedience, received joy in place of that first sorrow.

Einos, Eothina, and the Doxology

Noble souls which are accustomed to virtue and righteousness are not content to discharge their mere duty of confession of the Godhead, nor that of praise and thanksgiving to God for the abundance of his benevolences. Rather, because of their intense love, their warmth of faith, and their zeal to universalize the divine worship, they ask the greater good and the more persuasive beneficence. They pray for all people and call the whole of creation to join them in offering their veneration to God their Creator, as the three youths did while in the midst of the flaming fire, and as David also did.[1]

In accordance with this spirit of piety and this zeal, the holy Church instituted a hymn which she called *Einos (or Praise),* and in which she called upon every soul and every creature to join her in offering praises

---

[1] Dan. 3:52-90; Ps. 102:22; and Ps. 148.

and thanksgiving to God for his acts of mercy and love to mankind, which were especially revealed at the appearance of the Saviour on earth, the true Light of the world. For this reason, as we sing the hymns assigned for such praises we chant or recite the glorification with which the angels glorified God who was incarnate for the salvation of the world. By this we mean the Doxology which is the Great Glorification, "Glory be to thee, O thou who hast revealed the light", etc.

On Sundays the Church has assigned to this Glorification or Great Doxology the reading of Gospels, which are known as *Eothina* and mean *pertaining to the dawn.* They are eleven in number, symbolizing the eleven appearances of the Saviour to his Disciples after his Resurrection from the dead. These appearances were a confirmation to his Disciples of his Resurrection, as well as for the purpose of compassion on his followers, that they be not overcome by sorrow over a long period. Especially was this true of his Mother the Virgin Mary, to whom he appeared first (and who is referred to cryptically as the "other Mary, the Mother of James").[1] The second appearance was to Mary Magdalene alone at the tomb, the third to the same Mary and her companions on the way to Jerusalem, the fourth was to Peter, the fifth to the two Disciples Luke and Cleopas who were going to Emmaus, the sixth to all the Apostles, excepting Thomas, the seventh to the eleven Disciples, the eighth to seven of the Apostles who were at the shore of the lake of Tiberias, the ninth to more than five hundred brethren on a mountain, the tenth to James, and the eleventh to all his Apostles on the day of his Ascension.[2]

To the same end the Church ordained special hymns commemorating these holy appearances and called them *Doxas of the Eothina,* containing each the meaning of one of those appearances for that particular Sunday.

---

[1] St. Mt. 28:1 and St. Mk. 16:1.
[2] St. Jn. 20:11-16; St. Mt. 28:9; 20; St. Lk. 24:34; 1 Cor. 15:5; St. Lk. 24:13-36; St. Mk. 16:12; 14-18; St. Lk. 24:36-49; St. Jn. 20:19, 26; 1 Cor. 15:5; St. Jn. 21:1; St. Mt. 28:16; 1 Cor. 15:7; St. Lk. 24:50.

These Doxas of the Eothina were also the composition of Emperor Leo the Wise, the author of the Hypakoe.

After singing the Doxas of the Eothina; if it be a Sunday, or the Doxa of the Einos, if it be a great feast day, we sing the Troparion assigned for that day and begin the service of the Divine Liturgy. Otherwise we recite the petitions beginning with, "Let us finish our morning petitions to the Lord", and those that follow it. Then we recite the Stichera of the Oktoechos, known as the Aposticha, with its Stichoi. Then we say, "It is a good thing to confess to the Lord"; "Holy God", and what follows it, and the Troparion of the day. Then we recite the supplicatory petitions which are known as Ektene, "Have mercy upon us, O God, according to the multitude of thy mercies." Then we pray God to uphold our kings, and we conclude the service, and begin at once with the service of the First Hour.

The First Hour

God sent his Son a Light, a Guidance, and a Salvation to the world. However, while God expected confession of faith for his supernatural miracles, and faith in his sublime teachings, leading like a guiding light to the truth, in acordance with the utterance of the prophecies, the same prophecies which were entrusted to those for whose salvation he had especially come, behold, instead of faith they made him taste the most severe sufferings and the most bitter pains. They delivered him into the hands of oppressive judges, who, even in spite of all the lying, deceit, and false accusations of those who delivered him, found nothing in him to merit conviction.

In order that the holy Church may point to her children and remind them of the state of those cruel men, and of what happened to our Lord God and Saviour Jesus Christ in that hour, as he was in the midst of his struggles for salvation, she instituted the Prayer of the First Hour. In this service is unfolded the deceit, cruelty, and vileness of the Jewish high priests and their elders in their accusations against Christ. It also reveals Christ's guilelessness, his truthfulness, uprightness, and virtue, set against their iniquities, inventions, and envy, as the fifth Psalm referring to them, makes plain, and also the one hundredth Psalm, the second, third, and sixth verses of the same service.

Likewise, the holy Church intended in this prayer of the First Hour to urge her children to seek heavenly blessings and divine aid in order to facilitate their daily tasks and the labour of their hands, in accordance with the words of the Prophet, "Man goeth forth unto his work and to his labour until the evening. O Jehovah, how manifold are thy works! In wisdom hast thou made them all."[1]

The same may be gathered from the contents of Ps. 89:14, etc. This service was added with the Midnight Prayer in the fourth century to the collection of services that were in use in the first century.

The Third and Sixth Hours

Because of two events which took place in the third hour, the Church instituted the service of the Third Hour in commemoration of them. The first of these was the sentence of death passed by Pilate against our Lord God Jesus Christ. The second was the descent of the Holy Spirit upon the Disciples in the upper room of Zion.[2] And since this service falls in the early part of the morning, the Priest opens with, "Blessed be God our God", and what follows it. As for the service of the Sixth Hour, it was instituted by the Church in memory of sufferings and the Passion endured by our Redeemer when he was suspended on the Cross.

---

[1] Ps. 103:23-24.
[2] See Service of the Third Hour, Ps. 6:9-11; 24:16, 19; also 50:12-14, and the Troparion and the Prayer.

Typica: Antiphony and Makarizmoi

The Prophets foretold all the events of the coming of the Saviour, from the time of his Birth to his Ascension into heaven. They left out nothing of the sayings and doings of Christ, but they prophesied thereof, including those that took place up to the time of John the Baptist, when Christ had not yet fulfilled his offering of himself as a Sacrifice, nor given the form of his body as an oblation in the form of bread and wine, as the Holy Bible had symbolized that by the offering of Melchizedek, the manna of the Israelites, the lamb of the Passover, and other symbols that refer to it.

Up to the time of John the Baptist, therefore, the prophecies followed the course of the events in the life of Christ and his doings. And among the works of salvation was the offering of Christ himself as a Sacrifice, by giving his body, in the form of bread and wine, as an oblation.

In order to allude to the sayings of the Prophets with which they prophesied of the times up to John the Baptist, in which Christ was present but not appearing to many nor known by many as the Saviour and Redeemer, the Church instituted a service which consisted of Psalms and hymns, and which she called *Typica,* meaning *typical or symbolical.* And in this service the Church points out and explains the events of the time of John the Baptist, in which the holy oblations were present yet hidden in the Person of Christ. As Vilaras said, "The Typica is a symbol of the warnings of the forefathers and Prophets." A similar interpretation is given by St. Germanus, and also by Kavasella, where he says in the eighteenth chapter of his work, "The sayings of the Prophets which are sung refer to the time of John the Baptist."

The Typica applies to those prophecies, whether they consist of whole Psalms or of verses, or whether they are taken from verses of the Psalms, which are called in the rite of the service *Stichoi;* for they all come from the Old Testament. And since the Typica is sung by both choirs alternately, it is also called *Antiphony,* which means singing or chanting alternately. The Antiphony also is applied to whatever is sung alternately by the two choirs.

The first to institute the Typica, according to the authority of Photius the Patriarch of Constantinople, was the God-mantled Ignatius, the Bishop of Antioch, who was raised by the Apostle St. Peter and who was also a disciple of St. John the Evangelist, and one of the children who were brought to Christ to be blessed. But Philemon the Hebrew mentions in his history that the Antiphony was sung in his day in Alexandria before it was introduced by St. Ignatius in Antioch.

The Typica, or Antiphony, is divided into three stations, symbolizing three stages of the history of Israel, namely from Abraham to David, from David to the Babylonian Captivity, and from the Babylonian Captivity to Christ. It is usually performed after the service of the Sixth Hour. Later on there was added to this service the *Makarizmoi* or *Beatitudes,* consisting of verses from the Gospels, each of which begins with the word *blessed,* and of Troparia and of chanting, "O only-begotten, Son and Word of God", etc., alluding to the fact that the Son of God whom the Prophets foretold is the same who from the beginning of time was begotten of the Father, but who in time was born of the Virgin as Jesus, God and Man in one. He is one of the Holy Trinity, glorified with the Father and with the Holy Spirit, as Simeon the Thessalonian declares, "By these Psalms the Incarnation of the Son of God was foretold; but by the hymns the fullness of his grace is made manifest."

And in order that the Church may not deny the faithful a service which symbolizes in this fashion the forewarnings and prophecies of the Old Testament, and which alludes to the holy oblations hidden in Christ even before he instituted them, the Church ordained that the

Typica may be substituted for the service of the Holy Mass on days when the Mass is not served, either because of the absence of a Priest, or because he may not be prepared, or for some other reason. For this reason the Church took from the Mass of the Catechumens the one hundred and second Psalm, "Bless the Lord, O my soul", etc., which constitutes the First Antiphony, and the one hundred and forty-fifth Psalm, "Praise the Lord, O my soul", etc., and the Hymn, "O only-begotten Son and Word of God", etc., both of which constitute the Second Antiphony. These are followed by the Makarizimoi, or Beatitudes,[1] with the words of the penitent thief, "Remember us, Lord, when thou comest into thy kingdom," [2] following each Beatitude. To this service of the Typica, which is taken from the Mass of the Catechumens, the Church added something taken from the Mass of the Faithful, namely the Creed, "I believe in One God", etc., with the Prayer beginning, "Pardon, forego, and forgive, O God", etc., the Lord's Prayer, "Our Father, who art in heaven", etc., the Kontakion of the day or of the feast on which the service falls, and the thirty-third Psalm, "I will bless the Lord at all times", etc.

(For the rest of the service of the Typica see in its place. p. 120.)

THE DIVINE LITURGY AND THE OBJECT OF ITS INSTITUTION

All beings created by God achieve the goodness and benevolence of their Creator in so far as they are brought from naught into being, and in so far as God guides and preserves them; for the whole creation is God's possession and he is the Cause of its being. Yet the whole does not achieve this equally or in the same degree, but each according to his station received of the good gifts of God.

---

[1] St. Matt. 5:3-13.   [2] St. Luke 23:42.

Thus inanimate beings attain existence and the beauty thereof, and animals enjoy existence and the possession of life. But man was distinguished above all these in that he was created according to the form and likeness of God, and in that this sensible creation was created for his sake. God, therefore, created man because he loved him, and that he might enjoy God's love in more abundance, in so far as God singled him out immeasurably above all other creatures. Furthermore it was vouchsafed man, by his free choice, to unite with God.

But since man shared the likeness of God but did not preserve it, he fell under death and corruption because of his disobedience; and having lost the first birth which was free of suffering and consequence, he also lost the beauty that was first his, the splendour, the joy, the everlasting life, and the eternal bliss which were his through his union with God. The Creator, because of the abundance of his mercies and love, became like unto us and united with our weak and humble nature. He took unto himself a body from the ever-virgin Mary, and by his Birth, Baptism, Passion, and Resurrection he delivered our nature from the sin of our forefathers, restoring unto us what we had lost of everlasting life, which consists of beholding God and enjoying him for ever.

The flesh which the Word of God took unto himself from our human nature alone was sanctified because of its union with God, and he alone was filled with the divine gifts and in him alone dwelt the fullness of the Godhead, as it is written in the Holy Scriptures.[1] In order, therefore, that this sanctification and enjoyment of the divine gifts may not be limited to the First-born of our nature (the humanity which the Word took unto himself), but may pervade all those who desire this communion and this attainment through the second birth, free of the effects of passion, and through which we become the children of God, born unto everlasting

---

[1] Is. 11:1-2; St. Jn. 1:14; Col. 2:9.

life, God gave us a noble, holy, and undefiled birth, which is Baptism.

And because we are of dual nature, composed of spirit and flesh, Baptism also becomes dual, consisting of a material element and of a spiritual, divine power.

And since this birth is spiritual and supernatural, we demand a food which is also spiritual and supernatural, suitable for our birth which gives us everlasting life. This food is the invisible Body and Blood of our Lord in visible forms, which are the forms of bread and wine. By that birth, therefore, and by that food the natural Son of God made us children of God by adoption. He gave us himself as a symbol and example in all these things that we may follow his example and win the eternal gifts—life everlasting and endless bliss—which we had lost and which he restored to us.

This is the object of his Incarnation and of his Birth, of his granting unto us his holy Body as food, that he may make us through his Incarnation his chosen ones, through his Birth his companions, and through our nourishment by him inheritors of his kingdom.

He commanded us the living to be steadfast in our performance of this in remembrance of him,[1] and in remembrance of his benevolence to us until he comes again to judge the world. This is accomplished through faith by inheritance and by transmission from the living destined to die, to the dead who shall live again by regeneration, that salvation may extend unto all men.[2]

First Bishop over the First of the Churches of Christ

In view of what has been said above the Church instituted the service of the Mass, which is a fulfillment of the Sacrament of the Eucharist, or the Lord's Supper, in a way which reminds us, or embodies before us, the life of Jesus Christ on earth from beginning to end

---

[1] St. Lk. 22:19; 1 Cor. 11:23-26.   [2] 1 Tim. 4:10; St Jn. 4:14.

from his Birth of his virgin Mother to his Ascension into heaven.

This service of the Divine Mass, in its present arrangement, was transmitted to the Catholic Orthodox Church by St. James the Apostle, who was the first Bishop consecrated by Christ before his Ascension, to the throne of the church of holy Jerusalem, God's dwelling-place and throne, and the mother of all the churches of the world,[1] where Christ was born, where he came together with his Disciples, performed the sacramental Supper, and where the Holy Spirit descended on the Day of Pentecost.[2] The church of Jerusalem was followed by that of Antioch, the first seat of St. Peter. This same church was the house of Theophilus, which he endowed as a church after embracing the faith in Christ.[3] And it was Christ himself who taught his brother James the service of the Mass, having first appeared to him and later to him and the rest of the Apostles.[4]

First Appearance of the Divine Liturgy

The service of the Divine Mass before it was established by the Apostle James was very simple, as we may gather from the Acts and the Epistles of the Apostles; for after Christ had ascended to heaven the Disciples used to come together with the rest of the faithful, and meet in one of the houses of Jerusalem, particularly the upper room of Zion.[5] After lighting the lamps,[6] one

---

1 The throne of St. James remained in Jerusalem to the days of Eusebius, as he tells us in the seventh book of his History, chapter fifteen, where he says, "When the faithful fled from Jerusalem at the time it was besieged by Titus they took with them the episcopal throne of St. James.

2 See Nicophrus in his history, Book two Chapter three.

3 St. Luke 1:3 and Clement, Bk. one.

4 1 Cor. 15:7; John Chrysostom in his commentary on St. John 7:5, and Epiphanius in his book on Heresies, Chap. 87, where he says: "He (St. James) was the first to receive the Cathedra of a bishopric, and the first to whom Christ had delivered his seat on earth, as he was also known as the brother of the Lord. See also St. Mt. 13:55.

5 Acts 1:13.   6 Acts 20:7, 8.

of the Apostles would stand up and preach, teaching those present.[1] Then all would stand up, and one of them coming forward offers prayers and supplications to God with groanings which cannot be uttered, as the Holy Spirit would inspire him.[2] When he finishes the prayer the elder among them takes bread and wine mixed with hot water and blesses them, calling the Holy Spirit to change them into the undefiled Body and precious Blood of Christ.[3] After that he breaks the bread that has become transformed into the Lord's Body, and having first partaken of it and of the cup, he passes them to all those who are present.[4] At the conclusion of this Communion they offered prayers of thanksgiving to God. This constitutes the prayer of the Metalepsis.

Metalepsis

The word in Greek means *Communion,* and refers to the divine communion or the prayer of preparation for receiving the Communion and the prayer of thanksgiving which follows the Communion, as was the custom of the Jews; for those latter used to recite or sing, after consuming the Passover, the Psalms from 112 to 118, as is evident from the Holy Gospel, where it is said that the Disciples, having eaten the Supper, "sung a hymn", indicating the necessity of offering thanksgivings for having partaken of the holy Body and Blood of Christ. Accordingly the holy Church, in giving thanks to Christ for his benefactions and benevolences ordained special prayers for the communicants, and also the reading, for all, of the thirty-third Psalm, "I will bless the Lord at all times: his praise shall continually be in my mouth."

Koinonikon

Or hymn of Communion, which the Church ordained as an explanation and commemoration of his giving us

---

[1] Acts 2:42. [2] Ro. 8:26. [3] 1 Cor. 11:23-28. [4] Acts 2:42.

the Sacrament of his holy Body on the eve of his deliverance, and how the worthy and the unworthy (like
Judas) received this Sacrament. Hence we say in this
hymn, "Receive me today, O Son of God, a partaker of
the sacramental Supper", etc.

The Church kept the service of the Divine Liturgy
in its entirety as she received it from the undefiled Apostles.[1] But in time and in conformity with changing conditions, the Church, through the inspiration of the Holy
Spirit, introduced certain regulations and improvements
which are useful for the upbuilding of the faithful, assigning readings from the Holy Scriptures, and prayers, as we said before.

The Service of the Liturgy after the Saints, James Basil, John, and Gregory

The Liturgy of St. James the Apostle is used not only
by the Orthodox Church but also by churches which
are foreign to its doctrines, such as the Nestorian, the
Eutychian, the Armenian, the Syriac, and the Jacobite.
This universal compliance in all the ancient services of
the Mass, in the most significant part of the Eucharist,
testifies beyond doubt that this apostolic act and its delivery were as instituted on this particular subject.
It also testifies that the belief of the Catholic Church
of Christ is the same, and that it has not changed from
ancient times to the present. And because of the difficulty of communication among Christians in the first
three centuries, the order of the Divine Liturgy was not
the same in all the churches. For instance, the Christians in Jerusalem and the rest of Palestine followed
the Liturgy of the Apostle James, Bishop of Jerusalem;
in Alexandria and the rest of Egypt they followed
the Liturgy attributed to the Evangelist Mark, Bishop
of Alexandria; while in Rome and all parts of the west
they followed the Liturgy attributed to St. Clement of
Rome, and so on.

---

[1] 1 Cor. 11:23.

And due to the lengthy petitions in the service of St. James, which lasts for about five hours, and for fear that the congregation might grow weary and listless and unable to stand throughout all that time, the holy Fathers thought it wise to abbreviate or condense the lengthy petitions and prayers in that service, retaining passages appropriate and germane to the service. The first to do this, and to arrange a short service taken from St. James the Apostle was St. Basil the Great, whose service is known after his name as the Liturgy of St. Basil. In the same manner, St. John Chrysostom arranged a service from St. James the Apostle, and, this also became known as the Liturgy of St. John Chrysostom. Neither of these Fathers was content merely to omit parts of the Liturgy of St. James but they added certain prayers and petitions known by their names. The use of these two Liturgies spread throughout the east and west, along with a third Liturgy which was used in the days of the Great Fast (Lent), and which was known as the Liturgy of Presanctified Gifts. This latter was known in the east from the days of the undefiled Apostles by way of oral transmission. Then came St. Gregory, Bishop of Rome, known as Gregory Dialogus, who wrote down and introduced this Liturgy in the west in the sixth century, and it was attributed to him.

Assigning the Time of the Liturgical Services, and Their Origin

In order that the Church may preserve the unity of faith and divine worship in every place, she ordained that the foregoing Masses be celebrated at set times, as follows: The Mass of the Apostle James is celebrated on the day of his feast, on the twenty-third of October, and may be celebrated at other times, as the elder wishes. The Mass of St. Basil is celebrated ten times during the year (which see in his service). As for the Mass of St. John Chrysostom, it is celebrated through-

out the year except on Wednesdays and Fridays of Holy
Lent and on Monday, Tuesday, and Wednesday of Passion Week. The Mass of St. Gregory is celebrated on
the days of Lent, and it is called the Proegiasmena, or
the Presanctified Mass, because the gifts or oblations
used therein may not be transubstantiated again, having
already been consecrated in a previous Mass. However, the commemoration of the faithful is fulfilled in
this Mass, as mentioned in the service.

The first of these Masses, as we said before, is that of
St. James which had its origin in the first century. Then
followed the Mass of St. Basil in the fourth century;
then that of St. John Chrysostom in the fifth century,
and lastly the Gregorian Mass in the sixth century.
There is no difference in the essence of these four rites.

Divisions of the Mass

The service of the Divine Mass is divided into three
parts: the first part is the Offering, in which the oblations (gifts) of bread and wine are brought to the Altar
(Table) of the sanctuary to be consecrated by the Priest.
The second part is the Mass of the Catechumens, in
which of old the Catechumens were allowed to be present along with the faithful. The catechumens consisted of heathen who were preparing themselves to enter
the Christian religion through Baptism, and Christian
penitents who had fallen from membership in the
Church for one reason or another, especially those who
had denied Christ and were returning to the Faith. The
third part is called the Mass of the Faithful, which the
faithful only are permitted to attend. Hence, in ancient times, at the beginning of this part the catechumens and the penitents would leave the church.

These three parts which constitute the holy service of
Mass are securely united in such a way that it is not
possible to separate them one from another; for in the
first part the matter of the Sacrament of the Eucharist
is made ready; in the second part preparation is made

for the celebration of the Eucharist, and in the third, which is the most important, the Sacrament of the divine Eucharist is fulfilled, in that the bread and wine are transformed into the precious Body and undefiled Blood of Christ.

The first part of the divine service of the Mass is named from the fact that the faithful offer the bread and wine to the Priest to offer the bloodless Sacrifice, and for this reason the naming of this part as the Sacrifice prevailed among almost all Orthodox Christians.

The matter of the Sacraments of the Eucharist, which is thus prepared by the Priest, consists of bread and wine, as we said before. The first of these must come from clean wheat and must be leavened; the second from the pure juice of the vine of the color of blood, following the example of our Saviour Jesus Christ who delivered the Sacrament of the Eucharist under the forms of these two substances.[1]

The bread of the oblation, as is well known, should be in the form of a loaf, round, flattened, and thick. It is called an oblation because of its being offered for the bloodless Sacrifice. On the upper side of this oblation, exactly in the middle, is impressed the sign of the cross, surrounded by the Greek letters I Σ (which means Jesus), X Σ (Christ) and the word N I K A (conquer) as in the following diagram:

Thus the whole sentence would read, "In the sign of the Cross of Jesus Christ thou shalt conquer," which is

---

1 St. Mt. 26:26-29; St. Mk. 1:22-25; St. Lk. 22:7-20; 1 Cor. 11:23-26.

taken, as is well known, from the wonderful miracle which appeared in the middle of the skies to the great king Constantine before he embraced Christianity.[1]

In old times it was customary for Christians to offer for the divine Mass several pieces of bread, from which the Priest would choose the best for the celebration of the Sacrament. The rest then would be distributed to the poor and needy. But now it is considered sufficient to offer five pieces, commemorating the five loaves with which the Lord satisfied five thousand souls.[2] From these five the Priest selects one for the fulfillment of the Eucharist, or for the Sacrifice.[3] Hence this oblation is also called Lamb, in memory of our Lord and God Jesus Christ, the Lamb of God who taketh away the sins of the world.[4] As for the remaining four loaves, they are disposed of as follows: from the first is taken out a part for the Virgin; from the second, nine parts are taken for the saints; from the third, parts are taken for the living; and from the fourth, parts are taken for the dead, as you may see in the book of the service of Divine Liturgy.

Explanation of the Parts of the Mass
Kyron

Before beginning, the Priest takes *Kyron,* which means time or permission. When the Bishop is present this consists of simply kissing his hand, a sign of submission to him and in testimony that from his hand was the service received and by his hand fulfilled; for it is to the Bishop that the right of administering the Sacraments was given. Kissing the Bishop's hand also signifies that the Priest is duly ordained. Hence the Priest must take from the Bishop a *Kyron,* or permission to administer the service. In the Kyron when the Bishop is not present, the Priest stands in front of the Royal

[1] See account of his life May twenty-first in the Great Horologion.
[3] 1 Cor. 10:17.   [2] St. Jn. 6:9-13.   [4] St. Jn. 1:29.

Door, then kneels, repeating privately the prayer of the Kyron (which see in its place), indicating in it that under all conditions he is Orthodox, submitting and conforming to all the commandments of the holy Councils.

Kissing the Table

After that, the Priest enters the Holy of Holies, or Sanctuary, and kneels three times before the Table towards the east, worshipping Christ of the three Persons, and indicating his love of God and union with, and his sanctification from him.

Kissing the Vestments

The Priest then puts on his sacerdotal vestments, making the sign of the cross over each as he puts it on, indicating that the vestment is thus sanctified by the Cross, and that it grants its wearer sanctification.

Washing the Hands

This is followed by the washing of the hands, announcing thereby his own purity which he has attained for the performance of this service, and in preparation therefor, as Simeon the Thessalonian says, "For he that comes forward towards the pure One must be himself pure in his entirety." Similarly the beatified Germanus said, "The washing of hands among us Priests is a reminder unto us to purify, in the fear of God, our conscience, our mind, and our thoughts, which are like hands to our souls."

Moving the Oblation

This symbolizes the coming of Christ to the grotto. And after preparing the holy vessels the Priest resumes the order of the divine Sacrifice, as is stated in the service book of the Mass pertaining to the Priest.

Eisodos—Introit or Procession—The Cherubicon and the Litiya

The holy Church believes, according to what has preceded, that Christ's Death is the only true Sacrifice, which is the fulfillment of the Sacrifice in behalf of mankind. It also believes that Christ's all-pure and all-holy Body and Blood, while offered on the one hand for food and drink in the sacramental Supper, are offered on the other hand as a sacrifice unto God.

Hence the Church regards the Sacrament of the Eucharist not only as an all-holy Mystery (Sacrament), but also as a fearful mystical Sacrifice, acknowledging at the same time, in a procession before God, that this is being offered upon the holy Altar as a bloodless Sacrifice of thanksgiving for his abundant mercies and countless benevolences.

In order, therefore, to afford this expression of our faith a proper manifestation, and the holy Sacraments the honour of which they are worthy, we lift the Lamb in a procession, worshipping him as he passes by. This is what is meant by the Eisodos, or Procession with the oblations which are about to be transformed into the holy Body and the precious and undefiled Blood of Christ. This is what is known as the Great Eisodos, because it is the most characteristic part of the service, the greatest in the noble offering, since it is the object thereof and through it the faithful are sanctified and united with the Lord God. And for this reason the faithful remain standing throughout the Eisodos to the end of the Mass, reverently listening to the prayers and petitions.

This Eisodos or Procession which takes place amid the awe and reverence of the worshippers, this reception of the divine oblations in honour, fear, and worship, is an old institution which the Church received from the Apostle James, the Lord's brother, where he says, "Let all mortal flesh keep silence and in fear and trembling stand", etc. Said Coropalatis, the historian of

the great Church, "The pious kings of Constantinople
used to come forward in a procession of great reverence
before this Eisodos, symbolizing the taking down of
Christ's body from Golgotha by Nicodemus and its
burial in the tomb represented by the holy Table."

In sound doctrine, therefore, the holy Church ordained the singing of the Cherubicon, which means the
praise of the holy cherubim, when the oblations are carried in the procession, indicating thereby the entrance
of all the saints and the righteous, honouring him who
is the Sanctification of the saints, and the passing of the
cherubical powers before him: and with them is present
the Holy Spirit, beheld spiritually in the symbol of
fire and the sweet scent of incense. The Cherubicon
also signifies the casting away of every worldly care, in
imitation of the cherubim and all the ranks of angels,
as they stand in fear and trembling before the divine
throne, as is indicated in the words of the Cherubicon,
which had its origin, according to the historian Quad-
rinus, in the reign of Justinian the Orothodox, nephew
of Justinian the Great, and his successor in the year
565. The Cherubicon begins with the words, "Let us
who represent the cherubim mystically", etc. Speaking
in his history of the ranks in the royal palace, Coropalatis mentions that at the singing of the Cherubicon
the Archdeacon of the church steps forward and invites
the king, who comes forth, accompanied by the nobility
of his kingdom, and stands near the Altar, where the
sacramental Sacrifice is placed. There he dons, over
his royal robe, another one, gilded, and holds a cross in
his right hand; for it was the custom of kings, when
they placed their crowns on their heads, to hold a cross
in the right hand and the sceptre in the left. The king
then heads the Eisodos, surrounded by the nobility, and
as they reach the Royal Door all those in the procession stand outside the Sanctuary, or Holy of Holies,
except the king, who enters through the Royal Door,
where he finds the Patriarch standing. Each then bows

to the other, in brotherly love, the Patriarch from the inside and the king from the outside. In the meantime the Deacon, holding the censer in his right hand and the Patriarch's omophorion in his left, censes the king as he bows his head and in a loud voice says, "The Lord God remember the King's majesty in his kingdom for evermore", etc. And likewise say the rest of the clergy in the Eisodos, one by one, as they enter the Sanctuary. In the same manner they mention the Patriarch, as they say, "The Lord God remember your High Priesthood in his kingdom for evermore", etc. Then the Patriarch and the king greet each other, and the Patriarch lifts the gilded robe off the king and gives it to the church sexton, according to the established custom. The king then returns to his seat and sits down, nor does he stand up till the recitation of the Creed, "I believe in one God", etc.

It should be well kept in mind, howbeit, that nowhere in this Eisodos, or Procession should the adoration afforded the bread and wine be considered as worship.

The Little Eisodos (the Entrance)

Besides the Great Eisodos which we described above, there is another one, known as the Little Eisodos, which is accomplished by carrying the holy Gospels. This signifies the coming of the Son of God, and his holy entrance into the world. Hence the Bishop or Priest announces this procession by singing the Song of Triumph, as he enters to the Altar, saying, "Come let us bow down and worship Christ. Save us, O Son of God", etc., in accordance with the words of the Prophet, "All the earth shall worship thee, and shall sing unto thee; they shall sing to thy Name."[1] And likewise the Apostle, "And when he again bringeth in the first-born into the world he saith, 'And let the angels of God worship him.' "[2]

There is also a third procession with the branches of

---

[1] Ps. 65:4.   [2] Heb. 1:6.

palm trees. This takes place on Palm Sunday and signifies the reception of the triumph, and the joy in the
Saviour that is come.[1] Then there is the procession
around the church, as in the service of Easter Eve, signifying our expulsion from paradise because of disobedience. As we circle the church we beseech God to restore us to our old home, from which we were exiled.

As for the Litiya, it means a supplicatory hymn, or
processional which we sing in the narthex, or exterior
portico, of the church.

The procession with the cross also reminds us of the
joy of salvation which we received through the Crucified.

The Menaion

This is also known in Greek as *Panthekte* which
means all-inclusive. It is an ecclesiastical book of songs
which contains the services of all the dominical feasts,
the feasts of the Theotokos and of all the celebrated
saints, as well as the daily remembrances of the rest
of the saints throughout the twelve months. It is put in
rhyme, and was composed by several saints.

Needless to say that in poetical composition, in which
the composer has to preserve the meter and rhyme, although in the Greek language the latter is dispensed
with, certain things are permissible. Hence in the
Greek text of such a book often occur many words in
their symbolical or hyperbolical senses, and not the
literal one, such as the work *ousia,* which means essence
or element, for the word *phusis,* which figuratively
means nature, Synonyms and sometimes repetitions are
used in the same song, especially in the vocative case,
for no reason than the necessity of the rhyme.

Triodion

A great number of God-mantled saints, who sang of
divine things, were moved by the Holy Spirit and

---

[1] Lev. 23:40; St. Mt. 21:8; St. Jn. 12:13 and Rev. 7:9.

moved by divine longing, to write and compose hymns for the guidance of the faithful. Foremost among these was St. Cosma, the great composer; for this saint, realizing that glory and honour are meet unto the Holy Spirit, as they are meet unto the Father and the Son, invented the *Triodion,* which means a song of three odes, symbolizing the most Holy Trinity, the essence of life.

These odes are sung in the great and holy Passion Week of our Lord and God Jesus Christ. The composer originated the tunes after the opening words of the Troparia, after the naming almost of each day. Others of the Fathers, especially Theodore and Joseph, then imitated St. Cosma, composing hymns for the rest of the holy and great weeks of Quadragesima. These they delivered in their own monastery first, after they were put in the best order, as relating to the Odes and the quotations they made from the Fathers.

And since Sunday includes the first day, being the day of Resurrection, and the eighth and last, they did well in assigning to the second day, which is Monday, the first of the songs of praise, to the third the second, to the fourth the third, to the fifth the fourth, to the sixth the fifth, and the seventh, which is Saturday, the sixth with the two remaining songs, in which all the days in a more special way share. Then, too, the noble Cosma, composed a canon of four odes, which he designated for Great Saturday, even though the very wise King Leo ordered that this canon be completed by the anchorite Marcus, Bishop of Idropidus. This, however, only figuratively is called a Triodion, for it does not always comprise canons of three odes, but sometimes complete odes. Hence Nicepherus of Calithtus presumes that this nomenclature was adopted from the more prevailing name, or because of what takes place on Great Friday, as we said.

The object of the whole Tridion, therefore, which our holy Fathers had in mind was to remind us in a brief and figurative manner of the lovingkindnesses of

God, which accrued to us from the beginning: how we were created; how we disobeyed the commandment which was given us to observe; how we were expelled from the paradise of bliss; how we were kept afar because of the envy of the serpent, which is the foe, who is the source of evil since his downfall from heaven because of his haughtiness; how we were cast away and denied the blessings; and how we were led away by Satan. They also remind us how the Son of God and his Word had compassion on us, moved by anguish for us, how he bowed the heavens and came down, dwelling in the Virgin's womb, how he became Man for our sake, and by his undefiled conduct revealed unto us the ascent to heaven, first through his humility, through fasting, abstaining from evil, and the rest of his glorious deeds, how he suffered and rose and ascended into heaven, how he sent the Holy Spirit to his holy Disciples, how these preached him among all nations, that he was the Son of God and perfect God, and of what those divine Disciples did by the grace of the all-holy Spirit, in that they brought together from the ends of the earth, by their warning, all the saints, thus completing the upper world, which was of old the purpose of the Creator.

Synaxarion

The Holy Church, desiring to reveal to us the divine perfections which are commanded by God,[1] embodied by practise in the persons of the men of God, placed before the eyes of her sons the *Synaxarions,* which means a collection of the accounts of the saints of God. In this book the Church pictured the lives of the saints, and the content of each of their feasts, from which the purpose of the feast is clearly shown, and when and how it was appointed of old, along with the reason for this appointment, with special reference to what we have already said of the Triodions. The Synaxarions

---

[1] St. Mt. 5:48.

begin with the Sunday of the Pharisee and the Publican, and end with the Sunday of All Saints. (See the Synaxarions and the Sundays of the Triodion.)

SUNDAY

The Holy Book says that God the Father, by his Son, began on the first day, which is Sunday, with the creation of the sensible world, and ended his work on the sixth, resting on the seventh.

For this reason the seventh day was called sabbath, which in Hebrew (shabbath) means rest and quiet. This seventh day begins on Friday evening (sunset) and ends on Saturday evening, according to the Jewish custom.

Now since the whole of creation consisted of the purely spiritual, as the angels, and the purely sensible as matter, God united both by creating man of both. And since God created man partly of enduring and partly of unenduring elements, and this he did not for a temporal and transient end, but for an everlasting and permanent end, this being far superior to that, he made his soul especially after his divine likeness and holy image. He singled him out of all creatures for the honour of imitating him. And as a result of creating man's body, God appointed the Sabbath for rest.

Thus, God (may he be exalted) commanded man to do what is best in his eyes, which is to follow him and imitate him, and to rest from his works, as God rested from his, thus perpetuating the remembrance of his having been created and fashioned by him as well as the fact that God worked and rested from his work, which to God signifies the end of the work of creation. To man, however, it means actually rest for one day after six days of work, in order to find time for the fulfillment of spiritual activities, such as prayer, the various rites of worship and sacrifices and other religious duties. The rest on the sabbath is not an end of the commandment in itself, but was instituted for the added good of man, physically and spiritually. So that, having accomplished the duty of worship towards his Creator, he may be granted blessing and sanctification, in that God by blessing and sanctifying (hallowing) the seventh day, made those who keep it to be also blessed and sanctified,[1] until the time it was to be changed, as the Apostle said, "Which was a figure for the time then present, in which were offered both gifts and sacrifices, that could not make him that did the service perfect, as pertaining to the conscience; which stood only in meats and drinks, and divers washings, and carnal ordinances, imposed on them until the time of reformation."[2]

In addition to this, God later designated the sabbath as a symbol of the rest in the promised land.[3]

When, therefore, the beauty of creation was obliterated by submission to error, and the splendour of God's likeness was blotted out by disobedience, and the sanctify of the spiritual attribute was marred by rebellion, God the Father sent his Son, by whom he had made creation,[4] incarnate from an immaculate Virgin, in order to restore what had been obliterated and to renew what had been destroyed.[5]

But this renewal does not signify the creation of new things (for that had been done and accomplished, and God rested therefrom on the seventh day), but a work of love and providence, as he said, "My Father worketh hitherto, and I work."[6]

And in order to confirm the fact that he is the Creator, the Lawgiver, and the Commander of old and new, he said, "Ye have heard that it was said by them of old time. . . . But I say unto you."[7] Then concerning the sabbath and the annulment of its law, he said, "Or have ye not read in the law, how that on the sabbath days the priests in the temple profane the sabbath, and are

---

[1] See Gen. 2:3; Ex. 20:8; 31:13-14; Dt. 5:12-15; Ez. 20:12-26.
[2] Heb. 9:9-10.   [3] Josh. 22:4.   [4] St. Jn. 1:3; Heb. 1:2.
[5] St. Jn. 3:16; 1 St. Jn. 4:9.   [6] St. Jn. 5:17.   [7] St. Mt. 5:21-43.

blameless? [1] Then he added, "For the Son of Man is Lord even of the sabbath day." And that, "The sabbath was made for man." Likewise the Apostle, having observed this, said in contravening the keeping of the sabbath, "Let no man therefore judge you in meat, or in drink, or in respect of a holy day, or of the new moon, or of the sabbath days: which are a shadow of things to come.; for the body is of Christ." [2]

Yea, these things have become void with the existence of the new law of truth, "For", as the Apostle says, "if that which is done away was glorious, much more that which remaineth is glorious," [3] yea, infinitely more glorious.

This did Christ do and teach (to his Name be worship), in order to prepare the way for a new creation and a new law, as the Apostle also said, "Therefore if any man be in Christ, he is a new creature; old things are passed away; behold, all things are become new." [4] This is natural; for it was not possible to retain the old order when the new order had set in, as the Apostle says, "In that he saith, a new covenant, he hath made the first old. Now that which decayeth and waxeth old is ready to vanish away." [5]

Hence when he wished to begin the work of spiritual creation, the renewal of the likeness of the soul of man, which had been corrupted, and to restore it to the likeness of its former sanctification and the beauty of its splendour, to restore its unity with God its Creator in his heavenly kingdom, which he had prepared for it "from the foundation of the world," [6] he walked in the steps of his Father, "For what things soever he doeth, these also doeth the Son likewise." [7]

And as God the Father began the creation of the sensible world on the first day, which is Sunday, so the Son also began the work of the spiritual creation on the

---

[1] St. Mt. 12:5, 8; St. Mk. 2:27.   [2] Col. 2:16-17.   [3] 11 Cor. 3:11.
[4] 2 Cor. 5:17.   [5] Heb. 8:13.   [6] St. Mt. 25:34.
[7] St. Jn. 5:19.

first day, which is Palm Sunday, in which began his struggles of salvation. And as the Father was finished with creation on the sixth day and rested on the seventh day, so the Son finished the spiritual creation on the sixth day, Thursday evening, and rested physically in the tomb on the seventh day.

And again, as it was the Father's purpose in creating man to unite him with himself everlastingly, so it was the purpose of the Son in the renewal of man's creation to restore him to the state from which he had fallen, and to make him partaker of his eternal bliss and to enjoy him for ever.[1]

Now since the first rest of the sabbath took place after the creation of the sensible universe and later became a symbol for the rest of the promised land, so the rest of the second sabbath took place after the spiritual creation and became a symbol of the land of the meek in the heavenly homeland. Similarly as after the first creation and the first sabbath the old law was given, the old rites were instituted, and the Old Covenant pledged, so after the spiritual creation the law of the New Covenant, with all its new rites and institutions, was given; for it was on the Day of Resurrection, Sunday, that Christ said to his Disciples, "All power is given unto me in heaven and on earth: as my Father hath sent me, even so send I you. Go ye, therefore, into all the world, and preach the gospel to every creature. He that believeth and is baptized shall be saved; but he that believeth not shall be damned." [2]

The undefiled Disciples, therefore, in remembrance of this divine appearance on Sunday, on which the Saviour established the greatest doctrine of faith, belief in resurrection, proclaimed what he had commanded them; for it was on that day, too, that the perfection of human nature took place, as in the Incarnation of God the Word the grace of the remission of sins was

---

[1] 2 Cor. 4:16-18; Heb. 12:28.
[2] St. Mt. 28:18; St. Jn. 20:21; St. Mk. 16:15-16.

given; for it was by his Resurrection on the first day of the week, Sunday, that human nature was given the perfection of salvation, and life eternal in the world to come, as they had been assured before and had heard it from his teachings and now beheld it after his Passion, Death, and Resurrection.

Then to confirm to his Disciples the necessity of observing the first day as a remembrance of his Resurrection, and to assure them that the first day has been substituted for the sabbath, as the law of the New Covenant has been substituted for the old, he appeared to them again on Sunday, eight days after his Resurrection, thus reiterating the belief in his Resurrection, and reminding them of its great benefits,[1] commanding them to tarry in Jerusalem and to await there the descent of the Holy Spirit, as he had said, and according to the Father's promise.[2]

As for the Disciples, not knowing the day on which they were to receive the Holy Spirit, the Spirit of wisdom and understanding, the Spirit of power through which they were to preach his law, beginning at Jerusalem,[3] they continued in one accord with prayers and supplications, praising God and blessing him by offering the Sacrament of the Eucharist and the other Sacraments in his remembrance, as he had commanded them, when he said, "Do ye this in remembrance of me." At that same time they used to go frequently to the Temple.

Thus they waited and hoped for the Holy Spirit until he descended upon them fifty days after his Resurrection, which also falls on Sunday. Thus by his descent upon them on Sunday the Holy Spirit also imposed on them the keeping of Sunday. in confirmation of which we have sundry references and evidences. We shall now mention a few of these, recapitulating those we have already mentioned:

---

1 St. Jn. 21:31.
2 St. Jn. 14:26; 15:26-27; St. Lk. 24:47-49; Acts 1:8; 2:32; 3:15; 5:32.
3 St. Lk. 24:47.

God the Word, before his Incarnation, made creation on the first day, Sunday, then renewed it after his Incarnation by his Resurrection on Sunday. He proclaimed the joy of salvation to the women on Sunday, saying to them, "Rejoice", thus annulling the curse and sorrow of the fall of mankind. Then he appeared to his Disciples on Sunday, and commanded them to preach his New Covenant. Afterwards he sent to them the Holy Spirit on Sunday, confirming his own holy Resurrection, fulfilling his divine promise, and reassuring the hopes of his undefiled Apostles. At the same time he pointed out to them that the Jewish Passover has been fulfilled by his own Passover of salvation. In the same manner the Jewish Pentecost, which is the fiftieth day after the Passover, was fulfilled by the sending of the Holy Spirit on that day, fifty days after his Resurrection; for, as on that day the Jews eat bread made of new wheat, recalling their substitution of bread for manna and thus remembering their entrance into the land of promise,[1] so by partaking of the heavenly bread in our spiritual and bloodless Sacrifice, we commemorate our entrance into heaven by his Resurrection.

This being the case, Sunday, the day of the Lord's Resurrection, became known as the Lord's Day, of which the Psalmist sang, "This is the day which the Lord hath made; we will rejoice and be glad in it."[2] Yes, it is the first day in creation, the first in rank, the first in importance, the first in the gifts we received thereon, and first in the proclamation of God's love and mercy which became man's by the Resurrection of the Saviour, and by the attainment of human nature, the everlasting glory and kingdom.

For this reason the holy Apostles kept Sunday and sanctified it with the greatest sanctification, by using it for the teaching of the Faith,[3] celebrating the Sacrament of the Eucharist, consisting of the breaking of bread,[4] as they also carried on their works of mercy, love, and

---

1 Lev. 23:15-16.   2 Ps. 117:24.   3 St. Mt. 28:20.   4 St. Lk. 22:19.

bounty, and the partaking together of the undefiled Sacraments.[1]

In their path followed the holy Church after them. She commanded that Sunday be kept, ordaining for it special prayers, services, and rites. The Roman writer Pliny in his letter to Trajan Cæsar wrote that Christians had a custom of meeting on a certain day and of singing hymns to Christ as to a God. While Justin Martyr, wrote that on the Day of the Sun the Christian people of the cities and towns would meet and read the Epistles of the Apostles or the books of the Prophets, and after reading, an elder would preach a sermon, "Then we rise up together and pray; and after the prayer, bread and wine and water are offered, and the elder administers the Eucharist, while the people respond with, "Amen." Then Justin adds, "We meet on the Day of the Sun because it is the first day on which God made the world, and on it rose our Saviour from the dead." Later, King Constantine, who is equal to the Apostles, issued an edict throughout his kingdom forbidding litigation on the Day of the Sun, which is honoured by all, and calls upon the people to keep their holy vows and other religious duties. Then Emperor Justinian forbade litigation on the seven holy days preceding Easter, Passion Week, and the seven that follow it, the New Week, on Christmas, the Epiphany, the days of the Passion of the Apostles, and the days of the Sun which are celebrated every week, and which are truly called the days of the Lord. On all these days it was forbidden to hold trials whether before an arbiter or before a judge. Also officers in the army were excused from service on Sundays and other holidays; for Eusebius of Cæsarea mentions that Constantine the Great used to urge all his soldiers to keep the Day of the Sun, or Sunday; and those of them who were worthy to be participants in the divine faith he released in order that they might spend the vigils in

---

[1] 1 Cor. 16:1-2. Acts 20:7, 11.

the church of God, and should not stand in the way of their performance of religious services. Similarly he released day labourers and civil servants from their labours on Sundays. Thus all Christians who were employed in public offices were released from work on Sundays and holidays. And St. John Chrysostom calls Sunday the day of special benevolences, in relation to other days of the week.

PASSOVER (EASTER)

The most celebrated of Hebrew festivals was the *Passover,* which means literally the feast of passing over. In fact it represents two festivals, indicating two events, the first of which was the Passover itself and the other was the seven Days of Unleavened Bread. The Passover was a memorial of the deliverance of the first-born sons of the Israelites when the first-born of the Egyptians were killed by the angel of the Lord, as it was a symbol of the Sacrifice of the Saviour, which he fulfilled on the Cross. But the Days of Unleavened Bread were a memorial of the exodus of the children of Israel from Egypt, and their carrying their dough in a hurry before it was leavened.

The two events were comprised in the seven Days of Unleavened Bread, on the first of which they held the memorial of the deliverance of their first-born which was called Passover, or the passing over of the angel from the homes of the Israelites when the first-born of the Egyptians were killed, and their own first-born were saved.[1] Hence the holy Fathers ordained that Christians should not celebrate the same day of Passover as the Jews, neither on the day it fell, nor on the day preceding it, lest the reality come before the shadow, the true Sacrifice of Christ for salvation before the sacrifice of the Jewish paschal lamb.

---

[1] Ex. 12.

PENTECOST

This was a feast which the Jews celebrated on the sixteenth day of the month of Siwan (June), or the fiftieth day after the second day of the Passover which fell on the sixteenth of Abib, or April. They also called it the Feast of Weeks, because seven weeks from Easter passed before it came. The Greeks gave it the name *Pentecost,* which means the Fiftieth Day (after the Passover).[1] The Jews celebrated it in remembrance of the law which was given to them at the hands of Moses on that day on Mount Sinai. The Holy Church of Christ, however, celebrates it in remembrance of the descent of the Holy Spirit, fifty days after the Resurrection of Christ. The Arabic name, *Ansarah* is Hebrew in origin and means congregation, because on that day people congregated from distant places.

THE CHURCH BELL

The use of the bell in the holy Church to call the people to prayer was foretold in the use of horns by the Jews to call the congregation.[2]

LEAVE-TAKING OF FEASTS

The holy Church celebrates the Leave-Taking, as well as welcoming of the holy feasts, following the command which God gave his servant Moses, in that the beginning and the end of the festivals should be celebrated in a holy convocation.[3]

And unto God be thanks at the beginning and at the end.

---

[1] Dt. 16:10. [2] Nu. 10:2; Lev. 25:9. [3] Ex. 12:16; Lev. 23:7-8.

TABLE TO FIND THE SUNDAYS OF THE ENTIRE YEAR, 1938-1958

We have included in this Table the names of the months, the number of days in each month, the dates on which the Sundays fall, the sections for the Eptistle and Gospel which should be read on each Sunday during the Mass, the Tone, the Gospel of the Eothina, and what follows, the Exaposteilarion and the Glory as you will find them in their proper places.

TABLE TO FIND THE MONTH AND THE DAY OF THE

MONTH ON WHICH THE PASSOVER FALLS IN THE FOLLOWING YEARS

Year		Day of Month	Month
1938		11	April
1939		27	March
1940	Leap Year	15	April
1941		7	April
1942		23	March
1943		12	April
1944	Leap Year	3	April
1945		23	April
1946		8	April
1947		31	March
1948	Leap Year	19	April
1949		11	April
1950		27	March
1951		16	April
1952	Leap Year	7	April
1953		23	March
1954		12	April
1955		4	April
1956	Leap Year	23	April
1957		8	April
1958		31	March

Jewish Passover, April 5.   Holy Passover, April 11.   Latin Passover, April 4.

Months	Sundays	Epistles and Gospels		Tone	Eothina
January	3	Before Epiphany		5	8
Days 31	10	After Epiphany		6	9
	17	Twenty-nine		7	10
	24	Thirty-two		8	11
	31	Pharisee and Publican		1	1
February	7	Prodigal Son		2	2
Days 28	14	Meat Fare		3	3
	21	Cheese Fare		4	4
	28	The First Fasting		5	5
March	7	The Second Fasting		6	6
Days 31	14	The Third Fasting		7	7
	21	The Fourth Fasting		8	8
	28	The Fifth Fasting		1	9
April	4	Palm Sunday		—	—
Days 30	11	Holy Passover		—	—
	18	Thomas Sunday		1	1
	25	Ointment Bearers		2	4
May	2	The Paralytic		3	5
Days 31	9	The Samaritan		4	7
	16	The Blind		5	8
	23	Saintly Fathers		6	10
	30	Pentecost		—	—
June	6	The First		8	1
Days 30	13	The Second		1	2
	20	The Third		2	3
	27	The Fourth		3	4
July	4	The Fifth		4	5
Days 31	11	The Sixth		5	6
	18	Saintly Fathers		6	7
	25	The Eighth		7	8
August	1	The Ninth		8	9
Days 31	8	The Tenth		1	10
	15	The Eleventh		2	11
	22	The Twelfth		3	1
	29	The Thirteenth		4	2
September	5	The Fourteenth		5	3
Days 30	12	Before the Cross		6	4
	19	After the Cross		7	5
	26	17	18	8	6
October	3	18	19	1	7
Days 31	10	19	20	2	8
	17	Fathers' Sunday	21	3	9
	24	21	22	4	10
	31	22	23	5	11
November	7	23	24	6	1
Days 30	14	24	25	7	2
	21	25	26	8	3
	28	26	30	1	4
December	5	27	27	2	5
Days 31	12	Grandsires' Sunday		3	6
	19	Before Christmas		4	7
	26	After Christmas		5	8

Jewish Passover, March 25. Holy Passover, March 27. Latin Passover, March 27.

Months	Sundays	Epistles and Gospels		Tone	Eothina
January	2	Before Epiphany		6	9
Days 31	9	After Epiphany		7	10
	16	Pharisee and Publican		8	11
	23	Prodigal Son		1	1
	30	Meat Fare		2	2
February	6	Cheese Fare		3	3
Days 28	13	The First Fasting		4	4
	20	The Second Fasting		5	5
	27	The Third Fasting		6	6
March	6	The Fourth Fasting		7	7
Days 31	13	The Fifth Fasting		8	8
	20	Palm Sunday		—	—
	27	Holy Passover		—	—
April	3	Thomas Sunday		1	1
Days 30	10	Ointment Bearers		2	4
	17	The Paralytic		3	5
	24	The Samaritan		4	7
May	1	The Blind		5	8
Days 31	8	Saintly Fathers		6	10
	15	Pentecost		—	—
	22	The First		8	1
	29	The Second		1	2
June	5	The Third		2	3
Days 30	12	The Fourth		3	4
	19	The Fifth		4	5
	26	The Sixth		5	6
July	3	The Seventh		6	7
Days 31	10	The Eighth		7	8
	17	Saintly Fathers		8	9
	24	The Tenth		1	10
	31	The Eleventh		2	11
August	7	The Twelfth		3	1
Days 31	14	The Thirteenth		4	2
	21	The Fourteenth		5	3
	28	The Fifteenth		6	4
September	4	The Sixteenth		7	5
Days 30	11	Before the Cross		8	6
	18	After the Cross		1	7
	25	19	18	2	8
October	2	20	19	3	9
Days 31	9	21	20	4	10
	16	Fathers' Sunday	21	5	11
	23	23	22	6	1
	30	24	23	7	2
November	6	25	24	8	3
Days 30	13	26	25	1	4
	20	27	26	2	5
	27	28	30	3	6
December	4	30	27	4	7
Days 31	11	Grandsires' Sunday		5	8
	18	Before Christmas		6	9
	25	Christmas		—	—

Jewish Passover, April 13.   Holy Passover, April 15.   Latin Passover, March 11.

Months	Sundays	Epistles and Gospels		Tone	Eothina
January	1	Before Epiphany		8	11
Days 31	8	After Epiphany		1	1
	15	Twenty-nine		2	2
	22	Thirty-two		3	3
	29	Seventeen		4	4
February	5	Pharisee and Publican		5	5
Days 29	12	Prodigal Son		6	6
	19	Meat Fare		7	7
	26	Cheese Fare		8	8
March	4	The First Fasting		1	9
Days 31	11	The Second Fasting		2	10
	18	The Third Fasting		3	11
	25	The Fourth Fasting		4	1
April	1	The Fifth Fasting		5	2
Days 30	8	Palm Sunday		—	—
	15	Holy Passover		—	—
	22	Thomas Sunday		1	1
	29	Ointment Bearers		2	4
May	6	The Paralytic		3	5
Days 31	13	The Samaritan		4	7
	20	The Blind		5	8
	27	Saintly Fathers		6	10
June	3	Pentecost		—	—
Days 30	10	The First		8	1
	17	The Second		1	2
	24	The Third		2	3
July	1	The Fourth		3	4
Days 31	8	The Fifth		4	5
	15	Saintly Fathers		5	6
	22	The Seventh		6	7
	29	The Eighth		7	8
August	5	The Ninth		8	9
Days 31	12	Tne Tenth		1	10
	19	The Eleventh		2	11
	26	The Twelfth		3	1
September	2	The Thirteenth		4	2
Days 30	9	Before the Cross		5	3
	16	After the Cross		6	4
	23	16	18	7	5
	30	17	19	8	6
October	7	18	20	1	7
Days 31	14	Fathers' Sunday	21	2	8
	21	20	23	3	9
	28	21	24	4	10
November	4	22	22	5	11
Days 30	11	23	25	6	1
	18	24	26	7	2
	25	25	30	8	3
December	2	29	31	1	4
Days 31	9	27	27	2	5
	16	Grandsires' Sunday		3	6
	23	Before Christmas		4	7
	30	After Christmas		5	9

Jewish Passover, April 2.   Holy Passover, April 7.   Latin Passover, March 31.

Months	Sundays	Epistles and Gospels		Tone	Eothina
January	6	Epiphany		—	—
Days 31	13	After Epiphany		6	9
	20	Thirty-two		7	10
	27	Pharisee and Publican		1	11
February	3	Prodigal Son		1	1
Days 28	10	Meat Fare		2	2
	17	Cheese Fare		3	3
	24	The First Fasting		4	4
March	3	The Second Fasting		5	5
Days 31	10	The Third Fasting		6	6
	17	The Fourth Fasting		7	7
	24	The Fifth Fasting		8	1
	31	Palm Sunday		—	—
April	7	Holy Passover		—	—
Days 30	14	Thomas Sunday		1	1
	21	Ointment Bearers		2	4
	28	The Paralytic		3	5
May	5	The Samaritan		4	7
Days 31	12	The Blind		5	8
	19	Saintly Fathers		6	10
	26	Pentecost		—	—
June	2	The First		8	1
Days 30	9	The Second		1	2
	16	The Third		2	3
	23	The Fourth		3	4
	30	The Fifth		4	5
July	7	The Sixth		5	6
Days 31	14	Saintly Fathers		6	7
	21	The Eighth		7	8
	28	The Ninth		8	9
August	4	The Tenth		1	10
Days 31	11	The Eleventh		2	11
	18	The Twelfth		3	1
	25	The Thirteenth		4	2
September	1	The Fourteenth		5	3
Days 30	8	Before the Cross		6	4
	15	After the Cross		7	5
	22	17	18	8	6
	29	18	19	1	7
October	6	19	20	2	8
Days 31	13	Fathers' Sunday	21	3	9
	20	21	23	4	10
	27	22	24	5	11
November	3	23	22	6	1
Days 30	10	24	25	7	2
	17	25	26	8	3
	24	26	30	1	4
December	1	27	31	2	5
Days 31	8	28	27	3	6
	15	Grandsires' Sunday		4	7
	22	Before Christmas		5	8
	29	After Christmas		6	9

Jewish Passover, March 22. Holy Passover, March 23. Latin Passover, March 23.

Months	Sundays	Epistles and Gospels		Tone	Eothina
January	5	Before Epiphany*		7	10
Days 31	12	Pharisee and Publican		8	11
	19	Prodigal Son		1	1
	26	Meat Fare		2	2
February	2	Cheese Fare		3	3
Days 28	9	The First Fasting		4	4
	16	The Second Fasting		5	5
	23	The Third Fasting		6	6
March	2	The Fourth Fasting		7	7
Days 31	9	The Fifth Fasting		8	8
	16	Palm Sunday		—	—
	23	Holy Passover		—	—
	30	Thomas Sunday		1	1
April	6	Ointment Bearers		2	4
Days 30	13	The Paralytic		3	5
	20	The Samaritan		4	7
	27	The Blind		5	8
May	4	Saintly Fathers		6	10
Days 31	11	Pentecost		—	—
	18	The First		8	1
	25	The Second		1	2
June	1	The Third		2	3
Days 30	8	The Fourth		3	4
	15	The Fifth		4	5
	22	The Sixth		5	6
	29	The Seventh		6	7
July	6	The Eighth		7	8
Days 31	13	Saintly Fathers		8	9
	20	The Tenth		1	10
	27	The Eleventh		2	11
August	3	The Twelfth		3	1
Days 31	10	The Thirteenth		4	2
	17	The Fourteenth		5	3
	24	The Fifteenth		6	4
	31	The Sixteenth		7	5
September	7	Before the Cross		8	6
Days 30	14	Elevation of the Cross		—	—
	21	After the Cross		2	8
	28	2	18	3	9
October	5	2	9	4	10
Days 31	12	Fathers' Sunday	2	5	11
	19	23	21	6	1
	26	24	23	7	2
November	2	25	22	8	3
Days 30	9	26	24	1	4
	16	27	25	2	5
	23	28	26	3	6
	30	29	30	4	7
December	7	30	27	5	8
Days 31	14	29	28	6	9
	21	Before Christmas		7	10
	28	After Christmas		8	11

*The Gospel for the Sunday after the Epiphany is read on January 7.

Jewish Passover, April 10. Holy Passover, April 12. Latin Passover, April 12.

Months	Sundays	Epistles and Gospels		Tone	Eothina
January	4	Before Epiphany		1	1
Days 31	11	After Epiphany		2	2
	18	Twenty-ninth		3	3
	25	Thirty-second		4	4
February	1	Pharisee and Publican		5	5
Days 28	8	Prodigal Son		6	6
	15	Meat Fare		7	7
	22	Cheese Fare		8	8
March	1	The First Fasting		1	9
Days 31	8	The Second Fasting		2	10
	15	The Third Fasting		3	11
	22	The Fourth Fasting		4	1
	29	The Fifth Fasting		5	2
April	5	Palm Sunday		—	—
Days 30	12	Holy Passover		—	—
	19	Thomas Sunday		1	1
	26	Ointment Bearers		2	4
May	3	The Paralytic		3	5
Days 31	10	The Samaritan		4	7
	17	The Blind		5	8
	24	Saintly Fathers		6	10
	31	Pentecost		—	—
June	7	The First		8	1
Days 30	14	The Second		1	2
	21	The Third		2	3
	28	The Fourth		3	4
July	5	The Fifth		4	5
Days 31	12	The Sixth		5	6
	19	Saintly Fathers		6	7
	26	The Eighth		7	8
August	2	The Ninth		8	9
Days 31	9	The Tenth		1	10
	16	The Eleventh		2	11
	23	The Twelfth		3	1
	30	The Thirteenth		4	2
September	6	The Fourteenth		5	3
Days 30	13	Before the Cross		6	4
	20	After the Cross		7	5
	27	17	18	8	6
October	4	18	19	1	7
Days 31	11	Fathers' Sunday	20	2	8
	18	20	21	3	9
	25	21	23	4	10
November	1	22	22	5	11
Days 30	8	23	24	6	1
	15	24	25	7	2
	22	25	26	8	3
	29	26	30	1	4
December	6	27	27	2	5
Days 31	13	29	28	3	6
	20	Before Christmas		4	7
	27	After Christmas		5	8

Jewish Passover, March 30. Holy Passover, April 3. Latin Passover, March 27.

Months	Sundays	Epistles and Gospels		Tone	Eothina
January	3	Before Epiphany		5	8
Days 31	10	After Epiphany		6	9
	17	Thirty-second		7	10
	24	Pharisee and Publican		8	11
	31	Prodigal Son		1	1
February	7	Meat Fare		2	2
Days 29	14	Cheese Fare		3	3
	21	The First Fasting		4	4
	28	The Second Fasting		5	5
March	6	The Third Fasting		6	6
Days 31	13	The Fourth Fasting		7	7
	20	The Fifth Fasting		8	8
	27	Palm Sunday		—	—
April	3	Holy Passover		—	—
Days 30	10	Thomas Sunday		1	1
	17	Ointment Bearers		2	4
	24	The Paralytic		3	5
May	1	The Samaritan		4	7
Days 31	8	The Blind		5	8
	15	Saintly Fathers		6	10
	22	Pentecost		—	—
	29	The First		8	1
June	5	The Second		1	2
Days 30	12	The Third		2	3
	19	The Fourth		3	4
	26	The Fifth		4	5
July	3	The Sixth		5	6
Days 31	10	The Seventh		6	7
	17	Saintly Fathers		7	8
	24	The Ninth		8	9
	31	The Tenth		1	10
August	7	The Eleventh		2	11
Days 31	14	The Twelfth		3	1
	21	The Thirteenth		4	2
	28	The Fourteenth		5	3
September	4	The Fifteenth		6	4
Days 30	11	Before the Cross		7	5
	18	After the Cross		8	6
	25	18	18	1	7
October	2	19	19	2	8
Days 31	9	20	20	3	9
	16	Fathers' Sunday	21	4	10
	23	22	23	5	11
	30	23	22	6	1
November	6	24	24	7	2
Days 30	13	25	25	8	3
	20	26	26	1	4
	27	27	30	2	5
December	4	28	27	3	6
Days 31	11	Grandsires' Sunday		4	7
	18	Before Christmas		5	8
	25	Christmas		—	—

Jewish Passover, April 18. Holy Passover, April 23. Latin Passover, March 19.

Months	Sundays	Epistles and Gospels		Tone	Eothina
January	1	Before Epiphany		7	10
Days 31	8	After Epiphany		8	11
	15	Twenty-ninth		1	1
	22	Thirty-first		2	2
	29	Thirty-second		3	3
February	5	The Canaanite		4	4
Days 28	12	Pharisee and Publican		5	5
	19	Prodigal Son		6	6
	26	Meat Fare		7	7
March	5	Cheese Fare		8	8
Days 31	12	The First Fasting		1	9
	19	The Second Fasting		2	10
	26	The Third Fasting		3	11
April	2	The Fourth Fasting		4	1
Days 30	9	The Fifth Fasting		5	2
	16	Palm Sunday		—	—
	23	Holy Passover		—	—
	30	Thomas Sunday		1	1
May	7	Ointment Bearers		2	4
Days 31	14	The Paralytic		3	5
	21	The Samaritan		4	7
	28	The Blind		5	8
June	4	Saintly Fathers		6	10
Days 30	11	Pentecost		—	—
	18	The First		8	1
	25	The Second		1	2
July	2	The Third		2	3
Days 31	9	The Fourth		3	4
	16	Saintly Fathers		4	5
	23	The Sixth		5	6
	30	The Seventh		6	8
August	6	The Transfiguration		—	—
Days 31	13	The Ninth		8	9
	20	The Tenth		1	10
	27	The Eleventh		2	11
September	3	The Twelfth		3	1
Days 30	10	Before the Cross		4	2
	17	After the Cross		5	3
	24	15	18	6	4
October	1	16	19	7	5
Days 31	8	17	20	8	6
	15	Fathers' Sunday	21	1	7
	22	19	23	2	8
	29	20	24	3	9
November	5	21	22	4	10
Days 30	12	22	25	5	11
	19	23	26	6	1
	26	24	30	7	2
December	3	25	16	8	3
Days 31	10	26	27	1	4
	17	29	28	2	1
	24	Before Christmas		3	6
	31	Before Epiphany		4	7

Jewish Passover, April 7.   Holy Passover, April 8.   Latin Passover, April 7.

Months	Sundays	Epistles and Gospels		Tone	Eothina
January	7	After Epiphany		5	8
Days 31	14	Twenty-ninth		6	9
	21	Sixteenth		7	10
	28	Pharisee and Publican		8	11
February	4	Prodigal Son		1	1
Days 28	11	Meat Fare		2	2
	18	Cheese Fare		3	3
	25	The First Fasting		4	4
March	4	The Second Fasting		5	5
Days 31	11	The Third Fasting		6	6
	18	The Fourth Fasting		7	7
	25	The Fifth Fasting		8	8
April	1	Palm Sunday		—	—
Days 30	8	Holy Passover		—	—
	15	Thomas Sunday		1	1
	22	Ointment Bearers		2	4
	29	The Paralytic		3	5
May	6	The Samaritan		4	7
Days 31	13	The Blind		5	8
	20	Saintly Fathers		6	10
	27	Pentecost		—	—
June	3	The First		8	1
Days 30	10	The Second		1	2
	17	The Third		2	3
	24	The Fourth		3	4
July	1	The Fifth		4	5
Days 31	8	The Sixth		5	6
	15	Saintly Fathers		6	7
	22	The Eighth		7	8
	29	The Ninth		8	9
August	5	The Tenth		1	10
Days 31	12	The Eleventh		2	11
	19	The Twelfth		3	1
	26	The Thirteenth		4	2
September	2	The Fourteenth		4	3
Days 30	9	Before the Cross		6	4
	16	After the Cross		7	5
	23	17	18	8	6
	30	18	19	1	7
October	7	19	20	2	8
Days 31	14	Fathers' Sunday	21	3	9
	21	21	23	4	10
	28	22	24	5	11
November	4	23	22	6	1
Days 30	11	24	25	7	2
	18	25	26	8	3
	25	26	30	1	4
December	2	27	31	2	5
Days 31	9	28	27	3	6
	16	Grandsires' Sunday		4	7
	23	Before Christmas		5	8
	30	After Christmas		6	9

Jewish Passover, March 27. Holy Passover, March 31. Latin Passover, March 24.

Months	Sundays	Epistles and Gospels		Tone	Eothina
January	6	Epiphany		—	—
Days 31	13	After Epiphany		8	11
	20	Pharisee and Publican		1	1
	27	Prodigal Son		2	2
February	3	Meat Fare		3	3
Days 28	10	Cheese Fare		4	4
	17	The First Fasting		5	5
	24	The Second Fasting		6	6
March	3	The Third Fasting		7	7
Days 31	10	The Fourth Fasting		8	8
	17	The Fifth Fasting		1	9
	24	Palm Sunday		—	—
	31	Holy Passover		—	—
April	7	Thomas Sunday		1	1
Days 30	14	Ointment Bearers		2	4
	21	The Paralytic		3	5
	28	The Samaritan		4	7
May	5	The Blind		5	8
Days 31	12	Saintly Fathers		6	10
	19	Pentecost		—	—
	26	The First		8	1
June	2	The Second		1	2
Days 30	9	The Third		2	3
	16	The Fourth		3	4
	23	The Fifth		4	5
	30	The Sixth		5	6
July	7	The Seventh		6	7
Days 31	14	Saintly Fathers		7	8
	21	The Ninth		8	9
	28	The Tenth		1	10
August	4	The Eleventh		2	11
Days 31	11	The Twelfth		3	1
	18	The Thirteenth		4	2
	25	The Fourteenth		5	3
September	1	The Fifteenth		6	4
Days 30	8	Before the Cross		7	5
	15	After the Cross		8	6
	22	18	18	1	7
	29	19	19	2	8
October	6	20	20	3	9
Days 31	13	Fathers' Sunday		4	10
	20	22	23	5	11
	27	23	24	6	1
November	3	24	22	7	2
Days 30	10	25	25	8	3
	17	26	26	1	4
	24	27	30	2	5
December	1	28	31	3	6
Days 31	8	30	27	4	7
	15	29	28	5	8
	22	Before Christmas		6	9
	29	After Christmas		7	10

Jewish Passover, April 15. Holy Passover, April 19. Latin Passover, March 15.

Months	Sundays	Epistles and Gospels		Tone	Eothina
January	5	Before Epiphany		7	10
Days 31	12	After Epiphany		8	11
	19	Twenty-ninth		1	1
	26	Thirty-second		2	2
February	2	Seventeenth		3	3
Days 29	9	Pharisee and Publican		4	4
	16	Prodigal Son		5	5
	23	Meat Fare		6	6
March	1	Cheese Fare		7	7
Days 31	8	The First Fasting		8	8
	15	The Second Fasting		1	9
	22	The Third Fasting		2	10
	29	The Fourth Fasting		3	11
April	5	The Fifth Fasting		4	1
Days 30	12	Palm Sunday		—	—
	19	Holy Passover		—	—
	26	Thomas Sunday		1	1
May	3	Ointment Bearers		2	4
Days 31	10	The Paralytic		3	5
	17	The Samaritan		4	7
	24	The Blind		5	8
	31	Saintly Fathers		6	10
June	7	Pentecost		—	—
Days 30	14	The First		8	1
	21	The Second		1	2
	28	The Third		2	3
July	5	The Fourth		3	4
Days 31	12	The Fifth		4	5
	19	Saintly Fathers		5	6
	26	The Seventh		6	7
August	2	The Eighth		7	8
Days 31	9	The Ninth		8	9
	16	The Tenth		1	10
	23	The Eleventh		2	11
	30	The Twelfth		3	1
September	6	The Thirteenth		4	2
Days 30	13	Before the Cross		5	3
	20	After the Cross		6	4
	27	16	17	7	5
October	4	17	19	8	6
Days 31	11	Fathers' Sunday	21	1	7
	18	19	20	2	8
	25	20	23	3	9
November	1	21	22	4	10
Days 30	8	22	24	5	11
	15	23	25	6	1
	22	24	26	7	2
	29	25	30	8	3
December	6	26	27	1	4
Days 31	13	Grandsires' Sunday		2	5
	20	Before Christmas		3	6
	27	After Christmas		4	7

Jewish Passover, April 4.   Holy Passover, April 11.   Latin Passover, April 4.

Months	Sundays	Epistles and Gospels		Tone	Eothina
January	3	Before Epiphany		5	8
Days 31	10	After Epiphany		6	9
	17	Twenty-ninth		7	10
	24	Thirty-second		8	11
	31	Pharisee and Publican		1	1
February	7	Prodigal Son		2	2
Days 28	14	Meat Fare		3	3
	21	Cheese Fare		4	4
	28	The First Fasting		5	5
March	7	The Second Fasting		6	6
Days 31	14	The Third Fasting		7	7
	21	The Fourth Fasting		8	8
	28	The Fifth Fasting		1	9
April	4	Palm Sunday		—	—
Days 30	11	Holy Passover		—	—
	18	Thomas Sunday		1	1
	25	Ointment Bearers		2	4
May	2	The Paralytic		3	5
Days 31	9	The Samaritan		4	7
	16	The Blind		5	8
	23	Saintly Fathers		6	10
	30	Pentecost		—	—
June	6	The First		8	1
Days 30	13	The Second		1	2
	20	The Third		2	3
	27	The Fourth		3	4
July	4	The Fifth		4	5
Days 31	11	The Sixth		5	6
	18	Saintly Fathers		6	7
	25	The Eighth		7	8
August	1	The Ninth		8	9
Days 31	8	The Tenth		1	10
	15	The Eleventh		2	11
	22	The Twelfth		3	1
	29	The Thirteenth		4	2
September	5	The Fourteenth		5	3
Days 30	12	Before the Cross		6	4
	19	After the Cross		7	5
	26	17	18	8	6
October	3	18	19	1	7
Days 31	10	19	20	2	8
	17	Fathers' Sunday	21	3	9
	24	21	22	4	10
	31	22	23	5	11
November	7	23	24	6	1
Days 30	14	24	25	7	2
	21	25	26	8	3
	28	26	30	1	4
December	5	27	27	2	5
Days 31	12	Grandsires' Sunday		3	6
	19	Before Christmas		4	7
	26	After Christmas		5	8

Jewish Passover, March 24. Holy Passover, March 27. Latin Passover, March 27.

Months	Sundays	Epistles and Gospels		Tone	Eothina
January	2	Before Epiphany		6	9
Days 31	9	After Epiphany		7	10
	16	Pharisee and Publican		8	11
	23	Prodigal Son		1	1
	30	Meat Fare		2	2
February	6	Cheese Fare		3	3
Days 28	13	The First Fasting		4	4
	20	The Second Fasting		5	5
	27	The Third Fasting		6	6
March	6	The Fourth Fasting		7	7
Days 31	13	The Fifth Fasting		8	8
	20	Palm Sunday		—	—
	27	Holy Passover		—	—
April	3	Thomas Sunday		1	1
Days 30	10	Ointment Bearers		2	4
	17	The Paralytic		3	5
	24	The Samaritan		4	7
May	1	The Blind		5	8
Days 31	8	Saintly Fathers		6	10
	15	Pentecost		—	—
	22	The First		8	1
	29	The Second		1	2
June	5	The Third		2	3
Days 30	12	The Fourth		3	4
	19	The Fifth		4	5
	26	The Sixth		5	6
July	3	The Seventh		6	7
Days 31	10	The Eighth		7	8
	17	Saintly Fathers		8	9
	24	The Tenth		1	10
	31	The Eleventh		2	11
August	7	The Twelfth		3	1
Days 31	14	The Thirteenth		4	2
	21	The Fourteenth		5	3
	28	The Fifteenth		6	4
September	4	The Sixteenth		7	5
Days 30	11	Before the Cross		8	6
	18	After the Cross		1	7
	25	19	18	2	8
October	2	20	19	3	9
Days 31	9	21	20	4	10
	16	Fathers' Sunday	21	5	11
	23	23	23	6	1
	30	24	22	7	2
November	6	25	24	8	3
Days 30	13	26	25	1	4
	20	27	26	2	5
	27	28	30	3	6
December	4	30	27	4	7
Days 31	11	Grandsires' Sunday		5	8
	18	Before Christmas		6	9
	25	Christmas		—	—

Jewish Passover, April 12. Holy Passover, April 16. Latin Passover, March 12.

Months	Sundays	Epistles and Gospels		Tone	Eothina
January	1	Before Epiphany		8	11
Days 31	8	After Epiphany		1	1
	15	Twenty-ninth		2	2
	22	Thirty-second		3	3
	29	Seventeenth		4	4
February	5	Pharisee and Publican		5	5
Days 28	12	Prodigal Son		6	6
	19	Meat Fare		7	7
	26	Cheese Fare		8	8
March	5	The First Fasting		1	9
Days 31	12	The Second Fasting		2	10
	19	The Third Fasting		3	11
	26	The Fourth Fasting		4	1
April	2	The Fifth Fasting		5	2
Days 30	9	Palm Sunday		—	—
	16	Holy Passover		—	—
	23	Thomas Sunday		1	3
	30	Ointment Bearers		2	4
May	7	The Paralytic		3	5
Days 31	14	The Samaritan		4	7
	21	The Blind		5	8
	28	Saintly Fathers		6	10
June	4	Pentecost		8	1
Days 30	11	The First		1	2
	18	The Second		2	3
	25	The Third		3	4
July	2	The Fourth		4	5
Days 31	9	The Fifth		5	6
	16	Saintly Fathers		6	7
	23	The Seventh		7	8
	30	The Eighth			
August	6	The Transfiguration		—	10
Days 31	13	The Tenth		1	11
	20	The Eleventh		2	1
	27	The Twelfth		3	2
September	3	The Thirteenth		4	3
Days 30	10	Before the Cross		5	4
	17	After the Cross		6	5
	24	16		7	6
October	1	17	19	8	7
Days 31	8	18	20	1	8
	15	Fathers' Sunday	21	2	9
	22	20	23	3	10
	29	21	24	4	11
November	5	22	22	5	1
Days 30	12	23	25	6	2
	19	24	26	7	3
	26	25	30	8	4
December	3	26	31	1	5
Days 31	10	27	27	2	6
	17	17	28	3	7
	24	Before Christmas		4	8
	31	After Christmas		5	

Jewish Passover, April 1. Holy Passover, April 7. Latin Passover, March 31.

Months	Sundays	Epistles and Gospels		Tone	Eothina
January	7	Epiphany		—	—
Days 31	14	After Epiphany		6	9
	21	Thirty-second		7	10
	28	Pharisee and Publican		8	11
February	4	Prodigal Son		1	1
Days 29	11	Meat Fare		2	2
	18	Cheese Fare		3	3
	25	The First Fasting		4	4
March	3	The Second Fasting		5	5
Days 31	10	The Third Fasting		6	6
	17	The Fourth Fasting		7	7
	24	The Fifth Fasting		8	8
	31	Palm Sunday		—	—
April	7	Holy Passover		—	—
Days 30	14	Thomas Sunday		1	1
	21	Ointment Bearers		2	4
	28	The Paralytic		3	5
May	5	The Samaritan		4	7
Days 31	12	The Blind		5	8
	19	Saintly Fathers		6	10
	26	Pentecost		—	—
June	2	The First		8	1
Days 30	9	The Second		1	2
	16	The Third		2	3
	23	The Fourth		3	4
	30	The Fifth		4	5
July	7	The Sixth		5	6
Days 31	14	Saintly Fathers		6	7
	21	The Eighth		7	8
	28	The Ninth		8	9
August	4	The Tenth		1	10
Days 31	11	The Eleventh		2	11
	18	The Twelfth		3	1
	25	The Thirteenth		4	2
September	1	The Fourteenth		5	3
Days 30	8	Before the Cross		6	4
	15	After the Cross		7	5
	22	17	18	8	6
	29	18	19	1	7
October	6	19	20	2	8
Days 31	13	Fathers' Sunday	21	3	9
	20	21	23	4	10
	27	22	24	5	11
November	3	23	22	6	1
Days 30	10	24	25	7	2
	17	25	26	8	3
	24	26	30	1	4
December	1	27	31	2	5
Days 31	8	28	27	3	6
	15	Grandsires' Sunday		4	7
	22	Before Christmas		5	8
	29	After Christmas		6	9

Jewish Passover, April 18. Holy Passover, March 23. Latin Passover, March 23.

Months	Sundays	Epistles and Gospels		Tone	Eothina
January	5	Before Epiphany *		7	10
Days 31	12	Pharisee and Publican		8	11
	19	Prodigal Son		1	1
	26	Meat Fare		2	2
February	2	Cheese Fare		3	3
Days 28	9	The First Fasting		4	4
	16	The Second Fasting		5	5
	23	The Third Fasting		6	6
March	2	The Fourth Fasting		7	7
Days 31	9	The Fifth Fasting		8	8
	16	Palm Sunday		—	—
	23	Holy Passover		—	—
	30	Thomas Sunday		1	1
April	6	Ointment Bearers		2	4
Days 30	13	The Paralytic		3	5
	20	The Samaritan		4	7
	27	The Blind		5	8
May	4	Saintly Fathers		6	10
Days 31	11	Pentecost		—	—
	18	The First		8	1
	25	The Second		1	2
June	1	The Third		2	3
Days 30	8	The Fourth		3	4
	15	The Fifth		4	5
	22	The Sixth		5	6
	29	The Seventh		6	7
July	6	The Eighth		7	8
Days 31	13	Saintly Fathers		8	9
	20	The Tenth		1	10
	27	The Eleventh		2	11
August	3	The Twelfth		3	1
Days 31	10	The Thirteenth		4	2
	17	The Fourteenth		5	3
	24	The Fifteenth		6	4
	31	The Sixteenth		7	5
September	7	Before the Cross		8	6
Days 30	14	Elevation of the Cross		1	7
	21	After the Cross		2	8
	28	20	18	3	9
October	5	21	19	4	10
Days 31	12	Fathers' Sunday	20	5	11
	19	23	21	6	1
	26	24	23	7	2
November	2	25	22	8	3
Days 30	9	26	24	1	4
	16	27	25	2	5
	23	28	26	3	6
	30	29	30	4	7
December	7	30	30	5	8
Days 31	14	29	31	6	9
	21	Before Christmas		7	10
	28	After Christmas		8	11

* The Gospel for the Sunday after Epiphany is read January 7.

Jewish Passover, April 9.   Holy Passover, April 12.   Latin Passover, April 12.

Months	Sundays	Epistles and Gospels		Tone	Eothina
January	4	Before Epiphany		1	1
Days 31	11	After Epiphany		2	2
	18	Twenty-ninth		3	3
	25	Thirty-second		4	4
February	1	Pharisee and Publican		5	5
Days 28	8	Prodigal Son		6	6
	15	Meat Fare		7	7
	22	Cheese Fare		8	8
March	1	The First Fasting		1	9
Days 31	8	The Second Fasting		2	10
	15	The Third Fasting		3	11
	22	The Fourth Fasting		4	1
	29	The Fifth Fasting		5	2
April	5	Palm Sunday		—	—
Days 30	12	Holy Passover		—	—
	19	Thomas Sunday		1	1
	26	Ointment Bearers		2	4
May	3	The Paralytic		3	5
Days 31	10	The Samaritan		4	7
	17	The Blind		5	8
	24	Saintly Fathers		6	10
	31	Pentecost		—	—
June	7	The First		8	1
Days 30	14	The Second		1	2
	21	The Third		2	3
	28	The Fourth		3	4
July	5	The Fifth		4	5
Days 31	12	The Sixth		5	6
	19	Saintly Fathers		6	7
	26	The Eighth		7	8
August	2	The Ninth		8	9
Days 31	9	The Tenth		1	10
	16	The Eleventh		2	11
	23	The Twelfth		3	1
	30	The Thirteenth		4	2
September	6	The Fourteenth		5	3
Days 30	13	Before the Cross		6	4
	20	After the Cross		7	5
	27	17	18	8	6
October	4	18	19	1	7
Days 31	11	Fathers' Sunday	20	2	8
	18	20	21	3	9
	25	21	23	4	10
November	1	22	22	5	11
Days 30	8	23	24	6	1
	15	24	25	7	2
	22	25	26	8	3
	29	26	30	1	4
December	6	27	27	2	5
Days 31	13	29	28	3	6
	20	Before Christmas		4	7
	27	After Christmas		5	8

Jewish Passover, March 25. Holy Passover, April 4. Latin Passover, March 28.

Months	Sundays	Epistles and Gospels		Tone	Eothina
January	3	Before Epiphany		6	9
Days 31	10	After Epiphany		7	10
	17	Thirty-second		8	11
	24	Pharisee and Publican		1	1
	31	Prodigal Son		2	2
February	7	Meat Fare		3	3
Days 28	14	Cheese Fare		4	4
	21	The First Fasting		5	5
	28	The Second Fasting		6	6
March	7	The Third Fasting		7	7
Days 31	14	The Fourth Fasting		8	8
	21	The Fifth Fasting		1	9
	28	Palm Sunday		—	—
April	4	Holy Passover		—	—
Days 30	11	Thomas Sunday		1	1
	18	Ointment Bearers		2	4
	25	The Paralytic		3	5
May	2	The Samaritan		4	7
Days 31	9	The Blind		5	8
	16	Saintly Fathers		6	10
	23	Pentecost		—	—
	30	The First		8	1
June	6	The Second		1	2
Days 30	13	The Third		2	3
	20	The Fourth		3	4
	27	The Fifth		4	5
July	4	The Sixth		5	6
Days 31	11	The Seventh		6	7
	18	Saintly Fathers		7	8
	25	The Ninth		8	9
August	1	The Tenth		1	10
Days 31	8	The Eleventh		2	11
	15	The Twelfth		3	1
	22	The Thirteenth		4	2
	29	The Fourteenth		5	3
September	5	The Fifteenth		6	4
Days 30	12	Before the Cross		7	5
	19	After the Cross		8	6
	26	The Eighteenth		1	7
October	3	The Nineteenth		2	8
Days 31	10	The Twentieth		3	9
	17	Fathers' Sunday		4	10
	24	22	23	5	11
	31	23	22	6	1
November	7	24	24	7	2
Days 30	14	25	25	8	3
	21	26	26	1	4
	28	27	30	2	5
December	5	28	27	3	6
Days 31	12	29	28	4	7
	19	Before Christmas		5	8
	26	After Christmas		6	9

Jewish Passover, April 17. Holy Passover, April 23. Latin Passover, March 19.

Months	Sundays	Epistles and Gospels		Tone	Eothina
January	2	Before Epiphany		7	10
Days 31	9	After Epiphany		8	11
	16	Twelfth		1	1
	23	Fourteenth		2	2
	30	Fifteenth		3	3
February	6	Seventeenth		4	4
Days 29	13	Pharisee and Publican		5	5
	20	Prodigal Son		6	6
	27	Meat Fare		7	7
March	5	Cheese Fare		8	8
Days 31	12	First Fasting		1	9
	19	Second Fasting		2	10
	26	Third Fasting		3	11
April	2	Fourth Fasting		4	1
Days 30	9	Fifth Fasting		5	2
	16	Palm Sunday		—	—
	23	Holy Passover		—	—
	30	Thomas Sunday		1	1
May	7	Ointment Bearers		2	4
Days 31	14	The Paralytic		3	5
	21	The Samaritan		4	7
	28	The Blind		5	8
June	4	Saintly Fathers		6	10
Days 30	11	Pentecost			
	18	The First		8	1
	25	The Second		1	2
July	2	The Third		2	3
Days 31	9	The Fourth		3	4
	16	Saintly Fathers		4	5
	23	The Sixth		5	6
	30	The Seventh		6	7
August	6	The Transfiguration		—	—
Days 31	13	The Ninth		8	9
	20	The Tenth		1	10
	27	The Eleventh		2	11
September	3	The Twelfth		3	1
Days 30	10	Before the Cross		4	2
	17	After the Cross		5	3
	24	15	18	6	4
October	1	16	19	7	5
Days 31	8	17	20	8	6
	15	Saintly Fathers	21	1	7
	22	19	23	2	8
	29	20	24	3	9
November	5	21	22	4	10
Days 30	12	22	25	5	11
	19	23	26	6	1
	26	24	30	7	2
December	3	25	16	8	3
Days 31	10	26	27	1	4
	17	29	28	2	5
	24	Before Christmas		3	6
	31	Before Epipnany		4	7

Jewish Passover, April 3. Holy Passover, April 8. Latin Passover, April 8.

Months	Sundays	Epistles and Gospels		Tone	Eothina
January	7	After Epiphany		5	8
Days 31	14	Twenty-ninth		6	9
	21	Thirty-second		7	10
	28	Pharisee and Publican		8	11
February	4	Prodigal Son		1	1
Days 28	11	Meat Fare		2	2
	18	Cheese Fare		3	3
	25	The First Fasting		4	4
March	4	The Second Fasting		5	5
Days 31	11	The Third Fasting		6	6
	18	The Fourth Fasting		7	7
	25	The Fifth Fasting		8	8
April	1	Palm Sunday		—	—
Days 30	8	Holy Passover		—	—
	15	Thomas Sunday		1	1
	22	Ointment Bearers		2	4
	29	The Paralytic		3	5
May	6	The Samaritan		4	7
Days 31	13	The Blind		5	8
	20	Saintly Fathers		6	10
	27	Pentecost		—	—
June	3	The First		8	1
Days 30	10	The Second		1	2
	17	The Third		2	3
	24	The Fourth		3	4
July	1	The Fifth		4	5
Days 31	8	The Sixth		5	6
	15	Saintly Fathers		6	7
	22	The Eighth		7	8
	29	The Ninth		8	9
August	5	The Tenth		1	10
Days 31	12	The Eleventh		2	11
	19	The Twelfth		3	1
	26	The Thirteenth		4	2
September	2	The Fourteenth		5	3
Days 30	9	Before the Cross		6	4
	16	After the Cross		7	5
	23	17	18	8	6
	30	18	19	1	7
October	7	19	20	2	8
Days 31	14	Fathers' Sunday	21	3	9
	21	21	23	4	10
	28	22	24	5	11
November	4	23	22	6	1
Days 30	11	24	25	7	2
	18	25	26	8	3
	25	26	30	1	4
December	2	27	31	2	5
Days 31	9	28	27	3	6
	16	29	28	4	7
	23	Before Christmas		5	8
	30	After Christmas		6	9

1146 YEAR 1958

Jewish Passover, March 30. Holy Passover, March 31. Latin Passover, March 24.

Months	Sundays	Epistles and Gospels		Tone	Eothina
January	6	Epiphany		—	—
Days 31	13	After Epiphany		8	11
	20	Pharisee and Publican		1	1
	27	Prodigal Son		2	2
February	3	Meat Fare		3	3
Days 28	10	Cheese Fare		4	4
	17	The First Fasting		5	5
	24	The Second Fasting		6	6
March	3	The Third Fasting		7	7
Days 31	10	The Fourth Fasting		8	8
	17	The Fifth Fasting		1	9
	24	Palm Sunday		—	—
	31	Holy Passover		—	—
April	7	Thomas Sunday		1	1
Days 30	14	Ointment Bearers		2	4
	21	The Paralytic		3	5
	28	The Samaritan		4	7
May	5	The Blind		5	8
Days 31	12	Saintly Fathers		6	10
	19	Pentecost		—	—
	26	The First		8	1
June	2	The Second		1	2
Days 30	9	The Third		2	3
	16	The Fourth		3	4
	23	The Fifth		4	5
	30	The Sixth		5	6
July	7	The Seventh		6	7
Days 31	14	Saintly Fathers		7	8
	21	The Ninth		8	9
	28	The Tenth		1	10
August	4	The Eleventh		2	11
Days 31	11	The Twelfth		3	1
	18	The Thirteenth		4	2
	25	The Fourteenth		5	3
September	1	The Fifteenth		6	4
Days 30	8	Before the Cross		7	5
	15	After the Cross		8	6
	22	The Eighteenth		1	7
	29	The Nineteenth		2	8
October	6	The Twentieth		3	9
Days 31	13	Fathers' Sunday		4	10
	20	22	23	5	11
	27	23	24	6	1
November	3	24	22	7	2
Days 30	10	25	25	8	3
	17	26	26	1	4
	24	27	30	2	5
December	1	28	31	3	6
Days 31	8	30	27	4	7
	15	29	28	5	8
	22	Before Christmas		6	9
	29	After Christmas		7	10

Marriages

Births

Baptisms

Deaths